COMPUTERS IN EDUCATION

Proceedings of the IFIP TC 3
4th World Conference on Computers in Education – WCCE 85
Norfolk, VA, USA, July 29-August 2, 1985

edited by

KAREN DUNCAN
Health Information Systems
Los Altos, California, USA

and

DIANA HARRIS
University of Iowa
Iowa City, Iowa, USA

1985

NORTH-HOLLAND – AMSTERDAM · NEW YORK · OXFORD

ISBN: 0 444 87797 5

Published by:
ELSEVIER SCIENCE PUBLISHERS B.V.
P.O. Box 1991
1000 BZ Amsterdam
The Netherlands

Sole distributors for the U.S.A. and Canada:
ELSEVIER SCIENCE PUBLISHING COMPANY, INC.
52 Vanderbilt Avenue
New York, N.Y. 10017
U.S.A.

Library of Congress Cataloging in Publication Data

World Conference on Computers in Education (4th :
    1985 : Norfolk, Va.)
    Computers in education.

    1. Education--Data processing--Congresses.
2. Computer-assisted instruction--Congresses.
3. Computer literacy--Congresses. I. Duncan, K. A.
(Karen A.) II. Harris, Diana. III. IFIP Technical
Committee 3, Education. IV. Title.
LB1028.43.W66 1985   371.3'9445   85-10267
ISBN 0-444-87797-5

FOREWORD

This volume comprises the proceedings of the 1985 World Conference on Computers in Education. As such, the editors have included all refereed papers and summaries of all special sessions such as tutorials and panel presentations. To facilitate future reference to material relating to specific topics, the papers and summaries have been grouped according to the primary themes of the sessions as listed below:

Across the Curriculum
Design and Development of CAL
Pedagogical Tools and Techniques
Mathematics, Science, and Engineering Education
Humanities
New Tech, High Tech, and Using Technology
Computer Languages, Problem Solving, and Programming
LOGO
Graphics
Course and Curricula Recommendations
Computer Literacy
Non-traditional Education
Teacher Training
Issues and Ethics
National Systems and Policies
Non-curricular Aspects of Computing and Education
Computers in Research
Future of Computing and Education

The editors are grateful to the members of the WCCE '85 Program Committee for their timely and thoughtful selection of papers and special sessions for inclusion in the proceedings. We are especially grateful to Dick Austing for sharing the editors' workload in obtaining camera-ready write-ups for the special sessions, and for his assistance in elucidating the themes of the conference sessions. Thanks also to Stephanie Smit at North-Holland for her early guidance and patience when the proceedings document was beginning to take shape. Beth Collison's editorial assistance and Laurel Johnk's organization made our work manageable and smooth.

The editors have found the task of assembling the proceedings to be most gratifying — especially with respect to the opportunity to work closely with our educational computing peers. We trust you will find reading the papers and summaries as rewarding as we did.

Karen Duncan
Health Information Systems
U.S.A.

Diana Harris
University of Iowa
U.S.A.

MESSAGE FROM THE CHAIRS

This is the fourth IFIP (International Federation for Information Processing) TC 3 (Technical Committee on Education) World Conference on Computers in Education (WCCE). All of us involved with the conference believe that it will continue an outstanding tradition of fostering and promoting international cooperation in computer education.

The rich and varied program offered addresses virtually all areas of computers in education and encompasses most of the world. The quality of the program is a tribute to those who contributed papers, those who refereed papers, those who have agreed to serve as panelists, and to the thorough deliberation of the International Program Committee.

These proceedings represent a permanent record of what happened at WCCE '85. We are most grateful to Karen Duncan and Diana Harris for their splendid job in assembling this volume. It is difficult to even imagine the magnitude of such a task. Managing the receipt and reviewing of 300-plus papers was expertly handled by John McGregor.

WCCE '85 has also been fortunate to receive the full support and backing of the American Federation of Information Processing Societies (AFIPS). As co-sponsor, AFIPS has supplied the leadership and knowledge accumulated over many years of operation of National Computer Conferences in the United States. We are especially grateful to Rick Dobson, our AFIPS Headquarters staff liaison, and his staff, and to Sylvia Charp, who chaired the WCCE '85 AFIPS Steering Committee.

Additional notes of thanks go to Ted Sjoerdsma, who, in addition to serving as conference treasurer, brought us many years of experience from his work with the (United States) National Educational Computing Conferences, and to David Game, who took over local arrangements after Jerry moved from Virginia. Ralph Lee did an excellent job in organizing pre-conference workshops, as did Richard Austing in organizing the special sessions.

Finally, we must thank all of you who attend the conference or read these proceedings. Without you there would have been no purpose to this activity.

Gerald L. Engel
Chair, Organizing Committee

John W. Hamblen
Chair, International Program Committee

Organizing Committee

Gerald L. Engel, Chairman
John W. Hamblen, Vice Chairman and
   Program Chairman
Karen A. Duncan, Secretary and Co-Editor
Theodore J. Sjoerdsma, Treasurer

Diana Harris, Co-Editor
Ralph E. Lee, Workshops
David E. Game, Local Arrangements
Sylvia Charp, TC 3 Liaison
Richard L. Dobson, AFIPS Headquarters Liaison

Program Committee

John W. Hamblen, Chairman
Richard H. Austing, Vice Chairman and Special Sessions
John McGregor, Paper Review
Bernard Levrat, WCCE '81 Program Chairman

Australia, I.G. Pirie
Austria, H. Schauer
Belgium, R. de Caluwe
Bulgaria, T. Boyanov
Canada, R.S. McLean
Czechoslovakia, L. Uncovsky
Denmark, M. Koch
Federal Republic of Germany,
   R. Gunzenhauser
Finland, L. Fontell
France, J. Hebenstreit
German Democratic Republic, D. Schubert
Hungary, M. Hamori
India, V. Rajaraman
Iraq, Al-Tarafi
Israel, B.Z. Barta

Italy, P. Ercoli
Japan, S. Otsuki
Morocco, M. Najim
Netherlands, D.H. Wolbers
New Zealand, C.R. Boswell
Norway, A. Staupe
Poland, S. Waligorski
South Africa, G. Wiechers
Southeast Asia, S.C. Chan
Spain, R. Portaencasa
Sweden, H. Lawson
Switzerland, R. Morel
United Kingdom, J.L. Alty
United States, S. Charp
Yugoslavia, A. Madzic

TC 3/WG 3.1 Chairman, P. Bollerslev
TC 3/WG 3.2 Chairman, W.F. Atchison
TC 3/WG 3.3 Chairman, R.E.J. Lewis
TC 3/WG 3.4 Chairman, P.G. Raymont
TC 3/WG 3.5 Chairman, F.B. Lovis

WCCE '85 Program Advisory Group

These are individuals who have made oustanding contributions to the use of computers in education.

William F. Atchison
University of Maryland

David H. Ahl
Creative Computing

Judith Edwards Allen
Portland State University

David Bell
Acorn Computers Ltd.

Donald Bitzer
University of Illinois

Kenneth Brumbaugh
MECC - Minnesota

Ron Carruth
Minnesota School District

Kent Curtis
National Science Foundation

Dorothy Derringer
IBM Corporation

Robert Gillespie
Gillespie, Folkner, & Assoc.

William Gruener
Addison-Wesley Publishing Company

A.A.J. Hoffman
Consultant

Dustin Hueston
WICAT

Truman Hunter
IBM Corporation *(retired)*

Glenn Ingram
National Bureau of Standards

Stephen Jobs
Apple Computer

Thomas Kurtz
Dartmouth College

Joseph Lipson
WICAT

Arthur Luehrmann
Computer Literacy

Karl Karlstrom
Prentice-Hall, Inc.

Arthur Melmed
U.S. Department of Education

Andrew Molnar
National Science Foundation

David Moursund
University of Oregon

Lawrence Oliver
National Science Foundation

Richard Otte
National Institute of Education

Jesse Poore
Georgia Institute of Technology

Patrick Suppes
Stanford University

Bruce Thompson
Control Data Corporation

Don Thomsen
SIMS

LIST OF CONTENTS

ACROSS THE CURRICULUM

MATHEMATICS, SCIENCE, AND ENGINEERING EDUCATION

HUMANITIES

NEW TECH, HIGH TECH, AND USING TECHNOLOGY

COMPUTER LANGUAGES, PROBLEM-SOLVING, AND PROGRAMMING

COURSE AND CURRICULA RECOMMENDATIONS

COMPUTER LITERACY

NON-CURRICULAR ASPECTS OF COMPUTING AND EDUCATION

COMPUTERS IN RESEARCH

Computers in Educational Research

Educational Technologies Database Project

FUTURE OF COMPUTING AND EDUCATION

New Directions in Computer Education

Careers in Computing

CLOSING SESSION

Across the Curriculum

COMPUTERS IN EDUCATION, K. Duncan and D. Harris (eds.)
Elsevier Science Publishers B.V. (North-Holland)
©IFIP, 1985

INTEGRATING COMPUTERS INTO THE CURRICULUM--1

Glenn Fisher, Larry Hatfield and Mike Haney

International Council for Computers in Education

Panel participants will discuss successful approaches to using computers in math, science and music classes, K-12. Specific examples of curriculum   of training for implementation will be presented.

In each subject area, the key approach is to identify critical learnings, and then to see how a computer can assist with that objective. This approach has several benefits. Teachers focus on the idea of the computer as another instructional medium, rather than supplant or add to , an already overpacked curriculum. Teachers teach the curriculum they are used to, rather than having to redesign the course to accommodate computers. Teachers think about teaching, rather than about computers. Teachers' fears about computers and their use are reduced by seeing them in familiar patterns. The results are exciting.

Glenn Fisher, Chair
Alameda County Office of Education
Hayward, California

Larry Hatfield
The University of Georgia
Athens, Georgia

The impacts of instructional computing on mathematics education involve shifts in both the subject matter, content and its treatment. Epistemological, psychological, sociological and pedagogical perspective and rationales will be examined. Qualities of effective instructional computing in the mathematics classroom will be identified. Roles of the mathematics teacher, the mathematics student and the computer will be characterized from the viewpoint of multi-usage approaches to instructional computing. Strategies for integrating comprehensive computer use into the school mathematics curriculum will be discussed.

Mike Haney
The Blair Magnet School for Science/Math/
Computer Science
Montgomery County Public Schools, Maryland

If computers are to be used effectively, science teachers must understand their potential and not be enticed by the available packaged software. Teachers must remember that they are experts in science as well as science education. The best uses of computers in science education are those which let the students do science. Are there applications which help a student to formulate questions, design procedures, anticipate problems, carry out procedures, calculate, take measurements, analyze results, draw conclusions, construct models, research literature, reason, etc.? Yes, as long as the priority in science education is that computers should give students more time and resources to do science, and to do it better than was ever before possible. Students can use scientific tools like data bases, data manipulators, and simulators to: practice science in your classroom; make a classroom a lab for sampling, examining and concluding about nature; use statistical techniques which merge science, math and the computer; do research; extend your classroom beyond the school walls; use networks; maintain an in-house data base; and acquire data.

COMPUTERS IN EDUCATION, K. Duncan and D. Harris (eds.)
Elsevier Science Publishers B.V. (North-Holland)
© IFIP, 1985

INTEGRATING COMPUTERS INTO THE CURRICULUM--2

Glenn Fisher, Stephen Marcus, Beverly Hunter and Alan November

International Council for Computers in Education

Panel participants will discuss successful approaches to using computers in writing and social studies classes, K-12. Specific examples of curriculum and of training for implementation will be presented. In each subject area, the key approach is to identify critical learnings, and then to see how a computer can assist with that objective. This approach has several benefits. Teachers focus on the idea of the computer as another instructional medium, rather than as a daunting technical device to be mastered. Computers assist with, rather than supplant or add to , an already overpacked curriculum. Teachers teach the curriculum they are used to, rather than having to redesign the course to accommodate computers. Teachers think about teaching, rather than about computers. Teachers' fears about computers and their use are reduced by seeing them in familiar patterns. The results are exciting.

Glenn Fisher, Chair
Alameda County Office of Education
Hayward, California

Stephen Marcus
South Coast Writing Project
University of California at
  Santa Barbara

The usual approach to computer use in writing is to teach word processing. Preliminary research results indicate that, while students write more when using a word processor, they do not write better. When viewed from a curriculum perspective, as opposed to a computer perspective, this is not surprising--students aren't taught writing skills, but computer skills! The additional writing time is only partially spent in additional editing. The remainder is spent in formatting, which has no effect on content. When the focus is shifted to the writing curriculum, we can identify key skills and ideas and look at how computers (and word processors) can help with those skills. Specific lessons for using computers to teach writing will be discussed.

Beverly Hunter
Targeted Learning Corporation
Amissville, Virginia

In the United States, the three major areas of social studies curriculum include knowledge, democratic values and skills. The knowledge base is drawn from history, geography, government, law, anthropology, sociology, psychology, humanities and science--a vast amount of information. The skills move from acquiring information, to organizing, using and evaluating information, to participating effectively in society. Students now can use computer-based tools for data management, communications, data analysis and simulation, all of which directly support the goals of social studies. The tools enable students to become active researchers and participants who take control of information, rather than passive receivers of knowledge. This presentation will show examples of data base activities which illustrate the above points.

Alan November
Lexington Public Schools and Professional
  Development with Computers
Middleton, Massachusetts

I will present an overview of how to plan for the training of teachers in applying data bases, spreadsheets and word processing to the existing curriculum. Outlines, print materials, pre-designed disks and a practical list of DOs and Don'ts will be included.

COMPUTERS IN EDUCATION, K. Duncan and D. Harris (eds.)
Elsevier Science Publishers B.V. (North-Holland)
©IFIP, 1985

4

THE SECOND NATIONAL U.S. SURVEY OF INSTRUCTIONAL USES OF SCHOOL COMPUTERS

Henry Jay Becker, Johns Hopkins University, presenter
David Moursund, University of Oregon, session chairman

This session is devoted to a single presentation followed by audience questions. The subject is the Second National Survey of Instructional Uses of School Computers, conducted this past Spring in the United States at Johns Hopkins University. The presentation will provide the first release of data from the survey, and a discussion of the kinds of data to be made available in the coming months. Survey materials will be distributed.

A national survey, employing a probability sample of more than 2,300 U.S. elementary and secondary schools, gathered information from principals and more than 6,000 teachers in a complex design that will enable highly detailed descriptions and analyses to be conducted about how teachers of different grade levels and subjects are using computers in their teaching. The survey, conducted for the National Center for Education Statistics and the National Institute of Education by the Center for Social Organization of Schools at Johns Hopkins, is a follow-up to their 1983 survey. It was fielded between Febraury and May of this year.

This presentation is the first major discussion of the survey's results and will provide general information about the grade-level, subject-matter, and primary focus of teachers' instructional use patterns. Data from the survey will show how teacher involvement with computers differs according to school-level characteristics.

The presentation will include information about the kinds of descriptions and analyses that will be forthcoming from the survey data. Attendees will be provided with copies of some of the survey materials used in the study.

COMPUTERS IN EDUCATION, K. Duncan and D. Harris (eds.)
Elsevier Science Publishers B.V. (North-Holland)
© IFIP, 1985

TEACHING INFORMATICS IN HIGH SCHOOLS: A FRENCH EXPERIMENT

Jacques J. Arsac

Ecole Normale Superieure
Paris, France

This paper deals with the French experiment about optional teaching of
informatics in high schools started in 1981. The pedagogical objectives
are presented. Four ways of teaching programming are described, and
their fitness to pedagogical objectives discussed: empirical
programming, programming by schemas, projects, programming by
assertions. The last one has been used for teacher training in Paris,
and adapted to students in high schools in Paris. First results and
elements of evaluation are given.

1. THE FRENCH EXPERIMENT

In 1970, a symposium held in Sèvres,
France [7] recommended the introduction
of computer science in high schools. It
was said that children should run their
own programs on computers. This
activity would develop children's
algorithmic organizational and
operational aptitudes.

Ten years later, J. C. Simon presented a
report to the French government [8] on
computers and education. He also
recommended the introduction of
informatics in schools as a discipline.
The ministry of education decided to
follow that recommendation, at least to
a certain extent. An optional teaching
of informatics was started in twelve
French high schools in 1981, and is now
extended to some forty high schools. I
have been in charge of teacher training
in Paris, and of supporting their action
since 1981. I would like to present
here this experiment, and give some
indication on the results, although it
is too early for any precise evaluation.

2. PEDAGOGICAL OBJECTIVES

It is commonly agreed [7] that
programming should not be taught in high
schools for professional reasons.
Vocational training is now being given
in universities or in specialized
schools without any need for special
preparation in secondary school.
Nevertheless, jobs are rapidly changing
through the impact of new technologies,
primarily computer science. There is an
urgent need for an easy adaptation to
these technologies in a world of
underemployment. It may be important
for people to know something of

informatics even if they do not attend a
university.

More serious is the fact that the
informatization of society is a cultural
mutation. It affects our way of living,
but also our way of thinking. For
instance, instead of memorization, we
can query data bases. This is a deep
change which will certainly affect
education. Computer science is now a
part of the scientific culture, and it
is not desirable that future citizens be
illiterate in this domain. As he may
not attend a university, something of
computer science has to be taught in
schools. But this is not necessarily
programming [9].

The symposium in Sèvres [7] emphasized
the abilities developed by practicing
programming. There is now a general
agreement on the fact that programming
is mainly problem solving [10]. Thus,
teaching programming must develop
children's aptitudes to solve problems.
We propose to children concrete
situations in which the computer helps
to find the solution. The first
children's activity is reading a text,
and formulating or specifying a problem.
Then, they must analyze it and find a
way to solve it (an algorithm).
Finally, the algorithm is coded in a
programming language. All those steps
should be performed in a rational way,
so that children will be able to say how
their program works, and why it solves
the problem. Nevertheless, errors may
occur in the program, or may be made
while typing it on a keyboard. Children
must be able to detect and correct these
errors.

It is clear that those activities are

not the exclusive privilege of informatics. In humanities, children have to read and analyze texts. In mathematics, they have to solve problems in a rational way. We do not pretend to replace those disciplines, or even to succeed where they may have failed. It only happens that computers look interesting for a lot of children, who have a strong motivation to use them. Moreover, computer science is more concrete than mathematics. It can help children allergic to mathematics to develop problem solving abilities, and maybe to lose their aversion to mathematics. This is the context in which the French optional teaching of informatics in high schools has been developed. But there are several ways to teach programming. Some of them will be presented here, and their fitness to pedagogical objectives discussed. We restrict ourselves to imperative programming. To some extent, LOGO can be considered as an imperative language, and the use of recursion is of the same order as in PASCAL-like languages. We do not have enough experience with the use of object oriented languages [4] or logic programming [6] to say if they fit the above objectives, or what kind of objectives may be reached through teaching them.

3.   EMPIRICAL PROGRAMMING

This method was extensively used ten years ago. The programmer draws a flowchart to represent the analysis of the problem, then he codes it into an appropriate language. The course consists merely in presenting flowcharts, then describing a programming language (syntax, semantics). Several books about this kind of teaching have been published: Programming in FORTRAN, COBOL, BASIC, etc... The flowchart is a graphical representation of the sequence of actions in the program. It has the same meaning as the program, but puts the emphasis on the GOTO's. With this method, it is very difficult to write a correct program directly, and so the role of testing and debugging is essential. Program documentation may be difficult.

Considering the pedagogical objectives mentioned in section 2, this method should not be used. Nothing is done to help children to develop their problem-solving ability. This method insists on organizing and coding an algorithm, but says nothing on how to create it. As far as problem solving is considered, children are self-taught. Some of them

have a very good natural aptitude to discover a strategy to solve a given problem: they get very good results with computers. We hear a little too much about these little geniuses in the media. Some indications in France show that about 15% of the children taught this way can make good use of a computer. The other 85% give up more or less rapidly. It has been said that programming is interesting for children because it changes the relationship between children and teachers, and because errors are not penalized faults. Children need success to persevere.

It has also been said that this method is good for developing children's creativity. They are given a tool, and nothing else, and so their natural talent can express itself and grow freely. But there is a confusion between spontaneity and creativity. Most children need some guidance, some pedagogical support before being able to create a new algorithm by themselves. Let us be clear: we do not consider the ability of children to draw pictures on a screen with a computer as problem solving, unless they are explicitly asked to draw a non-trivial picture defined by an algorithm. Moreover, this method puts the accent on a particular language, which may be a source of trouble when a different language is needed or imposed.

4.   PROGRAMMING BY SCHEMAS

This method is derived from so called structure programming [5]. "Fundamental programming notions" are presented:

- sequential composition of statements
- alternative composition
     IF...THEN....ELSE....FI
- repetitive composition
     WHILE...DO....OD

Examples of algorithms using these control structures are given. Main data types in programming languages are described (integer, real, boolean, character), and also main data structures (arrays, files). Fundamental algorithms for these types or structures are given.

Children get a catalogue of predefined schemas. They learn how to translate them in an actual language [1]. To solve a given problem, they have to split it into smaller parts, through top-down programming. The simpler problems are solved using the general schemas of the catalogue. The catalogue is wide enough to cover most of the practical applications. When a problem cannot be solved this way, it is assumed that some ability to solve new problems has been gained through familiarity with known solutions for the problems of the catalogue.

This method fits better our pedagogical objectives. It limits the part of invention so that even those children without large imaginations can write programs. Instead of a 15% success rate with the empirical method, up to 70% has been observed in several French high schools. The aptitude to decompose a problem into smaller ones is essential (it is the application of Descartes's principle to computer science). Recognizing a given schema in an actual problem is also a good exercise, introducing abstraction.

Nevertheless, I personally consider that this method reduces children's creativity too much: they do not look for the solution of a problem, they look in a catalogue for a predefined solution. They do not get any support for solving problems outside the range of the catalogue. Extending this one is not a solution: if the catalogue is too wide, it cannot be memorized, and solving a problem becomes too difficult. The accent is not put on a specific language, which is a good thing, but rather on a schematic one in which the schemas are written. But often, this language looks like PASCAL, and many courses along this line were in fact PASCAL courses.

5. TEACHING BY PROJECTS

A difficulty of the previous method is that a relatively large part of the catalogue must be presented before children will be able to solve their own problems. They lack motivation to consider attentively the various schemas. A way to avoid this is to have children develop projects they have personally chosen. During the analysis, subproblems appear which can be solved using basic notions or schemas. These notions or schemas are given as an answer to an actual problem, and with better understanding by children.

The only difficulty is that the teacher loses control of pedagogical progress. Either the project is chosen by the teacher to guarantee a good progress (this is not a simple affair), and it is not obvious that children will accept this project, and all the benefit of the method is lost. Or the project is really chosen by children, likely with some guidance of the teacher, or in a

catalogue proposed by him. He must be prepared to face difficulties in random order.

We do not have significant evaluation of this method. Teachers in Rennes (France) tried it three years ago and more or less gave it up. To me, it is an indication that we have not yet mastered this method (at least with freely chosen large projects). It must be emphasized that children have some genius for choosing spontaneously difficult projects: they all want to start with a master's level chess player program.

6. TEACHING BY ASSERTION

Imperative languages are based on the assignment statement, written in PASCAL

$$I := I + 1$$

It describes the modification to be performed on a given variable (here, I is incremented by 1). Thus, an imperative program describes the sequence of transformations which will modify the situation of variables from the initial situation, that of data, to the final one, that of results. This is very different from functional programming which defines functions by composition of primitive or previously built functions, and of logic programming which describes relations between data and results, but says nothing of the way to change situations from the initial one to the final one.

The sequence of transformations described by an imperative program may be difficult to read, in the sense that nothing is said about the situations generated by these transformations. They have to be deduced from the semantics of statements: it is the reason why proving programs with assignments is so difficult. But this is only a consequence of our poor programming methods.

The sequence of actions described in a program should not be written according to some magic "creative" process. The programmer knows the initial and the final situations, specified in the problem. The only thing he has to invent is a sequence of situations between the initial and final ones. The actions needed to go from one situation to the next are generally obvious. Thus, creating a program is inventing a sequence of situations. This is true even for loops. There is in any loop a general situation which is encountered each time the loop is repeated. It

gives a very general guide for loop
design. Let us illustrate this on a
small example.

Let a[n] be an array of n elements. To
find the greatest element of a, we start
with proposing a general situation
according a standard way: part of the
work has been done. We are asked to
find the maximum of n elements: let us
assume that we have found the maximum of
the i first elements:

     a[k] is the greatest of a[1], a[2],
... a[i]

This is the creative step.

Now, we look for a condition under which
the problem is solved. We look for the
maximum of n elements, and we know the
maximum of i elements. It is finished
if i = n. Otherwise there are still
elements in the vector to be considered.

i is changed into i + 1. A new element
is introduced, which may change the
situation. If it is less or equal to
the previous maximum a[k], nothing is
changed, and the general situation is
still true. If not, then a[i] is the
new maximum, and k must be redefined as
i. We have thus a BASIC loop.

110 REM A(K) is the max of i first elem.

120 IF I = N THEN 200

130 LET I = I + 1

140 IF A(I) <= A(K) THEN 110

150 LET K = I

160 GO TO 110

200 REM A(K) is the max of the n elem.

If we enter line 110 with I and K such
that A(K) is the maximum of the I first
elements of A, I < = N, then it is clear
that we shall arrive at line 200 with
the wanted result. The only thing to do
is to invent an initial situation such
that this assertion is true, without
having too much work to do. If we
consider only the first element of A, we
do not have to look for the maximum: it
is the maximum. Thus, we can start with
I = 1 and K = 1, giving the
initialization of the loop

100 LET K = 1 : LET I = 1

Using this method, the successive steps
to build a loop are:

- to propose a general (invariant)
  situation, frequently like "part of
  the work has been done"
- to look for conditions under which the
  result is obtained
- when it is not finished, to advance
  towards the solution, and reach back
  the general situation
- to look for initial values such that
  the general situation be true, without
  too many computations.

This is wholly independent of the
programming language, and can be
implemented even with GOTO's (as the
example given here in BASIC). It is
more easily implemented in a language
with the DO....EXIT...OD loop statement:

```
    k := 1 ; i := 1;

    DO
      IF i = n THEN EXIT FI

      i := i + 1

      IF a[i] > a[k] THEN k :=i FI

    OD
```

This particular loop could have been
written using the WHILE statement,
because completion condition was given
by a single test. It is not the most
general case. This is the reason why
the WHILE loop is not the best fitted
for this method of loop design.

7. EXPERIMENTS WITH THIS METHOD

This method has been taught to several
teachers at Paris high schools in 1981.
They have adapted it to children, then
taught it in four high schools in Paris
from 1981 to 1984. Books illustrating
this method have been published [2]. I
have helped those teachers during these
years and visited their classes.

The method has not been presented in a
formal way. Teaching is done by
example, the accent being put on the way
in which the various problems are
solved. During the first exercises
performed by children, the teachers help
them by questions: "What general
situation can you suggest? Is it
finished? How can we go further..."
The method is gained by osmosis. Thus,
it is well accepted. Only some children
having started with the empirical method
(either in clubs, or at home) are
puzzled by this method. They feel that
they could find the solution more
rapidly, which is clearly true for the
first examples. More or less rapidly,
it happens that they do not succeed with

the empirical method, when other children supposed to be less clever write a correct program.

The optional informatics classes start in tenth grade. 60% of the children continue in the eleventh grade, but some external factors limit this number. Because a result is obtained with teaching by schemas, it means only that these methods have comparable success, far better than the empirical method.

In April 1984 I proposed an examination of the children in the optional classes in Paris. They were asked to form a character string representing the negation of a predicate given by another character string, with rules given in the exercise. The results have been extremely good. Although children had not had access to computers, I got a lot of correct answers, some of them using recursion. It means that most of the children master top-down programming correctly, that they are able to write correct programs from the first try. I did not take into account obvious syntactic errors, which would have been easily detected by a compiler, and corrected.

For the rest, I can only make some guesses. The method of assertion is less related to a specific programming language than any other. It is better fitted to our pedagogical goals: teach to children how to solve problems, not a programming language. Because the accent is put on situations rather than on actions, I think that this is good preparation for problem solving in a wider domain: children are trained to analyze situations, and to derive action from situation analysis. Very likely, children have to be more creative than when using catalogue of schemas. It could be an impediment for those with limited imagination of intuition. The creation of a loop through well defined steps is a help for them, allowing top-down programming to operate inside a single loop. I have been surprised to see what children in high schools are doing, and the results of the examination mentioned above.

8. CONCLUSIONS

Since our pedagogical objectives were to develop children's creativity and their aptitudes for analyzing and solving problems, it is very difficult to make any precise evaluation. Considering the kinds of activities they perform in computer classes, it seems impossible that part of these objectives should not be reached. It is clear that the

courses are well accepted, but this is not a positive observation: with the strong motivation of today's children for computers, even the worst teacher will interest them. What is more significant is that more than 60% of the children are interested and efficient. This is a higher ratio than with empirical programming.

We are trying to avoid teaching a programming language. We are insisting on the necessity of mastering by intelligence the process of programming: a child must know why his program works. These objectives were developed by Nicolas Boileau in his "Art Poétique" (1674).

Then cherish reason: may all your
                                writings
Only from reason derive lustre and price

He who never restrained himself
                never knew how to write

Often an evil feared
            leads to a worse one still

I try not to be long
            and I become obscure

There are some minds
                whose gloomy thoughts

Are always wrapped in a thick cloud:

The light of reason couldn't pierce them

So before you write learn how to think

What is clearly conceived
                    is clearly worded

And the words to say it come out easily

Hasten tardily and without losing heart

Twenty times on the loom
                start your work again

I do completely agree with Boileau's maxims. This method of teaching programming can only complement and enhance the teaching of any other discipline: teach children how to think!

Bibliography

[1] Autebert J.M., Beauquier J, Boasson L Kott L., L'informatique au lycée (Technique et vulg., Paris, 1980)

[2] Arsac-Mondou O., Bourgeois C., Gourtay M., Premièr livre de programmation (Cedic-Nathan, Paris, 1982)

[3] Arsac J., premières leçons de
    programmation (Cedic-Nathan, Paris
    1980)

[4] Bestougeff H., object oriented
    languages, a better way to teach
    programming, in Griffiths M. and
    Tagg E.D., the role of programming
    in teaching informatics (North
    Holland, Amsterdam, 1984)

[5] Dijkstra E.D., Structured
    programming (Academic Press, London,
    1972)

[6] Ennals R., The importance of Prolog
    in Griffiths M. and Tagg E.D., the
    role of programming in teaching
    informatics (North Holland,
    Amsterdam, 1984)

[7] Gass J.R., L'enseignement de
    l'informatique à l'école secondaire
    (publications de l'OCDE, Paris,
    1971)

[8] Simon J.C., l'éducation et
    l'informatisation de la société (la
    documentation française, Paris,
    1980)

[9] Hebenstreit J., Teaching programming
    to everybody: Why? to whom? What?
    in Griffith M. and Tagg E.D. the
    role of programming in teaching
    informatics (North Holland,
    Amsterdam, 1984)

[10] Griffiths M. and Tagg E.D., the
     role of programming in teaching
     informatics (North Holland,
     Amsterdam, 1984)

COMPUTERS IN EDUCATION, K. Duncan and D. Harris (eds.)
Elsevier Science Publishers B.V. (North-Holland)
© IFIP, 1985

A PROJECT TO INTRODUCE THE USE OF MICROCOMPUTERS IN THE FORMATION OF SCIENCE
TEACHERS AT THE PONTIFICAL CATHOLIC UNIVERSITY OF
MINAS GERAIS, BRAZIL
SIMÃO PEDRO PINTO MARINHO

Departamento de Ciências Biológicas
Pontifícia Universidade Católica de Minas Gerais
30.000 - Belo Horizonte/MG - Brasil

Looking for improvement on science teaching, through the better training of science teachers, and taking into account the importance of microcomputers in science teaching and learning, the Department of Biological Sciences of the PUC-MG is developing a project with a nucleus for science teaching applying informatics with the objectives of (a) organization of multidisciplinary teams for developing and adapting software to science teaching,(b) implanting the disciplines Logic of Programming Structure and Programming Language for Microcomputers and progressive introduction of more frequent use of microcomputers in other disciplines of the science teachers undergraduate program and (c) developing of science teachers-training programs for the use of microcomputers.

1. SOME GENERAL CONSIDERATIONS

In 1980 and 1981, SEI, MEC and CNPq/SEPLAN promoted two national seminars on informatics in Education with the objective of debating and looking into the position of Brazilian academic and scientific communities concerning the use of computer as an auxilliary tool in the process of teaching and learning (20).

With the purpose of introducing experimental research for the use of computers in education , looking for new solutions for our educational needs, SEI, MEC and CNPq/SEPLAN created,in 1983, the EDUCOM PROGRAM (4) with the general objective of encouraging the development of multi-disciplinary research in the use of informatics in the process of teaching and learning, through specific objectives :

a. establishing a nucleus for research and development of informatics in education;

b. establishing pilot centers in institutions with recognized capability in science and technology in the areas of informatics and education;

c. developing human resources needed to develop and implement the EDUCOM program in view of the requirements of the sector of educational informatics;

d. to follow up and to evaluate experiences developed in the pilot center created by the program;

e. to disseminate the results produced in those pilot centers.

The use of computers in education, with the use of educational programs developed by Brazilian teams, is one of the aims of MEC in establishing an informatics policy in education, culture and sports (3).

In Brazil, with the support of government's market reserve policy, there is a growing industry of computers, with a growing use, as seen in table I.
Of those computers, 80% are micro and mini-computers, produced by Brazilian enterprises.

YEAR	COMPUTERS IN USE	BRAZILIAN PARTICIPATION	VALUE (*)	BRAZILIAN PARTICIPATION
1980	8.844	17%	1.65	7%
1981	14.249	42%	2.14	14%
1982	23.000	50%	2.50	20%

(*) in US$ 1 million

TABLE I   (source: SEI)

However, we have a serious lack of educational (and other) software, a fact that makes the better implementation of this resource in our schools difficult. There are some emerging groups, mainly linked to universities, starting to develop science teaching software (1,14,18).

2. MICROCOMPUTERS IN BRAZILIAN SCHOOLS

As pointed out before (7), there is in Brazil a determination to introduce in our country,in the context of more developed nations, the use of the computer as an auxilliary tool in the process of teaching and learning. However,there is yet much discussion about this use, with its social, economic, psychological and other implications.
Actually, with the results of our economic policy being a large external debt, there is a great lack of funds for education. The resources

for the public schools, at all levels, are insufficient to support their normal operation and this situation is remembered by those who did not agree with the introduction of microcomputers in the schools. Many other reasons are also cited for not introducing this equipment in Brazilian schools.

On the other hand, there are groups that agree with this introduction for many reasons.

We can see in the experiences of other countries that the introduction of this educational resource requires a great investment. The greatest investment is made, however, in the training of adequate resources (20), certainly a good investment.

We think that the current lacks may not justify not introducing microcomputers in our schools , unless we accept the risk of creating problems for the future generations (11).

In Brazil, the use of microcomputers in the schools is a new adventure. They are being used just in some secondary schools belonging to private enterprises, those attended by the students coming from the highest social levels. This is too a critical situation, since we run the risk of accentuating, by the use of microcomputers, the existing social inequality, increasing a serious social problem, when the microcomputers are thought of as allowing the possibility of democratization in the school.

In those schools, however, and we see this as an subutilization of the machine, the microcomputer is being used mainly to introduce learners to the BASIC language, and not as an auxilliary tool to make learning more effective.

The more efficient use of microcomputers in Brazilian schools depends upon adequate software and trained human resources, these being achieved by the introduction of microcomputers in the training of new teachers and adequate teacher-training programs (12).

3. SCIENCE TEACHING IN BRAZIL

The main problems of science teaching in Brazil are not recent.The reasons for the increase of those problems are that laboratories are not adequate (when they exist) and that the science teachers are not prepared despite some(organized or not) efforts to introduce modern science teaching through laboratory classes that could allow the direct contact of the learners with its object of study (17).

Recently, the Federal Government created the PADCT, a program to support scientific and technological development as an instrument of execution of a national policy of science and technology (5).

EDUCATION FOR SCIENCE is one of the subprograms of PADCT (5), to be developed by CAPES/MEC. This subprogram has the objective of stimulating the implementation of new strategies and consolidating the current effective initiatives, with the aim of improving science and mathematics teaching through the development of a project with the following objectives :

a. identifying, training and supporting leadership at all school levels to ensure that the strategies and activities directed toward improving science teaching can have effects in the short and medium terms, while ensuring the continuity, diffusion and multiplication of realized efforts;

b. improving science and mathematics teaching mainly in the elementary school;

c. improving the training of science and mathematics teachers;

d. promoting the search for local solutions to improving science and mathematics teaching, stimulating the adaptation of these disciplines to the local conditions and to the level of the learners and an effective local coordination of the personal and institutional initiatives that contribute to improving science and mathematics teaching;

e. stimulating research and implementation of new methodologies to improve science and mathematics teaching.

This project must reach the proposed objectives through activities distributed in four areas :

1. research in science teaching : development of curricula and the implementation of pilot programs;

2. training of science and mathematics teachers;

3. science and mathematics teachers' - training programs in the schools;

4. extracurricular and out of school activities and science dissemination to the comunity.

4. MICROCOMPUTERS AND SCIENCE TEACHING

The knowledge of scientific method is fundamental to science teaching and requires that the learners participate in all the processes which characterize this method. The scientific method is a continuous alternation of reflections and experimentations (5).   To formulate questions, to propose and to test solutions for those questions, to separate complex problems in some more simple problems are common steps in scientific activity. Similarly, those are steps in the use of microcomputers, mainly in structured programming.Thus we think that computers may be useful in dealing adequately with scientific method. They require objectivity, capacity to reach decisions and creativeness in solving problems, abilities required in the scientific method.

The use of computers is important for the better development of creativity, through "solving problems" through programming. There are some reports that indicate that programming experiences lead to a better ability to solve problems (24). The capacity of solving problems is very important step in building a scientific mentality (15,19).

Microcomputers bring to classrooms simulations (9,10,16,24) developing and testing of models, allowing, as an auxilliary resource, a phenomenological approach, very important to materialize the relation : observation/ experimentation/theory.

Microcomputers have a significant pedagogic value in science teaching (2) and, we think, an important role in an urgent renovation on science teaching in Brazil.

5. THE TEACHERS

The use of microcomputers in Brazilian schools is very recent and there is a shortage of qualified teachers for their use, beyond the fact that their need is not clearly perceived. The introduction of microcomputers in schools requires qualified teachers (15), which is seen as a social and not only technological problem (20). We must remember too that the teachers will be responsable for developing educational software (6,20,21).

We think that the teacher-training programs for the use of microcomputers in the schools must not use only the teaching of programming languages and the demonstration of several uses of the machine (12).

The constant use of microcomputers in the schools brings deep changes in the process of teaching and learning, because it requires the compatibility of a sophisticated technology with a school level "workmanship" (19). Then, we think that the implementation of this new educational resource must rise from a deep debate about when, where and how to introduce it.

Our schools are not in a condition to support this introduction for many reasons, including the reactions of the teachers. They are conservative in outlook – and not only in Brazil (24) – and they have the tendency to keep their customs (13,22) although they always manifest a desire to change (23).

The teachers must be aware of the impact on students and on the process of teaching and learning and by this we think that the teachers' training for using microcomputers must take into account :

a. carrying them to a wide discussion about all aspects that involve the implementation of the microcomputers in schools, with its social, psychological, educational and other implications. The teachers must discuss the positive and negative aspects of this implementation and thus not see the computer as being imposed from above;

b. accentuating and exemplifying the auxilliary role of microcomputers in the process of teaching and learning, showing that it is not an end in itself;

c. allowing the critical analysis of better uses of microcomputers in education, through the knowledge of several uses, the question of software adjustment and portability and the cost/efficiency relation (15);

d. allowing the knowledge of programming languages, basic to the developing of educational software;

e. introducing some knowledge about hardware , giving some critical base in order to aid the choice for the best equipment for educational purposes;

f. more frequent use of microcomputers in the training of the teachers; avoiding the sporadic use of the machine;

g. critical use of educational software, including imported software, and a concrete analysis of their applicability and efficiency.

6. THE PROJECT

The DCB/PUC-MG decided to submit to CAPES/MEC a project in accordance with the subprogram Education for Science, of PADCT, taking into account its role in training science teachers. This project means the implementation of a nucleus for science teaching through informatics with the general objectives of :

a. progressive implementation of the regular use of microcomputers in our Biological Sciences licentiateship, both through specific disciplines (Logic of Programming Structure and Programming Languages for Micro-computers)and as a tool in other disciplines of the undergraduate program;

b. developing, adapting and evaluating educational software applied to science teaching;

c. developing science teachers-training programs in the schools.

The implementation and the action of the nucleus follow the schedule seen in Table II.

There is a considerable demand for portability

of software, so that the programs written for one
machine may be used on another. However, the
features of microcomputers are sufficiently
different to inhibit this portability.

We have in Brazil many different microcomputers
being bought and used in the schools. In our
nucleus we will use several types of microcomputers, all made in Brazil, that will allow
the adaptation of some software (some aspects as
graphic resolution, colors, etc. inhibit very
much the complete adaptation and portability)for
different machines.

We think that in three years we will have the
nucleus of science teachers-training program
using educational software developed and
adapted by our multidisciplinary teams.

We know that microcomputers will change in
Brazil, as in other nations, education - and
fast. Teachers and computer professionals must
work closely together to ensure that these
changes that are coming are for the better.

7. REFERENCES

1. ARGUELLO, C.A. 1984. Informática no ensino
   de Física. Cienc.Cult.,36(7)sup.:383.

2. BAYLOR, H.H. et alii. 1966. Computer
   simulation techniques. New York, Willey.

3. BRASIL. Ministério da Educação e Cultura.Se-
   cretaria Geral.Secretaria de Informática.
   1983. Diretrizes para o estabelecimento de u
   ma política de informática no setor educação,
   cultura e desportos. Brasília, MEC/SEINF.11p.

4. ____. Secretaria Especial de Informática.Mi-
   nistério Educação e Cultura. Conselho Nacional Desenvolvimento Científico e Tecnológico.
   Financiadora de Estudos e Projetos. 1983.
   Projeto EDUCOM. Brasília, SEI. 25p.

5. ____. Secretaria do PADCT. 1984. Informe
   PADCT. Brasília, PADCT. 10p.

6. GRAJEW, J. 1982. A microinformática e o futu
   ro da educação no Brasil. MicroSistemas, 10:
   32-35.

7. JÁBER, F. 1981. O futuro e a educação. Micro
   Sistemas, 2:8-10.

8. KLEIN, S.P. 1983. O desafio à educação fren-
   te ao avanço tecnológico. Tecnol.Educ., 52:
   44-46.

9. MARINHO, S.P.P. 1984. Uma aula sobre circui-
   tos elétricos. MicroSistemas, 30:72-74.

10. ____. Simulation in ZX-81. Eletric circuits
    I. (in the press)

11. ____. Microcomputador, um novo recurso na es
    cola (in the press).

12. ____. O microcomputador na escola e a forma-
    ção de professores (in the press).

13. MILLER, I. 1983. Os micros estão chegando.
    Brasília. MEC/SEINF. 4p.

14. NARDI, R. & JURAITIS, K.R. 1984. Tópicos de
    Física Básica: a instrução programada no mi-
    crocomputador. Cienc.Cult., 36(7)sup.:394.

15. OLIVEIRA, J.C.A. 1983. O computador como
    tecnologia educacional. Tecnol.Educ., 52:
    13-19.

16. PIAZZI, P. 1982. Aula de Física no TK-82C.
    MicroSistemas,12:30-31.

17. RAW, I. An effort to improve science
    education in Brazil. Apud: KRASILCHIK, M.
    Inovação no ensino de Ciências. In: GARCIA,
    W.E., ed. Inovação educacional no Brasil ;
    problemas e perspectivas. São Paulo,Cortez/
    Autores Associados, 1980. p.164-80.

18. RIBEIRO, A.M. 1984. Implantação na UFMG de
    um centro piloto de informática na educa -
    ção. Cienc.Cult., 36(7)sup.:395.

19. RIPPER, A.V. 1983. O computador chega à es-
    cola.Para que ? Tecnol.Educ., 52:40-43.

20. SEMINÁRIO NACIONAL DE INFORMÁTICA 1 E 2.
    Brasília e Salvador, 1981 e 1982. Anais.
    Brasília? SEI.

21. SOUZA,H.G. 1983. Informática na educação e
    ensino de informática : algumas questões.
    Em Aberto, 2(17):1-18.

22. STURDIVANT, P. 1983. Microcomputadores na
    escola. In:MEC/SEINF, ed. Informática e edu
    cação. Brasília, MEC/SEINF. p,25-30.

23. TAGLIEBER, J.E. & MAIA, I.R.R. 1979. Uma ex
    periência de ensino integrado. Educ.brasil.,
    3:247-55.

24. WAKER, P. 1982. Computer-assisted learning
    in the primary schools : now and in the
    near future. In : SACCE, Stellenbosch, 1982.
    Procedings. Stellenbosch(RSA), Steering
    Committee SACCE'82. p.525-33.

25. WEATHERALL, M. 1970. Método científico. São
    Paulo, EDUSP/Polígono. 282p.

8. ABBREVIATIONS

CAPES/MEC	- Coordination for improvement of Higher Education Personnal
CNPq/SEPLAN	- National Council for Scientific and Technological Development. President of Republic's Planning Secretariat
DCB/PUC-MG	- Department of Biological Sciences Pontifical Catholic University/MG
FINEP/SEPLAN	- Finance of Studies and Projects
MEC	- Ministry Education and Culture
NIEC/PUC-MG	- Nucleus for Science Teaching Applied informatics
PADCT	- Scientific and Technological Development Support program
PUC-MG	- Pontifical Catholic University/MG
SEI	- Special Informatics Secretariat

TABLE II
the chronogram of the nucleus

GOALS	STEPS
1. implantation of the nucleus	1. definition and adaptation of the physical area (in the campus of PUC-MG) for the instalation of the nucleus 2. buying and instalation of equipment (CPU, video terminals, disk drives, cassete recorders, printers)
2. activation of the nucleus	3. organization of teachers of PUC-MG in a group to discuss the questions that surround the introduction of computer in the school 4. training of teachers and some students of Department of Biological Sciences (PUC-MG) in logic of programming structure and BASIC language 5. organization of a multidisciplinary team (with teachers and students trained in step 4) to developing, adapting and evaluating of software to be used in science and biology teaching, in the secondary schools, colleges and universities 6. training of teachers of the Biological Sciences Licentiate ship for the regular use of microcomputers in their disciplines 7. evaluating of developed/adapted software in real condition of teaching 8. revision of tested software, if necessary, to ensure its success with many types of uses
3. the nucleus' team working together with science teachers in the schools	9. organization of seminars, lectures and other strategies to initiate the science teachers in the use of microcomputers in the schools, through a deep discussion about all the implications of this implementation 10. science teachers interessed in the use of microcomputers will be organized in groups to discuss this implementation and to follow up experiences in this use 11. training of science teachers in logic of programming structure and BASIC language

COMPUTERS IN EDUCATION, K. Duncan and D. Harris (eds.)
Elsevier Science Publishers B.V. (North-Holland)
© IFIP, 1985

ALPHA PROJECT: A PILOT PROJECT FOR THE INTEGRATION OF INFORMATION TECHNOLOGY IN THE
NATIONAL SECONDARY SCHOOL EDUCATIONAL SYSTEM IN URUGUAY

Jorge Grunberg   and Alberto Bolaña

COMPUTING CENTER
ORT INSTITUTE OF TECHNOLOGY
Cuareim 1451-Montevideo-Uruguay

The Alpha project is being implemented through a technical cooperation agreement
between ORT and the Ministry of Education of Uruguay, financial backing being provided
by IBM Uruguay. The main aim is the progressive and planned integration of information
technology into the secondary school educational system.
The operation is based in a selected state-run secondary school covering computer
literacy courses for students and teachers, and the development of educational software.
This paper describes the technical and pedagogical feasibility analysis, the operating
structure as well as strategic and operational objectives.

1. INTRODUCTION

This project was code named "ALPHA" after the
Spanish translation of "computer literacy"[1],
even though its actual content and purpose
exceeds the computer literacy issue.

The central purpose of this project is the
progressive and planned integration of information technology into the secondary school
educational system in Uruguay.
The field for development of the project is the
secondary school educational system existing in
our country, Republica Oriental del Uruguay.

Uruguay is a Latin American country, with a
population of 3.5 million, and 170.000 sq.km or
5 times the size of Holland.
With a long tradition of educational excellence,
its conservative attitude has made rather slow
the process of modernization of educational
methods and content.
Main characteristics of this system are the
following:

- A highly centralized planning of educational
  policy
- Illiteracy rate under 5%
- State-run free-of-charge public education in
  the Primary, Secondary and Tertiary levels
- Unrestricted access to the University of
  Uruguay
- Spanish as official language within the whole
  country
- An approximate number of 125.000 students
  taking secondary level studies (12 to 17 years)
  in 250 institutions (80% of these students are
  enrolled in state-run schools).

The Primary Education Cycle lasts six years;the
Secondary Cycle comprises a basic general period
(duration three years) and a higher specific
period, preparatory for the University, either
technical (duration four years) or general
(duration three years).

This project has been designed by WORLD ORT
UNION, a private, non-profit international
organization, dealing in technical education
and pedagogical research, founded in 1880,with
a student population of 100.000 a year and
operations in fifty-four countries all over the
world.

Carrying out the project is "Instituto Tecnolo-
gico ORT Uruguay", the largest private teaching
institution in the country dealing in technical
education, founded in 1949 with an annual
student population of 3.500. Its intramural
operations comprise tertiary level courses in
Computer Science and Electronics, together with
Pre-University courses in Electronics, Science
and Business Administration.
Extramural operations comprise technical cooperation and development of Joint projects,carried
out with both state-run and private organizations; one of these projects is "ALPHA", to
which we are referring.

Alpha project is being implemented by a technical cooperation agreement beetween ORT and the
Education Ministry of Uruguay.
Economic viability was attained through the
financial backing of IBM Uruguay. Phase 1 of the
project has begun in March 1984; it will last 2
years, with an update every 6 months.
Progress reports are evaluated by a technical
commission composed of Ministry of Education,
IBM and ORT representatives.
Phase 1 is being carried out in "Instituto Dáma-
so Antonio Larrañaga", a 5000 student-general
high school, considered a leader within the 150
schools of the public network.

2. ANALYSIS OF OPPORTUNITY AND RELEVANCE OF A PROJECT OF THIS KIND IN URUGUAY, A DEVELOPING COUNTRY

When starting out, this project met questions of
this sort:'Why spend time and money in Informa-

tics, when we lack chalk, teachers salaries are low and there is no library in the school?" (A school headmaster, Uruguay, 1983).

There are reasons lying in the realm of opportunities and relevance.

Whether a project of this kind is opportune should be analysed taking into consideration the technological advances in the field of micro-electronics at the beginning of the 80's, which brought up a total change in the price, portability and reliability parameters of software and hardware.

Reliability is a matter of particular importance concerning computer uses in education, because past experiences in the 60's and 70's have met the obstacle of hardware and software being not reliable enough for heavy interactive work. "Computers are not useful for education purposes because they are always out of order" was 20% of the answers in a survey of students involved in 1976 PLATO project[2]. Two further factors had influence on the opportunity factor: a national economic policy liberating import trade, not usual in the country, on one hand, and certain particular situations as parents' pressure and the press showing special interest in the matter, on the other.

Analysis of the relevance factor includes awareness of society's evolution process within the information age, and the need for an educational system which will train both the individual to fit accordingly in it and the student to be able to face a new type of tertiary level studies curricula. From a social point of view, the country has to take into account the need for a systematic exposure to these new kind of technologies and industries. Only nation-wide education networks have the power and are spread enough to involve the whole social body.

Uruguay has a scarse population, with a relatively high average standard of education and culture. Unions are well organized, the working population does not include large quantities of low paid, unespecialised manpower so typical of other developing countries, so the country needs an educational policy that would enable the citizen to integrate to the "information age industries".

From the strictly curricular side, society will expect more and more technological culture and skills from the highschool graduate.

Besides that, the University will have to assume in the near future that some computer and informatics skills are taught at the secondary level, because there will not be time available for this at the tertiary level.

3. GENERAL PRINCIPLES

Information technology as related to education is a matter of educational policy, as far as the strategic decision making process is concerned.

The basic duty of general secondary education in Uruguay is not the training of the student in the field of technology for the performing of professional jobs.

The approach to the process of integration of Information Technology to education must be a systems approach, since it operates on a system (the secondary school educational sub-system).

The educational system comprises, at least, the following:

- students
- teachers
- parents
- headmasters
- studies curricula
- technology

4. MAIN AIMS

Aims, classified in immediate, short term, and long term have been projected for each of the components of the educational system.

STUDENTS
-Immediate aims
    -To make them become computer literates (cultural aim).
    -To enhance their awareness of social implications of information technology (ethical aim).
    -To train them in basic computer uses (operational aim).
-Short term aims
    -To enable a natural use of the informatics laboratory.
    -To hasten the development of learning group dynamics and horizontal learning.
    -To develop mastery of algorythmic techniques for problem solving.
-Long term aims
    -To develop mastery of the systems approach for the enhancement of the ability to analyse situations.
    -To develop the ability to synthesise, make critical analysis and use interative problem solving techniques.
    -To make them aware of the need for self-education and continuous training.

TEACHERS
-Immediate aims
    -To attain their favourable opinion and disposition (strategic aim).
    -To make them become computer literates (cultural aim).
    -To train them in information technology essentials, so that interaction with computer professional technicians for courseware development can be implemen-

ted (operational aim).
- Short term aims
  - Development, selection and exploitation of informatics laboratory resources.
- Long term aims
  - Redefinition of the teacher's role.

The most urgent and significant question at the moment is to make teachers incorporate this new educational technology in their teaching resources, enabling them to implement new and diversified teaching strategies; this is also the greatest challenge to face in the future.
As every profession is expected to change, so will the teacher's; perhaps the best way to conceive the kind of teaching skills necessary for a society which is constantly changing would be "...I can show you how to fly, although I cannot follow your flying..."(Song by Alfredo Zitarrosa, Uruguayan poet and singer).

PARENTS
- Immediate aims
  - To make them become computer literates (cultural aim).
- Short term aims
  - To make them become involved in their children's education.

HEADMASTERS
- Immediate aims
  - To attain their favourable opinion and disposition (strategic aim).
- Short term aims
  - To make them implement the structural integration of the Informatics Laboratory.
- Long term aims
  - To develop new and redesigned evaluation techniques.
  - To look for new alternatives in education planning, methods and procedures.

STUDIES CURRICULA
- Short term aims
  - To attain higher operational efficiency in curricula implementation (operational aim).
  - To attain better distribution of resources and orientation in curricula implementation (logistic aim).
- Long term aims
  - To study the redefinition of content.
  - To shift the emphasis from content to method, research and continuous education.

TECHNOLOGY (USE OF INFORMATICS LAB)
- Immediate use
  - Computer Literacy.
  - Training.
- Short term uses
  - Application ("general use laboratory").
  - Training.
  - Computer literacy.
- Long term use
  - Research.
  - Application.
  - Training

- Computer literacy.

The Informatics Laboratory should become a resources providing center for each component of the educational system.

5. OPERATING STRUCTURE

The "Alpha" Project operating structure is composed of a central node at ORT headquarters in Montevideo, and a local node in the school where it is being developed.

Functions of the central node are:
General coordination of the project, research activity, publications and development of courseware.

The project leader is in close contact with the secondary school headmaster. He is in charge of project planning, control, technical considerations, budget and pedagogical follow up.

The courseware development team comprises a pedagogical advisor, a teacher of the corresponding subject and a professional in computer science. This team's duties are cost estimation, selection, standarization, control, distribution and design-implementation of local courseware.

Functions of the local nodes are:
Coordination in the school, administration of the informatics laboratory and teaching.

The coordinator provides teaching advice and manages the computer laboratory.

Laboratory assistants teach and should back up any computer projects students may be interested in.

The concept of the Informatics Laboratory is that it should tend to function as a general use, application and exercise laboratory for every subject.

6. HARDWARE AND SOFTWARE SELECTION

We consider the following the criteria for the incorporation of the technology which fits both the local environment and the available resources:

In selecting equipment costs, its application and use should be taken into consideration to act accordingly; this does not imply the highest or the lowest cost in the market.

Hardware and software should be of general use and application, well known, portable, easy to maintain locally and open to connections.

There is no reason to stick to isolated digital microcomputers; the use of analog controls, communications, networks, video systems, etc., should be considered.

Hardware should represent a maximum of 25% of

total investment.

Configuration must be appropriate to application, with a tendency to maximizing accessibility, (ratio of students per keyboard).

Graphic capabilities, fast response-time (in case of time shared computer resources), direct access magnetic media and user friendly software for immediate use (as word processing for instance) are elements not to be forgotten.

Colour monitors are not cost effective in our country since they can cost as much as another micro or terminal.

Communications are not widely used nor recomended on a national scale.

Strategic decisions should be taken as independently of specific hardware as possible.

7. TEACHERS TRAINING TRATEGY

The purpose of this section is to describe the development of a 3 year experience carried out in computer education for highschool teachers, and the present strategy to which this experience has led.

We will divide it in three main parts:
1. Past experience
2. New strategy outline
3. Present implementation.

1. Past Experience.
Three years ago, with the aim of providing teachers with basic education about informatics and computer uses, we designed a computer literacy course for highschool teachers.
We trained 60 secondary school teachers from almost every subject of the present studies curriculum.
The course was based mainly on an Introduction to Informatics and a crash course in Basic.
These 10-day, two hours a day, off-service courses put more emphasis on BASIC programming than in applications related to the specific subjects. As a result, few teachers actually became interested in the educational application to their particular subject. This led us to a large and complete reform of our teachers training strategy and its objectives.

Some of the biggest problems were:
-The course had no continuity. Most of the teachers forgot everything in a few months and they did not have the chance to operate and program a computer until the next off-service period.
-Emphasis was on programming rather than on the use and application of this new educational tool.
-The course was the same for all the teachers, regardless of the subject they taught.
-The evaluation techniques were not adequately designed.

The whole result was less than satisfactory and the conclusions that followed, led to the design

of a strategy outline which is described below.

2. Strategy outline.
1-We have to consider two main groups of teachers: those who will use the computers and software in instructional tasks; and those who will create or help to create the educational software, along with professional programmers and analysts in development teams. The needs will be different for each.
2-The largest group, that is the end-users, will receive a basic education in the use and applications of computers, software and courseware. They will be supported by laboratory advisors and teachers of the second group. This training will be given off-service.
3-The second group, selected teachers in specific subjects, will have training in-service, working closely with the project coordinators. The characteristics, objectives and contents of this course are as follows:
  a) To achieve the teachers' favorable disposition and positive opinion about the experience and the use of this kind of technology in general.
  b) To make the teachers computer literates showing them the whole range of possibilities that this new tool can offer them from a social and technical point of view.
  c) To give them the necessary abilities to use computational techniques to solve simple problems by themselves.
  d) To create a common language enabling teachers to interact witch computer experts in order to develop software and courseware to be used in the informatics laboratory.
Content:
1.-Introduction. Technological impact of informatics in the society.
2.-Historical perspective of the use of informatics in the educational process. Different methodologies, advantages and disadvantages of each.
3.-Introduction to educational software. Main characteristics and objectives.
4.-Problem analysis and solving from an algorithmic point of view. Workshop with applications to the secondary school curriculum.
5.-Introduction to systems and computer systems. Elements, peripherals, programs, languages.
6.-Development of simple application programs.
7.-Analysis and implementation of multi-disciplinary projects of educational software, test and evaluation.

8. BIBLIOGRAPHY

(1) "Programming the Second Literacy", by A.P. Ershov; Proceedings of WCCE 1981, North-Holland, 1981.

(2) "Learning and Teching with Computers", Chapter 3, page 97, by Tim O'Shea and John Self, Harvester Press, Brighton, 1983.

(3) "Run: computer education", by Dave Ahl, Creative Computing Press, 1980.

(4) "Learning with computers", by Alfred Bork, Digital Press, 1982.

COMPUTERS IN EDUCATION, K. Duncan and D. Harris (eds.)
Elsevier Science Publishers B.V. (North-Holland)
© IFIP, 1985

COMPUTERS IN EDUCATION AT ALL LEVELS AND FOR ALL DEPARTMENTS AT THE SENIOR TECHNICAL SCHOOL (MTS)

Antoon M.W. van der Linden

Senior Technical School (MTS)
Helmond, The Netherlands

After a summary about the educational system in the Netherlands the structure of the Technical Senior School is discussed.
Further the general philosophy, applications of the computer in the various departments of the school and the computer as an educational aid are discribed.
Finally some information about follow up courses for and contacts with the industry is given.

1. INTRODUCTION

The structure of the educational system in The Netherlands is as follows. After primary school students take a six year course, depending from their talents and interest. The basic choice is to opt for vocational or general education. Depending on the chosen educational stream, they may continue their studies in apprenticeships, secondary or higher vocational education or in universities. This article is confined to technical education, to be discerned in 4 levels, to wit :
- Lower Technical Education (LTS)
- Secondary Technical Education (MTS)
- Higher Technical Education (HTS)
- Universities of Technology (TH)
The MTS (=Senior Technical School) represents secondary technical education.

2. STRUCTURE OF THE SENIOR TECHNICAL SCHOOL (MTS)

Pupils are admitted with a certificate from either a 4-year intermediate secondary school course or a 4-year Lower Technical School (LTS) course, provided that their final exams included mathematics, physics and a foreign language (preferably english). The MTS has a four year course, of which the first and second year consist of full-time education at school, the number of lessons a week being 32. During the 3rd year, called "practical year", the student spends a minimum of 200 working days, equally spread in 2 or 3 firms. The purpose is to let the student gain practical experience and make him put to test what he learned in school. During the practical year guidance is provided by teachers at the school. During the final 4th year the students undergo their examination. The students attend 26 lessons a week at school. The certificate consists of 6 subjects, 3 subjects being compulsory and 3 subjects being optional. The MTS Helmond has 4 departments, to wit :
Construction Engineering, Electrotechnical Engineering, Electronics and Mechanical Engineering. Moreover the school has a further course (the 5th year) in Technical Informatics.

As for general subjects like languages, mathematics and social studies, the lesson tables are the same for all departments in the 1st and 2nd year. This is true also for the students who opt for these subjects for their school certificate. Technical and practical subjects are defined by department and by branch within the department.

COMPUTER APPLICATION IN MTS HELMOND

3. GENERAL PHILOSOPHY

The school tries very hard to integrate information technology in the educational process and therefore to make computer application possible in the various subjects. The educational purposes may be described as follows :
a. to give students an insight into computer systems;
b. to learn how to work with application packages and data bases; Computerization of machines and industrial processes by small "stand alone" microcomputer systems;
c. to recognize such problems in their specific disciplines which are suitable for processing by computer;
d. to be able to act as an interlocutor with computerization experts;
e. to write, test and document (simple) programs;
f. to get basic knowledge about the use of microprocessors;
g. to learn how to use P.L.C.'s in process control. Whenever possible the same computer systems are used in the various departments as those which the students got to know in their first year.

4. APPLICATION IN THE FIRST YEAR.

During the first year all students take one lesson a week in computing, i.e. about 40 lessons in total. During these lessons the students learn how to handle the computer, operate the key-board, get to know the surrounding configuration like monitor, floppy disc and printer and they learn how to input, use and read simple programs. The computer language being used is BASIC. Students always work in teams of two, having at their disposal a personal computer with an internal memory of 48 K Bytes, screen, printer and a floppy disc with a capacity of 315 KB.

During the last year the application of computers in the school has much increased.

5. APPLICATION IN THE VARIOUS DEPARTMENTS

The general philosophy as stated in chapter 3 works out in very different ways in the various departments.

a. Elektrical Engineering.
Attention is paid to the application of programmable components for controllable machines, appliances and industrial processes. The following subjects are dealt with :
- computer architecture
- analyses of processes
- designing of simple algorithms
- programming of logical building elements
- writing of simple software

    Microprocessors.
In 1977 the MTS obtained an evaluation kit for the MC 6800 microprocessor. After a one years' development phase a curriculum on the subject "microprocessors" was introduced in the second year in the "Electronics" department, both as a theoretical and as a practical matter.
The school's board of directors procured the money to purchase 14 training kits, thus giving the means to introduce the subject of microprocessors in the last year in the departments of Electrotechnical Engineering and Electronics. Following upon these developments it appeared feasible in September 1979 to start an evening course in "microcomputer technics" for workers of local and regional industries. Much of the development of this course is due to close co-operation between these industries and the University of Technology at Eindhoven. The quality of the developed curriculum and the actual know-how in the school made the ministry of education designate the MTS in Helmond as one of four schools in The Netherlands to start a one years' supplementary course "Technical Informatics".

b. Mechanical Engineering.
Here the application of information technology is aimed at the use of the computer, the microprocessor and the programmable logic controller (PLC) in control engineering and computerization of production processes. Introducing the computer changed the fitting-out of the workshop drastically. Numerical controlled (NC) and computer numeral controlled (CNC) machines like grinding and milling machines call for a totally different didactic approach of the method of teaching. Input of information into the NC-machines is done by punched tape. The punched tape is prepared off-location; the student feeds data into the computer, the computer translates the data into information for the NC-machine; this information is recorded on punched tape. Also here the outcome of the process may be simulated in order to restrict the chances of machine damage to a minimum. CNC-machines get their information directly (on line) from the programming location. Also information can be stored on cassette, to be fed into the machine at any time. Executing programs by cassettes creates certain risks, especially in the beginning phase.
In order to make the students familiar with the machines in as early phase as possible, the school has the use of instructional machines. The school has three grinding machines and one milling machine. With these machines goes a specially designed programming location, being fed by the industrial programming location. One of the programming locations is equiped with a colour monitor; CAD software for this system is available. Thus we are in a position to let our students get acquainted with the basic principles of CAD/CAM. The essential course of instruction is being developped. Lack of available time and insufficient funding by the Ministry hamper a sufficient progress. Computerized production asks for computerized production control. Therefore within the school a measuring instrument has been developped which confronts the students both with measuring and with didactic problems. The above mentioned developments have brought about a splitting up of the department of Mechanical Engineering into two subjects, to wit: Production Technology and Control Engineering.
In Production Technology emphasis is given to computerized production on NC- and CNC-machines. Preparing and workplanning is done by way of external computing systems and when designing a foundation is laid for the possible use of CAD/CAM and at the same time such items as flexible computerization come into the picture.
In Control Engineering emphasis is given to the sequence of events in the development of a mass-produced article, such as designing, maintenance, etc. Especially so to the application of a computer in process control and to the mechanical problems which have to be solved when computerizing process control.

c. Construction Engineering.
In the department of Construction Engineering the students are confronted with information technology both by writing programs themselves, further to be subjects taught in the 1st year, as well as by working with existing programs. As for writing programs, this activity is mostly confined to elaborating simple problems. However some students excell in these matters, also due to much extra time they spend in it.
The commissions issued are derived from subjects like architecture (constructions) and industrial planning. As for existing programs in the school are available :
calculation programs for architectural constructions;
programs for building physics;
networkplanning;
drawing of concrete constructions;
perspective drawing;
specifications and estimates.

6. PROGRAMMABLE LOGICAL CONTROLLER (PLC)

When using P.L.C.'s there is a distinction made between two control systems:
1) Self-contained control, mostly applied in smaller installations and in installations that are non-aligned. Information transfer between PLC and installation only takes place on the level of bits (1 or 0). Installation control therefore is functioning quite independently of the level of process control.
2) Aligned installations where distinction is made between two levels of information transfer.
a. Logic control signals, being also the signals for process control as mentioned before in 1).
b. information exchange with a computer and for other PLC's for production control.
In this case the computer has access to all PLC's by means of a separate databus. Information transfer takes place by parallel or serial data communication, not on a one-bit level.
One will often find PLC's in the workshop, as a means of replacing the traditional switch box. PLC is a flexible alternative for control systems that before were composed of switches, relays, logical and/or pneumatic circuits, etc.
In the departments of Electrical Engineering, Mechanical Engineering and Chemical Engineering the second year is well suited to teach the students how to put in "wiring" by means of software and in this way to realize switch functions (control).

7. PILOT PROJECT IN TECHNICAL INFORMATICS.

a. Starting the project.
In March 1982 the Minister of Education and Sciences of the Netherlands selected four Senior Technical Schools and charged them with the task to start a supplementary course "Technical Informatics" as an experiment as well as a pilot activity. Our school is one of them and the course started in August 1982.
b. Discription of the course.
The course aims making the modern technicians acquainted and familiar with methods of program system development, programming, user packages and the integration of hardware and software.
Pay attention to the formulated purpose, we come to the following design:
- knowledge and insight in the architecture of the programmable, busoriented digital systems
- applications of digital systems in controlling machines and industrial processes.
This comprises
analyses of processes, developing and choosing of algorithms, choosing hardware, building and testing interfaces, writing of software in assembler and pascal, integrating and testing of hardware and software and programming logical building elements.

8. THE COMPUTER AS AN EDUCATIONAL AID.

a. Homework control.
Using the computer as a means for homework control is not a novelty, so I will not dwell upon this subject too long. Every student gets a task which he has to elaborate independently. Task setting is the same for each student, but the parameters for each task are different. After the student has completed his task, the computer will indicate if he did so in the correct way. We have found the following advantages in working in this way :
(1) the student is obliged to execute the task; he can not copy;
(2) it takes less time of the teacher to correct the homework;
(3) the student gets the work marked right away.
A distinct disadvantage of this system is the time consuming aspect of formulating tasks in writing the necessary programs. These are also the reasons that development is rather slow.

b. Correcting papers and exams.
Multiple choice papers and exams are controlled by computer. The computer controls questions and tasks for their selection quality as well.

c. School administration.
With the exception of the time-table the whole administration is computerized, such as :
- students administration, containing all relevant data;
- admission data and all study results obtained in school;
- data about absents and late comers;
- information to be given to parents about results, absenteeism and tardiness;
- delivering data about classes like marks, lists and reports;
- financial annual report;
- postal traffic and its handling;
- wastages and educational output.
Programs are developed within the school.

9. FOLLOW-UP COURSES AND CONTACTS WITH INDUSTRY.

From the start (in 1966) the school has been striving for good relations with local and regional industry in the widest sense. This led to the development of many additional courses attuned to the needs of industries. Those more or less "tailor-made" courses almost all originate from demands by industries. Often, when the necessary know-how in the school is lacking, these courses are developed and given by experts coming from industry. The school acts as a service-institute offering location, inventory and other services. Apart from theory much attention is paid to practical skills. The length of the courses is as limited as possible in order to make them attractive for the students.

The length of courses varies from 10 weeks of three lessons each to 30 weeks of three lessons a week maximum.

The courses are mostly directed at:

(1) courses in modern technologies aiming at innovations in industry and at the application of information technology;
(2) training in modern management;
(3) refresher courses for employees, aiming at modern production technics.

To give an example

Basic electronics	10 weeks at 3 lessons	30 lessons
CNC control	25 weeks at 3 lessons	75 lessons
PLC	12 weeks at 3 lessons	36 lessons
Applying PLC	12 weeks at 3 lessons	36 lessons
Programming for CNC	20 weeks at 3 lessons	60 lessons
Measuring technics for machine building	10 weeks at 3 lessons	30 lessons
Elementary computing	20 weeks at 3 lessons	60 lessons
Programming in PASCAL	30 weeks at 3 lessons	90 lessons
Technical informatics	30 weeks at 3 lessons	90 lessons

10. HOW TO DEVELOP A COURSE.

A committee has been installed, the members of which are from industry, local authorities and local and regional vocational education. The committee may establish an existing need for a certain course. Also an industry may approach the committee and ask for a special course of its own. The committee will evaluate the demand and, if it is proven to be realistic, will charge a working party with the task to put the course into effect. Preparation and putting the course into effect follows a certain pattern, step by step.

Step 1.
A firm or a number of firms report which need for a course exists. Also the framework is drawn wherein the course shouls take shape. Furthermore directives for the course are formulated.

Step 2.
Description of the contents of the course and definition of the subject-matter. This is done by the working party, consisting of workers from the firm and, if need be, completed by people from education. They draft the curriculum and define the length of the course.

Step 3.
Drafting of a folder containing:
a. purpose of the course
b. target group
c. a brief description (abstract of the curriculum)
d. length of course
e. expenses of the course
f. exam and certificate
g. application form

Step 4.
Mailing of the folder to the firms; all firms in the region are informed about the new course. Registration is opened and this way the interest is gauged.

Step 5.
When there appears to be sufficient interest the working party will try and find experts for:
a. preparing of the subject matter and course material;
b. teaching the lessons.

Step 6.
Administrative tasks, like working out the subject-matter, enrolling the participants, preparing the time-table, fixing the dates, time-schedules and the date of the examination etc.

Step 7.
Presenting the course and taking the examination.

Step 8.
Evaluation of the course and, if need be, making of corrections and adjustments.

Final remarks :
Since 1968, when a modest start was made with this kind of refresher courses for workers in firms, about 4000 students passed one or more courses succesfully. In the field of quality control about 2000 people were trained this way during the past years. There is a growing interest in industry for this type of course.

11. COOPERATION WITH THE VOCATIONAL TEACHERS TRAINING CENTRE AT EINDHOVEN (NLO)

The broad interest at our school in computer applications in education and more specifically so in the applied methods in this field had as a consequence a close cooperation that has developed with the NLO at Eindhoven. Apart from being a pilot school where students of the NLO are gaining practical experience in teaching, our school puts specific computer materials and teacher capacity at the disposal of the NLO.

COMPUTERS IN EDUCATION, K. Duncan and D. Harris (eds.)
Elsevier Science Publishers B.V. (North-Holland)
© IFIP, 1985

EVALUATING AND IMPROVING INFORMATIC EDUCATION IN SECONDARY SCHOOLS BY MEANS OF PROGRAMMING CONTESTS[1]

Andreas Schwill

Informatik II, Universität Dortmund
Postfach 500 500, D-4600 Dortmund 50
Federal Republic of Germany

Based on a specification of the terms "informatic techniques and approaches" we give advice in this paper in a concrete way by which means these techniques can be imparted to the students. In detail we investigate which problems and programming languages support or inhibit the use of which informatic approaches. The results are based on a careful analysis of the total of approximately 440 contributions to three programming contests for students been organized in 1980/81, 1982/83 and 1984/85 in the FRG. This analysis covers the problem-solving process of students treating certain subjects and its relation to informatic techniques and programming languages involved.

1. INTRODUCTION

1.1. SURVEY OF THE CONTESTS

In 1980/81, 1982/83 and 1984/85 three programming contests for students (the first one being the national part of the worldwide IFIP-contest) were organized in the FRG by order of the Gesellschaft für Informatik e.V. (german association of computer science) which 113 participants with 119 contributions, 221 participants with 187 contributions and 150 participants with 131 contributions respectively took part in (3,4). The participants who might be at most 18 years old in the first two contests and at most 21 years old in the third contest had to solve a self-chosen problem with the aid of a computer and submit the solution together with a presentation of the problem, an outline of the solution method and its realization with the restriction that the programs might be at most ten pages (twelve pages at the third contest respectively) long. A survey of the structure of participants is given by the tables 1 - 3.

1.2. THE SUBJECT OF THIS PAPER

Since informatics was included in the lessons the teaching objectives are clearly laid down (1,11,12). As informatics is often designated as a science of techniques one important objective is to impart these techniques to the students. But since it is rarely mentioned in a concrete way what techniques it is about, we first specify the terms "informatic techniques and informatic approaches" in chapter 2. The formation of the lessons as to the contents with the purpose to achieve this objective efficiently is fairly open (hints are contained in (2,6,8,9) for instance). Advice of the following kind is desirable and conceivable: A student solving task X trains the informatic technique Y and furthermore he is motivated to learn technique Z.

In order to gain assertions concerning these topics and a survey of the students' methods to solve problems by computers, the approximately 440 contributions to the three programming

age	# participants 1. contest	%	# participants 2. contest	%	# participants 3. contest	%
21	not allowed	-	not allowed	-	7	4.7
20	not allowed	-	not allowed	-	14	9.3
19	not allowed	-	not allowed	-	37	24.7
18	33	29.2	87	38.9	49	32.7
17	42	37.2	75	33.9	24	16.0
16	19	16.8	27	12.7	15	10.0
15	13	11.5	22	10.0	2	1.3
≤14	6	5.3	10	4.5	2	1.3
	113	100.0	221	100.0	150	100.0

Table 1: Distribution of ages

field	# contributions 1. contest	%	# contributions 2. contest	%	# contributions 3. contest	%
games	20	16.8	48	25.7	14	10.7
mathematics	54	45.4	30	16.0	27	20.6
administration	4	3.4	28	15.0	29	22.1
computer graphics	0	0.0	20	10.7	15	11.5
informatics	0	0.0	19	10.2	17	13.0
physics	10	8.4	6	3.2	4	3.1
others	31	26.0	36	19.2	25	19.0
	119	100.0	187	100.0	131	100.0

Table 2: Distribution of fields.

programming languages	# contributions 1. contest	# contributions 2. contest	# contributions 3. contest
BASIC	88 (74%)	142 (76%)	71 (55%)
PASCAL	18 (15%)	26 (14%)	42 (32%)
machine languages	0	8	5
ELAN	1	3	7
FORTRAN	10	1	3
others	2	7	3
	119	187	131

Table 3: Distribution of programming languages

contests were investigated with regard to the following questions:

(a) What informatic techniques did the students use?
(b) Which relations exist between the fields of application of the students' programs and the informatic techniques used to solve the problems arising in these fields?
(c) How do programming languages influence the deal with certain informatic techniques?

Answers to these questions yield advice for the formation of computer literacy from the informatic point of view, too.

Results concerning these topics are contained in chapter 3. Chapter 4 gives a summary and conclusions.

2. WHAT ARE INFORMATIC TECHNIQUES AND INFORMATIC APPROACHES?

In literature it is often stated that informatics is a science of techniques and should therefore be included in the school domain (e.g. (6)). We take the view that the following 13 elements, referring to which the contributions were investigated, are characteristic informatic techniques and approaches (5,13):

(A) Methodical approaches and systematical proceeding in software development (structured programming, modularization, top-down and bottom-up approach)
(B) Thinking in successive and concurrent runs (algorithmic and functional approach)
(C) Specification of demands on the software to be developed
(D) Structuring and arrangement of objects (thinking in data structures)
(E) Definition of data structures by declaring possible operations and formal realization of their properties (idea of abstract data types)
(F) Verification of written software
(G) Understanding of syntax and semantics of specification and programming languages
(H) Investigation of the computational complexity of algorithms and increase of efficiency
(I) Recursion, parallelism, non-determinism and parametrization in data structures and algorithms
(J) Definition and use of virtual machines
(K) Implementation techniques (e.g. virtual memory management, segmentation of programs)
(L) Simulation techniques
(M) Teamwork (Overcoming the problem of complexity by modularization and interface definition)

3. RESULTS OF THE INVESTIGATION

3.1. RESULTS CORRESPONDING TO ALL CONTRIBUTIONS

While the evaluation of the contributions to the first and second contest allows only qualitative assertions (5), a modified refereeing procedure at the third contest (each contribution was evaluated by three referees among others according to the intensity the 13 techniques mentioned above

were used) enables a quantitative corroboration of the hypothesises.

The use of informatic techniques corresponding to all contributions and to team contributions of the third contest is shown in figure 1.

Although about 60% of the participants to the second and about 80% of the participants to the third contest gained informatic education (this number was not recorded in the first contest), the use of informatic techniques however does not rely on a basic education but on an advanced and experienced deal with the computer. The students were intuitively aware of the necessity of certain methodical proceeding, but the application of some techniques failed by the lack of basic knowledge. Elementary algorithms (e.g. quicksort) or data structures (e.g. trees) are rarely known.

Apart from the insufficient education, type and number of references to literature in the contributions may be a reason for this lack. Although in the second and third contest respectively more than 80% of the participants (this number was not recorded in the first contest) declared that they had gained their knowledge in informatics also by private studies; one third did not use any literature; two thirds quoted at least one computer instruction manual; only about one fifth refered to informatic textbooks and only about one fifteenth to other advanced (but not necessary informatic) literature. A lot of contributions show that the exclusive use of home computer manuals partially constricts the mental horizon, for the students often exchanged informatic techniques with "intelligent use of all functions of the computer". It is true that many instruction manuals describe the inner structure and all functions of the computer in detail but neither do they give information about standard algorithms and systematical design of programs or documentations nor do manuals usually contain references to basic informatic literature.

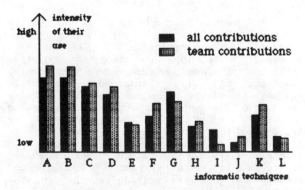

Fig. 1: Use of informatic techniques with respect to all contributions and team contrbutions (Basis: 3rd contest)

Very conspicious is the students' use of technique (M) "teamwork". The total of 41 team contributions was submitted to the three contests. However, an expected increase of the program complexity cannot be determined. To enable productive teamwork modularization with systematical definition of the interfaces is necessary. But the team programs only show a rather small lead by using techniques (A) and (B) (see figure 1). The cooperation seems to have mainly supported the communication and mutual help. The schools are certainly responsible for that, too, because they offer little opportunities to train teamwork and traditionally attach great importance to individual performances.

3.2. RESULTS CORRESPONDING TO DIFFERENT FIELDS OF STUDY

In this section we direct our interest to the relation between fields of study worked by the students and informatic techniques used to solve the problems arising in these fields. Assertions are only possible for the fields of games, mathematics/physics, administration, computer graphics and informatics due the small coverage of other fields (see table 2). Approach (M) is left out of consideration henceforth (see 3.1).

Before programming, one has to construct a model by defining systematically the data structures and the possible operations (techniques (A)-(E)). Some tasks do not require this model design, because the solutions are already available in an algorithmic form. Hence, such problems can be solved with common sense and do not force the use of informatic approaches.

In detail we gained the following results graded according to the number of informatic techniques involved:

(i) For the implementation of primitive screen games (e.g. pac-man) the knowledge of informatic techniques is hardly necessary. The implementation often degenerates to amateur construction (see figure 2).

Simple games can often be programmed in a straight forward way. The design of a model and methodical approaches are mainly inapplicable, because purpose and rules of the game (its specification in the informatic sense) are well-defined and their implementation is obvious. In contrast to strategy games (see below) special data structures are not required either. As the graphical output is usually in the foreground, difficulties with the hardware similar to problems in computer graphics (see (ii)) arise which can be solved by patient tenacity.

(ii) **Hardware-oriented problems (computer graphics for instance) make high demands on the tenacity in trying. Difficulties with the concrete computer equipment come into the fore to the disadvantage of informatic techniques (see figure 2).**

In the absence of suitable interfaces to higher programming languages, the solution of hardware-oriented problems (e.g. plotting by printers) often requires the use of subprograms in machine language because of the difficult synchronization and adaptation problems. Their solution seems to need so much "power" that there is no more time to use informatic techniques. The lack of approaches (E), (G), (I) and (L) is recognizable in the contributions. Due to the machine-orientation bit and byte are one of the most important data structures. Hence, especially the use of the elementary technique (D) ("data structures") is hardly necessary. Only very few students developed a program with tool characteristics that can be connected to other programs and extends the basic computer system (techniques (J): virtual machine).

(iii) **The programming of school problems of mathematics or physics hardly supports the use of informatic techniques. At most approaches (A) and (B) are required (see figure 2).**

Although hard mathematical problems were treated in some contributions from the informatic point of view the programs are mainly primitive, as they usually only transfer a formalized solution

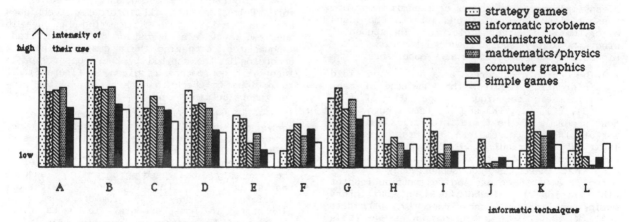

Figure 2: Use of informatic techniques in relation to different fields (Basis: 3rd contest)

already available into a programming language.
Example: To develop a program that determines
zeros of arbitrary functions by Newton's approximation method (problem frequently treated in
the contests) systematical proceeding (technique
(A)) is required in a high degree. A careful
analysis with respect to the convergency of
Newton's method, the continuity and differ-
entiability of the function is necessary. This
analysis has to be done on a pure mathematical
level and results in a set of mathematical formulae that can easily be converted into a programming language. The knowledge of the informatic techniques (E), (F), (I), (J) and (L) for
instance are not required.
As simple control and data structures (mostly
for-loops and arrays) usually suffice, the
students are not motivated or forced to apply
higher approaches.

**(iv) The knowledge of simple structured data
types (arrays, files) suffices to solve
common administration problems; specification, documentation and very simple virtual
machines are the most important informatic
techniques (see figure 2).**

Most submitted administration programs are to
maintain and process middle large data collections in the school domain, e.g. to calculate
and store the marks of the students or to manage
the school library, and are in use. Because the
programs have to fill a concrete application
frame and to meet legal regulations sometimes,
the participants attach great importance to a
specification covering the requirements (technique (C)). The programs provide an easy-under-
standable fault-tolerant user environment (part
of technique (J)) that enables also novices to
work with these programs. The documentations
contain comprehensive user manuals that explain
allowed inputs and instructions for error cases
in detail. From the program technical point of
view the programs are not so very complex. More
complicated data structures than arrays or files
are rarely used, although binary trees for instance are a more suitable structure to realize
search subroutines which are part of nearly
every administration program. Linear lists are
often implemented by arrays of records (possible
reason: lack of basic education). The used
algorithms are quite simple, too. The students'
programs mostly apply sequential search techniques and sort algorithms like bubblesort.

**(v) The design of programs assigned to the field
informatics requires the knowledge of many
informatic techniques, especially of (E),
(G), (I), (J), (K) and (L) (see figure 2).**

Most programs of the field informatics are software tools, e.g. assemblers, editors, compilers.
Their design requires extensive programming
activities from the participant which raised the
wish that these tasks be supported by the computer itself. In comparison to contributions of
other fields the students dealing with informatic problems used techniques (E), (G), (I),
(J), (K) and (L) in a higher degree. But it is
surprising that their lead of knowledge does not
extend to the application of the important

approach (D) ("data structures"). As already
mentioned the knowledge of higher structured
data types fails due to the lack of basic
education. Therefore several programs suffer
from low efficiency caused in the absence of
suitable data structures.

**(vi) The implementation of strategical games
(e.g. chess, gobang) highly requires
advanced knowledge of nearly all informatic
principles and in particular of techniques
(D), (H) and (I) (see figure 2).**

The programming of strategical games makes high
demands on the capability to use informatic
techniques. The application of the elements (A),
(B), (C), (D), (H) and (I) is recognizable in
the contributions in a very high degree. Without
the knowledge of the two most important
structures "(game-) tree" and "recursion" the
implementation of strategy games can hardly
succeed. Hence, the work of this subject forces
a very intensive deal with techniques (D) and
(I). Of course, the complexity of the program
development highly requires the use of techniques (A) and (B).
That strategy games are an excellent medium to
train informatic principles is also shown by the
following observation: Of all participants only
programmers of strategy games (they are directly
faced with the problem) investigated their programs under the aspect of computational complexity in a qualified way (technique (H)) and
tried to improve their efficiency.

3.3 RESULTS CORRESPONDING TO DIFFERENT PROGRAM-
MING LANGUAGES

In this chapter we investigate the influence of
programming languages on the relation between
subjects and informatic techniques used.

In the seventies it was often discussed which
programming language is most suitable for
schools. This controversy was settled by saying
that it all depends on the observance of the
correct systematic manner such that the transformation of a solution into a concrete programming language is only an automatic activity that
cannot influence the methodical proceeding any
more. But since not all informatic techniques
are supported by each programming language in
the same way (A classification of some important
languages by comparing their design principles
according to the capability they support our 13
informatic approaches is given in figure 3), it
is obvious to check this assertion by the contest contributions.

If the assertion would hold, it were to be expected that contributions in different languages
do not differ with respect to the intensity
informatic techniques are used. However, most
contributions show that this is not the case. On
the contrary, the used programming language
reacts upon the thinking and considerably
restricts or extends it. Programmers usually implementing in non-procedural languages close
their mind to certain informatic principles,
e.g. recursion, and problems the solution of

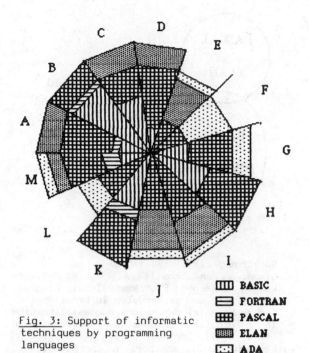

<u>Fig. 3</u>: Support of informatic
techniques by programming
languages

    [IIII] BASIC
    [≡] FORTRAN
    [⊞] PASCAL
    [▦] ELAN
    [⋮] ADA

quicksort) and data structures (e.g. lists,
trees) are fairly unknown. Possible reasons are
the lack of basic education and of access to
suitable textbooks. An expected lead of joint
contributions generally fails. Some participants
wasted a lot of time with problems that cannot
be assigned to informatics, for instance com-
puter-internal difficulties.

However, the main objective of our investigation
was to gain assertions about the relation between treated fields of subjects, informatic
techniques applied to solve problems arising in
the fields and programming languages involved.
The results could lead to a catalogue of problems that are suitable or unsuitable respectively to impart informatic principles to students. Such a collection of tasks would help to
form the lessons. We have seen that the necessity to use certain techniques depends on the
fields of application in such a way that some
problems can be solved without special knowledge
of informatic techniques, whereas other problems
require high experience in certain techniques.

which necessarily requires that principle, e.g.
typical backtracking problems (The Austrian phi-
losopher Wittgenstein summed it up: "The limits
of my world are the limits of my language".).
Details showing differences between the use of
informatic techniques are contained in figure 4,
where PASCAL and ELAN as representatives of the
structured and BASIC and FORTRAN as representatives of the unstructured language family are
combined.

As we pointed out in chapter 3.2, advanced
informatic techniques are necessary to solve
certain problems (e.g. informatic problems or
strategy games). An interesting question concerning the programming languages involved is:
Did the students choose those languages that are
most suitable to solve their problems, i.e. that
support the use of required informatic techniques best? Figure 5 gives a positive answer.
Programmers treating subjects demanding with
respect to informatic approaches used higher
programming languages relatively more often than
programmers working problems easy in the informatic sense.

4. SUMMARY, CONCLUSIONS AND PROPOSALS

In this paper we have investigated the problem-solving process, the knowledge of informatic
techniques and the use of programming languages
of students in secondary schools on the basis of
about 440 contributions which were sent to three
programming contests been organized in the FRG.

Many students are unfamiliar with informatic
techniques exceeding the design of simple virtual machines and a certain systematization of
software development. Basic algorithms (e.g.

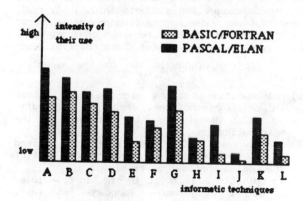

Fig. 4: Use of informatic techniques in
relation to different language
families (Basis: 3rd contest)

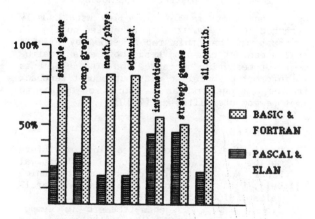

Fig. 5: Use of different languages in
different fields (Basis: all contests)

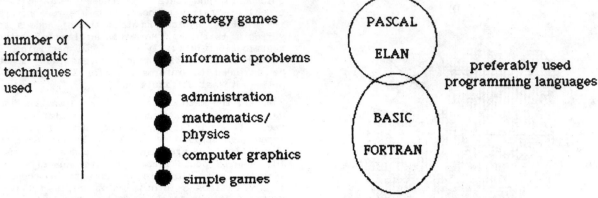

Fig.6: Relation between techniques, fields
and programming languages

Furthermore we have investigated the influence
of programming languages on the capability to
apply informatic techniques. In contrast to a
common view we found out that the use of informatic principles highly depends on their support
by the language. The students intuitively realized that and chose higher programming languages
if the treated problems required advanced techniques. Figure 6 summarizes these observations.

The following proposals sum up the essential
results:

1) Mathematical problems are unfit to impart
   informatic techniques. Therefore informatic
   education should not be included in the
   mathematics lessons.
2) Many informatic techniques are better trained
   by programming strategy games than by most of
   the common application problems.
3) To motivate and impart informatic principles
   a higher programming language (at least
   PASCAL) is necessary.
4) Basic textbooks should be made known. Producers of home computers should add those
   books to their equipment or at least refer
   to them in the instruction manuals.

Up to now contests for juveniles were usually
arranged in the FRG to support gifted pupils. In
contrast to that this report shows by example
that a contest can also serve both as an instrument for measuring successes and misdevelopments
in informatic education with subsequent feedback
to the lessons and as a source of advice to
improve computer literacy (7,10).

5. REFERENCES

(1) Bauer, F.L., Top-down teaching of infor-
    matics in secondary schools, Technical
    Report No. 7502, Technical University Munich
(2) Bell, D.H. and Simpson, D., Teaching paral-
    lelism, SIGCSE 14,2 (1982) 26-31
(3) Claus, V., 1. Jugendwettbewerb in Compu-
    Programmierung, LOG IN 2 (1981) 4-5 and
    Informatik Spektrum 4 (1981)
(4) Claus, V. and Fleischhack, H., Bericht über
    den 2. Jugendwettbewerb in Computer-Program-
    mierung, LOG IN 2 (1983) 13-15 and Informa-

tik Spektrum 3 (1983) 174-175
(5) Claus, V. and Schwill, A., Die Wechselwir-
    kungen zwischen Problemstellung, Program-
    miersprache und verwendeten Informatikmetho-
    den am Beispiel der beiden Bundeswettbewerbe
    in Informatik, Informatik-Fachberichte 90
    (1984) 87-91, Springer-Verlag
(6) Fleischhut, J., Koerber, B. and Riedel, D.,
    Didactical aspects of informatics education
    in secondary schools, Proc. of the World
    Conference on Computers in Education (1981)
    657-664
(7) Comer, J.R., Wier, R.R. and Rinewalt, J.R.,
    Programming contests, SIGCSE 15,1 (1983)
    241-244
(8) Ford, G., A framework for teaching recur-
    sion, SIGCSE 14,2 (1982) 32-39
(9) Kruse, R.L., On teaching recursion, SIGCSE
    14,1 (1982) 92-96
(10) Metzner, J.R., Proportional advancement
    from regional programming contests, SIGCSE
    15,3 (1983) 27-35
(11) Schneider, G.M., The introductory program-
    ming course in computer science - ten prin-
    ciples, SIGCSE 10,1 (1978) 107-114
(12) Turski, W.M. (ed.), Programming teaching
    techniques, Proc. of the IFIP TC-2 Conf. on
    Progr. Teaching Techniques 1972
(13) Wulf, W.A., Shaw, M., Hilfinger, P.N. and
    Flon, L, Fundamental structures of computer
    science, Addison-Wesley Publ. Comp. 1981

FOOTNOTE

1) This research was supported by the Minister
   President for Education and Science (BMBW) of
   the FRG under grant no. B3512.00B. The author
   is responsible for this publication.

COMPUTERS IN EDUCATION, K. Duncan and D. Harris (eds.)
Elsevier Science Publishers B.V. (North-Holland)
© IFIP, 1985

AN EXPERIMENT IN INTRODUCING THE BASIC CONCEPTS OF INFORMATICS

G. Olimpo, D. Persico, L. Sarti, M. Tavella

Istituto Tecnologie Didattiche, Consiglio Nazionale Ricerche, Genova

This paper describes an experiment in introducing informatics into basic education. This operation, developed in the context of the IRIS project, in coordination with the European Centre for Education, entailed the development of a teaching unit designed for the first two years of high school. The experiment is illustrated both from the point of view of the content and from that of the methods used, and the framework within which it was conducted, the working plan followed; the first results and prospects for the future are also described.
In particular, the robot Martino is introduced. This is a software instrument aimed at introducing the main basic concepts of the study of informatics.

1. INTRODUCTION

It is a widespread belief today that informatics is not only a specialized technical discipline, but also - and perhaps even above all - a method of thought to be put to use in a wide range of subjects and activities. To this concept of informatics, an educational value of great imortance is attributed. There are, however, contrasting points of view as to what the educational content of informatics actually is, and how it should be included in basic education.

The purpose of these notes is to describe a specific experiment in introducing the basic concepts of informatics into a high school context. The experience is described on the basis of the choice of contents and the means by which they may be transmitted, possible ways of conducting the experiment and the difficulties encountered, the first results obtained and future prospects. Within the framework of the experiment, the software instrument utilized was the robot Martino, a modified version "Karel the Robot" by R. Pattis.

The experiment was developed and put into practice by the Istituto per le Tecnologie Didattiche (Institute for Teaching Technologies) of the CNR (Italian National Research Council), in the context of the IRIS project, coordinated by the European Centre for Education, and conducted in several Italian schools. The IRIS project (Iniziative e Ricerche per l'Informatica nella Scuola - Undertakings and Research for Informatics at School) includes a series of parallel activities for introducing informatics into school at various levels.

2. PERSPECTIVE OF THE EXPERIMENT

2.1 Analysis of the context

It is widely believed today that an organic introduction to informatics is more and more urgently required in basic education. (19)

In some countries for some years now specific national projects have existed with the aim of stimulating and guiding a gradual process of introduction of informatics into school programs. Among the most representative of these, experiments carried out in the United Kingdom and the French national project should be mentioned. These two projects reflect different cultures and different school systems; however they are both the fruit of precise political decisions, based on the awareness of the strategic importance, in a modern industrial society, of spreading an "informatical" culture.

In Italy during the last few years, a variety of initiatives have been undertaken by teacher associations, cultural and recreational groups, single schools and single teachers.

There are also many "initiating" activities, originated by the publishing industry, the more important microcomputer manufacturers, hardware dealers and distributors. These activities are bent on supplying a prevalently technical outlook, of which the fundamental ingredients are computer structure and BASIC programming. They tend to satisfy the pressing market demand, creating an excessively technology oriented informatics culture, leaving out precisely those elements which have a greater potential for educational purposes and for linking the various subject areas.

Only recently the European Centre for Education, an independent organ of the Ministry of Education, founded the IRIS project. The experiment under reference, farther-reaching than the activities mentioned above, is part of this project and consists of a course, the scope of which is to introduce informatics into basic education.

Another significant aspect of the Italian situation is that of the limited spreading of an informatics culture among the teaching staff, and the difficulties of up-dating a school system distinguished by the inertia both of a part of the teachers and of the burocratic structures. This field, too, therefore, has to rely on the initiative of single teachers, spurred on by their own personal interest and by pressures from their students.

Difficulties of a technical nature are to be found in introducing informatics into the offical basic school programs, and are created by the lack of uniformity of the economic situation from one school to another.

2.2 Aims

The experiment under reference had the scope not so much of training specialists as of introducing informatics into basic education. The aims are therefore easily identified in those aspects of informatics which have a particular educational value, and make it easier for young people to fit into an informatics-minded society:

a) Encouraging the development of logic and cognitive capacities.

   The constant application of the informatic method encourages the acquisition of the capacity to face reality sistematically in an organic manner, both as far as concerns problem solving and in order to develop learning potential. In particular, the hierarchical decomposition method and the use of formal methodologies for describing realities increase the capacity to communicate, while the formulation of models and the abstraction of functions and data constitute the basis of abstract thought.

b) Improving the quality of learning.

   A large number of proposals and experiments carried out by teachers and research workers have contributed towards highlighting a wide range of educational advantages, some of which still undoubtedly remain to be discovered, to be achieved by introducing informatic methods and means into the teaching of non-informatic subjects. These advantages concern the possibility of widening and renewing the contents of each discipline, the possibility of giving knowledge a more concrete and operational form, and finally the possibility of improved, easier and more incisive communication in teaching, above all when referred to complex subjects.

   This object is of necessity complementary to the first, as problem solving and abstraction capacities, as a mental attitude sistematically adopted by the student are of course applied to any real context.

c) Educating towards life in an informatics-minded society.

   This objective implies the acquisition of a certain familiarity with the use of informatic means and their possible applications, spreading the concept of the computer as an instrument to exploit rather than to submit to, and debunking the idea of informatics as an inaccessible discipline.

2.3 Content

In line with the objectives stated above, it is possible to identify (24) a set of contents, based on the criteria already indicated above of privileging methods of thought of a general capacity rather than technologies of a contingent value.

Of course, varying degrees of completeness, of thoroughness, and of complexity, and a series of considerations which may condition a further selection within the framework of these contents, correspond to each scolastic level.

Two classes of contents are illustrated in greater detail, and the choices made are motivated herebelow.

a) Structured construction of algorithms and programs.

   Mastering the concept of an algorithm is a necessary condition in order to know the potentiality of the computer; acquiring the capacity to sinthesize algorithms means a great increase in one's own problem-solving capacities, in a general purpose sense, and consequently is particularly educational.

   But so-called structured programming is something more than the mere construction of an algorithmic and its coding in a programming language: it is a method of thought based on the capability to discover and build up the structure of what is real, and it uses definite tecniques in order to dominate the complexity and to guide organically the invention process.

   The pivots of this method of thought, intimately linked to one another, are the algorithimic concept, hierarchical decomposition (called "top-down") and function and data abstraction.

b) Education to access to information and to its handling by didactic use of preconstructed programs.

   In addition to the construction of algorithms and programs, also the use of preconstructed programs, such as data base, simulation programs, graphic editors, games and in general any didactic "environment" may constitute an educational factor of great importance.

   It entails, in fact:

   - getting used to considering a computer an instrument of work able to facilitate, improve or speed up production and cognitive activities;

   - getting used to modelling and formalizing situations and ideas which allow communication with informatic means and their functional integration into the activity being carried out;

   - the enrichment of teaching with computational capacities and the handling of otherwise inaccessible information;

   - a creative stimulus, thanks to the

fact that the student is able to make use of means which strenghten his or her expressive capacities.

As already stated at the beginning of this paragraph, the experiment under reference did not cover the whole area of content described here. Within the framework of the two classes mentioned, taking into account the scolastic level of the intervention and the requisites of compactness which the course itself had to comply with, a selection was made which led to a more detailed and restricted set of points, calibrated as far as concerns the degree of completeness, thoroughness and complexity, motivating factors, cultural links and links with the real context.
The first class of contents is present integrally in the course, since the algorithmic approach, the top-down process and functional abstraction were all considered to be indispensable and fundamental.
The second class is represented by the use of an operative environment and of a facilitated teaching environment in which the student may develop his first programs.

2.4 Methodological aspects

Coherently with the objects and contents described, it was decided to set up a teaching unit in wich the main characters were not, as is almost compulsory today, the structure of the computer and Basic language. This does not mean "poor" informatics, limited to the use of pencil and paper: all the conceptual aspects of the informatic method may take shape only by applying them to the solution of specific problems, and in conclusion through the construction of programs coded in a specific language and their execution on the computer.
The choices made as far as concerns the environment for the student to operate in are: Pascal language, the UCSD operative system, the robot Martino as the facilitated teaching environment, and the use of personal computers as a hardware support.

a)   The language.
      Many factors conditioned this choice: availability of the language, the age and scolastic level of the pupils, the knowledge of the teaching staff and so on. But rather than to these prevalently technical aspects, preference was given to the fact that each language has its own philosopy and subtends a different way of thinking, and Pascal in particular does not constitute merely a coding instrument, but even more an instrument of thought and ideation; it does not allow any elements to appear which depend on the specific architecture of the computer, and does not force the user to implement intrinsically simple logic structures in ways which are complex to carry out and to understand. Rather it adapts naturally to the applica-

tion of the conceptual instruments referred to.
b)   The harware and the operative system.
      The lack of uniformity in the economic situations of the schools involved prompted the use of personal computers as a hardware support, so as to allow schools with a limited investment capacity to acquire a smaller number of work stations, but not of a lower quality, as compared with schools having a higher budget.
      The choice of the UCSD operational system followed naturally the choice of a language and a hardware support to communicate it through, making it a de facto standard; it is also easy to learn and to use, even without being experts.
c)   Martino the robot.
      In order to temper down the difficulty of the contents, it was decided to utilize a software instrument such as the robot Martino, based on a variation of R. Pattis robot, Karel (17), able to facilitate the acquisition of informatic concepts and to strenghten the motivation of the students, thanks to the presence of play elements. The role of Martino is that of supplying a concrete reference at the moment of acquiring new concepts, and of inventing abstractions for the solution of a problem; an instrument for checking out the correctness of the solutions adopted; and finally a motivating play element.
      The world within which Martino moves consists of a network of "roads" orthogonal to one another (fig. 1).

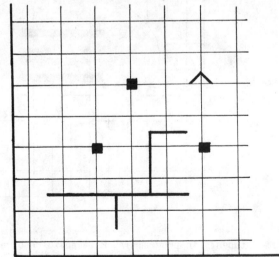

Figure 1.

The robot is represented by the arrow which indicates the direction in which it points. At the crosspoints there may be objects of a general nature (represented by a small full square) which Martino may pick up or put down. There may also be obstacles of various shapes and lengths, which represent limits to Martino's movements.

The only way for the student to communicate with Martino is to write a program according to which he carries out a specific task; in particular, it was decided to include in the Pascal language some robot control primitives: there are instructions which make Martino perform certain operations (forwards, right, left, pick up, put down) and predicates which provide information on Martino's situation (objectpresent, freeahead, freeright, north, south, and so on).

It should be noted that, unlike Karel the robot, a real language and programming environment are used to program Martino: UCSD Pascal.

In this way, it is possible to make Martino carry out certain specific operations in a particular "world", suitably configured by means of an actual Pascal program. For example, the task "go along the corridor, picking up any object present" may be resolved by a simple program such as the one illustred in figure 2.

the various concepts of informatics: algorithms, functional abstraction, procedures, control structures and top-down development. It is important to note that all these concepts may be introduced and made operational even without data. These are introduced during a later stage, with reference at first to Martino, and subsequently to problems of the real world. This represents a further simplification of the learning process, as it allows separate concepts to be learned in successive stages.

The structure of the contents reflects their conceptual priority criteria, introducing first of all, gradually, the elements considered to be more educational. Martino's world allows these concepts to be isolated, and permits the student to concentrate on them without being distracted by elements of a different nature and of lesser importance. For example, functional abstraction and the use of procedures are introduced almost immediately, even before control structures, while data is not introduced at all,

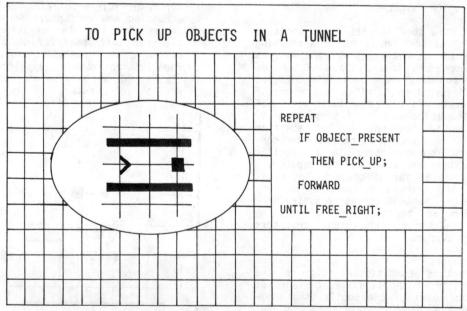

Figure 2.

In this way, the teacher may guide the students in programming Martino to resolve more and more complex tasks, and supply them with the "worlds" in which these tasks are to be carried out. The students build up Martino's programs in the form of normal Pascal programs and while they are being executed, Martino's actions are visualized by effect of the program they have built.

Martino's world is an extremely concrete reference for a gradual introduction of

thanks to the self-consistency of Martino's language, which allows a "clean" approach to the concept of algorithms as a sequence of steps required to carry out a predetermined task. This type of content structure is definitely different from the traditional sequence of introduction of contents: variables, control structures and finally procedures.

3. CONDUCTION OF THE EXPERIMENT

3.1 Course material

The experiment under reference constitutes, as already stated, a teaching unit of the IRIS project, and as such, it was developed in conformity with standards preestablished by the European Centre for Education: among these the modular structure of the course material should be mentioned, as well as the presence of a sequence of cards for the students and a teacher's guide.

The course material consists of a student's manual, a teacher's manual and several disks containing Martino's software, plus some test cards.

Martino accompanies the introduction of the basic concepts of informatics in five stages, each identified by a logically correlated set of contents:

Stage 1: Preliminary notions on computers
Stage 2: The first steps
Stage 3: How to define new instructions
Stage 4: If ... then ...
Stage 5: Repeat ... until ...

Each stage is articulated over activities framed in three differing contexts: in the class-room, at home and in the laboratory. While in the class-room the teacher introduces the new concepts, possibly utilizing the machine for short demonstrations, the activity at home consists of individual preparation of exercizes to be carried out in groups, on the computer, in the laboratory.

The subdivision into stages is present both in the students' cards and in the teacher's guide. The former, in line with the authors' conviction that the active participation of the students is necessary, really constitutes an interactive course, with frequent stimuli to perform exercizes and maintaining an interlocutory structure even when introducing new concepts.

The teacher's guide, which is indispensable considering the difficulties already mentioned in bringing teachers up to date, gives general indications with reference to the scope of the course, the contents, the times and means required, a plan for use of the material and the formalities for carrying out each stage. These five stages form the first part of an introductory informatics course, of which the second part, prepared by the Institute for Applied Mathematics of CNR (the National Research Council) leaves Martino's world to introduce data structures by means of a real example.

3.2 Characteristics

The experiment was carried out in a limited number of classes, in schools in various part of Italy (Genoa, Turin, Naples and Pavia). The students were first and second year high school students, and the average age was therefore about 14. It should be pointed out that the official study program for these classes did not include any subject of the informatics area.

The teachers involved in the experiment lent themselves on a voluntary basis, and with great enthusiasm. They already knew the students, as they are already teaching them various subjects within the normal study program, and got on well together. Generally speaking, none of the teachers had any previous experience of teaching informatics, indeed for some of them it was an experience quite out of their usual fields of interest: the teachers present were in fact from various fields, such as mathematics, physics, business administration, but also arts and history.

The problem of training the teaching staff was therefore particularly delicate, due to the fact that they did not possess the necessary knowledge and cultural background. The subject was confronted along two separate lines. On one hand, refresher courses were organized (lasting one week), utilizing as teaching material the unit which they would subsequently use with their own students. On the other hand, the "Teacher's guide" was prepared with particular care, and constitutes a real form of "direction" of the single lessons and exercizes, complete with suggestions for facing any critical situation and tips for possible applications. The hypothesis, which still remains partly to be verified, is that a guide of this type would make it possible even for teachers without any specific training to put the course into practice, turning it into a real self-refreshing instrument.

3.3 Control

Within the framework of the experiment, instruments were provided and used for collecting data as objective as possible concerning the progress of the students' learning:

- a questionnaire at the beginning of the course supplied useful information for classifying the students on the basis of their previous experience with computers;
- a "popularity" test compiled by the students at the end of each stage stressed elements of incompleteness, ambiguity or redundancy in the structure of each lesson;
- a rating test at the end of stages 3 and 5 was used to check that the basic contents of the course were being correctly acquired and consolidated by the students;
- a final test, consisting of the production of a program of a certain complexity and generality and put to the students in the form of an individual competition, in which the winner will be the author of the most correct and elegant program, allowed global evaluation of the progress of the whole course for each single participant.

Side by side with these sistematic controls, another less formal but directed form of check was implemented:

- before, during and upon completion of the experiment, meetings of the teachers involved with the authors of the teaching unit were held, leading to useful exchanges of opinions, suggestions, criticism;
- the course was run in some cases by the teachers, in other cases the authors worked side by side with the teachers, and in yet other cases replaced them completely.

This made it possible to evaluate the incidence of the "teacher" factor, and to obtain an immediate feedback of the impact on the students.

3.4 The first results

The control mechanism prepared beforehand, together with the sensations of the authors and teachers involved, provided a sufficiently accurate method of measuring the results of this first experiment.

The questionnaires filled in at the beginning of the course showed that none of the students had any previous knowledge of informatics or of programming. The "popularity" level of the various stages was in general very high, and increased considerably when Martino, the robot, was introduced, clearly due to the "play" motivations. The laboratory activities were also very much enjoyed, and the groups formed for these generally got on very well together. The only difficulties were noticed in groups containing too many students (due to the small number of machines available to some schools), or in situations where one of the elements of the group tended to emerge and become the leader of the group, monopolizing the use of the machine. In general it was found that the ideal group size was three people; however it must be kept in mind that one teacher alone cannot follow too many groups at the same time. The rating tests, together with the final test, showed very good language learning level and use of the operative system and of the computer in general. The rapidity and enthusiasm with which students of this age- group acquire the capacity to operate microcomputer were surprising. Their problem-solving capacities were undoubtedly strengthened, even though the short duration of the course did not permit, in some cases, a systematic method consolidation.

Separate thought should be given to the estimates which, in the teacher's guide, indicated the time necessary for the various types of activity. While these estimates proved to be mostly correct for class-room and home activities, the same may not be said for the time allocated to laboratory exercizes, which were often understimated, particularly in the case of numerous groups or hardware subject to frequent breakdowns.

4.   CONCLUSIONS AND PROSPECTS

To conclude, it may be said that the teaching unit under reference met with considerable success, both from the point of view of its impact on the students, who acquired rapidly the contents put to them and developed problem-solving capacities which they did not have at the beginning, and from the point of view of the teachers, and in spite of the absence of any form of official recognition of this activity, motivated not only by their personal interest but also by the pressure and enthusiastic responses of their students.

Some indications for second thoughts about the course material and content of the courses resulted from this experiment, and these are articulated along two different lines according to their incidence in time.

A series of very relevant suggestions put forward by the teachers or which came up during the direct meetings with the authors in the class- rooms or in the questionnaires and tests shall constitute the input for a review which should be completed within the end of the next academic year with a more complete and efficient edition of the material. Examples of these revisions are the extension of the functionality of the operative system, the use of interchangeable pages according to the type of computer utilized and so on.

As far as concerns the content, the intention is to lengthen the teaching unit, including, after the fundamental control structures, the data concept. This should allow, on one hand, a natural completion of the abstraction concept adding data abstraction to functional abstraction, and on the other hand an extension in time of the use of top-down methodologies, applying them to the data structuring process. This should provide a remedy to the problem already mentioned of the students not all getting used in a well-rooted manner to this method of thought.

At the present time, it is believed that the course modified as indicated above may be experimented during the 1984/1985 school-year, on a wider scale.

There are longer term prospects for the creation of a development and testing environment for concurrent programming, very similar to the present world of Martino, but containing more than one robot: Martino and his brothers.

5.   REFERENCES

(1) Andrews, G.R., Schneider, F.B., Concept and notation for concurrent programming, Computing Surveys. 15 (1983) 3-43.
(2) Various Authors, Introduzione all'informatica, Unità didattica sviluppata dagli Istituti Tecnologie Didattiche e Matematica Applicata del CNR, 1984.
(3) Bayman, P., Mayer, R.E., A Diagnosis of Beginning Programmers' Misconceptions of BASIC Programming Statements, Communications of ACM. 26 (1983) 677-679.

(4) Chen, P.P., The Entity - Relationship Model: Toward a Unified View of Data, ACM Transactions on data-base systems. 1 (1976).

(5) Clocksin, W.F., Mellish, C.S., Programming in PROLOG. (Springer Verlag, New York, 1981).

(6) Dijkstra, E.W., How do we tell truths that might hurt?, SIGPLAN Notices. 17 (1982) 13-15.

(7) Ferraris, M., Midoro, V., Olimpo, G., Petri net as a modelling tool in the development of CAL courseware, Comput. Educ. 8 (1984) 41-49.

(8) Fierli, M., Aspetti formativi dell'informatica di base, Atti della giornata AICA su Contenuti formativi dell'informatica di base, Padova, 1982.

(9) Gilbert, L.A., Microelectronics in education: two types of innovation, two strategies, Int. J. Man-Machine Studies. 17 (1982) 3-14.

(10) Killam, R., and others Computer Assisted Instruction in music, Pipeline. 6 (1981) 3-4.

(11) Kowalski, R.A., Logic as a computer language for children, Proc. European Conference on Artificial Intelligence. (Orsay, France, 1982).

(12) Jantzen, M., Structured Representation of Knowledge by Petri nets as an aid for teaching and research, in Net Theory and Application, (Springer Verlag, Berlin, 1980).

(13) Liskov, B.H., Zilles, S., Programming with abstract data types, SIGPLAN Notices. 9 (1974) 50-59.

(14) Moshell, M., Computer Power: a first course in using the computer (Gregg Div., Mc. Graw Hill, N.Y. 1982).

(15) Olimpo, G., Aspetti formativi del metodo informatico, Atti della giornata AICA su Contenuti formativi dell'Informatica di base, Padova, 1982.

(16) Papert, S., Mindstorms: children, computer and powerful ideas (Basic Books, Inc., New York, 1980).

(17) Pattis, R.E., Karel the Robot. (John Wiley & Sons, New York, 1981).

(18) Peterson, L., Petri net theory and the modelling of systems (Prentice Hall, Englewood Cliffs, 1981).

(19) Scotti, F., The conceptual schema as didactic tool, Atti di ACM- SIGSE Technical Symposium on Computer Science Education, Indianapolis, febbraio 1982.

(20) Slidel, R.J., Anderson, R.E., Hunter, B. Computer Literacy, (Academic Press, New York, 1982).

(21) The Open University, Micros in school: an awarness pack for teachers, Case studies, (The Open University Press, 1982).

(22) Wexelblat, R.L., The consequences of one's first programming language, Software-Practice and Experience. 11 (1981) 733-740.

(23) Woodhouse, D., Introductory courses in computing: aims and languages, Comput. Educ. 7 (1983) 79-90.

(24) Olimpo, G., Informatica nella formazione di base: obiettivi, contenuti e metodi, Proc. Simposio sobre Informatica y Educacion, Tucuman, 1984.

COMPUTERS IN EDUCATION, K. Duncan and D. Harris (eds.)
Elsevier Science Publishers B.V. (North-Holland)
© IFIP, 1985

TOWARDS A SELF-PACED LEARNING SUPPORT SYSTEM

Fumiyuki Terada, Ken Hirose and Tohru Handa

Department of Mathematics
Waseda University
Ohkubo 3-4-1 Shinjuku-ku
Tokyo 160, Japan

Present conditions of THE system which was presented in WCCE/81 are described and some facts and experiences in actual practice are reported.
THE system presents an interactive training and self-paced learning environment.
This report also describes plans for new trials.

§1. THE SYSTEM AND THE PURPOSE OF IT

1-1 THE system

"THE" system (Terada and Hirose Education System) was presented in (1) (WCCE/81) as a system offering, via a microcomputer-controlled videodisc system, an effective training course for high school mathematics.

The decision to combine computer and videodisc technologies was based on the fact that they appeared to be an ideal combination to realize the most effective self-paced CAI system.

The most distinguished feature of THE system is to offer self-paced learning environment which is impossible under regular classroom lessons. To realize this objective, we need sophisticated courseware. This is a tough problem and actually we encountered several difficulties. We needed a lot of response from learners as a feedback information for courseware strategy.

We constructed a proto-type THE system in 1980. Now we are experimenting with the 2nd version system.

And also, we are planning the 3rd version system for new trials.

1-2 Education that Copes with a
Variety of Mathematical Abilities

There are individual differences in the children's and student's speed and depth of learning; however to accomplish one of the aims of a study does not necessarily require the learning speed. What is required is the accomplishment of the study.

Not only the learning speed, but the response to the task of problem solving varies with students. An ideal education is to provide each student with enough time and suitable guidance.

An individual education such as this can not be expected from a classroom of 40 students. This is one reason why a good education system using new media is needed.

Moreover, the percentage of students going to upper secondary education in Japan has reached 95% as of 1985. The variety of the students' mathematical abilities is more of a problem in secondary education than in primary school.

1-3 Education for the Gifted Students

In mass education, gifted students are in a standstill. Gifted students aiming to specialize in mathematics in the future may be provided with good self-study books, but for gifted students, including students aiming to specialize in engineering and economics, a suitable guidance is desirable. So then, an efficient study can be given to the student.

A teacher at school can not look after in such a way. Also in Japan, "grade skipping" is not allowed and will not be for years to come.

THE system has a large influence to the future curriculum of mathematics in Japan.

The need for such a system in Japan was reported by one of the authors, Terada, in the 5th International Congress on Mathematical Education ("Core and Option Module", Aug. 24-29, 1984).

Mathematical education, especially secondary level, requires a system which can provide adequate voice explanations and a large amount of clear images. It also has interactive facilities and can store enough teaching materials.

Our system is a system which follow these requirements.

§2 THE COURSEWARE SYSTEM OF THE SYSTEM

The courseware system is composed of the following subsystems:

(i) Display system—a data base composed of illustrative still and/or motion picture and accompanying sound track.

A tutor, teaching students individually while encouraging the student, will using a methodology suited to the students' ability provide a lecture mainly in definitions and theorems and teach problem solving.

A tutor will teach a individual student a lecture on problem solving by providing mainly definitions and theorems, by using a methodology suited to the student's ability and encouraging the student. This subsystem performs such a tutor's task according to the control system.

(ii) Problem system—a data base of graded and classified problems and answers.

After a lecture, a tutor will provide a student with a suitable problem. A student will then attempt to solve the problem, check the solution and ask for the tutor's help on problem he/she could not solve.

(iii) Evaluation system—gives tests and evaluates the students based upon results and trends.

At suitable intervals, a tutor evaluates the student's total performance. He/she then selects about 10 problems from a "problem bank" and tests the student with them. From the test results, the student's degree of performance and trends are judged. This evaluation system is a subsystem based on this supposition.

(iv) Selection system—selects problems suitable to each student based upon results obtained from the evaluation subsystem.

A tutor will, on realizing that a student has a particular problem before hand, without delay take necessary steps to handle the situation. To do this, he/she prepares suitable materials in advance and pick out the required material any time.

Also when a problem is found to be too difficult, an easier problem must be provided and encourage the student. On the other hand, when a problem is too easy, a more chal-

lenging problem must be given and bring up the moral. This subsystem is used to achieve this.

(v) Control system—controls the above subsystems and records the results and trends developed from the individual student's evaluations.

For any version of THE system, our paradigm of courseware is shown as in figure 1.

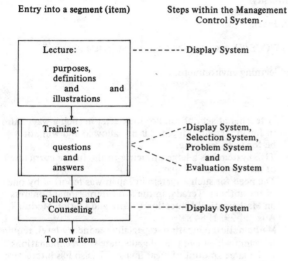
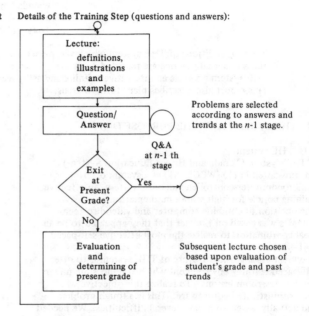

Figure 1.   Courseware paradigm

There are 2 types of courses which we built and provided to the monitors.

Type 1.   Suitable for beginners and is aimed at THE system mimicking the teacher's teaching methods.

The lesson starts with "lecture" which consists of introduction, explanation of the basics and examples. Next is "training" where about 2 problems are attempted and a measure of understanding is obtained.

This is an "item" out of a whole which has a "branch learning type" structure as shown in Figure 2. About 10 minutes is planned for a study of 1 item.

Type 2.   Study in a classroom is assumed and is aimed at supplementing incomplete parts and brushing up, mainly in problem solving.

The study starts with a survey of the students' performance and depending on those results initialized to either F (Fundamental), S (Standard) or H (High) as shown in Figure 3. A student does not know where he/she is positioned. The study of this course starts after the initialization.

In the study of this course, first required basic methods are shown and a standard problem for solving is given. Next according to F, S and H 5 to 6 problems are provided. A concluding study begins when attempts to solve this group of problems finish. This sequence constitutes an item and requires about 2 hours of studying time. During this period "Branch study" is not done.

When an item finishes and on the next day moving to the next item a branch occurs as in the following diagram.

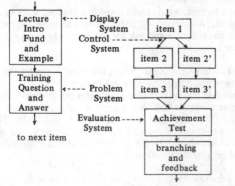

Figure 2, Type 1 Paradigm

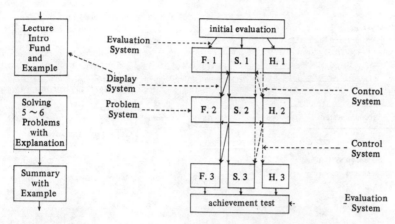

Figure 3, Type 2 Paradigm

In secondary mathematics, the study and accumulation of theories are important, so fine branching and feedback are not adequate. A mixture of the good points of the "liner" type study and "branching" type study is what is required. This is one of the characteristics of type 2.
Currently type 1 is only available as a upper secondary school level trigonometry and type 2 is as the core 14 chapters of the Japanese upper secondary mathematics.

§3 HARDWARE AND SOFTWARE
OF THE SYSTEM IN USE:

In comparison with 1st version system in WCCE/81, the hardware has been made much better at the request for THE system.
The present hardware configuration of THE system is a personal computer connected to a videodisc player as in figure 4.

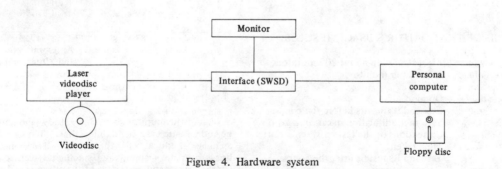

Figure 4. Hardware system

The personal computer used is an Universal Pioneer Corp. PX-7 and NEC-9801. Both have enough power to control the system and monitor the student's progress. The interface to superimpose synthesized image, which was presented as separated at WCCE/81, is now contained in PX-7.
Audio and visual information is recorded on the video disc. The video disc currently used is Pioneer's optical type LD500. This video disc stores 54,000 still images per side or a maximum of 5,400 events (1 event is a 28 sec. sound unit) of images plus sound per side.
SWSD (still with sound and data) is an voice synthesis inter-

face which was not available in the previous version of THE system. This has allowed more voice information to be obtainable incomparable to the previous system. Thus more versatility of the courseware is achieved. The previous system allowed 30 minutes of voice information per side, but due to SWSD a maximum of 42 hours per side of information is now available.
The courseware framework is realized through the software system and divided into the previously mentioned five subsystems. A schematic of these systems is shown Figure 5.

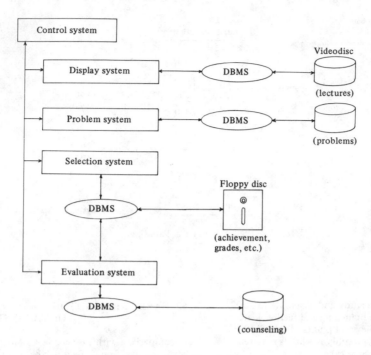

Figure 5. A schematic of the system

Using language to write the major part of the software, in PX-7 system, is MSX and, in NEC 9801 system, is UCSD-pascal.

after before	in favor	not in favor	total
enthu-siastic	63%	10%	73%
anxious or conser-vative	20%	7%	27%
total	83%	17%	100%

Table 1, An Opinion Survey before and after Computer Aided Study

§4. ANALYSIS OF THE MONITOR'S USAGE RESULTS

We have till now tested this system with about 200 monitors. The following data are obtained per monitor.

Before the Study	- Opinion survey
During the Study	- Test and its results before the course
	System modification questionnaire
	Corrections of the test answers
	Time taken
	Test and its results after the course
After the Study	- Opinion survey

* The monitors' tests and their results, problems and their marks and the time taken are all recorded on a floppy disk as a study log.

The data obtained so far will be reported.

4-1 An Opinion Survey on Computer Aided Study

This problem has been analysed before and after the monitor's study. Analysis of before the study has shown that 2 groups exist, a enthusiastic group and an anxious and conservative group. Also analysis of after the study has shown, as a matter of course, the existence of a group in favor of computer aided teaching and a group which is not. This distribution is as shown in Table 1.

Several of the monitors before the study who have stated to be enthusiastic have the opinion that, "A system like this has an image of education in the future". It is thought that since it is a futuristic system, an efficient study can be conducted. On the other hand, monitors of the anxious and conservative group have the opinion that, "There may exist an educational obstacle (especially the lack of humanity)" and that the operation of the system may be difficult.

Survey of the "favored" monitors' opinions after the study has shown that several monitors have expressed the merit of studying at one's pace and that the system is a futuristic educational material which can extend from mathematics to other fields of study. Those monitors not in favor have expressed that controlling the system is not easy as expected and machine learning lacks human touch.

From the point of view of human engineering, analysis of the monitors has shown that the ears (from headphones), eyes, shoulders and hips are strained in particular the eyes. These comments must be considered and hardware modifications to suit the user must be done.

4-2   Comparison with Other Educational Media
The system and the following 3 study methods have been compared from a survey of the students.

For a standard study method:
(A)   Lesson conducted by a teacher in a classroom;
      This approach has the drawback of ignoring each students own ability and studying pace.
(B)   Self-study using text books and reference books;
      The study can be conducted on the students own pace, however it easily becomes monotonous and errors can not be corrected immediately. Also the ordering of the materials may not be best suited to the student.
(C)   Study using mass media such radios and televisions;
      The drawbacks are that this completely ignores the students pace and no feedback is available.

The monitors were asked to choose between (A), (B) and (C) with THE system when studying and about 85% of them has chosen THE system in preference to (A), (B) or (C) (Table 2).

	THE is better	same	better than THE
(A)	85%	10%	5%
(B)	85%	15%	0%
(C)	86%	14%	0%

Table 2, Comparison with Other Media

4-3   Changes in the Attitudes Towards Learning
We surveyed the monitors, before and after the study, about the attitudes towards learning on the following 3 topics:

(a)   Has using THE system helped studying?
(b)   Has using THE system increased the inquisitiveness in mathematics as a whole?
(c)   Is there a significant increase in the understanding of the content studied using THE system?
The results were as shown in Table 3.

	increase	same	decrease
(a)	95%	5%	0%
(b)	80%	20%	0%
(c)	73%	27%	0%

Table 3, Changes in the Attitudes

4-4   Analysis of the Monitors' Study Log
The student's study log is automatically recorded on the floppy disk of THE system. We obtained the effects of the study from this and use them to control the student and improvement of the system.

Here we conducted the following analysis of the students who are still unsure with their knowledge after a normal school study. First 10 problems are given as a test. Next after the study is completed 10 problems similar to the ones given before are tested and the results of the tests are compared.

The mean of the difference between the number of correct answers of each monitor was 3. The details are provided in the graph below. If a dot appears above the dotted line, this simply means that the marks has increased; however from the distribution of the dots, the effect for the better of using the system can be deduced. For monitors, A and B, an unusual situation occurred during the study of a special treatment may be required (Figure 6).

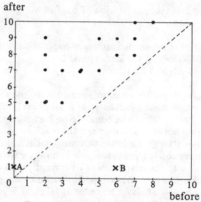

Figure 6, Monitors' Study Log

§5.   Future Directions of THE system
and plans for new trials

The main theme in the 1980's on mathematical education is concerned with problem solving. Not only should the lecture be understood, ambiguous points cleared and the problem solved, thinking along the lines of problem solving, mathematical thinking power advancement methods are required. Also we are very interested in the effects of the increasing power of the computers to the science curriculum and continuing to research in this area.
Whether it is attempting the problem solving course or improving the current THE system, what is needed is to solidify the logical aspects and to improve the man-machine interface, especially input. Also in general, the computing system is itself moving in that direction.
At present, THE system has limitations as follows:
(i)   Limitation of logical aspects.
This is the cause of
(ii)   Limitation to numerical calculations.
(iii) Lack of intermediate evaluation data:
       – This is improved as time goes on.
(iv)   Limitation of input problem, e.g. string manipulation, graph of functions, domain of sets:
       – These will be improve definitely in the near future based on the relative software and hardware improvement.

After all, improvement of man-machine interface and developments of the technologies which look after "logical aspect" should be most important to successfully achieve our purpose of THE system.

We are drawing up a plan to install theorem-proof checking apparatus in our system.

We have encountered several difficulties concerning with realization of proof checking apparatus.

We need just a proof checker. The system must check given proofs. Human-proofs are not always constructed as a sequence of immediate consequences.

Generally speaking, even though given human-proofs are complete in a sense, differences between formal proofs and human-proofs are not so small.

Thus we must make an attempt to come across formal inference rules in harmony with human proofs.

We are making a design of a logical system as a slight modification to NK ("natürlichen klassischer Kalkül" by G. Gentzen).

In this design, it takes utilization of the following (i), (ii), (iii) into account.

(i)   A part of ready-made formula manipulation system.
(ii)   The functions of the language APL.
(iii)   Methodologies of AI.

Furthermore, to preform a proof, prerequisite knowledge and lemmas must be made available as in a data base (perhaps a knowledge base). When one comes to an halt during a check, an interaction between the user and the machine will also be required. An attempt to create this man-machine interface seems to bring about a pessimistic view; however we are optimistic due to the development of current provers or proof checker systems, the cost performance of computers which is increasing at about an order of 10 every 7 years, man-machine interface system and tools.

REFERENCES

[1] F. Terada, K. Hirose and T. Ohno, Instruction technique on using videodisc system.
     IFIP, Proc. of 3rd World Conf. On Computer Education, pp 343-349, 1981

[2] F. Terada, K. Hirose and T. Ohno, THE system— Instruction Using Videodisc and a Microcomputer.
     Educ. Technol. Res., 6, pp 29-36, 1982

[3] H. Fujita and F. Terada, Mathematics Education in a society with High technology.
     Proc. of ICMI-JSME regional conference on math. educ., 1983, Tokyo.

COMPUTERS IN EDUCATION, K. Duncan and D. Harris (eds.)
Elsevier Science Publishers B.V. (North-Holland)
© IFIP, 1985

THE COVENTRY COMPUTER BASED LEARNING PROJECT 1982-1983

Margaret Bell

Coventry Computer Based Learning Unit
TOPSHOP, Greyfriars Lane
Coventry   CV1 2GY
ENGLAND

The Coventry Computer Based Learning Project is introduced and the lessons learned during this initiative are summarised.

A brief background to the project is given together with a project outline; there follows an assessment of the model established for the use of Computer Based Learning.   Then the courseware developed and the model used for this development are described.

Finally an indication is given of the progress that has been made since the completion of the project and the establishment of the Coventry Computer Based Learning Unit.

1.   INTRODUCTION

In December 1983 Coventry successfully completed its 2 year Computer Based Learning (CBL) Project using Control Data's PLATO system.   The Project was funded by national government to the extent of £1.1 million.

The Coventry PLATO Project was developed from a series of discussions during 1981 between representatives of the City of Coventry Local Authority and the Manpower Services Commission (MSC). These discussions centred on:

a   the most efficient means of ensuring youngsters obtained the skills necessary to compete in the labour market.

b   acceptable methods of compensating for 'gaps' in general education to enable youngsters to take full advantage of the training offered.

c   the introduction of youngsters to new technology.

d   the use of the latest and most advanced methods of training.

This paper summarises the lessons we learned during this joint project which studied the ways in which new technology can be integrated into established learning situations.   We investigated the management and organisation of a computer based learning system which must be integrated into the broader work patterns of a variety of institutions over multiple sites. We also established a method of producing computer courseware which is designed to meet specifically defined needs.

In April 1984 the Coventry CBL Unit was formed to build on the experience gained in this project and apply it to microcomputers.

2.   SUMMARY OF LESSONS LEARNED

Experience from this project has shown that at the present time **the most effective and efficient model for the management of Computer Based Learning (CBL) is obtained when the terminals are grouped together in a dedicated room** (which we have called a learning centre) under the supervision of a Learning Centre Administrator (LCA).

The sites chosen for these **learning centres should be within establishments that can allow the maximum possible usage; the site should not be restricted to the traditional school year and they should be open in the evenings and where possible also at the weekends.**

The room chosen for the learning centre should be large enough to accommodate the terminals and other resource materials and also provide space for students to work away from the terminals.

Ideally **each learning centre should have at least 10 terminals with at least two of them flexible enough to be used in other locations.** Every learning centre should have at least one printer capable of printing off student records including any symbols that are used and lesson screen displays.

During this project **no reluctance was shown by off-site users to travel to learning centres** as long as the learning centres had an adequate number of terminals. Several users did comment that in these early days of CBL it was a great advantage to use an existing and established learning centre to gain experience of CBL and to become familiar with the hardware requirements before investment was made into particular hardware or software on an individual basis.

The management problems caused by individual learning were highlighted in this project when attempts were made to integrate Computer Assisted Learning (CAL) with traditional teaching methods. **CAL should be used whenever possible within a structured learning management system.**

Computer Managed Learning can be used both to administer CAL lessons and to structure more traditional learning activities.

As time available for instructors to view lessons at a terminal is likely to be very limited it is important that information about lessons available, their content, objectives, style and structure, should be available in hard copy form. Instructors should be provided with familiarisation courses and be given the opportunity to become confident in the style and presentation material of a lesson before they use it with students.

A responsive system maintenance procedure should be established in order to ensure that the equipment is available for the maximum possible time. **It is extremely important that, when instructors have arranged to integrate CBL into their existing courses, the resource should be reliably available.**

The best applications of CBL made full use of the special characteristics of the medium:

a   **Individualised learning.**
b   **Automatic learning management.**
c   **Immediacy of the learning package.**
d   **Animation and graphic capabilities.**
e   **Privacy of the learning process.**
f   **Interactivity providing immediate feedback.**

We observed that CBL is attractive to students. **There is evidence from this project that students find the computer an acceptable medium through which to follow assessment procedures and testing generally.**

The use of the computer itself was found to be a stimulus for communication; the students spontaneously discussed amongst themselves their experiences whilst using the computer and if, as happened occasionally, two students used the same terminal, they discussed the questions that were asked and justified to each other the answers they wished to input.

CBL is particularly appropriate for those students who are wary of attempting to master learning objectives publicly.

The individualised nature of the lessons and the immediate feedback provided combine to increase the concentration level of those with learning difficulties and the variety of possible input methods make the learning process easier for those with co-ordination difficulties.

The courseware development model should combine the expertise in 3 areas:

a   **Instructors, teachers and lecturers** experienced in developing learning material within agreed subject areas for students of specified ability and age range.

b   **Support staff** experienced using and developing CBL material and in helping instructors to develop their ideas for learning material into formats suitable for computer presentation.

c   **Programmers** who are able to code designs and input them to the computer.

It is important that the Curriculum Working Groups are involved in the testing and validation of the lessons they have developed.

A detailed and comprehensive list of all courseware available should be on hand for those wishing to use the system; this should be cross-referenced by subject and topic.

3.   THE BACKGROUND

The Coventry PLATO Project grew out of the convergent interests of three major organisations. These were:

Coventry Local Education Authority
The Manpower Services Commission (MSC)
Control Data Limited

Because of the size and range of its Youth Programme and its wide experience of working closely with the MSC, Coventry was an appropriate choice to host this project and to organise the assessment and evaluation of computer based learning in a national context.

The system chosen by MSC for this project to investigate Computer Based Learning was Control Data's PLATO system. The PLATO system was run on a main frame computer in Barnet, London. Each of the 9 Coventry sites with PLATO terminals (52 altogether) had its own dedicated communication line.

4.   AN OUTLINE OF THE PROJECT

The general **terms of reference** for the project were as follows:

a   To use Computer Based Learning to provide high quality training in the Youth Opportunities Programme and associated programmes, leading into the Youth Training Schemes and other future initiatives.

b   To evaluate Computer Based Learning against other and more traditional methods in providing cost-effective training.

c   To develop a model based on the experiences of the Coventry project which may lead to the successful introduction of Computer Based Learning elsewhere.

At the outset of the project many decisions had to

be taken about issues around which there was little or no past experience to draw on.

It was decided to group the terminals in dedicated rooms which were called Learning Centres. The reasons supporting this choice were:

a   The terminals should be seen as a resource for everyone on the site.

b   It should be possible for people from other sites to use them on occasions.

c   Access to the terminals should be available to as wide a range of potential users as possible.

d   Terminal usage should be kept as high as possible.

e   It should be possible to allow terminal usage by individuals, groups or whole classes.

f   Terminals should be readily available for use by instructors to monitor and assess student progress.

Several factors were taken into account when the sites for the PLATO terminals were selected. The main ones were:

a   Different types of establishment should be represented: training workshops, colleges, schools, community centres.

b   Youngsters undertaking a wide range of MSC sponsored courses should be allowed access to the computer system.

c   Youngsters and adults outside training schemes should also have the opportunity to use the terminals.

d   The sites should be geographically well spread throughout the city.

As each new learning centre was opened a series of training courses was run and all staff on site were encouraged to attend.

The involvement of teaching staff in project activities was considered to be of major importance; they were encouraged to preview lessons, read information on the learning objectives and teaching strategies of the lessons and to access and monitor students' records.

There were basically 3 ways in which learning activities on PLATO were integrated into existing courses:

a   The instructor accompanied a group of students to the Learning Centre, supervised their PLATO usage and took them 'off-line' to discuss and resolve any problems that became evident.

b   The instructor supervised several learning activities in the Learning Centre, one of which

was PLATO usage; the students followed the PLATO lessons when appropriate in their course and on a rota basis if necessary.

c   A student used PLATO on a planned programme of work but with no teaching supervision present; instructors or teachers responsible for the student's course were encouraged to view the system and 'visit' the student during his or her PLATO access time.

The terminal in the library at one of the sites was used under the supervision of the librarian; she allowed students free access on a booking system but monitored very closely the type of lessons that were chosen and the progress made.

As their titles suggest the Learning Centre Administrators were originally employed to ensure the smooth operation of the learning centres, to administer terminal bookings, to ensure that users knew how to access lessons and records and to inform the engineers in the event of machine failure. None of the LCAs had any experience of programming, systems analysis, or computer operations nor had they any other experience of computers. It was clear from the start that they would be required to do much more than had been originally defined. Most importantly they had very quickly to become familiar with the lessons available so that they could advise instructors on those which might be appropriate for a particular course or to meet specified objectives.The role of the LCA expanded dramatically during the curriculum development phase of the project when each was expected to provide the technical support in analysis and design to one or more working groups and then to oversee the evaluation and implementation of the courseware.

The PLATO terminals were always considered to be a city-wide Coventry resource that happened to be based on 9 specific sites. After PLATO usage had been established in the host sites, other groups throughout Coventry were encouraged to use PLATO at a convenient site local to them. The terminal booking system became highly complex in order to provide the flexibility necessary to accommodate various user groups from distant sites with a variety of patterns of working.

In January 1983 members of the project Steering Group requested that Coventry special schools should be offered the use of PLATO.

The Coventry Project received several visitors from training departments within industry; they were interested in the Coventry models for using Computer Managed Learning and for producing computer courseware.

5.   ASSESSMENT OF THE MODEL

As the model for the use of Computer Based Learning in Coventry was implemented over time it was continually adapted in the light of the experience gained.

In most cases terminals were grouped together in learning centres; however, there were also circumstances when it was beneficial to have a terminal in the workshop.

We conclude that, in order to justify through adequate student usage the permanent placement of a terminal in a workshop, there must be sufficient courseware available which is directly related to the activities of that workshop. In many cases it may be a better option to develop a facility to move terminals into workshops as and when they are required.

The number of terminals available in a learning centre had a major effect on the way in which they could be used with students and on how the instructor could integrate their use into an existing course. All the sites with 4 terminals complained that more were needed; it was claimed to be extremely difficult to organise whole groups of students to use the system and, where an attempt was made fully to integrate CBL lessons as part of a course, it was often very difficult to provide the students with access to sufficient terminals at appropriate times. In some cases supervisors based at a 4 terminal site looked for opportunities to transport their students to an 8 terminal site to enable more to have hands-on access simultaneously.

The size of the learning centre was also an important factor in determining the way CBL was integrated into existing courses; it was easier to integrate PLATO into a course if the learning centre was large enough to allow other off-line activities to take place in the same room, enabling the instructor to supervise and help all the students together.

The sites varied in the amount of access time they could offer to potential users. Where PLATO was available outside normal working hours it provided the opportunity for less formal use. By March 1983 usage was established at about 5500 hours per month. In order to maintain the necessary element of flexibility and because of inevitable late cancellations this was considered to be the maximum average usage level that could be expected.

We are quite sure that it is crucial that, before the installation of terminals, the site management and all the teaching staff should be fully informed about the new resource, how training in its use will be made available to them, how it is envisaged they might use it and the extent to which it will be available to their students.

In general the initial response of the staff was cautious enthusiasm; understandably they did not want to introduce a new resource to their students before they themselves were confident in its use but, once introduced to the system, they were very quick to see its potential application.

A few staff showed concern at an early stage in the project that PLATO would mean a reduction in their professional workload. This was found not to be the case although **the use of CBL does change roles; staff spend more time in helping individual students follow personal learning programmes and in picking up and dealing with problems detected** than in class or group teaching.

It does seem that CBL **provides an ideal way of individualising learning.** However, in order that the students can benefit fully the computer must also supply management support; the teaching staff are then relieved of the burden of administration and are able to concentrate on the tuition required.

Some students were very apprehensive about using a computer and afraid they were going to be placed in a 'failure' situation; once they started using the lessons on the computer and were able to experience the frequent and positive feedback they were very confident about (and proud of) their use of PLATO.

There was no evidence that the initial enthusiasm for PLATO reduced with familiarity; many students followed lessons on PLATO throughout their 12 month course and showed no reluctance to continue their programmed access.

The students responded particularly well to the privacy and individual nature of the learning experience. The immediate and positive feedback given, the endless patience of the system and the opportunity for the student to work at his/her own pace combined to make the learning experience rewarding and stimulating. One of the characteristics of students using lessons on the computer most commented on by staff was the increase in concentration span.

In general students appeared to find the computer an acceptable medium through which to undertake activities about which they were normally reticent.

The attitudes of the children from special schools who used PLATO were similar to those of other PLATO users already described but more exaggerated. One Head made the following comment in a report he submitted to the Coventry team on his pupils' use of PLATO: **"Because the terminal provides a one to one relationship it is a situation in which the child with special needs thrives". We endorse this comment and regard it as a major advantage of CBL.** This experiment in the use of PLATO clearly demonstrated that **Computer Based Learning is particularly appropriate for children with special needs; it generates enthusiasm and motivation, it allows privacy and self progression.**

It was important that Coventry teaching staff should be familiar with using CBL and with different styles of computer-presented lessons before the Coventry Courseware development got under way. The lessons available at the beginning of the project demonstrated a wide variety of styles of presentation and teaching strategy. Some lessons demonstrated an extensive use of PLATO's facilities and proved to be a good application of

CBL; other lessons were examples of poor uses of CBL, often only 'page-turners' which did no more than a text book and did it less efficiently and effectively. It was important for both these types of lessons to be viewed and assessed in order for the worst mistakes to be avoided and the best ideas to be applied during the courseware development stage of the project.

6. DEVELOPMENT OF COURSEWARE

The purpose of **the courseware development model** was to focus staff with relevant experience and expertise on 4 main tasks:

a   Designing learning strategy for students of specified ability and age.

b   Curriculum development within agreed subject areas.

c   Designing and developing CBL courseware.

d   Programming.

In order to monitor and initiate the courseware development the Project Team established the Curriculum Development Group in January 1983.

This group was required:

a   To recommend to the Project Team areas for courseware development.

b   To control the development of courseware.

c   To construct a courseware development schedule and ensure target dates were met.

d   To assess the model for courseware development and recommend amendments where necessary.

e   To establish and maintain standards for Coventry courseware.

f   To ensure that the development process was well documented.

The following development areas were agreed:

a   Core Literacy.

b   English as a Second Language.

c   Health and Safety at Work.

d   Catering.

e   Electronics.

f   Mechanical Engineering.

g   Motor Vehicle Servicing.

h   Textile and Commercial Sewing.

i   Craft Design and Technology.

j   Student Centered Assessment.

The Curriculum Development Group was responsible for establishing a Curriculum Working Group for each area of courseware development that had been agreed. Many of the working group members were initially apprehensive because their knowledge of computers was limited or non-existent. They were assured that **it was their experience in teaching and their knowledge of the subject area that was valuable** and that their prime responsibilities were for good lesson design.

Although the same Curriculum Development Model was used for all the Coventry Courseware, each group's experience was slightly different either because of the composition of the membership or because of the peculiarities of the subject matter with which it was dealing. **It should be emphasised at this point that the flexibility of the model allowed the accommodation of such variations whilst maintaining quality and standards.**

In general the Curriculum Development Model used was extremely successful; the management of the project was impressed by the quality and quantity of courseware produced. **All those involved considered the model used to be an efficient way of using expertise and the best way to produce a product which would have credibility with the user group and meet its requirements, and which was also technically sound, reliable and robust.**

It was part of the responsibilities of the Curriculum Working Groups to initiate and monitor the validation of the Coventry Courseware.

The standardised validation methods collected information in four areas.

a   Student Performance.

b   Student Attitude.

c   Instructor Attitude.

d   Resource Implications.

Students stated that they found the instructions on the computer easy to follow and that any initial apprehension they felt about using a computer was replaced by a feeling of achievement. Many commented that where they were first introduced to skills on the computer and then were asked to apply those skills in a workshop situation they had more confidence in the practical application and felt they retained more information about the processes involved.

In general the attitude of the instructors to the integration of CBL into their courses was much more favourable in the case of Coventry Courseware than it had been when they were considering the courseware that had existed on PLATO originally. Some of this change in attitude could be attributed to the content of the lessons but some of the change was due more to the general credibility of the courseware and the fact that many of the instructors had been personally involved in its development or stood in a professional relationship with those who had been so involved.

7.   THE FUTURE

As a result of the PLATO project Coventry built up a rare concentration of experience in managing CBL on a large scale, integrating it into existing learning situations, monitoring the effect of CBL on students' attitudes , innovation and performance and developing high quality Computer Based Learning materials.   The Steering Group of the project recommended to the MSC that, "as a matter of urgency ways should be sought to build on the work which has been completed in this project.   The experience, expertise and commitment of teaching and workshop staff in Coventry and the training facilities of the LEA offer an immediate opportunity for further development to enhance the learning and training opportunities for those in employment, those out of work, and especially those young people who are preparing for the first time to face the challenge and the difficulties of the adult world".

A small bridging project, funded by the MSC, ran from 1st January to 31st March 1984.   It was established to consolidate the work of the PLATO project and to provide a transition period for the changeover from an on-line mainframe system to a system using microcomputers.

The CBL Unit was established in April 1984 to build on the work of the previous projects and to utilise the expertise of the CBL team in Coventry. The work of the Unit is progressing in two areas:

i   The provision of resources and support for the use of CBL.

ii   The production of new CBL materials.

COMPUTERS IN EDUCATION, K. Duncan and D. Harris (eds.)
Elsevier Science Publishers B.V. (North-Holland)
© IFIP, 1985

CORRELATIONS BETWEEN INSTRUCTOR, COURSE, AND CAI TUTORIALS

Avi Rushinek, Sara F. Rushinek, and Joel Stutz

University of Miami, Coral Gables, Florida

The present study evaluates the relationship among the EDP instructor and course evaluation and the use of Computer Assisted Instruction (CAI) software. This study identifies the "spill-over" effects. It concludes that these variables are highly and significantly related to each other. The understanding of such problems may be helpful for system resources planning and control.

1. INTRODUCTION AND OBJECTIVES

Romaniuk and Montgomerie (13) studied the use of Computer Assisted Instruction (CAI) as a supplement to a BASIC introductory computer course taken by first year computer systems students. Eighteen students took the course with CAI while another eighteen students took the course without CAI. Romaniuk and Montgomerie compared the performance and the time required to complete the course. However, much like other researchers (5-12), they did not evaluate the learning curve and its effects on the planning and control of CAI software.

Numerous other studies report on successful applications of CAI (1,2-3,4). However, none have examined the "spill-over" effect as it relates to BASIC programming for business. Accordingly, the hypothesis concerning user learning will be tested. This should help students, instructors, and CAI authors to better plan their work, as suggested by Rushinek et al. (14-18).

The main objective of this study is to evaluate the spill-over that takes place in learning to program in the BASIC programming language, using business applications. In addition, this study will make suggestions concerning the methodology of using the instructor evaluation survey to study the impact of CAI out of class, as well as in the classroom.

2. METHODOLOGY AND PROCEDURES

The subjects in this study were 239 novice computer users receiving instruction in the BASIC programming language via formal classroom lecture supplemented by CAI tutorials (Appendix B). The instructor had no part in the creation and implementation of the CAI programs or the study. Therefore, he had no vested interest in the outcome, except his consent to expose his students to this CAI experience.

This paper presents an evaluation of Computer Assisted Instruction (CAI). The basis for this evaluation are summated variables of items included in the Course Instruction Survey. Table 1 describes the definitions of these variables (V are the items on the questionnaire in Appendix A).

Table 1. Attitudinal Variable Definitions

Column A Variables Summated Rates	B Definitions from Variables (V) in Appendix A	C*D=E
Course =	V18+V19+V22+V24+V28+ V34+V36................	6*4=24
Instructor =	V21+V23+V25+V26+V27+ V29+V30+V32+V33+V35+ V37+V38................	12*4=48
Computer =	V40 through V63........	23*4=115
Tutins =	V66+V67+V68+V75+V76.....	5*4=20
Tutcom =	V69+V70+V71+V72+V73.....	5*4=20
Complain =	V64+V65+V20.............	3*4=12

C = Number of Questions
D = Neutral Value Per Question (4)
E = Indifference Total Per Variable

The first two variables in Table 1 are course and instructor. The variable Course, for example, is comprised of seven subscales, Items 18, 19, 22, 24, 28, 34, and 36 in the Course Instruction Survey. The variable Instructor is comprised of Items 21 through 38 and measures the students' attitudes toward their instructor. The variable called Computer, measures students' attitudes toward the computer. The variable Complain includes such items which indicate how students felt about waiting for the computer. Tutins reflects students' attitude towards the tutorial instruction, while Tutcom reflects attitudes towards the CAI. Finally, Complain reflects students' complaints.

Table 2 gives the number of valid cases and the mean and standard deviation of each variable. One may evaluate each of these means in regard to their location on the range of the distribution according to the definitions in Table 1. For instance, the mean of Tutins, 15.8787, indicates that the students have a definite overall positive attitude. It is substantially lower from the criterion of neutrality, 20, which is computed as the five variables times the attitudinal score of 4.000 (indifference).

Table 2. Mean and Standard Deviation
          of the Attitudinal Variables

Column A Variable Names	B Cases	C Mean Summated Rates	D Indifference Levels (from Table 1)
Course	239	19.51	< 24
Instructor	239	32.99	< 48
Computer	239	30.61	<115
Tutins	239	15.87	< 20
Tutcom	239	17.42	< 20
Complain	239	11.83	< 12

	E. Std. Dev.	F=D/Questions Average Rates Per Question	G Rank
Course	6.03	3.24	4
Instructor	10.22	2.75	2
Computer	8.52	1.33	1
Tutins	6.27	3.17	3
Tutcom	4.86	3.48	5
Complain	3.37	3.94	6

The comparison between the means (Column C) and the indifference levels (Column D) reveals that the mean values are much lower than the indifference values (for all variables except "Complain"). This indicates that the general attitudes were rather positive. Likewise, the complaints were close to indifference. The scales have been redefined in such a way that the lower scores (1-3) denote positive attitudes, the median (4) indicates indifference, and the higher scores (5-7) indicate negative attitudes.

Table 3 shows the results of the correlation between attitudes toward the tutorials versus attitudes toward the instructor (Tutins). The statistically significant correlations in Table 3 show that there is a definite spillover effect among these variables. Thus, one may assume that very positive attitudes toward the CAI may affect positively the instructor as well as the course evaluation. Therefore, since most of these variables are affected by using the CAI, as was previously demonstrated, the instructor evaluation is likely to be positively affected as well.

Table 3. Pearson Correlation of
          the Variable Instructor

Variable Pair	Coeff.	N	Sig.	Variance-Covar
Instructor-Course	.5952	239	.000	36.7416
Instructor-Computer	.3065	239	.000	26.7211
Instructor-Tutins	.3826	239	.000	24.5709
Instructor-Tutcom	.2330	239	.000	11.5942
Instructor-Complain	.1760	239	.003	6.0707

3. SUMMARY, CONCLUSIONS AND IMPLICATIONS

In summary, this study described how a modified instructor evaluation form can be used as a research instrument. The "spill-over" effect from CAI related variables onto the attitudes of students toward the instructor, the course and the computer was evaluated. The spill-over effect was found to be statistically significant and generalizable to the population.

It is concluded that the students who were using the CAI program enjoyed it and attributed it to the instructor, the computer and the course, although the instructor had nothing to do with the CAI except for having conceded to include the CAI as a homework assignment. It is also concluded that the instructor evaluation survey can be used effectively as a CAI research instrument.

The implications of this study are that the use of CAI to supplement classroom instruction significantly improves students' attitude toward the instructor and the course. This improvement is further dependent upon the attitudes toward the CAI used and the availability of proper computer facilities for using this CAI. Therefore, the improvement in instructor evaluation demonstrated in this paper is likely to increase due to improving CAI quality and the availability of facilities. However, these conclusions are restricted to the aforementioned population, namely, lower-division introductory computer courses for business college students. This methodology may be applied to other groups of students such as upper-division college students and high-school students as a possible extension to this study.

Moreover, instructors who would like to improve their student evaluation may try to incorporate CAI into their curriculum. This is especially applicable to instruction about the use of a computer. In the computer areas, the bonus will not only improve students' attitudes toward the instructor and the computer, but also improve the students' attitudes toward the course topic.

APPENDIX A

COURSE INSTRUCTION SURVEY

The objective of this questionnaire is to aid in improving teaching effectiveness. Results will provide the Business School with information which will assist in strengthening all aspects of this course.

For the results to be most useful, your answers should,

1. be based on your own individual thinking,
2. be as honest and objective as possible,
3. reflect overall performance rather than isolated incidents,
4. reflect a genuine and thoughtful response to each question independently, i.e., an answer that is not influenced by your other answers, or by your attitude toward other aspects of the course.

In addition, your comments on all aspects of the course and its instruction (whether reflected in the questions or not) are encouraged in the space provided. Specific written comments often provide the most valuable con-

structive criticism available to the College of Business Administration – Department of General Business.

INSTRUCTIONS: Please mark your responses to the following items on the separate answer sheet provided you! (Do not mark the question sheet.) Your responses will have no effect on your grade and will be kept strictly confidential.

Column #

1. Mark 4 in column 1.

2-10. Fill in your social security number in column #2 through 10.

11-17. Fill in your P.P.N. (Programmer Project Number) in columns #11 through 17.

18. The grade I expect to get for this course is:

     1. A   3. C   5. F
     2. B   4. D

19. In comparison with other courses my effort in this course so far is:

     1. Well above the average
     2. Above the average
     3. Average
     4. Below the average
     5. Well below the average

All items (20 – 39) use the same response scale, in which:

     1. Strongly agree
     2. Moderately agree
     3. Slightly agree
     4. Uncertain
     5. Slightly disagree
     6. Moderately disagree
     7. Strongly disagree

Column #

20. I appreciate this instruction evaluation survey as a useful tool to improve this course.

21. The instructor seems enthusiastic about the subject.

22. So far, I have found this course to be interesting.

23. The instructor seems well prepared for lecture and/or discussion.

24. This course seems very relevant to my own interests and goals.

25. The instructor seems informed of current trends and developments in the area.

26.   Assignments and presentations are usually worthwhile.

27.   So far, the instructor has been fair in his/her dealings with students.

28.   I think this course is unusually difficult for me.

29.   The instructor generally paces the course well.

30.   I generally enjoy attending this class.

31.   The instructor is generally accessible during office hours.

32.   I frequently feel confused during this class.

33.   The examples and illustrations used usually help me understand the subject.

34.   The objectives of this course are usually clear.

35.   The examination questions are usually clearly related to the subject material being covered.

36.   The assignments in this course are usually clear to me.

37.   The instructor's manner of presentation usually holds my attention during class.

38.   The instructor communicates his/her ideas clearly.

39.   The multimedia approach used in this course is superior to the traditional blackboard presentation.

For each pair of alternatives below (40 – 63) mark the number 1 – 7 which best describes your feelings about computers. For example on set number 40, if you think that the computer is powerful, mark one of the numbers between 5 through 7, where 7 represents greatest power. Likewise powerlessness is represented by numbers 1 through 4, with 4 being neutral.

40. powerless......   1234567   powerful
41. inefficient....   1234567   efficient
42. good..........   1234567   bad
43. useless........   1234567   useful
44. interesting....   1234567   boring
45. harmful........   1234567   harmless
46. understandable.   1234567   mystifying
47. difficult to use   1234567   easy to use
48. non-threatening   1234567   threatening
49. rewarding......   1234567   disappointing
50. strong........   1234567   weak
51. pleasing.......   1234567   annoying
52. fast..........   1234567   slow

53. tense..........   1234567   relaxed
54. fair...........   1234567   unfair
55. passive........   1234567   active
56. flexible.......   1234567   inflexible
57. discouraging...   1234567   encouraging
58. dangerous......   1234567   safe
59. subjective.....   1234567   objective
60. simple.........   1234567   complicated
61. indifferent....   1234567   sensitive
62. individualistic   1234567   not
                         1234567   individualistic
63. imprecise......   1234567   precise

FOR ITEMS 64 – 76, USE THE SAME RESPONSE SCALE AS FOR ITEMS 20 – 39.

64.   The computer lab proctors were helpful when I asked them questions.

65.   I had to wait too long for either a terminal or telephone line.

66.   I received individual attention from the tutorial.

67.   I enjoyed the flexibility given to me by the tutorial.

68.   I recieved objective performance evaluation by the tutorial.

69.   While using the computer I felt challenged to do my best.

70.   While using the computer I felt isolated and alone.

71.   I felt I could work at my own pace with the computer.

72.   Using the computer is an efficient use of a student's time.

73.   While using the computer I encountered disturbing mechanical malfunctions.

74.   I feel that classroom instruction supplemented with computerized instruction is superior to traditional classroom instruction only.

75.   My performance was evaluated fairly by the tutorials.

76.   I received immediate and frequent feedback from the tutorials.

77-   The grade I received on the last exam is:
79.   (please right justify the above)

APPENDIX B

(Beginning All Purpose Symbolic
Interactive Code)

BASIC TUTORIAL TOPICS

Please select one of the following modules in
sequence:

Tutorial 1	Review of Arithmetic Operators.
Tutorial 2	Introduction to System Commands.
Tutorial 3	Variable Names.
Tutorial 4	BASIC Statements.
Tutorial 5	Unconditional Branching and Arrays.
Tutorial 6	Additional BASIC Statements and System Commands.
Tutorial 7	Conditional Branching (if Statement).
Tutorial 8	Looping (For/Next Statements).

Please enter a tutorial number (1-8) and press
the return key.

REFERENCES

[1] Barr, A. and Others. "The Computer as a Tutorial Laboratory: The Stanford BIP Project." *International Journal of Man-Machine Studies*, Vol. 8, No. 5, pp. 567-596.

[2] Boyle, T. and G. Wright. "Computer-Assisted Evaluation of Student Achievement." *Engineering Education*, Vol. 68, pp. 1-5.

[3] Brown, B. R. "An Instrument for the Measure of Expressed Attitude Toward Computer-Assisted Instruction." *Experimentation with Computer-Assisted Instruction in Technical Education*, H. E. Mitzel and G. L. Bradon (eds.), (Semi-Annual Progress Report, Project No. OEC-5-85-074), University Park, Pa., The Pennsylvania State University, December 31, 1966.

[4] Bunderson, C. V. "The Computer and Instructional Design." *Computer-Assisted Instruction, Testing and Guidance*, W. E. Holtzman (ed.). Harper and Row, Inc., 1970.

[5] Buss, A. and G. Kearsley. "Individual and Small-Group Learning with Computer-Assisted Instruction." *AV Communication Review*, Vol. 24(1), 1976, pp. 79-86.

[6] Caldwell, E., D. Nix, and P. Peckham. "The Use of CAI to Provide Problems for Students in Introductory Genetics." *Journal of Computer-Based Instruction*, Vol. 3(1), August, 1976, pp. 13-20.

[7] Chandra, G. "A Study of the Consensus on Disclosure among Public Accountants and Security Analysts." *The Accounting Review*, Vol. 49, No. 4 (1974), pp. 733-742.

[8] Chizmar, J. and Others. "Assessing the Impact of an Instructional Innovation on Achievement Differentials: The Case of Computer-Assisted Instruction." *Journal of Economic Education*, Vol. 9, pp. 42-6.

[9] *Computer-Assisted Instruction in Programming: AID Project*, Progress Reports - Stanford Program in Computer-Assisted Instruction, July 1, 1968 to September 30, 1969.

[10] *Computer-Assisted Instruction in Programming: SIMPER and LOGO Project*, Progress Reports - Stanford Program in Computer-Assisted Instruction, July 1, 1968 to September 30, 1969.

[11] Dorn, C. "Computer Assistance in Veterinary Medical Education." *Journal of Veterinary Medical Education*, Vol. 3, pp. 7-21.

[12] Ellinger, R. and P. Frankland. "Computer-Assisted and Lecture Instruction: A Comparative Experiment." *Journal of Geography*, Vol. 75, pp. 109-120.

[13] Romaniuk, E. W. and T. C. Montgomerie. "After Implementing Your CAI Course--What's Next." Alberta University, Edmonton, June 1976. ERIC Ed. 151022.

[14] Rushinek, S., Rushinek, A. and Stutz, J. "Forecasting Interactive System Modification Used for Software Maintenance: An Empirical Investigation of User-Computer Interaction," *Journal of Educational Technology Systems*, Volume 12, No. 1, 1983-1984, 15-37.

[15] Rushinek, A., Rushinek, S. and Stutz, J. "Systems Quality Control Through Measuring Users' Attitudes," *The Journal of Data Education*, Spring 1983, 16-19.

[16] Rushinek, A., Rushinek, S. and Stutz, J. "A Methodology for Interactive Evaluation of User Reactions to Software Packages: An Empirical Analysis of System Performance, Interaction, and Run Time," *International Journal of Man-Machine Studies* (accepted for publication).

[17] Rushinek, A., Rushinek, S. and Stutz, J. "Development and Testing of a Discriminant Model for Measuring Changes in Instructor Evaluations due to Using Computer-Assisted Instruction," *The Journal of Computers in Mathematics and Science Teaching*, Vol. II, No. 4, Summer 1983, 17-25.

COMPUTERS IN EDUCATION, K. Duncan and D. Harris (eds.)
Elsevier Science Publishers B.V. (North-Holland)
© IFIP, 1985

SPECIAL PROJECTS IN COMPUTING EDUCATION:
BANK STREET SCHOOL OF EDUCATION

STEPHEN SHULLER, MODERATOR

This session will include presentations of current Bank Street activities related to the use of computers in education, followed by time for questions and discussion.

Bank Street has been active in computer education in a number of ways, including research, software and curriculum development, teacher education, and consultation and staff development activities with schools, school districts, and other educational agencies.

Through our Center for Children and Technology, (CCT), Bank Street researchers have been involved in several major projects concerning the use of technology in education. Current research projects include studies of environments which support the development of programming skills in children, uses for information management tools in education, networking, and interactive videodisk applications.

The Bank Street Media group develops software and print materials. Beginning with the Bank Street Writer, we have focused on the development of "tool" software which can expand students' powers to create and to manipulate computer-based tools for information management (the Bank Street Filer) and letter writing (the Bank Street Mailer), an environment for exploring mathematical relationships, and a program to facilitate telecommunications.

With the support of the U.S. Office of Education, Bank Street has been developing a multi-media learning environment in science and mathematics called The Voyage of the Mimi. This project is based around an adventure TV series, and includes print materials, computer software, and an interface for computer-monitored science laboratory equipment. Under the auspices of the National Science Foundation, our Mathematics, Science and Technology Teacher Education (MASTTE) Project is currently working with schools to effectively use the Mimi materials in classrooms.

The Bank Street Graduate School of Education has recently begun a masters degree program in education and technology. This program prepares teachers to use computers as educational tools, and to apply to the new technology the Bank Street approach of student-centered education.

Through its Computer Outreach Services, Bank Street has been working with several schools and school districts to use computers effectively in their educational programs. In addition, administrative applications, and staff and curriculum development. In 1984-85, we worked with 28 of the nation's largest school districts as one of two coordinators of IBM's Model School Computer Literacy Program.

PANELISTS

George Burns
Faculty Member, Computer Education Program
Bank Street Graduate School

Laura Martin
Research Associate
Center for Children and Technology

Regan McCarthy
Director
MASTTE Project

Stephen Shuller
Director
Computer Outreach Services

COMPUTERS IN EDUCATION, K. Duncan and D. Harris (eds.)
Elsevier Science Publishers B.V. (North-Holland)
©IFIP, 1985

THE IBM/ETS SECONDARY SCHOOL COMPUTER EDUCATION PROGRAM

Randy E. Bennett, Roger C. Kershaw, Martin B. Schneiderman, Brian M. Stecher

EDUCATIONAL TESTING SERVICE
Princeton, NJ, Los Angeles, CA

The IBM/ETS Secondary School Computer Education Program involved the donation of over 1500 IBM Personal Computers, a substantial amount of software, teacher training, and technical support to 101 schools in New York, California, and Florida. The program's major objective was to facilitate the use of computers in a wide variety of secondary school curricular areas, especially in such nontraditional computing areas as the humanities and social sciences. The software used to achieve this integration primarily fell into the category of applications programs: word processors, database management systems, spreadsheets, graphics and graphing tools, and telecommunications utilities.

Over the course of the program, participating schools were visited, questionnaire data were collected, interviews conducted, and narrative reports submitted by participating institutions. From these sources, a picture of how computers were actually used by program schools was constructed. This presentation will describe the program in terms of the hardware and software used, training provided, costs incurred by schools, and impacts detected. Problems encountered by educators in integrating computers into the secondary school curriculum will be described and recommendations for integration will be offered.

1. STAFF TRAINING

At the outset, we recognized that for the IBM Secondary School Computer Education Program to be successful, staff training would need to be a major focus of the program. ETS began by conducting an intensive two-week institute for a cadre of 24 teacher-trainers, two from each of the 12 participating teacher-training institutions. These educators, in turn, conducted month-long summer institutes that were attended by almost 500 high school teachers (representing 26 different subjects), school principals, and district administrators.

As part of the program, we conducted and documented site visits to all of the training programs, evaluated the institutes, and identified common characteristics of programs that we considered to be the most successful. As a result, we have developed specific recommendations for future staff training programs.

2. HARDWARE AND SOFTWARE

In selecting the hardware and software components of the IBM Secondary School Computer Education Program, ETS and IBM were strongly influenced by several discrete aims: a) promoting equitable access and use by minority groups and women; b) eliciting a sense of ownership in the program on the part of the schools; c) ensuring that school curricula would not be dictated, or perceived as being dictated, by ETS or IBM and; d) facilitating the continued use of the hardware and software in the schools beyond the 1983/84 school year. In addition, logistical considerations relative to shipping, setup,

installation and maintenance of 1500 PCs at over 100 institutions required special plans and procedures.

3. NETWORK SUPPORT AND PROGRAM IMPACT

Schools participating in the IBM/ETS Program were organized into geographically proximal clusters, or networks, supported by a teacher training institution (TTI). Beyond the initial training of teachers, it was the responsibility of the TTI to assist network schools in developing and implementing their computer education programs. ETS, in turn, took responsibility for supporting each of the twelve TTIs in the program.

Through their interactions with TTIs and schools, ETS staff members were able to construct a picture of how the program operated in participating schools. In addition, the program's effects were studied, including the degree to which overall program goals were attained, extent of unintended consequences for students, teachers, and institutions, and level of consumer satisfaction with the project.

4. UNANTICIPATED COSTS OF COMPUTER EDUCATION

Each school that participated in the IBM/ETS program received hardware and software valued at approximately $70,000, training for three or four staff members, and professional assistance during the school year. Yet, each still incurred additional costs for site preparation, security, staff participation, etc. We surveyed a sample of 21 schools in the program to determine the type and level of costs they incurred.

We compiled a list of cost categories that are
relevant to computer education, and analyzed the
distribution of costs in these categories among
schools in the program.   The analysis also
suggested relationships between program characteristics and costs which will be discussed.

COMPUTERS IN EDUCATION, K. Duncan and D. Harris (eds.)
Elsevier Science Publishers B.V. (North-Holland)
© IFIP, 1985

EXTRAPOLATION THEORY OF LEARNING AND COMPUTER-BASED EDUCATION

Boyan Lalov

Higher Institute of Mechanical and Electrical Engineering,
Department of Pedagogy, Sofia 1156, Bulgaria

The two traditional problems encountered by modern educational processes – the problem of forgetting and the problem of the enormous volume of educational information – can be successfully solved only on condition that the aims of education should be radically changed. As long as the main aim is acquisition of knowledge, time will always be short. In the present paper an attempt is made to formulate a system of principles which should reflect the objective laws of building up the mechanisms of thinking in the process of education.

Computer science is moving ahead of the scientific study of man. The concepts of classical pedagogy are not sufficient for the efficient utilization of the continously increasing possibilities of computer use in education. It is necessary to re-evaluateexisting concepts of education, having in mind the following two factors :

1. The contradiction between the fast growth of information created by society and the structure of the nervous system of individual human beings which is not able to perceive the intensive flood of information.

2. The experimental and theoretical results which reveal that learning is a fundamental scientific category equally affecting the problems of information processing both by natural and artificial systems.

With that background, characteristic of the interaction between man and machines during the second half of the 20th century, a universal objective law of human nature is outlined that connects education and thinking, activity and creativity; that objective law should be laid as the basis of modern education.

It is, in fact, the significant property of the nervous system to predict, to extrapolate the development of processes, thanks to information accumulated (though incomplete) during the interaction with the environment.

In the field of neurophisiology the problem of extrapolation (anticipation) has been widely discussed during the last decades, but in the field of pedagogy this problem has not been

sufficiently investigated yet.

The universal property of the nervous network to extrapolate is manifested on all levels in the hierarchy of brain. The figure 1 illustrates the extrapolation effect on the level of the optic cortex. The sides of the white triangle(a) occupying a central place in the figure, are not plotted but, nevertheless, it can be distinctly perceived. The boundary between the left and the right regions (b) is distinctly perceived as a continuous curve, although only separate points of this curve have been fixed.

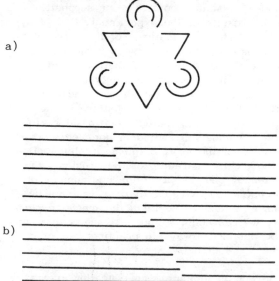

Figure 1 : Extrapolation Effect

In a similar way, on the basis of separate fragments, models of various phenomena that have not been observed and motions that have not been done, may be formed in the brain, broad regions of the sensor and motor cortex being involved. This is a process of a chain-like and avalanche-like formation of coalitions of excited nervous cells and their disintegration and suppression under the influence of other, newly-formed coalitions.

Some aspects of this process have been modelled by means of computer-aided simulation (1,2).

Thanks to the universal ability of the nervous system to predict, to extrapolate the development of phenomena, the objects in our subjective notions may be "subjected" to various effects : they can rotate, move together or away from each other. We can not only manipulate the model, but we can change its dimensions and shape. We can treat it with various substances, change the conditions of processing, prepare elements of arbitrary accuracy, of arbitrary strength, elasticity, relative weight, etc. Those mental manipulations with the objects of our thinking play an enormous, still unassessed, role in the process of education and creativity. The most characteristic feature of the subjective models (images) that are in our mental pictures or in our imagination is the fact that they are subject to additional and continous improvement. This means that we can correct, make precise or improve those models in the process of their utilization, while we constantly compare our suppositions with the results of the experiment. One of the most characteristic features of the extrapolating mechanisms of the nervous system is their multiplicational effect, i.e. their applicability in various situations and not only in those strict conditions under which they had been built. Still another essential feature is their ability to enter into mutual relationships, to combine themselves and form complete complexes in solving new, original problems. Depending on the character of the problem, the experience, and the precision and number of the constructed extrapolating mechanisms by means of which we perform the mental experiment, we can achieve unusual results that cannot be obtained always in practice, but may be checked indirectly.

The advent of computers in education created exceptionally favourable conditions for the development of the extrapolating properties of the human mind thanks to the interaction of the student with mathematical, phisical, chemical and biological objects on the basis of computer

simulation. Furthermore, objects and parameters can be simulated that cannot be really observed in the experiment but can be identified and assessed indirectly. Together with this, the student can affect some parameters which cannot be affected in a real experiment. In simulation, errors and inaccuracies in the final read-out, as well as auxiliary perturbating influences can be avoided; some other idealizations with a didactic purpose can be effected, e.g. changing the time scale, matching the mathematical curve of the process with the experimentally plotted curve, etc.

In the present paper an attempt is made to formulate a system of principles which should reflect the objective laws of building up the extrapolating mechanism of thinking in the process of education. The first principle of that system is the Principle of R e a s o n i n g, which implies the following : conscious activity is performed thanks to the mechanisms of predicting (extrapolating, anticipating) (a) the results of the development of the events and the planned actions; and (b) the conditions and actions for achieving certain results. The second principle is the Principle of I n s t r u c t i v e n e s s : each real act of education primarily represents constructing, expanding and final building up of the system for extrapolation of the events in research and pragmatic activity in pursuing the aims of life.

The two traditional problems encountered by modern educational processes - the problem of forgetting and the problem of the enormous volume of educational information - can be successfully solved only on condition that the aims of education should be radically changed. As long as the main aim is acquisition of knowledge, time will always be short. In the case when skills are being taught events are taking a more favourable turn. But this is not a satisfying solution either, because overlooking the scientific and theoretical training has a negative effect on the capabilities for adapting to arising new tasks and activities. Combining the two approaches - acquisition of knowledge and learning skills - is characteristic of the present stage of educational practice; it concerns computer-aided education as well.

Our observation on teaching physics, mathematics and other engineering subjects at high school and university level point to the following : the application of computers is directed towards transferring the contents of text-books and exercise-books onto the display of the microcomputer, aiming at individualizing and intensifying the educational process by means of programmed education. The capabilities of the computer are also used for vizualizing the processes. However, an approach to the educational process that is new in principle and different in quality is not being sought; such an appoach should secure the effective utilization of the great and constantly increasing capabilities of computers used in education.

The mastering of the mathematical and verbal description without rich extrapolating mechanisms having been built does not mean that the theory has been mastered. The knowledge of rules for action and algorithms for computation of parameters does not mean mastering of the theory either. All explanations and descriptions, all rules and algorithms become useless with the slightest change of the conditions under which a given technological process is carried out, or if new phisical phenomena arise. In such cases the specialist feels the necessity of fundamental theoretical thinking and tries to lean on the experience that he has already accumulated as a result of direct interaction with processes and phenomena. The extrapolating mechanisms that he has already built up can be used under new, most unexpected conditions as well. Unlike verbal and mathematical descriptions and prescriptions they are not forgotten even after years and decades. Even the most intricate theory can be easily understood and mastered if one has previously built up mechanisms of predicting the development of phenomena in a certian field of science by means of examples, problems and experiments. And vice versa, even the most simple relations about which we have no previously built-up visual, time-and-space, or sensor-and-motor notions will remain inaccessible for us inspite of the detailed descriptions and explanations that we are given in a verbal and symbolic form.

Words - those specific images of sound and speech - are a powerful instrument of thinking but they have no independent functions. This means that with incomplete spacial images, one cannot make adequate language formulations, nor can one achieve essential results by means of the conditions and regularities formulated by words. Treating the brain as a device which, similarly to the computer, processes symbolic information independently of the semantic basis will always lead to unsatisfactory results in education. The conception that scientific achievements lie in the verbal, graphic and symbolic

(mathematical) descriptions of objective laws and rules for action is not true. Without any rich and precise subjective models and extrapolating mechanisms reflecting the relations in the real world, the descriptions can neither be given meaning, nor can they be fully used and developed in future. In this sense, we can afford interpreting Newton's thought that the example is not less important than the theory, in the following way: theory is built upon the example, it is given meaning by the example and is used in concrete examples. The transfer of theoretical material from lectures on the computer, as our experience shows, is inefficient no matter how detailed the explanations are. This is so because the theory should not precede the experience. The traditional conception that the learning of the theory must precede the solving of problems should be abandoned. As the Soviet pedagogists A.A.Goldberg and L.A.Karasseva point out "the optimal learning of any theory consists in solving a chain of problems by relying on succinct instructions". At the same time we should mention that, as the American pedagogist J.Bruner emphasizes, everyone may suggest very difficult or very easy problems. It is necessary to find out the degrees, the varieties and the succession of their presentation.

The third principle of the system presented here-the Principle of A c t i v i t y - implies: in the process of education perception has a corrective role, and interaction with the environment plays a dominating role. As we place the educational process within the strict frames of activity and decision-making dialogue, we secure in fact the intensive interaction between the student and the environment. Figuratively speaking, he is subjected to its forming influence on condition that he is driven by sufficiently strong motives for participation, and that he has the possibility for a constant interaction with the objects that he studies. In that direction, we could give an example with the unusual success of teenagers in learning some games that require strong logics and complex activity involving analisis and sinthesis. Such is the case with chess and the recently polular game "Rubik's Cube", where adults are not often on a sufficiently high level to compete with children. Some young experts at the Rubik's Cube describe their skill as an ability "to see all six sides of the cube simultaneously", or as "an ability of the fingers to remember". According to D.Marx, in their endeavour to master the objective laws of the cube the children remind us of the research workers that during this century revealed the spectra of the various substances as well as the structure of molecules and atoms.

Is it possible that in the field of science and technology, the training of school-children should be organized so that we could witness unusual results ? In our opinion, this is possible only if we take into account the extrapolating abilities of the brain and construct the educational process on that basis. In that sense, the computer should resemble a magic cube for the child, which opens unlimited opportunities for interaction with nature. In order to achieve this, it is necessary to make it clear what the system of generating problems should be as well as the sequence of their presentation. Then only can we pass from the descriptive and prescriptive approach to the constructive approach in education.

According to Maxwell, physical researches reveal to us some new features of processes in nature, and we are compelled to find new forms of thinking, corresponding to these features.This means that we should speak not only about the formation of mathematical thinking, physical thinking, engineering thinking, etc., but also about the formation of mechanisms of thinking when dealing with vectors; other more diverse mechanisms of thinking when analysing mathematical functions; when effecting technical diagnosis of devices; when creating circuits in electronics; when mastering the algebraic transformations,etc.

From everything said so far, it follows that the educational process must be radically reconstructed; it should be organized not on the basis of traditional descriptions, explanations and prescriptions to be normally found in lectures,lessons and text-books, but on the basis of problems, operations, activities. Undoubtedly, the computer will play a decisive role in this reconstruction of education.

As a very good example in that respect we could point out the achievements of teenagers in studying programming. With the availability of personal computers, training in programming acquired the character of a direct interaction between the student and the computer. In the dialogue mode, each error made by the student is immediately indicated, each successful step is accepted by the machine right away. The multiple attempts lead to a fast and complete building-up of the mechanisms of predicting the response of the computer and the required actions that should be undertaken. The environment with which the student comes into interaction (in this case it is the computer) gradually "chisels", "carves" the system of

extrapolating mechanisms, thanks to which the teenagers being to create still more complex and more intricate programmes that make adults wonder, since they remember their slow first steps with traditional education in programming. The application of this approach in teaching physics, mathematics and other engineering subjects will lead to a level of training that is new in principle.

Of great importance for building up effective extrapolating mechanisms in the process of education is the "education" of the studied object from various points of view, its submission to various conditions, when it is acted upon in various ways, the effecting of a great number of "cross-sections". It is only in this way that the "enormous modeling device", as N.Amossov calls the brain, would be able not only to "read" a great number of positions and movements of the object, but it would also be able to grasp all characteristic features and relationships as well as the combinations in which they manifest themselves in the process of learning.

Maxwell wrote that "There is not a better way of conveying knowledge to the mind than its presentation in as many varied forms as possible.When the ideas that have penetrated our mind in various ways unite in the fortress of reason,the position they are in becomes inaccessible". These words reflect most distinctly the fourth principle, the Principle of Variation. The playing out of the great variety of versions is not aimed at securing in the future an action according to the well-known scheme, but on the contrary: the aim is that the nervous system should acquire such abilities as would enable it to find a solution during the multiple intermediate situations that have not been played out. The processes of the nervous system that "fill in" the missing information in the gaps between the separate versions have the character of "smoothing out", figuratively speaking. In this respect, the Latin root "polio" (smooth out, variate) of the word "extrapolation" acquires a new, still deeper sense.

In working out learning programmes and simulating models it is possible that the computer should take up the more elementary functions of generating versions, while the instructor should seek the direction of making the situations more varied. To illustrate the principle of variation, we would mention the computer-aided learning of a foreign language. The computer generates phrases on the basis of pre-specified paradigms or diagrams. For instance, only following the diagram: (He, she, Mary, John, the child)(has, hasn't) (a father, a mother, a brother, a sister, a friend) the computer can suggest 50 different phrases in a defined order or at random. During one lesson, 5 to 10 new words are being mastered that are included in different phrases. After a sentence has been given in his native language, the student should pronounce the same sentence in the foreign language, and he can get a confirmation by the screen and ear-phones. It is very important to find out the order of introducing the words, which from the very beginning secures a wealth of phrases and a successive mastering of grammar rules. A similar approach can be used in the field of mathematics, physics and engineering in order to generate a great number of problems after a pre-set diagram.

In creating a variety of problems, questions and situations, the question arises about the rules which should be observed in the process of education. In this respect, it is necessary to formulate in the first place the Principle of I s o l a t i n g that implies: "The new phenomena, processes, laws and activities are to be mastered at first under such conditions where the separate properties and relations manifest themselves independently".

In his famous "Geometry" Decartes wrote that in order to know the relations it is necessary to treat them "sometimes each one separately, and sometimes several at a time", and that "in each sequence of things we should be able to separate the simple ones and the rest of them will be known by comparing them to the simple things". Decartes expressed these ideas not incidentally, for they are an integral part of his complete scientific work "Reflections on the Method of Directing the Reason Well and of Seeking Truth in Science" which includes as an appendix the above mentioned "Geometry". From all four rules that lie in the fundametals of the method of Decartes, the first two refer to the above-mentioned Principle of I solating :

1. Reasoning should include only what would seem clear and distinct to the mind, so that there should not be any ground to put it to doubt.
2. Each one of the difficulties considered should be divided into parts which would allow one to come to the best solution.

To elucidate the connection between the Principle of Variation and the Principle of Isolating, we can consider the Principle of S a m e n e s s which implies: "When various operations and laws of cause and effect are successively mastered in the

process of education, the building-up of the system of extrapolating mechanisms runs slowly and painfully. Vice versa,"When one and the same operation or law is successively played out many times, the effect is much greater, the confusion and errors occur much more rarely".

In psychophysiology there exists the so called interferential theory of forgetting. As R.Klatzky notices, the distinction of the memory traces of one or another element decreases due to the entry of new elements into the short-term memory. Thus, the fading of the traces is determined not simply as time goes by, but because of the appearance of new information in the memory. To avoid the effect of interference, it is required that when new information is being mastered, sufficient time and attention should be paid to the corresponding element before we go on with another. The Principle of Sameness should not be understood as a requirement for uniformity of the examples and illustrations by means of which an idea is being mastered, but it refers to the requirement that the idea itself should remain "identically equal to itself" when its meaning is revealed by various means, examples and problems. Hence, the Principle of Sameness is to be applied together with the Principle of Variation. Thus, the effect of the "superposition" will act in such a direction that it will solidify the numerously repeated relationship that is present in all successively played out examples. In sports, in arts and science, in professional and labour activities, seeking versions within the requirements of the Principle of Sameness leads to virtuosity and mastership, to the development of capabilities for improvization and creativity.

The Principle of R e f e r e n c e : In the process of education, in solving problems or performing various activities, apart from the information which unambiguously defines the conditions of the problem or activity, it is also necessary to provide reference mechanisms. The reference can be of a physical or information nature. An example of modern device by means of which a physical reference is provided is an electronic device with a display used in language teaching on which the characteristics (phonograms) of the words are visually perceived with the aim of improving pronunciation. Similar devices have been recently applied in speech defects for correct articulation training.

When the reference is of a purely informational character, it is often reduced to a message which helps the student, by decreasing the non-determi-

nation of the problem. Instead of seeking and securing assistance by giving additional information
from the outside, it is necessary to secure the
slow, systematic and successive building-up of the
required extrapolating mechanisms and only then
can we offer the problem that seems unsolvable
without these mechanisms.

In learning how to read in English, the role of the
"reference" is played by the phonetic transcrip-
tion of words. This role can be played by two
accents : $\bar{a}, \bar{e}, \bar{u}$ = æ,ə,ʌ; á,é,í,ó,ú = ei,i,ai,ou,
ju. The independent usage of such an orthogra-
phic approximation at the beginning of education
in order to learn a sufficiently great number of
words, later leads to a comparatively easy transition to the original orthography. This is an interesting approach that is worth experimenting,
and it should be analysed more profoundly.

The Principle of G r a d u a l n e s s suggests such an
order of introducing the new elements in which
each new element in the process of learning is
correlated to the numerous elements that have
already been mastered and it causes new relationships and new problems to come into existence.
The solution of these problems must always precede the introduction of the next new element.The
violation of this requirement, causes the effect of
helplessness or the impression that the problem
cannot be solved. The problems that are hard to
solve are usually those that have been set at an
inadequate moment of the building-up of the extrapolating mechanisms. The most important thing
is to seek the intermediate cases, i.e. the problems which provide a transition from a more simple situation to another, more complex one.This
process can be repeated multiple times, inserting
other intermediate problems between the old and
the new ones.In psychophysiology, the consolidation of memory traces is considered to be information transition from the short-term to the long-
-term memory, which lasts for hours and days.
The attempts to built up new extrapolating mechanisms on the basis of this not yet completely digested information are connected with a greater
straining of attention, with a complex and not
sufficiently organized orientational activity. The
experimental facts and characteristics give the
ground to formulate the Principle of Fatigue:When
the extrapolating mechanisms have not passed
through a period of consolidation, their use in
complex situations is ineffective and leads to a
fast fatigue. An example of an obvious violation of
the Principle of F a t i g u e is sometimes the lec-
ture-type of education, in which within two academic periods, rather too many laws and procedures
can be presented, the next one being based on the

previous ones, without their having been mastered through exercises, and what is more, without allowing any time for the consolidation of the
memory traces. Computer-aided education
allows planning, experimenting and improving the
schedules in which the period of physiological
consolidation of the digested information is accounted for, thus opening the road to optimization
of the complete educational process.

The Principle of N e c e s s i t y requires the introduction of an enormous number of examples
initially, on the basis of which the idea is gradually formed, though not fully realized. The
gradually mastered relationships, the attempts
at extrapolation done, suggest its meaning. Then
the student can be asked to formulate various
versions of the respective law, principle or algorithm. Therefore, initially extrapolations are
connected with the investigation of the physical
aspects of the phenomenon, with the aprehension
of co-relationships, with out-lining the idea in a
purely sensory plan. In the final stage, extrapolations are in the domain of symbolic expression.
Only then can we make that formulation which
claims accuracy, completeness, logical rigour
and universality. In this case only the students
will be able to appreciate the qualities of the
suggested scientific generalization, and especially the necessity of having it.

The system of principles, considered here, reflects some basic laws in the process of education
treated as a process of building-up extrapolating
mechanisms. Some of the principles mutually
complement each other or partially overlap with
respect to the meaning they have. It is possible
that they can be more adequately named. Nevertheless, they lie in the basis of the extrapolation
theory of learning that is being built at present;
its evolution is closely connected with the effectiveness of present-day education and, in this
sense, with computer-based education.

REFERENCES:

1. Lalov B. Modelling Some Aspects of Learning
at the Level of Neutron Networks, Progress in
Cybernetics and Systems Research, Vol. XI,
Hemisphere Publ. Crp.,Washington, 1982.
2. Lalov B. Extrapolating Structures, Proc. of the
VI Intern. Congress of Cybernetics and Systems,
Paris, 1984. Thales Publications (W.O.) LTD.
England.
3. Lalov B. Methods of perfection and optimization of computer aided learning, Computers in
education, North-Holland Publ. Company, Amsterdam, 1981.

COMPUTERS IN EDUCATION, K. Duncan and D. Harris (eds.)
Elsevier Science Publishers B.V. (North-Holland)
© IFIP, 1985

COURSE INTEGRATION

David Woodhouse

Department of Computer Science
La Trobe University
Victoria, Australia

Computer use in schools should be the subject of long-range planning, with the twin aims of i. achieving its integration into the curriculum ii. avoiding constant revision of the curriculum as the discipline and technology evolve. This integration will require teachers of non-computing subjects to be somewhat more involved with computers. It is also observed that the assessment of programming work causes significant problems. A new approach to assessment could ameliorate the situation, and could also have more wide-ranging benefits.

1. TEACHING WITH COMPUTERS AND ABOUT COMPUTERS.

From the learner's point of view, the two main areas of impact of computers on education are in learning with computers and learning about computers (we shall not here be concerned with computer managed learning, or with the use of computers in school administration).

'Learning with computers' is denoted by CAL (computer assisted learning), and includes CAI and simulation. 'Learning about computers' ranges from elementary 'computer awareness' to advanced study of computer science, including programming and data structures. However, these two areas are beginning to overlap. Programming, especially in Logo or Prolog, is increasingly being seen as an essential part of learning with the computer: what one is learning is ways of thinking (Logo), and information storage and retrieval (Prolog). Furthermore, the use of the computer as a tool has been included in CAL, but it provides an excellent basis for learning about a computer.

This breaking down of the division between CAL and Computer Studies is entirely to be welcomed, as it makes for course integration.

Computers in education are still seen as rather special, whether as the subject or means of education. Being special and different can often be capitalized on, but on the whole it is a disadvantage as one is always having to make a special, separate case for staff, funds, equipment, timetable periods, curriculum slots, etc. What

is needed, therefore, is integration of both these areas and at all three levels of primary, secondary and tertiary education. This integration will be effected in various ways, as follows.

Teaching with computers will become a normal part of every subject (a larger part of some subjects than of others, of course). If this is to be achieved, significant developments will have to take place in teacher training, software production, and equipment provision.

Teaching about computers must be supported by work in other subjects, as mathematics supports physics, chemistry supports biology, physics and chemistry support geology, sociology supports history etc. Furthermore, computer study must be recognized as a genuinely experimental discipline: the early teaching with computers corresponds to preliminary laboratory work, while practical programming and other computer use sessions is effectively on-going laboratory work.

2. POLITICAL CONSIDERATIONS.

2.1 Empire-building.

Unfortunately, attempts by one subject teacher to change course patterns in a way which affects other subjects is often seen as empire-building. Many people are worried by the rise of computing, and fear that lack of knowledge will leave them vulnerable to being taken over.

A major problem with computers in education has been (and still is) their location outside the main stream of educational work.   Audio visual equipment was like this, but has now come in from the cold.   'We've always got on all right', runs the claim, 'Why do we need to change?' or even 'I know things could be better, but I haven't time to change'.

Change and integration require
    i. perception of need;
   ii. strong enough motivation to
       change; and
  iii. time to change

These all imply the need to plan ahead. Unfortunately, innovation has always been 'enthusiast-driven' and hence excluded from mainstream activities. We have now moved on somewhat from this situation - there are education authority-based computer committees, etc. - but in any school or other educational institution it still requires an enthusiast.

The stages of introduction are often
1. elective course   ⎫
2. computer club   ⎬ independence

3. part of the 'real   ⎫
   curriculum,' but an   ⎬ federation
   identifiably separate ⎪
   part   ⎭

4. a full participant in ⎫
   the curriculum, as   ⎪
   service course, served⎬ integration
   course, and teaching ⎪
   tool.   ⎭

Unfortunately, this takes time, and we are overtaken by events.   Therefore, we need to plan well ahead.

2.2 Conflicts.

There is a tension in course integration between the specialist computing teacher and the specialist teacher of subject x. Mathematics has had this problem for years: is mathematics for x best taught by the mathematics teacher or the x teacher?   In computing there are a number of conflicting currents.

   1. Computers or computer studies are introduced by the teacher of subject x.   Good: this should make for integration of at least the teaching of x with computer use - but what rapidly happens is that the x teacher becomes a specialist computer studies teacher, or the school's computer manager.

   2. Ad hoc users tend to use Basic first, and then come into conflict with the computer specialist who

feels s/he should be teaching the subject 'properly', with a 'proper' programming language.

   3. The computer specialist and/or initiator can adopt a proprietary attitude to computing, and disapprove of incidental, ad hoc use.   This is unfortunate, because in many cases it is incidental use that is more natural, and that will teach more about computers than formal courses.

2.3 Equity.

Integration is also necessary for enhancing social equality and equality of opportunity.   The tendencies for girls to opt out of computer work and for competence to be associated with parental capability to buy machines are more likely to be offset by integrated courses.   The more contexts in which the computer is presented, the more children are likely to benefit from it.

3.   FORWARD PLANNING (see Woodhouse,
     1984).

3.1 What is taught at any level of education at any time (and how it is taught) is determined by a number of factors.   The state of knowledge and understanding at that time affects what can be taught, while the political and cultural context affect what may be taught.   If curricula are to keep abreast of contemporary knowledge, they must change as the frontiers of knowledge are expanded.   However, it may not be easy to effect appropriate changes.   When knowledge remains static, of course, educators can study what was known yesterday, devise lesson plans for today, and be confident that it will be of use to their students tomorrow.   When it changes slowly, we have a similar picture, except that courses can evolve to match the evolution of knowledge.   Sometimes, however, a slow change in the knowledge base has proved to be a trap for the unwary educator who has failed to keep up with the change, until suddenly the discrepancy has become blatantly obvious. Then a 'course revolution' is needed, as, over a short time, major changes are made.

Sometimes knowledge changes more quickly and it is difficult to filter these changes down through the educational system fast enough.   Firstly the new knowledge is discovered through research, then it must be organized; then teachers learn it; then they devise educational strategies for teaching it; then they phase it into their courses;

and sometimes extensive advance warning of course changes must be given to organizing bodies and/or other educational institutions. Sometimes, knowledge is changing so fast that this process is irrelevant, as it cannot be completed before the knowledge is out of date. This is the current situation in many subjects, and is perhaps most obvious in subjects which relate to computers. Such rapid change in knowledge suggests a need for a radical change in our approach to education. What is needed is 'content-free' education in ways of learning, together with some content-specific work as a basis for future learning. Some of the content-specific aspects may be included as examples of the concepts and processes involved, but otherwise the content-free part can remain unchanged for some time. Many people feel that the computer can play a rôle in relieving the problems to which it is party, by assisting in the establishment of this 'content-free' education.

The inability to keep abreast of new ideas by filtering them down as they arise means that we must exercise some clairvoyance, plan courses for 1988 or 1990, and aim now for those. In this way, we shall make a quantum leap, and by-pass some stages of development. We see a similar phenomenon in societies that have come straight from the stone-age hunter-gatherer to industrial democracy, by-passing city-states, feudalism and the agricultural revolution. We must emulate them for a similar reason, namely that there is insufficient time to plod through each stage.

3.2 Quantum leaps in education.

We can identify at least three aspects of computer education that would benefit from a quantum leap.
    a. Computer literacy.
Any plans to introduce computer literacy courses should be abandoned in favour of learning about computers through computer topics into other courses.
    b. Secondary computing.
Secondary school computing is so new that it always includes introductory courses, whereas it should be planned to follow introductory work at primary level.
    c. Tertiary computing.
In a similar vein, the battle to have all tertiary students pursue at least one computer course should give way to a formal acknowledgement that soon all entering students will have prior computing experience.

3.3 Computer literacy.

Today's students are growing up into a world in which computers already play a major role, and are likely to play a larger one, so the school curriculum should include an introduction to computers. Furthermore, the student should actually use a computer if he or she is to gain a real understanding of a computer's capabilities and limitations, and the part played by the humans who pose the problems, devise the solutions and code the programs.

However, there are difficulties. Does everyone need to fight with the intricacies of a computer language? Won't this turn off as many as it helps? What language do we use? If we use Basic, are we prepared to confine ourselves to simple programs? If we are not, what will the average student do with his or her programming knowledge? Will the later teriary student have to re-learn programming in the context of structured programming? And even before we have finished with the philosophical questions, a whole lot of practical problems emerge: lack of equipment, lack of teacher expertise, lack of teacher continuity, pressure on timetable (is the new subject academically valid, and of sufficient value to displace existing subjects?).

Many people are still at the stage of fighting to establish a place in the curriculum for computer literacy. But this is a mistake. We do not give lessons in 'telephone awareness' or 'automobile literacy' for several reasons.

    i. Their use is taught outside the school, because there are sufficient knowledgeable people in the community.

    ii. Some schools do indeed offer 'driver education', but this builds on a generally-assumed knowledge.

    iii. The motor vehicle can appear in many subjects in integrated fashion: the car industry in economics; road laws in legal studies; impact of freeways in geography; effect of mobility in social studies; right down to actual experience when going on excursions in the school bus.

This third point indicates the right approach to take with computers, as can seen from a further exploration of the implications of the phrase 'computer literacy'. The phrase was obviously coined to indicate an analogy to literacy: literacy is the ability to read and write, and hence computer literacy is the ability to use a computer. However, this ability to use a computer is currently equated with the ability to write programs in a computer language. This is not a trivial ability, and is not directly related to an existing skill (in the way that reading and writing are related to using words in speech and responding to spoken words). Can we, then, really expect everyone to become computer literate? In an attempt to preserve an affirmative answer, the analogy of functional literacy is pressed into service. We do not expect someone to be able to read 'Principia Mathematica' or Salmond on Torts before we account them literate: we simply expect them to have the ability to function adequately in their daily lives. Hence functional literacy, and hence, by association, functional computer literacy. Unfortunately in the first place, the definition of literacy is often so diluted by this reinterpretation that it borders on illiteracy; and, even more importantly, the average person needs little computer use to function adequately from day to day - if they can press the buttons on the Easybank teller (and their account is in the black!) then they are satisfied. The problem is that computer literacy is not exactly analogous to literacy. We teach people to be able to read a bus stop notice so that they can read a bus stop notice. In a 'computer literacy' context, however, we do not teach people to use a computer so that they can use a computer but so that they can appreciate the effects of other people's use of computers in various contexts which affect them, such as in point of sale terminals or in the calculation of the electricity bill.

Thus, for functional computer literacy, it is best to learn about computers in context and to use them in context. The former may be achieved by integrating the teaching about computers into other subjects: the computer industry and industrial colonialism in economics; copyright and computer crime in legal studies; unemployment and the home office in social studies; representation of numbers and codes in mathematics; integrated circuits and electronics in physics; industrial and information revolutions in history; networks and weather forecasting in geography. All this will avoid the computer being considered in isolation. The latter aim, of integrating students' practical experience of computers, may be achieved by an increased use of computer assisted learning, teaching with computers, preferably in several different subject areas. This avoids the students' having to learn the details of a programming language as a starting point. Instead, they are offered modes of interaction with the computer which are designed to get the maximum response for a minimum of action, and which are designed to combine computer use with non-computing activities. The students are learning how to use the computer in order to be able to use the computer - but that very use will teach something about the effects of computer use. At a later stage, the students can study some of the programs they have been using, but this can be done without having to learn sufficient about the programming language to write in it. The interested students, of course, can go even further and write their own programs.

To summarise, we should forget the special 'computer literacy' or 'computer awareness' course, and concentrate on the introduction of CAL and the study of computers across the curriculum. It is worth remembering, too, that literacy has a second meaning, namely learned. (This clearly derives from when the only way to become learned was to read.) The analogy for computer literacy, would, I suppose, be an understanding of information, its representation, processing, storage, retrieval, interpretation and significance. It is worth bearing this in mind as a broader goal for 'computer literacy'.

3.4 Primary/Secondary computing.

When a completely new subject is introduced to the educational system, it is natural to introduce it at a high level. It may be a new, untried theory, inappropriate for lower level students who will regard it as fact. It may be the result of recent research, with a lot of prerequisite basic knowledge. And, in any case, the curriculum is more flexible at higher levels, and can more easily accommodate an extra subject, so the decision of what to evict is postponed. However, as knowledge advances, as the theory becomes accepted, as new prerequisites, which can be covered more quickly, are established, the new subject migrates down the system. Unfortunately, each such step downwards causes a discontinuity to propagate up through the system over the succeeding years. For example, if sequential topics A,B,C and D are taught in years 9,10,11 and 12 respectively, and topic A is moved down to year 7 in 1985, then in 1985 we need A taught to years 7 and 9; in 1986 topic B is taught to years 8 and 10; and so on.

The instance of this that concerns us here is that, just when the secondary school has been geared up to incorporate 'introductory computing', incoming students from primary level start appearing with computer knowledge. Then the secondary curriculum is inappropriate, and must be changed. To avoid this, we should look ahead and plan for an eventual coherent primary/secondary sequence. While we cannot foresee the whole pattern of computing education, and determine for all time what should be taught at what level, we can look further than 1985, when primary school computing is still regarded as the exception. Sensible discussion can take place on the feasible eventual extent of primary school computing, some provisional decisions be made, and secondary school planning be based on these assumptions. This approach will avoid a constant changing of curricula at all levels each year, as each cohort of students is treated differently. Clearly, temporary courses will be necessary, but these should be at the top, not the bottom.

3.5 Secondary/Tertiary Computing.

Similar considerations apply in the need to plan a co-ordinated secondary/ tertiary educational sequence in computing. For some time now, many people have sought to have computing widely available as a service subject at tertiary level. The majority of tertiary institutions accept this need for science students, and all their science students have at least a brush with programming (usually in Fortran), while many have a longer introductory computing course. Many institutions go further, and provide introductory computing for all students.

In many other places, this need has not yet been accepted. This is a matter of current concern, but looking ahead, it is clear that it will soon disappear: soon tertiary entrants will already be computer-literate, from work at school and/or home. A quantum leap will abandon the struggle, and plan tertiary courses on this assumption. This means that general courses for the non-specialist can be abandoned (if not immediately, then in the very near future). Courses for the specialist

must be carefully tailored to include both the illiterate (temporarily); the literate but incompletely learned; and the literate.

3.6 Tertiary Computing.

At La Trobe we have emphasized integrated courses for several years. Courses that have been mounted (in full or in part) or are planned, include the following.

1. Computer engineering. Mathematics, electronics, computer science combine in this course which is currently very popular, and is drawing recruiters from the other side of the world.

2. Cognitive science. Mathematics, psychology, linguistics, computer science, with an artificial intelligence emphasis, and theoretical study of systems prepare students for a 5th generation world.

3. Commerce. Meanwhile, mathematics, statistics, accounting and computer science is a standard but still popular and lucrative combination.

4. COURSE ASSESSMENT.
In contemporary education, with its increasingly relaxed and informal structure, course assessment is some-times an embarrassment. The problems with assessable courses include

    i. pressure to produce results, and
   ii. intimation of failure to those who are unsuccessful.

    i. Pressure to produce results. Sometimes the teacher does not explain the desired results clearly enough, and students have to go for overkill, and hope the desired result is included in what they have done. As deadlines approach rapid methods are sought, including the copying of answers. This is a particularly thorny problem in programming. In a small class, it would be difficult to pass off another's essay as one's own. A program uses a more formal language, and so it is easier, with a few judicious changes, to produce a plausibly different version. However, it is possible to plagiarise without the deliberate attempt to deceive. In various subjects, it is very valuable for students to discuss problems. Particularly is this so in programming, and professional prog-rammers use the same technique. So long as there results a mutual sharing of ideas, this is fine. However, a weak student can 'discuss' different aspects of a problem with four or five other students and hence obtain a satisfactory program! In either case, the desired skill - the whole point of the exercise - has not been acquired.

Finally, if the objectives and aims are inconsistent, even producing results may not develop the desired skills.

   ii. Intimation of failure.
This has been a major consideration of the last twenty years, and rightly so. The deleterious effect of examinations on those who fail has often been postulated (although not always substantiated) and many examinations have been removed or relaxed in consequence. Unfortunately, this causes other problems. Not only does it prevent the good student from demonstrating his or her ability; but also, ironically, the poor student's lack of ability is concealed, usually leading to a rude awakening at a later stage (a job interview or an application for entry to a course, for example).

The following approach to the problem of assessment may be worth considering (cf. Illich's ideas [Illich, 1971]). Divide courses into three groups.

   1. Essential skills - compulsory -
      non-assessable
   2. Relevant, but non-essential
      topics - compulsory - graded
   3. Qualifying courses - elective -
      pass/fail

   1. Many teachers are guilty of exaggeration. 'Please, miss/sir, why do we have to learn this?' 'Because you'll find it useful'. Will they really? This has been said about so many topics, that students have come to see it as a confidence trick to keep them working. Let us identify those skills which are <u>absolutely</u> essential to a satisfying life today, and make these compulsory, but do not assess them.
Such skills include
reading and writing, with a vocabulary of 5,000 words; handling numbers for shopping or measuring for house extensions, knowing where and how to find information. If they are really essential, almost all students will recognize this and work at developing them. Making them assessable, will simply result in some students achieving the results without the skills (see above), and convincing those who fail that they are social outcasts.

Programming and elementary computer structure and use should be included in this category, but with the emphasis on information access and handling, the computer being relevant as the most important information processor.

   2. In 10 years or more of formal education, other topics can be covered besides the bare essentials. These can be chosen to provide a 'rounded education' but need not be assessed as pass/fail. In this age of mass sport, many people have taken up running. Were they all to aspire to Olympic teams - or even an athletics club first team - most would 'fail'. However, most of these runners pace themselves, against the clock, and are happy to knock off a few minutes or seconds, even though they are many minutes or seconds slower than the best. So with these topics, it is suggested that results be available, but that these be as 'objective' as possible (preferably criterion-referenced), and that no arbitrary pass/fail level be specified.

This category should include further computer studies, computer applications, and visits to computer sites.

   3. Some students will want to go into jobs or other courses for which there is prerequisite knowledge or abilities, at specified levels of achievement. Many Year 12 courses are of this type. In such a case, it is sensible for the school to provide a pass/fail assessment that is indicative of the student's likely success/ failure to be employed or accepted for further study.

This category contains Year 12 computer science and any vocational courses, such as key punch operator or programmer.

5. CONCLUSION.

Computers have no rationale other than that of being used in a context. Therefore, they cannot be studied in isolation (until a higher level). The question is how the context is to be provided, whether by

   i. x teacher teaching computing
  ii. computer studies teacher
       including x,y,z ... examples
 iii. computer studies and x,y,z
       ... teachers teaching jointly.

It may be objected that this argument also implies that mathematics, another service discipline, should not be taught in isolation, either. In fact, it has been accepted that mathematics should not be taught entirely in isolation: the dry, academic problems at primary and secondary level have been replaced by work with maps and compasses, and with a host of other practical experiments and activities. However, there is a difference, because in computing we are talking about use of a machine.   It is easier to approach this experientially than it is so to approach the sine rule, for example.

Rushby (1979) classed CAL as instructional, revelatory, cojectural and emancipatory; Taylor (1980) saw the computer as tutor, tool, tutee.   In recent years, the emancipatory or tool mode has gained pre-eminence, as the computer has ceased to be the direct focus of the educational activity (tutor, tutee) and has become ancillary to it.   To give expression to this, it is necessary to integrate curricula. Furthermore, integration will enhance the learning about information technology itself (CERI, 1984).

However, if computing is to be integrated, teachers of other subjects need to know computing, so, paradoxically, we need an initial increase in special training.

6.   REFERENCES.

CERI (1984), 'International Conference on Education & New Information Technologies', Centre for Educational Research & Innovation, Paris.

I.D. Illich (1971), 'De-Schooling Society', Calder & Boyars.

N. Rushby (1979), 'Introduction to Educational Computing', Croom Helm.

R.P. Taylor (1980), 'The Computer in the School: Tutor, Tool, Tutee', Teachers College Press.

D. Woodhouse (1984), "Planning for the Day After Tomorrow', Computerisation Quarterly, Oct/Dec, 15-17.

COMPUTERS IN EDUCATION, K. Duncan and D. Harris (eds.)
Elsevier Science Publishers B.V. (North-Holland)
© IFIP, 1985

ADDRESSING FUNDAMENTAL PROBLEMS IN COMPUTER RELATED EDUCATION AND TRAINING

Harold W. Lawson, Jr.
Department of Computer and Information Science
Linkopings University
S-581 83 Linkoping, Sweden

Three fundamental problems that exist in academic curriculums, vocational training and pre-college programs as well, are identified and described. These problems are language, abstract and concrete thinking, and complexity. It is claimed that the "student" should be made aware of the sources and computer related significance of these problems at the beginning of the education or training process. Further, an approach to addressing these problems via the use of analogical reasoning, process abstractions and common denominator concepts that can be applied across all levels of computer systems hardwares, softwares and applications is presented. By the early identification and consideration of the fundamental problems, "students" stand a better chance to obtain a holistic view of computer systems and their applications instead of getting hung-up upon operational details. With a holistic view, the students can hopefully learn operational skills as required, primarily through self-study, which hopefully can lead to an elevation of the quality of and an eventual reduction in the quantity of computer related course offerings.

Keywords: Education Philosophy, Curriculum Development
Training Programs, Teacher Training

Introduction

The development of education curriculums and training programs in the computer field has, by and large followed (mirrored) the developments of the computer industry. New subject areas historically evolved such as programming languages, compilers and translators, operating and file systems, data base systems, computer graphics, computer networks, large scale integrated circuits, to name of few of the central non-application areas. One can observe that early courses tended to emphasize the operational details of the subject matter. In some cases, after several years, more structured approaches to presentation with an emphasis upon more fundamental aspects of the area evolved. However, we cannot say that we are close to any generally applicable uniform theory of computer related subjects that would correspond to theories of other well established disciplines. Even today, unfortunately much of our computer related education and training proceeds at the operational detail level and is highly partitioned into specialized subject areas with the computer field. Some "students" are successful in building a holistic view, determining what is fundamental and seeing the forest as well as the trees. However, they are generally the well motivated exceptions and for many of them, the view comes much later, after the educational or training process in the form of an "aha" experience.

It is important that computer education and training from the outset move in the direction of addressing "universal" common fundamental problems in the computer area, thus providing the students with a holistic view. In the lack of a universally accepted theory, the fundamental problems must be revealed at the beginning of the education or training process and

emphasized. These problems which are further addressed in the current paper are language, abstract and concrete thinking, and complexity. The problems apply universally in all computer related subject areas as well as in their intersections. Further, these problem areas are not unique to the computer field; they are fundamental in virtually all academic and technological fields. Many other fields (disciplines) have evolved approaches to dealing with these problems and we must find the methods and approaches to dealing with these problems in the computer field so that we can provide relevant education and training that will teach people to "learn" about computer systems and their utilization. A proper background should be provided to enable the "student" to master todays reality and be prepared to understand and live with future changes in concepts as well as in operational details.

Training Programs and Curriculum Development (Snapshots in Time)

In historically reflecting the "current status" of computer industry developments, both training programs and to a large extent academic curriculums have provided a snapshot in time of the "in vogue" areas at the time of program or curriculum development (ACM81, COS67). There have, fortunately been improvements in recent academic curriculum developments that suggest a move toward the early introduction of fundamental core knowledge rather than "in vogue" knowledge and skills. Peter Denning, in criticizing previous programming language dominated core curriculums, states the following:

"I believe that the time has come to seriously reexamine our approach to the core curriculum. In the process we can come to understand our own discipline better. Our core curriculum must be a clear statement, to ourselves and outsiders, of the nature of our discipline." DENN84.

This current article stresses the author's view of these fundamental education and training problems and suggests some avenues of addressing the problems.

In the long run, in this author's opinion, these fundamental educational problems will be solved or at least improved upon in the academic domain. However, at the primary and secondary education levels, many teachers have been exposed, due to the almost mass hysteria around computer system developments, to the operational details of application packages and/or programming languages. Thus, they have a narrow view of computer systems and their utilization. Therefore, it will probably take a long time before computer systems education and training programs at the primary and secondary educational levels can provide fundamental knowledge in the same manner as in other disciplines. Recent suggestions for teacher training, while appropriately stressing the importance of the utilization of computers, still seem to emphasize operational skills (ROGE84). Teachers are encouraged to "learn to use" rather than to understand. Thus their view of computers will be dominated by the tools they have learned to manipulate.

In the area of vocational training, emphasis is most often placed upon providing narrow operational skills in one or a few computer related fields. This limited education is in line with creating job specialization; however, it obviously creates communication problems amongst various specialists and contributes to propagating complexity. While computer related training of this form has importance for customer education as well as significant commercial education possibilities, the "students" are not provided with lasting knowledge that will help them in the long run. They tend to learn one or a few skills, after which, they

view the world of computing through their newly acquired skills.

In this author's opinion, we must start moving in the direction of emphasizing core knowledge by addressing the fundamental problems in respect to academic curriculums, pre-college programs and training programs as well. The approach used in achieving this goal in various education domains may vary somewhat; however, regardless of the domain, the existence and relevance of the fundamental problems should be made clear to the "students".

Fundamental Problems

We shall consider, in this section, the sources and computer related significance of the three fundamental problems mentioned in the introduction. These problems apply to all endevours in the computer field, whether it be in the usage of computers, in the design, development, marketing, installation or maintenance of computer system hardwares or softwares, or in studying any aspect of computer science or computer engineering. Consequently, they are

central to academic curriculums as well as vocational training and pre-college programs. The reader will observe that the three problems are highly interrelated.

As the reader considers these areas, keep in mind the attitude of many teachers and laymen of the field; namely, that you only need to "learn to use" the computer as a tool and do not need to understand anything about its underlying structure or "modus operandi". This is true as long as everything goes without problems in the utilization of the computer; however, it is when the first seemingly difficult problem arises that the naive user discovers the three problem areas and normally is forced to consult a "system guru" if one is available. Communicating with the guru about the problem brings these problems into focus.

Computer systems with their varieties of hardware and virtually infinite "add-on" software structures are, in fact, more sophisticated than automobiles, washing machines or coffee automats. Further, in the commercial environment, consider the installer or maintainer of computer systems hardware or software who runs into a significant problem. Suddenly, if not earlier, they have a rude awakening and discover the same fundamental problems. In fact, these problems are central to the entire life cycle of computer systems from product idea to utilization in various application environments.

Problem 1: Language

The natural languages we understand, speak, read and write are amongst our most important tools. We utilize our language, not only for communication, but in our dreams, fantasies, planning and for much of our daily problem solving. Language is manifested in terminology; that is, the jargon which must be comprehended in order to participate in intelligent discourse in a particular field. Further, language plays a central descriptive role in problem solving in the natural language domain as well as in the artificial language and professional language domains. Artificial languages are numerous, particularly in scientific and engineering disciplines where the artificial languages are utilized to describe physical or relational realities. Professional languages, which are all contained within some natural language, are used by various groups, for example, doctors, dentists, lawyers, linguists, economists, sociologists, bureaucrats, etc. A serious problem with artificial as well as professional languages is that they build barriers which isolate those who can from the rest of the world who cannot.

In the computer environment, the terminology and problem solving aspects of language are central to mastering the environment as a whole and in relating its constituent parts. In respect to the various computer related languages used to create hardware and software structures, we can observe that they definitely contribute to creating isolated specialist groups who can and the rest of the world who cannot.

The way of attacking these barriers, in respect to the computer field is not to rush in and learn the operational details of its languages. In fact, in computer education, as noted by Denning (DENN84), too much emphasis has been placed upon the role of a programming language and early courses tend to concentrate on non-essential programming language details. Unfortunately, many people tend to equate a detailed knowledge of a programming language with problem solving capability. Nothing could be further from the truth. Programming languages are, by and large, coding tools used to express a problem solution in terms that can be translated into operations understood by a processor (computer system). This point should be made clear at the outset of the education or training process.

Let us now consider another serious language problem resulting from early emphasis upon programming languages; namely, "the first programming language syndrome". That is, many beginners in the computer field, after mastering the details of their first programming language, never proceed to learn and utilize other programming languages. This is unfortunate because even if the programming language is for coding and not for fundamental problem solving, certain features of a particular programming language may prohibit effective and/or convenient computer based problem solutions. Thus clumsy coding solutions are constructed to overcome particular programming language shortcomings. There is no one best programming language; consequently, students should not be subjected, in their early education, to the details of a particular language. They should be taught the avenues of problem solving available in computer environments and be provided with the ability to learn the details of any appropriate programming language and/or computer system environment, primarily through self-study.

We should further illuminate the fact that in the computer system environment, programming languages are only one of several languages utilized in describing and creating the computer system environment. At virtually all levels of the software and hardware "architecture", there exist languages used to describe the processes of the level. Thus we have application languages, application generator languages, graphic languages, database languages, query languages, compiler writing languages, system programming languages, control languages, assembly languages, microprogramming languages and hardware description languages to be fairly, but not completely, exhaustive. With a knowledge of the relevant terminology and clear picture of problem solving principles, the "student" should also be able to grasp the details of all languages in a particular computer environment.

Problem 2: Abstract and Concrete Thinking

Creative problem solving with, as well as the understanding of, computer systems requires the ability to switch between abstract and concrete views of the problem to be solved, its representation in a language and the computer environment in which the problem is to be solved. In this author's long association with the computer field, he has observed that those people who are most successful are those who are able to think both abstractly and concretely and, in particular, are quite aware of when they are doing one or the other.

Language, of course, plays an important role in problem solving since, as described above, language is a primary tool that we utilize in accomplishing our mental tasks. Our problem solving skills with the use of the natural languages that we learn are extended by the artificial and professional languages that we learn as described above. It is interesting to observe how easily or difficultly people with different "native" language backgrounds learn artificial and professional languages and apply them to problem solving. During the authors sabbatical year of 1984, he studied the effect of natural languages upon people's ability and approaches to problem solving. It appears that Western languages, so-called agglutiated morphology languages, provide a background and way of thinking which supports detailed concrete thinking; whereas, Eastern languages of the isolated morphology category based upon graphic ideograms provide a background and way of thinking which supports abstract thinking. These observations are not universal; however they are tendencies. Further, language is not the only factor since the individuals psychological and physiological properties as well as the culture imposed by the societal environment also contribute. Kummel provides an interesting background discussion on the impacts of agglutiated vs. isolated morphology languages (KUMM79).

In the computer environment, we utilize elements which roughly correspond to the natural language agglutiated and isolated morphology delineations discussed above. Abstract representations of problems most frequently utilize graphical representations (normally some form of overall systems diagrams and flowcharts for algorithmic solutions); whereas concrete representations are accomplished via a programming language. Unfortunately, the main stream of language development efforts in the computer field towards providing problem solving tools have, by and large, concentrated on agglutiated language details. This encourages a digression into concrete thinking channels. We need to further develop the tools for abstraction in computer based problem solving so that we can enhance the student's ability to solve problems with the assistance of computer systems. The development of computer based graphic oriented languages for the utilization of computer systems as well as for design and programming is attracting greater and greater attention and should be the vehicle by which a better balance can be obtained.

Problem 3: Complexity

A solid foundation in the terminology and descriptive problem solving aspects of language as well as abstract and concrete thinking are prerequisites to developing an appreciation for and understanding of complexity. Our natural ability to handle complex situations, problems, etc. seems to be quite limited. When faced with complexity, a natural tendency is to divide and conquer; that is, to break the problem down into smaller subproblems which can be treated individually and then hopefully collect together (synthesize) the individual "local" solutions into an appropriate "global" solution. Attempts to solve complex global problems without decomposition into local subproblems are doomed to failure, whether it be in politics, economics, science, engineering, management, medicine or computer systems. Many individuals and organizations have learned this lesson the hard way. These problems with complexity should definitely be made known and if possible illustrated by citing concrete examples.

The decomposition of complex problems into processes and systems of cooperating processes is a fundamental abstract structuring mechanism that can be applied in problem solving in the computer environment and for that matter, in many other domains. In fact, it is wise to present the computer system itself as nothing more than several levels of systems of cooperating processes which we can consider to be the levels indicated in figure 1.

APPLICATION SYSTEM

GRAPHICS SYSTEM

DATABASE SYSTEM

LANGUAGE TRANSLATOR AND UTILITY SYSTEMS

OPERATING AND FILE SYSTEMS

NETWORK COMMUNICATION SYSTEM

TARGET (MACHINE LANGUAGE) SYSTEM

MICROARCHITECTURE

DIGITAL LOGIC

CIRCUITS

Figure 1 SYSTEMS OF COOPERATING PROCESSES

Not all computer system environments provide all of the levels indicated but a highly mature environment incorporates most of the levels. We can present this leveling as a hierarchy of systems of cooperating processes. Further, we can introduce the hierarchical relationship as a model of the computer system environment in two manners. Firstly, as a service model in a top-down fashion; namely, the higher level receives services from the lower levels. Secondly, we can view it as a support model (or builds-on model), in a bottom-up fashion where the lower level provides support to the higher levels. Both of these abstract views are correct and sometimes it is advantageous to view it one way or the other. To be completely honest with the students, it should be indicated that while the hierarchy provides a useful model, in real systems, the strict hierarchical structure is often violated where direct service or support frequently skips over adjacent levels.

The range of levels provides a seeming complexity for computer system environments and historically they have indeed been quite complicated. This complexity is to a large extent due to the fact that many different sets of people (specialists) have been involved in designing and implementing the various levels. The groups develop their own artificial languages, for the levels mentioned above, which unfortunately

creates barriers and prohibits meaningful inter-group communications. We desperately need to use abstractions across computer system levels to improve global understanding of computer system environments amongst all people involved in computer system life cycles from designer and developer to user.

Within the hierarchy of levels, we can speak of two types of complexity. Firstly, intra-level complexity which is complexity due to the inherent nature of the problem solving required at that level. We could possibly treat this as computational complexity with respect to the computational structures of the level. Secondly, there exists inter-level complexity which is introduced due to the mapping of level upon level. Obviously, during the design and development of a computer system environment to be made available to higher level Application System problem solvers and their "users", there is much discussion about what services (top-down model) or what support (bottom-up model) are to be provided and in what form. Thus an interface is formed between the coupling at each level. At this point a negotiated settlement of who (what level) shall handle the complexity is developed. Unfortunately, many times in the history of computer systems development, complexities have been migrated (passed) upwards in the hierarchy thus affecting more people and having larger economic consequences. Many complex problems have eventually been passed on to end users, frequently disguised as features, particularly by clever marketing people. A better decision, were possible, is to migrate the complexity downwards when appropriate lower level support can be provided thus avoiding exposing higher level users to the complexity. These computer related aspects of complexity should be clearly identified for the students.

Now that we have considered the sources and significance of these fundamental problems, let us consider at least one approach to addressing the problems.

An Approach to Addressing the Fundamental Problems

We need to find educational vehicles to illuminate and to address the problems of language, abstract and concrete thinking, and complexity. One pedagogical method which has been used by this author in addressing the three problem areas is the use of analogical reasoning. By utilizing analogical reasoning, we attempt to convey knowledge indirectly; that is, we find analogies (metaphors) which resemble the area of knowledge to be learned but which are already understood by the students. This vehicle has, of course, been utilized successfully by many teachers in many disciplines. It is also utilized effectively in problem solving and is, amongst other methods, the central concept of synectics introduced in the early 1950's (GORD61).

Further, the approach developed by this author, relies heavily upon the early introduction of common denominator concepts. That is, concepts which can be applied across the board in conveying the essential properties of computer systems hardwares, softwares and applications. Thus concepts such as process, processor (agent to execute processes), systems of cooperating processes, interruption of process execution, etc. are emphasized at the beginning. These concepts of process orientation help build an abstract framework for the student which we shall simply collectively identify in further discussions as the process abstraction. The common denominator properties of this abstraction were eluded to above in describing the various levels of figure 1.

The common denominator process abstraction concepts can be equated to many biological, organizational or human activity analogies. In attacking the language fundamental problem (particularly basic concepts and terminology), the author has successfully used the analogy of manual dishwashing and drying. This metaphor has certain nice properties, the best of which is that it is easily understood by virtually all students (LAWS82a,b,c). Further, it is conveniently extendible for introducing the notions of data (object) flow, control (both synchronous and asynchronous) and process logic (algorithms).

As mentioned above, analogical reasoning has been successfully applied, via such methods as Gordon's synectics, in many physical and organizational problem domains and is equally useful in the computer area. Again, the process abstraction is extremely useful for decomposing a problem in the analogical or real domain into constituent parts. Once the problem is understood abstractly as processes, the consideration of concrete implementation can be developed. The student should be exposed to various methods for process realization. That is, control oriented methods via procedural languages, data oriented methods via non-procedural, logic or functional languages, object oriented methods as well as higher level methods for application generation. The pros and cons of each method should be explained and demonstrated by well controlled hands-on experiments that avoid the problem of getting hung-up in the details of particular programming languages and computer system environments. The author is currently developing this approach to problem solving, via appropriate lectures and laboratory materials with significant "graphic" content, for introductory academic and vocational education courses.

As mentioned earlier, language and abstract and concrete thinking are prerequisites to mastering or at least learning to live with complexity. Again, process abstraction is the fundamental vehicle for understanding complexity. It shows the decomposition of the complex organization and allows us to deal with the individual process or individual system of cooperating processes in a hierarchy or in other topological forms. In the computer environment, it can be pointed out in relationship to the bottom up support model that each lower level system of cooperating processes, as denoted in figure 1, builds, in effect, the "processor" for the next higher level. Thus, a process is always bound in a pair relationship to a processor which is its execution agent.

The process abstraction is used quite successfully in the book "Human Information Processing: An Introduction to Psychology" (LIND77). The authors have described human psychological and physiological activities via process like abstractions. Certainly a complex area decomposed to fundamental activities. Material is also being developed along these lines for treating

complexity in the computer domain and some preliminary ideas have been reported (LAWS84).

In summarizing the approach, we find that it is the process abstraction developed by analogical reasoning and applied as a common denominator across all levels of computer systems hardwares, softwares and applications that provides the didactic backbone for addressing the three fundamental problem areas. It is quite likely that the investment spent in the early introduction of these problem areas will yield significant rewards in actually reducing the quantity of courses and course materials in academic education and training programs. Hopefully, operational details will be largely attained through self-study. Further, the reduction in quantity should be coupled with an increase in quality of the course offerings.

Historical Observation

The approach to education described above is for many quite obvious and even intuitive. Certainly, other educators have thought of and even utilized similar approaches. It is interesting to note that in fact, the use of common denominator abstractions for describing computer hardwares, softwares and applications was indicated in the first comprehensive book on computer systems (STIF50) as evidenced by the following quotation from the introductory chapter.

"THE TERM COMPONENT IS USED THROUGHOUT THIS SURVEY TO DEFINE ANY PHYSICAL MECHANISM OR MATHEMATICAL METHOD WHICH IS USED AS A TOOL IN AUTOMATIC COMPUTATION. THE TERM IS APPLIED EITHER TO AN ABSTRACT CONCEPT OR TO AN ITEM OF PHYSICAL EQUIPMENT. THE SCOPE OF THIS SURVEY INCLUDES NOT ONLY A TREATMENT OF THE DESIGN AND OPERATION OF PHYSICAL MECHANISMS BUT ALSO THE ARITHMETICAL AND ANALYTICAL PROCEDURES WHICH FORM THE BASIS OF SOLUTION OF PROBLEMS REDUCED TO NUMERICAL FORM."

If we substitute process for component, this quote is still quite suitable in the context of the current paper. What happened? Why did the fundamental notions get so confused? Have computer systems been so successful that the principle concepts got lost in the mass hysteria? Its time to get back on course.

Acknowledgements

The author wishes to thank Royal Professor Ungku A. Aziz, Vice-Chancellor of the University of Malaya, for his interest in the problems of computer education and for providing a sabbatical environment where the problem areas could be crystalized. Many of the ideas have influenced the "design" of an introductory "Computer Understanding" course which will eventually be required for all incoming students of the university. The reader should notice and now be able to appreciate the use of the word "understanding" instead of "literacy". Further, the author thanks Professor Tengku Mohd Azzman Shariffadeen, Dr. Mohammed bin Awang Lah, Dr. Mashkuri Hj. Yaacob, Miss Surender Kaur Bhart and Mr. See Wan Chee for useful discussions concerning the problem areas and in applying the ideas to course development.

References

ACM81. Committee on Computer Curricula for Computer Science and Information Processing Programs in Colleges and Universities, 1961-81, Association for Computing Machinery, New York, 1981.

COS67. Computer Sciences in Electrical Engineering, COSINE Committee, Commission on Engineering Education, National Academy of Engineering, Washington, D.C., September 1967.

DENN84. Denning, Peter J., Educational Ruminations, editorial appearing in the Communications of the ACM, Volume 27, Number 10, October 1984.

GORD61. Gordon, W.J.J., Synectics, Harper and Row, New York, 1961.

KUMM79. Kummel, P., Formalization of Natural Languages, Springer Verlag, Berlin, 1979.

LAWS82a. Lawson, H.W., Jr., Understanding Computer Systems, Computer Science Press, Rockville, Maryland, 1982. Translations or versions of this book are currently published in Swedish, Finnish, German, Dutch, Spanish and Bahasa Malaysia.

LAWS82b. Lawson, H.W., Jr., An Approach to Improving Computer Literacy, Training Informatics Courses: Guidelines for Trainers and Educationalists, edited by

H.L.W. Jackson, North-Holland Publishing Company, 1982, Proceedings of the IFIP WG 3.4 Working Conference on Updating Training for Teachers of Vocational Informatics Courses, Vienna, Austria, July 1981.

LAWS82c. Lawson, H.W., Jr., The Holistic Approach to Introducing Computer Systems, The Computing Teacher, Volume 10, Number 7, Eugene, Oregon, October 1982. Also published in a Japanese translation in Nikkei-Computer published by Nikkei-McGraw Hill, Tokyo, March 1982.

LAWS84. Lawson, H.W., Jr., Computer Architecture Education, A chapter appearing in the book containing lecture notes from the IBM Belgium sponsored International Professorship in Computer Science (1982), New Computer Architectures, edited by J. Tiberghien, Academic Press, London, 1984.

LIND77. Lindsay, P.H. and Norman, D.A., Human Information Processing: An Introduction to Psychology, Academic Press, New York, 1977.

ROGE84. Rogers, J.B., Moursund, D.G. and Engel, G.L., Preparing Precollege Teachers for the Computer Age, Communications of the ACM, Volume 27, Number 3, March 1984.

STIF50. Stifler, Jr., W.W., editor, Tompkins, C.B. and Wakelin, J.H., supervisors, High-Speed Computing Devices, McGraw-Hill, New York, 1950.

COMPUTERS IN EDUCATION, K. Duncan and D. Harris (eds.)
Elsevier Science Publishers B.V. (North-Holland)
© IFIP, 1985

MAKING THE COMPUTER WORK FOR YOU:
THE MECC COMPUTING AND INFORMATION COLLECTION

Karen Hoelscher

Software Designer, Minnesota Educational Computing Corporation

Information technology is changing the nature of
what needs to be learned, who will provide it,
and how it will be provided. Information processing skills are becoming basic skills. As technology evolves, we continue to evaluate current
methods of using information and to develop more
efficient methods of working with information.
MECC has developed a collection of software products designed to teach students in grades 4-]2
strategies for composing, accessing, and evaluating information using electronic technology.
This session will outline the project and provide an in-depth look at selected products in
the series.

Learning Outcomes: Participants will become
aware of the nature of electronic information
technology skills and the usefulness of the computer as a personal information processor for
students in grades 4-12.

Outline

I. Overview of the Computing and Information
    Project

    A. Composing With Information
       1) Products introduce and reinforce
       skills in using an electronic keyboard
       to create and edit documents, and to
       collect and display information using
       graphs

    B. Accessing Information
       1) Products provide experiences using
       data bases to create and maintain
       collections of information, searching
       data banks for information, analyzing
       that information

    C. Evaluating Information
       1) Students apply skills in completing
       an original research project with the
       use of electronic tools in collecting,
       synthesizing, evaluating, and present-
       ing information

II. Computing and Information in the Curriculum

    A. Scope and sequence
    B. Goals and objectives
    C. Using the collection in the classroom

III. Demonstration of Software

COMPUTERS IN EDUCATION, K. Duncan and D. Harris (eds.)
Elsevier Science Publishers B.V. (North-Holland)
© IFIP, 1985

CHILDREN IN CONTROL OF COMPUTERS

Richard Noss
Institute of Education
University of London

W Tagg
Advisory Unit for Computer Based Education
Endymion Road, Hatfield AL10 8AU, Herts.
England.

There is a good deal of so called educational software available today which is designed to deal with various learning difficulties. The authors believe that this often represents a negative approach to education which fails to exploit children's innate desire to control their physical and intellectual environment.
The work described here is based on the assumption that children have a fairly good grasp of the learning strategies that work for them, and that the successful teacher exploits this by helping children to build on their successes rather than by worrying about their failures.

1. INTRODUCTION

The Advisory Unit for Computer Based Education was established as a support service for schools in 1972. Since then the philosophy of the Unit has developed and matured, so that when we had been in existence for ten years it was an occasion to look retrospectively through the fifty issues of our newsletter. What surprised us at that time was that despite the huge technological changes, so much was still the same. The means of delivery had changed but not the message. This paper is about that message, about our experiences with real children, about our conviction that children should not be patronised by software that under-estimates their capabilities, and about what we are planning for the future.

In this paper we start by outlining the philosophy itself, and then go on to show its relevance in the classroom by drawing on our experiences from our Logo Project. However this was not where we started, and in any case learning to program is only part of the story. We shall therefore take the reader back to 1970 when our Information Retrieval project started. Our involvement in information handling skills is as big a commitment today as it was then and is the subject of a separate paper at this conference (Freeman and Levett). Our reason for including it here is because in its own but different way it similarly unlocks the computer's power for children.

There are only three pieces of software altogether that we want to talk about (indeed we almost feel that that is all that education needs or deserves); the third is the word processor. We shall show that here too we are talking about children in control, and re-emphasize that we are basing our opinions on what we have seen children doing.

Finally we draw the various strands together, look to the future and admit that perhaps after all there are one or two powerful ideas that we have left out. However each new idea does not need its own software; indeed we shall suggest that in the future, one piece of software (albeit a large one) may well suffice.

2. OUR PHILOSOPHY

The central tenet on which our approach has been founded has been to put the power of the computer into the hands of children. This has involved both the creation of software, and the development of applications of existing software within the classroom. Not surprisingly, our conception of that power has undergone continual change and renewal as machines and their capabilities have increased. More exactly, our vision of the power of the ideas which it is possible to offer to children has expanded with the technology. Nevertheless, there have been a number of general principles which have remained constant.

In the first place, it has always been important to us to allow children to control the machine. On a purely administrative level, this has involved a concentration on computer-based applications which focus on a child (or small group) interacting with the machine, rather than with, for example, whole-class teaching or demonstration. On a deeper level, it implies using the computer as a focus for playing with ideas, of using the computer as a focus for conjecture and trial-and-error, in Papert's phrase, as an 'object to think with'.

The second point is really a corollary of the first. Putting control into the hands of children necessarily shifts the axis of classroom power from the teacher to the children: the subordination of teaching to learning. This does not imply a necessary abdication by teachers from the learning process, but it does imply the necessity for teachers to stand back from their children's learning, and to consider (reconsider?) their own relationship to it.

Thirdly, it seems to us that a powerful use of the technology carries with it the opportunity for children to learn in their own way, to develop their own learning styles. Such an approach imposes demands on software-design. Besides ruling out the ubiquitous drill-and-practice programs which still dominate much of the educational scene, it also implies that the child, not the software, makes all the important decisions about what to do, where to go next, and how to get there. A further discussion of the implications of such an approach for software development can be found in Tagg (1981 & 1983).

Finally, our approach has been based on a commitment to the process rather than the product of computer-based learning. A child interrogating the census returns of an obscure Hertfordshire village may learn some history. More certainly she may learn to make guesses, to formulate and reformulate hypotheses, to follow-up leads and to modify approaches in the light of new information.

3. POWERFUL IDEAS AND LOGO

The most recent development over the past few years which comes closest to encapsulating the philosophy we have outlined has been the advent of Logo on affordable machines, and the accompanying vision of 'powerful ideas' as proposed by Papert (1980). This section will outline the framework of our research in this field, and draw together some implications both for the learning of Logo, and to provide a basis for the examination of other ideas embedded within computer-based learning.

In September 1982 the Chiltern Logo Project was set up and funded by the Government's Microelectronics Education Programme to investigate the way in which children (grades 3 - 5) learned to program in Logo. A specific focus of the research was to examine the potential of Logo to create a learning environment in which to do mathematics, or, as Papert (1972) claims, for children to 'be mathematicians'. The work has been divided into two phases. The first year involved 118 children in five classrooms (two inner-city, two suburban, and one rural) who learned to program in pairs as part of their normal curricular activity for about 90 minutes per week for each pair. Each classroom was equipped with a single computer, a printer, and a floor-turtle. The second phase included the gathering of case-study data on four pairs of children who had participated in the first year, in order to study more closely the difficulties encountered by children, and the development of a strategy for teacher intervention.

The children programmed within their classrooms, and were encouraged by their teachers to view Logo as a component of their normal activities.

This allowed an opportunity to assess the extent to which Logo work could take place alongside other non-computer work, observe the relationship between Logo and other classroom activities, and to integrate the teachers' role into the learning environment.

The programming was based on an unstructured approach in which the children posed their own programming projects. Within this framework, the teachers developed strategies for intervention which were appropriate to their own teaching style. During the first year, and after much heart-searching by the teachers, such interventions were minimised in order to maintain children's control over their own learning, and to assess the extent to which Logo's powerful ideas were accessible with minimal teacher-input.

In accord with our wish to observe the process of the children's learning, we have adopted a participant observation strategy which included the following data-gathering techniques:

1) Observation of children programming, and participation in the activity when necessary.

2) A printed record of every student/computer interaction.

3) Informal interviews with the children.

4) Children's written accounts of their work.

5) Audio-taped discussions with the teachers both individually and in meetings of the teaching team.

Details of our findings have been provided elsewhere. In particular, the strategies adopted by children in their earliest work have been described (Noss 1983), and the extent to which children were able to gain access to the powerful ideas of the language have been reported (Noss 1984a). In the context of this paper, it is relevant to consider just one aspect of our findings, namely that of the children's acquisition of Logo ideas.

Our findings suggest that children encounter the powerful ideas of Logo in three related contexts. These are:

1) The syntax and semantics of Logo (recursion, iteration, sub-procedures etc.) which form the fundamental building-blocks of the language itself.

2) The conceptual ideas embedded within the content of the relevant microworld. In a turtle-geometric context, these include the idea of turtle 'state' and the various turtle-theorems; in a broader context, we would include ideas such as variable and function.

3) The heuristics of Logo, such as debugging, breaking down problems into sub-problems etc.

responsibility and that they, the teachers, were ours. Two years ago, however, all that changed.

Computer based education came to UK primary education quite suddenly, and certainly before anyone was ready. At the time we were concerned because we knew that we could not cope (events have confirmed this). The great bonus to not coping, however, has been a greater involvement with children and a greater respect for them. We realised for instance that power is what the children wanted (which we believed) and that friendliness could if necessary be sacrificed. We learned that their ability to control the technology was quite outstanding and we now know that friendliness is essential for teachers (for themselves and because they sometimes believe it is essential for their children) but that for children it is merely a bonus.

Collecting, classifying, sorting, sifting, hypothesising, challenging and defending are clearly at the heart of all academic pursuits but to do all this we need software which has accessibility and power. Often accessibility for the first time user is made available at the expense of power, but over the last ten years we have been using a command driven rather than tutorial approach, and we have catered for the timid by providing as much on-line help as the technology permits.

Currently the majority of secondary and a very large number of primary schools in the UK are using our software and over 30 of the 109 local education authorities have bought licences for all their schools. Additionally, we are distributing a wide variety of associated data sets since not all our schools start at the beginning, i.e. by collecting their own data.

5. WORD PROCESSING

We cannot say much that is based on classroom trials here, because this work is still in its infancy for us, but we do know that the process of learning to write is extremely hard, much harder than learning to read for instance. Young children have the additional problem that their motor control is still underdeveloped. Listening to a six year old talking about what she is currently thinking and the ideas typically trip over each other to get out. By the time she is around eight she may be reading fluently as well but it will still be years before her pen can keep up with her brain (if it ever does).

There can be little doubt that learning to type is easier than learning to write (at least when it is so easy to edit) but for adults writing itself is a skill already acquired which the authors of word processor software exploit. However, even difficult-to-use text editors designed for programmers (as opposed to normal people) are improving the power that children have over the written word.

The reader will be aware, however, that nearly all word processor software is only a character processor whereas the word processor which we shall be providing for our primary schools later this year enables children to work with words *(their words)* as the building blocks to form into their ideas.

It is too soon to be able to report on our findings here but our feasibility study looks encouraging, and we shall report this aspect of our work more fully at the Conference.

6. CLARE

Our most recent project has been to develop an extension to Logo which will allow children (and adults) access to the largest microworld of all – the real world. CLARE (Control Logo And the Real Environment) consists of two components.

The first consists of a set of primitives loaded on top of an existing Logo which will operate in exactly the same way as existing Logo syntax, and will allow the user to communicate directly with the eight bits of the machine's user port either individually via commands such as TURNON [1 2 3], TURNOFF :BIT, or as a whole port as in SENDPORT 37. In principle, this will allow the user to communicate directly with her train set, her automatic hampster-feeder, or her toy robot arm.

However, preliminary discussion with a number of primary teachers has suggested that the real world is a rather daunting prospect for the beginner to control technology. We have therefore designed a second (optional) component, a 'mini-world', in the form of a compact box, with which beginners can gain access to the ideas of control. This will contain, among other things, lights, seven-segment displays, switches, and an analogue-to-digital converter, as well as sockets to plug in remote external devices. The user will be able to use the board (HELLOCLARE) or communicate directly to the rest of the world (HELLOWORLD) in exactly the same way.

Our objective has been to create a new microworld based around the idea of Control, in much the same way as the turtle has so successfully created a geometric microworld. The turtle may help the child to learn about geometry, but first and foremost it introduces the child to the idea of programming a computer. Similarly, we hope that CLARE will provide an introduction to the ideas of Control Technology, but we are more excited at the prospect of opening up a new approach to some of the more sophisticated aspects of Logo programming.

This aspect is particularly intriguing, since it seems that using lists is a natural way to turn bits on and off. In this way, we are

These categories are far from distinct. On the contrary, a central intention of the Logo environment is that the relationship between these different areas is exposed. For example the computational idea of a subprocedure connects with the heuristic of breaking a problem into more accessible parts. Similarly, the idea of logo 'inputs' to procedures may provide a powerful computational metaphor for the idea of mathematical variable. The extent to which such metaphors can be used as the basis for learning in a non-computer setting is the subject of current research.

We have attempted to illuminate the relationship between these categories of ideas, rather than simply to assess children's comprehension of particular categories as a result of learning Logo. In doing so, we have attempted to stress the process of learning rather than the product, to focus on understanding *how* children learn, rather than attempting to assess *what* they have learned.

While children have generally been able to learn key ideas from all three categories in an unstructured, largely unaided way, it has emerged that an important activity for the teacher has been to draw the links between the categories. There is a well-known meta-idea which states that the most powerful idea is the idea of a powerful idea. To this, we suggest the addition of a second: the (second) most powerful idea is the idea of connections between powerful ideas.

Essentially, the relationship between the three categories can be summed up by the diagram in figure 1.

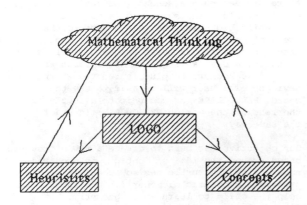

Figure 1.

Here the new element is 'mathematical thinking', by which we mean the process by which mathematicians do mathematics. The mathematician's behaviour is characterised by a concern with structure, pattern, and with relationships between the objects and processes of her domain. Of particular importance are the twin activities of conjecture and generalisation - forming links between pieces of knowledge, testing their limits, asserting and proving its generality. Much of this activity is not specifically goal-directed; we have similarly found much valuable 'exploratory' work in children's Logo learning (Noss 1984b).

In the remainder of this paper, we suggest ways in which this kind of activity can take place in a non-mathematical context. In one sense, we seek to justify a revision of figure 1, in which Logo is replaced (or augmented?) by other software, and in which the adjective 'mathematical' can be omitted.

4. INFORMATION RETRIEVAL

In 1972, very soon after the Unit was started, we were approached by a Geography teacher who had come back from a fairly typical field study with the usual untidy heap of data which she thought that the computer could tame for her. Our first approach (clearly mistaken) was to write her a bespoke piece of software which enabled her to do what she was prepared to specify. However all the usual problems about users changing their minds once they see what is possible emerged, and it soon became clear that it was going to be more productive if we tried to make facilities available to her in terms of a helpful framework rather than by responding directly to her demands. She learnt (grudgingly to start with) to fit her ideas into what we provided and eventually saw that new opportunities became available to her without her having to ask. At the same time, we learned the limitations of a purely algorithmic view of the world. It was from this time that we started to listen hard to what teachers were meaning as well as to what they were saying.

Much of our early work was concerned with making the computing environment friendly and it was several years before we realised that considerable care was needed if increased friendliness was not to be gained at the expense of power. Providing power over data, even untidy and inadequate data, was the task we set ourselves. That was what our customers wanted and increasingly we became excited by how many other people and disciplines got involved. If a criterion for good software is that the user starts to do things with it that the author never dreamt of, then we were certainly designing good software.

All this time we thought that it was the teachers who were our customer not the children. We took the attitude that children were their

hoping that CLARE, along with the control of
sprites, may provide an important introduction
to the power of Logo's list-processing.

7. CONCLUSION

It is clearly not entirely true to say that all
Computer Based Education is based on three
pieces of software. The whole world of C.A.D.
must surely be a candidate for at least one
other, but there are several others too. One
day children will write multi-dimensional
adventure games where today they write linear
stories, and we have not talked about spreadsheet software in the hands of children (but
we have seen it). We would like to see more
work with modelling using generalised simulation tools.

We are not for all this, advocating a proliferation of software products because our dream
is that one day we will be able to do all these
things within a single software environment.
The opportunities of this integrated approach
and of borrowing structures and methodologies
from one activity and applying them with no
unnecessary transformation to another are
obvious. Work on an integrated approach of
this kind is already in progress (see for
example Di Sessa 1982). However, such a solution
will not be available for a little while yet -
at least not on the machines that our schools
can afford. This need not be a cause for too
much concern: indeed the breathing space may
allow us to turn necessity into virtue, by
allowing the opportunity to help schools and
teachers to come to terms with what is on offer.

In the introduction to this paper we suggested
that there were only three pieces of software
that were needed by education. While we continue in the next few years to help teachers
and ourselves to come to terms with these
within a changing classroom context, we will be
continuing our attempt to reduce the number of
pieces of software to just one.

REFERENCES:

[1] Di Sessa, A., A Principled Design for an
    Integrated Computational Environment
    (M.I.T., 1982, unpublished).

[2] Levett, J., Freeman D., QUEST in the Learn-
    ing Environment: Computer Assisted Learning
    Information Handling as a Tool for Learning
    and Curriculum Development (to appear).

[3] Noss, R., Starting Logo: Interim Report
    of the Chiltern Logo Project (AUCBE 1983).

[4] Noss, R., Children Learning Logo Programming:
    Interim Report No. 2 of the Chiltern Logo
    Project (AUCBE 1984a).

[5] Noss, R., Explorations in Mathematical
    Thinking: Some Implications from Logo
    Classrooms (Proceedings of LOGO84 Confer-
    ence, M.I.T. June 1984b).

[6] Papert, S., Teaching Children to be Mathem-
    aticians versus Teaching About Mathematics,
    International Journal of Mathematical
    Education in Science and Technology 3,
    249-262.

[7] Papert, S., Mindstorms (Harvester 1980)

[8] Tagg, W., A Standard for CAL Dialogue
    (AUCBE 1981).

[9] Tagg, W., An Example of a Software Library
    and its Dissemination, World Yearbook of
    Education 1982/3 - Computers and Education
    (Kogan Page, 109-115, 1983).

COMPUTERS IN EDUCATION, K. Duncan and D. Harris (eds.)
Elsevier Science Publishers B.V. (North-Holland)
© IFIP, 1985

A COGNITIVE-CURRICULAR MODEL FOR TEACHING COMPUTER PROGRAMMING TO CHILDREN

Rafi Nachmias, David Mioduser, David Chen

The Computers in Education Research Lab.
School of Education - Tel Aviv University
Tel Aviv 69978 - Israel

This paper presents a rationale for the curriculum development for teaching a
programming language to children. A Theoretical Descriptive Model of required
skills needed by the naive programmer will be presented as a basis for the
curriculum development and as a tool for localizing, mapping and understanding
learners difficulties while acquiring a computer language. The guidelines and
principles of the curriculum, its scope and sequence and teaching strategies
will be listed. A description of the implementation and preliminary impressions
and a discussion will close this presentation.

1. INTRODUCTION

In Prof. Ershov's opening lecture at the last
WCCE (Laussane 1981), computer programming was
metaphored as "the second literacy" and
presented as a fundamental component in
everyone's culture. He forsees that: "we have no
choice but to include (teaching computer
programming) as operational congitive values
into the structure and content of public
education" [2].
Agreeing with this argument this paper presents
a way to cope with spreading computer
programming among the entire population.
The numerous problems related to teaching
computer programming to young children may be
divided into three areas:

The cognitive-research area

Computer programming is a rather complex
activity, requiring tehnical control of the
hardware, language acquisition ability, ability
to solve problems in an algorithmic or
procedural manner, and capacity for
understanding abstract mathematical concepts.
The knowledge of the cognitive skills and
thought processes required for performing this
activity by children is limited. We do not know
at what age children reach maturity and acquire
the various concepts of programming language,
and there is very little information regarding
the factors explaining the large variability in
achievements in the acquisition of a programming
language and the ability to apply it by
children.

The curriculum development area

The existing curricula is poor in quantity and
limited in variety: There are still only few
curricula for teaching programming to elementary
and junior high school children. The range of
alternative projects aimed at different age
levels, using different content and methodology
offered to schools to choose from, is not
sufficient yet. The large quantity of books and
magazines published in the last few years, which
reflects the existing high demand for popular
computing, is actually a
"Technological-leisure-time" industry that
doesn't satisfy the need for appropriate school
curriculum.

The School Implementation Area

The lack of curricula, rationale for its
implementation, and adequate teaching materials
and tools leaves teachers empty-handed while
coping with the everyday classroom problems of
computer programming teaching.

With these issues in mind, a rationale for the
curriculum development for teaching a
programming language to children will be
presented in this paper. This rationale was
developed at the "Computers in Education
Research Lab" in Tel Aviv University's School of
Education. A Theoretical Descriptive Model of
required skills needed by the naive programmer
will be presented as a basis for the curriculum
development and as a tool for localizing,
mapping and understanding learners difficulties
while acquiring a computer language. The
guidelines and principles of the curriculum, its
scope and sequence and teaching strategies will
be listed. A description of the implementation
and preliminary impressions and a discussion
will close this presentation.

2. RATIONALE FOR THE DEVELOPMENT OF A CURRICULUM FOR TEACHING PROGRAMMING LANGUAGE TO CHILDREN

2.1 Descriptive Model of required Skills needed by the Naive Programmer

The early seventies Pioneer works set the
fundamentals of a new interdisciplinary research
area: The psychology of computer programming
[13,10,9,5]. Through the last decade the number
of workers in this field has incresed
considerably and some theoretical models
describing computer programming as a complex
cognitive skill were developed. These models
offer a classification of the wide range of
skills and knowledge required for acquiring a

computer language into several main content
domains and its hierarchical organization.
In the issue of dividing subject matter into
main domains Shneiderman differentiates between
two major types of knowledge required for
programming: semantic knowledge, which includes
understanding the structure of a computer
program and its internal logic, and sintactic
knowledge comprising the syntax and vocabulary
of computer language [11].
Suggestions for the hierarchical organization of
programming language contents and skills appear
in Mayer´s eight level division of the Basic
language from machine level up to program level
[4], as well as in Shneiderman´s spiral approach
for teaching programming [12].
A characterization of the naive programmer´s
cognitive activity appears in Brook´s model,
according to him understanding the problem,
finding a method to solve it and coding the
solution into Computer language are the three
major activities of programming [1]. In a
similar manner, Green views programming as a
problem solving tool [3].
None of the described models may serve as
operational instrument in collecting,
classifying, mapping and organizing the required
programin_ basic skills during the course of an
empirical study. Therefore a need arises for a
model, which will serve as a basis for the
development of a curriculum for programming
teaching, and for locating and understanding the
difficulties encountered by the child in the
process of learning a programming language. The
following describes a Model that intends to
satisfy this need.

2.1.1 Hierarchical Five Content Domain Model

There are two dimensions at the basis of the
Model: the content dimension, dividing the
skills and concepts into five content domain;
and the hierarchical dimension, which
organizes the components of each content domain
hierarchically.

The five content domain

A. The technical skill of controlling the
machine (T): This includes a variety of skills
related to the ability to use the hardware:
keyboard, peripheral equipment, etc. These
skills may seem trivial; however, deficient
technical control of the machine may cause
difficulties during the acquisition of the
concepts of a programming language.

B. Mastery of the programming language (L): This
domain includes skills similar to those required
for the acquisition of a new language.
Programming language, like any other language,
has its own syntax, vocabulary (commands) and
grammatical rules. The programming student must
learn the exact manner in which each command is
written, and what it does, so that he may use it
later as a building block in the program as a
whole.

C. Understanding the structure of a computer
program (S): This series of skills is related to
understanding the structure of a computer
program, the order in which commands appear in
the program, and the ability to follow their
execution.

D. Understanding the logical dynamics of the
computer program (D): This centers around the
ability to follow the changes of values within
the variables of the program while it is
running, the ability to manipulate them and to
apply mathematical-logical rules to these
variables.

E. Various knowledge required, according to the
program´s topic (K): When writing a computer
program, specific knowledge related to the
discipline or topic at hand is necessary. For
example, when learning graphic programming it is
necessary to understand the carthesian axis
system; when dealing with musical programming,
one ought to understand basic concepts in music;
and in some areas of problem solving
mathematical knowledge is essential.

The hierarchical dimension of the model

The various skills and concepts may be arranged
hierarchically within each domain. This
hierarchy may serve to determine the order of
teaching. Each new skill will be based on
components of knowledge which have been learned
and mastered earlier.

A. The technical skill domain (T): The first
skill required here is basic use of the keyboard
and the ability to associate the specific key
and the character appearing on the screen. At
next stages the need to use special keys and
cursor movement keys and the ability to use
peripheral devices (diskettes, tape, printer,
etc.) may become important. At the most advanced
stages there is need for adding or changing ROM
and RAM cards, up to the level of a single chip.

B. The mastery of programming language domain
(L): An hierarchical order of learning commands
may be determined for each programming language.
For example, in BASIC the hierarchy may start
with elementary execution statements printing
and graphic statements, as well as program
operating commands; continue with assigning
values to variables, input, and loops; up to
complex programming statements such as
subroutines and mathematical functions.

C. Understanding the structure of computer
program (S): The continuum here starts with
understanding the order of statements in a
linear program: in which execution proceeds from
one statement to another, to the end of the
program. Then the concept of loop is introduced,
which leads to finite or infinite execution of a
part of the program; next should come the
follow-up of the order of statements in a
complex program, composed of several blocks
which are repeated according to specified

conditions; understanding nested loops and recursion up to internalizing the principles of the Top Down design.

D. Understanding the logical dynamics of the computer program (D): The hierarchical continuum begins with the ability to conceive the variable as a location for keeping changing values in memory, through the ability to change the values of the variable, usage of the variable as a parameter in programs with single parameter and multi-parameter statements; understanding logic of operation of assignment and condition statements; up to manipulation, follow-up and use of variables of different types. The ability to follow the variable values while the program is working becomes more difficult as the program becomes more complicated.

E. The pre-requisite knowledge domain (K): Here the hierarchy is dependent on the specific discipline which is related to the problem being solved.

2.1.2 The model as a tool for describing the process of acquiring a programming language, and as a basis for curricular development:

The division of the skills required by the programmer into five content domains and the determination of a hierarchy of programming concepts within each such domain as suggested in the model may serve two objectives: a content infrastructure for curriculum development on one hand and an operational instrument for describing the process of acquiring programming language by novices, and a tool for mapping and explaining the difficulties encountered by him, on the other hand. A curriculum was developed, its contents have been defined according to the hierarchical organization of the content domains and its principles and methods of teaching have been determined in agreement with the model. The activities of the learners and the difficulties encountered by them were mapped according to the content domains throughout a research and evaluation which have been carried out all through the curricular development. Within the conceptual framework of the model, one may describe two different types of learning each concept: the first is advancing in all the content levels in parallel, with regard to the hierarchy of concepts; the other is the integration of two or more levels into one concept.

2.2 The Principles of the Teaching Unit for Programming for Children

The Teaching Unit [6] is intended for grades 6 to 9, and in many cases parts of it may be taught as early as grade 4. It is based on Microsoft-Basic language, and is intended to be used in microcomputers with graphic and sound capability. (e.g. Apple II, Atari, Comodore 64, Spectrum, etc.).
Throughout the curricular development, special emphasis has been put on the following:

A. Hierarchical organization of the material: The material to be learned will be presented to the student hierarchically in all five content domains. Teaching the concepts and skills will be based on the components of knowledge which have been acquired and mastered earlier. Skipping over some skills which comprise a prerequisite, or advancing with the learning before mastery has been achieved, may cause difficulties later. For example, teaching the variable concept before teaching other basic concepts (as frequently seen in existing teaching programs) causes difficulties for beginner programmers, and children in particular. Each new skill will be presented in small steps, attempting to integrate it with the knowledge which already exists by practice and application of the subject studied.

B. Hands on experience:Learning will be accomplished by active work with a microcomputer, from the very beginning of the teaching and for most of its duration.

C. Softening the "mathematical blow": In most existing programs, all the examples, exercises and contents to be learned are taken from mathematics. This has remained from the days in which computer teaching was carried out by people who worked in the discipline of applied mathematics, and was intended mostly for mathematicians and those specializing in this discipline. This is the source of many difficulties for students who do not have mathematical background. The present program attempts to disconnect the teaching of programming as much as possible from the mathematical contents. The examples and excercises will not require mathematical knowledge which is not related directly to computer programming.

D. Variated application areas: In each stage of learning, the student will be requested to apply what he has learned using graphic, verbal and sound output. The student will create drawings, animations, sound effects, plan games, and write practical programs, related to his own world.

2.3. Scope and Sequence

The proposed curriculum for teaching a programming language to children may be divided into three main parts:

A. Basic blocks without variables:
Here students will write single-loop programs without variables, which perform simple tasks.

B. Basic blocks with variables:
This part will concentrate on the use of variables and learning the principles for composing branched programs.

C. Complex programming:
Combinations of the basic blocks into projects integrating the basic concepts studied in the two previous parts, and the acquisition of

principles of top-down design.
The following list presents the contents of the chapters of the teaching unit:

Part A
Ch. 0 : First acquaintance with the keyboard; learning how to operate the computer and peripheral equipment.
Ch. 1 : Basic graphic statements.
Ch. 2 : Computer program and its manipulation.
Ch. 3 : The random number and its use as a parameter for graphic statements.
Ch. 4 : Infinite loops.
Ch. 5 : High resolution graphic statements.
Ch. 6 : Printing statements.
Ch. 7 : The computer as a calculator.
Ch. 8 : Sound generation (dependent on the existence of suitable statements in the programming language).

Part B
Ch. 9 : Variables and their use.
Ch. 10: Manipulating variables.
Ch. 11: Input statements and various input devices.
Ch. 12: Conditioning and branching statements.
Ch. 13: Finite loops.

Part C
Ch. 14: Principles of structured programming.
Ch. 15: Building complex programs in graphic mode.
Ch. 16: Building complex programs in text mode.

The various content domains of the model are expressed in the above chapters. Each concept or topic are related basically to one content domain at least; it is also related in a secondary manner to other content domains. Table 1 shows the detailed representation of the

example, Ch. 11 which deals with input statements, describes the syntax of the Input statement (the language control level - L); stopping the program until input is supplied from the keyboard (understanding the structure of a computer program - S); the role of the input command for assigning values to variables (the logical dynamics of the computer program - D); and the various input devices are introduced

2.4 The Teaching Methods

The lesson's plan

The textbook presents the concepts and topics of each chapter, subdivided into 4 sections: The first explains the concept, its syntax and a simple example of its use; the second includes a large number of short computer programs demonstrating various applications and uses of the concept and the statement, together with explanations regarding their role in the program; the third includes tasks and excercises of increasing difficulty, related to the statement or concept; the fourth gives suggestions for some projects in which the use of the new concept, integrated with previous knowledge, is required.

The student's levels of activity and application

The learning of each concept is accomplished at five levels of activity and application:

Level 1 –PRACTICE: The student feeds the computer with examples and existing programs, runs them, practices the syntax aspects and notes the association between the concept or statement and the output.

Level 2 – CHANGING AN EXISTING PROGRAM: The student changes a statement or a parameter in an existing program, in order to achieve the

Table 1: Representation of Content Domains in the various chapters

Part	ch.	Chapter topic	Content Domains Main	Content Domains Secondary
	0	Learning to operate the computer	T	
	1	Basic graphic statements	L	T
	2	The computer program	S	L
	3	The random function	D	L
A	4	Infinite loop	S	L,D,T
	5	High resolution graphics	L	
	6	Printing statements	L	
	7	Computation	L	D
	8	Sound	L	
	9	Variables	D	L
	10	Manipulating Variables	D	S
B	11	Input statements	S,D,T	L
	12	Conditioning statements	D	L
	13	Finite loops	S,D	L
	14	Structured programming	S,D	
C	15	Complex graphics programs	S,D	
	16	Complex alphanumerics programs	S,D	

T - Technical skill domain
L - Mastery of programming language
S - Understanding the structure of computer program
D - Understanding the logical dynamics of the computer program

required result or output.

Level 3 - WRITING A SIMILAR PROGRAM: The student writes a program which is similar to the existing program, in a different medium. At this level the student moves from the ability to change a single command or parameter in a command, to changing an entire program.

Level 4 - WRITING AN ORIGINAL PROGRAM: The student writes an original program based on the idea, principle or mode of application presented in the existing program.

Level 5 - PROJECT: During the course the student carries out comprehensive projects which integrate several principles and concepts into one program.

For example, chapter 4 presenting the infinite loop includes an existing program which draws two eyes, with pupils moving from right to left (by drawing a point, erasing it and redrawing it, etc.). At the first level, the student runs the program, trying to understand the algorithm which is performed and the meaning of the infinite repitition of it. At the second level of application he is requested to change the colour of the pupil, change it from a point into a line, slow the pupil's movement, or increase the distance between the two moving points. At the third level of application he is asked to write a program in which a line or a form move downwards. The fourth level of application demands that the student write an original program based on the simple animation principle which has been presented, e.g. a traffic light changing colours, a clock whose hands move in four positions, a tennis ball moving from one racket to another, etc. When high resolution graphics have been learned, the movement will be integrated in a comprhensive graphics project, e.g. a figure doing excercises in several situations, or a program presenting a machine with moving parts.

Programming Environment

In a curriculum which centers around active interaction with the computer an appropriate program environment is of fundamental importance. The curriculum programming environment consists of the use of a microcomputer with graphic capacity, easy to operate and use, line interpreter, and a full screen editor which simplifies the debugging process. The materials provided for the student are a guide book, a demonstration diskette, personal worksheets, concrete models, and graphic planning sheets.

The learning framework

The learning may be carried out in class, in groups, or individually. Special care should be taken to ensure enough computer time for each child, not exceeding the ratio of 2-3 students per computer.

3. THE CURRICULUM'S IMPLEMENTATION

3.1 The Teaching and Research Scope

First impressions will be presented based on the teaching and research design that took place in the years 1982-1984.

The following groups were taught:
a) 10 classes of 7th-8th graders; b) 10 classes of 9th-11th graders; c) 2 classes of 6th grade disadvantaged children; d) 1 class of 6th grade gifted children

Parallely, two separate Research designs were implemented:

a) 6 case studies of children acquiring a computer language in optimal laboratory conditions - three 4th grade and three 6th grade aged children. Each child learned individually for approximately 50 hours having unlimited computer access time, a personal instructor and the developed instructional materials. As a result of close personal observation, detailed documentation of each child's learning process was obtained. A description of the research and its results appeared in a separate report [7].

b) An experimental study in which the curriculum was implemented in 4 elementary school classes: Two 4th grade and two 6th grade classes, for a period of 12 lessons (24 hours) in a regular school environment. A battery of tests was developed for each particular subject as well as a personal questionnaire summarizing students achievements. A detailed description of the research and it's results appears in a separate report [8].

3.2 Preliminary Impressions

Although research of computer language acquisition by children is far from complete, the author's findings may point to preliminary conclusions which will be described from three aspects: Cognitive, Affective and Curricular.

The Cognitive aspect

In the course of studies, significant differences were found between the age groups in acquisition of the computer language. As for 4th graders, most of them acquired the programming concepts presented in the first part of the currilum (basic programming without variables), but, almost all of them found it very difficult to understand the concept of variables which is the core of the second part. On the other hand, most of the 6th graders succeeded in the second part as well as the first.

The time needed to learn and apply concepts was significantly different between the age groups. In the given amount of time, some of the students in the eldest group (grades 9-12) reached successfully the objectives of the third part of the curriculum, whilst only a few of the 6th graders reached it. It may be possible that an addition of teaching time would have enabled more of the 6th graders to reach the same achievement, but probably not the 4th graders.

The analysis of students' achievements from the point of view of the model's content domains shows that the children, without almost any exception mastered the technical and syntactical aspects very rapidly. This observation was especially surprising among 4th graders that have not studied English yet (in Israel, English is learned as a foreign language starting at 5th grade). These students assimilated the new symbol system of the programming language and succeeded using it properly even without understanding the literal meaning of the statements. As an example, one of the 4th graders, while typing in (after 30 hours of instruction) a graphic program, misspelled the PLOT statement and typed "PLOTT" instead. When asked by his tutor to read his program to locate the mistake, the child answered astonished "But where am I supposed to know English from?!"

Difficulties were observed while acquiring the concepts of computer program and infinite loop that belong to the 3rd content domain, among most of the 4th graders and part of the 6th graders. As studies proceeded, most of the students in all ages succeeded to understand these concepts. The fourth domain's concepts were an unpassable obstacle for 4th graders, but passable, with difficulty for 6th graders.

The difficulties that arose in the course of the students' work may suggest about the nature of the cognitive process taking place while acquiring basic programming concepts and skills. The sources of difficulty can be divided into two parts: First – those caused by the increase of complexity and abstraction of concepts within a content domain. Second – the difficulty which arises from the integration of several content domains.

An example of the first type of difficulty is the transition from understanding an assignment of a value to a variable (x=5) to the ability to change systematically the value of a variable (x=x+1), in the logical dynamics of the computer program domain (D).

An example of the second type is the integration of random number generating and infinite loops. Students who understood how infinite loops work and applied this knowledge in their original programs, and also understood the concepts of random number generation found it difficult to integrate both concepts in one program.

The Affective Aspect

Motivation, enthusiasm and pleasure characterized most of the students' work, during all the studies. In response to the concluding questionnaires in the experimental groups, all the students without exception answered that they "enjoyed" or "enjoyed very much" the studies and would like to continue them, even in school.

The attitude of most of the students to the machine was positive and natural and their work flow was uninhibited, unlike some adults.

In spite of the high variance in achievements and application levels of concepts learned, the motivation of the weaker students was not lower than the stronger students. Each student succeeded applying what he had learned to his own capability and therefore was usually satisfied.

The Curricular Aspect

Time seems to be a dominant factor in the success of acquisition of programming concepts. The time allotted to each group, which varied between 24 to 40 hours, was not sufficient even for the best students, to fully apply and acquire concepts from the second and third parts of the curriculum.

The various levels of activity in practicing and applying the material at the computer were central in the learning process and took up two thirds of the learning time. To that, the variety of prepared programs and the assignments which appeared in the curriculum contributed greatly. Nevertheless, a shortage of practice time to enhance mastery of concepts learned in every stage was felt.

The use of graphics and application areas that are close to a child's world made the pleasant interaction between the child and the computer through programming activity possible. Graphics enabled concretization of abstract concepts, and helped young children, and children who are afraid of mathematics, to cope with mathematical contents.

4. CONCLUSIONS AND DISCUSSION

The hierarchical structure of the curriculum and the model of the student's working process, contributed in making the learning process more fluent and minimizing the difficulties which the student has to cope with.

Softening mathematics contents and the use of computer graphics in various applcation domains turn learning into a rich and creative process and enable lowering of the learning starting age. Hands on experience was central through the entire process. An essential condition in implementing such a program is to ensure sufficient computer time to each student.

Sixty hours seems to be a minimal period required for teaching properly all the three core parts of the curriculum. Because of the significant variance observed within and among the groups regarding required learning time, it is recommended to study this issue more particulary.

In order to implement successully the curriculum it is necessary to enrich the repertoire of demonstration programs and exercises adapting them to the wide range of student's ages and capacities. The model presented may serve as a sorting and classification tool.

Research findings correspond to the classical level categorization of Piaget's theory. The concrete operational level 4th graders do not succeed in acquiring the formal concepts of the second part of the progress, concepts that were understood and applied by part of the early formal operation level 6th graders. However, the computer as a tool that enables the concretization of formal concepts may contribute to the understanding of formal concepts by chidren in transition between stages. Concepts like random numbers, variables, and logical operations receive a different appliable meaning while programing, far beyond that which is received during mathematics lessons.

Because of the high variance between children's levels of achievement, one can not definitely determine the optimal age for teaching computer programming. The chidren's curiosity, which is not entirely fulfilled by the formal education system, the success of the 4th graders in acquiring and mastering concepts of technical and syntactical domains, and the beginning of maturity of the 6th graders in acquiring more abstract concepts should be taken under consideration, while determining the starting age.

The curriculum developers and the teachers should consider the obstacles and difficulties which the students of various ages will cope with, while developing and teaching computer programming. The model presented here may serve as an effective tool for their classification as well.

We hope that the model and the curriculum developed will contribute to a more adequate teaching of programming to the entire population.

REFERENCES:

[1] Brooks, R., "Towards a Theory of the Cognitive Processes in Computer Programming", Int. J. Man-Machine Studies 9 (1977) 737-751.

[2] Ershov, A.P., "Programming, The Second Literacy", in Lewis and Tagg (eds.), Computers in Education (1981) 1-8.

[3] Green, T.R.G., "Programming as a Cognitive Activity", in Smith, T.H. and Green, T.R.G. (eds.) Human-Interaction With Computers, (1980), 271-320.

[4] Mayer, R.E., "A Psychology of Learning BASIC", Communications of the ACM, 22 (Nov. 1979) 589-593.

[5] Minsky, M., "Form and Content in Computer Science", Communications of the ACM, 17 (April 1970) 197-215.

[6] Nachmias, R.; Mioduser, D. and Chen, D., Programming is a child's-game (Hebrew), Masada. in press (Israel, 1984).

[7] Nachmias, R.; Mioduser, D.and Chen, D., "A close look of how children acquire computer language: Six case studies", (Hebrew), The Computers in Education Research Lab. Research Report No. 5, (Tel-Aviv University, Israel, 1984).

[8] Nachmias, R.; Mioduser, D.and Chen, D., "Teaching programming at school: a 4th and 6th grade experience" (Hebrew). The Computers in Education Research Lab., Research Report, No. 6. (Tel-Aviv University, Israel, 1985).

[9] Papert, S., "Teaching Children Thinking", LOGO Memo No. 2, (MIT, 1971).

[10] Sackman, A. Man-Computer Problem Solving, Averbach (Princeton, N.J., 1970).

[11] Shneiderman, B., "Teaching Programming: A Spiral Approach to Syntax and Semantics", Computers and Education, 1 (1977), 193-197.

[12] Shneiderman, B., Software Psychology: Human Factors in Computer and Information Systems, Winthrop (Cambridge, Mass., 1980).

[13] Weinberg, G.M., The Psychology of Computer Programming, Van Nostrand Reinhold (New York, 1971).

COMPUTERS IN EDUCATION, K. Duncan and D. Harris (eds.)
Elsevier Science Publishers B.V. (North-Holland)
© IFIP, 1985

COMPUTERS IN SCHOOLS PLUS: THE BENEFITS OF EXTENDED OPPORTUNITIES

Elizabeth Farmer Schwartz

School District of Ladue
St. Louis County, Missouri

Making use of the district's computer facility beyond the school day has offered tremendous opportunities for increased staff development, testing and trying of new ideas, and public relations. Considerable revenues have been generated by offering courses for computer enthusiasts of all ages as well as training on a contract-basis for business/industry.

Ten-year-old Jason Henderson plays an interactive game, one that resembles numerous games children play in arcades coast to coast. But working on Saturday afternoons in a Ladue (Missouri) School District computer lab in St. Louis County, Jason has designed and executed this game himself using the new Sprite Logo available for the Apple computer. His class--which includes advanced Logo students grades 4, 5, 6, 7, and 8--is one of several hundred classes the district offers throughout the year on a tuition-basis after-hours. We're teaching computers to everyone from three-year-olds to adults in a program that costs the school system virtually nothing; makes efficient use of our system's computer laboratories, generates additional revenues enabling us to maintain state-of-the-art facilities and buy new products like the Sprite Logo; and best of all, provides numerous opportunities for staff development.

Five years ago, the Ladue School District (k-12; enr.: 3,200) offered no out-of-school classes of any kind. However, at the same time our in-school computer instruction was struggling to get off the ground. A few computers had appeared at elementary schools as gifts from PTA's and parents were looking to us to provide not only instruction for students on the computer but "programming" which many had heard would take their child to newer and greater heights. The fact of the matter was at that time there was not one elementary teacher in Ladue with the slightest knowledge of programming.

Secondary school computers were idle during off-school hours, so putting them to good use seemed like a great idea. What's more, we thought, an out-of-school program might not only alleviate the pressure on the elementary schools, but might serve as a useful way for us to experiment. We would be able to try different approaches to teaching children about computers that we didn't have time for during the school day; we could test software packages; we could try different program languages with different age groups to see which might be most appropriate.

But of course, before we could begin on an out-of-school basis, we had to have trained teachers. Our first step: we recruited our secondary teachers to teach small classes for younger children and used elementary teachers as their assistants. At the end of the first session, everyone had learned something new. Secondary teachers were surprised that young children could solve sophisticated problems, elementary teachers learned to teach the simple programming themselves, and more and more parents clamored for their children to learn BASIC. As the elementary teachers carried their new found skill back to the schools, additional teachers wanted to learn how to use computers and asked to assist in the out-of-school classes.

That was the beginning. The following year revenues from the program allowed us to hire an independent consultant to teach a group of teachers Logo. After the first Logo training session was completed the twenty-four teachers were encouraged to teach or assist in one of the newly launched Logo classes. Approximately 150 students signed up, and groups of 12 students were organized into numerous one-and-one-half hour classes. Initially three teachers were assigned to each group with no more explicit instructions than to put their heads together and develop Logo activities that they felt would be appropriate to the given age group. Lots of different approaches were tried, many creative activities. Teachers spent hours observing each other, and even more time incorporating what they learned from a colleague into something new and exciting for themselves.

In the summer of 1984 program revenues brought Logo trainers from New York to Ladue and eighteen Ladue teachers worked on ways to incorporate Logo into the curriculum. Over three hundred students of all ages provided opportunities for teachers to work with several versions of Logo, turtle robots, and new materials. Other teachers took advantage of the district's instructional planning center to write Logo materials to be shared in the schools. Five staff persons were sent to St. Paul, Minnesota, to take additional training, compare project development with St. Paul teachers and work first-hand with Seymour Papert.

During the school year 1984-85 Logo opportunities begin at the kindergarten level and continue through the seventh grade level during the school day for all district students. As teachers become more knowledgeable, it becomes clear that for our purposes Logo is a more preferable language to use in the elementary schools. Teachers are beginning to focus more on the problem-solving process as children write procedures in Logo rather than on the product. The use of Logo has allowed students to analyze their work and solve a multitude of mini-problems as they arise rather than solve a pre-defined problem in pre-determined ways as had been the case in earlier programming efforts. A concerted effort is being made to see that the learning which we believe results from Logo connects more specifically to other learning situations. Observable evidences are being documented as data is gathered for decision-making purposes and future experimental research.

But Logo is not all. Word-processing/creative writing classes began in the summer of 1983 with two interested members of the junior high English department. It was immediately apparent that there was an improvement in the quality of the student's writing due to their willingness and even eagerness to revise. Teachers found that the screen made the writing process observable, thus enabling them to facilitate as the student created his piece, rather than only comment on a final product. While formal research has not been conducted on word-processing in Ladue, the many evidences of increased motivation, editing, and length of writing projects has prompted the district to provide word-processing coupled with writing instruction for all students beginning at the fourth grade level. Word-processing is not confined to English departments in the secondary schools, but word-processing packages are available to all students and all departments as more and more emphasis is placed on writing across the disciplines. A new graduation requirement for the class of 1988 will include proficiency in word-processing. At least a fourth of the staff took one of several word-processing courses available last year. Currently two teachers are developing a project that hopefully will result in an area-wide creative writing magazine for teens utilizing the word-processor and tele-communications capabilities.

New thirty-hour student offerings in the summer of 1984 included an applications course built around the PFS family of software and Visicalc, telecommunications for elementary using Compuserve for younger students and Dow-Jones for

older ones, and a graphics course whereby the computer became an artist's tool. Various simulations were tried with different age groups to determine their viability for in-school use. Of course, numerous sections of Logo, BASIC and Pascal were available, too.

Summer of 1984 was also the beginning of computer courses designed specifically for educators which were taught by Ladue staff. Each sixteen-hour course carried graduate credit through the University of Missouri. Twelve courses included three levels of Logo instruction, word-processing for the composition teacher, an applications sampler, a course built around the PFS family--to name a few. Participants had the added dividend of observing student classes in each application at earlier times during the day.

Non-credit adult courses which began several years ago mainly for parents curious about what their children were doing have grown to include many applications on the Apples as well as business and professional courses on the IBMs. About one-half of evening instruction time is now purchased by businesses who send their employees to be trained in our center. This year the United States Defense Mapping Agency and the city's largest bank have purchased ten classes each. Other clients on the growing list include United Van Lines, DePaul Hospital, 7-Up, General Dynamics, Graybar Electric, to name a few. Special courses are set up each session for the Junior League, Council of Jewish Women and League of Women Voters, as well. With this increasing interest and demand by the business community, the district has contracted persons beyond its staff to teach many of the specialized offerings.

While all teachers in the district have taken advantage of some type of computer training (most is voluntary), at least 70% of the elementary staff have taught or assisted a more knowledgeable teacher in the summer or out-of-school programs. More and more secondary teachers are coming forth with new out-of-school computer offerings built around unique software packages or are experimenting with such things as IBM Logo. Teachers say such experience is a major contributor to their current level of expertise.

The district's computer-to-student ratio for the 1984-85 school year is 1 to 15, K-12, which is a direct reflection of the numbers of qualified teachers and comprehensive programs. The district's position is that ALL teachers are expected to use the new technologies to enhance the existing curriculum or improve the learning process.

As more and more emphasis is placed on computers during the school day, the direction and focus of the out-of-school program cannot remain the same. Since the program is designed as cost-recovery, annual planning must take into consideration the greater market, the number and availability of qualified teachers, the ability to offer a smorgasbord of courses that people are willing to pay for, and a well-conceived budget.

The fee charged to participants cannot be too high for obvious reasons. Our courses are generally $5 per hour of instruction, making a 12-hour course $60. Half-day summer courses and camps for students are less per hour. That's cheaper than commercially available courses in the St. Louis area and our student to teacher ratio never exceeds 12 to 1. The revenues must also allow for an hourly wage which will attract and retain qualified teachers. Our staff is paid from $15 to $24 per hour, depending on course offering and class size. Now that the program has grown to over 1000 participants per year, considerable hardware and software necessary for the classes and paid for by the program has been added to the district's facilities. Needless to say, these additions are most welcome to the regular school program.

While teachers enjoy earning an additional income, perhaps the greatest incentive to district teachers has been "the computer option", whereby teachers can apply the salary that they will receive for teaching computer courses toward the purchase of their own equipment. Buying in quantity, of course, means that the district can get a break on the price of computers and peripherals--better than what individual teachers could get walking into a computer store. Upon completion of a satisfactory letter of agreement, the teachers are able to receive their computer at the commencement of their work, allowing them to use the machine to practice and prepare.

Besides getting a great bargain on the price of the computers, teachers may get a tax break, because they use the computers in their work and for preparation at home. The IRS currently allows either a deduction or an investment tax credit and depreciation, depending on individual circumstances.

Approximately thirty-percent of the Ladue teachers now own their own computer. The advantages are obvious to the district. The more teachers use computers for their personal use, the more we will see computers used and used appropriately in the schools. As well, most of those teachers have paid for the computers by working with students enrolled in computer classes for many hours--thus increasing their experience and expertise.

For those teachers who do not have computers of their own, access to computers is available forty hours a week beyond the school day. In October of 1983, the district's newest and largest computer facility was opened at the high school. Not only is the center used from 7 to 4 p.m. for high school students, but now for the second year the center remains open until 10 p.m., Monday through Thursday, and on Saturdays from 9 a.m. until 4 p.m. With the exception of summer camps for children, the center is the site of all out-of-school offerings during the year. In addition, Ladue teachers may use computers, take any of the available courses free of charge, peruse software programs for any age, or observe the teaching of a colleague at almost any time.

The center which houses forty-eight computers, Apple IIes and IBM PCs, is organized very much like a library. While regularly scheduled classes may be going on in one or more teaching pods (twelve machines), at least one pod is available for individual users at all times. During the school day, students must present their library card when requesting machines and software; after hours a time card may be purchased enabling individuals to use computers and the library of software for fees as low as $2.00 per hour.

Software is loaned only to staff members, but journals, books, catalogs, and evaluations are available for all. The growing array of software is catalogued using the Dewey Decimal System and the information can be retrieved by computer as well as card catalog. Modems and support software make it possible to provide access to databases, a service useful to students preparing reports, projects, or term papers, to educational professionals involved in research, and to the general public interested in acquiring information on most any subject.

Some persons who visit our center and schools attribute our progress in computer education to the affluence of our community. While Ladue has certain advantages in this respect, I contend that the quality of computer education rests on much more than the acquisition of hardware even if there were "a computer for every child". With prices dropping daily and hardware manufacturers and grants providing equipment to schools across the land, computers will find their way into all schools eventually as has the marvel of the early seventies, the calculator. Therefore, in the long run, the gap that will separate will be caused not by the numbers of computers but how those computers are used. From my perspective, the crucial link will depend upon the quality of staff development and preparation, as well as curricular revision that must accommodate the new technologies.

Our experiences show that the more time teachers have "on-task" the better they are able to use computers, yet in many schools computers are turned off at many times during the day and rarely used by the staff after hours or in the summers. Our experiences show that with a growing number of teachers involved in computer

education a more varied and high-level use of
computers is possible for a greater number of
students, yet in many schools only one teacher
is responsible for the computer program and no
efforts are made to encourage or include others.
Our experiences show that it is not whether students know how to draw a square with Logo or if
the "trumpets of success" sound upon completion
of the drill and practice program, it is much
more important to look at the appropriateness
of the activity as it relates to the objective
we have for the child.

The teacher's goal is to motivate, facilitate
and guide the learning experience. A good teacher knows how to diagnose and prescribe. The
teacher must know that what he or she is doing
has value and translate that into a worthwhile
and meaningful experience for the student. It
is the teacher who stimulates ideas and works
with students to structure and expand those
ideas. Our experiences show that even when the
brightest students have the newest product like
Sprite Logo, the computer is far from an end in
itself. Thus, the role of the teacher remains
much the same.

I attribute the progress made in computer education in our district to Ladue's teachers, the
many individuals who have gone the extra mile.
They have spent countless hours beyond the
school day learning a new skill, working with a
child in a different way, observing or assisting
their colleagues, and rethinking their own way
of doing things. The way has been frustrating,
particularly since the development of new products and new generations of computers make us
ever aware that our quest has no end.

Each additional dollar spent by the Ladue Board
of Education and by members of the community who
frequent the center is directly related to the
quality of teaching and the value they have derived from the experiences. They want more of
each small success.

When we see ten-year-olds like Jason Henderson
create his game we know that the computer offers
unlimited opportunities for new levels of creativity to flourish, change to take place, learning to be enhanced and yes, powerful ideas to
emerge. We see Jason and we're pleased with our
progress in Ladue. But what should be happening for him in two years, in four years? What
will he be doing with computers when he is a
senior?

We have truly just begun.

COMPUTERS IN EDUCATION, K. Duncan and D. Harris (eds.)
Elsevier Science Publishers B.V. (North-Holland)
© IFIP, 1985

SERVICE COURSES IN SMALL POST-SECONDARY INSTITUTIONS

Moderator: John Beidler, University of Scranton, Scranton, PA

Panelists: Doris Lidtke, Towson State University
Richard Plishka, Penn State Worthington Campus
Rosemary Schmalz, University of Scranton

In the past, most services courses were simply programming languages courses. The content and structure of services courses in computing are changing. Today, students taking service courses expect information on word processing, electronic spreadsheets, graphics packages, integrated software packages, social issues, etc., which give them direct and immediate access to computing power without the need to write programs. This panel discusses the changing content and structure of service courses.

This session is divided into three parts. During the first part each panelist presents a selection of possible course topics (word processing, spreadsheets, graphics, social issues, copyright, privacy, systems concepts, problem solving, programming concepts, programming languages, etc.) with an emphasis on general concepts (i.e. teaching word processing rather than just the idiosyncrasies of a particular word processor like WordStar, PC Write, or any other specific package) rather than specifics.

In the second part, each panelist presents examples of specific implementations of service course along with the rationale for the selection of particular course topics and details about the specific software and hardware supporting these courses.

The session concludes with an open forum for comments, questions, and observations from the floor.

COMPUTERS IN EDUCATION, K. Duncan and D. Harris (eds.)
Elsevier Science Publishers B.V. (North-Holland)
©IFIP, 1985

SMALL COMPUTERS IN THE CLASSROOM: SELECTING HARDWARE AND LOCATING SOFTWARE

Dr. Lawrence A. Tomei, Montgomery, Alabama

One out of every four families in the United States already owns a personal computer. However, most educators have not gathered the fundamental tools necessary to exploit this capability in their classroom. Small **Computers in the Classroom** begins with an overview of the industry and its phenomenal growth within commercial, governmental, and educational disciplines. Small computer hardware is discussed in non-technical, layman's terms. The session presents a structured plan for successfully selecting the best machine at the best price. The session then turns its attention to the ABCs of evaluating software for student applications. Microcomputer languages, office tools, and computer-assisted instruction (CAI) are addressed. The session ends with a look at the future new innovations which will impact the classroom of the 1990s.

1. INTRODUCTION

One out of every four families in the United States already owns at least one personal computer; six out of ten elementary schools have implemented computer science classes using microcomputers as teaching aids. The phenomenal growth of the small computer within the commercial, governmental, and educational disciplines demands some degree of "computer literacy" and competency from its participants. Computer terminology alone can present a complicated, confusing barrier to the effective implementation of this newest computer technology in the classroom. Whether these machines are called microcomputers, personal computers, or small computers, this session will present the basics necessary for understanding the history, hardware, software, and classroom implications that this technology is bringing to the field of education.

2. HISTORY OF SMALL COMPUTERS

Nothing in the history of the microcomputer industry measures up to the introduction of the Apple II. Its first public showing was at the 1977 Computer Faire in San Francisco; the Apple booth was the main attraction. By 1979, the first piece of software that itself justified the purchase of a personal computer appeared on the market: the electronic spreadsheet VisiCalc. Dubbed the "most important new product of the year", its popularity was immediately apparent. Legitimacy was bestowed on the field in 1982 when IBM entered the market with its immensely successful IBM PC. However, things were to turn for the worse when Osborne, producers of the first portable computer, filed for bankruptcy. These five events exemplify the stellar growth of the small computer industry and its potential for both success and failure.

3. WHAT THE EDUCATOR NEEDS TO KNOW ABOUT SMALL COMPUTER HARDWARE

Today's micrcomputers sport very few visible "parts". Unlike their mainframe ancestors, the microcomputer houses basically a central processing unit, an array of addressable memory, a video display unit, a keyboard, and a mass storage system, plus a sophisticated operating system to make all the pieces work in unison. The central processing unit, or CPU, has advanced rapidly in recent years. The 8-bit CPU of the Apple II system has made way for the faster, more powerful 16-bit IBM PC. Advances in the microprocessor have been matched at every turn with the dramatic increases in internal memory; greater considerations in the ergonomic design of video displays and keyboards; geometric increases in the capacity of online storage devices; and, revolutionary advances in user friendly input and output devices.

4. CHOOSING THE RIGHT SMALL COMPUTER FOR YOUR CLASSROOM

Prospective users of these powerful tools must come to grips immediately with a method for choosing among over 450 manufacturers and suppliers of small systems. How about a tried and proven way? Choosing the best microcomputer involves the process of defining requirements (what you need, not what you want); obtaining vendor proposals (how to find that interested salesman); evaluating offers (the computer, the software, the services, and the vendor); and, making that final decision (and the winner is.....) By following a scientific approach, the problems of selecting the best small computer for your classroom is greatly simplified. Although no guarentees come with this process, it has proven successful in school districts around the country.

5. SOFTWARE PRODUCTS FOR TEACHING

Finding the right equipment is only half the task; combining the hardware with effective software for the classroom, the school plant, and the teacher is the ultimate determiner of success or failure. Software -- the programs that perform the required magic on the screen -- comes from a variety of sources. For the educator, the sources are even more varied than for business applications. With more than 30 million small computers in the United States, local users groups have emerged, centering their attention on either hobby, hardware, or general interests and most with extensive libraries of software readily available to its members. Software houses represent the growth industry of the 1980s. They specialize in custom-designed packages, aimed at a vertical marketplace such as education. Software brokers, relative newcomers to the small computer industry, provide a ready marketing source to software designers whose resources are otherwise limited by scope or funds; whose products would never see the "light of day" in the market without an intermediary. Some 105 brokers currently provide such service, offering a wide variety of software to their customers -- including the field of education. Computer stores, however, form the front line between the designer and the customer. Originally geared to support the somputer hobbyist, they have instead become the friend of the small user. Each of these sources of software has its strengths and weaknesses. The trick is in knowing the difference and exploiting each source to the advantage of the school and the student.

Three primary categories of software are appropriate to the field of education: curriculum development, administration, and instruction. Microcomputer languages are designed for the serious programmer who is developing an application from the ground up. Few of us have the time or expertise to take this approach. Our primary alternative rests with off-the-shelf office tools. User-oriented packages provide word processing, budgetary, data base management, and graphics capabilities for a fraction of the cost of in-house development efforts. In the classroom, small computer software provides a myriad of computer-assisted instruction (CAI, for short) applications where success or failure is a matter of knowing what you are buying versus whom you are teaching.

6. EVALUATING SMALL COMPUTER SOFTWARE PRODUCTS

Selecting the best software is a markedly different process then similar efforts to evaluate computer equipment. Luckily, a degree in computer science is not required to perform such an evaluation. If common sense principles are followed, it can be as easy as A-B-C.

A. Examine the Documentation. In many cases, there will be no need to proceed further. It is especially important to examine the manual prior to buying the software, even if it must be purchased separately. Without adequate documentation, it will be next to impossible to get the full value from any software. Moreover, poor documentation usually signals a poor program. Certain features tip the hand of good documentation. Error messages, a table of contents, command summary reference cards, and a troubleshooting section are key indicators of a sound user's guide. If a programmer had enough pride to prepare a solid manual, the battle is half won.

B. Evaluate the Support. If the documentation makes the grade, service and support from the vendor fall under scrutiny next. There is no such thing as an error-free program. Look for a company that will correct "bugs" and provide periodic upgrades and enhancements. Strong vendor support is evidenced by such extras as a hotline (preferably with a toll-free number), extended warranties, supportive users groups, newsletters, local dealer training, and
a liberal update policy for trading up to newer versions of the software.

C. Evaluate the Program Itself. Look for all the features specified on your shopping list (yes, you should have prepared a list of the desired features of the proposed software). As varied as this area might be, there are still characteristics common to any good program. They include English language messages, menu-driven operation, and standard user interfaces. Finally, be certain to evaluate the prospective software from the viewpoint of both the instructor and the student.

7. WILL SMALL COMPUTERS STAY IN THE CLASSROOM?

The most often asked question in the field of small computers is, "Will my equipment be obsolete in two or three years?" Very bluntly, given the present state of technological growth, the answer will undoubtedly be "yes". But perhaps the user, and especially the educator, is asking the wrong question. Perhaps the educator should be asking whether the small computer will meet my present and future requirements in the school plant, in the office, and in the classroom. If the answer to this question is an unqualified "yes" as well, your program is on sound ground. Congratulations.

COMPUTERS IN EDUCATION, K. Duncan and D. Harris (eds.)
Elsevier Science Publishers B.V. (North-Holland)
©IFIP, 1985

ISSUES AND PLANNING FOR EFFECTIVE COMPUTER USE

Glenn Fisher, Beverly Hunter and Don Rawitsch

International Council for Computers in Education

Panel participants will discuss critical aspects of planning, with examples of successful and unsuccessful approaches. Different uses of computers (programming vs. literacy vs. applications), training, and curriculum will be addressed.

Glenn Fisher
Alameda County Office of Education
Hayward, California

To successfully use computers, we must look at why other instructional technologies have not been successful and learn from their mistakes. One critical failure in introducing previous technologies was a lack of appropriate staff training. Extensive research on staff development supports experience with computers that, for effective use, the following conditions must be present:

1. Training is focused on the use, rather than on operation.
2. Training goals are tied to specific curriculum and teaching objectives.
3. Training occurs over a period of time, providing follow-up and long-term support.
4. Availability and use must immediately follow (or overlap with) training.

Most computer training currently provided, both preservice and inservice, focuses inappropriately on learning how to operate computers. One esteemed teacher training institution provides three hours of instruction on computer operation to its preservice teachers. Successful training, on the other hand, provides teachers with lessons and materials they can use that fit the current curriculum. Effective training focuses on learning to use and teach with appropriate software, not on programming. Inability to rapidly change our training pattern will provide inappropriate uses of computers and promote a backlash from overburdened teachers and disappointed parents.

Beverly Hunter
Targeted Learning Corporation
Amissville, Virginia

The Overlooked Variables in Planning. Planning for computer use in schools usually addresses matters such as equipment, software, teacher training and curriculum. Usually overlooked are the institutional and process variables that will determine success or failure of innovation. This presentation uses the framework from In Search of Excellence to examine characteristics of successful, innovative environments—characteristics such as a bias for action, small group collaboration, support for experimentation, tolerating failure, lack of rigid hierarchy, intensity of communication, autonomy and entrepreneurship, and the process of value shaping. Examples of these characteristics in planning for educational computing are drawn from 10 years of case study examples.

Don Rawitsch
MECC
St. Paul, Minnesota

Integration of computing activities into the school or district curriculum is a critical aspect of planning. This issue must be addressed both for new curriculum created by computers (such as computer science), and for computing activities with existing curriculum areas (such as reading). For use within existing areas, the key points are:

1. Computer use should be tied to the school's learning objectives.
2. Computer use can be planned by examining where computing activities are appropriate in the curriculum.
3. Careful planning will provide articulation and avoid repetition.

For new uses the key points are:

1. You must choose to implement computing as a separate subject or as part of all students' education (computer literacy).
2. Appropriate components of computing instruction must be identified.
3. An appropriate sequence must be developed.
4. Many computing activities can serve two purposes: subject area and computer literacy.

COMPUTERS IN EDUCATION, K. Duncan and D. Harris (eds.)
Elsevier Science Publishers B.V. (North-Holland)
© IFIP, 1985

YOUNG CHILDREN AND COMPUTERS

Sandra K. Morris, Marion C. Hyson, Dene G. Klinzing and Cynthia L. Paris
Computer Active Preschool Project
University of Delaware

Marilyn Church, Shirley Schwartz and June Wright
Computer Discovery Project
University of Maryland

Studies concerned with the young child's use of microcomputers have been conducted at the University of Delaware and the University of Maryland. Although these studies are not collaborative, they have been conducted from the developmental perspective of early childhood educators. Research at the University of Delaware has designed to examine educational, developmental and sociological implications of the young child's use of computers. Four studies in this presentation were conducted over the past two years in the University of Delaware Preschool, College of Human Resources. Studies at the University of Maryland center around the preschooler's use of microcomputers at school and in the home setting. Two studies, conducted during the past three years at the University of Maryland's Center for Young Children, will be presented.

The Computer as an Elicitor of Emotion in Young Children

Marion C. Hyson, Ph.D.

Concerns have been expressed about the emotional effects of early computer involvement. In this study four-year-old children were videotaped while using several kinds of computer programs and while watching television. Their emotional responses were assessed on the basis of facial expression data using a system that codes second by second occurrences of expressions such as interest, enjoyment, sadness and anger. Other nonverbal behavior was also coded from the videotapes. The results show that children's affective responses are, to some extent, related to the degree of personal control that a particular program allows.

The Effects of Direct Experience on Children's Concepts and Attitudes Concerning Computers

Marion C. Hyson, Ph.D. & Sandra K. Morris, M.S.

Despite our computer-dominated environment, children's ideas about computers may be vague or distorted. To what extent can experience with computers alter these beliefs, and to what extent are they resistant to change? Using a clinical interviewing procedure supplemented with pictures and an actual computer, researchers explored this question. Four-year-old children were interviewed twice, before and after a two-month period of computer use in a preschool classroom setting, and compared with another group who lacked this experience. Results highlight some major features of children's thinking about computers and suggest possible areas for educational intervention.

Interaction Patterns of Children in a Preschool Equipped with Microcomputers

Dene G. Klinzing, Ph.D.

In this program a report will be made on research which has examined the behavior of children in a preschool equipped with computers. The focus of this research has been children's choice of activity, verbal and social interaction patterns at various activity stations, and age and sex differences.

Peer Teaching and Helping Behaviors at Computers

Cynthia L. Paris, M.S. & Sandra K. Morris, M.S.

Teachers who are interested in integrating microcomputers into an early childhood classroom have expressed concerns over the affect computers may have on the established classroom environment. Will children spend time alone at the computer and fail to develop important social skills? Will the addition of the computer monopolize the teacher's time? Observations of children's helping and teaching behavior, and the implications of these findings to teachers and administrators of early childhood programs will be presented. Physical setting, teacher attitudes and behaviors, and related curriculum will be considered.

Center for Young Children: Disc Project Findings

Marilyn Church, Ed.D., Shirley Schwartz, M.Ed. & June Wright, M.A.

This presentation will report on a study of sixteen children, eight boys and eight girls, between the ages of three years, nine months and four years, ten months. All of the subjects were provided with microcomputer experiences on a voluntary basis at the Center for Young

Children, University of Maryland where a microcomputer was available two days a week in the
Discovery Room and two days a week in the classroom. The children were presented with two programs, a graphic arts program named "Scribbling,"
and a language arts program named "Picture Book
Fun." Actual results showed that there was a
significant difference between girls and boys in
the amount of time spent in the two settings,
but that there was no significant difference in
the preference for language arts and graphic
arts programs. Observational logs record other
interesting trends about the computer in the
classroom setting.

The kinds of experiences parents provide at home
as well as their expectations and values concerning the use of technology will affect children's
willingness to venture into new ways of learning.
Research at the University of Maryland's Center
for Young Children has been conducted to provide
information on children's experiences with microcomputers outside the school setting and parental attitudes toward the role of microcomputers
in their children's lives. Results of this research indicate that microcomputers are becoming
more common in preschool children's lives outside the school setting. Parents view their
children as part of the "new information age"
and have positive attitudes toward the incorporation of technological innovations in their children's educational experiences.

Design and Development of CAL

COMPUTERS IN EDUCATION, K. Duncan and D. Harris (eds.)
Elsevier Science Publishers B.V. (North-Holland)
© IFIP, 1985

DEVELOPING COURSEWARE FOR SCHOOLS IN WESTERN AUSTRALIA

Dr Nathan Hoffman and Mr Peter Skidmore

Education Department of Western Australia
Perth, Western Australia, Australia

This paper addresses a methodology used by the Education Department of Western
Australia to develop educational courseware by combining the skills of teachers with
the skills of programmers, but not expecting those skills to be found in the one
person.
The Education Department of Western Australia has been using these techniques for
several years now and the results of the combined talents of teacher and programmer can
be seen in the newer materials released under the WESOFT label.

1. INTRODUCTION

While this paper focuses on the process of software development, it may be helpful to review
some aspects of the development of computer
education in schools in Western Australia. For
those not familiar with Australian conditions,
education at the primary, secondary and
technical levels is the constitutional responsibility of the various State governments, which
operate under a Westminster system. The
Education Department of Western Australia is
responsible for administering a system spread
over approximately 2.5 million square kilometres. The population of the entire State
numbers only 1.3 million people, and there are
270 000 students engaged in primary and secondary education. The responsibilities of the
Education Department encompass more than 140
secondary schools (students aged 12-17 years),
and over 500 primary schools (students aged 5-12
years).

Western Australia has been fortunate in that
senior decision-makers within the Government and
the Education Department have recognized the
importance and potential of computers in
education and have been prepared to make a
commitment to support computer education.
Especially since 1977 the development of
computer education has benefited each year from
the commitment of significant resources.

A Schools Computing Branch was established
within the Education Department in 1977. The
purpose in establishing the Branch was, and is,
to provide an agency to co-ordinate the development of educational computing and to provide
policy advice to the Minister for Education and
the Director-General of Education. Currently
the Branch is headed by an officer with the
status of Inspector, has a full-time staff of
twenty and will have an annual budget in 1984-85
of close to $A1.5 million.

The basic philosophy underlying efforts in
Western Australia has been the recognition that
to utilize computers successfully schools will
require access to a high level of support services. These support services, which are
provided through the Schools Computing Branch,
include the provision of software, teacher
training, curriculum materials and hardware
maintenance, all of which are provided to
schools either free or at nominal cost. In
addition, primary and secondary schools have
access to financial assistance (in the form of a
dollar-for-dollar subsidy) for the purchase of
approved computer hardware. The subsidy was
provided with a view to ensuring that all
schools had the opportunity to gain access to
computer equipment. It is not a perfect mechanism for levelling out inequalities due to such
factors as the socio-economic status of a
school's community environment or the capacity
of the parents' organizations to generate funds
for the purchase of computer equipment, but it
is a start in this direction. The Schools
Computing Branch provides schools with additional
forms of assistance such as consulting and
access to information about research and development into new teaching techniques involving the
use of computers. A computing newsletter called
INTERFACE goes to all schools, and I would
welcome the opportunity for regular exchange of
copies of newsletters with educational
authorities elsewhere.

The experience in Western Australia has been
that the provision of a high level of support to
schools requires that there be some form of
standardization among the computer equipment
being utilized. In Western Australia we generally support only two or three different
systems. Currently the approved microcomputer
systems are the Australian-made MICROBEE
Advanced Personal Computer (with CP/M operating
system), and the ACORN BBC. It is not enough,
however, to see standardization simply in
terms of hardware. It is also necessary
to consider software. In Western Australia
we have acquired software from two main
sources; by purchase from commercial
suppliers and by in-house development within the

Schools Computing Branch. We have obtained some excellent software from commercial sources and have found that the policy of standardization offers considerable leverage in negotiating bulk purchase arrangements. We have found that, by and large, it is unrealistic to expect classroom teachers to produce much in the way of high-quality, original software. Therefore, our main source of high-quality software developed specifically for educational purposes has been the Schools Computing Branch. Fortunately, we have developed methods there which seem to work fairly well, and it is to those methods that I now turn.

The development of an educational courseware package is a complex task, involving a range of specific skills and a number of clearly defined stages. The production of courseware of an acceptable standard (both in educational terms and in programming and maintenance) requires a systematic approach. Such an approach is used by the Schools Computing Branch.

Any system used to produce courseware brings together the expertise and experience of the creative teacher and the expertise of the professional programmer in such a way that each member of the team has control over his or her respective area of expertise. This has meant that a method has had to be found for deciding, unambiguously, which tasks are programming tasks and which are the province of the designer.

Provision has also been made for the perusal of the design by other professionals, such as practising teachers and curriculum consultants. Their involvement must be meaningful - they should not be called in at the last minute and presented with a *fait accompli*. The designer also calls upon other professionals to assist with the preparation of the design, including graphic artists, publishing staff and subject experts from industry and commerce.

Allowance is made for the thorough trialling of the package in the situation for which it is intended to be used. In the case of classroom materials this means the involvement of students and teachers in a classroom situation.

Finally, the approach adopted is kept as simple as possible, in order to facilitate the development of courseware. It must not place an undue burden upon the design team. *It should make the job easier*.

Stages of Development

The process adopted by the Schools Computing Branch for the development of courseware is a result of over two years' experience in the preparation of educational courseware packages. During that time many alterations have been made to the design process and no doubt will continue to be made as more experience is gained.

The process can be divided into four broad areas: *idea generation, designing and programming, trialling and modification* and *publication*.

1. Idea Generation

    o Relationship to the curriculum
    o Suitability for implementation on a computer
    o Mode of intended use.

2. Designing and Programming

    o Preparation of a preliminary educational document
    o Preparation of a SCREEN - SEQUENCE design
    o Programming and coding
    o Preparation of teachers notes and student worksheets

3. Trialling and Modification

    o Trialling in schools, with feedback
    o Modification of the SCREEN - SEQUENCE, code, teachers notes
    o Retrialling

4. Publication

    o Preparation of illustrations, diagrams and artwork
    o Editing of teachers notes and student worksheets
    o Production of first copy and design of booklets
    o Printing

1. IDEA GENERATION

While each stage in the development of a piece of courseware is important, none is more important than the generation of a worthwhile idea. No amount of time or effort applied in the succeeding stages of development can form a useful program from a poor initial idea. This may seem to be obvious but my justification for stating it is the substantial percentage of educational packages which feature excellent graphics, sound, animation etc; but which are of little or no educational value. It would seem that additional time involved in the generation of good ideas is time well spent.

There are probably conditions under which this creative process might be enhanced. It is not my intention, however, to speculate on what they might be, but rather to suggest a few criteria that may be applied to those ideas which are suggested, with a view to eliminating those which are least likely to be useful.

Firstly, the courseware envisaged must be directly related to the curriculum. This means that the designers need to be thoroughly acquainted with the subject area and with the general capabilities of the students for whom the courseware is intended. Considerable teaching experience and an understanding of the learning theories upon which classroom practices are based are important prerequisites for the design of school educational software.

Programs must also be more than simply a translation of existing methods of learning onto a television screen. For example, there is little point in having students use computers to read novels, as books are a more effective and less costly method of dissemination of information. Similarly, the production of computer programs to take the place of manipulation of concrete objects in mathematics or to replace highly motivational 'hands on' experimentation in science, are of dubious value. If the aim of a piece of courseware can be achieved using existing methods such as film-strips, books, overhead projectors, lectures, experimentation, discussion etc, then the use of a computer is probably not justified or may only be justified on the basis of cost - at present an unlikely situation.

In considering the value of a software package from this point of view, it is often useful to attempt to list those features of the package which render it more useful than alternative methods of instruction. Will the courseware package assist students in ways that *you* could not? If so, in what ways?

Another useful criterion of a program's worth is the mode of intended use - a whole class, a small group or an individual. Designer-educators must keep in mind that most schools have a limited amount of computing equipment. Programs which involve a number of children using a computer simultaneously are in general, of more value to teachers than those which compel one student to monopolize the keyboard for long periods of time. Moreover, courseware which can be used in more than one of the modes mentioned above is particularly valuable to the teacher.

2. DESIGNING AND PROGRAMMING

2.1 Preparation of a preliminary educational document

Following the generation of the initial idea and its justification as a suitable package, the process of software specification begins. The first stage is the creation of a preliminary educational document which should provide a rationale for the development of the package and a general description of how the software will function, i.e. its *instructional design*.

Information is provided on:
  o the objectives of the package
  o the grade or year level and ability levels of the target group
  o the prerequisite skills or knowledge

not ordinarily possessed by the target group
  o a summary of the program, indicating the instructional design.

Although this document is useful for preparing the teachers notes after the program has been written, its main value is in clarifying in the designer's mind the educational rationale for the development of the package. Often, as problems arise in the succeeding stages of design, reference to these notes ensures that the initial intention is not lost as compromises are made.

The preliminary educational document is also a valuable source of information for the programmer, because it provides an overview of what is required and, in particular, a clear and concise explanation of *why* the program is being developed. With this information at hand the programmer is in a better position to provide what is required.

2.2 The SCREEN - SEQUENCE

Since the designers of the package are probably not the people who actually do the programming, it is essential that there be some way of conveying to the programmer exactly what is required. The programmer must have a complete and comprehensive understanding of how the program is to appear to students. The SCREEN - SEQUENCE approach is one method by which the designer specifies every detail of the program for the programmer.

The designer provides a sequence of screen displays which show in detail every image that might be presented to the user of the package. Figure 1 shows an example of one such sheet. Each contains an identifying number, a screen display, programming notes, sheet numbers from which control is passed to the current sheet, sheet numbers to which control is passed from the current sheet and any conditions to be met before control is passed. With this information the programmer should be left in no doubt as to what is required by the designer.

Each screen display is a representation, as accurate as is possible, of what is required. Text is positioned exactly, taking account of the character positions available for the screen mode selected and the sizes of text available. The text itself is specified after careful consideration of the target audience and the prerequisite skills needed and not left to the programmer to decide. Similarly, graphics are designed thoroughly and not left to the interpretation of the programmer. Cartoon character sizes and positions are specified at this stage, though exact shapes may be provided separately.

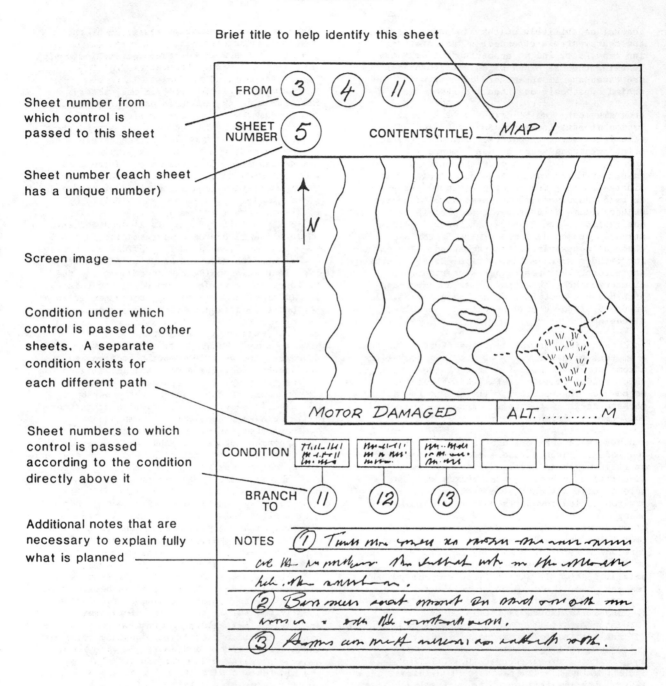

Figure 1 : Screen – sequence design sheet

The use of available colours is particularly important. Research suggests that colours can be very useful in enhancing not only the visual appeal of programs but in increasing understanding of the material being presented. There are, however, some dangers in the use of colour. There is some evidence that the use of colour can, in fact *reduce* student understanding, particularly if colour is not used consistently throughout a program.[1]

It can be difficult to show some sections of a design with purely static screen displays. In such cases, additional notes are added to each display, in an attempt to explain how the program is to work at that stage. Notes may also contain information on minor changes to be made to the screen display (under certain conditions) in order to avoid the tedium of designing a new display which is almost the same as the previous display. In general, notes contain sufficient information to explain any aspects of the screen display which may not be immediately obvious to the programmer.

A student moves from one display to another after satisfying one or more conditions. In the simplest case this may be the pressing of the return key. Often, depending on how the student responds, control passes to different branches of the program. Each sheet shows the conditions for transfer of control as well as the corresponding sheet numbers to which control passes. It should be possible, once the design is complete, for others (teachers, programmers, etc.) to step through each and every path in the program by following the design sheets.

In designing software using this SCREEN – SEQUENCE approach the designer necessarily develops a very clear and logical understanding of the program. All essential details of the software must be considered and specified. Any inconsistencies or errors of logic usually become blatantly obvious to designers as they progress through the process. It is also very easy (if the job is done properly) for other colleagues or consultants to view a design and suggest improvements at this SCREEN – SEQUENCE stage. Further, it is relatively easy to make worthwhile changes to the design by simply adding more sheets and replacing existing sheets.

It is much more preferable to make modifications at the SCREEN – SEQUENCE stage than to attempt to modify the computer code at some later stage. This is particularly true if changes involve major restructuring of the program. It is also important for the designer to discuss the software design with the professional programmer to ensure that what is intended is feasible. Ideally this contact occurs at several stages in the design process, beginning after the preparation of the preliminary educational document and continuing through the SCREEN – SEQUENCE phase. This liaison helps the programmer to become familiar with what is intended and, at the same time, can provide the designer with assurances about possibilities and impossibilities.

Designing must ensure that a program does not degenerate – as a result of programming and coding difficulties encountered – to the point where the original aims and objectives have been lost to expediency. A SCREEN – SEQUENCE, because it is such an accurate image of the program, serves as an excellent basis for logical, structured design of the code.

Experience has shown that a SCREEN – SEQUENCE is a much more useful document than a listing of a program. Often, courseware designed and programmed by teachers is valuable in terms of the educational idea, but the programming requires considerable improvement. Existence of the 'screen – sequence' and other documentation greatly facilitates further development of the courseware.

A SCREEN – SEQUENCE also provides valuable assistance to programming translating a program to other computers.

2.3 Programming and coding

When the designer is confident of the final screen sequence, both it and the preliminary educational document are handed to the programmer. During the programming stage the programmer almost certainly discusses aspects of the software, and changes may be necessary. Usually these changes are a result of insufficient detail in the design document or, much more rarely, the setting of an impossible programming task – resulting from an inadequate understanding of the limitations of the computer. The former problem can be overcome by careful, conscientious initial planning, while the latter can often be solved by the programmer suggesting alternative methods to achieve the objective.

It is essential that the programmer consult with the designer over any problems rather than making decisions which impinge upon the educational appearance of the software. It is this requirement that clearly separates programming tasks from design tasks. It is the designer's function to specify *what* is to appear to the students. *How* this is made to appear is the programmer's responsibility.

2.4 Preparation of teachers notes and student worksheets

Following programming and coding, a full set of teachers notes is prepared. These notes include all the material prepared for the preliminary educational document as well as a detailed description of how to operate the program, references to related curriculum materials and follow-up activities related to the courseware.

Depending upon the nature of the courseware, student worksheets or activity sheets, if appropriate, are prepared. These are designed to achieve the previously stated objectives of the courseware and to provide a stimulus for further investigation of the topic.

3. TRIALLING AND MODIFICATION

An essential part of any courseware development is trialling of the package with the age and ability group for which it is intended. Teachers notes and student booklets, as well as the software, are checked for ease of use and errors. Feedback is sought on any programming 'bugs', the ease of the use of the package, interpretation of the accompanying booklets and possible improvements to the materials. During the trial period (which may extend for several months) changes are made to the package, i.e. to the code and to the notes and worksheets.

The necessity to make major alterations to the package is avoided by thorough planning, discussion and alteration at the SCREEN - SEQUENCE stage when changes are relatively easily made. Occasionally, even with thorough planning, programs need major modification in the light of student and teacher reaction. When this occurs, trialling is stopped and the design process is recommenced, with the new ideas being incorporated at the 'screen - sequence' stage.

4. PUBLICATION

Publication of the printed material and the packaging to accompany the courseware is the final stage of production. This involves the preparation of artwork, cover designs, text correction and layout of the booklets. Much of this time-consuming stage is performed by specialist staff in liaison with the designer.

Within the Education Department of Western Australia much of this work is undertaken by the Publications Branch, which has the major responsibility for all publications prepared by the Department. Graphic artists ensure the teachers notes and student booklets and develop the necessary illustrations to support these documents. The Branch also checks the text material for clarity of expression and grammatical errors.

It is essential that careful consideration is given to the design and production of the packaging used with the courseware: it must be attractive, robust and at the same time, inexpensive.

CONCLUSION

In conclusion, I reiterate that courseware development within the Education Department of Western Australia is a team effort, with all members providing assistance and guidance within their own particular areas of expertise.

It is highly unlikely that the combined expertise of individual team members could ever be found in one person. Therefore I do not think that the development of good, educationally sound courseware should ever be the sole responsibility of either a programmer or a teacher. Teachers should concentrate on teaching and, in the case of computer-based courseware, on the design aspects of the materials. Programmers should concentrate on programming and on using the power and facilities of the particular computer to implement the educational design provided by the educators.

The methods outlined in this paper have been developed over a number of years, and naturally enough, are not perfect. The gradual development of these techniques is reflected in the software produced. The earlier primary school packages - Maths Drill, Spelling and Maths Number - illustrate the earlier stages of development; while the Science and Music packages, together with the soon-to-be-released Climate package, show the benefits of the SCREEN - SEQUENCE approach to design.

I invite you to take the opportunity to inspect some of this software and, in doing so, to note the changes in our approach that have taken place over a period of two years.

[1] Lamberski, R.J. and DWYER, F.M., The Instructional Effect of Coding (Colour and Black and White) on Information Acquisition and Retrieval, Educational Communications and Technology Jrnl. 31 (Spring 1983) 9-21.

COMPUTERS IN EDUCATION, K. Duncan and D. Harris (eds.)
Elsevier Science Publishers B.V. (North-Holland)
© IFIP, 1985

A MULTILANGUAGE TERMINAL FOR COMPUTER EDUCATION

M. Periasamy and M.V. Pitke
Tata Institute of Fundamental Research
Bombay 400 005

and

Centre for Development of Telematics
New Delhi 110 021

Countries having variety of languages and scripts need special computer terminals
to handle these scripts. Possibility of display of a mix of scripts, one of which is
the standard Roman Script, is an advantage. Design and implementation of an
input/output terminal for Devanagari script has been presented. A generalized
algorithm based on graphical approach has been implemented for use with any
computer system having graphic facility. The basic scheme can be adapted for a
variety of scripts. A standard ASCII keyboard with relabelled key tops meets the
requirements. Such terminals are expected to be very useful for promotion of
computer literacy in developing countries.

1. INTRODUCTION

In countries such as India which has a number
of well developed languages each with its own
script, communication with computer poses
special problems. Wide spread use of computers is possible only when it can accept commands and display/print in native languages.
Further, it is also necessary to have good
word and text processing capability in these
languages. We present here a low cost solution
based on microprocessor and other standard
hardware for this purpose.

Taking advantage of the similarity in character
sets and scripts, a common system serves a
group of languages. The main problem that
has to be tackled is with regard to the generation of characters on hard and soft copy
terminals. Graphical pecularities and complexity of character set of Indian languages
pose a problem that calls for a unique software
approach.

The system presented here has been developed
for Roman and Devanagari scripts. The implementation which enables the system for computer
education involves the development of

. Hardware

    . Typical graphics system
    . Multi-language key board
    . Auxilary storage interface

. Software

    . Character and compound character
      generation on soft/hard terminals

    . Dual text editor
    . Picture description instructions

The hardware and software could easily be
adopted for other Indian languages.

2. HARDWARE

The typical graphics hardware is built around
an eight bit microprocessor (Motorola 6802)
and its family chips. The hardware comprises
of three modules as shown in figure 1. The
microcomputer modules has 8 k bytes on
board memory alongwith the CPU, Monitor
ROM, Clock and the power on reset circuits.
The display controller module consists of a
display controller (MC 6847), 6 k bytes display
memory which gives the resolution of 256 x 192
dots, and an external character generator for
special purpose like using mathematical
symbols. The memory module has 32 k bytes
of RAM. The 4 k bytes of PROM serves as
Devanagari character generator and display
handler. This module alongwith the 5-1/4"
floppy disc provides the facility of creating
and editing files of any size, in both languages.

The above hardware and the text editor are
supported by the multilanguage keyboard
(figure 2). The keyboard is similar to standard
ASCII keyboard with key assignment for
Devanagari characters. The key assignment is
given in figure 3 alongwith the corresponding
ASCII characters.

3. CHARACTER GENERATION

The character set of Devanagari basically
consists of 12 vowels, 27 consonants and

16 matras (vowel modifier). The codes for these characters are arranged according to their graphical nature and the position of matras attributed to them. Though the standard dot matrix technique of character generation has been adopted here, the font selection for the Devanagari script is done keeping the software complexity in mind in view of its varying character sizes vertically and horizontally. The height of a script is fixed to 16 dots, whereas the width can be variable from 8 to 12 dots. So the Devanagari script is effectively displayed either in 16 x 8 or 16 x 12 dots. The display handler generates these variable compound characters and display them in a legible manner without any discontinuity between scripts. Each character which lends to form a compound character (script), has its equivalent ASCII code, and they are treated independently. So a fixed grammar for keying-in these character is advised to avoid confusion in creating or editing a file of these characters. The grammar is:

a) type the left matra, if any
b) type the consonant
c) type the bottom matra, if any
d) type the top matra, if any
e) type the right matra, if any

However, this grammar doesn't impose any limitation in character generation. Characters can be typed in any sequence and formed. This generalised variable character generation algorithm for Devanagari script could be used efficiently in computer system only if the system provides system and utility software

through this language. As a first step the 'Dual Text Editor' - a software tool which is an essential component of any computing environment has been developed.

4.   DUAL TEXT EDITOR

It is an editor which accepts commands in English and Hindi, performs all editing functions on materials as program statements, manuscript text, numeric data of both the languages, etc. and display the messages, if any, in the respective language.

Of the three major type of text editors (stream, line and screen editors), this one falls into the first category. Stream editors acts upon a text file as a single continuous chain of characters, as if the entire file were a single, indefinitely long character string, rather than act upon fixed length or variable length lines. The entire text is stored as a sequence of characters that are interpreted as lines by a filter than understands special line end delimiters.

All commands refer to an implied character pointer which is positionable within the text, and operate on a specified number of characters or complete lines ahead or behind this pointer. The Functional block diagram of the text editor is shown in figure 4.

4.1   INTERNAL STRUCTURE OF TEXT EDITOR

The editor considers a file as a few logical units called pages. The editor reads one page

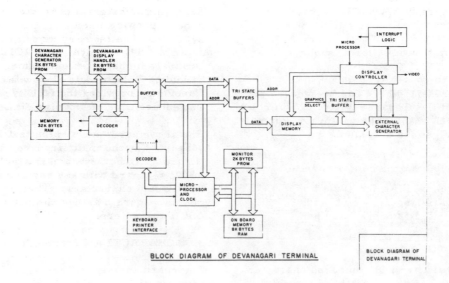

BLOCK DIAGRAM OF DEVANAGARI TERMINAL

Figure 1:

	0	1	2	3	4	5	6	7
0	NUL	DLE	SP	0	@	अ	रू	प
1	SOH	DC1	!	?	अ	ण	श्र	ा
2	STX	DC2	"	२	आ	त	र	ि
3	ETX	DC3	#	३	इ	थ	क	ी
4	EOT	DC4	$	४	ई	ध	ड़	ु
5	ENQ	NAK	%	५	उ	न	फ	ू
6	ACK	SYN	&	६	ऊ	प	ळ	ृ
7	BEEN	ETB	'	७	ए	ब	ल	े
8	BS	CAN	(	८	ऐ	भ	ह	ै
9	HT	EM	)	९	क्र	म	छ	ो
A	LF	SUB	*	:	ख	य	द	ौ
B	VT	ESC	+	;	ग	व	ठ	ँ
C	FF	FS	'	<	घ	श	ड	ः
D	CR	GS	–	=	च	ष	ढ	ं
E	SO	RS	.	>	ज	स	द	HALF
F	SI	US	/	?	द्य	क्ष	:	DEL

Figure 2: ASCII Equivalent Code Chart

of text at a time from the input file into the internal buffer where the page becomes available for editing. The memory area used by the editor is divided into three logical buffers as follows:

High Memory

| Save buffer |
| Free memory |
| Command buffer |
| Text buffer |

Low Memory

The text buffer contains the current page/s of text being edited and the command buffer holds commands string currently being typed at the terminal. These buffers are arranged to grow in opposite direction so that the size of each buffer automatically expands and contracts to accommodate the text being entered.

Figure 3: Keyboard Layout

The save buffer contains text stored with the save command which helps to move or merge text from place to other. The save buffer is released by the unsave command.

The control program of text editor comprises of three major procedures, namely:

i) the input handler
ii) the syntax analyser
iii) the command interpreter

The main functions of the input handler is:

- compute the start address of command buffer and check the limit
- accept the command string from the keyboard and store it into the command buffer
- handle the special function commands

The syntax analyser checks the command string for proper syntax. It checks for:

i) illegal commands
ii) illegal arguments
iii) level of nesting commands

The data for the syntax analyser is different for Hindi and English. The command string is passed to command interpreter if there is no syntax error. The command interpreter controls the execution of the command string. For each command of the command string, it forms the resultant argument, identifies the argument and passes control to the routine. Multiple iteration of the command string is also handled by this interpreter. The commands are broadly classfied as:

- commands for interaction with filing system
- input and output commands
- pointer relocation commands

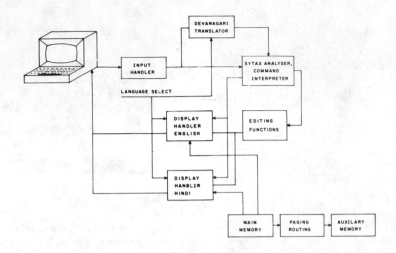

Figure 4:   BLOCK DIAGRAM OF DUAL TEXT EDITOR

- search commands
- text modification commands
- utility commands   (Appendix I)

4.2   EDITING DEVANAGARI TEXT FILES

The editing process for Hindi file text is the
same as for English text. Since the commands
are also in Hindi, it needs a separate syntax
analysis and command interpreter. But this
is solved by having a translator which converts
the Devanagari commands to equivalent English
command and the rest of the process is same.
The messages, which should be in the respective languages, is handled by the display
generator. All the error messages are
included in Appendix II.

The powerful commands like multiple iteration,
next page, save and unsave enables the user
to create, add, relocate, merge, delete and
modify the text of any size in these languages.

5. PICTURE DESCRIPTION LANGUAGES

Computer education may not be fully facilitated only with text. The combination of
picture and text can make the education
easier; especially in the school. So Picture
Description Language and the associated
graphics software have been developed. Since
pictures can be defined by various geometric
parameters, all the graphical primitives like
points, line, circle, ellipse are defined.
Jordan's eight points algorithm is used to
draw all these primitives. The user can

define the picture through a program using the
picture description language (PDL). This
instruction is a sort of assembly language for
graphics where the mnemonics specify the
primitive and whether it should be plotted or
erased, and the operands specify the parameters or the coordinates of the primitive.
For example:

* GR	Graphics mode
> ERS	Erase the screen
> CIR X,	Circle with origin X, Y and Radius
> ENG	End of graphics
* DEV	Devanagari mode
	Type the Devanagari test with
	End of text
* EN	English mode
- Computer	
- Z	English text is typed with end of text

If the above program is executed it plots a
circle with caption in English and Hindi. All
the instructions and their functions are given
in Appendix III.

With the help of the Dual Text Editor and the
Picture Description Language, this system
could be used for education purpose. Some of
the outputs obtained from the system are
shown in figure 5.

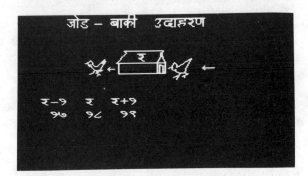

Figure 5: Sample Outputs

6. REFERENCES

(1) Van Dam and Rice
On line text editing
Computing Surveys, 3, 93 (1971)

(2) RT 11 - system reference manual
DEC Massachusetts (1975)

(3) Sequeira George L.R.
A dual text editor a microcomputer
M.Sc. Desertation work, University
of Bombay, 1983.

(4) Jordan, B.W. Jr. Lennon, W.J.
Holm, B.D.
An improved algorithm for the
generation of non parametric curves.

(5) Bown, H.J., O'Brien, C.D.
Sawchuk, W. & Storey
Picture Description Instruction for the
teledon videotax system
Communication Research Centre,
Dept. of Comm., Canada
Technical note No.699 E (1979)

APPENDIX II

LIST OF ERROR MESSAGES IN ENGLISH
AND HINDI

1. *CB FULL*   आदेश मध्यांतिक पूर्ण

     The Command Buffer is full. Delete one or more characters
to accommodate the terminating ESC character sequence.

2. ?ILL ARG?   अवैध कौशिक

     The argument specified is illegal for the command used. A
negative argument specified where a positive one was expected
or argument out of range.

3. ?ILL CMD?   अवैध आदेश

     Illegal Command.

4. ?EOF*?   संचिका समाप

     Attempted a Read or Next and no data was available.

5. ?*FILE FULL*?   संचिका पूरी

     Available space for an output file is full. Type a CTRL C
command and the CLOSE monitor command to save data already
written.

6. ?*FILE NOT FND*?   संचिका अप्राप्त

     Attempted to open a non-existing file for editing.

7. ?*FILE EXISTS*?   संचिका विद्यमान

     Attempted to open a file using a filename which already exists.

8. ?ILL DEV*?   अवैध यंत्र

     Attempted to open a file on an illegal device

9. ?*ILL NAME*?   अवैध नाम

     File name specified in EB, EW or ER command is illegal.

10. ?*NO FILE*?   संचिका नहीं

     Attempted to read or write when no file is open.

11. ?*NO ROOM*?   जगह नहीं

     Attempted to Insert, Save, Unsave, Read, Next, Change or
Exchange when there was not enough room in the appropriate
buffer. Delete unwanted buffers to create more room or write
text to the output file.

12. ?*NO TEXT*?   मूल नहीं

     Attempted to use U or T command when there was no text in
the Save Buffer.

13. ?*SRCH FAIL*?   खोज असफल

     The text string specified in the Get, Find or Position command
was not found in the available data.

14. ?" " ERR? "   " त्रुटि

     Iteration brackets are nested too deeply or used illegally or
brackets are not matched.

APPENDIX III

Graphic Picture Description Instructions

Mnemonic	Function	Parameters
EL	Draws an elipse based on its centre, major axis and minor axis.	4
PY	Draws a polygonal outline with 1+2 (number the number of vetices specified. Coordinates of vertices should follow the number of vetices.	1+2 (number of vertices)
PS	Fills a polygon with the number of vertices specified. Coordinates of vertices given in an anticlockwise direction should follow the number of vertices.	1/2 (number of vertices)
SCL	Provides scaling in X and Y directions. Parameters are direction of scaling and scaling in X and Y directions. Direction: 1 : positive scaling Not 1 : negative scaling.	4
RAC	Provides rotation in the anticlockwise direction by a specified angle 0. 0. 0 180	1
RCL	Provides rotation in the clockwise direction by a specified angle 0 0 0 180.	1
DLY	Provide delay after the display of part of the picture, the parameter is a representation of the amount of delay required.	1
NOP	No operation	0
ENG	End of graphics mode. Takes the user back to the create command mode.	0
RT	Draws a rectangle based left-hand lower corner, length and breadth.	4
REP-ERP	These allow repetition of a group of instructions enclosed between them. REP has 1 parameter specifying the number of repetitions. ERP has no parameters	4
N or S or E or W (Combinations) I	Draws a vector from the drawing position in the direction (north or South or East or West) or combinations of them) specified by the instruction, by the number of points specified as a parameter.	1
NTN, NRO, NSC	Initialises translation, rotation, and scaling parameters of the transformation matrix.	0
TRN	Provides translation in X and Y directions. Parameters are direction of translation, translation in X and Y directions. Direction : 0 : No translation 1 = Positive translation Not 0 or 1 : negative translation	
PT	Plots a point at the (X, Y) position specified	2
LN	Draws a line based on its end points	4
CR	Draws a circle based on its centre and radius	3
AC	Draws an arc of a circle based on an initial point, point on the arc and final point. Points should be given in an anticlockwise direction.	6

COMPUTERS IN EDUCATION, K. Duncan and D. Harris (eds.)
Elsevier Science Publishers B.V. (North-Holland)
© IFIP, 1985

IN-SERVICE TEACHERS' TRAINING IN CAL: AN EXPERIMENTAL RESEARCH

M. Ferraris[*], E. Sassi[+]

[*] Istituto per le Tecnologie Didattiche, Consiglio Nazionale Ricerche, Genova
[+]Dipartimento di Fisica, Università di Napoli, Napoli
Italy

In this paper we describe an experimental intensive course for in-service high school teachers aimed at providing an initial training both in informatics and in educational software use and production. The main aims of the activity were the specification of the various training needs (also on the basis of participants' reactions and attitudes) and the definition of a possible teachers training scheme suitable to satisfy the established requirements. The obtained results show the need of two different types of training courses: the first one aimed at supplying the capacity to select and utilize courseware (large audience, short course, no specific competence in informatics); the second one oriented to provide the basic elements in courseware design (small audience, long course, specific abilities in informatics).

1. INTRODUCTION

One of the consequences of the diffusion of computers in highly industrialized societies is the growing need on the part of teachers for information and training in the educational use of computers.
The range of requirements which is springing up is wide; however the following main themes may be listed:

- training in basic informatics;
- acquisition of the capacity to use courseware;
- acquisition of the capacity to produce courseware;
- acquisition of the capacity to train teachers in this field.

Although the above classification of training requirements is very schematic, the subjects indicated differ from one another, and each one has to be achieved by its own specific means. The great demand, the newness of the field, and the pressure of the market have often led to the creation of training activities which mix up various objects into unclear combinations. On the ground of these considerations, we decided to plan and experiment a training project in CAL, aimed at identifying a possible scheme of intervention to propose to the institutions responsible for teachers' training activities. This scheme would:

- be able to transfer instruments for a valid use of new educational technologies;
- be reproduceable and utilizable on a large scale;
- be easily modifiable (modular structure), as we are dealing here with rapidly evolving educational technologies.

This paper describes an experimental research in the development of training activities for the use of computers in schools. Its main features are:

- medium length intensive in-service training (80 hours over a period of four weeks);

- a population of high school teachers of scientific subjects (preferably not informatics), for whom previous knowledge of informatics was desiderable but not essential.

2. REFERENCE CONTEXT

The subject of in-service training of teachers in the field of courseware and, more in general, of informatics has been confronted during the last few years in almost all European countries. (1, 2) In some countries, and in particular France and the United Kingdom, this subject is one of the qualifying points of their national projects (MEP, SMDP, 100.000 micros...) launched to facilitate the introduction of computers in teaching activities.
Compared with this picture, the Italian situation has some specific characteristics (3) which make the transfer of training systems, already experimented in other countries, rather complex:

- there are no specific graduate courses for the training of teaching staff, not only in the subject of courseware, but more in general on educational technology;
- so far, there is no national project on CAL to uniform or, at least, to outline the intervention;
- the regional organisms (IRRSAE[1]) delegated to deal with updating and experimentation in the field of teaching have been working only for a short time, and have no consolidated experience;
- in-service training courses in CAL sub-

jects are in reality entrusted to spontaneous activities giving no incentives
(either economical or from a career point
of view).

Therefore the problem is that of meeting the
courseware training requirements with activities which are both valid and practicable in the
situation described above.
A first example of CAL training courses in
Italy was a living-in intensive seminar (one
month for about 160 hours), which took place in
1982 in Lecce (4) within the Informatics Summer
School planned and put into practice by the
"AICA-AED" workgroup(2) , which includes many
Italian groups involved in CAL research.
This first experience of training provided a
section for the acquisition of informatics
competence, a section with lectures and laboratory activities on CAL methodologies, and
another group-work section for guided production of courseware. As to the achievement of
the stated goals, the results of the course
were very satisfactory. However some problematic aspects did emerge, such as:

-   the difficulty of repeating the expe-
    rience, due to the total lack of ties
    between the course itself and the struc-
    tures delegated to take care of teachers'
    training;
-   the excessive work-load involved in
    organizing and running an intensive liv-
    ing-in course;
-   the difficulty of utilizing subsequently
    the competences acquired by the partici-
    pants (about 30 from all over Italy), as
    no local aggregations capable of encourag-
    ing the continuation of the activity were
    provided.

Taking into account these aspects and the
results of this first intervention, the training course described in this paper was planned
and carried out. This course maintains approximately the same contents and aims as the pre-
ceeding one, and differs from the latter in the
following:

-   it has a precise place in a context
    (IRRSAE) institutionally dedicated to
    training activities;
-   the local situation facilitates the
    creation of future groups of activity (the
    participants were all from the same
    region).

3.   STRUCTURE OF THE ACTIVITY

The main characteristics of the training
activity, planned and put into effect by
researchers of the DAE project, (5) of the
Faculty of Sciences, University of Naples, in
collaboration with the local IRRSAE, are
briefly described herebelow.
The basic idea was to create a course which
would provide at the same time an initial

training in informatics, on the use of courseware, and on the production of educational
software.
The specific aims and contents were articulated
over the following:
a)   basic CAL training (problems of the
     sector, analysis of teaching strategies,
     illustration of courseware examples and
     possible uses);
b)   first level training in informatics
     (elements of structured programming and
     Pascal);
c)   group-work experience on courseware design
     and production.

The organization of this work was planned as
follows:
-   participants: 25 in-service teachers,
    without incentives;
-   teaching staff: researchers of the DAE
    project, and some of the teachers who had
    attended the Lecce course in 1982.

Classes (80 hours over four weeks - 4 hours a
day five days a week) were distributed as
follows:
-   10 % of the hours for common activities as
    per point (a)
-   15 % of the hours for common activities as
    per point (b)
-   25 % of the hours for computer activities
    as per point (c)
-   50 % of the hours for group work as per
    point (c) (5 groups of 5 members each,
    each group with its own tutor).

4.   DESCRIPTION OF THE EXPERIENCE

The course was divided into a first part
consisting of lessons on CAL strategies and
elements of Pascal, a second section of operational application of the knowledge acquired
(construction of simple Pascal programs and
general purpose programs), and a third section
dedicated to the guided production of educational software.
Figure 1 is a scheme of the various stages of
the activities.
The decision to devote half of the work hours
to courseware design and implementation was
motivated by the firm belief that an operational group activity makes it possible to come
into contact with the multiplicity of the
problems, both of methodological and technical
nature, which had to be solved.
As this is the most significant stage of the
experience, it is worth describing the aspects
and the results of the group activity in
greater detail.
The participants divided themselves spontaneously into the five groups, each of which
worked under the continued coordination of a
tutor. At the beginning of the course a summary
description of the content of the projects on
which the groups were to work had been presented, in order to allow participants to choose
according to their personal interests and also

to foster further use of the produced course-ware.

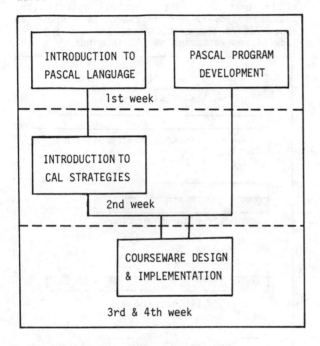

Figure 1: Stages of the course activities

The topics of the projects, chosen keeping in mind the type of degree of the participants and the subjects they were teaching at school, were the following:

1) data analysis with linear progression, building up input files, graphical search for the best straight line, examples of non-linear progression;
2) simulation of the movement of two masses, under gravitational interaction;
3) behaviour of real and ideal gases; study of thermodynamic transformation;
4) graphical study of geometrical transformations on a plane;
5) data acquisition and processing.

All the projects were set up as instructional material of a medium/high complexity (the suggested strategy was essentially that of simulation) destined to students aged 16 to 18. (6) Projects 1 to 4 were conceived as examples of courseware, consisting of software plus written material, while project 5 was conceived as courseware consisting of software and hardware (i.e. interface between a microphone and the computer).
This last project was proposed both in order to satisfy the specific requirements of a group of teachers from technical schools, teaching subjects such as automation systems, physics, electronics and so on, and also to gain experience on problems posed by the production of courseware which uses the computer also for

the acquisition and processing of data.
For the work on the projects, at the beginning each tutor produced a rough draft which included written notes and pre-programmed software; each group worked on the proposed materials, developing some parts. In general, at the end of the work, rough proofs were obtained, which needed to be completed and refined, though containing the main aspects of an educational software.
Problems were encountered in producing written material to support the software. In fact, during the lecture section this subject had not been gone into thoroughly, relying on the supposedly traditional ability of teachers to draw up notes. It should be pointed out that the participants had never had the opportunity to use courseware previously, and therefore had no familiarity with written material supporting educational software.
Another type of problem was the tendency, from those who were familiar with programming, to focus attention on the implementation stage, at times looking for sophisticated solutions without fully taking in the importance of the instructional design and of the validation stages.

5.   ANALYSIS OF THE RESULTS

As already mentioned in the introduction, the aim of this work was to identify a possible training scheme in the CAL field, which could be put into practice and generalized. The results were therefore evaluated on the basis of various elements, such as organization, acquisition of competences, and participants' attitudes and reactions. The information referred to these different categories was identified:

-   in an informal manner, by closely observing the activities carried out, and analysing the group works and the problems which emerged;

-   by means of more formal instruments consisting of pre and post course questionnaires, with the intent of verifying the knowledge acquired and, above all, of ascertaining opinions and attitudes in respect to the proposed themes.

The table in figure 2 indicates the key points used for drawing up the questionnaires.
The distinction between questions in an area of "knowledge" and in an area of "opinion", which may appear to be somewhat arbitrary, was based on the possibility of deciding with certainty whether the answers were correct or not. In order to clarify the difference between the various types of questions, figure 3 shows questions referred to both fields.

```
"KNOWLEDGE" AREA

- basic notions on computer science (I)
- computer program writing (I, F)
- hardware/software costs (I)
- CAL terminology (I, F)

"OPINION" AREA

- stages  and  competences  in  courseware
  production (I, F)
- educational value involved in programming
  language learning (I, F)
- comparison between computers and other edu-
  cational instruments (I)
- criteria for courseware evaluation (I, F)
- role of the teacher (courseware producer?
  user?) (I, F)
- ways in using computers in school (I, F)
- application to one's own particular subject
  (I, F)


I = initial questionnaire
F = final questionnaire
```

Figure 2: "Knowledge" and "Opinions" subject to
  verification

```
"KNOWLEDGE" AREA

If you already know a programming language,
write a program to determine the roots of
equations in the form ax  + bx + c = 0

Describe the meaning of the following terms,
using no more than four words for each one:
TUTORIAL,  SIMULATION,  DRILL  AND  PRACTICE,
COURSEWARE

"OPINION" AREA

Give your opinion about the following state-
ments:

    "a CAL package must be developed by the
    same teacher who will use it"

    complete                    total
    disagreement                agreement

    "in order to use courseware the teacher
    should know informatics"

    complete                    total
    disagreement                agreement
```

Figure 3: Examples of questions

Let us now look briefly (fig. 4) at the results
referred to the knowledge area.
These results confirm the widespread presence
of previous knowledge of informatics (this was,

on the other hand, a requisite for taking part
in the course), accompanied however by a lack
of information on its practical aspects (the
cost of hardware and software is unknown to
about 70% of the participants), and a declared
lack of understanding of CAL terminology.

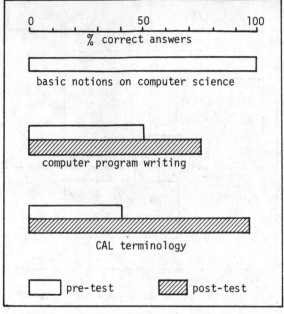

Figure 4: Results in the "knowledge" area

More than the "knowledge" aspects, however, the
opinion which resulted from the questionnaire
on some crucial aspects of CAL were of greater
interest for our purposes. In fact, the awareness of pre-existing attitudes and the changes
which may come about after a training course,
make it possible to pin-point the role the
teachers intend to, or may, fill in the present
school situation, and supplie indications as to
some of the contents which a training activity
in this field should include.
The analysis and comparison of the pre and post
course questionnaires, brought forth the
following teacher image:

-   A teacher who does not consider the use of
    previously prepared instructional software
    a limitation to his teaching activity.
    At the end of the course, more than 80% of
    the participants were of this opinion.
    This position represents a partial shift-
    ing of the original attitude, according to
    which about 60% of the teachers thought
    that the courseware should be entirely
    (22%) or at least partly (39%) developed
    by the teacher who is to use it.

-   He does not consider it essential that
    teachers acquire a particular competence
    in informatics in order to use pre-pro-
    grammed courseware; while at the beginning
    of the course 70% of the teachers believed

that competence in informatics was indispensable or at least desirable, at the end of the course, only 30% considered this competence useful (but not indispensable) for teachers to use educational software (and the percentage falls to 10% when referred to the knowledge required to the student).

Here again, there is a shifting of opinion, which is also very indicative of the possibility to organize CAL training courses in which the informatic content plays only a minor part.

- He has a very precise, and sometimes critical, opinion as to the role that computers should play in teaching activities.
  At the beginning of the course, 95% of the participants indicated the key role of the computer is providing a support to the activity of the teacher in class or with small groups.
  The idea of a computer as an instrument able to replace the teacher completely in giving lessons is considered in an entirely negative manner, exception made for exercises aimed at the recovery of abilities. These pre-existing opinions were confirmed by the answers to the final questionnaire, in which the examples of applications suggested by the teachers fall within the categories "drill and practice", "simulation" or use of a computer as a "tool" for the introduction of mathematical and physical concepts.

- He is aware of the wide range of competences required and of the complexity involved in courseware production.
  At the beginning of the course, almost all the teachers were unable to indicate what type of competences would be required in a production group (40%) or focused their attention mainly on informatic competences. By the end of the course, this attitude had changed considerably: most of the teachers recognize that courseware production requires various competences (informatics, instructional methodology, teaching experience and specific matter knowledge) and distributed them correctly among the various phases of courseware production.

- He feels that the main task of the teacher is being able to choose and integrate courseware into the subject taught.
  87% of the participants agreed on this point at the end of the course. This was however accompanied by a certain confusion and underestimation of the problem linked to the evaluation of courseware: the main qualities requested were "clarity", "ease of utilization", but very few included factors such as "correctness", "documentation", "supports for teacher and students" and so on.

These answers point out the need and the importance of courses aimed prevalently at supplying the capacity to choose and utilize courseware.

Part of the characteristics which emerged from the replies to the questionnaire were confirmed by the results of the informal observation of group activities. For example, the initial tendency of many of the participants to concentrate their attention on the informatics aspects of courseware production was modified by the end of the course, with an increase of awareness towards methodological aspects (documentation, CAL strategies, evaluation).

Globally, the courseware production stage, although closely guided as in the case under consideration, led to the acquisition of an awareness of the complexity of this type of work, and supplied elements of guidance for courseware evaluation.

6. CONCLUDING NOTES

The scopes underlying the activity described in this paper were the acquisition both of the capacity to use pre-existing courseware and an initial training in development of courseware.

With a duration of 80 hours, and without the pre-requisite of a previous training in computer programming, the targets proposed proved to be overdimensioned, and the participants asked to complete the experience during the following schoolyear.

On the basis of this experience, it seems possible to express schematically two different training requirements:

- integration into present school programs of pre-programmed courseware by teachers who have not had any prior training in informatics (utilization of courseware);
- production of CAL packages transferable to other contexts (production of courseware).

Intermediate needs are also present, for instance the teacher who produces specific CAL examples referred to the reality of a particular class by means of short-lived instructional material, which does not pretend to be either exhaustive or transferable. These situations evolve naturally and are present in such a variety of forms that they shall not be gone into for the scope of these notes.

It seems reasonable to conclude by laying down a proposal for two different types of training activity:

- UTILIZATION: aimed at acquiring the capacity to make use of pre-existing courseware, based on a widespread analysis of high quality courseware and the possibility of including them in present school curricula. No previous competence in informatics should be necessary, and the course might be accompanied by optional training in basic informatics.

- PRODUCTION: aimed at acquiring an initial ability in courseware development, based equally on training in informatics (a basic knowledge would be a pre-requisite for participants), and in "guided" courseware production on existing frameworks.

The first type of course may be limited to a duration of about 50 hours, while the second type will require about 150 hours.
UTILIZATION is of interest to a far vaster potential user market, and also acts as a vehicle for increasing the demand for qualified courseware.
PRODUCTION sparks off a training process for courseware authors and provides the basic elements for a profession which today is just beginning to exist.
The reference context in which these two types of training activity should be placed is shown schematically in figure 5.

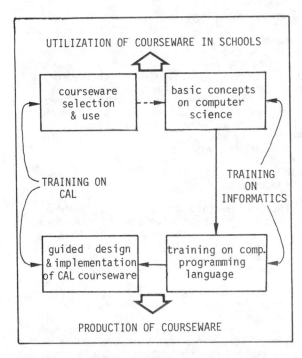

Figure 5: Training activities

The block called "courseware design and implementation" is to be taken as an activity for which multiple capabilities are required (summarized schematically as competences in the subject matter, in methodology, in informatics, in communication and so on), but rarely found all in the same person. A good opportunity for this type of activity might be, for example, the setting up of stages in Educational Technology Centres.
The last remark concerns the problem of linking up applied research, such as CAL research, with some service activities in the field of training. Continuous training of teachers, the

creation of courseware gathering centres, the production and distribution of courseware for adult education outside the scholastic context, are some examples of activities in which research and services are both found together.
It is necessary to create a two-way communication for the transfer of results, integrating functionally the different roles of educational research and in-service activities, without creating any confusion between the characteristics pertinent to each of these activities. The use of computers in teaching, considering the pressing demand and the lack of specific initial training for in-service teachers today, provides a very good opportunity to study situations with problems of linkage between teaching activities and research.
There is a great need for more clarification, and it is also from this point of view that the work here described was undertaken.

7.   REFERENCES

(1) Fothergill, R., J.S.A. Anderson and others Microelectronics Education Programme Policy and Guidelines, Information Guide 4 (CET, London, 1983).
(2) Various Authors, Actes du colloque national "Informatique et Einsegnement" (CNDP, Paris, 1983).
(3) Olimpo G., Sassi. E., Education and Training and New Information Technologies. A report on the Italian arrangements for exchange of information and experience. Technical Report of European Community (1982).
(4) Various Authors, Materiali del Seminario AED, Scuola Estiva di Informatica '82, Università di Lecce, in press.
(5) Avitabile G., Sassi, E., Applicazioni degli Elaboratori nella Didattica: il progetto DAE a Napoli Automazione e Strumentazione. 2 (1984) 113-120.
(6) Chioccariello, A., Olimpo, G., Sassi, E., Spadaccini, G., Production of CAL packages. A set of criteria and an example in the electric circuit field in National Research Council of Canada (ed.), Proc. 4th Canadian Symposium on Instructional Technology. (Winnipeg 1983).

(1) IRRSAE - Istituto Regionale per la Ricerca, la Sperimentazione e l'Aggiornamento Educativo (Regional Institute for Educational Research, Experimentation and Training)

(2) AICA - Associazione Italiana per l'Informatica ed il Calcolo Automatico (Italian Association for Informatics and Automatic Calculus)

COMPUTERS IN EDUCATION, K. Duncan and D. Harris (eds.)
Elsevier Science Publishers B.V. (North-Holland)
© IFIP, 1985

DESIGNING COMPUTER-BASED INTERACTIVE VIDEODISC INSTRUCTION

Kathie A. Fletcher, Daniel H. Hodgson, Nik Hughes, Kerry A. Johnson

Center for Instructional Development and Evaluation
The University of Maryland University College
College Park, Maryland 20742

During recent years, the new laserdisc technology has been combined with the micro-computer to form a new medium of instruction called computer-based interactive video (CBIV). Design of instructional materials for this medium requires an interdisciplin-ary approach involving instructional design, software development, video production, and implementation/evaluation. Each of these disciplines must be adapted to the CBIV environment.

A description of the instructional systems development model and a discussion of the ways this model has been applied in the CBIV environment will provide a springboard for a discussion of the principles involved in the actual creation of instruction. As part of this discussion, videodisc technology, hardware systems available, and software available for each hardware system, specifically authoring systems and authoring languages will be presented.

DESCRIPTION

The first section of the workshop will include a description of the instructional systems development model and a discussion of ways this model has been applied in the development of computer-based interactive video.

The second section will be a discussion of videodisc technology, available hardware systems that utilize both the videodisc and the computer, available software available for each hardware system, particularly authoring languages and authoring systems, and a discussion of the current limitations of the considerations specifically applicable to each characteristic of hardware and software discussed.

The third section of this workshop deals with the actual creation of screens and the message design principles involved in the process of designing screens and courseware.

COMPUTERS IN EDUCATION, K. Duncan and D. Harris (eds.)
Elsevier Science Publishers B.V. (North-Holland)
©IFIP, 1985

DESIGN, DEVELOPMENT AND USE OF COMPUTER ASSISTED LEARNING MATERIALS IN THE SCHOOL
CURRICULUM: THE CHELSEA (ENGLAND) EXPERIENCE

Chairperson: - Margaret Cox

Sophie McCormick, David Riddle, David Squires and Deryn Watson

Computers in the Curriculum Project, Chelsea College
Educational Computing Section, University of London.

This special session will take the participants through the stages of the design of Computer Assisted Learning materials within the constraints of the existing school curriculum, and currently available hardware; to the development process; the use of such materials in the classroom, and finally to new directions for a changing curriculum and expanding technological environment.

The objectives of the session are:

To show the participants the projects model for the successful design and development of computer assisted learning materials.

To demonstrate the limitations on CAL currently imposed by educational constraints, such as: examination syllabuses, traditional teaching methods, classroom organisation; and technological constraints, such as: limited hardware memory, screen definition and processing speed.

To provide new ideas of how CAL can be used to enhance and extend education in schools, with the existing constraints, and how these might change if some of the constraints are removed.

The session will be run in three stages:

Stage 1   Teacher designed CAL - Designing Computer Assisted Learning to enhance the school curriculum.

1 hour workshop on the design process (which involves teachers, subject specialists, software experts and curriculum developers) as used by the Project. Conference participants will investigate the design process by experiencing, first hand, the problems and considerations faced by a CAL design group.

Stage 2   Development of CAL - Stages and styles in the development of Computer Assisted Learning.

$1\frac{1}{2}$ hours practical workshop to illustrate the various stages and styles of developing CAL software. This workshop will include using software in Science, Humanities and Languages, to give the participants experience of the diversity of CAL and its current strengths and limitations. Participants will have an opportunity to contrast and compare simulations with modelling, role playing and decision making games across the school curriculum and to explore the exchange of ideas and teaching strategies between the different subject backgrounds.

Stage 3   Although there is an exponential growth in information technology, the microcomputers now available in education impose severe limitations on the CAL materials currently being produced for schools. This last one hour session will consider the current constraints imposed by educational tradition and the present technological limitations, with a glimpse of possible future directions.

Support materials such as CAL programs, handouts, worksheets etc will be provided for this special session.

Conference delegates will be involved actively throughout the three session stages.

COMPUTERS IN EDUCATION, K. Duncan and D. Harris (eds.)
Elsevier Science Publishers B.V. (North-Holland)
© IFIP, 1985

INSTRUCTIONAL DESIGN AND COURSE IMPLEMENTATION:
A CASE STUDY OF AN INTEGRATED APPROACH USING COMPUTERS

Thomas R. Earle,
School of Business Studies,
Darling Downs Institute of Advanced Education,
Darling Hts. P.O., TOOWOOMBA, QLD. 4350 AUSTRALIA

The paper describes the development and implementation of a course management system for teaching
computer programming in an undergraduate course. The problems of instructional design for computer based teaching are reviewed and a computer aided methodology, interpretive structural
modelling, used to develop the hierarchy of course content. Using the results of this methodology, a course management system was designed to integrate computers, study material and lecturers
in an effective instructional package. A CML system is used to monitor students progress and
their attention to the course. The evaluation of the system agrees with the conclusions of
previous studies which indicate that students show a strong positive attitudinal response to CML.

1. INTRODUCTION

The importance of computer based teaching programmes
has been emphasised continually in papers given at
previous WCCE Conferences as well as in the literature. Leiblum [1] (see also [2]) at the WCCE/81 summarised the general benefits of CAL (Computer
Assisted Learning); but also cautioned that because
many of the advantages attributed to CAL can be
achieved through other instructional methods, CAL
should be reserved for instructional problems that
CAL can solve in a unique and hopefully superior way.
Furthermore, since the initial flush of excitement
over computer based teaching programmes in the seventies, there is now a degree of caution being emphasised in the literature [3,4,5,6] e.g. lessons
learned from the earlier panaceas of teaching
machines and programmed instruction should not have
to be learnt over again with computers [3].

Part of the caution has been the recognition of the
importance of instructional design in computer based
learning techniques [7] rather than just computer
programming. Montague et al [4] concluded that "the
success of computer-based instruction depends not
only on the avalability of cheap computing power, but
on the development of methods and aids for designing
and implementing it."

Some authors have dealt with this problem of design
and development of instruction using computers.
Yngstrom [8] suggested a systematic approach based on
the theories of system analysis. Later, Merril [9]
suggested a similar, but more detailed set of components with his curriculum model of: need and constraints analysis; goal definition and discrepancy
analysis; specification of content and learning outcome development; sequencing and detailed analysis of
selected parts; test development; choosing learning
events and appropriate media; survey and procure existing materials; write and produce materials; pilot
test, field test; and exit analysis. Other authors
have examined individual stages in instructional
design for computer based teaching programmes e.g.
Kurtz and Bork [10] suggested a method for displaying
the structure and sequencing of the elements in the
instructional package.

In spite of the adoption of system design and
procedures, Montague et al [4] noted that these
procedures do not make up for the deficits in the
skills needed to devise quality instruction.
Furthermore, Montague et al [4] suggested improvements possibly could be obtained by the utilization
of computer-based aids for instructional design and
development.

The purpose of this paper is to address the problem
of instructional design in computer based teaching
and complement the above models of curriculum design
by reporting the application of a computer aided
method for developing the hierarchy (or sequencing)
of content which is a prerequisite to successful computer based teaching [11]. The first section of the
paper provides an overview of Interpretive
Structional Modelling and its application in developing a hierarchy of content for a third level
programming (Fortran) course to students studying a
computing major for a Bachelor of Business degree.
The second section will describe the development of a
computer managed learning system based on this
hierarchical model and the experience of the author
in applying it in the classroom.

2. COMPUTER AIDED INSTRUCTIONAL DESIGN

It is not the intention with this paper to review instructional design and learning theory in depth. The
reader is referred to such articles as Romiszowski
[12] and books by Briggs [13] and Gagne and Briggs
[14] for material providing a detailed background to
instructional design.

The relationship and sequence between individual objectives or content (as suggested by Gagne [15]) can
be described as a hierarchy with a strict sequential
dependence, one objective not being possible to
achieve until another objective has been learned or
as a hierarchy with a thematic relationship of a
looser character. If there are relatively few items
in the course then the construction of the hierarchy
is a simple matter. But in reality a course will
have a large number of content items or objectives
and therefore it is a substantial task [16] to

develop the hierarchy representing this complex structure.

Miller [17] and Simon [18] maintain the span of absolute judgment for the immediate memory of humans is of the order of seven times. Warfield [19] refers to this as the principle of bounded rationality which imposes severe limitations on the amount of information people are able to process. A hierarchy for course content will be of such complexity that it will be affected by this principle since there will be many linkages between elements resulting from the large number of contextual relationships. Such complexity may mean that one individual can do no more than contribute to the solution and therefore it requires a group process. A methodology used for determining course content needs to be able to cope with a hierarchy and the resulting complexity of large structures.

We can classify a hierarchy as a form of structural model since it employs graphics and words in a carefully defined pattern to portray the structure of a course curriculum. This differs from an adhoc model as there are specific rules for the formation of the structure which are dictated by learning theory (as suggested by Gagne [15]).

The structuring of the content of a course into a hierarchy should be iterative. New perceptions are gained from the initial structure and this may require alteration of the structure. This interactive process will continue until one is satisfied with the final structure.

Having to systematically establish the relationship between each element and the rest of the elements in the core to produce a hierarchy by manual methods is extremely time consuming and rather draconian. For example 100 elements would require 9,900 comparisons and decisions to be made and as such is generally beyond the limits of human endurance. A computer can make an important contribution here by helping the human preserve uniformity in the decision making of large structures by supplying substantive knowledge in such a way that assists him in preserving consistency.

Interpretive Structural Modelling (ISM) is a methodology which attempts to represent substantive content and its inter-relations diagrammatically, and through an interactive process it produces a hierarchical representation. The methodology of interpretive structural modelling was developed by Warfield [19] and extended by Carss [20].

A general overview of the ISM approach is shown in figure 1. Beginning with the perceptions of the group or individual, this mental model is translated into a representation system of a matrix model stored in a computer. This process called embedding is structuring the ingredients of the mental model from the information supplied by the developer. This matrix model can then be partitioned by the computer to form a multilevel diagraph. The next stage of substitution involves replacing the computer symbolism by ordinary language to achieve the interpretive structural model which is a hierarchy. This model is then validated by the human developers and may require further iterative steps before a satisfactory structure is achieved.

ISM requires two concepts to be identified by a user:

(a) the elements to be structured; and

(b) the type of relationship inferred by the hierarchy.

The methodololgy enables the coding of this information and the extraction of the hierarchy. The relationship between the n elements can be represented by a square matrix, M(n,n). The elements of the matrix are such that $M_{ij} = 1$ then element i is subordinate to element j. If $M_{ij} = 0$ then element i is not subordinate to element j. The following rules apply to the construction of the matrix:

(a) $M_{ij} = 0$ for all i = j
(b) $M_{ij} = 1$ then M $= 0$
(c) If $M_{ij} = 1$ and $M_{jk} = 1$ then $M_{ik} = 1$
    (i.e. transivity applies)

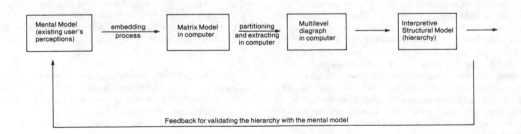

Figure 1. An overview of the ISM process

Therefore a connection in the hierarchy is indicated by 1 in the matrix element M_{ij}. The level of an element in the hierarchy is determined by summing the rows, that is $\sum_i M_{ij}$ gives the level of the element in the hierarchy where 0 indicates the highest level and 1 the next highest and so on. Carss [20] has adapted this procedure to an interactive programme. This programme has a sampling algorithm which minimises a number of questions required to obtain the hierarchy.

3. APPLICATION OF ISM

The above methodology of ISM was used in the instructional design of a computer programming course for final level undergraduate students in the School of Business Studies at the Darling Downs Institute of Advanced Education. As outlined by Merril [9], one of the first decisions was to establish the goals of the course. The next stage was to extract the elements of the course, which was done using the author's practical experience and the advice of colleagues in the area. The list was checked for redundancy and a final list of sixty-one elements was established. This set of elements was then structured into a hierarchy using the Interpretive Structural Modelling method. The resultant hierarchy was broken into vertical chain sections such that each chain represented a terminal behaviour with respect to each of the above goals.

The structure suggested by the hierarchy was significantly different to existing text books at the time of development and this suggests that previous text books in that area may have given little thought to a subject matter hierarchy based on Gagne's [15] idea of learning theory.

4. THE COMPUTER AS AN EDUCATIONAL AIDE

Despite a computer's remarkable capacity for storing, retrieving and manipulating data, computers cannot be warm, sympathetic or encouraging. Although artificial intelligence techniques [21] allow a computer to pretend to be, it is still just a pretence. Simpson [5] noted that it makes sense to use computers to support the teachers, not to replace or mimic them. Computers have generally been used in Computer Aided Instruction (CAI) or Computer Managed Learning (CML). Recent papers [1, 3, 4, 5, 6] have stressed the importance of a balance between the teacher, the students and the courseware. These papers indicate that various methods of instruction are appropriate in certain situations and that the teacher must manage all the various modes of instruction that are available to ensure that the optimum mix is attained for the student.

We can briefly define the choice of instructional package [22] in terms of a diagram. Figure 2(A), the traditional lecture mode indicates that the main flow of information occurs from the lecturer to student and that there is only a small flow from student back to the lecturer. Consequently, students have little opportunity for clarifying individual problems or assessing their competence. In figure 2(B), the traditional CAI approach ([22], [23]), the lecturer uses the computer to interact with the student. In figure 2(C), the CMI approach ([22], [23]), the student interacts with the computer to do progressive assessment and also interacts with some other form of instructional media, predominately printed notes, video recording, tape recording, slides etc. After the CMI system is designed, the lecturer predominantly interacts with the computer. Sometimes there is a combination of both the CMI and CAI approaches where the lecturer obtains feedback from the computer on the students' progress in the CAI situation.

This paper proposes that there should be a balance between these elements in the instructional situation. Figure 3 defines a course management system [24] which allows for interaction between all three elements, the lecturer, students and computer. The centre of the system is the student who has the opportunity to take advantage of interacting: (a) with the lecturer in terms of personal instruction, (b) with other courseware in terms of books, films, etc., or (c) with the computer in terms of a CAI or CMI approach.

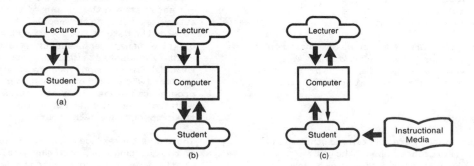

Figure 2. (A) Conventional instruction, (B) CAI, (C) CML.

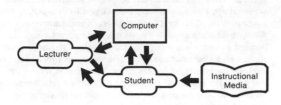

Figure 3. Course management system.

Therefore, a student can utilise the communication channel that best suits his/her particular needs at that point in time. Also the lecturer receives the benefits of being able to interact directly with the computer to determine the early warning signs of students who are in difficulty and need special assistance.

5.   COURSE MANAGEMENT SYSTEM

In a similar manner to Anderson et al [24], a course management system (CMS) was designed to integrate study notes, computers and lecturers in an effective manner. In the CMS, the students are expected to aquire their basic information and concepts primarily from individual readings of the study notes (Lay [3] noted that there was a superiority of the hard-copy over the computer presentation of learning material and that it is difficult to write CAL material so that it can be used as flexibly as most students use a text-book). The students progress is managed by a CML system called FORTQUIZ (Dixon and Judd [7] noted that CML had considerable savings in development and implementation over CAI while still retaining many of the advantages). The lecturer's time, saved because routine lecturing and formative testing was no longer required, was invested in one to one remediation in practical classes and in expanding the advanced concepts of the course. The basic elements of the course management system can be summarised as:

(a) study notes
(b) FORTQUIZ (a CML package)
(c) computer
(d) Formal class contact.

The overall structure of the course was based on the results of the hierarchy developed by ISM as described above which acted as a blue print plan for the study notes and the formative tests in the CML package.

(a) Study Notes

The study notes were written such that each chapter represented one of the goals of the course. Each chapter consisted of a series of modules which represented each element in the hierarchy. At the end of each module the student was directed to take a formative test based on that module using FORTQUIZ. At the end of each chapter there was a programming assignment

on the computer to test the accomplishment of the goal of the chapter.

(b) FORTQUIZ

The essential features of FORTQUIZ can be described as:

(i)   self pacing of students
(ii) interactive testing
(iii) immediate feedback
(iv) references for further study to overcome problems of understanding
(v)   mastery learning [25]
(vi) a lock-out of the system to ensure that students cannot repeat the test a number of times without first doing further study
(vii) a reporting system for the lecturer which includes individual reports on any student, class statistics, details of when students last accessed the system, etc.

The testing format in FORTQUIZ enables presentation flexibility e.g. the number of questions, the type of question format (multiple choice, individual answer, etc.) is chosen by the lecturer. Response types can be varied within a particular question batch.

Since each module relates to instructional objectives in the defined hierarchy, each question batch based on a module of the hierarchy must be mastered before the students proceed to the next module. Feedback is given to students on each question and in the case of incorrect answers the student is directed to the appropriate section of the study notes for revision.

FORTQUIZ has two main interactive sections: (a) Lecture interface; and (b) the student interface.

The lecturer interface allows for test construction, class registration, class maintenance, and management reports. At any time the lecturer can obtain management reports about the results of individual students on a test or a group of tests, and the overall results of any test or group of tests. Besides the percentage results for each test and the number of times a student attempts a test for the module, the program also records the date of last access by the student. Using the management reports, a lecturer can identify students at risk on any module and take remedial action. Using the date of last access, students who have dropped behind in their study program can be identified and course counselling with that student can be undertaken to reduce the drop-out rate in the course.

The student interface allows for multiple access to the questions file. Each time a student logs on, the program responds with the next set of questions for that student. The students are always under program control and never suffer the frustration of obscure computer related error messages. Upon completing the tests for a module, the student's results are evaluated. If the student has achieved 80% [26] or higher then the student is given access to the next module; however if the student does not master the module (that is the student test result is less than 80%) then the student is directed to further work in his study notes. In addition, the program locks the students out of the system for 30 minutes. This ensures the student does not attempt to sit at the terminal and continue to repeat the test without any further study. If a student fails to master a module after 3 attempts, the student is locked out of the system completely and referred to the lecturer for personal remediation. After this remediation session the lecturer can reinstate the student on FORTQUIZ to procede with the test in that module.

(c) Computer

The FORTQUIZ package has ben implemented on a HP3000 series III computer, which is the same computer on which the students are doing their practical programming. This ensures students do not have to change computer facilities and overcomes some of the difficulties described in previous papers [26].

(d) Formal Class Contact

A one hour session each week is reserved as an enrichment session for the course as well as for group communication. In addition there are up to 3 hours of practical laboratory sessions during which the lecturer holds individual discussions with each student on their progress with FORTQUIZ and the student's programming assignments are reviewed in detail. Thus the likelihood of unequal management of students is reduced [22]. Such personal contact was not possible under the traditional lecturer situation.

6. EVALUATION OF THE SYSTEM

Because the class size was relatively small, it was not possible to do a comparative study. Instead the system was evaluated in two stages.

In the first stage, the study notes were used over a two year period using the traditional methods. With this close involvement of the lecturer, weak areas in the notes were identified and improved. The question set was also administered during formal classes over a two year period to check on the reliability and validity of the questions to ensure their suitability for future use.

In the second stage, after the study notes and question sets were validated the FORTQUIZ system was implemented and a survey of participating students in the class was taken to determine their reaction to CML. Prior to this, none of the students were exposed to CML techniques in any other classes. 82% of the students who had completed FORTQUIZ agreed they would like to see CML implemented in other units.

This strong positive attitudal response agrees with other studies (eg. [24], [27], [28], [29]). Students listed a number of the traditonal reasons for using CML [7] as the advantages of using FORTQUIZ in the unit e.g. forces mastery learning, self-paced, immediate feedback, less time wasted in class, novelty approach, gives lecturer feedback on students' performance, better preparation for summative examination, reinforcement of concepts, keeps the students up to date with their study. 82% of the students agreed that the study notes helped prepare them adequately for FORTQUIZ.

The main criticism of FORTQUIZ was that 72% of the students agreed that they would like to see more feedback on wrong answers. This area of FORTQUIZ is currently being revised to provide more detailed feedback to students. Also 33% of the students suggested the question wording needed to be improved and this is also being investigated further.

The median time required to prepare for a module was 45 minutes, while the median time for module testing was 15 minutes.

The main advantages of using FORTQUIZ from the lecturer's point of view were:

(a) It considerably increased the lecturer's time for more personalised guidance and individualised instruction.

(b) The reports from FORTQUIZ allowed the lecturer to monitor the progress of students on a daily basis.

(c) The drop-out rate was not different to traditional teaching methods. This experience disagrees with previous experiences (eg. [27], [28]). This may be due to the fact that only 36% of the students reported any difficulties in getting to a terminal. (Terminal access has been labeled a problem by a number of others [27, 30]). In addition, it is suspected that the detailed student progress report enabled the lecturer to prevent a student dropping out because remedial advice was provided before they even reached the decision point to drop-out.

It was felt that the use of the computer not only improved the instructional design of the course but also enhanced the relationships between the lecturer and the students. By having easy access to information on each student the problems of individual students could be identified and followed up.

7. REFERENCES

[1] Leiblum, M.D., Factors sometimes overlooked and underestimated in the selection and success of CAL as an instructional medium, in Lewis, R. and Tagg, D. (eds.), Computers in Education (North-Holland, Amsterdam, 1981, 277-283).

[2] Hopper, R., Computers in science teaching - an introduction, Computers and Education 2 (1978) 1-7.

[3] Lay, R.W., Basic techniques for teaching 'BASIC', in Lewis, R. and Tagg, D. (eds.), Computers in Education (North-Holland, Amsterdam, 1981, 39-42).

[4] Montague, W.E., Wulfeck, W.H., and Ellis, J.A., Quality CBI depends on quality instructional design and quality implementation, Journal of Computer-Based Instruction 10 (1983) 90-93.

[5] Simpson, B., Heading for the Ha-Ha, British Journal of Educational Technology 14 (1983) 19-26.

[6] Charp, S. and Hebenstreit, J., Opening Session, in Lewis, R. and Tagg, D. (eds.), Computer Assisted Learning (North-Holland, Amsterdam, 1980, 1-2).

[7] Dixon, P.N. and Judd, W.A., A comparison of Computer-Managed instruction and lecture mode for teaching basic statistics, Journal of Computer-Based Instruction 4 (1977) 22-25.

[8] Yngstrom, L., A method for analysis and construction of interactive Computer-Based Teaching programmes, in Lecarme, O. and Lewis, R. (eds.), Computers in Education (North-Holland, Amsterdam, 1975, 37-40).

[9] Merril, J.R., A rational approach to the design of instruction, in A. Jones and H. Weinstock (eds.), Computer-based Science Instruction (Leiden, Noordhoff, 1977, 89-114).

[10] Kurtz, B.L. and Bork, A., An SADT Model for the production of Computer Based Learning Material, in Lewis, R. and Tagg, D. (eds.), Computers in Education (North-Holland, Amsterdam, 1981, 375-384).

[11] Spuck, D.W. and Owen, S.P., Individualized instruction: Its structure and management with computer assistance, Educational Technology 16 (1976) 35-43.

[12] Romiszowski, A.J., A new look at instructional design Part II, British Journal of Educational Technology 13 (1982) 15-55.

[13] Briggs, L.J., Instructional Design (Educational Technology Publication, Englewood Cliffs, 1977).

[14] Gagne, R.M. and Briggs, L.J., Principles of Instructional Design, Second Edition (Holt Rinehart and Winston, New York, 1979).

[15] Gagne, R.M., The Conditions of Learning (Holt Rinehart and Winston, New York, 1965).

[16] Countermine, T. and Singh, J.M., A Computer-Managed Instruction support system for large group individualized instruction, Journal of Computer-Based Instruction 4 (1977) 17-21.

[17] Miller, G.A., The magic number seven, plus or minus two: some limits on our capacity for procesing information. Psychological Review 63 (1956) 81-97.

[18] Simon, H.A., How big is a chunk, Science 182 (1974) 482-488.

[19] Warfield, J.N., Societal Systems (John Wiley and Sons, New York, 1976).

[20] Carss, B.W., Establishing priorities for inservice programmes through participative decision making using an ISM approach, Australian Council of Educational Administration, 4th National Conference (1977).

[21] Gable, A. and Page, C.V., The use of Artificial Intelligence techniques in Computer-Assisted Instruction: an overview, International Journal of Man-Machine Studies 12 (1980) 259-282.

[22] Splittgerber, F.L., Computer-Based Instruction: a revolution in the making, Educational Technology 19 (1979) 20-26.

[23] Belt, S.L. and West, S.F., Implementing Individually Guided Education (IGE) with computer assistance, Educational Technology 16 (1976) 40-44.

[24] Anderson, T.H., Anderson, R.C., Alessi, S.M., Dalgaard, B.R., Parden, D.W., Biddle, W.B., Surber, J.R., Smock, H.R., A multifaceted Computer Based Course Management System, in Lecarme, O. and Lewis, R., (eds.), Computers in Education (North-Holland, Amsterdam, 1975, 123-130).

[25] Federico, P., Individual differences in cognitive characteristics and Computer-Managed Mastery Learning, Journal of Computer-Based Instruction 9 (1982) 10-18.

[26] Carlson, J.G. and Minke, K.A. Fixed and ascending criteria for unit mastery learning, Journal of Educational Psychology 67 (1975) 96-101.

[27] Montanelli, R.G., Evaluating PLATO in the teaching of Computer Science, Journal of Computer-Based Instruction 5 (1979) 72-76.

[28] Ibrahim, R.L., Computer-Assisted Instruction in Kuwait: A Pilot Study, in Lewis, R. and Tagg, D. (eds.), Computers in Education (North-Holland, Amsterdam, 1981, 569-573).

[29] Schroeder, L. and Kent, P., Computer-Based Instruction in Dietetics Education, Journal of Computer-Based Instruction 8 (1982) 85-90.

[30] Jones, A. and O'Shea, T., Barriers to the use of Computer Assisted Learning, British Journal of Educational Technology 13 (1982) 207-217.

COMPUTERS IN EDUCATION, K. Duncan and D. Harris (eds.)
Elsevier Science Publishers B.V. (North-Holland)
© IFIP, 1985

Evaluation of Student Performance using the Microcomputer

Dr. John H. Dustman

Biology Department
Indiana University Northwest
Gary, Indiana

The use of microcomputer based technology to develop an integrated series of computer programs for complete classroom administration is discussed. The Classroom Administration System or CAS allows for test banking, examination production, examination scoring and analysis, and complete electronic gradebooking in a series of integrated and mutually interdependent programs for the Apple computer.

The use of microcomputers in support of education has received a tremendous amount of attention in the past decade. Most of this attention, however, has been focused on the areas of Computer Aided Instruction, and Computer Managed Instruction. Little attention has been paid to the area one could call Classroom Administration. Although the benefits of using the microcomputer in drill and practice routines, in simulations and game playing for educational purposes has generated a considerable amount of software support, far too little development has occurred in support of such functions as test construction, test grading, grade keeping, performance analysis, etc. Yet a significant portion of a teacher's time is committed to these functions at least at some level. Most teachers find that, without the aid of computer technology, these tasks are very time consuming even to complete only a minimal level of analysis and totally impossible at any higher level, and that few if any integrated series of computer programs have been developed to assist in this function. Many of the programs that do exist also tend to be "egocentric" in their analysis. I mean that these programs tend to analyze a test to see how good or bad the test was, and fails to analyze a test to determine student performance characteristics, which in reality was the original purpose of giving the test. This paper will describe a series of integrated computer program modules which have been designed to allow a teacher to upgrade their involvement in these teaching support areas and increase their efficiency as teachers

with a minimum time involvement; and how the use of such a system has change both teaching effectiveness and strategy.

C.A.S. SYSTEM OVERVIEW

A series of programs have been developed to operate on the Apple Computer System (both floppy and hard-disk based systems). The system called "Classroom Administration Systems" includes four functional subsystems which are: (1) Question Database System, (2) Examination Production System, (3) Gradebook System, and (4) Test Analysis System. Each subsystem is interconnected to the others for free exchange of information and compatibility.

The **"Question Database System"** allows for the development of files of questions in either a multiple choice, matching, true - false, completion, or essay type format. Each question file, with the exception of the matching type question files, may have up to 49 questions. Each question may have up to 1024 characters. In multiple choice questions the question text proper may be up to 230 characters in length, and each of five answer choices may be up to 160 characters in length. Essay and completion questions each may be up to 325 characters in length. There may be up to 1000 matching terms in each matching file with each entry containing two matched 32 character phrases or terms. All questions in the data base are fully norm referenced which includes the number of students attempting the question previously, the difficulty factor for the question, and when the question was last used.

The "**Examination Production System**" is designed to allow the teacher to produce complete, line justified, examination question ready to either give to a student or to mass duplicate. It allows the direct use of any an all questions included in the Question Data Base System as well as being able to add and mix new questions at the time the examination is being composed. The output of the system can either be in the form of printed text or the generation of text files designed to be read by a number of the apple specific word processors such as Applewriter, Screenwriter, Executive Secretary, etc.

When the test is being composed, answer choices are randomly sorted. Running the system twice using the same questions will produce two entirely different examination whose answer keys will have only between 22 and 26% overlap. In addition the system automatically produces a printed examination key for each examination and projects an estimated difficulty factor for the examination based upon previous norm referenced information which the database keeps on each question. The teacher then has the ability to compare current class performance levels with those of previous classes.   In multi-class or multi-teacher situations the norm-referenced aspect of the question database and the examination key allow for a mechanism of possibly evaluating teacher performance by comparing expected grade averages with the actual grade averages.

When using multiple choice questions, each individual question can be selected for use on the basis of difficulty factor or when last used, or the system can randomly pick a set number of questions from each question file. What is critical in the operation of the system is that the user develops the question files along restricted topic areas. The random choice of questions works best in criterion based examination systems where each question file covers a specific criterion or subject-concept area. If the question files are arranged according to concept areas, the norm-reference information on each question can generate a concept-area difficulty factor (i.e. average difficulty level for all questions in the file).

The "**Test Analysis System**" consists of a series of programs that will allow machine reading and grading of examinations containing multiple choice, True-False, and matching questions. This system is not able to grade essay or completion type of examination questions.

The grading of examinations requires the use of a card reader or scanner. The most commonly available units are made by Chatsworth Data Corporation, True Data Corporation, Mountain Hardware, HEI Corporation, Scan-Tron, and Zweig Corporation. Input into the microcomputer is either through an Apple specific Interface card or through an RS-232 Serial Interface card. The test analysis program will work with all of the previously mentioned card readers. Student examination cards or forms are scanned by the reader and the student score is recorded in an electronic grade file. If previous examinations have been taken by the student, the system displays what the students current average is and how far the current test score is above or below that average.

Following the entry of all examination cards for a particular test, the student responses can be analyzed in the following fashion: (1) Question Item Analysis, (2) Norm Reference Analysis, and (3) Division in subtest or concept specific subtest sets.

An item analysis of each individual question on an examination is the customary method of evaluating test performance. The system performs an item analysis on each question and includes the typical percentage having the question correct and percentages for those picking each individual answer choice, but also includes a 2 point biserial correlation value for each answer choice as compared to the correct answer, the average test grade for those students picking each answer choice and a Student´s t value for the difference between the test averages of those having the question correct and those having it incorrect. When more than one half of the class misses a question and when the ´t´ value is less than the significance level for the number taking the examination, a question is flagged as possibly being defective. Using the percentage correct as indicative of difficulty, the question database is automatically updated with this information and generates a self developing norm reference system. Using the previous systems to develop examinations and using the item analysis routine to analyze the data Kuder Richardson values above 0.8 have been consistently produced in three years of use and involving over 71 examinations.

The norm reference analysis is a specialized type of grade analysis developed through this system. In this analysis the response for each individual student are compared to that question's norm referenced history and numbers and percentages of answer correct and incorrect are generated for both previously used and never used questions. This information can be used to determine how dependent students are on old, circulating questions and how new questions compare, difficulty wise with new questions. The analysis also determines the difficulty questions for each question missed or answered correctly and gives an indication whether or not the student is missing consistently difficult questions or whether then performance is random and indicating a high dependence on guessing. Using this information the course instructor is better equipped to counsel students on how their study habits need to be changed. Without the use of the microcomputer, this depth of analysis would be totally impossible.

The third feature of test performance analysis is accomplished by allowing a test to be subdivided into subtests or sets. This allows the instructor to break an examination into concept areas or into performance criterion areas. Once the test is subdivided, grades are generated for each subtest. The student is then assigned multiple grades for each physical examination and each grade will reflect their relative performance in that area. Another application of this principle of subsetting which provides valuable information is where the instructor does two different subsetting of a particular test. One set of subtests is produced along concept areas covered, and a second according to the type of question utilized. If questions can be identified by using "Bloom´s" Taxonomy or some other system, scores can be identified as relating to questions dealing with memorization type questions, questions involving synthesis or deduction, etc. This information coupled with the traditional grading information can prove to be extremely powerful in distinguishing performance levels for each student.

The **"Gradebook system"** of this series of programs includes programs which allow the maintainence of grade records on students and an analysis of the student information for long-term counseling and planning. Included in this system is a Gradebook Program,

a Grade Reporter, a Grade Curver, and a Grade Analysis program. Each of the segments work from a text file containing student names and scores. Up to 30 scores may be kept on each student with as many as 800 students on a single disk file. The grade reporter, unlike a traditional teacher's grade record sheet, contains the ability to project performance levels needed to attain particular grade levels. Consequently, when accessing the electronic gradebook the instructor can also determine what the probabilities are for the student to attain a particular final grade and can advise the student accordingly. Most of the grades within the electronic gradebook are updated automatically when tests are machine graded; however, manual changes and updates are also possible. Among the items of information stored for each student is a code field containing up to 5 code levels. Each digit of the code field can be assigned to a particular area. Thus the teacher can have one gradebook file with all students recorded in it but identified by class period, etc. through the use of the code field. The Grade Analysis program within this system uses these code fields and will construct any analysis of grades by each of the codes used. Using this program has allowed an assessment of the performance of the various laboratory instructors and the impact or relationship of SAT scores to overall course performance. The coding of student major also proved valuable since the various program directors could easily see how their students were performing compared to students from other programs.

One difficulty in evaluating potential differences between student performance information from one year to the next is the fact that scores must be brought to a common base before comparison. The fact that one year the class average is 75 and the next year is 78 might only mean that the relative difficulty of the questions one year was different from that of the next, or it might mean that one class did in fact perform better. To avoid difference due directly to testing difference, the norm-reference information becomes vital. With the current system if a test is given which, according to previous norm-reference information should produce an average of 78, and the class averages only 72, it suggests some qualitative difference between the two populations.

If an SAT score analysis and/or a student major grade analysis is also performed, it can be determined whether the differences are attributable to either of these two factors. The data might also show, however, that the assigned laboratory instructors, which can change from year to year seems to have the greatest effect. Under these circumstances it would then seem appropriate to adjust the test scores to be directly comparable from one year to the next. In order to allow for such a transition, the system includes a variety of grade curving routines which allow grades to be standardized from one year to the next and to allow a more appropriate comparison.

Most instructors who choose to curve test grades really only adjust grades upwards through the expediency of dividing by a lower point total. This procedure is biased according to the position of the student within the grade scale. The curving module of this system allows for grade adjustment according to three different models. In one model, the mean and standard deviation set the grade scale and a C grade is assumed to be the mean plus or minus one standard deviation. The mean plus or minus 2 standard deviations establish the B and D ranges, and beyond 2 standard deviations the A and F ranges are established. In this model the user determines the desired final average and standard deviation and grades are curved to fit into those parameters so that each student retains their identical relative position within the A to F scale. The second model uses a 90, 80, 70, 60 grade scale and adjusts by standard deviations to that scale. The third model allows the user to set breakpoints for each grade level on both the uncurved and curved grades. Using any one of these models allows for a rapid manipulation of student scores to virtually any desired average. With the use of norm-reference information and projection of expected performance based upon the previous use history of each question, tests can be curved to equal previous or anticipated results. Doing this type of curving allows for an accurate determined of course difficulty from one year to the next.

One other factor which is vital to the exchange of information between teacher and student is the necessity to present to the student their grade information in such a form that it not only describes what their test scores are but where their weaknesses are and what they need to obtain a particular grade. A grade report module is included in this system which prints out test scores by the normal percentages/or/points, but also allows the subsetting of the individual tests, and the reporting of grades in terms of Stanines.

SUMMARY

The microcomputer can be used very effectively to reduce the work load of a teacher by performing many of the mundane, tedious tasks of classroom administration. The microcomputer, though the use of the "Classroom Administration System" has also allowed an expansion in the types of analysis performed on the student information, and has improved and made more effective the counseling of students. It has also allowed the development of automated test construction, and the utilization of fully norm-reference test banking with a wide range of question types. These changes have substantially affected the methods used in the classroom to evaluate student performance by allowing a level of analysis heretofore not possible.

COMPUTERS IN EDUCATION, K. Duncan and D. Harris (eds.)
Elsevier Science Publishers B.V. (North-Holland)
© IFIP, 1985

OMISSION DESIGN

David Benzie

The ITMA Collaboration
College of St. Mark and St. John
Derriford Road
Plymouth   PL6 8BH
United Kingdom

This paper is a crystalization of the experiences of ITMA over a period of time. It summarizes the aspects of a number of research programmes that relate to the design of educational software. In particular, the paper emphasizes the point that successful educational software invariably omits, in a controlled way, some activities and leaves them for pupils to carry out.

INTRODUCTION

Life is full of surprises and the idea that designers of computer based learning materials should, as part of their original design consideration, identify the things that will be omitted from the program may well be one of them. This paper, which is a crystalization of the experiences of ITMA[1] over a period of time, summarizes the aspects of our research which led to this proposition.

A major focus of attention for ITMA has been the search for ways of making qualitative improvements in the pattern of learning activities; we have been particularly concerned with those activities which relate to the acquiring of higher order skills such as reasoning and problem solving. These skills have traditionally proved to be exceptionally difficult to teach whilst being of immense value. To aid us in this search we have undertaken a number of major research projects.

The major study that produced evidence on the subject of this paper involved the systematic observation of about 200 mathematics lessons in a number of secondary schools over the course of a single term; the methodology and many of the findings of the study have been reported by Burkhardt (1). The teachers taking part in the study had access to a large collection of computer programs and it became apparent that the most successful pieces of software, in educational terms, were the ones where key things had been omitted and hence left for the pupils to do.

COMPUTERS IN CONTEXT

Any attempt to understand the success or otherwise of a piece of educational software must take an holistic account of the complex environment in which it was being used. It is a frequent mistake for those evaluating such software to attempt to make judgements in isolation from the educational context. Other elements in the analysis must be the pupils, teachers, books, blackboards and other resources that are made use of.

The role of the microcomputer in the classroom was comprehensively researched in the Mathematics Lesson observation programme (1) and this led to the production of a taxonomy relating learning activities to classroom roles. Full details may be found in a paper by Fraser (2) but they may be summarized as follows:

It is possible for teachers, pupils and suitably programmed microcomputers to adopt a number of different roles in the classroom. These roles are:

Manager: managing the learning activities
Explainer: explaining concepts, ideas, solutions...
Task setter: setting the tasks
Fellow pupil: working on the tasks together
Counsellor: helping others working on the task
Resource: available for the provision of further information

Whilst this taxonomy may appear to be something of a simplification it has, in practice, proved to be a useful framework for discussion. Some of the roles are traditionally assumed by teachers and some by pupils. However, there are great educational benefits (2) to be had from a change of stance by both pupils and teachers; the study found that suitably programmed microcomputers can help provoke this desired effect. Analysis of the observation records revealed that the most successful programs were those which refrained from some key activity.

There were a number of programs which fell into this category; a lesson involving one of them is described here.

EUREKA - AN OMISSION DESIGNED PROGRAM

EUREKA (5) is a program about graphical interpretation. It exemplifies the educational benefits to be had from the design decision to remove an activity that appears to be best done on a computer.

The program depicts a man taking a bath; the user can control the taps (on/off), plug (in/out) and man (in/out) by pressing single keys on the keyboard.

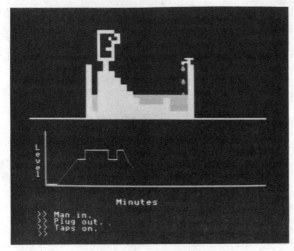

Figure 1. EUREKA

The effect of pressing the keys can be seen both on the graph and on the cartoon above it, as in figure 1. However, when used in this way there is little for pupils to do other than sit and watch - hardly the most effective of educational activities! For this reason, the program was also designed so that either the cartoon or the graph could be eliminated from the display. Further, the program also contains six pre-defined sequences which may be called up at any time by the user.

The effect of being able to omit either cartoon or graph is startling and has been observed many times. Here is a record of one such lesson (see also, Fraser (2)); Ⓣ Ⓜ Ⓔ Ⓒ Ⓕ & Ⓡ represent the six roles mentioned previously and t, c and p indicate whether teachers, pupils or the computer are playing them.

A LESSON WITH EUREKA

The lesson began, as lessons with EUREKA usually do, with the teacher using the program to demonstrate and explain what is involved in a cartesian graph. Both cartoon and graph are 'on'. The teacher <u>manages</u> a sequence, with comments from the class - plug in, taps on, taps off, man in, sings (some teacher comment here), an attempt to get the man out which failed because the singing is continuing, stop singing, man out, plug out. Pupils watch with interest.

Traditional didactive activities and roles, Ⓣ^t, Ⓜ^t, Ⓔ^t enlivened by the vivid scene setting Ⓔ^c of the program, whose humorous and very slightly risque personality maintains a high interest level. Pupils are passive.

Turning off the cartoon, leaving only the graph, the teacher uses the stored example 2, as shown in figure 2, to produce a graph on the screen. Still in exposition to the whole class, there is a lively discussion of what is happening. The example is replayed with the cartoon on, confirming the essential correctness of the class's conclusions.

Here the activity demands on the pupils changes, to problem solving with high level skills, though still at an easy level. The micro is thus <u>task setting</u> Ⓣ^c; the teacher still <u>manages</u> Ⓜ^t the task but discusses the various possible interpretations of the graph with definite signs of the <u>counselling role</u>. Ⓒ^t

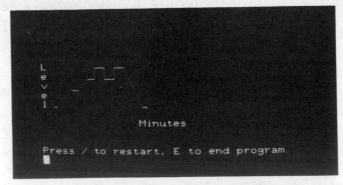

Figure 2. Example 2 from EUREKA

Next the teacher provides a worksheet divided into four sections and asks each child individually to write in the top section a story. (They are invited to use the screen prompts 'man in' etc., if they want - they all do.) They are then to draw in the second section the graph that represents what occurred. This produces lively interest and some discussion, with mixed but generally favourable results.

The computer is now switched off, having played its role as vivid scene setter $\textcircled{E}$ ^{c}, which persists by implication throughout. Teacher is <u>task setter</u> $\textcircled{T}$ ^{c} but <u>management</u> is now shared with the pupils $\textcircled{M}$P, whose learning activities are higher level involving image building, analysizing, abstracting and reflecting as well as symbolizing.

Each child is then told to fold over the paper so that the story is hidden, and to exchange with their neighbour who must then interpret the graph, writing the story as they see it in section 3 of the worksheet.

A similar balance of roles, with high level activities now also bringing in a problem solving element.

Checking back, the author then comments, in section 4 of the worksheet, on the interpretation in section 3, and on the accuracy of his graph in section 2. This works fairly well - though earlier conversations suggest other channels of communication than the graph may have played their part. The activity focusses detailed attention on the graph as a means of communication and discussion is lively.

Here reflecting, which is particularly elusive, is the centrepiece, with elements of proving involved through justifying what has been drawn on the graph.

The teacher finishes by promising other types of graphs for the next lesson, and by providing a worksheet of example 6, as shown in figure 3, for interpretation for homework.

A continuation of this high level activity is promised, involving additional resources contributed by the teacher, and an intriguing but difficult challenge is provided in example 6. Its interpretation will doubtless lead to later amusing discussions.

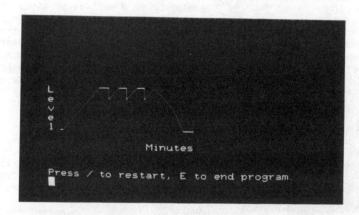

Figure 3. Example 6 from EUREKA

This lesson clearly demonstrates the value of the omission design concept in educational software. Designers of educational software commonly make the mistake of ignoring the talents and possible roles of other participants in the classroom and consequently attempt to force the computer to adopt either all of the roles or roles which are better left to others. A frequent effect of this serious mistake is that software forces an essentially passive and subordinate role on the pupil which in turn mitigates against the development of higher order thinking and problem solving skills. On the other hand, the omission of key activities from a program frequently leads to role swapping (when viewed from the traditional standpoint) and this has a beneficial effect on the quality of pupil activity (2).

THE LOCUS PROGRAM

Another perspective on the omission design principal can be gained by considering the program LOCUS (6); it was designed to help students explore and investigate loci produced by a moving point.

(a)

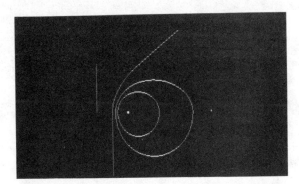

(b)

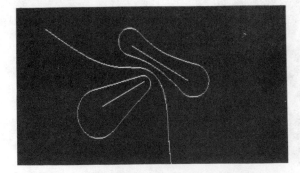

Figure 4. Two sets of loci produced by LOCUS

The program portrays on the screen the path of a point that moves in relation to some other object - some further points, or one or more straight lines. An example is shown in figure 4. Up to four such objects - points or lines - may be drawn on the screen; when the chosen objects have been placed on the screen in the desired position the computer may be instructed to trace out a locus. This locus is the path of a point moving in a fixed relationship to the object(s) on the screen; there are two possible relationships. When there is a single object, the point moves at a fixed distance from this object. When two objects are used, the point moves between them in such a way that there is a constant ratio of the distances between it and them. In both cases the user may select the values of the distance and of the ratio of distances.

From its inception, LOCUS was designed to be a catalyst for discussion in the classroom. It does not make any attempt to explain its own actions or to pose problems. These are left entirely to the teacher and the pupils and so there is great scope for the interchange of roles between pupils and teachers. In practice, the program has been used by a wide range of teachers with pupils aged between 10 and 18. In all cases there has been plenty of scope for thinking, hypothesizing and discussion at a level that suitably challenges the pupils.

FURTHER CONSIDERATIONS

There are yet more reasons why designers should concern themselves with the activities to be omitted from their software.

A program cannot, nor should it attempt to, prescribe the exact nature of the classroom activities that will be associated with it. Teaching styles vary widely - and most teachers also vary their style according to the pupils being taught. For this reason, designers need to be aware that they are creating a learning environment which should be capable of developing in a variety of ways. A program merely facilitates and provides a framework which can be coordinated, with other complex variables such as pupil and teacher behaviour, to produce the entity we know as a learning experience. Consequently, any attempt to provide a 'total learning experience' is almost certainly going to fail as it will subject both teachers and pupils to a level of constraint that is intolerable.

A further result of making decisions about what to omit from a program is the focussing of attention on the roles and activities that pupils and teachers will play. This, surely, is the correct educational perspective.

SUMMARY

When used in the classroom, computers are operating in a complex environment that includes teachers, pupils and possibly other elements. Teachers and pupils are the important ones; the designers of educational software must focus their attention on pupil learning rather than on computer activity.

The adoption of omission design principals leads to role imitation. This is valuable as it helps to promote the development of high order thinking and problem solving skills. Sensitively designed and developed software appears to offer us the possibility of making worthwhile progress in the attempt to introduce this type of activity to the classroom.

REFERENCES

[1] Burkhardt, H., et al, Microcomputers in the Mathematics Classroom, The Shell Centre for Mathematical Education, Nottingham University, U.K.

[2] Fraser, R., et al., Learning Activities and Classroom Roles, The Shell Centre for Mathematical Education.

[3] Petty, J., et al., Micros in the Primary Curriculum - The ITMA Approach, The Shell Centre for Mathematical Education.

[4] Coupland, J., et al., CAL in the Classroom - Analysis Techniques, The Shell Centre for Mathematical Education.

[5] ITMA Collaboration, The Micro as a Teaching Assistant, (A collection of 3 program teaching units, including EUREKA), Longman Micro Software.

[6] ITMA Collaboration, LOCUS (a program teaching unit), Longman Micro Software.

FOOTNOTE

[1]ITMA (Investigations on Teaching with Microcomputers as an Aid) is a Collaboration between groups principally at two institutions (The College of St. Mark and St. John, Plymouth and The Shell Centre for Mathematical Education, Nottingham University) who take a research based approach to exploring the potential of microcomputers in education. It was founded in 1978 by Rosemary Fraser following some earlier work with microcomputers in schools; it has grown since then and now encompasses people from a diverse range of backgrounds.

COMPUTERS IN EDUCATION, K. Duncan and D. Harris (eds.)
Elsevier Science Publishers B.V. (North-Holland)
© IFIP, 1985

A Teaching Support System for Information Processing for Large Numbers of Students

Susumu Horiguchi, Masato Abe, Yoshiyuki Kawazoe, Hisashi Nara[*]
Education Center for Information Processing and [*]College of General
Education, Tohoku University, Kawauchi, Sendai 980, Japan
and
Hiroshi Ichimura
Mitsubishi Electric Corporation, Kamakura, Kanagawa 247, Japan

This paper describes the computer-based teaching support system of the
Education Center for Information Processing, Tohoku University, Japan. The
system of the Center has been carefully designed and constructed so as to
meet efficiently the varied educational needs of a number of students. The
details of the system, the experience of its usage, the efficiency, and the
analysis of the logging information are discussed.

§ 1. Introduction

Tohoku University is one of the largest government supported universities in Japan and composed of ten faculties, a college of general education, and eight research institutes which have their own administrative systems. The university also has six other research and educational institutions. The number of students enrolled is about twelve thousand. The number of the university staff is about fifty-five hundred, of which twenty-five hundred are academic staff.

The Education Center for Information Processing, established in 1981, on Kawauchi campus, is responsible for providing all the students of the university with educational service of high quality. It is three and a half years since the Center started its educational service in March, 1982.

All the students of the ten faculties spend their first two years in the College of General Education on the same campus, which provides students with courses preliminary to their specialized studies. While in the college, the students are expected to accumulate information basic to their own specialities. They are also expected to make an effort to promote their understanding of the disciplines neighboring on their specialities and to extend and deepen their general education. In this respect, Tohoku University is particularly interested in providing all the students in the College of General Education with pertinent courses in the information and computer sciences.

Almost half of the whole student body of the university, namely about five thousand students, belongs to the College of General Education. In accordance with the students' educational needs, the College has been providing freshmen during each academic year with more than twenty classes in computer science. Each class normally accepts about 100 students. Among the other classes which the College opens, there are still about twenty where the students are able to use the computer system. Furthermore there are a number of classes in other faculties, and the number of total classes registered is

about 100 with more than 7,000 students. This situation is one of the reasons why we need a good teaching support system.

In this paper we describe the hardware and software system of the Education Center for Information Processing, Tohoku University. In particular we discuss the system of TESST (Teaching Support System, Tohoku University) [1] [2] and the experiences of those using it[3]. The system TESST which we constructed is management-oriented and has proved particularly useful in training classes with large numbers of students. This paper is organized as follows: After describing briefly the computer system of the Center in the next section, the system of TESST is discussed in detail in section 3. Section 4 is devoted to an analysis and evaluation of experiences of those using TESST for the past three years.

§ 2. Hardware System and Training Rooms

The host computer of the Education Center for Information Processing is a MELCOM-COSMO 900 II manufactured by Mitsubishi Electric Company. Its operation speed is about 6 MIPS, with 8 MB main memory and with 2.5 GB magnetic disk. One hundred and eighty-two TSS terminals of various types are connected to the host computer[4]. Among them 106 terminals are in the Center. The other terminals are distributed over four satellite stations on the other campuses. The system also accepts ten users via telephone call. The Center also has a mini-computer MELCOM 70/150 (1MIPS, 2MB), with twenty TSS terminals of 16bits personal computers(PC). This system is loosely coupled to the host computer via 9600BPS line. A schematic representation of the computer system is given in Fig. 1.

Training room I, in which there are 70 character display terminals and a line printer (LP), has a capacity to accept classes of up to 100 students. This room was specially constructed for large classes. Training room II contains various types of terminals and is used for smaller classes. The training room III contains 20 PC's controlled by the mini-computer,

and 5 serial printers for hard copy, and a LP.
In the open I/O room, there are many I/O devices
of various types, which are open for student
use. The four satellite stations are equipped
with character display terminals and hardcopy
units. Their numbers are   almost proportional
to the number of the students on the respective
campuses.

§3. Teaching Support System, Tohoku University – TESST –

The staff members of the Center are rather
few. There are only five full-time staff (three
academic and two technical) and four part-time
staff (two academic and two secretarial).
Therefore we have been forced to pursue
automatism and rationalization of the system to
the best of our ability. Some of the main
points to which we have attached particular
importance in designing TESST, are the following:

(1) rationalization of the system management,
(2) automated management of the seven training
    rooms including the rooms in the satellite
    stations,
(3) extensive support for a class teacher who
    is in charge of training a large number of
    students,
(4) construction of a data base which is easily
    accessible, to provide useful educational
    information.

TESST recognizes each class as a group to
which it gives various kinds of teaching support.
A group or a class consists of teacher(s) and a
number of students. The teacher of a group is
given a higher privilege status than his group
members. This higher status makes it possible
for the teacher to grasp at any time the
necessary information for student training.

The original version of TESST has been
revised several times and the present version is
a fully interactive one. In order to utilize
all the functions provided by TESST, the users
are requested only to remember the names of the
four processors: LESSON, CLASS, REPORT, and
LOG. This enables one to enjoy all kinds of
services by choosing interactively the appropriate branches from the menu offered by TESST.
In what follows we shall describe the outline of
TESST.

3.1 Registration Procedure

The registration procedure of a class at
the Center is schematically shown in Fig. 2. At
the beginning of a semester the registrations
are processed all together by using the marked
cards from the students. According to the
choice of the teacher, the same system resources
(the upper limits imposed on CPU time, size of
memory, region of magnetic disk, pages of LP
output, cost, etc.) are given to all the
students in the class. Additional registrations
may also be processed at any time.

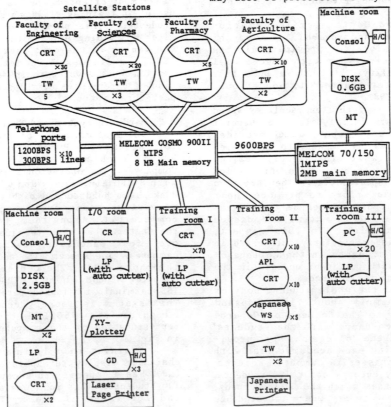

Fig.1 A schematic representation of the computer system.

3.2 Rationalized Supervision of Terminals in Training Rooms

The terminals in each training room are under the supervision of TESST according to the weekly timetable. When a training room is used by a class under the supervision of a teacher, the terminals in the room are set in a special mode, namely, the curricular mode. In this mode TESST prohibits a logging-on by students of any of the other classes. In the curricular mode, any terminal accepts logging-on's by up to two students, making a cooperative use of the terminal possible. Class attendance is automatically recorded by TESST. When the terminals are out of the curricular mode, any student can sit at one of the terminals at any time whenever the Center is open.

3.3 LESSON Processor

As is shown in Fig.3, the LESSON processor collects the useful functions of TESST in the actual class room training. Only the teacher has the privilege status to use these functions, and he is able to show a screen display or files of his own to all or a particular group of students. Monitoring, interruption, and compulsory logging-off are also possible. He may easily obtain information concerning present attendance. An example of using the LESSON processor is given below (underlined parts indicate the user inputs):

```
!LESSON
***** LESSON<TESST A01> HERE -12:38 7 28,´84 *****

1. DISPLAY PRESENT ATTENDANCE
2. COUPLING OR DECOUPLING
3. MONITOR - ON OR OFF
4. EXIT (END)

  KEY IN (1,2,3,OR 4) ?:3
1. MONITOR A PARTICULAR STUDENT´S TERMINAL
2. WHOSE TERMINAL DO YOU WANT TO MONITOR?
3. MONITOR - OFF

  KEY IN (1,2,OR 3) ?:1
  STUDENT´S ID NUMBER ?:3CA18053

ON 3F
  STUDENT´S LINE NUMBER ?:3F

  PLEASE INPUT DECHAIN 3F WHEN YOU WANT TO MONITOR - OFF !!
                    .
                    .
                    .
!DECHAIN 3F
```

3.4 CLASS Processor

The use of the CLASS processor is also restricted only to the teacher. The processor enables the teacher to present the assignments, to collect the answer files of the student assignments, to change the students' upper limit imposed on the system resources originally given to them, to find out the account number of a student by the user's name, and to obtain a list of the account numbers and the user's names of the students of his class. Some examples are given below:

```
!CLASS
***** CLASS<TESST A01> HERE -18:18 7, 28, ´84- *****
1. ASSIGNMENT PRESENTATION
2. ANSWER COLLECTION
3. CHANGE UPPER LIMIT OF COST
4. FIND OUT ACCOUNT NUMBER BY USER NAME
5. DISPLAY LIST OF GROUP MEMBERS
6. EXIT

  KEY IN (1,2,3,4,5,OR 6)?       :2
  KEY IN ASSIGNMENT NUMBER ?      :012
  KEY IN (1 RESULT OR 2 SOURCE) ?:1

3CA92001  3CA92003  3CA92004  3CA92005  3CA92009
***** CLASS<TESST> TERMINATED -18:18 7 28,´84- *****

!CLASS
***** CLASS<TESST A01> HERE -18:32 7 28, ´84- *****

  KEY IN (1,2,3,4,5,OR 6) ?:3

*** STUDENT´S UPPER LIMIT CHANGE ***
  1 ... DISPLAY DATA FOR UPPER LIMIT CHANGE
  2 ... CHANGE STUDENT´S UPPER LIMIT
  3 ... END

  KEY IN (1,2,3) ?:2
------------------------------------------------
PLEASE ENTER THE ACCOUNT OF STUDENT WHOSE
UPPER LIMIT YOU WANT TO INCREASE
------------------------------------------------
ACCOUNT ?:3TB58005

ACCOUNT  = 3TB58005 OK ? <Y OR N>:Y

PLEASE SPECIFY THE AMOUNT TO BE INCREASED IN
UNITS OF ¥100  ( MAX=10=¥1000 )

AMOUNT (1,2,....,10) ?:5

THE CHARGE TO BE INCREASED IS ¥500 OK ? <Y OR N>:Y
                    .
                    .
                    .
```

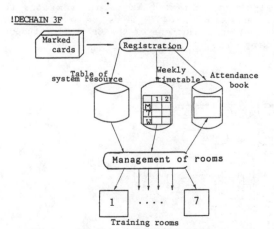

Fig.2 Registration procedure of a class.

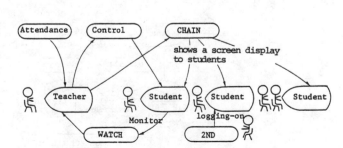

Fig.3 Functions of the LESSON processor.

3.5 REPORT Processor

When submitting reports of solutions to the assignments, students use the REPORT processor. The REPORT processor creates the answer files, by executing the source program (with data) coded by the student, in a unified format in the students' file region. If there are some errors, the REPORT processor gives the student error diagnostics instead of creating an answer file. Later teacher will collect the report files thus created into the teacher's file region (see 3.4 and Fig.4) to mark the answers. One of the important advantages of TESST is that the REPORT processor supports graphical outputs by a laser beam printer, contributing to a considerable reduction of the time consuming efforts by both students and teachers.

3.6 LOG Processor

The LOG processor is a useful tool to access the data base of various logging information collected by TESST.

ACCOUNT SUMMARY contains information about the actual consumption of the system resources by every student in the class. The account summary of each class is automatically renewed by TESST at the time of the initial program loading every morning. Each student can access only his own part of the account summary. ATTEND LOG displays the attendance records recorded by TESST. PROCESSOR LOG shows a record of the number of accesses of the various processors of the system. FLAG is a FORTRAN load and go processor, and the statistical error records committed by the students while using FLAG are easily obtained by using FLAG ERROR LOG. PASCAL ERROR LOG is also available.

All this information is indeed useful for teachers. By using it the teacher will be able to assess both the students' progress and the quality of the teacher's teaching program.

An example is given:

```
!LOG
***** GROUP LOG<TESST A01> HERE -16:01 7 28, '84- *****

1. GROUP ACCOUNT SUMMARY
2. ATTEND LOG
3. PROCESSOR LOG
4. FLAG ERROR LOG
5. PASCAL ERROR LOG
6. EXIT

   INPUT MENU NUMBER ?:1

   OUTPUT DEVICE (1.CRT,2.LP,OR 3.FILE) ?:1
                GROUP ACCOUNT SUMMARY        (7/28/84 16:01)

USER-NAME  ACCOUNT   COST CPU(S) ETIME(S) PLOUT LPOUT BJOB OJOB
B58001     3CA93000  486   47     8533    10    16    5    13
B58002     3CA93086  353   25     2276    0     21    3    1
```

§4. Results and Discussion

In this section, based on records accumulated within these three years, we will discuss the practical aspects of TESST. Especially we wish to stress a clear distinction, concerning the error distributions in FORTRAN programming, between the students of engineering and natural science majors and of humanities and social science majors.

4.1 Registration

In Table 1 we show the actual registration data in 1983 as an example of the number of registered students for each faculty. The contribution of the College of General Education is remarkably high. In most of the other big Japanese universities computer training classes start in the third year. In this respect we gain time in Japan.

4.2 Accumulated Data Base

TESST automatically accumulates various statistical data. Users can easily access this data base by using the LOG processor mentioned above, and can obtain necessary information. One of the most useful data may be the summary of the use of the processors. In Table 2, the higher ranked processors are listed. As is usual, the text editor, peripheral conversion language, and FORTRAN compiler have been used most frequently. Recently other languages like PASCAL, C, PL/I, LISP, and PROLOG have also been selected as standard languages in several classes, and the usage of these compilers or interpreters has grown considerably. All of the introductory courses are open for a half year schedule. To inspect the time development of the students, we can use LOG to sum up the FORTRAN error loggings. The topmost part of Fig. 5 shows the total error distribution within a half year. In the lower part of the figure, these errors are rearranged for every two months. In the first two months, elementary errors indicated as A, B, C, and D, amount to about 50%. After these two months this percentage falls to 35%. The error distribution of the students becomes much closer to that of trained people within a relatively short time. If we use batch oriented systems with a few terminals, it might take a full semester to achieve this level. This is one of the important contributions of the Center to student training.

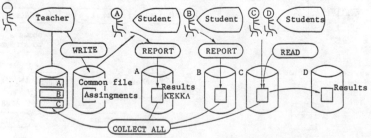

Fig.4 Functions of the CLASS and REPORT processors.

Table 1. Example of the registration data in 1983.

Faculty	Classes	Students	Number of Jobs	CPU Time (M)	Elapsed Time (H)
Economics	8	124	268	126.0	186.0
Sciences	32	1,392	13,255	1,850.3	5,262.7
Medicine	4	242	583	40.9	250.8
Pharmacy	7	116	1,619	110.7	885.6
Engineering	33	1,571	30,495	9,875.4	13,511.0
Agriculture	6	143	2,401	81.6	1,018.3
General Education	38	3,868	79,518	4,623.2	35,503.3
Total	128	7,456	128,139	16,708.1	56,617.7

Table 2. Higher ranked processors.

Processors	Percentage
EDIT : Text editor	25.5
FLAG : FORTRAN compile and go	21.0
PCL : Peripheral conversion language	19.1
LYNX : Linkage loader	5.3
FORTAN IV	4.2
Command Procedure	4.2
Others	19.2

4.3 Comparison between Students in Different Majors

Recent progress in computer hardware and software has made it possible for nonprofessional people to utilize computer systems in various fields. In response to this situation, university students, even in humanities and social science majors, feel a need to learn data processing by computer systems.

We selected two classes for engineering majors and two classes for social science majors. Almost the same lectures concerning data processing were given to them both. Following the introduction of simple FORTRAN programming by using the terminals in the Center, several assignments were given to them. We expected them to learn by themselves the details of FORTRAN grammer through working on the assignments. Examples of the error distributions of two classes are given in Figs. 6 (a) and (b). Considerable difference is noticed. Elementary errors occur very frequently in the classes for social science majors, and furthermore these errors do not decrease much in number within half a year. We checked this by performing correlation analyses for the four classes, and confirmed that there really exists a clear difference between the degrees of achievement of the students in different majors. Based on this consideration, we tried to teach in the next semester the FORTRAN grammer in detail to the social science majors. When we did this, the structure of the error distribution have changed drastically and became close to that of the engineering majors. However, within a half year semester only the simple introductory problems could be digested in these classes. This may be due to the fact that in general the social science majors do not have enough background to

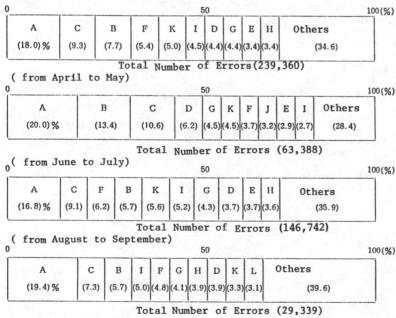

FLAG ERROR MESSAGE LIST

A : Unrecognizable statement
B : Invalid statement $
C : Undefined variable; xxxxxx
D : 1 or more invalid characters skipped
E : Missing statement : $ nnnnn
F : Non-dimensioned variable has subscript
G : Invalid expression
H : Invalid format syntax
I : Mismatched parentheses
J : Missing end statement
K : Missing operator
L : Invalid syntax
M : Missing format : $ nnnnn
N : No main program
O : Unterminated quote field
P : Duplicate statement $: nnnnn
Q : Unsatisfied DO : $ nnnnn
R : Misplaced declarative statement
S : Missing subprogram : xxxxxx
T : Invalid syntax in I/O list
U : Dimensioned variable has no subscript
V : Requested program : xxxxxx not found
W : Variable appears twice in dummy list
X : Statement must begin with a letter

Fig.5 Error distributions of FLAG for half a year.

accept courses in computer science. Thus, we may have a fundamental question as to whether it is really necessary or not to provide these students with training in programming, using standard high-level languages. We feel, on the contrary, that more important material for them to learn might be, not so much a complete knowledge of programming languages, as to handle data bases, to use statistical program packages, and to use graphic libraries.

The recent technological development in microcomputer systems and the enormous demand for them have made it possible to supply graphic and Japanese character terminals at relatively low cost. A number of PC's in the training room III are the very terminals of these kind. We have constructed a software system EGKS[5] (Educational Graphic Kernel System), which is a subset of the GKS[6][7]. We believe that the EGKS is most suited for student training in computer graphics in a world-wide standardized manner. We are presently comparing the advantage of the system with the existing one such as LOGO.

References

[1] S.Horiguchi, Y.Kawazoe, and H.Nara; "A Teaching Support System, Tohoku University - TESST- ,"(in Japanese) IECE Japan, Tech. Rep. ET82-5 pp.43-48 (Sep. 1982).

[2] S.Horiguchi, Y.Kawazoe, and H.Nara; "TESST for Large Numbers of Students and Its Practical Use," (in Japanese) IPS Japan, Tech. Rep. WGSE28-12 pp.67-72 (Feb.,1983).

[3] H.Nara, Y.Kawazoe, S.Horiguchi, H. Ichimura, Y.Matsumoto, and K.Inoue; "A Teaching Support System for Large Numbers of Students and Its Practical Use in a University Curriculum," (in Japanese) Jour. IPS Japan,vol.24, No.11,pp.1344-1353 (Nov.,1983).

[4] Y.Kawazoe, S.Horiguchi, and H.Nara; "The Computer System of the Education Center for Information Processing, Tohoku University," (in Japanese) Proc. Joint Electr. Eng. Tohoku Branch, Japan, 2F12 (Aug., 1982).

[5] S.Horiguchi, M.Abe, Y.Kawazoe, H.Nara, M.Tonomori, K.Inoue, K.Yoshida, and H.Ichimura; "A Study of Graphic Data Processing on Educational Computer Systems," (in Japanese) Proc. 28th Conf. IPS Japan, 6Q-5 PP.1605-1606 (Mar., 1984).

[6] "Information Processing Graphic Kernel System Function Description" Draft International Standard ISO/DIS 7942 (Nov., 1984).

[7] F.R.A.Hopgoog ; "Introduction to the Graphic Kernel System (GKS)", Academic Press (1983).

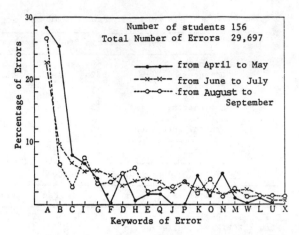

(a) social science majors

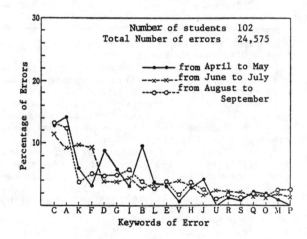

(b) engineering majors

Fig.6 Examples of the error distributions.

COMPUTERS IN EDUCATION, K. Duncan and D. Harris (eds.)
Elsevier Science Publishers B.V. (North-Holland)
© IFIP, 1985

151

TEACHER-ORIENTED EDUCATIONAL SOFTWARE

M.J. Coleman

Portsmouth Polytechnic
School of Information Science
Hampshire Terrace, Portsmouth PO1 2EG, England

As microcomputers become more widely used at the Primary (5-11 years) School level, design criteria for educational software are receiving close attention. Current developments seem to have focused on the requirements of the pupil; in this paper, however, it is argued that software design must give equal emphasis to the needs of the teacher.
An approach to the design of such software is suggested, and is illustrated by an example based on logic problems. The further development of the approach, so as to incorporate the use of a knowledge-base, is outlined.

1.   INTRODUCTION

In England it is intended that at least one microcomputer system will be installed in every Primary School by the end of 1984. Together with the formation of a national programme for microelectronics education the acceptance of the micro at this level is virtually complete. The debate is no longer about "why use computers?" but about "how should a computer be used?"

Perhaps the only certainty here is that there is no single answer to this question. Rather, to borrow a sales-cliche, the application areas are likely to be limited only by our own imaginations. Now herein lies a problem: every application is bound to need educational software, and primary school teachers will almost certainly not be in a position to write such software for themselves. They will not have the expertise; neither are they likely to have the time, or even inclination, to acquire such expertise.
This may not be so much of a problem if some professional support can be used for writing programs which the teachers specify; local arrangements [1] and the national programmes will help here. But, for the most part, a school's stock of software will have been gathered from a variety of sources with no design involvement on the part of the teacher. If the teacher is to have any design control, therefore, facilities for this must be built into the software itself: the software must be produced with the teacher in mind. "The whole history of curriculum development shows that the most vital and difficult task is to make useful material accessible to the teacher"[2]; software for the classroom is no exception.

2.   EDUCATIONAL SOFTWARE and the TEACHER

A report [3] identified six aspects of the teaching process which, it suggested, should be present in the classroom situation for all ages and abilities of pupils. Although the report was specifically concerned with the teaching of mathematics, the list is of general relevance:

(a) exposition by the teacher
(b) pupil/teacher and pupil/pupil discussions
(c) appropriate practical work
(d) consolidation & practice of fundamental skills and routines
(e) problem solving, incorporating everyday situations
(f) investigational work

Now whilst the computer can be used to support each of the above, it seems likely that educational software will concentrate on areas (c) thru (f). This is acceptable, but only if (a) and (b), exposition and discussion, will also be enhanced. To produce software that just splits the whole teaching process into two disparate sections is to court disaster.

But for the computer to be used in exposition and discussion requires a level of confidence that teachers appear not to have at present. Recent reseach [4] showed that whilst most teachers expect a substantial increase in schools computing usage in the coming years, over 75% felt that the microcomputer would not blend with their teaching methods. In other words, teachers believed that computers will strongly influence classroom instruction, but not in their classrooms!

Educational software design contributes to this dilemma. If the available software does not 'fit' into the lesson that the teacher wishes to give, then either the lesson has to be modified to accommodate the software, or else academic freedom is retained and the computer is not used at all. Both would seem to be educationally undesirable.

Similarly, discussion also depends on the teacher being confident with the software in use. A computer-based model, for instance, which incorporates local or nationally known elements, will promote the right sort of discussion. The teacher, after all, is concerned with prompting debate which is relevant to the subject in question; germane software lessens the ever-present danger of discussion drifting away from the topic and towards the computer itself ("What happens if I press this key Sir?").

It is contended, therefore, that a fundamental requirement for educational software is that it should lend itself to being 'tailored' by teachers to suit their own needs. Given our earlier supposition, however, that a primary school teacher will have minimal computing expertise, how might this objective be met?

3.   CODE AND DATA SEPARATION

It is not realistic to expect a teacher to modify the program itself. Documentation which suggests that different effects may be achieved by "changing lines x,y and z" really cannot be countenanced; the teacher, having little or no programming expertise, will have any confidence totally destroyed when a simple typing mistake brings a flood of incomprehensible error messages. This embargo immediately rules out educational software which has its data 'built-in' - such as DATA statements in a BASIC program.

A first step, therefore, is the separation of code and data. This is not a new idea, but one which is slow in gaining a general acceptance. Basically the idea is for the software to ask for its data to be input by the teacher as a precursor to its operation. A very simple example would be that of a spelling test program, for which the teacher inputs the words which are to be presented to the pupil. The system could be illustrated as shown in figure 1.

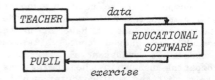

Figure 1: Data separation, teacher input

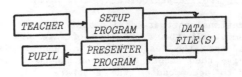

Figure 2: Data separation with SETUP program

Taking this approach further, an educational software package would comprise two programs, as shown in figure 2. The first, used by the teacher to create a data file, is termed a SETUP program; the second, which presents the data file to pupil users in some way, is termed the PRESENTER program.

Thus a single educational package may be used in different ways by different teachers, with each being able to introduce their own individual content and style to the presentation that the pupil sees. Moreover, by building a collection of data files, individual exercises can be applied for particular occasions (or pupils) by use of the one PRESENTER program.

It is thus intrinsic in the application of such teacher-oriented software that, in order for the system to be usable at all, data files must be created by the teacher. For this reason it is argued that the SETUP element of such a package requires a level of design no less sophisticated than that of the PRESENTER - for, again, the point has to be made that our teacher is a computing novice. A SETUP program must at least be:

* Simple and quick to use. If this is not the case then the hard-pressed teacher will be deterred rather than attracted.
* Self-validating. By ensuring that any data files produced are in the correct form for PRESENTER, embarassing failures in class are avoided - again to the benefit of teacher confidence.

It is no exaggertion to say that the whole approach will stand or fall on the design of this SETUP program.

4. AN EXAMPLE - LOGIC PROBLEMS

A Logic Problem is concerned with the evaluation of a number of 'clues' in order to determine relationships. As an example, given three children - Mary, John and Peter - and three ages - 8, 9 and 10 - the clues

    a) Mary is older than John
    b) Peter is not the youngest
    c) Peter is not 10 years old

define a Logic Problem, the solution to which is the matching of each child to its correct age. The above is a '2-object' problem (child & age). Additional complexity can be introduced by adding extra objects; a 3-object problem, for instance, might involve child, age and hair colour with clues of the form "Mary is older than John and her hair is not brown."

An educational software package to enable the definition and presentation of Logic Problems has been designed to the pattern suggested. That is, the package comprises a SETUP program and a PRESENTER program. The latter presents the problem and enables the pupil to derive a solution by completing a square grid. Figures 3 and 4 show the solutions to 2-object and 3-object problems respectively.

> Mary is older than John.
> Peter is not the youngest.
> Peter is not 10 years old.

	8	9	10
MARY	X	X	✓
JOHN	✓	X	X
PETER	X	✓	X

Figure 3: Solution grid for 2 object problem

> Mary is older than John and her hair is brown.
> Peter is not the youngest.
> Peter does not have fair hair; he is 12 years old.

	8	9	10	BROWN	FAIR	RED
MARY	X	X	✓	✓	X	X
JOHN	✓	X	X	X	✓	X
PETER	X	✓	X	X	X	✓
BROWN	X	X	✓			
FAIR	✓	X	X			
RED	X	✓	X			

Figure 4: Solution grid for 3 - object problem

The SETUP program is used by the teacher to define:

  * the objects of the problem (John, 10 etc)

  * the clues (Mary is older than John etc)

Also, in seeking to meet our criteria for a SETUP program - ease of use and self-validation - SETUP also provides the following facilities:

* Allows the specification of 2 or 3-object problems, so that the package can be tailored to different age levels.

* Evaluates the clues as they are input. In this way the data is validated, and the teacher can adjust the clues so as to generate solutions which are easier/harder to discover. Full capability for editing and backtracking of clues is available.

* Recognises a 'relationships' vocabulary comprising standard words (e.g. is, not, and, or, older, eldest ..)

* Permits the extension by the teacher of this vocabulary prior to the formulation of clues. In this way it is possible for the teacher to introduce new words and concepts to pupils through using the package.

* Ignores any word not in the known vocabulary. This enables clues to be embellished as appropriate - for instance, to provide some local colour.

Whilst SETUP is being used, the display screen gives a complete picture of the Logic Problem being formulated. As figure 5 shows, it presents a partially-completed grid, and the clues currently defined. As a reference check the available vocabulary is also on display. Both the clues and the vocabulary may be scrolled back and forth, and edited, by simple use of function keys.

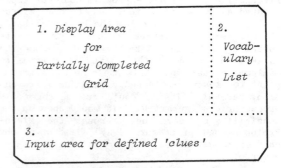

Both the Vocabulary List, and the currently defined 'clues', may be scrolled back and forth by use of simple function keys.   Area 3 is also employed for the output of any error messages.

Figure 5: SETUP program screen layout

5.   INTELLIGENT TEACHER-ORIENTATED EDUCATIONAL SOFTWARE

The package, and another [5] designed according to the same principles, have been evaluated by a number of primary school teachers. Responses have been very encouraging. In particular, teachers have welcomed the opportunity to stamp their own personality and style onto a piece of educational software. They have also made the point that, having created what amounts to their own software package, they are very likely to use it in the classroom.

Further research is now being conducted into ways in which the general principles of teacher-oriented software can be extended so as to encompass hardware and documentation [6]. One particular study is concerned with the use of a dual-processor British Broadcasting Corporation (BBC) Microcomputer system as the basic configuration to support educational software (see figure 6). The addition of a second processor board to what is by far the most common microcomputer system used in our schools is not expensive and opens up a number of very intriguing possibilities.

For instance, what if the second processor were used to support a descriptive language such a Micro-Prolog other than an imperative language such as BASIC? If this were the case then it should be feasible for the SETUP program running in the first processor (Figure 7) to use some form of knowledge-base via the Micro-Prolog in order to carry out a degree of 'intelligent tutoring' of the teacher. Previously the province of mainframe configurations, this type of assistance [7] could really bring the task of tailoring educational software down to a simple level.

Alternatively, the SETUP program could be implemented as a simple front-end to the Micro-Prolog processor supporting the knowledge-base. If this were so then the teacher would be able to define not only data items but also the rules to be used by the PRESENTER program to manipulate that data: this could be the starting point for teacher-oriented simulation software. Also, PRESENTER itself could run on the dual-processor configuration. This would open up the possibility of deriving, through the Micro-Prolog second processor, "Why" "How" and "Why not" explanations [8] as part of the PRESENTER repertoire.

At this point educational software starts to become really educational. Can the challenge be met?

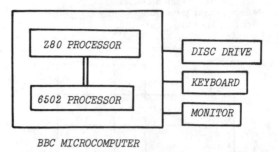

BBC MICROCOMPUTER

Figure 6:   BBC dual processor configuration.

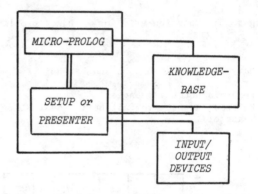

Figure 7: Knowledge-based Educational Software?

6.   REFERENCES

[1] Coleman M.J., Flynn G., Foster S.J., Ross N.A., Educational Software for Primary Schools - A Collaborative Approach, 2nd Educational Computing Conference, The City University, London, England (April 1983).

[2] Fraser R., et al, Designing Material for the Microcomputer and Teaching Partnership in the Classroom, Computer Education: Proceedings of the IFIP TC-3 3rd World Conference on Computers in Education, pp 303-9, North Holland, 1981.

[3] Cockcroft W.H., Mathemtics Counts (report of a Department of Education and Science enquiry into the teaching of mathematics in schools), H.M.S.O., 1982.

[4]   Stevens D.J., <u>Microcomputers: An Educat-</u>
      <u>ional Challenge,</u> Computers and Education,
      Vol 8 No 2 pp 263-67, 1984.

[5]   Humfryes J., <u>Logo Applications for Primary</u>
      <u>Schools,</u> Portsmouth Polytechnic B.Sc.
      Project Report, June 1984.

[6]   Coleman M.J., <u>Towards a Classroom Learning</u>
      <u>System</u>, Fourth International Microcomputer
      Applications Conference, Tokyo, Japan,
      May 1984.

[7]   Sleeman D., Brown J.S., <u>Intelligent</u>
      <u>Tutoring Systems,</u> Academic Press 1982.

[8]   Hammond P., <u>"Why", "How" and "Whynot"</u>
      <u>explanations,</u> Chapter 11 (Micro-Prolog
      for Expert Systems), of Micro-Prolog:
      Programming in Logic by Clark K.L., McCabe
      F.G., Prentice/ Hall International, 1984.

COMPUTERS IN EDUCATION, K. Duncan and D. Harris (eds.)
Elsevier Science Publishers B.V. (North-Holland)
© IFIP, 1985

PANEL SESSION

Maintaining Instructional Integrity with Quality Courseware

Chair: Larry C. Christensen, Brigham Young University

Panel: Alfred Bork, University of California
         George Gerhold, Western Washington University
         Donald Holznagel, Northwest Regional Educational lab

ABSTRACT

With the proliferation of computers in the educational environment, educators are now directing their attention to the software applications. It has been estimated that as much as 95 percent of the existing software is worthless or not suitable for use in the classroom. The panelists in this session will discuss the following questions:

How effective are software programs in the classroom?

Where can an educator look for quality courseware?

Will a seal of approval placed on software by educators promote high quality courseware?

What is the process for creating high-quality computer based material?

Is an authoring language the answer for producing software?

Can quality courseware be cost effective?

ABSTRACT Alfred Bork "The Quality of Computer Based Learning Modules"

A key to effective use of computers in education is a carefully thought out production system for producing quality software. The system of the Educational Technology Center, at the University of California, Irvine in producing sizable quantities of highly interactive learning units, will be addressed.

ABSTRACT George Gerhold "Quality Software with Authoring Languages"

There is no right process which will lead to high quality educational software; creativity cannot be generated by structuring a process. Quality can be increased, and cost can be reduced by involving the instructor-author as closely as possible in the production and editing of courseware. Authoring languages allow the instructor to be involved, and so they are part of the solution. Current work in authoring languages is making their use easier and more advantageous.

ABSTRACT Larry C. Christensen "Software Engineering and Psychology of Learning"

Past studies have questioned the effectiveness of some computer assisted instruction projects. With correct software engineering concepts connected to the psychology of instruction, the cost of such projects can be reduced, the effectiveness increased, and the learner benefits greatly enhanced. Some common mistakes in educational software engineering will also be presented.

COMPUTERS IN EDUCATION, K. Duncan and D. Harris (eds.)
Elsevier Science Publishers B.V. (North-Holland)
© IFIP, 1985

EXPERT SYSTEMS : TOWARDS CAI OF THE FUTURE ?

Maryse Quéré

Centre de Recherche en Informatique de Nancy
B.P. 239 - 54506 VANDOEUVRE LES NANCY CEDEX
FRANCE

This paper is a briefing on the apparent contradiction existing between the concept of courseware engineering and that of intelligent computer assisted instruction, and the interest in the new concept of expert systems. Two examples are used, one derived from the writing of a courseware program, and the other from a research project in progress.

I. INTRODUCTION

Computer Assisted Instruction is about 20 years old. A few significant features show it has just passed the teenage stage, others, on the other hand, tend to consider it as a child. Before speaking about its future, let's have a look at these two ages.

CAI is now recognized by teachers. Having for a long time been suspected of unfair competition it now has its proper place among teaching methods. Micro computing has made this financially possible. Many CAI interactive systems or author languages now available are supposed to help the teachers to write courseware more easily.

But what about courseware? We can estimate the quantity available in the world as a few thousands hours. We are also sure they are divided into classes that are incompatible with one another, the most important classes having at the most five hundred hours (1). And if we look more closely at this courseware, we notice that 80% are programmed teaching books transposed for the computer. That is to say : we can find graphics, colour, touch screens, music, etc., but they are simply multiple choice questions. Any teacher wishing to use CAI in a significant way would remain unsatisfied.

As it has no significant present, will CAI have a future? A great wave of interest can be seen in research, particularly in the artificial intelligence area, for its use in teaching. This is a relatively new area, and the few speeches about the experiments still in embryo give great hopes to teachers. Is that justified?

The aim of this paper is to describe CAI at the crossing of two roads - software engineering and knowledge engineering -, to show how artificial intelligence techniques can modify pedagogy, and how they can make the author's work easier, if a certain number of problems can be solved.

My reflexions are based upon an original experience with the three domains concerned in CAI :
- computer science research that feeds section V
- courseware production, that makes an example for section III
- the use of courseware at the teacher training center I have been in charge of for many years.

II. CAI, SOFTWARE ENGINEERING, ARTIFICIAL INTELLIGENCE

In this paper, CAI keeps it restrictive meaning : courseware is a dialogue between a student and a computer. This dialogue is meant to allow the student to achieve a specific goal that can be measured in terms of knowledge and "savoir-faire".

This section shows how CAI has helped software engineering, without leaving the frame of limited pedagogical functions. The following section shows the contribution of AI required adding new pedagogical functions, that unfortunately decreased the generality of programs. And from there the apparent contradiction is pointed out that would reveal a breaking point in the courseware production.

II.1. In the beginning were FORTRAN and COURSEWRITER

The first tools the authors had to write courseware with were languages of the FORTRAN family. Fortunately, the courseware written then was multiple choice questions and this tool was quite sufficient. By skillfully making up the instructions with "significant" words (qu, ca, cb, wa, wb, ty, br) the first author-languages were created (14).

---

(1) PLATO library, CNDP library, CONDUIT project

Many author-languages have been used since. If their functions have grown as far as graphics, answer analysis, CAI management (CAN 8 !), etc., they still are languages of the FORTRAN family, and so haven't profited by the evolution of programming languages resulting in software engineering tools.

II.2. Then came the editors, the types, the modularity

The "programming" aspect of the use of the author-languages made them difficult to use for authors who didn't have any knowledge in computing. That is why computer specialists had the idea of writing - for the authors - easy to use interactive tools, allowing them to introduce their own courseware into the machine.

These tools had the characteristics of those made for the non-specialist end-user, making no distinction between a teacher, a secretary or a designer. They used the editor concept (for text, graphics, sound...)(10).

Meanwhile type and modularity concepts (PASCAL, ALGOL 68, CLU, ADA...) were being developed. These concepts, applied to the pedagogical domain, led in 1981 to the specification of the functional editor of the DIANE project (6,7,12). This editor is characterized by both

- modularity: courseware is split into three hierarchy levels - courseware, dialogue, pedagogical situation -, each level containing elements of an inferior level in a structured pseudo-French of the PASCAL type (1,6) and

- type aspect : all the pedagogical objects are typed (including answer analysis, answer judgement) and can be created and modified with the help of a specific sub-editor. All the named objects can be re-used. Such an object data base is the beginning of a workshop for "courseware enginee ring".

II.3. Management, spreading, portability

In the introduction it was noted that a great obstacle to an intensive use of CAI is the incompatibility between the different production and utilisation systems of courseware. Some firms have, inside their own system (PLATO, CAN 8), provided for spreading organization: to the credit of the DIANE project, moreover, it has proposed an answer to the portability problem (12).

II.4. Assessment

We can consider that the whole "functional editor + management tools + spreading tools" of

the DIANE project has raised CAI up to the level of modern tools of software engineering.

But which CAI are we talking about? Of course, we have gone beyond the stage of multiple choice questions, thanks to a more and more sophisticated answer analysis that allows a "free" answer (cf EGO or IMG). The students are free to use requests. The students' paths are more and more individualized thanks to the memorization of most of the student behaviour.

But the author has provided for everything as the computer does not show any intelligence at all (13) :

- all steps are completely pre-defined : the computer will never make up an exercise;
- the solution to an exercise is final, not the reasoning that got us there. The analysis is made by comparing the student solution with the author solutions : the computer can never solve the problems it gives;
- the requests the student can use are set (help, calculator, dictionary, backward...) : the student can't ask his/her own questions hoping that the computer will help with the answer.

II.5. Meanwhile, artificial intelligence...

The introduction of artificial intelligence techniques date from the SCHOLAR program (5), the aim of which was to teach South American geography. Besides having an inner representation of geography knowledge and no pre-recorded texts, this system added an new initiative that no longer belonged only to the program concerned.

In the field of repairing electronic circuits, the SOPHIE program's (4) goal was to break down reasonings, its strong interface in natural language allowing it to understand and criticize the student propositions.

A first characteristic of ICAI (1) software is its specialization in one matter, often in a very specific field.

Understanding is made easier - the computer is an expert - whereas generalizing is lessened. Shall we then write an ad-hoc software for each field?

A second characteristic is the natural language interface. But if we look more closely at the techniques used in existing programs (ATN, semantic networks) we notice that understanding and language generation are closely linked to our study. Will there be tools to "parameter" the writing of such interfaces?

---

(1) Intelligent Computer Assisted Instruction

The last characteristic, finally, is the initiative the students is allowed, as a consequence of the "understanding" of the program's interventions and of the fact that the program "knows" the subject and the way to treat it, instead of presenting only memorized cliches. But how can we get this knowledge into the computer?

These three questions sum up the situation of AI in CAI : to write a program, we need a team consisting of specialists of the subject matter, specialists in natural language, and computer specialists. And as they are very busy, don't try to ask them to use graphics, colour, videodisc, sound, many character sets, etc.

II.6. Author position

The courseware author's position, as I have observed , is very confused, and the disparity of the equipment and software doesn't help.

The author who has only learnt a little about computers and CAI tends to aim too low or too high as far as dialogue-specification is concerned because he/she doesn't understand what production systems can do. The author can leave the work of writing the program to computer specialists, or do the work himself, and make the mistake of writing in a non specialized language, whereas an interactive system would be perfectly suitable. As he can't write programs, the result is feeble. Unfortunatly, this happens to many teachers who were given computers by student-parents associations or the town council; these computers don't usually have specific software for CAI.

The author who has studied computers and is interested in artificial intelligence sees no reason to use existing production tools and so writes in his own non-specialized language. He manages quite well, generally, but it takes a lot of time.

The next paragraph is about an actual experiment by a few such authors and sheds light upon today's evolution.

III. AN ACTUAL EXPERIMENT FROM A GEOGRAPHY PROGRAM

For 3 years I have been in charge of a group of teachers in differents subjects (arts, German, mathematics) whose goal was to produce courseware to give teachers an approach to computers. We had to say what computing is by showing the way to use it in schools.

All these people had had 9 months minimum of training in computing and have acquired a lot of experience at work, within the frame work of the French Experiment (12). Two of them started studying the various techniques used for writing programs that help write, for the same theme, completely different dialogues from a

pedagogical point of view.

The question of production tools didn't arise here, as the authors had written the program in the LSE language.

The theme is that of determining a climate from the data concerning temperature and rainfall. In the initial courseware (CNDP library) the research is guided by the program. The computer asks the student questions about the characteristics of the climate he must identify, in an order specified by the author, completely programmed with conditional instructions and access to the climate data base. As the data are entered, the determination gets more precise, and after a certain length of time the computer gives its diagnostics. The student has only to input the data and we hope that after several iterations of doing this, by imitating the model the student will have assimilated the determination algorithm.

The first variant consists in leaving the initiative to the student. He tries to determine a climate (the characteristics of which he doesn't know) and asks, in any order and natural language, questions about these characteristics. The computer analyses the questions and gives the data. When he wishes to, the student proposes diagnostics. The computer evaluates the diagnostics and gives the proof. The research, here, is non-directing and after a good training, the students learns "on site" the right determination algorithm.

The second variant uses the formalism of expert systems and permits the previous two steps. When the student has the initiative, he puts into the computer a certain number of characteristics interpreted as facts by the system. After a certain length of time, the computer signals that it has determined the climate. The student can, if he wishes to, make a proposal, and the computer sends the solution it has found with the corresponding reasoning. When the computer has the initiative, it asks questions of the student, who answers them in the same way. The end of the session is the same. By combining both steps (first passively, then more and more actively) the student learns the algorithm of determination.

In this second variant the geography teachers - who were advisers - were very interested in seeing how easy it was to modify the determination rules (courseware can be adapted to the acquired competence and be used at different levels of studies by simply modifying the rules set). On the other hand this technique could be used whatever the subject, and a courseware on mycology or geology could easily be created.

That is the point, among others, to be developed in the next section.

IV. CONTRIBUTION OF EXPERT SYSTEMS TO CAI

Expert systems form only a small part of artificial intelligence, but they seem full of promise. Subjacent concepts are emerging, techniques are decanting and improving (8,9) and the applications to pedagogy are becoming more and more numerous.

IV.1. Contribution of "declarative programming" and inference mechanisms

As seen in the previous paragraph, declarative programming which consists of specifying rules and facts, eventually meta-rules for a better use of the latter, and letting "shift for itself" the inference mechanism, permit introducing into AI a dimension of software engineering : incremental aspect, easy to modify, change from one subject to another. Moreover we now talk about knowledge engineering for the whole of these techniques. No one can see why a non computer-specialist teacher shouldn't be able to produce AI-type courseware, if he introduces the necessary knowledge, just as he used to do with an ordinary dialogue in an interactive CAI system. At the present time, an inference engine without variables, named PENELOPE, has been built on the equipment for French schools and the teachers are beginning to get used to it.

IV.2. Facilitating role for spliting the three functions : expertise of the domain, understanding and generating of natural language, guidance (2)

Since the computer can reason independently of knowledge, it's logical to apply to it the three functions that manage the dialogue :

- when the student gives a problem to the computer, it must first "understand" the problem and analyze it based upon language (more precisely upon the specialized language of the field, plus a certain number of general mechanisms);
- when the problem is being solved, the computer analyzes based on the knowledge of the field;
- when it changes from one problem to another, the computer analyzes the response based on the learner's mastery of the domain.

So, several experts are set to work. They transmit to one another information that forms the data base of the system. Each expert has its own set of rules and meta-rules.

This is the approach that a small research group in my laboratory took with the MEDIAN project (3), discussed in the next section.

V. RECONCILIATION BETWEEN IA AND COURSEWARE ENGINEERING : THE MEDIAN PROJECT

The object of the MEDIAN project is to show the feasability of courseware engineering tools permitting authors who are not computer-specialists to write problem-solving CAI dialogues. A whole set of such tools would form a problem-solving partner (PSP).

V.1. Interesting subjects

The independence of the PSP with regard to domain is proved by the choice of two totally different subjects :

- solving arithmetic problems (in primary school);
- learning the flow of book-keeping records of the activity of firms (at the end of secondary education).

V.2. Expertise compilation

We are working with primary teachers from a school in the suburb of NANCY. We are also in contact with psychologists who have studied the understanding and reasoning mechanisms and the causes for learning error with children.

As far as book-keeping is concerned, we are using three expert teachers. The phase of expertise compilation can be considered to be completed.

V.3. Realized functions

As we are writing this paper we have achieved :

- an understanding of the specification of arithmetic problems (100 rules)
- the solving of book-keeping problems (60 rules)

An understanding of the specification of book-keeping is more difficult because we are dealing with documents when time and space must be considered and which are applied to a micro world.

The solving of arithmetic problems is trivial.

The explanation modules are well advanced.

The "pedagogue" is just beginning but forms the most interesting part as it is the least explored until now in parallel research (11).

V.4. Medium-ranged goals

We wish to use a unique inference engine for the whole functions, to write rule editors common to both fields, a "general" pedagogue in addition to specific "didacticians". We will then have made a progress towards our general goal.

VI. CONCLUSION

In this paper we haven't described an experiment, as we can't experiment with tools that don't yet exist. We hope that at the next conference, many teams from many countries will come to the briefing, after this experiment, on current CAI expert systems.

VII. ACKNOWLEDGEMENTS

My acknowledgements to

- René DIETSCH and Maryse SACCO, for the many hours they spent on the "climate" courseware, and for the interest they showed in AI;
- the French AGENCE DE L'INFORMATIQUE, which sponsors the MEDIAN project, Ammar BOUDJOGHRA and Agnès MEDVEDEFF who are participants in this project;
- Daniel COULON and Monique GRANDBASTIEN, who are my advisers in my laboratory, respectively on natural language processing and expert systems;

and all the teachers and students, thanks to whom my interest in CAI does not decrease.

VIII. REFERENCES

(1) ADI, Rapport EAO, 1981. ADI, Tour Fiat, Cedex 16, 92084 Paris la Défense.

(2) A. BONNET, G. FAFIOTTE, et M. QUERE. L'utilisation des ordinateurs dans l'enseignement. Actes de la journée de synthèse, congrès AFCET, Gif sur Yvette, 1981.

(3) A. BOUDJOGHRA, A. MEDVEDEFF et M. QUERE. EAO : vers un partenaire de résolution de problèmes utilisant plusieurs experts. Le projet MEDIAN.
Journées "Systèmes experts", AVIGNON, mai 1984.

(4) R. BURTON, and J.S. BROWN. An investigation of computer coaching for informal learning activities, International journal of Man-Machine studies, 1979, 11, pp 5-24.

(5) J. CARBONELL. AI in CAI, An artificial Intelligence approach to computer-assisted instruction, IEEE transactions on man-machine systems, vol MMS-11, dec 70.

(6) Projet DIANE. DIANE création : l'éditeur fonctionnel. ADI, Paris, avril 84.

(7) D. COULON, J.P. FINANCE, R. MOHR, J.M. PIERREL, M. QUERE, F. SIMONOT. ECRIN, Fonctionnalités d'un système d'EAO. Publication CRIN n° 82-R-021.

(8) J.P. LAURENT. Les moteurs de systèmes experts : typologie, comparaison et guide du concepteur. Journées "Systèmes experts", Avignon, mai 84.

(9) J. LAURIERE. Représentation et utilisation des connaissances. TSI, vol 1, n°1, 1982.

(10) J.L. LEONHARDT, R. ZEILINGER, A. DELEGLISE et P. MADDALENA. Rapport final de contribution à la phase I du projet TELEMAQUE, IRPEACS, LYON, 1982.

(11) T. O'SHEA. Rule based computer tutors. Expert systems in the Micro-Electronic age, 1979.

(12) M. QUERE. Computers in Education : the French Experiment. ICCH 83, Raleigh, 1983.

(13) M. QUERE. Langages d'auteurs d'hier et d'aujourd'hui. Journal de l'EAO et de la Formation Continue, Paris, octobre 83.

(14) M. RORPACH. Langages et systèmes d'implémentation de cours en enseignement assisté par ordinateur, Publications de l'IREM de Nancy, 1974.

COMPUTERS IN EDUCATION, K. Duncan and D. Harris (eds.)
Elsevier Science Publishers B.V. (North-Holland)
© IFIP, 1985

MUMEDALA - AN APPROACH TO MULTI-MEDIA AUTHORING

Philip G. Barker
Interactive Systems Research Group

Department of Computer Science
Teesside Polytechnic
County Cleveland, UK

The MUMEDALA (MUlti-MEDia Authoring LAnguage) system is an authoring facility that is designed to enable the creation and control of a sophisticated interactive learning environment. Such an environment might contain a variety of channels that enable (1) the presentation of instructional material, and (2) the capture of student response and monitoring data. The latter provides the means of achieving highly individualised instructional schema based upon the use of a range of teaching media. This paper presents an overview of the MUMEDALA system, its design features and the progress being made towards its realisation.

1. INTRODUCTION

If it is to be used effectively, any form of instructional technology that is based upon a computer system must possess some of the basic attributes of conventional human teachers. It is thus important to understand the basic objectives and mechanisms of teaching and to appreciate which tasks can be delegated to a computer controlled system. The introductory section of this paper therefore discusses some of the pedagogical factors that should influence the design and construction of sophisticated multi-media workstations (or learning centres) for use in an educational environment.

1.1 The Nature of Educational Dialogue

There is a variety of different forms of human dialogue. Undoubtedly, from the point of view of their educational implications the most important of these are those that enable large amounts of knowledge transfer (and thus teaching and learning) to take place. Teaching and learning play a vital role in modern society. They are people orientated activities whose purpose is to instill the knowledge and skills necessary to facilitate human survival in a variety of different environments. The basic mechanisms by which these objectives are achieved involve both the transfer and the subsequent assimilation of information.

Information transfer, or communication, involves the movement of information from one location to another. When two humans (such as a teacher and a student) communicate with each other (see figure 1) they exchange information by means of several different communication channels - the spoken word, writing, drawings and ideograms; through facial expressions and a multitude of gesticulative actions (1). Each communication channel is characterised by a bandwidth (that is capacity for information transfer) and may be used in parallel with any of the other available channels in order to achieve an optimal exchange mechanism.

During these processes of communication it is likely that two basic types of mental modelling (and hence, information transfer) take place. In the first of these, the communicating partners each build up a model of the other's knowledge states, mental attributes and state of mind. The second type of modelling involves the construction of models to represent those concepts and ideas that are to be transferred between the communicating agents. The synthetic processes (perception, cognition, etc) involved in building each of these types of model are of fundamental importance since they significantly influence the dynamic course and outcome of the communication processes between those who are involved in knowledge transfer.

An understanding of the basic nature of the interaction that takes place between two people during an educational dialogue is imperative. Without such an understanding the feasibility of using a computer based system as an effective teaching tool (see figure 2) is questionable.

1.2 Mechanisms for Human-Computer Dialogue

If computers are to be used to implement any form of educational dialogue, two basic types of information flow must be supported. Firstly, from a teacher (or author) to/from the computer; secondly, from the computer to/from the student. This paper is primarily concerned with the first of these - although it must be realised that the two cannot be totally separated and isolated from each other.

In almost all conventional approaches to human-computer dialogue the visual display unit (see figure 2) or VDU (or some variant of this) has provided the primitive hardware mechanism that enables information flow to take place. Only two basic communication channels are used: input via a variety of tactile keyboard operations; and visual output via the CRT display. The VDU permits a minimal range of sonic effects to be produced. As will be described in the next section, there is nowadays a move towards more

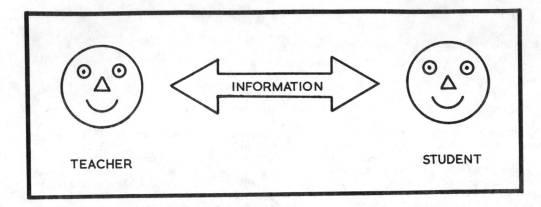

Figure 1   An educational dialogue between humans.

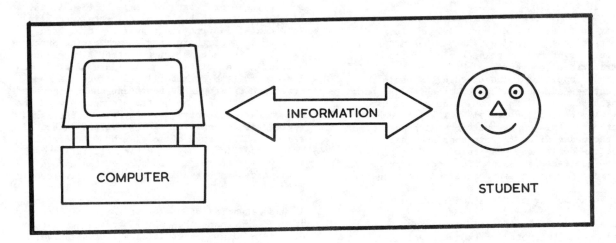

Figure 2   A human-computer dialogue.

sophisticated types of interaction environment
in which the CRT/keyboard combination represent
just two of a large selection of communication
channels.

Those involved in the preparation of computer
based learning resources (or courseware) have
utilised one or other of three basic software
development methodologies: (a) self-use of a
conventional programming language; (b) self-use
of a special purpose authoring facility; and/or
(c) use of a programmer who is expert in one or
other of (a) and (b). Each of these approaches
to courseware development have been described
elsewhere (2).   While programming languages
are probably adequate for the implementation
of simple VDU-based human-computer dialogues,
it is highly unlikely that they will meet the
input/output requirements placed upon them by
the complex nature of the interactions involved
in a multi-media workstation.   Furthermore,

and of more importance, the end-user interface
necessary for the employment of such languages
(3) is likely to present a significant barrier
to those who have limited knowledge of computer
programming and hardware interfacing. For this
reason we believe that author languages of the
type described in this paper will offer significant benefits to courseware developers.

1.3   Multi-media Interaction Environments

When students use computer terminals for the
purpose of learning they are said to be interacting with the operational courseware contained
within the system.   Collectively, the facilities
that a terminal provides, in order to support
this process, are said to constitute an interaction environment.   As was suggested in the
previous section, the number of channels
supported by an ordinary VDU (and, hence, the
total communication bandwidth that is available)

is quite minimal. In view of this, in order
to enhance information transfer and (hopefully)
learning, it would seem desirable to want to
increase the number of communication channels
that exist between the computer and the learner.

The many different types of channel that are
available to facilitate human-computer data and
information transfer have been described in
detail in another publication (4). Some of
the more important of these are summarised
below:

- text generation/analysis,
- sound production,
- speech recognition/generation,
- image production/analysis,
- tactile and electrical stimulation, and
- the analysis of bio-signals.

The devices that may be used to accomplish the
above types of operation are many and varied.
They include conventional keyboards and CRT
screens (see figure 2), hand print terminals (5),
touch sensitive keyboards (6), high resolution
graphics equipment (7), and a variety of special
aids for the disabled and handicapped learner
(8).

When the basic facilities of a VDU are substantially enhanced by the addition of some of the
ancillary types of communication channel listed
above, the end-product is said to constitute a
multi-media learning environment. An example of
such an environment is provided by the currently
popular computer-controlled interactive video
systems (3). In a system of this type there
are usually two CRT screens available (one for
the display of computer generated images and a
second to enable the viewing of images derived
from an optical laser disc). There are also
audio channels available as well as a variety
of keyboard systems.

Multi-media interaction environments will
undoubtedly form the basis of the more acceptable and effective individualised computer-based
instructional systems of the future. For this
reason we have been studying the problems
involved in attempting to construct an author
language (MUMEDALA) that is designed to provide
its user with the necessary facilities to
control complex interaction environments of
the type outlined above. Some of our earlier
experimental work in this area has been described elsewhere (9).

1.4 Problems of Generating Interactive Courseware

Many of the current approaches to generating
courseware for the control of interactive multi-
media workstations are thwarted with difficulties
that arise from a number of different sources.
Three of the most significant of these are
(a) the inadequacy of currently available
courseware authoring tools; (b) the difficulty

of integrating instructional resources onto a
common storage medium; and (c) the problems
inherent in sharing and distributing instructional resources. Each of these problems has
been debated in more detail in reference (3).
This paper deals only with item (a).

Conventional programming languages such as
PASCAL or BASIC have been extensively used for
generating courseware for multi-media learning
centres (3,10). Unfortunately, their use is
time consuming, requires a significant amount
of technical knowledge, and often results in
courseware that is not transferable between
workstations that are based upon different types
of computer hardware. Similarly, attempts at
modifying existing author languages such as
PILOT (11) or MICROTEXT (12) often result in
programming systems that have ad-hoc and often
ergonomically unsound end-user interfaces.
Unfortunately, there have been very few attempts
to present any radically new approaches to
author language design specifically for the
control of workstations that incorporate the
latest developments in information storage and
communication technology. Three notable
exceptions to this state of affairs will be
found in the work of Brandt and Knapp (13),
DELTAK Inc. (14) and Owl Communications (15).
Our own approach to the solution of the author
language problem is briefly outlined in the
following section of this paper.

2. THE MUMEDALA SYSTEM

The MUMEDALA system is an experimental test
vehicle that is intended to provide a framework
in which to conduct those hardware, software and
interfacing experiments that we believe are
necessary in order to produce a successful
solution to the problems inherent in multi-media
authoring. This section outlines some of the
important features of the system (16,17).

2.1 Design Considerations

When the requirements specification for the
MUMEDALA system were originally formulated, a
number of items were considered to be of prime
importance. Some of the more important of
these design criteria are listed below. It was
thought that the system must be capable of:

(a) operating in both an autonomous mode
    and a networked environment,
(b) supporting a variety of human-computer
    interaction techniques,
(c) providing both frame and line orien-
    tated dialogues - see reference (18),
(d) providing good frame editing facilities,
(e) presenting animated sequences,
(f) providing highly end-user orientated
    interfaces, that is, it must be user
    friendly and easy to use,
(g) providing adequate data base support
    facilities,

(h) capturing broadcast (radio and TV) material from global distribution system,

(i) supporting a variety of information storage media,

(j) constructing dynamic models of individual students and of using them to produce highly individualised instructional schema - see reference (19).

(k) incorporating standards (where they exist) in order to facilitate the exchange of instructional material.

(l) producing material that can be easily modified to meet different requirements,

(m) providing an extensible environment capable of absorbing unforeseen advances in technology and user requirements,

(n) being made highly reliable and of being easily maintained by local technicians,

(o) permitting facile control of the learner's interaction environment.

The growing importance of both global and local area communication networks - see references (20) and (21) should mean that the dissemination and exchange of educational material might, in the future, be more easily accomplished than it has been in the past. We therefore believe that educational workstations that are unable to exploit networking facilities of this type will be of limited applicability - particularly in situations where it is required to access archived material from a remote (or semi-remote) data base system. Another extremely important design feature for the system is the requirement to be able to capture (and, subsequently, modify and/or 'cut and snip') material transmitted via radio and TV broadcasting networks (such as the UK's BBC and Open University). Unfortunately, the problems inherent in manipulating multi-media data bases - see reference (22) - impose severe restrictions on what can currently be achieved in this context.

The storage facilities that need to be provided must cater for, amongst others, both video and digital information. For example: (a) flexible and hard magnetic discs; (b) video read and read/write stores - as are provided by optical disc and video cassette systems; and, (c) ancillary static image stores of the type made available through slide collections and microfiche equipment. The introduction of a single all-purpose storage medium - see reference (23) - will undoubtedly be a major step forward as far as multi-media instructional technology is concerned.

Requirements in the area of modelling and the provision of a mechanism (author language) to enable the facile control of the learner's interaction environment were briefly outlined in the introduction. The remainder of this paper is now devoted to a description of some of the work that has been done with respect to the provision of authoring facilities to meet the requirements outlined above.

2.2   Modes of Usage

A schematic illustration of the MUMEDALA interaction environment is presented in figure 3. The system is primarily a frame based one in which CRT frames, video frames (from a VCR and/or optical disc), and/or slide frames are used to facilitate the output of instructional material to the user. Users may belong to either of two broad classes: learners and authors. From the point of view of the latter there are three general modes of interaction: (1) frame generation, (2) lesson creation, and (3) system interrogation. Only CRT frames are generated during live on-line interaction with the system. The other types of frame are produced externally and then pre-loaded into the workstation or made accessible to it via a suitable back-end data base and communication network.

When in frame generation mode the author creates a series of numbered VDU frames. These may belong to any of five primitive classes: instructional, remedial, reinforcing, testing and help. Once created and numbered the frames are stored in a local data base (and possibly archived on a remote computer system). The VDU frames may be supported by ancillary sound and graphic units or diversions to on-line equipment. As soon as some instructional frames exist the author may enter lesson creation mode. During this part of the authoring process the author specifies the order in which ancillary resources are to be controlled in order to support the learning process. Once a lesson becomes operational the third mode of interaction - system interrogation - may be invoked. Using this mode it is possible for the teacher/author to determine the progress being made by individual students and the way in which the instructional resources are being used. Further details of each of these authoring modes are given in reference (16).

The authoring facilities to achieve the above objectives are realised through the use of a keyword based command language. This uses two basic types of command: direct and indirect. When the system is loaded and executed (in authoring context) the author is placed in direct command mode. When in this mode the author may issue any of the MUMEDALA direct commands (see table 1) to the terminal control program. Each of these commands causes the system to pass into other states that enable the CAI author to perform certain standard types of operation.

An instructional unit with which a student interacts will usually consist of a control element and the associated set of frames upon

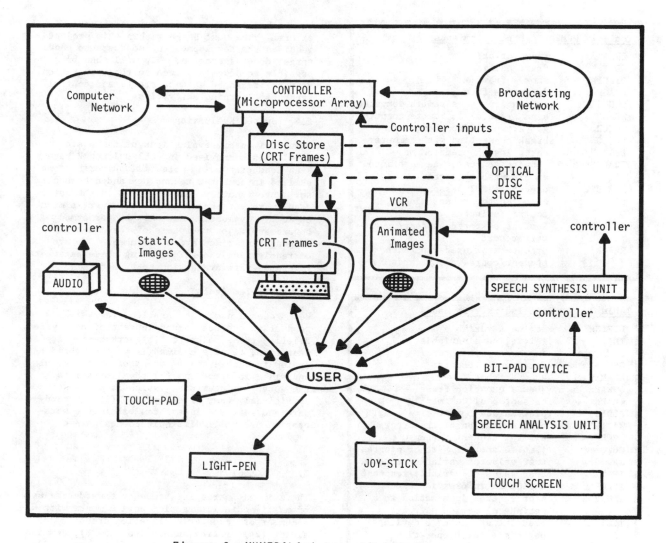

Figure 3   MUMEDALA interaction environment.

which it operates. The control element for a
lesson is defined in terms of the indirect
commands made available by the MUMEDALA system.
A MUMEDALA source program consists of a file
containing a series of these commands. In order
to convert this file into an executable control
unit, the source program must be translated into
an appropriate target code – at present BASIC
is used for this purpose.

Generally, an indirect statement will contain
four basic parts: (a) a label, (b) a command
keyword, (c) an operand list, and (d) a comment
field. Of these, the label and comment field
are optional. Some commands may not require
an operand – in which case this field will be
absent from the statement. The allowed command
keywords are listed in table 2. Details of the
structure of the operand lists and specifica-

tions of the parsing algorithms for analysing
and checking the validity of individual statements are given in reference (17).

2.3   Towards an Implementation

The major implementation effort to date has
been devoted to two basic areas: (a) the
development of a command interpreter to handle
direct commands, and (b) the design and programming of algorithms for the statement
analyser for handling indirect commands. In
case (a) the system hardware is based upon an
ETHERNET local area network (LAN) with (as a
future development) gateway connections to a
number of remote computers. Software development for the command interpreter has been
mainly concerned with the code needed to handle
CRT frame creation and editing at the work-

Table 1	MUMEDALA Direct Commands
CREATE	frame creation
EDIT	frame editing
DISPLAY	show a frame
ERASE	destroy a frame
CONNECT	form a link to a remote computer
SEND	send frame(s) to remote computer
FETCH	get frame(s) from computer
DISCONNECT	break connection with computer
LESSON	enter lesson creation mode
TRANSLATE	convert source statements into an executable lesson
EXECUTE	execute a CAI lesson
SET	allow author to set global control switches
INSPECT	look at a stored student/courseware record
REPORT	produce a printed report on student/courseware records

Table 2	MUMEDALA Indirect Commands
DEFINE	define a variable
INIT	initialise a variable
INC	increment a counter
DEC	decrement a counter
FRAME	show a frame
QFRAME	show a question frame
SLIDE	present a slide image
AUDIO	play an audio recording
WAIT	halt execution of the program
ACCEPT	await a student response
GOTO	jump to another part of program
IF	test value of variable/response
IFNOT	test value of variable/response
INFOBLOCK	define an information block
CONTROL	send control information to a peripheral device
TEST	test the status of a device
MATCH	perform a match operation
SCREEN	make a screen active for information display
SCREENSEG	define screen segmentation
PIPE	define an information flow line from a device to a screen or screen segment
CANCEL	previously defined information flow and display assignations
SET	set program switches or values of system variables
SPEEK	message to voice synthesiser
STOP	terminate execution of program
ANIMATION	show sequence from optical disc
MESSAGE	send a message via a device
MONITOR	set student monitoring options
END	end of MUMEDALA program file

station with subsequent storage of the frames both within the workstation and in a local back-end data base connected to the LAN.   In case (b), the statement analyser is now complete thereby enabling complete MUMEDALA programs to

be checked for syntax and (some) semantic errors.   The next stage within this project requires the development of software to handle target code generation.   It will then be possible to down-load code to the workstation so that it can be used to create and control students' learning activities.

2.4   System Evaluation

Some rudimentary evaluations of the basic facilities summarised in tables 1 and 2 have been conducted using potential authors - some skilled in computer technology and others not so.   Unfortunately, the results (in the latter case) were not encouraging.   However, a more objective evaluation must now be performed before any major revisions of the end-user language interface are undertaken.   We are currently involved in designing the experiments to enable this evaluation to be made.

2.5   Problem Areas

We foresee a number of problem areas with respect to the future development of our system. Briefly, these relate to (1) workstation implementation, (2) the availability of a hybrid LAN system to enable the movement of both digital and video information, (3) the limitations of the author's interface - which is still not sufficiently user friendly, and (4) the hardware and software interfaces within the workstation are still difficult to design and implement.

3.   CONCLUSION

There is an increasing tendency towards the use of multi-media interaction environments within a number of computer application areas.   Job aiding (24), office automation (25-28), command and control systems (29-30), and education (31) are but four examples.   Because of the importance of this aspect of human-machine interaction a considerable amount of research and development effort still needs to be devoted to the production of a user friendly dialogue programming system for use in a multi-channel interaction environment.

In this paper one approach (MUMEDALA) to meeting this need has been described.   Unfortunately, our initial investigations into the acceptability of the MUMEDALA system would suggest that this language interface may still be too complex for the non-specialist user.

4.   ACKNOWLEDGEMENTS

The author is indebted to Pat Croft (Durham University) for typing the manuscript and to Tim Skipper (Teesside Polytechnic) for programming support.   He also acknowledges the various forms of financial support provided by

Teesside Polytechnic, the British Council, and the Council for Educational Technology.

5. REFERENCES

(1) Goffman, E., Interaction Ritual - Essays on Face-to-Face Behaviour, Penguin Books, 1967.

(2) Barker, P.G. and Singh, R., Author Languages for Computer-Based Learning, British Journal of Educational Technology, Volume 13, No. 3, 167-196, October 1982.

(3) Barker, P.G., Video Disc Programming for Interactive Video, Electronics and Wireless World, Volume 89, No. 1574, 44-48, 1983.

(4) Barker, P.G. and Yeates, H., Chapter 1: Using Computers for Education and Training, in Introducing Computer Assisted Learning, Prentice Hall, 1985.

(5) Barker, P.G., Data Base Interaction Using a Hand Print Terminal, International Journal of Man-Machine Studies, Academic Press, Volume 17, 435-458, 1982.

(6) Barker, P.G., Experiments With a Touch Sensitive Keypad, Electronics & Computing Monthly, Volume 1, Issue 7, 20-24, December 1981.

(7) Barker, P.G. and Jones, P.S., Syntactic Definition and Parsing of Molecular Formulae, Part 2: Graphical Synthesis of Molecular Formulae for Data Base Queries, The Computer Journal, Volume 21, No. 3, 224-233, 1978.

(8) Barker, P.G., A CAI Interface for the Disabled, Working Paper, Interactive Systems Research Group, Department of Computer Science, Teesside Polytechnic, County Cleveland, UK, January 1982.

(9) Barker, P.G., Some Experiments in Man-Machine Interaction Relevant to Computer Assisted Learning, British Journal of Educational Technology, Volume 13, No. 1, 65-75, January 1982.

(10) Yeates, H., Some Experiments in Man-Machine Interaction Relevant to Computer Assisted Learning, M.Sc. Thesis, University of Durham, UK, 1981.

(11) Barker, P.G. and Singh, R., A Practical Introduction to Authoring for Computer Assisted Instruction - Part II: PILOT, British Journal of Educational Technology, Volume 14, No. 3, 174-200, 1983.

(12) Barker, P.G. and Singh, R., A Practical Introduction to Authoring for Computer Assisted Instruction - Part III: MICROTEXT, British Journal of Educational Technology, Volume 15, Issue 2, 82-106, 1984.

(13) Brandt, R.C. and Knapp, R.H., Video Computer Authoring System, Department of Physics, University of Utah, Salt Lake City, Utah 84112, USA, 1979.

(14) Delta Vision - Computer Enhanced Multi-Media Training Systems, Product Specification No. 9P2404A, DELTAK Inc., 1220 Kensington Road, Oak Brook, Illinois 60521, April 1981.

(15) Gardner, P.M., Authoring Package Combines Microcomputer and Viewdata Techniques in Interactive Laservision System, Owl Micro-Communications Ltd., The Maltings, Station Road, Sawbridgeworth, Herts, CM21 9LY, UK, March 1983.

(16) Barker, P.G., Skipper T. and Singh, R., MUMEDALA - An Approach to Multi-Media Authoring (System Overview), Working Paper - Version 3.3, Interactive Systems Research Group, Department of Computer Science, Teesside Polytechnic, County Cleveland, UK, October 1982.

(17) Barker, P.G. and Skipper T., MUMEDALA Statement Analysis, Working Paper - Version 6.1, Interactive Systems Research Group, Department of Computer Science, Teesside Polytechnic, County Cleveland, UK, October 1982.

(18) Barker, P.G., Frame Programming in BASIC, Working Paper, Interactive Systems Research Group, Department of Computer Science, Teesside Polytechnic, County Cleveland, UK, March 1983.

(19) Self, J.A., Student Models and Artificial Intelligence, Computers and Education, Volume 3, 309-312, Pergamon Press, 1979.

(20) Haefner, K., The Concept of an Integrated System for Information access and Tele-communications (ISIT) and its impact on Education in the 80's, 973-978 in Information Processing 80, (Ed: Lavington, S.H.), North Holland Publishing Company, 1980.

(21) Boutmy, E.J. and Danthine, A., TELEINFORMATICS '79, North Holland Publishing Company, 1979.

(22) Barker, P.G. and Yeates, H., Problems Associated with Multi-Media Data Bases, British Journal of Educational Technology, Volume 12, No. 2, 158-175, May 1981.

(23) Kane, G.R., Leonard, W.F. and Nashburg, R.E., CAVI - A Microcomputer-based Tool to Enhance Flexible-paced Learning, 160-166 in Proceedings of the 10th ASEE/IEEE Frontiers in Education Conference, (Eds: Grayson, L.P. and Biedenbach, J.M.), 1980.

(24) Towne, D.M., The Automated Integration of
     Training and Aiding Information for the
     Operator/Technician, in Proceedings of the
     Third Biennial Conference on Maintenance
     Training and Aiding, 53-63, Orlando, FL,
     1979.

(25) Barker, P.G. and Najah, M., Pictorial
     Interfaces to Data Bases, Working Paper,
     Interactive Systems Research Group,
     Department of Computer Science, Teesside
     Polytechnic, County Cleveland, UK,
     February 1985.

(26) Barker, P.G., Najah, M. and Roper, J.S.,
     User Experiences with a MICROPAD, Journal
     of Microcomputer Applications, Volume 7,
     19-39, 1984.

(27) Forsdick, H.C., Thomas, R.H., Robertson,
     G.G. and Travers, V.M., Initial Experience
     with Multimedia Documents in Diamond,
     Database Engineering, Volume 7, No. 3,
     25-42, 1984.

(28) Christodoulakis, S., An Experimental Multi-
     media System for an Office Environment,
     Database Engineering, Volume 7, No. 3,
     43-48, 1984.

(29) Friedell, M., Barnett, J. and Kranlich, D.,
     Context-sensitive, Graphic Presentation of
     Information, Computer Graphics, Volume 16,
     No. 3, 181-187, 1982.

(30) Kramlich, D., Spatial Data Management on
     the USS Carl Vinson, Database Engineering,
     Volume 7, No. 3, 10-19, 1984.

(31) Barker, P.G. and Yeates, H., Chapter 4:
     Multi-media CAL; and Chapter 5: Approaches
     to Multi-media CAL, in Introducing Computer
     Assisted Learning, Prentice-Hall, 1985.

COMPUTERS IN EDUCATION, K. Duncan and D. Harris (eds.)
Elsevier Science Publishers B.V. (North-Holland)
© IFIP, 1985

PERCEIVED DIFFICULTIES IN LEARNING AN AUTHORING LANGUAGE SYSTEM

Clifton S. Harris

The University of Texas at Dallas
P. O. Box 830688
Richardson, TX   75083-0688   U.S.A.

The perceived difficulties encountered by practicing school teachers in becoming
reasonably proficient with an authoring language system are outlined. The authoring
system facilitated the actual preparation of computer-based lessons as an integral
part of the study.
The objectives of the study were (1) to develop a scheme for representing the
primary authoring commands in meaningful chunks, (2) to devise a technique for
encoding functional knowledge of the command structure in long-term memory, (3) to
observe actual strategies used in learning the authoring system, and (4) to analyze
the resulting protocol-type data to yield consequences and insights.
Participants showed a strong drive to learn by doing as a necessary confirmation of
memory. Cognitive difficulties centered around retaining command-type instructions.
Technical difficulties included manipulating the display to accommodate graphics and
text.

Learning an authoring language is viewed as a promising way for practicing teachers to begin to create computer-based materials for classroom use. Creation of appropriate courseware by teachers is thought to be an effective means of providing greater utilization of microcomputer systems in schools in the U.S. Teachers, however, display a lack of confidence and competence in modifying commercial courseware. The study being reported here deals with the issues of confidence and competence.

An authoring language provides a needed alternative to the traditional computer languages in that it encourages and permits teachers to undertake the creation of instructional materials for precollege level instruction. An innovative approach to teacher master of authoring systems holds substantial promise to enhance teacher confidence and competence in creating such materials. Facilitation of teacher mastery of a powerful authoring language should increase the scope and quantity of good courseware and thereby provide more effective utilization of the rapidly growing microcomputer installations in schools throughout the world.

Only recently have educational psychologists and computer scientists begun to study teaching methods specifically geared to programmer education.[1] Nonetheless, there is some consensus that much can be done to improve training of novice and experienced programmers by applying the principles of educational psychology to teacher knowledge and skills needed to develop computer-based materials.[2] In fact, a movement to make the entire software environment more friendly to novice programmers is gaining considerable momentum.[3]

Authoring language systems have been developed as a means of creating computer-based instructional materials with greater ease and with considerable saving in time. In fact, the claim is made that the time required to write computer-assisted lesson materials can be reduced up to 90 per cent with the use of the authoring feature.[4] Obviously, a tool of this kind is quite a boon for teachers who do not have sophisticated programming skills.

This author agrees with Sheil[5] that most innovations in programming languages and methodology are motivated by a belief that they will improve the performance of the programmers who use them. Even though studies of software engineering, or more specifically "programming tasks," leave much to be desired in terms of experimental treatments such studies are needed to shed light on the complex psychological behavior associated with programming skill. Results from studies such as the one reported here are useful in that they provide guidance for system designers, psychologists, and educators selecting topics for more detailed study.

OBJECTIVES OF THE STUDY

In order to achieve the primary goals of developing an innovative mechanism to facilitate mastery of an authoring language system by precollege teachers, the following objectives were defined. The first objective was to develop a scheme for representing the primary authoring commands in meaningful chunks (configurations) which can be more easily accommodated in working memory. Second, a technique for encoding functional knowledge of the command structure in long term memory (LTM) to alleviate restrictions on short term memory (STM) capacity for programming lesson content needed to be devised. And third, observation of the actual strategies used in learning the system including difficulties encountered and the kinds of mistakes made was obtained through an interview process. Assuming that the above objectives could be achieved, a fourth and final objective was the analysis of resulting data to yield consequences and insights which could be used as a basis for (a) describing better the cognitive processes involved in learning an authoring language and (b) structuring more effectively (logically) the authoring commands.

LITERATURE RELEVANT TO THE STUDY

An investigation of this nature relies on three primary assumptions that are crucial to a study of this kind: First, various memorization techniques are key to encoding and organizing procedures that are capable of permitting researchers to deal directly with cognitive representations of information which need to be retrieved from memory. Secondly, the verbalizations of human subjects can be a reliable source of data about cognitive processing. Third, the individual human strategies used in learning new information observed by researchers can be used as a valid basis for developing a model of the learning mechanism. The results of systematic investigations appear to support affirmatively these assumptions.

For example on the first issue, Gagne and White[6] have noted that research on all learning techniques must assess to a greater degree than in the past the nature of the memory representation of the learned material. In addition, Belleza[7] contends that memorization techniques employed in training adults in techniques such as mnemonic strategies for learning lists and prose material are well substantiated.

With regard to the second issue, Ericsson and Simon[8] have provided substantial evidence that verbal reports of human subjects can be used as objective data when such reports are elicited with care and interpreted with full understanding of the circumstances under which they were obtained.

Evidence speaking to the third assumption is available from Anzai and Simon[9] who have demonstrated the validity of utilizing individual strategies employed by human subjects to learn problem-solving tasks as a basis for developing a model of learning mechanisms.

Additionally, recent research leading to a construct of spreading activation has delineated the distinction between learned facts (declarative memory) and specific steps of what to do (procedural memory).[10] This distinction appears to be particularly useful in authoring tasks which call for permanently stored (we hope) knowledge of basic commands to be retrieved from LTM and placed in working memory where production (authoring) conditions can be matched.

PROCEDURE AND METHOD OF INVESTIGATION

A total of 18 teachers representing various disciplines, ethnic groups, grade levels, and types of schools, who were interested in becoming competent with an authoring language system, participated in the study.

The participants (subjects) were rapidly briefed on human factor issues particularly those related to human-computer dialogue as a variable for investigation: such dialogue includes performance (programming) with the assistance of an authoring language system. The subjects were then oriented to a scope of the authoring language system, specifically the Apple Super PILOT authoring language.

The orientation to the system featured a familiarization to the system commands organized by the author into the following meaningful chunks:

1. Editor Chunk (Allows author to create words, graphics, sound effects and special characters)
2. Control Chunk (Facilitates author control in lesson text editor)
3. Data Chunk (Accommodates most frequent author instructions)
4. Program Manipulation Chunk (Helps author manipulate student responses)
5. File Chunk (Accommodates rather specialized uses)
6. Data Processing Chunk (Facilitates basic computations)

Subjects were asked in advance to provide some strategies they thought they might employ in learning the system. Later, after some actual experience with the system they were asked to delineate actual strategies used. In an interview procedure, used throughout the study, subjects were queried concerning the kinds of mistakes made and the difficulties encountered in their experience with the system. Responses obtained to the above two categories provided the data for subsequent analysis.

ANALYSIS OF DATA

Analysis of the responses obtained were grouped into two categories: The perceived difficulties encountered and the kinds of mistakes made in the process of becoming reasonably proficient with the authoring system.

The perceived difficulties encountered were further divided into two categories: A cognitive category that is generally concerned with matters related to retention. For example subjects had difficulty in remembering order, function, and relationship of programming commands in spite of efforts to "chunk" the command structure into functional and semantic groups to facilitate retention in long term memory. A second category can be labeled technical in that the difficulties were specialized:

i.e., they were characteristically "how to" terminology. For instance, how to get all text and graphics on screen, how to shape the initial sequence of statement, question, response, etc.

It was possible to divide the information obtained through the kinds of mistakes made into a general and a specific category, according to the subjects' choice of terminology. The subjects experienced frequent mistakes in manipulating the screen in order to display graphics and text in proper relationship. Another frequent source of mistakes was that of learning to relate commands to each other; this could be a consequence of the more general failure to perceive the flow of logic throughout the program. A further frequent source of mistakes was the attempt to address too many objectives and to include too much content in a single program. It appears that only with an actual authoring experience does a teacher perceive that computer-supported instruction is so detailed and time constrained that small slices of content are required for effective presentation in a tutorial format.

CONSEQUENCES OR LESSONS LEARNED

One of the first consequences discovered in this study was that novice programmers have a strong drive to learn an authoring language "by doing" as opposed to reliance on a memory however facilitated by semantic and mnemonic chunks. Chunking of commands although useful, and undoubtedly more helpful than reliance on thumbing through reference manuals was not as useful as envisioned by the author. It is also believed that a part of the psychological behavior of novice programmers is to be typically insecure with reliance on memory until that memory has been supplemented and confirmed "by doing" programming tasks. Knowledge of results achieved in actual attempts "to make it work" appear to be necessarily reassuring. Educators in teaching roles and developers of authoring systems need to be conscious that the two levels of memory of <u>learned facts</u> (commands in this case) can be mastered in a rote or meaningful manner, but the more demanding task is that of aiding <u>procedural memory</u> to relate properly commands to each other.

Another lesson learned was that perceived difficulties encountered reveal both a cognitive (general) and a technical (specific) concern or problem. The cognitive difficulty centers around the issue of retaining command-type instructions and transferring a given command to a new or novel application.

Foremost among mistakes involving technical difficulties was the matter of manipulating the screen display in order to accommodate graphics and text. Such matters as shaping text first then drawing graphics within or about text was a common display problem. Although this mistake is readily overcome with experience, it is believed that it can be mitigated with prior instruction. The next most frequent mistake was the failure to relate commands to each other; this mistake is essentially a failure to perceive the continuity or flow of logic in programming. It is believed that this failure can be minimized with a special emphasis in the orientation and illustration phase of instruction. The third most frequent mistake was the tendency to address too many objectives and too much content in the instructional design phase of programming. It is difficult to convince a practicing teacher that developing computer-supported instruction is so detailed in terms of tutorial branching that considerably less content can be accommodated than in the typical lecture/discussion format of instruction. This author believes that only programming experience can adequately confirm this reality to a novice programmer.

Subsequent studies of learning an authoring language system might well contemplate the objective process involved, insecurity with reliance on memory of commands alone along with the other cognitive processes (declarative memory and procedural memory) at work. Logical structuring of the authoring commands in some chunking arrangement is helpful at the outset, but development of a facile way to relate procedurally commands to each other is needed. Incorporation of these two features in the orientation and familiarization phase of instruction promise to diminish some of the difficulties encountered and resulting mistakes made.

REFERENCES

[1] Mayer, R.E., Comprehension as affected by structure of problem representation, Memory and Cognition. 43(1976) 249-255.

[2] Schneiderman, B., Software Psychology--Human Factors in Computer and Information Systems (Winthrop, Cambridge, 1983).

[3] du Boulay, B., O'Shea, T. and Monke, J., The black box inside the glass box: presenting computing concepts to novices, International Jrnl of Man-Machine Studies. 14(1981) 237-249.

[4] Schleicher, G. Authoring systems can save time in development of CAI, Electronic Education. 2(1982) 20-27.

[5] Sheil, B. The psychological study of programming, ACM Computing Surveys. 13(1981) 101-121.

[6] Gayne, R. and White, R. Memory structures and learning outcomes, Review of Educational Research. 48(1978) 182-222.

[7] Belleza, F.S. Mnemonic-Device Instruction with Adults, Pressley, M. and Levin, J. (eds.), Cognitive Strategy Research (Springer-Verlag, New York, 1983).

[8] Ericsson, K. and Simon, H. Verbal reports
     as data, Psychological Review. 87(1980)
     215-221.

[9] Anzai, Y. and Simon, H. The theory of
     learning by doing, Psychological Review.
     86(1979) 124-140.

[10] Anderson, J. R. Spreading Activation in
     Anderson, J. and Kosslyn, S. (eds.)
     Tutorials in Learning and Memory
     (W. H. Freeman, San Francisco, 1984).

-0-0-0-

COMPUTERS IN EDUCATION, K. Duncan and D. Harris (eds.)
Elsevier Science Publishers B.V. (North-Holland)
© IFIP, 1985

Interactive, On-Line Design of Educational Software in the Smalltalk-80 Environment

William F. Finzer
Department of Mathematics, San Francisco State University

Laura Gould, National Secretary
Computer Professionals for Social Responsibility

Computer systems based on high-resolution interactive graphics provide a powerful new medium for the presentation of educational material. However, the cost of developing applications in such systems is very high and the results are, for the most part, disappointing. In the development cycle, programming consumes an inordinate amount of time, overshadowing and even undoing the effort expended on careful design. There tends to be too little involvement on the part of those people with the best understanding of how people learn, and too much involvement from those immersed in the workings of the computer.

The work presented in this tutorial is based on the belief that it should be possible to place interactive, graphical systems in the hands of creative curriculum designers, those with an understanding of the power of such systems but not necessarily able or willing to write programs to control them. Given this belief, our task is to provide an environment in which it is possible (even pleasant and stimulating) for such designers to implement their own interactive, graphical conceptions, without having to hire a professional programmer to do it for them.

The tutorial will include a videotape demonstration of a research prototype design environment called Programming by Rehearsal, a hands-on experience in design using a more primitive design tool implemented on a micro-computer, and a presentation of a project in which teachers are being trained as designers of educational software.

I. Programming by Rehearsal

The Smalltalk-80 programming environment, created at the Xerox Palo Alto Research Center, provided the authors with the tools needed to create a curriculum design environment. A potent metaphor, based on the theater, emerged from the fact that Smalltalk is an "object-oriented" language; this means that a programmer writes a Smalltalk application by choosing, or defining, an appropriate set of objects and teaching them to interact with one another. Smalltalk objects are not generally visible on the screen and the effects of code that a programmer writes are not necessarily immediately apparent. The authors undertook to concretize Smalltalk's abstractions in the form of *performers* who participate in a *production* and to ensure the the designer's efforts would always result in immediate action on *stage* much as would the requests of a director rehearsing a theater company.

The videotape to be shown in the tutorial session demonstrates many of the features that make Programming by Rehearsal a prototype for design environments that will become accessible to curriculum designers in the next decade. Such environments should significantly improve the quality of educational software by allowing creative educators to specify their designs directly on the screen. Since the educators will be the 'programmers,' the cost of experimentation should also be lowered considerably.

The Layout Editor

While Programming by Rehearsal runs only on fast, expensive hardware, the Layout Editor runs on micro-computers and has been used for the past year by a group of teachers to design interesting, simulation-oriented, educational software. Not a complete design environment, the Layout Editor requires substantial programmer assistance to turn screen layouts into working programs; nevertheless, it significantly speeds the development of working prototypes that can be tested in classrooms.

Participants in the tutorial will be led through a ninety minute, hands-on, exercise in design using the Layout Editor.

The Computer Curriculum Cadre

Twenty master teachers, from kindergarten through high school have been learning the art of designing educational software and teaching other teachers to use computers effectively in their classrooms since January, 1983. Their work in curriculum development has been supported by the Layout Editor tool described above and by student programmers at San Francisco State University. The results of their design efforts have high payoff, not only through the software they have developed, but through their increased critical awareness of the problems of using software in a classroom. This work has been supported by the Fund for Improvement of Post-Secondary Education, the California State Technology Fund, and Apple Education Foundation.

Pedagogical Tools
and Techniques

COMPUTERS IN EDUCATION, K. Duncan and D. Harris (eds.)
Elsevier Science Publishers B.V. (North-Holland)
© IFIP, 1985

INTERACTIVE MODULES TO TEACH SPREADSHEET ANALYSIS

B. Ibrahim, A. Bork[*], J.-C. Courbon, S. Franklin[*], C. Kuehni, B. Levrat

Centre Universitaire d'Informatique
University of Geneva
24, rue du General Dufour
1211 GENEVE 4, SWITZERLAND

A Computer Based Learning project aimed at developing support material for a first course in the use of computers for a large population of students in Economics is presented. The conception and implementation tools which are described involve a production technique for multilingual computer material.

Some of the learning modules are presented to illustrate interactivity, help sequences, answer analysis in free form text input and menu exploration. Evaluation by the French speaking students is also described. The material covered teaches the use of a Spreadsheet program, in French, Italian and English.

1. INTRODUCTION

In the world of tomorrow, most university graduates will enter professions whose routine tasks can be accomplished only by those familiar with using computers. Some graduates will have to become familiar with programming languages but the vast majority will find that a working knowledge of text processing, electronic mail and Spreadsheet programs is sufficient to give them access to the computing resources they need.

Such software is often advertised as "friendly" and "easy to use" for beginners even though its use requires the assimilation of knowledge found in thick manuals that many potential users are reluctant to study in detail. More importantly, such manuals may cover only distinct mechanical manipulations and fail to present any coherent view of the purposes for which the software is useful. Intensive seminars, such as those organized for private corporation managers, appear impractical in universities where we must reach a large number of students with diverse backgrounds, tight schedules and limited resources. Taking advantage of of experiments done at the University of California, Irvine, and of the tools made available to us, our group at the University of Geneva decided to develop a number of computer based learning modules for all business students either as part of a formal course or as individual study.

The first modules have been designed, implemented and tested with a group of students. This paper describes the current state of the project, briefly describes the tools it has used, and outlines our plans for the future.

2. AIMS

Although it is easy to state on paper that designing and implementing CBL (Computer Based Learning) material is well within the reach of present technology, our team felt a need to demonstrate its capacity to produce portable, high quality, interactive modules in several languages, free from limitations in text manipulation, graphics and student answer analysis. We also want to be able to use as delivery stations a whole range of personal computers as well as the terminals of the future University of Geneva network [1]. Only after the programs have been thoroughly tested, should they be made available to a much larger community of users.

For a first experiment, we chose a first year course in the department of "Sciences Commerciales et Industrielles" where 350 business administration students are taking an introductory course in the use of computers. With such a large number of students, it is difficult to provide staff to supervise hands-on laboratory work. On the other hand, the same students will be confronted with the use of personal computers in their professional life. We chose in the introductory course to combine formal lectures and our computer based learning modules about the use of a Spreadsheet program as exercises.

Good CBL material should offer a stimulating presentation of the subject matter, allow students to work at their own paces, give them some control of the material they want to study and provide meaningful help sequences. If the teaching staff wants it, evaluation (grading) of student progress should not be at the expense of the "user friendly" aspects of the system. Such material cannot be developed without a close involvement of experienced teachers of the subject matter who participate in the pedagogical design of the modules as well as in their testing and and evaluation.

3. SOFTWARE TOOLS

The programming environment was dictated by the requirement that the Geneva material remain compatible with modules produced at the Educational Technology Center at Irvine [2]. All work is currently being done in UCSD Pascal [3], versions of which exist for most micro-computers. Although the project started with Terak computers, the modules presently run on Victor 9000/Sirius, DEC Rainbow, IBM PC and compatible computers.

Mentioning a programming environment implies that standard tools are readily available. A number of separately compiled "units" with well defined interfaces handle such things as displaying text and images, random access files and matching students' answers against patterns defined in the pedagogical design. The string intrinsics of the UCSD Pascal system are used throughout the programs. The modules can run on any computer with graphics capabilities and with a current version of the UCSD p-system.

3.1 MULTIPLE WINDOWS ON THE SCREEN

A general set of screen handling tools has been developed at the University of California, Irvine [4], enabling the programmer to define on the screen as many windows as the pedagogical design has specified. Some will show text, others will display vector or bit-map graphics, or accept student answers.

Text is presented at a speed controlled by the user. Line breaks are done on word boundaries. If the whole text of a given message does not fit in a single window, the programmer can generate scrolling automatically or under user control. When an answer is typed by the student, echoing is done in the appropriate window with some editing facilities available before the RETURN key is pressed. Prompting occurs if the student fails to type anything or forgets to press RETURN after a predetermined time.

Graphics facilities include clipping, horizontal and vertical scale adjustment, and changing the line appearance. Text and graphics can be displayed in the same window limited only by the ability of the personal computer to display high quality text images on a graphics screen. For speed, one can display bit-map images in the predefined windows.

3.2 ORGANIZING THE INFORMATION

Each module entails substantial amounts of text and graphics information. At the start, we decided to separate the logic which consists of instructions written in Pascal from the information to be displayed to the user, which can be stored on disk and called when needed. Each message, text or graphics, has a meaningful name which becomes a key to a random access file on the disk.

File and message names can be handled by the programs, providing for great flexibility. Under program control, users can access their own files, temporary or permanent, consult the directory when appropriate or receive meaningful diagnostics if a requested file is not present.

We take advantage of these features in adapting our software to different languages. The message names, referenced by the program logic remain unchanged while their contents are translated in the desired languages. The corresponding files are given different postfixes, which will let the program know which languages are available and let the user choose one of them.

In the following example, we assume that module 1 extracts its messages from a file named MOD1.KFIL (KFIL characterizes the random access or "Keyed FILes"). It has been translated in English and Italian and the 3 files are present on the same floppy disk with the names:

MOD1.F.KFIL   MOD1.E.KFIL   MOD1.I.KFIL

When the program is started, it examines all files prefixed with MOD1 and presents the following line to the student:

F(rançais)   E(nglish)   I(taliano) ?

After "F", "E" or "I" is selected, all messages come in the specified language. We plan to have all the modules running in German and Spanish in addition to the three languages already mentioned. Other languages can be added easily.

3.3 ANALYZING STUDENT ANSWERS

Multilingualism can be achieved easily if it is possible to separate the analysis of the content of an answer from the actions of the program: the logic depends on matching answers with one of the situations envisioned by the designers. The anticipated answers are coded in the form of grammar rules that the input string must verify. The syntax of the rules is very simple and adapting them to respond to unanticipated student reactions requires nothing more than editing the current rules with a normal text editor.

The rules corresponding to each situation is stored under a unique message name. When the material is translated or simply tailored to a different environment, the message name remains the same but its contents are adapted to the new situation. Consider the question in figure 4; the answer "another one has changed" was accepted, but "it is different", or "New Result" would have also been recognized. It is the combination of good pedagogical design, clean writing of the specification rules, and evaluation with students followed by improvement which gives these programs their power and flexibility.

4. LEARNING MODULES

B. Kurtz and A. Bork have outlined the several phases which occur in the development of good computer based learning material [5]. After the initial planning which sets the goals, teachers, familiar with the material to be taught, should work together with specialists in using the computer for learning to provide the pedagogical design. This involves a systematic decomposition in lessons, each covering a precise theme. Each lesson is then broken down into tasks, each of which constitutes a necessary step in understanding the material.

For each task, a scenario or script is then prepared which will provide the coder with a complete specification of the dialog which is to take place between the computer and the user. In parallel, information about what to display and how to display it must be prepared. Coding and testing may raise questions which require revising some of the specifications. Good programming practices, code reviews and field testing ensure the quality of each module.

The design phase was completed during a three month period that A. Bork spent at the University of Geneva, from October to December 1982. A number of technical issues relating to graphics, performance, file organization and multilingualism were resolved when S. Franklin came in the Spring of 1983.

4.1 THE SPREADSHEET PROGRAM

The first piece of software needed in the project was a Spreadsheet program which had all the important features of the major commercial programs of the same kind, work at an acceptable speed, and at the same time, be organized as a "unit" which the different teaching modules could invoke and control closely.

For readers who have never seen VisiCalc, Multiplan, Lotus 1-2-3, or similar programs, let us state briefly that a Spreadsheet program handles two dimensional tables of "cells" whose contents can be specified interactively by the user. Each cell holds either text (label) or a numeric value. This numeric value is determined by a character string interpreted as an algebraic expression, which can consist of a simple numerical constant or an expression involving operators, parentheses, functions and (most importantly) references to other cells. When a cell is changed, the values displayed in each cell of the table are updated. Global functions allow the user to reformat rows or columns, to define several windows, to edit the contents of a given cell, to duplicate a cell or a region, etc. It is also possible to save tables on disk and to retrieve them. Spreadsheet programs are very popular because they are easy to use in forecasting, financial planning and simple data analysis.

Our approach is to use the interactivity of the computer to present the many possibilities of a Spreadsheet program without giving long textual explanations. As much as possible, concepts are introduced by asking questions which will bring the student to experiment and discover the underlying principles. Interactive help sequences are offered if the student cannot master the current topic.

It is important for the student to discriminate easily between actions taken by the Spreadsheet program and those which are part of the pedagogical environment also stored in the computer. We facilitate this by splitting the screen into four windows. The top of the screen displays the Spreadsheet while the bottom has three windows: question and answer windows on the left; on the right, a window to display explanations, comments, suggestions and encouragement from the teaching modules (see figure 1). The program displays different cursors to show students whether they are supposed to manipulate the Spreadsheet or to type something in the answer port.

4.2 GETTING STARTED

The first lesson familiarizes the user with the basic notions of a Spreadsheet: cells can be reached by pressing the arrow keys; their contents can be changed; the current window can be moved to show cells outside the area currently displayed. The first task is reading values from a table.

Different prompts appear when a student fails to press RETURN or does not even attempt to press a key after a reasonable amount of time. In case the student cannot give the right answer, the program slowly goes through a graphic help sequence, blinking two rectangles on the screen (figure 2) and writing the

Figure 1   The spreadsheet is displayed at the top. The question window asks the student to enter a number in the box below where a cursor is blinking. The help window at the right displays a gentle prompt.

A1   (L) Population of swiss cities   5907W

	A	B	C	D	E	F
1	Population	1965	1970	1974	1975	1976
2	Zurich	438.50	426.90	404.30	395.80	387.90
3	Basel	214.90	213.40	201.00	195.60	191.50
4	Geneva	173.50	174.80	164.30	158.90	155.40
5	Bern	166.30	162.50	156.10	152.20	148.60
6	Lausanne	132.10	135.60	137.40	135.30	133.90
7	Winterthur	87.50	92.30	92.00	90.30	88.70
8	St. Gall	79.30	81.00	80.90	79.20	77.30
9						

What was the population of Winterthur, in thousands of inhabitants, in 1970?

and finaly we find the population of Winterthur in 1970.

There were 135.6   thousands of inhabitants

Figure 2   The learner's answer (135.6) is wrong. This figure shows a snapshot of a sequence which gave help finding a value in the table. The rectangles were part of an explanation in that sequence; they are not part of the Spreadsheet simulation.

A1   (L) Population of swiss cities   5907W

	A	B	C	D	E	F
1	Population	1965	1970	1974	1975	1976
2	Zurich	438.50	426.90	404.30	395.80	387.90
3	Basel	214.90	213.40	201.00	195.60	191.50
4	Geneva	173.50	174.80	164.30	158.90	155.40
5	Bern	166.30	162.50	156.10	152.20	148.60
6	Lausanne	132.10	135.60	137.40	135.30	133.90
7	Winterthur	87.50	92.30	92.00	90.30	88.70
8	St. Gall	79.30	81.00	80.90	79.20	77.30
9						

What was the population of Basel, in thousands of inhabitants, in 1976?

The keyboard of a computer has numbers on the top row.
Next time type
         1   instead of l
         .   instead of ,
         0   instead of o

There were 191,5o   thousands of inhabitants

Figure 3   Although the Spreadsheet program doesn't allow the use of letters for numbers, the user gets only a warning at this early stage.

value found at their intersection in the answer window. The exercise is then repeated using the same table with another randomly chosen year and city pair.

We also take this opportunity to remedy the frequently observed misuse of the keyboard to enter numerical values which comes from typewriters: the letters "l" and "O" are used instead of the digits "1" and "0". Spreadsheet programs are very unkind to such mistakes, but we give only gentle warnings (figure 3).

After a help sequence, the student must correctly work two consecutive exercises before continuing; otherwise, additional help sequences are offered. If there are still difficulties, the student is advised to seek help from a human teacher.

A second task shows that the screen displays only part of the spreadsheet. To do this, we "zoom out" until each cell is a thin line with the Spreadsheet cursor a rectangle around that line. The window is a larger rectangle and the user sees what happens when the cursor crosses the limits of the window.

The third task returns to normal dimensions and asks the user to move to a cell which lies outside the screen when the question is asked. If the student isn't successful, a help sequence does it for him and a new question is asked.

The fourth and fifth tasks consist in modifying a numeric value and a label, respectively, in a given cell. An example will show how to proceed and the student is asked to modify the content of a cell chosen at random. We check that the correct change is made at the right place. The last task of this lesson checks that the user can create a table.

4.3 INTRODUCING FORMULAS

The main task of lesson 2 is to introduce the concept of relationships among cells through the use of algebraic formulae. A much smaller table is used to focus attention on the third column which exhibits the dependencies (figure 4).

We change one of the numbers in the first two columns and we ask the user what else has changed. The user can indicate in many ways that something has changed in the third column. We strongly feel we must handle in natural language any of these forms of answer to this and other simple questions; the scheme outlined in 3.3 has proven to be very satisfactory.

The next task requires the student to write explicitly the formula for one cell to receive the average of two other cells and for another, their product. Note that we have not yet formally introduced the student to the to the syntax of algebraic expressions. We make this "omission" consciously because the syntax is that of common use and because the diagnostics of out Spreadsheet program are explicit and friendly enough to catch any mistakes.

4.4 MENU EXPLORATION

It is a challenge to guide the student through an already explicit menu. We decided to encourage the student to explore the different commands appearing on the screen, offering explanations along the route followed through the command tree (figure 5). Students are given suggestions about how to start. If nothing happens after a predetermined time, the program takes the initiative, completing an unfinished command or demonstrating one which has not yet

B2   (U) 86   6546W

	A	B	C	D	E	F
1	Value 1	Value 2	Result			
2	40.00	86.00	126.00			
3	8.00	2.00	10.00			
4						
5						
6						
7						
8						
9						

```
we changed a number.
What ELSE happened?
```

```
Very good!  You've got it!!!
```

```
another one has changed too
```

Figure 4 The user is prompted for a text answer to go in the answer window.

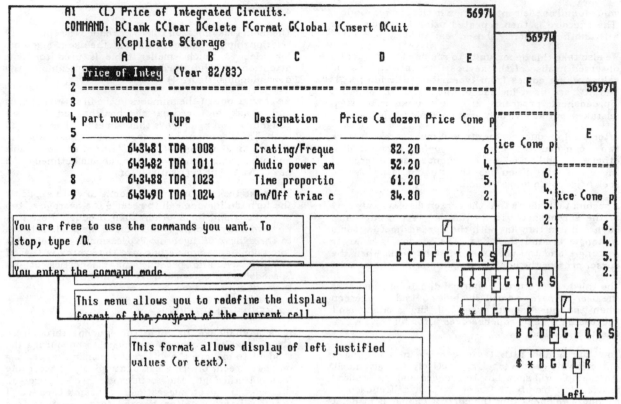

Figure 5   The screen pictures which are shown here will appear one at a time. Note the tree which builds up in the message window as the user tries the options.

been tried. If there is no visible effect on the screen, the student is told why and is given suggestions on what to do to achieve a particular goal.

4.5 OTHER MODULES

There are a few more modules which complete the project:
- An introduction to the micro-computer and its keyboard.
- A module to teach about duplication of cells and regions.
- Some quizzes about model building with the help of the Spreadsheet.

We plan to build similar modules to teach the basics of text processing, document preparation and electronic mail. Computer based material for teaching programming in Pascal or in Ada could be also integrated in our environment.

5. EVALUATION

About 30 students have gone through the modules described above. They spent between one and four hours on a purely voluntary basis, then they filled a questionnaire which expressed their desire to go on (94%), their satisfaction about the method (62%), the rhythm (62%) and the fact that they learned something about computing (69%). Their main complaint was about getting lost (69%) and not knowing what to do; this happened mostly with the menu exploration. We consider the evaluation very positive and an encouragement to use the material on a regular basis.

6. ACKNOWLEDGEMENTS

This project has been possible through the help of the National Swiss Fund for Scientific Research (grants 2.433-0.82 and 2.881-0.83). The gift of 4 IBM PC by IBM Switzerland and the loan of equipment by DEC are gratefully acknowledged.

A number of people have helped in the coding and the evaluation. They are X.Comtesse, A. Cosatti, M.Mornacchi-Pichon, D. Secco and J. Xydas to whom we are deeply indebted for their time and dedication.

7. REFERENCES.

[1] Nouveaux services informatiques pour l'Université de Genève, V. Zakharov, in Courrier Informatique, University of Geneva, April 84.

[2] Learning with Computers, A. Bork, Digital Press, 1981.

[3] Beginner's Guide for the UCSD Pascal System, K. Bowles, McGraw-Hill, 1980.

[4] Support Software for Computer Based Learning Materials, Bork, A., Franklin, S., et al. Technical Report. Information and Computer Sciences, University of California, Irvine, 1984.

[5] An SADT model for the production of computer based learning material. B. L. Kurz and A. Bork in Computers in Education, R. Lewis & D. Tagg editors, North-Holland, IFIP 1981.

COMPUTERS IN EDUCATION, K. Duncan and D. Harris (eds.)
Elsevier Science Publishers B.V. (North-Holland)
© IFIP, 1985

CAE - COMPUTER AIDED ENVIRONMENT
CASE STUDY: Programming system PMS that makes Pascal easy to learn!

Tomasz Müldner, Ivan Tomek

School of Computer Science, Acadia University
Wolfville, BOP 1X0 Nova Scotia, Canada

We describe an implementation of a Computer Aided Environment for
the teaching of Pascal that provides an integrated syntax-driven
full screen editor and an interpreter with windows into the
executing program's memory. Syntactic correctness of programs is
checked during editing. The interpreter features the highlighting
of the current instruction and constant updating of changing
values of variables during interpretation. This integrated
environment greatly simplifies the teaching and learning of
programming and allows the student to get a very concrete
understanding of programming concepts.

1. INTRODUCTION.

The question of how to teach
beginners programming is a vital one and
has been approached in many ways:
using CAI packages to provide lessons
and check students' knowledge by
presenting multiple choice questions; by
teaching a pseudocode with precise,
abstract semantic description; or by
introducing the student to a real
programming environment. Each of these
approaches has some virtues and some
drawbacks. CAI, as it has been mostly
used for teaching so far, has little, if
any, advantage over a book and a
scribbler.

Pseudo-code is, by definition, a
nonexisting language, generally non-
implemented and so the students do not
get any practice following abstract
(virtual) computations using a pen-
and-pencil technique. Using a real
programming environment tends to
complicate the initial stages of
learning since the technical issues of
editing, compiling, linking, and
executing obscure the programming
issues.

PMS is an attempt to combine and
automate the three methods, and provide
what we would like to call CAE -
Computer Aided Environment, rather then
Computer Aided Instruction. By CAE we
mean an integrated programming
environment that can be used for both
teaching and learning a programming
language: an instructor can take
advantage of this computer aid during
the classes (perhaps using large
monitors), while students can get
practice using the system in the privacy
of their terminal labs or at home. Thus

our proposal is:
**Use computers to teach
and learn programming.**

More precisely, a computer is used a
simulator of a programming environment
consisting of an editor, a compiler and
a run-time system. Thus the user is from
the very beginning exposed to a real
programming environment while the
complexity of the system is limited. The
latter goal is achieved by dividing
system into a number of separate
subsystems.

With this approach much of the textual
information can also be on-line and thus
the need for manuals is minimized.

Our teaching environment has two basic
components:

- a syntax driven editor,
that is an editor which "understands" a
given programming language, and provides
full static error checking simulataneou-
sly with editing;

- an interpreter
which interprets programs and provides
windows into the executing program's
memory so that the user can follow each
step of the program's flow.

One of our beliefs is that to
understand the behaviour of programs one
has to follow the steps of the
computation (that is to use operational
semantics). Of course, this does not
apply to non-Von Neumann languages,
like functional languages (for
example, LISP [2] or FP [3]) or descriptive languages (like PROLOG [4]); they
will require a different approach.

Our interpreter also provides full
dynamic (multi-level) error type
checking.

Another question in addition to how to teach programming is which programming language should be chosen to become the first language students learn. We like many others believe that Pascal currently is the best choice for a core language. In the past BASIC was frequently used but its various problems have resulted in a decline in its use even in high schools [1].

On the basis of these considerations we have decided to build a Pascal CAE, called PMS (Pascal Make Simple). Note, however, that PMS is just an example of what we mean by CAE.

To be able to show interactions between the editor, the compiler, and the run-time system, PMS provides an interpreted Pascal implementation. For pedagogical reasons we have decided to divide the full Pascal into a number of minilanguages, each of which concentrates on a specific issue, such as control structure, terminal and file input/output, data structures, and so on. The minilanguages are called: MINI (so many Pascal features that it forms a "mini-Pascal") NUMBERS, RECORDS, STRINGS, VARIANTS, etc., so that their names reflect their purpose.

The rest of this paper is structured as follows:
Section 2 provides a description of the PMS editor, section 3 describes the interpreter. Section 4 gives detailed examples of the operation of some of the minilanguages. In the conclusion we describe the current state of the implementation.

2. PMS EDITOR.

When a beginner is exposed to a real Pascal environment he may be quite confused - he has to learn how to use an editor to create a file, then how to compile a program, how to link it with libraries, and eventually how to execute it. UCSD [5] and TURBO [6] Pascal implementations make one step towards an integrated Pascal programming environment - they provide an editor consolidated with the compiler, and so the switching back and forth between the compiler and the edi- tor is easier.

PMS goes even further and provides a "syntax-driven" editor that translates the program as it is being typed. To our knowledge, this is a novel approach - the only similar system is a Cornell synthetiser, which, however, provides the user with "templates" of Pascal programming constructs rather than letting him type the program in the usual linear way.

In doing translation, the PMS editor converts lines of the program entered by the user into an intermediate code for future execution by the interpreter.

As an example, of the use of PMS, consider a beginner who wishes to write a program to display

"Hello, world!".

Typing MINI (the name of the first minilanguage that provides, among others features, file i/o) the user enters the first PMS minilanguage and finds himself in the editor environment. The screen of his terminal now is shown in Figure 1.

As you can see, the screen is divided into four sections:
- the top line is the **message line** used as an interface between PMS and the user (the message READY means that PMS is expecting a command);
- the left section of the screen is called the **program screen**, and contains the text of the program when the user is editing one, and during execution;
- the right section of the screen is called the **memory screen**, and will be used in the interpretation phase; it will display identifiers that are used in the program, their types and current values;
- the bottom section of the screen is called i/o **screen**, and will be used during interpretation to show the

```
ready
------------------------------------------------------------------
                                  *               MEMORY
                                  * Identifier Type      value
                                  *
                                  *
                                  *
                                  *
********************************************************************
```

Figure 1 : Initial setup of a screen.

program's output and echo what the user types in (note that this is the only response the user of a conventional Pascal system would see on the screen during the execution).

The editor is fully customizeable, the default setup is WordStar-like.

Suppose that our user was exposed to the WRITELN statement and knows that it outputs its argument values. He wants to test it and types:

WRITELN(Hello world)

PMS will change the display to the state shown in Figure 2.

The PMS editor recognized that a PROGRAM line required by Pascal is missing and displayed the message: PROGRAM expected.

The user can immediately correct this error by inserting the line:

PROGRAM test1;

in front of the current line.

As soon as he hits the Return key after typing the line, the part of the program that has been entered so far will be retranslated. In our example, the first line is correct, and so PMS will wait for the user's next command. If the user moves the cursor to the following line (containing the WRITELN statement) and hit the Return key, this line will be retranslated, and the user will get another error message explaining that apostrophes are required around the string constant. The user can get even more help at any time: typing an appropriate key (^J by default) will move him to the help subsystem, with brief explanations of PMS commands.

Once a complete program is entered PMS informs the user that the translation phase is terminated, and he or she can either start the second phase - interpretation, or if he or she wishes so, reedit the program.

It is obvious that a syntax-driven editor gives the user great advantages since he gets immediate (and continuous) help on whether his programs are syntactically correct. You may wonder why so few such editors have been developed so far? Perhaps the catch is that this technique slows down editing? Not to our knowledge: PMS is so fast that we have not been able to type fast enough that the computer (IBM PC, TI PC) could not catch up with translating. (By the way, if the user becomes bored with Pascal and wishes to write a letter, there is a toggle to turn translation off, so a syntax driven editor becomes a simple screen editor.)

3. PMS Interpreter.

The interpreter gets as input a translated and executable form of the Pascal program so that interpretation is quite fast (the speed, however, is not our concern at all, as the purpose of PMS is to show the flow of control and changes of variable values).

The PMS interpreter differs from other interpreters in that it provides specialized windows into the program's memory. One can also think of this component of PMS as an enhanced debugger. During interpretation the user can see not only the current state of all the variables changing during the execution but also the flow of control: the instruction which is currently being executed is displayed in a different color (inverse video on the monochrome monitor). This arrangement implies some limitations on the number of variables the user can declare in his program, but one should not forget that the main purpose of PMS is a system for teaching (and is thus aimed at beginners) and demonstration of concepts rather than development of large programs.

To demonstrate how the PMS interpreter works let us consider a simple fragment of a Pascal program in Figure 3 (on the next page).

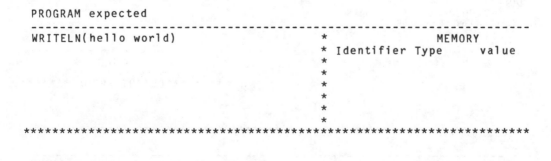

```
PROGRAM expected
----------------------------------------------------------------------
WRITELN(hello world)                    *              MEMORY
                                        * Identifier Type     value
                                        *
                                        *
                                        *
                                        *
                                        *
                                        *
*********************************************************************************


----------------------------------------------------------------------
```

Figure 2 : The state of the screen after the incorrect statement is entered.

```
HALT: File has not been assigned.
---------------------------------------------------------------------
program files;               *                MEMORY
var s:string[10];            * Identifier Type     value
    f :text;                 *
begin                        * s            STRING
  reset(f);                  * f            TEXT
  readln(f,s);               *
end.                         *
                             *
*********************************************************************
```

```
----------------------------------------------------------------------
```

Figure 3 : Pascal program to read from a file.

(In the black and white version of PMS, the highlighted current instruction is displayed in inverse video; in the color version it is displayed in a different color.)

As you can see from the error message at the top of the screen, the PMS interpreter helps the user can understand the cause of some run-time errors. Execution is aborted as in a real system and, additionally, the user is informed what is the cause of the abortion. Note that most existing Pascal implementations provide quite limited run-time error checking (have you ever spent a long time before discovering that your program is not executing, instead it has just died, for example because you tried to read beyond the end of file? PMS produces a run-time error for it.)

Let us mention two more of the many run-time error checks of PMS that are not supported by most existing systems:
- range of enumerated types is enforced; as in:

```
        var x:1..5;
     x:=2;
     x:=x+4;  { out of range }
```

- variants of records have limited access:

```
var R : Record
           Case b : Boolean of
           False : (x:Char);
           True  : (y:Char);
        End;
     R.b := True;
     R.x:= '?';  { not accessible !!! }
```

The PMS interpreter will regonize these errors and help the user correct them by producing appropriate messages at run time.

More examples of the PMS interpreter's actions are given in the following section.

4. Minilanguages.

This section gives a couple of examples of programs from various Pascal subsets implemented in PMS, here called **minilanguages.** It also shows some differences between individual PMS interpreters specialized in showing various aspects of Pascal constructs.

```
-------------------------------------------------------------
ready for execution
-------------------------------------------------------------
program arithmetic;          *                MEMORY
var r:real;                  * Identifier Type    value
begin                        *
  r:=0.001;                  *
  writeln(r+r:10:5);         *
  writeln(2*r:10:5);         *
end.                         *
                             *
                             *
                             * ********OUTPUT FORMAT*******
                             *
                             *
                             *
*********************************************************************
```

```
-------------------------------------------------------------
```

Figure 4 : A program to test accuracy of real arithmetic.

We have already seen some examples of minilanguage MINI (with terminal and file i/o operations). Let's therefore start this section with an example of a program from the NUMBERS minilanguage which presents various aspects of real arithmetic. The state of the screen just before the start of the execution is shown in Figure 4.

Two options are available to show that "computer" arithmetic differs from "theoretical" arithmetic. The two options are called High-Precision-Arithmetic and Low-Precision-Arithmetic. Running the above program under the first option (after executing the first two statements) the user will eventually get the following display shown in Figure 5.

The additional window (at the bottom of the memory region at the right) called the OUTPUT FORMAT shows the format of the output specified in the WRITELN statement: the value 0.00210 is displayed in a field of length 10, starting at position 3 (7 digits, left justified).

Running under the second option results in a distorted results:
0.00214, and 0.00210.
This shows the student that in computer arithmetic r+r does not necessarily equal 2*r (lack of space prevents from showing the PMS display).

Pascal's control structures are presented in the MINI minilanguage.

Every programmer probably remembers the hard time he initially had with nested loops! Consider the program given in Figure 6. It shows an intermediate state of execution of the loop. Stepping through successive stages of execution the user can get a good understanding of how a FOR statement works.

Other control statements handled by this minilanguage are conditional statements (IF), loops (REPEAT, WHILE, FOR), and selective choice (CASE).

```
-----------------------------------------------------------------
program arithmetic;          *          MEMORY
var r:real;                  * Identifier Type      value
begin                        *
 r:=0.001;                   * r         REAL  1.00000E-03
 writeln(r+r:10:7);          *
 writeln(2*r:10:7);          *
end.                         *
                             *
                             ***********OUTPUT FORMAT******
                             *   0.00200
                             *0987654321
                             *1
*****************************************************************
   0.00200
   0.00200
```

Figure 5 : Output produced by the program testing accuracy of real arithmetic.

```
-----------------------------------------------------------------
program test;                *          MEMORY
var i,j:integer;             * Identifier Type     Value
begin                        *
   for i:=1 to 5 do          * i         INTEGER    4
   begin                     * j         INTEGER    5
     for j:=i to 5 do        *
     write('X');             *
     writeln;                *
   end;                      *
end.                         *
                             *
                             *
*****************************************************************
XXXXX
XXXX
XXX
X
```

Figure 6: A program showing an execution of a FOR statement.

```
program arraytest;                 * f     10      11      12      13
type i=integer;                    * j              1
var f:array[1..4] of i; j:i;       *
begin                              *
    for j:=10 to 13 do             *
        f[j-9]:=j;                 *
  for j:=1 to 4 do                 *
    f[j]:=f[f[j]-9]+1;             *
end.                               *
                                   *
                                   *
                                   * f :  col = 1
**********************************************************************
```

Figure 7: A program showing operations on arrays.

Pascal data types are illustrated in a several minilanguages: ARRAYS, SETS, RECORDS, FILES, and VARIANTS; this division into several modules is due mainly to different graphical representations used to show these constructs.

Let us take a look at a program from the ARRAYS minilanguage (Figure 7).

This program is rather tricky but PMS graphics shows exactly what is going on: the diagram shows the screen reached after several steps of execution when the second loop is executed, and the first column of the array f is being processed (therefore you can see an additional window "f : col = 1".) The memory screen simultaneously shows the current value of the components of array f.

Lack of space prevents us from showing other examples, in particular, examples of the PROCEDURES minilanguage (which demonstrates procedures and functions including recursion, parameter passing, the dynamically changing scope, stacking of calls, and dynamic use of available memory space).

4. Conclusion.

It is our hope that PMS, as an example of a CAE will contribute to much faster learning of programming. There is a growing number of people who will learn programming (Pascal in particular) and so there is a great demand for better tools to make the learning process easier. We believe that PMS is a step in this direction, and our limited experience confirms that students find it very helpful.

One of the important advantages of PMS is that it can be introduced in the class (or even through a TV) and then the user can enjoy working with PMS on his own, repeating examples as many times as required, but always under the control of the system! PMS has so far been implemented on the IBM PC and TI PC (other implementations are under way).

References.

[1] The Recent Advance Placement Advanced Placement course description. Computer Science; College Entrance Examination Board, 1982.

[2] McCarthy, J. and others, LISP 1.5 Programmer's Manual. The MIT Press, Cambridge Mass. 1962.

[3] Backus, J. Can Programming be Liberated from the Von Neumann Style, CACM 21, 8 (August 1981).

[4] Clocksin, W. F. and Mellish, C.S., Programming in Prolog. Springer-Verlag 1981.

[5] Grant, C. W. and Butah, J. Introduction to the UCSD p-System. SYBEX 1982.

[6] TURBO Pascal Reference Manual. Borland International. 1983.

COMPUTERS IN EDUCATION, K. Duncan and D. Harris (eds.)
Elsevier Science Publishers B.V. (North-Holland)
© IFIP, 1985

THE COMPUTER-ASSISTED RESEARCH PAPER

Lynn Veach Sadler, Wendy Tibbetts Greene, and Emory W. Sadler

Methodist College, Fayetteville, North Carolina

A&T State University, Greensboro, North Carolina

"A Computerized Guide Through the Construction of the Research Paper," which is being developed for the IBM PC, teaches research writing as <u>process</u>. The audience is the college and high school student, who selects applicable disciplines (Education, Humanities, Sciences, Social Sciences) and branches (e.g., to access such on-line search facilities as "Dialogue" and "BRS After Dark"). The twelve sections are "Choosing and Narrowing the Topic," "Finding the Approach: Asking the <u>Right</u> Question," "Finding the Essential Sources," "Taking Notes," "Answering the Question: Drafting a Controlling Statement," "Outlining the Research Paper," "Writing in <u>Sections</u>," "Integrating Quotations and Paraphrases," "Arranging the <u>Whole</u>," "Preparing the Footnotes and Bibliography," "Becoming the Critic: Reviewing and Revising," and "Finalizing."

Teaching and writing the research paper have frequently been perceived as onerous tasks by teacher and student, respectively. With the assistance of Emory Sadler as programmer, Lynn Sadler and Wendy Greene are developing, out of their own classroom experience and as a complement to their program in computer-assisted composition, software that uses word processing to teach the art of research writing as a <u>process</u>. It eliminates much of the frustration students experience using the traditional methods when they encounter such problems as losing their note cards or finding that they have failed to record citations in full.

AUDIENCE AND NATURE

The program, called "A Computerized Guide Through the Construction of the Research Paper," is being developed for the IBM PC, with adaptations to other computers planned for the future. The audience is the college and high school student--both the novice and the adept or semi-adept who wants a systematized approach and an efficient method of mastering and retaining the sources used. The software is general-purpose in intent but allows the user to select what is individually applicable from the four basic categories of disciplines--Education, Humanities, Sciences, and Social Sciences--as, for example, in the section on basic research sources. It also has different tracks or branches for the student who has access to such on-line search facilities as "Dialogue" and "BRS After Dark" (the use of which will themselves serve to focus and narrow the topic) and the one whose library lacks on-line research capabilities.

DIVISIONS

"A Computerized Guide Through the Construction of the Research Paper" is divided into twelve sections that lead the student through the process of creating and constructing the pro-

duct. Those divisions, sketched below, with "Taking Notes" (Section Four) demonstrated, are "Choosing and Narrowing the Topic," "Finding the Approach: Asking the <u>Right</u> Question," "Finding the Essential Sources," "Taking Notes," "Answering the Question: Drafting a Controlling Statement," "Outlining the Research Paper," "Writing in <u>Sections</u>," "Integrating Quotations and Paraphrases," "Arranging the <u>Whole</u>," "Preparing the Footnotes and Bibliography," "Becoming the Critic: Reviewing and Revising," and "Finalizing." While the process of construction is emphasized, the more confident student can opt to omit some sections and tutorials and call up those that ask questions whose responses build the fabric and structure of the research paper.

THE STUDENT'S INITIATION

The program opens with a short, interactive tutorial on the nature of research writing-- comparing and contrasting it with composing in the traditional rhetorical modes, demonstrating the difference between true research writing and "scissors and pasting," cautioning that the latter often ends in plagiarizing, and stressing the importance of the objective style in research writing. The intent here is to build the student's confidence: "You are probably familiar with constructing the standard five-paragraph essay. Well, writing the research paper basically enlarges on that process and enables you to find out what knowledgeable people have thought about your topic. . . ."

"A Computerized Guide Through the Construction of the Research Paper" aids the student whose teacher has not provided a list of suggested subjects for the paper, the writer who is having difficulty choosing from such a list, and the writer who has a topic and is ready to begin preparing the research paper. The student is first asked to enter the letter of the appropriate category:

     A. I have the topic for my research paper.
     B. I have topics to choose from but need
         help selecting from the list.
     C. <u>Please</u> help me find a topic!

If the choice is <u>A</u> ("I have the topic for my
research paper."), the student is asked, "Do
you need to narrow your topic?" and is also
given the opportunity to test <u>whether</u> the topic
is narrow enough. If the student chooses not
to test for that narrowness, the computer cannot resist becoming slightly acidic: "All
right, but fair is fair. Don't blame me if
your teacher pans the whole paper because the
topic is too broad!"

If the choice is <u>B</u> ("I have topics to choose
from but need help selecting from the list."),
the computer suggests that "we" (the writer and
the computer in tandem) perform an interest-
level analysis of as many of the topics on the
list as necessary until the student is satisfied that the topic settled upon not only grips
him/her but that provocative lacunae exist in
his/her knowledge of that subject. The computer tells the student, "I won't let you waste
our time. You have to convince me that you are
really committed to this topic."

SECTION ONE: "CHOOSING AND NARROWING THE TOPIC"

If the student has no topic (Choice <u>C</u>, above),
the computer, after reassuring him/her that it
likes to work with open-minded people, branches to Section One, "Choosing and Narrowing the
Topic," and suggests that a proper way to begin
is by having the writer execute a series of
selections that progressively narrow in range.
For example, the student could, through a
series of choices, move from the <u>Social
Sciences</u> to <u>Psychology</u> to <u>Developmental Psy-
chology</u> to <u>Adolescent Psychology</u> to <u>Adolescent
Sexuality</u> to <u>Adolescent Sexual Fantasies</u> to
<u>Male Adolescent Sexual Fantasies about the
Mothers of Friends</u> (or <u>Female Adolescent
Sexual Fantasies about the Fathers of Friends</u>)
to . . . . At present, each of the four major
discipline categories (Education, Humanities,
Sciences, Social Sciences) yields at least
twenty (narrowed) subjects for a research paper. As in response to <u>B</u> above, the computer
inventories the interest and knowledge level
of the student in the topic chosen. When the
subject for the research paper is agreed upon,
the computer suggests:

          The next screen is going to be
     one of those <u>tabula rosae</u> your teach-
     ers are always talking about. Take
     the opportunity--this is the only time
     in the history of computers in this
     country (and perhaps the world) that
     a student has been allowed to have a
     blank screen!--to jot down everything
     you know or think you know about _____

_____ (the
chosen topic).[1]
          You can, by the way, use up
     as many screens as you want.
     Against my better judgment, I am
     also letting you skip this exercise
     if you prefer to.

SECTION TWO: "FINDING THE APPROACH: ASKING THE RIGHT QUESTION"

Section Two, "Finding the Approach: Asking
the Right Question," again reminds the writer
that there is an analogy between the research
paper and the accustomed rhetorical essay:
"You have written essays in many so-called
rhetorical modes (e.g., argumentation, narration, description, process, definition). You
can also take different <u>approaches</u> to the
material in your research paper. We have to
establish your approach before we proceed, and
I want you to be as committed to that approach
as to the topic itself." The computer then
asks questions designed to gauge the interest
level in a particular approach:

          Your topic is (Richard Wright's
     <u>Savage Holiday</u>).
     Do you want to
          1. find out everything there is to
              know about _____?
          2. prove, demonstrate, or conclude
              something about _____?
          3. convince your reader of something
              about _____?

Whatever choice is made by the student, the
computer briefly (and interactively) outlines
the differences among #1 (the investigative
report), #2 (the proposition or thesis paper),
and #3 (the persuasive proposal) and ascer-
tains that the writer has a firm sense of the
sub-<u>types</u> or sub-<u>genres</u> of research papers.
The computer also discusses the sophistication
level of each approach and emphasizes the
writer's self-involvement in #2 as contrasted
with the audience involvement of #3. It
finally leads the student to think through
and input the central/controlling question
posed by the topic and the approach chosen.

SECTION THREE: "FINDING THE ESSENTIAL SOURCES"

Section Three, "Finding the Essential Sources,"
surveys the basic research resources by
discipline (e.g., Education to sub-categories
such as Child Development or Vocational/
Technical Education or Special Education to
journals and indexes, as the <u>Current Index</u> to
<u>Journals in Education</u> and the ERIC series).
The individual student is routed on the basis
of the topic chosen and can request a printout
of the recommended starting points for research on that topic. The student who will
use on-line search techniques can omit this
section.

SECTION FOUR: "TAKING NOTES"

The section of "A Computerized Guide Through
the Construction of the Research Paper" called
"Taking Notes" directs the student to handle
the sources gathered in a <u>systematic</u> way. It
is presented below with broken lines used to
indicate screen changes.

Taking Notes

Now that you have books and articles that
appear pertinent to your central/controlling
question, you are ready to survey these sources
and take notes.

As much as anything else, this is a <u>problem-
avoiding</u> session. I am determined to prevent
your
    1. losing track of which source said
       what.
    2. being unable to find a title, an
       author's name, or a page number.
    3. forgetting the contribution of an
       individual source.

ADVICE: Learning to check your entry against
the text before moving on will save you problems and "professionalize" your efforts.

Let's begin with your books. <u>Arrange</u> <u>them</u> <u>in</u>
<u>the</u> <u>order</u> <u>in</u> <u>which</u> <u>you</u> <u>will</u> <u>consider</u> <u>them</u>, be-
ginning with the book that you suspect will be
<u>most</u> <u>important</u> to your research project, the
second most important, and so on. A perusal
of the table of contents and index will help.
If you cannot determine which books are likely
to be paramount, consult the <u>copyright</u> <u>date</u> (as
opposed to the date of publication, which may
represent a reprint) and consider the most recent first.

There were quite a few <u>tips</u> on that last screen.
Let's make sure you absorbed them. On the upcoming screens, enter the letter representing
the correct response.

The best order in which to consider book
sources is
    A. least to most important
    B. random
    C. most to least important.

If you cannot decide the relative importance
of your books, consult
    A. the copyright date
    B. the most recent publication date
    C. the author's date of birth.

To help determine the importance of a book,
look at
    A. the title page
    B. the index
    C. the table of contents and the index.

Good. We're ready to begin entering your data.
Go to the title page of your first book.
Enter the name of the author, using normal
order. In the case of multiple authorship,
input all of the authors, separated by commas
and in the order in which they appear on the
title page. If there are more than three
authors, use only the first, followed by the
Latin abbreviation for "and others," e.g.,
<u>Thomas</u> <u>B.</u> <u>Martin,</u> <u>et</u> <u>al.</u> Check your spelling
against the text. Press ENTER when you have
completed the entry.

Next, give the complete title of the book;
check your entry against the text; press ENTER
when you have finished.

Enter the publisher, the city of publication,
and the date of publication, using a colon (:),
followed by two spaces, after the city, as in
the example below.
    New York: G. P. Putnam, 1984
We'll talk about exceptions in the section on
footnoting and bibliography. Press ENTER when
you have checked the entry against your text.

Look at the table of contents. Find the
chapter(s) centrally relevant to your controlling question. Turn to the chapter(s) and list
the number, title, and page numbers.
    EXAMPLE: Chapter Nine, "Computers in
          Special Education," pp. 189-94.
Press ENTER when you have checked your entry.

Think of several key words to check in the index. If I were researching "Dogs in Mediaeval
Literature," I would try "Middle Ages,"
"literature, Mediaeval," "dogs," "canines,"
"animals, dogs" and perhaps some specific kinds
of dogs. Use your imagination and knowledge.
Cerberus is a famous Classical dog who might
well appear in Mediaeval literature, but Nana,
the nurse-dog in <u>Peter</u> <u>Pan</u>, obviously couldn't.
(I might kick your fingers off my input keys

if you made such a blunder!) Press ENTER when
you're ready to move on.

List each key word you find in the index, follow it with a comma, and then list the page
numbers provided. Use a separate line for
each key word.
      EXAMPLE: "literature, Mediaeval,"
                pp. 29-35, 45-51
                "animals, dogs," p. 114
Check your entries and press ENTER.

(The computer next instructs the student how to
request a printout of the entries made for each
book.)

With the printout of your entries before you,
concentrate on each book in turn. Skim the
pages you have entered, noting on your printout those that you need to reconsider carefully.
After that reconsideration, briefly (one-two
sentences) enter the book's point of view and/
or information about your topic or central
question. When you are satisfied that you
have mastered the data, press ENTER.

Besides entering a book's thesis or summarizing
the relevance to the central question, the
student can enter up to three direct quotations
and three paraphrases for each source.

Articles and non-book materials are approached
in the same way, with the order of consideration based on those most recently published.
A paraphrase of the thesis or a statement of
the relevance to the topic and up to three
quotations and three paraphrases are allowed
for each.

SECTION FIVE: "ANSWERING THE QUESTION:
                DRAFTING A CONTROLLING STATE-
                MENT"

By the time the student has taken notes on the
sources, he/she has an idea of what stand to
take on the central/controlling question and
knows how to make use of sources that disagree
as well as agree with that position. Through
a series of questions, the computer leads the
writer to formulate the controlling idea or
central statement of the research paper so as
to forecast the directions of that paper and
demonstrates how that aim would be phrased
differently for each of the three major approaches (the investigative report, the pro-
position/thesis paper, the persuasive proposal). To make sure that the process of
writing the research paper is reemphasized, the
computer, once the student has reentered and
honed the controlling statement, now provides a
tree diagram of the route from broad to nar-

rowed topic and from controlling question to
controlling statement. The student is thus
readied for the task of outlining the paper.

SECTION SIX: "OUTLINING THE PAPER"

"Outlining the Paper," Section Six, helps the
student break the thesis into the pieces that
will constitute the major sections of the
research paper. The computer reminds the
writer that each section, although made up of
a varying number of paragraphs, nonetheless
corresponds to the structure of the five-
paragraph essay; that is, the research paper
must have an introduction, a conclusion, and
at least three middle sections that constitute
the "body" or "meat and potatoes" of the
structure. It suggests that this body consider
the opposing sources first and then move to the
citations of the evidence and finally insists
that the writer go beyond the sources to express his/her own opinion and conclusions
about the controlling statement. Finally, the
section on outlining has the student call up
the source citations that have been entered in
Section Four ("Taking Notes") and have them
listed in the appropriate section of the outline to be expanded and integrated later.

SECTION SEVEN: "WRITING IN SECTIONS"

The student can call up and work on any section, but the computer indicates that the
Introduction and the first and second sections
of the Body (the opposing sources and the
citation of the evidence, respectively) are
the most logical starting points. Indeed, it
recommends doing a brief introduction that can
be refined later and going on to the matter
of the sources, which have already been allocated to the appropriate portions of the
structure in the section on outlining.

Aside from suggesting that a logical procedure
is Introduction to Presentation of the Opposition to Citation of the Evidence, the computer
helps the writer to decide on the most appropriate method of developing the remaining
sections. Depending on the topic chosen, for
example, the writer may need to follow a time
sequence, present events, use a chronological
progression, or prove by logic.

SECTION EIGHT: "INTEGRATING QUOTATIONS AND
                PARAPHRASES"

When the student is ready to work on the body
sections related to sources, the computer
provides an interactive tutorial on quotations
that stresses the importance of embedding
them contexually and teaches the summary of
the content of a quotation in different words,
the indirect use of a complete quotation, the
use of partial quotations, the direct use of
complete quotations with interpolations, the
use of a quotation already cited in the
sources, and the use of ellipsis. The student
can avoid this section after having gone

through it once or can return to it as often
as is desired.

SECTION NINE: "ARRANGING THE WHOLE"

For the first time, in Section Nine, the student gets to see--arrayed as part of the
whole--the sections that have been developed
individually. The first draft suddenly appears;
and the writer, with the aid of the computer,
takes inventory to see that all of the parts
are accounted for, tests for the kind of
development employed in each section, and is
tutored (as the need arises) in the art of
moving paragraphs or sections around.

SECTION TEN: "NOTES AND BIBLIOGRAPHY"

The computer assures the writer that, given
the new technology, this section is now the
easiest part of preparing the research paper
and talks briefly about the citational rap-
prochement of the disciplines precisely because of the increasing use of computers.
While the program teaches a standard form for
footnotes (in parentheses in the text of the
paper) and bibliography, it allows the student
to branch to the specific requirements of his/
her own discipline if necessary and teaches,
interactively, the differences among "Bibliography," "Annotated Bibliography," and "A List
of Sources Cited." Footnote and bibliographical
entries are drawn from the section on "Taking
Notes" such that the student does not have to
re-enter the information but adjusts the pagination, chooses between footnote and bibliographical form, and indicates whether, in the
case of the footnote, the citation must be in
full.

SECTION ELEVEN: "CRITICAL REVIEW AND REVISING"

The computer tells the writer that even the
beauty of print without smudges and strike-
overs--the professional look of the computer-
assisted research paper--cannot make up for
grammar and spelling infelicities. It now
exacts that the writer become critic-reader
and go through the draft again and again, each
time examining the paper from another specific
aspect and enjoying the ease of revision, which
is treated as an integral element of the process of composing the research paper. It
urges the use of programs that assess spelling,
grammar, and style.

SECTION TWELVE: "FINALIZING"

When the computer is satisfied that the writer
has gone through the paper at least three times,
it informs him/her of entitlement to a title;
helps to prepare the title page; and indicates
how an outline (if required) can be accessed
from Section Six and how the pagination, heading, and margins can be set as specified by
the instructor. Ultimately, it congratulates
the student's success with the research paper,
urges that a copy be printed for the writer

as well as the teacher, and hopes that the
student will now request a printout of what
he/she knew about the subject originally to be
compared with the knowledge found in the
finished product.

----

[1]The computer continues: "I'm going to
store this information in my memory and not let
you have access to it until the final, beauti-
ful copy of your paper has sped from my printer. Then you can print out this information
dump and compare it with how much you know
about _____ (the chosen topic)
after our sessions together."

COMPUTERS IN EDUCATION, K. Duncan and D. Harris (eds.)
Elsevier Science Publishers B.V. (North-Holland)
© IFIP, 1985

A FIRST STEP IN COMPUTER-BASED LEARNING OF MOLECULAR EMBRYOLOGY AT THE UNIVERSITY AND FIRST ACHIEVEMENTS

Jacques Fiszer, Nicole Bernard-Daugeras, Colette Favard-Séréno and Michel Lauthier

OPE-Biologie - CNEAO
Université Paris 7 - Université Paris 6
2, place Jussieu
75251 PARIS Cedex 05, France

A new set of Biology computer-based pedagogical materials is worked out, built up on a great number of small-size units, which are autonomous and can be interlinked. Their concatenation is, under appropriate circumstances, to be left to each student's initiative. The pedagogical materials deal with some aspects of gametogenesis, in terms of Molecular Biology, and their consequences on embryonic development. These facts and concepts are not easily integrated by students in their knowledge of embryogenesis. The main purpose of the new pedagogical products is to achieve such an integration. With this design, a group of three units is achieved for a first exploration of specific features of chromosomes during gametogenesis: characterization – chemical constitution – biosynthetic activity, of these chromosomes.

1. INTRODUCTION

The OPE-Biology project has been developed since the end of 1968 (OPE= *Ordinateur pour l'Enseignement*, i.e.: Computer for Education).

The OPE-Biology research is devoted to study of specific didactic problems concerning Biology, at the University, and to the contribution of computers to Biology education. More particularly have been defined and investigated some pedagogical possibilities of computer use in the field of Fundamental Biology, especially training in *logical reasoning* (deductive as well as inductive reasoning) and in *experimental methodology*.

This research, initiated in 1969-1970, resulted in an important series of computer-based dialogues, dealing with experimental analysis of main embryogenetic processes (3-4-5-13-14).

These pedagogical materials have been running through a specific CAI system: the OPE system (1).

The different OPE-Biology computer-based dialogues were practised by over 8000 students, coming from different Universities.

In 1982, the research took a new step forward into a new direction, on the ground of quite a new pedagogical procedure.

2. A NEW PEDAGOGICAL PROCEDURE

A previous paper gives full description of the design, structure and detailed particulars of our new pedagogical procedure (15). The main features of this procedure are as follows.

. The whole set of new pedagogical materials is built up on a great number of small-size elements, at present denominated *units*, which are autonomous or semi-autonomous and which can be interlinked in a variety of ways. During a two hour session, for example, a student will be in a position to practise at least 3 or 4 units, at most about 12 units among all existing units.

. The concatenation of different units is, to a large extent, to be left to each student's initiative, or it can be brought about by the student's specific needs, difficulties, errors, and so on.

. The different concatenation possibilities are regulated through a system of indicator elements, acting as some kind of multiple-pin connecting plugs, or *connectors*, respectively located at the entry point (*inlet*, or *input*) of each unit and at its end (*output*).

. An output connector contains various sorts of codified marks, indicators, parameters and counter values, giving specific information about the work which was accomplished by the student while practising the unit, about the objectives which were attained.

An inlet connector contains, among others, information about requisite conditions which should be fulfilled prior to the practice of the unit.

. At the completion of a given unit, the student has free access to any other unit which can be linked up, i.e. any unit whose inlet connector matches the output connectors of units which were previously practised by the student.

. Some units, closely related to each other, may constitute a definite group, a sort of *module*, possessing its own characteristic input and output connectors. But if a student does not want to work throughout the whole group of units, he is free to practise only one or a few of them - provided the relevant conditions are satisfied.

. When a student decides to practise a new unit, or a new group of units, a correct conformity between previous output connectors and the new inlet connector allows the dialogue to begin straight away. If such a conformity does not exist, the student may have to pass an appropriate test, in order to estimate whether he is able to accomplish a profitable work in the chosen unit or group of units. As a matter of fact, there is no obligation whatsoever, for any student, to practise all units allowing to fulfill the prerequisite conditions prior the entrance into a new unit or group of units. The student is admitted into the unit, or into the group, if he had acquired the appropriate knowledge through his regular lectures, tutorials, practical work - and this is what the mentioned test is for. On the other hand, in the course of a unit, if a student labours along, encounters difficulties he is not able to overcome, the dialogue may be switched on to another unit, or group, in order to study the proper knowledge, facts, concepts, methods.

. Such a procedure should ensure the best adaptation to each individual student, according to his knowledge, his wishes, his needs.

For a given subject matter, the student-computer dialogue may commence, at will, with any one out of all available units or groups of units, under proper conditions. And, through the successive units he is selecting, each student may direct his attention and his efforts to the topics he is most concerned in. No student is constrained to spend his time on some point, should it be an important point, if he has already got a thorough knowledge of it, or if his concerns at that moment are different.

Besides, on a given subject matter,

the contents of different courses often show a great diversity between different Universities, different teaching Departments and subdivisions. With this new procedure, each student will be in a position, for instance, to practise, or not, some definite unit, dealing with some definite fact, aspect, concept, technique, according as the courses he had taken went, or not, into deep details.

. In addition, a few key features of OPE-Biology pedagogical products and the way they are used should be briefly reminded.

These dialogues run in plain French language and can be practised by any French-speaking Biology student. The OPE system, owing to its various characteristics, functions, resources, did turn out to be rather an elaborate and refined system of analysis and treatment of student answers, messages, requests, paths. So that could be performed a *student-computer dialogue* of a fairly good standard, so long as no attempt is made to simulate a whole conversation between actual human beings. At the terminal, each student is, to a large extent, in a position to express himself as he wishes, as he feels it necessary, using the words and expressions he has in mind, and the sorts of denominations and formulations he is accustomed to or which he was taught - these, in Biology, often show an important variability.

Before practising the OPE Biology dialogues, the students must already be acquainted with the subject matter - whatever their regular courses and handbooks may be.

To each terminal is connected a slide projector, operated by the computer. At any time in the course of the dialogue, the student may call back any of previously projected slides. And, at any moment, he may look up a word or an expression in an automatic dictionary.

All students'answers, messages, requests, paths, are automatically recorded and sorted, with various specifications, and printed on statistical documents which can be delivered by the computer after each session.

3. SUBJECT MATTER AND DIDACTIC PROBLEMS
3.1. General outlines

Like all former OPE Biology dialogues, the new computer-based pedagogical materials are designed for University students, and more particularly for first and second year Medical and Biology students. For these students, an important part of teaching is devoted to Biology of Reproduction and embryonic Development. The study of embryonic Development (animal, human) includes not only a

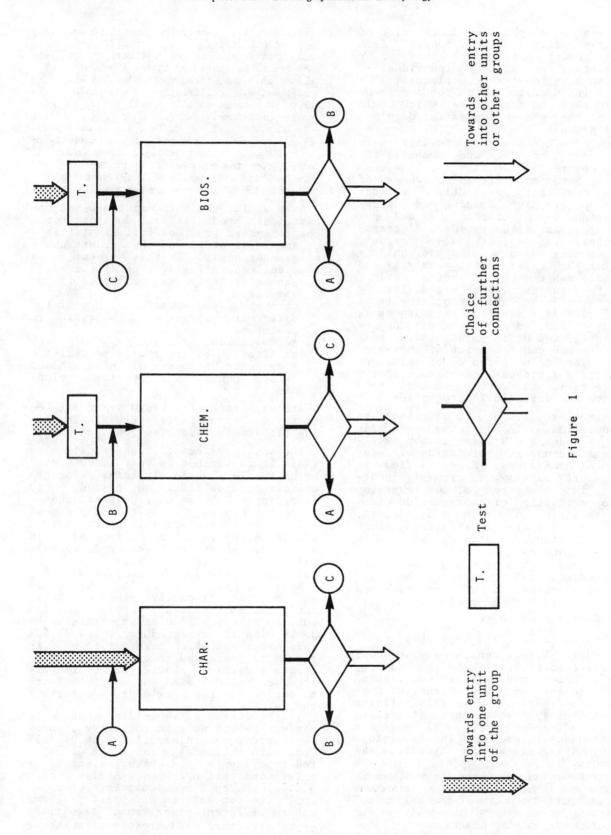

Figure 1

step-by-step morphologic description of successive stages of development - from fertilized egg until late embryonic or larval stage and new born individual - but also an extensive experimental analysis, intended to search for and identify factors and mechanisms which could explain the whole sequential developmental process.

Often enough, students readily make every effort to learn and memorize the whole description part, which means: learning and memorizing sequences of stages and their respective designations, progressive arising and differentiation of diverse tissues and organs, relevant illustrations, diagrams, with their legends, symbols, arrows, conventional colours, and so on.

As for the experimental analysis and the whole range of intellectual activities it requires, which are definitely not confined to just memorizing facts, data, methods, results, this aspect is not easily and, in any case, not completely integrated by the students in their knowledge and comprehension of embryogenesis. The main purpose of previous OPE Biology dialogues, mentioned above, is precisely to secure such a progressive and methodical integration.

A third level is now to be taken into consideration. It concerns *Molecular Biology* and the new bases it may provide for a deeper interpretation of developmental mechanisms. Students find it particularly uneasy to properly incorporate, into their general comprehension and representation of embryonic development, this kind of facts and concepts, which are of quite a different nature and which involve studies at quite different scales.

The general goal of the new pedagogical products is to attain the best possible integration of the mentioned three aspects of Embryology:

descriptive - experimental - molecular.

3.2. Main themes and purposes

Molecular Biology denotes a vast scope of current scientific research, the results of which may procure new lights, in particular, on embryogenetic processes (6-8-9-10-11-18). This definite area of Biology, sometimes referred to as *Molecular Embryology*, is more and more frequently present in Embryology courses as well as in treatises and handbooks.

The first part of an embryonic development, triggered off by fertilization, was beforehand prepared, inside the oocyte (mother cell of the ovum) by an intensive synthetic activity of its genome (set of genetic factors existing in a cell nucleus), during an important period of gametogenesis, namely the *growth phase*. This synthetic activity results in different macromolecules which, for the most part, accumulate and are to be stored up inside the ovum.

Later on, the stored macromolecules are to be progressively utilized by the developing embryo, in accordance with a well scheduled metabolic programme.

In a male organism, during the *growth phase* of gametogenesis, the biosynthetic activity of spermatocytes (mother cells of spermatozoa) is also, for the main part, a preparation for events which will occur later on: specific differentiation of spermatozoa and fertilization.

As a whole, the new computer-based pedagogical products are designed for a comprehensive study of full signification and implications of the growth phase of gametogenesis. In this respect, we have defined following general themes:
. genome activity in mother cells of gametes;
. chronology and precise nature of the different sorts of biosynthetic processes;
. accumulation, storage and ulterior utilization of the stored products;
. programmed sequence of biosyntheses in the course of embryonic development.

And each student should eventually come to a comprehensive synthesis involving all studied processes and concepts.

The whole system of pedagogical materials is to include a very large number of units. This obviously means pedagogical elaboration for a long period. But, according to the main principles underlying the system, a unit or a group of units can be brought into operation and available for students as soon as it is achieved, as there is no need to wait until other units, to which it is to be connected later on, are completed.

Besides, it is out of the question to work out an exhaustive study of every fact, datum, concept, involved in the subject matter. The ones which are to be dealt with in our computer-based dialogues are those which turn out to be difficult to learn and to completely understand, and which should be thoroughly acquired and mastered as a prerequisite to get to further knowledge, to further concepts.

In the course of these dialogues, each student has to work in an active manner - observe, reason, conclude by himself (but with guidance) - carry out simulated experiments - conceive, select, formulate and test hypotheses - draw main Biology concepts and manipulate them - apply the concepts to different problems and to different experimental situations - re-structure and re-organize these concepts and incorporate them in his knowledge. No student is asked to learn and memorize any experimental demonstration: he has to undertake the demonstration by himself. The dialogues, which do not supersede any other teaching activity, are chiefly meant to stimulate each student's reflection activity, and to contribute to his comprehension, mastery, modelling of main biological concepts and mechanisms.

All these different circumstances always require a thorough, deep and very long analysis of the subject matter.

4. FIRST ACHIEVEMENTS

4.1. Definition and specifications

Owing to the general principles of the whole pedagogical procedure, actual realization of computer-based materials could have started by almost any theme, any topic, among those which are to be treated. By analysing the subject matter, we considered that, when the entire system of interconnected units is available, most students, whatever the themes they began to work at may be, are very likely to come, soon or later, to a specific theme which, in a way, appears like a sort of cross-roads; and this is the theme we decided to start with. It concerns chromosomes as they can be observed during some time in the course of the gametogenesis process. On account of their very particular aspect during that time, closely related to the way they are functioning, they are currently referred to as *lampbrush chromosomes* (2-7-17).

A group of three units is now achieved for a first exploration of some major features of lampbrush chromosomes.

Figure 1 is a diagrammatic representation of this group of three units, respectively dealing with *characterization* (CHAR.), *chemical constitution* (CHEM.) and *biosynthetic activity* (BIOS.) of lampbrush chromosomes, and shows the way this group can be utilized.

There is no prerequisite of entrance into this group of units - apart from the general rule that students *must* have already studied the subject matter. But there is some reservation.

If a student chooses to begin with the CHAR. unit, he may do so. But if the first chosen unit is either of the two others, the student has to pass a preliminary test (T.), a short one, in order to make sure that his knowledge of Meiosis, in particular, is adequate (concerning one specific aspect or consequence of meiotic process); failing which he would not be able to proceed successful-

ly in the unit, and he is then advised to learn carefully the subject, Meiosis, before practising this unit, or to try some other unit.

The preliminary test *is not* in operation, and the dialogue in the unit begins immediately, for a student who already completed any other unit of the group (working throughout the CHAR. unit, for example, clears up the mentioned critical points concerning Meiosis, so that, in this case, the test is useless).

When elaborating such a group of units, once we agree as to the outlines of each unit and its chief aims, we draw up, for each unit, a list of a limited number of precise pedagogical objectives, in accordance with the general purposes. Then, we define the methods and means which should be the more appropriate to reach the different objectives. Thereafter begins the actual work of realizing the pedagogical materials, from writing and drawing till coding and implementing.

4.2. Units on lampbrush chromosomes

4.2.1. *Characterization unit*

At the completion of this unit, the student will be able to:

. unambiguously locate lampbrush chromosomes in the sole type of cells in which they can be observed;

. determine and delimit the exact period during which such an observation is possible;

. given a pair of lampbrush chromosomes, specify the number of chromatids actually present in each chromosome (chromatids are sister strands issuing from splitting of a chromosome at the beginning of a cell division process);

. get a correct notion of the overall size of lampbrush chromosomes and evaluate the dimensions of some of their constituent parts.

These objectives are to be attained through close observation of various cells, nuclei and chromosomes shown on projected slides (photographs taken at different magnification power, schematic drawings, and so on) - logical reasoning - measurement - calculation.

4.2.2. *Chemical constitution unit*

In this unit, each student is in a position to search for, identify and precisely locate the chemical constituents of a lampbrush chromosome.

This is chiefly done by means of simulated biochemical experiments, performed by the student in his own way, with the use of specific enzymes. Each student has to pay close attention to the methodological principles underlying the experiments he carries out.

4.2.3. *Biosynthetic activity unit*

At the completion of this unit, which
is a first approach to some basic aspects of gene activity in lampbrush
chromosomes, the student will be able to
do the following:

. determine, among the different macromolecules
which are present in a chromosome, which kind
of macromolecules are actually being synthesized in lampbrush chromosomes, and which ones are
not;

. find out which configuration of the chromosomal strand is necessarily correlated to biosynthetic activity;

. recognize, in lampbrush chromosomes, the precise structural elements which are the revealing outcomes of biosynthetic activity;

. specify the kind of enzyme which is involved
in the biosynthetic process;

. determine the exact direction of the enzyme-
controlled synthetic process alongside the
chromosomal strand, by inferring it from the
ordered arrangement of definite structural
elements;

. determine the proper origin of proteins which
combine with the macromolecules being synthesized;

. state what happens next to newly manufactured
macromolecules, and what happens to the chromosomal strand when the whole biosynthetic process is over.

To attain these objectives, the student has not only to make observations,
but mainly to carry out various experiments and to carefully analyse and interpret experimental results.

Among other problems, one pedagogical
problem we have to cope with lies in the
fact that many a student has a propensi-
ty to jump to conclusions, which he is
not yet logically entitled to infer from
the information in his possession.

A brief example, taken out of the *biosynthetic activity unit*, is schematically represented in Figure 2, by a simplified and abridged flowchart. In this
part of the dialogue, the point in question is whether a definite kind of ma-
cromolecule, usually designated by the
symbol RNA, is being synthesized in
lampbrush chromosomes and, if so, where
this is done, precisely. For such a purpose, an appropriate technique is *auto-
radiography*.

Radioactive chemicals, acting as *precursors*,
may be utilized by a living cell and incorporated into macromolecules which are being synthesized by the cell. The high specificity of some precursors makes it possible to identify and
locate precisely the biosynthetic process inside the cell, by means of photographic detection
of radioactivity.

In an earlier part of the dialogue,
the student had to choose the specific
radioactive precursor which should be a-
dequate to the case. This experimental
search must be carried out by degrees.

First, slide No. 3 (V3) shows autoradiographic results, and the student has
to decide whether they actually reveal
any RNA synthesis (question No. 9: Q9),
which is the case. If there were none,
there would be no need to continue that
search any further. Students making mistakes, or asking for help, are given some clues, which may guide their observation and reflection activity.

But these results, obtained with the
use of a light microscope, do not allow
anyone to tell which parts of the lampbrush chromosomes are actually radioactive, thus signalling synthetic activities. Therefore comes a second degree,
at a different scale. Slide No. 4 (V 4)
shows more detailed autoradiographic documents, obtained with the use of an e-
lectron microscope this time. And the
student has to determine (question Q 10)
which particular region of the chromosome is the seat of RNA synthesis. Such
particular regions are usually called
loops. The flowchart represents various
pathways, referring to students who
would make different kinds of errors,
confusions, oversights, or who would unduly jump to inappropriate conclusions.
According to the case, students are given further information, basic keys for
methodical observation and logical reasoning, more detailed questions, and are
shown other types of documents, illustrations, schematic and interpretative
drawings (V 5,... V 8).

A third degree is still necessary.
Other documents (V 9) present a limited portion of one loop of a lampbrush
chromosome. By analysing these documents, the student should be able to
specify that radioactivity, therefore
RNA synthesis, is connected with the a-
xial strand of the loop as well as with
typical slender filaments, namely *fibrillae* (this is the purpose of question
Q 11, the flowchart of which *is not* represented herewith).

Later on, further necessary experiments, including control experiments,
are performed, with the use of inhibiting substances (chosen by the student
himself) which can stop specifically one
definite kind of biosynthesis and not
others. At the completion of this gradual, methodical analysis, the student,
from now on, *and from now on only*,
should be in a position to draw definite
and reliable conclusions, and to designate indisputably *fibrillae* as outcomes
of RNA synthesis in progress.

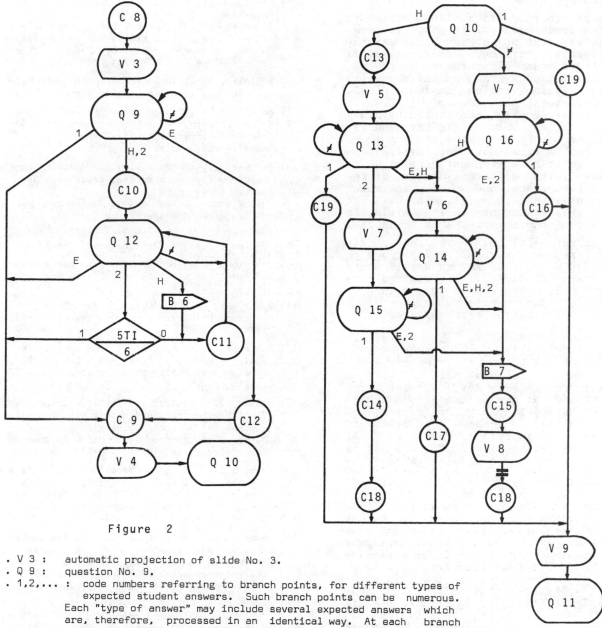

Figure 2

. V 3 :   automatic projection of slide No. 3.
. Q 9 :   question No. 9.
. 1,2,... : code numbers referring to branch points, for different types of
            expected student answers. Such branch points can be numerous.
            Each "type of answer" may include several expected answers which
            are, therefore, processed in an identical way. At each   branch
            point, the student is given an appropriate comment,   even when
            this is not separately mentioned in the flowchart.
. ≠   :   branch point for other types of answers as well as for unexpected
            answers.
. C 8, C 9,...: specific treatments, comments, and so on.
. B 6 :   sixth binary path indicator. When an indicator is set, its value
            is 1; otherwise, its value is 0.
. 5TI/6: fifth test of path indicators. In this particular case, the test
            is about just one indicator, which is path indicator No. 6.
. A double bar across the flow line denotes a pause. The dialogue will
            proceed when the student decides so.

5. PROSPECTS

Among other units in view, covering all mentioned general themes, are several units relating to lampbrush chromosomes again, for much deeper analysis of all different biosynthetic processes. Also is planned a group of units dealing with a distinct region inside the cell nucleus, namely the *nucleolus*, which is the seat of highly important biosynthetic activities, not sufficiently understood and mastered by many students.

Besides, several sorts of *utility units* are to be worked out, dealing, for example, with different types of methods, techniques, and so on, and which can be utilized at will, in case of need, by any student while working in any part of the entire system of units.

Different units may have to be modified later on, amended, brought up to date, on account of future developments of research in Biology. The limited size of each unit should make it possible to bring about any necessary change in it within a reasonable period of time.

The new achievements, as well as all previous OPE-Biology computer-based dialogues, should be in operation by means of the new French national CAI system (12-16) specifically developed for pedagogical use at the instance of A.D.I. (French National Agency for Informatics) and which is to embody most of typical features, functions, resources of former OPE system, in addition to a great deal of improvements and innovations.

REFERENCES

(1) Adam, F., Jacoud, R., Jacques, M., Kessis, J.J., Pelletereau, J.J., Penné, J., Rambaut, J.P. and Toulouse, J.P., A current CAI project: the O.P.E. system, in *Information Processing 74* (North-Holland, Amsterdam, 1974), 875-879.

(2) Alberts, B., Bray, D., Lewis, J., Raff, M., Roberts, K. and Watson, J.C., *Molecular Biology of the Cell* (Garland, New York, 1983).

(3) Anxolabéhère, D., Daugeras, N., Favard-Séréno, C., Fiszer, J., Lauthier, M. and Périquet, G., Entraînement au raisonnement logique et à une méthodologie expérimentale par l'emploi de l'ordinateur dans l'enseignement des Sciences biologiques, in Lecarme, O. and Lewis, R. (eds.), *Computers in Education* (North-Holland/American Elsevier, Amsterdam/New York, 1975), 643-647.

(4) Anxolabéhère, D., Bernard-Daugeras, N., Favard-Séréno, C., Fiszer, J., Lauthier, M. and Périquet, G., A contribution of the computer to Biology education at the University, *European Journal of Science Education*, vol. 2, No. 4 (1980), 377-394.

(5) Anxolabéhère, D., Bernard-Daugeras, N., Favard-Séréno, C., Fiszer, J., Lauthier, M. and Périquet, G., The OPE Biology educational project: current trends and new developments, *European Journal of Science Education*, vol. 6, No. 4 (1984), 349-360.

(6) Balinsky, B.I., *An Introduction to Embryology*, 5th ed. (Saunders, Philadelphia, 1981).

(7) Berkaloff, A., Bourguet, J., Favard, P. and N. and Lacroix, J.C., *Biologie et Physiologie cellulaires*, vol. IV: *Chromosomes* (Hermann, Paris, 1981).

(8) Brachet, J., *Introduction to Molecular Embryology* (Springer Verlag, Heidelberg/New York, 1974).
In French: *Introduction à l'Embryologie moléculaire* (Masson, Paris, 1974).

(9) Browder, L.W., *Developmental Biology*, 2nd edition (Saunders, Philadelphia, 1984).

(10) Davidson, E.H., *Gene activity in early Development*, 2nd ed. (Academic Press, New York, 1976).

(11) Denis, H., *Précis d'Embryologie moléculaire* (Presses Universitaires de France, Paris, 1974).

(12) Dubreuil, F., Projet DIANE: conception d'un dialogue sous l'éditeur "FORME LANGAGIERE", *Enseignement Public et Informatique*, No. 33 (1984), 74-95.

(13) Fiszer, J., Possibilités, rôle, limites de l'utilisation de l'ordinateur dans l'enseignement des Sciences biologiques, in *Problems of Programmed Instruction 73* (Moscow University Press, 1973), 113-123.

(14) Fiszer, J., Quelques problèmes relatifs à l'emploi de l'ordinateur dans l'enseignement de la Biologie à l'Université, in *Problems of Programmed Instruction 79* (Moscow University Press, 1979), 54-68.

(15) Fiszer, J., Bernard-Daugeras, N., Favard-Séréno, C. and Lauthier, M., Une autre conception du didacticiel en Biologie: unités interconnectables, *Enseignement Public et Informatique*, No. 35 (1984), 75-84.

(16) Landry, P., DIANE, *Enseignement Public et Informatique*, numéro spécial: "Pour une introduction aux langages d'auteur" (1983), 98-119.

(17) MacGregor, H.C., Recent developments in the study of lampbrush chromosomes, *Heredity*, vol. 44, part 1 (1980), 3-35.

(18) Malacinski, G.M. and Klein, W.H. (eds.), *Molecular aspects of early Development* (Plenum Press, New York, 1983).

COMPUTERS IN EDUCATION, K. Duncan and D. Harris (eds.)
Elsevier Science Publishers B.V. (North-Holland)
© IFIP, 1985

IMPROVING BASIC SKILLS IN ENGLISH WITH CAI TECHNIQUES

Enrico Borello* and Mario Italiani**

*University of Turin, Italy
**University of Milan, Italy

Work in the field of CAI was begun at the University of Turin in 1978 with the aim of testing the didactic effectiveness of these techniques in applied linguistics.

It is in the area of error diagnosis and presentation of the learning materials where CAI is very useful and where the computer's full potential is exploited. This paper describes some years of experience with CAI applied to teaching English to adults with a course designed and tested at the University of Turin.

1 INTRODUCTION

During the past decade the manner in which computers have been used to enhance learning in many subjects has undergone important transformations.

As Bell says /2/ in a few years CAI has been greatly extended into new areas and now students can communicate with computers in a flexible manner while early CAI programs were very rigid in their control of students.

Eventhough the present CAI systems still exercise significant control over students and provide for a somewhat limited variety of responses, they do give students considerably greater control over the learning environment than was permitted by the early attempts.

This fact has determined transformations in didactics and, as a result of this, also the role of teachers is changing remarkably.

This is true even more so if we think of the humanities, since the majority of the existing structures in many subjects must be modified to meet the potentialities of computers.

The introduction of computers in teaching has led to diversified uses, among which modelling and simulation and data banks. Modelling and simulation are commonly applied to scientific subjects such as chemistry, phisics, mathematics, while data banks are mainly used in medicine, economics: so, in these years a lot of tested materials have became available and students can learn many scientific subjects through CAI programs.

The case of the humanities is quite different because initial experiments were concerned with quantitative subjects (e.g. statistics for linguists) and experimental works commenced very late in the teaching of art subjects (see Allen /1/). However also in the humanities some projects have been planned and one area which seems to hold great interest is that of foreign language teaching. Computers are principally used to present learning materials, such as spelling drills and grammatical problems, which give students the opportunity for response. In this form of interaction, the computer simulates much of the behaviour of the skilled teacher and may add some qualities which even the skilled teacher does not possess, e.g. virtually unlimited memory of the past performances by individual students and a store of instructional alternatives which may be the product of a team of instructional strategies. It is in the areas of error diagnosis and presentation of the learning materials where CAI is very useful and where the computer's full potential is exploited. This paper describes some years of experience with CAI applied to teaching English to adults with a course designed and tested at the University of Turin.

2 COMPUTER BASED TECHNIQUES IN LANGUAGE TEACHING

Eventhough most language teaching programs are designed only to teach the basic language skills, many teachers have noticed that students were discovering how language operates and thus obtaining correct sentences with words and structures they had never learnt before (see Frizot /8/).

Interestingly enough, this type of behaviour has not been experienced when teaching is along traditional lines.

This fact is not surprising because traditional textbooks often present too many descriptive rules, and the reason teachers emphatisse grammar in conventional methods is because they cannot adequately control the error making process.

Audio-visual and communicative methods on the contrary limit themselves to produce the model and renforce it by drills.

Since the student is never asked to find out how the model operates and since he rarely experiments its limits of validity, he accumulates learning structures which he seldom uses because he does not know what to do with them, unless the teacher gives him the proper indication.

This dependence on the teacher explains why some students can be fluent in class and totally inept in a more real situation, whereas others not so good in class, can communicate with a native.

Students do change when they are given the opportunity to play an active part in how they are going to learn: the gradually acquired rigor and methodology of CAI methods is appreciated by most and it is very helpful in diagnosis and treating frequent mistakes which too often remain unnoticed in conventional teaching. It has been so often noticed that elementary mistakes in foreign languages cause so many students to fail simply because the basic notion has never been assimilated and tested. With CAI it is much easier to know the profile of each student. Given a specific grammatical problem, before the time the student enters this class it might have been explained to him in five different ways. If he still makes mistakes, he will rightly conclude that a sixth explanation will not work and his attention will be elsewhere.

A tutorial approach to the same problem will show him the source of the error and the means to remedy it: further, it will give him immediate feed-back on his work without the embarassment of oral in class.

Given these potentialities computer based techniques should be used not only to drill grammatical rules but more to make students deduce frequent language models.

To this end we think that more meaningful results may be obtained by applying linguistic models which contain a highly formalized language treatment to the preparation of didactic material. In fact we think that computers should be used either to check the students' grammatical knowledge and spelling abilities or to guide them through the analysis of a text, and the students will be able to question these data freely in order to work on.

3 IMPROVING BASIC SKILLS WITH CAI

Work in the field of CAI was begun at the University of Turin in 1978 with the aim of testing the didactic effectiveness of these techniques in applied linguistics.

To this end at Turin and Pavia Universities a small group of researchers in Computer Science and Linguistics has carried out a first course on generative grammar, which is a very important part of modern theorical linguistics, implemented by means of Coursewriter language and tested with LANCAI interpreter (see /4/). The course has been tested with some students and relevant interest has been shown by teachers and students in this type of teaching techniques.

CAI has proved to be an efficient aid, and we saw that the lack of enthusiasm for new technology amongst language teachers was, perhaps, understandable in the light of the poor results achieved withother teaching aids as the language laboratory and the current vast range of audio-visual.

Technical aids in fact can be of great value but they can only be efficiently utilised if the range of the courseware which can be used on them is both varied and of high quality, and "it is an unfortunate fact of life that advances in the development of hardware are much quicker than in the development of software" (see /6/). There is nothing inherently wrong with technical aids such as language laboratory, slide projector or videotape recorder, but there is, however, a tendency for teachers to dismiss the hardware because the software is inadequate. This is particularly true of the microcomputer. In fact, the microcomputer has been noticeably slow to gain a foothold in language teaching in spite of the fact that moderately priced hardware has been available for some years, and good quality teaching material is generally hard to find.

As has been shown by all experiments which have been carried out, there are three important factors necessary in order to increase effectiveness in language learning:
- the student's need for mastering a foreign language;
- a systematic plan with objectives set forth by linguists;
- appropriate instruction and teaching methods

displayed in the classroom.

The CAI course projected at Turin University has been developed and applied taking into account each of these three factors.

The course has been designed to teach some English grammar rules to students who cannot attend regular courses.

The system is aimed at teaching a language to adults who have already obtained a certain level of proficiency in English.

These students have as their incentive the necessity of developing skills until they are fluent in every aspect.

In learning foreign languages receptive skills (understanding and reading) do not necessarily lead to productive skills (speaking and writing).

Our course aims primarily at developing the first set of skills with drills and exercises on the computer, but we encourage students to develop simultaneously the second set by using the language laboratory.

In order to develop the above mentioned skills, drills have been adapted for the classroom for personal training.

After some years of very different language training, students do not have a common background upon which the teacher can draw on. It is therefore essential to review immediately the basic structures to establish a minimal working knowledge on which to build up.

From an educational point of view, it is very important to determine what the student does not know or knows incorrectly.

Misconceptions of the student can often be detected by errors made. Some misconceptions are incidental (slips) or accidental (mistakes), others appear systematically (bugs); some are simple (mistakes), others represent complicated patterns of behaviour.

Unlike mistakes, bugs seem to be complex, intentional actions reflecting mistaken beliefs about the skills (see /3/).

The diagnosis of misconceptions is extremely important for an effective design of remedial strategy.

For these reasons, a series of preliminary tests are given at the beginning of the course (see fig.1). For an adequate simulation of the teacher in a teacher-student CAI dialogue, we must simulate the idea the teacher has about the student's knowledge (the student's model). A first diagnosis is drawn for each student which serves to select the lessons according

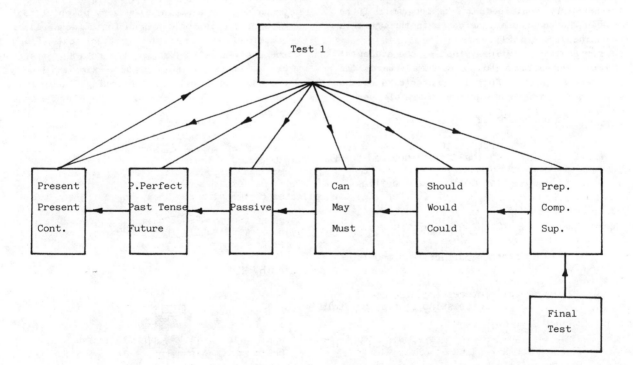

Figure 1: Course Content

to his level. Achievement scores and notes on
the difficulties encountered are kept (on the
file "Student" and studied by the teacher).
Even at this stage the program provides most
of the help needed by the students who will
use the teacher as last resort.
The final test checks the level of knowledge
achieved about the arguments treated in the
course, and if the student doesn't answer
correctly 80% of the questions, he has to
repeat the lessons. Besides the initial and
final tests, the course is provided six
separate, related lessons regarding the
following arguments (see fig.1):

1 Present and present continuous;
2 Past tense, present perfect and future;
3 Active and passive forms;
4 Defective verbs: can, may, must;
5 Should, would, could;
6   Prepositions-adverbs(position)-
    comparative

The lessons cover the essential   structures
and vocaboulary of modern English and are
designed to be course-independent in order to
attract a wide range of users.
Each lesson begins with an optional grammar
review, followed by a checking routine to
ensure that the student is familiar with the
vocaboulary contained in the program. If he
knows the vocaboulary he can skip through this
routine very quickly.
Error analysis routines pinpoint the students'
errors and attempt to guide them towards the
correct response. So the computer's reactions
to the various inputs are on the whole very

useful. The teachers who have designed the
course have anticipated a great number of
common errors for each question. The student
is normally allowed three attempts at each
question and a review of all incorrectly
attempted questions takes place at the end of
a sequence.

The Course programs are written in OLIMASTER
(with the inclusion of BASIC routines inside
Messages and Questions) and run on Olivetti
M20 or M24 computers with PCOS operating
system and 160 K core memory.
At present we are working on SDX, an Author
friendly system designed and implemented
during 1984 by the Research group on CAI of
the University of Turin under the coordination of Prof.Lionello Cantoni.
The most attractive characteristic of SDX, in
comparison with Olimaster (and other CAI
languages) is the drastic reduction of the
ratio: time of implementation/time of
employment of courseware due to the complete
absence of any kind of intermediation between
the author and the computer (neither the help
of EDP specialists nor a language of any kind
are requested) and the aids offered by several
easy-to-use subsystems like graphics, flowcharting, etc.
Graphics, for example, is a very powerful tool
of SDX: the author can draw inside messages or
questions paintings and written texts using
the arrow-keys of M20 and the options offered
by a menu that includes simple lines,
rectangulars, ellypes, painting, deleting,
writing text, recording drawings. (See Cantoni

Si osservino le seguenti frasi:

   I repair the car
         The car is repaired by ME

My sister collects butterflies
             Butterflies are collected by HER

You hunt Moby Dick
      Moby Dick is hunted by YOU

My brother collects car models
             Car models are collected by HIM

We tell interesting stories
      Interesting stories are told by US

They drive the car
      The car is driven by THEM

Figure 2: Graphics Sample

/6/).

Colour is used extensively to highlight verbs and adjectives, to pinpoint errors or to draw attention.

Graphics is used where appropriate, in presentations and in exercises: for example a man under a tree to draw attention to the preposition "under". Representations of simple objects -a car, a table, a human face or figure- are interspersed throughhout the package(see fig.2).

Animation of words is another feature: for example to emphatise syntactical points such as the position of prepositions in relation to the verb or certain adjectives.

The order of phrases creates some problems for students and we had felt that it would be easier to show the learner what is happening if the phrases could be seen to move. Clearly this cannot be done with traditional teaching aids. We therefore decided to design a series of programs incorporating animated sequences to illustrate and reinforce aspects of phrase-order. Animated sequences avoid the boring presentation style which characterises so many CAI programs.

Questions are of two types:
1 the student is asked to give the answer he believe to be correct;
2 multiple choise answer.

An example which guides the students is shown in fig.3. The flow-chart -which is taken from

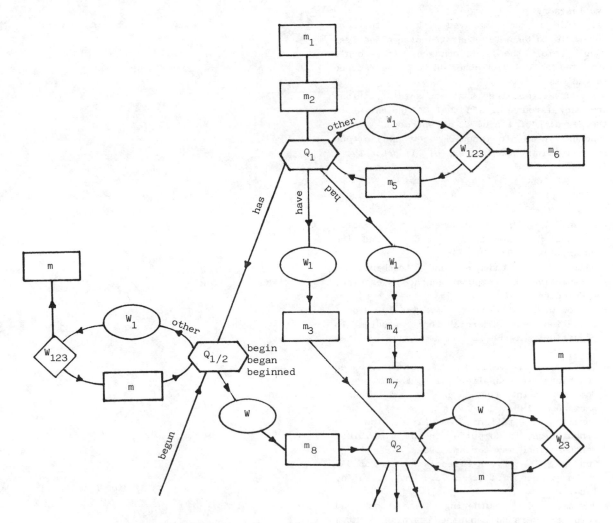

Figure 3: Flow chart of the phrase: "school already (to begin)"

a course realised by Marilyn Costa and Penelope Hatch of the University of Turin-foresees the eventual errors which a student can make.

Q1 is the question, which must be written in two parts: if the student answers correctly, he goes to Q1/2. In the other cases he follows a backing-up exercise.

The question of open-ended responses is a very difficult one: one area in which responses are inevitably open-ended is translation.

4 CONCLUSIONS

Noone can doubt that the computer is particulary good at a sort of work like to present and test points of grammar and vocabulary, but greater immagination on the part of the teacher can reveal a number of exercises which are much more stimulating for the learner.

CAI could be much improved with immagination, but it is to be noted that teaching objectives should remain the first concern, if we don't want to see CAI and other aids to be reduced to gadgets.

Our course demonstred that students' reactions are very favourable and that CAI potential in the learning of languages is enormous.

Teachers need to acquire new skills and imagination in order to exploit it properly.

5 REFERENCES

1 Allen,J., The development of computer courses for humanists, computer and the humanities 8(1974)291-305

2 Bell,F.H., Students and teachers: a perspective on computer-enhanced learning, EDUnineteen, 2-7

3 Bobrow,D.G. & Collins, A.M.(eds), Representation and understanting: studies in cognitive science, (Academic Press, New York, 1975)

4 Borello, E.-Italiani M. Computer-based teaching in applied linguistics, in Computers in Education, North-Holland, Amsterdam, 1981

5 Borello, E.-Italiani, M. CAI Techniques in Linguistics, in Computing in the Humanities, North-Holland, Amsterdam, 1982

6 Cantoni, L.-SDX: A Friendly System for CAI Authors, Dept. of Comp. Sc., Un. of. Turin, 1984

7 Davies, G. Authoring Techniques and Computer-Assisted Language Learning, Intus 2, 1982, pp. 49-56

8 Frizot, D. Teaching English with Computer Assisted Learning, in Computers in Education, North-Holland, Amsterdam, 1981

COMPUTERS IN EDUCATION, K. Duncan and D. Harris (eds.)
Elsevier Science Publishers B.V. (North-Holland)
© IFIP, 1985

AN EXPERIENCE IN DEVELOPING AND USING A
TIME-DOMAIN INTERACTIVE EDUCATIONAL PROCEDURE

G. M. Dimirovski

Electrotechnicki fakultet, P.O.B. 574
University "Kiril and Metodii," 91000 Skopje, Yugoslavia

This paper surveys the three stages of an experience in developing and
using a time-domain, interactive, educational methodology and its
package aimed at teaching and self-tuition in non-linear multi-variable
control and technological systems. Control engineering, human-
behavioral, cognitive and computing aspects are discussed. Student-
computer interaction is closely investigated. Both positive and
negative elements and users evaluation are reported.
Keywords: Interactive package, non-linear multi-variable systems, man-
          computer dialogue, postgraduate users, symbiotic systems.

1. INTRODUCTION

The recent tremendous development of
computing tools and fast decrease of
their prices has brought into our
everyday life and work an almost total
spread of computers, although this
process is much slower in developing
countries. It is widely acknowledged
that education may not and must not be
out of this process of change. However,
this process has given rise to many new
and complex problems, some of them
unknown so far and some known to a
rather restricted number of countries,
institutions, and even individuals
(e.g., problems associated with man-
machine systems). Among them are the
basic ones: how should we change over
to computer-assisted education, which
also implies adequate, programmed
literature; what are appropriate ways of
doing it with respect to educational
level, area, and different subjects;
what are appropriate approaches of doing
it with respect to cultural traditions
and general state of country
development; and how to cope with the
fast override of this technology in,
generally, unprepared society
environments. These questions have
forced us toward some research in the
aspects of concern and some practical
work in the case of computer-assisted
education (CAE) in control engineering.

The experience which is discussed in
this paper has gradually led to certain
conclusions and closer understanding of
real problems associated with the
development, implementation, and use of
interactive computer-assisted teaching.

It was not without misses. An
additional feature is that it has been
gained partially through research visits
to the Postgraduate School of Control
Engineering (SCE) at Bradford
University, U.K., and partially with the
Faculty of Electrical Engineering (FEE)
at Skopje University, Yugoslavia.
Originally, this work has been inspired
by remarkable achievements in both
process computer control and computer-
aided methodologies in research and
education at Bradford SCE, where a
number of research projects on these
subjects have been accomplished during
the past decade (in some of which this
author also has been involved). In
recent years, however, in addition to
regular work, aspects discussed in here
have been of continuing concern in our
work in Skopje FEE so that they reflect
more an experience from a developing
country and a transfer of knowledge and
technology. This paper surveys their
development, including the package CSNCS
aimed at research and teaching and/or
self-tuition of university students, as
a computerized tool. It traces the
three stages of aforementioned
development: 1977-1978, 1979-1982, and
1983-present, and summarizes the present
view and conclusions on the discussed
subject.

2. EARLY DEVELOPMENT-ENTHUSIASTIC
OPTIMISM AND MISSES

By now it has been widely noted that
interactive computer-assisted techniques
in education to a large extent have
emerged from interactive packages for

research, at least in early days
/23,15,26/. Also it seems that the
control engineering area has been
leading the way. Although with a
relatively limited number of
contributions, the 1st IFAC Symposium on
ACE in 1977 has clearly shown several
basic aspects which should be recalled
/26/: (i) development of such packages
has been biased with needs to serve
research; (ii) they include quite
advanced methods of systems and control
theory, transparent to a limited number
of individuals, but this is exactly what
enhanced interests within industry;
(iii) such packages have been used
mainly at postgraduate level and/or for
final student projects, which has
contributed to their quick further
development, extensions and additional
support from industry; (iv) particularly
successful subjects have been process
computer control and identification, and
this has contributed to laboratory
automation. In the case of developing
countries, some problems have been
pointed out: shortage of competent
staff, insufficient funds, lack of
interest within under-developed
industry, lack of text books, etc.
However, it turned out that most
important educational aspects of
interactive CAE, which emerge from the
fact of being man-machine systems
oriented, then have not been recognized.
These were the general circumstances
when our early contribution to computer-
assisted education techniques took place
/6-8/.

There were present and available several
very useful (and, to the author's
opinion, important) sources of knowledge
and experience on which our work at that
time was directly based, namely
references /1-5,15,16, and 20/. In
particular, the successful use in both
research and education of the previous
interactive methodology of Gough and
Thiga, called CAIAD and aimed at MIMO
linear systems, with a M.Sc. course in
Control at SCE was encouraging /15/.
Having well understood the nature of
real-world systems, technological ones
particularly, and the importance of
clear distinction of manipulating models
and operating real systems, our work was
entirely devoted to the classes of MIMO
non-linear systems with additive non-
linearities and/or time-varying gain,
and with or without time-delay. The
approach adopted was the same - input-
output and time-domain - because of
their direct real-world tangibility to
practicing engineers, students and
novice users. As a result of this
applied research a package called CSNCS

(Computer-aided Study of Non-linear
Control Systems) came out, providing
certain research capabilities (reported,
including /9/) and an interactive
graphics educational procedure
(reported, including /8/). It was seen
later (Automatica, 1979) that almost all
recommendations concerning such packages
known to control engineering people,
working on computer-assisted
methodologies have been respected within
CSNCS. Requirements such as the essence
of linearity hypothesis and easily
reachable theoretical aspects of systems
and control visualization of difficult
notions and concepts, simulation
capabilities, easy comparison of models,
short response time, consistent
indications, robustness to user's
errors, clear and simple dialogue,
flexible and expansible segmented and
documented programs, etc. were met.
Also CSNCS application for research and
for simulation purposes, not available
before, was soon well demonstrated. Yet
its educational application has not been
practically accepted, and moreover
several doctoral level colleagues have
found it to be difficult in spite of all
facilities. Similarly have ended
attempts to transfer this computer-
assisted methodology to Dhahran Systems
Engineering (which for linear systems
was successful and CAIAD-II was
developed, /17,18/) and to Skopje FEE.
Our first explanation for this was found
in the nature of non-linear systems,
which require a considerable theoretical
knowledge in mathematics, systems
science and control, and empirical
knowledge of engineering. It turned
out, however, that then we missed the
very basic necessary premises from an
educational point of view - the
symbiotic man-machine system created
with CSNCS interactive graphics to
operate in an extended real-time.

3.   THE DEVELOPMENT AND EXPERIENCE OF
     CSNCS-II

It has been stated even in our reports
from the early stage that what was
sought by any interactive computer
methodology actually was a special
"soft" system in the form of lasting
man-computer interaction. Then this
issue was neither completely understood,
nor elaborated and argued. However,
following the gained first experience,
particularly the negative one in
educational application, it was
challenging to find out what were the
real reasons. The discussion of
Rosenbrock on man-computer aspects in
his paper "The future of control"

(Automatica, 13, 389-392, 1977) gave a hint to research for results in human factors engineering and man-computer systems, which has led us to Rouse's paper /24/. Although operator and analyst man-computer stereotypes have been investigated there, and not the student man-computer stereotype, we found the main point we missed in our first design of CSNCS. Indeed, in the case of on-line interactive systems a special purpose man-computer system, which combines compatible capabilities of computer's power in information processing and man's power in heuristic ability, arises which is not as straight-forward as it looks.

Using Rouse's conceptual structure for man-computer interfaces in on-line interactive systems in the case of analyst stereotype, from summer 1979 to summer 1981, the first design of our package has been revised and the improved CSNCS-II produced /10,11/. Apart from a significant improvement of the facility for estimation of induced system/subsystem norms while in operation /6,10/, the whole design of man-computer interaction has been revised and many man-computer dialogues changed so that a full on-line guidance (instructions, hints, cautions) and possibility to skip over parts of it have been included. Also the organization module is being altered so that a reasonably free choice of running sequence of application modules has been enabled. Certain constraints on the way the user runs particular modules have been imposed for the sake of efficient guidance and instruction in the self-tuition mode of usage (although this has slowed down the CSNCS-II research run). In addition, basic model transformation into frequency domain has been included in a later version, because it was noticed that student comprehension needs some standard, well understood teaching material in hand all the time.

There has been a limited number of users of CSNCS-II: a few author's colleagues, and two graduate and several postgraduate students because the package requires a considerable understanding of linear and non-linear systems. However, this version has been found to clarify notions and concepts such as: linear superposition principle decomposition, signal norms and system norms, Minkowski, Holder and Cauchy-Schwartz inequalities, input magnitude dependence of non-linear system behavior, the gap between real-world system responses and model responses, inertial and delay behavior of real technological systems, system interaction and decoupling, control system integrity, self-sustained and forced oscillations, operating regimes under stochastic inputs, influence of typical non-linearities and time-varying gain, and relationship between system models in state equations and in impulse and frequency responses. Although this was considered only as a possible conclusion, it was encouraging to persist with this work on interactive educational methodology. Therefore we tried to summarize additional experience in CSNCS-II assisted teaching and self-tuition:

The student-computer stereotype is very close to that of the analyst-computer stereotype in problem solving.

Its nature during teaching is basically environment-event-driven while during self-tuition is self-paced, and therefore operationally belongs to extended real-time.

Although he may have considerable knowledge, since he is not trained, he does also scanning of the VDU and tries to associate features seen with his background and experience in his long-term memory, and this takes most of the time.

Student's motivation enhances remarkable perception power and at the same time actuates inductive as well as deductive reasoning if a visualized interaction, proper organization of information displayed, and clear and quick dialogue are provided.

Nice ding-dong signals at appropriate points throughout student-computer dialogue enhance his perception.

Graphical information should not be overwritten with too much alpha-numerics, unless it is most necessary, because pictorial information has greater impact on his perception and comprehension.

Information display should be consistently organized on the VDU considering a human is a parallel information processor generally and integrates his perceptions at the time. Only relevant information should be displayed.

The computer should respond quickly or should provide noticeable feedback in the case of an unavoidable delay.

Students should have an opportunity to choose thorough or partial on-line guidance, for they are quite imaginative. However, a prescribed, pedagogically consistent direction for the novice user should be provided.

The student should be assigned a coherent series of tasks in both the teaching and self-tuition modes of package usage, which make him well aware that he has been given a computer-assisted methodology to save him time and actuate his creative resources, and not just to reduce his workload.

The package should be organized in three groups of programs-modules: (i) organization, information-flow and data-base controls; (ii) man-machine communication; and (iii) the "educational material."

The interactive graphics system should be accompanied by adequate programmed textbooks.

4. ON THE THIRD DESIGN OF CSNCS

It is quite common that experience will enhance some further development to a forseeable extent. During the last few years a further advance of interactive methodologies is evident, which is due mainly to the following reasons: (i) the range of computing capacity of minis and micros today as opposed to that of five years ago; (ii) remarkable achievements of software engineering; and (iii) fast advancement in the knowledge and practical results of artificial intelligence. It was not unexpected that some postgraduate students wanted to re-write CSNCS-II on their personal computer, since such a development already happened with CAIAD-II /18/ and, very likely, to many similar dedicated packages. In addition, recently most of our own observations, including those summarized in the previous section, have found confirmation and been completed by reported results on knowledge-based man-machine systems and human-computer dialogue /14,22,25,27/.

In 1983 our work on further development of CSNCS-interactive methodology started, following a newly defined and structured secondary school education in control /12/ and an adequate adaptation of university education in control at our FEE. To give a general idea of the latter we present the relevant part of the undergraduate syllabus structure (postgraduate being part-time with a flexible syllabus) in automatics-informatics at FEE: (a) automatics - fundamentals of automatic control, discrete-time control systems, non-

linear control systems, computer control of technological processes, automation of technological systems, instrumentation for process automation, design of process control systems, analogue and digital simulation; (b) informatics - fundamentals of FORTRAN programming, logic circuits and automata theory, digital computer architecture, system software, applications software, process computers. These current circumstances and our intention to introduce regular use of the interactive graphics system in undergraduate as well as postgraduate courses have had considerable impact on the projection of CSNCS-III.

In their considerations of human-computer dialogue design, Williges and Williges /27/ have pointed out certain main principles defined as compatibility, consistency, flexibility, brevity, immediate feedback, and human workload, and thoroughly studied all aspects of HELP information retrieval. Investigating the interactions between the user and computer until he obtains the desired information by reaching his goal, Ohsuga /22/ has proved through his system KAUS that the user's gain is enhanced by realizing appropriate model building and handling on the computer via appropriate language. Within his project INFORM, Fischer /14/ gives a thorough discussion on a concept of a symbiotic, knowledge-based information manipulation system aimed at developing human-oriented support computers, and has stressed the importance of cognitive science views and of such concepts as convivial, knowledge-based and information-manipulation systems.

Now a brief scan of the projected model of the CSNCS-III interactive methodology /13/ will be presented, together with some detailed information on features inherited from previous CSNCS designs and their functioning to provide a minimum of illustration. First of all, the new educational objective requires inclusion of classical continuous and discrete control systems, of basic digital modeling, identification and realization methods and of basic stochastic control. In addition, since a direct relation between linear time-domain and frequency-domain multivariable models has been established /21/ related methods should be included. Also, fundamental aspects of large-scale systems are needed now. This way an integrated, computer-aided approach to identification, modeling, and analysis of control systems, together with certain design methods, which combines time-domain and frequency-domain concepts and classical, modern, and heuristic methods, would be obtained. Although developments toward personal computers are likely to occur, CSNCS-III is aimed at implementation on the IBM 4331 and on the DEC VAX 780. In its previous development, the package was written in HP FORTRAN, required a minimum of 23 K words and external disc memory support, was organized in 66 overlay segments and implemented standard feedback-feedforward control system structures as defined by the IEC Document /19/. Due to 18 different types of non-linearities, 4 deterministic and 2 stochastic signal generators (all typical inputs with Gaussian and uniform noise), multi-variable PID controllers, linear dynamic subsystems with or without time-delay, and user's definition of control system composition, several hundred types of control systems are easily implemented. In addition, it contains facilities for performance indices calculation, interaction measure, structural linear system properties, induced system norms estimation, oscillatory regimes, sector linearization, Leissajou figures, system integrity and decoupling study, and graphics for pictures versus time and input-output mappings, and their magnification. Fig. 1 presents the package and current work on its improvement, and Fig. 2 shows an operational block diagram. The rest of figures (taken from a case-study on an SS decoupling PID multi-variable DDC of a three-tank system) illustrate types of graphics provided.

Without going into more detail, the third design of CSNCS is defined taking into consideration our observation and recent results on symbiotic, knowledge-based man-computer systems which use a combined conversational and command driven mode. The following main modules should be noticed: (a) knowledge base, (b) data base, (c) procedure base, (d) conversational alternative, (e) program executor, (f) input executor, and (g) output executor.

5. CONCLUSION

Through surveying the experience in developing and using a time-domain educational methodology aimed at non-linear multi-variable systems, it has been demonstrated that an effective realization of human-computer symbiosis in a training process requires simultaneous respect for control

engineering, human-behavior, and cognitive aspects. Hardware is usually determined by other processes, and therefore the problem reduces to software and man-computer stereotype in a teaching/learning process. With respect to control engineering aspects, it seems that a conceptual plateau is being reached which may be described as an integrated computer-assisted approach to identification, modeling, and analysis which combines time-domain and frequency-domain concepts and basic classical, modern and heuristic methods. The development of this interactive methodology has been brought to a status which promises successful use at the postgraduate level, and in its last concept in the undergraduate course as well.

ACKNOWLEDGEMENTS

This research was made possible through collaboration between the Universities of Bradford and Skopje, a recent BC visiting grant, and by Professor M. G. Mylroi's endeavors in support of this collaboration. The author is indebted to Professor S. Barnett for his continuing encouragement and valuable help in systems research. Professor N. E. Gough's guidance in the early development of the CSNCS package is also acknowledged. Particular gratitude is due to the SRC of Macedonia.

6. REFERENCES

/1/ Barnett,S.,Matrices in Control Theory (Van Nostrand Reinhold, London,1971).

/2/ Barnett,S.,Introduction to Mathematical Control Theory (Clarendon Press, Oxford,1975)

/3/ Cooke,R.G.,Infinite Matrices and Sequence Spaces (Dover,New York,1955).

/4/ Desoer,C.A. & Vidyasagar,M.,Feedback Systems: Input-Output Properties (Academic Press,New York,1975).

/5/ Dimirovski,G.M.,Lecture Notes on Nonlinear Automatic Control (in Macedonian). University "Kiril and Metodii" (Faculty of El.and Mech. Eng.,Skopje,1975).

/6/ Dimirovski,G.M.,Barnett,S.& Gough,N.E.,Principles of the input-output approach to computer-aided study of MIMO nonlinear control systems. Rep.R326-Control Eng.,University of Bradford (Bradford,1977).

/7/ Dimirovski,G.M.,The CSNCS package for computer-aided study of MIMO nonlinear control systems. Rep.R331-Control Eng.,University of Bradford (Bradford,1977/1978).

/8/ Dimirovski,G.M.,Interactive computer techniques in the teaching of systems theory and automatic control (in Serbo-Croat).Proc. JUREMA 26, 4,pp.23-24 (Zagreb,1978).

/9/ Dimirovski,G.M.,Barnett,S.,Kleftouris,D.N. & Gough,N.E.,An input-output package for MIMO

nonlinear control systems.Prepr.2nd IFAC/IFIP
Symp.on SOCOCO,2,paper C.IX (Prague,1979).

/10/ Dimirovski,G.M.,The CSNCS-II package and case-
studies/The CSNCS-II user's guide. Reps.R340/
R341-Control Eng.,University of Bradford
(Bradford,1979/1982).

/11/ Dimirovski,G.M.,Barnett,S.and Gough,N.E.,
Interactive program packages for teaching
and self-tuition in the theory and application of modern methods of control engineering.
Proc.4th Int.Symp."Computer at the University", pp.129-136 (Cavtat,1982).

/12/ Dimirovski,G.M.,Džekov,T.,Kamilovski,M.,Shu-
tinovski,G.,Arsov,G. & Gugulovska,T., New
course structure and curricula for secondary
school education and professional training
in instrumentation and control.Special rep.,
Faculty of EE and Inst. for Advancement of
Education of SR Macedonia (Skopje,1983).

/13/ Dimirovski,G.M.,The third design of CSNCS
package for education and research (in Macedonian). Rep.EF/ZA/CAS-1,Faculty of EE,Uni-
versity "Kiril and Metodii",Skopje(in prepar.).

/14/ Fischer,G.,Symboitic, knowledge-based computer support systems.Automatica 19 (1983)
pp.627-636.

/15/ Gough,N.E. & Thiga,R.S.,A computer-aided
procedure for teaching control system analysis and design to university students.R274-
Control Eng.,University of Bradford (Bradford,1975).

/16/ Gough,N.E.,Lecture Notes on Discrete Control
Systems.Bradford University Press (Bradford,
1976).

/17/ Gough,N.E.,Computer-assisted study of systems
using TSB: Pt.1-Continuous systems, Pt.2-Dis-
crete systems,Pt.3 - Convolution algegra. Reps.
SE/CAD/1,4,and 11 - Systems Eng.,University
of Petroleum and Minerals (Dhahran,1978/1979).

/18/ Gough,N.E. & Thiga,R.S.A.,Small-computer procedures for training control engineers.Proc.
5th Int.Symp."Computer at the University",
pp.75-82 (Cavtat,1983).

/19/ IEC Document Dispatch Advise Note TC-65/84,
The IEC Bureau Central (Geneva,Swiss,1982).

/20/ King,R.E. & Williamson,D., Time domain matrix
analysis of hybrid control systems.Proc. IEE,
111 (164) pp. 1607-1614.

/21/ Kouvaritakis,B. & Kleftouris,D., The characteristic sequences method for multivariable
systems: a time domain approach to the characteristic locus method.Int.J.Control,31 (1980)
pp.127-152.

/22/ Ohsuga,S.,Knowledge-based man-machine systems.
Automatica, 19 (1983) pp. 665-691.

/23/ Rosenbrock,H.H., Computer-Aided Control System Design (Academic Press,N.York-London,1974).

/24/ Rouse,W.B., Design of man-computer interfaces
for on-line interactive systems,Proc.IEEE, 63,
(1975) pp.847-857.

/25/ Simon,H. The Sciences of the Artificial (MIT
Press, Cambrdige/MA, 1981).

/26/ Special Section on Automatic Control Education, Automatica 15 (1979),pp.101-121.

/27/ Williges,R.C. and Williges, B.H., Human-computer dialogue design considerations. Automatica, 19 (1983), pp.686-773.

COMPUTERS IN EDUCATION, K. Duncan and D. Harris (eds.)
Elsevier Science Publishers B.V. (North-Holland)
© IFIP, 1985

KODÁLY, COMPUTERS AND THE CLASSROOM -
the development of a flexible music education teaching aid program
for young children

Colin Wells, Music Education Centre, Microtechnology Unit,
University of Reading School of Education, Reading, UK.,
and Michael Stocks, Local Education Authority, Somerset, UK.*

This paper will describe the various stages in the development of a computer aided
learning program which was specifically designed as an aid for the class teacher.
It will describe the program in detail explaining how it was designed to be both
flexible and easily controllable and will indicate some of the range of educational
possibilities for which it could offer help.

A. BACKGROUND

Prior to the first meeting of the two authors in
July 1983, Colin Wells had been the Technical
Director of the "Investigations on Teaching with
Microcomputers as an Aid" Collaboration - a
group involved in many aspects of research,
program and teaching unit development, in-
service training and information work connected
with the uses of computers in education. He had
begun some specific research and development
work in the field of microcomputers in Music
education, building on his varied background as
a qualified Music teacher and Computer
Scientist. Of particular interest, was the
development of flexible "resource" programs
which could be used by teachers as an aid in
teaching a variety of topics to a wide range of
age groups and abilities and as an aid to
demonstrate links between these topics when they
exist.

Michael Stocks, the Inspector for Music in
Somerset, had no previous experience in using
microcomputers, and although he had been
somewhat interested by what he had heard about
the use of computers in Music education, he
could see little of immediate relevance to the
particular approach that he was developing in
the County. This approach was based firmly in
singing and solfa work, and although it had
strong links with the methods developed by
Zoltán Kodály in Hungary (Refs 1-6), English
song material was used. Thus, without any
serious expectations of any materials being
developed, Michael arranged with Colin to meet
for a day to discuss how computers could be used
in Music education, and whether there might be
any possible applications to suit his scheme.

B. INITIAL PLANNING

At the first meeting Colin showed Michael some
of the published and pre-release development
programs for Music education which he had
collected over the previous months. Michael

later admitted that seeing these programs was a
rather "mind-blowing" experience. He had not
previously comprehended the potential power of
intermingling text, graphics, sound, colour and
animation within the interactive framework of a
computer program. Although he didn't find any
one program which he would use as written (the
only SOLFA program being a straight drill and
practice exercise), he clearly saw many exciting
elements from several programs which
demonstrated the potential of the computer.
Still struggling to come to terms with
implications for his scheme in Somerset, Michael
suggested that Colin should now visit some
schools in Somerset to see his "Growing up with
Music" scheme in operation so that any further
discussion could continue within a recognizable
framework.

Accordingly two Somerset primary schools were
visited by Colin, and it was his turn to have
somewhat a "mind blowing" experience! The two
groups, one with children aged about 6 and the
other with children aged about 9, were engaged
in many varied singing and rhythmic activities
responding to their teachers, and without the
use of any instruments apart from their voices.
The strong impressions were that they were all
very confident about their voices; they were all
enjoying singing and were developing a high
degree of competance for their age in terms of
both performance and aural memory, and in understanding musical concepts and notation. For
example the group of 9 year old pupils could
sing back a new 8 bar tune sung by the teacher
but could not only achieve this starting after
the teachers had finished, but also starting
after the teachers first 4 bars - thus requiring
them to sing from memory whilst listening and
remembering new notes!

After this experience and further discussions
with the Area Music Tutor for Somerset, Andrew
Maddocks, it was decided to form a working party
of 9 teachers and advisers to try and design a
program suitable for the scheme in Somerset.

---

*This paper reports on work started while Colin Wells was directing research into music education
and computers with the ITMA Collaboration at the College of St Mark and St John, Plymouth, UK.

C. DEVELOPING IDEAS INTO A WORKING PROGRAM

The working party met for the first time in October 1983, and as most of the members had no experience in the use of computers, the first session was spent viewing previously written programs and discussing their relative merits.

After this initial acclimatization, the group began to focus in a particular area of interest and started to list requirements for a program as follows:
- need to be able to display tunes in rhythm only, rhythm solfa or staff notation, and with or without sound.
- the tunes need only be the short (4 or 8 bar) tunes from the Growing Up with Music repertoire, and indeed this link with familiar tunes was heavily desired.
- if facilities could be provided for entering new tunes, then the rhythmic aspect should be a rhythmic activity, i.e. not just selecting from keys labelled with different time values as was commonly seen in music editor programs.
- need to provide a choice of clefs e.g. to mark doh or soh only, as an intermediate step between solfa and fixed pitch staff notation.
- need to have at least a few musical keys e.g. G, D and C, for the tunes to accommodate the range of tunes in the repertoire, and also some chromatic notes especially fi and ta.
- need a choice of time signatures for simple and compound time.
- need ample opportunities for child performance e.g. singing or clapping.

Initially the group conceived of definite pre-planned sequences illustrating various points they might want to make using these facilities, but gradually began to see that much greater

flexibility could be achieved by providing a superset of all the required facilities and leaving the sequencing control firmly in the hands of the teacher/user during the lesson.

Accordingly the program, named REPLAY, (7) was designed for the BBC microcomputer (as in Somerset schools), to meet all of the above requirements and to cope with any key and a full chromatic 2 octaves.

Throughout the next few months when the program was going through various draft versions, the main work of the group was to select an easy user interface with easily memorable keys in logical positions to try and maintain the correct balance between flexibility and controllability. Wherever possible the keys were used for one purpose only, for example the control key was used to mean "NOT" i.e. to turn off a feature; and the shift key was only used to signify a compound time. The option selection was done by selecting a series of single keys as desired by the user, rather than going through a series of possibly distracting menus of choices on the screen. A particularly large discussion point was the method of keyboard tune entry - whereas some other music programs had used 2 rows of the QWERTY keys to mirror a chromatic scale, this fundamentally fixed this in the key of C major. So, as the pitch entry required was in SOLFA, which is key independent, the chromatic keys were laid out in one straight line. This had the added spin-off that music intervals were directly related to distance - which isn't true on a piano keyboard for example.

The final keyboard layout for "special" keys was as follows:

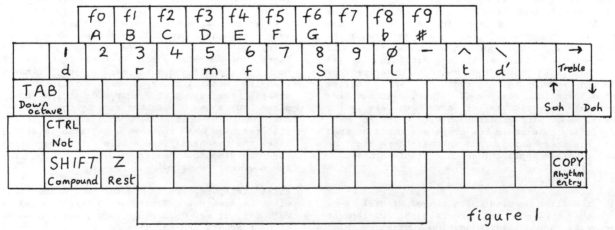

figure 1

By May 1984 the program was operational as described in the next section.

D. PROGRAM DESCRIPTION

On starting the program, the screen will show the prompt "OPTIONS?"

These options select the source or filing arrangements for the tunes, and how they are to be played and displayed. A full screen display is shown below.

OPTIONS ?

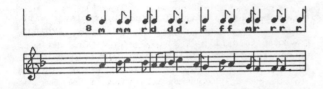

Options

Options are chosen by one or more single key presses as follows:

(a) Source of tune. This can be

    B* - Begin (a new tune from the keyboard) or
    L - Load (a file from tape)

(The * signifies the option which is automatically in force at the start of the program).

(b) Choice of clef. This can be

    → Treble
    ↓ Doh or
    ↑ Soh

(The Doh or Soh clefs place the letter d or s at the appropriate place).

(c) Notes and stave display. This can be

    N* Notes on or
    cN Notes off

(The c here signifies pressing the "Control" key together with the letter N).

(d) Rhythm line display. This can be

    R* Rhythm on or
    cR Rhythm off

(e) Solfa display. This can be

    S* Solfa on or

    cS Solfa off

(f) Sound output. This can be

    V* Volume on (normal pitched output) or
    cV Volume off (i.e. silent) or
    M   Monotone

(g) Time signature. This can be

    2* 2 simple beats or
    3   3 simple beats or
    4   4 simple beats or
    sh 2 2 compound beats or
    sh 3 3 compound beats or
    sh 4 4 compound beats

(h) Time signature display. This can be

    T* Time signature on or
    cT Time signature off

(i) Playback - this will normally be automatic and play straight through the tune, but can be played under manual control by typing

    C Controlled speed.

(j) Choice of key (or position of doh). This option should be chosen last and uses the red function keys as in figure 1.

    e.g. to select C#, press f2 and then f9.

OPTIONS ?

To end the selection of options - press RET

All choices of option except those in (a) and (i) will remain in force until changed.

File loading

If the L - Load option is selected, then after the RET key is pressed, you are asked

    File name?

Enter the required file name followed by RET .

When the file is loaded, it will immediately be displayed according to current display option settings for clef, notes, rhythm, solfa, volume, and time signature.

The time signature and key used will be those saved with the file unless superceded by new values. E.g. a tune saved in a file in the key of G will be displayed in the key of D by selecting options:

    L f3 [RET]

After loading a file, it can then be replayed in any different mode as usual using the options.

Beginning a new tune

After selecting option B, (or at the start of the program if neither L or B are pressed), and pressing [RET] , you reach: "ENTER RHYTHM' and the screen will flash to indicate whole beat pulses. These beats will be simple or compound depending on the option choice selected.

Tap in your required rhythm in time to the flashes, using the "Copy" key for notes or the z key for rests. You can end the rhythm at any time by pressing [RET] to complete the last note, and the screen will stop flashing. If the Rhythm option is on, the rhythm line will be displayed while you are entering the rhythm, but will be a note behind as the length of notes is not known until the next is played (or ended).

If you end the rhythm in the middle of a beat then that beat is automatically filled with quaver rests to avoid notation problems later. However incomplete bars are not filled in.

After [RET] is pressed to end the rhythm entry, you are prompted: "ENTER SOLFA'. Here the row of keys as in figure 1 is used for the chromatic notes doh to doh'.

Pressing these keys on their own selects notes from the top octave, and if the "Tab" key is held whilst pressing the keys, the lower octave is used.

Unpitched noises can be entered by pressing X.

If a mistake is made, the "delete" key will clear back to the last note which was on a beat.

When all rhythm notes have been allocated a Solfa pitch, the options prompt will return.

The entered Solfa will result in notes and/or Solfa being displayed according to the options selected.

After a tune is entered it can be replayed with different options or kept in a file by typing:
K - Keep in a file
which is the 3rd option as an alternative to L and B.

Keep in a file

After selecting K and pressing [RET] , you are asked: File name?

Enter the required file name (up to 7 characters) followed by [RET] .

After filing the tune will still be loaded and can be replayed as desired.

Drivechart for the program

The operation of the program as described above can be summarized by the following simple diagram called a "drivechart", which acts as a quick reminder sheet for the teacher or other user:

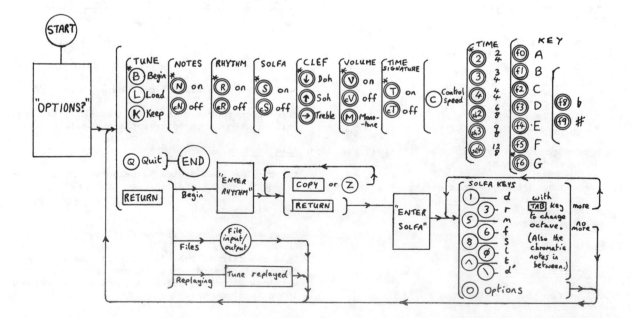

E. TEACHER TRAINING AND SUGGESTIONS FOR CLASSROOM USE

After the program had been tried and discussed by the development team, two training sessions were planned for the class teachers in six trial primary schools from various parts of Somerset, including one infant (5-7 year old) school.

The first session of three hours was devoted to familiarizing the teachers with the operation of a microcomputer, and the operation of the REPLAY program as given in the last section.

A selection of tune files were provided with the program so that the various program options could be explored initially without needing to enter new tunes from the keyboard.

By the end of the session, the teachers had largely overcome their initial doubts and fears, and were able to take the programs away for the following week to continue the familiarizing process on the machines in their own schools.

A week later these teachers returned for the second 3 hour training session, which was firmly based on educational aspects and ideas for use in the classroom.

The following four short "lesson" examples were first demonstrated by Michael using the teachers as the class of pupils:

1. Reading of pitch names from solfa letters. Adding rhythm element to arrive at rhythm-solfa. Introduction to time signatures

PREPARE	cN	CR	S	cV	4	cT	f2	B	RET

Enter ♩ ♩ ♩ z │ ♩ ♩ ♩ z ‖
(No Rhythm visual)

Enter s l s   s l s

"Let us sing this short melody. Now sing it with your own handsigns."

PREPARE	B	RET

(No Rhythm visual)
Enter s s l l s   s   s l l s

Enter s s m   ss m   s m m s

"Let us sing this melody. Now with our handsigns. Notice how these solfa letters are grouped, suggesting rhythm. Let us look at the rhythm symbols which fit these letters."

PREPARE	R	RET

"Now we can see the rhythm clearly as well as the pitch. Do you notice where the

rests come? This time, as we sing the melody touch your shoulders when we come to a rest."

"Now let us ask the computer to play the melody."

PREPARE	V	RET

"How many pulses to a bar? Listen again."
"Can you tell me the time signature we should use?"

PREPARE	T	RET

2. Reading from rhythm-solfa

PREPARE	cN	R	S	cV	4	T	B	RET

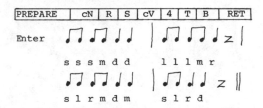

s s s m d d   l l l m r

s l r m d m   s l r d

"First, let us tap (speak) the rhythm. Now we shall sing as a melody."

"Now we shall listen to the computer play the melody."

PREPARE	V	RET

3. Introducing s l m in staff notation. The constant pitch relationship as d changes.

PREPARE	R	S	cV	4	T	f3	B	RET

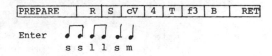

s s l l s m

"Let us sing this short melody."

PREPARE	N	RET

"Here is the same melody in staff notation. Note how s relates to l, and how s relates to m. Let us sing this melody."

PREPARE	f2	RET

"Now we have a new position for d, so all the notes adjust in the same way. Their relationship to each other, however, remains the same even though s and m are now on lines and l is in a space."

4. Reading from staff notation

PREPARE	cN	R	S	cV	4	T	L-ENGINE	RET

"Without using your voice, who recognises this tune? Let us all sing it from rhythm-solfa. Copy this melody into your books. How many phrases does this melody have? What can you tell me about the rhythmic phrases? We have recently been practising our reading from staff notation."

| PREPARE | N | cR | cS | f5 | RET |

"Let us sing this to solfa. Notice that we
start on the note s.   Let us change our d
and sing it again."

| PREPARE | f2 | RET |

"Now here is a new melody to read which you
have not heard in advance."

| PREPARE | B | RET |

Enter

                    (No visuals appear)
Enter   s s m m r r d   s s m m r r d

       m m r r m m l   s s m m s s d
       (Staff notation appears)

"Let us sing this melody. The rhythm is the
same as 'Engine', but the pitch is different so the melody is different. Now let us
compare our melody with the computer's
playing of it."

| PREPARE | V | RET |

Following these demonstration lessons and
discussions on them, the teachers, working in
pairs, were asked to prepare one (or more)
different short examples of use for demonstration about an hour later.   Each pair managed at
least one example, and these were all different
and some quite innovative.   One presentation,
for example, used a tune whose first 4 bars were
inverted to form the concluding 4 bars.   This
was used as a discussion point to highlight the
fact that solfa notation does not in itself
clearly show the pattern for an inverted tune,
whereas standard notes on a stave do show the
inverted pattern, to reinforce the aurally
perceived inverted tune.

Other ideas discussed (which show the scope of
the program for older children) were:
- the effects of different key signatures on the
same staff notation e.g. between D and D flat
- the use for pitch, rhythm or combined dictation exercises
- the   use for sight singing, using the
controlled speed key
- the possibilities of demonstrating enharmonic
key changes sounding the same but written
differently e.g. changing key from D flat to C
sharp
- the way notes are grouped in simple   or
compound time and the effects on pulse and
musicality, as could be shown by quickly
changing a continuous quaver tune from 3/4 time
to 6/8.

By the end of these two training sessions, these
teachers were beginning to grow in confidence
about the programs use; had a lot of starting
points for class lessons, and would be able to
begin to prepare a wealth of lesson ideas on
their own whilst becoming even more confident
and familiar with the program.

It must be stressed again here that the use of a
flexible program, such as REPLAY, in the classroom is demanding for the teacher, but with
adequate preparation and confidence, this can be
far more rewarding and useful than many other
more structured (but less demanding) programs.
In other words "it's worth the effort!"

F. SCHOOL TRIALS

The main set of trials are taking place in the
Autumn Term 1984, and Spring of 1985 initially
in the schools represented at the teacher training sessions described above.   As the program
will be used in conjunction with the well
defined "Growing up with Music" scheme, with its
development scheme of skills and concepts, it
should be possible to not only evaluate the use
of the program as such, but also to directly
compare the advantages and disadvantages of its
use with comparable classes and schools in
Somerset not using the computer.   Full results
of these trials, (and of the trials in other
areas of the country not using the Growing up
with Music Scheme, and with other age groups)
will be provided and discussed when the paper is
presented.

References

1. Kodály's Principles and Practice by Erzsébet
   Szőnyi. Published by Corvina Press, 1974.
2. 333 reading exercises by Zoltán Kodály.
   Published by Boosey and Hawkes, 1972.
   (revised edition)
3. The selected writings of Zoltán Kodály.
   Published by Boosey and Hawkes, 1974.
4. Solfege according to the Kodály concept by
   Erzsébet Hegg.
   Published by the Zoltán Kodály Pedagogical
   Institute of Music, Kecskemet, 1975.
5. Musical reading and writing 1-111 by Erzsébet
   Szőnyi. Published by Boosey and Hawkes,
   1974, 1978, 1979.
6. The land without Music by Bernarr Rainbow.
   Published by Novello, 1967
7. Micros and Music by the ITMA Collaboration.
   Published by Longman Microsoftware, 1985.

COMPUTERS IN EDUCATION, K. Duncan and D. Harris (eds.)
Elsevier Science Publishers B.V. (North-Holland)
© IFIP, 1985

MODELLING THE SPHERE OF EDUCATION

Květa Kronrádová, Bohumil Miniberger, Jaroslav Polák

Charles University Computing Centre
Prague 1, Malostranské nám. 25, Czechoslovakia

The Modelling of the sphere of education is outlined in order to assist improvement in school management with two models, which are described: an aggregated model and a deaggregated one. Both are formed using the system dynamics method.
When models are used, evolutionary trends can be determined and possible evolutionary disproportions can be treated ahead of time.

1. Introduction

Education has a great influence on the activity of the whole national economy. The education a worker has acquired is utilized for tens of years, so that unsuitable decisions concerning education can have a negative effect on national economy for a long time. Nowadays, with growing scientific and technical progress, it is even more so. In order to assist improvement in school management, we have begun constructing a system of models for the information system of education. These models are formed by the system dynamics method /see e.g. $[2]$, $[3]$, $[4]$, $[5]$ /.

While constructing a system of models, we began with a model for the acquisition and utilization of professional skills. Teaching students is certainly the most important activity of a university while a sufficient number of well trained workers with university degrees in all regions of our economy is a necessary condition, though not a sufficient one, for introducing the most progressive results of science successfully into practice.

In the first stage a basic model illustrating, in an aggregated form, the processes of acquiring professional skills and their utilization in the national economy was formed /see $[6]$ /. We will briefly inform you about this aggregated model and then describe the deaggregated model. In both models we will leave out less important details to make them simpler.

In the description of this model we will use the same denotation for a reservoir and for the variable describing the number of its elements, similarly a canal and the variable denoting its flow /i.e. the number of elements which flow through the canal during 1 period/.

2. The aggregated model

The aim of creating the model was to gain a device for the conceptual management of university education, especially to determine the number of

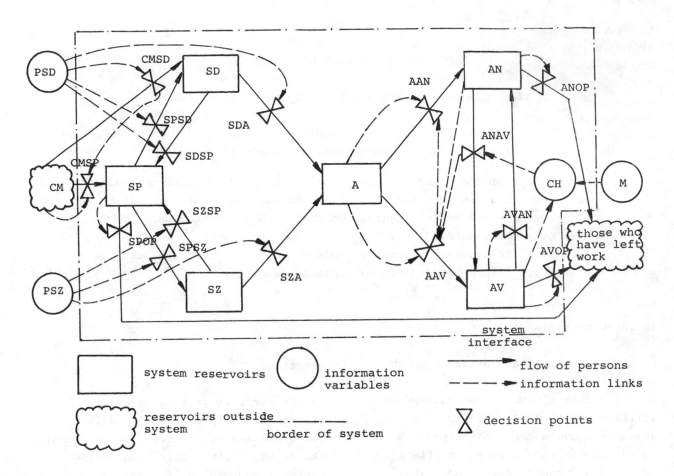

Figure 1: Basic model for acquisition and utilization of professional skills

students to be admitted to universities in relation to the needs of national economy. The graphic model is in Fig. 1. The period is one civil year.

High school graduates from the reservoir CM flow through the canal CMSD into the reservoir SD /containing regular day students at the university/ and through the canal CMSP into reservoir SP /containing employed high school graduates not counting extra-mural students/. From the reservoir SP newly enrolled day students flow through canal SPSD into the reservoir SD and newly enrolled extra-mural students through canal SPSZ into reservoir SZ /containing extra-mural university

students/. Day students leaving universities go from SD through the canal SDSP into the reservoir SP; extra-mural students leaving universities depart from SZ by the canal SZSP back into the reservoir SP. Day study graduates go from the reservoir SD by the canal SDA into the "reservoir" A; extra-mural study graduates proceed from SZ by the canal SZA into "reservoir" A. The "reservoir" A is not a reservoir in the original meaning of the word; elements do not accumulate in it, but pass in and out of it in the same period. From A graduates flow either through canal AAN into the reservoir AN /containing university graduates without qualified jobs/ or through canal AAV into the reservoir AV /containing university - level graduates with qualified jobs/. Through the canals ANAV and AVAN graduates are shifted between AN and AV. When retiring from work, high school graduates pass through the canal SPOP and university - level graduates from the reservoir AN through the canal ANOP and from AV through the canal AVOP out of the system.

How the system will behave is affected by the exogenous variables PSD /number of enrolled day students/, PSZ /number of students enrolled for extra-mural studies/, CM /number of high school graduates and M /number of jobs in the national economy, suitable for university - level graduates/. An important variable which characterizes the state of the system is CH /the number of planned positions requiring university - level qualification, not occupied by a university-level graduate/.

The mathematical model consists of these equations:

$$SDSP_t = 0,15.PSD_{t-1}+0,06.PSD_{t-2}+0,02.PSD_{t-3}$$
$$+0,04.PSD_{t-4}+0,04.PSD_{t-5}+0,002.PSD_{t-6}$$
$$SZSP_t = 0,25.PSZ_{t-1}+0,14.PSZ_{t-2}+0,05.PSZ_{t-3}$$
$$+0,04.PSZ_{t-4}+0,01.PSZ_{t-5}+0,01.PSZ_{t-6}$$
$$SDA_t = 0,22.PSD_{t-4}+0,43.PSD_{t-5}+0,08.PSD_{t-6}$$
$$SZA_t = 0,37.PSZ_{t-5}+0,14.PSZ_{t-6}$$
$$A_t = SDA_t+SZA_t$$
$$AVAN_t = 0,03.AV_{t-1}$$
$$ANAN_t = 0,07.CH_{t-1}$$
$$AAV_t = \frac{ANAV_t}{0,79.AN_{t-1}} . A_t$$
$$AAN_t = A_t - AAV_t$$
$$ANOP_t = 0,07.AN_{t-1}$$
$$AVOP_t = 0,001.AV_{t-1}$$

$$SPOP_t = 0,04.SP_{t-1}$$
$$SP_t = SP_{t-1}+CM_t-PSD_t-PSZ_t+SDSP_t+SZSP_t-SPOP_t$$
$$SD_t = SD_{t-1}+PSD_t-SDSP_t-SDA_t$$
$$SZ_t = SZ_{t-1}+PSZ_t-SZSP_t-SZA_t$$
$$AN_t = AN_{t-1}+AAN_t+AVAN_t-ANAV_t-ANOP_t$$
$$AV_t = AV_{t-1}+AAV_t-AVAN_t+ANAV_t-AVOP_t$$
$$CH_t = M_t-AV_t$$

The values of the parameters included in these equations were estimated so that the behaviour of the model would differ from reality of the years 1971 to 1980 as little as possible. As a measure of the difference between the model and reality, the weighted mean of Theil's inequality coefficients [7] were chosen for those variables of the model for which either their actual value or at least qualified estimates of their values were known. This weighted mean was minimized by Fletcher-Powell's method [1].

Testing the model on retrospective data turned out to be satisfactory, so that the elaboration of five different variants of prognoses /for 1981 until 2000/ was undertaken. These variants show that the evolution so far tends to deepen the inconsistency between the acquisition of professional skill and its utilization, for the number of university graduates who do not have jobs to suit their qualification grew quickly while the number of jobs suitable for graduates and occupied by unqualified persons still stayed large.

A fundamental deficiency of the aggregated model is its inability to map the variances stemming from the unsuitable structure of subjects of study. That is why, in the next phase, the model was deaggregated according to groups of subjects.

3. Deaggregated model

According to state statistic codes, specializations studied at university level are divided into 17 groups:

10 natural sciences
21 mining and geology
22 metallurgy
23 mechanical engineering
26 electrical engineering
28 technical chemistry
29 foods
31 consumer goods industry
36 building
37 communications
39 other technical specializations
40 agriculture
50 medicine
62 economics
76 teacher training
79 other social sciences
80 arts

For each group of subjects /except group 37 for which data were not available/ an individually functioning partial model was constructed. All of these partial models have similar graphic models; one of the possible examples /with 4-year day studies and 5-year extra-mural studies/ is in Fig. 2. The set of equations is also similar, differing only in the values of parameters used in the equations and the initial values of stock variables and values of exogenous variables. The interval is again one civil year.

The system contains the region of university education /i.e. the region supplying qualified staff/ and the region of posts requiring university graduates /i.e. the region of demand for staff/.

The region of university education consists of the region of day studies which is most important and the region of extra-mural studies. Day studies are 4,5 or 6 years long /according to specialization, while in some cases the number of years can change in time/. In one group of subjects there sometimes exist different lengths of study - the graphic model must then include all the possibilities. Extra-mural studies are usually 1 year longer but for certain subjects they do not exist. They can take 5 or 6 years.

As far as specialists are concerned, we have utilized these facts /exceptions can be eliminated for the model/: Individual establishments at which specialists are employed /i.e. firms, offices etc./ cannot make their own decisions how large their staff will be. This is determined centrally with regard to a plan which every organization receives from the State Planning Committee via its ministry. A whole series of institutions takes part in preparing this plan. They must take into account the claims and needs of the employers as well as population evolution, demographic and other data from the state system of statistics. That is why we assume that each establishment is given a precise number of planned staff for which educational requirements and the range of pay are determined in qualification catalogues. While constructing the model further we shall assume, if a planned post requiring qualification from a certain group of specializations is occupied by

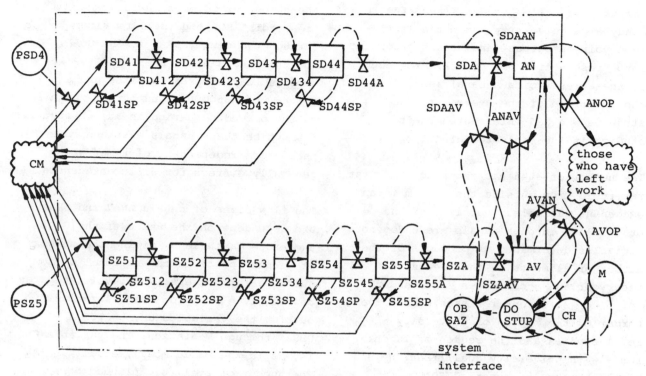

Figure 2: Extended model for acquisition and utilization of professional skills
/example for a group of subjects, for which only 4-year day study and
5-year extra-mural study exists/

a university graduate of a specialization from this group, that it is occupied by a qualified person /not taking into account other requirements/, otherwise it is occupied by someone without professional skills. Every establishment tries to have as large a planned staff as possible because its payroll is in accordance with this number. Some jobs requiring university - level education can in justified cases be occupied by high school graduates with long practice. This is not generally so and in some domains it is completely impossible e.g. medicine, teaching etc. We can further assume that post-graduate students of a certain group of specializations are already employed at planned posts requiring university - level education in this group or that they shall take

such a job during their studies.

A part of the expanded model describing university - level day studies or extra-mural studies of a certain length has a simple form. It consists of some reservoirs $SD_{i1}, \ldots, SD_{ii}$ or $SZ_{i1}, \ldots, SZ_{ii}$ following each other and containing students in the individual grades of the given specialization; the reservoirs are denoted SD_{ij} for day studies and SZ_{ij} for extra-mural studies, where $i = 4,5,6$ means the length of study in years and $j = 1, \ldots, i$ is the order of grade. The reservoirs are joined to each other by canals through which students flow to higher grades. The first reservoir is entered by canals PSD_i and PSZ_i respectively from outside the system.

Through these flow students accepted to study at a university. From the last reservoir an output canal takes graduates into "reservoirs" SDA or SZA. From each of these reservoirs a canal leads into the interface of the system, taking students who had interrupted their studies in the indicated grade.

The number of students entering the first reservoir from outside the system is an exogenous variable. The sizes of the other flows through canals are endogenous variables determined as products of the number of elements in the preceding reservoir and a parameter /independent of time/ different for each canal. The border of the region of university - level studies and the region of labour force with university qualification is formed by the "reservoirs" SDA /containing graduates from day studies of the given group of specializations/ and SZA /containing graduates from extramural studies of the group of specializations/. Again they are not reservoirs in the original meaning of the word.

Forming the region of labour force with university - level qualification was more dificult, especially because the data were hard to reach and less reliable. The reservoirs were the same as in the basic model /they only concern university - qualified workers of the given group of specialization/. The "reservoir" SDA and SZA form a source from which new workers flow into the reservoirs AN and AV through the canals SDAAN, SDAAV and SZAAV. The rest of the canals are again analogous to the basic model.

The flow size through canal SZAAV equals the number of persons in the "reservoir" SZA, and the flow size through the canal SDAAN is SDA-SDAAV. For the canals AVAN, ANOP and AVOP we suppose that their flow sizes are equal to the product of the number of workers in the preceding period in the reservoirs from which these canals exit and some parameter /independent of time/ which generally differs for different canals.

The flow sizes of canals ANAV and SDAAV are dependent on the value of the exogenous variable M /giving the number of planned posts in the national economy suitable for university - level graduates of the given group of specializations/, but for the variables CH, DOSTUP and OBSAZ through mediation. The variable CH is, as in the basic model, equal to M-AV. The number of available planned posts for which university - level education of the given group of specializations is necessary, i.e. the number of jobs that can be occupied in a certain period, are determined by the variable DOSTUP, which is the sum of three addends. One of them is the number of new posts, another the number of posts vacant because qualified persons who held them are leaving altogether or taking jobs not requiring qualification, i.e. AVOP + AVAN, and the third is the number of jobs occupied by unqualified workers and vacant for the same reason, i.e. part of CH - the size of the part is determined by a parameter /independent of time/. Part of the reachable posts are occupied by qualified persons; their number is stated by the variable OBSAZ, the rest by unqualified workers. We assume that the ratio of these parts differs only slightly from the ratio AV:CH, i.e. of all occupied planned posts requiring university - level qualification in the given group of specializations. The modified ratio is determined by using a parameter /independent on time/. SDAAV+ANAV = OBSAZ holds. We suppose that the ratio of flow sizes through canals SDAAV and ANAV is approximately equal to the ratio of the numbers of elements in the reservoirs SDA and AN, partially improved for SDA. The modified ratio is determined by using an independent parameter. That is to say we assume that part of the workers in AN is satisfied with their job and is not keen on finding a post suitable to their education level, whereas fresh graduates all want to obtain posts for which their qualification is necessary.

The equations of the mathematical model are drawn from the facts we have stated in the description of the graphic model and from the law of retaining the number of elements for equations describing the behaviour of reservoirs. The parameters included in equations were estimated /independently for each group of specializations/ analogously to the basic model by minimizing the weighted mean of Theil's inequality coefficients /for the years 1971-82/ for those variables of the model for which their actual values or at least their qualified approximations were known.

A model thus constructed was, however, satisfactory only for some groups of specializations. For other it was not possible to achieve a consistency of the model with reality. This is specially the case of groups of specializations where data are less accurate. Bad reachability and low reliability of some data were the chief limiting factor in the constructions of these models.

4. Utilization of the model

The model enables simulating the behaviour of the region of university - level education and the region of qualified labour force, i.e. to quantify the inequality between the "supply" and "demand" for workers with professional skills using the variables AN and CH. The model also enables trying out different management strategies in advance and choosing the most satisfactory one. It is, e.g., possible to try different algorithms for determining the number of students to be accepted to study at university-level and to choose the number that best corresponds to the needs of our national economy. For instance the following algorithm was tested for the basic model:

$$PSD_t = 0,26 . CM_t$$

$$PSZ_t = 0,02 . /CH_{t-1} - 0,79 . AN_{t-1}/.$$

5. Bibliography:

[1] Fletcher, R., Powell, M. J. D.: A Rapid Descent Method for Minimization, Computer Journal 2 /1963/ 163-168

[2] Forrester, J. W.: Industrial Dynamics /Wright-Allen Press, Cambridge 1961/

[3] Forrester, J. W.: Principles of Systems /Wright-Allen Press, Cambridge 1968/

[4] Forrester, J. W.: Urban Dynamics /Wright-Allen Press, Cambridge 1969/

[5] Forrester, J. W.: World Dynamics /Wright-Allen Press, Cambridge 1971/

[6] Miniberger, B. et al: A Model for Acquirement and Utilization of Professional Skills. Comp. Center of Charles Univ., Prague /1982/

[7] Theil, H.: Principles of Econometrics, Amsterdam, /North Holland, Amsterdam, 1971/

COMPUTERS IN EDUCATION, K. Duncan and D. Harris (eds.)
Elsevier Science Publishers B.V. (North-Holland)
© IFIP, 1985

TEACHING PROBLEM SOLVING IN COMPLEX SITUATIONS USING SIMULATION MODELS

José J. González

Department of Computer Science
Agder Regional College of Engineering
N-4890 Grimstad, Norway

Human actions occur in coupled dynamic systems of overwhelming complexity. Both everyday experience and laboratory studies suggest that man's problem-solving behaviour is inappropiate when dealing with complex dynamic systems. It is argued that neither factual knowledge about phenomena, regardless of whether belonging to natural, economic or social sciences, nor a synthesis of such in the form of global models (world models, urban models, etc.) is a sufficient strategy in dealing with real complex systems. The more modest aim of introducing decision-making training in computer simulated models as part of the curricula of engineers and planners is likely to prove more effective. Teaching experiences are briefly reported. Criteria for construction of simulation models for use in higher education are proposed. Finally, current work on a multiexecutive simulation model is described.

1.   INTRODUCTION

Human actions, whether industrial, agricultural, financial, social or political in origin, affect very complex systems. Although those systems may greatly differ in particular details they have nevertheless common global characteristics. They are dynamic and highly coupled. They have an overwhelming richness of components: it is hardly possible to identify most of them, and even harder to keep track of their full interactions. Actions may fail to achieve the intended effect and, more often than not, they have unexpected repercussions; the picture is further complicated due to time lag by propagation of effects[1]. The coupled dynamic and intransparent nature of systems is a formidable challenge even to modern computerized society. The world today certainly abounds in man-made crises (political, economical, ecological) due to inappropiate actions. But it is usually overlooked that positive spin-off effects equally often arise. When this occurs, insufficient understanding of systems prevents us from having the ground prepared for these shoots to grow under optimal conditions. A case in point: in most countries society has failed to prepare for optimal use of computers in education although the snowball has been rolling for decades and has become an avalanche by now.

The availability of modern computers has given a boost to system dynamics. Powerful tools have been developed to simulate and analyze more or less general systems. With regard to the generality of the systems, the efforts culminated with the world models of the Club of Rome [1]. While it is difficult to overestimate the importance of system dynamics as such, the prophecies of the Club of Rome can hardly be taken literally (and perhaps never were intended to). Many questions have been posed about the validity of the models chosen. A crucial objection is that world models play determinism[2], in that key future developments are predicted based on given initial conditions. However, it is an impossible task to ascertain more than a tiny fraction of the relevant initial conditions. Indeed, one can safely assume that one does not know more a small subset of the crucial natural, social and economical laws, thus making the question of sufficiency of initial conditions a futile one [2]. The same objections apply mutatis mutandis for less general global models[3].

2.   HUMAN PROBLEM SOLVING IN VERY COMPLEX SITUATIONS

While system dynamics is concerned with modelling reality, and its aim is to provide more or less accurate simulations of some object situation, the cognitive psychologist Dietrich Dörner took a different approach [3]. He wanted to study the problem-solving behaviour of individuals and groups who are facing very complex dynamic systems. For this

objective he constructed scenarios that
did not necessarily resemble reality in
specific details but in global characteristics such as overwhelming richness
of components, intransparency, dynamic
behaviour and degree of interaction
among the components. Dörner's seminal
work was the simulation model "Tanaland"
(1975&1978) where he operated with an
african scenario with two different tribes and its flora, fauna and ecological
characteristics. An interactive computer
simulation program allowed twelve independent volunteers each to play the
role of benevolent dictators by being
able to determine actions during a fairly long "time" interval. The volunteers
were carefully chosen among university
students of different faculties and,
according to psychological criteria,
they provided a better than average selection. The point with an african
scenario was to avoid preconceptions
which could have arisen if the benevolent dictators had been confronted with
a familiar situation. The volunteers
could choose among a rich gamut of agricultural, industrial and social actions.
Each one was given the task of bettering
the lots of his/her fictitious subjects.
During the "reign" of every volunteer
his/her performance and lines of reasoning were closely watched by Dörner and
coworkers through observation, interviews and monitoring of the results.
Although the volunteers did intend to
better the living standard of the tribes
in Tanaland, the results were devastat-
ing: only one out of the twelve benevolent dictators succeeded in this task
while all the others created chaos.
According to Dörner one could identify
several types of inappropiate behaviour.
The most important were: insufficient
definition of aims; particular attention
toward parts of the system to the de-
triment of the whole; disregard of secondary effects (i.e., unintended consequences of actions); overmanaging;
"authoritarian" behaviour [3].

3.   TEACHING PROBLEM SOLVING IN
         COMPLEX DYNAMIC SYSTEMS

Observation of typical patterns of inappropiate problem-solving behaviour
led Dörner to suggest strategies for
problem solving in complex dynamic systems [4]. Indeed, if inappropiate behaviour towards complex dynamic systems is
as widespread as factual crises and
Dörner's laboratory experiments seem to
suggest, it is imperative to educate
would-be decision-makers in this field.
This means that engineers, economists
and social scientists ought to get
thorough training in systems theory and

practical experience in problem solving
as decision-makers in simulated scenarios. To gain this experience in complex
dynamic systems the scenarios need only
loosely resemble real situations. One
may assume that general experience in
managing complex dynamic systems will be
an asset when confronting reality. (This
point will be further discussed in the
next Section). Now, Tanaland and similar
scenarios invented by Dörner and others
can easily be implemented on medium size
and even small size computers. This is,
of course, very important for availabi-
ity at educational institutions[4].

During the last eight years I have regularly taught a course in Strategic
Problem Solving for engineers and
economists at Agder Regional College of
Engineering. The course introduces system dynamics at a very general level.
The Tanaland scenario and Dörner's findings are thoroughly discussed. Finally,
the students have the opportunity to
play the role of benevolent dictators in
"Doriland", an african scenario differing from Tanaland in many details. The
performance of most of the students as
decision-makers in Doriland is usually
reasonably good. Since Tanaland and
Doriland are quite different scenarios,
one is tempted to conclude that an exposure to general problem solving in
complex dynamic systems helped students
to implement more appropiate decision-
making behaviours. At the same time, the
very fact that students of this course
managed to perform reasonably well made
it possible to observe other traits. An
interesting finding was that most succesful students did not take advantage
of positive spin-off effects, thus staying far below the optimum level.

Although the problem solving behaviour
of the participants of my course was
quite satisfactory, care must be exer-
cised when interpreting the results. Indeed, Tanaland and Doriland, though different, still were similar in many respects. The reason for better performance
in the latter case may be due to similarities of the scenarios rather than to
knowledge of appropiate problem-solving
strategies.

4.   MULTIEXECUTIVE SIMULATION MODELS

Both Tanaland and Doriland are single-
executive models, i.e., they involve one
decision-maker. This person plays a dictatorial role towards a simulated scenario. One cannot exclude the possibility that Dörner's findings may partly be
due to the special dictatorial role. I
am hinting   that there may be a

psychological law behind Lord Acton's dictum that "power tends to corrupt and absolute power corrupts absolutely". But there is a more fundamental reason to proceed from single-executive to multi-executive models, i.e. those involving several decision-makers. This has to do with what Hayek calls the fragmentation of knowledge: the fact that each member of society can have only a small fraction of the knowledge possesed by all, and that each is therefore ignorant of most of the facts on which the working of society rests [5]. One may add, that fragmentation of knowledge cannot be overcome by groups no matter how organized, even if in posession of an optimum database. At no point will any human being have more than a very restricted knowledge of facts. Another point to remember is that even the sum total of human knowledge is but a fraction of the total facts. Accordingly, the way civilization works is by utilization of knowledge which is and remains widely dispersed among individuals. Furthermore, for human actions to be succesful they must observe rules which are adapted to many other facts that one does not know [2,5].

Simulation models reflecting fragmentation of knowledge, division of labour and complexity of design comparable to any existing situation are unthinkable. But one should aim at developing simulation models for educational purposes containing the crucial features in a nutshell. In the following, a general proposal is put forward and in the next Section a concrete example is discussed. A minimum requirement would be that simulation models for teaching problem solving in complex dynamic systems ought to reflect the facts mentioned above by consisting of several units interacting with each other both through internal properties of the system and through executive actions. Each unit represents an environment where a human executive can act, for instance, a factory, an institution, a bank, etc. The system should also contain subsystems that can interact with most of these units, e.g., the ecological subsystem. The total system can be affected by actions from several independent executives who, alike reality, know many though not all facts about a particular environment and can influence the system through actions which in most cases operate within this particular environment or units interacting with it. The actions of the executive attached to this environment will mostly be unpredictable for people standing outside because these actions will be based on knowledge of facts that they do not share. Every unit of the

simulation model will still be a formidable problem even to the attached executive. Furthermore, through the interaction with other units and confrontation with their unexpected behaviour, each executive will face the system as in real situations: a complex dynamic system operated by several intelligent beings each contriving to solve problems related to their part of the whole. However, the aim should not be to design complex systems for their own sake but to achieve effects known from systems in modern civilization where widely dispersed knowledge can be utilized through interaction between several units. At the same time, one would expect unpredictable ecological, social and economical effects due to repercussion of actions. Altogether, this would provide a setup for research about appropiate problem-solving strategies according to integrated ecological, economical and social criteria.

5. A CONCRETE CASE OF A MULTIEXECUTIVE MODEL

At Agder Regional College of Engineering my collaborators, the economist Dag Aasland, the students Bodil M. Myhra and Liv R. Rasmussen and myself started 1982 an interdisciplinary project aimed at implementing a simulation model consisting, to begin with, of 1-2 factories , a bank, consumers and political authorities. The final aim is to have an operational system for educational purposes and research where each unit is operated by an attached executive[5]. In its final version the system will be implemented on several small (128K RAM) computers connected in network, each unit operating on one computer. On running the simulation model, a tutor will play the important role of judicial authority, i.e., the tutor will care that agreements and the rules of the game are observed. The tutor will additionally operate a console computer taking care of the start of the simulation and of the interactions between the units and with other subsystems. We intend the system to have the following properties:
1) Production of commodities and services. We do not aim at make-believe but at simulating them in a way that can be used by buyers for their aims.
2) Development and invention of new commodities and services.
3) Competition and cooperation, both among units and with a simulated external world.
4) Social interactions. Later on ecological interactions as well.
5) It will be possible to operate the model in different ways. One interesting

possibility is allowing other units to be represented in the group playing the role of the authorities-unit such that the decisions of the latter be taken in a democratic way.

In designing models like this it is desirable to achieve a product resembling some would-be piece of reality, not necessarily emulating some existing system. In this way, it is possible to cut down the size of the model to something manageable by a network of small computers. Furthermore, it is desirable to model each unit (i.e., a factory, a bank, etc.) so that they present a challenge to and demand qualified actions from students of management or economy (or engineers with sufficient training in these fields). Very little is known about how to combine simplicity with model realism in this sense. Therefore, we have taken the following heuristic approach: to begin with, we concentrate the functions of the consumers, of the authorities and of the tutor in a superexecutive being able to act on behalf of all of these. (Needless to say, the role of the tutor-superexecutive will be played by a qualified teacher). Thus, during an intermediate test phase we devise a simpler model consisting of three interacting units, the other two being a factory and a bank. Furthermore, during this phase we open up the system by allowing the tutor at any time to interphere and readjust parameters as deus ex machina whenever it is necessary for the system to behave in a sensible way. In this way, experience will help us to incorporate desired features into the model until we end up with a satisfactory version. Work is in progress and we expect to have a working prototype around spring 1985.

Finally, I want to stress that the criteria and heuristic principles for the construction of simulation models proposed here must be subjected to careful scrutiny. We do hope to get feedback and constructive criticism from any others who are working along similar lines.

ACKNOWLEDGEMENT

I am very grateful to professor Dörner for the starting idea of Doriland and for useful conversations and discussions.

FOOTNOTES

(1) As an example of unintended consequences and time lag effects one has atmospheric pollution. The far away transport of pollution was detected by observant people already in the infancy of industrialization. In Ibsen's drama

"Brand" (1866) the principal character gives a vivid account of atmospheric pollution of british origin in Western Norway (Act V). Noxious effects of transported pollution became apparent for scandinavian countries since the nineteentwenties when fish populations started to disappear in lakes. However, it was not until the nineteenseventies, when extensive damages in middle european forests were detected, that most people became aware of major ecological implications.

(2) The question whether socio-economical systems are indeterministic does not need to be debated here. The essential point for practical purposes is that very complex systems display unpredictable behaviour.

(3) These remarks should not be taken as derogatory toward system dynamics. There is no doubt that system dynamics has contributed enormously to our understanding of the behaviour of systems and that it is a valuable tool for modelling systems. All I am trying to say is that limitations of knowledge about both laws and facts (initial conditions) severely restrict the class of systems which can be modelled faithfully.

(4) Indeed, it is feasible to implement illustrative scenarios on usual school computers of 64-128K RAM thus making important ideas of system dynamics accesible to secondary or even primary education.

(5) In the classroom situation an executive may mean a group of students in charge of the unit in question.

REFERENCES

[1] Meadows, D.H. et al., Limits to growth (1972).
    Forrester, J.W., World dynamics (1973).
[2] von Hayek, F.A., Law, legislation and liberty, Vol. I: Rules and order (Routledge & Kegan Paul, London, 1973).
[3] Dörner, D., Psychologisches Experiment: Wie Menschen eine Welt verbessern wollten und sie dabei zerstörten, Bild der Wissenschaft 2 (1975) 48-53.
    Dörner, D. & Reither, F., Über das Problemlösen in sehr komplexen Realitätsbereichen, Zeitschrift für experimentelle und angewandte Psychologie XXV (1978) 527-551.
[4] Dörner, D., Vernetztes Denken - Strategien zur Problembewältigung, Bild der Wissenschaft 3 (1977) 97 - 102.
    Dörner, D., Kreuzig, H.W., Reither, F. and Stäudel, T. (eds.), Lohhausen - Vom Umgang mit Unbestimmtheit und

Komplexität (Hans Huber, Bern, 1983).

[5] von Hayek, F.A., The constitution
    of liberty (Routledge & Kegan Paul,
    London, 1960 & 1976), especially
    Ch. 2. See also [2].

COMPUTERS IN EDUCATION, K. Duncan and D. Harris (eds.)
Elsevier Science Publishers B.V. (North-Holland)
© IFIP, 1985

COMPUTER SIMULATIONS AND COGNITIVE DEVELOPMENT

Klaus Breuer

Universitaet-GH Paderborn
Fachbereich Erziehungswissenschaften
Warburgerstrasse 100
D-4790 Paderborn
FR of Germany

A model of computer simulation uses in social-science classes is outlined. It is based on an approach to learning and teaching from cognitive psychology. On this basis computer simulations can become a central
part of meaningful complex learning environments. From theoretical
assumptions can be predicted that learning in such environments should
result in the development of cognitive and of learning strategies as
opposed to mere content learning, and thus forster cognitive development. Experiences from formal classes are reported and will be complemented by statistical results at the conference.

1. COMPUTER SIMULATIONS AND INSTRUCTION

The use of computer simulations in instruction is part of the early recommendations for computer applications in
education (13,34). And there are powerful demonstrations for the simulation of
complex natural laws, like the simulated
mutation of the drosophila fly in genetics, for example (11). With the development of special simulation languages, a
shift from the mere use of simulation
programs to the active development of
models and their simulation by students
has become possible (26). Today the
microcomputer has given new flexibility
to the use of computer simulations in
education. On this basis the assumption
of a growing use of computer simulations
in instruction on all levels of teaching
seems a valid one, though there is still
a lack of educational theory which could
explain for significant learning processes fostered by computer-based simulations (33). This status in return does
not allow for systematic planning and
evaluation of computer simulation uses
within educational contexts.
This paper tries to contribute to the
closure of this gap reporting on a two
years experience with the "theory related development and evaluation" of
teaching (31), founded on computer-based
simulations in social science classes
within the German vocational school
system. The approach is based on
- the general assumptions of cognitive
  psychology (30),
- the theoretical framework of cognitive
  complexity(4,19,24,29), and
- the results from new approaches to
  problem-solving research, based on
  the simulation of complex dynamic
  environments (9,10,27).

2. BASIC ASSUMPTIONS OF COGNITIVE PSY-
CHOLOGY

The cognitive paradigm in psychology has
overcome the behavioral stimulus-respon-
se models of learning by taking into
account human information processing in
reference to learning and cognition
(2,8). One of the widely shared assumptions within cognitive theories is
that of structure of memory. The cognitive system is considered to be made up
from three major, interrelated components (30): content structure (knowledge
of what), cognitive strategies (knowledge of how), and learning strategies
(knowledge of how to proceed).

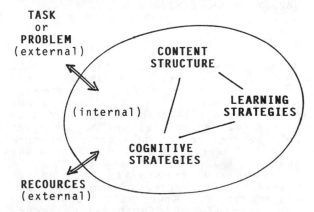

Figure 1. Basic components of the cognitive system (mod. from 31)

In the content structure concepts and
attidues are stored and linked within
semantic networks. The controlling components of the content structure, the
cognitive strategies, allow the application of existing concepts, the adaption
of concepts to new situations, and the

setting up of interrelations between existing components in reference to given problems. Learning strategies can become operative if there are no appropriate concepts and/or strategies available in a given stituation, which is the case of a cognitive conflict. Learning strategies organize the processes of selection and the embedding of all new information into the cognitive system.

From this general model of the cognitive system there are at least two important implications for teaching:

* It is necessary that instruction provides students with concepts and attitudes as well as with strategies of thinking and learning. SCHRODER, KARLINS & PHARES (25) refer to this position by stressing the need for more "process learning" in opposition to the traditional mere "content learning".
* Meaningful learning, as opposed to root-memory learning, arises from cognitive conflicts. Instruction can induce such conflicts by confronting students with problems. Such problems first have to allow to be linked to exiting components within the cognitive structure of students (1); they secondly have to be neither trivial (induce no conflict) nor too hard (arise tendency of avoidance) (31).

A more detailed description of information processing within problem-solving activities is available within the concept of cognitive complexity sensu HARVEY, HUNT, SCHRODER & STREUFERT.

3. THE CONCEPT OF COGNITIVE COMPLEXITY

Within the works on the concept, labeled conceptual complexity too, there are two basic aspects. The first gives a model of the cognitive system, the second explains the situational characteristics of information processing. They both can only be scetched roughly here; for more details the reader should refer to the sources (19),(22),(24), and (29).
The cognitive complexity of a person represents the degree to which the cognitive semantic space is differentiated and integrated. Differentiation stands for the number of semantic dimensions a person can apply in the perception of a problem. Integration refers to the combinatory rules by which different dimensions can be interrelated and combined in the development of perspectives for judgement. Thus a cognitive less complex, or simple person has a smaller number of dimensions which are not highly discriminated in themselves, and a

smaller and less flexible set of combinatory rules for the processing of scale values on the dimensions in a certain content area.
A cognitivly more complex person is able to refer to more dimensions and to make finer distinctions on them. The scale values developed can be organized to different perspectives towards the given body of information. They themselves can be judged again for their appropriateness and be applied in final judgement.

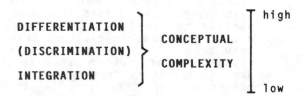

Figure 2. Basic elements of conceptual complexity theory

Between the endpoints of high and low conceptual complexity individuals, and groups also, can be rated in respect to their levels of complexity (15,24).
The situational levels of information processing are considered to be based on the interaction between a person's cognitive complexity and the characteristics of its environment. In this position the authors of the concept (14) refer back to a psychological orientation which already has been expressed by LEWIN (17) in the formula $B = f (P , E)$; that is, somebody's behavior results from a function interrelating the person and its environment. The level of information processing is depicted by a reverse U-shaped curve. Both a low and a high level of environmental complexity reduce it.

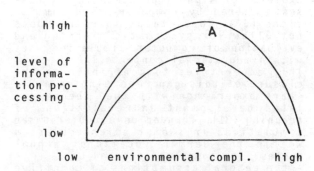

Figure 3. Situational levels of information processing (from 23)

A maximum level is reached at a medium level of environmental complexity. Within this relation conceptually more complex individuals (curve A) reach higher levels of information processing than

simpler ones (curve B).
In reference to the general model of the cognitive system given above, the concept of cognitive complexity stresses the components of content structure and of cognitive strategies. Content structure is depicted by differentiation and discrimination, that is concepts and attitudes and their degree of refinement. Not yet contained is the idea of a semantic network between the different elements (7,12), which however seems to be compatible to the concept. Cognitive strategies are embedded in integration, the set of combinatory rules for interrelating concepts and the higher order ones for judging the appropriateness of the interferences drawn (18).
Learning strategies are not referred to expressively, though there is little doubt that conclusions and interferences developed in problem-oriented information processing and found reliable, that is in other words suitable to solve an existing cognitive conflict, can become embedded into the cognitive system. This way learning can result in:

* the refinement of existing concepts or attitudes, enhancing discrimination,
* the embedding of new concepts or attitudes in content structure, enhancing differentiation, and/or
* the refinement of existing and/or embedding of new rules for interferences and evaluation, enhancing integration,
* which alltogether contributes to the development of cognitive complexity as a domain specific trait (31).

The three varieties of learning-results can be considered as different levels on a continuum between concrete and abstract knowledge. The establishment of interrelations between these levels is import in respect to both perspectives; that is, sometimes concrete facts given have to be generalized to global principles, and the other way around, some situations demand the processing of concrete facts which are in accordance with principles at hand.
Educationally relevant implications from the theoretical considerations terminate in two proposals. The first is process learning, stressing the development of an encreased flexibility in information processing (15, 25). The second is conceptual level matching, stressing the improvement of student-environment-interaction in teaching in respect to forster cognitive complexity (14, 16).

4. CONCEPTUAL LEVEL MATCHING AND PROCESS LEARNING

To match the complexity of the learning environment to the levels of cognitive complexity of students is a direct application of the assumptions on the situational characteristics of information processing stated above (compare Fig. 3). The simple rationale is: The lower the level of cognitive complexity of students, the more structured should be the learning environment (14). At a low level teaching should be "clearly organized within normative structure", at a high level teaching should become multilateral interdependent (20).
Practical application is forstered by grouping students according to their conceptual levels into homogenious subgroups within classes. In such groups the levels of interaction while working on problems should offer a maximum of stimulation to the information processing activities of each individual and avoid the confrontation with arguments on the subject matter much below or too much above each member's level of complexity. In this respect the idea of conceptual level matching is in accordance with KOHLBERG's "plus one" thesis from moral education (32). The theoretical assumptions have empirically been found valid in our recent research (6). The intra-group interaction in problem-solving situations contributes to cognitive development presumably by the fact that the individuals are confronted with different interpretations on the given facts from different group members. This way new interrelations between existing concepts can be established, alternative integrations to a given problem can be detected, and higher order rules for judging their validity can be developed. It makes up the need for information processing activities which, within the cognitive system, are part of the components of cognitive and of learning strategies. This effect of intra-group interaction is in correspondence with the request for more process-learning already (25). The attributes of learning environments which are necessary for its stimulation are:

1. Opportunity of choice to the individual student.
2. Chance to work alone - "to search, inquire, hypothesize, try out, and to create a product of his own." (ibid)
3. Chance to work "... as a member of a team in solving significant societal problems; to recognize, accept and respect differences among individuals, and to develop via mutual understanding." (ibid)

4. Offer of "... special process educational materials developed   to give
the child practice in information
search, information   utilization
/forming concepts, testing hypothe-
ses/, and the use of feedback for
modifying the ways he codes the environment." (ibid)

An example for the realization of "process educational material", from the
authors' opinion, has been the talking
typewriter developed by MOORE and ANDER-
SON (21). They have labeled their device
for the self-directed study of reading
and writing an example of an "authotelic
environment", which stands for meaning-
fullness, responsiveness and riskless-
ness to the students. The three features
go along with the requirements for meaningful learning given already at the
beginning of the paper. And this allows
to come back to the potentials of compu
ter-based simulations in reference to
cognitive development now.

5. PROCESS LEARNING AND COMPUTER-BASED SIMULATIONS

Regarding the theoretical considerations, and our first experiences too,
computer simulations offer an outstanding chance for the development of process educational teachware to be used as
part of authotelic environments. The
three basic components are:

1. The statement of a meaningful, complex problem. It describes a decision-making situation, giving the
   social context, the starting conditions of the system, the set of variables, which can be influenced, and
   a global goal for students' coping
   within that situation (compare 28).
2. The simulation program, representing
   a model of the decision- making situation, which can calculate the new
   status of the system after each decision period and give feedback on its
   parameters to the students.
3. The students work in small-group
   teams on the problems given.

The students have to analyze the situation, to work out a conceptualisation of
the system, to define the specific goals
of their coping with the problem, and to
define the set of decisions which is to
be entered into the simulation program.
The feedback they receive from the program defines a variation of the starting
situation and asks for the iteration of
their activities.

The requirements for such uses of simulation programs are:
a) The program is a model of a complex
segment of reality. Examples are given
by the simulations which have been developed in problem solving research in
recent years in Germany and in the United States. They for example depict
- the economic system of a municipality
  which is to be improved by the "town
  council" (9),
- the microeconomic system of a company
  which is to be run by the "manager"
  (35),
- the flood control-system within a
  county which is to be operated by an
  "executive" (27), or
- the living conditions of an African
  tribe which should be improved by an
  "advisor" (10).
All these worlds are part of everybodys'
all-day knowledge, and most of us have
already been critics of the poor actions
of experts. In "real" action our knowledge however proves to be not differentiated, discriminated, and/or integrated
enough for successful decisionmaking and
thus gives rise for cognitive conflicts.
b) The models are dynamic. They depict
processes with, without actions from the
decisionmakers, collapse after some time.
That is, the tribe vanishes from starva-
tion, the company gets in the red, and
so on. This stresses the need for decision-making, and as a necessary prerequisite the solving of a good deal of
cognitive conflicts, that is learning.
c) The models are responsive. After each
period of decision-making the new status
of the system is reported to the students. This allows to test the adequacy
of the present conceptualisations of the
system, and most times results in the
need for their revision, that is in
cognitive conflicts again. This way the
statuses of the system give feedback to
the levels of information-processing by
the students. In addition the open definition of the problem, there is a global
goal only, keeps information-processing
on the level of problem-solving and
prevents the decrease to mere application of rules.
d) The decision-making processes within
the model and the learning environment
are free from physical and psychological
risks. All decisions are made on a symbolic level and the simulation programs
calculate symbolic results only. This
neither theatens the beings within the
simulated environment nor the deciosin-
makers themselves. For this reason none
of the problems contains features of
competion.
e) The decision-making processes are
based on small-group interaction within
the teams. Conceptual level matching is
practiced by forming homogenious groups

according to the individual levels of cognitive complexity. Within each team this results in the confrontation with different integrations from the members, the need for argumentation, and for adoption which all requires the application of cognitive and of learning strategies. Matching of structure within the learning environments has not yet been practiced. Present works aim at the development of program-features which can adopt feedback to the working-groups according to their different levels of cognitive complexity.

6. EXPERIENCES FROM CLASS

Present experiences go back to several singular applications of three different simulation environments and to one year of formal teaching within a class of a vocational school. Within that class three simulations have been applied in the topics of third world aid, of managing a company, and of global economic development. In total the lecturing time spend on the simulations within the classes comes up to 20 hours of teamwork.
Empirical analysis is based on a control-group design in which the research class is accompanied by a control-class. Dependent variables are
- the levels of individudual cognitive complexity,
- the decision-making behavior in a posttest simulation, and the
- attitudes of the students towards their learning experiences.
The corresponding analyses are not yet finished. At the time of the conference they will be available, including the results from two more classes with formal teaching during an equivalent period. Qualitative results from informal observations may already be stated, in respect to the acceptance of the learning environments by the students, and their engagement in learning.
Before we give these final statements, there is one necessary information on the German vocational school system and the relevancy of politics/economy classes for students within vocational schools: students are aged 17 to 21 years; they have to attend school for one or two days a week, while being trained in a company for the remaining days. Main subjects are technology, technical math and technical drawing. Religion and politics/economy classes are obligations with negative perception from most students. Within that context the work within the simulation environments has been surprising: students have been highly engaged in the decision-making processes; they have been busy for all the lecturing time without any

hints to reluctance or any kind of destructive behavior. They habe been able to influence the systems by their decisions in a way that most teams finally attained developments towards a positive trend.
The grouping procedures have been accepted without any denials, and from our observations there have been effective intra-group communications.
It would be surprising to find divergent results from the formal analyses.

7. REFERENCES

(1) Aebli, H., Zwoelf Grundformen des Lernens (Klett, Stuttgart,1983).
(2) Anderson, J.R., Language, memory and thought (Erlbaum, Hillsdale, NJ., 1976).
(3) Breuer, K., Computerunterstuetztes Lernen auf der Basis eines Informationsprogramms (Arbeitsgemeinschaft fuer Hochschuldidaktik, Hamburg, 1981).
(4) Breuer, K., Personen und Medien in Interaktion, Schulpraxis 4 (1983) 22-25.
(5) Breuer, K., Assessing training for problem-oriented information retrieval, in Rijnsdorp, J.E. and Plomp, Tj. (eds.), Training for tomorrow (Pergamon, Oxford, 1984).
(6) Breuer, K. and Reising, D., Innere Differenzierung nach kognitiven Niveaugruppen, Typoscript, Universitaet Paderborn (in preparation).
(7) Doerner, D., Kognitionstheoretische Aspekte der Darbietung von Lerninhalten, in Frey, K. (ed.), Curriculum-Handbuch, Bd. II (Piper, Muenchen, 1975).
(8) Doerner, D., Problemloesen als Informationsverarbeitung (Kohlhammer, Stuttgart, 1976).
(9) Doerner, D. and coworkers, Lohhausen (Huber, Bern, 1983).
(10) Doerner, D. and Reither, F., Ueber das Problemloesen in sehr komplexen Realitaetsbereichen, Zeitschrift fuer experimentelle und angewandte Psychologie 25(1978) 527-551.
(11) Eichmann, E.H., Simulationen im PLATO System, in Brunnstein, K., Haefner, K. and Haendler, W. (eds.), Rechner-Gestuetzter Unterricht (Springer, Berlin, 1974).
(12) Evans, S., The structure of instructional knowledge: An operational model, Instructional Science 2 (1974) 421-450.
(13) Eyferth, K. and coworkers, Computer im Unterricht (Klett, Stuttgart, 1974).

(14)   Hunt, D.E., Person-environment in-
       teraction: A challange found wan-
       ting before it was tried, Review
       of educational research 45 (1975)
       209-230.

(15)   Hunt, D.E. and coworkers, Asses-
       sing conceptual level by the para-
       graph completion method (Ontario
       Institute for Studies in Educa-
       tion, Informal Series/3, Toronto
       1977).

(16)   Krohne, H.W., Kognitive Struktu-
       riertheit als Bedingung und Ziel
       schulischen Lernens, Zeitschrift
       fuer Entwicklungspsychologie und
       Paedagogische Psychologie 9 (1977)
       54-75.

(17)   Lewin, K., Principles of topologi-
       cal psychology, (McGraw-Hill, New
       York, 1936).

(18)   Luer, G., Anwendung von Problem-
       loesungsstrategien im Unterricht,
       in Frey, K. and Lang, M. (eds.)
       Kognitionspsychologie und natur-
       wissenschaftlicher Unterricht
       (Huber, Bern, 1973).

(19)   Mandl, L. and Huber, G.L. (eds.)
       Kognitive Komplexitaet (Hogrefe,
       Goettingen, 1978).

(20)   Miller, A., Conceptual matching
       models and interactional research
       in education, Review of educa-
       tional research 51 (1981) 33-84.

(21)   Moore, O.K. and Anderson, A.R.,
       Some principles for the design of
       clarifying educational environ-
       ments, in Goslin, D.A. (ed.) Hand-
       book of sozialisation theory and
       research (Rand McNally, Chicago,
       1969).

(22)   Seiler, T.B., Kognitive Struktu-
       riertheit (Kohlhammer, Stuttgart,
       1973).

(23)   Schroder, H.M., Conceptual comple-
       xity and personality organization,
       in Schroder, H.M. and Suedfeld, P.
       (eds.), Personality and informa-
       tion processing (Holt, Rinehart &
       Winston, New York, 1971).

(24)   Schroder, H.M., Driver, D. and
       Streufert, S., Human information
       processing (Holt, Rinehart & Win-
       ston, New York, 1967).

(25)   Schroder, H.M., Karlins, M. and
       Phares, J., Education for freedom
       (Wiley, New York, 1973).

(26)   Simon, H. (ed.), Computer-Simula-
       tion und Modellbildung im Unter-
       richt (Oldenbourg, Muenchen,
       1980).

(27)   Streufert, S., Flood-Simulation
       Program, Penn. State Univ. (perso-
       nal demonstration 1983).

(28)   Streufert, S., The stress of exe-
       lence, Across the board 20 (1983)
       8-16.

(29)   Streufert, S. and Streufert, S.,
       Behavior in the complex environ-
       ment (Winston, Washington, 1978).

(30)   Tennyson, R.D. and Breuer, K.,
       Cognitive-based design guidelines
       for using video and computer tech-
       nology in course development, in
       Zuber-Skerrit, O. (ed.), Video in
       higher education (Kogan Page, Lon-
       don, 1984).

(31)   Tulodziecki, G. and Breuer, K.,
       Zur Entwicklung von Unterrichts-
       konzepten, in Tulodziecki, G.,
       Breuer, K. and Hauf, A., Konzepte
       fuer das berufliche Lehren und
       Lernen (Klinkhardt und Handwerk u.
       Technik, Bad Heilbrunn u. Hamburg,
       1984).

(32)   Turiel, E., An experimental test
       of the sequentiality of develop-
       mental stages in the child's moral
       judgements, Journal of personality
       and social psychology (1966) 611-
       618.

(33)   Wedekind, J., Unterrichtsmedium
       Computersimulation (Lexika, Weil
       der Stadt, 1981).

(34)   Zinn, K.L., An evaluative review
       of uses of computers in instruc-
       tion, Project CLUE final report,
       Univ. of Mich. (3rd ed. 1973).

(35)   Putz-Osterloh, W., Ueber die
       Beziehung zwischen Testintelligenz
       und Problemloeseforschung, Zeit-
       schrift fuer Psychologie 189
       (1981) 79 - 100.

COMPUTERS IN EDUCATION, K. Duncan and D. Harris (eds.)
Elsevier Science Publishers B.V. (North-Holland)
© IFIP, 1985

DATA COMMUNICATION AND COMPUTER NETWORKS:

"A PROPOSAL FOR A CURRICULUM AND A SURVEY OF DIFFERENT PEDAGOGICAL AIDS"

A.C. Derycke [*] - C. Nora [**]

[*] Université de Lille I - C.U.E.E.P 59655 Villeneuve d'Ascq Cédex - France -
[**] Ecole Nationale Supérieure des Télécommunications

46 rue Barrault - 75634 Paris Cédex 13 - France -

This paper focuses on the development of data communication and computer network
education. The first part presents the chosen approach to undertake this problem: the
constitution of a working group, for which the main goals are the definition of a
curriculum, the inventory of the possible pedagogical aids, and a list of
recommendations to develop further aids. The second part presents special courseware at
the introductory level, which matches the previous requirements.

1. THE PROBLEM OF DATA COMMUNICATION EDUCATION

Microcomputers are spreading quite rapidly
everywhere; data processing is part of any
industry now. With them, the need for
communication is growing tremendously.

At the same time, new kinds of applications are
developing with the arrival of new services,
based on telecommunication networks, like
electronic directories using videotex terminals.

With these technological evolutions, it seems
quite impossible now to continue training e.d.
professionals without any instruction on network
and data communication.

For a few years, training of telecommunication
specialists has already greatly emphasized
computers. This trend progressed quickly and
easily according to the evolution of the
telecommunication industry with the arrival of
electronic switching, numerical transmission and
so on.

To introduce communication topics in the
computer curriculum requires more attention (6).
First of all, in many universities, institutes
or colleges, the teachers of data communication
must also teach communications; they must be
trained first, since they will be the future
teachers.

And secondly, even if they could afford to
receive the help of such specialists, there are
not enough of them now to meet the needs of
industry and education.

On the other hand, several institutes or
universities were given the chance to develop
such curricula according to their main
objectives to their local environment.

This is the case, for instance, of our two
institutions. For one of them, the Ecole

Nationale Supérieure des Télécommunicatons,
which, in particular, is in charge of the
education of engineers for the PTT
administration, one of its main objectives is
the training of top specialists in
telecommunications, computers and electronics in
computer networks. The second one, the
University of Lille, is involved in a very large
program of continuing education. As such, it
must fulfill the increased needs of local
industry; for example, the main French mail-
order companies, for which network communication
is a capital feature, are based near by.

Considering such necessities and to try to help
develop courses in data communication, several
steps were taken; one of them was to gather some
specialists to define a suitable curriculum and
another one was to develop some computer
courseware.

2. THE OBJECTIVES OF THE WORKING GROUP

Sponsored by the "Agence de l'Informatique," a
governmental agency, a working group was
organized bringing together specialists in
network education and persons from the
telecommunication administration. This group
was given four main objectives.

2.1 The definition of a curriculum

The first aim was to specify a complete
curriculum encompassing a basic knowledge of
electronic transmission for the organizational
and human aspects of telematic applications.

Instead of a true curriculum, an exhaustive
treatment of the different topics of the field
was preferred. Furthermore, according to the
weight of normalization, the use of the ISO
model was also included. The main chapters
cover:

- the basic communication elements

- the OSI Model of ISO
- the organization and design of networks
- the services and networks available for public uses
- the services and networks available for private uses
- network management and exploitation
- some specialized applications.

This curriculum is mainly a guideline for teachers' new courses that can be structured according to their objectives.

Figure (1) organizes the main fields and their possible relationships with connecting subjects, like operating system...

Figure 1 legend:

⬡ Computer Network Modules

▭ Connecting Subjects

⬡ Advanced Topics

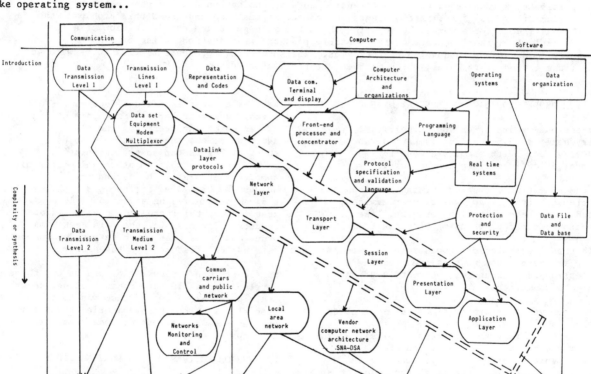

FIGURE (1)

2.2 An inventory of the main pedagogical aids

This may help both new and old teachers. The tools range from text books, slides, and courseware to software and hardware used by network specialists, and which are a necessity to fulfill professional training, such as simulation software, network analyzer and so forth.

2.3 A survey of some examples of existing courses

These examples are seen as an illustration of

how it is possible to use the curriculum and the inventory, given the pre-requisites and the known objectives of the course.

2.4 Some recommendations for developing new pedagogical aids

A first result, which may already be seen, is the lack of materials, due to many problems: the overload of the various specialists and particularly of the teachers, the rapid evolution of the technology and of its normalization. For these last reasons, many materials quickly become obsolete.

Among these recommendations will be the development of CAI tools. One of these is shown in the next part.

3. COMPUTER ASSISTED INSTRUCTION FOR DATA COMMUNICATIONS SYSTEMS AND NETWORKS

3.1 Main goals

The goals were to realize a set of modules of courses in the area of data communications and computer networks by using Computer Assisted Instruction. The requirements were:

- to be open at the undergraduate level for students who have just a basic knowledge of data processing (e.g., a first approach in programming)

- to be consistent and allow for self paced learning

- to obtain a large target population to cover the development cost.

Therefore in the exhaustive inventory of the topics described above, it was necessary to identify a minimum curriculum (the core of the various degrees).

3.2 The core of the CAI courses

The core was divided into seven chapters, each being spread over one of two modules. Figure 2 gives a description of each chapter and the goals, in terms of know-how.

3.3 The development of the CAI system

With members of the working group, a team was constituted. Because none of them had a great experience in the CAI domain, the methodology which was adopted for the development of these courses was similar to the methodology for the development of a classical data processing application. Four phases were identified: the detailed pedagogical analysis (equivalent to the analysis and systems specification in data processing); the writing of pedagogical scenarios and dialogues (structured design); implementation of the courseware; and finally the test and evaluation.

3.3.1 The detailed pedagogical analysis

Each member prepared papers on the topics, the organization and the prerequisites for each chapter. These papers were debated during several meetings. The discussions were often very animated and long particularly on the problems of terminology, on the relative importance of some sub-topics, and on the emergence of new domains like the integrated service digital networks and local area networks.

CAI Course Core

The core	Example of desired student capacity
	Able to
Chapter 1 Data transmission and information theory	. evaluate the required date rate for specific applications . express the relation between data rate and bandwidth
Chapter 2 Taxonomy and topology of computer and communication networks	. compare network topology in terms of routing, reliability, etc. . compare circuit, message and packet switching networks
Chapter 3 From data set equipment to front end	. for a given configuration, determine and characterize the right data set equipment . explain the use of the digital junction (RS 232-V24)
Chapter 4 The several layers approach of the computer network: the OSI model	. give the function and services of each layer . simulate a protocal like BSC
Chapter 5 Public network and Vendor Network architecture	. choose an appropriate carrier network for a given application . fill out a subscription form for a public packet network
Chapter 6 Telematic services	. choose among different possible products for a special kind of application like "electronic mailing"
Chapter 7 Design, Management and exploitation synthesis in an organization	. build a particular network

Figure 2

Three major problems have appeared:

- the first problem was related to the place and the importance of signal processing and information theory in the core. After discussion it was decided that this chapter must be kept to a minimum level which would correspond to the prerequisite of other chapters.

- the second problem, and the most fundamental one, was related to the OSI model of reference of the ISO (1,2). Several questions were asked: should the OSI model be presented as an introduction to the course; could it be placed at the beginning of the curriculum for its use as an analysis tool, or at the end of the curriculum for the purpose of introducing some advanced courses later? Finally it was decided that the OSI model must be presented even if it raised some difficulties due to the abstract nature of the model and to the layered and hierarchical approach of the data communications which are sometimes controversial (3).
However, this model is presented after the module on the taxonomy and the topology of computer networks and after the module on data communications lines, the line equipment (modems, multiplexor, ...etc.) and digital interfaces (e.g., V24). In fact it appears difficult to present the ISO model as the first topic to students who have never been introduced to the domain of computer networks.

- the third problem was in relation to the nation-wide services of the PTT for computer networks and Telematics. Several methods could be used to present these services. One is to distribute these services along the whole course to illustrate each concept or technique presented. Another is to create a specific module for all the services. It is this latter way which was chosen because it allows some comparisons between classes of services (for example leased lines versus packet networks), especially in the economic domain. This also gives some facility to update these services: introduction of news services, changes in the characteristics or in the tariff, etc. In order to make this module more attractive, some case studies are proposed to the students who are required to determine the right service, from both technical and economical considerations, for a specific application. For example, the student is asked to fill in a form on the screen of the terminal for a subscription to Transpac, the French X25 packet network.

3.3.2 The writing of dialogues

For each module a detailed pedagogical scenario was established which gave the contents of the "screens," the nature of the interactions, answer analysis, etc. In a pragmatic way several CAI techniques were used: the tutorial

mode for the presentation of some parts of the course, the drill and practice mode with synthesis exercises, interactive simulation to illustrate and explain some fundamental mechanisms of computer network and protocols, and lastly, case studies used to enforce the synthesis of several modules. The path followed by each student in the module is not directed by the tests. The student is able to choose freely the sequence which interests him and can organize his own progression. For each module three modes (only the "materials") the self evaluation mode (only synthesis and case studies); and finally the normal mode where the whole content is presented.

3.3.3 Implementation

The microcomputer chosen for implementation was the Bull 90/50 (similar to the IBM PC) because this microcomputer was chosen by the French University and the Ministry of Education to equip the first cycle (undergraduate studies). At the time of implementation of these courses no author languages for this class of equipment existed. So in order to simplify the implementation, the pedagogical data (e.g., texts and pictures) are dissociated from the learning program management and the interaction.

For the texts, sequential files are created using a good commercial screen editor. Special characters are inserted, when editing, to divide it into screen and subscreen. A small utility program builds a reference table to allow direct access to a given "screen" in an efficient manner. For the graphics we have chosen to express them in the form of abstract data types. A specially developed graphic editor allows the interactive construction of pictures and the ability to divide these pictures into several segments which can be displayed separately with controlled timing in order to animate the picture. We have developed a library of procedures that can be used in every module and which hide the details of execution and structures of graphical data from the module designers. These procedures are related to the pointing to a picture of a given identification number, and to displaying a segment of this picture or to erasing a segment, etc.

For programming CAI modules the Pascal language was selected (Pascal MT+ on CP/M 86.TM) because it was compiled, structured, easily readable, and it gives the possibility of a pseudo-separate compilation via "modules" which allowed us to implement abstract types, reusable in most CAI modules.

Correction of text or picture with this method of implementation is easy and does not require a new compilation. However the development time is long and the modules result in large files. For example, chapter II on the taxonomy and topology of networks take 74 K for the program itself with three overlays, 30 K for the text and 40 K for the picture. This is due, partly, to the expansion factor of this class of Pascal compiler (4) and of the lack of efficiency of this Pascal to store composite graphic structures.

3.3.4 Evaluation

Since spring 1984 seven modules have been completed, and this allows an evaluation of the courseware. A first technical phase was conducted with the help of instructors who are not involved in the project, to track all the typographical errors, check the validity and placement of pictures and sometimes to reduce the text of some of the "screens."

The second phase, now starting, is a pedagogical evaluation of this CAI system: some experiments will be taking place during summer 1984 in a special summer school for teachers and during the next school year with several groups of students.

Upon issuing this first evaluation, a second release will be realized with an author system (DIANE (5)) in order to transport these courses to a wider variety of microcomputers.

4. CONCLUSION

The study, which is actually done, must allow specifying different courses in this field, in relation with the needs of the industry and the emergence of the different kinds of jobs: network architect or designer.

As it seems quite impossible to satisfy the growing need for education by traditional ways, the use of computer based education must be developed. Moreover, it seems already obvious that some complete achievement can't be fulfilled by classical CAI courseware and so, a first attempt to use an expert-system for teaching network design has been completed.

5. ACKNOWLEDGEMENT

This study was possible with the participation, in the working group, of J. Botrel, V. Delebarre, Guillemot, F. Lefebvre, S. Motard, G. Pujolle, Pilon, D. Seret, S. Tohme, P. Tonon, M. J. Varloot.

6. BIBLIOGRAPHIE

(1) ISO "Basic reference model for Open Systems Interconnection" ISO-7498-1983.

(2) Proceeding of the IEEE "Special issue on open systems interconnection (OSI) - Standard architecture and protocols," Vol. 71 No. 12 - December 1983.

(3) D. COHEN - J. POSTEL "The ISO reference model and other protocol architectures" Information processing 83, Editor REA Mason-North Holland, pp. 29-34

(4) J. GILBREATH - G. GILBREATH "Erathosten Revisited" Byte January 1983, pp. 283-326.

(5) Système AUTEUR DIANE: manuel de l'utilisateur, Agence de l'Informatique

(6) W. BRACKER, Jr. B. KONSYNSKI III, D. SOKOLOV "Ranking data communication in today's classroom", Data Communications, April 1984, pp. 133-137.

TM: trade mark of Digital Research)

COMPUTERS IN EDUCATION, K. Duncan and D. Harris (eds.)
Elsevier Science Publishers B.V. (North-Holland)
© IFIP, 1985

DIAGNOSTIC EVALUATION IN LEARNING PROCESSES

M. Ferraris[*], V. Midoro[*], G. Olimpo[*+], D. Persico[*], G. Sissa[*]

[*] Istituto Tecnologie Didattiche, Consiglio Nazionale Ricerche, Genova, Italy
[+] Dipartimento Informatica Sistemistica e Telematica, Università di Genova, Italy

This paper presents a methodology and a system for computer assisted design and delivery of diagnostic tests. The methodology relies upon a hierarchical model of contents and leads to highly individualized tests, which provide a detailed measure of achievement minimizing at the same time the workload imposed on students by the test. DELFI, the system which has been developed in connection with the methodology, assists authors in designing and implementating diagnostic tests by supporting some activities, such as item formulation, and by fully automatizing some others, such as the production of code for test delivery. A non toy example of test design using DELFI is provided in the paper, concerning the arithmetic operations on complex numbers.

1. INTRODUCTION

The term "diagnostic evaluation" refers to any possible kind of test procedure capable of providing a precise and detailed description of the student's achievement in connection with a specific learning process. The motivating factors for diagnostic evaluation are the possibility to build truly adaptive, individualized learning processes and the possibility to have a detailed formative feedback upon implemented courses. In fact, to individualize means to teach what a student does not know starting from what he or she knows; and to validate and correct a course means to know which are its less successful parts in terms of achievements: both require a detailed map of student's achievement to be used directly to orient the learning process in the former case; and to be used in terms of average performances in the latter. However, truly diagnostic test are not widely used because:

a) a diagnostic test should be built upon a detailed structure of the subject matter referred to by the test, which may imply a hard work for test design;

b) test delivery may become a heavy burden both for students and teachers because of the need to assess the usually large set of knowledge and skills which belong to the content domain to be tested.

This paper presents a specific methodology for test design and delivery which helps to lessen the above mentioned problems in several ways:
- by providing a methodological framework to test design
- by supporting test authors in their work by means of an actual computer assisted test design
- by using the computer for test delivery
- and, finally, by adopting a delivery strategy which minimizes the load imposed on students by the test.

The methodology is based upon the assumption that the content domain may be represented by a hierarchical model, which is especially fitting for subjects of a procedural nature. In the following, the methodology and the software system named DELFI are described in detail, and a fragment of a simple, yet meaningful example of test design is presented concerning arithmetic operations upon complex numbers.

2. DESCRIPTION OF THE METHODOLOGY

2.1 Basic hypothesis

Our approach is based upon a few fundamental hypotheses:
- The diagnostic test and the related instructional process must be based upon the same contents' structure. This allow to give a proper meaning to the test which can be defined as a procedure to detect which part of the structure have been achieved by a student as a result of a specific instructional process and which have not; or to detect which part of the structure corresponds to a low average achievement in order to have a corrective feedback on the related parts of the instructional process.
- The content representation must be of a hierarchical type (4), where each node of the hierarchy corresponds to a well defined student skill. This means that the approach lends itself very well to subject of a procedural nature often, requiring skills of a algorithmic nature; while for subjects of a higher taxonomic level, the approach may become arbitrary or difficult to use. However it should be noticed that in many cases the hierarchical model is less restrictive than it seems, since also more general representations of the subject matter based upon network models such as entailment meshes (7) or Petri Nets (2, 5) can always produce hierarchical representations if considered from a specific point of view.

2.2 Subject Matter Representation

We assume that the subject matter structure consists of a hierarchy of nodes, each of which corresponds to a specific item of knowledge and to a specific skill.

From the point of view of testing, the skill associated to each node of the hieararchy may be interpreted as a class of tasks, and it can be considered achieved if a student is able to accomplish successfully any task of the class.

Actually, there are two possible types of dependence between a node A and its sons (i.e. the nodes directly dependent from it in the hierarchy):

a) if the accomplishment of any task related to the node A (fig. 1) implies the achievement of each son of A, it can be said that B, C and D are bound by an and link;

b) if the accomplishment of any task of A implies the achievement of only one son of A at a time it can be said that the link between B, C and D is of type or.

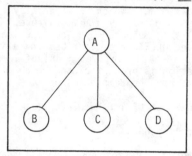

Figure 1: A simple hierarchy

It should be noticed that it is also frequent to have links of a mixed type, i.e. the accomplishment of a task A may imply, for instance, the accomplishment of (A and B) or C.

It must be noticed that the definition of the hierarchy is a very critical point in the overall process of instructional design. In fact, as it will be clearer later, a consistent hierarchy is the very basis for test reliability and, of course, for the effectiveness of an instructional process to. On the other hand, to develope a consistent hierarchy requires a deep analysis and several professional competencies among which a good knowledge of the subject matter, a deep teaching experience of that subject matter and a strong methodological know how.

2.3 Test delivery strategy

In order to assess the student's knowledge and to minimize the burden imposed upon him or her by the test, the following top-down strategy has been adopted.

It is assumed that if a student answers correctly the test items associated with a node N of a hierarchy, he has to use all the subordinate skills, i.e. he is tested not only on N but, indirectly also on all its subordinate nodes.

It should be noticed that this assumption holds only if the test items for N have been properly selected in number and type so as to involve all the subordinate nodes (skills). On this basis, test administration can start with the items related to the highest node; this maximizes the information about student learning because it allows indirect verification of the achievement of all the nodes of the hierarchy. If the student answers correctly to the first set of items, the test ends. If the student answers incorrectly, the node N is considered failed and the test goes deeper into the hierarchy presenting the student with the items pertaining to the appropriate subordinate nodes of N. The test goes on recursively until all nodes of the hierarchy have been, directly or indirectly, assessed. The output of the test is the detailed indication of which nodes have been achieved.

It should be noticed that this strategy of test administration is very hard to handle manually and, anyhow, requires the use of a computer for both test delivery, data collection, and results presentation. For more details about the methodology, other possible testing strategies, and CAL, we refer to (3).

2.4 Items formulation

This phase aims at defining the test items required for testing each node in a hierarchically represented content domain.

The selected criterion is that of associating to each node a minimum set of items whose correct answer guarantees the achievement of all subordinate nodes. Notice that the nature of the links (and, or) changes both the structure of the test and the related "item table" indicating the number of items and the features of each of them. The author can use the item table as a guideline to items formulation.

For example, in the simple hierarchy of figure 1, we have two different test structures according to the logic link between B, C and D which can be of the and type or of the or type. Figure 2 shows the corresponding item tables.

	and LINK
TEST ITEMS	NODES INVOLVED
A 1	A B C
B	PRIMITIVE
C	PRIMITIVE
D	PRIMITIVE

	or LINK
TEST ITEMS	NODES INVOLVED
A 1	A B
A 2	A C
A 3	A D
B	PRIMITIVE
C	PRIMITIVE
D	PRIMITIVE

Figure 2: Two different items tables

Note that in the case of an <u>or</u> link, three items are necessary for a thorough testing of A.

3. THE DELFI SYSTEM

The test methodology which has been presented implies for test authors various activities of different nature; some of them, such as hierarchy definition or test items formulation, require in any case a heavy human intervention while others, such as the production of the control code for test delivery, can be easily automatized.
The DELFI system has been designed and implemented to ease the work of test authors and can be referred to as an actual system for computer assisted test design. It gives assistance and support to the author in performing the most conceptual phases of test design and fully automatizes the production of the code for test delivery, so freing the author from a complex task devoid of conceptual content and extremely error prone.
Figure 3 shows the main functions of the system.
The input of the system is the hierarchy representing the content domain, and is interactively supplied by the author. On the basis of the hierarchy and of the logic links the system generates the item table, that is, the table reporting the number of the test items necessary for the assessment of the hierarchy nodes and, for each of them, the nodes (skills) to be involved in the corresponding questions.
The purpose of the item table is to help the author to define the structure and the content of each individual item. This activity together with hierarchy construction is the only phase which cannot be fully automatized and requires of the author:

a)   the selection of the item type suitable for verifying the skills involved by a given node and the formulation of the item on the basis of the involved skills;

b)   the implementation of a procedure which handles each item with regard to question presentation, answer acquisition, answer analysis and data collection.

The last phase of test development concern the automatic generation of the code for actual test delivery according to the top-down strategy described in section 2.3.
Moreover, the system can supply a scheme of the delivery strategy, which can be helpful for both verifying its inner coherence and coding the test in different programming languages.
It should be noticed that the code produced by DELFI includes also the storage of test results in a file which can be subsequently used by suitable programs oriented to individual feedback, course feedback or individual remedy.

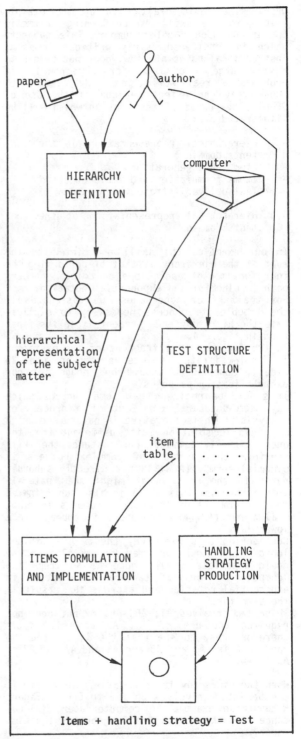

Figure 3: The phases of test design

4.   THE TEST ON COMPLEX NUMBERS

This section aims at exemplifying the application of the methodology and the related use of

DELFI. The topic dealt with by the example refers to the skill of performing aritmetic operations upon complex number. This subject, which is considered fairly critical from the instructional point of view, does not originate a very large or complex hierarchy; however it provides a real world, non-toy case which should give an effective idea of the use of DELFI. The phases of test design which will be illustrated are:

- Hierarchical representation of the contents domain
- Item table generation
- Items formulation and implementation
- Test delivery strategy generation

4.1 Hierarchical representation of the contents domain

In our example, the skill associated to the root of the hierarchy is that of performing the four fundamental operations on complex numbers both in binomial and exponential notation.
For the sake of conciseness we disregard all the troublesome process necessary to explicitate the hierarchy and present it in its final form in figure 4.
In the figure only a fragment of the hierarchy is displeyed (its complete version includes 26 nodes); however it should be enough for our examplification purposes.
It should be noticed that some choices which may seem unnatural come out of a process of analysis which is iterative in nature and which may lead to solution quite different from the ones initially devised. For instance the skill "perform the product of complex numbers in binomial form". (A23) Is not directly subordinated to the root as it might seem natural. This is because this skill is also subordinated to "perform the division upon numbers in binomial form" (A2), and therefore it appears it a lower level.
Considering this hierarchy, the meaning of the logic links (and, or) may become clearer. We could associate to the node A1 an item like "compute the sum of two complex numbers in exponential notation and express the result in the same form".
This item involves A1, A5, A6, A7 but does not requires the use of A2, A3 and A4. It is therefore easy to see that the link among the sons of A is (A1 and A5 and A6 and A7) or A2 or A3 or A4.

When the hierarchy is in a satisfactory form, it can be interactively supplied to DELFI. Figure 5 shows an example of computer/user dialogue concerning the input of a fragment of the hierarchy.

4.2 Item table generation

This phase aims at building a table characterizing the test items associated to each node of the hierarchy.

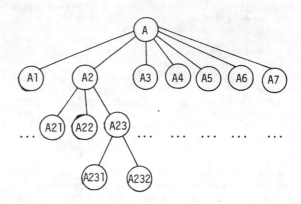

A : to perform the four arithmetic operations on complex numbers both in binomial and exponential form.
A1 : to perform the sum upon numbers in binomial form.
A2 : to perform the division upon numbers in binomial form.
A3 : to perform the multiplication upon numbers in binomial form.
A4 : to perform the division upon numbers in exponential form.
A5 : to convert from exponential to binomial form.
A6 : to convert from binomial to exponential form.
A7 : to detect the need to convert from exponential to binomial form (when summing complex numbers in exponential form).
A21 : to find the conjugate of a complex number.
A22 : to detect the need to multiply both numerator and denominator for the conjugate of the denominators (when dividing complex numbers).
A23 : to perform the product of complex numbers in binomial form.
A231 : to calculate the product of two binomials.
A232 : to know that $J**2 = -1$.
. . . .

Figure 4: An example of hierarchy for the skill "To perform the four arithmetic operation upon complex numbers"

```
ROOT: A
SONS: (A1 & A5 & A6 & A7) ^ A2 ^ A3 ^ A4
NODE: A1
SONS: A11 & A12
NODE: A2
SONS: A21 & A22 & A23
NODE: A23
SONS: A231 & A232
NODE: A3
. . . . . . . .
```

Figure 5: Interactive input of the hierarchy

After the input of the hierarchy, DELFI allows the automatic generation of the item table. This table supplies the minimum number of items to cover the hierarchy as well as the indication, for each of them, of the subordinate nodes to be involved. The item table for our example is displayed in figure 6.

ITEMS TABLE

```
A 1     : A A1 A5 A6 A7 A11 A12 A51 A52 A61
          A 62
A 2     : A A2 A21 A22 A23 A231 A232
A 3     : A A3 A31 A32 A33 A34 A35 A36
A 4     : A A4 A41
A1 1    : A1 A11 A12
A2 1    : A2 A21 A22 A23 A231 A232
A3 1    : A3 A31 A32 A33 A34 A35 A36
A4 1    : A4 A41
A5 1    : A5 A51 A52
A6 1    : A6 A61 A62
A23 1   : A23 A231 A232
A11     : PRIMITIVE
A12     : PRIMITIVE
A21     : PRIMITIVE
A22     : PRIMITIVE
A231    : PRIMITIVE
A232    : PRIMITIVE
A31     : PRIMITIVE
A32     : PRIMITIVE
A33     : PRIMITIVE
A34     : PRIMITIVE
A35     : PRIMITIVE
A36     : PRIMITIVE
A41     : PRIMITIVE
A51     : PRIMITIVE
A61     : PRIMITIVE
A62     : PRIMITIVE
A7      : PRIMITIVE
```

Figure 6: The items table

From it, it turn out that, for instance, the node A requires four items to be thoroughly tested, e.g. A1, A2, A3, A4. For each of them the item table provides the subordinate nodes to be involved in the corresponding question.

4.3 Item definition

The item table acts as a basis for item definition. Unfortunately it provides only a structural reference, and many aspects of the item definition, including the actual invention of the question to be put to the student, are left to authors' immagination, experience and common sense.

For instance, if we consider the entry A1 of the item table, we obtain from it the information that the question will involve:
- aritmetic operations upon complex numbers (A)
- the sum in binomial form (A5)
- the conversion from binomial to exponential form (A6)
- the decision to convert from exponential to binomial form (A7)

From this indication the author must build a suitable question, which in our case could be the one of figure 7.

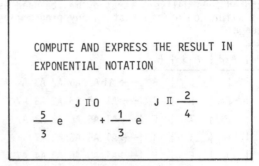

Figure 7: An example of item

As already mentioned, this is one of the most critical phases of test design.

Some of the related problems are listed below:
- The formulation of an item activating all the nodes indicated in the item table can lead to a twisted, scarcely comprehensible, and forced formulation. This difficulty arises particularly in the case of items concerning the highest nodes of large hierarchies.
  This element does not affect so much the case we are dealing with here because the hierarchy is small and has been developed in a way oriented to minimizing the problems arising during items' definition.
- Questions can be put following different styles: multiple choices, concealed multiple choices, open questions and so on. The choice should be made on the basis of the nature of the skill being tested, of the possible difficulty in descriminating conceptual errors from simple distractions, etc.
  In our case, to minimize the chance of computation errors in open questions the student has been provided with a simple desk calculator simulated or a section of the screen for a quick and safe computation of trigonometric functions.

4.4 Test delivery strategy

The top-down testing strategy tipically leads to a very complex delivery control flow due also to the presence of the or links which may sensibly increase the number of test items and, consequently, the number of different paths.

Figure 8 displays a fragment of the test delivery strategy automatically produced by DELFI from our hierarchy.

Since supplying a global picture of the flowchart would produce in most cases a very complex diagram, DELFI output deals with a node at a time providing for each possible result (achieved, not achieved) of the items associated with that node the next possible nodes to test. The test start from node A and, if the answers to A1, A2, A3, A4 are correct, it ends immediately. If, for instance, only A1 and A2 are achieved the process must go on testing nodes A3 or node A4 and so on. As already mentioned this delivery strategy may be used as a basis for coding the test in any programming language.

A 1	A 2	A 3	A 4	
F	F	F	F	--->A1 A5 A6 A2 A3 A4 A7
F	F	F	T	--->A1 A5 A6 A2 A3 A7
F	F	T	F	--->A1 A5 A6 A2 A3 A7
F	F	T	T	--->A1 A5 A6 A2 A7
F	T	F	F	--->A1 A5 A6 A3 A4 A7
F	T	F	T	--->A1 A5 A6 A3 A7
F	T	T	F	--->A1 A5 A6 A4 A7
F	T	T	T	--->A1 A5 A6 A7
T	F	F	F	--->A2 A3 A4
T	F	F	T	--->A2 A3
T	F	T	F	--->A2 A4
T	F	T	T	--->A2
T	T	F	F	--->A3 A4
T	T	F	T	--->A3
T	T	T	F	--->A4
T	T	T	T	--->EXIT

A1	
F	---> A11 A12
T	---> EXIT

A5 1	
F	---> A51 A52
T	---> EXIT

A6 1	
F	---> A61 A62
T	---> EXIT

Figure 8: A fragment of the test delivery strategy

Finally a very useful feature of DELFI is that of producing automatically from the above strategy the Pascal control code for test delivery. Though conceptually uninteresting this facility is extremely helpful for the author especially in the case of very large hierarchies. It must be noticed that the automatic coding facility

produces also the code for collecting data about student performance. This data are subsequently analysed by a suitable program which presents the test results in a friendly form very close to a natural language communication.

```
 _____
|                  TEST RESULTS                   |
| YOU DON'T KNOW HOW TO PERFORM THE FOUR ARITH-   |
| METIC OPERATIONS ON COMPLEX NUMBERS BOTH IN     |
| BINOMIAL AND EXPONENTIAL FORM BECAUSE YOU       |
| DON'T KNOW:                                      |
|                                                 |
| -    HOW TO PERFORM THE SUM UPON NUMBERS IN     |
|      EXPONENTIAL FORM                            |
|                                                 |
| -    HOW TO DETECT THE NEED TO CONVERT FROM     |
|      EXPONENTIAL TO BINOMIAL FORM, (WHEN        |
|      SUMMING COMPLEX NUMBERS IN EXPONENTIAL     |
|      FORM)                                       |
|_____|
```

Figure 9: An example of test results

In figure 9 an example of results output is presented corresponding to the case:
                    A1 failed
                    A2, A3, A4 achieved
                    A7 failed

5.   CONCLUSIONS AND PERSPECTIVES

The use of DELFI for design, realization, and delivery of diagnostic tests has made apparent the advantages and the limitation both of the methodology and of the system.
The methodology is particularly effective for rather small hierarchies dealing with algorithmic topics. It allows to save considerable time when assessing a test and provide a precise description of the student's knowledge.
An important side-effect of the methodology is that of bringing into evidence possible inconsistencies within the hierarchy. (6) This suggests, as a methodological guideline for instructional design, that of designing the test as a form of feedback to the content structure before the actual design of the tutorial sections.
Concerning a further development of the methodology, it is worth observing that it is possible to modify the delivery strategy in view of objectives other than the test, leaving unchanged both the content structure and the criteria for items' design.
For example, it is possible to associate to diagnostic tests a remedial sequence meant to lead the student from a state of "partial knowledge" to that of "total knowledge" in a particular content domain. During this activity each node can be interpreted as a teaching procedure to get the student familiar with the topic referred to. The delivery of this remedial sequence could be based on different strategies (top-down or bottom-up) according to the nature of the subject being taught or to the student psychological characteristic.

6.   REFERENCES

(1)   Brien, R., Laganā, S., Flowcharting: a
      Procedure for Development of Learning
      Hierarchies, PLET. 14 (1977) 305-314.
(2)   Ferraris, M., Midoro, V., Olimpo, G.,
      Petri Nets as a Modelling Tool in the
      Development of CAL courseware, Comput.
      Educ. 8 (1984) 41-49.
(3)   Ferraris, M., Midoro, V., Olimpo, G.,
      Diagnostic Testing and the Development of
      CAL Remedial Sequences, Comput. Educ. 8
      (1984) 407-414.
(4)   Gagné, R., The Conditions of Learning.
      (Reinhart and Winston, N.Y., 1965).
(5)   Jantzen, M., Structural Representation of
      Knowledge by Petri Nets as an aid for
      Teaching and Research, in Net Theory and
      Applications. (Springer Verlag, Berlin
      1980).
(6)   Okey, J.R., Developing and Validating
      Learning Hierarchies. AVCR. 21 (1973)
      87-108.
(7)   Pask, G., Conversation Theory Applications
      in Education and Epistemology. (Elsevier,
      Amsterdam, 1976).

COMPUTERS IN EDUCATION, K. Duncan and D. Harris (eds.)
Elsevier Science Publishers B.V. (North-Holland)
© IFIP, 1985

AN EXPERIMENT WITH COMPUTER-AIDED LEARNING IN THE DANISH SAVINGS BANKS

B.SC(Econ) Jens Chr. Hauge
Sparekassernes Datacenter (SDC)
Borupvang 1, DK-2750 Ballerup
Copenhagen, Denmark

The Danish savings bank sector has during the last 3 years carried on a pedagogical experiment with computer-aided learning (CAL). The principal aim is to examine whether the employees in the savings banks can by means of CAL-material keep up with the technological development in an appropriate way. The CAL-project is far advanced in Denmark and it is now possible to draw some conclusions about the pedagogical, technical, and financial circumstances which are associated with the production of CAL-material.

1. INTRODUCTION

Since february 1982 the Danish savings bank sector has investigated the possibilities of computer-aided learning.

This article will give a description of the development since the start of the project, discuss some special points and touch on the future aspects of the project.

2. BACKGROUND

The Danish savings bank sector consists of 100 autonomous savings banks with approximately 1350 branch offices and 12,000 employees.

The level of education in the Danish savings banks is generally very high. This applies for the basic education as well as for the fine possibilities of further education. During the last 3 years approximately 5,000 computer terminals and 1,500 mini computers of the brand Olivetti have been installed in replacement of a functionally and technically worn out Datasaab equipment.

The environment in which the savings banks are operating is changing so rapidly that there is a growing need for training and education programmes that allow for individualization, flexibility and decentralization.

I would like to give following comments on these:

Individualization refers to the need for training that is adaptable to the needs and background of the individual employee.

Flexibility refers to the desirability of reducing the time span between the time when a training need is established and the time when an appropriate training activity is or can be made available. In traditional training activities this time span is often considerable.

Decentralization refers to the wish to make training available in or at least near the branch office in which the employee is working.

When the new Olivetti equipment was put into operation, it became possible to educate by means of computer terminals. The savings banks decided to launch a CAL-project to investigate this topic.

The CAL-project has two aims:

* A pedagogical aim:

    To gain experience in developing and using computer-aided learning materials in courses relevant to savings bank employees.

* A technological aim:

    To investigate the possibilities of using a computer terminal system (Olivetti) which is presently installed for computer-aided learning purposes or personal computers.

3. PEDAGOGICAL AIMS

The education of the employees in the savings banks is for one thing based on the traditions in the Danish school system. In this connection I would like to stress the pedagogical freedom of method in Denmark where the individual teacher is responsible for the choice of the relevant education material. Furthermore there is traditionally a free debate in connection with the education. In the further training of adults group work is used considerably.

The savings banks have used programmed education in book form and have gained some experience with this kind of education material. It has not been very successful. This is undoubtedly due to the fact that this kind of education is too bo-ring.

The basis of the CAL-project is finally to be considered in the light of the advanced on-line milieu in which the Danish savings banks have been working during the last 10 years. This means that the general opposition against tech-nology is not very widespread among the em-ployees.

Early in the CAL-project the pedagogical prin-ciples were set up as a contrast between a huma-nistic and a more traditional technological pe-dagogy. Figure 1 shows these contrasts.

The pedagogical objective of the CAL-project has resulted in a set of pedagogical demands on a good CAL-material which can be used in the fur-ther education of the employees in the savings banks.

Pedagogical demands:

*   The programmes should be structured in such a way that the student can choose his way through the material according to his own needs - which means that the programmes should not imitate traditional programmed instruction.

*   The programmes should be flexible and should give easy access to all parts of the programme and easy paths of transition from one part to another.

*   The programmes should provide the student with the opportunity of testing his know-ledge and skills.

The CAL-material is constructed in a parallel structure with theory, examples, and tests. A dictionary is always available if the student encounters words or concepts that he is not fa-milar with. See figure 2 and figure 3.

You may however build in a "way" in the material to support the doubtful student. At the same time the student should always be free to choose this offer or not.

The contrast between a humanistic pedagogy and a more traditional technological pedagogy described briefly:	
Pedagogical aims of the CAL-project	The traditional technological pedagogy
1. The student is a subject who evaluates and chooses.	1. The student is an object who is in-fluenced and led in an appropriate direction.
2. The student is critical to the subjects.	2. The author knows "the truth" which the student has to learn.
3. The student is responsible for what he/she learns.	3. "The informative label" of the mate-rial contains information about gua-ranteed learning.
4. The student chooses the method and determines the course.	4. The author chooses the method and determines the course.
5. The CAL-material is transparent.	5. The material is not transparent.
6. The student asks the questions and the computer answers.	6. The system asks the questions.
7. The student deals with unities and elements as parts of unities.	7. The student deals with elements which are imperceptibly linked up as unities.
8. The student evaluates the learing.	8. The system evaluates the learning of the student.

Figure 1: Pedagogical principles of the CAL-project

Figure 2: <u>The Parallel Structure</u>

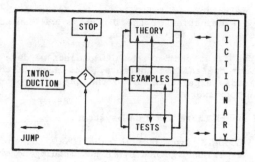

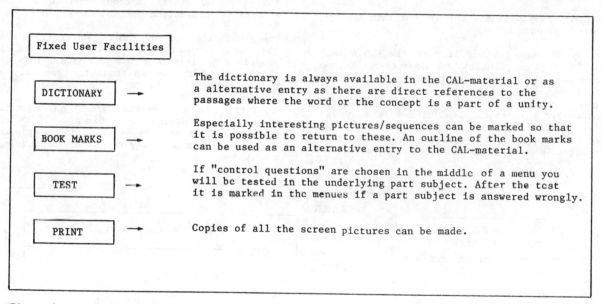

Figure 3: Fixed User Facilities

4. TECHNOLOGICAL AIMS

The decision basis for the selection of hardware and software formed an important part of the first CAL-project.

The selection of hardware followed a strategy for the purchase of personal computers in the savings banks, which was determined in the autumn of 1983.

This strategy recommended that the savings banks should purchase IBM PC or other compatible personal computers, among these especially Olivetti M24.

Furthermore great importance was attached to the fact that personal computers can be used for other administrative purposes in the savings banks. This means that a purchase of "educational computer terminals" was not taken into consideration.

Finally it was stressed that it is possible to integrate the CAL-material with other existing standard software to the IBM PC e.g. the integrated programmes with text processing, calculation programmes, data base, process work and communication. And at the moment we are endeavouring to establish an integration between the on-line system and the personal computers.

The selection of software is based on a thou-rough examination of the Danish as well as the foreign market for education software.

In the first part of the CAL-project we develo-ped our own edition software. This gave us con-siderable experience as to the qualities of re-levant software.

In Denmark there are 2 CAL-systems:

* COMCATS from DUS INTERNATIONAL, based on experience gained by "Århus Tandlægehøjsko-le" (Dental College of Århus) and "Jydsk Telefon" (The Telephone Company of Jut-land).

* COMUS, developed by a relatively small con-sultant firm, whose owners have a back-ground in the public education system.

In connection with the CAL-project both CAL-sy-stems were examined.

Partly through a study tour in the U.S.A. and partly through contact to Courseware Europe in Holland we learned about EnCore/TenCORE from the Computer Teaching Corporation in the U.S.A. Since the spring of 1984 the CAL-project group has worked with EnCORE/TenCORE and is very sa-tisfied with this software. In the spring 3 ma-jor CAL-materials were finished: financial cal-culation, budget system and documentary credit.

5. WORKING HYPOTHESES IN THE CAL-PROJECT

The CAL-project has not yet been finished and there are naturally no complete conclusions on the many questions raised in the course of the project.

In the following I will underline some problems on the basis of the many discussions in the CAL-project.
It is important to know the subjects which are suitable for transformation into CAL-material?

The project has up till now dealt with further education of employees who have already a good basic education. CAL-material is suited for the learning of minor subjects that are often being changed e.g. expansion of existing EDP-systems. It is also important that the CAL-material is brought into relation with pedagogy. This means that the CAL-material becomes part of a major educational connection. See figure 4.

The combination of educational material is ano-ther great subject for discussion. It seems ap-propriate to integrate the CAL-material in the traditional education in about the same way as written material.

An integrated multi-media educational material with video, slides, audio equipment, books and CAL-material is not the solution in my opinion. This will demand too many resources for develop-ment and maintenance.

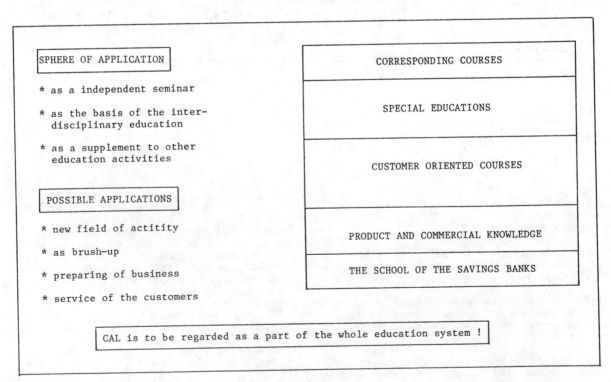

Figure 4: The Position of CAL in the Education System

The project has included many experiments on the separation of the processes and structure of the CAL-project. The basic opinion is that the student himself is responsible for his activities. It is not especially relevant to establish a great control instrument to ensure that the student does not deceive the CAL-material.

Example: the correct answer to the question "Which city is the biggest in Denmark?" It is not interesting to be able to sort out following answers:

* It is not Copenhagen.
* I am not sure whether it is Copenhagen.
* I wonder if it should be Copenhagen.

The aim is to ensure a structure in the CAL-material so that the student has a good starting point for an independent process with the subject. It is decisive that the student is given the possibility to find the relevant informations and to link them up in a meaningful connection.

It has been discussed how to construct the ideal project group.

We can recommend a group with these three kinds of expertise:

* subject expertise which can often be obtained from someone who is not engaged in education or data processing in their daily work.

* pedagogical expertise which can often be found in a specialized staff function.

* data processing expertise which can be found in the edp-department.

6. CONCLUSIONS

Pedagogical Conclusions

An external evaluation of the CAL-material has been made since the beginning of the experiment. It occured that many students regarded the material as very interesting but also as a kind of plaything. It was difficult to draw a conclusion on a possible positive result on a long view by means of this kind of education. It was obvious that the students missed the social milieu known from the traditional seminars.

However, the evaluations showed that education in well-defined subjects is acceptable.

Technological Conclusions

We found that the development of our own edition software demands considerable resources and that an accelerated introduction of CAL in the savings banks would make the purchase of an effective edition system necessary.

The work with IBM PC/Olivetti M24 and TenCORE has given good results. A large number of CAL-materials now has to be produced before the question of new software will be of current interest.

We discovered that the present technical equipment is sufficient to attain our end. More sophisticated equipment, e.g. video-discs might come later. But there is no need to wait for better equipment - it is already here!

Financial conclusions

In the first part of the CAL-project (1982 - 1984) we made a rough cost/benefit analysis according to which the relation between the development and accomplishment of residential seminars and a CAL-material results in following break even:

* minimum 30 students if CAL should be able to compete with residential seminars

* minimum 200 students if CAL should be able to compete with non-residential seminars

It is however not quite fair to compare a residential seminar with a CAL-material. It would be more reasonable to compare a CAL-material with other forms of materials as for instance correspondance colleges materials or compendium materials.

7. THE FUTURE ASPECTS

In the future - which is very near - we have proposed these objectives for ourselves:

(1) During the next two years about 20 CAL-materials are to be developed in three development centres.

(2) To find a suitable way of communication to all Danish savings banks.

(3) In the first six months of 1985 the results of this extended test period are to be evaluated and a new recommendation is to be made. During this period the programmes will have been used by a large number of employees.

REFERENCES

(1) Jakobsen, Leif Kvistgaard, An Experiment in
     Computer Learning - a Case Study: Denmark
     (ISBI 1983).
(2) Dean, Christopher and Whitlock, Quentin, a
     Handbook of Computer Based Training (Kogan
     Page, London, 1984).
(3) WCCE'81, Preceedings of the IFIP TC-3 (Lau-
     sanne, Switzerland, 1981).
(4.) Steinberg, Ester R., Teaching Computers to
     Teach (Lawrence Erlbaum Associates, London,
     1984).

Additional remark

The references hold only literature in English.
A good deal of literature in the Scandinavian
languages has however been published.

ACKNOWLEDGEMENT

I would like to thank Mr. Torsten Alf Jensen for
the inspiration to the description of the pedagogical principles and many fruitful discussions
on the topic.

COMPUTERS IN EDUCATION, K. Duncan and D. Harris (eds.)
Elsevier Science Publishers B.V. (North-Holland)
© IFIP, 1985

USING DATA BASES IN THE CLASSROOM

Toni Downes

Catholic Education Office, Sydney,
P.O. Box 217,
Leichhardt, N.S.W. 2040 Australia

It is the author's view that putting computers into classrooms to support current educational practices is not the solution to the problems associated with the Age of Information Technology. A more valuable approach would be to channel computing power into learning experiences that develop skills for surviving in today's rapidly changing world. This presentation describes a novel approach to using Data Bases in the light of Bev Labbett's work on Handling Information in the classroom.

"The introduction of the computer into any problem area, be it medicine, education, or whatever, usually creates the impression that grievous deficiences are being corrected, that something is being done. But often its principal effect is to push problems even further into obscurity - to avoid confrontation with the need for FUNDAMENTAL CRITICAL THINKING." (Joseph Weizenbaum, Sydney Morning Herald, 21 April 1984)

It is a truism to say that computers are being introduced into schools at an ever increasing rate. There is at least one computer in most secondary schools in Australia with many schools having numbers of computers. A similar trend is evident in primary schools. What seems to be lacking is the "fundamental critical thinking" about their use. It is my belief that computers in schools will not contribute towards the solution of the problem of the "age of information technology" until there is much more thought and discussion about the fundamental problems facing education.

What sort of education is needed to develop our future adults, adults who should be "characterised not only by the possession of knowledge and skills, but by independence of mind and a willingness to become involved in issues which each sees as worthwhile" (NSW Aims of Primary Education, p.7 reprinted 1984)? These adults will be faced with a complex, rapidly changing and exciting society but one fraught with many new types of problems, only some of which have their source in the Information Technology Revolution. Are our traditional methods of education equal to the task?

Stonier (1984) addresses the two-fold issue of how to live in this age and how to educate for living most eloquently. He argues that there first needs to be "a shift in objective from making a living to learning how to live". He continues:

"There are two major aspects in learning how to face life in the 21st or any other century. The

first involves understanding the world, the second involves understanding oneself ... Understanding the world requires not only exposure to traditional disciplines ... which allow students to understand the natural and social world in which they live - but it must also have a more global focus. We are all members of the human race living on an isolated planet floating in a hostile space. We need education for environmental responsibility, and, even more crucial now, education for developing harmonious relationships within global society. This means a downplaying of ethnocentric and nationalistic values and an expansion of a more humanistic, anthropological approach. Our young people must learn to enjoy cultural diversity and integrate with it.

"Apart from improving relationships within the immediate community, the major problem confronting our young people today is to close the gap between the rich and poor nations of the world. If that cannot be accomplished within a reasonable period of time, it can only set the stage for nuclear violence ...

"At the more individual level we need to teach a whole series of skills on how to survive in this world. Most of these are either not taught at all or relegated to a minor position in the curriculum: how to deal with government bureaucrats; how to get the most out of interviews with physicians; how to be successful teenagers; how to be good lovers; how to be effective parents; how to grow old gracefully; how to face death. Most of the really important decisions made in life are not based on information acquired during formal education. Why not? ...

"It has always been the dream of educators to develop critical faculties so that students are able to understand concepts and develop them on their own. This should be expanded not only to foster more creative imagination but to foster artistic, physical and social skills.

"... We must educate for the constructive use of leisure time: between the early 19th century and the late 20th, the work week has been cut in half. This trend will accelerate. Education itself must become one of those pleasurable activities.

"There is another more vital aspect: in the future, obtaining and organising information will become the dominant life activity for most people. It is that which one enjoys learning most which one learns best."

If educators are to meet the challenge of the 20th and 21st centuries they must:

- systematically explore the ever-changing implications of technological and other developments within our complex social system,

- continually unlearn assumptions about priorities in learning,

- maintain a balanced perspective of the overall aims of education, and

- develop an integrated response to changes needed in the education system.

No longer does a grounding in the basic facts provide a base for lifelong learning. This is not to deny children's need to develop basic skills and knowledge. Rather, to extend this list of "basics" beyond the "easy to teach" and "easy to test" bits of knowledge and skills to include such things as organising ideas, expressing feelings, solving problems, clarifying values, seeing other points of view, initiating ideas, etc.

"In the world of the information explosion, where the total sum of information is doubling every two or three years, the ability to ask the right question is likely to be more important than the provision of answers. Information retrieval machines can supply the latter when and where required. Perhaps that is what children should be doing - if they do not see the question where is the need to have an answer?"
(Longworth, 1974)

Jones (1982) suggests that a more appropriate classification of the essential skills taught in schools might include competence, creativity and co-operation.

Competence - Learning how to learn (including framing questions, being resourceful and literate in information skills, being able to communicate ideas and feelings and being able to make decisions).

Creativity - Valuing creative thinking and positive attitudes to learning and leisure.

Co-operation - Adopting co-operative problem-solving approaches and learning styles (including effective listening and communication).

Thomas O'Brien (1983) defines some of the behaviours that a "competent" person might display:

" - to respond to situations flexibly,
  - to take advantage of fortuitous circumstances,
  - to make sense of ambiguous or contradictory messages,
  - to recognise the importance of different elements in a situation,
  - to find similarities between situations despite differences that may separate them,
  - to draw distinctions between situations despite similarities that may link them,
  - to synthesise new concepts by taking old concepts and putting them together in new ways, and
  - to come up with novel ideas."

Other authors - Longworth (1982), Labbett (1983) - refer to the need for "flexible and adaptable thinkers".

There are many aspects of current classroom and school practices that mitigate against the development of such skills, one being the concentration on mechanical aspects of learning. When bringing computers into the classroom we have to ensure we are not enshrining such practices even more.

There is a number of ways computers can be used in classrooms to develop such skills as competence, creativity and co-operation. Logo and word processing are two such areas. A skilful teacher working in such environments can create many learning experiences to help children develop these skills. The purpose of this paper is to explore a third possible approach: using data bases in classrooms.

Computers excel at storing, sorting and retrieving information. Giving a child a tool such as a computer can liberate the child, leaving him/her free to analyse, synthesise and evaluate information while developing his/her own knowledge and conceptual structures. Data bases are used educationally in a variety of ways but not all of these develop such skills as competence, creativity and co-operation. Because their use in Australian classrooms is not yet widespread, we have time to sit back and reflect on ways that teachers might use them to develop these skills. This paper will outline one such approach in depth. In this approach the teacher has two main roles:

1. As a space creator, creating learning experiences in which children are encouraged to experience the problems of handling information,

2. As classroom historian, assessing the information pupils have created.

These roles originated in the work of Bev Labbett (1983) on developing children as flexible and adaptable thinkers. Labbett's work is particularly relevant to the themes developed so far. Not only does his approach provide an environment in which children can develop competence, creativity and co-operation it also accurately mirrors real world experiences that the children are likely to have. One example is the making of decisions in the face of uncertainty, lack of immediate feedback and lack of a right/wrong dichotomy. These are the type of parameters that characterise the major social, moral, political and personal issues of Stonier's world.

Because of the importance of Labbett's ideas to the understanding of my approach to the use of data bases in classrooms they will now be described in some detail (passages in the following discussion are direct quotes from Labbett's work).

In Labbett's approach, the fundamental aim is to develop children as "flexible and adaptable thinkers". He looks carefully at the activity of handling information in the classroom. This activity is not seen as a means to an end. It is both a means and an end. It includes:

" - the activity of making false starts,
 - the activity of entering and escaping from blind alleys,
 - the activity of ordering and reordering words as the information-maker drafts and redrafts primary location information into first this pattern and then that pattern,
 - the activity of distilling the relevant from the irrelevant and jettisoning the latter,
 - the activity of rejecting one way of presenting information on the basis of advice that the future user(s) will not be capable of understanding it,
 - the activity of experimenting with chapter headings and titles before deciding on the most appropriate ones,
 - the activity of devising ways of holding information collected from here and there for later use, and
 - the activity of privately not getting it right till the fifth go."

THE TEACHER AS A SPACE CREATOR

In this model the role of the skilful teacher .. as a space creator is to:

"- devise tasks that involve the activity of handling information,
 - create the space for individuals to experience problems as they engage in the activity of handling information,
 - get himself/herself involved in the activity of handling information other individuals in the classroom provide, in ways that s/he judges promotes rather than inhibits flexible/adaptable thinking. Within this approach the teacher makes, provisionally, the following assumptions:
 - that it has not been necessary to predefine with precision what flexible and adaptable thinking is about in order to make an abstraction of it for teaching purposes. The significant questions will be - how has flexible and adaptable thinking revealed itself in the classroom work that has taken place?,
 - that the future of such a lesson will be unpredictable. There will be no significant questions, no significant concerns beyond those created by the individuals as they engage in the activity of handling the same information,
 - that the words, numbers, symbols, physical objects and the action of other human beings, which individuals will encounter in these lessons, be accorded no status higher than sources of information to be handled, and that there is a range of ways in which sources of information may be handled,
 - that creating the conditions for promoting flexible/adaptable thinking will be helped by devising classroom tasks based on such criteria as:
   i) tasks that do not have one correct answer nor one correct way of handling them,
   ii) tasks sufficiently loosely specified, to create the space for individuals to proceed in differing directions (another way of saying that is .. for individuals to proceed in directions that are not centrally defined),
   iii) tasks so worded that they support the individuals inferring differing significances,
 - that it is reasonable to prefer in this lesson to create the space for individuals to experience problems rather than invading their space on the basis of claiming to know what they need to do,
 - that promoting flexible/adaptable thinking

necessarily involves individuals experiencing uncertainty as they engage in the activity of handling information,

- that it requires skilful teacher action to create space for individuals to experience uncertainty, without making the space so wide that uncertainty descends into inertia or disaffection,
- immediate supportive feedback from another individual on whether an action was the right or wrong one is not available,
- that acting as the definer of the correct and the incorrect, the right or the wrong, will not necessarily promote flexible and adaptable thinking,
- that it will be helpful to place a higher premium on individuals announcing their own errors, their own mistakes on this lesson,
- that the long-term educational aims will be helped by preferring to support individuals as they explore avenues out of the fixes they get themselves into, even if one believes that those avenues will prove un- productive,
- that maintaining the space created for individuals to experience problems will be helped by declaring a preference for the activities of listening, questioning, spec- ulating rather than the activities of assisting and explaining,
- that the sensitive neglect of individuals as they engage in the activity of handling inf- ormation is not necessarily an abdication of teacher responsibility. It may be seen as helpful in a curriculum concerned with the activity of handling information. It makes easier the task of assessing the information individuals have created, for one cannot claim to know what those individuals set out to do,
- that, beyond announcing the task there is no prior content to be transmitted in this lesson
- that the existence of any content presupposes individuals having engaged in the activity of handling information,
- that the traces left behind by individuals (the work done) after ending the activity of handling the same information now constitutes the significant lesson 'content',
- that it will be helpful to accord this 'content' the status of results or 'the place we've got to in the time available', rather than the status of final answers,
- that the traces (or work done by individuals) be seen as classroom-generated curriculum materials for further study, but recognising that presenting all the individuals in the class with the results of each group's work raises the issue of privacy,
- that where individual pupils in this lesson engage in the activity of handling informat- ion created by others, the teacher is faced with the challenge of handling discussion in ways that, by preference, promote flexible and adaptable thinking,
- that assessing the traces left behind by individuals who have engaged in the activity

of handling information will be helped by provisionally assuming not to know how they have handled that information."

The above framework is not an easy one for teachers to work within. Many teachers have difficulty in not defining ideas as "right or wrong" as so many of our other classroom prac- tices are enshrined within this conceptual framework. Recent moves by teachers away from a content approach to a process approach to curriculum issues reduce the over-reliance of teachers on the role of arbiter of the correct/ incorrect.

Those teachers already involved in "conferenc- ing" in process approaches e.g. process writing, problem solving with Logo, inquiry approaches to social studies etc. have already grappled with some of the issues described in the above quote, e.g. "sensitive neglect" - knowing when not to intervene in the process, when not to identify errors so that children have sufficient space to develop their own error detecting cap- abilities.

I believe that many of the desirable teacher behaviours put forward by Labbett fall within the bounds of "conferencing", a skill some of today's classroom teachers are beginning to develop. I also believe that in order to prov- ide a nurturing environment for flexible and adaptable thinkers, an approach such as Labbett's is necessary when handling all types of information in the classroom, e.g. child- ren's stories, pictorial information, historical information and even mathematical information.

THE TEACHER AS A CLASSROOM HISTORIAN

Normally when teachers assess the results of pupil's work they assume that through conversa- tion with the child they can gain a knowledge of the processes that the child has gone through. However, no matter how skilful teachers may be at "conferencing" they should be careful not to place too much emphasis on what pupils actually say. Labbett cautions:

"There is no necessary relationship between the way pupils talk about the activity of hand- ling information and the way they did in fact handle it."

Furthermore:

"When pupils talk about the work that they have done, there seem to be two possible problems - the first is the recalling of a past now over, finished, maybe not particularly enjoyed and therefore unmemorable. But now, more import- antly the recalling hinges crucially on their experience with using appropriate language to depict the activity they have engaged in. The following story testifies most eloquently to this problem of language:

" 'I must have been ten years old at the time. The class teacher had set what she had already described to us as a very difficult maths problem. Towards the end of the lesson, I had solved the problem and took my solution to her. She looked at my working and she said "How did you work it out?" If only I had had the vocabulary I have now - but my first response to her was "I guessed" and, at that, she dismissed any further response that I wanted to make. I'm sure if I had been able to say to her "I estimated the range within which the answer could fall and then worked towards refining the answer to the point that I had proved that it was the correct one" then she would have been quite accepting. But she dismissed me and implied in her dismissal that I had in fact cheated. Only one other member of the class actually solved the problem and was given great approval for having done so. And I have to say, even now, I am extremely irritated and feel that I have been cheated of some sort of recognition - just because of that one event. It's funny.'

"In fact, exercising judgement of worth on the basis of the descriptions pupils give of the activity they have engaged in can be a hazardous enterprise."

A further problem with the teacher assuming that s/he knows the processes the child has gone through is that s/he will be much more likely to jump in and provide suggestions or define what is "correct" etc. with a risk of taking the problem out of the grasp of the child. Such behaviour on the part of the teacher is unlikely to promote flexible and adaptable thinking in the student.

Labbett suggests that in order to promote flexible and adaptable thinking, teachers might when assessing children's work consider assuming the role of the historian "who when encountering information (a document) is unable to get in touch with the individual who created that document. Such an approach provides the opportunity for teachers themselves to engage in the very process they have encouraged their pupils to use: inferring, speculating and question-making on the basis of the traces pupils have left behind of their own efforts at being historians. In order to act as an historian in the face of pupils' writings or sayings, consideration must be given to the nature of the tasks specified by the teacher in information handling lessons. Tasks should not be phrased as questions to be answered but as instructional directives to pupils. Pupils should be asked to:

- provide a range of interpretations ..
- provide a list of questions ..
- provide alternative but plausible stories ..
- defend someone else's interpretation ..
- co-operatively reconstruct stories ..

The presentation will illustrate how some of these concerns might be translated into classroom practices using existing Australian data bases. The emphasis will be on the practical aspects with activities, lesson plans and appropriate teacher behaviours being demonstrated.

REFERENCES

JONES, R., "Study Text", Micro Primer Pack, MEP Primary Project, 1982.
LABBETT, B., "Flexible and Adaptable Thinking in the Age of Information Technology and the Activity of Handling Information".
LONGWORTH, N., Education Guardian, Tuesday, 18 June, 1974.
LONGWORTH, N., "Today's Development for Tomorrow's World - Educating for the Information Society", Computer Education, June 1982.
O'BRIEN, T., "Five Essays on Computers in Education", Phi Delta Kappan, October 1983.
STONIER, T., "The Revolution in Education", Quick, No. 13, March 1984.

COMPUTERS IN EDUCATION, K. Duncan and D. Harris (eds.)
Elsevier Science Publishers B.V. (North-Holland)
© IFIP, 1985

TPSA: TEACHING OF THINKING IN A COMPUTER ENVIRONMENT

Joseph Regev

Computation Center
Ben-Gurion University of the Negev
Beer-Sheva, Israel

Abstract: Children in schools have only few occasions where they are required to handle problems in unknown situations. The TPSA educational program was built to make children face situations where they do not know what to do at the beginning. The situations are all in a computer environment. The children are required to write programs in BASIC and in LOGO, to win in computerized strategy games, to perform creativity exercises, to analyse computer games, to write new computer games and to solve mathematical problems with the help of the computer. The program is designed to enhance motivation, creativity and decision-making capabilities. The activities and the principles of TPSA are described, along with its difficulties. TPSA stands for True Problem Solving Approach.

Teaching and Problem Solving

In this paper the question of why we teach problem solving will not be dealt with. In (Holt 1964 and Glasser 1969) one can find the basis for this educational approach. The emphasis on information which comes from teachers and from books, information which must be learned until one can prove knowledge in an examination - this emphasis causes the children to come out of the educational system with very few tools and capabilities for handling problems. Problems in this context are situations where it is not clear what to do, where it is not enough to put the numbers in the formula. What are the characteristics of such problems?

1.   There is information which is connected somehow with the problem.
2.   Not all the information is relevant to the problem.
3.   Some information may be missing and may require looking for it in some other source or getting it by "Trial and Error".
4.   One cannot solve the problem just by reading the problem carefully nor from the information found at hand.
5.   One has to decide what is irrelevant and to discover the missing information. Only then can one start to arrange everything, as with a jigsaw-puzzle, in order to get a solution.
6.   A solution may prove to be wrong so that the whole mental process may have to be restarted .

Because the term problem-solving may mean many things (e.g. Grogono & Nelson 1982), our approach is called the True Problem Solving Approach. Many an educational program does include in its rationale the phrase "problem solving" but usually, the above-mentioned elements are not easily discerned in these programs.

Computers

Computers are the best battle field for teaching in such an approach. One can easily create such somewhat confusing situations as required. These situations will be described later in this paper. Computers allow the pupil to try things, to fail without causing any damage and to make wrong decisions with minimum embarassment and frustration. One can easily recover from such a failure and start anew. In the game the child may be killed one minute and in the next he is back in business again. The subject of computers is rather new so that a teacher is not necessrily bound by the heritage of former generations of teachers and educators.

Computers may be taught in a descriptive approach, the way one would normally teach gardening (Anderson 1966). They may be taught in the Computer Literacy Hands-On Approach (Luerhmann 1982). One may teach the subject in an algorithmic approach which is typical to universities (Francis & Amir 1972). One may use the data approach (Jolley 1968) where computers do not play the major role. Finally, one may teach or rather use computers in the LOGO approach (Papert 1980) which has many elements in common with TPSA. Needless to say, one can even "teach" the subject in the old-fashioned approach where the teacher writes something on the blackboard and the children copy it onto keyboard, without understanding what is going on.

The TPSA approach has to do with the teaching of the subject of computers but it is not just that. The information on how one uses a computer or writes a program - that information is acquired in the process of handling the problems but it is never learned for its own sake and it is given as needed for the solution of the problems.It's a process-oriented teaching and not a product-oriented one. No one is required to learn it by heart - only to know how to find it in the folder which is always at hand. Actually the pupils may learn very little about computers and computer programming, compared to a normal class studying computers, but the mental effort is great.

The TPSA program has been developed in the last 8 years by the teachers in the "Science for Youth" program in the Ben-Gurion University of the Negev. The teachers are: Ofra Lidda, Shay Abramson, Shoshana Kott and William Farjun, with the author being both a teacher and an advisor for the other teachers. The TPSA program has been used many times, mainly with gifted children ages 11 to 15.

Principles of TPSA
The first principle is that of creativity. We try to encourage the children to create new entities which didn't exist before (namely ideas for new computer programs). From this principle stems another point: there are many solutions to any given problem. This point is emphasized again and again. There isn't just one solution to a problem - there are many ways to do it.

The second principle is termed efficacious thinking. We try to accustom the children to that kind of thinking which is divergent in the beginning, when the problem is not clear, but changes over to convergent thinking when a solution is deemed feasible.

The next principle is that of decision-making. The children are afraid to make their own decisions. They are accustomed to having their decisions always made by teachers (or by parents) and fear the responsibility. We try to get them to make independent decisions even though the area is limited to computer programs.

Motivation is our next goal. We try to make things as interesting as possible. We tend to design problems which are known to the children and whose solution is something they would like to achieve. Games are very good in this respect and we will show later how we avoid "bad" games and how we use those games which serve the problem-solving purpose.

The last principle is simply fun. There is a lot of fun in dealing with computers and there is no reason to suppress it. The graphics and the color are fun. After having strained their minds for two hours (without a formal break), they are allowed to change the activity to a lighter one (which is actually still in the problem - solving realm), for half an hour.

Some teachers claim the prize of solving problems is the feeling you did it. We think fun is a prize in line with our approach and we know the children are waiting for it anxiously.

Activities
The above-mentioned principles materialize in the form of activities which are described here:
Creativity Exercises: In a creativity exercise the teacher tells the children that a new computer laboratory will allegedly be opened in their school. The computers may be used by the teachers, the pupils, the head-master, the nurse and the janitor. They are given 5 minutes to think up ideas that can be implemented on these computers. After 5 minutes, the teacher stops them, asks each one how many ideas he could find and then allows each pupil, in a round-robin fashion to present just one of his ideas at a time. Each idea is written on the blackboard and discussed. At the end, the teacher points out those ideas which haven't been raised before and describes ideas from former years.

Printer Pictures: Although better pictures are created later, we do have the children, at an early stage of the program, create pictures on the printer using alphanumeric characters only. A 3-dimensional cube, a house, the star of David, the American flag, a face, a man etc. It's not easy to get them right on the screen and later on the printer, but it is always a nice problem.

Opinion & Jokes Programs: The problem is to write a program which, when given a name, will give the opinion of the programmer on that person (and will say "I don't know" to any unknown name). It's a simple exercise in the IF statement - but what enthusiasm! They bring their friends to see what the computer says. A similiar problem is to write a program which will tell a joke for every topic or every number. This one also results in high motivation. Another one in this group is a telephone directory program (no arrays involved).

Everyday Problems: Preparing grade certificates for pupils out of grade sheets of teachers is a good exercise in arrays. Preparing an invoice in a grocery is a similar problem.

Educational Programs: Writing a "Little Professor" program is a nice problem which has to do with the random number generator. Writing a quiz program in any preferred subject is both a problem in programming and in the subject-matter. Writing (or rather modifying) a program which creates a story according to the pupil's choice, out of a prescribed list at each turn, may be termed an exercise in creativity although it's not really all that creative.

Create Your Own Problems: That may seem a nice idea but it's not. The children usually cannot invent completely new ideas. It's too indefinite for them. Every year, every course, in many sessions we keep telling the children: "Invent your own problems". The only good one we got was: Write a program to output ancient (Biblical) Hebrew characters from normal (modern) Hebrew input. The boy didn't get far with the idea.

GAMES
Games play a major part in our program. Not only are they used as the last part of every session but the same games are used in many places in the main ("learning") part of the sessions.

There is a library of games specially built for this program. Some of the games are well known such as Nim, Matches, Tic-Tac-Toe, Lemonade, Reversi and Wumpus (Levy 1983). Some have been invented by us as RED OR GREEN and a special 7-oriented version of GUESS MY NUMBER. To these we added many simple computer games to make the library big enough so that the children would like to go on playing with it. The library was written originally on the CDC CYBER main-frame which was used by us at that time (Regev 1981). Later it was converted in part to the PET COMMODORE and now it is being converted again to the APPLE IIe which we use now. They are all in Hebrew, of course.

The games are mostly strategy games and not Arcade games. Most of them have been designed to fit the philosophy of TPSA. At the beginning, the player is confused by the synthetic environment and by the clues of the game. As he goes on playing, he learns how to behave, what is the meaning of the clues, and how to use them. Each game can be won by the player, but it takes quite a number of rounds to learn the algorithm to do that. The game is not too easy, so as to pose a real problem, and not too difficult, lest it cause frustration, which would defeat our educational purpose.

One interesting point which should be discussed here is the question of Transfer. Whatever the educational purpose of a game may be, the child seldom is able to transfer his learned capabilities from the game to other activities. In one conference a story was told which may highlight this point. Somebody took a group of children and let them play again and again with "SPEAK & SPELL" or a similar toy. When all

children could spell all words properly, they were taken to another room where a teacher gave them an oral dictation. To the surprise of all people involved, the children as a group failed in the dictation which contained the very same words they knew to type correctly on the toy! It's not clear whether this experiment was really performed or whether it was devised by the distinguished speaker. Our experience tends to confirm this story. The children knew how to win the games but had difficulties in doing the some basic operations outside the closed world of the game. They had difficulties in the formalization of the algorithm they used. Even its verbalization was not easy. We have reason to believe that a discussion after the game about what happened in the game enhances its educational value.

After playing with the game and after analysing what went on, the children take the computer program and try to learn how it is built and how it performs what it is supposed to do. Later, most children like to write their own versions of the same game. Although limited and not so perfect, it's their own.

Mathematics
We are quite cautious in bringing Mathematical Problems to these children. Some computer teachers were former Mathematics teachers and tended to bring together these two different subjects causing the computer to look like a powerful number-handling machine. Mathematics and computers require different modes of thinking. Mathematics has to do mainly with abstract thinking while computers have to do with multi-stage thinking. Some children (even gifted) due to bad past experience with some Mathematics teachers, tend to close their ears once Mathematics is mentioned.

Mathematical problems are presented at a later stage of the program. Following Dr. Eli Maor (Maor 1980) we give them problems such as: Ulam's hypothesis, Happy numbers, the continued sum of digits of a cube of an integer being always 1,8, or 9, and also the calculation of the digits of π. These problems have very little to do with the formal curriculum in Mathematics.

LOGO
Some of the groups use LOGO in an educational program designed by Liron (Liron 1983). Many children keep asking for BASIC, because they have seen it in the home computers at the homes of their friends, their own homes or at their schools. Also we weren't too happy with LOGO number-handling and text-handling statements (compared to its graphic statements and its logical structure). The result was a compromise: LOGO was included as a small module

which comes after the printer pictures and before IF. In this module we teach only the FD,BK,RT,LT,TO statements and the simple commands of the editor. This module was very successful. LOGO is immediate. Whatever the child does, he sees the results immediately. LOGO is clear and direct. The connection between the program and the outcome is clear, while in BASIC the connection is usually quite difficult to perceive. LOGO is nice; the pictures created are aesthetic. We were warned by other teachers that the LOGO editor, being different from the DOS editor, would confuse the children. This didn't happen. LOGO gave them a heightened appetite for computers and for problem solving and they went readily back to BASIC.

What we learned from our pupils
The TPSA program evolved over 8 years. We started from the official high school program (Pelles 1975) but got farther and farther from it. We are not ashamed to say that we learned how to do it properly with and from our pupils.

The first point we learned is that unlike our preconception, people learn from errors and not from smooth application of what was taught. If everything went right it was "easy come, easy go". If the pupil had errors in his program, he saw it as a "slap on the face" and he learned the lesson. Having learned this strengthened our emphasis on problems and on ambiguous situations. If one explained everything beautifully and left no cause for difficulty and for mental effort - one did the wrong thing philosophically and methodically.

We learned to build tasks gradually. We start with a simple problem, easy to solve, and step by step make it more complicated. Otherwise it may be too difficult to solve and we defeat our purpose: to show the child that unclear problems can be solved. All the problems appear in a folder, together with examples. A solution page is given to the pupil if requested after the pupil has tried seriously to solve a problem (even if he didn't succeed).

As mentioned before, we don't teach our pupils the syntax of BASIC statements and DOS commands or any other important fact. We supply them with those details of BASIC, LOGO and DOS as required for the solution of the problems. The problems keep advancing with the parallel material in a formal curriculum but much more slowly. We don't see it as our duty to cover any material. We keep emphasizing the point that there are many solutions to any given problem (in our program) by making each child present his or her particular solution.

There are two difficult points in our program. The first is the narrow gap between lack of knowledge how to solve a problem and a total lack of understanding of what the problem is all about. A teacher has to be very careful not to pass from one state to the other and he must go back whenever the need arises. The simplest problem may sometimes seem unfathomable to a group of kids and one must be on guard all time.

The second difficulty lies with the teacher himself. In TPSA the teacher doesn't teach any more. He doesn't stand in the podium, presenting the pupils with his wisdom. He becomes a guide, a consultant with whom the pupil can discuss his difficulties. That different state of affairs may be hard to accept for most teachers. When a child asks you a question while solving a problem, the easiest thing in the world is to tell him how to do it. One must restrain oneself to giving minimum help, sometimes saying "try it and see what happens" or "I'm sure you can find the solution by yourself. Keep trying".

The TPSA program is in Hebrew. The games are in Hebrew. But BASIC, LOGO and DOS are in English. This poses a problem which is typical to non-English speaking countries. LOGO because of its immediate nature, causes the least problems in this respect. (It's also the shortest in number of letters in each statement). BASIC and DOS do cause difficulties. For several years we had at our disposal a Hebrew BASIC programming system which made things much easier. But this system is available on the CDC main-frame only, which we no longer use.

The philosophy of TPSA is used also in a formal programming course given to students in Ben Gurion University (Regev 1984) . With CAI (Regev 1980) it forms the basis for Project PETAKH .

Conclusions
In this paper an approach was described which used the appeal of computers and the stampede to learn about computers in order to improve the ability of children to solve unclear problems and to handle unknown situations. Computer programming problems and computer strategy games are used to that end. The children keep coming in to participate in this program. Every year, we have to open 7 groups of 20 children each, because of the pressure. There are groups for beginners, 2nd year pupils, and for children who, after two years, want to work on advanced projects. The teachers keep improving the program. Recently the Ministry of Education decided to support this program and make it available to every

interested teacher in the informal educational sector in Israel.

Bibliography

1. Anderson, Decima M.: Computer Programming, FORTRAN IV. (1966) Prentice-Hall, Englewood Cliffs N.J.

2. Francis, Nissim & Amir, Gideon: FORTRAN, Theory and Practice (1972) Academon, Jerusalem (in Hebrew)

3. Glasser, William: Schools without Failure (1969) Harper & Row. N.Y.

4. Grogono Peter & Nelson, Sharon H.: Problem Solving & Computer Programming (1982) Addison-Wesley. Reading Mass

5. Jolley, D.L.: Data Study (1968) World University Library, London

6. Holt, John: How Children Fail (1964) Dell. N.Y.

7. Levy, David: Computer Gamesmanship (1983) Century, London

8. Liron, Uri: Some Problems in children's LOGO Learning in Hershkowitz, R. (Ed.)Proceedings of the 7th International Conference of Psychology of Mathematics Education.Shoresh(1983) Weizman Institute,Rehovoth. pp. 346-351

9. Luehrmann, Arthur & Peckham, Herbert: Computer Literacy, A Hands On approach, for the Apple (1982) McGraw-Hill, N.Y.

10. Maor, Eli: A Summer Course with the TI57 Programmable Calculator. Mathematics Teacher, 73, 2 (Feb. 1980) pp.99-106

11. Papert, Seymor: Mindstorms: Computers and Powerful Ideas (1980) Basic Books

12. Pelles, Yona: Computer Literacy in Israeli High Schools, in Lecarme, O. & Lewis, B. (Eds.): Computers in Education, IFIP (1975) North-Holland, Amsterdam. pp. 743-748

13. Regev, Joseph: FLUID/MASHOV - a CAI System Based on Games, Dialogue and Feedback, J. of Comp. Based Instruction, 7, 1 (Aug. 1980). pp. 8-11

14. Regev, Joseph: Games or the Fun of Using Computers in Learning, in Lewis, R. & Tagg, E.D. (Eds): Computers in Education, WCCE81 (1981) North-Holland, Amsdterdam. pp. 806

15. Regev, Joseph: FORTRAN Course in the True Problem Solving Approach; Data Base: Exercises and Examples. 10th Revision (1984) Ben-Gurion University, Beer-Sheva (In Hebrew & FORTRAN)

COMPUTERS IN EDUCATION, K. Duncan and D. Harris (eds.)
Elsevier Science Publishers B.V. (North-Holland)
© IFIP, 1985

TEACHING ANALYTICAL AND DESIGN SKILLS TO BUSINESS INFORMATION SYSTEMS STUDENTS
GIVEN TIGHT CONSTRAINTS ON TIME AND RESOURCES

Judith D. Wilson

Information Systems
University of Cincinnati
Cincinnati, OH   45221-0130

A pivotal course in a business information system program has been modified in an attempt to upgrade the program given tight constraints on time and resources. The course modifications are explained, and the benefits and problems experienced while teaching the modified course are discussed.

INTRODUCTION

The complexity of applications programming requires willingness on the part of applications programmers to tackle large scale problems and the skills to succeed. The fluid job market for systems analysts and software engineers requires use of skills that cannot be entirely anticipated. Adequate preparation for these conditions includes mastery of analytical problem solving and design skills as well as structured programming techniques. All are needed to solve problems of even moderate logical complexity, where a number of interdependent conditions must be accounted for at any given time.

The applied emphasis of business programs in every area including information systems, however, encourages omission of courses that focus on general conceptual understanding and development of analytical skill, the ability to determine the salient features and underlying structure of situations, whether arguments or enterprises. In addition, tight budgets discourage curriculum development beyond what is deemed the essential or "core" set of courses if additional faculty and equipment resources might be needed.

The recent DPMA and ACM Information Systems curriculum recommendations, however, include analytical and design skills among their objectives, although greater emphasis is placed on analysis of specific types of applications than on analysis as a general problem solving skill (1,4). And, in one apparently successful case, L. Cassell (2) finds that business students can benefit from an information systems course patterned after a core computer science course recommended in the Association for Computing Machinery's Curriculum '78. The objectives of the ACM recommended CS8, "Organization of Programming Languages", is to develop an understanding of the structure and behavior of higher level languages, and the consequence is that business information systems students are given a better understanding of the application programmer's primary tool and of the programming environment.

This paper reports on my experience with a course redesign which attempts to satisfy some of the need for more analytical training of information systems students, given tight constraints on time and resources.

AN INFORMATION SYSTEMS PROGRAM

The Students.

My experience teaching software concepts and practices to undergraduate business information systems students at the University of Cincinnati for the past several years has found that these students tend to be gregarious, that they like to work with others, to share ideas, and prefer to work in a supportive, cooperative environment than a competitive one. I have also found that these students do not tolerate complexity well, that they prefer to work with small, manageable problems and are generally poorly equipped analytically to manage software complexity even in advanced (second and third year) courses.

S. Papert of the Massachusetts Institute of Technology is reported to have identified three types of programming "style" which seem to have implications for programming performance (6), the "artistic", where direction is discovered in the course of implementation, the "extremely structured", where implementation follows a carefully thought through plan, and the adventureous or daring where the the main interest is in exploring the limits of the machine. Two of these styles, the artistic and the extremely structured, apply to students in the information systems program at the University of Cincinnati. Most of these students begin as "artistic" programmers, while a few of the more successful emerge as "extremely structured" programmers. The pragmatic inclination of the information systems students in general would favor the "structured" style but most students have trouble mastering the techniques necessary to make "extremely structured" programming possible.

This phenomenon is due in part to the applied emphasis of the business curriculum, but it may also be due to underlying attitudes and motivations of business information systems students. This has been suggested by a study that compared attitudes and motivations of information systems and computer science students regarding computers (7). The two samples used in the study were selected from the information systems program at the University of Cincinnati and the computer science program at Western Michigan University and were controlled for size, sex, experience and distribution across the academic programs. The study found that information systems students are less inclined to trust computers in important situations or to describe computers in terms of human qualities than are computer science students, and that considerations of high pay and job security, factors extrinsic to computers and computing, are more likely to motivate information systems students than computer science students to pursue careers in computing. The study also found that the information systems students tend to value well-documented programs more than do the computer science students, and are more likely to consider it important for computer professionals to be practical. These results are summarized in table 1 (see Appendix, table 1).

The study suggests that information systems students are typically well-suited attitudinally to work within business organizations and to work with people but that they do not appear to be technology-focused, and may not be highly motivated by "nature" to master technical computing skills.

The Program.

The undergraduate Information Systems program at the University of Cincinnati operates within rigid time constraints. The academic year is organized into three ten-week quarters and a nine-week summer quarter. In addition, the BBA degree offered by the parent college, the College of Business Administration, is considered a generalist degree, and so degree programs that exceed 30 quarter hours in the major field of study are discouraged.

The objective of the Information Systems program is to prepare students for careers as applications software engineers and systems analysts. The program currently consists of four lower level courses that teach programming and structured programming concepts which students usually take in the sophomore year. Courses that teach software engineering techniques (using team projects) and database concepts (a two course sequence) are offered in the second year of the program. The second year courses expose students to more complex data and file organization concepts and more demanding programming projects.

The first course in the major, IS221, teaches programming using the Pascal language. Students are also required to submit designs of their programs using a full-English pseudocode, but the course is programming-intensive (a program each week) and so students focus on coding and debugging rather than on designing and testing, and although students are aware that they are writing pseudocode "designs", they do not understand how to use this tool to actually design algorithmic problem solutions before implementation. As a result, design concepts are not carried over into the other courses, one of which is IS250.

The Course: Original Organization.

IS250 is often taken as the second course in the Information Systems major. It was originally designed to teach PL/I which is used in second and third year courses and to introduce students to static data structures (linear lists and tables) and searching and sorting algorithms.

As originally taught, the course consisted of several short programming assignments and a larger programming project introducing students to disk I/O and external routines. Again, time restrictions forced IS250 to be programming-intensive placing emphasis on coding and debugging and encouraging a trial-and-error or "artistic" style of programming. The project, which involved I/O bound programming using IBM Job Control Language, actually discouraged attention to procedural design problems. Design and testing strategies were discussed in class and in the primary text for the course, Problem Solving and the Computer by J. Shortt and T.C. Wilson (5), but these techniques were poorly understood by students, rarely used, and never tested. Consequently, those who passed the course knew something about a subset of PL/I syntax but understood little about the design and testing principles that would be required to complete the more complex programming assignments of second and third year information systems courses. These students generally had difficulty bridging the gap to the second year courses and were often forced to abandon the program after the first year.

The Course: Redesigned.

Students were discovering late in the Information Systems program that they were unwilling to, or could not, handle the requirements of moderately complex programming environments, and those who survived probably did so without the full repertoire of software development skills they would need later. IS250 needed to be changed to minimize these problems, but the tight restrictions on time and resources at that time could not be changed.

The course was redesigned within these constraints to
(1) maximize exposure to design problems and techniques without significantly reducing exposure to PL/I implementation of input, searching and sorting algorithms, and

(2) encourage a more analytical approach to programming problems.

The course as originally organized could be described as program-driven while the redesigned course is topic-driven (see Appendix, figure 4).

To satisfy the design requirement, students are required to submit designs of some of their programs well in advance of program due dates (see table 2). The analytical requirement is satisfied by a more abstract focus in class discussions due to the use of design tools to introduce and explain algorithms, and by assignment of a term project that involves less system complexity and greater procedural complexity.

The Design Component

The importance of design is stressed from the beginning. A detailed design of the first assignment which requires the use of both selection and looping structures is due nearly a week before the program. The design tool used for this purpose is a modified version of the Jackson structure chart (3) since it forces modular or blocking design and graphically supplements emphasis in the first two weeks of the course on modular programming concepts and top-down design methodology (see figure 1).

A detailed design using pseudocode is required for a later programming assignment a week before the program itself is due. Since heavy emphasis is placed on program documentation in the Information Systems program, and IS221 requires full-English pseudocode designs, students tend to associate pseudocode with documentation rather than design functions (see figure 2). Thus a standard pseudocode, that is easier to read and write than PL/I code, has been adopted for IS250 in order to encourage its use as a design tool (see figure 3).

The term project has two design phases. Students are required to submit a general design using a modified structure chart showing the "upper level" modular structure of their proposed solution three weeks before the project program is due. A detailed design using pseudocode is required approximately 10 days later. This two-stage, two week design process redirects interest from coding to structured planning, and provides an opportunity to show how different design tools might be appropriate for different phases of the top-down design process.

The Analytic Component

Emphasis on I/O bound programming tends to draw the programmer's attention from procedural problems to computer system problems, such as Job Control Language syntax and 'midstream'

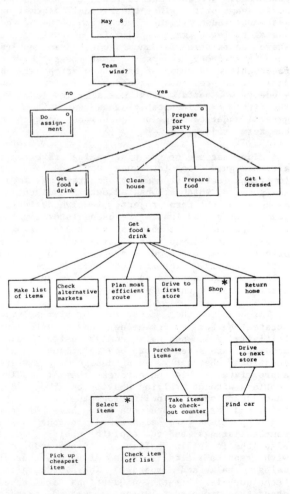

Figure 1. An example of the structure chart used as a design tool in IS 250. Vertical bars within a process box indicate that the box is expanded elsewhere. '*' and 'o' in the upper right corner of a box indicate a repeated process and a selected process respectively. No circuits are permitted. This example is only partially expanded.

Table 2. General schedule for IS250 showing due dates for programming assignments (PAs) and designs. Programs are usually due on fridays and designs are due early in the week.

Week	Designs (Due Days)	Programs
1		
2	Detailed design for PA1 (Mon)	PA1
3		PA2
4		PA3
5	Detailed design for PA4 (Wed)	
6		PA4
7		PA5
8	General design for Project (Wed)	PA6
9	Detailed design for project (Mon)	
10		Project

system software changes, which are typically
solvable only with specific technical help.
Advanced information systems students need to
learn when and how to use system support people,
but the focus for beginning students should be
on learning how to help themselves.

This was one of the problems with IS250 as
originally designed. Students were, in effect,
learning more about how to find help in a
specific context than about how to solve
problems themselves. At the University of
Cincinnati, academic computer center consultants
provide the necessary technical system support,
and student frustration and motivation had
become clearly tied to the quality of this
technical support.

The revised course has reduced reliance on
system support personnel by requiring students
to solve a procedurally non-trivial problem for
their project that uses minimal system
resources.[1] Students are allowed to work alone
or in teams of two since the typical information
systems student likes to work with others, and
seems to learn more rapidly in an environment
where cooperation is encouraged. Exam results
show that both members of most teams have a
reasonably good grasp of their project program's
data structures and procedural logic. Even
students who perform at a generally low level on
the final exam inevitably show enthusiasm and
general understanding on questions concerning
the term project.

The last one or two programming assignments
are designed to introduce students to an
important feature of modular programming. These
assignments, which are handed out and discussed
along with the term project, involve designing
and testing modules to be used later in the
final project. The modules are tested using a
"test harness" or driver routine that is to be
discarded when the modules are shown to perform
satisfactorily. The tested modules are then
"black boxed" and stored as object modules for
later linkage with the project program.

Throughout the course, problem-solving
strategies for programming assignments are
initially discussed using only design tools.
Students are asked to propose solutions or ask
questions abstractly, using design tools where
appropriate. This encourages them to solve
problems without relying heavily on PL/I code,
thus reducing the inclination to program by
trial and error. Students who have program
logic problems are also asked to put aside
source listings and to explain their general
algorithm in plain English or pseudocode and
with graphical aids (such as structure charts)
using chalk and board. The pedagogical
technique is Socratic. Questions are asked
about the proposed solution in such a way that
the student comes to see, without being told,
whether the method can achieve the objective and
avoid undesired side effects. These tactics
have been observed to yield positive results.

Except for a few intractable cases, students
spot potential problems and answer their own
questions. They are then able to correct their
source code without further help.

EVALUATION OF THE REDESIGNED COURSE

In its original form, IS250 introduced
students to the PL/I programming language. The
redesigned course now satisfies CIS2 and about
50% of CIS3 of the DPMA Model Curriculum, and
helps comply with the ACM Information Systems
Undergraduate Curriculum Recommendations by
satisfying P1 (topics 2 and 3) and IS2 (topics 1
and modest parts of 2 and 3). The course
redesign has had both positive and negative
consequences, however, and whether or not the
new design is to be recommended depends on the
relative value placed on these benefits and
problems.

```
0  Input and Store a List of Values.

1  Set initial values.

   1.1  Set the list counter to 1.

2  Read the first value.

3  While values remain and the counter is less than the maximum list
   size

   3.1  Increment the list counter by 1.

   3.2  Store the value at the location indicated by the list counter.

   3.3  Read the next value.

4  End of Input and Store a List of Values.
```

Figure 2.   This is an example of full-English pseudocode used in
IS221. Some variations are typical for a problem such
as this where an array of items is stored internally.
The problems in IS221 are extremely simple, however,
and all values are global within the programs and the
designs.

```
PROCEDURE INPUT_LIST(LIST,#ITEMS,MAX_SIZE)

  /* Values are read from an external source of indeterminant
     size and stored as a list  */

  PARAMETERS:
     LIST = List to be built from input values.
     #ITEMS = Number of values actually input.
     MAX_SIZE = Upperbound on list size.

  LOCAL VARIABLES:
     K = Selects successive list locations.

  K  <-- 0

  READ First Value

  WHILE More Data & K < MAX_SIZE  DO
     K  <-- K + 1
     LIST(K)  <-- Value
     READ Next Value
  END WHILE

END INPUT_LIST
```

Figure 3.   This is an example of the pseudocode conventions
adopted for IS250. Students were encouraged to
document their designs and to differentiate between
global and local variables and parameters.

Beneficial Results

1. Increased General Understanding.

The use of structure charts as a design tool allows focus on general modular structure which is critical for top-down testing. The amount of time students previously spent using trial and error and brute force methods or consulting help to find program bugs has been noticeably reduced. Students who request help with a problem during the last half of the term typically have made headway in isolating the problem source using reasonable strategies such as procedure "stubs" and selective dump traces, and have formulated hypotheses about what to do next. In some of these cases, the problem has not been either syntatic or logical in nature (VAX-11 PL/I compiler "bugs" or system anomalies have been showing up with some frequency).

The use of pseudocode permits early and natural introductions to the concepts of external procedures, parameters, and user-defined functions. In one lecture, late in the quarter, pseudocode is used to design a problem solution with the objective of showing how Boolean (logical) functions can be suggested naturally by the design process. It is then shown that these functions would streamline the PL/I code. This approach can both explain and motivate the use of such exotic tools.

Student work can be more effectively tested by examinations that require the use of design tools to show the logical structure of a program, permitting detection of the student who can reproduce on an exam code designed and written by another. This also enables examinations to test for understanding of algorithms without the encumbrance of PL/I syntax. It is not easy, for example, to test a student's ability to spot logical problems in an algorithm expressed in PL/I without the distracting background considerations of possible compile time errors or runtime problems due to compiler features (such as type conversion restrictions and array bounds checking). The student's understanding of procedural logic can be unproblematically tested, however, when pseudocode or structure charts are used.

2. Better Program Quality.

Although the rate of success on programs has not been affected by the course modifications, program quality has improved, particularly in the case of the more complex term project. Students who take the design phase seriously tend to finish early and typically write programs with fewer lines of source code (the number of lines of code ranged from 450 to 3800 with an average around 1200 in Fall 1983), and better program performance (in terms of functional richness, user-friendliness, and strategic flexibility). Satisfactory performance on the project design phases has

been shown to have a reasonably high positive correlation with satisfactory performance on the project program for several sections of IS250 since its redesign (table 3).

3. Long Range Benefits.

Students who have completed the revised course have recently begun to enter second year courses in the program, but it is still too early and the numbers are still too small to obtain reliable measures of performance impact. A preliminary attempt to test for significant changes was done with a small number of students in the first course of the two-course database sequence. The results show a higher positive correlation between the term averages in the database course and IS250 after revision than between those in database and IS250 prior to revision, and thus that performance in the revised course may be a better predictor of performance in later courses (table 4).

Problematic Results

1. The New Course is Work-Intensive.

The redesigned course is work-intensive. The analytical and design focuses require time and effort, some of which will not produce immediate concrete results. While this may be accepted as routine by students in the sciences and humanities, it is not easily tolerated by business students. Consequently, many students fall behind and have to drop the course. The normal drop rate is close to 25%, while the drop rate for this course has approached 45%.

Course Factor	Correlation
Project program designs	.6000
Cumulative quiz score	.2218
Final exam score	.4097
Term average for IS250	.6672

Table 3. Correlations of IS250 grade components with the project program score for the redesigned course.

Course Organization	
Original	Redesigned
.5584	.8631

Table 4. Correlations between term averages for IS250 and IS321 ("Principles of Database") for students who completed the original and redesigned versions of IS250.

Comments of those who have withdrawn from the course have included, "I've discovered I don't really enjoy doing this as much as I thought I would." and some have added, "I want to work more with people." while others, more wistfully, have admitted, "I don't know what I want to do, but I now know this isn't it!" These are discoveries that should be made early, not late, and they are made by students who otherwise would probably leave the program in the second year (as juniors). The pace and focus of the course, however, risk losing students who might be able to handle these factors later. For this reason, it might be desirable, resources permitting, to move some of this material into a later course at the first year level.

2. Resource Demands.

Although a low level course, IS250 cannot be taught by graduate teaching assistants without careful supervision, nor can the designs, or design-based examination questions, be marked by undergraduate graders. The course requires well-trained instructors, and thus will tend to reduce departmental flexibility with regard to teaching assignments.

3. Instructional Demands.

IS250 is time-consuming to teach. Assignments, examples, and examinations must be carefully constructed. Feedback on the designs should be immediate and sufficient to explain problems so that they will not recur in future work, and this often requires pain-staking traces through logic that is often idiosyncratic and occasionally very clever.

CONCLUSIONS

The course as redesigned satisfies a programmatic need. Students who complete the course have a better grasp of design tools and analytical techniques and of the programming process than did their predecessors. Several students have openly expressed excitement when it first becomes clear that they are now in control of the programming process and no longer have to await step by step direction. Finally, many of the project programs are fine examples of analytic problem-solving. Whereas past projects were regarded as obstacles to be mechanically and expeditiously overcome, many students in the revised course are obviously proud of their work and excited about what a fairly simple computer program can be made to do.

On the other hand, a course like this one requires from the instructor considerable expenditures in time and physical and psychical energy preparing, explaining and grading assignments and examinations. The design focus means greater student involvement in assigned problems, and the anxiety and excitement that this can generate may prove time-consuming outside of class. But, of course, these kinds of demands can be their own rewards.

FOOTNOTES

[1] A master file inventory update problem using sequential files has been replaced by problems such as moving a simple robot through a maze in search of treasure, or implementing a user-friendly tic-tac-toe game with the computer as adversary.

REFERENCES

[1] Adams, D.R., and Athey, T.H., Eds., DPMA Model Curriculum for Undergraduate Computer Information Systems Education (Data Processing Management Association, Park Ridge, Illinois, 1981).

[2] Cassel, L.N., "Organization of Programming Languages for Business Information Systems Majors," ACM SIGCSE Bulletin, Volume 15 (February 1983) 228-231.

[3] Jenson, R.W. and Tonies, C.C., Software Engineering (Prentice-Hall, Inc., New Jersey, 1979).

[4] Nunamaker, Jr., J.R., Couger, J.D., and Davis, G.B., "Information Systems Curriculum Recommendations for the 80s: Undergraduate and Graduate Programs," Communications of the ACM, Volume 25 (November 1982) 781-805.

[5] Shortt, J. and Wilson, T.C., Problem Solving and the Computer: A Structured Concept With PL/I (PL/C), Second Edition (Addison-Wesley Publishing Co., Reading, Massachusetts, 1979).

[6] Turner, J.A., "Programming Style Can Identify Student Hackers, Expert Says," Chronicle of Higher Education, Volume 27 (Nov. 16, 1983) 16.

[7] Wilson, J. D., and Braun, G. F., "Psychological Differences in University Computer Student Populations," ACM SIGCSE Bulletin, Volume 17 (March 1985) 160-172.

APPENDIX

Table 1. Differences in attitudes regarding computers and motivations for taking computer courses between information systems and computer science students. (Group means and standard deviations are shown. Differences were tested for significance using separate or pooled two-tailed t tests where appropriate.)

Attitude or Motivation	Student Groups	
	BIS	CS
Category 1		
Coding: 1 - agree strongly to 5 - disagree strongly	n = 136	n = 115
	mean (St. Dev.)	mean (St. Dev.)
Computer professionals should		
be very practical.	1.9632 (0.9060)	2.2174 (0.9623)*
not be interested in making lots of money through their work.	3.6176 (0.8525)	3.3478 (0.9370)*
have a high mathematical aptitude.	2.4559 (1.0878)	1.9739 (1.0127)***
Attitudes about Computer programs:		
Efficiency is more important than documentation.	3.5073 (1.0399)	3.3565 (1.2008)
It's reasonable to sacrifice documentation to enhance storage efficiency.	3.5441 (1.0246)	3.2000 (1.1255)*
Category 2		
Coding: 1 - high to 5 - low	n = 136	n = 115
Attitudes about computers:		
Trusting	3.5245 (0.7011)	3.0985 (0.7621)***
Anthropomorphic	3.1185 (0.9023)	2.8739 (0.8373)*
Category 3		
Coding: 1 - high to 4 - low	n = 135	n = 115
Motivation to take computer courses:		
Enjoyment of programming and computers	1.7037 (0.5336)	1.6348 (0.5393)
Job Security and high pay	1.6889 (0.6043)	1.8608 (0.6836)*

*p < .05
**p < .01
***p < .001

WEEK	PL/I TOPICS	DESIGN and ANALYSIS
1	- Program layout - Identifier names & declarations - Simple I/O - Assignment statements - Arithmetic operators & expressions - Interactive (VAX) PL/I	- Modular program design: Structure charts - Program documentation
2	- Simple Data Types - Logical Expressions - Control structures: selection & iteration - ON ENDFILE - DO groups	- Algorithm for finding the largest of a set of values - Common problems when using structure charts
3	- Procedures: Defining and calling Local & Global Variables - Edit I/O - Iterated DO - External data Files - 1-dimensional arrays: Input algorithms	- Types of program errors - Debugging programs: Clues from program output Using selective dumps
4	- 1-Dimensional arrays: Bubble sort, tag sort	- Selecting program modules: Size considerations Functional independence Data independence - Formal introduction to pseudocode
5	- 1-Dimensional arrays: Sequential searching - Multi-dimensional arrays - Structure variables	- Algorithms & programs - Binary search algorithm
6	- Character manipulation - VERIFY function	- Top-down coding & testing: Procedure stubs
7	- Procedures: Parameter mechanisms Arrays as parameters External procedures	- External routines - Modular progam development: Coding & testing modules independently Achieving data independence
8	- Functions, logical functions	- Compiling & linking external routines - Using functions in pseudocode
9	- Recursive procedures	- Iteration & recursion - Appropriate uses of recursion
10	- Review	

Figure 4. Topic syllabus for IS250

COMPUTERS IN EDUCATION, K. Duncan and D. Harris (eds.)
Elsevier Science Publishers B.V. (North-Holland)
© IFIP, 1985

TEACHING BUSINESS COMPUTING - A TOP DOWN APPROACH FROM DOWN UNDER

Kate Behan

Business Faculty
Swinburne Institute
John Street
Hawthorn
Victoria 3122
Australia

INTRODUCTION

In this paper, the author argues that we should
teach those skills relevant to future 'end-users'
in our introductory computer courses. Topics
such as application generators which, if they
are discussed at all, appear near the end of
a computing course, should become the starting
point for all students - not the finishing
point for future professional computerists.

Imagine that you are a driving instructor about
to take a keen young student out for a driving
lesson. You both settle into the front seats
of the driving school's automatic transmission
automobile. The student is excited and highly
motivated to learn to drive this machine. The
student is aware that driving skills will open
up many new opportunities. But you know that
the student should not rush head-long into the
modern driving era - automatic transmissions,
automatic ignition, power steering and so on.
You have a responsibility to ensure that the
student can appreciate the historic developments
that have taken place since the automobile was
invented.

You begin this first driving lesson by explaining that driving was not always this easy - the
first drivers had to crank the engine. You
show the student a book which has photographs
of a person cranking up an old T-model Ford.
"See", you say "this is what used to happen."
And you continue to trace the development of
engine ignition devices.

Then you have to cover transmission developments
leading up to automatic transmission as we know
it today - the braking system and the steering
system have yet to come. By the end of the
third lesson there has been no time to actually
drive the automobile - but much has been taught!

By the end of the sixth lesson you have explained in detail how each component of the car works
- after all, drivers had to be mechanics in the
old days before we had service stations - there
has not yet been time to actually drive the automobile.

The student's motivation is now very low - the
desire to be able to drive remains but there
is no excitement left. The student does not
even arrive for the seventh lesson - becoming
a motor mechanic was never one of his or her
career options!

How many computer educators would accept the
above scenario as a legitimate approach to teaching driving skills? Very few, I believe.

Yet how many computer educators take precisely
the same approach to introductory computer
courses?

Many "introductory computer" courses have the
following outline:

- Computer technology, past and present.

- Basic computer concepts.

- Hardware.

    . Number systems.
    . Binary arithmetic.
    . CPU.
    . Input devices.
    . Storage devices.
    . Output devices.

- Software.

    . System software.
    . Application software.
    . Flowcharting and programming and
        languages.

- Systems concepts.

    . Life cycle for in-house development.
    . Packages.

-   Management implications of computers.

The length of the course seems irrelevant - each
topic usually expands in proportion to the time
available and the area of expertise of the course
leader. It is not a coincidence that most introductory computer texts also follow the same
tired, but well-tried and trodden formula.

The publishers of the 1984 vintage of introductory computer books display a greater knowledge of modern colour printing technology than
the authors do of modern business computing
technology!

Many of the students currently enrolled in introductory computer courses will not undertake
further formal computer studies.

Almost all of the students currently enrolled
in introductory computer courses will be "computer users" in their chosen professional
careers.

A small number of the students currently enrolled
in introductory computer courses will choose
to become computer professionals and will undertake further extensive computer studies.

It is surely time that we took a new look at
the content of introductory computer courses.
The only thing that students enrolled in an introductory computer course have in common is
that they will all be computer users (drivers)
of the future.

We may well ask "how much of our introductory
computer courses is really relevant to students
who will become end users"? Is a half hour
on number systems and binary arithmetic likely
to have any value, or will it merely cause confusion? What relevnce does flowcharting have
today? Is the technological past really worth
studying at this level?

We need to start afresh and design introductory
computer courses that meet the requirements of
future end-users.

Gordon B. Davis, in an excellent paper (Ref. 4)
provides an overview of end user computing.

'The importance of end-user computing is apparent
from rapid development of information centres
to support it and the forecasts of experts who
have studied it. For example, Bob Benjamin of
Xerox estimates that by 1990, end-user computing
will take 75 per cent of corporate computer
resources. Rockart and Flannery estimate a
growth rate of 50 to 90 per cent per year in
companies promoting end-user computing; this
is contrasted with a growth of 5 to 15 per cent
in traditional data processing.

The computer resources that support end-user
computing include hardware, software, and organization:

- The hardware support can vary depending on
  the organization. The following may be
  used individually or in combination:

  - Terminals to external time-sharing
    system

  - Terminals to mainframe

  - Stand alone microcomputers

  - Microcomputers in network

- The software support for end-user computing include the following:

  - Planning languages and spread sheet
    processors (examples are IFPS, EXPRESS,
    VISICALC, etc.)

  - Procedural languages such as BASIC and
    APL

  - Very high level languages for programm-
    ing and query. Examples are NOMAD,
    FOCUS AND RAMIS

  - Statistical analysis software. Examples
    are SAS and SPSS.

  - Database management system

- The organization for end-user computing
  may use one or more of the following
  options:

  - Information centre with analysts who
    program to user specifications

  - Information centre with analysts who
    assist users to utilize the facilities
    and provide training and consultation

  - Analysts assigned to user areas who
    assist users by doing the work or by
    aiding users with the facilities

  - A policy supporting end-user computing,
    but no direct support organization

  - No policy or support

  - Policy that there will be no end-user
    computing

The last item in the organizational options
makes clear that some organizations are not
happy with the idea of end-user computing and
especially user-developed systems.'

We should design courses that

- develop the ability to use such software

- develop an understanding of the implications of using such hardware alternatives

- introduce the organizational issues.

Let's look at a different form of introductory
computer course. It should cover the following
areas:

- The nature of the computer as a data
  management device.

- The relevance of computer sizes i.e. micro
  vs mini vs mainframe

- The different ways that applications can
  be developed.

- What makes a successful computer system.

The major purpose of such a course is surely to motivate the future user to want to use the system properly and to instil confidence that the task is within the user's capabilities.

To achieve this, the course must

. use examples that are meaningful to each student.

. provide hands-on use of some good data management tools.

. be designed so that the student ends up with a good understanding of the man/machine interface.

Introductory hands-on sessions early in a course mean we have to be very careful how we sequence exercises.

Coming face to face with a computer system for the very first time a person has to undergo several quite distinct learning experience - these include the following:

1. keyboard skills

2. computer concepts

3. using specific software

It is important to keep these in mind as separate learning experiences, for if the instructor does not design exercises that progressively develop the confidence of the student then all is lost.

An opening gambit of "Let's log on and invoke the editor and then we'll create a data file", is an example of how easy it is to forget the number of totally new concepts involved in what is to most of us in a fairly simple procedure.

The naive student needs to know

. what is logon

. why you logon

. how you logon

. where to find the space bar

. how to start a new line

. upper or lower case

. whether spaces are needed

. what invoke means

. who the editor is

. what a data file is

. why we need to create one

. how to create it.

We have been developing a new approach to our introductory computer course at Swinburne Institute over the past two years. We have a Prime 2250 with 9 terminals running INFORMATION Prime's Pick-style operating system. We use an application generator called SIMPLE. But even with the right resources it is very easy to fall into old ways.

Let's look at the main menu for a system called SIMPLE INFORMATION and consider how easily a very "simple" end-user system can be made either complex or "simple".

```
A  -  New file setup
B  -  Dictionary definition
C  -  Data entry (or inquiry)
D  -  Display a report
      . . . . .
E  -  Print a report
F  -  Print a Dictionary
G  -  Display list of all SIMPLE files
H  -  Print list of all SIMPLE files
I  -  Use another file
J  -  Print Documentation
K  -  Show the Introductory Instructions
L  -  Print the Introductory Instructions
M  -  Customize a screen
N  -  Display list of screens
O  -  Custom Report definition
P  -  Print Custom Report(s)
R  -  Reset video display type
X  -  Cross reference a file
```

It is a good chance that the average instructor will start off by explaining what each item in the menu means - starting at A and working through to X. Having discussed each briefly, the instructor will then show how to do A, followed by B and so on all the way to X. This would be as bad as existing introductory courses!

A far better approach is to start at the most easily understood item - in this particular case, data entry or enquiry, which is C. If the instructor has done some homework, a file will already have been created and several records entered. The potential user can see what is being discussed and can browse through the file.

This is a good place to enhance keyboard skills. The file chosen as an illustration should have only a few items but the student should understand the significance of having such data available. A sample "tutorial management system" is shown in Appendix A.

Once students feel confident that the data is in the system, get them to enter some new records with particular values in one item. Then select D and show them how to display a report selecting the items they have just entered.

Having experienced all these activities the student is now confident that computers are not very difficult to use and hopefully will be very keen to apply what has been learned to a new data management need.

Also, having experienced C and D, the student is much better prepared in order to understand what happens in A and B. Just reflect upon the length of time it would take you to explain all those things that the student has not only experienced but also understood. As usual, "doing it" is more interesting than being told about it. The student is now much more receptive to the concepts of data files, records, item names and item contents.

Appendix B shows a sample system developed for use in Australian schools. Such an approach is a valid introduction to data processing - regardless of the specialist disciplines that the student may subsequently pursue.

James Martin (Ref 7) has said that "data processing to a large extent will consist of:

   . creating good data base

   . extracting information when needed from these data bases

   . generating applications that use the data bases

   . creating and controlling input to the data bases."

Such basic data management exercises should give the student a good understanding of why computers are so useful.

In 1982 James Martin (Ref 7) said "a decade from now the DP profession will be greatly changed. Progressive DP organizations are making those changes now."

If we, as computer educators, ignore the directions that our industry is taking we may very well produce graduates whom no one wants.

Already we see signs of this. A Datamation article (Ref 1) gives an intersting idea of the direction being taken by progressive companies.

"....the management training program began to recruit liberal arts graduates directly out of college. These people typically have no prior computing training or experience, and therefore no pre-conceived notions of how systems should be built or which languages should be used ..... we have found that they often tend to write better programs, and sooner, than a more experienced person who attempts to write COBOL-type program using APL or Natural. The latter just dosen't work."

In July 1984 I received 4 new introductory computer books. Long (Ref 5) has 27 pages on computer history and 16 lines on application generators; Mandell (Ref 6) has 14 pages on computer history, 0 lines on application generators but 1 colour photograph of PASCAL'S adding machine; Stair (Ref 8) has 15 pages on computer history and 21 lines on fourth generation languages; Capron and Williams (Ref 3) has 16 pages

of computer history and 21 lines on non-procedural languages.

Also in July 1984 I received the Summer 1984 Guide to Software Productivity Aids (Ref 2). It listed over 85 products in the application generator category and approximately 720 other productivity aids ranging through Screen Generators, Test Data Generators, Pre-compilers etc. - if our introductory computer texts are any guide these products don't even exist! The Xephon Buyers Guide (Ref 9) provides an in depth comparison of 29 on-line application generators that run on IBM equipment. In the majority of educational institutions the only students who will learn about the computing tools that they will most likely use are those who specialize in computing subjects.

CONCLUSION

The approach taken in many introductory computer courses does little to prepare the student for life as an "end user" in the late 1980's and 1990's. There is ample evidence from industry that "end users" are successfully achieving good results from the computer systems that they help develop. We should re-think our approach to teaching computing and teach from the fourth generation down, rather than the first generation up.

REFERENCES

(1)   Abbey, Scott G. COBOL DUMPED Datamation January 1984.

(2)   APPLIED COMPUTER RESEARCH, GUIDE TO SOFTWARE PRODUCTIVITY AIDS: SUMMER 1984.

(3)   Capron & Williams, COMPUTERS AND DATA PROCESSING Benjamin Cummings Publishing Company.

(4)   Davis, Gordon B., CAUTION: USER DEVELOPED SYSTEMS CAN BE DANGEROUS TO YOUR ORGANIZATION.
      IFIP-ACS JOINT INTERNATIONAL SYMPOSIUM ON INFORMATION SYSTEMS April 1984.

(5)   Long, INTRODUCTION TO COMPUTERS AND INFORMATION PROCESSING Prentice-Hall 1984.

(6)   Mandell, COMPUTERS AND DATA PROCESSING TODAY WITH BASIC West Publishing, 1983.

(7)   Martin, James, APPLICATION DEVELOPMENT WITHOUT PROGRAMMERS, Prentice-Hall, 1982.

(8)   Stair, PRINCIPLES OF DATA PROCESSING, Richard D. Irwin, 1984.

(9)   XEPHON BUYERS GUIDE: DEC. 1983; ON-LINE APPLICATION GENERATORS.

APPENDIX A

TUTORIAL MANAGEMENT SYSTEM

DATA DEFINITIONS

We will use NUMBER AS THE RECORD-ID

Item Name	Type	Length	Decimal	Description
NUMBER	NUMBERS	6	0	Student Number
SURNAME	TEXT	20	-	Student Surname
NAMES	TEXT	20	-	Given names
SEX	TEXT	1	-	Student sex
TUTOR	TEXT	20	-	Name of tutor
TUTE. DAY	TEXT	9	-	Day of tutorial
TUTE. TIME	NUMBERS	4	2	Start time of tutorial

TEST DATA FOR TUTORIAL MANAGEMENT SYSTEM

NUMBER	SURNAME	NAMES	SEX	TUTOR	TUTE-DAY	TUTE-TIME
831000	BLOGGS	FRED	M	ADRIENNE	MONDAY	1.00
832000	OSOPHICAL	PHIL	F	KATE	WEDNESDAY	11.00
833000	ANDREWS	HARRY	M	ED	TUESDAY	3.00
834000	KELLY	NED	M	HU	FRIDAY	5.30
835000	O'SHEA	NELLY	F	KATE	TUESDAY	11.00
836000	SOPHICAL	THEO	M	ED	TUESDAY	3.00
837000	O'SHEA	HARRY	F	ED	TUESDAY	3.00

Produce the following reports:

a)   a list of all students.

b)   a list of all students in ED's tutorials.

c)   a list of all female students.

d)   a list of all male students.

e)   a list of all students in Kate's Wednesday tutorial.

The following example is provided to assist you in getting your reports.

If you want a list of all male students you would enter

    SURNAME   NAMES   SEX   PHRASE   WITH   SEX   EQ   'M'

Using the test data above, determine the correct answer before you produce the report.

APPENDIX   B

During information technology week in 1982 the first fleet data base was made
available to any school in Australia - it is available for several common brands
of micro computer.

The FIRST FLEET database contains information about each of the 777 convicts
sent to Australia in 1788.

EXAMPLE CONVICT RECORD:

GIVEN NAME:	Mary
SURNAME:	Allen
SEX:	F
SHIP:	Lady Penrhyn
AGE:	22
TRADE:	Service, prostitute
PLACE OF TRIAL:	Old Bailey
DATE OF TRIAL:	25-Oct-86
CRIME:	Highway Robbery
VALUE (in shillings)	72
TERM (in years)	7
SENTENCE (Death or Transportation):	T

EXAMPLE REQUEST:

o   In response to the menu offering choices 1 to 15, type 2 for "enquiry by
     name".

o   Type JONES as the surname about which you're requesting information.

o   You'll receive a list of JONES's with some information about them including
     a unique identification code (I.D. number).

o   If you'd like more information about one of them, note the I.D. number
     and type Y in answer to "Do you want a full enquiry?"

o   Type the I.D. number and all the information recorded about that convict
     will appear on the screen.

o   If you want to look in full at another convict, type the I.D. number over
     the top of the previous one, and the computer will replace the screen
     with the new information.

o   Press the ESC key twice and the RETURN key once to get back to the menu
     to do further enquiries.

"THE BIRDS OF ANTARTICA" DATABASE WAS DEVELOPED FOR INFORMATION TECHNOLOGY MONTH
IN 1984.

COMPUTERS IN EDUCATION, K. Duncan and D. Harris (eds.)
Elsevier Science Publishers B.V. (North-Holland)
© IFIP, 1985

Portability of Computer Based Learning Materials across machines and across natural languages

Stephen D. Franklin

Bernard C. Levrat

Educational Technology Center
Information and Computer Science
University of California
Irvine, California 92717

Centre Universitaire d'Informatique
University of Geneva
24, rue General Dufour
1211 Geneve 4

Portability of computer based learning materials across machines and across natural languages is important for both educational and economic reasons. Based on our experience writing, maintaining and transporting such materials, this paper discusses the problems that must be addressed and presents strategies and tools which have proved critical. Among other topics, this paper pays particular attention to input/output, graphics and text presentation, analysis of student responses, and maintaining the quality of the original material when it is translated into foreign languages.

1. Life cycle of computer based learning material

The development cycle of good computer based learning (CBL) materials from initial conception through detailed design, programming, debugging, field testing, evaluation, revision and distribution is best measured in years, not weeks or months [1]. Once such material has been developed, the intellectual investment in it and the educational context in which it must fit argue that a good CBL program should be around almost as long as a good book. Given the rapidly changing technical and economic basis of computers, such longevity is attainable only if CBL materials can be transported to new machines as they become available. All too often, changes in technology or marketing have forced us to choose between abandoning computer based materials or reprogramming them at at substantial expense.

Fine interactive learning material has disappeared with the particular time- sharing systems which supported it. This represents a real loss which should be avoided in the future. Unfortunately, we are beginning to see the same phenomenon on personal computers for much the same reasons: hardware dependence, system specific software, and failure to balance long term costs against short term economies.

To help insulate CBL material from the vagaries of the computer marketplace, it should be written so that it is readable by others than its original developers. It must also be easily transportable between different machines that have substantially the same functional capabilities. Moreover, good
educational material should be designed so that it can be adapted to take advantage of new technological possibilities without expensive modifications affecting the logic of the program.

2. Software requirements for portability

One obvious requirement for portability is that the programming language(s) used be widely available in reasonably standard form on a variety of machines. Another is that any language used should directly support modern programming practices such as structured programming, modular design, powerful data description facilities, and a strong emphasis on program readability and maintainability. Modern programming practices are essential in order to have programs which reflect closely the pedagogical design of the authors, which encourage imbedded documentation and which can be easily read and maintained by software specialists. These considerations exclude COBOL, FORTRAN, PL/I, the multitude of BASICs, and any language supported by only one vendor.

In fact, our work has used Pascal although others of ALGOL's descendants such as Ada and Modula-2 would also be suitable choices once the implementation base has grown [2]. To avoid Pascal's well-known limitation on separate compilations and the continual recompilation of common routines that this limitation fosters, we have used the UCSD Pascal implementation of the language. (UCSD Pascal is a trademark of the Regents of the University of California.)

"Units" in UCSD Pascal provide strong type checking accross separate compilations which in turn allows encapsulation in such "units" of the routines and data structures necessary to handle all input and output. These "units" serve the same functions as Ada's packages and Modula-2's modules: at the same time as they present a uniform interface to programs using them, their implemetation can be modified to adapt to different hardware or operating system configurations, even if this entails the use of assembly language.

3. Software strategies for portability

In our work, two general strategies have proved particularly effective in implementing portable software without compromising educational or aesthetic quality:

1) have a standard package for input and (multi-window) screen display,
2) separate program logic from program data and make as much of the program as possible data rather than logic.

The Educational Technology Center has developed a standard package, called "Ports," which both our groups use for all keyboard input and screen output [3]. It presents to a CBL program an interface which does not vary from one system to another (it has been implemented on over half a dozen). It handles variations in keyboards (e.g., what codes are emitted by cursor movement keys), accepts both text (character string) and graphics (positional) input, allows a program to define multiple windows each of which can be used for both text and graphics, for both input and output, and contains features which make it particularly well suited for CBL materials. These features include learner adjustable writing speed, learner controlled scrolling when a window "overflows", robust (i.e., will not "crash" at "wrong type" of input) timed input with gentle prompting for answers, and other capabilities that make it easy to display and selectively erase (when the learner is ready to go on) portions of the screen formatted to attract the learner's attention. Ports provides these facilities even to novice coders with no more than a course or two in Pascal. On the other hand, educational design is not limited by it because it also has more advanced (i.e., flexible) facilities.

Ports has been used extensively at ETC for the implementation of computer based courses in physics, in general science observation and a variety of dialogs on a number of subjects related to computer science [4] [5]. They made life easier in Geneva during the design and implementation of an introductory course for business administration students and were invaluable tools in the development of a LOGO interpreter which runs in 4 languages (English, French, German and Italian) on 3 different microcomputers (DEC Rainbow, IBM PC and Victor Sirius).

Turning to the separation of program logic and program data, an obvious approach is to put the data into files which the program code reads. The logic of good CBL material is rarely purely sequential and thus the data files must allow random access. (Although standard Pascal does not provide random access files, many current implementations do and this capability is currently under study for inclusion in the next version of the standard [6].)

Our groups use an implementation of "keyed files" developed at ETC: a "keyed file" consists of messages (each with its own mnemonic name or "key"); a program uses a "key" to specify which message it wants next. Messages can contain display information, data used to analyze learners' responses (see section 5 below) or data for any other purpose. "Display information" includes the actual text to be output, positioning and formatting information including the location and characteristics of windows on the screen, and information which drives graphic displays. This breadth in our definition of what constitutes messages and display information is how we follow the strategy "make as much of the program as possible data rather than logic."

Field use has demonstrated the soundness of these techniques, that they can be used by different people in different environments and that they offer significant gains in productivity. Programs can be implemented so that relatively simple tools suffice to handle a number of common "fine-tuning" changes (e.g., spelling correction, rephrasing messages, limited graphics changes, screen reformatting) without having to recompile the program. These simple tools include a standard text editor and a program which converts between standard text files and keyed files of messages, as decribed above. An interactive graphic editor which produces a file of "graphics" messages is extremely useful but not indispensable.

4. The portability of graphics

Providing portable and powerful input and display facilities for text is considerably easier than doing the same for graphics. The "Ports" unit both our groups use has considerable graphics capabilities: each window has its own programmer-chosen coordinate system, there are line and arc drawing primitives with automatic clipping, drawing can be done in a variety of modes including "erase" and "invert" (i.e., switch foreground with background color for each point drawn), it allows positional input using arrow keys. On this last point, the chief problems are "echoing" the position on the screen before the learner completes the selection and handling keyboard auto-repeat. More "sophisticated" hardware such as joy sticks, track balls and mice where the hardware automatically provides an on screen echo during selection are actually easier for the software to handle.

While Ports currently supports only line oriented graphics in two colors, there are many educational uses for more sophisticated graphics capabilities including color, area filling, bit-map block drawing, and display list processing. Some of these can be done without seriously compromising portability although there may be other trade offs (e.g., typically, adding color decreases text capabilities). Others, such as bit-map block drawing, can mean that the only portability is in recoding or even redesigning whatever part of a program uses that capability. Unfortunately, there are times when one must use such capabilities knowing too well the price that will have to be paid to transport the code. This situation is not likely to improve until there is substantial commercial support, both software and hardware, for graphics standards such as GKS [7] and NAPLPS [8].

5. Analysis of student answers in natural language

In contrast to the thorny problems of graphics, introducing some semantic interpretation of students' answers turns out to be relatively easy. One considers a student's response as matching an anticipated response whenever it satisfies one of the acceptance rules relating to that particular situation.

The rules used to parse the answers to a given question can be stored in a keyed file under a meaningful name and retrieved by the answer analysis unit which then applies it to student input.

The answer analaysis uses simple string comparisons to determine if the input string (representing the student's response to a question) matches an expected response as specified in the rules written by the designers of the material. These rules, described below, are written in a form which can be understood easily by teachers participating in the original design, by those translating the materials into another (natural) language, and by teachers who may have to modify the rules to handle situations overlooked in the original design.

In spite of the simplicity of the answer analysis algorithms (string comparisons) and the rules for specifying a correct answer (given below), interactive programs using these tools usually seem to behave "remarkably intelligently." The intelligence, however, lies not in the algorithms but in the careful simultaneous design by skilled educators of the questions and the specifications of rules for expected responses. At the moment, those specifications are built from only three sets of recognition rules.

5.1 Specifying recognition rules for analyzing student responses

For the question "Would you like another example?", "YES", "OK", "SURE" or "PLEASE" should be considered synonymous. These alternatives will appear in a recognition rule as follows:

```
_YE|_OK_|O.K.|_SURE|PLEASE
```

The "_" symbol is used as a "sticky blank" to indicate that nothing but a word separator can appear in its place. Once the learner's response is converted to upper case, "Yessir" or "surely" will be accepted but "okay" would not.

While this rule will cover other variations in "YES" such as "YEP" or "YEAH", additional entries may be needed for misspellings such as "PLEEZE":

```
_YE|_OK_|O.K.|_SURE|PLEASE|PLEEZE
```

If the simultaneous presence of more than one component is needed, "|and|" is used to join the specification of each of the components into a single test which must be on its own line:

```
_YE|_OK_|O.K.|_SURE|PLEASE|PLEEZE
```
```
_OF_|and|COURSE
```

This specification matches any of the substrings given in the first line and also matches "OF COURSE" or "OF COURSE", but not "OFF COURSE".

This specification also interprets "OF COURSE NOT" or "PLEASE QUIT" as positive answers. "|not|" indicates that the following alternatives must not appear:

```
_YE|_OK_|O.K.|_SURE|PLEASE|PLEEZE|and|not|_NO_|N'T|STOP
```
```
_OF_|and|COURSE|and|not|_NO_|N'T
```

5.2 Monitoring and improving answer recognition

A key to developing good CBL material is a thorough understanding of the responses a learner is likely to give to various questions. Even the best of CBL designers, however, do misjudge likely responses at times. Some responses are anticipated which never occur in actual use; this is of minor import. A much more serious condition occurs when the answer analysis fails to recognize or erroneously interprets a response. Data has to be gathered on the paths that students take through the course material and also on the precise wording of their answers. In some

situations, it is also reasonable to gather other information such as timing data.

Collecting this data can be facilitated by various forms of networking or file sharing. Analyzing it is most easily done using the hardware and software resources typically found on time-sharing systems. The results of the analysis are valuable to designers, who want to improve the quality of the materials, and to teachers, who want to know where their students are having trouble.

6. Moving from one natural language to another

By following the practices outlined above, we can have well structured programs which implement carefully prepared pedagogical designs to teach a range of subjects. The data presented by the programs are to be found in "keyed files" along with the rules for analyzing the students answers. An intelligent translation of the content of the "messages", keeping all the "message" names unchanged will then allow the programs to be available in different languages.

There are also practices and methods to help the translation process maintain the quality attained in the original language. For example, the translator must know the subject matter and the intended audience. There must be extensive testing of the student interaction using the same tools as for the original development. This necessitates the translation taking place near some user location. Ideally, the translator should be able to communicate with the original developers. In this situation, translation becomes a cooperative effort bringing insight and enrichment to the participants. There are also technical details which can ruin the translation if not handled properly.

6.1 Influence on screen design.

Rarely will a sentence in one language be translatable into a sentence in another language of exactly the same length. The screen control unit, Ports, automatically breaks a sentence at word boundaries (to conform to the window in which it is displayed) and continues it on the next line. Under some circumstances, this may force scrolling of the text within the window which can cause its own type of problems.

For example, an English speaking designer decides to display a question in a carefully placed window 7 lines high and 20 columns wide on a screen containing other information. The message, aptly named 'ChooseOne', reads as follows:

```
Please point to which of the following toys
cannot reasonably use a microprocessor
   -- a baseball bat
   -- a record player
   -- a doll
```

A French translator produces the following :

```
Veuillez indiquer, s'il vous plait, lequel des jouets
ci-dessous ne peut raisonnablement utiliser un
micro-processeur
   -- une batte de baseball
```

```
    -- un tourne disque
    -- une poupee
```

Here is part of a program using the message and the display produced.

```
...                            +----------------------+
VAR QuestionPort : Port;       |Please point to which | 1
BEGIN                          |of the following toys | 2
    ...                        |cannot reasonably use | 3
    PtErase (QuestionPort);    |    a microprocessor  | 4
    TxpSelect (QuestionPort);  | -- a baseball bat    | 5
    TxpDisplay ('ChooseOne');  | -- a record player   | 6
    ...                        | -- a doll            | 7
                               +----------------------+
```

(Boundaries and numbers are shown
for the reader's convenience and
do not appear on the screen.)

The same program run with the message in French fills the "QuestionPort" entirely, breaking the lines nicely at word boundaries.

```
+----------------------+
| Veuillez indiquer,   | 1
|   s'il vous plait,   | 2
| lequel des jouets    | 3
| ci-dessous ne peut   | 4
|   raisonnablement    | 5
|     utiliser un      | 6
|   micro-processeur   | 7
+----------------------+
```

Unfortuately, there are not enough lines in the window to accomodate all of the translated text.

If QuestionPort was defined to scroll four lines at a time, a message will appear at the bottom of the entire screen telling the student to press the spacebar to continue and when the student does this, QuestionPort will scroll four lines removing the meaning of the question.

```
+----------------------+
|   raisonnablement    | 1
|     utiliser un      | 2
|   micro-processeur   | 3
| -- une batte de      | 4
|     baseball         | 5
| -- un tourne-disque  | 6
| -- une poupee        | 7
+----------------------+
```

The translator can try to rephrase the message in French retaining the full meaning and tone but using fewer and shorter words. If the keyed files containing the messages to be displayed also contain the screen layout information, a capability supported by the Ports unit, the translator can even try to rearrange the screen. Neither of these approaches is simple or always satisfactory. The translator might even wish that the original designers had not used such a small window. The fact is that translators must, in certain cases, address some of the same problems which faced the original designers.

6.2 "Low level" system messages.

System software itself produces messages; for example, the message about pressing a space bar given above. Part of translating CBL materials involves making sure that such messages appear in the appropriate language. This task is among the easiest parts of translating educational materials if the software being used was designed with this in mind; otherwise, it can be extremely painful. We describe how the Ports unit handles this problem.

The Ports unit displays its own messages and directly interprets responses to them. Internally, all language dependent information is stored in string variables which are initialized to the appropriate English values. Each of these string variables is identified by a mnemonic tag (a single character) and Ports contains routines which allow each to be set and queried individually by the program. Typically, these variables are reset as soon after the start of a program as it can determine which natural language is appropriate either by asking the learner directly or checking an "environment" file.

6.3 Managing national character sets

Most European languages use characters with accents or diacritical marks not present in the English alphabet. Although all these characters can be accomodated in an 8-bit code and although almost all current personal computers use such a code, the assignment of 8-bit codes to characters not in the normal U.S. character set can vary from one computer family to another.

The measures necessary to maintain portability in the face of this lamentable situation are more bothersome than difficult. Characters not in the normal U.S. set should NOT be represented by literals. The most general solution is to use character variables which can be initialized in a system dependent way to achieve a system independent effect: the value of the identifier eGrave is always "e". Using named constants is another approach (e.g., in Pascal, "CONST eGrave = 'e'"), but it requires editing the program before recompiling it and goes against the general strategy of moving as much data outside the program logic as is possible.

Even though a personal computer may have a keyboard and display which faithfully handle an "extended" character set, the learner may well not use these capabilities fully but instead type "e" uniformly for "e," "e," "e," or "E." Thus, the analysis of learners' responses is generally simpler to specify and more accurate if the response has been transformed so that all these alternatives have been mapped onto a single character (say, "E") before comparing the response with a similarly normalized anticipated response.

7. Adapting to different cultural environments

Translating CBL material into a foreign language and making it work with a keyboard which is using the special characters of that language is no small accomplishment. To make it usable requires much more than that. An understanding of the mentality of the students, of their cultural background and their current speech idiosynchrasies is also needed. In the example given above, a French student who has not been to the United States is unlikely to know what a baseball bat is. Some substitution will have to be attempted, but it is hard to be sure that the original pedagogical design is preserved.

The only way to carry material across several cultures is to engage actively in cooperative ventures, showing future users that the designers can offer an immediate response to their suggestions and criticisms. If one doesn't like the phrasing of the questions, then one should be able to have it changed. Answer analysis entails semantic assumptions that simple translation cannot be expected to capture since this analysis embodies the expectations of experienced teachers about anticipated student responses. Other teachers will know what is to be expected in a different environment and they must be given the means to express their expectations.

The problems of portability are not easily solved and there will always be parts of the "solution" that are weak and less than satisfactory. Nonetheless, portability is not an unattainable or unreasonable goal. Indeed, it is unreasonable not to try to attain it. The Geneva-Irvine experience shows that a relatively modest investment of human and material resources can produce results considerably more quickly than almost any other method of transfering CBL design knowledge. Leaving aside the personal satisfaction felt by all involved, from the original designers to their colleages who used the tools described above to transport the materials, the fact remains that the cost of not building portability into CBL materials is to doom them to a limited period and extent of use. This is a waste we cannot afford.

Acknowledgements.

The concepts, techniques and work described in this paper are a product of collegial efforts at the Educational Technology Center, University of California Irvine, founded and directed by Professor Alfred Bork, and at the University of Geneva. The authors are indebted to their colleagues at both institutions who have contributed to different parts of the software and helped clarify many of the concepts used in the article: Bertrand Ibrahim and Christiane Kuehni at Geneva, Steven Bartlett, Alfred Bork, Augusto Chioccariello, Martin Katz, Barry Kurtz, Tim Shimeall and David Trowbridge at UCI.

The project was supported by the Swiss National Research Fund through grant 2.881-0.83, by US NSF grant #78-06471, and by US FIPSE grant #G008200987. The gift or loan of equipment by IBM and DEC are gratefully acknowledged.

References

[1] Kurtz, B. and Bork, A., " An SADT model for the production of computer based learning material" in Computers and Education, R. Lewis and D. Tagg Ed., North-Holland, IFIP, 1981.

[2] Franklin, S. and Kurtz, B., "Techniques in Pascal for developing computer-based learning materials", Proceedings of the 1980 Western Educational Computing Conference, 1981.

[3] Bork, A., Franklin, S., et al., "Support Software for Computer Based Learning Materials", Technical Report Information and Computer Sciences, University of California Irvine, 1984.

[4] Bork, Alfred, Learning with Computers, Digital Press, 1981.

[5] Bork, A., Franklin, S., Trowbridge, D., Feibel, W., "Current Projects at the Educational Technology Center", AEDS Monitor, v.22, no. 1, 2, 1983.

[6] Joint ANSI/IEEE Pascal Standards Committee, "Forward to Candidate Extension Library", SIGPLAN Notices, v. 19, no. 7, 1984.

[7] ANSI Technical Committee X3H3, "Draft Proposed American National Standard Graphical Kernel System", Computer Graphics, v. 18, special issue, 1984.

[8] Fleming, J. and Frezza, W., "NAPLPS: A new standard for text and graphics", Byte, v. 8, no. 2-5, 1983.

COMPUTERS IN EDUCATION, K. Duncan and D. Harris (eds.)
Elsevier Science Publishers B.V. (North-Holland)
© IFIP, 1985

QUEST IN THE LEARNING ENVIRONMENT:

Computer Assisted Information Handling as a tool
For Learning and Curriculum Development

Diana Freeman and John Levett

The Advisory Unit for Computer Based Education
Hatfield, Herts, U.K.

Information technology should be an integral part of the existing curriculum in Primary and Secondary schools in England and Wales. The information handling program QUEST forms a basis for two research projects which the authors are currently co-ordinating. A model of information handling is proposed in which a 'common core' of information skills can be elaborated by computer approaches within any subject discipline. The design, interrogation and evaluation of data files are discussed in relation to the restraints imposed by the child's stage of development and the nature of the software employed. In conclusion, the implications of computer-related information handling for curriculum design and children's learning are briefly discussed.

Introduction. This paper intends to propose that information technology can be an integral part of the existing curriculum of primary and secondary schools in England and Wales. The information handling program QUEST, which allows teachers and pupils to insert, interrogate and manipulate information in numerous ways, forms the basis of this proposal. The authors are currently investigating the use of QUEST in the curriculum in selected primary and secondary schools in the Chiltern Microelectronic Education Programme Region.

There are three main functions of QUEST : first, the program has an editing function. This allows previously structured information about items (RECORDS) to be entered into the program under headings (FIELDS) : secondly, items can be interrogated by matching attributes within one or more fields using a flexible, but precise, QUERY language : thirdly, there are utility programs that can classify, graph, map or re-order the data, results or a selection of the results. This presents teachers with a powerful tool that can be fitted into any subject area within the curriculum because the program is content-free and is able to reflect an individual teacher's style, approach and philosophy.

It is proposed to outline the following for consideration:

  (i)   The nature of the two information handling projects.

  (ii)   Development of a model of information handling based on skills and concepts which can be elaborated by computer approaches.

 (iii)   Interpretive and stage development restraints on the design, interrogation and evaluation of datafiles.

  (iv) The future: can we identify the effects of computer-related information handling on both curriculum design and children's learning?

(i) (a) The Chiltern MEP Region Information Handling Project (April, 1984 to March, 1986). The project aims to discover the extent to which QUEST can be used within the existing humanities curriculum in the 11 to 19 year age range. Five Local Education Authorities elected to join the project – Buckinghamshire, Bedfordshire, Cambridgeshire, Hertfordshire and the London Borough of Harrow. Project teachers in the five schools have been provided with a microcomputer by their LEA. This would be a departmental resource; four of the project schools also have a room with computer network of up to 8 stations which are also available to the teachers. The schools and project teachers were selected because of the nature of teaching and learning that took place in the school within the humanities. Because QUEST requires skills and techniques of information handling, history and geography courses that are skills - based, rather than content - based, or that encourage enquiry learning, rather than factual recall, would most readily assimilate a computer aided approach. So, the project schools were chosen from those that use the Schools Council Geography or History courses. Three of the schools have Humanities Departments which have already established a cross-curricula approach.

The aims of the project are : to identify skills and techniques of information handling that are common to both subjects; to help teachers and pupils become familiar with these techniques within the classroom; to apply these techniques to appropriate parts of the humanities curriculum; to produce sample datafiles and support materials that may be helpful to other teachers ; to identify the nature of learning that takes place through information handling on computer.

(i) (b) The Hertingfordbury Project (January,
1984 to December, 1985)
The Project is being conducted within six Primary
Schools in a single Education Authority. The
participating schools were selected to provide a
balance of characteristics: size, age, location,
socio-economic intake of pupils, internal
organisation, curriculum content, teaching style
and computer availability. It was intended, in
establishing such a balance, to reflect the
varied circumstances of working environment
current within the majority of English Primary
Schools.   The schools encompass the full Primary
age range of 5 to 11 years.
Under the 1983/1984 Government Department of
Trade and Industry initiative of providing
financial assistance to Local Education
Authorities to equip every Primary School within
the United Kingdom with a microcomputer each
school within the Project was in possession of at
least one computer. Certain schools had
voluntarily increased their own hardware support
with resulting computer/pupil ratios varying from
1 to 15.1 to 1 to 69. It was decided to increase
hardware support within certain schools at
appropriate times according to the demands of the
Project.
The general terms of reference for the Project
were to document the nature and content of
investigations undertaken with the assistance of
computer storage, interrogation and retrieval of
information i.e. as it is applied to current
studies and those that prompted by the
facilities of a particular program. Particular
reference is made to the QUEST program and
investigations of its appropriateness for
curriculum activities pursued by Primary age
children. Further note will be taken of teacher
development, strategies for in-service education
of teachers and the influence ofcomputer-assisted
information handling upon curriculum development.
Generally, the methods to be adopted within the
Project are those of child/group/teacher case
studies to establish developmental and curriculum
influences and formal procedures for establishing
strategies employed in software use.

(ii) **A model of Information Handling.** If we
identify the concepts that are generally accepted
to underlie learning they can broadly be divided
into concrete operations and formal operations.
Concrete operations include concepts of
classification, succession, magnitude and
relationships between items and are developed in
primary schools. The children are also beginning
to develop skills of reading, writing, numeracy,
observation, listening and personal
communication. It is proposed that availability
of information handling on computer can give
children the power to seek, organise, question
and draw conclusions from data. These conceptual
developments are generally accepted to belong to
the realm of formal operations through the
hypothetico-deductive model, and are not fully
applicable until 12+ to 15+, but we propose that
this model is central to a model of Information
Handling on computer.

The hypothetico - deductive scientific model
contains the framework within which information
handling resides. Most teachers now identify
this model with a logically sound method of
inference. In this way one's perceptual
experiences help to form an image of the real
world. The formal presentation of this image
creates an 'a priori' model, a hunch, a guess, as
to the real image. A hypothesis can then be
postulated and an experimental design envisaged
whereby the hypothesis can be tested. The
experimental design starts with the 'a priori'
and sets about defining criteria by which the
hypothesis can be fully tested. Decisions about
what data to collect, how to measure, define,
structure and classify that data all have a
bearing on the hypothesis. The danger lies in
collecting data only to satisfy the hypothesis,
and not looking at wider issues. The hypothesis
is tested by means of verifying data that has
been collected. This can be by statistical tests
which synthesise and summarise data and so enable
a hypothesis to be accepted or rejected. (Figure
1)

Information handling on computer allows for data
to be more elaborately analysed. Data can be
ordered and reordered, made into lists or
diagrams, selected, or matched, so that any
relationships can be fully explored. Analysis
and explanation can be based on full evaluation
of the data rather than a statistical summary so
that attempts to provide answers or explanations
to support the hypothesis have a much firmer
foundation. This is much more satisfactory in
the social and environmental sciences where
generalisations are much more difficult to
achieve and normative theories are more common.
Handling data on computer means that the richness
of individual items is still apparent.
Information handling on the computer allows more
effective exploration of these two methodological
aims by allowing both quantitative and
qualitative evaluation.

It is our contention that this route to enquiry
is common to all disciplines. If we follow this
argument further, then the skills of information
handling and those of handling data on the
computer are also common to all disciplines. It
is apparent that information handling on the
computer is a common core within the curriculum
and is subject independent. Nevertheless this
core is embedded within a subject specific
context. Images of the real world,
identification of sources of study about
phenomena, and finding and extracting information
from these sources are firmly related to subject-
specific skills. For instance, historical
enquiry specifically requires skills in using
archive materials such as transcribing,
translating and searching for original sources.
In a scientific context the requirements may be
observation, recording, measuring or using
instruments to collect data. These are skills,
among many others, that are taught in different
disciplines as a means of collecting information

Figure 1:

The relationships between the hypothetic - deductive model, skills of information handling generated by this model and additional skills exemplified by information handling on a computer.

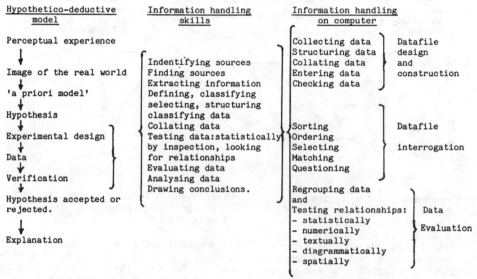

Hypothetico-deductive model	Information handling skills	Information handling on computer	
Perceptual experience ↓		Collecting data Structuring data Collating data Entering data Checking data	Datafile design and construction
Image of the real world ↓	Indentifying sources Finding sources Extracting information Defining, classifying selecting, structuring classifying data		
'a priori model' ↓			
Hypothesis ↓			
Experimental design ↓	Collating data Testing data:statistically by inspection, looking for relationships Evaluating data Analysing data Drawing conclusions.	Sorting Ordering Selecting Matching Questioning	Datafile interrogation
Data ↓			
Verification ↓		Regrouping data and Testing relationships: - statistically - numerically - textually - diagrammatically - spatially	Data Evaluation
Hypothesis accepted or rejected. ↓			
Explanation			

towards achieving greater understanding of the world. Deciding what data to collect and how to collect it is an important part of this process and reflects the methodology of individual subjects.

Once data has been collected it can be structured to enable the hypothesis to be fully tested. The structure depends on the hypothesis, but it should be flexible enough to allow for a multi-faceted approach. Design and construction of a datafile is a common core activity related to all subject areas. These are additional skills of information handling on computer, but essential if full interrogation of data is to take place. Datafile interrogation and evaluation are the key factors. Once the datafile has been created, the skills of computer interrogation, sorting, ordering, selecting, matching and questioning allow both generalisations and serendipitious revelations to be made. The methods of the enquiry dictate the nature of the result. Preliminary evaluation can take place on the computer because of the capacity to regroup data and test relationships in a variety of different ways. So many methods may be tried in a short space of time that give different perspectives to the data that they provide a sound basis for conclusions to be made and full analysis to take place.

The methods are chosen from a wide range of data evaluation available on computer, but the final analysis and conclusions reflect subject methodology. The relationship of information handling on computer to common core and subject specific skills can be shown in Figure 2.

It is therefore apparent that information handling is a fundamental part of a child's learning process. This paper attempts to show some of the ways in which early researches by two information handling projects, one in secondary schools and one in primary schools, demonstrate that process. We believe that information handling on computer should not be taught as a separate subject, or to elite groups, but that it is essential in all subjects and to all children.

(iii) **Child / Computer interface.** It is proposed that the instantiation of a computer program for the purposes of information handling imposes certain restraints regarding the form of data capture, its encoding within the confines of the program and the utility of the available method of interrogation. It is equally suggested that restraints arise by virtue of the learning context and specified instructional outcomes.

The term 'restraints' is defined as factors inherent within a computer program which inhibit the child in achieving desired goals as defined by the child, articulated through whichever agency (software restraints) or factors which inhibit the child in utilising the available utilities of a computer program (stage developments restraints).

The two types of restraints may be further refined. Software restraints refer to the attributes of the program and thus may appropriately refer to the style of the program (command/menu), the syntax of the command structure, and the demands upon coding and/or abbreviating information as made by the specifications of data files.

Figure 2:

A common core of information handling by computer (the 'cracker' model)

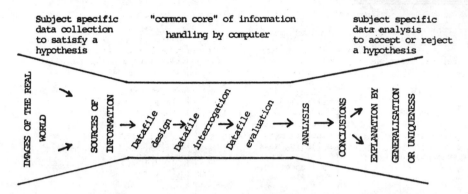

Subject specific
data collection
to satisfy a
hypothesis

"common core" of information
handling by computer

subject specific
data analysis
to accept or reject
a hypothesis

Stage development restraints refer to the attributes of the child; the computer program is made available to the child to the extent that the child is in possession of the skills/concepts implied by the facilities of the program. One may include, for example, such factors as the ability of the child to appreciate, to the extent that it facilitates the process of an enquiry, the way in which information is stored, handled and retrieved, the ability of the child to pose questions which form a valid basis for an enquiry and the ability of the child to select from the stored information an output that is appropriate for evaluation purposes.

Software related approaches. The activity of information handling can be described as follows: i) Approaches defined (confined) by the software (software related approaches). ii) Approaches defined (confined) by the intellectual, social and psycho-motor development of the child (information skills approaches).

Before further considering software related approaches it is important to define certain terms more closely. i) Collection refers to the assembly of data from primary and/or secondary sources, its arrangement into a form appropriate for inclusion in a data file, the design of the file, the input of data and its amendment, addition, maintenance and preparation for use. ii) Interrogation refers to the retrieval of data of required characteristics from the file for specified purposes. iii) Evaluation refers to the relating of displayed results of interrogation to the enquiry which prompted it, the refinement of queries and assessment of the need for future action.
Each stage is influential in constraining subsequent stages. Thus, the structure of the program and the form of file design restrain the form within which data is collected; the form of collection restrains the freedom to interrogate data; the methods of interrogation restrain the ease in evaluating the result in terms of the

desired end. Equally the nature of the interrogation progress will influence the process of data file design.

Information skills approaches. In considering information skills approaches reference is being made to the capacity of the child to undertake enquiries of an investigative nature. Such approaches are categorised as follows:
  i)   Ethical / Social / Relational : those attributes which are conditions of the child being able to engage in activity in a social context and relate to the different roles required during social activity;
  ii) Verbal / Linguistic : those attributes which indicate that the child is disposed to ask questions, engage in investigations and communicate findings;
  iii) Representational / Spatial / Mathematical : those attributes which are required to interpret and represent observations relating to different sources;
  iv) Organisational / Logical : those attributes that indicate that a child can evaluate the context of an enquiry and engage in such within a self-defined or pre-defined scheme.
The basis for the validation of such categories is as follows:
  i)   observation of the behavioural responses evident in responding to the demands of an enquiry in a social environment;
  ii) the specific verbal / linguistic skills / concepts implicit in, and required by, interrogation of related sources and communicating responses to it;
  iii) the specific spatial / mathematical skills / concepts implicit in, and required by, the organisation, interpretation and representation of data in related areas;
  iv) the implied cognitive and affective responses required in relating ii) and iii) above to the propose and desired

aims of an enquiry.
The dwell in the acquisition of the skills /
concepts / attributes related to each category
can impose limitations upon the achievement of
desired goals if such goals are to be pursued by
the implementation of a computer program. This
relates specifically to the child's perception of
the structure of the data and the processes
adopted by the program in handling such data or,
alternatively, the creation of appropriate
metaphors to compensate for invalid perceptions.
Further limitations will be imposed according to
the ability of the child to categorise and
classify data, the response of the child to
constraints regarding field / record size, the
ability of the child to recognise the properties
of data and recognition that file design imposes
restraints upon interrogation.

Restraints imposed by information skills
approaches at the evaluation stage of information
handling are of a different nature in that their
relationship to a computer program relates less
to the content of data files than to the format
of the output. Restraints at the evaluation
stage are valid to the extent that a child
appreciates certain elements of the output. In
this respect one would note the ability to
recognise patterns and trends in results, the
ability to distinguish fact from opinion in
conclusions and the disposition to propose
further enquiries to confirm such conclusions.

Stage development restraints. It has been
suggested that the computer-assisted information
handling is constrained by two factors, - the
attributes of a computer program and the
attributes of the child. It is now proposed to
outline those elements of the child's development
which influence the child's acquisition of the
appropriate qualities to both use a computer
program for purposes of information handling and
engage in investigative activity.
Three elements are proposed:
  i)   physical : related to psycho-motor
        development and the ability of the child
        to acquire appropriate skills;
  ii)   emotional : related to the capacity of
        the child to respond to the social
        demands of peer relations and to the
        positive / negative aspects of
        expectations regarding the pursuit of
        enquiries.
  iii) intellectual / conceptual : related to
        definable mathematical / spatial
        generalisations and appreciations and the
        ability of the child to make logical
        relations between different classes of
        ideas.

It is not proposed to enter into a debate
regarding the validation of stages and/or their
content as the evidence in relation to
information activities is inadequate at this
stage of the current projects. It is
appropriate, however, to outline those areas to
which attention will be given, namely: the

content of, chronological relations to and
pedagogic implications of stages and their
validation in terms of experiences qualitatively
different i.e. information activities generally
and those undertaken specifically by virtue of a
computer program. The latter point is of
interest as it is questionable whether or not the
qualititive nature of a computer program resets
the boundaries within which validation of stages
and their constituents is established.

Data file design. It is now proposed to consider
in further detail the practical and conceptual
issues relating to data file design,
interrogation and evaluation and to outline those
questions with which the current projects are
presently concerning themselves.
Matters relating to data file design might
conveniently be grouped as follows: i) Sources
of data; ii) File content; iii) Pedagogic
issues.
Whether or not the child is involved in the
collection / creation of data from direct
activity or the rearranging of previously
collected / collated data according to a
different purpose raises matters regarding the
proximity of the user to the sources. The issue
of children's appreciation of the 'shape' of
information within a file is frequently cited in
support of introducing file design through
initial experience of interrogation. Proponents
of this view argue that children will recognise
certain features and conventions of file
construction fundamental to good practice which
can be incorporated into their own design, that
familiarity with the demands and restraints of
interrogation will influence design, that future
data may be recognised in a familiar form, and
that, as file design directly influences data
collection, familiarity with the structure of the
program is essential if data collection is to be
undertaken in a purposeful manner. In reply it
can be noted that instructional objectives
relating to file design are as readily
accomplished through refinement of children's own
files as through interrogation of those of
others.
Discussion of data sources leads to consideration
of the nature of enquiries suitable for computer-
assisted information handling. The predominent
criteria would appear to be as follows: the
nature of the data to be handled (considered
quantitatively and qualitatively), the specific
instructional objectives, the stage of
development of the child and the skills /
concepts demanded by, and the investigative
nature of, the enquiry. There is insufficient
evidence to abstract any valid generalisations
regarding the nature of the investigations which
are appropriate for computer-assisted information
handling but certain features are discernible,
namely: identity between the creator and user of
files, the predominance of numeric data elements,
creation arising from personal / direct
observation of phenomena containing many
variables and file design arising from questions
of relationship between variables.

The first issue for consideration of file content is that of restraints upon design. Design can be considered as both a function of use and of purpose: 'use' relates to the activity of file creation from the point of view of the creator / user (the specific intentions for which the file was created and the implications of these for interrogation); 'purpose' relates to the specific instructional objectives that can be related to the file. Each function creates related restraints.

A computer program will offer certain facilities to prepare and operate upon data. Such facilities require the input of data in a form capable of being handled and a uniformity of input between fields and between records and, also, between files if such are required for comparison. Restrictions of field and record length determine loss of information as a feature of file design, where the form and size of collected data may be inappropriate for inclusion, with concomitant requirements for consistency in abbreviating and coding data : consistency with accepted conventions, consistency within the file and between files if data is of a similar nature and / or designed for other than the creator of the file. Consideration must also be given to incorporation elsewhere in the file of details of such coding. Equally, interrogation of numeric data requires an appreciation, not only of the nature of the data, but of its characteristics and the inclusion of such details (maximum / minimum values, standard deviation, mean, median, etc.) within the file is a further responsibility of the designer.

Amongst the pedagogic issues relating to file design are those which concern the nature of the investigations that prompt the design. Such investigations can be categorised according to the nature of the learning environment as closed (restrictive) or open (speculative). Restrictive investigations are those which are designed to accomodate a specific determined use while speculative investigations refer to those which are designed with a view to establishing a relationship between the various elements. Such open enquiries contain considerable implications for file design. Files of this type may require extensive maintenance and demand certain predispositions towards seeing / seeking relationships between variables within the data. Similarly investigations involving large numbers of variables require a sophisticated appreciation in selection of data the validity of which will only be apparent at the interrogation / evaluation stage. It may equally be true that within such investigations there is a bias towards obtaining a positive result which may be inappropriate given the nature of the data. The value of computer activity for this type of enquiry is influenced by the extent to which the child can recognise the validity of representative samples and compensate accordingly at the evaluation stage for inadequate samples. A similar distinction might be drawn between

teaching styles. A didactic approach is more likely to relate data file creation to previously specified instructional outcomes while a heuristic approach is more likely to fashion instructional outcomes to the issues that arise from data file creation. The validity of either approach lies, however, not within the response to file design but in the nature of the learning environment which it creates and its encouragement of appropriate prerequisities for design. Such prerequisites, or predispositions, would include the ability of the child to undertake an enquiry, to appreciate that there are different ways of investigating, the ability to pose questions likely to be answered by investigation, the capacity to pursue relevant lines of enquiry and relate methods of approach to a defined purpose, the ability to propose appropriate methods for collecting, classifying and coding information and the ability to organise information according to different purposes.

Data file interrogation. Issues relating to the interrogation of data files can be conveniently be discussed under the following headings: i) command syntax; ii) presentation of output. The use of a computer program for the purposes of data handling requires certain conventions. Such conventions might be responses to the character of the hardware, to those universally, or nationally, accepted in relation to data handling or to the nature of the data. Our concerns here are those of the conventions of command status syntax and the general implications of command status approaches.

The distinction between menu and command-driven programs requires brief comment.

Menu-driven programs create a question which can be answered by positive or negative responses or by reference to the contents of the file which has been created; command-driven progams employ a user or non-user defined vocabulary and a non-user defined syntax. Frequently preference is expressed in favour of the former, in terms of ease of achieving instructional objectives, over the latter where concerns are raised that the syntax, which does not universally correspond to children's experiences, must be learnt. It would appear that in order for children to employ such syntax for their own purposes the conditions in which it is first encountered is crucial. Thus it is important that the child can relate the command to the result that corresponds to a stated request of data (a mental picture) and that the child can form a substitution for the syntax (a metaphor).

Questions of design are different to those of interrogation to the extent that in designing a file the child is aware of the universality of the data being compiled when with interrogating it the unit of data (the field) and its relations (the record) can be divorced not in the actuality but in terms of presented output. The commands which summarise a) questions relating to one or a number of fields and the b) requested output are QUERY and PRINT. In such conditions the child is required to appreciate that a QUERY is made of a field but that PRINTed fields can be other than those interrogated. The child's response to this appears to be hierarchical. In early experience of data handling the child recognises that the data relating to a need is contained in particular fields, PRINTs the required fields, sorts the fields thus output and then attempts to relate the data from the output of these sorted fields. The child thus makes a distinction, by preference, between PRINT and QUERY; in the former the child is required only to specify the source of the result but in the latter must specify possible values. This is appropriate for the child. The question of establishing relationships via a QUERY statement which relate fields and their elements presupposes a predisposition for seeking relationships; establishing the same via PRINT statements may encourage such a disposition arising from the nature of the output. It might similarly be argued that a QUERY statement presupposes a predisposition for seeing a relationship in that values for the QUERY need to be specified; a PRINT statement presents possible values for consideration.

The apparently random nature of children's early experiences of file interrogation serves a valuable purpose: it enables familiarisation with the nature of the stored data, it establishes the qualities of particular fields and their relationship to other fields and encourages recognition of similarities or divergencies between records. Note must also be taken of the apparent encouragement that is derived from printer in preference to VDU output and from numeric in preference to string data.

Datafile evaluation Once results of a QUERY or PRINT statement have been obtained they do not constitute the 'answer' but merely a yardstick from which to judge and intrepret the data. The child can make inferences, reject or accept a hypothesis, or wish to further interpret the results before a definite conclusion can be drawn. The results may be one step on the way to a conclusion.

There are opportunities to reorganise the results appertaining to one field graphically in barcharts, histograms and pie charts. Relationships between two fields can be found by correlating items graphically. Numeric descriptions of the variance and frequency of results can be obtained. Certain simple statistical tests, such as correlation or deviation may be applied. Results may be analysed textually for key words or phrases, or be displayed as a map to show the spatial relationships between data items. All these opportunities are present, and it requires skill and judgement to choose the appropriate methods for displaying results on the computer so that logical inferences may be drawn.

The ease by which the data can be transformed very rapidly between different methods of display or analysis means that methods can be tried out to see if they are appropriate. The child has the capability of choosing, but also of testing and trialling. There are obvious limitations which the child will discover : restraints of string and numeric methods of display such as the discovery that numeric data has far more opportunities for transformation and description. There are also restraints on spatial data, which must have accurate, numeric description of each point to which it belongs. Thus a child learns that there are limitations of transforming the results, and can thus select, test and choose within these constraints. Seeing their own data made into another form helps children want to interpret the results more fully. It is more motivating to leave the computer with a printed copy of a diagram that has been carefully chosen and then spend more time thinking about what conclusions to draw from it, than to spend a long time on the lower level task of drawing a diagram. It gives children the opportunity to become familiar with more techniques and so make more rational judgements.

(iv) **Further questions.** In conclusion, it is pertinent to outline those questions to which further attention might be directed. Having considered information handling in relation to the skills / concepts / attributes it implies / demands and the restraints computer-assisted activity imposes consideration might also be given to its subject matter.

There might exist a dichotomy between the overlay of skills / concepts inherent in the activity of information handling upon defined disciplines and the methodology prescribed or described by such disciplines. Is it the case that the use of a computer program encourages a methodology in the handling of sources which is at variance with the methodology of the disciplines? In this connection it might be said that such conflict is more likely to arise in those disciplines in which consideration of the nuances of the validity of sources and their subsequent validation by reference to factors unrelated to their actual content is paramount (e.g the validation of historical data is of a different order to that of chemical data).

Equally, it is appropriate to ask if there exists a common core of information handling skills which are independent of the methodology of that of individual disciplines? Investigation of the curriculum might reveal parts of individual syllabuses which are free of a large content base and activities which, by the nature of their sources, are implicitly suitable for computer-assisted data handling.

A related matter is that of the implications of confining data within a file. It might be asked whether or not there exists a liability, in defining a boundary of a data base, to consider the data base as representing a universal set ignoring significant factors outside the boundary and factors unclassifiable in terms of a data field. Such factors, combined with a possible bias towards obtaining a positive result from interrogations, have significant implications for proposed enquiries.

COMPUTERS IN EDUCATION, K. Duncan and D. Harris (eds.)
Elsevier Science Publishers B.V. (North-Holland)
© IFIP, 1985

PRINCIPLES FOR INTERFACES BETWEEN YOUNG CHILDREN AND COMPUTERS

Csaba J. Egyhazy and Barbara Hutson

Virginia Polytechnic Institute and State University,
Departments of Computer Science and Education
Falls Church, Virginia

In designing human/computer interfaces, it is important to begin by considering characteristics of the task. This paper examines (1) elements
in the communication system which includes child and computer; (2) the
nature of the young child's learning, (3) the ideal characteristics of
an interface, given those learning characteristics, and the expanding
possibilities in software and input/output devices. By designing systems
to fit the child and his/her tasks, it should be possible to create
interfaces that are not only sturdy and safe, but permit easy, direct,
and consistent manipulation of graphics, text and other modes, providing
immediate, dynamic feedback. Such systems should adapt to changing levels
of skill and allow exploration as well as direct instruction.

1. INTRODUCTION

Interest in human-computer interfaces began
just over a decade ago. Thomas Martin (1)
defined interface as "a physical/conceptual
structure both channeling and facilitating
communication" (p. 203). The first major publication in the field was James Martin's Design
of Man-Computer Dialogues (2). Intended to
be a comprehensive guide to the development
of human-computer interfaces, the book addresses
interactions with traditional CRTs as well as
graphics terminals, voice units, and alternative
I/O devices. It also considers user psychology
as related to computer systems, quite a novel
idea just over ten years ago. Many of the ideas
and recommendations put forth in this book are
still highly applicable today. He said, for
example, that design of man-machine interface
should begin with characteristics of the task
and the human. The importance of the human-
computer interface is greatly emphasized in
Ben Schneiderman's book on Software Psychology:
Human Factors in Computer and Information Systems
(3). As Schneiderman suggests, technological
advancement is encouraged by understanding and
incorporating fundamental principles of human
behavior.

A few journal articles dealing with effective
interface design also began to appear in the
mid-seventies. Papers by D. R. Cheriton (4),
T. C. S. Kennedy (5), and J. Foley (6) enumerated
several ways in which both textual and graphics
interface components could be made more human-
oriented.

Today, entire issues of journals are being dedicated to research developments in this field.
Specifically, such areas as the psychology of
human-computer interaction (7) and human-factors
in computing (8) have each received the attention of special issues of a major periodical.

Additionally, articles have been devoted to
authoring systems, a form of interface (9),
and the design of software for children (10).

There is emerging interest, both theoretical
and practical, in facets of the interface between
young children (age 3-7) and computers. Up
to this point efforts have been made to stretch
an adult model to fit children -- e.g., making
programming languages a little simpler (10),
making the appearance of the computer more
appealing, making possible more direct access
to graphic displays. Yet children are not just
small, primitive adults. A model of human/
computer interface designed for adults (and
rather sophisticated adults) is not well-
designed for 3-year olds. There is need for
radical rethinking about the ideal characteristics of computer-based learning systems for
young children. More specifically, there is
need to consider how young children learn, and
the implications such learning principles bear
for child/ computer interfaces.

With this goal in mind we will ask: What are
key elements in such interfaces? What are some
considerations in young children's learning?
What are the ideal characteristics of interfaces
between young children and computers? What
are some recent and emerging developments in
I/O devices and related software?

2. KEY ELEMENTS IN INTERFACES BETWEEN YOUNG CHILDREN AND COMPUTERS

A complete computer-based learning system
includes all the elements and relationships
such as child, caretaker, hardware, software,
instructional design, input/ output devices,
knowledge base, data structure, etc. We will
focus more narrowly upon the immediate interface
between child and computer, represented by the
input/output devices and the software linking

these devices on one hand to the main (computer)
processor and on the other to the young human
information processor.

This interface may be thought of as a communication system. The child may initiate communication or may respond to a message (in any mode)
from the computer. The child communicates to
the computer by any of a variety of input
devices, such as key press (including in some
cases typing verbal messages), mouse, light
pen, joystick, touchpad, and potentially, panels,
optical scanner for graphics, or voice recognition devices. The computer processes this input
and responds either directly or after some input
analysis algorithm, by storing the data, recording it for later playback, and/or displaying
either the translated message or some response
to it. The message or response may be displayed
on output devices such as screen (text or graphics), voice or music synthesizer, movement,
etc.

Critical elements in this interface include
not just the visible elements of child, computer,
input and output devices, but the software that
links the I/O devices to the CPU. Design of
optimal computer-based learning systems for
young children should be based on fitting to
the child's needs and abilities not only the
physical characteristics of the input/output
devices but the software linking them to the
processor. We will, therefore, focus on basic
learning principles that most directly affect
the design of interfaces between young children
and computers. Furthermore, these principles
about young children's learning will form a
background for identifying ideal characteristics
of interfaces between young children and computers.

3. CONSIDERATIONS IN PLANNING LEARNING
    EXPERIENCES FOR YOUNG CHILDREN

The generalizations that we will present are
in part principles drawn from the fields of
learning and development and in part reflections
of our own biases and speculations. While they
may later be refined, they seem adequate to
guide this preliminary discussion.

Goals. Goals for learning include both
objectively defined mastery and subjectively
defined sense of mastery and efficacy, both
convergent and divergent learning. For the
young child, age 3-7, access to the computer
should initially require little planning,inte-
gration, or skill in use of symbols. Joyce
Hakansson, interviewed by Van Tyle (11), for
example, states that software for children should
be "as natural, as intuitive, as barrier-free
as possible." Goals, however, include increase
in pattern recognition, prediction and planning.

Motivation. Where possible, motivation should
be based on sense of efficacy, a mild challenge

at the edge of one's present level of competence. Where overlearning is required, social
reinforcement or other extrinsic means of
reinforcement may be helpful. Knowledge of
results may be useful not just as a source of
motivation but as a guide to differentiation
of concepts and to the effects of one's actions.

Conditions for Learning. Although we will talk
as though the child were alone with the computer,
it is likely that initial learning and new
combinations will be entered as part of a social
unit of child and caregiver (parent, teacher,
older child, grandparent), that the child's
progress will be monitored and his/her pleasure
and discoveries shared with others, and that
the child will at times engage with others in
cooperative projects or competitive games.
Tom Snyder (11) urges the design of software
that will intrigue and involve the parent with
the child.

The conditions of learning for a young child
require sturdy, safe equipment. This is not
just a long-range economy or a basic precaution
but makes it possible for parents or teachers
to say "Please touch," maximizing the child's
freedom to explore.

During initial stages of learning, structure
and relatively narrow limits can both simplify
learning (12) and provide a sense of safety
that facilitates exploration. These limits,
however, should progressively expand (at the
learner's option or through computer analysis
of responses) as the learner's knowledge and
confidence increase. The option of returning
to an earlier level, though, should always be
available, particularly when the learner wants
to explore new combinations or to analyze more
explicitly concepts previously learned intuitively and implicitly.

Thomas Martin (1) says that "training should
take place in increments, starting with the
simple and moving to the complex. The interface
itself should be designed so that the interaction sequences learned by a beginner prepare
him for more sophisticated interactions." Simple
initial concepts can be expanded (a.) by horizontal expansion of applications to new content
of comparable structure and difficulty; (b.)
by vertical expansion to include new levels
of difficulty; and (c.) by hierarchical linking
of concepts.

4. IDEAL CHARACTERISTICS OF INTERFACES
    BETWEEN YOUNG CHILDREN AND COMPUTERS

The child should initially be able to feed input
directly, simply, and concretely to the computer,
but he/she should be helped to gain control
over less direct and more abstract (symbolic)
means of communicating with the computer. In
line with this goal, early learning should
include efforts to establish correspondence

between various symbol systems, including not only familiar ones such as the correspondence of shape to name but the relationship of physical movement to symbol. It is also desirable that the child, through his actions, should be able to cause objects or simulated objects to move.

As noted earlier, though, the means of input would ideally change as the child grows more sophisticated, gradually shifting to more symbolic and indirect modes. Even for adults, novice users who prefer an interface that is descriptive and easy to learn may become expert users who prefer a rapid, efficient interface (13). This notion of expanding levels, useful for adults, is critical for designing interfaces for children.

Output from the computer to the child should be congruent with the child's current level of knowledge, logical ability, interests, and preference for various modes. In early stages the most useful modes of output to the young child are auditory and graphic. Dynamic features in messages from computer to child are attractive, but perhaps less critical (except in learning activities that are not intrinsically motivating) for output than for input from the child. Again, the form of the output can gradually change as the child shows readiness.

Insofar as possible, basic formats should be consistent across all modes. That is, the child shouldn't have to learn one set of commands and messages for text and another for graphics or numbers. The same notion applies to consistency across various levels -- the initial commands and formats should not so much be changed as expanded when new options are opened.

There is an interaction between difficulty of concept (relative to an individual's current level of concept and comfort in a given concept or skill) and optimal manner of presentation and response. The more difficult or complex (for a given learner) a cognitive process is, the easier the input and response should be. Once a concept or cognitive process is well established, though, it can serve as a base for new complexities of input or response. (This same principle has been found useful in introducing adults to complex programs, by introducing to novices simple metaphors or models that become increasingly sophisticated).

The nature of the learning task as well as the nature of the learner will make some forms of input and response more natural beginning modes for a given concept than are other forms (14). Miller and Thomas (15) address the same issue for adult users in terms of the "functional capability" required for various tasks. For example, a joystick may be useful to simulate certain kinds of movement, while a light pen can be useful for others. Ultimately, though, any form of information can be translated, either by the child or by the computer, to another form.

These considerations, in sum, imply that the interface between child and computer should be safe and sturdy; simple and direct in initial input requirements but capable of expanding to more complex levels; dynamic and immediate in response; initially graphic and auditory in mode of presentation to the child, but gradually moving toward text and other abstract representations. In addition, it should be motivational, and should invite exploration as well as active participation in directed learning experiences.

A few years ago, no child/computer interfaces responded to these requirements. A sophisticated adult with highly specialized training fed abstract symbolic information into a mainframe computer by means of abstruse and indirect programs and received equally abstract paper printout of symbolic information or undecipherable error messages. The arrival of smaller computers spurred attempts to make systems easier to use, both for adults and for children. Even though considerable progress has been made, few real systems fully match the ideal specifications for child/computer interfaces.

The ideal interfaces between young children and computers should be based on identification of the essence of what should be communicated to the young child, the manner in which it should be presented, and the ways in which he/she can best respond. The determination of the minimum hardware and software combination necessary to facilitate this communication is one of the primary design decisions to be faced by computer scientists.

After discussing recent and emerging developments in input and output devices and related software, we will conclude with some general observations in planning optimal computer based learning systems for children.

5. INPUT/OUTPUT DEVICES -- EXPANDING POSIBILITIES

Recent and emerging features of software for input and output devices have greatly expanded possibilities for meeting children's needs. We will focus on four aspects: integration and consistency, ease of manipulation, voice, and graphics.

5.1 Integration and Consistency.

Over the past few years emerging software has enabled the novice adult and/or teenager to solve complex problems with relative ease. Examples of this software are Visicalc, Wordstar, Lotus 1-2-3 and so on. Today software developers attempt to integrate worksheets, graphics, and word processing, producing sets of products that address a larger set of user needs (though there's still more promise than delivery). Generally, the current integration effort includes one of the following: concurrency, shared technology and functional integration. Concurrency means that different software products reside in the computer's memory at the same time. Shared technology means that a single product handles not only numbers but words and pictures, all at the same time. Functional integrity means that the result of one product can be fed into another for further manipulation. Creative Computing (16) pointed out (p. 5-8) that there are not only integrated programs but integrating programs that link software from different suppliers. For example, the package Press 'n' Plot can combine text from one program with graphs from another, then move, rotate, clip or scale the images. This software development approach will undoubtedly further the cause for developing software that links I/O devices and CPU in a way congruent with the stated principles for the design of young child-computer interfaces.

Integration makes possible consistency, which may be the single most important ingredient in the development of children's software, and in adult's software, for that matter. Michael Crichton (17), for example, stated that business users want programs "to be internally consistent and simple to learn" (p. E) and to be so well integrated that they can perform a variety of applications operations in a single environment with interchangeable files and similar, simple commands across all types of data and all types of operations. Unless a program is totally consistent in its displays (words and/or pictures), error detection, keystroke assignments, help messages, option lists, and so on, its users will not be able to relax enough to allow fun and learning to occur.

5.2 Ease of Manipulation.

The interface technology encompasses developments in hardware and software that essentially reduce the number of things a user must remember in order to use a system directly and more effectively. On the hardware side, pointing devices such as mice, touchscreens, and high-resolution graphics displays simplify communication between the user and the system.

The most important and revolutionary aspect of the new interface technology is the software. This makes it possible to produce many types of systems with the hardware devices mentioned in the previous section. There are three obvious components of this special software: multiple overlapping windows, commands issued by selection from menu options using a pointing device, and programs that can communicate information to other programs simply and consistently. The use of windows and pointing devices is the most

obvious improvement over older systems. Moving an object to a different window can be accomplished in the same way for a sentence, a graphic image, or a block of numbers from a math program. First the object is selected (as done in Lisa and Macintosh), then the verb "cut" is sent to the object, cutting it out of the window it currently lives in. Next, a new location for the object is selected, with a pointing device, and a command such as "paste" is sent. At no time does the user have to worry about whether or not the object moved is text, graphics, or numbers.

The pointing device is the input counterpart of the graphics display. Without a pointing device, menus can become an endless series of delays for the user who already knows what he/she wants to do and how to do it. Of pointing devices that are widely available (refer to Table 1), the mouse is often the preferred one when using multiple windows.

Extension of this technology should incorporate the means by which a young child could manipulate multiple windows for purposes, for instance, of creating stories with known or imaginary characters.

5.3 Voice.

Voice is the most natural form of human communication, and it is, in most cases, the communication mode children acquire first. In addition, psychologists and learning specialists believe that listening to information may speed and improve retention.

One of the major disadvantages of voice as a form of input is the large quantity of data that has to be stored. Recording just a few minutes of voice interaction can easily require more than a megabyte of data to be processed, compressed, and stored, all in real time. In addition, children's changing articulation and speech patterns make recognition more difficult for the computer.

System output can also be enhanced via voice. To aid adults in learning to use sophisticated features, most systems today offer Help functions that provide textual information. Since most children do not become skilled at reading until later, an audio Help facility would be an ideal interface between young children and the computer.

Further out on the horizon are direct speech-transcription systems. The idea of such a system interface is to produce ASCII text from spoken inputs, thus allowing users to interact with the computer without using the keyboard. One of the major obstacles to overcome is the intimidation that some young children feel when presented with a microphone.

5.4 Graphics.

Computer generated visual reproduction, controllable by young children, would be one of the
most important technological breakthroughs in
meeting children's needs. The Touch Tablet
represents one of the first input interfaces
designed with the above capability in mind.
Electronic fingerpainting, using a Powerpad
(18), is an example of the kind of application
realizable.

The future of computer graphics holds a number
of exciting possibilities; animation combined
with movement is certainly one of them. Thus,
it is conceivable that a young child will
eventually be able to create a computer-animated
story, exercising not only creativity, but the
capacity to fantasize.

6. CONCLUSIONS

Use of some of the features just described,
plus application of features now available
primarily in systems for adults, should make
it possible to design child/computer interfaces
that are not only sturdy and safe but easily
and directly manipulable, consistent, addressable through various modes, and allow immediate,
dynamic response. With plannning, it will be
possible to design systems that more effectively
adapt to the child's changing levels of skill
and understanding, allow exploration as well
as direct instruction, and are consistent across
many subprograms. While there's been promising
work on voice and graphics, there's room for
more work to suit them to the young child.

There is still need for some technical advances
and for design of learning systems that employ
both maximally effective I/O devices and developmentally appropriate organization of learning
experiences. These advances should further
ensure that we can concentrate on how children
and computers can work together.

REFERENCES

[1] Martin, T. H., The user interface in
    interactive systems in Cuadra, C. A. (ed.,)
    Annual Review of Information Science and
    Technology 8 (1973).

[2] Martin, J., Design of man-computer dialogues
    (Prentice-Hall, Inc., Englewood Cliffs,
    N. J., 1973).

[3] Schneiderman, B., Software psychology:
    human factors in computer and information
    systems (Winthrop Publishers, Inc.,
    Cambridge, Mass., 1980).

[4] Cheriton, D. R., Man-machine interface
    design for time sharing systems, Proceedings
    of ACM Annual Conference (1976).

[5] Kennedy, T. C. S., The design of inter-
    active procedures for man-machine
    communications, Int. J. of Man-Machine
    Studies 6 (1974).

[6] Foley, J. D. and Wallace, V. L., The art
    of natural graphics man-machine conversa-
    tion. Proceedings IEEE Vol. 62 (4) (1974).

[7] ACM Computing Surveys, Special Issue on
    The Psychology of Human-Computer
    Interaction 13 (1) (March 1981).

[8] IBM Systems Journal, Special Issue on Human
    Factors Vol 20 (2 & 3) (1981).

[9] Kearsley G., Authoring systems in computer
    based education. Communications of ACM 25,
    7 (July 1982).

[10] McKeag, R. M., Eves, A. and Rooney,
     E. J., Designing software for children,
     Software-Practice and Experience 14 No 5
     (May 1984).

[11] Van Tyle, S., Is there a Wufflegump in
     Your House? Creative Computing (October
     1984).

[12] Piestrup, A., Game sets and builders,
     Byte (June 1984).

[13] Chafin, R. L. and Martin, T.H., A man-
     computer interface study for command and
     control computer systems. Proceedings
     of the IEEE International Conference on
     Cybernetics and Society (1979).

[14] Card, S. K., English, W. K. and Burr, B. J.,
     Evaluation of mouse, data-controlled iso-
     metric joystick, step keys, and text keys
     for text selection on a CRT. Ergonomics 21,
     No. 8 (1978).

[15] Miller, L. A. and Thomas, J. C., Jr., Behav-
     ioral issues in the use of interactive
     systems. Man-Machine Studies 9 (1977).

[16] Integrating programs vs. integrated
     programs. Creative Computing (October
     1984).

[17] Crichton, M., Making software softer or
     the programmable program. Business Week
     (September 1984).

[18] Holden E., Chalkboard's Powerpad and
     Leonardo's Library. Byte (March 1984).

COMPUTERS IN EDUCATION, K. Duncan and D. Harris (eds.)
Elsevier Science Publishers B.V. (North-Holland)
© IFIP, 1985

COMPUTER ASSISTED TESTING BY QUESTIONS AND ANSWERS[1]

J. CHASTENET de GERY[2], J. Ph. DROUARD[3], B. DUMONT[3],
S. HOCQUENGHEM[2], D. LACOMBE[3], G. SOL[3]

Advantages and inconveniences of computer assisted tests will be examined under their different aspects. We will first specify our method of creating them, with the complete preparatory work the importance of which could not be under-estimated. Second we will present, as an example, the study of our mathematical tests set, which has been elaborated in Paris (France) on a large scale. We will then conclude on the possibilities opened by this kind of work and on the conditions of their development.

1. MAIN ADVANTAGES AND INCONVENIENCES OF USING THE COMPUTER TO TEST STUDENTS

First it has to be noted that computer assisted tests can be constructed as measures for students' knowledge (for exams, contests, orientation or self-evaluation), as a way for them to participate in their learning or training, or finally as pedagogical researches.

Using the computer to test students, of course, has all the advantages of a mechanical process:

- the possibility, when the system is achieved, to deal quickly with large numbers of students in an autonomous way of working (including an individual amount of "thinking" time), but involving comparatively a small staff;

- the objectivity of the machine in front of the student, the responses of which can be reproduced if the students react in the same way to the program. Of course, if the author wants it, some random variations can be provided for the response of the computer to identical stimuli of the students;

- the possibility of going further than a simple MCQ (multiple choices questionnaire) with either hidden MCQ (where the answer is compared with a list hidden from the user) or arithmetical or logical calculations of the student's answer;

- the adaptability of the machine to different categories of people with different switching points depending on the student's answers to the last question or to previous ones. This opens numerous and personalized ways to go through the program;

- the possibility of using an autonomous microcomputer (taking into account the limits of its small memory) or a centralized and more powerful system;

- an automatic record and an analysis of the answers on a personal as well as on a statistical basis.

With the computer it is possible to keep the student anonymous, though leaving him the possibility of stopping anywhere in the program and starting again later where it was interrupted (for example using a code, known only by the student).

The test can be marked (or not) and the mark can be given to the student (or not), at the end or during the examination.

The length of the test can be measured or limited to the full set of questions or question by question; it can also be timed for notation.

The previous choices are not neutral; they depend on the context, and their influence on the results can be analysed with the help of the computer.

Among the inconveniences, one can quote:

- the high price of the machine (which is decreasing though: computers are going to be quite cheap and always more powerful) and the problem of "transportability": i.e., using a given program on different kinds of computers,

- the great investment in time of people well qualified in the subject matter and in using computers (this financial problem could be solved if the product was used by a lot of students); the author-languages are helpful but not for writing high-performance programs,

- the long time between the decision to build a test and the realization of the project,

- the contact between the student and the computer, even if it is obviously neutral (it is not a judge), may not be as friendly as one can imagine; very often the student has difficulties expressing his/her answers or making remarks about the program, especially in mathematics. But a good program having also the qualities of a good teacher has perhaps not gone out of our dreams yet.

2. SOME PROBLEMS OF METHODOLOGY[4]

The preparation of the test begins with the definition of the considered field and continues with a pedagogical study the aim of which is to choose the important points which are to be controlled by this program.

To be useful, the tests must help to determine the knowledge, or lack of knowledge, and the misunderstanding of the testee as precisely as possible, not forgetting that they are always related to a particular situation and a certain approach (computers, indeed, allow such a project).

A set of topics has to be created and, for each point of each topic, a set of relevant and discriminating exercises, i.e., such that the answer alone shows which path has been chosen by the student.

To create such exercises we have to know what kind of errors and false reasonings the students typically make, the frequency of these mistakes and in what conditions the students are more tempted to reproduce them.

That is the reason why we always begin our research with an inquiry on a very large sample (several thousands of students chosen at random in various French Provinces) to get all (or almost all) the possible answers to our questions. The frequency of these answers results in a hierarchy among them. In the meantime, we try to understand the methods by which the students await their incorrect results (for example, by reading students' drafts or asking verbal questions if possible).

It is necessary to experiment with different variants of questionnaires; on the one hand to avoid cribbing as often as possible and on the other hand to see the influence of different parameters (size and place of the numbers, place of the different exercises on the copy, choice of the answers in a MCQ, phrasing of the questions, ...).

It is even possible to see some effect of a priori useless parameters (e.g., a question finishing too close to the right margin got a large percentage of non-answers).

After such an inquiry, the test has to be ordered, structuring the different important notions and organizing the questions in a "ramification" able to arrive as quickly as possible at the testees' misunderstandings.

At last the test is put into the computer and technically verified. Then two experiments still have to be done: one on a small sample under the control of an observer and, after a first set of modifications according to the reaction of the first users, another one on a large sample recorded by the computer.

It is clear that all this work represents a very heavy investment in time if one wants to take the lowest risk of error in evaluating the students in this situation where there is no real contact between student and teacher and where, in the end, the machine is going to judge the student.

This kind of work, to be useful and safe for the testees, must be done by a team of competent and experienced researcher-teachers.

The result will be all the better to the extent that the authors are prepared for this kind of work and used to criticism (eventually toward themselves). It is also possible to imagine that such a team would sometimes need a help from some programming engineers.

3. AN EXAMPLE TO ILLUSTRATE OUR METHODOLOGY: A computer assisted test on fractions

1. The aim

The aim is to diagnose incorrect methods of calculating the fractions through a few exercises which must

- give students the opportunity to make mistakes revealing some misunderstanding of the correct rules and/or a belief in false rules,

- discriminate in such a way that one false result does not proceed from two different sources of error.

2. The target and the sample

Our tests concern every student above 15 years: teen-agers, non-scientific students, adults involved in professional training ... ; but for our preliminary inquiry (pen and paper) we took 150 French schools at random:

- 50 classes of "3èmes des Collèges" (average age: 15)[5]

- 50 classes of "3èmes des L.E.P." (average age: 16)[6]

- 50 classes of "1ère A des Lycées" (average age: 17).[7]

3. The topics of our study

- Addition, multiplication, and division of two fractions or of one fraction and one integer,

- Simplification of fractions to arrive at their lowest terms,

- Problem of a zero denominator.

4. The wrong rules and the favoring parameters

Examples:

(1) <u>for addition</u> (see N.B in fine)

(a) Problems with "1":

For $\frac{1}{3} + 1$, we obtained answers such as
$\frac{1}{3}$ or $\frac{1}{4}$ that we did not find with: $\frac{2}{3} + 5$.

(b) Particularities of the numbers:

For $\frac{7}{3} + \frac{3}{7}$, 17% of the "colleges" students gave 1
or $\frac{10}{10}$ as an answer but none of them gave $\frac{11}{28}$ for
$\frac{5}{7} + \frac{6}{21}$.

(2) <u>For simplification</u>

(a) We use $\frac{3 \times 11 \pm 5 \times 7}{5 \times 11 \pm 3 \times 7}$ which is a "trap" to
drive the students to wrong simplification (by
11 or by 7 more obviously, or by 3 or by 5), or

to cut this fraction into $\frac{3 \times 11}{5 \times 11} \pm \frac{5 \times 7}{7 \times 7}$. "1"
was given by 19% of the "colleges" students as
an answer for $\frac{3 \times 11 + 5 \times 7}{5 \times 11 + 7 \times 7}$ and 6% of them
answered $\frac{34}{15}$, i.e.: $\frac{3}{5} + \frac{5}{3}$.

(b) We use another kind of "trap" fraction, for
example: $\frac{6900 + 63}{1400 + 63}$ which was an inducement to
reduce by dividing by 100 and/or neglecting 63.

The possible wrong results are shown in
Figure 1.

We obtained 20% of the "colleges" students and
10% of the "1ère A" students who answered $\frac{69}{14}$.
But no one gave: $\frac{2300 + 9}{200 + 21}$ or $\frac{23 + 9}{2 + 21}$.

5. Variants

All our exercises are set up with variations, as
we said above; for example $\frac{6900 + 63}{1400 + 63}$ is an

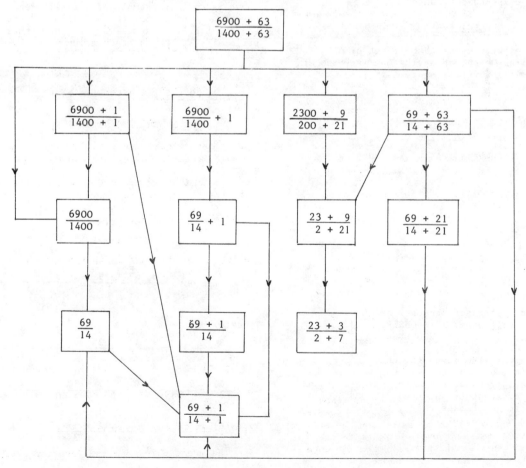

Figure 1.   Incorrect Result Paths

exercise belonging to the form: $\frac{X + Y}{Z + Y}$.

It has two kinds of variants:

- one on the place of X, Y and Z:

$$\frac{6900 + 63}{1400 + 63} \quad \frac{6900 + 63}{63 + 1400} \quad \frac{63 + 6900}{63 + 1400} \quad \frac{63 + 6900}{1400 + 63}$$

- one on the value of X, Y and Z (X<<Y, X~Y, X>>Y)

$$\frac{99 + 1515}{55 + 1515} \qquad \frac{63 + 45}{35 + 45}$$

(the numeric values have been chosen to make the possible false results different).

Our experiment has shown that placement does not have a great effect on the results.
Nevertheless the numeric values involved a different behavior between the "colleges" students who react the same way whatever kind of exercise it is, and the students of the literary section who made the wrong simplification $\left(\frac{X+Y}{Z+Y} = \frac{X}{Z}\right)$ when X>>Y and Z>>Y, i.e., when Y is negligible compared to X and Z.

6. The pen and paper tests

We sent to every chosen school a set of 42 questionnaires, each one having one exercise of each of the eight following types:

Type 1

$\frac{X + Y}{Z + Y}$ with 5 sets of numeric values and 4 positions for numbers so: 20 variants, plus another: $\frac{728 - 63}{618 - 63}$.

Type 2

Sum of fractions

two as $\frac{a}{b}$ (a≠0, b≠0), one as $\frac{0}{a}$ (a≠0),

one as $\frac{a}{0}$ (a≠0), one as $\frac{0}{0}$.

For the two last cases students had the possibility to choose: "IMPOSSIBLE ☐"
                          or "NONSENSE ☐".

This choice was also given for the 7 other exercises in order not to make too obvious what the right answer was. For this reason we found that a log of students answered "IMPOSSIBLE" or "NONSENSE" for exercises where, in fact, the calculation was possible.

For Example:

(a)

$$\frac{\frac{1}{2} + \frac{1}{3} - \frac{5}{6}}{\frac{1}{2} - \frac{1}{3} + \frac{5}{6}}$$

	0 (correct answer)	IMPOSSIBLE NONSENSE	No answer
Collèges	65 %	13 %	1 %
L.E.P	21 %	5 %	16 %
1ère A	73 %	14 %	2 %

(b) Division of a fraction by an integer (or vice versa)

	Correct answer	IMPOSSIBLE NONSENSE	No answer
Collèges	75 %	5 %	1 %
L.E.P	41 %	11 %	12 %
1ère A	81 %	2 %	1 %

Above is another example of the difference between the behavior of the "colleges" students and the L.E.P.'students who are, nevertheless, officially at the same education level.

Type (3)

$$\frac{13}{25} + \frac{7}{25} \quad \frac{9}{7} - \frac{6}{21} \quad \frac{5}{3} - \frac{35}{21} \quad \frac{1}{5} \pm \frac{1}{7} \quad \frac{1}{3} + \frac{4}{7} \quad \frac{5}{4} - 1$$

$$\frac{1}{3} + 1 \quad \frac{4}{5} - 1 \quad \frac{2}{3} + 5 \quad \frac{7}{12} - \frac{6}{12} \quad \frac{5}{7} + \frac{6}{21} \quad \frac{7}{3} + \frac{3}{7}$$

Type (4)

$$4 \times \frac{3}{7} \quad \frac{3}{7} \times 4 \quad 5 \times \frac{3}{7} \quad \frac{3}{7} \times 3 \quad 7 \times \frac{3}{7} \quad \frac{4}{7} \times \frac{3}{7} \quad \frac{2}{3} \times \frac{7}{3}$$

$$\frac{6}{7} \times \frac{6}{5} \quad \frac{20}{3} \times \frac{21}{5} \quad \frac{3}{20} \times \frac{5}{21} \quad \frac{1}{9} \times \frac{3}{5} \quad \frac{21}{35} \times \frac{20}{12} \quad \frac{3}{7} \times \frac{7}{3}$$

Type (5)

$$\frac{\frac{3}{5}}{\frac{3}{7}} \quad \frac{\frac{5}{3}}{\frac{7}{3}} \quad \frac{\frac{3}{7}}{\frac{5}{3}} \quad \frac{\frac{2}{9}}{\frac{2}{9}} \quad \frac{\frac{3}{5}}{\frac{5}{7}} \quad \frac{\frac{3}{5}}{\frac{5}{3}} \quad \frac{\frac{3}{7}}{\frac{2}{5}} \quad \frac{\frac{7}{9}}{\frac{1}{4}}$$

Type (6)

$$\frac{\frac{2}{3}}{5} \quad \frac{\frac{9}{3}}{7} \quad \frac{\frac{2}{7}}{10} \quad \frac{2}{\frac{3}{5}} \quad \frac{9}{\frac{3}{7}} \quad \frac{2}{\frac{7}{10}}$$

Type (7)

$$\frac{9 \times 7 \times 40}{21 \times 30} \quad \frac{21 \times 30}{9 \times 7 \times 40} \quad \frac{6 \times 14 \times 55}{20 \times 21 \times 11}$$

Type (8)

$$\frac{3 \times 11 \pm 5 \times 7}{5 \times 11 \pm 3 \times 7}$$

7. Analysis of the results of the preliminary inquiry

We received 3223 questionnaires back:

1107 from the "collèges",
809 from the L.E.P.,
1307 from the "1ère A."

We can thus be sure the sample was representative, i.e., we can be sure that:

- the mistakes appearing with a non-negligible frequency are not negligible,

- the mistakes which did not appear or which seldom appeared can be negligible (maybe temporary) for the program.

For example:

(a) In a C.A.I. program for students at the L.E.P. level (by Régie RENAULT on the Plato System), the wrong expected answers for $\frac{a}{b} + \frac{c}{d}$ are, among others, $\frac{a}{b} \times \frac{c}{d}$, $\frac{a}{b} \times \frac{d}{c}$ but not $\frac{a + c}{b + d}$.

But our inquiry has shown that the misunderstanding between addition and division or multiplication almost never appears while the sum of numerators and denominators is done by, grosso modo, 16% of the L.E.P.'s students.

(b) Moreover, our preliminary inquiry has displayed some mistakes which were not expected, for example, the presence of "1" involves an exception to the rule: $\frac{a}{b} + \frac{c}{d} = \frac{a + c}{b + d}$, as we have seen with $\frac{1}{5} - \frac{1}{7}$ where the answer $\frac{1}{2}$ was given by 9% of the L.E.P.'s students and 0 by less than 1% while, for $\frac{9}{7} - \frac{6}{21}$, the answer $-\frac{3}{14}$ was given by 13% of the L.E.P.'s students.

8. Discovering the wrong path, given the wrong results

Even if the values of the parameters of our exercises have been well chosen to be discriminatory, we have to recognize that a lot of wrong results remain unexplained; for example, with $\frac{6900 + 63}{1400 + 63}$, we were not able to explain 17% of the results given by the students (each of these results was given by less that 1% of the students).

That is why we began to try and use Artificial Intelligence methods (Expert system). It seems that a great part of these students don't think of the meaning of fractions but use them only like some graphic signs, following both true and false rules; the latter ones are sometimes very sophisticated and sometimes depending on the "context," i.e., on the numeric values used in the calculus (problem of "1" and "0" for example). Nevertheless, in almost every case these rules can be expressed as rewriting rules, for example: $\frac{a}{b} + \frac{c}{d}$ $\frac{a + c}{b + d}$.

The analysis of the results of the preliminary inquiry has given us about 20 rules of that kind which can be put in a computer.

The first step of our present work was to build an A.I. program able to receive rules for rewriting algebraic formulae:

- to transform a given fraction to a given aim (i.e., another fraction) or to find several or all the results which can be obtained by using some rules,

- to find the path followed between the first fraction and the results.

In a second step it would allow us to use this program in order to build an "intelligent" C.A.I. program.

9. Organization of the program

We have built the first part of our program on the fractions on the type No. 1 (see above) with $\frac{6400 + 17}{1300 + 17}$ and $\frac{99 + 1515}{55 + 1515}$.

In fact the first one is not exactly of type 1 because of the absence of "crossed simplification" (between 6400 and 17 or between 1300 and 17) but, as we have seen in our inquiry, these simplifications don't appear. We have taken these numbers because the correct simplification is simple.

The scheme of the program is given below at the last page but we will describe it now.

– PRELIMINAIRES –

For this program we use an "editor" allowing the author and the student to write fractions on the screen in their usual appearance; that is why we begin teaching the students how to use the keyboard. Then we specify our terminology on what we call a "écriture fractionnaire standard" (standard fractionnary writing) and a "écriture fractionnaire irréductible" (fractionnary writing at its lowest terms) to insist on the fact that irreducibility is a property of representations of rational numbers and not a property of numbers themselves.

At the beginning of the first exercise, the student is asked to calculate F = ... giving the answer as an integer or as an "écriture fractionnaire irréductible," or to type "IMPOSSIBLE."

- SYNTAXE CORRECTE -

If the answer is not correctly given in its form (dot, comma, letters other than IMPOSSIBLE, ...) a specific "error message" is written on the screen; after five trials the program stops.

- IMPOSSIBLE -

The first time the students are told that they could at least make the addition at the numerator and the denominator level.

The second time we try to guess why it looks impossible. If it is because the result of the division of the numerator by the denominator is not an integer we tell the students that they can answer by giving a fraction. Then we ask the first question again. If it is because of another problem, the students are invited to express their reasons which are recorded for a later analysis. Then they have to decide to go on to anther exercise or not.

- NOMBRE ENTIER -

If the answer is an integer (and a wrong answer in this case):

- if it is the integer part of the rational F the answer is corrected (emphasizing the fact that F is not equal to its integer part). The previous question is then repeated;

- if not, the answer is analysed like an ordinary answer (see below: "page choix").

- REECRITURE, CONFIRMATION -

At this point the program tells the students that their answer means two things:

1. F is equal to their answer
2. their answer is an "écriture fractionnaire irreductible."

That is to make clear that there were two parts in our question. Now the students have to confirm their answer or to change it. They can do this no more than 10 times. Each answer is recorded to be analysed later on.

- RESPONSE EXACTE -

If the answer is equal to F the computer tests the irreducibility of the answer. If it is correct the students are gratified. If not they are asked to correct their answer; in this case, the answer is analysed as a new one (ETIQ.4).

If the answer is not equal to F, the computer tests the irreducibility of the answer and it is automatically corrected by the computer (which gives the students the number to divide the numerator and the denominator to achieve the fraction in its lowest terms).

- PAGE CHOIX -

At this point, the students have given a wrong answer. First the correct simplification is shown to them. Second they see two different answers: theirs (F1) and the computer's (F2), and they have to choose among four possibilities:

(1) F1 and F2 are correct
(2) F1 is correct and F2 is wrong
(3) F1 is wrong and F2 is correct
(4) F1 and F2 are wrong.

(2) and (4) can be interpreted as: the students cannot even recognize a correct calculation; they must come back to their teacher or an appropriate math book. However, we think that this exit has to be used only if the students agree. If they don't, some help has to be available and the program can continue with the second exercise.

(1) two ways are given to the students to show the possibility of F1 = F2 = F

- with an approximation of F1 and F2,

- with the "crossed multiplication proof."

Then the "page choix" is given again but only with the choices 2, 3 and 4, with the same pattern.

(3) If the wrong answer F1 was an expected one, it is corrected, eventually by asking the students which way they have chosen; here are for example two different ways expected to arrive at:

(a)
$$\frac{6900 + 63}{1400 + 63} = \frac{690\!\!\!/0 + 63}{140\!\!\!/0 + 63} = \frac{69 + 63}{14 + 63} = \frac{69}{14} + \frac{63}{63} =$$
$$\frac{69}{14} + 1 = \frac{83}{14}$$

(b)
$$\frac{6900 + 63}{1400 + 63} = \frac{6900}{1400} + \frac{63}{63} = \frac{69}{14} + 1 = \frac{83}{14}$$

In case (a) there are two mistakes to be corrected and only one in case (b). Each expected error is corrected by specifying the wrong process which has been used and an example with small numbers is given to point out the mistake and to try to convince the students.

If the answer is not expected the computer records it and a special message is given to the students.

After the correction of the last answer, each previous recorded wrong answer is shown again. Students can see the correction if they want to.

Then the program arrives at the second exercise

which aims to verify the effect of the previous correction; if a student makes a mistake already seen in the first exercise he/she will receive a special remark emphasizing this problem and the false rule used.

(This program is used on a MICRAL-G and is written in Basic; it has been used experimentally by some "collèges" students and will be tested on a bigger sample next year).

N.B: in French schools, writings like $3\frac{1}{2}$ instead of $3 + \frac{1}{2}$ are not taught; this is why we did not look for this kind of errors, but, of course, inquiries with such exercises would be quite useful in Anglo-Saxon countries.

1. This work has been supported by a Research Convention with the French Ministry of the National Education.

2. Centre de Recherches et d'Expérimentation pour l'Enseignement des Mathématiques (CREEM), Conservatoire National des Arts et Métiers (CNAM), 292 rue Saint-Martin, F. 75141 PARIS Cédex 03 France.

3. Unité d'enseignement et de Recherche de Didactique des Disciplines, Université PARIS 7, 2 place Jussieu, F 75251 PARIS Cédex 05 France.

4. Part 3 will be an illustration of this part.

5. "3ème des Collèges" in the French system of education corresponds to the fourth year of high school.

6. L.E.P.: Lycée d'Enseignement Professionnel (technical school).

7. "1ère A des Lycées" correspond to the last year of high school (literary section).

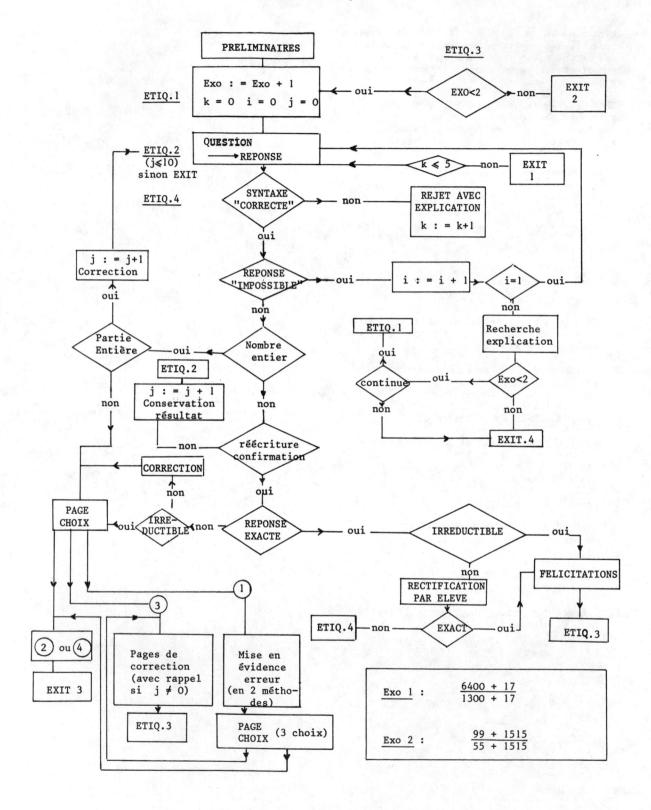

COMPUTERS IN EDUCATION, K. Duncan and D. Harris (eds.)
Elsevier Science Publishers B.V. (North-Holland)
© IFIP, 1985

CONTRIBUTIONS OF COMPUTER-BASED EDUCATION TO THE EDUCATION OF GIFTED CHILDREN

M.M. Malan

Bureau for University and Continuing Education
University of Stellenbosch
Stellenbosch, Republic of South Africa.

Computer-based education, specifically with the microcomputer, has the potential to contribute significantly to the education of highly gifted children. These children usually find it difficult to progress in an ordinary classroom situation, for various reasons. The microcomputer can contribute to the education of gifted children in a number of ways: The microcomputer
- involves the gifted child more actively in the learning process by providing varied sensory and conceptual learning modes,
- eliminates unnecessary mental drudgery which frustrates the faster learning gifted child,
- provides learning experience suitable to the child's level of development,
- contributes to the achievement of goals like creativity, problem solving, abstraction and generalization and
- stimulates social development of children.
These benefits can only be achieved if the development of courseware and the training and retraining of educators in computer-based education receive high priority.

1. INTRODUCTION

One of the most pressing problems in education today is to provide education in which the unique potential of all children, also the highly gifted are realised and developed to the full. The past two decades have seen the emergence of a growing interest in the specialized education required to provide for the needs and expectations of highly gifted children. A second trend in education which has exciting possibilities for the education of gifted children, is the use of the computer/microcomputer as a teaching aid (usually called Computer Assisted Learning(CAL) or Instruction(CAI) or Computer-Based Education(CBE)). This development is of the utmost importance and significance with regard to the micro-electronic era which we are about to enter.

The purpose of this paper is to investigate ways in which the microcomputer can contribute to the special educational needs of highly gifted children. To be able to give an answer to this question, the special educational needs of these children must be identified. Then the characterictics of computer-based education which can contribute to these special educational needs, will be identified.

2. SPECIAL EDUCATIONAL NEEDS OF HIGHLY GIFTED CHILDREN.

2.1 Education strategies for gifted children.

Gifted children are "... the most versatile and complex of all human groups, possibly the most neglected of all with special educational needs" (21).

This was, and in many cases still is, the attitude because educators in the past believed gifted children could provide for their own needs and that the educators should rather direct their attention to the less able children, the possible failures. Fortunately this viewpoint is changing, albeit slowly.

To develop teaching programmes tailored to the educational needs of gifted children is a challenging task, mainly because of the many different definitions and viewpoints that exist for giftedness. Another factor which contributes to the complexity of the challenge is that gifted children are not a homogeneous group, but a very heterogeneous group, for example mentally gifted children, academically gifted children (children with specific academic abilities) and creatively gifted children (10).

As far as the teaching of these children

is concerned, three teaching strategies
are usually implemented.
1. The first strategy is *acceleration*,
   where gifted children are moved faster through the channels of education.
2. The second strategy is *enrichment*,
   which involves special procedures and
   content for the gifted, usually in
   the normal classroom situation.
3. The third strategy, *ability grouping*,
   means that gifted children are segregated into seperate (more or less)
   homogeneous groups, where they receive special education, which usually amounts to acceleration and/or
   enrichment.

These strategies usually entail much additional work for the already overloaded
teacher.

In the next paragraph the characteristics
of gifted children will be dealt with
briefly, and then the role that the microcomputer can play in solving some of
these complex issues will be discussed.

2.2   Characteristics of Gifted Chil-
           dren.

2.2.1   Gifted children are usually characterized by their superior intellectual ability. This ability can be expressed as a general intellectual ability
(high achievement in a broad spectrum of
subjects and activities), as a specific
academic aptitude (in a specific subject)
or as creative or productive thinking.

These children are sharp and alert, and
have a strong desire to learn. They have
wide interests and the potential to produce new knowledge and to excell in various areas. They show independent judgment and are keen thinkers (23).

Children with high intellectual ability
are usually able to grasp easily concepts
of greater difficulty, they are able to
acquire a knowledge and understanding of
symbols, they are able to deal with abstractions, and they are quick with
sound generalizations (10).

2.2.2   Many gifted children very often
show excellent leadership abilities.

2.2.3   Some gifted children excel in
the visual and performing arts.

2.2.4   Other gifted children possess
well developed psychomotor abilities and
excell in sport.

2.2.5   Gifted children usually have a
very strong task commitment. Most of them
have high standards and set high goals
for themselves. They tend to blame them-

selves excessively when they make mistakes (5).

2.2.6   Gifted children often face social
difficulties with their age peers. They
are seldom fortunate enough to find an
intellectual peer in their own age group.
From a study of schools in Oxfordshire
(quoted by Behr(2)), it would seem that
"... unusually gifted children had to
hide their brilliance if they wanted a
smooth passage in school."

Tannenbaum noted that, in the United
States of America, the brilliant student
is "... an exceptionally prominent target for teenage pressures and that there
is a danger of his deliberately masking
his talents in order to relieve these
pressures" (qouted by Behr(2)).

2.2.7   Very often gifted children are
under achievers in school. According to
Harris and Baskin (11), "... a significant factor in their underachievement is
boredom."

3.   CONTRIBUTIONS OF COMPUTER-BASED
           EDUCATION TOWARDS THE SPECIAL
           EDUCATIONAL NEEDS OF HIGHLY
           GIFTED CHILDREN.

3.1   Computer-based education makes
           more active learning possible.

Learning of all kinds is improved when
learners can do something while learning
or with which they are learning. They
must be able to see the results of their
learning activities, they must receive
feedback on their attempts (29).

The computer is well equipped to do just
this, because computers are interactive.
A computer is much more than a machine
that merely presents learning materials
to the learner or than a medium of expression for the student. The computer
is able to process the student's response
and determines in a split second the direction in which the student should proceed.

The computer also has the capability of
allowing students much practice in such
complicated mental processes as interpreting data and results, analyzing data
and results, synthesizing, applying and
evaluating data and results (28). To this
list the following activities, for which
the computer is well suited, may be added:
predicting the outcome of certain actions
or decisions, planning of logical sequence, the development of original ideas
(18).

The interactivity of computer-based education allows the student to control

the pace and level of instruction (24) - which is often a source of strong motivation to the student.

Is is in these learner controlled activities, where the learners are afforded maximum control, that the greatest benefits to intellectual development are produced, because these activities encourage the development of algorithms and problemsolving strategies, make possible real world application and facilitate the development of learning skills (5). It seems then that the interactive nature of the child's involvement with the computer in learning or teaching situations has the possibility of enhancing more active learning, of contributing to the development of the higher - order mental activities and of improving the motivation.

3.2 Computer-based education provides more varied sensory and conceptual modes.

The computer is a very versatile teaching aid. It can display letters in a great variety of simple shapes and sizes, and in a number of colours. It can play single tones of varying pitch, duration and loudness. It will accept input from a variety of devices, for example a typewriter keyboard, game paddles, joysticks, light pens or digitized drawing pads.

The computer can also be connected electronically to any device that can respond to or generate an electrical signal; for example videotape, videodisc players, electronic musical instruments, physiological monotoring equipment and almost all household appliances.

This is of great significance for the education of gifted children, because it opens up a whole new world of possibilities to experiment with. The higher - order mental activities mentioned in the previous paragraph (3.1) can be put to test in a variety of situations, learning can be individualized to a much greater extent and learning experience will be more "real-life" orientated. The gifted can only benefit from this characteristic of the computer (29).

3.3 Computer-based education makes learning possible with less mental drudgery.

Under mental drudgery is understood doing things that you can already do and that therefore becomes boring (29). The traditional classroom abounds with situations which can be described as mental drudgery, especially as far as gifted

children are concerned. Examples of drudgery are the endless oral repetition of multiplication tables, the learning of rows and rows of spelling words or vocabulary, the carrying out of intricate calculations involved in scientific problems or the balancing of a budget, the endless rewriting and retyping of drafts and the long hours spent in searching through library card catalogues or indexes (29).

In many cases, especially when gifted children are involved, the solution to a problem takes place in a few minutes (even seconds) but the tedious calculations to arrive at the correct answers may take many minutes. Often unnecessary arithmetical mistakes are made, because the pupils become frustrated by and impatient with the mental drudgery. Very often they lose interest because all motivation has been lost.

The computer can contribute greatly towards improving this situation. Once the youngsters have mastered the underlying principles of scientific calculations, they can use the computer to do the laborious calculations, while they themselves can concentrate on higher-level mental activities.

3.4 Through comptuer-based education the rate of learning can be accelerated.

Learning content presented to the learner at exactly the right pace is an exhilirating experience. The learner's attention does not wander, nor does he fall behind. The train of thought being imparted is followed without effort.

Unfortunately this happy match is seldom experienced in the classroom. The presentation of learning content is usually too fast for the slow learner, much too slow for the gifted child, and just right for only a few (if any) (29).

In this case, the computer can be a useful teaching aid, because when properly programmed, computers can match the pace and timing of a presentation to a learner's requirements at a given moment. The result amounts to an average time-saving factor of one-third when computer-based education is compared to conventional teaching methods.

Through computer-based education one key goal of education, namely individualized rates of learning, becomes attainable as a matter of routine.

3.5   Individually tailored learning is
       possible through computer-based
       education.

In contrast to books, films, television
which are mass media - they deliver the
same message to all users - the computer,
well programmed, can cater for the individual needs and tastes of its users (29).
The ability to individualize teaching and
learning is one of the most significant
contributions of microcomputers to education, because pupils at all levels,
from the highly gifted to the very slow,
can benefit from this. It frees the student from rigidity and inflexibility of
group instruction.

In the conventional classroom situation
one serious problem arises when attempts
are made to cater for the gifted children,
namely how to implement the acceleration
strategy. Acceleration can be achieved
by computer managed instruction, whereby
the student is enabled to control his
own progress. Through the feedback received from the computer, the student can
determine when he has mastered a certain
facet of the learning content and is
ready to move on to the next topic.

The computer can also be used for many
administrative functions in support of
gifted programs. Individual diagnostic
and prescriptive programs can assist teachers in determining which objectives
have already been realized, which objectives need additional instruction and
practice, and which resources and activities are available to reach each objective. Computers can also generate
tests, score them and keep records on individual students.

Computer networks enable pupils to retrieve information from distant locations.
Networks may also reduce some of the isolation that many gifted children feel and
provide motivation and stimulation to expand beyond their current resources (28).
The pupil can also determine on which level he wants to work. Well written computer programs usually contain several levels of difficulty from which the pupil
may choose. Some educators see in the
computer the ultimate learning tool, because it can go in any direction at any
place and to whatever depth the student
wants to take it (5).

3.6   Computer-based education fosters
       more independent learning.

Two problems with independent study, that
is study without guidance from other persons, are verifying progress and sustai-
ning motivation. Computers offer new

possibilities for independent verification of a student's progress, as programs
can be written to monitor progress during lessons, note errors and offer
extra instruction or extra drill where
needed (29).

Papert (25) postulates that while interacting with the computer, the student
assumes the role of the teacher, and in
teaching himself something, inevitably
learns it better. Computers also increase motivation, because students work
on stimulated real world problems which
are rendered more relevant. Reluctant
learners often become more responsive,
active and interested in their schoolwork. These motivational factors make it
possible that computers can be an aid in
stimulating under-achieving gifted children toward developing to their full
potential (5).

3.7   Computer-based education provides
       better aids to abstraction.

3.7.1 Programming

The writing of computer programs can
play an important role in the development of abstract thinking. When writing
a program, complicated processes are represented precisely and directly (29).
Many benefits may be derived from teaching gifted children programming skills.
In the first instance programming is an
excellent activity for increasing cognitive and creative skills. It can promote
logical, deductive thinking; it promotes
problem-solving abilities. Finally it
enables students to think about thinking
(7).

To become familiar with the computer and
to dispel existing fears of it, gifted
children may be introduced to the computer by several hours of games playing
(28).

The value of these educational strategy
games is that the player must develop
successful strategies in order to complete the game. The player must be able
to analyze the game situation, to predict the results of possible moves.
These results must then be evaluated
before deciding on a particular move.
After the move, the situation must be
re-evaluated. These activities involve
memory, analysis, evaluation, logical
thinking and flexible thinking (7). After this initial introduction period,
programming skills should be taught next,
starting with elementary PRINT statements and progressing to branching
statements, loops, strings, arrays and
graphics. It is important that after a

student has been introduced to a concept, he should be given ample opportunity to apply it. Every effort should be made to help students to develop their own programs, because it is here that the unique talents of the gifted may begin to surface. The question of which programming language to teach gifted children, is a difficult one to answer. BASIC is a very popular language, because it is the language used by almost all microcomputers. LOGO, PASCAL and BASIC are very suitable for training and practice in logical analytical processes and as outlets for creativity (7).

It should be stated here, however, that as far as gifted children are concerned, learning to program is not advanced, it is fundamental. Programming itself is not a major challenge to the gifted. Once the gifted have developed programming skills, they are prepared to apply their skills to projects that can correctly be labelled "advanced" (16).

3.7.2 Creativity

A serious lack in the conventional classroom situation is the difficulty to provide situations in which the creativity of pupils can be developed.

In view of the fact that gifted children usually have exceptional creative talent, this is an extremely serious shortcoming. Computers could be a powerful tool to solve this problem.

Logic and creative programs can take several different forms; for example the child must design a logical step-by-step solution to a problem posed by the computer; the child poses a problem and must also write a program to solve the problem. The child may also use a light pen to create computer art by other means than writing a program. In these creative activities the following thinking actions might be used by the child:
- applying knowledge to new situations - using principles of logic to transfer learning from prior experiences to new problems.
- Interpreting - evaluating data for validity or interpreting the solution the computer gave to the problem.
- Cooling - learning computer languages and applying them in writing a program, thereby making the child aware of the relationship between the thought process and the written word.
- Designing projects or investigations - in writing and executing a program, the child plans ahead before actually using the program.

These logical and creative programs are

by far the most difficult and pose a great challenge in terms of problem-solving. Problem-solving abilities are improved by careful and correct programming (32).

3.7.3 Problem-solving

Teaching children sound problem-solving techniques is another area in education which is rarely fully exploited in the conventional classroom setting. A problem always consists of three basic components.
- A set of given information (description of the problem);
- A goal, or description of what would constitute a solution;
- A set of operations (actions) which, when followed closely, would lead to the goal (or solution) (2).

These three components are inherent to programming, therefore problem-solving has much in common with programming. Small wonder then that programming is seen as an ideal vehicle for developing the problem-solving abilities of gifted children.

Computers aid and encourage children in problem-solving endeavours by permitting them to explore alternative solutions freely without the inhibiting possibility of penalty for possible failure. Children can always rerun a program to try different strategies. Pupils are encouraged to use their capacity for discovering relations. Variables are easily manipulated, thus clarifying the relationship of a particular variable to the outcome of the problem (32).

3.8 Computer-based education and socialization of gifted children

Gifted children often face social difficulties as a result of their advanced intellectual development. Their social peers are often not on their intellectual level and contact between the gifted child and his own age group is often lacking. Computers can be useful in providing positive social experiences and developing interpersonal skills among gifted children. Research suggests that computers enable children to share their experiences and promote co-operative behaviour in groups (5). This is achieved by focussing on group interaction through group problem-solving and programming, through co-operative and competitive game-playing, through aids for writing letters in school newspapers, and through peer tutoring and consulting with experts.

Until recently most computers were independent, stand-alone machines, isolating people. This situation is rapidly changing as local and global networks and powerful databases provide computer links. It is possible to have access to libraries and other sources of information from classrooms, homes and offices (30). The gifted child is therefore no longer isolated from his intellectual peers. The computer is therefore able to make a significant breakthrough in this field as well.

4.   CONCLUSION

The world is on the threshold of an exiting new era, and the age of the computer, specifically the home-computer or personalized computer, is with us. It is most likely that gifted children, who have the potential to bring a powerful store of talents to their interaction with computers, will make a significant contribution to the continued development of computer technology. It is therefore the duty of educators to see to it that the inclusion of computer activities in differentiated curricula for the gifted should receive high priority in educational planning for this group.

The computer ia a very powerful and versatile aid in the teaching of highly gifted children. At lower levels of intellectual activities, students have access to instant instruction through complex multi-level branching programs in the tutorial mode. In the drill and practice mode they can master, at a rate suitable to their abilities, necessary facts and principles, and they can master necessary skills like arithmatic operations. At higher levels, via simulations and programming, they might gain access to knowledge and experience that might be outside their realm of experience but not beyond the level of their ability(ies). There are also affective benefits to be gained by working with computers. Computers enhance self-confidence and curiosity, they stimulate exploratory behaviour and motivation and they foster positive attitudes towards learning. In the computer age the role of the teacher will change from an answer-provider and drill-master to a director of teaching and learning experiences. To a great extent teachers will be freed from mundane tasks and will have more time to concentrate on more creative activities.

Although computer-based education offers exiting possibilities in the education of gifted children, some problems do exist. There is a serious shortage of sophisticated software for use with gifted children. A second serious problem is an acute shortage of trained teachers in computer literacy. A third problem area centres around the development of enrichment programs involving computers.

Despite these and other problems the computer is already reasonably well established as an educational tool. An exiting future awaits us if we have the courage to open our eyes to the promising role that the computer can play in providing suitable educational experiences to that special, but up to now neglected group of children - the highly gifted.

REFERENCES

1) BEHR, A.L. (ed.), Teaching the gifted child, Publication Series of the South African Association for the Advancement of Education (SAAAE), 1983.
2) BEHR, A.L., Educating the gifted - some psycho-didactical considerations, Behr, A.L. (ed.), 1983: 105-134.
3) BOYD, G.M., Four ways of providing computer assisted learning and their probable impacts, *Computer Education*, Vol. 6, 1982: 305-310.
4) DE JAGER, N.J., Onderwysvoorsiening aan begaafde leerlinge, Behr, A.L. (ed.), 1983:71-89.
5) DOVER, A., Computers and the gifted: Past, Present and Future, *Gifted Child Quarterly*, Vol. 27, no. 2 Spr. 1983: 81-85.
6) DWYER, T.A. & CRITCHFIELD, M., Multi-computer systems for the support of inventive learning, *Computers and Education*, Vol. 6, 1982:7-12.
7) EDWARDS, L., Teaching higher level thinking skills through computer courseware, *Association for Educational Data Systems Monitor*, Vol. 21, no. 11-12, May-June 1983:28-30.
8) ELRON, O., Teaching with computer simulations, *Science and Children*, Vol. 20, no. 8, May 1983:13-17.
9) FORD, M.S., WALKINGTON, P.A., BITTER, G.G., Gifted Education - Enrichment or Acceleration? - Computers provide both!, *The Journal of Computers in Mathematics and Science Teaching*, Fall 1981:18-19.
10) GOUWS, M., A description, definition and categorization of gifted children, Behr, A.L. (ed.), 1983:35-59.
11) HARRIS, K. & BASKIN, B., Reading guidance for   gifted children, *Top of the News*, Vol. 38, no. 4, Sum. 1982: 308-311.
12) HEDBRING, C. & RUBENZER, R., Integrating the IEP and SOI with educational programming for the gifted, *Gifted Child Quarterly*, Vol. 23, no. 2, Sum. 1979:338-345.
13) HEID, M.K., Characteristics and

special needs of the gifted student in mathematics.*Mathematics teacher*, Vol.76, no. 4 Apr. 1983:221-226.

14) HILL, J.S., Rekenaarondersteunde onderrig, *Kurr-i-kom*, Vol. 8, no. 4, Jul-Aug. 1982:2.

15) JOINER, L.M., MILLER, S.R., SILVERSTEIN, B.J., Potential and limits of computers in schools, *Educational Leadership*, Vol. 37, no. 6, Mar. 1980: 498-501.

16) KOETKE, W., Computers and the mathematically gifted, *Mathematics Teacher*, Vol. 76, no. 4, 1983:270-272.

17) KOTZE, J.M.A., Voorsittersrede SAVBO, 1983: Begaafdekindonderwys: enkele probleemareas, Behr, A.L. (ed.), 1983: 1-14.

18) LEIMBACH, J., Spotlight on computers: Students in control, *SLJ School Library Journal*, August 1982, 37.

19) LEWIS, R., Education, Computers and Micro-electronics, *Technological Horizons in Education*, Vol. 8, no. 7, Jan. 1981, 47-49, 59.

20) LINVILL, J.G., University Role in the Computer Age, *Science*, Col. 215, 12 Feb. 1982:802-806.

21) MEYER,P.S., Die onderrig van begaafde kinders en die mannekragsituasie in Suid-Afrika, Behr, A.L. (ed.) 1983: 15-33.

22) MILLER, C.L., & DRAGER, L.B., Authorising for Computer-based Training. *NSPI Journal*, Nov. 1979:13-17.

23) NEETHLING, J.S., The indentification of the gifted and talented, Behr, A.L. (ed.), 1983:61-69.

24) NELL, D.J., Education and Information Science - an approach, *Mentor*, Vol. 63, no. 5, Nov. 1981:204.

25) PAPERT, S., Mindstorms. Children, computers and powerful ideas, Brighton, The Harvester Press, Ltd.

26) STEELE, K.J., BATTISTA, M.T. & KROCKOVER, G.H., The effect of microcomputer assisted instruction upon the computer literacy of high ability students. *Gifted Child Quarterly*, Vol. 26, no. 4, Fall 1982:162-164.

27) STROM, R.D., Expectations for education of the gifted and talented, *The Educational Forum*, Vol. 47, no. 3, Spring 1983:279-310.

28) TASHNER, J.H., Using computers with gifted students, *Top of the News*, Vol. 38, no. 4 Sum. 1982:318-324.

29) WALKER, D.F., Reflections on the educational Potential and limitations of microcomputers, *Phi Delta Kappan*, Vol. 65, no. 2,Oct. 1983: 103-107.

30) WEYER, S.A., Computers for communication, *Childhood Education*, Vol. 59, no. 59, no. 4, Mar./Apr. 1983: 232-236.

31) WRIGHT, D.G., & CUNNINGHAM, C.H., A model summer program for gifted children, *Gifted Child Quarterly*, Vol. 23,

no. 3 Fall 1979: 538-542.

32) ZEISER, E.L. & HOFFMAN, S., Computers: tools for thinking, *Childhood Education*, Vol. 59, no. 4, Mar./Apr. 1983: 251-254.

COMPUTERS IN EDUCATION, K. Duncan and D. Harris (eds.)
Elsevier Science Publishers B.V. (North-Holland)

COMPUTER ASSISTED LEARNING AND THE WEAK PUPILS IN MATHEMATICS

Kim Foss Hansen

Danish National Institute of Educational Research
Copenhagen, Denmark

1. INTRODUCTION DELIMITING THE CONCEPTS SPECIAL EDUCATION AND THE WEAK PUPILS

In Denmark 13% of the pupils of a school year are registered as pupils in the special education, and municipal accounts show that at some time or other 20-25% of all pupils receive special education in some form or other.

In this article the main stress is laid on the special education of pupils unable to keep up with the ordinary instruction in mathematics, i.e. pupils who have difficulties over the subject. Mathematics is the subject referring the second largest number of pupils to special education. Danish is the subject referring the largest number of pupils.

In general, special education is defined as an education specifically based on the qualifications, needs, and motivations of the individual child. However, this includes, at the same time, a definition of the ordinary education from which the pupil is referred. In other words, special education is a relative concept.

What usually indicates special education is the concept 'difficulties' of some kind or other. This is a practical concept which makes sense only when the difficulties are seen in relation to and in connection with a specific educational system and with the methods and textbooks of this system.

The special education in mathematics is a mirror image and an expression of what, why, and how things are done in the ordinary class. There is a close and complex connection between special and 'ordinary' education, a connection which is often disregarded.

1.1 The ordinary education

Class teaching is the most prevailing teaching method in the mathematics education. The education is structured in such a way that the teacher finds the pupils divided into a group of normal performers, a group of exceptional performers - and a group of weak performers. Generally the group of weak performers is unable to keep up with the rest of the class. The potential pupils for the special education are found in this group which usually comprises abt. 1/5-1/3 of the pupils of the class. This is true of all regions of the country and also of middle class schools as well as lower class schools. This clearly indicates that the need of assistance and support is created in the individual group - in the class. The structure of the teaching (viz. a short phase of correction, a phase of going through by the teacher, and a phase for the pupils to work independently with written problems) together with the contents and structure of the textbooks (spiral organization) are the things determining this. Practice indicates special education for part of the pupils in the group of weak performers.

1.2 Reference to special education

Only rarely is the reference to special education effected on the basis of tests. In most cases it is effected on the basis of the ordinary teacher's evaluation of the pupil in question, which is usually very undifferentiated and very general. Thus the evaluation of pupils referred to special education during grade 1-3 typically includes characteristics like: childishness, immaturity, lack of concentration, lack of motor skill, and inattentiveness. Only in very few cases, difficulties concerning the subject as such are specified. The most frequently mentioned difficulty in connection with the subject is "difficulty in abstract thinking" which means that the pupil has difficulty in solving problems within the areas: theory of sets, logic, statements, and equations. In other words, these difficulties are often so implicit that they need no special mention. As far as the evaluation of pupils in grade 3-7 is concerned, it is characteristic that the list of reasons for difficulties also includes - often very specific - difficulties concerning the subject. These are almost always difficulties within one or more of the four basic arithmetical operations. This is an important issue, as the Danish mathematics education includes a much larger variety of disciplines than just these four operations. At all levels the education includes instruction in algebra, geometry, calculus of probability, combinatoric, and statistics. The evaluation of the weak performers in grade 8-10 is seldom very specific. The most frequent evaluation states that the pupil is weak in all areas within the subject. It is easier to state what the pupil knows than what the pupil does not know!

Although the reasons for the reference to special education include some form of evaluation of the pupil in relation to the subject - an evaluation which might indicate that the abilities of the pupil were decisive of his/her profit by the subject - it clearly appears from interviews with teachers that the reference is sooner carried out on the background of the teacher's own limited possibilities of assisting these pupils. When the teacher feels it difficult to consider this group of pupils properly, he/she tries to obtain more time for the members of the group by referring pupils from the group to special education.

1.3 The organizatory forms of the special education

The special education in mathematics is effected under different organizatory forms which are of paramount importance for the pupil's possibilities to enter the middle group of the ordinary class after the special education.

Generally the special education is given for a period varying from two months to the rest of the pupil's schooling. This article gives prominence to the most frequent special education which implies that the pupil spends 1-3 of the 4 periods of the subject in a special education class of 3-6 pupils from 2-3 different grades.

The periods not spent in the special education class are spent in the ordinary class. One would assume that the pupil would participate in the ordinary education of the class just like he/she did, before he/she was referred to special education. However, this is seldom the case; in most cases the pupil is given problems supplied by the special teacher or problems at levels below the level on which the other pupils are working. Usually these are problems which will not cause the pupil in question so great difficulties that he/she will have to draw on the teacher's assistance to any large extent. Add to

this that the 'ordinary' teacher often feels that the responsibility for the education of the pupil concerned has now passed to the special teacher.

The general estimation of this special education is that it is rarely successful.

2 SURVEY OF THE USE OF THE COMPUTER IN THE SPECIAL EDUCATION IN MATHEMATICS IN DENMARK

Several experiments with computer aided instruction have been carried out in the special education in Denmark. In most cases the purpose has been to clarify:
1. whether the computer offers greater possibilities of individualization and whether it can advantageously conduct an education planned in advance;
2. whether the computer will form a natural (not disturbing or isolating) part of the daily education;
3. whether the computer will form part of the education in a more dynamic way than traditional educational material;
4. whether the motivation is increased, as questions and answers follow each other in rapid succession;
5. whether the pupils are able to transfer the skills from individual problems, e.g. in drill and practice form;
6. whether the computer affects the function between teacher and pupil.

Furthermore, it has often been the purpose of the experiments to establish whether the teacher obtains greater possibilities of individual education and group education of the pupils who are not instructed by means of the computer (it is assumed that the pupils spend only a smaller part of the period at the computer).

2.1 The contents of the instruction

In the above-mentioned experimental instruction the following types of programs were used:

1. Addition $a + b = ?$
2. Addition $a + ? =$ sum total
3. Addition $a + ? = 10$
4. Addition   e.g. $23 + 12 = ?$
                   Does it make 37 or 35 or 45?
5. Subtraction $a - b = ?$
6. Subtraction $a - ? =$ difference
7. Subtraction,   e.g.

$$\begin{array}{r} 10 \\ 36 \\ -\ 18 \\ \hline 18 \end{array}$$

8. The sequence of numbers, e.g.
   What comes after 3?
   What comes before 8?

What comes before
and what comes
after 17?
9. Practice in addition tables
10. Practice in subtraction tables
11. Practice in multiplication tables
12. Practice in division tables.

In most programs the pupil is given a certain number of attempts (2 or 3), and then the correct answer is given. The last programs allow for teacher menu (e.g. statistics).

3. CRITICAL COMMENTS ON THE USE OF THE COMPUTER UP TILL NOW

As appears clearly from the above, all the programs include drill and practice exercises. No explanation has been coded, the only explanation from the computer to the pupil being the correct answer.

The subject area is very limited in relation to the usual curriculum of the instruction in mathematics. Therefore, the pupil will hardly be able to cope with the instruction of the ordinary class, if only, because of lack of instruction within the disciplines constituting the contents of the ordinary instruction.

In relation to the purposes of the experiments it is demonstrated that the reporting is extremely modest, not to say inadequate, the evaluation building exclusively upon the statements of the participating teachers. No control groups have been involved, and no impartial examination of the learning progress of the pupils has been carried out.

3.1 The value of the learning

In the judgment of the participating teachers, the concentrated method of work of the pupils has a positive effect on their practising of the handling of figures. Further, in their judgment, the fact that they (the teachers) promptly discover possible shortcomings on the part of the pupils within the areas of the programs and thus are able to go through the problem again with the pupils is of a positive value to the learning of the pupils.

In other words, what is evaluated as having a good effect on the learning is an increased concentration during the short intervals when the pupils are working with the computers, together with the possibility of a prompt feedback. However, the questions whether this effect is really present and whether it is a lasting effect are not investigated.

The purpose mentioned under item 5 is not examined either.

3.2 Does the pupil derive advantage from the computer work?

The participating teachers consider it an advantage that the pupils see only one problem at a time on the screen, and that immediately after having solved a problem they are presented with a new. It can be said that the teachers find it positive that the pupils concentrate on the specific problem to be solved and cannot be diverted by other problems, solved or unsolved.

Moreover, it is pointed out that the work with the computer offers a change in the paper and pencil work which otherwise comprises the periods, and that no pupil is tempted to crib from the neighbour, because the problems are never alike due to the pupils' different speed in working.

The advantages to the pupils can be summarized as follows:

The pupils do not have to work with those books which were part of the reason why they were referred to special education; the teachers express this by saying that the pupils who work unattentively with books show a more concentrated and independent method of work at the computer.

3.3 Does the teacher derive advantage from the computer work?

The teachers underline the fact that much of the final output of the program offers a favourable possibility of following the development of the pupils in the subject. This means a.o. that written tests to be corrected by the teachers are rendered superfluous. Moreover, the teachers state that when computers are available there will never be a shortage of extra problems for the quick pupil, and, furthermore, that the computer helps the teacher make inattentive pupils concentrate more on the problems.

Apart from the above-mentioned critical points, the following ought to be pointed out:
1. The computer is applied within the most narrow area of the instruction in mathematics, viz. the practice in handling of figures within the four basic arithmetical operations.
2. The computer is used purely as a practising device according to the best behavioral principles.
3. It has not been attempted to use the computer as a means to give the pupils understanding/comprehension, in-

sight and behaviors for problem-solving.

4. It has not been attempted to incorporate the computer as a means in concection with the conceptualization of the pupils.
5. The computer has been equipped with familiar practice problems within a very narrow field of the subject.
6. The use of the computer in the special education does not give occasion for a changed method of instruction or a changed teacher role.

To sum up: The use of the computer in the special education has not caused a special education different from the general, and it has not caused a change of the ordinary education. When a stop is put to the computer with programs of practice, the ordinary education is presented with a great possibility of avoiding changes.

4. STARTING POINTS FOR A FUTURE USE OF THE COMPUTER IN SPECIAL EDUCATION

First of all we must put a stop to the present use of the computer in the special education, because here it is used to present an instructional content in a way which is far from the usual way of presenting mathematics and far from the intentions expressed in the curricula of the subject. The computer programs of today have a strong resemblance to the teaching materials used 30-50 years ago - which would be rejected by the pupils if presented to them in book form.

We must look into the possibilities of the computer within the following main areas:

1. Would the use of the computer prevent the reference of pupils to special education?
2. Would the use of the computer enable the pupils to be integrated in the ordinary education again?

Re: 1. Before this question can be answered, an experimental education will have to be established, aiming at:

a. a change of the role of the teacher from a deducting to a coaching role;
b. a change of the controlling function of the textbooks in the education;
c. a change of the working method of the pupils from a passively receiving and revising method to an actively examining and researching method.
d. education on the actual learning level of the individual pupil.

This is the basis upon which the application of the computer must be evaluated.

Re: 2. Before this question can be answered positively, a special education must be organized, including at least the two following educational tasks in relation to the weak pupil:

a) the education must bring about an improvement of the deficiencies of the pupil, a remedy of the pupil's difficulties within the subject, and
b) the education must include the subject matter which the pupil fails to obtain, while he/she is in the special education.

In other words, the special education must be both ordinary education and special education at the same time.

This is the basis upon which the possibilities of the computer must be evaluated.

5. THE PROBLEMS OF THE WEAK PUPILS IN RELATION TO THE ORDINARY EDUCATION

The main point of this section is that the education taking place in the ordinary instruction in mathematics is not aimed at the actual learning level of the weak pupil.

The actual learning level can be described as the level on which the pupil is able to absorb new subject matter and connect it with the previously acquired subject matter, or, to put it otherwise: the stage when the pupil is able to include new experience and new knowledge in a complex of experience wellknown and familiar to the pupil, thus raising his/her knowledge to a higher level.

The subject matter within a given mathematical discipline is presented in the textbooks in accordance with the spiral organization introduced a.o. by Jerome Bruner, which means that it is presented in a still more complex way, starting on a low level of abstraction and increasing towards a still higher level of abstraction.

In order that the pupil can profit by the instruction, it is of the utmost importance that the spiral level on which the instruction is effected is in accordance with the pupil's actual level of learning.

As mentioned above, the predominant teaching method is class teaching. This method consists of three phases, mentioned below in relation to the group of weak pupils:

1. Problems which the pupil is able to solve independently.
2. Problems which the pupil is unable to solve independently.
3. Problems which the pupil is able to solve without assistance.
4. THE ACTUAL LEARNING LEVEL. Problems which the pupil is able to solve, if he/she receives a little help and instruction.
5. Problems which the pupil is unable to solve, unless he/she receives much help and instruction.
6. Problems which the pupil is unable to solve, no matter how much help and instruction he/she receives.

The pupil is working without being able to receive any assistance.

Problems within a given subject area arranged according to increasing degree of difficulty.

The pupil is able to receive assistance.

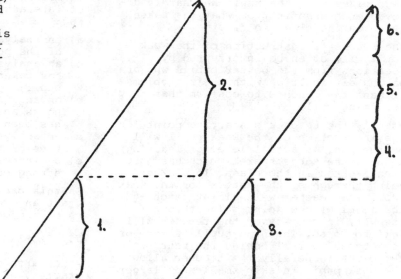

5.1 Phase 1: Phase of correction

In this phase, which is most frequently at the beginning of the period, the problems of the pupils are corrected verbally, and if the majority of the pupils have solved a problem wrongly, the teacher will go through the problem. If only a minority have not solved the problem correctly, this minority are asked to contact the teacher after the phase of going through, i.e. in the phase when the pupils are working with independent problem-solving.

This way of correcting problems means that only the most difficult problems will be gone through for the group of weak pupils, whereas the 'easy' problems will not be gone through (although these pupils were unable to solve them independently).

5.2 Phase 2: Phase of going through

In most cases the going through of a type of problem or of a new subject area is carried out in the form of a dialogue between the teacher and the individual pupils of the class. Characteristically, the weak pupil is seldom involved in this dialogue. This is due to the fact that the contents and progress of the going through have not been organized so as to consider the weak pupil. There are several reasons for this; the most central reasons are the following:

- the teacher feels that it may be difficult for him/her to keep to the subject;
- the going through will be too long;
- many pupils will not be able to concentrate their attention on the central point of the phase;
- the teacher feels that the weak pupil should not be involved, as he/she cannot be expected to be able to answer the questions satisfactorily;
- the weak pupil must be saved from suffering defeat in front of his/her

class-mates.

The teacher brings the phase of going through to an end, after having evaluated how well especially the middle group of pupils will be able to tackle the problems which the textbooks provide in connection with the subject just gone through.

5.3 Phase 3: The phase of independent problems

In this phase the actual education of the weak pupil takes place. The teacher recognizes that the pupil has hardly derived much benefit from what has taken place in the class so far.

The teacher's instruction of the weak pupil will often be interrupted by questions from the better pupils who are having difficulties with their problems or want the teacher to confirm that they are doing well.

Usually the teacher's starting point for the instruction of the weak pupil will be the pupil's actual level of learning and not the subject area which has just been treated in the class. In his/her going through of the matter for the weak pupil the teacher will aim at reaching the level of the joint going through; however, in most cases the teacher will fail to do so. Thus the pupil is more or less bound to fall behind the rest of the class. Generally the teacher allows the weak pupil to skip smaller or larger parts of the matter, in his/her efforts to keep the pupil inside the framework of the class instruction. Class instruction is based upon the impression that it is possible to let the pupils start more or less jointly each time a new lesson is commenced. This is an illusion as far as the weak pupil is concerned, but the illusion is concealed exactly through the skipping of the more difficult areas and problems. The subjects with which the pupil will thus be concerned are, in fact, the subjects within the four basic arithmetical operations.

Summing up, the following should be underlined:

1. The weak pupil's profit by the phase of correction is unsatisfactory;
2. The weak pupil's profit by the phase of going through is unsatisfactory, because this phase does not include the actual learning level of the pupil;
3. The instruction of the weak pupil during the phase of independent problems is not sufficient to compensate for the deficiencies of the two previous phases.

The application of the computer must be evaluated in this light.

6. COULD THE COMPUTER BE USED IN CONNECTION WITH THE SOLVING OF THE ABOVE-MENTIONED PROBLEMS?

To examine the possibilities of the computer in connection with the education of weak pupils it is necessary to clarify the reasons why this group of pupils has come into being, in other words, the interaction between the pupils of a class, their teacher, and the educational materials applied. Such an analysis of interaction must include the following:

a) an analysis of the previous education of the pupil;
b) an analysis of the interaction which has taken place between teacher and pupil;
c) an analysis of the system of textbooks according to which the pupil has been instructed;
d) an analysis of the teacher's priorities of the subjects;
e) a diagnosis of the pupil's weak and strong points, respectively.

On this background it is possible to start an evaluation of the potentialities of the computer.

7. CLOSING REMARKS

A research of the above subject has been started, and I hope to be able to tell more about it in my presentation.

COMPUTERS IN EDUCATION, K. Duncan and D. Harris (eds.)
Elsevier Science Publishers B.V. (North-Holland)
© IFIP, 1985

COMPUTER ASSISTED READING AND MATHEMATICS PROGRAM

Debra J. Glowinski and E. Wayne Roberson
National Diffusion Network Division
United States Department of Education

Sheila L. Cory and Margie Walker
Chapel Hill-Carrboro City Schools, North Carolina

Two projects related to reading and mathematics will be discussed. First, the Computer Assisted Diagnostic Prescriptive Program (CADPP), an exemplary computer management program for reading and mathematics, will be presented by the original co-authors of the system. This will be followed by a presentation of a large-scale computer literacy implementation funded through a Chapter II Competition Grant from the State of North Carolina.

The CADPP is a computer management program in reading and mathematics, which was validated by the National Institute of Education and the United States Office of Education in the fall of 1979. Since that time, the CADPP has been funded by the National Diffusion Network, under the United States Department of Education, to provide materials and in-service training to educational service providers in replicating its program.

The National Diffusion Network, or NDN, is a federally funded system that makes exemplary educational programs available for adoption by schools, colleges, and other institutions. It does so by providing dissemination funds to exemplary programs for two purposes: (1) to enable the programs to make public and non-public schools, colleges, and other institutions aware of what they offer, and (2) to enable the programs to provide in-service training, follow-up assistance, and in some cases, curriculum materials to schools and others that want to adopt them.

To summarize, the CADPP is a data-based management system which allows a user to load: (1) learning characteristics of individual students to include age, instructional level, and identified learning modality, if applicable; and (2) skill-oriented characteristics of available instructional materials to include readability level, interest level, and modality utilized, into a computerized filing/retrieval system. Once these files are loaded, the CADPP cross-references these files to match similar student characteristics to instructional material characteristics, and produces customized prescriptions (personalized educational plans) for each participating student, based upon the reinforcement skills requested by the instructor.

In addition to generating prescriptions, the CADPP tracks an individual child's yearly activities and can produce cumulative reports for: skills instructed and skills mastered with date of mastery indicated; a total listing of all instructional materials utilized during the year; and additional summary reports for the instructor's planning/grouping for instructional reinforcement.

To date, the CADPP user's group consists of over 500 schools in 35 different states.

The CADPP program operates on Apple II Plus and IIe microcomputers; the Radio Shack TRS 80 Models II and IV microcomputers; and the Franklin microcompters. An 80 column card, two disk drives, and a printer are also required.

The Chapel Hill-Carrboro City Schools project is designed to answer basic research questions about the feasibility of implementing a large-scale computer literacy curriculum in grades K-12, and also to assess the utility of such a curriculum in terms of student knowledge, skill, and attitude outcomes. In addition to answers to research questions, this project will produce a field-tested set of materials for use with Logo and Bank Street Writer in the classroom, and a set of field-tested staff development materials that will relate directly to the curriculum materials.

This project places a 15-Apple lab in each elementary school in our school system for one-third of a year. The labs are used to focus on two major computer literacy objectives and two major traditional curriculum objectives. One focus of effort is (1) to develop programming skills and (2) to positively affect math attitude for all students in the fifth grade through use of the computer language Logo. A second focus of the effort is (1) to teach tool use of the computer and (2) to improve writing skills for all students in the sixth grade. Bank Street Writer is the software used. Instruction to students is provided by the classroom teacher, with assistance through modeled lessons, staff development, curriculum development, and assessment provided by a lab helping-teacher.

Curriculum materials and staff development materials have been produced. Curriculum materials consist of 6 student workbooks for Logo, and a guide to the Bank Street Writer and a set of creative writing activities that give step-by-step directions for use of a word processor. A project evaluation design has been developed, a very experienced lab helping-teacher has been hired, hardware has been ordered, and a great deal of motivation exists to use this project to learn a great deal of value for future decision-making.

Mathematics, Science, and Engineering Education

COMPUTERS IN EDUCATION, K. Duncan and D. Harris (eds.)
Elsevier Science Publishers B.V. (North-Holland)
© IFIP, 1985

COMPUTERS IN PRE-COLLEGIATE MATHEMATICS EDUCATION

Sheldon P. Gordon

Suffolk Community College
Selden, NY 11784

This session is designed to highlight some of the new and innovative ways in which computers are being used in pre-collegiate mathematics education. The primary focus of the presenters be on the effects that such activities will have on the mathematics curricula. In addition, actual demonstrations of typical software for implementing the ideas will be presented.

Professor Willard Baxter will discuss the results of a National Science Foundation-funded project involving secondary teachers and curricula development. The goal of the project is to familiarize the teachers with computers and their applications through a series of summer workshops with the primary emphasis being on the individual's subsequent development of appropriate courseware. The presentation will describe the outcomes of this project. In particular, the presenter will discuss the variations that can exist between the anticipated goals of such a project and the actual results of its implementation.

In addition, Professor Baxter will broaden the context to make some general observations about the mathematical backgrounds necessary for students to do very meaningful computer-related assignments while at the same time learning a computer language. These comments apply freshman mathematics majors as well as to secondary teachers.

Dr. Leo H. Klingen will discuss the implications of computer usage in the school curriculum. Rather than a reduction of classical mathematics in the curriculum, his thesis is that the computer can actually provide for a far richer mathematical experience for the students and better applications of the mathematics that is taught.

Among the examples he will present are such things as the use of Euclid's algorithm for finding the greatest common divisor instead of decomposition into primes, Heron's algorithm for quadratics, Horner's method for evaluating polynomials and for synthetic division, algorithmic approaches to logarithms and other numerical techniques. In turn, the introduction of such topics and methods into the curriculum then allows for the consideration of other important concepts and questions, such as convergence of iterative methods and properties of functions.

In addition, he will show that teachers can enrich their lessons by incorporating many new demonstrations such as graphical methods on the screen, simulations in probability theory and construction of mathematical models with systems of difference equations. The result is the use of the computer as a discovery tool in mathematics education.

Dr. Peter Schmidt will discuss the results of Project SCHUMA to develop programs which (semi-)automatically solve school tasks and which may give explanations referring to the solution. The tasks include mathematical story problems in such areas as motion problems, distribution problems, trigonometric problems and vector algegra problems. Two approaches are used to solve such story problems. One proceeds from a program that can cope with story problems in a restricted input language having the capability of allowing the student to reword the given task in an appropriate form. The other system puts a tree of questions to the student so that the system can collect the relevant information in the story.

The methods used are predicated on a student having learned the solution method, but needing more exercises. The research behind them focuses on the didactics of the subject, the response-sensitivity of the program and on giving the student free-play.

Finally, the presenter will discuss the potential impact that formula manipulating programs or computer algebra may have on mathematics curricula.

Professor Sheldon P. Gordon will present some examples of how computer graphics can be used to enrich mathematics classes at the algebra and trigonometry level. All too often, computer applications focus on reinforcing manipulative skills in classes at this level. However, there are a variety of particularly simple mathematical models for some very interesting phenomena which use just the mathematics taught in such classes. As a result, the students can see the usefulness of the mathematics as more than just a manipulative skill or the means of solving traditional word problems. Among the cases which will be discussed and demonstrated are population growth models for one species, population growth among competing species (predator-prey model) and an arms race model between competing nations.

Furthermore, the speed and ease with which the computer can generate the solutions, both numerically in a table and graphically, allows the teacher to turn the computer into a exploratory tool akin to the microscopes and telescopes of scientists. In this way, the students are able to see immediately what happens if values of the quantities involved are changed in any desired way. In turn, this is a nice way to involve all the students in a class and to excite them with the thrill of discovery.

PRESENTERS

Willard E. Baxter
University of Delaware
Newark, DE 19716

Leo H. Klingen
Helmholtz-Gymnasium
Bonn, West Germany

Peter Schmidt
Universitat Bonn
Bonn, West Germany

Sheldon P. Gordon
Suffolk Community College
Selden, NY 11784

COMPUTERS IN EDUCATION, K. Duncan and D. Harris (eds.)
Elsevier Science Publishers B.V. (North-Holland)
© IFIP, 1985

COMPUTERS IN UNDERGRADUATE MATHEMATICS EDUCATION

Sheldon P. Gordon

Suffolk Community College
Selden, NY 11784

This session is designed to highlight some of the new and innovative ways in which computers are being used in undergraduate mathematics education. In addition, the presenters will also focus on the effects that such activities will have on the mathematics curriculua.

Professor Howard Penn will address the use of computer graphics in the calculus sequence as applied to the topic of sketching polar coordinate graphs, an area that many students have difficulty mastering. To overcome this, he assigns to his computer calculus class the problem of writing a program to graph polar coordinate equations. The program is simple and can be written on any system which has graphics. After the students practice some of the standard equations, they are asked to graph some unusual curves and to come up with at least one original graph. Many of the graphs presented in the talk were first submitted by the students.

With this approach, the students get to see many more graphs which increases their ability to sketch the standard curves. Furthermore, writing the program increases their awareness of several factors about polar coordinate curves, including the parametric nature of the equations and the conversion from polar to rectangular coordinates.

Professor Florence Gordon will discuss how the use of computer graphics can dramatically enhance student understanding of the main concepts and methods of elementary probability and statistics. Particular topics to be covered include graphical simulations of the binomial distribution, the Central Limit Theorem and the random walk phenomenon. In addition, there will be graphics demonstrations involving the normal distribution, the binomial distribution, the t-distribution, confidence intervals for means and/or proportions, hypothesis tests and linear regression.

The programs to be demonstrated can be used either by the instructor in the classroom environment or by individual students. In either approach, these programs have proven exceptionally successful in increasing student understanding

and providing additional motivation. This has been particularly true in introductory, non-calculus based statistics and probability courses where the students typically are not mathematically mature and so require all possible conceptual aids.

Professor P. K. Wong will describe an NSF-supported project designed to develop and implement a series of modules on the computational and geometrical aspects of linear algebra. The topics in linear algebra which are particularly well suited to this type of treatment include linear independence and basis, matrices as mappings, geometry of eigenvalues and eigenvectors, projections and least squares approximations, use of matrices in computer graphics and rotations of a four dimensional cube and projections of it onto two space. The programs can be used either in the classroom or in a laboratory setting.

Professor Sheldon Gordon will discuss the potential effects that symbolic manipulation packages such as MuMath and MACSYMA and their descendents will have on the undergraduate mathematics curriculum. He will first give a brief demonstration of the capabilities of one of these systems. He will then consider their implications for undergraduate mathematics education. On the one hand, such systems can prove to be a blessing in terms of forcing the mathematics community to totally reexamine the content of its courses with a view towards eliminating many manipulative topics which may no longer be relevant. The consequent streamlining of these courses would then permit either greater emphasis on student understanding or additional time to introduce additional topics or both. On the other hand, these systems may prove a curse in terms of totally eliminating all manipulative skills from forthcoming generations of mathematicians, scientists and engineers with the concommitant loss in insight.

PRESENTERS

Howard Penn
U. S. Naval Academy

Florence S. Gordon
New York Institute of Technology

P. K. Wong
Michigan State University

Sheldon P. Gordon
Suffolk Community College

SPONSOR: CIMSE - National Consortium on Computers in Mathematical Sciences Education

COMPUTERS IN EDUCATION, K. Duncan and D. Harris (eds.)
Elsevier Science Publishers B.V. (North-Holland)
© IFIP, 1985

DISCRETE MATHEMATICS

Martha J. Siegel, Towson State University, Chairperson

Participants: John F. Dalphin, Norwich University
Gerald L. Isaacs, Carroll College
Elliot B. Koffman, Temple University

DISCRETE MATHEMATICS IN COMPUTER SCIENCE PROGRAMS

John F. Dalphin, Norwich University, Northfield, Vermont 05663

Digital computers perform two main functions: symbol manipulation (epitomized by word processing and graphical displays) and discrete numeric computation. To best understand the specific numeric principles and data structures necessary to symbol manipulation, a grounding in discrete structures is necessary for computer science students. In addition, there are some side-effects of discrete mathematical study which benefit the mental maturation of the student: enhancement of problem solving techniques; development of mathematical bases for advanced study; experience handling problems which are nonintuitive. Discrete mathematics is as important to study in the computing sciences as the calculus is to engineering.

THE ROLE OF DISCRETE MATHEMATICS IN SMALL COLLEGE COMPUTER SCIENCE PROGRAMS

Gerald L. Isaacs, Department of Computer Science, Carroll College, Waukesha, WI 53186

This section will address the impact of the addition of discrete mathematics into curricula of the small college. This addition will affect small college in a wide variety of ways. Some of which may be subtle and very political.

The following areas and how they will be affected by the addition of discrete mathematics will be addressed: the traditional calculus sequence, the mathematics major, the dual computer science/mathematics major, the computer science curriculum, the flexibility of students and their elective courses, the Mathematics Department and its faculty, the Computer Science Department and its faculty and lastly the faculty in traditional humanist or liberal arts areas.

THE ROLE OF DISCRETE MATHEMATICS IN CS1 and CS2

Elliot B. Koffman, Department of Computer Science, Temple University, Philadelphia, PA 19122

The task force on CS1 and CS2 of the ACM (Association for Computing Machinery) Curriculum Committee has recommended a course in Discrete Mathematics as a prerequisite for CS2: the second course in programming methods. The task force also recommended that Computer Science students take the Discrete Mathematics course concurrently with CS1. Some relevant discrete mathematics concepts include functions, Boolean algebra and logic, axioms, proof techniques (including induction), sets, positional notation, number bases, and mathematical models. This talk will address the relationship of these concepts to topics in CS1 and CS2.

DISCRETE MATHEMATICS IN THE FIRST TWO YEARS

Martha J. Siegel, Mathematics Department, Towson State University, Towson, MD 21204

There have been some radical changes in the way mathematics departments in the colleges and universities of the United States have been viewing their traditional courses in the first two years. The introduction of courses in discrete mathematics at the elementary level has become a reality. Discrete mathematics is good mathematics. In fact, many in the mathematical community object to the implied dichotomy of discrete vs. continuous mathematics. Such separation is neither real nor helpful. However, pragmatism forces us to write syllabi which will fit gracefully into existing programs. The Mathematical Association of America along with ACM and the American Society for Engineering Education established a panel of mathematicians and computer scientists to address the issue of discrete mathematics in the first two years. This talk will focus on the recommendations of that panel.[1] The course we have proposed is independent of, but at the same level as, the calculus. Its goal is to increase mathematical maturity through problem solving, algorithmic thinking, the nature of proof, and the power of abstract mathematical structures.

[1] Mathematical Association of America, Panel on Discrete Mathematics in the First Two Years: A Preliminary Report, November, 1984.

COMPUTERS IN EDUCATION, K. Duncan and D. Harris (eds.)
Elsevier Science Publishers B.V. (North-Holland)
© IFIP, 1985

PROGRAMMING IN MATHEMATICS EDUCATION:
AN ESSENTIAL COMPONENT IN THE DEVELOPMENT OF REASONING SKILLS

Karen L. Jones and Dr. Charles E. Lamb

Department of Curriculum and Instruction
The University of Texas at Austin
Austin, Texas

A rationale for the utilization of computer technology in mathematics education is presented. The roles of the computer as a teaching tool and aid to instruction are discussed and concerns are addressed.
The heuristic processes of problem solving are examined and descriptions of inductive and deductive reasoning skills relevant to programming exercises are provided.
The paper concludes that incorporation of programming stategies in mathematics instruction is an essential component in the development of reasoning skills.

The impact of computer technology in education is probably greater in the area of mathematics education than in any other discipline. Aside from the obvious uses of the computer as a teaching tool and as an aid to instruction, there exists a responsibility on the part of mathematics teachers to incorporate programming instruction into existing mathematics curricula. Through design, coding, revision and debugging of a computer program, students engage in mental processes which develop deductive reasoning skills and problem solving techniques. The programming experience for students of all levels of ability can be a rewarding educational endeavor and, more importantly, learning computer programming techniques may be a better and more efficient way of developing certain crucial thinking skills.
The need to educate the public cannot be denied. Dr. J. C. R. Licklider of Massachusetts Institute of Technology, in a report to the National Science Foundation, points out that:

Education is not only missing a great opportunity, it is failing to discharge a crucial responsibility. The world is rapidly moving into the "information age". In order to make the transition wisely and well, the public must understand information science and technology. People must master technology or be mastered by it. (Licklider, 1979)

It is the question of 'missing a great opportunity' that the authors of this paper wish to address. If one examines the capabilities of machine technology and considers educational experiences related to and made possible by such technologies, one realizes education is on the threshold of such advances never before possible.

It was with these views in mind that the National Council of Teachers of Mathematics issued An Agenda for Action: Recommendations on School Mathematics For the 1980's. (NCTM, 1980) The publication establishes the suggested modifications of the curriculum for the decade. Throughout the eight recommendations and subtopics, implications of utilizing computer technology are both explicit and implicit.

The third recommendation specifically addresses the role of computers and calculators in the mathematics classroom. It states "Mathematics programs must take full advantage of the power of calculators and computers at all levels." The subtopics of recommendation 3 state that not only must students learn about the role of computers, most students must be prepared to use them by learning to communicate with them.

Although this recommendation supports the use of computers and calculators for computer literacy and computer science courses, computer usage must not be limited to only those topics. It can be shown that the computer, specifically via programming strategies, can be used to facilitate many aspects of the remaining seven recommendations. (Jones, 1983) By examining the recommendations, the effectiveness of computer programming courses as a means of meeting the outlined goals becomes evident.

The first and foremost consideration should be the role of computer programming in addressing the first recommendation which states: "Problem solving must be the focus of school mathematics in the 1980's." By developing problem solving skills, the individual is preparing to deal with day-to-day experiences. In the process of revising the mathematics curriculum, computer programming courses may be considered as a method to facilitate the development of problem solving skills.

In an position paper submitted to Technology in Science Education: The Next Ten Years, John Seely Brown encouraged the use of computers in problem solving:

> Teaching students problem-solving skills has long been a deep concern within the education community. With the advent of computers, the task of constructing and debugging programs has provided an ideal domain for students to develop their problem-solving skills.

It can be shown that programming strategies are exemplary of problem solving heuristics. (Jones, Lamb, Silverman, 1982) In the steps of program development, the programmer must understand the problem, analyze the given data, determine the relevancy of the data and formulate different approaches to the solution. He must then select a feasible approach and formulate an algorithm for the solution. A flowchart is an acceptable outline of the algorithm, as is psuedo-code. After coding and keying-in the program, the execution will determine the success or failure of the algorithm and coding. The process of debugging is in itself heuristic.

The steps in programming coincide with the four steps of heuristic processes generalized by Polya in How to Solve It (1973). Those steps include: 1. understand the problem, the unknown, the data, the conditions, etc. and be able to put the problem into suitable notation; 2. devise a plan (flowcharts and/or psuedo-code are encouraged because they are natural organizers); 3. carry out the plan and 4. examine the results to see if they are reasonable and just. In addition, often after these steps are accomplished the student continues working and changing the program 'just to see what happens'. In this sense students are learning by true discovery methods and are able to internalize processes, thus gaining a more thorough conceptual understanding.

Utilizing algorithms in programming can be viewed from at least two perspectives. The student must have an understanding of a solution type and know where to apply that solution. In this way the student would master a certain solution type and seek similar problems that could utilize that type. In addition, the student must expand his repertoire of solution types or develop a generalized scheme of problem solving heuristics in order to find a solution that is applicable. It is one thing for a student to recognize an application of something that is known to him and proceed with a solution utilizing that which is known. On a higher level, it is another thing for a student to examine a problem, realize the solution is at that point unknown to him and set about discovering a solution. The difference is the ability of the student to induce a formula or algorithm unfamiliar to him as opposed to simply applying a known formula or algorithm.

Polya (1973), in describing the heuristic approach to problem solving, explained the difference between inductive and deductive reasoning:

> Studying the methods of solving problems, we perceive another face of mathematics. Yes, mathematics has two faces; it is the rigorous science of Euclid but it is also something else. Mathematics presented in the Euclidean way appears as a systematic, deductive science; but mathematics in the making appears as an experimental, inductive science. Both aspects are as old as the science of mathematics itself. But the second aspect is new in one respect; mathematics "in statu nascendi," in the process of being invented, has never before been presented in quite this manner to the student, or to the teacher himself, or to the general public.

The uniqueness of the computer as a learning tool is discussed by Arthur Leuhrmann (1979) in a position paper appearing in Technology in Science Education: The Next Ten Years:

> The computer is unique among

information technologies in that it permits intelligent interaction with the learner. All previous information technologies have been one-way paths for distributing facts and ideas. This is true of printed books, audio recordings, and broadcasts of recorded television. The computer alone permits the learner, at his own pace, to interact either with his efforts--to construct a problem--or with a teacher's programmed dialogue. The computer is also unusual in that an individual can learn to use it constructively and creatively as an aid to conceptualizing and solving problems. When a person writes a computer program he is expressing an idea, and when he runs a program he is testing the idea against an expected outcome. Assessment and critical facility are required in testing logic. On a small scale, debugging a computer is similar to intellectual processes used by researchers in any field. Writing for computers has intellectual dimensions in the same sense that writing essays or solving mathematics problems does.

Teachers of mathematics have long heralded courses in geometry for the development of logical reasoning skills. Aspects of computer programming have many of these same attributes. In creating computer programs, one is engaged in deductive reasoning processes. Once a given function, formula, or algorithm is learned, the programmer sees individual uses and applications for it. A repertoire of rules closely akin to geometric theorems is internalized. The programmer learns general rules and discovers specific applications for those rules. More importantly, the programmer must also apply inductive reasoning. Strategies evolve from specific cases. The programmer finds individual instances where certain functions, formulae, and algorithms work. The generalization of their applications can then be tested. Perhaps one of the greatest advantages in programming is to be able to start with a very simplistic algorithm and develop it into a very complex program by expanding its applications. Due to the nature of programming, statements, functions, and subroutines can be added to make programs more specific or more general.

In addition, development of logical sequencing skills is a natural outcome of programming. Because the computer is a machine dependent on the programmer's ability to set the statements and commands in order, the flow of the program reflects that order. If the order is not as the programmer intended, the steps must be reordered. Often the reordering procedure is 'guess and test'; however, the programmer begins to induce the correct order to produce the desired flow.

Teachers of mathematics have also contended that learning geometric concepts and creating logical proofs does in fact develop deductive reasoning skills. The question of development of inductive reasoning skills should also be of concern. This should not be confused with the inductive proof which is a process to prove that if 1) a formula holds true for one specific value and if 2) it can be proved that if it holds for one value then it must hold for the next consecutive value, then it must hold true for all values. True inductive reasoning should involve more than proving formulae. Rarely is one blessed with such a neat problem to solve. Rather life is full of specific problems, the solutions to which lead to generalizations of a global nature. In teaching geometry, the importance of inductive reasoning skills is most often slighted.

This is not to say that geometry is an obsolete course. On the contrary, geometry is a very necessary course which should be augmented by the instruction of programming stategies; however, it must be noted that many students do not have the opportunity to take geometry in secondary school. For these students, the experiences of programming may be the only lessons in logical reasoning skills available to them. At present, mathematics education is overburdened with 'back-to-basics' computational skills. The curricula for remedial or non-college bound mathematics courses have become test oriented with the primary objective of raising standardized test scores. Little task time is available for discovery learning and experimentation. The emphasis on rote computational skills tends to squelch creative thinking skills. With the incorporation of programming into the curriculum, both could be emphasized.

The question has been raised concerning the ability of certain students to program. In the strictest sense, anyone who writes even a simple statement is a programmer in that he has communicated an instruction to the computer. The complexity of the programming is dependent not only on the individual, but also the computer time available, the instruction prior to the task, the assistance during the task and the evaluation procedure once the task is complete. The language chosen is a critical factor for some groups. It would be unwise to expect a ninth grade remedial mathematics student to create a complex FORTRAN or COBOL program; however, it would be reasonable to expect that student to create a LOGO program.

Aside from problems encountered when trying to make computer hardware available for all students of mathematics rather than a select few, the question of how to incorporate programming instruction time into an already comprehensive curriculum arises. By selecting assignments that deal with components of an existing curriculum, one can utilize the computer to teach that component. For instance, when covering the concept of primeness, students can write a program to generate prime numbers. Not only must the student understand the concept, he must be able to communicate the algorithm to the computer. A superficial understanding will not suffice. Students truly comprehend when they are able to verbalize the concept, in this case to a computer.

The use of the computer as a problem solving tool lends itself to the varying abilities of students. The extent to which students are inclined to work is not inhibited by the computer. On the contrary, individuals may delve more deeply into problems that were once too tedious or time consuming to be feasible endeavors in the traditional classroom. They use their time and energy to expand their understanding of mathematical concepts rather than on rote computational tasks. As an example, when introducing statistical concepts such as probability, it is virtually impossible to gather enough data by hand to demonstrate such things as dice rolls or card draws and then pictorially display bell curves, bar graphs, pie graphs, etc. It is a relatively simple process requiring a program of less than fifteen statements to demonstrate one thousand (or any other number) dice rolls and print the bell curve of the results on the screen. Other concepts

such as randomness and integral values can the be explored.

In addition, concepts involving advanced computational skills no longer inhibit students once they have mastered communication with the computer. For example, when covering the concept of graphing linear equations, finding the x-intercept is a relatively easy task. When graphing polynomial equations the task is more complicated, in fact, impossible for the less capable student. It is possible using iteration to determine the x-intercept with an accuracy of, for instance, .000001 and even graph the equation on the computer. In addition, students can explore perturbed equations in this manner. Perhaps a more profound example of using the computer to gain accuracy and provide a better understanding is an investment problem. Consider a man who has two hundred thousand dollars to invest. He can invest in gold mine stock and the chance of a return of ten times his investment is twenty-five percent while the chance of losing the investment is seventy-five percent. If he only invests one hundred thousand dollars at a time, what is the probablity of his making ten million dollars? Using a nested loop, the student can simulate any number of simulated investments and calculate the probability of success, which is not intuitively obvious.

The advantages of computer implementation in mathematics curricula is manifold. As previously stated, programming can incorporate traditional mathematics concepts in a logical structure demanding both deductive and inductive reasoning skills. The heuristic approach to problem solving becomes habitual. Also, concepts which previously were too time consuming or too tedious to cover are now possible through computer programming. The fact that students must communicate their concepts and thus internalize them is of utmost importance.

More importantly, the computer is a natural motivator. Unfortunately, mathematics probably has the dubious honor of being number one on the list of most hated courses in elementary and secondary education. Although Polya (1973) was not addressing computer usage in How To Solve It, he made a point well worth remembering:

Thus the teacher of mathematics has a great opportunity. If he fills

his alloted time with drilling his
students in routine operations he
kills their interest, hampers their
intellectual development, and
misuses his opportunity. But if he
challenges the curiousity of his
students by setting them problems
proportionate to their knowledge,
and helps them to solve their
problems with stimulating
questions, he may give them a taste
for, and some means of, independent
thinking.

REFERENCES:

[1] Brown, John Seely, Fundamental
    research in technology in science
    education, Technology in Science
    Education: The Next Ten Years
    (1979).

[2] Jones, Karen L., Electronic Learning
    Devices and the National Council of
    Teachers of Mathematics Recommen-
    dations for the 1980's, A position
    paper presented to the Third Annual
    Texas Conference on Technology and
    Education, Austin, Texas (1983).

[3] Jones, K., Lamb, C., and Silverman,
    F., Using machine technology to
    enhance problem solving in the
    middle school classroom, Math
    Monograph #7, Mathematics Council
    of The Alberta Teachers'
    Association (1982).

[4] Licklider, J. C. R., Impact of
    information technology on education
    in science and technology, Techno-
    logy in Science Education: The Next
    Ten Years, National Science Founda-
    tion (1979).

[5] Luerhmann, A., Technology and
    science education, Technology in
    Science Education: The Next Ten
    Years, National Science Founda-
    tion (1979).

[6] National Council of Teachers of
    Mathematics, An Agenda for Action:
    Recommendations for School
    Mathematics of the 1980's, Reston,
    Va. (1980).

[7] Polya, G., How to solve it,
    Princeton University Press,
    Princeton, N.J. (1973).

COMPUTERS IN EDUCATION, K. Duncan and D. Harris (eds.)
Elsevier Science Publishers B.V. (North-Holland)
© IFIP, 1985

MICROCOMPUTER DIAGNOSTIC TESTING IN ELEMENTARY MATHEMATICS CLASSROOMS

Robert W. Janke and Peter J. Pilkey

Strongsville City Schools
Strongsville, Ohio U.S.A.

A microcomputer program was developed by the authors to identify student errors in whole number computational problems. Eighty errors could be identified for solutions generated by students. A study was conducted with 376 students to determine whether the microcomputer diagnostic information helped teachers to improve student achievement. The diagnostic information helped teachers to significantly improve student achievement.

1. INTRODUCTION

Diagnosing student errors in mathematics is an imperative (Suydam, 1984) and difficult task for which many teachers are poorly prepared or lack sufficient classroom time to conduct (Sovchik and Heddens, 1978). Microcomputer diagnostic testing has been proposed as a potential tool to help the teacher more effectively manage classroom instruction by allowing the teacher to focus the limited available time upon planning and teaching (Bright, 1984a, Hill, 1983).

However, using microcomputers to diagnose errors in mathematics is limited by the lack of adequate diagnostic programs (Bright, 1984b). Efforts to date have been limited in scope of errors or mathematical operations, not developed for microcomputers, not capable of diagnosing the errors in answers generated by students, and/or lacking sufficient empirical validation of ultimate improvement in student achievement.

Travis (1978,1984) wrote a mainframe program that was able to classify the multiplication errors of community college students into six categories. Students receiving the error information multiplied better than students who did not receive the information. Woerner (1980) also wrote a mainframe program and analyzed the responses of high school students to adding fractions. Errors were classified and the students receiving the error information added fractions as well as those students who were not given the error information. Brown and Burton (1978) developed a mainframe program called BUGGY which replicated the error algorithms used by junior high school students in solving subtraction problems. Barclay (1980) reported that a class of 13 year old students had a favorable reaction to playing BUGGY, but no data were reported about whether student achievement increased because of the use of the program. Signer (1982) developed a microcomputer diagnostic program which only identified the concepts failed rather than the errors made.

The latest National Council of Teachers of Mathematics Yearbook (NCTM, 1984) focused upon the application of microcomputers to mathematics instruction. Several features were described as necessary for an effective diagnostic program of which the most important are as follows: a) comprehensive diagnosis, b) immediate diagnosis, c) diagnosis based upon generative student responses, d) individualized test construction, and e) provision of useful classroom reports which can score tests and group students with similar errors.

The authors developed a microcomputer which meets each of those requirements. The remainder of this paper describes the software capabilities, the results of a classroom validation study, and suggested applications.

2. SOFTWARE CAPABILITIES

Eighty specific algorithmic errors in the whole number computational operations were incorporated into the software. These errors are in the lists of errors published over the last 60 years of which Ashlock (1982), Brueckner (1930), Cox (1974), and Reisman (1978) are representative. The errors identified by the software are approximately 95% of the actual errors made by students (Brueckner, 1930; Cox, 1974). Including specific errors rather than categories of errors as reported by Engelhardt (1977), Janke (1980), and Roberts (1968) was done to maximize the specific diagnostic information available to the teacher.

The specific error made on a problem can be identified within three seconds. If the answer to any problem was consistent with several error algorithms, then each was listed for that student.

Errors were identified from among the great variety of potential answers generated by the students than from a forced multiple-choice selection of an answer. This capability permits the identification of a large number of errors with a few test problems.

The error analysis was given for any test item with any number combinations that the teacher wished to construct subject to the following constraints: three addends each with three digits, four digits in subtraction, three digits in the multiplier and four digits in the multiplicand, and three digits in the divisor and five digits in the dividend with and without a remainder. Many individualized tests could be constructed and administered on the microcomputer to the student or the answers from an entire class on a paper and pencil worksheet could be entered into the microcomputer for diagnosis.

The reports about classroom and student performance given to the teacher included the following information: a) the average test score for every student, b) the class average, c) the number of students passing each test item, d) the specific error made by each student on each test item, and e) the listing of students by the type and frequency of errors made. User prompts were included so that a support staff member could enter the student answers and obtain the reports without the involvement of the teacher.

The important issue with any software is if it contributes to improved student achievement. A study was done to test the hypothesis that the diagnostic classroom reports generated by the software helped teachers to improve student achievement to a greater degree than when teachers were not given the diagnostic error information.

3. METHOD

3.1 Subjects

The sample was 376 students in grades 2-6 in two schools within the same suburban school district. One school was randomly assigned as the experimental group and had 218 students while the other school was assigned as the control group and had 158 students. The regular teacher continued their assignment during the study. The average ability percentile of the experimental and control groups was 69 and 70, respectively, as measured by the Educational Ability Series published by Science Research Associates (SRA).

3.2 Procedure

Each student was tested once every four weeks for a 12 week period and the test results were given to the teacher. Control group teachers were given the student and the class average and the experimental group teachers were given the reports described in the software capabilities section of this paper. No corrective or remedial teaching strategies were given to the teachers. Three forms of an approximate 20 item test were given to each grade level and each measured the whole number computational objec-

tives of the SRA Achievement Series for that grade level. One test was used as both the pretest and the posttest. Students generated their own answers on a worksheet and the answers were entered into the microcomputer by either the authors or a parent volunteer. The pretest average for the experimental group was 86.8% and was 87.2% for the control group. An analysis of covariance with the pretest as the covariate and the posttest as the criterion was used to test the hypothesis.

4. RESULTS

As predicted, there was significantly improved achievement when teachers were given the diagnostic classroom compared to the control group, F (1,373) = 5.253, $p < .05$. The posttest average of the experimental and control groups were 93.2% and 91.1%, respectively. The difference between the average of the experimental group and the average of the control group increased after each testing and were -.4, 1.1, 1.4, and 2.1 percent. The difference between the groups in improved achievement was greatest in grades 2-4 where the pretest-posttest score of the experimental group was 84.3% to 95.2% and of the control group was 87.7% to 93.3%.

5. DISCUSSION

Microcomputer diagnosis of errors does help teachers to improve student achievement. The teachers suggested several reasons for such a result. First, the diagnosis was specific so that the teachers felt that they could understand the incorrect algorithm used by the student. Second, the comprehensiveness of the error identification was greater than the teacher could perform. Third, the option of having support personnel or students enter the answers removed the burden of diagnosis from the teacher and allowed the teacher to concentrate upon planning and teaching. Fourth, the diagnostic classroom reports helped the teacher to more effectively group students for remedial instruction.

Empirical information about which teaching methods will correct which errors has remained as elusive as Cox (1975) reported. The teachers did judge a general teaching strategy to be most effective in correcting the errors. The method was to describe and demonstrate the error to either the individual student or to a group of students making the same error. The teachers felt that the specificity and the comprehensiveness of the diagnosis gave them a unique chance to understand the student's error and to explain to the student why the answer was an error. Physical manipulatives were not judged to be as effective as a verbal or a cognitive explanation. Much research needs to be done to discover the best remedial instructional strategy for each error.

The high pretest average seemed to reduce the potential for showing even larger posttest differences between the groups. Students who were below the average showed the largest gains, but the potential range for improvement for even these students was limited. A more difficult test may have given a greater opportunity for showing larger differences between the groups in posttest achievement. The diagnostic error information does appear to have particular use for below average students who may need remedial mathematics instruction.

The larger differences observed between the groups in the early grades suggest that the diagnostic error information may be most useful when students are in the initial stages of learning a mathematical operation. The error diagnosis may help the learner to modify their solution strategies before the error becomes deeply ingrained. Conclusions about the particular effectiveness of the error information for the early grades is confounded by the classroom teacher variable in the study.

The software used in this study appears to have several applications. First, the classroom diagnostic reports give the teacher valuable information to individualize instruction. Second, the individualized testing and report options can provide the student with unlimited practice and instant feedback of the errors made which can be particulary useful in a tutorial situation where the tutor can provide an immediate description and explanation of the error to the student. Third, the teacher may wish to generate a list of potential errors to textbook or workbook problems and use the list of errors to diagnose errors at the student's desk while the problems are being solved.

The software used in this study can be used on the Apple II series and also on the TRS-80 Model III and Model IV. A user notebook has been made with directions, descriptions and illustrations of the errors, and samples of all reports. The software is now being distributed by the Scholastic, Inc. A more comprehensive analysis of the data was not possible within the time limitations given for submission of this paper. An expanded analysis is being conducted and will be reported at a later date.

Please contact the principal author at the following address for further information:

Robert W. Janke
17959 North Inlet Drive
Strongsville, Ohio 44136
U.S.A.

6. REFERENCES

(1) Ashlock, R.B., Error patterns in computation (Merrill, Columbus, Ohio, 1982).

(2) Barclay, T., Buggy, Mathematics Teaching.92 (1980) 10-12.

(3) Bright, G.W., Real-time diagnosis of computation errors in CAI, in Cheek,H.N.(ed.), Diagnostic and prescriptive mathematics issues, ideas, and insights (Research Council for Diagnostic and Prescriptive Mathematics, Kent, Ohio, 1984a).

(4) Bright, G.W.,Computer diagnosis of errors, School Science and Mathematics 84 (1984b) 208-219.

(5) Brown, J.S. and Burton, R.R.,Diagnostic models for procedural bugs in basic mathematical skills, Cognitive Science 2 (1978) 155-192.

(6) Brueckner, L.J. Diagnostic and remedial teaching in arithmetic (Winston, Philadelphia, 1930).

(7) Cox, L.S., Analysis, classification, and frequency of systematic error computational patterns in the addition, subtraction, multiplication, and division vertical algorithms for grades 2-6 and special education classes, (University of Kansas, Kansas City, 1974).

(8) Cox, L.S. Diagnosing and remediating systematic errors in addition and subtraction computations, The Arithmetic Teacher, 22 (1975) 151-157.

(9) Engelhardt, J.M. Analysis of children's computational errors: a qualitative approach, British Journal of Educational Psychology 47 (1977) 149-154.

(10) Hill, S.A. The microcomputer in the instructional program, The Arithmetic Teacher 30 (1983) 14-15: 54-55.

(11) Janke, R.W. Computational errors of mentally retarded students, Psychology in the Schools 17 (1980) 30-32.

(12) National Council of Teachers of Mathematics. Computers in mathematics in education (National Council of Teachers of Mathematics, Reston, Virginia, 1984).

(13) Reisman, F.K. A guide to the diagnostic teaching of arithmetic (Merrill, Columbus, Ohio, 1978).

(14) Roberts, G.H. The failure strategies of third grade arithmetic pupils, The Arithmetic Teacher 15 (1968) 442-446.

(15) Signer, B. Math doctor, M.D.--microcomputer adapative diagnosis, The Computing Teacher 10 (1982) 17-20.

(16) Sovchik, R. and Heddens, J.W. Classroom diagnosis and remediation, The Arithmetic Teacher 25 (1978) 47-49.

(17) Suydam, M.N. What research says: helping low-achieving students in mathematics, School Science and Mathematics 84 (1984) 437-439.

(18) Travis, B.P. The diagnosis and remediation
     of learning difficulties of community
     college students developmental mathematics
     students using computer technology, Disser-
     tation Abstracts International 39 (1978)
     2115A.
(19) Travis, B.P. Computer diagnosis of algo-
     rithmic errors, in Hansen,V.P.(ed.), Com-
     puters in mathematics education (National
     Council of Teachers of Mathematics, Reston,
     Virginia, 1984).
(20) Woerner,K.L. Computer based diagnosis and
     remediation of computational errors with
     fractions, Dissertation Abstracts Inter-
     national 41 (1980) 1455A.

COMPUTERS IN EDUCATION, K. Duncan and D. Harris (eds.)
Elsevier Science Publishers B.V. (North-Holland)
© IFIP, 1985

AN EXPERIMENT IN INTERACTIVE COMPUTERIZED TEACHING OF A TOPIC FROM ADVANCED CALCULUS

Bev Marshman

Department of Applied Mathematics
University of Waterloo
Waterloo, Ontario
Canada N2L 3G1

An experiment is discussed in which part of a second year calculus class was taught the concept of uniform convergence of a sequence of functions by an interactive computer model, while the remainder was taught in traditional lecture mode. An outline of the teaching techniques used in the module is followed by a comparison of the performances of the two groups on a pre-test, post-test, mid-term, and final examination. Finally, an attempt is made to evaluate the significance of any differences in performance, and the assets and liabilities of computer-aided teaching for this type of material in general.

1. INTRODUCTION

During the period from January 1975 to April 1978, the University of Waterloo and International Business Machines jointly conducted an experimental project called COMIT (Computerized Multi-Media Instructional Television). As part of this project, the calculus module discussed herein was developed by the author, ably assisted by L.J. Makela, then a graduate student in the Department of Computer Science, who took charge of the programming.

Our principal aims were twofold. First, we wanted to see if the graphics capabilities and interactive nature of the COMIT facilities[1] could be used effectively to convey as complex a mathematical concept as uniform convergence to second-year calculus students. Secondly, we wanted to compare the performances of the students who learned through CAI (computer-assisted instruction) with that of the rest of the students on tests for both short-term and long-term retention of the material, to see if there were any statistically significant differences.

2. DEVELOPMENT OF THE MODULE

The subject material of the module, uniform convergence of a sequence of functions, was chosen for a variety of reasons: it is most easily interpreted geometrically, and would thus utilize the graphics capabilities available; it is a concept which frequently gives students difficulty, and hence, we hoped, would truly test the system as a teaching device; finally, it is about the right length for an experimental module, being equivalent to about two one-hour lectures.

The first stage in our approach to the development of this CAI course segment was to establish three sets of objectives:

(i) entering objectives, which define what the student needs to know <u>before</u> starting,

(ii) intermediate, or enabling objectives, which define what the student should be able to do at the end of each of several steps in the lesson, and

(iii) terminal objectives, which define what the student should be able to do at the end of the module.

---

[1] Specifically, these were: terminals consisting of a standard Sony colour television receiver and an IBM 3270 Keyboard (or an acoustic pen, which we did not use), an IBM System 7 computer linked to the University of Waterloo IBM 370/158, and various software packages (such as graphics) developed by IBM specifically to assist in course ware development.

Thus the topic was organized into a
hierarchy of distinct steps, each building on
the previous ones, leading ultimately to the
'terminal objectives'. Figure 1 illustrates
the basic structure of the module as a flow
chart through the various objectives.

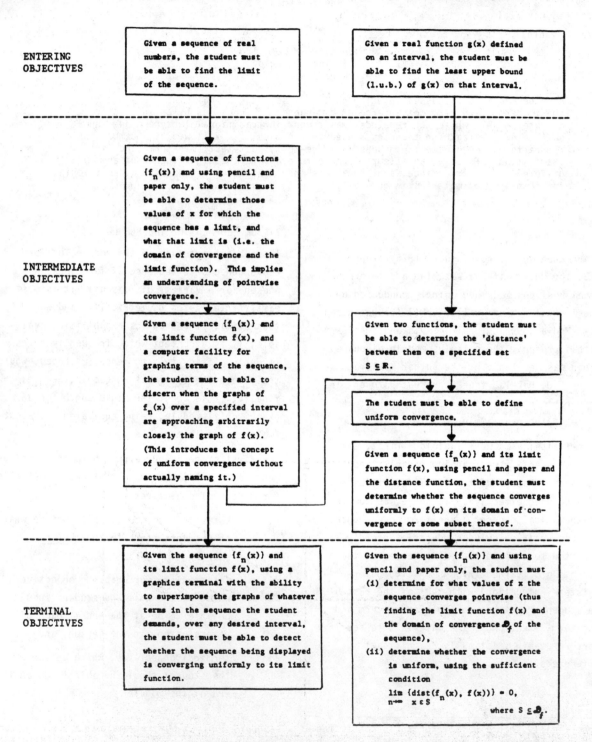

Figure 1

Once this structure was established, each step was further dissected, and the actual content of the module - text, examples, illustrations, quizzes - was designed. This was followed by several months of coding, testing, and debugging until the module was finally ready for student use.

A discussion of uniform convergence of a sequence $f_n(x)$ of functions involves several non-trivial mathematical concepts: convergence of a sequence of reals, convergence of a function set $f_n(x)$ at a specific $x = x_0$, a measure of 'distance' between two functions over an interval, and finally, convergence of a set of graphs to a fixed graph over an interval. It is certainly not our intent here to 'teach' these ideas; however, a brief look at how some of them were treated in the module will serve to illustrate our techniques. (Anyone not interested in the actual content of the module can safely ignore the balance of this section; it is not essential to the remainder.)

Our first task was to establish the nature of point-wise convergence of a sequence of functions. Consider, for example, an old favourite, $f_n(x) = x^n$, $n = 1, 2, 3, \ldots$ In the module, the student was initially allowed to simply plot any term(s) of the sequence (for example, $f_3(x) = x^3$), on any desired interval of x-values. Thus if terms $n = 1, 2, 3, 4, \ldots, 12$ on the interval $[-1.1, 1.1]$ were requested in turn, the screen would ultimately contain (in the appropriate window) the set of graphs shown in Figure 2, with the latest choice highlighted in white, and the previous ones dimmed to pale green. Then, to convey the idea of a point-wise limit, the student was invited to <u>fix</u> $x = x_0$, and the values $f_n(x_0)$ were displayed as a vertical row of dots. If, for example, the points $x_0 = -1$, $x_0 = -1/2$, $x_0 = 1/2$ were successively picked, the final graph would show up as in Figure 3; the oscillatory behaviour of $(-1)^n$ is depicted by the two dots at $(-1,1)$ and $(-1,1)$, while the convergence of $(-\frac{1}{2})^n$ and $(\frac{1}{2})^n$ to zero is clearly seen as the dots for those x-values approach the x-axis.

Once the concept of pointwise convergence had been presented, the student was allowed to 'play' with several other examples of sequences, using the graphics capabilities of the system to assist in finding the set $\mathscr{D}_f$ of x's for which the sequence coverged, and

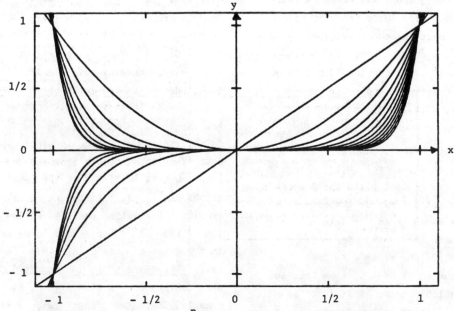

Figure 2: The graphs of x^n for $n = 1, 2, 3, \ldots, 12$ are shown.

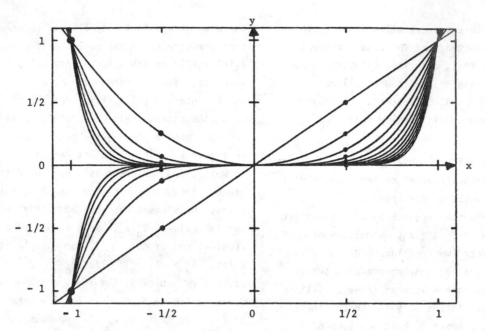

Figure 3:   The behaviour of the sequence x_o^n for $x_o = -1, -1/2$, and $+1/2$
is indicated by corresponding sequences of dots in a vertical
line through each of these values.

hence to what limit function $f(x)$, which is just $f(x) = \lim_{n \to \infty} f_n(x)$ for $x \in \mathcal{D}_f$. Then the notion of 'distance' between $f_n(x)$ and $f(x)$ was introduced, and lastly, the concept of uniform convergence, by inviting the student to determine whether the graphs of $f_n(x)$ approach the graph of $f(x)$ across a given interval, i.e. the least upper bound of the distance function approaches zero. Throughout this progression, the students' grasp of the material was constantly monitored by a variety of questions (including some multiple choice), with immediate feedback on the proper reasoning when errors were made.

Consider, for example, the sequence of functions $nx/(1 + n^2x^2)$ on the interval $[0,1]$. The student would first request plots for several different n's to get a feel for the general behaviour of the sequence on the interval. Figure 4 a) illustrates $f_n(x)$ for $n = 1,2,3,4,5,10,30,100$, along with the specific behaviour at $x_o = 1/4$, $x_o = 1/2$, and $x_o = 3/4$. To establish the limit function $f(x) = 0$ on $[0,1]$, some work with pencil and

paper would likely also be necessary, since this sequence is not monotone, and it is not immediately obvious that $\lim_{n \to \infty} f_n(x) = 0$ for values of x near $x = 0$. The 'distance' between $f_n(x)$ and $f(x)$ could then be requested for any value of n; this was displayed graphically by vertical lines whose lengths are just $|f_n(x) - f(x)|$ at each x, as shown in Figure 4) for $n = 30$, with $f(x) = 0$. In this case, a few such illustrations were generally sufficient to convince the student that the least upper bound of these distances on $[0,1]$ is always .5, no matter how large n, thus violating the formal definition of uniform convergence, which demands that this bound approach zero. To show how this is linked to the behaviour of the graphs of $f_n(x)$, the student was asked to examine the limiting position of the graphs of the $f_n(x)$ as n gets very large as opposed to the graph of $f(x)$, the limit function itself. These are shown in Figures 4 c) and 4 d); when convergence is non-uniform, as in this example, these two graphs always differ.

The brief outline above hopefully gives the flavour of what we attempted to do in the module. Anyone interested in the details of the program will find complete information in [1].

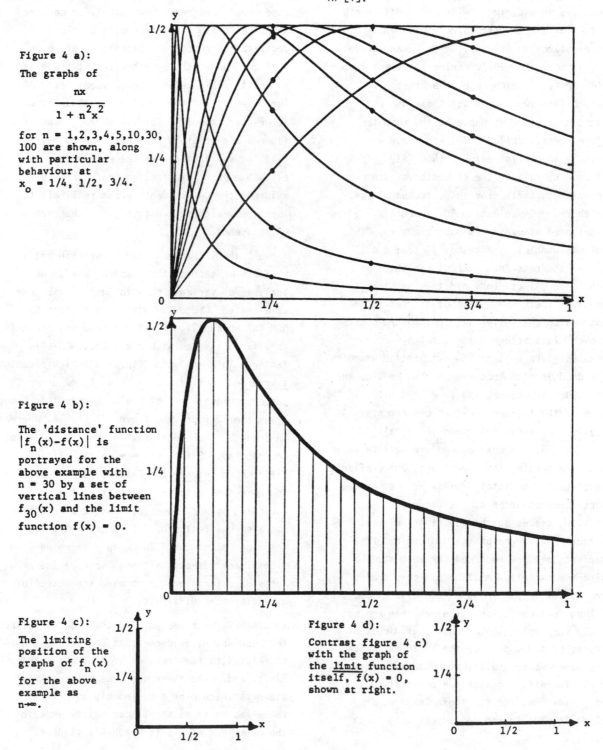

Figure 4 a):
The graphs of
$$\frac{nx}{1 + n^2x^2}$$
for n = 1,2,3,4,5,10,30, 100 are shown, along with particular behaviour at x_o = 1/4, 1/2, 3/4.

Figure 4 b):
The 'distance' function $|f_n(x)-f(x)|$ is portrayed for the above example with n = 30 by a set of vertical lines between $f_{30}(x)$ and the limit function f(x) = 0.

Figure 4 c):
The limiting position of the graphs of $f_n(x)$ for the above example as n→∞.

Figure 4 d):
Contrast figure 4 c) with the graph of the <u>limit</u> function itself, f(x) = 0, shown at right.

3. STRUCTURE OF THE EXPERIMENT AND
STATISTICAL ANALYSIS

Once the module was functioning reliably, we
conducted an experiment with three different
classes of second year calculus students
(herein labelled Group 1, Group 2, and Group
3) in the winter 1977, spring 1977, and winter
1978 terms. In each case, the class was
divided into two segments: those who would be
taught uniform convergence by the computer
module (herein called CAI), and those who
would be taught in lectures (NON-CAI). This
was done by ranking the students in each class
according to their previous calculus grades,
and then simply selecting 10 students
distributed as evenly as possible across this
ranking; with class sizes of 30, 32, and 27,
the CAI students formed about one-third of
each. The CAI students did the computer
module on their own time, but did not attend
lectures on that material; the NON-CAI portion
of each class attended identical two-hour
lectures given by the author. Similar examples
were used in both lectures and the module, and
all students received the same hand-out
notes on the topic of uniform convergence. As
a measure of their prior knowledge, all
students wrote an unannounced pre-test in the
lecture preceding the experiment, and similarly,
a post-test immediately following, to measure
short-term retention of the material. In
addition, grades on the questions relevant to
uniform convergence on the midterm and final
examinations were recorded for each student
(with the exception that no mid-term grades
were available for Group 2) to serve as measures
of long term retention, although they are not
likely very reliable indicators of direct
effects of the module or the lectures, since
many other factors will have come into play by
then. These four grades, on pre-test, post-
test, mid-term, and final examination, are
called T1, T2, T3 and T4 respectively in this
analysis.

Table 1 illustrates the performance of CAI
and NON-CAI students on the pre-test and post-
test, the measures local (in time) to the
experiment, and hence most likely to measure
direct effects. The figures in brackets
indicate the number of students expected in
that cell under the hypothesis that there is
no relationship between the student being CAI
(or NON-CAI) and the fraction of students with
T2 greater than T1. For all three groups, the
figures are consistent with this hypothesis;
that is, any differences are well within the
allowable error, indicating that there is no
evidence the CAI students are more likely to
improve over their pre-test grade than are NON-
CAI students.

Table 2 shows the mean grades for each set of
students on each of the measures used. An
analysis of variance on - ℓn (grade) was done
as a nested factorial with main factors CAI,
NON-CAI versus T1, T2, T3, T4, and the students
as a factor nested within the CAI, NON-CAI
factor. This analysis displayed a significant
time effect only, in both Group 1 and Group 3;
the predominant part of the time effect in Group
1 was the T3 improvement over T1 and T2, whereas
in Group 3, the sudden fall from T3 to T4 also
contributed. But there were no significant
differences between the CAI and NON-CAI sets
in their time patterns, indicating that,
according to our evidence, long-term retention
was also unaffected by CAI versus NON-CAI
teaching techniques. In Group 2 there were no
significant effects, although some of the error
terms were large enough to make the detection
of differences difficult.

In summary: our analysis of the data we collected , showed no evidence that CAI versus NON-CAI
is related to the fraction of students with
T2>T1, and while there was some evidence that
students learn over time (no big surprise!)
there was again no significant difference in
the behaviour of CAI from NON-CAI students in
this resepect.

Type of Student	GROUP 1			GROUP 2			GROUP 3		
	Number with T2>T1	Number with T2≤T1	Totals	Number with T2>T1	Number with T2≤T1	Totals	Number with T2>T1	Number with T2≤T1	Totals
CAI	7 (6.7)	3 (3.3)	10	6 (5)	4 (5)	10	7 (6.7)	3 (3.3)	10
NON-CAI	7 (10.3)	13 (9.7)	20	10 (11)	12 (11)	22	11 (11.3)	6 (5.7)	17
TOTALS	14	16	30	16	16	32	18	9	27

Table 1:   Comparison of CAI versus NON-CAI student performance on pre-test and post-test. No statistically significant effects of CAI were found.

	MEANS FOR GROUP 1				MEANS FOR GROUP 2			MEANS FOR GROUP 3			
	T1	T2	T3	T4	T1	T2	T4	T1	T2	T3	T4
CAI	.729	.821	.821	.780	.494	.594	.630	.538	.713	.787	.480
NON-CAI	.607	.655	.869	.663	.632	.639	.564	.479	.686	.719	.414

Table 2:   Comparison of mean scores for CAI and NON-CAI students on pre-test (T1), post-test (T2), mid-term (T3) and final examination (T4). Significant <u>time</u> patterns exist for groups 1 and 3, but they are the same for both CAI and NON-CAI students, again indicating no significant differences between CAI and NON-CAI. Group 2 showed no significant patterns of any sort.

4. DISCUSSIONS AND CONCLUSIONS

Our primary aim, that of testing the capabilities of CAI as a teaching device for mathematical material, was fully achieved, and with great success. Aside from some complaints about the response time of the computer, over which we had no control, student reaction to the module was very favourable. The following is a selection of typical quotes from the written comments handed in on completion of the module.

"I feel that seeing the graphs and being able to experiment with various n's and x's greatly helped me understand the concept of uniform convergence .... Another advantage of this teaching method is that it requires active participation of the student, where in a class, full attention is not always given."

"...I was forced to respond to questions all the time and thus take part in what was going on...."

"The graphical aspect certainly added to the comprehension....."

"Being able to go at your own pace and having things repeated when you didn't catch a concept was helpful. The use of examples with immediate feedback and explanations of how to do the questions was good also."

"The advantage was that I had to be on the alert all the time and thus I learned more about the topic. In class I normally feel sleepy somtimes.....The idea of asking questions after each section was a good one. It tested the student's ability to retain the work."

The principal advantages of an interactive medium are the ability of the teacher to monitor and control the student's progress (right answers lead to the next stage of development, wrong answers lead to explanations, review, and further examples), and reciprocally, the ability of the student to control the presentation of material (parameters can be varied, more examples done, review or further explanation requested). Active participation is constantly demanded of the student. In addition, for mathematical topics, the graphics capabilities of CAI are a strong enhancement. It is interesting to note that nearly all these positive aspects are mentioned in the above comments.

Some of the students thought even more examples should have been included; some would have preferred two one-hour sessions rather than one two-hour, as their attention flagged towards the end. It should also be pointed out that the novelty of the situation probably contributed somewhat to their enthusiasm. It is the feeling of the author, however, that the immediacy of the participation and feedback is a truly valuable asset of computer-aided instruction; one does not ever learn much in mathematics by listening to someone <u>talk</u> about something; one learns by trying things out, making errors, correcting for them, and trying again. It is in this aspect that an interactive system excels.

Regarding our second aim, that of comparing the performances of CAI versus NON-CAI students, the statistical results speak for themselves: any differences are well within allowable error. The post-test grades, which are certainly the measures most closely related to the material presented in the module, were obtained on a ten-minute quiz, and it could be questioned whether such a quiz could test anything in depth. Nevertheless, it was designed to test whether their knowledge was at a level acceptable for that topic in that particular course, and as such represents as extensive a direct performance test as would ever be required. It is worth noting that, as regards T3 and T4, the probable reason for T3 being the highest score is that uniform convergence comprises about one-third of the material on that particular mid-term, hence merits much studying at that time, whereas it is only worth 10-15% of the final examination, and is often given short shrift in favour of the

remainder of the course material. Overall then, we conclude that using CAI did not produce significantly better performance (at least as we measure it) by the CAI students over the NON-CAI students. Whether that means they did or did not understand the concepts more fully is quite another question!

ACKNOWLEDGEMENTS

I wish to thank G. W. Bennett for assistance with the statistical analysis of results, L. J. Makela for programming the module and for valuable feedback on the method of presentation throughout, and the students themselves for their co-operation and enthusiasm.

REFERENCES

[1] Makela, L. J., "CAI on COMIT: The Development and Implementation of a Computer-Assisted-Instruction Course Segment for Use with Math 230B", master's thesis, Department of Computer Science, University of Waterloo, November 1977.

COMPUTERS IN EDUCATION, K. Duncan and D. Harris (eds.)
Elsevier Science Publishers B.V. (North-Holland)
© IFIP, 1985

L.E.G.O. — AN INTERACTIVE COMPUTER GRAPHICS SYSTEM FOR TEACHING GEOMETRY

Norma Fuller, Przemyslaw Prusinkiewicz, Gerard Rambally

Department of Computer Science
University of Regina
Regina, Sask., Canada S4S 0A2

L.E.G.O. (LISP-based Euclidean Geometry Operations) is an interactive graphics system for creating, manipulating and viewing two- and three-dimensional figures. Figures are objects of the language. They can be referred to by names, passed as arguments to functions and result from function calls. This is consistent with the Euclidean approach to geometry and contrasts L.E.G.O. to systems based on the Cartesian approach. L.E.G.O. is particularly useful when teaching or studying areas difficult to grasp without good visual aid; for instance, geometry in three dimensions or recursive concepts in geometry.

INTRODUCTION

In the classroom, certain simple two-dimensional illustrations can often be sketched with sufficient precision for student understanding. However, it is difficult for even the most talented instructor to sketch three-dimensional objects and complex two-dimensional figures in real time, using a chalkboard or transparencies, with enough precision to enhance the learning process. The students' understanding must therefore evolve totally from abstract symbolism without an adequate visual model.

Many studies have been conducted to supplement the teaching of mathematics using interactive computer graphics. Statistics was one of the first fields in which interactive graphics packages were utilized to supplement the teaching process [7, 17]. Most of the research, however, focused on the development of graphics packages which allowed students to manipulate mathematical functions. Utilization of these packages ranged from high school mathematics [6] to first year courses in calculus [2, 4, 13] to advanced mathematics classes in Fourier series and differential equations [3, 11, 12].

The LOGO project [9] was first presented as a conceptual framework for teaching mathematics. The concept of *turtle geometry* introduced in LOGO can be thought of as an instrument for studying geometry [1]. However, this approach demands considerable programming competence to generate complex figures.

This paper describes a system called L.E.G.O. (Lisp-based Euclidean Geometry Operations) which is a tool for creating complex geometric figures in real time, in order to reinforce concepts taught. L.E.G.O. is characterized by the following features:

- Geometric figures are objects of the language. They can be referred to by names, and used as arguments or obtained as results of functions. This approach is diametrically opposite to the previous approaches in which a user basically manipulates equations, and geometric figures are but visual representations of these equations. L.E.G.O. follows the Euclidean approach to geometry, as opposed to the Cartesian approach found in other systems.

- Functions are defined interactively *by examples*. Before starting a geometric construction it is possible to specify particular figures (points, lines, etc.) as parameters. When the construction is finished, it can be recalled using a different set of parameters.

- Function calls can be nested, allowing the user to easily define recursive geometric objects, such as Peano curves [8].

- Three-dimensional objects can be defined, manipulated and viewed.

As a consequence of the above features, definition of complex geometric constructions or objects in L.E.G.O. requires little or no programming experience.

THE L.E.G.O. SYSTEM

From the viewpoint of language design, L.E.G.O. is an extension of LISP. At the present time, L.E.G.O. is written in Franz Lisp [5, 18] running under Berkeley Unix 4.2 on the Vax 730. An alphanumeric terminal and a high-resolution vector graphics monitor are used for man-machine communication. This configuration was chosen as the most convenient for developing the concept of the system. Transportation of L.E.G.O. to microcomputers is foreseen.

L.E.G.O. introduces four data types with geometric interpretation: points, lines, circles and planes. Variables of the geometric types are stored in a symbol table maintained by L.E.G.O. and independent from the LISP symbol table. A number of functions referring to variables of the geometric types, and patterned on the primitive operations of Euclidean geometry, are predefined.

In the two-dimensional case the following functions are available:

(**point** *x_coordinate y_coordinate*)

    - creates a point given coordinates;

(**line** *point_name point_name*)

    - creates a line given two points;

(**circle** *point_name line_name*)

    - creates a circle given its center and radius;

(**intersection** *name name*)

    - creates the point or points of intersection between two lines, a line and a circle, or two circles.

When a geometric function is called, it displays the corresponding figure on the graphics screen and asks for its name on the alphanumeric screen. After the name has been typed in, it is displayed near the figure. More than one object can be named as the result of a single function call; for instance, two points of intersection between a circle and a line. These names can be subsequently used in the program, when referring to the objects they denote.

Example 1. Usage of predefined geometric functions, interaction with the system and the form of the graphic output are illustrated in figure 1. The problem being solved is to bisect a line *L* defined by points *A* and *B* with a line *P* perpendicular to *L*. ~

A geometric construction can be defined as a function by using function definition functions: **define_function** and **end_function**. In this case it is usually preferable not to display construction lines and irrelevant names, when the function is called. Visibility of figures and names is controlled by functions: **visible, invisible, named** and **unnamed.**

Example 2. In order to specify the construction from the previous example as a function, the following statements would be used:

(**define_function** *bisect A B*)

    .
    .
    .

(**end_function**)

These statements should be entered at points α and ω of the man-machine dialogue shown in figure 1.

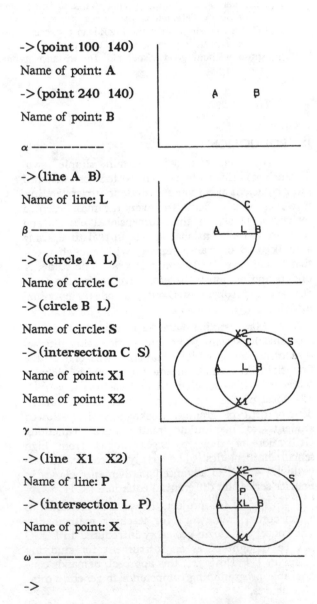

Figure. 1 Bisecting a line in L.E.G.O.: Interaction with the system and samples of the construction in progress.

In order to make the construction lines and their names invisible, the statements

    (invisible)
       .
       .
       .
    (visible)

should be entered at points β and γ. A call to the function defined in this way is illustrated in figure 2.

->(point 125 100)

Name of point: P

->(point 300 200)

Name of point: Q

->(bisect P Q)

Name of line: M

Name of line: N

Name of point: T

->

Figure. 2 Example of a function call.

    Both predefined and user-defined functions can be used in subsequent function definitions. For instance, the **bisect** function can be used in a construction of the circumcenter and the circumcircle of a triangle. Thus, complex geometric constructions can be described using hierarchies of subconstructions, rather than in terms of primitive geometric operations.

    L.E.G.O. allows for recursive calling of functions.

Example 3. The left side of figure 3 presents the recursive definition of the Sierpiński gasket [8, 14]. Function **midpoint** used in the definiton of the gasket is similar to the function **bisect** from example 2; however, the perpendicular bisecting line is made invisible. **Distance** is a predefined geometric function returning the distance between two points. Construction of the gasket in progress is shown on the right side of figure 3.

    L.E.G.O. also provides the ability to define and manipulate three-dimensional objects, and to display their projections. For this purpose the following predefined three-dimensional functions are available:

(**point_3** *x_coordinate y_coordinate*
                  z_coordinate)

    - creates a three-dimensional point given its coordinates;

(**ppp_plane** *point_name point_name*
                 point_name)

(**pl_plane** *point_name line_name*)

(**ll_plane** *line_name line_name*)

    - these functions create a plane defined by three points, a point and a line, or two lines respectively;

->(point 200 200)

Name of point: A

->(point 800 200)

Name of point: B

->(point 500 700)

Name of point: C

->(define_function gasket A B C)

* (unnamed)

* (midpoint A B)

Name of point: C1

* (midpoint B C)

Name of point: A1

* (midpoint C A)

Name of point: B1

* (cond ((>(distance A C1) 25)

    (gasket A C1 B1)

    (gasket C1 B A1)

    (gasket B1 A1 C)

    ))

* (end_function)

->

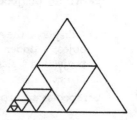

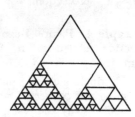

Figure. 3 Creating the Sierpiński gasket in L.E.G.O. Note the changes of prompt (* replaces ->) when in the "**define_function**" mode.

(**current_plane** *plane_name*)

> - specifies the plane in which a two-dimensional construction will be subsequently carried on. Use of the **current_plane** function is essential when creating circles on planes other than the default Oxy.

Functions **line** and **intersection** can be directly used in three-dimensional constructions. Notice that the three-dimensional intersection may create not only points but also lines (resulting from the intersection of two planes).

Projections of three-dimensional objects onto the surface of the screen can be accomplished using functions:

(**parallel_projection** *plane_name*
>   *line_name*)

> - displays the parallel projection of the object under construction given a projection plane and a direction of projection.

(**perspective_projection** *plane_name*
>   *point_name*)

> - displays the perspective projection of a three-dimensional object, given a projection plane and a center of projection.

Example 4. Figure 4 shows three views of a construction related to the following problem taken from [16].

> "Midpoints of six pairwise skew edges of a cube are connected with line segments in such a way that each line lies on a face of the cube. Describe the polygon formed by these line segments."

The construction is illustrated in figure 4a. Figure 4b suggests that the polygon under consideration is planar. Figure 4c suggests that it is a regular hexagon. Notice that L.E.G.O. has made it possible to quickly formulate a hypothesis, which otherwise might be difficult to find.

ADVANTAGES OF THE L.E.G.O. SYSTEM

Learning theories suggest that education should expose students to various cognitive styles of learning. The more modes of communication used in the classroom, the greater the students' chances of success with the material.

Geometry is a discipline in which the visualization process is extremely important. Mathemat-

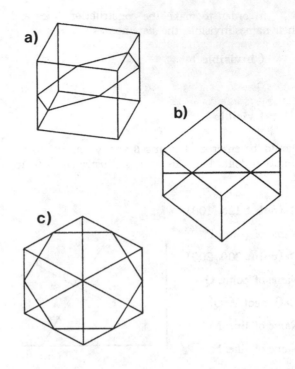

Figure. 4 Viewing a three-dimensional object in L.E.G.O. Different views help in the formulation of a hypothesis.

ics educators such as Polya [10] and Steinhaus [15] have consistently advocated the drawing of figures and the building of physical models to aid the problem solving process. It is needless to mention the tedium and difficulty involved in building three-dimensional models. Such tedium and difficulty is absent when using L.E.G.O. Students and teachers can easily construct *complex figures* in *two or three dimensions*, as illustrated in the previous section. Due to the *speed and accuracy* of computer calculations, exact drawings can be obtained almost instantly. This is in contrast to the slow and very approximate drawings made at the chalkboard and sometimes found in textbooks.

Geometry is a deductive science, starting with primitives and using them to specify axioms and to prove theorems in a bottom-up manner. L.E.G.O. reinforces this *structured approach to problem solving* by allowing users to build and store functions for later use in the development of more complex constructions. Compounded with this advantage is the opportunity for different users to build unique sets of functions, making the system highly *flexible*.

Interactivity is one of the most important features of the system. Students can experiment with geometric constructions and study them under a variety of conditions. This feature can be used to view a three-dimensional object from different points, or to repeat a construction with modified data. A student can ask "what if..." type questions, and get an immediate visual response. This helps in the *formulation of hypotheses* (c.f. Example 4), and in the investigating of the *domain of discourse* of a construction. (For example, the construction of a triangle given one edge and two adjacent angles will fail if the sum of the angles exceeds 180 degrees.)

Yet another advantage of L.E.G.O. deals with time. Diagrams do not have to appear instantaneously as in textbooks, but can gradually develop in a step-by-step mode, allowing for the simultaneous explanation of the underlying constructions. This *temporal aspect of constructions*, combined with the *simplicity of the recursive definitions*, makes L.E.G.O. a very powerful, instructive and enjoyable tool for studying recursive concepts in geometry (c.f. Example 3). Notice that these concepts are usually difficult to grasp without good visual aid.

Diagrams in books often have many details which distract students and make it difficult to identify the essential elements. L.E.G.O. allows the instructor to include as many details as necessary in a particular construction, and to select the *relevant visual information* to be displayed.

CONCLUSION

Few instructors can accurately sketch complex geometric objects in real time on the chalkboard. While textbooks normally provide adequate two-dimensional illustrations, few books supply precise, accurate and easy to understand presentations of three-dimensional objects. Students must therefore rely mainly on verbal communication and symbol manipulation, with insufficient visual models. It is quite likely that many students who are "failures" in the current education system could be successful if better visual reinforcements were used in the learning process.

The purpose of L.E.G.O. is to facilitate the manipulation and visual presentation of geometric constructions and objects. Pilot tests indicate that these goals are met, and that the system is very powerful, simple to use (despite the LISP syntax) and attractive. However, large-scale implementation and "field testing" have yet to be done.

ACKNOWLEDGMENT

This research was supported in part by a grant from the Natural Sciences and Engineering Research Council of Canada.

REFERENCES

[1] Abelson, H. and diSessa, A., *Turtle Geometry: the computer as a medium for explaining mathematics* (MIT Press. Cambridge, 1980).

[2] Abraham, R. et al., Visual Math: a fantasy for the future of education, *SIGCUE Bulletin* 14 No. 1 (1980) 2-10.

[3] Barnes, B.H. and Stocker, F.R., Computer generated aids to teaching geometric concepts, *Creative Computing* 2 No. 6 (1976) 66-71.

[4] Chastenet de Gery, J. and Hocquenghem, S., Collective use of a microcomputer with graphics to illustrate the mathematics lesson, in Lewis, R. and Togg, E.D. (eds.), *Computers in Education, Part 1* (North-Holland, Amsterdam, 1981).

[5] Foderaro, J., *The Franz LISP Manual* (University of California, Berkeley, 1979).

[6] Forcheri, P., Lemut, E. and Molfino, M.T., The GRAF system: an interactive graphic system for teaching mathematics, *Computers and Education* 7 No. 3 (1983) 177-182.

[7] Gentlemen, J.F., Interactive graphics in a terminal-equipped classroom, *Communications in Statistics - Theory and Methods* A5 No. 10 (1976) 949-967.

[8] Mandelbrot, B.B., *The Fractal Geometry of Nature* (W.H. Freeman, San Francisco, 1982).

[9] Papert, S., *Mindstorms: children, computers and powerful ideas* (Basic Books, New York, 1980).

[10] Polya, G., *How To Solve It* (Princeton University Press, Princeton, 1971).

[11] Porter, G., Computer graphics as a lecture aid in undergraduate mathematics, *Proceedings of National Educational Computing Conference (NECC) 1979* (University of Iowa, Iowa City, 1979)

[12] Raggett, G., Computer graphics for numerical analysis tuition, *International Journal of Mathematical Education in Science and Technology* 9 No. 2 (1973) 182-191.

[13] Shneiderman, B., A computer graphics system for polynomials, *Mathematics Teacher* 67 No. 2 (1974) 111-113.

[14] Sierpiński, W., *Sur une courbe dout tout point est un point de ramification*, Comptes Rendus 160 (1915).

[15] Steinhaus, H., *Mathematical Snapshots* (Oxford University Press, Oxford 1983).

[16] Straszewicz, S., *Zadania z Olimpiad Matematycznych - Tom II* [Problems from Olympics in Mathematics - vol. II] (Państwowe Zakłady Wydawnictw Szkolnych, Warsaw, 1961).

[17] Wegmen, E., Computer graphics in undergraduate statistics, *International Journal of Mathematical Education in Science and Technology* 5 (1974) 15-23.

[18] Wilensky, R., *LISPcraft* (W.W. Norton, New York, 1984).

COMPUTERS IN EDUCATION, K. Duncan and D. Harris (eds.)
Elsevier Science Publishers B.V. (North-Holland)
© IFIP, 1985

TRIG - AN INTELLIGENT DRILL-AND-PRACTICE SYSTEM FOR INTRODUCTORY TRIGONOMETRY

Peter Piddock

Faculty of Education,
University of Birmingham,
P O Box 363, Birmingham B15 2TT,
United Kingdom

TRIG is a drill-and-practice system for elementary trigonometry. It uses a diagram or topic map to allow selection of topic; it generates a problem and an appropriate diagram, for the selected topic; it has a calculator mode, with display features such as indices and square root signs, which presents expressions to the user in a familiar format; it offers a wide range of help on request; it keeps records of the user's actions for the teacher to use later for diagnosis and progress-checking. It has been implemented on a British Broadcasting Corporation Model B using disc overlays.

1. INTRODUCTION

This system is not a package in the usual sense. Rather, it is a toolkit with which the user may select topics of study in elementary trigonometry and solve problems on them. It generates problems, displays their associated diagrams, and offers help in the selection of the next goal to be achieved. Records are kept for the student's teacher to use for diagnostic and progress-checking purposes; this feature could easily be interfaced to a computer-managed learning system.

The TRIG system is intended to display the following characteristics of the computer as a learning device which are among those cited by Bork:(1)

> interactive learning;
> individualisation;
> student control over pacing;
> student control over content;
> testing as a learning mode.

It was decided to use various parts of the screen display consistently for various purposes. As Jenkin (2) says: "....the student knows which regions of the screen to concentrate on for dialogue, which to study at length, etc. ....". (Figure 1)

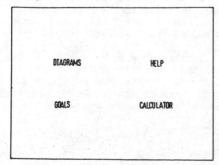

Figure 1

2. FEATURES

2.1 Topic Selection

The selection of the 'topic map' option in the main menu causes a diagram to be displayed (Figure 2). Most of the boxes and connecting paths are displayed as dotted lines and these and the text are in cyan. The current node (initially 'Introduction') and current arc (initially pointing to sin) are shown in solid lines in red and the text of the current node is also in red, in reverse video. Pressing the space bar rotates the choice of selected arc clockwise by one; pressing any key other than 'return' makes the node pointed at by the current arc into the current node; pressing 'return' causes the selection of the topic indicated by the current node and control is returned to the main menu. (The use of solid and dotted lines and reverse video as well as different colours ensures clarity of use on a monochrome monitor). Although at a considerably lower level of detail, the topic map attempts to provide an analogue of Pask's entailment structures(3) and seems to have similarity to features of TICCIT.(4) 'Help' works at the main menu level because the goal selection mechanism is set to 'topic map' by default until overridden by either an explicit goal selection (or a new call to the topic map system). It provides a brief explanation of changing arc, changing mode and confirming a choice.

2.2 Problem Generator

Every node in the topic map involves the generation of a triangle. These may be of three types: obtuse, acute or right-angled. The angles may be lettered as A, B and C, with corresponding opposite sides a, b and c. Other combinations of letters are possible, and these and the size of angles are selected by pseudo-random number generation. Additionally, the triangle may be oriented at any angle to the horizontal. (This is generally only of importance in right-angled cases, where there is an

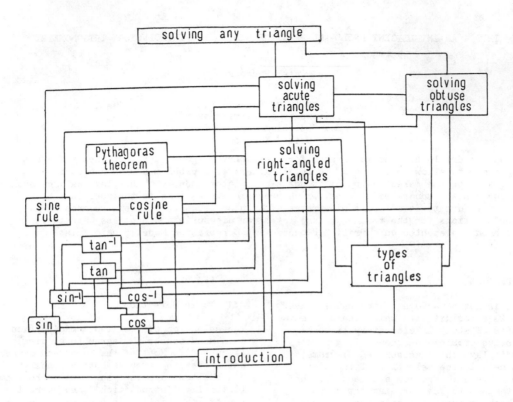

Figure 2

implied degree of difficulty of solution according to whether this angle is 0°, 90°, 180°, 270°
or some random value (5, 6).

Care has been taken to ensure that no angle is
ever less than 20°, simply to prevent awkwardly-
squashed diagrams being generated. Also, only
integer values are ever used for angles. These
are always generated first, before the lengths
of sides are calculated.

Once the triangle data has been generated, the
extent to which this information is revealed to
the student is determined by the type of problem.
Thus, a problem about sin would generate a
right-angled triangle with (say) angles A, B, C
and sides a, b, c. Assuming that B is the right
angle, the size of angles A, B and of side b,
would be revealed and there would only be one
goal to be satisfied, namely side a. If the
problem concerned solution of a general triangle,
the information revealed might be two sides and
an included angle, three sides, three angles and
one side, etc. with all the 'unknown' sides and
angles appearing as solution goals for the user
to achieve.

2.3 Diagram Display

The upper left-hand quarter of the screen is
used to display the diagram appropriate to the
problem to be solved. This is always a triangle,
although its orientation may be varied according
to the nature of the problem. The circumscribing

circle of the triangle is concentric with a
second circle of larger radius, the difference
in radius being the diagonal of a screen character.

Once the triangle data has been generated by the
problem generator, the coordinates of the vertices of the triangle may be calculated straight-
forwardly and the triangle drawn. The characters
lettering the three vertices are then displayed.
They are centred on a third concentric circle
midway between the two already described, on the
intersection of this circle with the angle bisectors of the triangle. The lower-case letters
which name the sides are sited on the perpendicular bisectors of these sides, produced beyond
the sides by an arbitrary distance (in practice
found to be about a character's width) away from
the centre of the circle, and with appropriate
correction being made in the case of obtuse
triangles to ensure that the letter appears on
the 'outside' of the triangle.

When the triangle has a right-angle, this is
marked with the conventional 'square' symbol.
The resulting diagram is thus of a type familiar
to the student and is always scaled to occupy the
maximum space in its window. (See figure 3).

2.4 Help Systems

There are two levels of help system available in
TRIG, although the user is unaware of the
difference. Within the scope of individual

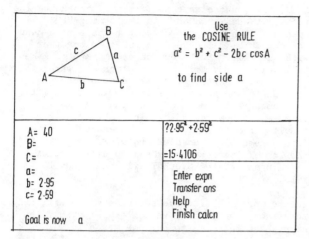

Figure 3

The help system uses the upper right-hand quarter of the screen.

2.5 Calculator Mode

The calculator mode permits the student to use the computer as a powerful desk calculator, with all the usually required functions available (circular, inverse circular, square root, squaring, exponentiation, common and natural logarithms). When this mode is entered from the main menu, the computer uses as a window the bottom right-hand quarter of the screen. The calculator menu offers a choice of: Enter expression, Transfer answer, Help, or Finish calculation. Expression entry is effected with considerable reliance on the ten programmable function keys, labelled F0 to F9. When, for example, F0 is depressed by the user 'sin (' appears in the box which forms the upper third of the calculation window. The user may then enter a number or an arithmetic expression as the argument of the sine function. It is the user's responsibility to provide the right closing bracket where it is needed, and multiplication has to be explicitly represented by *, as in Basic. Each of the 'usual' Basic trigonometric functions is represented in this way (sin, cos, tan). Inverse functions arcsin, arccos and arctan are provided. These are represented as $\sin^{-1}$, $\cos^{-1}$, $\tan^{-1}$ respectively. Log10 is represented as log and $\log_e$ as ln. The square root function is displayed as a '$\sqrt{}$(' combination, using the user-defined character facility of the BBC machine. This facility is further exploited by causing the F2 + shift combination to enter the index 2, for squaring. (The index -1 is used to indicate inverse functions, again through the user-defined character mechanism, but is not possible for the user to enter this character directly on its own. Exponentiation with other powers is represented by the conventional Basic notation using "↑"). The net effect of these features is largely cosmetic, ensuring that the expressions which the user enters look rather more like mathematics than Basic. A good example occurs with an attempt to use Pythagoras' theorem to find the third side of a triangle:

Basic: SQR (3↑3 + 4↑2)
Calculator: $\sqrt{(3^2 + 4^2)}$

When the user invokes one of these built-in functions, an appropriate sub-string, such as 'SQR(', or 'FNsin(', is appended to a string variable, as is each 'normal' keypress which the user makes. When the user indicates that the end of the expression has been reached, by pressing 'Return', the accumulated string is evaluated by a call to the EVAL function, another of the BBC machine's powerful features. Syntax errors and use of 'illegal' characters (like variable names, although future versions may accommodate these) are trapped by the software and return the user to the calculator menu. The result of a successful expression evaluation

modules called from the main menu, help is provided about the operation of the module in question. This is of a fairly rudimentary nature. For example, calculator 'help' describes the use of the function keys and the operation of the calculator menu. However, at the outer level (the main menu) the outcome of 'help' is seen as a function of the current goal and the previously-satisfied goals associated with the current problem. Thus, if the problem being tackled is the solution of a general triangle, ABC, the user may have been provided with the initial information A, b and c. If the user now attempts to select anything other than a as the current goal, the goal selection module will prevent this without a full explanation. 'Help' will result in a sequence of one or more screens of information (which may be interrupted or aborted) giving the supporting theory which is needed to satisfy the next achievable goal. Thus, in this example, the first screen displayed by the help system would suggest that when two sides and an included angle are known, the cosine rule (unstated) can be used to calculate the value of the third side. The next screen spells this out as a formula. Since the student is obliged to choose actively to continue to look at further screens in the help sequence, and these choices are recorded by the performance monitor, the teacher can examine the student's degree of reliance on the use of the help system to provide the necessary theory, and the way in which this reliance may be changing with continued use of the system. Any formulae used by the help system are expressed in terms of the variables being used in the current problem, so that the cosine rule may appear as:

$a^2 = b^2 + c^2 - 2bc \cos A$ for triangle ABC,

but as

$p^2 = q^2 + r^2 - 2qr \cos P$ when the triangle is PQR.

appears at the bottom of the upper box preceded by =. This result remains visible when subsequent attempts are made at expression evaluation, until one of these succeeds.

The result of an expression evaluation can be transferred to the current goal as an attempt to 'answer' this part of the problem. At present the software merely checks that the putative answer lies within a given (teacher-definable) tolerance of the 'correct answer' and responds appropriately. (Future versions will attempt to diagnose the more obvious faults, such as inverted rational expressions, which may occur.) Whether or not the goal is thus achieved, control returns to the TRIG main menu. 'Help' produces a description of the use of the function keys, and 'Finish' forces a return to the main menu.

All trigonometric functions use degree, not radian, arguments as these are much more commonly encountered by students at this level. The combination CTRL+FO allows entry of letters, so that the user can type in SIN, COS, etc. with their usual Basic (radian) interpretation if this is required. This feature has to be invoked for each expression for which it is required, as it is cancelled when the evaluation attempt is made.

2.6 Goal Selection

The nature of the goals to be satisfied (i.e. the values of angles and sides which are to be found) depends upon the topic selected, and on the degree of difficulty, which is also at the student's option. The system displays the values of variables which constitute 'given' information, together with a list of available (as yet unsatisfied) goals, in the bottom left-hand quarter of the screen. The currently selected goal appears in this list in reverse video. When the student invokes the goal selection process from the main menu, the system checks that the proposed new goal is achievable from the present state of knowledge of the values of the variables in the triangle. If it is possible to achieve the new goal, it becomes the current goal; if not, a message informs the student that the goal cannot be achieved at present. (For example, if all that is known of triangle ABC are angle A and sides a and b, it is not possible to calculate angle C until angle B has been determined by use of the sine rule.) At this point the student can invoke the help system which will suggest which new goal is appropriate and, if required, how its value may be calculated.

2.7 Performance Monitor

When the program is started it first looks for a file called STUDENT. If this is present, it is used to obtain the student's name and the session number to reset the time on the system clock to the value which it had on the last exit from the system. If STUDENT is not present, the program requests the student's names so that the file can be created at the end of the session.

A new file, whose name is formed by appending the two-digit session number to the string "LOG", is opened. Each time the student makes a main-menu choice, this is recorded in the file together with the time. Such records are marked to make them readily identifiable by other software, and a random-access technique is used to append records to the end of the file, closing it after each amendment. Most of the student's keypresses are now recorded. In practice this only results in a file of a few thousand bytes, even from a session of an hour or two in length. At the end of the session, the student's disc will contain an updated STUDENT file and a new LOG file.

Future work will include software which will help the teacher to monitor and interpret such files. At present this has to be done manually.

3   IMPLEMENTATION

The TRIG software began its life as a Lisp implementation, (using MicroSoft's muLISP on the Research Machines 380Z). For numerous reasons, it was decided to switch to a version which would run on the British Broadcasting Corporation (Acorn) computer. Considerations of space and development difficulties dictated the use of Basic, which is present in ROM on this machine. Even so, extensive use has been made of overlaying (7) in order to squeeze a large piece of software into a relatively small memory (32k). It remains true that some aspects of the task of implementing TRIG would have been made much easier if it had been possible to use LISP, although the demands of floating-point arithmetic and trigonometric functions make the proprietary Acornsoft interpreter unsuitable as it stands. Future versions are planned which will be able to make use of these types of facility by accessing the arithmetic routines in the Basic ROM(8). The problem of extending muLISP to include graphics and floating-point arithmetic has already been solved(9), so that an RML380Z version is technically already feasible and exists in parts. The chief drawbacks, from the research viewpoint, of using this machine are the lack of an internal clock which can be used to time the entries into the LOG files and the need to provide an expression evaluator for the calculator subsystem.

4   REFERENCES

(1) Bork, A., Interactive Learning, in Taylor, R. P. (ed.), The Computer in School, (Teachers' College Press, New York, 1980).

(2) Jenkin, J. M., Some principles of screen design and software for their support, in Smith, P. R. (ed.), Computer Assisted Learning, (Pergamon, Oxford, 1981).

(3) Entwistle, N., Styles of Teaching and Learning (Wiley, Chichester, 1981).

(4)   Morrison, F., Planning a large scale
      computer assisted instruction installation:
      the TICCIT experience, in Lecarme, O. and
      Lewis, R. (eds.), Computers in Education
      (IFIP 2nd World Conference), (North-Holland,
      Amsterdam, 1975).

(5)   School Mathematics Project (1971) SMP Book
      F - Teacher's Guide (Cambridge University
      Press, Cambridge).

(6)   School Mathematics Project (1972) SMP Book
      G - Teacher's Guide (Cambridge University
      Press, Cambridge).

(7)   Quick, P., Overlays saving bytes, Acorn
      User 16 (Nov. 1983) 67-69.

(8)   Christensen, D., Mapping out the Beebon,
      Personal Computer World 5, 7 (July 1982)
      91-99.

(9)   Piddock, P., Extended muSIMP/msMATH for
      teaching and learning mathematics (to be
      published in 1985).

COMPUTERS IN EDUCATION, K. Duncan and D. Harris (eds.)
Elsevier Science Publishers B.V. (North-Holland)
© IFIP, 1985

A CERTAIN EXPERIMENTAL COMPUTER AIDED COURSE OF LOGIC IN POLAND

Marcin Mostowski and Zinaida Trybulec

The Warsaw University, Bialystok's Branch, Department of Logic,
Bialystok, Swierkowa 20, Poland

This paper describes an experiment conducted in Poland: a correspondence course of logic with the help of the Mizar-MSE system. This system was designed to verify the correctness of mathematical proofs. It is the computer aided system of natural deduction for the first order language. This paper contains: a few words about the ideology of teaching logic, the description of the experiment, the short description of the Mizar-MSE system.

INTRODUCTION

For three years now logic courses using the Mizar-MSE language have been provided at the Warsaw University. These courses are held on an interactive basis. In 1983 the author of the Mizar language and the editor-in-chief of the "Delta" magazine decided to publish a correspondence course of the Mizar-MSE. "Delta" is a Polish popular science monthy aimed at students of the secondary schools. The MIZAR course experiment had in view the verification of the attractiveness and effectivity of Mizar as a tool for teaching logic to students; also it gave them an opportunity of contact with a computer (unfortunately indirect). Before we get down to details, a few words about the ideology of Mizar-MSE and of teaching logic.

1. CAN FORMAL LOGIC BE A TOOL OF THINKING?

The fact that logic is a tool of thinking is often used as an argument for teaching logic in higher or secondary schools. But logic, at least as it is formulated in the majority of modern handbooks of mathematical logic, is not a tool of thinking at all - at least not for human beings. This objection is not new. For some time now many people have noted the abyss between formal proof theory and the practice of reasoning. Two known papers devoted to this problem were published in the same year, the first written by G.Gentzen [1], the second by S.Jaskowski [2]. Both have formu- lated systems of the so called natural deduction. The handbook of logic by J.Slupecki and L.Borkowski [3] was based on Jaskowski's ideas. It is worth noting, that this handbook has for a long time been used as a basis for the logic course at the Philosophical Departament of Warsaw University.

The search for a practically sound proof theory meets with natural obstacles. Logical steps in a proof can not be too large, because the correctness of reasoning must be practically decidable for human beings - otherwise, the formalization can be superfluous. It has been shown, that larger reasoning steps caused essential difficulties in checking the correctness of the reasoning. Particularly, the currently used deductions are too complicated for any simple checking method. However, what is too complicated for men can be very simple for computers.

Computers make possible an essential progress in the search of a practically sound proof theory. Recently in Poland, A.Trybulec was the promotor of such investigations; his group created a series of "logic information" languages under the general name Mizar. The first such fully efficient language is Mizar-MSE (MSE means Multi - Sorted with Equality). It is a multi - sorted language of Predicate Calculus with equality, used for recording reasonings and equipped with programs (in Pascal) checking the syntactical correctness of texts and logical correctness of reasonings. Mizar-MSE is destined mainly for teaching of logic. Other, more universal, languages of this kind are being prepared.

With Mizar-MSE we can record mathematical proofs posessing legibility and size of deductions similar to these encountered in mathematical textbooks for beginners in higher schools. This proves that formal logic can be not only helpful for teaching reasonings, but it can also be an efficient tool of reasoning. As professor W.Marciszewski has remarked, Mizar-MSE combines the neatness of formulations with real algorithmic verifiability of logical corectness of reasonings.   It is its main advantage over hitherto known proof-systems.

2.   THE COURSE OF MIZAR-MSE IN "DELTA"

The course of the Mizar language started in September (9) number "Delta" (1983).
On one hand the course was an opportunity to show a new language and the main proving techniques, on the other it allowed the students who were interested in the course to learn the techniques of working with a computer.   Direct work of students with the computer was not possible (because of lack of computers in schools) so solutions of the exercises had to be hand-written, then they were sent to "Delta" and finally they were processed by the SM-4 computer (a Russian copy of the PDP 11/40) by the Mizar team.   The printout of the solutions together with appropriate comments were sent to the participant.   Therefore the cycle of processing the exercises was prolonged about three weeks.

This course did not present all the possibilities of the Mizar language (for example it did not present the Mizar as a multi-sorted language).

To show the proving techniques with the help of Mizar a fragment of the elementary theory of the ordering of rational numbers was chosen.   The course was divided into ten parts (the school year lasts ten months in Poland).   The English version of the course text can be found in Mizar-MSE Primer [4].

On the whole we have received 241 solutions: part 1 - 70 solutions, part 2 - 60 solutions, part 3 - 35 solutions, part 4 - 27 solutions, part 5 - 22 solutions, part 6 - 12 solutions, part 7 - 9 solutions, part 8 - 6 solutions.   We also received letters containing questions and requests for explication of certain problems which appeared during the attempts of solving the exercises.   Up to the tenth number inclusively we also enclosed offprint with correct solution of exercises.

One of the parts of the Mizar-MSE system is a Pascal program verifying the logical correctness of justifications, called the checker. The decision to postpone its description in the last chapter of the Mizar course was a mistake. This was already evident in the solutions of exercises concerning the second part of this course (the attempt to justify an existential statement).   We were forced to give additional explanatory remarks concerning the checker in advance.

Two matters especially two matters required clearing up: 1.   the way the checker treats equalities, 2.   why does the checker accept certain sentences as obviously true.

There were three kinds of errors: 1.   syntactical errors (incorrect Mizar notation), 2.   logical errors, 3.   consequences of lack of knowledge of the checker.

The first part of the course caused no difficulties; they started with the second as was demonstrated by the obtained solutions.

ad 1.   Syntactical errors were relatively numerous but in our opinion they were insignificant.   If the Mizar student could directly interact with the computer (which was the case of Mizar aided logic instruction at our university), he would be able to eliminate these errors himself.   Therefore we corrected syntactical errors ourselves and we informed the student about it.

ad 2.   Logical errors followed from insufficient knowledge of logic. It seems that the most difficult to assimilate is the law of transposition.   Inequality was also incorrectly interpreted as transitive. This error could be a result of lack of distinguishing between true sentences in a model and correctness of the inference.

ad 3.   Most errors resulted from the lack of the knowledge of the checker. They concerned mainly the following: a.   the way the checker treats equality, b.   why more than one universal sentence can not be in thesis jusification, c.   sentences obvious to the checker which were not tautologies of the propositional calculus, d.   justification of existential sentences.

The conclusions which seem to be significant are as follows:

1.   Mizar-MSE is a rather attractive tool for teaching logic, but the correspondence method of teaching is not the best one.   The proce- ssing of the obtained solutions is too extended in time, a student had no direct contact either with computer or with his teacher, hence the correct solutions of the exercises required too much time.

2.   The students who sent the solutions proved to have mastered a high level of logical competence.   This fact is

the more astonishing in view of the fact that course of logic at the secondary schools practically does not exist.

3. The teaching of the art of proving was attempted without providing the students with the rules of game, this being due to the lack of the description of the Mizar checker. In fact, the method employed was that of imitating the examples of proofs contained in the course. This imitation method might be good if direct access to computer was provided but it proved to be inefficient in the described case.

4. The most general conclusion drawn from an extensive discussion and from experiences obtained in teaching logic for humanities students is as follows: Mizar as a tool of teaching how to prove theorems provides us with an attractive and efficient method. However, teaching logic with its help should be done only after our students have obtained a training in mathematics. This training would enable them to work on interpretations instead of certain abstract objects.

It seems that logic should be taught on the basis of the students' acquaintance with a particular disciplin in which it is characteristic of the proofs that they are, so to speak, concrete proofs. This stage of practical training in the skill of deductive reasoning should be followed by the teaching of abstract rules of deduction as stated in formal logic. Then the student is able to read logical laws in the correct way and he does not meet with any difficulties even when dealing with non-trivial cases.

While starting our course we were not aware of these methodical presuppositions but they became more and more apparent to us in the course of successive experiences. These presuppositions turned out to be right provided that the students have enough opportunities to make the transition from concrete pieces of reasoning to abstract logical rules. In the case of our course these opportunities were too small to ensure a full success. Nevertheless, we can safely speak of a considerable success, since our students who at the start had no education in logic, at the end proved able to perform elementary mathematical proofs.

3. THE SHORT DESCRIPTION OF MIZAR-MSE

Here is a short description of Mizar-MSE. The typical Mizar-MSE text has the following form:

ENVIRON

(predeclarations, that is preliminary determination of types of variables (X_{ij} is of type T_i))

LET $X_{11},...,X_{1i1}$ **DENOTE** T_1;

....

LET $X_{n1},...,X_{nin}$ **DENOTE** T_n;

(introduction of individual constants (A_{ij} is of type S_i))

GIVEN $A_{11},...,A_{1m1}$ **BEING** S_1;

....

GIVEN $A_{m1},...,A_{mbm}$ **BEING** S_m;

(axioms)

B1: β_1;

....

Bj: β_j;

BEGIN

C1: γ_1 (theorem C1)

PROOF (of theorem C1) . . . **END**;

.....

Ct: γ_t (theorem Ct)

PROOF (of theorem Ct) . . . **END**;

Names of types, labels (Ai,Bi,Ci), individual constants, and variables, and predicate symbols are represented as strings of characters and digits.

$\alpha_i, \beta_i, \gamma_i$ correspond to sentences constructed by means of variables, individual constants, predicates symbols, parenthesis, commas, and logical constants (variables must be bounded).

Here we give the translation of logical constants of Mizar-MSE into standard logical symbolism:

"FOR x ST α EX y ST β" corresponds to $\forall x (\alpha \rightarrow \exists y \beta)$, "FOR x EX y ST α" corresponds to $\forall x \exists y \alpha$, "FOR x,y ST α HOLDS β" corresponds to $\forall x \forall y (\alpha \rightarrow \beta)$, FOR x HOLDS α corresponds to $\forall x \alpha$, EX x ST α corresponds to $\exists x \alpha$, NOT, IMPLIES, OR, &, IFF denote known

logical connectives; = is an equality; <>
is unequality.

In the text part enclosed by the
words ENVIRON and BEGIN we introduce a
language and axioms (with respect to
variables, types, locally defined
individual constants and predicate symbols
the language remains open). Logical
correctness is checked only after BEGIN.

Every variable must have a definite
type (sort); instead of fixing the type of
a variable x before BEGIN by the statement
"LET x DENOTE T;" we can later write, for
instance:

FOR x BEING T ST α HOLDS β

Individual fully defined constants
can be introduced only before BEGIN by
means of the construction GIVEN ... BEING
...; .The type of a predicate and its
arity is defined by its occurrence. That
is, for instance, if the statement

FOR x BEING T EX y BEING S ST P[x,y]

appears in the text, then here P
denotes a binary predicate with first
argument of type T, and second one with
type S (different predicates having
different sorts can have the same
identifiers). Any type is defined by the
first occurence of its identifier. Types
are individualized by their identifiers,
that is types having the same identifiers
are identical.

Every Mizar-statement ends with a
semicolon, with an important exception.
If after a sentence there follows a proof,
then this sentence can not end with a
semicolon, otherwise the Checker will try
to treat it as logically obvious. When it
is not obvious then Checker annouces a
logical error. A proof begins with the
word PROOF and ends with "END;".

Every sentence can have a label. A
label has to precede a sentence and must
be separated from it by colon. Axioms
particularly ought to have labels, because
we include them only for references.
Labels are used for references.

Commentaries must be preceded by ==
at the beginning of lines. Every line,
which begins with this symbol, is ignored
by Mizar-MSE.

Here we present an exemplary correct
text in Mizar-MSE:

ENVIRON

LET X,Y,Z DENOTE RATIONAL;

REFLEXIVITY: FOR X HOLDS NG[X,X];
TRANSITIVITY:
FOR X,Y,Z ST NG[X,Y] & NG[Y,Z]
    HOLDS NG[X,Z];

GIVEN A,B,C BEING RATIONAL;

Z1: NG[A,B];
Z2: NG[B,C];

BEGIN

T1: FOR X EX Y ST NG[X,Y]
  PROOF
    LET X' BE RATIONAL;
    NG[X',X'] BY REFLEXIVITY;
    HENCE THESIS
  END;

T2: FOR X ST NG[X,A] HOLDS NG[X,C]
  PROOF
    ASSUME NOT THESIS;
    THEN CONSIDER X SUCH THAT
    1: NG[X,A] & NOT NG[X,C];
    NG[A,C] BY Z1,Z2,TRANSITIVITY;
    HENCE CONTRADICTION BY 1,TRANSITIVITY
  END;

LET in the statement "LET X' BE
RATIONAL;" is used to introduce a locally
defined constant which will be generalized
at the end of our reasoning. We can also
use statements such as

"LET X' BE T SUCH THAT α(X');".

This statement is equivalent to

"LET X' BE T; ASSUME α(X');".

Both the constructions LET and ASSUME
are determined by our thesis - that is by
what we have to prove (a sentence which
remains to be proven now can be
abbreviated as THESIS).

When our thesis is "FOR X BEING T ST
α(X) HOLDS β(X)", then we can use
the statement "LET Y' BE T SUCH THAT
α(Y');", in this case the term THESIS
obtains the same meaning as "β(Y')".

When our thesis is "FOR X BEING T
HOLDS α(X)", then we can use the statement
"LET Y BE T;", now our thesis is "α(Y)".
We can also construct an indirect proof
using the statement (as in the proof of
T2) "ASSUME NOT THESIS;", now our thesis
becomes identical with the "CONTRADICTION"
(CONTRADICTION is the logical constant
representing logically false sentence); a
similar construction can be used in every
case.

When our thesis is "α IMPLIES β",
then we can use statement "ASSUME α;", and
now our thesis is identical with "β".

To introduce locally defined constants we have another construction, namely CONSIDER ... . This construction is independent from our thesis. When the existential sentence "EX X BEING T ST α(X)" can be correctly justified by sentences with labels E1,...,En, then we can introduce a new constant A such that α(A) holds by the following statement: "CONSIDER A BEING T SUCH THAT E: α(A) BY E1,...,En;". The label E is necessary if we want to refer to the sentence α(A), because through using CONSIDER similarly as ASSUME THAT we can introduce a list of sentences with labels thus breaking up the suitable sentence into its conjuncts. In this case we can refer to all such sentences only using their labels.

Instead of "ASSUME EX X ST α(X); THEN CONSIDER A SUCH THAT α(A);" we can write "GIVEN A SUCH THAT α(A);".

A useful way of referring to other sentences is to use the word THEN, which is used to justify a sentence by the preceding one. The conclusion of reasoning must be preceded by the word THUS (or when we want to refer to the previous sentence by the word HENCE).

Every separate sentence after BEGIN must be followed by its justification (when it is not obvious to the Checker). We can justify by reference (in this case we use either the word BY and labels or the words THEN,HENCE) or by proof. When a sentence is not followed by a proof then and only then it must end with a semicolon. By proving sentences occuring in other proofs we obtain nested proofs of any degree.

In some cases a proved sentence does not have to be formulated explicitely, it can be reconstructed by Mizar-MSE. For the reconstruction constructions like LET, ASSUME, THUS, HENCE, and GIVEN are used (these constructions form the so-called skeleton of a reasoning - a proved thesis must be in agreement with the skeleton of its proof). To introduce a reasoning without an explicitely formulated thesis we use the word NOW. In such reasonings the term THESIS is defined only if it is defined before NOW.

Now we must say something about the Checker. When α is justified by β1,...,βn (through labels or otherwise), then this justification is checked as follows:

1. a formula γ it is constructed equivalent to β1 & ... & βn & not α;

2. γ is formulated in normal disjunctive form, where elementary components are atomic formulas or general formulas (formulated in terms of negation, conjunction, and general quantifier, with elimination of any even number of successive negations). At this stage all identities beyond of scope of quantifiers are eliminated by the identification of some constants;

3. from any disjunct γi of γ the Checker tries to obtain a contradiction, which can be done in two ways:

first, by comparing conjuncts of γi and investigating if one of them is a negation of another,

second, by investigating any positive general conjunct of γi and finding out whether a contradiction can be obtained by substituting constants occurring in γi for generally bounded variables in this conjunct. Obviously if there is such a conjunct then γi implies contradiction.

In both cases some simple properties of identity under quantifiers are used.

REFERENCES

[1] Gentzen, G., Untersuchungen ueber das logische Schlieszen I, Mathematische Zeitschrift 39 (1934) 176 - 210.
[2] Jaskowski, S., On the rules of supposition in formal logic, Studia Logica 1 (1934), 5 - 32.
[3] Slupecki, J. and Borkowski L., Elementy logiki matematycznej i teorii mnogosci (PWN, Warszawa 1963).
[4] Prazmowski, K. and Rudnicki, P. Mizar-MSE Primer, ICS PAS Reports n. 529, Warszawa 1983.

COMPUTERS IN EDUCATION, K. Duncan and D. Harris (eds.)
Elsevier Science Publishers B.V. (North-Holland)
© IFIP, 1985

SOLVING OF GENERAL PROBLEMS AND PROBLEM-CLASSES

Dr. phil. Leo H. Klingen

Helmholtz-Gymnasium

Bonn, Federal Republic of Germany

About ten years after the beginning of computeroriented work in German Grammar Schools ("Gymnasium") a newer use of software tools is emerging in some schools: Packets with abstract datatypes and corresponding operators are producing greater flexibility for problem-classes instead of single programs adapted only for one problem. Especially packets for symbolic datahandling in linear and quadratic algebra (solution of equations, tranformation of terms) are able to handle nested applications in natural- and social sciences. This has consequences for the mathematics curriculum.

Introduction

Pupils are accustomed to using computers to solve many special problems; each pocket-calculator will give values of the sine-function as well as values of the log-function with more digits than in the former school-tables. If special software is inserted or a special PROM is implemented, it is possible to solve integration-problems, chess-problems, as well as automatic syllabication etc. by simple commands with microcomputers. However there are more general problems and also classes of coherent problems which can be addressed by means of the computer. We will look for corresponding software-tools.

Abstract datatypes and corresponding operators

Adaption to commonly utilized notations is a helpful instrument for problem-solving. For example, children, who learn to use fractions, want to operate with fractions on the screen if possible in the same manner as with fractions in their exercise-books. Thus abstract datatypes are necessary, as well as infix-operators upon them, and special procedures working with them. In geometry they need points, internally represented as sets of coordinates, lines and planes, internally represented as sets of coefficients, and procedures as "draw" or "combine" or "intersect" etc. Let us consider a typical example in physics :

Electrical resistances are shunted in series or parallel to form complex connections. The total resistance can be described by

```
RESISTANCE VAR  r1, r2, .....r6,
                rtotal ;

get(r1); get(r2); ..... get(r6);

rtotal := ((( r2 SER r3) PAR r4 PAR
         r5) SER r1) PAR r6;
```

Its value is obtained by a simple

```
put (rtotal)
```

if you have inserted the following packet, which only contains the simple laws of Kirchhoff and the definition of input/output and assignement :

```
PACKET resistance-handling DEFINES
RESISTANCE, :=, SER, PAR, put, get :

  TYPE RESISTANCE = STRUCT (REAL ohm) ;

  RESISTANCE OP SER (RESISTANCE CONST
                  r1,r2) :
    RESISTANCE VAR result ;
    result.ohm := r1.ohm + r2.ohm ;
    result
  END OP SER ;

  RESISTANCE OP PAR (RESISTANCE CONST
                  r1, r2) :
    RESISTANCE VAR result ;
    result.ohm := r1 * r2/ (r1 +  r2) ;
    result
  END OP PAR ;

  OP := (RESISTANCE VAR r1,
         RESISTANCE CONST r2) :
    r1.ohm := r2.ohm
  END OP := ;

  PROC get (RESISTANCE VAR r) :
    put ("Resistance in Ohm ?");
    get (r.ohm)
  END PROC get ;
```

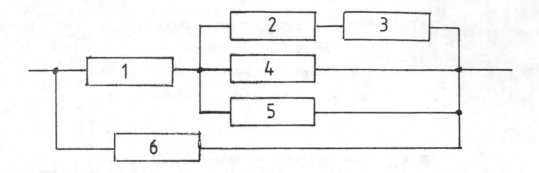

Figure 1. Connection of various resistances

```
PROC put (RESISTANCE CONST r) :
   put (r.ohm) ;
   put ("Ohm")
END PROC put

END PACKET resistance-handling .
```

It is interesting to examine the same subject by changing from direct to alternating current; the corresponding packet with the abstract datatype

```
TYPE ACRESISTANCE = STRUCT (COMPLEX
                           value)
```

can use exactly the same detailled formulations as above, if another packet for calculation with complex numbers has been inserted previously. In a sequence of packets each new packet can use the software-tools of the earlier inserted packets and the main program as the last one can use them all. Here the possibilities of an elaborated computer-language (ELAN) remain close to the abstraction given by the scientific model.

In a similar manner it is possible to write packets and operators for fractions, set theory, theory of probability, Boolean algebra, graph theory, constructive geometry etc.
Also inserted standard procedures (in the EUMEL-operating system for ELAN about 400 standard procedures) have to be seen in this context; the success of LOGO .for first manipulations on the screen by a simple call of inserted procedures has the same fundament.

Symbolic algebra as a general tool

A packet for symbolic algebraic processing is a powerful instrument for solving a wide range of problem-classes, and not only in mathematics. In a project, in the last year of a 3-year-syllabus of computer science, some pupils have constructed such a packet (with about 700 lines in ELAN) similar to a subset of professional software as muMATH. This algebraic processing is able to transform algebraic terms (fractions with general rational terms included) and to solve equations of first or second degree as well as systems of two or three linear equations. (In brief: the packet handles algebra like a perfect 15-year-old pupil).

Examples:

```
transform ("(a + b) **3")

produces the output  a**3 + 3*a**2*b
                        + 3*a*b**2 + b**3
                     ;

solve (" x = x + 1 ", "x" )

produces the output    no solution;

solve ("(ay + 1)/y = 3a/8","y")

produces the output    y = - 1.6* a;

solve (" x*x + p*x + q = 0", "x")

produces the well known formula

x = -p/2 +- raiz (p**2/4 - q)    .
```

If the raiz contains concrete values, follows also a concrete algorithm (Heron) for the quadratic raiz.

Finally

solve ("(x+a) / (x-a) =
       (b+x) / (b- x)", "x")

produces the output

    x = raiz (a * b)
and x = - raiz (a*b).

You can apply the packet naturally to much more complicated algebraic problems, even those in French exercise-books, which are not normally solved by German pupils. It's an advantage, that the number of blancs and the existence of the multiplication-symbol "*" doesn't matter.

Applications for general problem-solving.

In a first approach for real aplications of this algebra-packet we solved equations in physics as

s = v * t   of kinematics or
p * v = R* T of gas-dynamics :

The call   solve("p*v = R*T", "T") produces the output T = p * v / R.

Soon the pupils proposed an input-mask for concrete values of given magnitudes; and the computer had to find the output-variable and its value.
In the continuation of this work, we attempted small systems of two equations solvable by substitution, for example

1/g + 1/b = 1/f and b/g = B/G in geometrical optics.

If you give the values of 3 of the 5 variables, you can automatically obtain the values of the other 2 variables as output by using the packet. Finally, we completed this beginning to a full and extendable system of problem-solving for problem-classes which are typical at school. The input-mask asks for the subject:

e.g. kinematics, series, commercial
     calculation, volumes and weights,
     electrotechnique
     or: new subject.

Then a description is given on the screen of typical problems and also the formula-base of the discipline in standard-notation, further on a warning that describes what problems are not solvable. Sometimes a subdivision is requested, for example for the subject "series" "arithmetical serie or geometrical serie?" Then the corresponding specific formula-file is automatically called, the input of concrete magnitudes automatically produces a search for accessible output-variables (if necessary by little systems of 2 or 3 simultaneous equations with the same variables) and the automatic processing and solving with the help of the algebra packet is realized. The values of the outputs are transformed to normal magnitudes by the transformation of units, which are in corresponding tables of additional files. Also material constants (for example specific weights or specific resistances) are available.
If a new subject is chosen in the input-mask, the computer asks for subdivisions, for formulas, for textual description, for tables of units and for tables of material constants. Then the possiblities of the solving system are augmented by the new subject for following uses. Also an amplification by trigonometric transformations, symbolic differentiation or symbolic integration in union with numeric integration in certain cases seems possible.
Finally it should be pointed out that there are problem-classes, which can be described better in a special language, as for example dynamic processes by "DYNAMO". If a school possesses a DYNAMO-Compiler, pupils can learn not only in artifical small samples (models of few variables and linear constraints) but also with the 42 variables of the world-model of Forrester.

Conclusion : Educational objectives

The educational goal of this work is not simply to provide pupils of informatics with an extended project. Also it should not be the first educational consequence to expose pupils to drill-practices (CAI) with numerous exercises to solve equations because the existence of symbolic algebra-processing permits the opportunity and gives self-control. A better way has been shown in Europe by art teachers: 50 years ago the majority of pupils could not paint and remained so for the whole of the time they spent at school. Today, by very different means, almost all pupils have been enabled to do creative art. Neither is the main purpose to provide an approximate idea of artifical intelligence, when machines "understand" the text of a problem in a mathematical sense, by interpreting the meaning of the symbols, thus offering an example of an expert system. There are other non-cognitive educational objectives:
Transformations of this type in mathematics and problem-solving of this kind in science are typical for more than 80% of the relevant schoolwork in the

lower grades. It is important for pupils to see that a machine can only do
this reproductive and deductive work
and that the few remaining problems receive the brilliance of creative work.
These latter activities cannot be done
by machines and require real human labour, the real art of teaching and,
above all, goodwill and engagement on
the part of youth.

COMPUTERS IN EDUCATION, K. Duncan and D. Harris (eds.)
Elsevier Science Publishers B.V. (North-Holland)
© IFIP, 1985

COMPUTER DIALOGS FOR DEVELOPING CONCEPTS OF PHYSICS

David Trowbridge*
Augusto Chioccariello

Educational Technology Center
Information and Computer Science
University of California
Irvine, CA 92717
(714) 856-7452

A collection of computer based learning modules has been developed at the Educational Technology Center to aid introductory physics students. Development of the modules has been based on research results concerning students' naive conceptions of physics and upon master teachers' experiences working individually with students. The computer aids consist of graphic interactive dialogs that treat topics of introductory kinematics and dynamics which are known to be particularly troublesome for students.

Introduction

A problem shared by many introductory general physics courses is that large numbers of students drop out before completing the course. Often, this course is a major obstacle for students. Causes for this phenomenon have been attributed to various student weaknesses, including misconceptions, lack of general problem solving skills, poor mathematical backgrounds, and inadequate reasoning skills. In this paper, we discuss a project which uses the computer to target these areas of student difficulty and provide remediation.

In some cases, student difficulties could be remedied by instructors working directly with students one-on-one. Teaching through questioning can be an effective means for uncovering specific difficulties and helping students to overcome them. Some teachers do engage their students in Socratic dialog, when time permits. But this is a very time-consuming effort which is not usually feasible, especially in courses with large student enrollments.

One of the problems associated with a large lecture format course is that in each content area of the course, the instructor must assume a minimum background among students. Unfortunately, in most cases, students come to the course with widely varying backgrounds. Ideally, we would like to provide instruction tailored to each student's background and needs.

Computer based learning materials may be able to provide some aid to students in this regard. Well designed computer programs can make the expertise of the master teacher available to a large audience, while preserving one of the most valuable qualities of the master teacher/student relationship: interactivity. Highly interactive Socratic dialogs can mimic some of the roles of a skilled tutor such as teaching through inquiry. (See, for instance, Bork 1984.)

This paper describes a project at the Educational Technology Center which is producing computer based learning materials to aid students' development of conceptual understanding and problem solving skills relevant to the content of the first semester of the introductory course on the physics of motion. The project is a three-year project funded by the Fund for the Improvement of Post-Secondary Education (FIPSE, grant no. G008200987).

We do not attempt to provide comprehensive coverage of introductory kinematics and dynamics, but only to provide aid in areas that have been found to be particularly troublesome to students. We draw upon relevant research results and use strategies for instruction which are used by master teachers.

*current address:

Center for Design of Educational Computing
Carnegie-Mellon University
Pittsburgh, PA 15213
(412) 578-7641

We illustrate in this paper how research results and instructional strategies are incorporated into the learning material by describing two of the dialogs, "Motion With and Without Friction", and "Problem Solving in Kinematics." The first dialog draws from research which has revealed several common naive conceptions about motion among introductory physics students. The second draws from the experience of instructors that students display common difficulties in solving elementary kinematics problems, and that these difficulties can be remedied by certain kinds of individual tutorial assistance.

Research on Students' Conceptions of Dynamics

Recently, a number of research studies have investigated students' conceptual difficulties. For instance, common preconceptions and alternative conceptions of dynamics have been studied by Clement (1977, 1982), diSessa (1981), White (1983), Lawson (1984). Several of these studies have explored students' conceptual understanding of motion before, during and after formal study of the physics of motion. These findings have been replicated and now considerable consensus can be found about students' naive conceptions of motion.

Each of these studies has invoked a clinical interview format in which students' understanding of the material is probed by presenting a task which is carefully designed to reveal the existence of certain misconceptions. Typically, the investigator asks the student to make a prediction, to perform the task and then to explain the outcome.

Early work was conducted by Clement (1977), who used a simple paper and pencil task to explore students' conceptions of dynamics. Students were asked to sketch the trajectory of a spaceship whose engine delivered a short blast along a line perpendicular to the initial velocity of the ship. A large fraction of first-year university students displayed one or both of the following errors: (1) the velocity of the ship would always be in the same direction as it was being pushed by its engine, and (2) after the engine stopped firing, the ship would resume the motion it had prior to the engine blast.

diSessa (1981) investigated naive conceptions using a computer microworld. A small triangular object, called a "dynaturtle," was displayed on a computer screen. The student used keys on the keyboard to change the orientation of the "turtle" and deliver

small "kicks" to it. When given a kick, the turtle would change its velocity in the prescribed direction by a fixed magnitude. In the absence of kicks, the turtle would continue to move in a straight line at a steady speed, according to the rules of Newtonian mechanics. diSessa found that young adolescents expected the turtle to move toward the target when they kicked it toward the target.

Several of diSessa's findings were replicated by Lawson (1984) among first-year university students in a general physical science course. Using a dry-ice puck on a glass table, students controlled the puck by delivering small blasts of air to it. Results from interviews using the physical equipment were similar to those of diSessa.

White (1983) investigated the development of stategies for solving some simple tasks in the dynaturtle world. She catalogued the difficulties they had and then designed a series of games to help students develop an intuition of Newtonian mechanics (White, 1984).

A naive conception revealed in all of these studies was that: "Objects move in the direction they are pushed." While this is a useful concept in our usual everyday experience, it causes difficulty when trying to learn Newtonian mechanics. An interactive, graphic computer dialog was designed to deal with this difficulty in a direct and systematic manner. Following is a description of the computer dialog, "Motion With and Without Friction" which confronts this notion.

Motion With and Without Friction

The dialog has two goals: (1) to develop students' intuition of motion in a friction-free Newtonian world, and (2) to provide analytical tools for interpreting motion in that world.

A simple task, "Docking a Space Ship" is presented which can be solved either by trial and error (to develop intuition) or by use of velocity vectors (to practice an analytical approach). In the first instance, the task is presented as a game to dock the spaceship in a space port by controlling it with an engine that delivers short bursts or "kicks" to the ship. Through trial and error, the student learns to maneuver the ship to the vicinity of the port and then to bring it to rest inside (Figure 1). A requirement to do this by using the least amount of fuel adds an element of competition to the task. In the second, the students are asked to solve the task analytically, by calculating the kicks necessary to

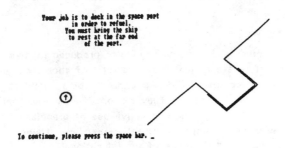

Figure 1. Space Docking Game

send the ship in the prescribed direction, and then to bring it to rest at once, without trial and error.

A series of three activities concerning the concept of friction is provided to help students connect their everyday experiences with motion in a friction-filled world to the interpretation of motion in a friction-free, Newtonian world. Then a sequence of six activities introduces the concepts of velocity vector and change in velocity vector. The dialog emphasizes three aspects of velocity vectors in one dimension: algebraic sign, numerical value and physical units. Students are given practice in computing changes in velocity for arbitrary initial and final velocities and in giving verbal interpretations of changes in motion. The program contains a facility for constructing vector diagrams in both one and two dimensions. Diagrams drawn by the students are checked for accuracy by the program and help is provided when necessary. Each case, consisting of an initial velocity and a final velocity is illustrated using animation of the space ship.

Problem Solving in Kinematics

Instructors of physics are familiar with the difficulties students have with the problem of one-dimensional projectile motion. The dialog "Problem Solving in Kinematics" represents an attempt to incorporate the experience and expertise of skilled instructors into an interactive computer program. A team of four teachers designed the program, implementing on the computer approaches they might use in their office working with individual students who are developing skills in solving mechanics problems.

This problem is a rich source of topics which, though conceptually simple, provide several stumbling blocks to the typical first-year physics student. Among these are the ideas of establishing a coordinate system, applying an operational definition of acceleration, and using the kinematical equations with proper regard to sign and value. Since these are aspects which are important to a wide class of kinematics problems, the example of an object projected vertically in a gravitational field was chosen for extensive and detailed treatment in this dialog. A series of general problem solving steps is introduced, and students are given practice in applying them. These steps include (1) Classifying the problem, (2) Identifying the knowns and unknowns, (3) Identifying the appropriate mathematical tools, (4) Drawing a diagram, (5) Choosing a coordinate system, (6) Solving the equation for the unknown, (7) Substituting values for all the known quantities, and (8) Computing the answer.

The one dimensional projectile problem is actually a problem skeleton or generator, into which certain object names and numerical values are chosen at random and placed in the statement of the problem by the running program. Thus each time the program is run, a different "problem" is presented to the student (Figure 2).

The program provides several special features such as a means for identifying knowns and unknowns by pointing to words in the problem, a capability for constructing a diagram on the screen, a facility for substituting values into the equation, and a means for doing algebra on-line in order to solve an equation for a single variable.

A stone is tossed straight up with a speed of 35 meters per second. This experiment takes place on the planet Achilles where the gravitational acceleration is 20 meters per second per second. Problem: Find the position at time 1.5 sec.

How would you begin this problem?

Figure 2. Finding Height of a Projectile at Time t

Field Testing of the Modules

Initial versions of the software were tested by ten college sophomores and thirty high school seniors from the Irvine area. In all cases the students had already completed an introductory mechanics class. Students worked as individuals or in groups of two or three. Detailed notes were taken on the range of student responses to tasks and answers to questions. Each session took about one hour.

A major purpose of the field testing was to establish whether the answers the design team anticipated actually matched those the learners gave. The success of the learning experience depends on this match so it is important to ensure that the program is prepared for the learners' answers. Minor or major revisions may result from this field testing.

For example, in the dialog "Problem Solving in Kinematics" the following question was asked, "Let's classify the problem. What type of problem is this?" The writing team had anticipated several answers and designed an analysis based on the following patterns:

(a) (ONE or 1) and (DIMENSION)

(b) (FREE and FALL) or (CONSTANT and ACCELERATION)

(c) MATH or PHYSICS or MOTION or SCIENCE

(d) HARD or IMPOSSIBLE or DIFFICULT or EASY or SIMPLE

The answer is considered correct if it contains the patterns defined in (a) and (b) above. The purpose is to get the student to think about the problem; if the student gives the correct answer the program goes on to new material; otherwise, it gives help.

Most college students used the vocabulary anticipated, but some referred to "gravity." The majority of high school students identified this as a "word problem." Both answers were unexpected but typical. The first suggested to the authors a way to improve category (c). The second was an indication that the students needed some help with skills of classifying problems on motion.

Even though our observation of student behavior did not lead to any conclusion about the effectiveness of this material, the dialog worked well with both individuals and groups. A consistent result was that groups tended to make fewer mistakes than individuals working alone, apparently due to the discussion that was stimulated among members of the groups.

Conclusion

Altogether, the thirty-one modules produced by this project take a typical learner a total of about ten hours to complete. (See Appendix A for a complete list of the materials.) They run on the IBM Personal Computer. They make extensive use of graphics. They were developed in UCSD Pascal (tm). Using the underlying software of the Educational Technology Center, the modules are transportable to other machines which support the p-System and which provide comparable graphics capabilities. The dialogs are usable without any additional manual or instructions.

The development of highly interactive computer material based on sound educational research and the experience of expert teachers is a complex and difficult task. It requires a production system which allows for a team approach to design and implementation. The production system of the Educational Technology Center typically involves three or four authors on the design team and a dozen or so coders on the programming staff (Bork 1984). Additional information about the production system is available from the Center at Irvine.

Acknowledgment

In addition to the authors, the following people participated in the design, review and revision of these programs: A. Arons, A. Bork, J. Clement, W. Feibel, A. Fernandez, L. Hojsholt, J. Pitre, R. von Blum, B. White, and W. Wollman. We would like to thank those people and members of the ETC programming staff without whose expertise, patience, and creativity these materials could not have been produced.

References

Bork, Alfred, Personal Computers for Education, Harper & Row, 1984.

Clement, John, "Catalogue of Students' Conceptual Modes in Physics: Movement and Force", working paper, Department of Physics and Astronomy, University of Massachusetts, November, 1977.

Clement, John, "Students' Preconceptions in Introductory Mechanics", American Journal of Physics 50, 66-71, 1982.

diSessa, Andrea, "Unlearning Aristotelian Physics: A Study of Knowledge-Based Learning", Cognitive Science, 1981.

Lawson, Ronald, "Student Understanding of Single Particle Dynamics", doctoral dissertation, Department of Physics, University of Washington, June, 1984

White, Barbara, "Sources of Difficulty in Understanding Newtonian Dynamics", <u>Cognitive Science</u> 7,41, 1983.

White, Barbara, "Designing Computer Games to Help Students Understand Newton's Laws of Motion", <u>Cognition and Instruction</u>, 1, 1984.

Appendix A

I. GRAPHS & MOTION
   1. Graphs of Position
   2. Reading a Graph
   3. Comparing Speed
   4. Comparing Slopes
   5. Position and Velocity Graphs
   6. Speeding Up
   7. Instantaneous Velocity
   8. Curved Position Graphs
   9. Acceleration

II. MOTION WITH AND WITHOUT FRICTION

   A. MOVING & PUSHING
   1. The Coasting Car
   2. Rubbing Effect
   3. Stopping a Space Ship

   B. VELOCITY VECTORS
   1. Speed and Velocity
   2. Velocity vectors in one dimension
   3. Change in Velocity
   4. Exercises with change in Velocity
   5. Velocity vectors in two dimensions
   6. Changes in velocity in two dimensions

   C. DOCKING A SPACE SHIP
   1. Space Docking Game
   2. Using Vectors to Dock a Ship

III. PROBLEM SOLVING

   A. AIDS FOR SOLVING PROBLEMS
   1. Reading Carefully
   2. Using Tables
   3. Obtaining Needed Information
   4. Evaluating Problem Solutions

   B. SOLVING PROBLEMS IN KINEMATICS
   1. Height of a Projectile at Time t
   2. Acceleration of a Planet

IV. SCALING
   1. Size of Squares: Integer Factors
   2. Size of Squares: Non-Integer Factors
   3. Rectangles
   4. Scaling Exercises
   5. Areas of Arbitrary Shapes

COMPUTERS IN EDUCATION, K. Duncan and D. Harris (eds.)
Elsevier Science Publishers B.V. (North-Holland)
© IFIP, 1985

INFORMATION TECHNOLOGY AND FIELD STUDIES

Geoffrey Strack

Advisory Teacher in Computer Education for the London Borough of Haringey, United Kingdom.

The use of Information Technology to enhance Ecological studies is introduced. The various ways in which electronic devices and computers can be used to support and accelerate the learning experience in this area of the curriculum, will be described. An illustrated account will be given to set the scene and participants in the workshop will have the opportunity to enter data and fully experience the range of software. It is planned to discuss the values and implications of the transportability of data between the programs.

Whilst the pervasion of Information Technology in education for younger children has been rapid, the introduction for older children has been comparatively much slower. There have been many reasons for this, but the most important has been the lack of acceptance by teachers that what there is on offer, can significantly improve on their current practices without considerably increasing their own work loads. As with almost all initiatives for older children, successes have been confined to relatively narrow areas of the curriculum, and by focusing initially on Ecology, I believe that we are making a contribution to resolving this problem.

In the writing and use of computer software for use in Field Studies we have had the following objectives in mind :-

To reduce the time needed for the analysis of data and thus make much better use of the limited time available on a field trip.

To provide students with a means by which they
can manipulate statistics with a greater degree of confidence.

To enable students to become familiar with a greater range of statistical tests that are relevant to their data.

Through using the different statistical tests and as a result of growing confidence in their use, be better able to select the individual tests most appropriate to their data.

To provide the facility for transporting data and using it relevantly in as many different programs as possible.

To enable teachers and students to experience an effective use of the computer and as a result of what they see to be a worthwhile activity become more confident in the use of the microcomputer.

Sampling from an oligotrophic stream

The items that we have included in our programme are :-

i). ECOSOFT, a fully interactive suite of programs written by myself and a colleague that enable a number of graphical and data analysis manipulations to be performed quickly, accurately and with the minimum of difficulty.

ii). A data base called QUEST which provides the facility for maintaining detailed data lists for each habitat visited. Information from these can be accessed and displayed in a variety of ways.

iii). A wordprocessor provides students with the opportunity to produce well set out,well presented accurate accounts. The use of this facility has often been the last to be used on a field trip, but once having used it, students (and teachers) use it continuously.

iv). A program that functions as a binary tree, helps students to practise the construction of keys for identification purposes and gain some insight into animal and plant classification.

v). The use of an electronic data capturing device provides the opportunity to measure a variety of physical parameters at regular intervals over a 24 hour period. On returning to the laboratory the device is interfaced to a computer and the data can be played back and displayed graphically.

The response to our programme in the United Kingdom has been very encouraging and the confidence that teachers have developed as a result of their involvement in this use of Information Technology is clearly playing a significant part in the pervasion of the microcomputer to other areas of the curriculum.

COMPUTERS IN EDUCATION, K. Duncan and D. Harris (eds.)
Elsevier Science Publishers B.V. (North-Holland)
© IFIP, 1985

TEACHING MATHEMATICAL STORY PROBLEMS

Peter Schmidt

Institut für Informatik, Universität Bonn,
5300 Bonn, West Germany

One goal of the SCHUMA-project is to develop programs which (semi-)automatically solve school tasks and which may give explanations referring to the solution. The tasks include mathematical story problems. Another goal of the project is the development of intelligent tutoring systems that present tasks to the student. The material basis is the secondary school curriculum. This paper contains didactic reflections and some concepts for an intelligent tutoring system for a special type of story problems, the motion tasks.

1. The SCHUMA - Project

Our institute for computer science is currently starting a research project in the field of school mathematics.

It is one goal of the project to develop programs which are able to solve the tasks that students of secondary schools have to perform. The tasks are mathematical story problems and problems which are formally defined in a scheme. The student presents a problem to the system, he gets a solution of the problem, and he may ask for further explanations referring to the solution.

It is not easy to write a program which automatically solves story problems. To cope with the difficulties in understanding natural language we pursue two directions:

(i) The student has the possibility to word the story in a form with restricted input sentences.

(ii) The system puts a tree of questions to the student so that the system can collect the relevant information in the story.

In both cases the system has to know the type of the task.

Such a system may be a useful help in a student's every day school life.

Another goal of the project is to develop intelligent tutoring programs. We do not plan to develop complete courses. Such activities are surveyed in [1]. We assume that a student has learnt a task type in the school and that he wants to solve more problems as an exercise. [2 and 3] contain descriptions of special intelligent tutoring systems.

The material basis of the work is the secondary school curriculum. The educational basis is the didactics which emphasize the importance of identifying the goals of the learning task.

The ongoing research will focus on the didactics of the subject, the response-sensitivity of the programs, and on giving the student free play.

2. MATHEMATICAL STORY PROBLEMS

Story problems describe a real situation. The ability to know how such realistic problems can be tackled by mathematical methods and the ability to solve such problems are essential for understanding mathematics.

It is typical of the solution of story problems that

i) different ways of solution may be successful,

ii) the order in which one extracts the relevant information is optional, and

iii) there are different ways to represent the information in a solution scheme.

These observations lead to some requirements for a system that presents mathematical story problems:

- The system ought to know the different possible solution methods.

- The system should allow the student to collect the information in an optional order.

More general requirements for educational software are collected in [4].
[5] studies students' errors in the process of solving story problems.

We start our investigations with a special type of story problems, the motion tasks.

3. MOTION TASKS AND DIDACTIC REFLECTIONS

3.1 Motion Tasks

Motion tasks are stories which describe the motion of two objects and ask for further information about the motion.

An example is: A freight train, which covers 40 km per hour, leaves the station at seven o'clock. A fast train, which moves by an average speed of 60 km/h, follows at eight o'clock. When does the fast train pass the freight train?

3.2 The Solution of Motion Tasks

Tasks of that type can sometimes be solved at a glance. A systematic way of solving those tasks consists in setting up one equation or a system of linear equations which relate the known and the unknown quantities. A graphic representation is useful for an approximate solution and facilitates the solution of such problems. The motion of an object is represented by a straight line. It is recommended for instruction to use a graphic representation whenever it is possible.

3.3 The Steps of Solution

A detailed solution of such tasks comprises the following steps:

a) Choose units in a system of coordinates fitting the problem.

b) Read the text and extract the information about the points and/or the gradients of the motions.

c) Draw the straight lines which represent the motions. Infer the approximate solution of the problem from the graphic representation.

d) Set up equations to solve the problem numerically. Solve the resulting system of linear equations.

3.4 Foreknowledge

To solve tasks of that type in the above described way a student needs to know about the use of a system of coordinates, about equations of straight lines in a system of coordinates, about the fact that stright-line motions with constant speed can be represented as straight lines in a system of coordinates, and about the solution of a system of liear equations.

3.5 Goals of Learning

The main goals of learning are to understand a story problem, to extract the relevant information, to describe the problem in mathematical terms, and to solve the problem.

4. THE SYSTEM

4.1 The Instructional Strategy

a) At the beginning of the instruction the system presents a task and gives a model solution. This model solution and especially the graphic representation are the basis for the communication of the student and the system in natural language.

b) The student then may ask questions about the problem and the solution. The system will test the foreknowledge of the student.

c) The system presents tasks of increasing difficulty to the student. If the student has solved all the problems, he is versed in solving tasks of that kind.

d) When a student is good and quick in solving the tasks, the system offers him two possibilities to increase his working speed: i) The system skips tasks so that the student need not solve all the stored problems.   ii) The student need not solve all the problems step by step in dialogue with the computer. He can solve the problems on his own with pencil and paper and present the results to the system. If the solution is correct, the system presents the next problem. If the solution is incorrect, the system tries to find the mistake working backwards together with the student. If the equations are correct, the student has to find his computing error. If the equations are incorrect, the points and gradients which led to the equations are tested.

4.2 The Model Solution

The system presents the model solution for the simple task of section 3.1. A short version of the model solution is as follows:

<u>Step 1:</u> Units in a system of coordinates.

We choose a system of coordinates in order to represent the motions as straight lines. We choose one hour as the unit on the time-axis. We choose 10 km as the unit on the space-axis.

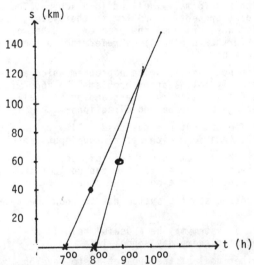

Figure 1: Graphical solution

<u>Step 2:</u> Points and gradients of the motion.

The freight train starts at seven o'clock from the station. Therefore 'x' is a point of its course. The freight train covers 40 km/h. At eight o'clock it is 40 km from the station. Therefore 'o' is a point of its course. The connection of the points shows its course. Analogously for the fast train.

<u>Step 3:</u> Graphical solution.

The point of intersection is the point where

the trains meet. The fast train passes the freight train at about ten o'clock. The distance from the station is about 120 km.

Step 4: Equations.

The equation $s=4t$ describes the course of the freight train. The equation $s=6t-6$ describes the course of the fast train.

Step 5: Numerical solution

(t_0,s_0) is the meeting point.
We solve the system of equations

$s_0=4t_0$, $s_0=6t_0-6$:

$4t_0=6t_0-6$, ... , $t_0=3$, $s_0=12$.

Step 6: Problem Solution

The fast train passes the freight train at ten o'clock. It is 120 km from the station.

4.3 The Set of Tasks

The motion tasks vary with regard to several aspects: The unknown quantities (for example meeting point, speed, starting point); known quantities that can be stated absolutely or relatively; the direction of the motions; quantities that can be stated explicitly or implicitly.

Such tasks can be ranked according to the degree of difficulty. The tasks are connected with each other by the items in which they differ. If a student has solved a task and if he has difficulty solving the following task, the system can bring the new task in relation to the former one. In this way the system can give helpful comments to the student.

4.4 The Dialogue

If a student wants to solve a task step by step, the system makes a request for every step of the solution - for example: Choose the units of the system of coordinates or set up the equations. The student has free play within the steps of the solution. For example, he is free to choose the units and he is free to choose the order in which he interprets the text of the task. For each step of the solution there exists a list containing possible students' mistakes and the origin of the mistakes. The system interprets the mistake and gives the student that information, so that the student can correct himself. If this information does not suffice, the student gets helpful hints and at last the correct answer.

4.5 Parts of the System

Figure 2 shows the main parts of the system.

The 'dialogue within a sitting' controls the presentation of the tasks. It utilizes the student's knowledge, the progress of learning and the student's wishes for its decisions.

The 'dialogue within a task' controls the single steps of the solution and tests the student's answers.

The heart of the system is its knowledge. Like a human teacher the system has different sorts of knowledge: The knowledge about the tasks and their connections, the solution methods, the possible student's mistakes and their causes. In a concrete situation pieces of the different areas of knowledge come together to form a sensible action.

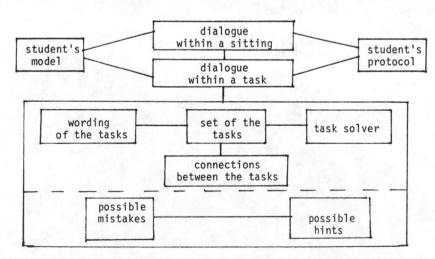

Figure 2: Parts of the system

5. CONCLUSION

The paper contains outlines of the SCHUMA-project and a short description of an intelligent tutoring system that teaches motion tasks.

The SCHUMA-project is in its beginning. Ten students are recently beginning to work in the project for the purpose of a diploma.

We pursue the above mentioned subjects in prototypical investigations.

An important part of the work will be the test with German students. Gagné and Briggs formulate in [6]: 'Even experienced designers have learnt to expect imperfections with their first efforts. It is this very recycling, based on empirical testing of the system that leads to its later effectiveness.'

REFERENCES

[1] Chambers, J.A. and Sprecher, J.W., Computer-Assisted Instruction (Prentice-Hall, Inc., Englewood Cliffs, New Jersey, 1983).

[2] Barr, A. and Feigenbaum, E.A. (ed.), The Handbook of Artificial Intelligence, vol. 2, (Pitman Books Limited, London, 1982).

[3] Sleeman, D. and Brown, J.S. (ed.), Intelligent Tutoring Systems, (Academic Press Inc, London, 1982).

[4] Diepold, P., Kriterien für Unterrichtssoftware, in Arlt, W. and Haefner, K.(eds.), Informatik als Herausforderung an Schule und Ausbildung, GI-Facgtagung, (Springer-Verlag, Berlin, 1984).

[5] Polster, J., Fallstudien zu Mathematisierungsprozessen beim Lösen von Textaufgaben, Dissertation, Universität Frankfurt, (1983).

[6] Gagné, R.M. and Briggs, L.J., Principles of Instructional Design, (Holt, Rinehart and Winston, New York, 1979).

COMPUTERS IN EDUCATION, K. Duncan and D. Harris (eds.)
Elsevier Science Publishers B.V. (North-Holland)
© IFIP, 1985

FINITE STATE MACHINES: AN INTRODUCTORY ENRICHMENT EXPERIENCE FOR GIFTED CHILDREN

Harold Reiter
Dept. of Computer Science
University of Maryland
College Park, MD 20742

Judy Muntner
Montgomery County Public Schools
Gifted and Talented Office
850 Hungerford Drive
Rockville, MD 20850

In recent years, mathematics educators have realized that some ideas and concepts which had been considered too deep for inclusion in the elementary curriculum not only are learnable by children, but in fact often provide a very positive and exciting intellectual experience. This paper relates the experiences of the authors in initiating and teaching several sessions based upon just such a concept. It is the story of a very positive mathematical learning experience. This positive feeling was shared by both the 20 nine, ten and eleven year old learners and the two "overaged" teachers.

BACKGROUND

During a sabbatical year spent in the University of Maryland Computer Science Department, Harold Reiter had the opportunity to teach a sophomore level course in discrete mathematics which included the topic of finite state machines. His nine year old daughter Ashley noticed some of the transition diagrams and she inquired quizzically about their meaning. He told her the definitions and gave an example. Surprisingly, she was quickly able to construct some useful examples and even solve some problems from the course exam.   Three natural questions immediately came to mind:

1. What are the difficulties in learning the elementary ideas in the mechanics of finite state machines?
2. Furthermore, if it is possible to teach these ideas to 5th and 6th graders, should we?
3. Finally, if such ideas are learnable by some elementary school students, who are they?

Upon reaching the conclusion that the essential skill needed for basic understanding of finite state machines (for the definition see the last paragraph of this section) is sequential processing of elementary bits of information, Harold Reiter contacted Judie Muntner, one of his daughter's teachers, and presented the germ of the idea and his questions to her. It was agreed that one reasonable way to answer question 2 was to test it in the classroom. As a test population for trying out these ideas an ideal solution presented itself: the group of 20 gifted and talented (g-t) 5th and 6th grade students Ashley

worked with one day a week. These students are a part of a special program in the Montgomery County Maryland School System called T.O.K., Thinking Opportunities for Kids. They leave their regular classroom and school one day a week to work with other identified g-t students and a special g-t teacher in a resource room environment especially designed for them. This group of students was felt to be a good test population for several reasons. First, in teaching gifted students teachers have more latitude in their choice of strategies. If one method doesn't work, another can be substituted. The teacher can mentally regroup, change approaches and not be overly concerned about "turning off" the students. They have "staying power". Second, g-t students are generally beyond Piaget's concrete-level-of-thinking stage so they are able to deal with conceptual ideas.

Third, gifted students, by virtue of the characteristics that identify them (see Table 1), learn faster and with less effort and retain more information than their peers. Thus, they are an ideal population for educators to work with in determining learning activities appropriate to the general school population.

Several higher level thinking skills, as identified by Bloom [1] would be called upon by these students in their study of finite state machines. These include analyzing, generalizing, evaluating, synthesizing, abstracting, and generating hypotheses. Bloom [1] urges teachers to have g-t students spend more time engaged in activities that involve the three thinking skills of analysis, synthesis and evaluation, skills he identified in his hierarchal pyramid.

Table 1. Characteristics of Gifted Children

1. Sensitivity to, awareness of, and curiosity regarding quantity and the quantitative aspects of things.
2. Quickness in perceiving, comprehending, understanding, and dealing effectively with quantity and quantitative aspects of things within the environment.
3. Ability to think and work abstractly and symbolically when dealing with quantity and quantitative ideas.
4. Ability to communicate quantitative ideas effectively to others, both orally and in writing; and to readily receive and assimilate quantitative ideas in the same way.
5. Ability to perceive mathematical patterns, structures, relationships and interrelationships.
6. Ability to think and perform in quantitative situations in a flexible rather than in a stereotyped manner.
7. Ability to think and reason analytically and deductively; ability to think and reason inductively and to generalize.
8. Ability to transfer learning to new or novel "untaught" quantitative situations.
9. Ability to apply mathematical learning to social situations, to other curriculum areas, and the like.

(From Weaver and Brawley, 1959, pp. 6-77)

We agreed to hold three 45 minute sessions. We hoped to answer three questions during the study. First, are finite state machines an appropriate topic for g-t elementary school students? Second, would these ideas have a place in the elementary school curriculum? And third, how would students react to this experience?

Rather than beginning with the general notion of finite state machines, we agreed to discuss only the class of such machines called finite state acceptors. A finite state acceptor (FSA) is a collection of five objects (S, Σ, S_0, F, T) where S is a finite set of states, Σ is a finite set of input symbols, S_0 is a special member of S called the start state, F is a subset of S called the "favorable" states, and T is a transition table which determines the next state as a function of the current state and the current "scanned" input symbol.

The First Session

Instead of attempting to discuss this definition, however, we began by presenting several examples (of diagrams) of FSA's. We hoped that the students would decide for themselves the different parts of the machine, thus "discovering" the definition. The first example presented at the board was

Fig. 1

Translating the symbols $\mid\rightarrow$ and $\sqrt{}$ into start and favorable provided the first link between the diagram and the formal definition. We were ready to discuss the action of the machine on the "input string" 1 0 1 0 0 1 1 0. We start by "processing" the left most input symbol. The arrow labeled 1 pointing from S_0 to S_1 is followed so that the machine goes into state S_1 after one transition and scans the 2nd input symbol, a 0. We follow the arrow labeled 0 leaving S_1 (this arrow is called a "loop") and this leads back to S_1. Continuing in this manner we obtain the sequence $S_0 S_1 S_1 S_0 S_0 S_0 S_1 S_0 S_0$.

Since the final state S_0 is checked, we accept the input sequence 1 0 1 0 0 1 1 0. Before looking at the FSA's action on other input strings we decided to give the students a chance to help us single out the components of the machine. We agreed that the machine had two locations which we called "states", two types of arrow labels which we called "input symbols", and some other symbols "$\mid\rightarrow$" and "$\sqrt{}$". What was not clear to them was the importance of the relationship between the arrows, the input symbols, and the states. At this stage we distributed worksheets with the diagram of figure 1 at the top and the partially completed list below:

States: S_0, S_1
Input Symbols:
Start State:
Favorable State(s):
Transition Table:

	0	1
S_0	S_0	S_1
S_1		

The youngsters had very little trouble completing the list. At the bottom of the worksheet was another table:

Input String	Decision
1 0 1 0 0 1 1 0	Accept
1 0 0 1 0 0 0 1	
1 1 1 0 0 1 1	
0 1 1 0 0	
0 0 0 0	
0 1 0 1 1 0 1 1 1	

Again we asked the students to complete the table. They did so quickly and enthusiastically. Finally we got to the fundamental question: What is it about the accepted strings that differentiates them from the others? We asked them to develop hypotheses about the characteristics of the accepted strings. When a child developed an hypothesis, we either checked it out as a group with examples of strings satisfying the hypothesis or asked the child to come up with a few new strings he could use himself to check his hypothesis. One child noticed that among the accepted strings in the table, those with any 1's at all have a pair of consecutive 1's. So we agreed to test 101. Realizing that his hypothesis did not do the job he eagerly went "back to the drawing board." Several students soon realized that the location and the number of 0's in the string has no effect on the decision since it has no effect on the current state (actually 0 can be viewed as the identity function from $\{S_0, S_1\}$ to itself). According to Krutetskii (3), this ability of "curtailment", the elimination of intermediate steps in the thinking process, is one of the three major abilities used to distinguish mathematically gifted children. Before long almost all the children realized that the accepted strings of 0's and 1's were those with an even number of 1's. Many reached this conclusion on their own, but a few others required more input strings than those provided on the worksheet.

Next we asked what input strings would be accepted if the √ is changed from S_0 to S_1. A few were able to reason abstractly here that the complement of the previously accepted set of strings would be accepted here. Others needed to work through this example just as they had for the first FSA. As each new diagram was presented, the students excitedly and eagerly began to question and analyze the problem. Many questions were "what if...?" and "can it have...?". Each new diagram began with a concrete discussion and analysis: what are the states?, the input symbols?, the start state?, the favorable states?, and the transition table? We followed this up by asking them to determine the acceptance or rejection of several strings, both our previously constructed ones and their spur-of-the-moment strings. In response to questions about the limits of what constitutes an FSA, we presented a complicated machine with states identified by upper case letters and input set composed of several lower case letters. Some other questions generated during this session were: Is there an upper or lower limit on the number of states, the number of input symbols or the size of an input string?

The third example was the three stat FSA whose diagram is given by

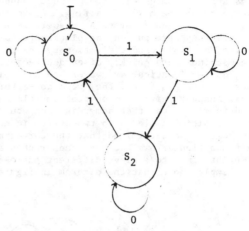

Fig. 2

Again, the children were asked to fill out on their worksheets the list of machine parts, this time with no help from us. Several were able to do this very quickly.

States: S_0, S_1, S_2
Input Symbols: 0, 1
Start State: S_0
Favorable State(s): S_0
Transition Table:

	0	1
S_0	S_0	S_1
S_1	S_1	S_2
S_2	S_2	S_0

At this point some children jumped immediately to the question of characterizing the accepted strings without first considering the sample input strings given on the worksheet. In other words, they were able to attack the general problem and then to regard each sample string as a special case. Most children still needed to work through a few examples before reaching a conclusion about the decision rule.

We had planned the work up to this time to constitute our first session of approximately 45 minutes. However, because the students grasped the ideas and learned to apply them so quickly, we still had almost half our session left. Their responses showed the excitement and pleasure they felt being involved in what they perceived to be a real-life problem solving situation involving mathematics. Clearly it was time to quickly regroup and decide how best to proceed.

We decided to present the students with a problem of constructing a FSA of their own which
accepts a certain collection of strings (and
none others). The problem: to construct a machine which accepts (precisely) those strings of
zeros and ones which have two or more consecutive ones somewhere in the string. Again they
worked quickly and eagerly. As answers were developed, they were put on the blackboard for
testing, analysis, and evaluation by the group.
Some machines were quickly discarded because
they had two identical arrows or had incomplete
transition tables (i.e., they were non-determini-
stic). Another fairly common problem related to
non-determinism was that some diagrams would
have transition tables with two states in certain boxes. We determined that the corresponding transition arrows had been constructed at
different times to achieve different purposes.
For example, note that the diagram in figure 3

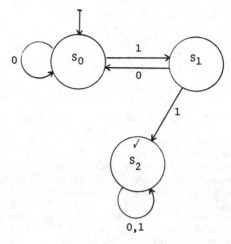

Fig. 4

such strings of 0's and 1's by the name "binary
strings" but in introducing the term binary
string, we tried to make sure the children did
not confuse binary string with the (integral)
binary representation of a positive integer,
the latter of which must have a 1 in the left-
most position.

The first session was an unqualified success.
The students had advanced faster and further
than we had believed possible in view of previous experiences working with college students.
It was exciting to see their enthusiasm.

The Second Session

Several students showed up the next week with
their finite machines designed and tested. Greg
presented his solution to the problem involving
0's at the end of the string at the board:

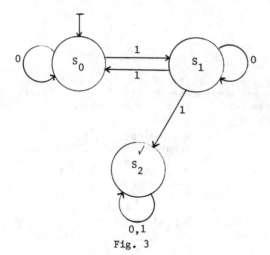

Fig. 3

has two transition arrows leaving S_1 labeled
with 1. Although this situation is not allowed
for a FSA, the intention of the student was to
go back to S_0 when the 0-loop at S_1 has been
used and to go to S_2 when it hasn't since in
that case two successive 1's would have appeared.
As a group we attempted to find a general method
for eliminating this problem. We realized that
in this particular problem, our intention should
be to start over whenever a 0 is scanned unless
two successive 1's have already been scanned.
Therefore, a solution to the problem (there are
other solutions) is the FSA whose diagram is
given in figure 4.

We pointed out several times that a FSA could
fail in either of two ways. It could accept
some strings it should reject and it could reject some strings it should accept. Thus in
testing a FSA, we must use both strings with the
acceptance property and those without it. We
ended the session by presenting a challenge for
the following week. Design two FSA's, one which
accepts strings of 0's and 1's which begin with
two 0's and one which accepts strings of 0's and
1's which end with two 0's. We had begun to call

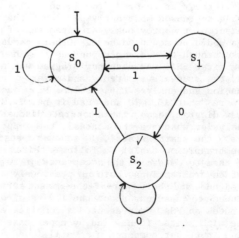

Fig. 5

The group quickly analyzed this solution. Was it truly (the diagram of) a FSA? Yes, O.K. let's test it out with some strings. O.K., so far, so good. Now let's reason through it. If the string ends in two 0's, must it be accepted? Yes. Now, if it ends with 01, 11 or 10, must it be rejected? Yes. He did it! Now, some of the students like Greg were given the choice of working on other machines or staying with the group to design the solution to the other part of the challenge. As it turned out, the children did both. They chimed in and joined in the group design work as well as completing their individual tasks. The group began by analyzing the problem -- where did they want to stay? ... to wind up? Then they worked to fill in the missing elements. In working through the problem of accepting strings which start with a pair of 0's, it was clear that the decision to accept or reject must be made once and for all after the second symbol is scanned. We decided to use the word "trap" for a state which cannot be left. Note that some traps are favorable and some are not. The group had little trouble designing a machine to accept (exactly) those binary strings which begin with a pair of 0's.

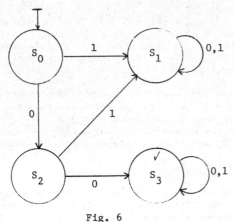

Fig. 6

This group work was designed to provide a review of the previous week's session. However, as we proceeded the questions and responses from the group indicated this to be unnecessary. A rather remarkable thing happened during this group session. Bobby, one of the brightest children in the group, had been out sick during the first session. Yet, after just 20 minutes of discussion with little mention of states or transition tables, he showed he knew intuitively exactly what a FSA is. Does this mean that the notion of FSA is a natural conceptual forerunner of the digital computer? After all, it is deterministic, it has input, it has (a kind of) memory, and we can think of it as having output (0 when the final state is unfavorable and 1 when the final state is favorable).

Our last activity involved asking students to make up their own rule and to design and test a FSA for it. After accomplishing this task they

were asked to fold down the top of the page, hiding the decision rule but exposing the diagram. Papers were exchanged and students were asked to develop an hypothesis for the rule, test it and work until they successfully identified the rule. As usual, each child could choose to work alone or with a partner. About a third were able to complete this task successfully. Others needed help in thinking of a rule to begin the task. This activity allowed for a great deal of peer sharing and discussion. Interested students were again invited to present their diagrams on the board. Some of the decision rules for which FSA's were constructed were (for binary strings):

1. Accept if (and only if) the third symbol is a 1.
2. Accept if (and only if) there are two or more consecutive 0's.
3. Accept if (and only if) there are only 1's in the string.
4. Accept if (and only if) there are at least two 1's.
5. Accept if (and only if) the number of 1's is a multiple of 4.
6. Accept if (and only if) the final symbol is 0.

One student tried to design a FSA which accepts binary strings having an equal number of 0's and 1's. We had some difficulty explaining that there is no FSA which accomplishes this decision rule. We pointed out that a more powerful machine would be required to recognize such strings.

The Third Session

During this very short session we simply asked the students to comment on the value of the experience. Why should we bother to learn about finite machines? What, if anything, was neat about them? Some of the responses were:

... It gives another view of math.
... It develops patterns of thinking.
... It will help me with my computer work.
... It was fun.
... It's binary.

Although we did not pursue it, there is a large store of construction problems for FSA's associated binary and ternary arithmetic. If students have studied binary numbers, problems of this type would nicely reinforce their understanding. Here we use as input strings binary (ternary) representations. Students can be asked to construct machines which accept the following collections:

1. The representations of the positive even integers.
2. The representations of multiples of k, where k is a fixed integer bigger than 2.
3. The ternary representations which do not contain the digit 1.

CONCLUSIONS

Although students were enthusiastic about their new learning experience, we got the impression that they would not have described it as mathematics. Thus, one positive effect that we had not considered previously was that it gave rise to an expanded view of what mathematics is. Many of them told us that they just couldn't wait to get to college and take math courses like discrete structures.

Can this topic be taught to the g-t students and should it be? We would respond "yes" unreservedly. It is an appropriate topic that demands use of higher thinking skills. It also provides both acceleration and enrichment simultaneously. Can and should finite machines be introduced to our regular elementary school population? Again, our experience tells us that this is possible. It is a topic that would allow these students to see and do mathematics in a new light. This group may not learn as quickly and some may not be ready for the more in-depth experience of designing their own machines, possibly preferring to stay at the analysis level (trying to find strings which are accepted and rejected and then finding the decision rule).

Another potential use for this topic is diagnostic. Since very few children have ever been exposed to the mechanics of FSA's, it would make a helpful tool for differentiating capable mathematics students from those who are truly gifted. In any case, the elementary school mathematics teacher with a penchant for learning mathematics will find it very rewarding to share this excitment and thought provoking learning experience with his/her class.

[1] Bloom, Benjamin S., Taxonomy of Educational Objectives, Handbook I: cognitive domain (McKay Publishing Co., New York, 1956).
[2] Weaver, J. Fred and Cleo F. Brawley, Enriching the elementary school program for more capable children, Journal of Education 142 (Oct 1959) 6-7.
[3] Krutetskii, V. A., An investigation of mathematical abilities in school children, in Kilpatrick, Jeremy and Izaak Wirszup (eds.), Soviet Studies in the Psychology of Learning and Teaching Mathematics, Volume II: The structure of mathematical abilities (University of Chicago, Chicago, 1969).

COMPUTERS IN EDUCATION, K. Duncan and D. Harris (eds.)
Elsevier Science Publishers B.V. (North-Holland)
©IFIP, 1985

PROGRAMMING ICONS AND CREATING MATHEMATICAL GAMES

Marlene Kliman

MIT and Edinburgh University

MIT Educational Computing Group

545 Technology Square

Cambridge, MA 02139

USA

This paper discusses PI, an iconographic, joystick-driven programming language designed for young and handicapped children. Partly based on Logo turtle graphics, PI provides a set of language primitives and game shells that give children enough structure to create interactive mathematical games and enough freedom to feel that their work is original and meaningful. Testing has shown that PI is a viable system for young children to use for both structured and open-ended mathematical work.

1. Introduction

PI (Programming Icons) is an icon-based, joystick-driven programming language that was developed to fill a gap in the range of mathematical software available for young children. Although mathematical software for young children abounds, much of what is currently available may be difficult to use, or is somewhat restricted. There is little that very young or mildly handicapped children can readily use for open-ended mathematical investigations.

Difficulties may arise when children lack skills required to interpret and manipulate the software. Often skills such as letter or word recognition, memorization of commands, or location of keys on a keyboard must be mastered before use of a particular piece of software can proceed fluently and without outside help. Learning to use such software can be frustrating for some children, especially those who cannot read well or easily use a keyboard.

To avoid some of these problems, touchpads [4] and other special devices [8] have been used as input systems for Logo [1] and other software. These input systems are easier to use than keyboards, and can be overlaid with a transparency that represents commands as letters or symbols instead of as words. Unfortunately, most of these systems, however helpful, are also limiting. They are usually not versatile enough for anything but very elementary and restricted work. For example, since most touchpads cannot display information sent from the computer, they cannot be used for representing new or changed information.

In addition to restrictions imposed by the input system, the design of the software itself may also impose serious limitations on what can be achieved by very young users. Relatively complex rules or syntax, commands with ill-chosen names (or symbols), and limitations of the software may prevent young children from reaching a level of proficiency in which they can feel that they are doing anything very interesting or creative. For example, writing interactive programs, which can be highly motivating, is usually not possible with simple systems.

PI addresses both software limitation and input problems. Because PI users need no ability with reading, typing, or numerals (although at advanced levels, numeric input may be desirable), PI has very wide accessibility. PI provides a way of using a very concrete version of turtle geometry for designing and playing mathematical games. Beginners as well as advanced users can create games which they find interesting and challenging.

2. Description of PI

Figure 1 shows the screen used for programming with PI. On the left is a menu with icons for the PI primitives FORWARD, RIGHT, PENCOLOR, and CLEAR SCREEN (a LEFT primitive may be added in the future). These icons are compatible with Bliss [3], an international iconographic communitcation system used with the handicaped. At the lower left center is an icon for saving procedures, and in the center is a grid of large squares on which a turtle shaped like a grid square with an arrow in it can move. As the turtle moves and draws on the grid, an icon-sized representation of the picture on the grid is automatically created next to the procedure-saving icon. This icon can be saved and added to the menu. It can then, in turn, be used in creating new procedures.

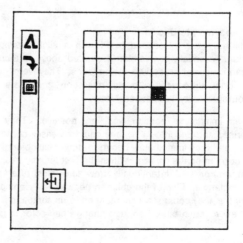

Figure 1: The Screen for Programming with PI

PI is operated with a joystick that has a lever and at least one button. The lever is used for selecting the icon to be executed, and the button is used for executing icons. Additional joystick buttons can be used to control additional turtles. Since commands can be entered in any order and there is no chance for entering a misspelled or incorrect command, syntax errors are impossible.

Mathematical games of a wide range of complexity and difficulty can be created and played by using one of the game shells in conjunction with the PI grid, turtle, primitives, and user-defined procedures. Games are played by loading any of a "game board" (pre-designed picture drawn with PI) onto the PI grid, special icons (representing procedures programmed with PI) onto the menu, and sets of game rules. Rules may constrain how and where the turtle moves and the colors with which it draws, and may assign point values to various moves or combinations of moves. Game shells are frameworks for determining the various parameters of games - boards, icons, and rules. Each game has a separate "rules screen" in which the parameters of the game can be set.

3. The Pilot Study

3.1. Testing Conditions

In the spring of 1984, a version of PI was implemented on an Apple II microcomputer and was tested in a pilot study [6, 7]. In the pilot study, seven children worked with PI for an average of five 40 minute sessions each, alone or in pairs, over a period of about three weeks. The children's ages ranged between 5 and 9: one was 5, three were 6, two were 7, and one was 9. Four of the children were from non-professional backgrounds and had never used a computer before.

Pilot testing was mainly concerned with making sure that PI is a viable system for young users and developing some activities for beginners. Additional testing will further refine some of the game shells and look at the types of things children of different ages and abilities create with PI over a longer period of time.

3.2. Learning to Use PI

Children were introduced to PI with a slightly simplified version, essentially the version described above, without the screen clear and procedure saving icons. They were given a very brief introduction to its operation and were then encouraged to try it out themselves.

Their immediate reaction was very positive. They were surprised and delighted that they could so easily control the turtle, and they immediately began to draw multicolored lines and corners on the screen. Within the first ten minutes, all of them, unprompted, intentionally drew all or most of a square or a rectangle. Five of the children became fairly competent users (i.e. they could state an intention to do something, such as draw a line in blue, turn, and change pen color to green,

and then do it) within the first five to fifteen minutes. The other two children did not master the commands until the second session.

3.3. Pre-Designed Mathematical Games

After initial exploration, many of the children seemed to lack the confidence and the initiative to continue to discover on their own what could be done with PI. Although they were able to suggest pictures and patterns that they might draw with PI, the children did not, in general, feel ready to approach these projects with confidence or plans. At this point, the children were, however, very interested in and challenged by a series of pre-designed games involving guiding the turtle through various paths, including mazes and obstacle courses. These games were successful in building up children's confidence, weaning them on to more creative and original mathematical work with PI, providing a context in which they could gain fluency with PI, encouraging simple mathematics such as counting, comparing, and measuring, and engendering a cooperative spirit.

A typical game is shown in figure 2. The picture on the grid is meant to represent a body of water with two islands in it. Children were asked to move the turtle to the purple squares in the upper left corner (shown with diagonal stripes in figure 2) without straying from the blue water (shown clear). Point values were later added to each color in the picture, so that each time the turtle landed on a square of a particular color, the child's score would be raised accordingly. Children were then asked to move the turtle to the purple squares while collecting as few points as possible.

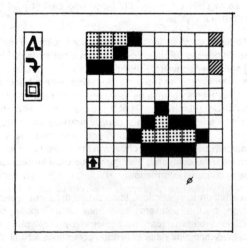

Figure 2: A Pre-designed Game

One of the features that seemed most motivating about the games was the on-screen tally of points. Although children were given the option of playing the games without scoring, they invariably chose to use the tally. Use of the tally promoted enthusiasm by encouraging the children to look for shortcuts and patterns, so that they could achieve a better score. Although at first some children tended to be competitive, and simply tried to get a better score than the others, they soon became curious about what others did to achieve better scores. They began to work together to find the smallest number of moves needed to follow a particular path or get through a particular maze. In this way, they discovered that it was possible to traverse some paths in more than one way, with the same number of moves, and that four 90 degree turns bring the turtle back to its original orientation.

3.4. Original Mathematical Games

3.4.1. Overview

After working with pre-designed games for between one and two sessions, the children's confidence and facility with PI increased greatly, and they began to talk about what they would do if they could make up their own games with PI. At this point, the game shells were gradually introduced.

Designing and playing mathematical games fostered a cooperative atmosphere. Children enjoyed playing each others' games, and usually the game designer watched intently, offering or denying hints and suggestions, as others played his or her game. Sometimes the game designer would not tell the player the rules, and would instead insist that the player discover them. Often a game would be suspended while children discussed how to make the game easier, harder, or more interesting, or talked over the advantages of a particular move. Occasionally, children gave conflicting rules and had to debug their games. They considered how the various rules interacted to prevent the game from proceeding as they had intended and tried to figure out a way of changing the rules so that the game worked properly. Sometimes they noticed and rectified the conflict right away, but often they did not realize that there was any problem until they actually started playing the game.

3.4.2. Board

The first game shell to which children were introduced was Board. With Board, a natural extension of the pre-designed games they had been playing, the children used PI to draw multicolored game boards on the grid and made up rules to go along with them.

Most of the games that the children first created with Board were quite simple. These games centered on moving the turtle to a particular goal square (i.e. "the blue square in the corner", or "the yellow square in the middle"). With each move, one point was added to or subtracted from the total score, depending on the color of the square on which the turtle landed. Over time, however, children created Board games with much more intricate rules and goals. Typical rules created after children had worked with Board for one or two sessions involved adding and subtracting numbers other than one - for example "if you land on red, you lose two points, if you land on green, your score goes back to zero." Some of the more advanced rules had more than one part - for example, "if you land on red, you lose three points and you have to go back to the beginning." Examples of the more complex goals developed include completing spirals or geometric figures, putting the missing color into a pattern, and filling the entire grid with one color.

In order to win at these more complicated Board games, children developed strategies for maximizing scores. Typical strategies included landing on grid squares of particular colors to get more (or fewer) points or an automatic move to a more advantageous position, or avoiding squares of those colors that would produce less favorable results when landed on. Many of the more complicated games required that children do quite a bit of mathematics when creating game boards. For example, in creating boards for games that involved completing spirals or filling the missing colors into a pattern, children counted squares, compared side lengths, and looked at boards from different orientations.

3.4.3. Tiles

A different game shell, Tiles, was designed specifically to encourage this kind of geometric and spatial work. Using Tiles, children could create games involving tiling all or part of the grid with particular shapes. Children could pick the shapes with which they wanted to try to tile the grid from a pool of pre-designed shapes (in the future, children will be able to program these shapes themselves), and either try to fill the grid in a haphazard way or decide on a structure for the game. A typical game might require that two players, each with a turtle assigned to draw a particular shape in a particular color, work together to fill the grid by alternating tiles of different colors.

Figure 3 shows a screen layout for a Tiles game that several of the children played. An icon representing a square and one representing an L-shape have been added to the menu. When one of these icons is executed, the turtle draws the corresponding shape on the screen in the appropriate orientation. A toggle can be set so that shapes cannot overlap. In figure 3, the grid has been partially filled, and the counters in the lower right indicate how many of each has been used.

Tiles games directly influenced the type of patterns and shapes that the children drew as Board game boards, and encouraged much discussion about grid-filling, and rotations and orientations of shapes. For example, after spending some time filling an eight by eight grid with different-shaped tiles made up of four squares, a 7 year old child, described by his teacher as average in mathematics, announced that sixteen of one type of any such tile (given that tiles can wrap around the grid) will always fill the grid "because there will always be

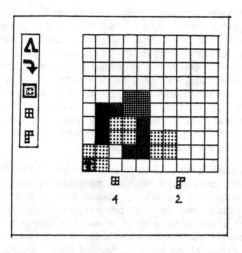

Figure 3: A Tiles Game

sixty-four little squares." Excited about his discovery, he then went on to consider how many of tiles composed of various numbers of squares would fill the grid.

3.4.4. Chase

The Chase game shell provided a particularly apt context for addition and subtraction, graphing, and visual thinking. With Chase, one or two players use turtles to try to "trap" a square moving around the grid in a geometric pattern. Each time a player moves or turns, the square moves one step in its pattern. Players must determine the square's path and then figure out how to intercept it so that they can land on the same grid square as the moving square. As with Tiles, Chase could be used for free play, or children could create rules determining more specific game rules such as the number of players, scoring, etc.

Some children using Chase found it helpful to first make a "map" of the square's path on a piece of large-squared paper. They located the square by using the screen grid as an X-Y coordinate system (e.g. counting out a position "four across and three from the bottom"), then found and marked the corresponding position on the squared paper. When the children numbered the positions in the square's path, they could tell where the square would be in a certain number of moves by counting up (or adding on) the number of moves from the number representing the square's position.

3.4.5. Programming with PI

While most of the testing sessions were spent working with mathematical games, three children spent much of one session writing programs with PI. They had been told beforehand that they were going to be able to write programs next time. They were very excited about this, although they had little idea of what it entailed. When first programming with PI, the children all recognized that a miniature version of whatever was being created on the grid appeared at the lower left of the screen. They found the icons sensible and meaningful representations of the procedures they created and had no trouble remembering that executing the icons caused a similar picture to be drawn on the PI grid.

The children were amazed that the turtle was able to reproduce their patterns. Two of them spent much of the session running one or two procedures that they had created over and over again in different colors and orientations, intrigued with the variety that could be achieved. The third child worked at a more complex level. He did not merely use PI to create procedures out of primitives, he also combined procedures and primitives into higher-level procedures.

4. Discussion

Pilot testing showed that PI provides a natural context in which young children can do mathematics. In free play with PI and in designing and playing mathematical games, children measured, compared, counted, added, and multiplied in order to draw shapes, to determine how many of a certain move would bring the turtle to a particular grid square, or to figure out how the best score could be achieved. PI also provides a motivating context for logical and visual thinking. Children frequently invented and tested hypotheses, debugged games and programs, and worked with rotations and spatial orientation of shapes.

One likely reason that PI is so captivating is that it allows children to play an important part in constructing and manipulating their learning environments. Using PI, children can set their own goals and choose the rules by which and the context in which the goals can be attained. For example, when a game board became too familiar, children sometimes changed the board on which the game was played, but kept the same rules and objective. When a game became too easy, children sometimes changed the rules slightly to make the game more challenging. As observers of human nature, children enjoyed watching their friends navigate through the rules and constraints they had created, eager to determine what others found easy or difficult. As amateur scientists, children set down rules, formed hypotheses, and conducted experiments to discover specific and general properties of the rule-based systems they had created.

PI's potential as a teaching tool is promising [5]. Unlike mathematical teaching aids such as Cuisinaire rods and Dienes blocks [2], PI does not simply give children concrete objects on which to perform mathematical operations without introducing them to the corresponding mathematical notation. Since PI allows use of counters, repeat factors, numbers and numeric expressions, children can begin to establish for themselves that formal arithmetic can be a useful and meaningful shorthand. Of course, a teacher's intervention in introducing appropriate symbolic notation, helping children to generalize and formalize their experiences with PI, and guiding and structuring the kinds of explorations and games created can also be extremely useful, if not crucial for some children.

A system such as PI could not have been created without computer technology. Besides being scorekeeper, rule book, referee, playground, and construction kit, the computer also eliminates a great deal of tedium, thus, helping children maintain interest in their work. The structure of a game can be altered significantly in less than a minute by changing several rules, and a game board can be redesigned easily in a very short time as well. Because of the power of the computer, great variety can be achieved within the constraints imposed by a language simple enough to be used by very young children. By providing a carefully designed set of language primitives and game shells, PI gives even beginners enough structure to create mathematical games and projects, but also provides enough freedom so that no two games need be alike, so that original and unique games can be created, and so that older children are challenged as well.

5. Summary

Pilot testing has shown that PI is a viable context for children's creative mathematical work. Future testing will involve using PI as an educational tool for children of a variety of abilities and backgrounds, and will also focus on PI as an environment in which to study formation and changes in children's simple mathematical goals, plans, and debugging strategies. Cross-cultural research with PI could easily be performed, as, unlike most educational software, PI makes no assumptions about the user's native language or language abilities. Future research should shed light on how children fare in learning environments in which their work is structured and guided by the constraints of the environment itself, but within those constraints, children are largely free to engage in self-directed and original work. This is the sort of learning environment that is made possible with computers.

Acknowledgments

I am very grateful to Andy diSessa at MIT, as many of the ideas in PI grew out of discussions with him. I would also like to thank the head teacher, students, and staff of St. Patrick's School, Edinburgh, for their cooperation in this project, and those people at MIT and Edinburgh who read and commented on drafts of this paper.

References

1. Abelson, H.   *Apple   Logo.*   BYTE/McGraw-Hill, Peterborough, NH, 1982.

2. Dienes, Z.   *An Experimental Study of Mathematics Learning.* Hutchinson, London, 1963.

3. Hehner, B. (ed).   *Bliss Symbols for Use.* Blissymbolics Communication Institute, Toronto, 1980.

4. Howe, J.   Using Computers in Special Education. Department of Artificial Intelligence Research Paper 148, Edinburgh, 1980.

5. Kliman, M. A New Approach to Infant and Early Primary Mathematics. *Primary Contact* (1985 - to appear). Published by Manchester Polytechnic, Manchester UK.

6. Kliman, M. Programming Icons. Department of Artificial Intelligence Research Report 229, Edinburgh, 1984.

7. Kliman, M.   Sprite Logo, Icon-Style: Sprite Logo for Educational Simulations. *Your 64* , 2 (August 1984).

8. Perlman, R. Using Computer Technology to Provide a Creative Learning Environment for Pre-school Children. *Logo Memo* 24, MIT, 1076.

COMPUTERS IN EDUCATION, K. Duncan and D. Harris (eds.)
Elsevier Science Publishers B.V. (North-Holland)
© IFIP, 1985

405

Macintosh: Rethinking computer education for engineering students

Andrew U. Frank

Department of Civil Engineering
University of Maine at Orono, Orono, Maine 04469

Computer education for engineering students is an open problem. The advent of a new type of affordable hardware, the Apple Macintosh, which introduced a new concept for the user-machine interface opens new possibilities for computer education. This paper discusses (1) the possible goals of computer education for engineering students, (2) a new concept for introducing computers, and (3) how the Macintosh is being used to achieve those goals at the University of Maine.

1. Introduction

Education in computer usage, i.e. how to use a computer to best advantage to solve applied problems, has become a problem in many science and engineering departments. Most students take an introductory programming course early in the curriculum. Because of the unforgiving nature of the mainframe systems usually employed, they spend enormous amounts of time on trivial assignments and little is left for more realistic and complex problems. When they are later asked to use computers for solving technical or scientific assignments, they are ill prepared. As a result, computers are not used to full advantage in our present educational system.

Modern personal computers, which are easier to operate, allow students to concentrate more on the essential goals, and to minimize extraneous problems related to idiosyncrasies in complex operating systems. The new Apple Macintosh is perhaps the most outstanding example of an easy to use machine. The Macintosh incorporates for the first time the concept of 'direct manipulation' in a machine in the price range of a personal computer. It uses novel hardware, (i.e. a powerful 16-bit microprocessor and a high resolution, bit mapped graphics screen) combined with innovative operating system software to provide the first low cost system with an effective 'visual interface'. Operations inside the computer are made graphically visible for the user which does not only help the experienced user, but dramatically reduces the beginning students problem of understanding and using the system [9].

This paper describes a serie of two courses offered by the Civil Engineering Department of the University of Maine at Orono, as a new approach to the challenge of more effective computer education for engineering students. The department is a typical civil engineering department with approximately 250 students. It is part of the University of Maine at Orono, a smaller land grant university with about 11,000 students. The course discussed in this paper is considered to be an experiment within the College of Engineering and Science. If the course is successful, we expect it to be duplicated in other engineering departments. Moreover, we feel that these ideas can be effectively applied to computer education in other fields as well. We advocate that others critically examine their present offerings in this area,

and develop similar courses to better respond to the needs of their students.

2. Goals of education in computer usage

Everybody asks for computer literacy. However, no generally accepted definition exists. The following is a list of what we see as important goals for computer education for engineering students. Computer education should enable students not only to use today's computer efficiently, but also to understand the basic principles involved so they will be able to stay abreast of future changes. It is thus obvious that an effective course must do more than teach a computer language. The course must concentrate on the general principles which are unlikely to change rapidly, and use present systems only to illustrate these principles in computers. Students must understand which parts of the computer environment they will find similar on other machines, and which are particular for the machine used for instruction.

2.1 Understanding computers – It seems necessary that students understand the hardware components of today's computers, their functions, limitations and advantages. It is equally important to know the basic principles of software; not only the operating system, but also the compiler, linker, editor and other utilities.

2.2 Information and data – To understand how computers may be used to solve problems is facilitated by understanding the characters of information and data. Such knowledge may prevent the widespread confusion about what computers can (easily) do and what operations are (still) reserved for human beings.

2.3 Communication – Communication of ideas and exchange of data are becoming more and more important. The principles that apply both to communication between machines (networks), and to the effective use of output for human understanding (print, screen, graphics, voice) must be understood.

2.4 Programming – All engineering students should learn at least one programming language and become familiar with it. We do not assume that most practicing engineers will write their own programs; instead, we foresee general use of software packages, produced by specialsts. Nevertheless, teaching a programming language seems essential in order to provide the student with a framework to explore and apply the more abstract topics mentioned thus far. Additionally, students must be able to apply programming in order to solve problems put forward in later courses.

We do not agree with the approach taken in [4] which provides the students with finished programs and discusses the mathematical principles only; it appears too easy for students to gloss over problems, and they are not exposed to the task of converting a mathematical idea for a solution to a program.

3. Insufficience of 'Introductory Programming' courses

Judging from the available textbooks, the average computer course today is an introductory course in the use of a programming language; usually FORTRAN in engineering programs. This approach is insufficient for several reasons:

3.1 Batch orientation - Many books still assume that the student will use punched cards even though punched cards are now seldom used in practice and will disappear completely in the immediate future. All aspects of interactive programming are left out in most books (a noteable exception is [2]). This makes it difficult for the student to understand and assess the interactive programs she will later use.

3.2 Concentration on 'programming language' - The course introduces students to the use of a programming language alone. Most often the use of the operating system and the utilities are explained only as far as absolutely necessary for the development of small programs. Students are not explicitly told how to use the computer for other problems, nor are the principles of the operating system explained to them. This greatly hinders future use of the computer in advanced courses.

3.3 Examples unrelated to engineering - Examples in general text books are unspecific in order to be understandable to students from all fields. They are often simplistic and do not relate to students of engineering. Furthermore, the examples do not prepare the student for the type of programs she will later see when applied to her field. Programming has become so broad an activity that very different knowledge is necessary to work in a specific field of application. This can not be achieved by a general course.

4. Integration of computer usage in the curriculum

If we want to equip our students with a sound understanding of the best use of computers in their profession, we must integrate computer usage in their curriculum. An independent course little related to the rest of the curriculum can not achieve this as it remains an unconnected topic in the students experience (and much too often an unpleasant one).

Discussions in our college have shown that students can achieve proper experience with computers only if each student takes at least one course with a strong computer usage component **each semester**. This means that we have to follow the introductory course (in first or second year) with applied courses (e.g. an engineering design course) that include some use of computers. Such a component may be built into most practical or design courses without taking time away from the principle subject. Quite the contrary, we experience that many topics may be

studied in more depth if computer simulation is available or if more design alternatives can be explored.

5. Modern personal computers and their use in teaching

If we analyse what is difficult for students when they deal with the traditional mainframe computer, we can better assess the improvements possible with the newest personal computers.

5.1 Invisibility: computers handle objects like files, records, etc, which are invisible to the user. It is difficult for a beginner to keep track of the multitude of objects of different kinds she operates on with commands. Eventually, users understand and develop a feeling for these things - as all of us have done - but this is very time consuming and entails many 'trial and error' situations and disappointments.

5.2 Inconsistent interfaces: a specific action - say erase an object - is expressed in very different ways, depending on the class of the object and the situation (not only a different command, but also different syntax).

For example, compare the difference between how you delete a file and how you delete a line in a file in the system you are familiar with. The problem is aggravated as each utility and application program presents another type of interface. Again, users may eventually become proficient in their use, but the program behaviour is baffling to the beginner.

5.3 Overly complex systems: most general purpose multi-user mainframe computers now in use provide extremely versatile command languages. However, their functionality is much larger than students normally need, and students have difficulty selecting the subset they need. They may encounter problems if they inadvertently use an unfamiliar mode. Typically manuals are several large binders with over 500 pages each, written by specialists for specialists - a language completely incomprehensible to the beginner, and unfortunately often specific to the manufacturer.

5.4 Difficult to get started with: starting to use a general-purpose mainframe is made additionally difficult by the provisions in their operating system for tailoring them to the users need. Very often, beginners have to deal with the "naked" operating system until, much later, they have created their set of 'macros' to abbreviate command sequences often used.

We may conclude that a machine suitable for teaching computer usage must be simple to use for the beginners. To judge a machine to this end may be difficult as all experienced computer users have developed considerable skills to deal with even the most intricate machines. The following properties seem to be important:
- visible interface: the user's actions should cause visible reactions on pictures of the objects manipulated (also called 'direct manipulation').
- consistent interface: a similar operation should be performed with similar commands and similar syntax.
- a limited operation system with the necessary functionality, but not providing too many additional features which only confuse beginners.

- let the user select or adapt a proposed command in lieu of asking him to produce the command [13].

Several attempts to realize these goals have been made previously. Notable in the past are the Waterloo Environment to reduce complexity of the IBM operating systems on the mainframe side. Single user workstations have been produced by Xerox (Star), Apollo [3] and Apple (Lisa and Macintosh). The last one offers the necessary features for the lowest price (around $2000 per personal computer).

Selection of a computer for use in a computer course is similar to other selections of computers: decide which qualities are essential and select the one that has them. The danger lies in being tempted to buy a machine with more features than necesary. Such features are never free, they may perhaps not increase the price, but they will invariably increase the complexity of the user interface and make the machine harder to use.

6. Guidelines for the new course sequence "computer usage"

This chapter will discuss the main assumptions and guidelines we use in the course and present the outline of its contents.

6.1 Reduce complexity
We assume that complexity of the task is the major impedient in any programming course. Complexity can be reduced mainly by introducing new topics one at a time only, and have the student exercise this topic before anything new is added [6].

6.2 Reduce problems not related to the present goal
Beginning programmers have to deal with a great deal of detail, especially in order to gain access to the mainframe, control the invisible environment there, edit, compile, link and run their programs. Single user systems can be made simpler as they serve for a smaller selection of tasks. Personal computers, like the Apple Macintosh with its visible interface, further reduce the amount of knowledge and experience a beginning user needs in order to write a program.

6.3 Fast reaction of the system
The time lapse between a user's action and the system's reaction, for example during debugging a program, are critical. If response time is extremely fast - say in less than ten seconds between editing an error and seeing the change in the output from the running program - program development for beginners is much faster. Not only does each step take less time, but the involvment with the problem is not interupted and facts are remembered in the learner's short time memory. We believe this fast response enhances learning by helping the user to assimilate patterns in a way similar to the assimilation of typical patterns of behaviour in ordinary life.

6.4 Reduce technical details
The Pascal Interpreter for the Apple Macintosh (made by Think Technology Inc.) is an integrated system, providing a language specific editor together with advanced debugging tools in one package with a uniform interface. The editor checks the syntax of the program during input and signals errors immediately; it also indents the program according to standard rules (prettyprinting)
This should especially help beginners who often have problems

with some of the minute details of Pascal syntax (especially semicolons and begin - end pairs). Eliminating these hinderances will allow increased concentration on the essentials of program design.

6.5 Include interactive programming
Design of interactive programs is cumbersome on most mainframes, at least for the beginner. There are always several system idiosyncrasies to be considered so textbooks usually do not discuss these areas. The input procedures of the Apple Macintosh are quite simple to use (lazy I/O).

6.6 Include graphic output
The high resolution screen built in the Apple Macintosh, together with its high performance bit mapped graphic routines allow integration of graphic output without adding much complexity. Graphics can help enormously to make the user visualize the dynamic behaviour of programs and lends itself to many rewarding simple programs (see the publications of the LOGO group [7] [10]).

7. Teaching methods

7.1 Program plans
We assume that the problem of programming does not lie primarily with the syntax and vocabulary of the chosen programming language, but in the difficulty of devising a plan to solve a problem. Experienced programmers have accumulated a number of plans that they have used previously. When they have to solve a new problem, they choose from a stock of basic ideas, which are then adapted to the specific situation (often by copying the previous program and editing: changing is easier than inventing [13]). Beginners, however, are asked to create solutions from the void - an immensely more difficult task.

7.2 Programs are for reading
Programs must be considered primarily as accurate and formal descriptions of an algorithm, and should be readable by humans. The additional benefit of programming languages that algorithms can be executed by a computer should not influence the design and notation [5].

7.3 Reading assignments
Reading one's own programs as well as programs written by others must be an integral part of teaching programming.

7.4 No initial optimization
Algorithms should be described as clearly as possible and at first no effort should be spent on optimizing (neither for run time nor for storage utilization). Optimization invariably makes a program more difficult to understand. This is not to advocate inefficient algorithms, but to avoid optimization tricks that obscure the meaning of a program. If a program later is running too slowly, program transformations can be used to speed it up.

7.5 Programming style
Students should not only learn to write a program that produces the correct results, but to compose a well written program. This is not an end in itself, but experience shows that clumsy programs seldom work correctly, are difficult to debug and impossible to change later. It is a disservice to the learner not to insist on programming style.

7.6 Reasoning about programs
The mathematically founded methods for reasoning about programs, as used in formal proofs [5] [15] [6], must be introduced early to the students.

7.7 Modularization
Even small problems are too big for the beginner, and students should learn from the very beginning how to split a problem into smaller problems which are easier to solve. Our personal experience is more with the data abstraction technique (also called abstract data types or initial algebra) [11,12] than with procedural abstraction, and we feel that it is important to understand and apply these methods even in cases that seem too simple . It is too late to learn new techniques when complex problems are calling for them. Personal experience with writing large and complex programs has shown that routines that are very small and embody only one idea are easy to write and seldom contain an error (by our standards, routines with more than 10 executable statements are considered long!).

7.8 Functional programming style
Small routines designed using the principles of data abstraction lend themselves to being written as functions. Functional programming languages and functional programming style were quite successful in the past and – at least applied with judgement – seem to lead to programs easy to understand. Moreover, the idea of a function is well established with university students and this allows us to exploi previous knowledge.

8. The outline of the course

The goal of the course is to have students understand computers and become familiar with their use. The first goal is achieved through the later – 'learning by doing' is the catchword. Therefore a great number of small assignments are given to the students, two each week and – if one is done after the other – each taking about two to three hours to fullfil. Many of them will be assignments to change an existing program. Some assignments may form a sequence, where the program written in the previous assignment is expanded over several steps. This should provide the students with experience in building programs using stepwise refinement [15].

The books used for the courses are the following:
- Systematic Programming' by N. Wirth[15], which is one of the few introductory texts, which discuss programming in general and are not concerned only with syntax and vocabulary. It is also the only book I found that introduces formal reasoning about programs.
- 'Numerical Methods Using Pascal' by L.Atkinson and P. Harley [1] for the numerical part.

We also recommend the following addional texts to students who are interested in further reading:
- 'Mac: The Apple Macintosh Book' by C. Lu[9] for more details about hardware.
- An introductory text in Pascal about non numeric programming if they feel they need it.

A lab is set up with 8 Apple Macintosh for exclusive use by students of this course, yielding a 1 in 8 ratio between students and machines. The lab is open every weekday from 9 a.m. till 9 p.m. We encourage the use of the Macintosh for work related to other courses.

The course is divided in three parts:

8.1 Familiarize students with the Macintosh
The first week is used to familiarize the students with the interface of the operating system and the editor to write short documents. We assume that students will, on their own initiative, also explore the graphics editor (MacPaint). The consistency of the interface across all programs should make this period short; nevertheless, two assignments will insure that all students get the necessary practice before the next step. Lectures will be used to discuss the hardware parts and the first presentation of the task of the operating systems .

8.2 Introduction to programming
Several weeks (three to five) will be devoted to the general idea of programming. Students will be presented with complete, running programs to read and change. Only a limited part of the Pascal vocabulary will be used, not with the intention of subsetting, but rather by excluding all but the most obvious constructs (including functions with value parameters).
We start with the 'triangle example' from [7] and motivate the introduction of procedures and functions as abstractions (abbreviations) of repeatedly used task. This leads in a natural way to recursion, and we did not observe any problems with students understanding this.
The next group of examples are operations on number systems (integer, rational numbers, complex numbers and ultimately polynoms). This provides us with mathematically clean algebraic examples for abstract data types. The idea can then be expanded and applied to less 'clean' practical applications. Assignments in this phase are program reading and small changes as well as writing larger sets of subroutines. This period concentrates theoretically on the idea of abstraction and layered architecture of systems.

8.3 Programming language Pascal
When the students have gained some experience with programs, the time is ripe to introduce them to the details of the Pascal language in a systematic way. We present the language in a logical order and explain details which either have not yet been covered or have been covered incompletely. Here the stress is on showing the students the systematic construction behind programming languages in general, and Pascal as a specific example. Programming assignments will be split between reading and writing, with examples preferably showing some building blocks often used (e.g. filling and searching arrays). All constructs of Pascal but pointers are introduced in the first semester.

8.4 Programming for engineering application
The second half of the first semester and the first half of the second semester will be devoted to building a library of modules useful for building application programs in engineering and science. Topics to be treated include:
- handling polynomials, including derivatives and integration, finding zeros and maxima/minima, and graphical output
- dealing with arbitrary functions, including finding zeros, differentiation and integration, using numerical methods
- advanced matrix operations, i.e. solution to systems of linear equations, inversion of matrices, eigenvalue and eigenvectors
- simple cases of systems of (non linear) equations
- introduction to numerical solution of differential equations.

Numerical methods take a large share of time, but we will also treat at least one example of calculations related to networks (either flow or critical path) in order to introduce the techniques applicable in this area [14]. This is also the occasion to explain the use of pointer variables in Pascal.

8.5 Transition to the mainframe and FORTRAN

Starting in the second semester, students are gradually introduced to use the mainframe (IBM under VM/CMS). The goal is to enable the users to decide for themselves when to use what machine, and to become aware of the relative advantages of each. An introduction to FORTRAN is also included which should enable students to use and possibly adapt existing programs written in FORTRAN. According to [8] students do not encounter problems when moving to the mainframe, and the skills they learned first are transported easily.

9. General changes in the curriculum

A computer usage course with the contents explained above can show mathematics in a new, more applied light. During development of the course, we looked carefully at the use of mathematics in engineering disciplines, especially civil engineering, and compared it with the present contents of the compulsory mathematics courses.

9.1 Calculus and differential equation

Calculus is the foundation of modern mechanics, and therefore of prime importance for most engineering sciences. Nevertheless, it should be asked if the present nearly exclusive concentration on calculus in our mathematics introduction is justified. The present contents often seems to be more directed towards mathematical proofs and results of theoretical value but very seldom motivated by the way calculus is applied in engineering sciences. In my opinion, the reason for this is that most applications of calculus in engineering lead to problems which can only be dealt with using numerical methods (eg. most integrals defy formal integration, most differential equations of interest to engineers can only be solved approximatively). However, numerical methods have become accessible only now, using computers and programming.

9.2 Algebra

Data abstraction – a very important method in specifying and designing computer programs – is directly connected to abstract algebra. Understanding the abstract properties of algebra and being able to look at problems using these methods are helpful.
The basic concepts of set theory should be available to all students. Such concepts are applied in many cases of programming and provide powerful tools to analyze the operations of programs (and some programming languages include sets as basic data types and provide the necessary operations).

Boolean algebra (including predicate calculus) must be introduced to students to enable them to reason about conditional statements in programs.

Further, the generally used number systems (integers, rational numbers, reals and complex numbers) should be understood as forming different algebras with some differences in their axioms. A theoretical understanding here will help to understand the peculiarities of the number systems used by computers with their limited precision (this will increase in importance as the new IEEE standard for real operations is used more often).

9.3 Topology

Many branches of engineering science deal with topological structures (electrical and other water networks, critical path, etc.). The Computer Aided Designing systems now available to manipulation of geometric or graphical structures rely (open or covered) on topological principles.

9.4 Theory of formal languages and automatons

Programming languages and, in general, all user interfaces to computer programs can be considered as formal languages. Theory can supply us with a few basic tools to describe a formal language (production rules, generally in the form of syntax diagrams), and to classify formal languages according to criteria of prime importance when the program to interpret the language is written. Similarly, some fundamental concepts from the theory of finite state automatons, the background for most theoretical studies in computer science, can furnish better models to illustrate computers' operation.

We do not propose that all these subjects from the more abstract parts of modern mathematics should be included. We do propose that we should critically examine the role of mathematics in the engineering curriculum. When we reconsider the place of computers in the curriculum, it is obviously appropriate to reconsider mathematics as well. We would advocate a much closer relationship between the two, and assume that computers can help students solve complex mathematical problems and, therefore, foster learning.

10. Conclusions

This paper presents a philosophy of computer education for engineering or science departments. It should be clearly noted that we do not advocate a single software, hardware or teaching technique, nor an isolated change in the curriculum. Such simple solutions are never adequate to coping with such complex a problem as integrating computing into education. We hope that we have convinced the reader that the measures we have taken are promising, namely:

- integrating computer usage in many courses so that students take at least one course with a strong computer usage component each semester
- expanding the introductory course from a 'programming language course' to a general course about computers and the principles of computer science
- teaching a programming language and a program development method which can be used for solving large technical problems
- selecting examples while teaching the programming languages that are related to engineering and science and form useful building blocks for the student for later use in problem solving.
- use interactive systems and computer graphics to make complex abstract topics visible (which is only possible on the most modern personal computers with the 'visible human interface' [9] and a consistent and simple command language).

Experience so far shows enthusiastic response from students and faculty in the course, but longterm success or failure of the experiment will depend on the faculty of following courses enhancing their teaching with computer related assignments.

References:

[1] Atkinson, L.U.; Harley, P.J.; An Introduction to Numerical Methods with Pascal, International Computer Science Series, Addison–Wesley Publishing Co., London, 1983

[2] Bowles, K.L.; Franklin, S.D.; Volper, D.J.; Problem Solving Using UCSD Pascal, Springer Verlag, New York, 1984 (2nd Edition)

[3] Brown, Marc H.; Sedgewick, R.; Technical Report CS-83-28, Brown University, R.I.,1983

[4] Chapra, S.C., Canale, R.P., Numerical Methods for Engineers, McGraw Hill, 1985

[5] Dahl, O.J.; Dijkstra, E.W.; Hoare, C.A.; Structured Programming, Academic Press, New York, 1972

[6] Dijkstra, E.W.; A Discipline of Programming, Prentice-Hall, Englewood Cliffs, N.J., 1976

[7] Feurzeig, W.; Lukas, G.; Lukas, J.O.; The LOGO Language, 1973

[8] Garlan, D.B.; Miller, P.L.; GNOME: An Introductory Programming Environment Based on a Family of Structure Editors, ACM Software Engineering Notes, Vol. 9, No. 3, May 1984

[9] Lu, Cary; Mac: The Apple Macintosh Book, Bellevue, Washington, Microsoft Press, 1984

[10] Papert, S.; Mindstorms: Children, Computers and Powerful Ideas, Basic Books, New York, 1980

[11] Parnas, D.L.; A Technique for Software Module Specification with Examples, Communications of ACM, Vol. 15, No. 5, May 1972, p. 330

[12] Parnas, D.L.; On the criteria to be used in Decomposing Systems into Modules, Communications of ACM, Vol. 15, No. 12, Dec. 1972, p. 1053

[13] Smith, D.C.; et al; Designing the Star User Interface, Byte Magazine, Vol. 7, No. 4, April 1982

[14] Syslo, M.; Deo, N.; Kowalik, J.; Discrete Optimization Algorithms with Pascal Programs, Prentice Hall, Englewood Cliffs, N.J., 1983

[15] Wirth, N.; Systematic Programming: An Introduction, Prentice Hall, 1973

COMPUTERS IN EDUCATION, K. Duncan and D. Harris (eds.)
Elsevier Science Publishers B.V. (North-Holland)
© IFIP, 1985

A COST-EFFECTIVE USE OF LIMITED COMPUTING RESOURCES IN TEACHING ENGINEERING DESIGN

J.R. GREENE

Department of Electrical & Electronic Engineering
University of Cape Town, Private Bag Rondebosch 7700 Cape
South Africa

This is a proposal for a simple and inexpensive way of using the computer to assist in the teaching of engineering design skills. The approach features a minimal hardware requirement (a single microcomputer can service a class of up to 100 students) and rapid and simple programming. It is believed to be widely applicable, but is illustrated here with reference to its use in teaching Electronic Circuit Design at second and third year undergraduate level at the University of Cape Town. The paper describes the method in detail, presents the results of informal evaluations and discusses possible extensions.

1. INTRODUCTION

The idea that instruction in the art of engineering design should lie at the very core of engineering education finds widespread acceptance. Yet, in practice, such instruction tends to play a marginal role, often being relegated to little more than a token presence in the curriculum. Most engineering curricula place a heavy emphasis on analysis rather than problem-solving and creative synthesis, perhaps because we are very unclear as to how to teach the latter effectively. Moreover, to meet even the minimal goal of student fluency in the basic vocabulary of design concepts and techniques is extremely arduous and time-consuming, and the assessment of student work poses serious problems. In order to gain the fluency and confidence required the student needs a great deal of practice in making actual design decisions. Close monitoring of the work is needed in the early stages, with detailed and carefully considered criticism of the emerging design. Since no two design solutions will be identical, the problem of adequately assessing completed designs alone may place an intolerable burden on the instructor of a large class. In the light of these problems, the existing gap between intentions and practice comes as no surprise.

In such a situation it is reasonable to enquire whether the use of the computer can help. For two decades much has been said about the promise of the computer in individualising teaching, and this is precisely what is needed in teaching design.

In practice, however, many of these hopes have failed to materialise and, certainly, little if any instructional use of computer based education (CBE) seems to have been made in design education. Again it is not difficult to see why: the usual modes of CBE do not readily lend themselves to so open-ended an activity. It is of course true that the computer can be (and often is) effectively used as a powerful tool in the design process. This is an important aspect of educational computing but it can contribute little to the problem being addressed here - that of assisting an instructor to introduce his class to the rudiments of the actual art of design. Tutorial-mode Computer-Aided Instruction (CAI) may have a marginal role to play, but it seems particularly ill-matched to the open-ended complexity of the design task - an opinion that is supported by the lack of published material and commercial software for the purpose. Moreover the cost of providing sufficient hardware for an adequate degree of student interaction would be very great, and would probably be dwarfed by the costs of writing the software required. The author has addressed this problem in a previous paper[1] and suggested various remedies and the present paper is an elaboration of the most successful of these in pilot trials at the University of Cape Town.

This paper proposes a mode of CBE appropriate to introductory education in engineering design. The method is a simple, low-key one, readily implemented with minimal resources. Although the technique is flexible and could be adapted in many ways, the version implemented by the author was developed subject to the constraint of a single microcomputer being available for the use of a class of about 70 students. Time available for software authoring was also severely limited. Despite these constraints (or perhaps even on account of them) a viable method was developed and subjected to three informal pilot trials in the author's own discipline - that of electronic circuit design. Student acceptance of the method was universally enthusiastic and the result of the informal evaluation has been very encouraging. More formal evaluation poses serious difficulties if reliable data are to be gained, though clearly this must be attempted. The method appears to be readily generalisable in terms of both level and subject matter and may have applications in non-academic technical training and the development of basic design skills at school level.

2. GENERAL DESCRIPTION

The essence of the method is that students are
assigned a simple structured design task, and
the computer is used to mediate a kind of
dialogue between student and instructor.
Detailed guidance is given to the student to
refine and correct his or her design until a
formal target specification has been met. Thus
the process is, in a sense, an interactive one,
but the interaction is not in 'real time'.
Communication from computer to students takes
the form of 'hard copy' printout. This is the
reason for the minimal hardware requirements -
each student spends no more than a minute or two
at the computer keyboard entering the data defining his or her current design proposal, then
detaches the printout containing the computer's
response.
Most of the work is done away from the computer.
The final assessment of the design is also
carried out by the computer.

It is obvious that in order to make this
possible several constraints on the 'designer's'
freedom of choice are inevitable. The simplest
approach is for the form and structure of the
design solution to be a 'given'. The student
must be set the task simply of making choices
from a finite repertoire of alternatives, and/or
choosing a set of numerical values for the
general design parameters so that the formal
performance specification is met. Clearly, this
is less than a simulation of actual 'real-world'
design but it does in fact realistically reflect
a great deal of low-level design activity in
which the basic form of a design solution is a
fait accompli, is specified by a superior, or
taken from a "handbook". In any event, it seems
likely that such a structured approach is
desirable in the early stages of design education.
It does at least allow the student to make
choices and discover the consequences, as well
as demanding a meticulous attention to detail
that is easily omitted in other approaches.
There can be little doubt that such an approach,
involving active participation by the student,
is a significantly better preparation for real
design than one which depends heavily on
analysis of textbook examples. In the author's
contention, it is also preferable to one in
which the student is "thrown in at the deep end"
and allowed to flounder.

Undoubtedly some students profit from such
treatment, but many simply "sink", and regretfully conclude that they are not cut out to be
designers, while others develop "hit or miss"
approaches to design which all too readily
become habitual.

The basic technique is capable of elaboration in
many ways, some of which are discussed below,
but in the author's opinion its greatest merit
lies in its essential simplicity. Design tasks
can be prepared quickly and easily, and the
programming required is very simple (BASIC is
more than adequate for the purpose as a pro-

gramming language though there may well be advantages to the instructor in using a better
structured one.) Where appropriate the programming task can be further simplified (or
perhaps more complex design tasks accommodated)
by incorporating existing analysis packages.
The hardware requirements are minimal:virtually
any computer (micro, mini or mainframe) can be
used, provided there is provision for alphanumeric hard-copy printout. A version could
even be implemented using a sophisticated
programmable calculator.

3. A PILOT STUDY

In order to complement the rather abstract
description of the technique given above, and to
provide the results of an informal evaluation of
its effectiveness, an account will now be given
of a pilot implementation of the method, involving 70 students of the University of Cape
Town's Department of Electrical and Electronic
Engineering, as part of a third year, single
semester course in electronic circuits. Eight
design tasks were given, graded from very simple
to moderately complex. The major goal was to
instruct the students in the art of the
systematic design of circuits so as to achieve
a precisely stated formal performance specification (taking into account "worst-case" combinations of circumstances.) Component tolerances
were specified, together with realistic limits
on parameters. Examples of a simple and a more
complex design will be given in the appendices
to this paper.

The following protocol was adopted:

i. The students were given a "problem sheet"
    containing a fully-specified, realistic re-
    quirement and asked to submit within three
    days, the schematic diagram of a circuit
    that would meet the requirement. A solution
    in broad outline was required, without, for
    example, specific component values. No use
    was made of the computer during this phase.
    Its purpose was to encourage the student to
    think seriously (and perhaps even originally)
    about the problem, and to attempt to place
    it in a realistic context. The presentat-
    ion of the problem also attempted to convey
    something of the 'flavour' of real engineer-
    ing design - in particular a sense of the
    open-endedness and the enormous possible
    variety of design approaches. This seemed
    particularly important in view of the
    rather narrow artificial constraints
    necessarily imposed during the computer-
    aided phase of the design.

ii. The instructor then collected the proposed
    designs and subjected them to a cursory ex-
    amination, primarily to ensure that some
    individual work had been done by each
    student - 'copying' being very easy to de-
    tect at this stage - but also to obtain
    general feedback on the level of competence
    of the class, prevailing misconceptions etc.

and perhaps also to be inspired by some clever solutions!).

iii. The instructor then handed out, (in skeleton form, without component values) an "approved" solution, stressing carefully that it is by no means the only possible approach, nor even necessarily the best one. (It was found that a number of students would vigorously argue for the superiority of their own designs. This in itself is a valuable learning experience, both for student and instructor!). The task set the students was now to adopt the proposed design, and complete it by supplying suitable numerical values for the components so as to realise in detail the specified performance characteristics, taking into account worst-case combinations of possible component variation.

iv. Each student, having completed this task, would then log on to the computer and enter the proposed values in response to a series of prompts (programmed by the instructor). The computer then computes the performance of the circuit using the students' values and compares it with the limits set by the instructor (which, of course, correspond to the performance design specification).

If any aspects of the specification are not met, the fact will be indicated on a hardcopy printout, together with additional messages constituting specific guidance to the student. Obviously, providing appropriate and useful messages in response to errors is an art, and the author has found that one improves rapidly with practice. Some of the most useful messages are ones which simply alert the student's attention to aspects of the state of the circuit that might easily be overlooked. Typical printed comments might be as follows:

Transistor Q1 is saturated.
Current in R1 (23mA) is excessive:
Input impedance is lower than 1KΩ
at 1 MHz.
You have ignored the +80%-20% tolerance on C7 (typical for electrolytic capacitors).

If you are having difficulties contact J. Greene in Room 411.

v. The student does not attempt to rectify matters there and then but detaches the printout and reworks the problem away from the computer. When s/he believes that the problems have been overcome the new data are entered into the computer which once again evaluates the design and prints out appropriate comments.

vi. This process may be repeated as often as needed. When the design fully meets the performance specification, a congratulary

message is printed. The student then detaches the printout, (as evidence that the design has been achieved and providing a record of the values entered), appends it to a completed design sheet and hands it in to the instructor.

4. RESULTS

Evaluation of the method has so far taken the form of a student questionnaire at the end of each trial, together with careful and critical but informal observation of student activity. Student reaction, as evidenced by the responses to the questionnaire, has been unanimously positive - all the 60 students who responded said that they believed the experiment to have been successful and their understanding of electronic circuit design to have been significantly increased. The only negative comments related to accessibility of the computer - many students felt that the use of a single computer for so large a class had led to excessive congestion. (In the two later trials two and, occasionally three, HP-85 computers were used and this appeared to solve the problem.)

For the author, the most striking observation was the degree of interest aroused. Students clustered around the computer, which tended to become the focus for heated discussions concerning the design.

Early fears that students would simply copy sets of values proved groundless. Students felt challenged by the problems and invariably began by choosing their own sets of values. They then became committed to their initial arbitrary choices and determined to 'debug' their own designs. Although there was intense discussion and interchange of ideas, there was very little tendency to copy actual values (a process which is difficult, in any event, due to their high degree of "connectedness" and mutual interdependence). An exception to this exists in the earliest examples in the sequence. Here it is desirable to avoid overwhelming the student, by setting very simple examples - for example a potential divider or coupling circuit, requiring perhaps no more than two or three components to be chosen - and the likelihood and undetectability of copying is significant. This problem was overcome by writing a separate program to randomly individualise the problems, printing a unique individual problem sheet for each student in the class.

5. MODIFICATIONS

The basic scheme could be adapted and elaborated in many ways. Perhaps the most significant addition would be the inclusion of elements of Computer Managed Learning, in the form of a detailed record-keeping system which would maintain a file of each student's activity and progress. If all the design evaluation programs were maintained on disc, students could then work their way through them at their own pace.

Although the calculations involved in the design evaluations need be of only the simplest kind - the substitution of numerical values into preprogrammed expressions - there would be much to be gained by more sophisticated processing. Standard engineering analysis packages could be used for the purpose, either co-resident with the CBE program or available on a second disc drive and called as required. Extensive use could also be made of graphics in providing feedback to the student.

6. CONCLUSION

A method has been presented of using very limited computer resources to assist in instruction in the art of engineering design. It has been implemented on a trial basis as a part of courses in electronic circuit design. Student response has been enthusiastic and informal observation suggests that it has been successful and has a real contribution to make. It is a simple and low-key method which may offer an easy entry route to those who wish to make a start in the difficult and problematic area of computer-based education.

REFERENCE

[1] Greene, J.R., The cost-effective use of the Computer in Engineering Education and Training, National Conference on the Computer in Education and Training, Pretoria, South Africa, March 1985 (to be published).

APPENDIX

Four examples of design studies will be given. In each case the original problem statement and proposed skeleton solution will be given, along with a representative selection of the printed comments which afford guidance to the students.

1. A Transistor Inverter.

Design a simple single-transistor inverter circuit using an NPN BJT with a current gain in the range 50 to 500. Assume that in the worst case, and taking into account ambient temperature variation, Vbe(ON) is in the range 0,4 to 0.8V. Use a 1Kohm collector resistor.

The transistor must be guaranteed to be OFF for an input potential of less than 0.8V and any input greater than 4 volts must be certain to saturate it.

The circuit is to be supplied from a single SV positive rail. Use only standard resistors from the E12 range of preferred values.

The following skeleton circuit was supplied after the students had submitted their attempts:

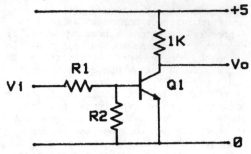

Here is a selection of the kind of comments provided by the computer:

"When Vbe is high and the current gain at its lower limit the transistor will fail to saturate with an input of 4V."

"A BJT with low Vbe will fail to turn OFF with these values."

"Your solution is formally correct but the resistor values you have specified are absurdly low. Moreover they do not conform to preferred values in the E12 series (i.e. decimal multiples of 10 12 15 18 22 27 33 39 47 56 68 82)."

2. A Simple Voltage Regulator.

A piece of electronic equipment requires a stabilised supply potential of 5 -0 +0.25V. It draws a current varying from 0 to 20mA. The primary power source is a battery which has an emf of 10V when fresh, but the equipment must continue to operate until the battery voltage falls to 7V.

In the circuit supplied, the Zener diode has a minimum potential of 5V at a current of 10mA, a slope resistance of 15ohms and a maximum allowable dissipation of 200mW. Choose a suitable value for R and specify its required power rating.

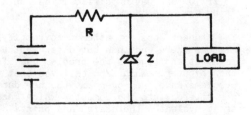

Typical printed comments:

"On full load when the battery is low the output voltage falls to 4.6V which is out of tolerance".

"When battery is fresh and load current is zero, dissipation in the Zener diode is 318mW which exceeds the allowable rating."

"You have specified a 2MW power rating for R which is absurd!"

"If you are still having problems come and discuss it with me in Room 411 between 2 and 5 pm."

3. Design a single-stage BJT amplifier having a midband gain of 30dB, an input impedance of at least 10Kohm, an output impedance no greater than 1Kohm and single dominant break frequencies at 100Hz and 20KHz. A sinusoidal output swing of at least 1V peak is required.

The amplifier is to run off a single 10V supply rail, from which it must draw a quiescent current of no more than 5mA. The active device is a BJT with a static current gain in the range 50 to 500 and an Ft of 300MHz.

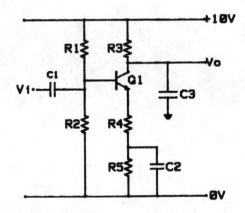

Typical comments:

"A high-gain version of Q1 would saturate in your circuit."

"You seem to have overlooked base current loading of the base potential-divider circuit when a low-gain transistor is used."

"Gain is low (26dB). Have you overlooked intrinsic emitter resistance?".

4. An Electro-Optic Intrusion Alarm

Phase 1: Draw a carefully specified BLOCK DIAGRAM of an electro-optic intrusion alarm using synchronous rectification for narrow-band detection of the returning light.

When you have completed the block diagram, give a proposed circuit realisation of each module. It is suggested that the source of radiation be an infra-red LED modulated at about 1KHz. No component values are required at this stage. Use operational amplifiers rather than discrete devices where possible.

Phase 2: Complete this design: (see diagram overleaf).

Data:

BJT static current gain 50 - 500

LED: Von = 1.5V ; Imax = 60mA

Photodiode: sensitivity 0.5A/W

Ambient illumination on diode <1mW

Opamps: Ibias< 1nA ; Vout(max) + -10V

Resistors 20% E12 preferred values

Design specifications:

Modulation frequency 1KHz ±200Hz
System bandwidth   10Hz
Base saturation overdrive factor 10
LED ON current 50mA ± 10%
5V dc out for .05mW optical signal

Typical comments:

"The photodiode will saturate on ambient illumination."

"Insufficient base drive for reliable saturation of Q1".

"C2/R5 too small giving excessive tilt on 1KHz square wave".

"Overall gain is insufficient".

"Excessive transimpedance gain - opamp will saturate".

"Drive frequency is 42% high".

J.R. Greene

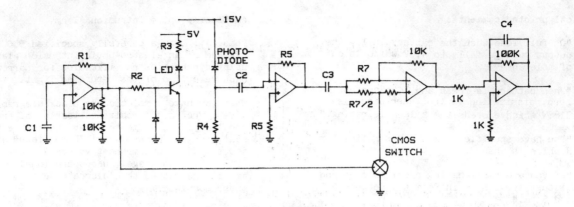

Circuit for Design Study 4
A prototype Electro-Optic Intrusion Alarm

COMPUTERS IN EDUCATION, K. Duncan and D. Harris (eds.)
Elsevier Science Publishers B.V. (North-Holland)
© IFIP, 1985

THE ROLE OF COMPUTING IN ENGINEERING EDUCATION

William J. Rasdorf, P.E.* and Olaf O. Storaasli

* Assistant Professor
Civil Engineering and Computer Science
North Carolina State University
Box 7908, Raleigh, NC 27695
United States

The role of computer science is increasing in nearly every engineering discipline. One of the dilemmas in engineering education today is how future engineers can best assimilate the advanced, yet fundamental, knowledge of computer science appropriate for their professional engineering career. This paper suggests that the role of the academic community must be to prepare engineering students to use computer methods and applications as a part of their fundamental engineering education. It is the responsibility of colleges and universities to incorporate contemporary computing fundamentals into their academic curriculum to improve the professional qualifications of their engineering graduates.

INTRODUCTION

The rapid advances occurring in interactive microcomputing and computer science have provided the engineer with a powerful means of processing, storing, retrieving, and displaying data. This has made computer science a growing and essential part of nearly every engineering discipline. Applications of existing computer science technologies are spreading and are giving engineers a sophisticated means of rapid access to a wide variety of information, solutions to complex problems, and ways to model complicated engineering systems. More advanced computer science technologies in such areas as data management (3, 8), artificial intelligence (9, 18), concurrent processing (13), and graphics (16) are also being explored. The effective use of computer technology in engineering processes and applications is recognized by many as the key to increased individual, company, and national productivity.

In the future, an integrated combination of computer-aided analysis and design techniques will need to be developed for all types of engineering design problems (6). This will require applying computer science principles and practices to a variety of engineering systems in order to determine their response to external influences. The implications of this requirement for the academic community are clear: we must prepare our students to use computer methods and applications as a part of their fundamental education.

The low cost and ready availability of computer hardware has removed the financial barrier that formerly limited the use of computers by many small and medium sized engineering firms (19, 20). In addition, the software industry has made available a growing supply of useful engineering and administrative programs. Satisfying the special needs of engineering organizations, however, often requires in-house software development. As a result, engineering graduates are sought whose training has included a study of the fundamentals of computer science. Unfortunately, the number of graduates who have received this education has not kept pace with the demand, and has therefore limited the number of qualified applicants (5).

The potential of low cost interactive computing, computer-aided design, and computer graphics in engineering has been demonstrated (19, 20). It is now the responsibility of colleges and universities to prepare their students to make use of this potential. By incorporating contemporary computing fundamentals in their academic curriculum, colleges and universities can significantly improve the professional qualifications of their engineering graduates. These graduates will then be able to provide their expertise to the engineering profession in an area of great importance to its future. Although the academic curriculum must be upgraded to meet this challenge, many engineering schools are currently making the changes necessary to enhance their students' knowledge of the fundamental concepts of computer science.

Purpose

One of the dilemmas in engineering education today is how future engineers can best assimilate the advanced, yet fundamental, knowledge in computer methods and technology appropriate for their specific engineering discipline (12). It may be enlightening to note that many of the most successful results have come from engineering schools which contain their own computer science departments or where individual engineering departments offer their own computing courses geared specifically to their discipline (e.g. C-MU, NCSU, RPI, MIT). The common thread among these programs is the ready availability to engineering students of computing facilities and computing expertise. This paper examines these issues and describes:

- the need for engineers to gain a sophisticated understanding of advanced computer science techniques that will have a significant impact on the engineering professions;
- current educational practices (and their drawbacks) regarding computing in engineering; and
- the impact into the 1990's of new computer technology.

Emphasizing computer science as an integral part of an engineering student's education depends on many factors - educational practices, student needs, school and university computer acquisition plans, faculty support, research needs, available funds, and so on. This paper addresses two of these issues: educational practices and student needs. It describes those aspects of computer science, related to computer software design, development, management, and use, that would enable engineering students to perform effectively in their subsequent classwork, in graduate school, and in their careers.

The ideas presented here can be used as a guide by educators who wish to enhance the computing aspects of their engineering curricula. The paper will also be of interest to engineering firms that are evaluating the educational profile of new graduates to locate those who possess, in addition to their engineering skills, both the ability to evaluate and use production software and the ability to organize and supervise the development of in-house software.

CURRENT EDUCATIONAL PRACTICES

At many institutions the importance of an in depth knowledge of advanced computer science techniques within engineering departments has not been recognized. The traditional, undergraduate engineering curriculum has generally contained only an introductory course. The fundamental objectives of the course are to teach students the use of a programming language (more often than not that language has been FORTRAN, although Basic, Watfiv, and PL/1 have also been commonly used), an operating system, and a text editor. Additional goals include teaching students to represent the logic of the problem-solution process using flowcharts or algorithms, to write programs that efficiently implement the logical representation, and to compute resulting values with varying input.

Unfortunately, the results of this educational experience are often limited; students learn to draw flowcharts and they learn the mechanics of a programming language. The novelty of the concepts and the unforgiving rules of language syntax, combined with unfamiliar editors and long debugging sessions, leave the student with little time to achieve the remaining goals of the course. As a result, many fundamental topics remain only partially discovered or completely unaddressed. Fortunately the faculty can, by establishing an appropriate choice of objectives, effectively incorporate these topics into subsequent courses.

Both industry (IBM, DEC, etc.) and agencies of the U. S. government (NSF, NASA, etc.) have recognized the need to improve the computing education of engineering graduates and offer incentives (equipment donations, consortiums, free software, grants, etc.) to do so. Despite the successes of their programs, these groups have had a limited impact on this major problem simply because of its magnitude. The greatest impact must come from within the colleges and universities themselves (4). But to achieve the objectives stated herein will require significant infusions of experienced faculty, computer hardware and software, and high-level support. Fortunately, close cooperation between academia, industry, and the government has been developing and is resulting in programs aimed at alleviating the perceived problems.

EDUCATIONAL OBJECTIVES

An understanding of problem solving as an engineering activity is an essential part of each students educational program. Students can use the computer to solve engineering and scientific problems either by independently developing their own programs or by using existing application software and library routines.

The needs of students with respect to developing new and using existing software are particularly important. Regarding new program development, students should have a thorough working knowledge of at least one scientific programming language, be able to use the computer to solve any problem requiring computation in any course in which they are subsequently enrolled, and be able to verify that their program is working properly and providing correct answers (2). When using existing programs and subroutines that apply to the problems and topics covered in engineering courses, students should:

- know the pertinent criteria to select the best program for the problem at hand;
- understand the associated user manual from both a user and system viewpoint;
- verify the accuracy of the program by using test-case problems that have known solutions; and
- consistently and correctly interpret the results.

Beyond dealing with application oriented software students must:

- understand the use of computer-aided design, interactive analysis and design, and optimization techniques;
- be familiar with the use of state-of-the-art computer hardware including micro, mini, and mainframe computers, terminals, printers, plotters, and data acquisition units;
- be familiar with the use of state-of-the-art software including operating systems, editors, text processors, and electronic mail and other communications systems; and
- be familiar with the integration of multiple applications into a comprehensive engineering system.

Accomplishing all of these objectives at an early stage in the students' educational program may at first seem to be an insurmountable task. However, a careful analysis of the curriculum may illuminate many resources already in place and indicate subsequent steps that can be taken to achieve the objectives.

A Note of Caution

Although computer science is being discussed in this paper and computer programming is emphasized, it must be remembered that the student's primary goal is to learn the principles and practices of engineering (11). Students must first understand the concepts and techniques of the solution method before laying out the algorithms and implementing them in code. In that regard, the emphasis on computer science should assume a subordinate, although decided, role in the engineering educational program.

REINFORCING AND ENHANCING COMPUTER USE

A number of approaches can be taken to enhance the engineering student's knowledge of computer science (15). The first approach is to enable the student to continually use, in his engineering courses, the knowledge obtained from his introductory computer science course. Doing so requires that the faculty encourage regular and frequent use of the computer. The engineering curriculum should be structured so that it continually builds on the introductory computing course by integrating computer-aided analysis and design techniques into upper-level courses.

While learning the fundamental principles of engineering, students will have frequent opportunity to apply computational skills in completing homework, laboratory, and special project assignments. Programming solutions to problems in all of these different settings should be encouraged. To develop the student's computational dexterity, faculty should develop assignments that require the student to write original programs in addition to using existing programs.

Another approach to increasing the engineering student's knowledge of computer science is to introduce new courses that stress the advanced computing methods and applications that are specific to engineering. Such courses should include an emphasis on advanced programming language topics, data storage and use, and program organization and control.

Sommer suggests an even broader approach to computer-aided engineering education composed of three distinct systems: the instructional system; the problem-solving system; and the experimental system (17). Used as an instructional system, the computer provides information about a particular engineering subject - including text, figures, and tables - and prompts the student with questions and exercises. As a problem solving system, the computer offers the student an engineering problem, sets of possible steps to its solution, and justification for each step in the solution process. The student obtains the solution by learning the correct sequence of steps. In an experimental educational mode, the computer can be used to monitor experiments and acquire and analyze data, or it can be used to simulate experiments without the use of laboratory facilities (17).

A further development is the proposed Computer-Aided Teaching (CAT) System described by Baecher (1). The system is designed to give the student an understanding of fundamental engineering concepts, an intuitive feel for mechanical behavior, and the ability to model complex physical systems. It comprehensively deals with conceptual and preliminary design stages, modeling, and optimization, as well as with analysis and detailed design. The CAT system makes use of graphics and database management and expert system technologies to provide a computer-enhanced educational environment for engineering students that addresses knowledge building, knowledge reinforcement and testing, and knowledge synthesis (1).

Each of the above aspects of computer use lies well within the realm of engineering educational objectives; each merits attention.

However, the focus maintained in this paper is on the fundamental knowledge necessary to enable engineers to design, develop, manage, and use software and to understand its relationship to the engineering problem solving process.

TOPICS OF INTEREST

Proper computer program design requires that the student have a sound knowledge of software engineering - the application of language-independent engineering principles and practices to the development of large computer programs. Topics of primary importance are data structures, program control, and program organization.

Data Structures

The study of data structures is too often incomplete because instruction in using higher level data structures, including tables, lists, trees, graphs, networks, etc., is usually neglected in engineering curricula. As a result, engineers are often unaware of the conceptual basis for these data structures, of the availability of algorithms for processing them, and of the means whereby they can be implemented in FORTRAN and other languages.

This instructional neglect is of particular concern because many engineering applications can be readily represented by higher level data structures. Networks and network processing techniques, for example, can be used in finite elements, framed structures, hydraulic systems, transportation systems, construction scheduling, and surveying. Regardless of the application area the engineering student should be taught to recognize the type of data structure that most precisely represents the problem he is modeling and be aware and capable of using the facilities available for processing the data structure.

The underlying motivation for emphasizing data structures is the important role that data plays in the design process. The design process is highly data generative. It begins by the designer determining the values for basic data items which reflect early design decisions. Using a structural engineering example, these might include describing a structure, facility, or component's configuration (topology and geometry (14)) and applied loads. From this basic data additional data is derived by the designer and by application programs, and is stored in the database. An analysis program, for example, generates forces, moments, and displacements using geometric and loading data. A design program subsequently uses the analysis results to determine required member properties, etc.

When all of the data needed to represent the structure has been derived, the design is complete. Its final, external representation consists of a combination of project specifications, design calculations, and drawings, each of which can be obtained in an automated manner with a computer-aided design system. The role that data plays in the design process is extensive, and its proper representation and use is an important ingredient in the success of computer-aided design systems. The ability to recognize how data is structured and to store, retrieve, and manipulate it with software designed to do so is an engineering necessity. It is therefore imperative that the engineering student understand this role and the relationship between program data structures and the design process data items they represent.

Program Control

Structured programming is the process of developing and organizing computer programs by using well-formed control constructs. Control in programs is the means of directing the flow of operations and is achieved by sequential execution, iteration, recursion, conditional execution, and selection. All computer languages provide a built-in set of constructs to directly implement some, all, or combinations of these forms of control (7, 10). The engineering student should fully understand each form and be able to build equivalent structures from what is available in his language if the appropriate forms do not already exist. The proper use of programming control constructs is necessary for developing efficient and well-structured programs.

Program Organization

Program organization stems from structured programming. Control constructs play a role in program organization, but subprograms are the major organizational component. The proper combination of subprograms, as well as the prudent selection and use of local and global variables, must be carefully considered by software designers. Each program should be divided into well-defined modules, supporting data abstraction, each with a clear purpose and specific interfaces to the remainder of the program. Such practices can readily be achieved if the engineering graduate recognizes them to be a direct outgrowth of an organized approach to the more global engineering problem solution process (15). Just as data structures reflect the composition and development of the physical structure, programs must accurately reflect its evolution through the engineering design process.

Other Concerns

A variety of other topics should be included from the software engineering perspective. Among them are problem-oriented languages, user-program interfaces, basic machine operation, defensive programming, debugging techniques, and documentation.

Students should be made aware, for example, that good documentation means much more than inserting internal program comments after a program has been written. Comprehensive documentation includes developing user manuals and technical documentation manuals, as well as inserting internal comments during program development. The similarity of these practices to documenting design calculations and developing engineering reports should be pointed out.

Another example, defensive programming, is a means of dealing with unexpected or unanticipated program operation. The unexpected invariably leads to errors, and debugging is required to eliminate them. Practice and familiarity with the programming language, combined with the use of a good compiler, will expedite the removal of syntax errors. On the other hand, removing semantic errors which deal with the meaning and logic of the program is more difficult. These are most efficiently removed by using special debugging programs provided by the operating system. To become accomplished at using these debugging programs, students can be required to debug with them as an integral part of their programming assignments.

Programming Assignments

Student homework assignments that involve writing computer programs should relate directly to an engineering problem. Ideally the assignments should demonstrate an analytical solution process, incorporate programming control and organization concepts, and integrate data structuring concepts.

Each programming assignment should be designed to include a reasonable number of new computing concepts and practices. It should provide students the opportunity to practice the concepts presented in the lectures, handouts, and textbook by implementing them in programs. For example, a student should learn to understand the usefulness and scope of good documentation by writing the documentation himself. However, despite the fact that comprehensive documentation is mandatory in all engineering programs, it is not necessary to require its incorporation into every programming assignment. Such repetition reduces the time available for the student to spend on new assignments and may negatively influence his opinion of the repeated material.

Judging Student Performance

Programming assignments alone are not a sufficient measure of student performance. Without additional incentive, students tend to concentrate on coding and debugging, neglecting lecture material and helpful programming techniques that require additional thought and practice. To ensure that the concepts presented in the lecture are well understood, non-programming assignments based on lecture notes, handout material, and the textbook are imperative. Periodic tests covering all of the material presented will provide additional reinforcement.

THE IMPACT OF ADVANCES IN COMPUTER TECHNOLOGY

A number of computer hardware and software innovations will soon have a significant impact on engineering education. Memory, processor, storage, and software advances are among those that will continue to provide lower costs and greater availability of computing facilities.

The trend in memory is to continue quadrupling capacity (4K to 16K to 64K, etc.) with 4MBit chips likely in the 1990's. The trend in processors is more computing power and greater speed. Already the first wave of 32 bit microprocessors (including the 68000, 32032, 432, and 99000) has appeared and is being replaced with versions that run faster (some twice the original speed) and require significantly less power (CMOS). At the same time, size reductions are permitting additional functionality, including memory buffers, addressing, floating point, and some operating system features, to be incorporated directly onto the silicon processor chip.

Secondary storage costs continue to drop rapidly with floppy, hard (winchester), and optical disk technologies each vying for an increased market share. Floppy disk size is being cut in half while its storage capacity is being doubled. Hard disks, initially considered to be expensive, now cost less than floppy disks did when they were first introduced. Optical disk technology has been proven and commercial products are on the market. Although the effects of this technology on the engineering student's education will be gradual, they will manifest themselves in the form of rapid access to a wide variety of engineering information.

Similar advances have occurred in software. After years of establishing a wide variety of operating systems some fundamental, although informal, standards (e.g., UNIX) have now emerged. In addition, the adherence to national standards in compilers and languages (e.g., FORTRAN 77) has reduced the burden on the user of verifying the portability of his applications to different machines. At the same time, it removes the computer manufacturer from software development issues, resulting in the introduction of advanced technology at a lower cost and a more rapid rate.

We can thus expect that in the future, fast, powerful, and inexpensive computing capabilities will be available to the engineering profession and to the educational institutions which support and contribute to it (16). Because of the potential impact of such machines on engineering problem solving and operations, it is critically important for engineering students to receive an educational background that supports their effective use of these capabilities.

CONCLUDING REMARKS

This paper addressed the increasingly important role of advanced computer science techniques in engineering education. Current educational practices and their shortcomings were discussed as well as new options to reinforce and enhance the role of computing in engineering. The key ingredients, operating system fundamentals, data structures, program control and organization, algorithms, and computer architectures (emergence of concurrent processing) were discussed.

The proper tradeoff between engineering fundamentals and computer science is changing with many of the concepts of engineering now being packaged in algorithms or on computer chips. Even though computer science is not the primary focus of engineers, significant increases in knowledge of computer science can continue to make significant benefits to the engineering profession.

The paper suggested that to convey the essentials of computer science to future engineers requires, in part, the addition of computer courses to the engineering curriculum. It also requires a strengthening of the computational content of many others so that the student comes to treat the computer as a fundamental component of his work. Indeed this is a major undertaking but the benefits of advanced computer knowledge by new engineering graduates promises to provide significant future innovations in the engineering profession.

REFERENCES

[1]   "Computer-Aided Teaching Facility for Design of Constructed Facilities," An ATHENA Project Proposal, Constructed Facilities Division, Department of Civil Engineering, Massachusetts Institute of Technology, December, 1983.

[2]   Beck, C. F., Committee Chairman, "Ethical Considerations In Computer Use," Journal of the Technical Councils, American Society of Civil Engineers, Volume 105, Number TC2, Pages 415-427, December, 1979.

[3]   Blackburn, C. L., Storaasli, O. O., and Fulton, R. E., "The Role and Application of Data Base Management in Integrated Computer-Aided Design," Journal of Aircraft, American Institute of Aeronautics and Astronautics, Volume 20, Number 8, Pages 717-725, August, 1983.

[4]   Cain, J. T., Langdon, G. G., and Varanasi, M. R., "The IEEE Computer Society Model Program in Computer Science and Engineering," Computer, Volume 17, Number 4, Pages 8-17, April, 1984.

[5]   Comfort, W. J., et. al, "Technology Transfer and Development of Computer-Aided Engineering with the University Community," Presented at the Winter Annual Meeting of the ASME Technology and Society Division, American Society of Mechanical Engineers, Washington, D.C., November, 1981.

[6]   Elias, A. L., "Computer-Aided Engineering - The AI Connection," Astronautics and Aeronautics, Volume 21, Numbers 7/8, Pages 48-54, July/August, 1983.

[7]   Fenves, S. J. and Schiffman, R. L., "Quality Assurance of Engineering Software," Journal of the Technical Councils of ASCE, American Society of Civil Engineers, Volume 105, Number TC1, Pages 57-74, April, 1979.

[8]   Fenves, S. J. and Rasdorf, W. J., "The Role of Database Management Systems in Structural Design," Proceedings of the IABSE Colloquim on Informatics in Structural Engineering, International Association of Bridge and Structural Engineers, Bergamo, Italy, Pages 229-242, October, 1982.

[9]   Fenves, S. J., Maher, M. L., Sriram, D., "Knowledge Based Expert Systems in Civil Engineering," Proceedings of the Third Conference on Computing in Civil Engineering, American Society of Civil Engineers, Pages 248-257, April, 1984.

[10] Hughes, C. E., Pfleeger, C. P., Rose, L. L., Advanced Programming Techniques. A Second Course in Programming Using FORTRAN, John Wiley and Sons, New York, NY, 1978.

[11] "Computer Utilization by Undergraduates in Civil Engineering," North Carolina State University Department of Civil Engineering, Committee on Undergraduate Programs Report, February, 1982.

[12] Noor, A. K., Storaasli, O. O., and Fulton, R. E., "Impact of New Computing Systems on Finite Element Computation," Impact of New Computing Systems on Computational Mechanics (Noor, Editor), ASME Special Publication H00290, November, 1983. Also in State-of-the-Art Surveys on Finite Element Technology (Noor & Pilkey, Editors), ASME Special Publication, November, 1983.

[13] Ransom, J. B., Storaasli, O. O., and Fulton, R. E., "Application of Concurrent Processing to Structural Dynamic Response Computations," Proceedings of the NASA-GWU Symposium on Advances and Trends in Structures and Dynamics, October, 1984.

[14] Rasdorf, W. J., "Relational Database Modeling of Building Design Data," Proceedings of the Third Conference on Computing in Civil Engineering, American Society of Civil Engineers, Pages 364-371, April, 1984.

[15] Rasdorf, W. J., "Civil Engineering Educational Computing - Beyond an Introduction," Proceedings of the Third Conference on Computing in Civil Engineering, American Society of Civil Engineers, Pages 134-142, April 1984.

[16] Rehak, D. R., "The Use of Powerful Personal Computers in Engineering Education," Proceedings of the ASEE Annual Convention, American Society of Engineering Education, Vol. 1, Pages 165-169, June, 1983.

[17] Sommer, H. T., Wernfer, B. D., Howie, G. R., "Computer-Aided Engineering Education," Mechanical Engineering, Pages 38-40, December, 1982.

[18] Sriram, D., Maher, M. L., Fenves, S. J., "Applications of Expert Systems in Structural Engineering," Proceedings of the Conference on Artificial Intelligence, April, 1983.

[19] Storaasli, O. O., "On the Role of Minicomputers in Structural Design," Computers and Structures, Volume 7, Number 1, Pages 117-123, February, 1977.

[20] Storaasli, O. O., and Foster, E. P., "Cost-Effective Use of Minicomputers to Solve Structural Problems," Journal of Aircraft, American Institute of Aeronautics and Astronautics, Volume 16, Number 11, Pages 775-779, November, 1979.

Humanities

COMPUTERS IN EDUCATION, K. Duncan and D. Harris (eds.)
Elsevier Science Publishers B.V. (North-Holland)
© IFIP, 1985

A HUMANITIES AND SOCIAL SCIENCES ORIENTED CURRICULUM

Gary Strong, Diana Woodward, Parto Dehdashti and Wayne Zachary
John Hall, Moderator

College of Information Studies,
Drexel University
Philadelphia, Pennsylvania

The purpose of Information Systems curricula is to educate those who will design and manage information systems. These information professionals need more than a thorough understanding of the limits and capabilities of their primary tool, the computer. They need an understanding of the purposes and values of the information system's end-user. Information professionals need a social sciences background that will enable them to understand the behavioral aspects of any individuals or organizations they hope to help. From the humanities, information professionals need good critical thinking and communication skills, an understanding of the nature of knowledge and cognitive structures, and a sensivitity to the social, political, economic, and ethical issues raised by the new information technology. A humanities and social sciences oriented information systems curriculum will prepare students to design and manage systems that are not only powerful and efficient, but also designed to please the user.

The Behavioral Sciences and Information Systems

The human behavioral aspects of information systems are increasing in importance. Consider the rise in interest in information ethics, human factors, and the organizational setting of the information system. This is due to a shift in emphasis from the computer and software to the role of information itself in information systems applications. This shift is motivated by lower constraints imposed by new computer hardware and software and by increased understanding of information flows in organizations and between human and computer. A curriculum to deal with these changes must bring the humanities and social sciences back into computer education.

Gary Strong

The Humanities and Information Systems

Successful design and management of information systems requires communication and critical thinking skills developed through studies in the humanities. This paper details which humanities courses are of special use to which information systems professionals: database designers, systems analysts, information center managers, information retrieval specialists, etc. The humanities perspective is also desirable for information professionals dealing with such issues as plagiarism/copyright/ownership of information, privacy/freedom of information, censorship versus information security, confidentiality, liability for the failures of information systems, and a host of political, social, and economic values challenged by the new information technology.

Diana Woodward

Social/Behavioral Issues in Information Systems Curricula

This paper reports on a study to develop an undergraduate information systems curriculum organized primarily around social and behavioral themes. Beginning with interview and documentary data, a set of social and behavioral thems were developed to integrate the various technical topics in undergraduate information systems education. Bibliographic searches and other methods were then used to develop a common set of examples and case studies that exemplify the various themes and that can be used across several courses to provide continuity of social/behavioral concerns. The relationship of this social/behavioral curriculum model to existing DPMA and ACM models is also discussed.

Parto Dehdashti
and
Wayne Zachary

COMPUTERS IN EDUCATION, K. Duncan and D. Harris (eds.)
Elsevier Science Publishers B.V. (North-Holland)
©IFIP, 1985

428

WORD PROCESSING IN PRE-HIGH SCHOOL EDUCATION

Nancy Lee Olsen, Worthington, Ohio
Cathy Conlin, Norton Glebe Primary School, United Kingdom

The session will be divided into three segments:
the definition, mechanics, and benefits of word
processing; a study of several different word
processing programs successfully implemented
with different student groups including gifted
and learning disabled students; and a question
and answer period.

First, we will look at the concepts of word
processing, how it is accomplished, some of the
differences between various word processing
packages, and hardware requirements. Selecting
a word processing package depends on the type of
writing expected of your students, the features
to be included, and the type of computers and
monitors available at your school. We will
examine both the advantages and disadvantages of
word processing and how it can help a student
improve his/her writing.

The next segment will include overviews of several word processing programs which have been
successfully used with students from 4 to 12
years of age. The first case study will be
Cathy Conlin's creative writing program at the
Norton Glebe Primary School in Cleveland County,
England. The second study is a program by Patty
Went and Nancy Olsen with learning disabled
students at an elementary school in Worthington,
Ohio. The next part will be the implementation
of a program with a third grade class, and the
concluding study is report writing with gifted
sixth grade students.

The final part of the session will be devoted to
questions and answers on word processing.

Mrs. Nancy Lee Olsen is a writer and author of
two books from Worthington, OH who for four
years has worked extensively using microcomputers with students from the first through the
sixth grade.

COMPUTERS IN EDUCATION, K. Duncan and D. Harris (eds.)
Elsevier Science Publishers B.V. (North-Holland)
© IFIP, 1985

COMPUTERS AND WRITING: VARIATIONS ON A THEME

Stephen Marcus, Ph.D.

South Coast Writing Project, Graduate School of Education, University of California
Santa Barbara, CA 93106 USA

Respondent: Valerie Arms, Ph.D.
             Department of Humanities
             Drexel University
             Philadelphia, PENN 19104 USA

    Software for computer-assisted writing instruction (CAI/writing) can be described in terms of
"generations." From the earliest, single-activity, drill-and-practice software to the notion of
"idea processors" and author stations, the historical development of CAI/writing courseware provides
a useful framework for describing the resources now available for elementary through college levels.
Additionally, there are philosophical, psychological, and sociological dimensions to be considered
when designing and using computer-based writing activities. This presentation will provide
such perspectives and help define issues relevant to current and future definitions of computer
literacy in CAI/writing.

COMPUTERS IN EDUCATION, K. Duncan and D. Harris (eds.)
Elsevier Science Publishers B.V. (North-Holland)
©IFIP, 1985

USING COMPUTERS TO TEACH LITERATURE

Chairperson
Nancy M. Ide, Vassar College

Participants
Frank L. Borchardt, Duke University
Bates L. Hoffer, Trinity University
Lance Miller, IBM Corporation

This session, sponsored by the Association for Computers and the Humanities, is intended to show how computers have been successfully used in teaching literature at the undergraduate level and to provide demonstrations of software tools that are particularly well-suited to this task. Thus the attendee should gain both an understanding of the possibilities for computer assistance in exploring theme, content, and style in literary works as well as familiarity with programs designed for text analysis of this kind.

CONCORDANCING SCHILLER WITH A KURZWEIL OR HOW TO USE A $150,000 MAGIC MARKER

Frank L. Borchardt

Beginning with printed texts, scanning same on an optical character reader, cleaning them up in a wordprocessor, and running concordance programs on them, a class in German Drama at Duke brought the German dramatist, Friedrich von Schiller into the electronic age. The literary exercise (as opposed to the electronic one) was traditional. The set tasks were idea and motif studies. The evidence was positivistic: the surface occurrence of lexical items. The work could have been accomplished with highlighters of varying colors. John Smith's ARRAS program permitted the establishment of word and idea "fields" and the identification of their locations across the texts. "Word-fields" applied in this exercise with fair to excellent results. Certain congruences (e.g. between "lust" and "power" word-fields in Schillers _Fiesco_) are otherwise not evident upon super-ficial reading of the text.

COMPUTERS and the ANALYSIS of STYLE and STRUCTURE in LITERATURE

Bates L. Hoffer

The simple sentence and paragraph structure of writers such as Hemingway, Salinger and Malamud is often varied at critical points in plot structure. Students can use available programs to locate aberrant sentences and paragraphs as a first step in structural analysis. Other uses of computers in teaching literature include quick location of similes with like/as/seems, and so on, to analyze patterns of analogy in writers like Shakespeare and Poe.

Another use is location of the 1/2 and 3/4 points of stories by e.g., Poe and Hemingway, who usually have important structural elements such as turning point and climax at those locations.

DISCUSSION AND DEMONSTRATION OF THE EPISTLE and TUPLES PROGRAMS

Lance Miller

-Abstract Unavailable-

COMPUTERS IN EDUCATION, K. Duncan and D. Harris (eds.)
Elsevier Science Publishers B.V. (North-Holland)
© IFIP, 1985

WHAT HAS CAI DONE FOR THE HUMANITIES?

Joseph Raben, Chairperson
Professor emeritus, Queens College
CUNY
Director, Paradigm Press

Glyn Holmes
Professor, Language Labs
University College
University of Western Ontario

Donald Ross
Professor, Department of English
University of Minnesota

Michael Arenson
Professor, Department of Music
University of Delaware

Since the arrival of the microcomputer, humanists have been able to fulfill a commitment made two decades ago: to employ electronic technology in the further understanding of those subjects, such as language and music, which are unique human creations. Much that was learned through research on clumsy mainframes and with punched cards is now being applied to student instruction in writing, foreign-language acquisition, and the understanding of music. Three pioneers in this field--Donald Ross, Glyn Holmes, and Michael Arenson-- report on state-of-the-art developments in their disciplines.

Donald Ross

A program called ACCESS, developed for computer-aided instruction in composition, lets writing teachers develop complex exercises and assignments for college juniors and seniors. The teachers do not have to know any programming or programming languages, since ACCESS exercise structures are defined in English, and their contents are typed in through a simple word processor. After one teacher has developed an exercise, others can edit it, restructure it, or use all or part of it in the same non-programming environment. Ross will illustrate his talk with samples of exercises that have been used in the classroom.

Glyn Holmes

This part of the session will examine the types of programs now available for foreign languages: the skills that they help develop, the place of these skills in the total language curriculum, and the impact that CAI has had on the profession. Certain trends, such as the development of increasingly intelligent and substantial programs, may, if they continue, lead to the expansion of CAI in the language curriculum.

Michael Arenson

Under a grant from the National Endowment for the Humanities, fourteen institutions have been working together since 1981 to create a Videodisc Music series consisting of four two-sided discs that can be used either in the classroom for individualized instruction in music appreciation, history, or theory classes. In addition to the actual performances of the works, the discs contain analyses and related slides. This talk will include detailed information on the Videodisc Music series itself, on software being written for the series, and on the potential of videodisc technology in music instruction.

COMPUTERS IN EDUCATION, K. Duncan and D. Harris (eds.)
Elsevier Science Publishers B.V. (North-Holland)
©IFIP, 1985

COMPUTER-BASED INSTRUCTION IN MUSIC EDUCATION

Michael Arenson

Dept. of Music, University of Delaware

Computer-based music instruction (CBMI) started in the late 1960's
with developments by Earl Hultberg at SUNY Potsdam, Wolfgang Kuhn
of Stanford, Ned Deihl at Penn. State, as well as a few other
pioneers. This tutorial will begin with a discussion of these and
other important people and events in the history of CBMI, followed
by a description of the major software and hardware available
around the country for CBMI. Participants will then receive
information about strategies used in the design, production, and
testing of music courseware. Lastly, they will be given a
demonstration of other state-of-the-art CBMI software and hardware.

New Tech, High Tech, and Using Technology

COMPUTERS IN EDUCATION, K. Duncan and D. Harris (eds.)
Elsevier Science Publishers B.V. (North-Holland)
© IFIP, 1985

ROBOT AWARENESS PROGRAMS

Frank Slaton
Director of Computing
California State University, San Bernardino

This paper describes a highly successful robot awareness program and provides details on how it was planned and conducted. The author shares his personal experiences with the 1984 ROBOT OLYMPICS, an internationally recognized event held at California State University, San Bernardino.

You may ask "Why is an awareness program necessary ?" Normally, how are our students learning about robots ? They can read a science fiction book, watch television or go to a Hollywood movie. The portrayals are often a far cry from reality. A robot awareness program can help dispel myths, remove mysteries and reduce fear of the unknown. These very points are the purposes of technological education.

Where do you find robots today ? They are used in manufacturing, most noticeable in the automobile industry. They are used for welding, painting and some assembly operations. They are particularly suitable in an undesirable environment associated with radioactive materials, extreme heat or hostility. The space program used robots in moon exploration, satellite repair and will some day use them for mining in space. Once we realize that robots are useful and versatile we begin to see the need for an "awareness event".

Because schools were still equipping classrooms with microcomputers, it did not seem logical to establish competitions utilizing the existing classroom resources. We thus began to identify a robot awareness program outside the classroom. There were several historical experiences to learn from. Science fairs feature: physical objects, appeal to spectators and innovative subject matter. Spelling bees feature: performance before an audience, a zeal to excel and multi-tier competitions. Speaking of competition, consider interscholastic sports, with their competition, school spirit, cheering sections and awards. When you think of school competitions you know the amount of practice that is involved to achieve recognition. In most of these competitions the learning experiences involve many teacher and parent involvements before public fame is achieved.

Would it be possible to wrap up all of these features into a robot awareness event outside the classroom ? Because the event was being molded in 1983 in the shadow of the 1984 Los Angeles Olympics, it seemed only natural to design a ROBOT OLYMPICS.

Who would you expect to host such an event ? Many institutions of higher education have had computer awareness programs for years. Our University was no exception. Taking the lead in robot awareness seemed a natural progression.

In the balance of this paper you will learn how the first ROBOT OLYMPICS was conceived and what planning was necessary for its success. Even if you are not interested in robots, the discussion is relevant to the planning of other school events. Note particularly the community involvement and publicity.

During development of the initial concept, the theme was set as "A Unique Education Experience". Participation by all ages would be emphasized. The setting would provide for spectators, including other students and the public.

With this theme established, a national call for participation was issued, distributed initially at the June 1983 National Educational Computing Conference in Baltimore. Manufacturer names were gleaned from various publications. National magazines ran the event in their calendars.

Participation would be sought from schools within the University's service area, a two-county area in Southern California. This includes Riverside County and San Bernardino County -- the largest county in the United States. These two counties have 500 K-12 schools. Other schools would be allowed to participate, but not be 'solicited'.

It was decided to schedule the ROBOT OLYMPICS concurrently with a computer festival that had been so successful a year earlier. This would provide two revenue sources -- fees charged to exhibitors and fees charges to workshop participants. Three co-sponsors had already identified with the festival.

Publicity began six months ahead of the planned event to each of the 500 schools and the 70 Chambers of Commerce in the two-county area. A monthly ROBOT OLYMPICS Newsletter announced the forthcoming event and suggested robot related education activities. Reading lists were provided. Products and their dealers were identified.

A workshop for teachers was held three months before the event. Two dealers participated and demonstrated robots. Schools represented at the workshop provided the nucleus for the ultimate robot competitions.

A key element of the publicity was the establishment of a speakers' bureau. University staff responsible for organizing the ROBOT OLYMPICS visited schools, museums, service organizations and chambers of commerce. The speaker would take along one or more robots, usually provided by a cooperating robot dealer. Copies of the current ROBOT OLYMPICS Newsletter would be distributed.

The ROBOT OLYMPICS Newsletter provided a list of robot articles in current periodicals and a list of books. The manufacturers contacted were cooperative and helpful, furnishing literature and providing the names of dealers. Reviewing this literature identified the available education robots. These robots had to be reasonably priced, yet demonstrate robot principles. There turned out to be three types of education robots available.

(1) A mobile "android-like" robot that sometimes needed an accompanying computer. You may recognize brand names like HERO, RB5X, and TOPO.

(2) Robot "arms" that needed a computer or a teaching pendant.

(3) Robot "turtles" that needed an attached computer and might have drawing or speaking ability.

Kits were available for under $100 and the assembly activity brings in other skills and the opportunity for team activity.

A Buyers Guide was included in the

ROBOT OLYMPICS Newsletter, summarizing the results of the literature review. Robot features, prices and dealers were shown for twenty-two models from ten manufacturers.

The United States Small Business Administration helped publicize business workshops. Area Chamber of Commerce meetings provided a chance to show robots to school and business representatives. Keep in mind that most of these people had never seen an educational robot. The robot awareness program began here. Publicity was provided to businesses in the Chamber Newsletters.

The Region 13 Teacher Education Computer Center serving the University's service area is one of fifteen State-funded regional training centers. This center periodically holds teacher in-service training on the University campus and publishes a Newsletter for schools. The Center assisted with publicity and helped identify resources.

The importance of planning cannot be over emphasized. Details were in place six months in advance, and a status report was provided to top University administrators. In order to reduce publicity costs, it was decided to concurrently schedule the ROBOT OLYMPICS with two previously held annual activities. The two revenue sources mentioned earlier comprised a Computer Festival dubbed the ME Festival -- microtechnology for everybody. Rock show historians may recognize the genesis of "ME", recalling the 1982 and 1983 "US" Festivals held nine miles north of the campus of California State University, San Bernardino.

A three-person ROBOT OLYMPICS Committee was established to manage the three major components.

(1) ROBOT OLYMPICS

(2) Workshops

(3) Exhibits and Entertainment

Entertainment for all ages had traditionally been part of an annual Campus Open House. Additionally as a feature attraction a high-tech theme attraction was added - a computer controlled animated whale.

Exhibit booths sized 10' X 10' were laid out in the gymnasium, with electricity provided each booth by reusable extension cords. Admission to the exhibit area was free and hours were 11:00 a.m. to 6:00 p.m. on a Friday and Saturday.

Workshop categories covered education, business and general interest. Volunteer workshop leaders included University faculty and staff, school resources and vendor representatives. One area author led a workshop for a book sale guarantee.

Because this was the first ROBOT OLYMPICS, the events themselves had not ever been defined. A scant three months before the event the following event criteria were published in the periodic ROBOT OLYMPICS Newsletter mentioned earlier. A ROBOT OLYMPICS event had to:

Demonstrate capabilities found on one or more available robots.

Be within skill levels of most students in one of the following grade categories: K-6, junior high, or high school.

Be able to be set up, run, and area cleared within 30 minutes.

Have clearly defined objectives which can be measured for judging.

Be challenging to contestants.

Not pose a safety hazard.

Run on a plywood floor, indoor-outdoor carpet, or tabletop.

Be appealing to spectator audience.

Have minimum expense for props.

Not be sensitive to wind or outdoor temperatures.

A ROBOT OLYMPICS Newsletter published two months before the event announced that a copy of the "Official ROBOT OLYMPICS Rule Book" was available free to any school considering entering competition. The rule book included a registration form (no fee required). School teams were scheduled on a Friday during school hours.

The rule book described the six different events as follows:

Robot Dash: Robot will travel out a specified distance, turn right or left, travel around an obstacle, and return to starting line.

Figure Tracing: Robot will draw one of specified letters in ´CAL STATE´. Letters will be capitals in square-block format, at least two feet high.

Robot Slalom: Robot will travel out a specified distance, pass the first obstacle on a specified side, travel around second obstacle in a specified direction, pass first obstacle again on opposite side, and return to starting line.

Robot Biathlon: Robot will travel out to three specified locations on competition grid while avoiding an obstacle on the grid, knock over a target at each location, and return to starting line.

Robot Maze: Robot will traverse an unknown maze consisting of two right turns and two left turns in random order.

Robot Construction: Participants will assemble robot from designated kit. Participants will operate robot according to required program.

Events were held in a rented circus tent, with four stages and bleachers. Authentic circus music was provided by a restored turn-of-the-century card-programmed Gavioli band organ. School groups had the chance to view a twenty-two foot replica of a whale, controlled by an Apple computer, transported from University of Maryland Baltimore County.

All participants in the competitions received a free T-shirt and winning schools got free trophies. Official statistics were reported in a news release. Dozens of newspaper and magazine articles provided publicity for the participants, their schools and the University.

In 1985 the University involved more schools by holding preliminary ROBOT OLYMPIC events throughout the two county service area. The ROBOT OLYMPICS Newsletter and speaker bureau activities are continuing on a year-around basis.

COMPUTERS IN EDUCATION, K. Duncan and D. Harris (eds.)
Elsevier Science Publishers B.V. (North-Holland)
© IFIP, 1985

THE IMPLEMENTATION OF HIGH TECHNOLOGY IN LARGE URBAN SCHOOL DISTRICTS

Patricia A. Hamilton

Training and Technology
1800 Old Meadow Road, Suite #112
McLean, Virginia 22102
United States of America

This study was conducted for the Council of Great City Schools during the 1983-84
school year and describes in general terms the range of computers that large city
schools are now using for administrative and instructional purposes. Of necessity,
the results comprise a status report only. The use of computers and other high technology equipment has seen unprecedented growth over the last three years. The purpose
here is to provide information on how districts are implementing the technology.

Computers in schools have become, in a few short
years, a complex and highly controversial field.
Various national commission reports on the
status of American education have hailed,
damned, or ignored the entire movement. On
Capitol Hill, the nation's lawmakers have proposed implementing tax deductions for computer
donations but remain unsure whether such a move
would help or hurt the drive for excellence.
Companies producing computers continue to manufacture and sell equipment to schools, often
faster than such large bureaucracies can adjust.
At the local level, confusion appears to be the
order of the day as no one is clear on exactly
how to respond to community and national pressure to place computers in the classroom.

What is becoming clear, however, is that the
computer may not be another passing educational
fad. Report after report has emerged this year
describing America's technology gap in our
schools. It is becoming far more evident that
using computers in the classroom will be increasingly important as the United States
attempts to keep pace with other nations.

Such clarity begins to fade when questions
emerge about what the technology will be used
for, how many and what jobs can be secured by
such training, what is to be taught and how,
how to plan for future programming in such a
fast-changing field, how to assure equal access
to the benefits of computers, and how to manage
and pay for the privilege of using them.

This report will examine some of these issues
indirectly by examining how our nation's urban
schools are responding to the computer challenge. A look at how city school systems are
now planning to install computers, how they are
managing the planning, purchasing, and evaluation

of equipment, what equipment is actually being
purchased and with what criteria, which courseware is being used to operate the systems, what
computer languages are being taught, and how all
of it is being financed and maintained will be
presented.

Because of the wide range of topics covered here,
not all issues are examined. For instance,
neither the instructional software used in the
classroom and its effectiveness, nor the management problems associated with such extensive
purchasing, have been covered. The field itself
is not only extremely technical and detailed,
but cuts across school cyctem responsibilities
for curriculum, finance, procurement, personnel
training, materials evaluation, research and
development, student records, and classroom
teaching.

The information for this report was obtained
directly from personnel in 28 of the largest
urban school districts across the United States
which have primary responsibility for computer
technology. A list of these districts can be
found at the end of the report. Superintendents
in each district were asked to identify the
person(s) responsible for this important area.
Each person, usually of Associate Superintendent
to Program Director rank, was interviewed at
length on the topics covered in this report.
Written descriptions of each district's program
were sent to those who were interviewed for
corrections and modifications to ensure accuracy.

A. **District-Wide Planning**

The fast-growing interest in computer technology
has significantly increased the importance of
local planning. The millions of dollars spent
on hardware, courseware, and training has

dictated such planning, but the planning itself is often lagging behind the dollar investment. Forty-eight per cent of the districts in this survey have approved some sort of district-wide plan in the last three years (most of these within the last year). Another 41 per cent are now in the process of developing a plan. Only three of the districts did not have any kind of plan for high technology on the drawing-board.

All of the plans that have been developed include goals for instructional technology, and about ½ also include finance/business and central administrative data management matters. The instructional plans normally included issues such as staff training, procurement and disbursement of hardware and software, maintenance of equipment, computer literacy, computer science and computer-assisted instruction (CAI), and management and organizational problems.

Most district plans were developed by committees comprised of administrators, teachers, parents, and consultants. Some districts used consultants to develop specific recommendations and proposeals for plans. The use of consultants was especially prevalent with planning for the administrative applications of computers. In-house expertise was drawn on more often for instructional applications.

In the course of this study, only a small number of districts that mentioned designing plans for computers for vocational or special education were encounterd. Albuquerque, New Mexico and Milwaukee, Wisconsin appeared to be ahead of other districts in this area. In addition, it was found that most planning was done on three-to five-year cycles. This would correspond to planning cycles in other areas, including federal programming. Minneapolis, Minnesota has a five-year plan in instructional technology and general school improvement that could serve as a prototype for other school districts.

What seemed most apparent from the interviews was that districts like Boston, Massachusetts, Detroit, Michigan, and Denver, Colorado, which had older plans (i.e., plans that preceded the purchase of equipment), had evolved further both in the planning process itself and in the direction in which the school system was moving.

B. Management of High Technology

The management of high technology historically has been handled by school districts dealing with central business/finance and/or data processing. This traditional organizational structure has begun to change over the last few years. Over 60 per cent of the districts in this survey now have two distinct managment directions: 1) the original office(s) with a relatively large staff with responsibilities for data processing, finance, personnel, and payroll, and 2) a newer office (or new duties within an older division) that coordinates

instructional purchases, curricular standards, and in-service training. The latter division now appears to have prime responsibility, in many cases, for reviewing and approving instructional hardware and courseware, purchasing, surveying inventory, repairing equipment, consulting with teachers, and maintaining courseware libraries. In most cases, this instructional track has been in existence only a few (usually fewer than three) years and has only one to three people assigned full-time responsibilities in this area.

Only 21 per cent of the districts in this survey still had just one division in charge of all technology. On the other hand, approximately 17 per cent had three or more diivsions, usually with prime responsibilities for audio-visual equipment, personnel and Chapter 1 (ECIA). Normally, the person in charge of instructional technology, whether in administrative or instructional divisions, also chaired a district committee on technology comrised of representatives from data processing and various curricular fields and grade levels.

The type and brand of hardware and courseware purchased is managed at the central office level in 72 per cent of the districts. The remaining districts allowed individual school principals to make purchasing decisions. Only about 20 per cent of the districts require the purchasing of specific brands of equipment or that courseware be centrally approved.

In districts with centralized authority, management problems include not only which equipment to buy but how to disburse it to the individual schools and which staff to train in its use.

C. Computer Equipment and Courseware

1. Instructional equipment. Microcomputers manufactured by the Apple Corporation are the most frequently used (40 per cent) instructional computers in the big city schools. This preponderance of Apple computers appears to be due in part to the availability of compatible software through the Minnesota Education Computing Consortium (MECC), the most popular source for courseware (see section on Courseware). Radio Shack TRS 80's and Commodores are the next most frequently purchased micros (see Table 1). IBM-manufactured equipment appears to be gaining increasingly large shares of the market, compared to other brands, although it is found now in only seven per cent of the Council districts. DEC, Atari, and Hewlett-Packard terminals also have a small segment of the urban school market. Franklin, Dolphin, Data General, and Texas Instruments euqipment complete the remainder of the microcomputer instructional equipment found in these city schools.

TABLE 1.   Instructional Computer Equipment

Manufacturer	Share of Great City Market
Apple Corporation	40%
Radio Shack	23%
Commodore	17%
IBM	7%
Digital Equipment Corporation	5%
Hewlett-Packard	4%
Atari	3%
Other	1%

2. Administrative equipment. The most frequently used equipment for administrative applications is ibm and Honeywell, with Burroughs
computers used less than half as often. Data
General, Hewlett-Packard, and Digital Equipment
Corporation (DEC) computers are found less often
in central administrative functions.

3. Courseware. The school systems participating
in this survey most frequently cite the Minnesota
Education Computing Consortium (MECC) as the
most valued source for instructional courseware.
The attractiveness of this software appears to
be based on its being carefully previewed,
tested, and validated, and on its generally low
price. It should be noted here that the MECC
programs are compatible only with the Apple computers at this time, although efforts are now
being made to rewrite the software for Atari and
IBM machinery.

While MECC courseware most often receives high
praise, the most frequently purchased software
is from the publishers. Many school systems
prefer courseware from publishers over that
provided by MECC because the former is reputed
to be more relevant to curricular goals and basal
textbooks. Other education agencies, both local
and state, and vendors supply courseware much
less often than MECC and the publishers. Only
four districts reported developing some of their
own courseware, and in only one district was
in-house courseware found to comprise the bulk
of the system's courseware library.

4. Additional forms of technology. In addition
to traditional mainframe computers for administrative use and the new microcomputers for
instructional purposes, city schools are insti-
tuting other forms of technonlogy (see Table 2).
The majority of city schools now have or plan
to have in the near future cable capacity. Most
urban schools in major media markets now receive
cable services when franchises are awarded.

In addition, electronic mail is reported to be
in use in about ½ of the city districts, and
about 2/3 expect to begin or increase this
capacity in the near future.

Only five of the reporting school systems have
video disc players at this time, but nearly ½
expect to have them in the near future.

Similarly, few districts are now experimenting
with robotics, but several expect to become
more involved in the near future. By contrast,
computerized word processors are found in all of
the districts in this survey, and some now operate their own television stations and internal
telephone systems.

TABLE 2.   Additional Forms of Technology

Technology	% of Districts with Technology	% Planning to Have Technology
Cable	66%	66%
Telecommunications	78%	22%
Electronic Mail	44%	70%
Video Disc	19%	48%
Robotics	7%	22%
Optical Scanners	70%	7%
Word Processors	100%	100%

D.   Equipment Maintenance

The area of computer maintenance in city school
systems is changing rapidly. Almost ½ of the
districts were doing some or all of their own
maintenance or were planning to do so soon.
Currently, staff are being trained, maintenance
centers are being opened, and some districts
(such as Denver) are forming maintenance consor-
tia with neighboring school districts. For the
moment, however, most school systems rely on
the purchasing of extended maintenance warranties
while in-house capacities are being developed.
Most warranties are purchased directly from the
manufacturers, but a number of districts are
contracting out maintenance agreements through
competitive bidding processes. Almost all
school systems use at least two of three
general maintenance strategies (i.e., in-house
repair, manufacturer warranty, and competitive
maintenance contracts). The fastest-growing
approcah appears to be to develop in-house
capabilities because of the lower cost and
greater speed of repair.

E.   Number and Uses of Computers

1. Administrative applications. At the central office levels, computers have been used
for many years for business/finance, personnel,
student records, scheduling, testing and research, and budgetary or payroll functions. It
is in this area that city schools seem to have
the edge on other kinds of school systems in
terms of the numbers and sophistication of
computer applications. This edge should not
be surprising, given the size of the districts
and the range of operations. More recently,
central offices have begun computerizing
library books, transportation routes, food
services, curricular information, and energy
usage patterns. Again, the sheer size and
complexity of these districts dictate greater
computerization for management purposes.

The most recent innovations for administrative applications are at the school building level. Here, principals, teachers, librarians, and counselors are purchasing or developing their own hardware and software to: manage courseloads, track library books, and manage grade reports, student records, test results, and Individual Education Plans (IEP) for handicapped students. Another fast-growing application of the computer is the linking of individual schools to portions of the central office mainframe computers. Dade County, Florida appears to be breaking new ground in this area. Table 3 shows the number of responding school districts which use many of these administrative applications at the central and school building levels.

TABLE 3.   ADMINSTRATIVE APPLICATIONS*

Student Academic Records	Central	Bldg.
Class Schedule	23	12
Grade Report	21	10
Test Scoring	22	10
IEP Records	17	8
Others (list)	-0-	-0-

Student Non-Academic Records		
Vocational Counseling	12	10
Health Immunization	15	3
Psychological Test Results	14	4
Others--Attendance	2	-0-

Transportation Functions		
Passenger Lists	17	2
Route/Driver Scheduling	13	-0-
Vehicle Performance and Maintenance	12	-0-
Others (list)	-0-	-0-

Food Services		
Free/Reduced Price Lunch	19	2
Elegibility Lists	17	2
Menu Planning	7	1
Inventory	20	1
Others (list)	-0-	-0-

Library Functions		
Book Inventories	16	1
Book Orders	15	1
Book Checkout	3	4
Overdue Notices	1	7
Others (list)	-0-	-0-

Public Relations Areas		
Mailing Lists	24	4
Staff Directories	23	2
Pupil Directories	17	2
Others (list)	-0-	-0-

Co-Curricular Activities		
Income/Expenditures	17	3
Eligibility Lists	9	2

Research and Development		
Testing	23	2
Research	22	1

Budget Planning	Central	Bldg.
Collective Negotiations	16	-0-
Planning	21	2
School Boundary/Census Information	20	-0-
Enrollment Projections	17	1
Others (list)	-0-	-0-

Scheduling Functions		
Class Schedules	23	9
Staff Schedules	17	6
Building/Classroom Utilization	18	4
Others (list)	-0-	-0-

Personnel Functions		
Salary Information	25	-0-
Employment Files	21	1
Leave Records	21	-0-
Certification Information	22	1
In-Service Information	9	-0-
Others (list)	-0-	-0-

Business Functions		
Payroll	24	-0-
Receipts/Spending/Accounting	25	-0-
Appropriations Information	18	-0-
Inventory Reports (Federal, State, Board)	22	1
Others (list)	-0-	-0-

*Numbers represent numbers of school districts responding that use computers for one of the designated purposes.

2. Instructional applications. The use of computers to teach students is the fastest growing role for this important new field, but a use that continues to lag behind administrative applications for most big city schools. About 88 per cent of the secondary schools and 57 per cent of the elementary schools in the responding districts had at least one microcomputer or terminal for instructional purposes. The range of schools having microcomputers is very wide, with at least one district reporting that computers were in only one per cent of their elementary schools and one district reporting computers on only 40 per cent of their secondary schools. In November, 1983, six of the 27 reporting districts, or 22 per cent, had computers in every elementary school, whereas 17 of the districts, or 61 per cent, had computers in all of their secondary schools (see Table 4). While many school buildings appear to have at least one terminal for instructional purposes, in some cases that is all they have, and the ratio of students to computers is large. This survey found that the ratio of students to computers in the elementary grades (K-6) in these schools is about 863:1, or one computer for every 863 pupils. The range is very wide--97:1 through 4000:1. At the secondary grade levels (7-12), the ratios are somewhat better--one instructional computer for every 186 pupils, with a range of 40:1 through 473:1 (see Table 5). Ratios were computed by dividing the number of elementary (K-6) and

secondary (7-12) students by the number of micro-computers or terminals used for instructional purposes at those respective grade levels. The highest and the lowest ratios were omitted before computing the average.

TABLE 4.   Per Cent of Schools with Computers

Schools with Computers	Percentage
Elementary Schools with Computers	57
Secondary Schools with Computers	88
Districts with Computers in Elementary Schools	22
Districts with Computers in Secondary Schools	61

- - - - - - - - - - - - - - - - - -

TABLE 5.   Ratios of Students to Computers

Grade Level	Low	High	Adjusted Average
Elementary (K-6)	97:1	4000:1	863:1
Secondary (7-12)	40:1	473:1	186:1

The uses to which instructional computers were put were also explored by this survey. Districts were asked to identify either computer literacy courses or courses in computer science according to their own definitions of each. Many districts reported that they did not have a computer li-teracy course for students per se, but rather that literacy was infused throughout the curri-culum as part of their computer-assisted in-struction (CAI) plan. Only a small number of districts have courses in computer literacy at the elementary grade level. In general, it was found that about 50 per cent of the districts had at least one computer literacy course on the secondary grade level, but many had none at all. Recently, Washington, DC Public Schools insti-tuted requirements for a ½-credit course in com-puter literacy for high school graduation.

Course offerings in computer science tend to be more prevalent. While only five districts had computer science courses at the elementary level, all districts except one offered such courses at the secondary level. In fact, the average district offered seven different computer science courses.

In general, these course offerings in the com-puter sciences are courses in programming or in computer theory. Instruction in BASIC was of-fered in almost 90 per cent of the elementary schools having such courses, and in all of the secondary schools. (BASIC is the most common and least technical of all the major computer languages). LOGO is the next most commonly taught computer language in grades K-6 while PASCAL is the next most common at the secondary level (see Table 6).

Unfortunately, most districts could not estimate the actual number of students enrolled in these courses. Of those eight districts that could, only about 2600 elementary students and about 3060 secondary students were enrolled per district.

TABLE 6.   Computer Languages Taught in
Great City Schools

Elementary Grades

Language	Percentage
BASIC	88
LOGO	66
Others	11

Secondary Grades

BASIC	100
PASCAL	77
COBOL	59
FORTRAN	55
LOGO	37
PILOT	30
RPG	30
Others	15

F.   Staff and Teacher Training

Most training of staff in computer usage or literacy is done in-house, but other education agencies and vendors also provide instruction. All but one of the reporting districts had pro-vided training for administrative and instruc-tional staff. The number of teachers trained ranged from 50 to 6000 per year and the number of administrators trained ranged from 11 to 2000 per year. Most districts were unable to provide data on the total numbers of teachers trained to teach computer literacy or computer sciences, but of those that could, an average of 158 elementary teachers, 113 secondary teachers, 22 special education teachers, and 14 vocational education teachers were trained to some level of proficiency. Only three dis-tricts reported teacher-certification in computer literacy: Albuquerque, New Mexico and Boston Massachusetts have local certification, and Dade County, Florida complies with a state-level certification requirement.

G.   Budget

About ½ of the reporting districts in this sur-vey had funds specifically designated for in-structional technology and the other ½ purchased computers and courseware from their instructional materials and equipment budgets. Outside funding was contributed most frequently by local PTA's, but very little by the private sector. However, in a few districts, such as Detroit, Michigan, Columbus, Ohio, Minneapolis, Minnesota, and Washington, DC, and California schools, the private sector has taken a very active role in providing equipment. The districts that have specific computer funds had allocated amounts ranging fromm $55,000 to $3,000,000 (averaging about $790,000) for instruction in 1982-83, and from $270,00 to $3,500,000 (averaging about $1,970,000) for business and administration applications. Figures were not available for 1983-84.

H. Conclusions

From the results of this survey, a number of
very general conclusions and trends emerged.
First, it was apparent that the computer movement has made itself most prominent in the secondary rather that the elementary grades. While
a small number of districts indicated in their
plans that computer familiarity should begin in
the early grades, most districts had, in fact,
begun at the secondary level. Perhaps the reasons
or this lie in the easy connection one can make
between such secondary-level training and available jobs, and in the difficulty of altering
curricula. Computer courses at the elementary
level usually require more broadly-based curriculum revisions that at the seconsary level.

The issue of curriculum revision brings up the
second major point. It was disturbing to find
that, in some few cases, the purchasing of equipment on a large scale had preceded the actual
planning of what to do with it. Such purchases
in some cases appeared to be driven more by
computer vendors than by distric-wide planning.
It would be unusual for schools to purchase
textbooks with no thought of the courses in which
they might be useful, but this appears to be
what has happened with computer-buying in some
districts. It is also evident that the software
used, while state-of-the-art, is more likely to
shape the curricula than vice-versa. This seemed
particularly true with packaged mass-market programs. The highest levels of praise for computer
courseware came from districts that had developed
their own to match local needs and curriculum
objectives. Unfortunately, it is much more
difficult and costly to develop courseware in-
house, which is why districts must turn to outside sources.

Third, most of the training now done with computers is fairly isolated in particular secondary
schools in courses designed to teach sepcific
computer skills. This may be a temporary phenomenon as time will be needed to build the supply
of computers, develop general computer familiarity, and mesh the current hardware into the
overall district curriculum. It was somewhat
surprising to see such scant offerings in general
computer literacy, but a closer look at the
districts' long-range plans shows that such instruction, along with CAI, was the direction in
which most schools were moving. Such fundamental
change in how to present traditional academic
material through computers will take a great
deal of time and planning. Hopefully, the
enormous effort required will pay off in increased achievement, although it remains to be
seen whether computers in the classroom will
actually enhance learning.

A fourth conclusion deals with equity and equal
access to computers and the benefits they may
bring. Very few insatnces were observed in
which districts reviewed computer hardware and
courseware for the same racial and gender bias
with which they review textbooks and standardized tests. In addition, the concentration of
language-minority youngsters in city schools
makes it very important to consider the implications of computers for bilingual programs.
Software in Spanish and Vietnamese, for instance,
still lags behind, and few computer manufacturers
have included specialized keys to accomodate
bilingual children, e.g., the inverted question
mark for Hispanic students. These issues take
on enormous importance in city schools because
of the populations they serve. If access to the
technologies of the future is limited in these
areas, then it will be that much more difficult
to find gainful career employment later on and
computers simply evolve into one more gate-keeper.

The fimal comclusion is based on the comparison
of the results found in this study with those
found on other surveys on the same issue. In
the spring of 1982, the NCES Fast Response Survey
howed that the number of microcomputers available to public school students tripled between
the fall of 1980 and the spring of 1982--from
40,000 to 120,00. At that time, 22 per cent of
the elementary schools and 65 per cent of the
secondary schools had at least one microcomputer.

Henry Jay Becker of Johns Hopkins University
conducted a survey of over 2000 schools and
reported that in January of 1983, 42 per cent
of the elementary schools and 77 per cent of
the secondary schools had at least one microcomputer. In the summer of 1983, Market Data
Retrieval of Westport, Connecticut conducted
a telephone survey of every school district in
the country. They found that 62 per cent of
the elementary schools, 81 per cent of the
junior high schools, and 89 per cent of the
senior high schools nationwide had at least one
microcomputer. Although the Hamilton survey
found that 57 per cent of the elementary
schools and 88 per cent of the secondary schools
had computers, it must be remenbered that these
figures were gathered more recently than those
in the other two surveys.

City schools do not fare well when one compares
the number of students to the number of computers. Becker found an average of 183:1 in
elementary schools while Hamilton found and
863:1 ration. At the secondary level, Becker's
survey found 88:1 while Hamilton's showed 186:1.

If course offerings in computer literacy and
computer science are compared, it can be seen
that large cities are doing as well as or better
than other kinds of school systems. Becker found
that 51 per cent of the high schools taught
computer literacy and 64 per cent had courses
in computer science. The districts in the
hamilton survey have computer science courses
in virtually all of their high schools and
computer literacy instruction in 51 per cent
of these schools.

Because the acquisition and implementation of
computers are growing so rapidly, it is difficult
to construct comparative data. It is clear,
however, that although city high schools have
computers in almost every building, and courses
are now available, the number of computers available to meet the needs is far from sufficient.

- - - - - - - - - - - - - - - - - -

LIST OF SCHOOL DISTRICTS PARTICIPATING IN THE
               STUDY

ALABAMA   MINNESOTA
  Birmingham   Milwaukee
                             Minneapolis
CALIFORNIA
  Los Angeles   MISSOURI
  Oakland   St. Louis
  San Francisco
                           NEW YORK
COLORADO   New York City
  Denver
                           OHIO
DISTRICY OF COLUMBIA   Cleveland
                             Columbus
FLORIDA   Toledo
  Dade County
                           OREGON
GEORGIA   Portland
  Atlanta
                           PENNSYLVANIA
ILLINOIS   Philadelphia
  Chicago   Pittsburgh

LOUISIANA   TENNESSEE
  New Orleans   Memphis
                             Nashville
MARYLAND
  Baltimore   TEXAS
                             Dallas
MASSACHUSETTS
  Boston   VIRGINIA
                             Norfolk
MICHIGAN
  Detroit   WASHINGTON
                             Seattle

COMPUTERS IN EDUCATION, K. Duncan and D. Harris (eds.)
Elsevier Science Publishers B.V. (North-Holland)
© IFIP, 1985

CLASSROOM BEHAVIOR RECORD:
Videodisc Development for Teaching Observation Skills

Lynn Johnson, M.A.
Joan Sustik Huntley, Ph.D.
Computer Assisted Instruction Laboratory
Weeg Computing Center
University of Iowa
Iowa City, IA 52242

Technological innovations have permitted novel applications of computers in education. This article summarizes the process used to develop an interactive videodisc package that teaches behavioral observation using the Classroom Behavior Record. Standardizing the instruction yields a higher degree of inter-observer reliability than previous methods.

THE PROBLEM:

Effective July 1, 1983, the State of Iowa required systematic observations of overt behaviors of all children referred as potentially having behavior disorders. The Classroom Behavior Record (Nichols, Robinson, Fitzgerald, 1979), a paper-pencil observation scale, developed at the University of Iowa fulfilled this requirement. However, an efficient and effective method of training reliable observers was lacking.

In the five years since its development, the Classroom Behavior Record has been taught to over 18 observers throughout the state of Iowa. It took 40 to 60 hours of trainee time and 30 to 50 hours of trainer time to develop the desired level of reliability. Observer training included memorizing the terms and definitions of 32 behavior codes, working videotape to recognize behaviors, practicing with the code in live classrooms, and learning to record and summarize data.

While greater efficiency was possible through small group training, travel, with its associated time and costs, and scheduling conflicts often prohibited this approach. This demonstrated the need for an individualized training package that would be readily available statewide.

The interactive videodisc, a visual storage medium, enhances the advantages of computer based instruction. Its random access capabilities merge a full color display, motion, and sound with computer managed instruction, self-pacing and branching to create an interactive learning environment. It offered the technical capabilities to individualized instruction of the Classroom Behavior Record.

PACKAGE DESCRIPTION:

Content: The content of the Classroom Behavior Record is stored on both the videodisc and the computer disk. The videodisc contains narrative descriptions, motion samples, and documented still examples and non-examples of each behavior. Section heading stills, glossary information, short practice sessions for learning each behavior code and extended cumulative practices are also included on the videodisc. The computer program responds to users' input, controls the sequence of videodisc material, presents additional content information, and generates graphics to orient the user regarding their location within the program. Numerous option points enable the student to "look up" code definitions in the Glossary, review a unit, examine related information or repeat a segment.

The video information was gathered over 3 1/2 months. The behaviors of 22 children, ages 4 to 14, in classrooms at the Department of Educational Services, Child Psychiatry Service at the University of Iowa were recorded on one inch videotape. Some of the extreme behaviors, rarely exhibited in classrooms, were not demonstrated during the initial taping. This video information was therefore staged by six student actors. In total, 17 hours of recorded tape were edited to comprise approximately 25 minutes of videodisc motion.

Hardware: The learner views two television screens and communicates via an Apple II microcomputer keyboard and graphics tablet. One television screen displays motion segments and documented stills from the Pioneer LDV-4000 videodisc player; the other displays computer generated output. A PowerPad graphics tablet with a coded plastic overlay simulates the clipboard and pencil recording techniques normally used in the classroom. The microcomputer scores the individual codes students enter via the graphics tablet and provides feedback.

CONTENT OUTLINE:

The content is organized into an overview, six behavior groups, six procedure concepts, and four extended practices.

A. Overview: The student is introduced to the Classroom Behavior Record, presented the observation routine and factors regarding precedence in coding.

B. Behavior Group:

    1. On/Off Task: behaviors most commonly seen in the classroom - deals with attending or non-attending to task behaviors.

    2. Positive/Negative Interaction: behaviors in which the student is relating to either peers or staff.

    3. Student as Object: those instances in which the student is acted upon by peers or staff.

    4. Comply/Non-comply: behaviors displayed when a student does or does not fulfill staff's requests.

    5. Learning Activities: behaviors seen in an individualized or group instruction situation.

    6. Disruptive Behaviors: exhibited when a student is being angry, noisy, or self-focused.

C. Procedure Concepts:

    1. Observation Routine: one instance of coding a student's behavior.

    2. Rules of Precedence: when two codes conflict - which has precedence.

3. Alternating Variables: to compare a student's behavior with the entire class, alter observations between the student and peers.

4. Setting Specificity: behavior appropriate to one setting may be inappropriate to another.

5. Intensity: always code the most severe and intense behavior.

6. Open Intervals: a means of coding behavior unique to an individual.

D. Extended Practices: Four extended sessions, each of increasing length, reinforce previous learning codes.

DESIGN DECISIONS:

Using a computer-controlled videodisc as a delivery system, the following design decision needed to be made:

1. How should the half-hour of videodisc space be used? Should it be spent entirely on teaching codes or a combination of teaching and practice? We used documented stills to illustrate examples and non-examples of each behavior, freeing approximately 15 minutes of videodisc motion for practice segments.

2. What information should be presented by the various system components? We made the following decisions:

Videodisc:
    motion - classroom examples of behavior; practices

    still images - title frames; glossary definitions; sample coding sheets; documented examples and non-examples

    audio tracks - introduction to student to the program; describe behavior codes; provide classroom sound accompanying motion samples

Computer:
  text - information about a video
       still; directions for locat-
       ing a specific child to
       observe; menu options; feed-
       back and additional
       informational text

  graphics - orient students to
           their location in the
           program

VIDEODISC DEVELOPMENT:

Development Team: A videodisc
package is developed through the coordinated efforts of many people. The
personnel for this project included:

1. Instructional Designer - coordinate
    staff; establish feasible goals;
    manage the development process; as-
    sist in major design decisions.

2. Content Expert - write the grants
    for funding; organize the content;
    write the instructional script.

3. Video Specialists - tape the
    behaviors; log the tapes; select
    the video; generate video stills;
    edit the one-inch master tape.

4. Computer Programmer - interface
    hardware and software; program the
    computer according to the script's
    specifications.

5. Graduate Assistant - assist with
    the instructional design; script
    writing and editing; programming.

TOOLS:

To aid with the complex process of
videodisc development the staff of the
Computer Assisted Instruction Lab at
the University of Iowa developed the
following software tools:

SCRIPTOR: A large amount of information needs to be available to the
development team - video and computer
screen content, narration, feedback,
learner control, and branching all must

Figure 1

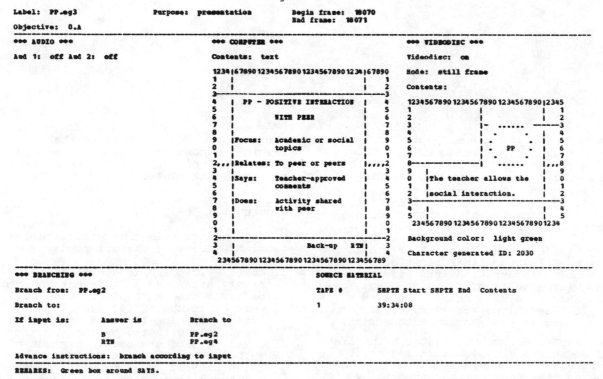

Figure 2

```
Label: PP.prac.video      Purpose: question       Begin frame: 18084
                                                   End frame:   19163
Objective: 8.A
───────────────────────────────────────────────────────────────────────────────
*** AUDIO ***                  *** COMPUTER ***            *** VIDEODISC ***

Aud 1: on                  Computer: screen off       Videodisc: on
Aud 2: off
                                                      Mode: motion
Length: 36 seconds
                                                      Length: 36 seconds
Contents: Classroom sounds.
                                                      Description: Classroom scene.
───────────────────────────────────────────────────────────────────────────────
*** BRANCHING ***                          SOURCE MATERIAL

Branch from: PP.sheet                      TAPE #    SMPTE Start SMPTE End  Contents

Branch to: PP.feed.imed                       4      02:15:00    02:21:00   PP - High beep
                                              4      02:21:00    02:27:00   PP - Low beep
Advance instructions: auto-advance            4      02:27:00    02:33:00   PP - High
                                              4      02:33:00    02:39:00   IL - Low
                                              4      02:39:00    02:45:00   IS - High
                                              4      02:45:00    02:51:00   AT - Low
───────────────────────────────────────────────────────────────────────────────
REMARKS:  Computer generated beeps at the end of each six second segment.
```

Classroom Behavior Record   Group 2 - POS-NEG INTERACTION   - 20 -

be thoroughly discussed and implemented. To keep track of this information efficiently, we designed "Scriptor" using a minicomputer text editor. Scriptor prompts the user for audio, computer and video information, and then formats this information so that it is easy to read in hardcopy form as shown in figures one and two. Also included are "labels" or titles for each instructional occurrence, branching information, and videotape and videodisc identifiers. Because of the ease of making changes on a text editor, revisions are simplified, resulting in a higher quality script.

VIDMASTER: Before "Vidmaster," the list of audio and video (motion and still) information to be included on the one-inch master tape was constructed by cutting and pasting scraps of paper together. Fingers were crossed in the hope that nothing was left off the videodisc. With Vidmaster, a database managing 54,000 records, all required information is entered directly from the script. Figure three is the result - a complete list of video and audio from which the Video Center can construct the master tape.

PROBLEMS:

Any project this size will have its problems. Some of these include:

1. Cost: Videodisc development is simply expensive. It is not unheard of for a single 30-minute side to cost a minimum of $60,000 (Seger, 1984). Funding for this project was creatively gathered by the developers of the code. A grant of $9,000 from the Video Center, the University of Iowa, provided person-nel and materials to tape classroom behaviors, generate stills, tape the audio narrative, and edit the master tape. The Department of Public Instruction, the State of Iowa, granted $20,000 for logging tapes,

Figure 3

PAGE 76						CBR PROJECT			15:16:19 09/26/84	
FRAME	HAS_SEPTE	CONTENT	EDIT_LEN	CUT	ID			LABEL	BEG-SEPTE	END-SEPTE
22058	12:15:08	S	00:00:02	•••••	1080	VIDEO : AUDIO-1 : AUDIO-2 :		DG.CLOSING		
22059	12:15:09	S	00:00:02	. . .	1045	VIDEO : AUDIO-1 : AUDIO-2 :		PI.TITLE.11.C		
22060	12:15:10	S	00:00:02	•••••	1045	VIDEO : AUDIO-1 : AUDIO-2 :		PI.TITLE.11.C		
22061	12:15:11	B	00:00:04	. . .		VIDEO : AUDIO-1 : AUDIO-2 :				
22064	12:15:14	B	00:00:04	•••••		VIDEO : AUDIO-1 : AUDIO-2 :				
22065	12:15:15	B	00:06:01	. . .		VIDEO : AUDIO-1 : AUDIO-2 :		PI.VIDEO.1 PI.VIDEO.1	8 47:16:20 8 47:16:20	8 47:22:20 8 47:22:20
22245	12:21:15	B	00:06:01	•••••		VIDEO : AUDIO-1 : AUDIO-2 :		PI.VIDEO.1 PI.VIDEO.1	8 47:16:20 8 47:16:20	8 47:22:20 8 47:22:20
22246	12:21:16	B	00:00:04	. . .		VIDEO : AUDIO-1 : AUDIO-2 :				
22249	12:21:19	B	00:00:04	•••••		VIDEO : AUDIO-1 : AUDIO-2 :				
22250	12:21:20	B	00:06:01	. . .		VIDEO : AUDIO-1 : AUDIO-2 :		PI.VIDEO.2 PI.VIDEO.2	9 05:22:15 9 05:22:15	9 05:28:15 9 05:28:15

writing the instructional script, hiring a design and technical consultant, programming, and pressing the videodisc. Weeg Computing Center, the University of Iowa, provided the technical and programming support necessary to complete the project. Completing the project with such a low capital outlay was possible only through a great deal of volunteer staff time during the script writing process. The content expert, instrumental in the project's success, <u>donated</u> all of her time and services.

2. **Personnel:** The skills of individuals on the development team complemented each other. However, because of the tight budget, secretarial help was unavailable and many clerical duties were performed by the graduate assistant. This was not an optimal use of expertise.

3. **Using Actors:** Although efforts were made to videotape spontaneous behaviors, the amount of taping required to obtain the few infrequent behaviors was cost prohibitive; thus student actors staged them. While lacking in realism, these staged segments maintained fidelity and kept costs down.

4. **Technical:** With the computer programming incomplete, technical problems have emerged. Much programmer time was spent on generalized utilities. This application requires upper- and lowercase for the Apple II, text combined with color graphics, rapid input via a graphics tablet, timing controlled by an external clock, and the videodisc software. The programmer had to refine these before the instructional code could be written.

RELIABILITY:

The overall purpose of this project is to develop a package that will train behavioral observers to record and report student classroom behaviors. To determine if this implementation is effective, a reliability study has been proposed. After training, observers will code a variety of videotaped classrooms, and the results statistically analyzed. Only through a reliability study can the instructional value of this package be determined.

REFERENCES

Huntley, J. S., "Writing Scripts by Computer," E-ITV, (1), 54-57, 1984.

Nichols, P., Robinson, M. D., and Fitzgerald, G., Classroom Behavior Record Instruction Manual. (Title I Project No. 02802), Washington, D.C., 1979.

Seger, K., "PC & Video: Working Partners," PC World, (9), 200-206, 1984.

CAPTIONS FOR FIGURES

Figure 1. A Scriptor example, illustrating a videodisc still with corresponding computer text.

Figure 2. A second Scriptor example showing a videodisc motion segment.

Figure 3. An example of Vidmaster's organization of audio, motion, and still information necessary for editing the master tape.

COMPUTERS IN EDUCATION, K. Duncan and D. Harris (eds.)
Elsevier Science Publishers B.V. (North-Holland)
© IFIP, 1985

INTERNATIONAL NETWORKING

Daniel J. Oberst, EDUCOM, Princeton, NJ, USA

Prof. Dr. Gerhard Krueger, Institut fur Informatik III, Karlsruhe, West Germany

Prof. Paul Gilmore, Computer Science Department, University of British Columbia, Vancouver, Canada

There are now several thousand computers representing hundreds of academic institutions around the world that are now linked by one or more computer networks. This panel will describe several of these national and international networks. Included will be an overview of the scope of each, institutions represented, protocols, and applications of computer networking in each. Future plans for development and support of the networks will be described, along with a status report on efforts to link the various networks through gateways.

Computer Networks in the US Academic Environment

Dan Oberst, EDUCOM

Starting with the ARPANET, this talk will trace the growth of the several major academic networks in the US, including BITNET, CSNET, MAILNET and UUCP. EDUCOM's role in promoting computer networking in higher education will be described along with current efforts in integrating and interconnecting these networks. Activities of the BITNET Network Support Center, a joint activity of the City University of New York and EDUCOM,will also be outlined.

DFN, Deutsches Forschungsnetz, the German Research Net

Prof. Dr. Gerhard Krueger

A status report on the DFN will be presented, including a description of the protocols adopted for use in the DFN. The role of the DFN in relation to EARN (the European component of BITNET) will also be discussed, along with a report on the strategies required for the interconnection of these networks.

CANADANET (CDNNET) and EAN

Prof. Paul Gilmore

The EAN project, out of the University of British Columbia, is part of an effort to establish a Canada-wide message network for the research community (CDNNET). EAN also represented one of the first implementations of the recent CCITT recommendations (X.400 series) for computer message handling systems. The presentation will describe the current status of CDNNET and EAN, as well as efforts to link with other X.400-based message systems in Europe and Japan.

COMPUTERS IN EDUCATION, K. Duncan and D. Harris (eds.)
Elsevier Science Publishers B.V. (North-Holland)
©IFIP, 1985

RELEVANCE OF EXPERT SYSTEMS TO COMPUTER BASED EDUCATION

J.L. Alty

Department of Computer Science, University of Strathclyde,
Glasgow, Scotland

ABSTRACT

Expert Systems are a development of Artificial Intelligence which provide a formalism
for storing the knowledge of an expert within a computer system in an explicit form
which can then be used in a consultative session to advise or guide a person with
less expertise in the domain of interest.   Since Education involves the transferral
of expertise from teacher to pupil, expert systems will clearly have a key role.
This tutorial session will give a brief overview of the methodology of Expert
Systems and highlight its relevance to computer based education.

DESCRIPTION OF PRESENTATION

The nature of expertise will be explored
and some general conclusions drawn about key
features of expertise which will need to be
represented in any computer-based expert system.
Techniques for storing expertise and methods of
inferring new knowledge will be outlined.
Examples will be given of successful
applications of the methodology both in
computer-based education and other fields.
Existing expert system building tools will be
briefly discussed as will the relevance of
Artificial Intelligence programming languages
such as LISP and PROLOG.   The session will
conclude with a summary of potential benefits
and possible drawbacks to the approach.

COMPUTERS IN EDUCATION, K. Duncan and D. Harris (eds.)
Elsevier Science Publishers B.V. (North-Holland)
© IFIP, 1985

PANEL SESSION

KNOWLEDGE-BASED SOFTWARE IN SUPPORT OF CAI

CHAIRMAN: Gordon E Stokes   Brigham Young University

PANELISTS: Patrick Raymont   The National Computing Cntr.
                Lewis Johnson   Yale University
                Robert E.J. Lewis   St. Martin's College

This session will present research results and experience with systems
that are designed to act as tutors and evaluators in a CAI environment. Yale University's PROUST system featuring intention based
program debugging will be discussed. Brigham Young University's
ELROND project will be presented with a discussion of the Lab Tutor
system and the Algorithm evaluator for use with the introductory
programming class. Research being conducted on intelligent tutoring
systems for use with a variety of subjects at the National Computing
Centre for Information Technology will be presented.

A discussion on the place of knowledge-based systems in CAI courses
will explore the feasibility, magnitude, and benefits of the
development of these systems.

ABSTRACT   Patrick Raymont
An important ingredient in many
instructional programmes is tutored
practice in some procedure which has
been already taught. A human tutor
has the ability to
-    generate variations of problems
     and procedures.
-    analyze student responses and
     compare them with the correct
     response.
-    identify student problems and
     issue appropriate tutorial advice.
-    decide when mastery has been
     achieved.
A suitably constructed "expert system"
can go some way towards simulating the
capability of the human tutor in these
respects. Some tentative experiments
in this direction will be described.

ABSTRACT   Lewis Johnson
The PROUST program will be described.
PROUST does on line analysis and
understanding of PASCAL programs
written by novice programmers.
PROUST takes as input a program and
a description of the program's
requirements, then finds the most
likely mapping between requirements
and code. This mapping is in essence
a reconstruction of the design and
implementation steps the programmer
went through in writing the program.
Bugs are discovered while relating
requirements to code. This allows PROUST
to give deep explanations of program
bugs by referring to the intentions
underlying the program.

ABSTRACT   Gordon Stokes
The ELROND system will be briefly
described. ELROND is a two semester
hour computer based introductory
programming course. A tutoring
system will be discussed that does
not require a knowledge of a student's
program but will serve as a lab
assistant does and help the student
discover where their program bugs
are. The use of an evaluator system for
grading student programs that looks at
logic flow and assigns partial credit
for programs that do not work right will
be presented.

COMPUTERS IN EDUCATION, K. Duncan and D. Harris (eds.)
Elsevier Science Publishers B.V. (North-Holland)
©IFIP, 1985

COMPUTERIZATION OF CAMPUSES

Session Chairperson:

Jesse H. Poore
Georgia Institute of Technology

(Other participants to be identified later)

This session offers a panel discussion of strategies and techniques for creating sophisticated, computer-supported learning environments conducive to university-level instruction in science and engineering.

The discussion will focus around plans at Georgia Tech and other schools for programs of research on the design, development and testing of professional-level and upper-division computerized learning tools. In order to capitalize on the most significant achievements of modern professional practice in a variety of academic disciplines, these programs sponsor a broad array of activities which will explore and extend the educational uses of state-of-the-art developments in expert systems, decision making, and distributed intelligence.

With the ever-increasing power of modern information processing devices, it will become increasingly possible to "capture" and summarize the experience and judgment of the best authorities in a given field or specialty, thereby allowing an individual practitioner to test his own thoughts against the cumulative wisdom of his profession. The impressive capabilities offered by expert system techniques need to be expanded and made available for the improvement of higher education.

Education for a world of rapid change and high technology must be sophisticated enough to allow the learner to become an active participant in his own education. Passive rote-learning is not sufficient for the education of tomorrow's leaders. Learners need to be given the tools to test their decisions, designs, and hypotheses on large and significant problems, and to see the consequences of their actions. Although a large body of computer software exists for providing professionals with decision-making support in many fields of engineering, science, and medicine, there needs to be a major development effort to make this software usable in academic settings.

A key to providing appropriate and responsive information processing power to an individual learner will be the optimal use of computer communications and networking. Careful management of a broad array of devices and techniques is essential in order to be able to distribute intelligent systems capabilities throughout the learning environment.

COMPUTERS IN EDUCATION, K. Duncan and D. Harris (eds.)
Elsevier Science Publishers B.V. (North-Holland)
© IFIP, 1985

MINDPAD: A System to Support Knowledge Acquisition during Problem-solving

M J Coombs

Department of Computer Science
University of Strathclyde
Glasgow   G1 1XH
Scotland, UK

The MINDPAD project concerns the design of a system to help experts solve problems
which fall at the junction of their expertise and that of some adjacent subject. This
necessitates the acquisition of knowledge from the adjacent area during problem-solving
and its integration with existing knowledge. MINDPAD supports these functions by
providing users with a domain specific "language" for modelling problem states and
transformations, which are then critiqued by the system. Responding to the critique,
users extend and refine their understanding of the concepts covering the problem, and
by so doing, achieve a solution. The debugging of PROLOG database programs forms the
task domain for the prototype system.

1.   The Problem

Experience from setting up exert system projects
within the very different application areas of
paint selection for industrial machinery and
computer-user guidance has indicated that
professional problem-solvers seek two major
benefits from expert systems. First, they look
to a system when the problem is complex to help
them organize their problem-solving. The system
is expected to ensure that all relevant
information is collected, that it is correctly
weighted and combined, and that the reasoning
process is public and open to review. Secondly,
they seek support when the knowledge required
for problem-solving interacts with some domain
outside their main area of expertise. In this
case, they expect the system to help them
identify the additional knowledge required, and
to help them understand it in the context of
their problem (Basden, 1983).

While the first role falls well within the
capability of current systems, the use of
tranditional knowledge-based problem-solvers as
learning aids has been less successful (Clancey
and Letsinger, 1981). However, the need for
close interaction between the two functions
makes the solution of employing separate
specialist problem-solvers and tutorial systems
undesirable. It is therefore important to
develop a design for a knowledge-based system
which can effectively integrate the support of
both problem-solving and learning.

The need for such a system has become particularly
accute with increasing specialization in many
disciplines, professionals frequently finding
themselves required to solve problems which
fall between their expertise and that of some
adjacent specialty. To do this they need to
interact with some knowledge source, be it
textual or another human expert, in order to
acquire new concepts related to the problem.

Having acquired them, they must learn to apply
them correctly. The context for knowledge
acquisition and the criteria for judging
effectiveness are thus determined by the problem.
Knowledge acquisition must therefore be both
focussed and bounded by the problem and not
simply by general factors related to the subject
domain. The MINDPAD project is concerned with
the design of a system to support such problem-
oriented knowledge acquisition.

2.   A Theoretical Framework

When an expert attempts to solve a problem in
which relevant goals, facts, rules and procedures are located in a complementary domain, the
problem may be said to be "ill-structured" (from
the expert's point of view). Moreover, learning
is required to convert the problem to a "well-
structured" form, with precisely defined goals
against which to test solutions, with sufficient
facts and rules to develop a solution path, and
with some appropriate control regime for their
effective application.

The process of "ill-structured" problem-solving
has been characterized by Simon (1973). Simon
argues that the expert must first impose
structure before attempting a solution. Indeed,
it is more important that some structure (any
structure) is imposed rather than investing much
effort in seeking the correct structure. This
is because the process of imposition will
generate its own feedback and so help the
problem to be refined. Moreover, the structuring of a problem will critically involve
learning: the expert will seek new facts and
rules to give the problem structure; he will
learn how the facts and rules may be obtained
and applied; he will learn to understand the
domain concepts from which the facts and rules
are composed. With experience, he will come to
recognize well-structured problems within ill-
structured problems, and thus will be able to

make appropriate transformations algorithmically rather than heuristically.

Simon argues that this involves two types of activity: analytic processing, of the form represented by classical problem-solving programs (e.g. expert systems); synthetic "noticing and evoking" processes which access mental models from long-term memory and collect information from the external environment with the goal of formulating a well-defined problem to put forward for solution. The synthetic stage is primarily concerned with shaping a problem (e.g. defining a set of starting conditions, defining a goal and defining a knowledge domain within which the problem is located); the analytic stage is concerned with applying some control structure to the predefined problem to generate some result. If this result is not an acceptable problem solution, the synthetic stage may use this information to generate a new version of the problem.

The primary concern of the MINDPAD project has been to seek a computational paradigm for exploring the synthetic aspects of problem-solving. This should be suitable for implementation as the system control structure and should also provide an acceptable framework within which the user can reason about his problem.

The paradigm adopted has been influenced by a "mental modelling" view of cognition, principally Pask's work on learning (1976) and Johnson-Laird's work on the psychological basis of reasoning (1983). Related research within A.I. includes that of qualitative reasoning and envisionment (deKleer, 1982; Kuipers, 1982).

The idealized reasoning processes implemented in MINDPAD are best described in terms of the manipulation of explicitly represented "mental-models". This involves: 1) the construction of finite models of the domain of interest; 2) the formulation of putative conclusions on the basis of them; 3) the search for models of the domain which are counter-examples to such conclusions.

The mental processes required are as follows. The expert must first retrieve from memory, the world or some textual source, facts and rules which might fall within the scope of the problem. From these facts and rules, the expert will create a model which is believed to support some conclusion of interest. Within the model, objects will be represented symbolically in some way which is likely to be constructed to minimize the effort required to compute the conclusion(s). These computational processes are assumed to involve the calculation of truth functional relations between objects and are seen as closely related to the classical problem-solving procedures already modelled by A.I.

The search for counter-examples also involves model building. However, what is required is that the objects within the model must be rearranged, or reinterpreted so as to preserve the critical truth relations between facts and rules but destroy the truth relations required by the conclusion.

The procedures required for effective model building may fail in a limited number of ways. An expert may:

-- fail to access appropriate facts and rules to use in creating his mental model;

-- fail to find a way of symbolically represent-ing facts and rules;

-- fail to specify a model at the correct level of detail or abstraction;

-- fail to "understand" the implications of some change in his model for the truth relations which previously held (the model may contain contradictions).

While the MINDPAD system is expected eventually to enhance both model construction and the search for counter-examples, the current research is focussed upon the model building stage alone. This is because it is the logically prior function and because the psychological requirements for its support are better understood (e.g. see Green, Sime & Fitter, 1981). However, it is expected that systems built during the project will permit experimentation with aiding model evaluation. Facilities for supporting model building implemented in the prototype MINDPAD include:

-- a content-oriented query system for accessing facts and rules within the problem domain;

-- a domain specific "language" for building models of the problem domain (at various levels of detail) and for specifying conclusions.

The system itself is required to evaluate the user's models to ensure that they are correct and that conclusions drawn from them are valid.

It is clear from the above criteria, that MINDPAD differs significantly from a conventional expert system. Notably it does not follow Feigenbaum's (1977) proposal that expert systems derive their power from the domain knowledge they possess rather than from the representational formalisms and inference systems employed. MINDPAD's effectiveness in supporting the synthetic stage of reasoning is critically dependent on the language provided for the external representation of mental models (and on the procedures available within the system for their evaluation).

3.   The MINDPAD Program

The prototype MINDPAD system is designed to support the debugging of PROLOG programs by help-ing users understand the procedural aspects of execution. True to our interest in problem-solving across domains, it is assumed that the user is an expert in subject area related to his problem. Furthermore, he must cast statements about this area into a set of PROLOG clauses which execute to yield some desired result. Given the predicate calculus basis of PROLOG, it is argued that the transition between propositions about the world and PROLOG clauses is relatively direct. However, the set of clauses must obey the procedural constraints imposed by the PROLOG interpreter (top-down, depth-first search).

The prototype MINDPAD is programmed to be expert in PROLOG execution and to help the user understand just those aspects of execution which underly some error in his program. It is assumed that some error has already occurred before MINDPAD is called and that MINDPAD's task is to help the user understand why the program produces the results it does (not how it might be amended to produce the results desired). This is the first simplification imposed on the prototype system.

Further simplifications concern the decision to concentrate upon supporting model building rather than the search for counter-examples. First, the topic of PROLOG execution is sufficiently restricted to ease the task of devising a "modelling language". Secondly, the task of evaluating models is simplified both by the deterministic nature of PROLOG execution and by the use of the interpreter itself to generate a single, critical model to compare with the user's.

Prototype MINDPAD provides the user with four facilities (see Fig. 1):

-- a domain specific knowledge-base concerning PROLOG execution;

-- a "modelling language" derived from the object and relation terms used in the knowledge-base;

-- a system to evaluate user models and conclusions drawn from them;

-- a knowledge "interpreter".

The basic MINDPAD procedure is as follows. The user is first given free access to the knowledge-base, being invited to explore concepts he believes to relate to his problem   via a flexible query system. Knowledge of PROLOG execution is itself represented as a database of PROLOG clauses. This format is exploited by the query system, which interprets query types in terms of truth-conditions which should hold in the domain. The query language gives appropriate procedural interpretations to quantifiers, terms of causation, etc. The queries are applied to the knowledge-base by the "knowledge interpreter" which is in reality an especially crafted PROLOG interpreter.

Having explored the knowledge-base, the user is invited to test his understanding of the execution of his bugged program, using the "modelling language". The user states his PROLOG query, the expected solution and the chains of implication which he believes makes a given solution true.

The evaluation system now uses the "knowledge interpreter" to test the user's account of execution (his model of execution) and to identify faulted, or wrongly applied, concepts where it is not correct.

The system proceeds by building its own model of execution in the same language as the user. If any discrepancies are identified between the user's model (representing the user's "understanding") and that generated by the system, they become the focus of activity aimed at identifying understanding difficulties. The prototype system only attempts a shallow analysis of the user's understanding difficulties, doing little more than identifying the PROLOG concepts covering faults in the user's model of execution. While it was initially expected that effective user modelling would be important in MINDPAD, the design of the "modelling language" has proved more significant. This has therefore provided the main focus for our effort.

With the prototype, knowledge about the causes of failure are represented as sets of discrepant definitions of relations and terms, including a few higher level relations between individual errors known as "fault syndromes". These discrepant definitions are interpreted by the "knowledge interpreter" in an attempt to generate the user's discrepant model. Sets of error rules which reproduce, or partially reproduce, the user's model are recorded and scored, using heuristics collected from expert PROLOG programmers. The highest scoring set is then communicated to the user. He is then charged to correct his model, the corrections being evaluated and the results of the evaluation being taken as further evidence of the source of his difficulty.

4.   An Example

Given below is the user's first model of PROLOG

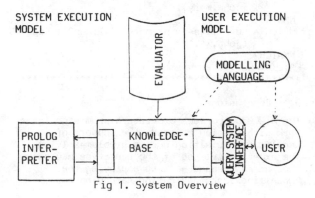

SYSTEM EXECUTION MODEL   USER EXECUTION MODEL

Fig 1. System Overview

execution relating to a program which fails to support the query ?-likes(wine,mary) contrary to expectation. The "modelling language" describes PROLOG execution at three different levels of detail, and the user may make his discriptions at a mixture of levels. This feature has proved important both for analysis and for helping the user develop his understanding (e.g. it enables the user to control memory load by exploring the extension of one concept at a time, and without affecting the truth relations of other concepts defined at a different level).

```
     likes1:likes(john,mary).
     likes2:likes(john,X):-human(X),likes(X,wine).
     human1:human(mary).
QUESTION: ?-likes(wine,mary)
RESULT: PROVED yes          RUN: FAIL no
*************************************************
CALL - PROC:likes, GOAL likes(wine,mary).
 MATCH-GOAL:likes(wine,mary).,likes2:likes(john,X).
 INSTANT - X mary
 CALL - PROC:human, SUBGOAL:human(mary).
  MATCH-SUBGOAL:human(mary).,human1:human(mary).
 CALL - PROC:likes, SUBGOAL:likes(mary,wine).
  SUCCEED
*************************************************
```

Given the above model, the system notes that it is incomplete at the top procedural level. There are three procedure CALLs but no EXITs or FAILs. It thus begins the analysis by parsing for possible procedure exits and marks these in the explanation. To achieve such parsing, the system must make reference to constraints operating at the lower level of PROLOG description. With the present example, this would provide the additional information that an incorrect result of the MATCH operation had been declared on the first call. It is also noted that the user has failed to indicate that PROLOG would first attempt a match to likes1, which would fail. However, this would not necessarily indicate that the user did not understand the matching process: he could have simply decided to abbreviate the explanation. As a result of this analysis the following annotations are written into the explanation text and denoted by exclamation marks.

```
*************************************************
!!!Missing MATCH to likes1;possible abbreviation!!!
CALL - PROC:likes, GOAL:likes(wine,mary).
 MATCH - GOAL:likes(wine,mary).,likes2:likes(john,X).
 INSTANT - X:mary
!!!MATCH would not SUCCEED!!!
!!!Likely FAIL; suspect user considers EXIT!!!
CALL - PROC:human, SUBGOAL:human(mary).
 MATCH-SUBGOAL:human(mary).,human1:human(mary).
!!!Missing indication of whether MATCH SUCCEEDS;
    suspect user considers SUCCEEDs!!!
!!!On previous assumption, assume user considers
    EXIT!!!
CALL - PROC:likes, SUBGOAL:likes(mary,wine).
 SUCCEED
!!!No indication of the HEAD MATCHed; SUBGOAL
does not MATCH any FACT or RULE, therefore the
CALL would FAIL!!!
*************************************************
```

The above pattern points to a lack of understanding concerning the topic MATCH. The user is therefore directed to query this concept and to amend the model.

```
*************************************************
CALL - PROC:likes, GOAL:likes(wine,mary).
 MATCH - GOAL:likes(wine,mary)., likes1:likes
         (john,mary).
 NMATCH
 MATCH - GOAL likes(wine,mary).,likes2:likes
         (john,X).
 INSTANT - X:mary
 CALL - PROC:human, SUBGOAL:human(mary).
  MATCH - GOAL:human(mary)., human1:human(mary).
  SUCCEED
 EXIT
 CALL - PROC:likes, SUBGOAL:likes(mary,wine).
  MATCH - SUBGOAL likes(mary,wine)., GOAL:likes
          (wine,mary).
  SUCCEED
  EXIT - PROC:likes
EXIT - PROC:likes
*************************************************
```

The model is again incorrect, although, there is additional evidence. First, the user has now included correctly the initial failed match with likes1. However, given a complete understanding of the topic, there is a contradiction with the result of the match with likes2. Secondly, the final match is not declared as being between a subgoal and a clause head, but between a subgoal and goal. Thirdly, it is declared as being successful. Even if one of the elements was a clause head, the match would have failed because the constants in the arguments of the two predicate structures are reversed. This pattern is sufficiently close to a fault syndrome linking the concepts of HEAD, GOAL and SUBGOAL by an attempt to work backwards from an assumed match with a structure in the tail of a clause for this to be communicated to the user.

The correct model is given below.

```
*************************************************
CALL - PROC:likes, GOAL:likes(wine,mary).
 MATCH - GOAL likes(wine,mary)., likes1:likes
         (john,mary).
 NMATCH
 MATCH - GOAL:likes(wine,mary)., likes2:likes
         (john,X).
 NMATCH
FAIL - PROC:likes
*************************************************
```

5.   Conclusions

The MINDPAD approach provides a promising framework within which to study the support of knowledge acquisition during problem-solving. The experimental use of the prototype has shown that users respond well to employing the "modelling language" during debugging and

identify basic conceptual difficulties faster.
Moreover, there is some evidence that the system
helps users make smoother transitions between
the declarative and procedural readings of
PROLOG clauses and that it inhibits the learning
of erroneous models of the language.

There is, however, much work to be done. It
takes users longer than is acceptable to learn
to use the "modelling language". The system
would also benefit from a powerful error
modelling facility which was able to identify
the cause of user misunderstandings and omissions
(e.g. why a user continually fails to apply a
concept in a given context). Nevertheless,
both the theoretical and implementation approach
appears sound and suitable for further development.

References

Basden, A. (1983). On the application of expert
systems. International Journal of Man-Machine
Studies, 19, 5, 461-478.

Clancey, W.J. & Letsinger, R. (1981). NEOMYCIN:
reconfiguring a rule-based expert system for
application to teaching. Proceedings of IJCAI-7,
829-836.

Coombs, M.J. & Alty, J.L. (1984). Expert
systems: an alternative paradigm. International
Journal of Man-Machine Studies, 20, 1, 21-44.

deKleer, J. (1982). Foundations of envisioning.
Proceedings of AAAI-82, 434-437.

Feigenbaum, E.A. (1977). The art of artificial
intelligence: themes and case studies of
knowledge engineering. Proceedings of IJCAI-5,
1014-1029.

Green, T.R.G., Sime, M.E. & Fitter, M.J. (1981).
The art of notation. In M.J. Coombs and J.L.
Alty (eds), Computing Skills and the User
Interface. London: Academic Press.

Johnson-Laird, P.N. (1983). Mental Models.
Cambridge: Cambridge University Press.

Kuipers, B. (1982). Getting the envisionment
right. Proceedings of AAAI-82, 209-212.

Simon, H.A. (1973). The structure of ill
structured problems. Artificial Intelligence,
4, 181-201.

COMPUTERS IN EDUCATION, K. Duncan and D. Harris (eds.)
Elsevier Science Publishers B.V. (North-Holland)
© IFIP, 1985

Intelligent CAL System Based on Teaching Strategy and Learner Model

Setsuko OTSUKI and Akira TAKEUCHI

University Computation Center
Kyushu University
Fukuoka, Japan

This paper proposes a computer assisted learning system called BOOK, which allows learners to study freely and independently through natural language dialogue and offers teachers facilities for authoring coursewares and knowledge.

The major portion of the paper is devoted to the intelligent aspect of the system and is classified broadly into the following two subjects.

1) A proposition of the multi-hierarchical model of the knowledge representation for natural language dialogue and a language for implementing the model.

2) A proposition of the strategy graph and the learner model which give courseware the foundation of a method to judge the learner's state of comprehension and to offer the suitable learning environment for each individual learner.

1. INTRODUCTION

One of the difficulties remaining unsolved in the field of CAL (Computer Assisted Learning) is to make mixed initiative feasible through natural language dialogue between coursewares and learners. In other words, one must develop a generally applicable method that would make it possible for both the courseware and the learner to control the presentation of the material. The system should permit learners to ask questions freely whenever they arise. Through natural language intercourse with the learner the system should have the capacity to judge the learner's comprehension. On the basis of this information and the author's teaching strategy, it would create the most suitable learning environment for each individual.

Although several papers concerning CAL coursewares, e.g. (1-5), capable of understanding and answering the learner's questions in natural language have been published within this decade, a general mechanism capable of providing the above type of mixed initiative in CAL has yet to be investigated. Perhaps this is due to lack of experience in the authoring and application of such an intelligent CAL courseware.

This paper presents a unified CAL system "BOOK" which aids in learning, authoring and managing coursewares and provides a mechanism for mixed initiative through natural language dialogue according to both learner's understanding and to author's teaching strategy.

Except for the intelligent aspect of the BOOK system, this system has already been reported at the last WCCE/81 in (6). Only the special features about the last paper are summarized along with the intelligent characteristics in section 2. A multi-hierarchical model of knowledge representation for natural language dialogue and a language for implementing the knowledge model are described briefly in section 3. A detailed description on this subject is given in (7). In section 4, the data structure

and the method for implementing mixed initiative are proposed. A dialogue excerpt along with an explanation about the alternation of the initiative to direct the flow of dialogue between a learner and a courseware produced by the BOOK system are presented in section 5. Discussion and conclusions are given in section 6.

2. CHARACTERISTICS OF BOOK SYSTEM

The BOOK system was designed to help in learning, authoring and managing coursewares in the following manner.

2.1 As a Learning Aid

Facilities (1)-(3) are offered.

(1) The external appearance of a produced courseware has a structure composed of a title, a table of contents, contents and index, just like a book to which we are accustomed from childhood.

(2) All coursewares, together with the knowledge part, are classified automatically according to titles, fields, authors and indexes, like in a library, so that they may be called or retrieved in natural language dialogue.

(3) While a courseware is in use, the system always complies with the learner's request, e.g. learner's questions in natural language, learner's request to change the subject, etc.

2.2 As an Authoring Aid

Facilities (4)-(6) are offered.

(4) An authoring language called "BOOK" is designed by appending statements proper for CAL to a frequently used programming language like Basic, Pascal, Fortran.

(5) The authoring process is modularized by separating it into three parts; drawing pictures on the display screen by using the picture editor, writing programs in BOOK language by using the BOOK text editor and defining constituents of knowledge about the scene in the form of tables, natural language sentences or Prolog clauses by using

the knowledge editor.

(6) All the author has to do is merely to write down these three parts separately for each unit of a courseware called "page" (see section 4.1). All the other work such as editing these three parts together into one courseware according to the table of contents, making the produced courseware enter into the database, forming the knowledge representation for natural language dialogue, etc. are done by the BOOK system.

2.3 As a Managing Aid
    Facilities (7)-(10) are offered.

(7) All pictures, BOOK programs, produced coursewares and knowledge parts are kept under the supervision of the system.

(8) Records about registrations, modifications and cancellations of coursewares and various kinds of statistics concerning the use of the coursewares are also supervised by the BOOK system.

(9) Information concerning each learner's understanding is also collected and managed through the BOOK system (see section 4.3, 4.4).

(10) The system plays the role of a librarian by presenting coursewares or their parts pertaining to a subject designated by the learner. If so desired the table of contents of any courseware may be displayed.

2.4 Structure of BOOK System

Three kinds of editors, i.e. BOOK program editor, picture editor and knowledge editor, are prepared for authoring. The BOOK compiler edits these authored articles into one complete courseware. The BOOK manager and three kinds of databases, i.e. courseware database, problem database and learner database, are used for learning.

3. NATURAL LANGUAGE DIALOGUE

3.1 Multi-hierarchical Model for Knowledge Representation

Figure 1 shows the knowledge structure for natural language dialogue. Because of the following reasons the model consists of two parts; the conceptual part and the language part.

(1) One word may have a syntactic function in the language part but a semantic function in the conceptional part. For instance, while the word "why" in the language part represents a part of speech, connective relation, etc., in the conceptional part it evokes a rule calling for the logic of a sentence just spoken.

(2) The language part needs different syntactic

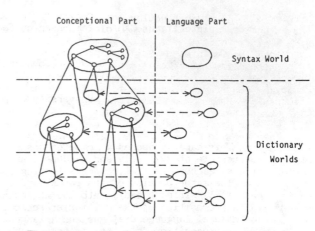

Figure 1. Knowledge Structure for Dialogue System.

rules and dictionaries for different kinds of languages, while the conceptional part may be used commonly amongst them.

(3) The syntactic rules in the language part may be generally applied to many dialoging systems with different subjects. However the conceptional part is particular to a subject or an author of a courseware.

(4) The language part is used to analyze and to synthesize a natural language sentence. On the other hand, the conceptional part is used to verify a concept obtained from natural language analysis or to draw a logical conclusion by inference from that concept.

The circles in figure 1 represent knowledge worlds. In the conceptional part, the worlds are located hierarchically according to the scope of their implications (For a concrete example, see section 4.1.). Each world in the conceptional part has a precise one to one correspondence with a dictionary world in the language part. Knowledge in a world is usable only when the world is active. When a world is activated, its ancestor worlds are also activated so that the knowledge in higher rank worlds may be usable.

Figure 2 shows the outline of dialogue analysis. The two rectangles labeled "the language part" and "the conceptional part" respectively, represent the activated worlds in each part.

3.2 Implementation of Multi-hierarchical Knowledge Representation

Knowledge is described in a language called

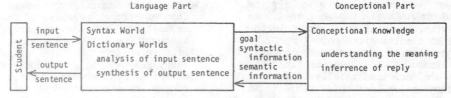

Figure 2. Outline of Dialogue Processing.

˙Prolog-S˙. The basic function of Prolog-S is the same as that of well known Prolog languages, e.g. (8-10). However it also has two other functions accompanied by built-in predicates in order to realize the model stated in the previous section. Being implemented on Lisp, Prolog-S has facilities to both invoke its interpreter from Lisp functions and to invoke Lisp functions from Prolog-S clauses.

3.2.1 Manipulation of Multiworld Hierarchy

Each knowledge world has its own name. Knowledge is expressed by Prolog-S clauses. Each clause written in Prolog-S belongs to one of the worlds. The hierarchical relationship between worlds is also knowledge. Five built-in predicates are prepared for handling multi-hierarchical worlds; ˙new_world˙ for creating a new world, ˙init_world˙ for activating a designated world and its ancestor worlds after inactivating previously active worlds, ˙open_world˙ for activating a special world in addition to currently activated worlds and ˙change_world˙ for inactivating each active world in language/conceptional part after activating corresponding worlds in conceptional/language part.

The Prolog-S interpreter uses clauses only in activated worlds. If more than one activated world has the same predicate name, the interpreter invokes them in the reverse order of activation because the most recently activated world is likely a current topic of dialogue.

3.2.2 Introduction of Transit Variables

A transit variable is introduced to share information between clauses with different top level goals or clauses in different worlds. This variable, distinguished by its first symbol, ˙$˙, is implemented as a stack and used both for natural language processing as shown in the following section and for transmitting the learner's state of understanding as shown in the section 4.3. If a transit variable appears in a clause, the Prolog-S interpreter replaces the transit variable by the top value of the stack just before unification occurs unless they are quoted (the same meaning as Lisp).

There are four built-in predicates to change values of the transit variables, i.e. ˙init_state˙, ˙push˙, ˙pop˙ and ˙set˙. The effects of push and pop are recovered if backtrack takes place; however, the effects of init_state and set aren't eliminated even if backtrack occurs.

3.3 Natural Language Dialogue

The process of natural language dialogue is divided into three steps: analysis, understanding and synthesis of natural language. We consider understanding of a natural language sentence to be equivalent to obtaining a new goal, which expresses the meaning and is going to be used for natural language synthesis, by means of inference in the conceptional part using the old goal obtained from sentence analysis. Then both analysis and synthesis are considered as a conversion between a natural language sentence and a goal with its accompanying values (i.e. syntactic information like tense, voice, mood, modality, adverbial phrase, etc.) saved in transit variables.

DCG described in (11) which can be directly converted into Prolog-S clauses is compatible with the idea of converting natural language into goals with corresponding values of transit variables or vice versa. Therefore notation of syntax in the language part is described by DCG with many expressions added to meet our requirements.

For instance, at the analysis step, a sentence
˙I can't catch the meaning of P20403 in the first line˙
is converted into the following set of values of transit variables in the language part.
$goal=catch(I meaning(P20403 *mean $place))
$tense1=present $tense2=nil $voice=active
$modality=can $negation=negative
$mood=statement $adverbial=in(line_1)
$place=class1(line_1)
$topics=[P20403 meaning(P20403 *mean $place)]
At the understanding step, the goal ˙catch(I meaning(P20403 *mean $place))˙ is unified with the following two clauses in the conceptional part.
catch(I meaning(*x *y *z)):-
    if equal($negation negative)
    then meaning(*x *y *z),push($output be(*x *y)),push($modality nil), push($negation affirmative).
meaning(P20403 program_name class1(line_1)).
At the synthesis step, a new goal ˙output(*sentence $output)˙ and a set of accompanying values, i.e.
$goal=output(*sentence
            be(P20403 program_name))
$tense1=present $tense2=nil $voice=active
$modality=nil $negation=affirmative
$mood=statement $adverbial=in(line_1)
are converted into a sentence
˙In the first line P20403 is a program name˙.
In the above example a Prolog variable is expressed by its first symbol ˙*˙.

4. MECHANISM OF MIXED INITIATIVE

4.1 Courseware Unit ˙page˙ and Knowledge
    Representation in Courseware Database
In order to facilitate free and independent study, learners had better take the initiative in advancing the courseware within some defined limits. On the other hand, coursewares are often composed of many series of scenes and procedures which the author wants the learners to work with continuously without interruption in order to explain some concept. ˙Page˙ is introduced to make these discrepancies compatible with the BOOK system by assigning the following five roles to *pages*.
(1) During the execution of a *page*, it is not possible for a learner to interrupt, while at the end of a *page* free dialogue is welcomed.
(2) *Page* is a learning unit for a learner.
(3) *Page* is a descriptive unit for an author.
(4) *Page* is an editing unit for the BOOK system.
(5) *Page* is also a unit of learner's understanding model (see section 4.4).

Figure 3 gives an outline of the conceptional part of knowledge structure consisting of four levels of worlds represented here by rectangles. The upper most level, called BOOK world, contains knowledge for the courseware hierarchy in the form of a directed acyclic graph whose nodes correspond to worlds in the second level. Each second level world correspond to a courseware containing knowledge for hierarchical relationship of page worlds located in the third level. Worlds in the lowest level contain knowledge for pictures presented to learners while learning a *page* in the third level.

4.2 Strategy Graph in Courseware Database

In the BOOK world of the conceptional part, every node of the BOOK hierarchy will have a set of prerequisites along with the educational objectives of that particular courseware. Likewise in the courseware world, every node in the page hierarchy has its prerequisites and educational objectives.

In general, when some of the educational objectives of one *page* form part of the prerequisites of another, the former *page* must be allocated in advance of the latter *page*. But this is not always the case. Sometimes the relation of prerequisites and educational objectives forms a loop and prevents from putting

pages in order. A table of contents is a totally ordered graph which the author arranges according to the author's teaching strategy. So if necessary, the above loop can be eliminated by adjusting the order of *pages* in the loop in accordance with the table of contents. In this way a courseware can be expressed by a semi-ordered graph, in which every node is attached the educational objectives of a *page* pertinent to that node.

This is called strategy graph. Strategy graph is used to show the sequence of *pages* necessary to learn a designated concept in conformity with a definite courseware.

4.3 Evaluation of Learner's Understanding

The problem database is made up of an aggregate of problems, each of which is composed of a name, scenes, a BOOK program, a knowledge world and a set of prerequisites and educational objectives. All of these entities are produced in the same way as courseware *pages* and may be invoked from any courseware *page* for use by the problem name or by designating sets of prerequisites and educational objectives.

In the design of a problem's BOOK program there may be a set of reference numbers expressed as real numbers in the interval [0.0,1.0] which correspond to different levels of the learner's understanding about the educational objectives. Besides this evaluation, another number between [-1.0,0.0) is given as an indication of learner's level of comprehension evaluated on the basis of questions put forth by the learner that deal with material already covered in some part of the courseware and used as a prerequisite knowledge in the problem. These numbers are called comprehension grades in this paper.

4.4 Learner Model in Learner Database

When a learner finishes studying a *page*, the educational objectives and prerequisites of the *page* are stored in the learner database together with comprehension grades, courseware name, page name and the time of study in the form of Prolog clauses. These data are collected for each learner.

If the names of a learner and a courseware are identified, a learner model is immediately formed by copying the strategy graph of the same courseware in the courseware database and attaching the learner's comprehension grades to each node if defined in the learner database. Comprehension grades for nodes that have not been studied by the learner remain undefined. This learner model expresses the learner's state of understanding and learner's history of study for any theme included in the courseware. Furthermore, since the model expresses the themes a learner has not yet covered or comprehended as well as the necessary sequence of study to achieve understanding of them, it can evaluate the learner's understanding and suggest the best way to study any chosen theme in the courseware. Besides, the model is also useful for reviewing the teaching strategy by examining the statistical results of the comprehension grades, criticizing the quality of coursewares by a comparative study of the learner model, etc.

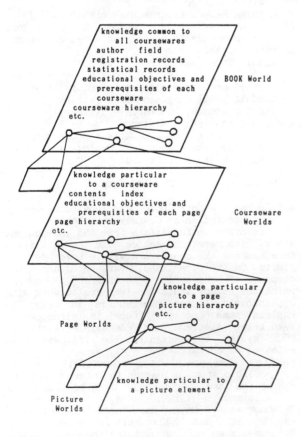

Figure 3. Knowledge Structure of Conceptional Part in BOOK System.

4.5 The Initiative in the BOOK System

In traditional CAL instructions have always been initiated by the courseware. However, as intelligent coursewares are able to recognize learner's requirements stated in natural language by means of inference of knowledge, the learner has a chance to take the initiative so as to ask questions, replace coursewares, alter the learning sequence, etc. In such a case, how does the courseware harmonize the learner's independent requests with author's teaching strategy for effective study? This section presents an attempt to solve this problem.

4.5.1 Role of the BOOK Manager

Besides the roles described in 2.3, the BOOK manager includes an inferring mechanism of Prolog-S as stated in 3 so that it may by able to select a courseware, a *page*, a problem, a learner model etc. from databases in the following manner.

1) Courseware selection is achieved through dialogue with a learner in the BOOK world. In this process the learner may call for a specific courseware by name if known, or review the contents of coursewares to determine their suitability by designating key words or looking over their respective tables of contents. Thus the learner has full control over courseware selection.

2) Once a courseware is selected, the selection of a *page* to begin with is the BOOK manager's next task. In this case, the learner's request is again given the highest priority. If a learner hasn't any concrete request, the BOOK manager, referring to the learner model, locates a subgraph including more than one node for which the comprehension grade is lower than some predefined threshold value and then begins with a node having the most basic educational objective for which the comprehension grade is lower than the threshold value or undefined in the subgraph. If all the comprehension grades exceed the predefined threshold, the BOOK manager selects the most basic educational objective of all with undefined comprehension grade.

4.5.2 When the Learner Directs Dialogue

In the following three cases, a learner has the opportunity to direct the dialogue in a CAL courseware.

L1) Any time when the courseware prompts a learner to pose a question by displaying a prompting message like ˙Have you any questions?˙.

L2) In the execution of a *page* when the courseware asks a learner to answer some given question, the learner is allowed to ask another question without answering the given question. After the learner's question is settled, the original question is repeated again by the courseware.

L3) At the end of a *page* a prompt signal is displayed allowing the learner to proceed as desired.

4.5.3 When the Learning Process is Directed by the System

In the following three cases the BOOK system controls the direction of the dialogue

What values are assigned to B and X in the following program?

```pascal
program P20403(output);
  var a,b,x:real;
  begin
    a:=2.5;
    b:=2e-14;
    x:=a+b;
    writeln(x)
  end.
```

Figure 4-a. Example Problem.

```
Educational Objectives
    notation(constant real)
    significant_digit(real)

Prerequisites
    program_heading
    variable_declaration(real)
    assignment_statement(primitive_type)
    terminal_output
    simple_program structure
```

Figure 4-b. Example of Educational Objectives and Prerequisites.

within a CAL courseware.

B1) The *page* of a courseware is executed according to the fundamentals of the BOOK program and the dialogue is controlled accordingly.

B2) At the end of a *page* if a learner doesn't initiate further dialogue by either asking a question or changing the subject, the BOOK manager decides the *page* to be studied next through employing method 2) stated in 4.5.1.

B3) If the learner's solution to a problem doesn't achieve some predefined level, the manager will exhort the learner to solve another problem if the prerequisite themes of the former problem are understood, if not it will select *pages* which teach the prerequisite themes.

5. EXAMPLE OF DIALOGUE IN NATURAL LANGUAGE

Figure 4-a is an excerpt from problems used in a courseware named ˙Introduction to Pascal˙. Figure 4-b shows sets of educational objectives and prerequisites of the problem, respectively.

The following is an example of the mixed initiated dialogue in natural language, after displaying the figure 4-a to a learner. In the dialogue, B means an output from the BOOK system and L means an input by the learner.

B   Any questions?   [B1]
*L   I can't catch the meaning of P20403 in the first line.   [L1]
B   In the first line P20403 is a program name.
L   What is the program name used for?

B   O.K. I'll show you a page explaining
       the program name.
       {*after displaying the explanation, it comes
       back to this scene again.*}
*B   Any more questions?   [B1]
L   No.
B   Now, please answer.
L   2e-14, 2e-11.5.
B   Your answer is incorrect. Then what is
       the value of B?
*L   What does 2e-14 mean?   [L2]
B   e-14 in the expression means the -14th
       power of 10, and 2e-14 means twice of
       e-14.
*B   Then what is the value of B?   [B1]
L   It is 0.00000000000002.
B   Right. Can you work out the value of X?
L   Yes, X equals 2.50000000000002.
B   No. Do you know how many digits are
       included in a real variable?
L   No, I don't.
B   14 digits are included in a real varia-
       ble. Significant digits of a real number
       is 14. Now answer the value of X.
L   2.5
B   Good. Then let's try another problem.[B3]

Sentences which are directing the flow of
the dialogue are not indented, while indentation
is used to indicate that the sentence is in
response to the previous sentence. The symbol
"*" indicates that either the BOOK system or the
learner has taken control of the dialogue and
the characters in [ ] on the right give the
reason why.

6. DISCUSSION AND CONCLUSIONS

This paper is based on the experience of
the first version of the BOOK system, in which
two main aims are pursued; one is to lighten the
author's burden in making a courseware and the
other is to allow learners study freely and
independently.

The main subject of this paper also comes
from these two aims. That is to say, the subject
of this research is how the BOOK system can
lighten the author's burden of writing knowledge, how the author can realize his own teaching strategy effectively in a courseware endowed
with natural language dialogue, when and how
learners can ask questions (even when not
directly related but necessary for general
comprehension) and in what way learners' independency and the author's teaching strategy
become compatible.

All of the above is made possible by the
adoption of two models; the multi-hierarchical
model of knowledge representation stated in 3.1,
4.1 and the learner understanding model stated
in 4.2, 4.4. The multi-hierarchical worlds are
able to allow the author to fully concentrate on
the knowledge he is presenting by releasing him
from worrying about the discrepancy of the
expressions of knowledge or polysemy words
between different worlds. The author's teaching
strategy is easily expressed in the form of a
table of contents with relevant sets of prerequisites and educational objectives and plays a

role of the original form of the learner model.
The learner model plays a role of making
learner's independency and individuality coexist
with the teaching strategy. That is to say, the
basic decision of courseware selection is in the
hands of the learner, within each courseware the
author's teaching strategy offers the fundamentals of presenting the material and within this
framework learners are allowed to study freely.

This version of the BOOK system is being
used on a trial basis, and the experience of
this trial has taught us that all aspects of the
learner model graph must be carefully explored
case by case. For instance a too high threshold
makes learners bored because the learning point
on the graph stays on the same node. Or the
method described in 4.5.1 that determines which
page to begin with does not always produce the
best choice. Exploring the subgraph in the
reverse order sometimes gets good results
because studying an advanced subject first often
makes learners recall items they have forgotten
or makes ungrasped concepts in the basic subject
clear, so that it may become unnecessary to
study the basic *pages*.

REFERENCES

[1] Carbonell, J.R., AI in CAI, IEEE Transac-
     tions on Man-Machine Systems, Vol.MMS-11,
     No.4 (1970) 190-202.
[2] Brown, J.S., Burton, R.R. and de Kleer, J.,
     Pedagogical, Natural Language and Knowledge
     Engineering Techniques in SOPHIE I,II and
     III, in Sleeman, D. and Brown, J.S. (eds.),
     Intelligent Tutoring Systems (Academic
     Press, 1982).
[3] Davis, R., Buchanan, B. and Shortliffe, E.,
     Production Rules as a Representation for a
     Knowledge-Based Consultation Program, Artif-
     icial Intelligence, Vol.8, (1977) 15-45.
[4] Goldstein, I.P., The Genetic Graph: A Repre-
     sentation for the Evolution of Procedural
     Knowledge, in Sleeman, D. and Brown, J.S.
     (eds.), Intelligent Tutoring Systems
     (Academic Press, 1982).
[5] Clancey, W., Tutoring Rules for Guiding a
     Case Method Dialogue, Int. J. of Man-Machine
     Studies, Vol.11, No.1, (1979) 25-49.
[6] Otsuki, S. and Takeuchi, A., A Unified CAL
     System for Authoring, Learning and Managing
     Aids, Proc. of IFIP WCCE 81, (1981) 249-256.
[7] Otsuki, S. and Takeuchi, A., A Model of
     Natural Language Dialogue and its Applica-
     tion to CAI, Trans. of Information Process-
     ing Society of Japan, Vol.25, No.4 (1984)
     665-673.
[8] Kowalsky, R., Predicate Logic as Programming
     Language, Proc. of IFIP 74, (1974) 569-574.
[9] Pereira, L.M., Pereira, F.C.N. and Warren,
     D.H.D., User's Guide to DEC-10 Prolog(1979).
[10] Nakashima, H., Prolog/KR User's Manual,
     Dept. of Mathematical Eng. and Instr.
     Phys., University of Tokyo (1981).
[11] Pereira, F.C.N. and Warren, D.H.D., Defin-
     ite Clause Grammar for Language Analysis,
     Artificial Intelligence, Vol.13, (1980)
     231-278.

COMPUTERS IN EDUCATION, K. Duncan and D. Harris (eds.)
Elsevier Science Publishers B.V. (North-Holland)
© IFIP, 1985

EXPERT SYSTEM COMPONENTS FOR INTELLIGENT COMPUTER AIDED INSTRUCTION

John Morris, Ph.D.

IIT Research Institute
Turin Road, North
Rome, New York   13440

This paper describes components of an expert system to extend an existing CAI system, such as PILOT. It permits a course writer to use an expert system as a resource in preparing a script with some of the characteristics of Intelligent Computer Aided Instruction (ICAI). All commands in PILOT remain available to the course author, so that commands for messages to and from the student, conditional branching, and so on, can all be used without modification. ICAI capabilities are invoked simply by typing the appropriate commands as part of a PILOT script.

Structurally, the expert system and the system that controls it are separate from PILOT. They are written in LISP. PILOT generates calls to the expert system when required by a command appearing in the script. For example, in a course for institutional dieticians, the ICAI system might contain rules for planning meals for various diets (diabetic, ulcer, etc.), and allow the student to experiment with menus. Criteria for costs, nutrients, and other evaluation factors would be entered as rules. The student is able to try out plans, have them critiqued by the program, and eventually learn an effective approach to meal planning. The student would not necessarily learn the rules as such; he or she would be learning meal planning by actually planning meals under the supervision of an intelligent tutor.

For the course writer, the principal problem with this approach is developing, coding, and debugging the rule set. In expert systems, this job is usually performed through consultation between an expert and a "knowledge engineer." It can require a year or more of development to obtain the required degree of consistency and completeness in the rules. Our goal is to provide a system that can be used by a qualified teacher to enter and test his or her own rule set, within a reasonable amount of time. "Reasonable" means that the approach will be cost-effective -- that the extra time required will be outweighed by the greater effectiveness of the resulting course.

The design of the instructor interface is critical. The instructor faces a difficult problem that he or she may never have considered before: the logical organization of the subject matter. The instructor's purpose is to show the student how to proceed --how to solve problems, how to do a job correctly. The system is intended to provide the instructor with help in building the required logical structure, which is expressed in the form of rules.

The specific role of the course writer is a combination of:

1. Instructional Designer (the person who develops the course outline and the specific strategies to be used)

2. Subject-Matter Expert (the person who knows the techniques and background information required for the topic)

3. Knowledge Engineer (the person who can translate knowledge into the forms required for effective processing)

We assume that the course writer can play the first two roles. Our job is to make it as easy as possible for him or her to play the third role, by making it easy to input rules and facts, and to test them for completeness and accuracy.

For the student, the experience of using this kind of system should be like that of getting a new machine or tool and learning how to use it. He or she should have the chance to experiment with new approaches and ideas, to see how the machine will respond to them. The instructional program should be more like a computer game in structure than like a piece of traditional instruction. The student should be able to try out different responses until he or she becomes an expert.

1.0 USER COMMANDS

The formats shown here are based on the system developed in Winston and Horn (1). The formats could be modified to make them more "user-friendly," but the critical problem is getting the rules themselves specified, testing them for consistency and effectiveness and using them in a working system.

1.1 RULE

Format:

RULE:(<rulename>(IF (<clause >1) (<clause 2>), ... (<clause n>))(THEN (<consequent 1>) (<consequent 2>) ... (<consequent m>)))

The system will look through its list of FACTS to determine whether clause 1, clause 2, etc., are matched by any of the FACTS. If all of the n clauses are matched (i.e., if the MATCH function returns T for all of the n clauses), then all of the m consequents are added to the list of FACTS.

In the DIAGNOSE mode, an attempt is made to apply a rule when any of its consequents have been added to the HYPOTHESES list. The system performs the following operations:

o   First, it reads the next hypothesis on the list of HYPOTHESES. If the list is empty, then no hypothesis has been confirmed, and the search ends.

o   If the hypothesis is on the list of FACTS, then it is immediately confirmed, and the successful search is reported.

o   If not, then the system next determines which rules, on the RULES list, contain the hypothesis as a consequent. If there are no such rules, then the hypothesis cannot be confirmed, failure is reported, and the hypothesis is removed from the list.

o   The antecedent clauses of each of the relevant rules are examined to determine whether they are on the list of FACTS. If all clauses are true -- that is, if all clauses are matched by elements of the FACTS list -- then the rule fires, and the consequents become FACTS.

o   If an antecedent clause is not on the list of FACTS, then it becomes a hypothesis to be proved.

This process continues until the original hypothesis has been added to the list of facts -- in other words, until it has been proved -- or until all applicable rules have been tried unsuccessfully.

The rules may be modified easily. Routines for adding and deleting rules simply add the new rule to the RULES list, or delete the old one. An instruction for deleting a rule has the following format:

REMOVE: (<rulename>)

In a more sophisticated system, it would be possible to perform a search when a new rule is added, to locate possible conflicts among the rules. These might occur if two rules had the same set of antecedents, but different consequents. If the two sets of consequents were in conflict (i.e., one consequent contradicted another), then the two rules would be incompatible. It would be particularly difficult to detect if the incompatibility were indirect -- for example if (ANIMAL CHEWS CUD) were one of the consequents of one of the rules, while (ANIMAL EATS MEAT) were a consequent of one of the others.

A more sophisticated system might also perform a check whenever a rule is deleted, to determine what FACTS are no longer supported.

1.2 FACT

The course writer can also include any number of facts, which are stored in a list called FACTS. These represent the more-or-less transient knowledge of the system. They are entered in the form:

FACT: (ANIMAL HAS BLACK STRIPES)

When a fact must be removed from the list of FACTS, the course writer writes:

DELFACT: (ANIMAL EATS MEAT)

Routines for adding and deleting facts are available to the course writer. If these same routines were available to the student, they would make it possible for him or her to add facts to the list. Of course, the system might be testing the student's factual knowledge, determining whether he or she knows if an item is on the list of facts. In this case, the student would not be allowed to change the lists of facts.

DIAGNOSE prints a message like this:

((IS THIS TRUE?) (ANIMAL CHEWS CUD))

If the student types T, then the system remembers the fact, and can use it in later inferences. This approach ensures that the format of the fact precisely matches the format of the antecedent of the rule. If the student were permitted to type in the fact, using his or her own words, there would be no guarantee that it would match the form in which it appears in a rule. That is, the student might have typed ANIMAL CHEWS ITS CUD, with the result that the extraneous ITS would cause a mismatch.

The MATCH function makes this process somewhat more tolerant.

1.3 MATCH

MATCH is a command that determines whether one sting of symbols matches another string. An exact match is simply the EQUAL function in LISP, which determines whether each character in one expression is the same as the corresponding character in the other.

As currently written (in LISP, based on Winston and Horn), the MATCH function permits the rule to include wild-card symbols at any point:

o The symbol > will match any one symbol. Thus (THE > DOG) would match (THE LARGE DOG) but not (THE LARGE BROWN DOG) or (THE DOG).

o The symbol & will match zero, one, or more symbols in the target string. Thus (THE & DOG) could match (THE LARGE DOG), (THE BROWN DOG), (THE LARGE BROWN DOG), or simply (THE DOG).

This type of MATCH facility gives the course writer more flexibility in writing rules. At the same time, it does not involve natural language processing, with the problems of syntactic and semantic analysis that natural language systems require.

It is also possible to use the MATCH function to perform more elaborate processing on an input to permit rules that say something like:

((IF (DESTINATION IS WITHIN 50 MILES OF HOME)) (THEN (DISALLOW MEAL DEDUCTION)))).

Both the antecedent and the consequent of this rule require rather extensive processing. A circle search routine or table lookup is needed for the first, and a set of procedures for checking the deduction is required for the second.

The MATCH routine can determine whether an input contains any of a list of words, as well as perform the other matching functions described.

2.0 SYSTEM USE

The set of rules in the demonstration system represents a simple classification of animals (2). The specific RULES, FACTS, and HYPOTHESES in this system can easily be modified, or a completely different set could be substituted for them.

The system can be used in a number of modes:

o The DEDUCE routine will go through the RULES and the available FACTS to see what further FACTS can be derived.

o The DIAGNOSE routine starts with a list of one or more HYPOTHESES. It checks to see whether the FACTS will support any of them.

DEDUCE does "forward chaining," which means that it goes from rules and facts to find out what additional facts can be confirmed. When new facts are added to the FACTS list, DEDUCE can be used to determine their effects -- what additional knowledge we now have.

A teaching system might ask the student, "What additional inferences could you make if you knew that (ANIMAL HAS STRIPES)?" The student might type in "(ANIMAL IS ZEBRA)". The DEDUCE routine could then show what actual results follow from this new knowledge. ("You can deduce (ANIMAL IS TIGER)".)

In a more practical application, the question might be, "What additional inferences could you make if you knew that (MAIN BEARING IS CORRODED)?" The student could be given a list of possible outcomes from which to choose.

The student might be given a list of options, which could be added as facts, with the student guessing the possible outcomes from each fact that he or she chooses to add. In this way, the student can explore the problem space, learning the interconnections among facts.

The system can randomly select a number of possible facts, asking the student to pick one or more of them. (The selection would be made from the antecedents of the existing RULES.) After picking a fact, the student can be asked to specify the effect of this fact, on other facts, using the rule base. Each new fact can be added incrementally, in order to find out exactly which facts are required to reach a specified goal.

Another approach, using "backward chaining," uses the DIAGNOSE routine. It is given this name because it starts with results (such as diseases), and attempts to determine whether the observed facts (or symptoms) will confirm them. If we produce the hypothesis that (ANIMAL IS PENGUIN), the DIAGNOSE routine looks for the facts that would be needed to support this conclusion. It asks ((IS THIS TRUE?) (ANIMAL HAS FEATHERS)) and waits for a reply from the student.

The system is very purposive, asking only the questions that are relevant to the conclusion. Once the student thinks that he or she knows this portion of the subject area, the system can ask irrelevant questions as well, attempting to mislead the student.

The course writer makes use of these facilities in the following ways.

First, a set of RULES, together with FACTS and HYPOTHESES, are entered.

Control programs (based on Winston and Horn) are available to do forward and backward chaining --that is, to go from rules to consequences and from consequences (in the form of hypotheses) to the rules that entail them.

The student can be presented with a list of facts -- in the form of short sentences -- to select and type in. The dialogue could be:

You want to find out whether (ANIMAL IS PENGUIN) is true. Which of these facts would help to show that it is true?

    A. (ANIMAL HAS FEATHERS)

    B. (ANIMAL EATS GRASS)

    C. (ANIMAL HAS FORWARD-POINTING EYES)

Please type A, B, or C.

This would be trivial if it were set up simply as a multiple choice question. What makes it interesting is the possibility that each of the elements in parentheses is variable -- the program itself can pick out the hypothesis to include in the question slot, and the alternatives to put into the three answer slots. In this way, the system can generate a large set of questions from the database with a single program.

What makes expert systems difficult, complex, and interesting is the need for matching conditions that are not simple character-by-character matches of two strings. An example was given above:

    (DESTINATION IS WITHIN 50 MILES OF HOME)

Processing of this criterion is conceptually simple enough. You obtain the values for DESTINATION and HOME. You have the value of 50 for the distance between these two points. Distances between cities might be contained in a table, and you would perform a table look-up, hoping that both cities were included in the table. If not, you try to find an indication of the location of each of these points, such as a latitude and longitude pair. Once these values are found, the distance can be computed, using a special-purpose function. If the distance is less than 50 miles, then T (for TRUE) is returned.

For this type of question and answer, the course writer can call on a LISP programmer to write the support programs. This is far more effective than attempting to write some kind of general-purpose natural language system that would be capable of recognizing the large number of forms that a rule could take.

Another type of question is:

You know that (ANIMAL HAS WINGS) (ANIMAL IS BLACK AND WHITE) (ANIMAL SWIMS WELL). On the basis of this knowledge, which of the following hypotheses could you prove?

    A. (ANIMAL IS GIRAFFE)

    B. (ANIMAL IS PENGUIN)

    C. (ANIMAL IS TIGER)

The system has the ability to generate large numbers of test questions like this, without further programming by the course writer.

Another mode in which the student can use the system is in an exploration of the consequences of various actions. The student can select a set of hypotheses to be confirmed and the system determines which facts are needed to confirm them. This can be performed in an interactive dialogue, with the system asking questions in the form:

    ((IS THIS TRUE?) (ANIMAL HAS BLACK STRIPES))

In this way the student learns what kinds of facts are relevant to a given problem. Alternatively, the student himself or herself could add new facts to the FACTS list.

In a more practical application, the questions could take the form:

    ((IS THIS TRUE?) (WARNING-SYSTEM HAS BEEN DISABLED))

All that is needed is a new set of rules in order to create a system that would perform this function.

3.0 PROGRAM REQUIREMENTS

The purpose of this section is to show the additions to PILOT that are required. The expert system based on Winston and Horn is used as a model. A more sophisticated expert system would be able to support more functions than these. As noted in Section 2, simple extensions of the expert system would be required for some functions and are described below.

To permit the student to enter hypotheses and to explore their consequences, the HYPOTHESES list can be set to include the requested hypothesis:

    HYP: < hypothesis >

For example, if the student wants to explore the hypothesis (ANIMAL IS PENGUIN), he or she writes the command:

HYP: ANIMAL IS PENGUIN

PILOT then translates this into the LISP command:

(SETQ HYPOTHESES < hypothesis >)

Then the DIAGNOSE program is called with the command:

(DIAGNOSE)

When the hypothesis has been confirmed, or when it is determined that no hypothesis can be confirmed on the basis of the current rule set and the student's responses, the DIAGNOSE program will exit. Control can be returned to PILOT at this point.

The system maintains two functions, HOW and WHY. HOW answers the student's question, "What rules were used to deduce the fact that ...?" HOW replies with a list of the appropriate rules. If the fact was given, it says so. If the fact does not appear on the list of FACTS -- i.e., if it is not known to the system -- it reports this. To call this function, PILOT generates the LISP command:

(HOW < fact >)

Where < fact > is whatever the student typed.

Similarly, WHY can be used to answer the question, "Why did you need the fact that ...?" WHY returns a list of the facts that depend on the given fact. If the fact was the hypothesis, WHY reports this. If the fact is not part of the current deduction, WHY says so. PILOT generates a LISP call as follows:

(WHY < fact >)

Where < fact > is what the student has typed.

The student could add a new fact to the list of facts. This could then be tested to determine what new consequences would follow. In the PILOT language, the command is:

FACT: < fact >

For example, the student might write:

FACT: (ANIMAL HAS FEATHERS)

To add this new fact, PILOT generates the LISP command:

(REMEMBER < fact >)

Where < fact > is the new fact that the student adds. The function DEDUCE will expand

the list of FACTS to include whatever can now be derived from the given facts, the new fact, and the rules. The course writer writes the command simply as:

DEDUCE:

REMOVE simply runs through the list of FACTS, recursively calling on itself until it finds the fact to be removed, and then returning the remaining facts. This, or an equivalent function, could be called by PILOT when a student wanted to delete a fact from the FACTS list -- perhaps because it had been included in error. The LISP call from PILOT might be:

(DELETE-FACT < fact >)

Where < fact > is whatever the student typed in.

To insert a new rule, the course writer types:

RULE: < newrule >

For example:

RULE: (RULE IDENTIFY16

(IF (ANIMAL FLIES) (ANIMAL HAS
      FEATHERS))

(THEN (ANIMAL IS BIRD))

PILOT translates this into a LISP command:

(SETQ RULES (CONS < newrule > RULES))

The course writer also has the ability to delete rules, using the command:

REMOVE: < rulename >

For example:

REMOVE: IDENTIFY16

PILOT then translates this into a LISP function resembling the one given for deleting facts, using a LISP command:

(DELETE-RULE < rulename >)

Following addition or deletion of a fact or a rule, the course writer might want to call on DEDUCE to show the result of this change.

At some point, the course writer might want to start over again, by deleting all current knowledge from the system. The PILOT command is:

DELFACTS:

This generates the LISP command:

(SETQ FACTS NIL)

Similarly the PILOT command to delete rules is:

DELRULES:

This generates a LISP command:

(SETQ RULES NIL)

At some point, the student might wish to test out a hypothesis. The system generates a list of available hypotheses for him or her by collecting all the conclusions of the rules. This would be feasible if there were only a small number of rules in the system, but if there were much more than a dozen rules, the number of hypotheses would be too large to display.

In this case the system goes through the list of rules, picking off the conclusions to each rule, and displaying them one at a time for the student to select or reject.

If the student chooses to write his or her own hypotheses, it is easy to add them to the list of current hypotheses. The PILOT command is:

HYP: <hypothesis>

This generates the LISP command:

(SETQ   HYPOTHESES   (CONS   <hypothesis> HYPOTHESES))

A call to the DIAGNOSE routine determines whether the new hypothesis can be supported by the current set of rules and facts, and, if not, what additional facts are needed.

A PILOT command like this:

DELHYP: <hypothesis>

Can be used to delete a hypothesis from the current set, using a LISP routine:

(DELETE-HYP <hypothesis>)

The MATCH routine was described briefly in Section 2. This is a set of existing LISP routines, based on Winston and Horn, which extends the power of the system to compare two strings.

MATCH includes the following special symbols:

> matches any single word

& matches one or more words (it should probably be modified to match zero or more words)

>X matches any single word and saves the word in the variable X

&Y matches one or more words and saves them in the variable Y

RESTRICT > < a predicate > matches any expression which meets the criteria stated in the predicate (where the predicate is a LISP function returning T or NIL)

The RESTRICT operator is particularly powerful, since the predicate that it references can be arbitrarily complex. It may be difficult to use, however, since the course writer or a programmer would have to write the predicate function.

Nevertheless, if a rule took the form (IF (DESTINATION IS WITHIN 50 MILES OF HOME) ...), then RESTRICT could be used to generate a call to a function --call it NEARHOME -- that would return the correct value. More generally, some such approach as this is required if the expert system is to approach the sophistication of an ICAI system.

The MATCH function does not require any specific commands from the course writer, other than the use of >, &, or RESTRICT in a rule.

REFERENCES

[1] Winston, P., and B. Horn. LISP. Reading, Mass.: Addison-Wesley, (1981).

[2] Webster, R., and L. Miner. "Expert Systems: Programming Problem-Solving." Technology, (Jan.-Feb., 1982).

COMPUTERS IN EDUCATION, K. Duncan and D. Harris (eds.)
Elsevier Science Publishers B.V. (North-Holland)
© IFIP, 1985

THE SIMULTANEOUS CONTROL BY MICROCOMPUTER OF SEVERAL MECHANICAL SYSTEMS
USING A SINGLE FIBRE OPTICS LINK

Dr. E.W. Reed, Leeds Polytechnic, Leeds, England, LS1 3HE
Emma E. Hellawell, Sarah D. Hill, Mrs. C.D. Cleverley,
Leeds Girls' High School

This paper falls into two parts. The first part deals with a liaison
between a girls' school and a polytechnic in the field of computer
studies particularly in the control of mechanical sytems. One result
of this liaison was the participation in a TV show of two girls controlling
robots and a short video of this is to be presented. The second part
describes one girl's particular project involving the control of multiple
systems via a single fibre optics link. Small items of equipment have
been selected especially so that they can be transported to the USA for
demonstration. The paper is to be presented by two schoolgirls.

BACKGROUND

For the last five years there has been
collaboration between Leeds Polytechnic and
Leeds Girls' High School initially helping
to introduce staff and girls to the use of
microcomputers. This started because of
family connections.

Of special interest has been the field of
microcomputers applied to mechanical
engineering. This has led to several projects
including robots (ref. 1), fluid power (ref. 2)
and now the control of multiple systems by
fibre optics.

It is unusual for girls in the UK to become
engineers. This is for deeply-rooted social
reasons. So much so that 1984 was designated
WISE year (Women in Science and Engineering).
This involvement by girls of the school in
engineering has caused a great deal of interest
nationally and a number of lectures and
demonstrations have been given by girls in
such places as Lancaster and Loughborough
Universities (refs. 1 & 2) and for the
Institution of Mechanical Engineers in London
and Birmingham. The 1982 and 1984 Christmas
Lectures were given for the Council of
Engineering Institutions. Two girls
participated in a programme for South West TV
and a video is presented.

Without doubt, girls who partake in these
activities do gain a great deal of confidence.
Staff and girls alike find it a stimulating
experience which broadens their horizons.

One girls in the video, Sophia, subsequently
won £3,000 worth of computing equipment for
the school by writing a winning essay on her
views on the effect of microcomputers on the
World. She is now reading Engineering at
Oxford. The other girl, Frances, is reading
Law at Cambridge.

Now that computers are being much more widely
introduced into schools and being used to assist
in the teaching of so many subjects, it is
hoped that schools will not experience the
inter-departmental rivalries faced by the
Univesities and Polytechnics when the microcomputer was first introduced. Competition
was usually between the Computing and
Electronics departments which with hindsight
is now seen as a nonsense.

We have collaborative contacts with several
places including establishments in Denmark
(ref. 3) and France and we know of other
collaborative ventures. Our experience has
been that collaboration between people from
different establishments works very well without
any of the aforementioned rivalry.

If anyone reading or hearing this paper wishes
to contact us - even if it is just to come
and see what we do - we would be pleased if
they would so so.

THE PROJECT

As part of the School's extra-mural activities
girls are given a week in which to do work
experience and this has been a further
opportunity for a few girls to work with
Dr. Reed. This project is the result of one
of these work experience weeks in July 1984.

The object was to use a microcomputer to switch
a number of machines, each independent of the
other over a relatively long distance, say
across a workshop. Long wires connected to
microcomputers act as aerials and can not
only introduce spurious information but can
actually damage microcomputers. Electro-
mechanical devices, typically electric motors,
create a great deal of interference. Fibre
optics are a way of overcoming this, but being
expensive the need is to transmit parallel
data through a single link in serial form.

Emma with her handiwork

1. Port
2. U.A.R.T.
3. Fibre optics transmitter
4. Fibre Optics link

5. Fibre optics receiver
6. U.A.R.T.
7. Transistorised relays
8. Solid state relays

9. Motorised doll
10. Motor 1
11. Motor 2
12. Mains solenoid

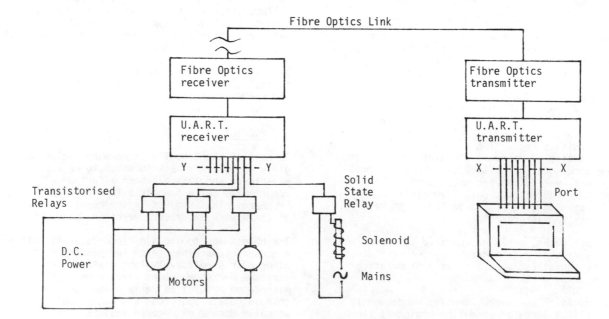

NB   The information at YY is the same as at XX

Figure 1 - Layout of Control Sytem

<u>Parallel Port</u>. An input/output part of a microcomputer widely used for control purposes. A port typically has 8 parallel connections, each used for input or output according to preset conditions.

<u>U.A.R.T.</u> Universal Asynchronous Receiver Transmitter
It enables parallel data to be converted into serial form and vice versa. Universal because it can act as receiver or transmitter. Asychronous because a receiver and transmitter pair will still work together even if the timing of each is not precise. An anology is morse code where words (parallel data) are transmitted in dots and dashes (serial form); the rate of transmission of serial data is known as the baud note.

<u>Fibre Optics Transmitter</u> Voltage pulses are converted into light pulses.

<u>Fibre Optics Link</u> A flexible glass or plastic tube through which light passes losing virtually no energy because of total internal reflection.

<u>Fibre Optics Receiver</u> Light pulses are converted into voltage pulses.

<u>Transistorised Relay</u> A transistor controls a solenoid which is part of a relay. The relay in turn switches a power supply. This is a very common and widely used arrangement.

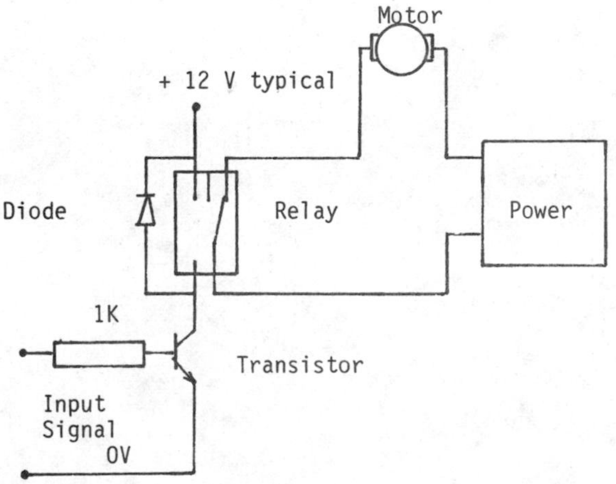

It can be seen in Figure 2 that the relay physically separates the large power source (which could be mains electricity) from the microcomputer which could save the latter from damage should there be a malfunction.

Relays come in all shapes and sizes. They consist of a solenoid which, when energised, closes or opens a pair (or several pairs) of contacts. NB A diode is usually added as shown as a protection against damage by back electro motive force (emf) when the solenoid is switched off.

The making-up of a transistorised relay as shown here is a very nice and useful pupil project. Relays can be used to switch many things e.g. electric motors as demonstrated in this paper. Judith made such an interface (ref. 2).

<u>Solid State Relay</u> A family of devices is now available which are very simple to use and are generally replacing normal relays. They are called solid state relays. Physically they are small blocks with just 4 terminals and are connected as shown in Figure 3.

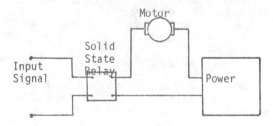

Figure 3 - Circuit Using Solid State Relay

They are an elegant way of interfacing but are sometimes rejected for several reasons. They are more expensive than normal relays and they are silent. One can hear a normal relay clicking over as it works. They will fail completely when overloaded; a normal relay's contacts would become pitted but would probably still work. They cannot operate several pairs of contacts at once. However, since they have no moving parts they should function indefinitely.

In this project a solid state relay is included to switch a mains driven solenoid.

Figure 2 - Circuit Using Transistorised Relay

SOFTWARE

A valuable part of the project was to be able
to develop software and a whole range of
programmes were developed. A simple one is
included here. It is written in BASIC. The
programme allows an operator to switch on
and off any of the three DC motors or mains
driven solenoid shown in Figure 1. Each
device behaves quite independently.

```
10 OUT  #4B, #0F;  Configure Port as Output
20 PRINT  "  TO SWITCH  MOTOR 1    ENTER 1"
30 PRINT  "             MOTOR 2          2"
40 PRINT  "             MOTOR 3          4"
50 PRINT  "             MAINS            8"
60 INPUT A
70 B = IN ( #4A)
80 A = AXORB
90 OUT  #4A, A ;  Give data to port
100 GOTO 20
```

COMMENT

This demonstration used an actual fibre optics
link costing about £80 or $80. U.A.R.T.'s
cost only a few pounds. A less costly
arrangement giving the same effect could be
devised using just a pair of wires and
photo-couplers. It would of course be
subject to interference.

CONCLUSION

To Emma the project was a valuable experience.
It gave an insight into engineering and the
connections and gulfs between it and school
subjects. When the project was defined the
initial reaction was to feel daunted but this
gave way to feelings of pleasure and
satisfaction as things developed and were
understood. She learnt that it was not
necessary to know everything about each
device and indeed such a task would be
impossible. She also saw that the laboratory
she worked in was full of people each relying
upon one another for knowledge and experience:
nobody knew enough. "No man is an island"
(or girl for that matter). Hence the value
of such conferences as the one this paper
is written for.

If there is any shortcoming to the
collaboration and project work described here,
it is that only a few girls can get
involved at any time. However, this is better
than none at all. It is good for staff
development and pupils and students generally
benefit in the end.

Ref. 1
REED, Frances, LANGLEY, Sophia, CLEVERLEY,
Mrs. C.D., WARD, R.L., and REED, E.W.,
"Microprocessor control of a robot as a
Polytechnic-School linked project".
Conference. Involving Micros in Education,
University of Lancaster and International
Federation for Information Processing,
March 1982.

Ref. 2
REED, Stephanie, EVANS, Judith, CLEVERLEY,
Mrs. C.D., and REED, E.W.,
"A School-Polytechnic linked project,
describing microcomputers controlling robots
and fluid power, to include a T.V. performance"
Conference. Micros in Education. University
of Loughborough and Council for Educational
Technology, April 1984.

Ref. 3
PAEGOGISK FORSOGS - OG UDVIKLINGSARBEDJE MED
DATALAERE SOM OBLIGATORIKS FAG PA 5-6
KLASSETRIN, OG SOM VALGFAG PA 8-9 KLASSETRIN

COMPUTERS IN EDUCATION, K. Duncan and D. Harris (eds.)
Elsevier Science Publishers B.V. (North-Holland)
© IFIP, 1985

FACULTY WORKSTATIONS: A NEW KIND OF COMPUTING

Donald D. Sharp Jr. and Gerald A. Knezek

Department of Computer Sciences
North Texas State University
Denton, Texas 76203

Several American universities are now requiring that all incoming
freshman purchase a personal computer. Other universities are strongly
encouraging their students to have access to a personal computer.
Before this trend sweeps the country, it is imperative that university
faculty members become more familiar with these personal computers so
that they can integrate them into their curriculum and use them in
their research. This paper presents the approach that the Computer
Science Department at North Texas State University has taken to provide
workstations for faculty use.
Each Computer Science faculty member at NTSU has been provided with a
Texas Instruments Professional Computer for his/her office to use as a
stand-alone computer or it may be used as a terminal to one of the
larger computers on campus. These workstations are typically used with
commercially available word processing software to write memos, technical papers, books, and course outlines. Spreadsheet software packages
are often used for such purposes as preparing research proposal budgets
and for keeping track of each student's grades in each class. The use
of standard software packages and the ability to have stand-alone
computing power as well as access to a larger computer would seem to
make this type of faculty workstation useful not only for Computer
Science faculty but also for any other university faculty.

1. INTRODUCTION

Several American universities are now
requiring every incoming freshman to
purchase a personal computer or to
show that they have access to a personal computer [Osgo84]. Clarkson
University issues each incoming freshman a Zenith Z-100 microcomputer and
increases tuition each semester to pay
for the computer. At Stevens Institute
of Technology, all freshman in the science and systems planning/management
program are required to buy an Atari
800 computer. Incoming freshmen at
Dallas Baptist College are required to
buy a Radio Shack Model 100 portable
computer. Drew College of Liberal Arts
issues Epson QX-10 microcomputers to
each freshman and allocates tuition
funds to pay for the computers.

All freshman at Dartmouth College are
required to purchase an Apple Macintosh
personal computer and all freshmen at
Drexel University are required to have
access to a Macintosh computer [Smit83,
Thur84]. According to current plans,
by 1986 all freshmen at Carnegie-Mellon
University will be required to buy a
very powerful personal computer that
will become an integral part of their
education [Osgo84, Slac83].

Many other universities, even though
they do not yet require every student to
have a personal computer, strongly encourage their students to purchase a
personal computer [Osgo84]. Many
universities provide sizeable discounts
on the purchase of selected personal
computers by students and faculty.

Before this trend towards requiring all
university students to purchase personal
computers sweeps the country, it is imperative that university faculty members become more familiar with these
personal computers so that they can integrate them into their curriculum and
use them in their research. It appears
that most universities are just now
beginning to plan for providing personal
computers to faculty members so that
they can learn to use them for their
various academic purposes. Two leaders
in this area are Stanford University's
Project Tiro which has provided almost
every professor in the Humanities Department with an IBM Personal Computer
[Litt83] and Brown Univeristy's scholar's
workstations [Brow83,Ship83].

This paper presents the approach taken
by the Computer Science Department at
North Texas State University (NTSU) to
provide personal computers for each

Computer Science faculty member to be used as a faculty workstation. Even though this project is currently only for Computer Science faculty, the results seem to indicate that this approach is a viable one for any faculty member at a large or medium-sized univeristy.

2. Hardware and Software

The key element in the faculty workstation approach is a powerful personal computer which is usually located in each faculty member's office. At NTSU, this computer is a 16-bit Texas Instruments Professional Computer (TIPC) [Texa 83] with a color monitor, 256K of random access memory, two floppy disks, a 3-plane graphics option, and communication capability. The TIPC is largely compatible with the IBM Personal Computer. Many programs and most data diskettes can be used interchangeably between the two computer systems.

Each faculty workstation is also provided with software packages including two word-processors, a spreadsheet program, and several programming languages. The word-processing software packages are Wordstar and Easywriter II. Most of our faculty members prefer using Wordstar. The spreadsheet program is Multiplan. Languages which are available to every faculty member are MS-Basic, MS-Pascal, MS-Fortran, and MS-Cobol. All of this software runs under the MS-DOS Operating System which is the same as the PC DOS Operating System which is used on most IBM Personal Computers.

Some faculty members have obtained other software in addition to this basic package which is available to everyone. Other software packages used by some of the faculty members are: Lotus 1-2-3, PC-File, Turbo Pascal, MicroRIM, Dbase II, Visicalc, UCSD p-System Pascal, and IQ-Lisp. There are almost 500 software packages which are now available for the TIPC [Texa84].

In the administrative area of the Computer Science Department there are two more TIPC's which are identical to the ones in the faculty offices except that each one is connected to a letter-quality printer. These two machines are used by the departmental secretaries for word processing and by the faculty members to obtain hard-copy. If a faculty member has something to print like a memo or a paper, it is usually composed on the TIPC in the faculty member's office and the floppy disk containing the data is then taken to one of the TIPC's in the administrative area to be printed.

In addition to having the power of a personal computer available to a faculty member when he needs it, the TIPC also can be used as an intelligent terminal to the large mainframe computers on the campus via a broad-band local area network. This is accomplished by using a communications package called VTERM [Satu83] which was secured under a mass purchase agreement and is licensed for use with all TIPC's on campus. NTSU has three large time-sharing computers supporting instruction and research, two DEC VAX 11/780 super-minicomputers and a NAS 8040 mainframe, the later of which is comparable to an IBM 3083 computer.

The 23 faculty workstations in the Computer Science Department as well as more than 100 other faculty/staff personal computers and terminals at NTSU can access any one of these large systems simply by entering the command CALL A780, CALL B780, or CALL 8040, depending on the system desired. Currently, 38 of the 54 buildings on campus are connected to the Sytek broad-band local area network, with potential expansion to all buildings, numerous host computers and up to 2000 workstations.

In addition to the hardware listed above for faculty use, the Computer Science Department also has many other computers which are primarily for student use. These include 32 Texas Instruments 99/4A home computers with color monitors, 32 Apple II and IIe personal computers, 20 IBM Personal Computers, 3 Texas Instruments Professional Computers, and two Texas Instruments 990 minicomputers connected to 24 terminals. There are also about 200 "dumb" terminals on the campus which have access through the broad-band network to the VAX and IBM-compatible machines. 64 of these terminals are located in the Computer Science Department.

3. Using the Faculty Workstation

Most faculty members use the workstation primarily for word processing using Wordstar. The biggest advantage of word processing on a personal computer is the speed with which changes can be made. Although the departmental secretaries are trained to do word processing, most faculty members find it quicker and easier to do their own word processing for most documents. The faculty member does not have to wait for secretarial help and then proof and correct the output. Much "boilerplate" often can be copied from other documents. Several faculty members wrote chapters for a

book which were typeset directly from
the output of the Wordstar word processor.

Also, by using a personal computer the
faculty member does not have to worry
about access restrictions to a large
computer through a terminal or the computer not being available because of
hardware or software problems or routine maintenance. In the unusual case
when there is a problem with the faculty
member's personal computer, there is
normally an identical computer available
in a friend's office or in the administrative area. Repairs are made on
campus in the Computer Science Department's maintenance shop.

Many faculty members like to use the
Multiplan or Visicalc spreadsheet program for recording each student's grades
in a class. The spreadsheet program can
keep track of each student's grade for
each test, paper, project, or exam. For
example, if each test is worth 10%, each
paper 15%, and the final exam 30%, then
the spreadsheet program can easily generate the final grade for each student
in a manner of seconds.

Many faculty members also use the faculty
workstation as an intelligent terminal to
access the larger computers and perform
tasks that are too big for the personal
computer. Typical uses are to run a
statistical package which will analyze
large amounts of data or a simulation
involving many events. Using the personal computer as an intelligent terminal as well as a stand-alone computer
makes the faculty workstation much more
powerful than either a separate personal
computer or a terminal to a large time
sharing computer could be.

The main uses of the faculty workstation
listed thus far are certainly not restricted to Computer Science faculty. In
addition to the general uses listed
above, each Computer Science faculty
member has his/her own unique uses of
the computer as would any other specialist. Some of these uses include working with different languages to create
specialized computer programs, using the
color graphics capability of the personal computer, or using the personal computer as a terminal to one of the VAX
computers to build larger systems, run
simulations, etc.

4. Training of Faculty Members

Little formal training has been necessary to enable the Computer Sciences
faculty to fully utilize their work-

stations. Typically other faculty
members in the department provide im-
promptu instruction to a colleague who
is less skilled in a particular application. The large size of the department (21 full-time professional academicians) creates a high probability that
at least one department member will be
skilled in virtually every area.
Identical faculty machines throughout
the department aid in the rapid transfer of hardware and software knowledge.

The informal training provided for computer scientists probably would not be
adequate for university faculty in
general. Other methods such as structured seminars, newsletters, and telephone hot-line support might be necessary for those academicians whose disciplines are not directly involved with
computing.

5. Evaluation

Most of the faculty of the Computer
Science Department feel that the faculty workstation is a big improvement over
the time-sharing terminals which they
previously had in their offices. They
are not bothered by slow response, lack
of available ports, or downtime on the
time-sharing computer. They find the
faculty workstation to be more user
friendly with less strange commands to
learn and use. They like the privacy
of data that the personal computer provides. For example, they can keep
student grades on their own private
diskette as opposed to using a disk
file on the time-sharing machine.

Word processing on the personal computer
is quicker and easier than on the time-
sharing machine and printed output is
much easier to obtain. Most faculty
members now bypass the departmental
typing pool in most cases because it is
quicker and easier to type something
yourself rather than to have a secretary
type it. If access to one of the large
time-sharing systems is still required,
then the faculty work station can act
as a terminal to that system.

The personal computer also can do some
things that were not possible with a
time-sharing system. For example, the
TIPC has excellent color graphics
capability which was not previously
available. Software for producing
spreadsheets was not available on the
time-sharing computers. The personal
computer also can be carried into the
classroom to assist in teaching.

6.   Conclusions

The use of a powerful personal computer
as a workstation attached to a network
containing at least one larger computer
seems to be an increasingly popular way
to configure computer systems. The
ability to have stand-alone computing
power as well as access to a larger
computer makes the faculty workstation
more useful than either a separate
personal computer or a terminal to a
large time-sharing computer.

Most of the uses of the faculty workstation which have been presented in
this paper are not restricted to Computer Science faculty but would seem to
be useful to faculty in any other
department of the university. It is
not necessary for the faculty member
to be a computer programmer to use a
faculty workstation.

REFERENCES

Brow83   Brown, Marc, Meyrowitz, Norman,
         and van Dam, Andries. "Personal
         Computer Networks and Graphical
         Animation: Rationale and Prac-
         tice for Education". Proceed-
         ings of the Fourteenth SIGCSE
         Technical Symposium on Computer
         Science Education, Orlando,
         Florida, February 17-18, 1983,
         reprinted as ACM SIGCSE
         Bulletin, Volume 15, Number 1,
         February 1983, 296-307.

Litt83   Littman, Jonathan. "Computing
         the Classics". PC World, Volume
         1, Number 6, September 1983,
         266-274.

Osgo84   Osgood, Donna. "A Computer on
         Every Desk: A Survey of
         Personal Computers in American
         Universities". Byte, Volume 9,
         Number 6, June 1984.

Satu83   ---. "VTERM User's Manual".
         Saturn Consulting Group
         Incorporated, June 1, 1983

Ship83   Shipp, William S., Meyrowitz,
         Norman, and van Dam, Andries.
         "Networks of Scholar's Work-
         stations in a University
         Community". Proceedings of
         the Twenty-Fifth IEEE Computer
         Society International Confer-
         ence (COMPCON'83), Arlington,
         Virginia, September 25-29, 1983,
         108-122.

Slac83   Slack, Keith, Morris, Jim, Van
         Houweling, Douglas, and Wishbow,
         Nina. "The Future of Computing
         at Carnegie-Mellon University".
         Proceedings of the Twenty-Fifth

         IEEE Computer Society Inter-
         national Conference (COMPCON'83),
         Arlington, Virginia, September
         25-29, 1983, 94-99.

Smit83   Smith, Allen L. "Suppose Every
         Freshman Owned a Microcomputer".
         Proceedings of the Twenty-Fifth
         IEEE Computer Society Interna-
         tional Conference (COMPCON'83),
         Arlington, Virginia, September
         25-29, 1983, 123-126.

Texa83   ---. Personal/Professional
         Computers: How Can They Help
         You? Dallas Texas: Texas
         Instruments, 1983.

Texa84   ---. "TI PC Software Guide:
         Almost 500 Packages for the
         PC". DirecTIons (The Official
         Magazine for the Texas Instru-
         ments Computer Users Group),
         Volume 1, Number 8, June 1984,
         8-13.

Thur84   Thury, Eva. "Drexel's Brave
         New World". MacWorld, July/
         August 1984, 122-127.

COMPUTERS IN EDUCATION, K. Duncan and D. Harris (eds.)
Elsevier Science Publishers B.V. (North-Holland)
© IFIP, 1985

COMPUTER SCIENCE EDUCATION BASED ON MICRO-OPERATIONS

Ken Ishikawa and Nobuo Baba

Faculty of Education, Utsunomiya University,
Utsunomiya, Japan

An instructional technique based on a micro-operation scheme was hypothesised in order to teach data flow and computer programming. For effective teaching, a micro-operationable computer system called EDCOM has been developed and implemented. The EDCOM system provides a concrete data flow model that substitutes memory boxes, calculation boxes, buses and gates for five computer units. To study the control mechanism with actual feeling, the gates can be operated directly by the learner. To evaluate its effectiveness, EDCOM was applied to the machine (assembly) language programming courses of various kinds of schools. There was virtually no deviation in EDCOM's success regardless of the type of school or age of student. Results show that learning can be achived in 33% shorter time and with less misunderstanding.

1. INTRODUCTION

Introductory computer science and programming courses have been offered to various kinds of schools[1]. In this trial, how to increase the learner's scientific understanding of computers and computer programming has been studied.

Up to now a number of educational aids have been developed for teaching the principles of computers. However, these aids still need improvement, because of the following:

a. Educational computers indicating logical elements of actual computers are too complicated for novices because of their too detailed configuration.

b. Hardware logic trainers, that consist of SSI, MSI, and LSI require the understanding of hardware, thus, are not suitable for junior high school students.

c. Simulation of the data flow and control mechanism of computers by the interactive terminals linked to a central computer or by micro computer systems is difficult to understand with actual feeling.

The EDCOM (EDucational COMputer) was designed and implemented to solve these difficulties. The design principles of the EDCOM system are the following [2]:

i) The system provides a data flow model that performs the micro-operation, i.e. the gates between the registers and the buses can be operated manually by the learner. In addition, the gates can also be controlled automatically in the same way as an actual computer.

ii) The system provides an approachable concrete data processing model that substitutes the four components (memory boxes, calculation boxes, buses, and gates) for the usual five computer units.

To evaluate the effectiveness of the instructional technique, the EDCOM was applied to the machine (assembly) language programming

lessons for junior high school students (age 14) in an Industrial arts course, and for medical technology students and undergraduate engineering students (age 20) in an Introductory computer science course [3],[4],[5].

2. TWO DESIGN PRINCIPLES OF THE EDCOM

2.1 A micro-operation scheme that simulates the control mechanism in the computer

Figure 1 shows the example of micro-operations with the relation among the machine instructions, assembly language instructions, and high-level language instructions. In previous teaching methods, high-level language programs or assembly language programs were converted into machine-level object codes in order to explain the functions of each instruction. But it was difficult to understand the instruction's function. However, a micro-programming scheme [6] enables students to control the gates of the hardware, and the control timing of the gates directly. This is a reasonable scheme for teaching the data flow and control mechanism of the computer more clearly.

Based on this scheme, we made the gates of the EDCOM operative in order that the learner could open or close the gates manually in the same manner specified by the micro-instruction. Thus, a machine instruction can be executed in a sequence of micro-operations operated by the learner himself, and the learner can obtain "hands-on" experience in constructing the machine instructions.

The gates can also be controlled automatically by the control signals from the control unit as a wired-logic computer. The wiring between the control unit and gates may be performed by the teacher or learner according to the functions of the machine instructions they define. In addition, this flexible gates control mechanism of the EDCOM allows the teacher to teach the

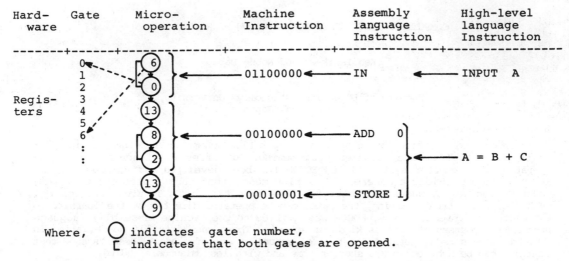

Figure 1. Relation between the micro-operations and High-level
language instructions

concepts of micro-programming computer systems
by substituting the memory units of the EDCOM
for the control memory unit.

2.2 An approachable concrete model for studying the functions of the computer

So as to stress learning by function rather than
by unit name, it is assumed that the computer
is made up of four main components which
comprise the basic functions of a computer:

   i) Memory boxes: The boxes keep the data
and output the same data which are inputted into
the boxes (Registers and Memory cells).

   ii) Calculation boxes: Each box outputs the
result of each calculation according to the data
which is inputted into that box (Adder, AND, OR
and NOT).

   iii) Buses: The data paths from one
register to another.

   iv) Gates: The gates are set between the
registers and buses, and control the data flow
from the registers to the buses or from the
buses to the registers.

The data flow and control mechanisms are
explained by operating the gates and by using
those boxes. After understanding the micro-
operations, the student is taught machine
(assembly) language programs that have the same
function as the sequence of micro-operations
already learned. After completing these lessons,
high-level language programming (BASIC) is
taught.

3. CONFIGURATION OF THE EDCOM

Based on the above two design principles, the
EDCOM was designed and implemented as shown in
Figure 2.

3.1 Layout of display panel

The display panel of the EDCOM is divided into
two sections; one is a data flow panel and the
other is a control panel. Each panel is 1.2
meters in height and 0.9 meter in width. The
data flow panel consists of sub-panels handling
Input, Output, Arithmetic and Logic Unit (ALU)
and Memory units. Each unit performs its own
function independently and is connected to buses
A and B. The control panel consists of the
Control unit only. These features enable the
learner to recognize the functions of each unit
independently and clearly. The register's
state in each unit is displayed by 8 or 4 lights
emitting diodes (LED's) representing its state
in a binary manner. The status of the
controllable gates is also displayed by a LED's.
Therefore, the learner can understand what is
going on inside the computer by observing these
LED's.

3.2 Gates control mechanism

Figure 3 shows the logic diagram of a gate. The
8-bit data in the register is sent to Bus B
when the manual gate control switch is on or
when at least one control signal input terminal
is activated. The control signal input terminals
receive some control signals from the control
unit connected by the patch-cord according to
the machine instruction definitions. A delay
circuit is added to the gate circuits to
eliminate the noise picked up by the long wires
and the chattering of the manual gate control
switches.

3.3 Functions of the five computer units

i) ALU: The ALU consists of gates, an 8-bit

Accumulator referred to as a memory box, and calculation boxes (such as ADD, logical AND, logical OR, logical NOT, and a Comparator). The Accumulator register receives data from the Memory unit and Input unit via Bus B by opening gate 0. The Accumulator register also receives the calculated result of one of the four calculation boxes by opening gate 2,3,4, or 5. The data of the Accumulator register can be stored in the Memory unit and Output unit via Bus A. These ALU functions are necessary but represent only a minimum configuration which can perform basic logical operations and the four fundamental rules of arithmetic. Table 2 shows that these programs can be executed in a maximum of 12 steps by using the machine instructions shown in Table 1.

ii) Memory unit: The Memory unit consists of gates and two memory boxes, one consisting of Memory cells totaling 16 bytes and another a Memory address register.

iii) Input unit and iv) Output unit : The Input unit and Output unit also consist of gates and registers, referred to as memory boxes.

v) Control unit: The Control unit consists of gates, an Instruction register and a Program counter, which are referred to as memory boxes, and a Control signal generator referred to as a calculation box.

3.4 Relation between the data flow panel and the control panel.

The data flow panel alone can be used as a micro-operationable educational computer system. When Bus B is connected to the Instruction register in the Control unit and the control signals are connected to the appropriate gates in the data flow panel, a wired-programming computer can be constructed.

Table 1 shows the example instruction formats

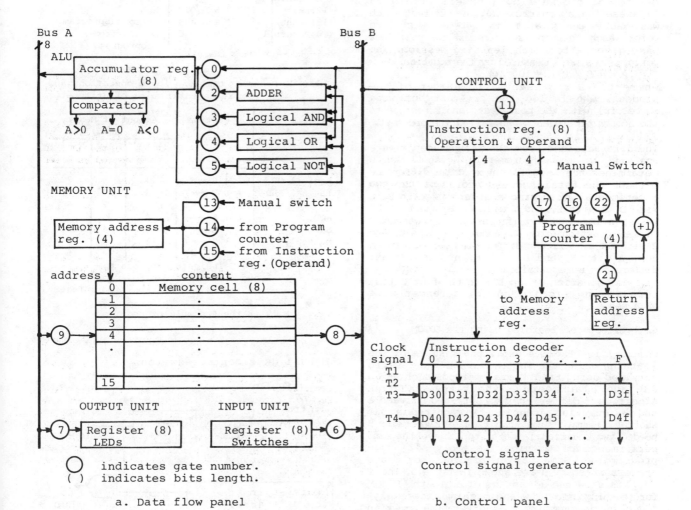

Figure 2. Layout of the EDCOM.

that cover the basic computer instructions. The connections between the control signal output and gates are flexible. The function of the instructions can easily be defined by the learner. In this example, the Load instruction is defined by connecting Control signal D30 to gate 15 and 8, and Control signal D40 to gate 0.

4. EVALUATION

4.1 Machine (assembly) language programming

The evaluation was performed from the view points of the effect of the EDCOM itself, experience of the teacher, age of the learner, and the type of school, as shown in Table 3 [3],[4],[5]. Table 4 shows the experimental results obtained in 7 question tests of five subject groups (A, B, C, D, and E). The questions are divided into three groups: I) The sequence of micro-operations, II) Machine (assembly) language programming, and III) Methods of programming (answers within 25 Japanese "Kana" characters). The pre-test which was exactly the same as the post-test was given before each learning session and the post-test was given after each learning session. The performances were measured by the equation,

$$P = (S / F) * 100 \ (\%)$$

where the S represents the number of the students who failed the pre-test but were successful with the post-test, and F represents the number of students who failed the pre-test.

The data obtained from these experiments were analyzed by the nonparametric U-test [7] which determines the significance of the difference between the total success scores of the two experimental groups: comparisons A with B, C with D, A with E, and C with E. In the four U-tests, a level of significance of 0.05 was used.

 i) Question group I: A compared with B, and C with D, significant differences were obtained. But, A with E, and D with E, no significant differences were obtained.

 ii) Question group II: In the four U-test results, no significant differences were obtained.

4.1.1 Effects of learning using the EDCOM

Column A in Table 4 shows the results of the learning using the EDCOM. B shows the results obtained using traditional methods such as an OHP and blackboard without the EDCOM. A significant difference was obtained between A and B (question group I). A required a 33% shorter learning time than that of B, because B needed two additional hours to achieve the same performance of machine (assembly) language programming. Some failure factors for wrong answers given by B are shown in Table 5. These results show the advantage of using the EDCOM for teaching data flow and machine (assembly) language programming in shorter time and with less misunderstanding.

Table 1. Instruction Formats

Instruc-tion	Format 7 6 5 4 3 2 1 0	Operation
(0) Load	0 0 0 0 address	Load from memory into reg.
(1) Store	0 0 0 1 address	Store reg. in memory.
(2) Add	0 0 1 0 address	Add memory to reg.
(3) And	0 0 1 1 address	Logical AND.
(4) Or	0 1 0 0 address	Logical OR.
(5) Not	0 1 0 1 0 0 0 0	Logical NOT.
(6) In	0 1 1 0 0 0 0 0	Load from input unit into reg.
(7) Out	0 1 1 1 0 0 0 0	Store register in output unit.
(8) Branch	1 0 0 0 address	Branch.
(9) If A>0 Branch	1 0 0 1 address	Branch if A>0.
(10)If A=0 Branch	1 0 1 0 address	Branch if A=0.
(11)If A<0 Branch	1 0 1 1 address	Branch if A<0.
(12)Halt	1 1 0 0 0 0 0 0	Halt.
(13)Gosub	1 1 0 1 address	Go to subprogram.
(14)Return	1 1 1 0 0 0 0 0	Return from subprogram.

Table 2. Programs of basic logic operations and the four fundamental rules of arithmetic.

Program	Operation	Amount of Memory (byte used)		
		Instruction	Data	Total
Logical OR	A | B → C	4	3	7
Logical AND	A & B → C	4	3	7
Logical NOT	A̅ → C	4	2	6
ADD	D + E → F	4	3	7
Subtract	D - E → F	6	4	10
Multiply	D * G → F	11	5	16
Divide	G / H → F	12	4	16

where, A, B and C indicate 8-bit data.
 D, E and F indicate 8-bit 2'complement.
 G and H indicate 7-bit positive integer data.
 H is in the Accumulator reg.

Manual gate control switch

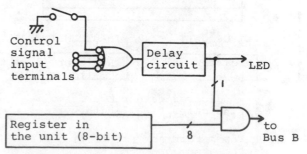

Figure 3. Logic diagram of a gate.

Table 3. Features of the subject groups.

Subject groups	A	B	C	D	E
Use of the EDCOM	used	not used	used	used	used
Teacher's computer experience	expe-rienced	expe-rienced	expe-rienced	inexpe-rienced	expe-rienced
No. of students tested	18	16	20	26	39
Year	1983	1984	1982	1983	1983
Type of school	Medical technology school		Junior high school		Undergraduate engineering
Age	20		14		20

Table 4. Learning performances.

Question group	Subject groups / Questions	A	B	C	D	E
I	1. Micro-operations of data transfer	94.4% 17/18	93.8% 15/16	88.9% 16/18	79.2% 19/24	91.0% 30/33
	2. Micro-operations of add	100.0% 18/18	81.3% 13/16	85.0% 17/20	45.8% 11/24	84.2% 32/38
	3. Micro-operations of subtract	94.4% 17/18	37.5% 6/16	65.0% 13/20	25.0% 6/24	82.1% 32/39
II	4. Machine programming of add	94.4% 17/18	100.0% 16/16	89.5% 17/19	100.0% 25/25	73.0% 27/37
	5. Machine programming of subtract	100.0% 18/18	87.5% 14/16	84.2% 16/19	88.0% 22/25	86.1% 31/36
III	6. Method of Multiply	94.4% 17/18	93.8% 15/16	100.0% 19/19	45.8% 11/24	71.8% 28/39
	7. Method of Divide	94.4% 17/18	93.8% 15/16	89.5% 17/19	37.5% 9/24	51.3% 20/39
Total sessions (hours)		4	6	4	6	4

The upper number of each block indicates P (%) and the lower indicates S / F

Table 5. Failure factors of group B

Failure factors	Question number		
	2	3	5
1. Two values were loaded into the Accumulator Reg.	25.0%	31.3%	6.3%
2. Erroneous usage of the Accumulator Reg.	18.8	6.3	0
3. Void data was loaded into the Accumulator Reg.	12.5	0	0
4. Lack of data for dyadic operation.	25.0	0	0
5. Two values were flowed on the Bus.	12.5	0	0
6. Memory access without address specification.	48.8	0	25.0
7. Erroneous selection of arithmetic circuit.	0	0	12.5
8. Erroneous method of subtraction.	-	31.3	31.3

The percentage data reflects failure factors involved in each problem.
Therefor more than one failure factor was found in some cases.

4.1.2 Effects of the teacher's experience

Column C in Table 4 shows the results of learning taught by an experienced teacher who has used computers for ten years. D shows the results of learning taught by an inexperienced teacher who has studied only a basic computer science course (2 units) at a college before this trial. The EDCOM was used for teaching both C and D. A significant difference was obtained between C and D (question group I). Even an inexperienced teacher can gain the same performances of machine (assembly) language programming (question group II) as a well experienced teacher by using the EDCOM in additional two hours (total six hours). After these sessions, the teacher of D group said that the EDCOM was useful in understanding the computer mechanism for the teacher himself.

4.1.3 Effect of grade level and types of school

Column E in Table 4 shows the performance of learning using the EDCOM on an undergraduate engineering class. As a result, no significant differences were obtained between A and E, and C and E (question groups I and II). These results show that good results can be achieved in a variety of levels and kinds of schools using the EDCOM. But, in question group III, E could not achieve as good a performance as A and C, because the undergraduate students tried to answer the too detailed descriptions with only 25 "Kana" characters.

4.2 Influence of the EDCOM on high-level language programming.

After the high-level programming (BASIC) lessons of the four fundamental rules of arithmetic and sorting, the question "Did you recall or think of the data flow represented by the EDCOM while you were programming?" was asked to the experimental group C. As a result, only 10% of the students remembered the EDCOM. On the other hand, after programming the computer controlled cargo system, 65% of the students remembered the EDCOM. Moreover, the students who had remembered the EDCOM had a better completion of the programs (See Figure 4). These experimental results show that the EDCOM is also useful for high-level language programming, especially when the process requires input/output operations between the Input/Output unit registers and the external medium.

5. CONCLUSION

Two instructional techniques were performed for effective learning:

i) The instructional strategy based on the micro-operation scheme with manually operative gates were set up to make learner understanding of the data flow and control mechanisms easier.

ii) From the view point of computer functions, the five computer units were substituted for four basic functions as memory box, calculation box, bus, and gate.

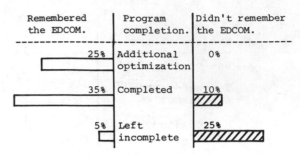

Figure 4. **Relationship** between the program **completion** and remembrance of the EDCOM.

This was realized in the EDCOM as the learner could understand the machine (assembly) language programming and high-level language programming effectively.

ACKNOWLEDGEMENTS

We wish to thank Prof. T. Baba of Utsunomiya University, S. Murata of Ministry of Education, Science and Culture, for their valuable comments and suggestions on our research.

REFERENCES

[1] Baba, N., Ishikawa, K., Murata, S. and Masubuchi, S., Computer Education at a Junior High School, Paper of technical group, ET82-6, IECE Japan (Oct. 1982).
[2] Ishikawa, K., Baba, N. Murata, S., A Model Computer for Educational Use, Paper of technical group, ET82-6, IECE Japan (Oct. 1982).
[3] Ishikawa, K., Baba, N. and Murata, S., Evaluation of Computer Science Education at a Junior High School (1), Paper of technical group, ET83-3, IECE Japan (Jul. 1983).
[4] Baba, N., Ishikawa, K. and Murata, S., Evaluation of Computer Science Education at a Junior High School (2), 7th Conf. of Japan Soci. of Science education (1983).
[5] Ishikawa, K., Inagaki, S., Baba, N. and Murata, S., Evaluation of Computer Science Education at a Junior High School (3), Bulletin of Educational Technology Center, Faculty of Education, Utsunomiya Univ. (April 1984).
[6] Baba, T., Ishikawa K. and Okuda, K., A Two-Level Microprogrammed Multiprocessor Computer with Nonnumeric Functions, IEEE Trans. Comput., Vol. C-31, No. 12 (December 1982).
[7] Freund, J. E., Modern Elementary Statistics (Prentice-Hall, 1963).
[8] Mayer, R. E., A Psychology of Learning BASIC, Commun., ACM 22 (1979).
[9] Mayer, R. E., The Psychology of How Novices Learn Computer Programming, ACM Computing Surveys, Vol. 13, No. 1 (March 1981).

COMPUTERS IN EDUCATION, K. Duncan and D. Harris (eds.)
Elsevier Science Publishers B.V. (North-Holland)
© IFIP, 1985

COMPUTER SYSTEMS FOR SMALL POST-SECONDARY INSTITUTIONS

Moderator: R. Waldo Roth, Taylor University

Panelists: Names not available at the time the session was developed

The cost of keeping up with rapidly changing technology is increasingly difficult for liberal arts and smaller community colleges. This session focuses on two issues:

1.   What can be expected from vendors in the way of support for high tech programs at these institutions?

2.   What other sources of funding exist for these schools?

This session is sponsored by ASCUE (the Association of Smaller Computer Users in Education). Panelists include representatives from major computer manufacturers spanning the spectrum from microcomputer systems through minicomputers to large mainframes.

COMPUTERS IN EDUCATION, K. Duncan and D. Harris (eds.)
Elsevier Science Publishers B.V. (North-Holland)
© IFIP, 1985

Structuring Learning Networks:

The Possibilities for Networked Software

Jo Ann Wilton
Ontario Institute for Studies in Education
252 Bloor Street West
Toronto, Ontario, Canada M5S 1V6

Increasing numbers of classroom microcomputer networks create opportunities for new computer learning environments - network environments which can vary in terms of i) the amount and nature of communications between individual members of the group, ii) the extent and independence of action allowed each student and iii) the degree of consensus or competition needed for the final task outcome. This study of learning networks involves three aspects: the hardware and system software needed to create the network, the communication patterns which describe the group task and specific examples of software which uses these strategies.

The introduction of computers to education is often justified by their ability to individualize the learning process. The frequent role of computers in the classroom to date has involved the direct and exclusive interactions of student and software. Yet research strongly suggests that students who work in groups perform better on tasks and are more committed to that task than those who work alone (Garibaldi, 1980). Educators should ensure that students do have suitable cooperative and competitive group experiences which involve group interactions - the trading of ideas, the development of attitudes and the training of interactive skills. While a wide range of classroom strategies offer these opportunities, similar experiences can be gained by balancing individual work at computers with small group, side-by-side computer-supported activities. On the other hand, the recognized importance of group dynamics justifies an investigation of the possibility of creating group experiences through the use of computer networks in the classroom. It is the latter of these two computer-supported group structures that focuses the work of this paper.

Group tasks are not automatically successful for learning and in certain circumstances some of the dangers can be avoided by computerization of the group process. In ordinary groups, students "will diffuse the responsibility for a cognitive task" (Petty et al 1980). This finding would apply equally well to settings in which a group share a task at a single computer or terminal. However, in a networked situation, each student would have to be involved, either as a 'known' participant or anonymously. The work of Hirokawa (1980) suggests that more effective decision-making groups are those in which there is considerable information exchange and where the group members agree on procedures. The environment of a computer network could be controlled to either force or merely to make available more interaction and information before decisions are made.

This brief introduction to the educational research on group behaviours is not exhaustive but serves to identify areas of concern for software designers. Tasks should not be networked just because they can be. Although he was not specifying his comments for computerized learning activities, Johnson (1981) cautions that more research is needed to show "how and when cooperation can maximize learning" and "which types of tasks are most appropriate for particular goal structures".

The study of learning networks involves three aspects: the hardware and system software needed to create the network, the communication patterns planned by the courseware writer which describe the group task and the process of the activity, and finally, the environment of each student in terms of the perception of the 'world' as presented by the computer, the uniqueness of the task and the amount and direction of information available to the individual.

This article reviews the major issues involved in establishing networks of microcomputers and then concentrates on the nature of the learning experience that can be expected from the use of local networks in the classroom environment.

Microcomputer Networks

Since so many variations on the theme are evolving, the term 'network' is becoming a generic name. At the earliest stages, computer networks involved a series of time-sharing terminals linked to a mainframe computer. The cost of computer power and the expertise needed to keep a system running made a time-sharing network ideal for business and large institutions such as universities. It was the advantage of independent computing power, the real-time response and local peripheral control which highlighted the case for stand-alone mini or microcomputer use in many settings. Now, networks of microcomputers attempt to regain the strengths of the shared capacity: access to high quality peripherals and the variety of communication paths without losing the best of what the microcomputer offers.

Microprocessor networks have taken various directions. In the university setting, where mainframe or large minicomputers already were available, networks could be devised which linked microprocessors to the larger unit. In a different setting and with a different objective, a mainframe-micro network could be structured. In this case, a classroom of microcomputers could be linked to a mainframe computer. The mainframe would become part of the network rather than the central point. Linked microprocessors would be able to access the storage capacity of the mainframe and use its computational space. The larger system's printer would also be available to the micro user. The peripherals of the microcomputer classroom would continue to be able to be accessed and communications directly from any node on the bus to any other node including micro to micro would be possible.

A network composed just of microprocessors and their peripherals has more immediate usefulness to most educational environments. In this case, the emphasis is on the communication capabilities rather than on additional power or capacity. Attempts to establish such a network have taken different approaches. In a throwback to the earliest network structures with all the power in a central location, one configuration had the microprocessor boards for all user terminals housed in the same box as the common controlling processor (Saal, 1981). The common processor was the route to all peripherals and between user nodes. Users did have the independence of their own processor, but had no independent access to peripherals or to each other.

In the most simple of microcomputer networks, disc multiplexors can be used to queue the users and avoid 'collision' of messages. No central processor is acting as an intermediary but links between users must go through disk files and, therefore, really limit the types of multi-user and inter-user activities. Nevertheless, this is as close as most educational environments are presently capable of achieving with available equipment.

The technology, both the physical structure and the necessary system software, does exist now for a more useful type of network for microcomputers. A bus, of coaxial cable, links any number of nodes so that all have equal status on the bus. Nodes may be independent microcomputers, printers or extra storage units. In one such example, Ethernet, the communications protocol, sends messages onto the bus in packets with destination and origin in a header, the message content in 256 bytes all followed by an error-detector or check-sum. The protocol uses a method called carrier-sense multiple access with collision detection for handling simultaneous entries to the bus. In this type of network, each node is independent and handles its own affairs (Mier, 1984).

An application of the Ethernet-like communication procedures is the Cluster/One/Model A network involving Apple II computers. In the configuration, network servers have been introduced to the linear-bus structure. A 'file server' would be a microcomputer

linking several storage facilities to the bus. Currently the cost of the Ethernet technology is prohibitive for most educational settings; but, the promise of a less expensive format has been made and the development of appropriate courseware would make the cost seem more acceptable.

Using a different networking standard from Ethernet, the new ICON microcomputer, produced by CEMCORP in Ontario and distributed by Burroughs essentially for the educational market, is designed specifically as a networked system. All user stations in the network (up to 32) get their operating system (QNX), languages and files from a 10 megabyte hard disk fileserver. The hardware linkages are essential; but, the communications protocol - ARCNET, a ring structure using a token passing strategy for collision prevention - is what makes learning networks possible. The IBM PC Network uses a strategy very similar to that for the ICON - a protocol selection which may favour ARCNET over Ethernet as the most common standard (Mier, 1984). The characteristics of efficiency, error-resistence and invisibility to the user are key to the usefulness of such networks by the applications-oriented educational community.

From the educator's viewpoint, the technical aspects of microcomputer networks are interesting; but, the key issues are how available are appropriate systems, what types of information flow are possible through the network and, as a result, how can the network be used to address learning objectives.

A Communications Topology

Network topology in terms of microcomputer systems has been discussed by several authors (Wallace, 1978; Dwyer, 1981, and Saal, 1981). Their work has been amalgamated here into five categories of major network structures (Figure 1).

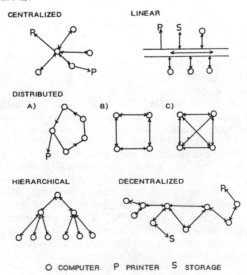

O COMPUTER   P PRINTER   S STORAGE

Figure 1: A Topology of Network Structures

The centralized pattern can represent a central computer with terminals and service nodes controlled from it, or a linking of several computers to a central monitoring node. The central node could be a computer or an independent disc drive in which case, the service devices could either exist as nodes to the central linking unit or be attached to a specific user computer and therefore not available to the rest.

A distributed network has the participating microcomputer units independent and linked among themselves rather than through or to an intermediary. In the first diagram for a distributed network, (a), the movement of information is around the circle in one direction. Each user station takes in only those packets routed to it; but, all of the network has to be 'awake' for any messages to pass. Other distributed networks have internodal linkages either as a limited bidirectional circle pattern (b) or in a more fully accessed pattern with all internodal connections possible (c).

The very flexible linear pattern allows for full linkages for all active units and more user or service nodes can be added without affecting communications through the system. If one of the nodes was designed to interpret between systems, ie. a "gateway", one network could be linked to another in spite of the number 'awake' on each system. It is this arrangement which is made possible by protocols such as Ethernet and ARCNET.

The hierarchical formation is a pattern that could carry CAI packages or distributive communications. Information moves upward or downward through the system but not laterally. The intermediate nodes in the vertical route may download a package from the top level, distribute it to the user level and then upload the results for record keeping. Alpert (1981) discusses a microcomputer network at the university level which was created by linking microcomputers to a mainframe for CAI and classroom uses.

This type of network would also be represented in the teacher-controlled classroom network used in some Ontario schools where a microcomputer sends the same program to all machines in the room. Although not involved as a learning medium, a hierarchical network also was used in a classroom to record student 'covert' reactions to the instructional process (Clark and Rogers, 1980).

A decentralized network allows a series of computers to communicate but each of these computers centers its own system of storage, printer and other service nodes in addition to one or more users. The printer of one grouping is not accessible to the users on other systems unless by means of an awkward format which would involve taking over the second computer and dedicating it to accessing its own printer for the user on the first system.

This topology represents the network linkages. Software can make some of these patterns emulate other network structures and thereby look, to the user, as if only

particular communication routes are possible. A more flexible system such as the linear pattern can be made hierarchical in function by the type of software that is loaded at the different nodes. However, software can not overcome limitations in all systems and many communication connections will be made impossible or extraordinarily convoluted.

Learning Networks

In the educational environment, what is important is the communications world that the software package builds for the student. By the initial instructions given when the program begins or by the nature of the task to be performed, software can mold that interaction between the user and the computer to be whatever type of environment is appropriate for the desired learning activities. Designers of computerized learning materials are more interested in a topology of learning networks than the hardware links, except to the extent that the latter places constraints on what can be done (Figure 2).

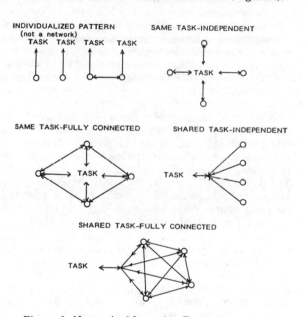

Figure 2: Networked Learning Environments

In the more traditional learning structures involving the learner and the computer, each student interacts with a task individually and exclusively. The duo of learner and computer may be networked to a common source or even the same program but the action of one learner neither affects nor is even known by other learners.

If network capabilities are present, new possibilities for learning environments are open to the teacher. In the 'individualized pattern', students may work at the same task but their actions do not influence the task for others. Communication between learners is possible; but, any change in action that results would influence the way each learner approached the individual task and no cooperation or conflict is transferred to the task. If the network is entirely in the classroom, the inter-user communications would not really qualify as a learning network - the computers may be networked but the learning is not.

If the results of the work of one student influence the nature of the task for other students, new types of learning networks are described. In 'same task-independent' designs, the students are accessing the same task. Because of the action of one, the model would not remain the same for the other users. For example, in a stock market model, each user could play the role of a stock broker. The market conditions change constantly as a result of the transactions made by the users. Many real world networks are of this nature including airline reservations and inventory control. These types of networks provide opportunities for students in a classroom environment; but, the structure does not really need other simultaneous users since they are decision-independent and the changes in the task model produced by the user could be simulated.

The learning networks become more interesting when communications between users are possible and the result of that communication influences the process of the task. The results of that interaction would affect the way in which either or both proceeded with their input to the central task.

Another set of learning networks is possible if the task is dependent on the cooperation of all users. Each has to fulfill a task before the others can proceed. In some way the work of one influences the success of the group in performing the task. The Solo/NET/ works example, N-TREK, where each user played a role in the spaceship and all systems had to work for survival, is a first in what will no doubt be many applications of this type of learning network (Dwyer, 1981; Dwyer and Critchfield, 1982).

The 'shared-independent' model illustrates the uniting of effort for the task and where users do not communicate except as they see the results of the group. Individual performance feedback may be group-wide or known only to each person. Another option would allow users either to be anonymous or be known by name to the whole group. In a final structure, users have the capability of communicating with other users perhaps to share a part of the task or just to exchange information for their separate roles.

In most cases, a learning activity would be designed for only one of these types of interaction. But, just as there might be more than one strategy employed in developing a lesson objective, the network conditions might alter the task as it unfolds. Students may be asked to respond to a challenge without group input or cooperation; and, at a later stage have the network conditions change to allow interaction of some kind between users.

In devising networked activities for a computerized classroom, educators must be aware of the type of learning they want to have happen and to structure the software to present those opportunities. Since computer communications can disguise or block out some of the human aspects of direct social contacts, teachers must be careful to set the use of these computerized group activities into an appropriate classroom environment. A debriefing session could allow student to share their experiences from the role-playing or to further discuss attitudes they developed during the task performance.

Applications for Learning Networks

Classroom networks open up many possibilities for imaginative and useful software packages. Four examples are suggested here based on the way in which the software and the student interact.

i) Self-representation

As suggested earlier, one of the reasons for selecting a learning network as the strategy may be the desire for anonymity. It is appropriate that students interact with their ideals and ideas and student-student activities is the appropriate setting (Johnson, 1981). But in many instances, the peer pressures, social structures or group dynamics can block the learning experience.

By using a computer network, the student can react to and have input to the attitudes of other students and be forced, at the same time, to formalize their own attitudes to the same stimuli. Because the computer returns to all members, unidentified, the results of the group, no personalities or group positions can add weight to any arguments or opinions. It is acknowledged that students must be able to cope with attitudinal discussions on a face-to-face basis; but, like many skills, the skill of analysis and cognitive process needed for affective group participation can be practiced in isolation from the total experience.

A preliminary attempt to translate those steps into a learning network produced the MAKE UP YOUR OWN MIND package discussed later in the report. The program was designed to offer the students a chance to independently and anonymously assess their own and the group's initial attitudes to a controversial topic. Each then has the opportunity to study information on the topic, a review paced by the individual learner. The careful interpretation of the information is encouraged by the need later to tell the group, through the computer, about their reactions to the details learned. Once again the group reactions are disseminated to all students. Before the attitudes are reassessed, all group members have the chance to make a statement for all to read. The results of a re-vote on the original stimulus is again displayed for the whole group.

In this classification, the activity may have identified differences but there was no attempt to force consensus and there was no task, as such, to be performed based on the learned material either by individual or group.

ii) Role-Playing (Shared-independence)

In this model, students have tasks to perform according to

the roles assigned them by the network. Their tasks, however, are independent - they can not share a decision or modify their responses by between-user communications. In other words, they follow the shared-independence model of the learning network topology.

Different examples of applications could depend on the importance of each group member's actions on the success of the group task. In a slightly different setting from N-TREK, the game MATSRCH also described by Dwyer, has each student computer operating a spaceship. The actions of one must be recognized and responded to by other group members - each member has the same role. The same structure used in another Solo/NET program has one half of the students acting as pilots, each with a plane to control. The other half of the group play the roles of air traffic controllers who try to land the planes using a variety of simulated display and control equipment.

The work of Dwyer and his associates uses network structures very effectively but intergroup communications remain at the level of responses to the observed performances of others. No conscious group communications are involved.

iii) Role-playing (conflict-consensus)

The rules of the simulated group task can be set to place the group members in competition. They may have a common task but have quite different personal goals in determining the way in which the task is performed.

The outline of an idea for such a group learning activity is based on the need for government sponsored improvements in an agricultural village in India. Each student is assigned the role of one member of a village committee established to spend a sum of money given by the government.

The computer can give each user different background information according to the role each is assigned plus the task data common to all. As in the full communication, shared-dependence model, users can try to influence the other members before different stages of the final vote is taken. A debriefing after the exercise would show, by computer printout, the pattern of decision-making taken by the group. Direct group communication could help to assimilate some of the attitudes developed by the role-playing.

A final example is already computerized but not networked. KOMET is an interactive management game whose objectives involve business informatics as well as management methods. Several students coordinating the running of different departments in a company would add cooperation skills as another objective (Marti and Vogel, 1981).

iv) Role-playing (Independent-diplomacy)

In this type of learning network, each user has a task to perform - perhaps to survive; but, communications between users would allow a sharing of information or

corresponding decisions. The results of the group task could be reported in terms of individual achievement or system status.

An excellent example of such a simulation is presented as S.O.S. Pollution. (Orbach, 1979) S.O.S. Pollution is a very sophisticated process emphasizing the nature and direction of communications through the system. Each player is a businessman in a small community. They buy and sell goods and are otherwise involved in the economic life of the community. All of their actions have a pollution price, a factor which is not immediately known to the players. They can share information and make joint decisions. The winner is the one with the greatest income but no one wins if the air and water pollution rise above crucial levels.

Working Examples of Networked Software

A draft form of a program, MAKE UP YOUR OWN MIND, was prepared three years ago by this author to exemplify the application of a learning network to a lesson involving attitudinal objectives. The learning network was applied to a group of five microcomputers linked to a common disc drive. Ideally, there would be a disc multiplexor system to arbitrate disc access requests but the preliminary work was set for a system where cooperation is used to manage the accessing.

A partial implementation of a previously outlined design HUMAN SETTLEMENTS (1984) represents the "share task - independent" style of software network. The program was produced as part of the Ontario Ministry of Education software development project. In the simulation part of the package, users on a network are given separate roles to play. Each is supplied with information containing both shared and unique data about the route alternatives for a highway in an urban planning decision-making task. The original network, C64s and multiplexor, prevented the obvious extension to a fully connected software network on which users could interact directly and exclusively with other roles to share information or lobby their cause.

The recent arrival of the ICON microcomputer has stimulated interest in classroom networking uses for software communications in Ontario. No doubt, other educational microcomputers will also be linked in patterns permitting this type of software development. IBM is field testing the use of a similar network for classroom use in selected schools in the province. However, current work is being focused on the ICON system where programs like HUMAN SETTLEMENTS are being translated and improved and other new simulations are being implemented.

The ICON network allows direct communications between a student station and any node on the system or among a number of student stations. The latter instance is the more interesting because it makes it possible for several students to be linked by a program in such a way that they have a common action space where the task is presented. As a result of the sharing structure, the moves of one student appear immediately in the action space of all others. Synchronous messaging either between specific students or to everyone in the group can parallel the activity related to the action spaces.

For use as an experimental tool as well as a classroom activity, an existing strategy game involving a spatial analysis problem, frequently known as Blackbox, was restructured to be played by up to four players linked on an ICON network. The resulting program, NET/PROBES, has both a shared game board (completely interactive through use of a trackball) and two message pads on the screen at each terminal - one message pad for sending and one for receiving comments from team mates. Since each student has control of a subset of the information and the controls needed for problem solving, plus the capability for open messaging, NET/PROBES fits into the shared task - fully connected model of the learning networks typology.

A series of questions related to the nature of the user behaviour in networked problem solving and the educational potential of such activity has prompted a field study using NET/PROBES as the experimental task. Somewhat similar investigations have been conducted with respect to computer conferencing and the group communications involved in those interactions (Kiesler et al, 1984). However, the current work being done by the author places the issues in an educational setting and combines two dimensions of synchronous communication - the shared action space and messaging.

Five areas of observation form the focus of the study: the role of each participant on the network in terms of the task performance, the level of participation as compared to the level in side-by-side tasks, the type and amount of communication by messaging, the way in which the shared action space becomes part of the communications system which the group develops and the way in which the group structures itself to solve the problem. It is anticipated that the results of this study will be reported at the conference in August, 1985.

Beyond this initial investigation, further thoughtful research should go into the best designs for the type of learning activities such networks should support. The most important factor is the characteristics of the environment that the computer creates for each user. The nature and extent of learning offered will depend on the students' perception of the 'information space' within which they are operating. A good part of that experience is determined by the structure of the task and the routes of communication built into the model.

REFERENCES

Alpert, E. "Moving Instructional Computing from a Mainframe to a Shared Storage Microcomputer System". Computers in Education, Proceedings of the IFIP TC-3 3rd World Conference on Computers in Education, Lausanne, Switzerland. Lewis, R and Tagg, D. (eds.), North-Holland, 1981, p.397-401.

Clark, D.C. and Rogers, D.H. "The Study of Student Covert Behaviors with the Aid of Microcomputers". Educational Technology, November, 1981, p.46-49.

Dwyer, T.A. "Multi-Micro Learning Environments: A Preliminary Report on the Solo/NET/works Project". BYTE, January, 1981, p.204-216.

Dwyer, T.A. and Critchfield,M. "Multi-computer Systems for the Support of Inventive Learning". Computers and Education, Vol. 6, 1982, P.7-12.

Garibaldi, A.M. "Affective Contributions of Cooperative and Group Goal Structures". Journal of Educational Psychology, Vol. 71 (6), 1979, p.788-794.

Johnson, D.W. "Student-Student Interaction: The Neglected Variable in Education". Educational Researcher, Vol. 10 (1), 1981, p.5-10.

Hirokawa, R.Y. "A Comparative Analysis of Communication Patterns Within Effective and Ineffective Decision-Making Groups". Communication Monographs, Vol. 47, 1980, p.81-91.

Kiesler, S., Siegel, J. and McGuire, T.W. "Social Psychological Aspects of Computer-Mediated Communication". American Psychologist, Vol 39(10), 1984, P.1123-1134.

Marti, H. and Vogel, J.S. "The Value of A Top Management Game in the Education of Production Engineers". Computers in Education, Proceedings of the IFIP TC-3 3rd World Conference on Computers in Education, Lausanne, Switzerland. Lewis, R. and Tagg, D. (eds.), 1981, p.115-121.

Mier, E.E. "The Evolution of a Standard Ethernet". BYTE, December, 1984, p. 131-142.

Orbach, E. "Instrumental Simulation Games as Systems of Communication". Journal of Educational Technology Systems, Vol. 8 (1), 1979-80, p.67-93.

Petty, R.E., Harkins, S.G. and Williams, K.D. "The Effects of Group Diffusion of Cognitive Effort on Attitudes: An Information-Processing View". Journal of Personality and Social Psychology, Vol. 38 (1), 1980, p.81-92.

Saal, H.J. "Local-Area Networks: Possibilities for Personal Computers". BYTE, October, 1981, p.92-112

The work described in this paper was conducted at O.I.S.E., but the author's business address is: Coordinator of Computer Education, Peel Board of Education, 73 King St. W., Mississauga, Ontario, Canada L5H 1B5

COMPUTERS IN EDUCATION, K. Duncan and D. Harris (eds.)
Elsevier Science Publishers B.V. (North-Holland)
© IFIP, 1985

ALABAMA EDUCATIONAL COMPUTING
RESEARCH AND DEVELOPMENT NETWORK

James D. Burney, PhD

School of Education
University of North Alabama
Florence, AL 35632-0001

Bernard J. Schroer, PhD
William Teoh, PhD

Johnson Environmental and Energy Center
University of Alabama in Huntsville
Huntsville, AL 35899

ABSTRACT

This report details the formation and implementation to date of the Alabama Educational Cooperating Research and Development Network between the University of Alabama in Huntsville and the University of North Alabama. Included in the report are the philosophy of the project, project history and organization, development of the CAI software, and programs to date.

INTRODUCTION

In June 1984 the Alabama Legislature appropriated funds to the University of Alabama in Huntsville (UAH) and the University of North Alabama (UNA) for the purpose of developing the Alabama Educational Computing Research and Development Network. The philosophy of this network is predicated on the idea that individual study using CAI techniques is an effective way to remediate specific deficits in academic performance. Furthermore, it is postulated that the most effective way to provide the appropriate software is by custom designing each CAI program to meet specific objectives, rather than trying to match objectives with previously written programs available in the marketplace.

HISTORY OF THE PROJECT

The Alabama State Department of Education has identified a set of 232 competencies[1] essential for all students to master prior to graduation. Any competency not successfully met in testing must be remediated through additional instruction. Specifically, the state competency testing program requires children in the third, sixth, and ninth grades to pass a set of competencies. If a child fails to pass the ninth grade competencies, he cannot receive a high school diploma upon completion of the twelfth grade. Teachers are required by law to provide remedial instruction for competencies not passed and to document all remedial instruction activities.

This project has taken these State Department of Education competencies as instructional objectives. Individual CAI packages are being developed for each of the 232 objectives, covering math, language arts, and reading. This approach is unusual in that prior efforts to integrate CAI into remedial instructional programming have attempted to identify commercially available or public domain software to meet the various objectives. By developing software specifically designed to meet already stated objectives, a more parsimonious solution to the effective implementation of CAI is possible. A secondary benefit from this approach is to insure consistency in program format and response methods so that children have less difficulty adapting to the idiosyncrasies of the programs.

The second area of uniqueness in this project is that it is being implemented through the partnership of two universities, a state department of education, and various public school systems. The Alabama State Department of Education has contributed the competency objectives and continuing consultative support; the University of North Alabama is providing expertise in educational curriculum development and remedial programming; the University of Alabama in Huntsville is providing technical, engineering, and programming expertise in converting program protocols into finished code and developing the communications software and interfaces for the statewide network. And last, but of great importance, three local school systems are currently working with the project in field testing the programs and in using the communications network.

OBJECTIVE

The objectives of this project have led to the formation of a consortium between two universities working with others to impact upon the problem of poor academic performance in the public schools through the application of modern technology. This project is concerned both with the development of effective CAI software and with the development of a state-wide delivery system for the dissemination of the software. This delivery system consists of informing school systems of the availability of the materials, training teachers to use the programs, establishment of an on-line storage system for software that can be accessed by schools across the state, and provision of programs on disk for schools not desiring to download them directly.

ORGANIZATION

The Alabama Educational Computing Research and Development Network functions under the consultative leadership of the State Department of Education with each university contributing faculty and resources to the project under a consortium agreement. Each university has appointed a project director who works with the other principals on a cooperative basis to achieve the objectives set forth in the consortium agreement. This arrangement is unique in the State of Alabama where interuniversity competition is the rule and cooperative endeavors are seldom encountered.

The makeup of the partners in the consortium is of interest because of their diversity. The University of North Alabama School of Education is the more prosaic in that its mission is education. The importance of microcomputers in education was realized early at UNA. One of the first educational computing laboratories in the state was established there in 1982. Since then all education majors are required to complete a course in educational computing prior to graduation. Also of benefit to the project was the educational technology orientation and expertise of the UNA participants inthe areas of concept and task analysis as they apply to remedial education.

The University of Alabama in Huntsville Johnson Environmental and Energy Center is the other participant. Extensive educational programming has been done here in the past through the development of an energy education software series for the Alabama Department of Energy. This experience, coupled with a large pool of manpower having high technical and programming capabilities and an interest in education, equipped them to provide a unique contribution to the project through both software and hardware development.

NETWORK HARDWARE/SOFTWARE

A systems overview of the hardware and the communication interfaces of the network is given in Figure 1. This hardware supports the Network Laboratory at UAH, the Development Laboratory at UAH, and the remote terminal accesses. In the second year of the project a duplicate network laboratory will be installed at UNA to serve the northwest region of the State with the UAH laboratory serving the northeast region. Also during the second year additional remote terminal accesses will be added to the project.

The hardware for the Network Laboratory consists of:

° Server - IBM PC with 256K, DS/DD disk drive, Zenith monitor, and Epson MX 80 printer

° Nodes - IBM PC with 128K and DS/DD disk drive (two)

° On-line storage - Iomega dual 10 MB disk drive with removable disk cartridges

° Modems - UDS 212 A 300/1200 baud autoanswering (two)

° 3COM Etherlink/IBM PC interface boards for DOS 2.0 (three).

The hardware at the three pilot schools consists of:

° Terminal - Apple IIe starter system with serial interface card

° Modem - UDS 212A 1200 baud.

In addition to the pilot schools, remote access to the UAH laboratory will be installed in the UNA computer laboratory, the UNA Kilby training school, and the Alabama Department of Education.

The system software supporting the Network Laboratory at UAH consists of:

° IBM DOS 2.0 disk operating system

° 3COM Ethershare IBM PC server software

° Terminal communications software

° Bulletin board software.

The 3COM Ethershare software permits multiple users to share the hard disk on the IBM PC network server. The shared hard disk then operates identically to diskettes or local hard disks. Network security is maintained to

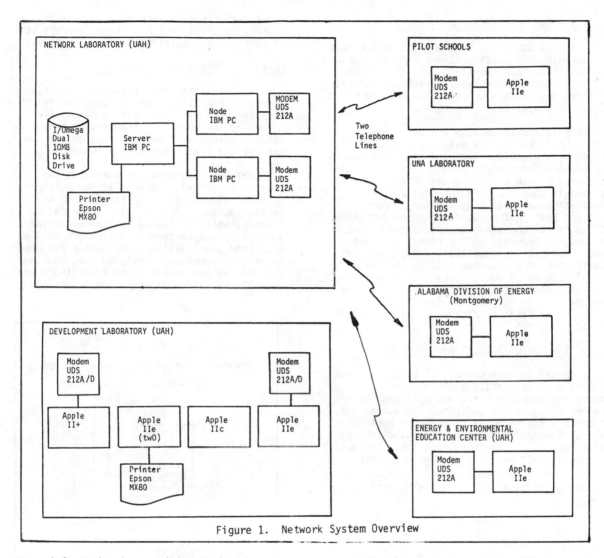

Figure 1. Network System Overview

protect information by requiring passwords before users have access to the shared disk. To access other data requires additional passwords, therefore providing control for all programs and data. Through the software no user can access information or change data that they have not been authorized to use.

The terminal communications software was written by UAH rather than purchased commercially available software. This approach allowed multiple copies of the software to be readily distributed to any school wanting to access the network. In addition, the effort to write this software was relatively minimal.

The bulletin board software was also written by UAH using several public domain packages as a basis. Unique features of the bulletin board are download capability of CAI modules and communication with other schools, universities, and agencies of the network.

CAI SOFTWARE DEVELOPMENT

The following phases were defined in the development of the remediation CAI software:

Phase I   - Specification definition/review
Phase II   - Software development
Phase III - Software verification/validation
Phase IV   - Field testing.

These phases are being closely followed to assure content accuracy and consistency and software reliability and quality, and to minimize interface problems since multiple institutions and agencies are involved in the project.

Phase I - Specifications Definition/Review

The UNA School of Education is responsible for defining the specifications for the remediation software. The staff consists of curriculum development specialists with the majority of these specialists graduate students in the School of Education.

Module specifications are being written for each of the State's basic competencies listed in the Minimum Standard and Competencies for Alabama Schools[1]. Table I lists these competencies by subject and grade level. A typical module specification includes pretest, remediation and post test sections. Each pretest and post test consists of three questions. If any two of the three questions are missed the program branches to the remediation section. The module specification includes the details for each computer display including the actual text which would appear on the monitor. A general description of the graphics for the program is also included in the package. A typical specification package consists of 30-50 and 50-60 screen.

Phase II - Software Development

The UAH Johnson Center is responsible for writing the remediation software. Undergraduate engineering students have been trained to write the software. To assist the students a programmer's guide and program disk have been prepared containing machine language utilities, character fonts, and basic subroutines. Also included on the program disk is a sample remediation program which illustrates the use of these aids in writing an application program.

In addition, a variety of commercially purchased software and peripherals are available to expedite the software development. Some of the more frequently used items are:

° Apple Mechanic, Typefaces for Apple Mechanic, Alpha Plot, Utility City, and Double Take from Beagle Brothers Microsoftware Systems.

° The Complete Graphics System II, the Graphic Magician and Special Effects from Penguin Software.

Phase III - Software Verification/Validation

The verification and validation of the software is performed by both universities. The lead programmer at UAH weekly checks the progress of each module by running the program and comparing the displays with the program specifications in Phase I. Also, each module is loaded onto the network for UNA to download and perform a similar verification procedure.

The finished modules are also sent to the Alabama Department of Education, where a team of curriculum specialists review the modules.

Phase IV - Field Testing

The field testing of each module is performed by UNA using their Kilby training school and the three pilot schools in Huntsville, Florence, and Cullman. Teachers at these schools have been trained by the consortium in the use and evaluation of the software.

During the summers for the first two years, classes will be held at the University of North Alabama to train teachers in the use of the system. Additionally, technical training will be offered to persons in the various school systems so that there will be qualified staff available to handle the more technical aspects of participation, such as downloading and reproduction of software and modem installation and maintenance.

Table I.

MINIMUM STANDARDS COMPETENCIES FOR ALABAMA SCHOOLS

- Software Modules -

Reading			
	Grade Level		
Standard	3rd	6th	9th	Total
I	8	5	2	15
II	9	12	1	22
III	5	5	2	12
IV	--	--	14	14
V	--	--	1	1
VI	--	--	1	1
Total	22	22	21	65

Language			
	Grade Level		
Standard	3rd	6th	9th	Total
I	5	5	3	13
II	1	2	3	6
III	1	1	1	3
IV	1	1	3	5
V	2	1	2	5
VI	2	2	1	5
VII	1	1	1	3
Viii	1	2	6	9
IX	1	4	1	6
X	5	3	1	9
XI	2	1	--	3
XII	1	1	--	2
XIII	1	--	--	1
Total	24	24	22	70

Mathematics			
	Grade Level		
Standard	3rd	6th	9th	Total
I	4	8	9	21
II	5	7	7	19
III	1	3	4	8
IV	3	7	7	17
V	1	3	3	7
VI	4	6	15	25
Total	18	45	45	97

PROGRESS

During the summer of 1984, three demonstration CAI modules were completed and circulated within the educational community for comment. The feedback received and experience gained in preparing these programs were invaluable in setting the pattern for the programs to follow. The three demonstration modules were:

- Math Standard: I
  Competency: 1
  Level: 3rd grade
  Associate numbers from 0-100 with numerals and word names.

- Math Standard: II
  Competency: 2
  Level: 3rd grade
  Read thermometer to nearest degree on Celsius and Fahrenheit scales.

- Math Standard: III
  Competency: 1
  Level: 6th grade
  Read and interpret bar, circle, and line graphs.

Figure 2 contains the teacher guide for the second module. Figure 3 outlines the structure of the software for the module. Figure 4 outlines the program logic for the module.

CONCLUSIONS

At this time the following progress has been made and conclusions can be drawn:

- The formal agreements have been concluded between UAH and UNA and the State Department of Education.

- The joining of a School of Education and a technical research center each at different universities has received praise from state officials. More importantly such an arrangement is working in the interest of both universities.

- The Network and Development Laboratories at UAH are operational and on-line.

- Three CAI modules have been completed, peer reviewed and received favorable comments.

- Initial response indicates that individual study using CAI is an effective way to remediate specific academic deficits.

- Considerable interest has evolved in custom designing each CAI module to meet specific objectives rather than trying to match objectives with commercially available software.

- Undergraduate engineering students with programming experience are ideal for writing the CAI software, especially when provided a well defined specification.

- Some of the reviewers of the software have indicated that software is ideally suited for initial learning experiences and for student enrichment.

REFERENCES

[1] Teague, Wayne, Minimum Standards and Competencies (Reading, Language, and Mathematics for Alabama Schools (Alabama State Department of Education, 1979).

MATH STANDARD II. COMPETENCY 2.

Read thermometer to nearest degree on Celsius and Fahrengeit scales.

Objective: This program is designed to teach the basic skills necessary to read temperatures on liquid thermometers using both Celsius and Fahrenheit scales.

Structure: Because of the remedial nature of this program, all basic skills making up the ability to read liquid thermometers are included. The program is divided into four sections: 1) identifying thermometers, 2) characteristics of Celsius and Fahrenheit thermometers, 3) reading temperatures at freezing and boiling, and 4) reading temperatures at any point on both types of thermometers.

Each section is preceded by a pretest. If the child correctly completes the pretest, that section is skipped and the pretest of the next section is presented. If the pretest is not successfully completed, the child is moved into a tutorial section covering the skills for that section. At completion of the tutorial, a posttest is presented. If the child does not complete the posttest correctly, the program recycles through that tutorial. If the posttest is correctly completed, the child goes to the pretest for the next section. The program logic is shown in the attached chart.

Design: The overall objective of the program was task analyzed to identify scope and sequence. Within each sub-objective a concept analysis was conducted to identify critical attributes. A mastery-learning approach is incorporated requiring successful completion of each sub-objective before the next may be attempted, preventing the possible omission of critical concepts. Each pretest and posttest is designed so that the child must correctly answer at least 2/3 of the questions to go to the next section.

Using the program: The program is designed to run on an Apple II+ or IIe computer with 64K memory and a single disk drive. A color monitor is recommended but not necessary. Insert the disk in the drive, turn on the computer and monitor, and follow prompts as they appear on the screen. Reading level of text has been controlled as much as possible in light of the subject matter being presented. Children should be instructed before beginning the program to always read all the text on a frame before responding, and to always press the SPACE BAR to go to the next frame. Several frames of credits will appear when the program is first run. If the computer is not turned off, and a second child is to use the same program, these credit frames will be skipped the second and following times through the program. We suggest that before you begin to use the program with children, you go through the entire program to familiarize yourself with it. To do this you must intentionally miss the items on each pretest to enter the intervention sections. There are no identifiers to mark items as pretest, posttest, or tutorial, but you will have no trouble recognizing these parts.

In case of problems: Every effort has been make to make this program as problem-free as possible. If, however, you should have a problem or wish to make suggestions about improving the program, please contact Dr. James Burney, School of Education, University of North Alabama, Florence, Alabama, 35632-0001. You may call (205) 766-4100, Ext. 229 for immediate assistance in case of emergencies.

Figure 2. Typical Teacher Guide

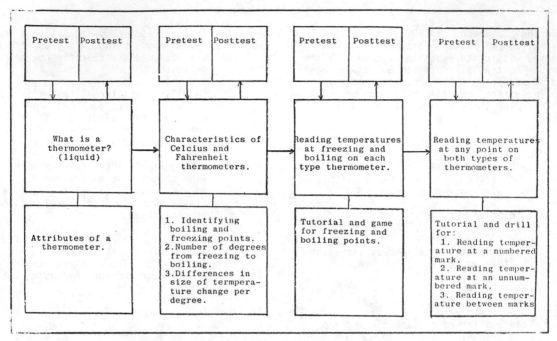

Figure 3.   Typical Module Structure

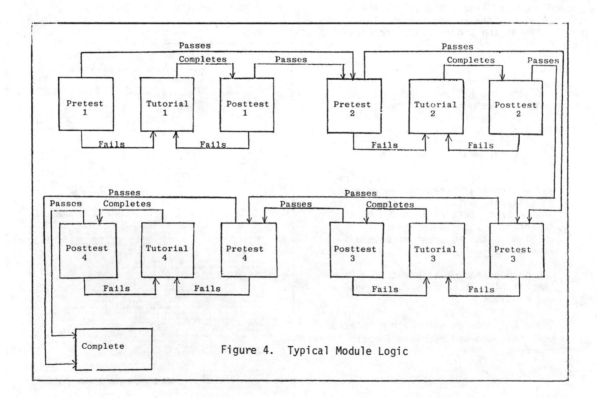

Figure 4.   Typical Module Logic

COMPUTERS IN EDUCATION, K. Duncan and D. Harris (eds.)
Elsevier Science Publishers B.V. (North-Holland)
© IFIP, 1985

ELECTRONIC CONFERENCING AND FACULTY/STUDENT CONTACT TIME

Estelle Brown and Jane Sullivan

Glassboro State College
Glassboro, New Jersey 08028
United States

This study investigated whether electronic conferencing would provide the needed
instructional support system for students involved in a field experience. Results
indicate that given the opportunity, students in higher education would find
electronic mail systems a convenient and not too complicated means of contacting
instructors. While they do not all see it as the primary means of contact with
instructors, they do view it as a viable supplement.

1. INTRODUCTION

The United States is in the process of shifting
from a labor- to an information-intensive
society. To make the shift, students must
learn to use computers to access and analyze
vast amounts of information. One area of
expertise expected of college graduates will
involve practical management of information.

Computer conferencing, which involves the integration of computing and information technologies in business environments, has proven to be
an effective approach to information management
for it augments the effectiveness of professionals in processing, retrieving and communicating information. Electronic conferencing,
messaging and data management has already been
used effectively on the college campus. The
University of Calgary, Canada, for example,
maintains a 24-hour Multics system that
accommodates 120 simultaneous users. Their
system was so heavily used, day and night, that
a "rationing scheme" needed to be devised to
accommodate the demand. Students use the computer to access course information as well as to
perform class assignments.(1) At The New
Jersey Institute of Technology, an electronic
conferencing system (EIES) linked twelve small
colleges, located throughout the United States,
to a computer network that enabled them to
communicate with each other as well as with an
instructor who delivered lectures electronically
to all the connected campuses.(2)

Electronic conferencing can function differently
in different settings; yet there are certain
components common to all systems. Conferees use
computer terminals linked together to form a
computer-communications network. Programs and
data bases enable users to pass information to
each other as well as to access the available
data bases. Thus a user is able to send a
query to a group of users. The memo is stored
in a "Bulletin Board" data base accessed and
responded to by appropriate users. A user can
then return to the computer at a convenient
time and call up the answer to the memo sent

earlier. Messages can be as brief as one word
or as lengthy as an hour lecture, depending upon
the protocols of the system.

2. STATEMENT OF THE PROBLEM

There is a particular place in the Teacher
Education curriculum where electronic conferencing is especially applicable. Pre-service
teachers, faced with a class assignment such
as tutoring, feel a particular need for
immediate feedback from their instructors.
Questions arise--What skill should I teach next?
Where can I find material for practice in this
skill? Why did my lesson fail?--that demand
an "ASAP" answer. The conference between
student and instructor is critical to the
success of the tutoring experience. Yet,
instructors who teach the field experience
must be supervising at the school-tutoring
sites much of the time during the day and so
are not available for office conferences. As a
result, while the need for faculty/student
contact increases, the possibility of it
decreases.

This project was designed to investigate
whether electronic conferencing, with its
interactive and storage capabilities can provide the needed instructional support system
to students involved in a field experience.

3. PROCEDURE

3.1 Population

Students from four sections of reading methods
courses were selected as subjects for this
study, two sections of the course "Advanced
Teaching of Reading" (ATR) for elementary
education majors, and two for the course
required of special education majors, "Reading
for the Handicapped" (RFH). One section of
each course was randomly selected as the
experimental group. The other two sections
served as the control group. The experimental
group contained 43 subjects while the control
group contained 34.

3.2 Testing Instruments

There were two instruments used as comparison measures for this project.

3.21 Cagney Reading Methods Test

A 33-item multiple choice test, developed by Cagney,(3) was used to assess the subjects' knowledge about methods for teaching reading. The Reading Methods Test was administered as a posttest during the last week of class.

In the test, ten classroom situations are described and respondents are required to make decisions about testing, grouping and instructing students under given conditions.

3.22 Electronic Mail Survey

The researchers developed a six-item Likert-type scale to assess subjects' attitudes toward the use of electronic mail for requesting information about tutoring pupils in reading. The items in the survey examined attitudes on the use of such a system for communicating with the instructor. The survey was administered to both groups before and after the study was conducted. The intent was to observe changes in subjects' perceptions of the complexity as well as the productivity of electronic conferences. Responses to items on the attitude survey were assigned weights of 0-4, with 0 indicating "strongly agree" and 4 representing "strongly disagree." A list of the survey items can be found in Figure 1.

1. Learning to use the computer to exchange messages about methods and materials for tutoring is too complex.

2. Assessing information about methods and materials for tutoring from the computer makes one more independent than obtaining the information from the professor.

3. In-person conferences pertaining to methods and materials for tutoring are more productive than conferencing through an electronic mail system.

4. The electronic mail system simplifies the process of obtaining information about tutoring.

5. Using an electronic mail system to obtain information about methods and materials for tutoring is too impersonal.

6. The electronic mail system should be used only in addition to in-person conferencing.

Figure 1:   Items included in the electronic mail survey

3.3 Electronic Mail System

The electronic mail system that was used for the study was "Yalectronic Mail." Yalectronic Mail is available to subscribers of Bitnet, which links computers at Yale with those of other Universities by means of high speed telecommunications. NJECN, the computer system servicing the nine state colleges of New Jersey, is a subscriber to Bitnet. With Bitnet and facilities on VM/CMS, users are able to exchange messages, memos and files with any user or group of users on the network.

By creating "Standard Nickname" files, the investigators were able to send memos to individual students by name, to each of the classes as a whole and/or to each other.

The system allowed users who received memos to send a response to that memo immediately. There were also provisions for saving copies of memos that were sent as well as transmitting copies of the memo to other users. Whole documents, created off line, could be loaded as files and shipped to other users. The length of the text sent was only restricted to the amount of space on the diskette allocated to the particular user ID.

Rather than a full screen editor, users were required to access a line editor, a system that made correcting text errors rather cumbersome.

3.4 Method

The survey instrument was administered to both groups at the start of the project. Results indicated that there were no significant differences between the groups on any of the items with respect to their attitudes toward the use of the computer.

The experimental group was then taught how to use Yalectronic Mail. Subjects needed to learn how to sign on to the system, how to access Yalectronic, how to send and receive memos, and how to use the line editor. Three 65-minute class periods were used for these instructions.

In place of the three periods devoted to electronic mail instruction, control group subjects listened to lectures on topics about microcomputers included in the course syllabi.

Once the experimental group subjects had mastered Yalectronic Mail, they were expected to use it regularly. They had access to fourteen terminals located in three different areas on the college campus. These terminals were available six days a week, from 8:30 a.m. until 9:30 p.m. Seven terminals were Decwriters, which printed hard copies of the memos and seven were Hazeltines, terminals that delivered messages via video screens. All terminals were connected directly to the NJECN system.

The experimental subjects were also taught how to use a data base of tutoring materials stored on Profile III+, a file management system available for Radio Shack Model III micro-computer. There were six of these micro-computers available for subjects' use.

Subjects were instructed to check their "mailboxes" at least once every forty-eight hours, thus insuring that they would have at least one contact with the instructor before each tutoring session.

The instructors read their messages and responded to them daily. In these responses they answered questions, directed students to the data base for additional information, gave specific instructions and made comments on the progress of the tutoring. Instructors also posted general announcements to students when necessary.

Each of the control groups was instructed to follow the usual procedures for seeking guidance in tutoring. They were told to sign up for appointments with the instructor at which time they could discuss the specific problems they had encountered in their tutoring. It was during these in-person conferences that the subjects of the control groups were given the same kind of individual instruction that experimental subjects were receiving through the electronic mail system.

The four classes that made up both the experi-mental and control groups met once a week for a 65-minute period. During these class meetings instruction following the general syllabus for each course was conducted, with the exception of the three class sessions used for instruction in computers vs the electronic mail system as described above.

All subjects, both experimental and control, were required to submit detailed lesson plans for tutoring. Each plan was graded, with written comments on the content of the lesson included regularly.

At the end of ten weeks, a posttest was adminis-tered to both groups. Subjects were asked to respond to the same survey form used for the pretest. In addition, all subjects took the Cagney Reading Test described above.

4. ANALYSIS OF DATA

The effectiveness of the electronic conferencing system was assessed by comparing the experi-mental and control classes on selected dependent variables.

4.1 An analysis of variance was performed on the Cagney Reading Test scores. The results of this analysis, presented in table 1, revealed no significant differences between the experimental and control groups.

Table 1. Summary of Analysis of Variance of Cagney Reading Test

Source	Mean Square	F
Class	8.401	0.573
Treatment	8.068	0.551
Class X Trtmnt	7.159	0.489

There was one degree of freedom for each F Test.

4.2 Student affective responses to the elec-tronic conferencing system were compared for significant differences by using a three-way analysis of variance. A summary of the analysis of variance is presented in table 2.

Item 1 of the survey asked subjects to consider how complex learning to use the electronic mail system would be. Differences between the experimental and control groups were signifi-cant (p .05) with the control group considering the task more complex than the experimental group.

In Item 2, subjects were asked if receiving information via the computer rather than directly from the professor would make them more independent. There were no significant differences between the groups with respect to the responses on this item.

In Item 3, subjects were to contrast electronic conferences with in-person conferences. There were no significant differences between the responses of the two groups. Means of both groups indicated that they found the in-person conferences more productive.

Item 4 asked subjects whether they agreed that an electronic mail system simplifies the process of obtaining information. F-test values indicated that there was a significant treatment by class interaction (p .01) for this item. To identify the variable responsible for the interaction, post hoc one-tailed t-tests were performed. Results of these tests indicated that differences between the experi-mental and control RFH groups were significant (p .05). Differences between ATR and RFH classes were also significant (p .05). There was also a class by pre-posttest interaction. The authors attribute this to differences between group means in the pretest survey.

Item 5 asked subjects to indicate whether use of electronic mail was too impersonal. Differences between the treatment groups were significant (p .001) with the experimental group disagreeing with this item to a greater degree.

In Item 6, subjects indicated whether electronic

Table 2.   Summary of Analysis of Variance
of Electronic Mail Survey

Items	1	2	3	4	5	6
Source	F	F	F	F	F	F
Trtmnt	4.00*	1.35	1.83	0.28	12.8***	1.15
Class	0.92	0.00	0.31	0.27	1.46	6.69*
Pre/Pst Tst	3.02	2.33	0.27	3.07	2.79	0.00
Trtmnt by Class	0.14	1.14	1.64	8.23**	0.83	1.54
Trtmnt by Pre/Pst	2.53	0.82	0.74	4.66*	0.33	2.13
Clss by Pre/Pst	0.16	2.14	0.22	0.01	0.12	0.12
Trtmnt X Class X Pre/Pst	0.06	0.01	1.74	0.26	0.81	0.33

*p .05
**p .01
***p .001
All analyses were done with a three-way ANOVA.   There was one
degree of freedom for each F Test.

mail should be used only in addition to
in-person conferencing. Classes (ATR vs RFH)
differed significantly (p .05) in their
response to this item with ATR subjects agreeing
to a greater degree than RFH subjects.

5.   INTERPRETATION AND DISCUSSION

The analysis of the Cagney Reading Test results
revealed no significant differences between the
two groups. The mean test scores indicated
that subjects from both groups were able to
make judgments regarding reading instruction
adequately. It would appear that the electronic mail system did not increase the
decision-making ability of the experimental
group. However, neither did it lessen that
group's knowledge of reading techniques.

The question in Item 1 of the survey attempted
to measure attitudes of students toward the
additional task of learning to use the computer
as a means of requesting and receiving essential
information about tutoring. Results of the
ANOVA would indicate that the experimental
group did not consider the system too burden-
some to learn. Findings from the Cagney
Reading Test, indicating, as they did, that the
mastery of course content and the acquisition
of tutoring skills were not diminished by class
time that was taken to train experimental
subjects in the use of the electronic conferencing system, would appear to support this
finding.

Results of the analysis of Item 2 responses
suggest that neither group perceived the method
as contributing to a sense of independence.
These results, again supported by the results

of the Cagney Reading Test, can be interpreted
in several ways. It may be that using an
electronic mail system does not foster independent learning. Students commented that they
felt less bound by time constraints when they
could go to the computer and pick up their
messages. They also appreciated having a hard
copy of suggestions from the instructor. They
felt that the memo served as an accurate
reference when they were planning their next
day's instruction. On the other hand, the
tutoring experience itself requires decision-
making on the part of the student. Seen in
this light, any effect electronic mail might
have had on developing independent thinking may
have been overshadowed by the effect the
overall experience had on it. Future research
is needed to clarify this finding.

Subjects' attitudes toward the efficiency of an
electronic mail system were measured by Item 3.
They were asked to determine if the conferencing system would produce the quality and
quantity of information that could be obtained
in an in-person contact with the instructor.
That is, could they learn as much about
teaching reading and solving tutoring problems
through instructor memos as they could through
in-person conferences? Both groups agreed that
in-person conferences were more productive.

Results of the analysis of Item 4 responses
indicate that at the end of the study RFH
subjects found electronic mail to be a more
convenient means of requesting and receiving
assistance than did ATR subjects. This difference may be the result of one or more factors.
Classes were taught by different instructors.
Teacher differences may also have been a

contributing factor to the difference in attitude. The groups themselves differed in their
goals. One group intended to work with regular
class children while the other group were being
trained to work with special children. This
difference in career goals as well may have
contributed to the differences in the way the
two classes responded to this item.

Persons inexperienced in computers tend to feel
that computers decrease the number of human
contacts; therefore, personal interaction may
be seriously reduced. The investigators
attempted to measure the extent to which this
feeling existed among subjects in the experiment through Item 5. The significant differences between the responses of the two groups
would indicate that the students who used the
electronic mail did not judge it to be too
impersonal.

The researchers assessed student attitudes
toward the electronic conferencing system as:
1) the sole means of student/instructor
consultation, 2) as part of a dual access
system involving computer conferencing and
in-person contact with the instructor. When
the results were analyzed, significant differences were noted between the two classes.
Elementary education majors felt more strongly
that electronic mail should be used only in
addition to in-person conferencing. These
results, considered along with those of Item 3,
where subjects found in-person conferences more
productive, would suggest that, at least with
some students, electronic mail should take the
direction of a supplementary, rather than a
primary, means of instructor-student contact.

In summary, this study investigated whether
electronic conferencing would provide the
needed instructional support system for students involved in a field experience. Results
indicate that given the opportunity, students
in higher education would find electronic mail
systems a convenient and not too complicated
means of contacting instructors. While they do
not all see it as the primary means of contact
with instructors, they do view it as a viable
supplement.

While the question of protection of privacy,
a concern that many technologists share with
respect to networking, was not addressed by
this particular study, it should certainly be
considered if the technique is to be extended
to material that is of a confidential nature.

REFERENCES

(1) Computer power at Calgary, T.H.E. Journal,
     January (1982) 40.

(2) Savin, William, NJIT-EIES: Building net-
     works, paper presented at the Conference
     on Computeracy: Computing Education in
     New Jersey, k-12 (April, 1983).

(3) Cagney, Margaret. Cagney Reading
     Methods Test, Department of Reading/
     Speech Correction, Glassboro State
     College (1982).

COMPUTERS IN EDUCATION, K. Duncan and D. Harris (eds.)
Elsevier Science Publishers B.V. (North-Holland)
© IFIP, 1985

Face Robot for Pacemaking in Classroom Work

Keizo Nagaoka [*]   Issei Shiohara [**]

[*] Faculty of Education, Kobe   [**] Shiohara Girls' Senior
University, Kobe, Japan   High School, Kobe, Japan

Mailing Address: Faculty of Education, Kobe University
3-11 Tsurukabuto, Nada-ku, Kobe 657, Japan

The purpose of the Face Robot system is the pacemaking of classroom work. The principle of the system consists of pacemaking theory with analysis of the response curve (the learners' time required to do an exercise) and dynamic representation of the face method. The face method has been adopted as a man-machine interface between the microcomputer and the teacher. Practical trials of the system were performed in a high school. Some results are obtained, e.g.: Enabling the teacher to know obviously the learning condition of the learners, thereby not wasting time on finished learners, or not cutting the time short for unfinished learners, etc. The Face Robot is not a commander to the teacher, but an aid offering the information for pacemaking.

1. Introduction

This paper reports on the Face Robot system that one of the authors has developed, the purpose of which is the pacemaking of classroom work. Although the majority of computer applications in education aim at individual instruction, the classroom work as a whole (to be reffered to simply as "classroom work" in the following discussion) or simultaneous group instruction is an important format of instructional process in the classroom. It trains the learners in the mutual communication between them and benefiting from the other learners' way of thinking or learning styles, as the discussion in the former paper by one of the authors presented at WCCE81 (1). Since the most popular instructional format in Japan today is the lecture or classroom work, the research and development for classroom work appear very useful.

The principle of the system consists of a pacemaking theory with analysis of the response curve and dynamic representation of the face method. Response curves can be obtained by monitoring the learner's time required to do an exercise using a response analyzer (abbreviated as R.A. in the following). The face method has been adopted as a man-machine interface between the microcomputer and the teacher. The main purpose of this system is not to increase the efficiency of instruction 10% or 20%, but to provide the learners with the optimum pacemaking activity of the teacher in the classroom, which concerns the effectiveness of and the motivation for learning.

2. System Construction

The system consists mainly of an R.A. and a microcomputer, and the construction is shown in figure 1. The Face Robot system is divided into three subsystems, as shown in the upper part of figure 1. They are
1) Data Acquisition
2) Data Analysis
3) Face Display
The Data Acquisition subsystem faces the lear-

ners to acquire data. The acquired data are analyzed by means of calculation of indexes and estimation of parameters with probability model in the Data Analysis subsystem. In the Face Display subsystem, the face as an expression of the learning process of the learners is represented on the CRT.

The discussion in this paper is concerned with the practical trial of this Face Robot in the actual high school classroom. The Data Acquisition subsystem consists of an R.A. and an interface that connects the R.A. and a microcomputer. In addition to the above practical mode, there are two other modes in this system: simulation mode and general mode. The simulation mode of the system is discussed in the paper presented at ETIC84 (2); the data are acquired by means of generation of random variables with the probability model stored in the microcomputer. In the general mode, the Data Acquisition subsystem can deal with any data of time series.

3. Response Curve

The situation is supposed to be such that the teacher shows an exercise and gives instruction to the learners to respond by operating R.A. button in the classroom when they have finished the exercise. A response curve that indicates a transition of response rate with time is obtained shown in figure 2.

The notation used for the response curve is also indicated in figure 2. The symbols are
ts: time point of start
tr: time point of start of response
te: time point of end
Td: time interval of no response (dead time)
Ta: time interval of response (answering time)
Now let us see the data in figure 3 with the aid of this notation which explain the difference of pacemaking between trained teachers and student teachers. The trained teachers end the exercise dynamically corresponding to Td, but student teachers end statically, or uniformly,

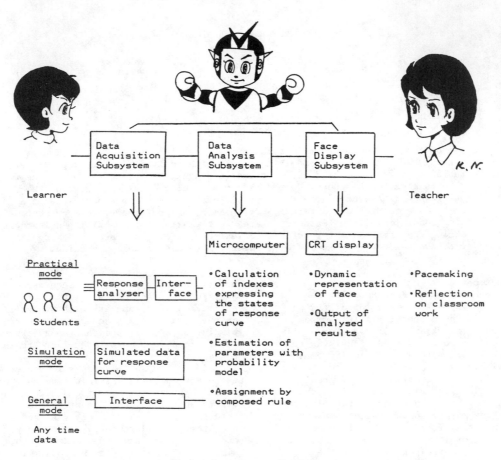

Figure 1.　System Construction

in fixed time length in spite of the various
length of Td.

4.　Theoretical Distribution of Response Time
The simplest assumptions for the response time
model of a group of learners are:
1) There is a physically minimum response time
   t_0.
2) There is also a mean response time τ.
3) The group is homogeneous and then the theoretical distribution of response time maximize its own entropy, i.e.

$$\int_{t_0}^{\infty} f(t)\log f(t)dt \rightarrow max.$$

If the above assumption is made, the cumulative
exponential curve will be derived as the response curve by means of calculus of variations
as follows:

$$F(t)= \begin{cases} 1-\exp(-(t-t_0)/\tau), & t \geq t_0 \\ 0, & t < t_0 \end{cases} \quad [1]$$

In the case of an exercise that includes n-
subordinate factors that are independent of one
another and the response curves　　which have

the same τ, the response curve will be the
cumulative Gamma distribution with parameter n.
The curve increases more slowly than [1] at
first and become S-shaped according to the
value of n.　On the other hand, in the case of
n-subordinate factors that are dependent on one
another, and the τ　　which are the same, the
shape of the curve is the same as that of [1],
but elongated n times.　It is supposed that the
former response curve corresponds to an exercise which consists of multiplex contents, and
the latter corresponds to simply increased but
homogeneous contents.　This result is useful
for observing the response curves.

5.　Pacemaking with Response Curve
The pacemaking behaviour of the teacher in the
learner's exercise or problem solving process
explained above is limited here as follows:
a) When should the teacher let the learners
   stop the exercise?
b) When should the teacher give a hint to the
   learners?
It has been known from actual experiences that
the points to be noted in pacemaking by observing a response curve are as follows:
1) To end when the response rate has arrived at
   an appropriate level, not too low and not

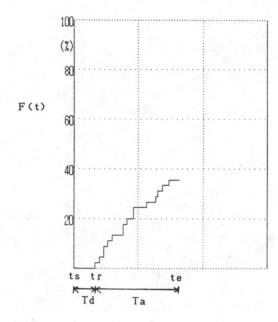

Figure 2.   Notation of the Response Curve

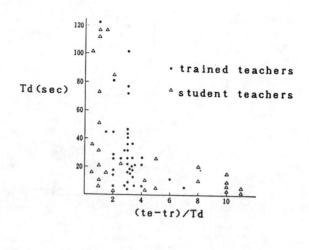

Figure 3.   Td and Corresponding End Time

high.   The level is often set at 80%.
2) To end when an appropriate length of time
   has passed, not too soon and not too late.
   The time is often set at Ta= 2∿3 Td (See the
   data of trained teachers in figure 3).
3) To give a hint when the response rate does
   not increase for a while, or the response
   curve becomes flat.
With respect to the analysis of response curves
to estimate the parameters, the Weibull distribution function is preferred here, because
there are some previous results on the fitting
of the Weibull distribution model to response
curves (3).

6.   Representation of Face
It is important to arrange a sophisticated man-
machine interface between the information of
the response curve and the observation of the
teacher, because teacher, during instruction in
the classroom, does not normally have the time
to evelute quickly various numerical results
from the microcomputer. For this need, the
face method that was proposed by Chernoff (4)
was adopted and the Face Display subsystem was
organised. In the system, the face is represented not statically, but dynamically, quite
different from most former uses.
Five examples of the face currently adopted are
shown in figure 4. The face has seven factors
of expression, and the corresponding indexes
are indicated in table 1.
In table 1, t is the current time, t_i is the
time of last response (i-th response), $t_{(i-4)}$
is the time of the (i-4)th response, Ta80 is
the estimated time for 80% responses, and
INT( ) is the integer function. The grade of

values is translated from the values of indexes.
The translation formulas are also shown in
table 1. The seven values are expressed as a
vector $[x_1, x_2, \ldots, x_7]$, where x_i is the value
of the factor i that is the factor number in
table 1. In figure 4, the face A is all-nine
expression [9,9,9,9,9,9,9], B is all-one [1,1,
1,1,1,1,1], C is the mean [5,5,5,5,5,5,5]. The
face D and E in figure 4 are the typical faces
of actually observed response curves, which are
also shown in the figure. D is an example of
an expression at the time point when a high
response rate is reached in a short time for an
easy exercise, so that the face seems joyful
and vivid. E is an example of expression for a
difficult exercise. The low response rate in
spite of waiting for a long time causes a
puzzled expression. In this case the teacher
must give a hint for the learners, or end the
exercise if there is no suitable hint.

7.   Practical Trial in the Actual Classroom
Practical trials were performed seven times in
the 12th grade classroom of a high school. The
subjects taught were English and mathematics,
the number of classes was three, and the number
of students was 45 for each class.
Photo 1 shows the classroom where the Face
Robot is installed. The switch box with five
buttons provided under each learner's desk is
shown in photo 2, but here now only one response button is being used to indicate the
finish of exercise. In photo 3 the teacher is
showing an exercise and is simultaneously depressing the keys of the microcomputer to
start the system. Photo 4 shows the face and
response curve on the CRT set on the teacher's

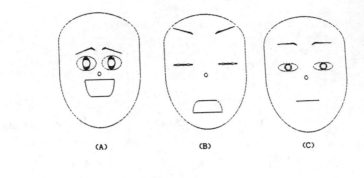

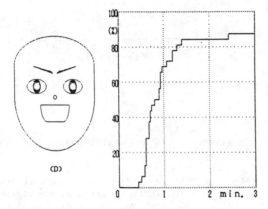

The corresponding exercise in English: "Change
the voice of the sentence --- My father gave
this book to me."

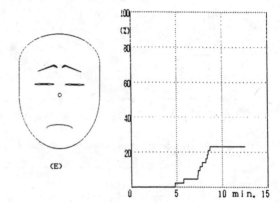

The corresponding exercise is math.: "Find the
value of x ---

Figure 4.   Example of Face

desk.
There were four teachers who participated in the
practical trial.
Figure 5 shows a typical pacemaking by one of
these teachers using the Face Robot. The succe-
sive motions of face can be depicted corresponding to the dynamic changes of response curve.
Three faces were represented at three different
time points $(1) \sim (3)$. The first response (t=ts)
occured at about 20 seconds after start (t=tr);
Td=20 sec. The response rate increased quickly
approaching the time point (1) and after 1.5
minutes, gradually began to change slowly.
There came presently a plateau the length of
which was about 2 minutes. Then the curve
suddenly rose again immediately after the time
point (2) when the teacher had given a hint for
the learners who had not finished the exercise
yet and the learners had become responsive with
this timely hint. At the time point (3), the
response rate rose fairly high. It is supposed
to be possible to identify the three faces from
one another corresponding to each state of the
response curve.

6. Discussion

Some results are obtained with respect to the
advantages of the Face Robot.
1) Enabling the teacher to know obviously the
   learning condition of the learners, thereby
   not wasting time on finished learners, or
   not cutting the time short for unfinished
   learners.
2) Enabling the teacher to grasp the learning
   condition at a glance, thereby concentrating
   on teaching.
3) Enabling the teacher to be experienced by
   looking at the many possible faces representing various data, thereby cultivating the
   teaching skill for pacemaking.
The points to improve are as follows.
1) Until the teacher is familiar with the
   method, it is difficult for him or her to
   derive the information only by looking at
   the face.
2) When the teacher walks among the learners to
   teach individually, it is not possible to
   see the face display on the teacher's desk.
The Face Robot is not a commander to the teacher, but an aid offering the information for
pacemaking. Educational machine, including the
Face Robot, must not snatch the decision making

Table 1. Factors of Expression and Indexes

No. of Factors	Factors of Expression	Indexes of Response Curve	Translation Formula	Means of Indexes
1	Shape of Mouth	Response Rate	$INT(F(t))+1$	Performance of Responses
2	Distance of Eyeblows and Eyes	Estimated Weibull Shape Parameter	$INT(9(m-1))+1$	Degree of Multiplexity
3	Distance of both Eyeblows	Length of Plateau	$INT(\frac{t-ti}{Td/40})$	Evaluation of Plateau of Learning (absolute)
4	Distance of Mouth and Nose	Changing of Response Curve	$INT(\frac{4(t-ti)}{t-t(i-4)})$	Evaluation of Plateau of Learning (relative)
5	Shape of Eyeblows	Estimated Time of 80% Response	$INT(Ta80/2)+1$	Prediction of Performance
6	Shape of Eyes	Normalized Estimated time of 80% Response	$INT(\frac{Ta80+Td}{t/9})+1$	Normalized Predictive Performance
7	Distance of both Eyes	Time Normalized with Td	$INT(9t/5Td)$	Time Scale Normalized with No-Response time

Photo 1. The Classroom installed the Face Robot

Photo 2. The Switches of R.A.

Photo 3. The Teacher starts the system

Photo 4. The Face and Response Curve on the CRT

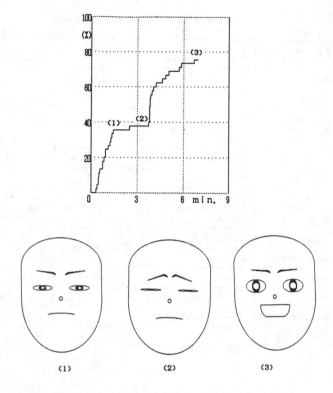

Figure 5.   Pacemaking using the Face

capability away from the teacher; it should also
contribute to the training of teachers' skill
in the classroom.

Acknowledgment
The authors wish to thank Mr.K.Naka and Miss
H.Iwakiri for trying out this system in thire
classroom, and Kazuo Seko for his helpful
assistance.

Reference
(1) Nagaoka,K. and Fujita,H., Computerized
    Training System of Discussion, Proceedings
    of WCCE81, Lausanne, Switzerland (1981).
(2) Nagaoka,K., Face Robot with Response Analy-
    ser in the Classroom, Proceedings of ETIC84
    (Educational Technology International Con-
    ference'84), Bradford, U.K. (1984).
(3) Fujita,H., Educational Informatics
    (Shokodoh, Tokyo, 1975).
(4) Chernoff,H., The Use of Faces to Represent
    Points in k-Dimensional Space Graphically,
    J.Am.Stat.Asoc., Vol.68,361-368 (June 1973).

COMPUTERS IN EDUCATION, K. Duncan and D. Harris (eds.)
Elsevier Science Publishers B.V. (North-Holland)
© IFIP, 1985

HANDS-ON MEASURES FOR HANDS-ON LEARNING*

Gary Marchionini

College of Library and Information Services
University of Maryland
College Park, Maryland 20742 USA

Hands-on experiences are recommended for students in introductory computer courses at all levels. Hands-on instruments for measuring student success should be based on instructional practice, and thus include hands-on components. Instruments for measuring affective and cognitive success in an introductory computer course were developed and compared to traditional paper and pencil instruments. Interactions across personality type and other individual differences were also studied. Mode of testing was not a factor in predicting success on the affective or cognitive criteria. Instructors are encouraged to include hands-on tests in designing and executing these courses.

INTRODUCTION

Interest in computers is presently so great that elementary through graduate schools offer versions of introductory computer training. The common intent of these courses is to provide initial experience with an important and rapidly emerging intellectual tool. This seems certain to continue for the next five to ten years until the populace is generally computer literate via the environment and instructors in traditional disciplines develop the expertise to integrate computers into their courses.

It is commonly accepted that introductory training should provide maximum hands-on experience. The ancient dictum, "I hear and I forget, I see and I remember, I do and I understand" is often used to reinforce this notion. In recommending an exemplary introductory computer science course for secondary schools, Rogers and Austing (5) cite "practice in making appropriate use of computers as tools for problem solving in a variety of circumstances . . ." as a primary goal of the course. Hands-on experience is considered so important that they suggest: "Serious consideration should be given to postponing the implementation of a computer science course if adequate facilities are not yet available in a school" (p. 51).

Just as it is reasonable to provide hands-on experience in introductory computer courses, it is also good educational practice to evaluate students on the material they have studied. Moreover, it is reasonable to evaluate student learning using the same methods and media that were used in the instruction. From a

theoretical perspective, Salomon (6) argues that the mode of media (symbol system) explored by a learner determines the mental skills applied and therefore the knowledge-skills learned. The most direct way to measure the skills and concepts learned through hands-on experience is to use hands-on instruments. Although matching testing mode to instructional methods is often difficult to do in traditional settings, the particular attributes of computers and the excitement of an emerging discipline provide an opportunity to develop and use hands-on evaluation strategies. The purpose of this paper is to report the results of a controlled comparison of hands-on and paper and pencil tests for an introductory computer course. Both affective and cognitive instruments were evaluated and interactions with selected human factors variables were examined.

METHOD

An exploratory experiment was conducted with 31 graduate Library Science students enrolled in an introductory computer course during the summer of 1984. The course was designed to introduce students to microcomputers and included four major content strands: principles of hardware and software; applications of microcomputers in libraries, schools, and homes; programming in a high level language (BASIC); and issues and social impacts related to computers. Students completed several hands-on assignments during the term, including: modifying and writing programs, and using a personal filing program. Various labs were required for other hands-on work like graphics programming, Logo programming, word processing, and spreadsheet use.

The central question of the research was whether mode of testing had an effect on the level of success attained by students. Thus, mode of testing was the primary independent variable for

---

*This research was supported by the University of Maryland Graduate Research Board.

the experiment. It was hypothesized that scores would be equivalent for hands-on and paper and pencil versions of tests.

Previous research in introductory computer courses has suggested that success is related to individual human differences. Mathematics and science ability (3), cognitive style (7), and spatial memory and age (1) have each been related to performance in introductory computer situations. To explore the interactions between mode of testing and individual differences, seven human characteristic variations were considered in the experiment. These were: personal rigidity, age, sex, high school performance, undergraduate performance, work preference (people, data, or things), and task preference (verbal or quantitative). Personal rigidity was selected as a personality variable because it was hypothesized that students who were resistant to change--rigid--would be most affected by alternative testing modes. The Rehfisch Rigidity Scale (4) was administered on the first day of class and used to stratify the sample into high, average, and low rigidity groups. Other individual difference data were collected via self-report on a student survey administered the first day of class.

The dependent variable, success in becoming "computer literate," was divided into affective and cognitive dimensions. These dimensions were measured using instruments which were paper and pencil (PP) or hands-on (HO). For the affective dimension, a semantic differential attitude scale having ten responses (2) was used for measuring student attitudes toward computers and change. A hands-on version of the scales was developed. Students responded to the scales via two simple cursor controls and the carriage return. Students were randomly assigned to complete the scales the last day of class in either the paper and pencil or hands-on format.

Cognitive measures were treated in a different manner. Although hands-on experience clearly reinforces understanding of concepts about computers, the experiences are particularly useful in developing skills in actually using computers and executing procedures. Two separate instruments were used to measure the learning of concepts and the learning of skills. To measure concept learning, things students could have learned in discussion or reading, a part of the Minnesota Educational Computing Consortium Computer Literacy Questionnaire was administered to all students on the last day of class. To measure skill learning, a hands-on, nine-step procedure was developed which all students executed individually, on the computer, under the guidance of a graduate assistant. This was also administered on the last day of class. The procedure included "booting the system," cataloging a disk, loading, running, and modifying a program, and then saving and verifying the results.

For the attitude criterion measures, two-way analyses of variance crossing each of the seven individual characteristic variables by mode of testing were performed to test for main effects and interactions. Since two achievement criterion measures (HO and PP) were taken for each student rather than randomly assigning them to mode of testing, correlation coefficients were examined for individual characteristics and the respective test scores.

RESULTS AND DISCUSSION

Attitudes. Student attitudes were very positive toward computers and positive toward change. For the attitude scales, the possible range of scores was 10 (extremely positive) to 70 (extremely negative). Attitudes toward computers had an overall mean of 21.1. Means for the HO and PP subgroups were 20.9 and 21.3 respectively. Attitudes toward change had an overall mean of 28.8 and the means for the HO and PP subgroups were 26.6 and 30.9 respectively. Although results for the HO subgroups were more positive on both scales, the differences were not statistically significant at the .05 level. Results of the seven pairs of analyses of variance crossing individual characteristics with mode of testing are presented in Table 1. None of the main effects were found to be statistically significant for attitudes toward computers. The large F value for interaction between task preference and mode of testing is likely due to sampling error since only four students selected quantitative tasks.

Table 1
F Ratios and Probability Levels for ANOVAS

Effects	Computers		Change	
	F	P	F	P
Mode of testing	1.06	.81	2.03	.17
Rigidity	1.96	.16	.22	.81
interaction	.54	.59	2.65	.09
Mode of testing	.02	.89	2.03	.17
Sex	.66	.43	1.94	.18
interaction	.18	.68	.00	.96
Mode of testing	.43	.52	1.57	.31
High school perform.	1.32	.29	.90	.42
interaction	1.85	.44	.92	.41
Mode of testing	.61	.44	4.13	.05
Undergrad. perform.	1.11	.37	1.49	.24
interaction	.13	.72	.03	.87
Mode of testing	.02	.89	1.84	.19
Work preference	.19	.83	.10	.91
interaction	.31	.78	.56	.58
Mode of testing	.03	.87	2.19	.15
Task preference	.69	.41	1.31	.26
interaction	12.23	.002	2.88	.10

Undergraduate performance seemed to be related to attitudes towards both computers and change. Although not statistically significant for either case, undergraduate performance subgroups from low to high had increasingly more positive attitudes. The failure to find statistically significant attitudinal differences between modes of testing or across individual differences suggests that equivalent results can be obtained from HO and PP testing.

Achievement. Results for the achievement tests were generally very high. The mean score for the PP test (49 possible) was 45.4. The mean score on the HO test (20 possible) was 18.3. The Pearson correlation coefficient for HO and PP scores was .50 (p .002). This strong relationship between scores on the HO and PP tests supports the hypothesis that success is independent of testing mode. Correlation coefficients for the individual characteristic variables and the two achievement results are presented in Table 2.

Table 2
Correlation Coefficients of Individual Characteristics and Achievement Results

Characteristic	Hands-on		Paper and Pencil	
	R	P	R	P
Rigidity	-.21	.13	-.13	.25
Age	-.12	.26	-.02	.45
Sex	.26	.08	.33	.04
High school perform.	-.54	.001	-.41	.01
Undergrad. perform.	-.24	.10	-.36	.02
Work preference	-.14	.23	.08	.35
Task perference	.01	.49	.18	.17

Note: R values for rigidity and age are Pearson, others are Spearman.

Weak relationships for rigidity and achievement were found. For both HO and PP tests, high scores on the rigidity test (high personal rigidity) were related to lower achievement scores. Whether personal rigidity is a predictor of performance bears further research. The fact that HO and PP results reflect parallel trends tends to support the equivalency of mode of testing. Age and achievement were not found to be related for either mode of testing. Females scored higher than males on both modes of testing. The mean HO score for females (n=15) was 18.4 and 17.8 for males (n=6). The mean PP score for females was 45.9 and 43.3 for males. Although these results were not statistically significant, they are interesting since they are contrary to previous results (2) and the concerns of many authors (see April 1984 issue of The Computing Teacher). Statistically significant relationships were found for past academic performance and both modes of testing. For both high school and undergraduate performance, the higher the performance (1=excellent,

2=above average, etc.), the higher the score on both the HO and PP test. That high past academic performance leads to current high performance is not surprising. What is interesting, however, is that past performance which was most likely based exclusively on PP tests is still a predictor for HO performance. Preferences for working with people, data or things, and type of intellectual task were not strongly related to achievement on either mode of testing. Overall, students achieved comparable levels of success on both modes of testing.

CONCLUSION

The use of hands-on tests in introductory computer courses is appealing from a theoretical view, and the results of this study support this theory. No gross differences were found between student performance on hands-on and paper and pencil tests in the affective or cognitive domain. Individual characteristics were not found to strongly influence student performance in general, and those that had some effect had consistent effects for both hands-on and paper and pencil measures. The sample used in this experiment was predominantly female and verbally oriented--both characteristics which have been negatively correlated to use of computers. The high level of success achieved by students may serve to amplify the findings since these subjects could have been expected to be highly affected by hands-on testing. On the other hand, the high level of success may have been due to achievement instruments that were too easy, thus not allowing discrimination among the personal characteristics to be detected. Further study is recommended.

The use of hands-on tests should be explored by instructors at all levels. The results of this study demonstrate that hands-on tests produce comparable results to paper and pencil tests. The experience of hands-on tests may itself be valuable, especially in courses aimed at naive users. The potentials for standardization and ease of administration and scoring, are similar to the potentials of computer based instruction. Research on optimal designs for hands-on tests should be supported, and packages for easily generating tests should be developed. Individual instructors can and should in the interim develop and personally administer hands-on tests in their courses.

REFERENCES

[1] Egan, D. and Gomez, L. Characteristics of
     people who can learn to use computer text
     editors: hints for future text editor
     design and training, Proceedings of the
     ASIS Annual Meeting 19 (1982), 75–79.

[2] Marchionini, G. Computer enhanced practice
     and introductory algebra, Ph.D. disserta-
     tion, Wayne State University, 1981.

[3] Peterson, C. and Howe, T. Predicting
     academic success in introduction to
     computers, AEDS Journal, 12 (2), 1979, 182–
     91.

[4] Robinson, John and Shaver, Phillip (eds.),
     Measures of social psychological
     attitudes, Ann Arbor, Michigan, Institute
     for Social Research, 1973.

[5] Rogers, Jean and Austing, Dick, Computer
     science in secondary schools: recommenda-
     tions for a one-year course, In Topics
     computer education for elementary and
     secondary schools, Washington, D.C., ACM,
     1981.

[6] Solomon, Gavriel, Interaction of media,
     cognition, and learning, San Francisco,
     Jossey-Bass, 1981.

[7] Stevens, D. Cognitive processes and
     success of students in instructional
     computer courses, AEDS Journal, 16 (4),
     1983, 228–33.

COMPUTERS IN EDUCATION, K. Duncan and D. Harris (eds.)
Elsevier Science Publishers B.V. (North-Holland)
© IFIP, 1985

LOW COST HAND-HELD COMPUTER IN CLASSROOM INSTRUCTION

Charles E. Barb, Jr., Ph.D.

School of Civil Engineering and Environmental Science, and
Department of Regional and City Planning
334 Carson Engineering Center
The University of Oklahoma
Norman, Oklahoma 73019

Since Fall 1984, Freshmen entering the School of Civil Engineering and Environmental
Science at the University of Oklahoma are required to own a personal hand-held computer for use in their undergraduate courses. The Oklahoma program represents a
leading example of an evolving trend to personal computers in colleges and universities today.

The paper briefly describes the rationale and objectives of the program, the
hand-held computer prescribed, initial experience in computer programming and substantive topic instruction with hand-held computers in the classroom, initial experience in developing instructional software, and implications of this innovation.

1. INTRODUCTION

The University of Oklahoma School of Civil Engineering and Environmental Science (OU/CEES)
computer requirement differs from other pub-
licized programs at Carnegie Mellon, Drexel and
Clarkson Universities, among others, in its
prescription of a less expensive hand-held computer and the intent to integrate their use in
classroom lectures, laboratories and exams.
The other universities require students to purchase desk top computers, costing $1000 to
$4000, which are not portable or adaptable
broadly to classroom instruction. The hand-
held computer initially prescribed in the
Oklahoma program is the calculator-sized Sharp
1261 with CE 125 Printer/Microcassette Tape
Recorder which combined retail for about $200.
The computer and printer/tape recorder are both
battery powered.

1.1 Background

Computer programming instruction in engineering
at the University of Oklahoma was included in a
freshman "Introduction to Engineering" course
featuring instruction in FORTRAN 77. In the
Spring of 1983 the College of Engineering Faculty dropped programming instruction from the
introduction course and deferred instruction to
a Junior level, one credit course replacement.
At this time the Civil Engineering and Environmental Science Faculty currently the hand-held
computer requirement with the objective of expanding computer application in their curricula. Hand-held computers were accepted as a
viable curriculum requirement due to the similarity of their BASIC language to FORTRAN 77
their reasonable cost; and an assessment that
potentially 80% to 90% of student computing
needs in undergraduate Civil Engineering,
Environmental Science and Pre-Architecture

curricula could be met with a hand-held computer. And, most significantly, with all students
owning a portable computer, their use could be
incorporated in classroom instruction.

During the Summer and Fall of 1983, the author
taught two experimental sections of the traditional "Introduction to Engineering" course exploring computer programming instruction in
BASIC on hand-held computers, and use of hand-
held computers in lecture presentation of substantive engineering topics. The instruction
was successful and elicited considerable student enthusiasm. During the Fall of 1983, students from the two courses organized a Hand-
held Computer Club which has assembled a library of published hand-held computer software
and began developing "courseware", that is,
computer software for use in engineering
courses.

1.2 Program Objectives and Implementation

The OU/CEES hand-held computer program has
two objectives:

1. Introducing computer programming and
    drilling students in programming to a
    skill level, and stimulating students to
    adapt computing as a personal tool for use
    in their education.

2. Implementing hand-held computer-supported
    instruction in the classroom as part of
    lectures, labs and examinations in the
    three School curricula.

The cornerstone of the program for student
training will be CE 1111, Introduction to Hand-
held Computers, a one semester credit hour BA-
SIC programming course required of first semester freshmen and all transfer students. In-

struction includes all programming features of the hand-held computer including subroutines and program chaining, and emphasizes program specification, structured program design, documentation and testing. The course is taught concurrently with a revised College "Introduction to Engineering" course from which engineering computer programming applications are derived.

2.   HAND-HELD COMPUTERS

Portable hand-held computers today are of two types: pocket-sized computers similar to pocket calculators, and larger "lap" computers that are the size of a textbook. The OU/CEES program prescribes a pocket, calculator-sized computer. Lap computers are judged less suitable because of their cost, unnecessary features beyond those basically needed for computation in undergraduate engineering courses, and the fact that printer and program/data storage devices commonly are not battery-powered and thus portable.

Pocket-sized hand-held computers are similar to programmable scientific pocket calculators with the significant exception that they are more conveniently programmed in BASIC. The computers are battery powered, have a calculator-sized keyboard and one to four line liquid-crystal display, and they commonly interface to a battery-powered printer and tape recorder. They generally have 1K to 16K RAM memory; however some more expensive models also feature plug-in additional memory. Pocket-sized hand-held computers were first introduced in 1980 by Radio Shack. Currently there are more than a half dozen different hand-held computer models available from manufacturers, including Hewlett-Packard, Texas Instruments, Panasonic, Sharp and Casio. Radio Shack also markets Sharp and Casio hand-held computers under the Radio Shack name. The computers currently cost from $70 to $600. Printer and tape recorder attachments cost extra.

A considerable library of software, primarily in the form of books of program listings, is available for hand-held computers ranging from games to statistics, business and engineering applications. As will be noted later, however, this software has proven to be of little instructional utility.

The computer currently selected for the OU/CEES program is the Sharp PC-1261 with CE-125 Printer/Microcassette Tape Recorder. The computer currently retails for about $110; the interface for about $120. It is recommended based upon price, its 10.2K RAM memory capacity, and the compactness and convenience of the printer/microcassette tape recorder attachment. The computer has an EXTENDED BASIC that includes all common computer language features (including two dimensional arrays) and a full assortment of scientific functions and tape re-

corder control commands. The computer also has very convenient line editing.

3.   COMPUTER PROGRAMMING INSTRUCTION WITH HAND-HELD COMPUTERS

Experimental instruction, as previously mentioned, was conducted within the context of "Introduction to Engineering". The course traditionally represented 2 credits or 10 to 12 semester weeks of FORTRAN 77 instruction using the College's DEC PDP 11-70 minicomputer in time share mode, and 1 credit of instruction in engineering topics. As taught by the author, FORTRAN was introduced through subroutines and structured narrative program design, program integrity, internal and user documentation was emphasized. Programming exercises included menu branching, statistical computations, sorting, computer printer graphics, and a term programming project of student choice.

The first full experiment in hand-held computer programming instruction was a three week "Intersession" short course offering of "Introduction to Engineering" in May-June 1983. Course experimentation continued during Fall 1983 with a regular semester offering of same introduction course. Both course offerings included the full content of the traditional introduction course, however, less time was required for programming instruction.

In the course, initial BASIC programming instruction was completed in six class days, or six semester weeks. Programming topics included computer familiarization and use as a scientific calculator, programmed computations and input/output statements, loops, branching and program design and documentation. Each topic included homework programming assignments generally highlighting introductory engineering topics such as the computation of mean, median and standard deviation statistics, and the summation of two-dimensional vectors. Programming skills were further reinforced through a term programming project of student choice representing an initial program library for a recent or concurrently enrolled course. Students developed program libraries for courses in physics, chemistry, calculus, surveying, structural analysis and solid waste management (a transportation algorithm for trash truck routing).

Student response to both experimental courses was uniformly favorable and grades were above average.

3.1   Principal Findings

Several findings regarding computer programming instruction with hand-held computers were derived from the course experimentation.

1.   Hand-held computers programmable in BASIC are viable for teaching fundamental programming concepts including structured

techniques and documentation.

2. Using BASIC and hand-held computers, fundamental computer programming instruction can be reduced to five or six weeks, or one semester credit, from ten to twelve weeks needed to similarly teach FORTRAN 77 on a minicomputer.

3. A variety of hand-held computers programmable in BASIC can be accommodated in one class and students with "off brands" can follow the instruction without difficulty.

4. In using hand-held computers in the classroom, the sequence of programming topics did not change but topic presentation changed from chalkboard lecture to structured exercises in which students explored given lines of code with their computers. In this format the instructor became less of a lecturer and more of a programming consultant.

5. Classroom instruction with hand-held computer exercises elicited greater student classroom attention and understanding of programming concepts while in class. The transition from classroom to homework assignment was less awkward.

6. Students are more motivated to learn programming and use their hand-held computer because they have invested in its purchase and they see its use in other courses. (However, casual observation of course graduates suggest that possibly only 30% of the students adopt computing as a personal tool. Reinforcing assignments are necessary in follow-on courses.)

7. Student development of program libraries for use in other courses is a useful exercise representing a realistic goal for the course; however, the courseware developed typically is crude and not useable for distribution.

3.2 CE 1111: Introduction to Hand-Held Computers

Based upon the experiments and findings above, a one semester credit course was designed as a core requirement in the Civil Engineering, Environmental Science and Pre-Architecture curricula. The course was first taught Fall 1984. Content of the course is the same as that described above; however the course format is different.

The course is organized as a laboratory course which meets for an hour and a half, twice a week. Generally, the first lab session each week is used to introduce a weekly programming assignment and related programming concepts. Programming assignments are submitted in two parts. Programs are first designed in terms of

a program specification, input-output examples, user instructions and a program narrative -- students are discouraged to attempt to program a solution before its thorough design. Program designs are due the second lab session of the week at which time a design solution is distributed and discussed. The final, fully operational program is due the following week when again a solution is distributed and discussed.

Initial student response and achievement in the course has been good.

4. TOPIC INSTRUCTION WITH HAND-HELD COMPUTERS

Using the hand-held computer to support substantive engineering topic instruction also was explored in the above reported experimental "Introduction to Engineering" sections. To extend understanding of elementary statistics, students wrote a program to compute mean, median and standard deviation statistics. To extend their understanding of vector arithmetic, they wrote a two dimensional vector summation program. The exercises proved effective in reinforcing understanding of the computations but were more challenging and time consuming than was anticipated.

Alternatively, least squares regression programs for linear, exponential, geometric and logarithmic curve fitting, and a program for engineering economic computations were distributed to students to support introduction of regression statistics and engineering economy. Classroom topic lectures were organized around an introduction to the programs and structured examples of their use. The software was used in homework assignments and subsequent course examinations.

4.1 Principal Findings

Five principal findings regarding the use of hand-held computers in substantive engineering topic instruction were drawn from course experimentation.

1. Using computer programming exercises to reinforce understanding of computations should be selectively employed and well planned because of the student time potentially required.

2. In using hand-held computers with distributed software for topic instruction:

   A. The sequence of topic instruction did not change but the method of topic presentation did. Presentation changed from chalkboard lecture with an emphasis upon mathematical computations to a structured learning exercise based upon software features. More emphasis was placed upon interpreting typical engineering problems, planning their solution with the software, exploring the input/output sensitivity of computations with graphing, and validating computer answers derived.

B. Students were more attentive and participated more in class through computer exercises.

C. A broader range of student homework problems were possible as a result of time-saving courseware.

3. While there is a considerable library of software available for hand-held computers, it commonly includes separate short, stand-alone program routines not integrated, organized or adequately inclusive to support common text book introduction of engineering topics. Furthermore, students' efforts in developing courseware as term project programs suggest that effective courseware will require considerable design, testing and documentation, and that useful programs will be those that perform non-trivial computations and save student time.

5. INITIAL COURSEWARE DEVELOPMENT

With recognition that courseware is not available to support undergraduate Civil Engineering, Environmental Science and Pre-Architecture curricula, and that casual, ad hoc student efforts cannot lead to distributable, curriculum-wide libraries, the author initiated courseware development efforts during the Summer of 1984 with a faculty colleague. The effort received university support during Spring semester 1985 to the extent of a quarter time faculty release time and a quarter-time student programmer to begin software development for two sophomore level Civil Engineering courses: surveying and statistics. At this writing, the nature of useful courseware, the scope and scale of courseware development and an approach to courseware development is understood, and prerequisite software design techniques and standards have been defined.

5.1 Principal Findings

Four principal findings have been drawn from initial courseware development.

1. Typical useful courseware in an undergraduate Civil Engineering, Environmental Science or Pre-Architecture curricula is computationally-oriented and related to fundamental analysis and design computations taught in courses. The computations are generally well within the memory constraints of available hand-held computers and they seldom need to be presented graphically or in the fashion of an arcade game to retain student interest and attention.

2. Analysis of the three School curricula suggests 22 courses or topic areas warrant a courseware library and each library likely will have seven to eight program modules. This is a significant undertaking and one that is generally beyond the resources of the university.

3. Courseware development includes five steps:

A. Topic by topic evaluation of a course to identify computational topics that represent: (a) viable student programming assignments as an alternative to traditional pencil computation exercises, and (b) meaningful, non-trivial computations in a topic courseware module that should be developed to enhance or extend instruction.

B. From the above list, program specifications are drafted for each library module. Specifications include definition of the instructional environment and use of the courseware. Once specifications are developed for all library modules, they are reviewed and integrated into a course library.

C. From the above specifications, detailed problem examples are developed illustrating program input and output design. From these designs a program narrative design is developed.

D. Programs are written from the program narrative and thoroughly tested for performance accuracy and integrity.

E. The courseware is verified in classroom application and courseware features are redesigned as appropriate.

Courseware will require the close collaboration between an experienced course instructor and a software development professional.

4. Considerable thought must be applied to the ergonomic design of the software to its instructional application.

6. INSTRUCTIONAL IMPLICATIONS AND ISSUES

Adaptation of hand-held computers in the classroom for computer programming and substantive topic instruction has several instructional implications.

6.1 How Programming Instruction Will Likely Change

While programming topics or the sequence of their instruction won't change, topic delivery will. The traditional deductive lecture, first introducing programming concepts followed by chalkboard coding examples, will change to a more inductive structured learning approach in which students are led through selected programming experiments with their computer and then broader concepts are highlighted in summary. Lecture preparation will become the planning of effective sequences of classroom coding exercises.

Use of hand-held computers will elicit closer student attention and greater participation in class, and it will introduce students to personal inquiry of "what would happen if?" questions now posed to instructors in traditional lectures. The physical use of the computer will cause students to better grasp concepts and coding details introduced in the classroom, and more successfully transfer them later to outside-of-class homework.

Students will work more independently on their homework programming assignments than when they cluster in computer terminal rooms. This will result in less informal instruction between students but conversely more self-reliance, original work and sounder student understanding.

6.2 Substantive Topic Instruction Changes

In adapting hand-held computer analysis and design software to substantive lectures, again course topics and the sequence of introducing topics likely will not change, but topic presentation will. The traditional lecture emphasizing chalkboard computations will change to more of a structured learning approach using the computer and software in a planned sequence of classroom exercises. Emphasis will change from calculating answers to interpreting problems and planning their solution with their computer, exploring the input/output sensitivity of the underlying computation (found effective with graphing), and logical validation of computer derived answers.

6.3 Instructional Issues

From the changes sketched above, several issues become evident. These are issues beyond the question of BASIC versus FORTRAN or COBOL and hand-held versus desk top computers. The BASIC-FORTRAN/COBOL question is really grounded in prejudice. Professionals today are proving that any of the languages may be profitable used, and modern structured programming and documentation concepts can be adapted to BASIC. The hand-held versus desk top question is really a question of costs, capacity perceived to be necessary versus capacity available, and portability which portends classroom use.

The significant instructional issues relate to what is "learned" by a student, instructor investment and ego, and student "academic freedom" to employ hand-held computers.

The traditional concept of what is "learned" is challenged by hand-held computers in the classroom. As noted above, using hand-held computers with software in topic instruction likely will change the emphasis of instruction. Whether students will acquire as _sound_ a basic understanding of topics using hand-held computers is the instructional challenge; whether students will acquire a _broader_ understanding through computer applications is the instructional opportunity.

For faculty to adapt hand-held computers to classroom instruction will obviously require an investment in learning the device and its programming, and acquiring and learning or developing necessary courseware. Due to the current memory limitations of available hand-held computers, some rescaling of examples also may be necessary. But, by and large, paper and pencil scale computations currently used in the classroom are well within the memory capacity of a 10.2K computer.

A more significant dimension to faculty adaptation may be the change in professional role from "font of knowledge" lecturer to "consultant" in structured student inquiry. This may cause an emotional challenge for both faculty and students brought up in a "lecture and two exam" educational tradition. For students it may mean a transfer of responsibility for performance in a course from the professor and his presentation style, a familiar rationalization, to the student and his initiative to explore.

And last, how should faculty respond to students with initiative to apply hand-held computers in courses -- what degree of "academic freedom" will faculty allow students in using the technology? Not many years ago faculty were faced with the advent of pocket calculators. Some faculty dealt with the issue by prohibiting or restricting their use. Is a blanket exclusion of computers an enlightened or realistic response to the technology -- or a responsible response to students who, beyond college, will have to adapt to new technology to remain professionally competitive?

7. SUMMARY AND CONCLUSIONS

In summary several conclusions warrant highlighting:

1. The essence of the hand-held computer is its ready accessibility and portability which affords a unique opportunity for in-class application both in instructing computer programming and introducing substantive topics.

2. Hand-held computers programmable in BASIC are a low cost, practical alternative to instructional computing in many undergraduate curriculums today and the purchase of a $200 hand-held computer is a reasonable

student requirement.

3. The hand-held computer is a logical cor-
    nerstone in a mix of computing facilities
    (main frame, mini and desktop micros) that
    need to be organized to support instruc-
    tional needs in a contemporary engineering
    education.

4. To achieve broad student adaptation of
    computing as a tool, students must be sol-
    idly trained in programming and computer
    use must be reinforced throughout a cur-
    riculum or application will be as narrow
    as programmable calculators are used to-
    day.

5. Adaptation of computing in the classroom
    has significant instructional implications
    both in approach and what is "learned".

But, most significantly, the University of
Oklahoma program underscores that the development of a full library of courseware upgrading
undergraduate instruction in Civil Engineering,
to the computer age is a significant undertaking both pedagogically and in terms of time
and money. One that is overdue but one that is
now feasible with the hand-held computer in the
classroom.

COMPUTERS IN EDUCATION, K. Duncan and D. Harris (eds.)
Elsevier Science Publishers B.V. (North-Holland)
© IFIP, 1985

VOICE SYNTHESIS: AN UPDATE AND PERSPECTIVE

Randall L. Gull

Director, Curriculum Development
Jostens Learning Systems Inc.

We live in a verbal world. Over 90% of our daily communication is accomplished by voice. Voice is the most expedient and, in many circumstances, the most effective means of communication.

Can you imagine how complex your life would become should you lose your ability to speak? All communications would be done by sign or by letter. Many individuals, due to physical limitations, have been placed in this position. While most have been able to adjust and live productive and fulfilled lives, certainly the absence of voice has posed a major challenge to them.

The ability to communicate verbally is more than a convenience; skills of speaking and listening have a significant impact on our cognitive abilities. In terms of chronological human development, listening and speaking serve as a foundation for learning the skills of reading and writing. It is all too evident that children with impairments often have difficulty speaking and writing. Research has also named listening as a primary skill in learning to think logically and sequentially.

Different cognitive skills are used in response to auditory and visual stimuli. Visually an image is received in a composite picture; such cognitive skills as focus, discrimination and interpretation are used to respond. In contrast, auditory stimuli are received sequentially in units; such cognitive skills as sequence, recall, and assimilation are used to respond.

Therefore, the sensory channels used to receive, process, and assimilate information have a direct impact on the learning process. In many cases the challenge placed on the various sensory modes is as important as the content of the learning experience.

Based on these observations, it would appear that the incorporation of voice output with microcomputers used for educational purposes is far more than a "nicety" or "gimmick." The inclusion of voice with computer-based instruction is crucial to the development of many of the high level thinking skills that many of today's programs claim to promote and enhance. Requiring a student to read and respond to a CAI program in a total visual environment is not only unnatural, but possibly interruptive to the learning process. One could use the analogy of a two-legged stool to represent many of today's

microcomputer learning centers. Yes, the programs are interactive and visually complete, but the auditory function, a primary sense and skill, is being neglected. Fortunately, technology has advanced to allow the third leg of the stool to be added. Voice synthesis, the artificial production of voice, is now available at a reasonable cost.

Digitized voice synthesis has made great strides in the last two years. Recent technology, using a development process known as linear predictive code (LPC), has made it possible to realistically emulate the human voice and at the same time to require small amounts of memory. Prior to LPC, a consumer was forced to make a hard decision between the available technologies of phonemic-based or wave form-based voice synthesis. Phonemic-based systems are memory efficient, but the voice output sounds robotic. Wave form-based systems are very humanlike, but require an inordinate amount of memory. Certainly, in education only humanlike voice is acceptable, and the nature of a microcomputer demands a memory efficient system; LPC technology answers both these needs.

The time has come for educators to step back and evaluate the need to include voice with their microcomputer learning centers. An awareness of the various modes of learning and a sensitivity to the cruciality of verbal communication emphasize the obvious importance of voice inclusion. Now technology has made it both possible and affordable.

NOTE: During the presentation I will demonstrate the three synthesis technologies: phonemic, wave form, and LPC. I will discuss the strengths and weaknesses of each.

Computer Languages, Problem-solving, and Programming

COMPUTERS IN EDUCATION, K. Duncan and D. Harris (eds.)
Elsevier Science Publishers B.V. (North-Holland)
© IFIP, 1985

A Structured Pedagogy for Programming Courses

Frank W. Connolly
College of Public and International Affairs
The American University
Washington, D.C.

This paper shares the author's experience with Structured Programming techniques as a pedagogical base in conducting program language courses and in grading students projects in language-oriented courses.

I. Introduction

Structured Programming is a philosophy of system design and development that has been extensively researched and documented during the past decade. Its merits are explained in many programming and most systems development texts in use today. The benefits include reduced development and maintenance costs as the result of top-down design supported by standardization of program design and coding. In seeking to teach these concepts the author happened upon a teaching approach (Introduction to Computer Programming Structured COBOL by Shelly & Cashman) that proved unworkable, but provided the grist for incorporating structured programming techniques as teaching tools to provide students focused learning experiences that foster both good programs and good programming habits.

In professional environments, Structured Programming tenets call for program development teams to facilitate writing "proper" programs that are well documented and easily maintainable. Classroom restrictions and the need to expose all class members to rudimentary structured techniques (as well as syntactical rules of a langiuage) dictate modifications to industry's implementation. The challenge is to modify the logistics of implementing structured programming, without compromising the philosophy that underlies its adoption.

II. The Benefits

Introducing students to the concepts of Structured Programming via lecture on the merits and benefits of top-down design and proper documentation is not enough. Students should have the opportunity and requirement to work in an environment that requires developing programs using structured techniques, and their work should be evaluated in a manner that both encourages and rewards proper use. Such a learning environment not only teaches the precepts of Structured Programming, it aids the development of programming habits that are essential. Structured programming becomes the expected approach, rather than an arbitrary requirement.

Fostering a structured classroom environment has numerous benefits:

1. Milestones for logic and code development provide students with the incentive to work on developing a program in an interative manner, rather than waiting until the night before a program is due and pulling an "all-nighter" in hopes of getting done;

2. Peer review (via Walkthrus) increases peer pressure on students to complete tasks in a timely fashion;

3. Just as industry studies show the cost benefits of early detection of errors, so to students learn the "grade benefits" of logic and code reviews that detect errors in the early stages of program development;

4. Students are exposed to the problem solving approaches of other class members, and come to understand and appreciate alternate approaches to the same problem. In addition they experience the benefits of standards in documentation and design materials

as they struggle to understand another's proposed solution, or to defend their own;

5. Peer teaching takes place naturally, as strong students assist weaker ones;

6. Students devlop an empirical appreciation for program development as an iterative process -- a step-wise refinement moving along logical paths toward a solution;

7. Collective problem analysis improves the problem-solving skills and abilities of the individual students; and,

8. Students are actively involved in classroom activities, learning, defending, assisting, and researching solutions.

III. The Techniques

The tools for implementing this structured teaching include:

1. Detailed standards for documentation materials (Hierarchy charts, I-P-O charts, and pseudocode);

2. Detailed standards for program code;

3. Student conducted Walkthrus of design materials and code; and,

4. A grading strategy that fosters adherence to the standards and completon of the defined program development steps.

A. Documentation Standards
A detailed description of the expected materials used for program development and documentation is distributed to each student. These reflect commonly accepted standards for Hierarchy charts, I-P-O charts and pseudocode. These standards are the basis for students critiqueing the format of materials required for the walkthrus, and the instructor's final review of documentation materials submitted at the completion of the programming project.

B. Code Standards
As with the Documentation Standards, these reflect coding standards that are commonly used in the industry (e.g. naming conventions, indentation rules). These, too, are used by students in reviewing program code as part of the

walkthru process. They form the basis for the instructor's final review of the completed project.

C. Walkthrus
The concept of egoless programs and code is fostered in industry by using programming teams -- librarian, lead programmers, project leaders, etc. Students' skill levels are fairly homogenious, so that lead programmers and project leaders are not available. Despite these limitations, walkthrus provide a unique opportunity for student learning.

For each project students are assigned to a project team (dyads for large projects, triads for smaller ones) and must participate in two walkthrus: a review of program design; and, a review of written program code. Both of these walkthrus are completed in class, prior to any program testing.

For the Design Walkthru, students are expected to arrive at class with completed Hierarchy Chart, I-P-O charts and pseudocode. Each student in turn presents his/her materials to other team members who review the submitted materials focusing on two questions:

1. Will the logic setforth in the Hierarchy Chart, I-P-O charts and Pseudocode fulfill the project requirements?

2. Do the materials presented adhere to the established standards for the course?

Team members are limited to pointing out shortcomings or potential problems in the logic. They are encouraged NOT to suggest corrections or improvements, only to identify problems. The presenting student has the responsibility to search out corrections. Further, reviewers are instructed not to compare their logic design with that of the presenting student. The emphasis is on each student developing a workable solution, not on reaching a consensus, nor on achieving a common solution. Using the reviewers' feedback, each student corrects the design materials and translates the resulting logic into program code.

In the Code Walkthru each student brings to class the updated version of their design materials (i.e. Hierarchy Chart,

I-P-O charts and pseudocode), and an error-free, compiler-generated listing of their source code. To avoid a discussion of grammatical issues of the language, handwritten code and code that includes syntactical errors are not acceptable (that eliminates listings that have not been generated by the compiler). As in the Design Walkthru, each student presents and defends his/her code to the other team members. Reviewers compare the corrected design materials (Hierarchy and I-P-O charts, and pseudocode) to the presented code. Assuming that the design materials are correct, Reviewers focus on two critical questions:

1. Does the code accurately translate the corrected logic for solving the problem (i.e. does it accurately translate the design materials)?

2. Do the materials adhere to the course standards?

Individual students are responsible for correcting identified errors. Then they move into a traditional program testing sequence. After the Code Walkthru the instructor releases the data and control language to test the program.

During the Design and Code Walkthrus the instructor concentrates on three tasks:

1. Collecting grading records;

2. Identifying questions and the appropriate response for same; and,

3. Ascertaining topics in need of clarification or follow-up.

The instructor moves from team to team identifying students who came to class fully prepared for the Walkthru. Although this can be done surreptitiously, directly asking each student the status of their materials increases peer pressure.

Project teams slide into a passive mode, seeking the quick and easy way out by asking the instructor for assistance or clarification. Some questions cannot reasonably be answered by team members and the instructor must handle these. But, questions that can be answered by other team members are reflected back to the team, occassionally with suggestions for where to find the appropriate material in manuals or the text.

Listening to team discussions identifies problem areas or topics that require fuller presentation or clarification. When several teams are struggling with the same problem it may indicate a need for clarification or even recovering previous lecture material. If a team asks a question that focuses attention on a technique that the entire class should hear, the answer is directed to the entire class. Responses can be deffered until the walkthru is complete, or the process of the walkthru can be interrupted to present the concept. Although interrupting the walkthru disrupts the teams' train of thought, it allows the small groups to collectively analyze and reflect upon the newly presented concept.

D. Grading Strategy

Studies of the development life cycle of a program and structured programming have focused attention on the multiple phases of program development, the step-wise refinement process. In the development process students need to develop the habit of properly focusing their attention for each step of the process. Roger Pressman points out in Software Engineering: A Practitioner's Approach that discipline is required to restrict one's attention to a single, specific level at a time. Jumping from major design phases into detailed concerns about code is distracting and wasteful. Since the program development skills being taught have multiple phases, grading student work should foster and reward this concentrated focus. For that reason, project grading is broken into components which reflect the steps involved:

1. Logical design;

2. Code development;

3. Successful execution of the program; and

4. Adherence to code and documentation standards.

The grading procedure is designed to integrate the concern for structured techniques with the requirements of evaluating student mastery of the concepts and their use.

For a project to be considered complete a packet of materials must be submitted. The packet includes:

1. Source listing from the clean compilation;

2. Correct output (i.e. format specifications have been met exactly, and the results are arithmetically and logically correct);

3. Accurate and current I-P-O charts;

4. Accurate and current pseudo-code; and,

5. Accurate and current Hierarchy Chart.

When students submit the completed project packet, the first task is for the instructor to review the program generated output. Projects with incorrect output are returned to the student without reviewing the documentation materials or code. Students make the corrections indicated and resubmit all materials.

When the program generated output is reviewed and found to be correct, the Hierarchy Chart, I-P-O charts and pseudocode are reviewed, and the program code is evaluated. The documentation materials are evaluated for

1. Adherence to the documentation standards, and

2. The documentation's accuracy in reflecting the final program solution.

The program code is evaluated for:

1. Adherence to standards, and

2. Utilization of techniques and procedures included in the recent course materials (e.g. if single dimensioned arrays were the focus of lectures and the purpose for the programming project, has the student used that technique in completing the problem?)

To foster attention to each phase in the development process, each aspect of the project is graded separately, and each contributes to an overall project grade:

Design Walkthru: I-P-O charts, pseudo-code and Hierarchy Charts must be prepared for the Design Walkthru. Students receive 2 points toward their project for coming to the Walkthru with the material ready. No attempt is made on the instructor's part to review or evaluate the design materials at this stage. Project team members are responsible for reviewing. The instructor verifies that a student was prepared or not.

Code Walkthru: Each student is to have a complete, error-free program listing of the assigned program for the Code Walkthru (i.e. no errors, no cautions, no warnings) in addition to corrected versions of their design materials (H-I-P-O charts and pseudocode). Students earn 3 points toward their project grade by coming to class with the appropriate materials. The project team members are responsible for review and critique of the materials; the instructor's task is to record whether or not a student came to the Walkthru prepared.

Completed Program Materials. Once programs successfully execute, students hand in the completed project packet (i.e. source listing, the output generated by the program, and the finalized version of their design materials).

From zero (0) to six (6) points are earned for program completion, based upon a specified completion date. Six points are earned for completion by the defined deadline. This award is reduced by one point point for each class period the program is late.

To encourage careful examination of program output, there is a penalty of one (1) point for handing in a program that generates incorrect output. If errors are found in output the entire submitted package is returned to the student, without evaluating or reviewing the design materials or code.

Technique and Style: Only after programs are accepted as correct, the design materials and program code are reviewed and evaluated by the instructor. This review covers Hierarchy Charts, I-P-O charts, pseudocode, and program code. Each student earns from zero (0) to four (4) points based upon their adherence to code and documentation standards, and their use' of current coding techniques.

Students earn from zero (0) to fifteen (15) points for each project. Letter grades are assigned as follows:

Points	Grade
14-15	A
11-13	B
8-10	C
4-7	D
0-3	F

A balance in grading is built into the system to reflect the importance of design and documentation along with adherence to time deadlines. The scheme proposed here reflects the author's emphasis on program documentation and design:

1. Six (6) points (40%) of the grade is based on getting the program running by the deadline;

2. Five (5) points are gained by being prepared for walkthrus (33.3%); and,

3. Four (4) points for adherence to standards (26.6%).

Being prepared for walkthrus and adhering to standards can assure a student a minimum grade of C (9 points). Skipping the walkthrus means that the highest grade possible is also a C (10 points maximum). Total disregard for programming and documentation standards limits a student to 11 points (a maximum grade of B).

Grades are assigned for each phase of program development at the time the milestone occurs. Using an open and accessible grading system allows each student to measure his/her progress at any time. This regular feedback not only keeps the student apprised of their progress, it reenforces the cyclical nature of program development by reflecting the importance placed on each phase.

IV. Summary

Programming is a developed skill which assumes normal intelligence, but which is honed by experience and personal discipline. Research has resulted in the development of techniques for improving efficieny in program and system development. This paper describes one strategy for using some of these same techniques as teaching strategies in undergraduate programming classes. For students these techniques offer realistic, interesting learning experiences. For teachers, these techniques can be a framework for developing exercises through which students are taught less, but learn more.

COMPUTERS IN EDUCATION, K. Duncan and D. Harris (eds.)
Elsevier Science Publishers B.V. (North-Holland)
© IFIP, 1985

DEVELOPING PROGRAM READING COMPREHENSION TESTS FOR THE COMPUTER SCIENCE CLASSROOM

Lionel E. Deimel, Jr.* and Lois Makoid**

*Department of Computer Science
**Department of Psychology
North Carolina State University
Raleigh, North Carolina 27695
U.S.A.

A methodology for constructing program reading comprehension tests is discussed and illustrated. Emphasis is on multiple-choice tests used with realistic reading passages. Item writing employing a classification of question types developed by the authors and a program comprehension model developed by Ruven Brooks is recommended.

1. THE CASE FOR TESTING READING COMPREHENSION

Although it may seem axiomatic that requiring programming students to write programs or parts of programs on examinations is the ideal form of testing in an introductory course, such is not necessarily the case. The mechanics of administering composition exercises are troublesome. A number of authors have pointed out these difficulties and have suggested that asking students to read and answer questions about programs or program fragments represents an attractive alternative to the more obvious testing strategy using code writing (1, 2). Moreover, "programming" involves skills other than program writing, the ability to read programs being one of these. Not only is program reading ability intrinsically valuable to the programmer, but reading programs may be a useful way of sharpening one's programming skills (3).

Lemos has made a particularly strong case for the use of reading exercises on examinations (4). He argues that composition questions require the student to work in an artificial environment, that grading is arbitrary, subjective, and time-consuming, and that meaningful but tractable problems are hard to construct. Relying on programs written outside of class for evaluating student progress is not fully acceptable, as there is no way to insure that students do their own work or work with acceptable efficiency. Using results from two experiments (5, 6), Lemos concludes that results of grammatical tests do not correlate strongly with the ability to write programs, but that there is a moderate correlation between the results of reading tests and the ability to write programs (as measured by writing questions on examinations). Given the greater tractability of reading tests, Lemos suggests that they represent efficient testing instruments (measured in terms of instructor investment) and that more effort should be put into developing reading tests "with a high linear relationship to writing ability."

Program reading comprehension questions then may be justified on two grounds—they test a skill which programming students need to develop, and they represent a potentially attractive way of testing for knowledge required for writing programs. Program reading and writing are different activities, however, and we should not expect them always to be equally developed in individuals, any more than natural language reading and writing abilities are correlated.

2. GENERAL CONSIDERATIONS FOR TEST CONSTRUCTION

In what follows, we will suggest techniques and guidelines for constructing reading comprehension tests and illustrate with examples how these suggestions may be applied. By a comprehension test, we mean any examination instrument for which the student must read and understand either complete programs or program fragments in order to answer the question asked. Such questions may be multiple-choice or free-response. Typically, the student is given a passage to read and is asked a question about it, although it is also possible to ask the student to select one of several passages as the answer to a question. Possible forms are illustrated by the three simple examples below:

1. What is the apparent purpose of the code below?

```
TEMP := A;
A := B;
B := TEMP;
```

2. What is the apparent purpose of the code below?

```
TEMP := A;
A := B;
B := TEMP;
```

   (a) Set A, B, and TEMP all to the same value.
   (b) Sort the values of A, B, and TEMP.
   (c) Exchange the values of A and B.
   (d) Sort the values of A and B.

3. Which of the following fragments correctly

and efficiently exchanges the values of A
and B?

```
(a) T1 := A;      (b) B := A;
    T2 := B;          A := B;
    B  := T2;
    A  := T1;

(c) TEMP := A;    (d) T1 := A;
    A := B;           T2 := B;
    B := TEMP;        A := T2;
                      B := T1;
```

We recommend use of the multiple-choice format.
Multiple-choice tests can be made highly reliable and can be graded objectively and quickly.
Admittedly, the effort required to construct a
good multiple-choice test is substantial, but
the reward of scoring ease often justifies the
investment, particularly in the large classes
now typical of introductory programming courses.
Over time, a pool of test items (questions) can
be developed, further reducing the investment in
the administration of individual tests. (See (7)
for a discussion of the advantages of multiple-
choice testing.)

Presenting separate passages for each question
has the advantage of allowing diverse questions
on the same examination, but there are disadvantages. In order to provide sufficient contextual information to answer more advanced questions, passages may become lengthy. The amount
of reading may then make the time required to
answer a series of questions excessive. The
reading overhead can sometimes be reduced by
supplying contextual material for many questions at once. For example, at the beginning of
the examination, certain variables may be declared, and these identifiers can be used over
and over in succeeding questions wherever variables of their types are required.

It is attractive, in fact, to ask many questions
about a single passage. Such a passage can be
relatively long, as the time devoted to reading
it can be amortized over the full set of questions. This allows use of complete, documented
programs or procedures and places the student in
a realistic situation wherein he must separate
the relevant from the irrelevant and misleading.
More importantly, questions can be asked which
probe deeply the student's understanding of programming. Questions based on only a few lines of
code may require only rudimentary knowledge of
the programming language and not test more complete and comprehensive understanding of programs required of the professional programmer.

Ruven Brooks (8, 9) has provided a useful model
of program comprehension which is useful (a) in
understanding why more extensive and realistic
fragments are important in testing comprehension
and (b) in providing criteria to be used in making decisions about the kind of questions to be
asked. A program, he suggests, is understood as
a succession of knowledge domains representing
the problem being solved, the mathematical model

used in the problem analysis, the overall program organization, particular algorithms and data structures, the programming language, and the
host machine. Total program comprehension encompasses not only relevant knowledge in each of
these domains, but understanding of how individual domains relate to one another. Obviously,
providing the reader with only a few isolated
lines of code cannot force him to demonstrate
facility in dealing with the complexities inherent in real programs. If more complete passages
are available for reading, however, the test
writer can consciously select questions posed in
particular knowledge domains or questions which
require relating specific domains to one another. Too many comprehension tests fail to demonstrate the test taker's full competence because
most questions are taken from the same knowledge
domain, most often that of the source language
domain.

We will emphasize use of the single passage with
multiple questions because we think its advantages are significant and because it is an often
overlooked technique. Undoubtedly many programming instructors are reluctant to use reading
comprehension testing as a measure of student
competence because the examples of such testing
they have seen lack variety and seem to tap the
more trivial aspects of the code being read.
Multiple-choice comprehension testing may seem
especially unattractive, as items are hard to
construct and often seem unduly simple to answer. Certainly many poor examples of comprehension testing appear in textbooks, teacher's
manuals, and technical papers on computer science education and software psychology. We intend to show, however, not only that there is
great variety in the kind of questions that can
be asked, but also that the instructor can construct questions, if not mechanically, at least
systematically.

3. CLASSIFYING COMPREHENSION QUESTION TYPES

In (10), we offered a list of question types
which can be used on program reading comprehension tests. The list is not exhaustive, but
suggests that the test writer has many options.
To structure the list, we used the taxonomy of
behavioral objectives in the cognitive domain
proposed by B. S. Bloom and widely used for operationally defining educational objectives (11,
12). Other organizing principles could have been
applied, though Bloom's scheme is surely ser-
viceable. A revised version of our taxonomy appears in (13).

Bloom defines six levels of educational objectives, which he calls <u>knowledge</u>, <u>comprehension</u>,
<u>application</u>, <u>analysis</u>, <u>synthesis</u>, and <u>evalua-
tion</u>. Bloom claims that these levels order cognitive behaviors from the simple to the complex.
The levels are arranged hierarchically, in
fact--the objectives of one level requiring and
building upon the behaviors found in previous
levels. By classifying types of comprehension
questions within these levels, we are able, at

least generally, to enumerate particular measurement tools in order of increasing cognitive complexity. So that the reader can better appreciate this ordering, we will describe the six levels as they relate generally to the measurement of programming competencies. Recognize that there is ambiguity in these levels and evidence that the ordering of the first four is more certain than the positions of the last two (14).

Tasks requiring responses at the knowledge level call for definitions, recognition, simple identifications, etc. of terminology, conventions, structures, functions, procedures, or processes. At this level, the student basically only gives back information which he has learned or read.

Comprehension (Bloom's terminology) refers to "the lowest level of understanding." Questions at this level require the student to paraphrase or summarize information without necessarily being able to see all its implications. Comprehension may be shown by translating programs from one form to another (for example, into flowcharts or data structure diagrams), by interpreting the function of a section of code, or by displaying a simple execution trace.

The third level is application. This level involves the use of abstractions or concepts (rules, methods, conventions, procedures) in particular and concrete situations. The student may be required to trace complex program behavior, understand program behavior in modified environments, or indicate how program modules can be used in non-obvious ways.

Analysis refers to the ability to understand not only the workings of individual components of a program but also to understand the relationships among those components and the implications of those relationships. Test questions at this level require recognition of unstated assumptions, both inductive and deductive reasoning, recognition of errors in reasoning, etc. The student may be asked about the elements of a program, how they are organized, how they work together, or what range of program behavior is possible.

Synthesis refers to the ability to put parts together to form a new whole. This may involve a revision of a program, documentation of a newly encountered program, rearrangement of segments of a program to alter function, modification of a program's form without change of function, etc. (Program writing is the most obvious form of synthesis in programming, but is not relevant to reading comprehension testing, of course.) Although this level stresses creative behaviors and the formation of some "product," the product need not be source code. Synthesis questions can elicit original thinking on a complex problem, the derivation of relationships, the formation of hypotheses, or the planning of a course of action. They may require modification of a program, development of test strategies, or generation of test data.

Finally, we come to the level of evaluation. Evaluation behavior involves the employment of criteria to render a (qualitative or quantitative) judgement, decision, or selection (15). Test questions designed at this level are at the highest level of cognitive activity because they involve elements of all other categories plus conscious judgements based on clearly defined criteria. The student may be required to judge various aspects of software quality (efficiency, correctness, maintainability, consistency of style, etc.). Test questions can include asking students to justify the use of a particular algorithm, criticize poorly written code, compare and contrast two programs on some basis, or prove a program correct.

4. TEST ITEM CONSTRUCTION

Construction of a reading comprehension test must begin with a determination of what the test writer is testing for. The first step must be an identification of subject matter—the use of particular data structures or algorithms, scope rules, etc. Next, and here is where our taxonomy becomes useful, the type of mastery expected should be defined. In beginning classes or in more advanced classes dealing with new and difficult subjects, relatively low level skills, represented by knowledge- and comprehension-level behaviors, are probably as advanced as the instructor can reasonably demand. In more advanced courses or in beginning courses dealing with more familiar material, analysis- and synthesis-level behaviors may appropriately be sought. (Remember that higher level behaviors generally require skills from lower levels.) Our classification suggests the types of questions which may be appropriate.

We can offer no magic formula for finding an appropriate passage to be read, the next step in the test-construction process. The test writer must rely on skill, intuition, and experience. Appropriate texts may be written especially for the test or chosen from a collection of programs. The test writer should not overlook the possibility of using programs written for other purposes, programs written by students in previous terms, or examples from textbooks. Whether constructed or selected, however, the passage must contain the proper elements for the test, admit of the right sort of questions, and satisfy other pragmatic constraints of length, language features, application area, and style. The style issue may be complex, for style may be manipulated in many ways which affect testing. For instance, incorrect indentation may be introduced to see if students understand particular control structures, and comments may be included or excluded in order to lower or raise the level of difficulty of a particular question by providing or withholding information from the reader. Nearly every passage selection represents a compromise, just as programming assignments seldom contain all elements sought by the instructor in precisely the right mix. It may be helpful to begin the selection process by trying

to construct a programming assignment whose ful-
fillment would yield an appropriate text for
reading.

The actual writing of multiple-choice items must
be done with great care. The stem, the question
or the statement to be completed, should cue the
reader as to the subject matter and nature of
the cognitive activity required. This obviates
searching through disparate answers and having
to eliminate them one-by-one. "The programming
technique illustrated on line 45 is called" is a
better stem for an item requiring the identification of a recursive call than "Procedure EX-
AMPLE is." The correct answer should be a gra-
matically proper answer for or completetion of
the stem. It should also be derivable from the
reading passage and the stem. Keep Brooks's model in mind when phrasing questions, as it is often possible to pose equivalent questions in
different domains. Questions can be phrased in
terms of a specific identifier, for example, or
in terms of the function performed by an unspec-
ified variable. Where students are expected to
show thorough understanding of programs, questions should be taken from as many knowledge domains as possible and should require transfer of
knowledge between domains.

The most difficult part of writing items is making up distractors, the plausible but wrong answers which must be included. There should be
neither too many nor too few of them, lest the
reading of the question take too long or be too
susceptible to guessing. Offering 4 answers is
typical. Miller, et al. (15) suggest guidelines
for writing distractors:

1. Write nonsense answers in technical jargon.
2. Write sensible but irrelevant or trivial
   answers.
3. Write answers that are correct for related
   questions.
4. Write answers that are partially correct but
   exclude components that make other responses
   more correct.
5. Occasionally use "none of the above" or "all
   of the above," remembering that students
   will select the latter more often than the
   former.

Answers should be randomly ordered unless there
is some obvious logical progression among them.
It should be made clear whether a "correct" answer or the "best" answer is required. Many
testing experts caution against questions requiring that several answers be selected, as
this format complicates scoring. If this format
and the use of too few distractors are avoided,
there is general agreement that adjusting scores
to account for guessing is unnecessary.

There are additional aspects of test construction to consider. The wording of questions
should not cue the answers to other questions.
To ensure this does not happen, questions without their reading passages, can be given to an
assistant. Any question which can be answered

should be eliminated. All questions should not
be of equal difficulty, as it is important to
make adequate discriminations among students of
various abilities. If only hard questions are
presented, for example, the test writer will
learn little about the many students who get
most of the items wrong. It is helpful to present questions from easiest to most difficult.
Students sometimes give up after encountering
difficult questions early or are left with insufficient time to answer later questions they
can answer. Basing the ordering on difficulty
ratings from at least two assistants is desirable. Assistants can also identify possible am-
biguities or questions with no correct answer.

5.   SOME ILLUSTRATIONS

We now illustrate the foregoing guidelines with
questions adapted from a reading comprehension
test constructed by the authors and colleagues
and given to students completing their second
programming course in Pascal. The reading passage consisted of a set of global declarations
and a fully-documented list-processing procedure. (The passage, along with the complete comprehension test, appears in (16).) There were 11
multiple-choice items on the test, selected to
maximize variety not only of question type, but
also knowledge domains tapped. This was consistent with our objective of measuring students'
reading comprehension, broadly construed. No
knowledge-level or evaluation items were used,
as they were considered, respectively, too easy
and too hard.

4.   Which diagram best represents the major data
     structure on which procedure UPDATE oper-
     ates?

(a)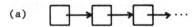

(b)

(c)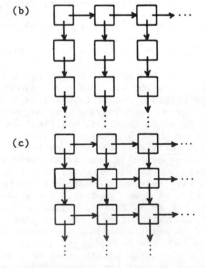

This question requires translation of a data
structure into pictorial form. The correct an-

swer is (b). This question is not difficult and is an example of what we have called <u>translation</u> at the comprehension level. The distractors represent reasonable linked-list structures, but are easily dismissed by a reader who understands record and pointer declarations.

5. On a single call to procedure UPDATE, once ERCODE is set to a value other than OKUPDATE, is it ever changed?

   (a) Yes, it can be set to another value other than OKUPDATE.
   (b) Yes, it can be reset to OKUPDATE.
   (c) Yes, it can be set to any value of type ERRORTYPE.
   (d) No, it cannot be set to another value.

The answer to question 5 is (d), which may be determined by searching through the code for instances of ERCODE and tracing various execution paths to see what can happen to it. Notice that no special knowledge of data structures or the application is needed to answer this question. It is not a straightforward tracing question and therefore is classified as a <u>prediction</u> question under level 3, application. Compare this to the superficially similar next item. Notice that the cases which must be considered in question 6 are not immediately obvious from the code itself.

6. When UPDATE is called, suppose the fields of INREC have the values indicated below:

Field	Value
CNAME	´503´
SECT	´002´
SNAME.LAST	´JONES´
SNAME.MIDDLE	´A´
SNAME.FIRST	´JOHN´
FLAG	T2
GRADE	88

What might the procedure do? (Circle <u>all</u> that apply.)

   (a) Update test 2 grade in course 503 section 1 for JOHN A. JONES to 88.
   (b) Set ERCODE to NOFIELD.
   (c) Update quiz 2 grade in course 503 section 2 for JOHN A. JONES to 88.
   (d) Set ERCODE to NOSECTION.
   (e) Update test 2 grade in course 503 section 2 for JOHN A. JONES to 88.
   (f) Set ERCODE to NOSTUDENT.
   (g) None of the above.

This item violates our suggestion of avoiding multiple-answer questions and required less straightforward grading than we prefer. (See (17) regarding such questions.) It proved to be a difficult but discriminating item, however. Mere tracing of the code is not sufficient here; the student must consider possible states of the data structure upon entry and trace the consequences of each. The item is thus classified as an <u>analysis</u> one under the analysis level. Notice

that the student must relate the problem domain answers to the data structure domain. The answers are (d), (e), and (f).

7. Which of the following are apparently assumptions of the procedure?

   (a) If two courses (each with students enrolled) have the same name, their sections must be different.
   (b) All sections for the same course are represented consecutively.
   (c) Every section contains at least one student.
   (d) No student is in two different courses.

There is no basis in the code for answers (b) or (d), but there is a test to handle a section with no students, a fact which eliminates (c). If two courses had the same names and sections, only student records in the first could be updated. There is no evidence to suggest this is an intended feature of UPDATE, so that (a) expresses the most likely assumption of the programmer. This is an analysis-level item employing <u>inference</u>. Note that the answers are all written in the problem domain, which requires the student to relate the code to higher-level concepts.

8. Which one of the following statements best describes the effort required to change the WHILE loop beginning at line 85 to a REPEAT loop, with the understanding that the function of UPDATE is to remain unchanged?

   (a) The change is easily made by substituting REPEAT for lines 85 and 86 and following the body of the loop with UNTIL (ERCODE<>OKUPDATE) OR (STUDPTR^.NAME=SNAME).
   (b) The change requires the introduction of a new Boolean variable.
   (c) The change requires the introduction of an IF statement.
   (d) The change requires the introduction of a new Boolean variable and an IF statement.
   (e) The change requires restructuring the code in ways other than those described above.

This question illustrates how a synthesis question, in this case a <u>modification</u> one, can be made into a good multiple-choice item. The correct answer is (c). Were the body of the WHILE loop always executed at least once, (a) would describe a satisfactory change, but a proper understanding of the procedure leads to the realization that this cannot be guaranteed. An IF is necessary to bypass the loop in this case. Answer (b) describes a technique often necessary for loop restructuring but unneeded here. Both (d) and (e) are plausible. Notice that the student must actually construct the modification to be certain of picking the right answer. This question requires use of information from several knowledge domains and is quite difficult.

6. POST-TEST ITEM ANALYSIS

Even the best of test writers sometimes create items which are unsuccessful. To be sure test items have accomplished their purpose, post-test item analyses should be performed.

If computational resources are available for item analysis, the most important type of analysis for an achievement test correlates each item with the total test score. Correlations near zero indicate the item is too difficult, ambiguous, or unrelated to what the test writer intended to ask. Low correlation indicates the item does not well relate students getting it correct to students getting high overall test scores. Correlations of .5 or above are desirable.

A related type of measure which can be computed easily by hand is the index of discrimination. Order all the tests by overall score and select the top 1/3 and bottom 1/3 scorers. Count the number of students getting the item correct that are in the top 1/3, subtract the number getting the item correct in the bottom 1/3, and divide this number by 1/3 of the total students. Items with values of .4 or above are very good, between .4 and .2 satisfatory, and below .2 poor.

Another indication of the worth of an item is the index of difficulty. This is simply the proportion of students who answer the item correctly. Test items should have an average difficulty of 50% for maximum discriminating power. (See (17) for additional discussion.)

On the basis of these analyses, one can scrutinize items which are poor discriminators. The test writer can question if an item is poorly designed, not accurately measuring what was intended, not clearly stated, or of an inappropriate difficulty level. One can also ask if the students' educational experiences are different from what was expected, and if so, why. From this information, items can be redesigned or eliminated from the test or item pool, or students can be given additional experiences necessary to acquire the desired skills.

7. POSTSCRIPT

We have intended to show that program reading comprehension testing is useful and that tests can be constructed and evaluated systematically. A question classification scheme which relates question types to instructor objectives and a model for program comprehension are cornerstones of this methodology. Although their usefulness does not depend upon their being completely "right," it is desirable that refinements be made wherever possible. We are constantly revising our taxonomy and invite the recommendations of others.

REFERENCES

[1] Trombotta, M, On testing programming ability, SIGCSE Bulletin 11 (Dec. 1979) 56-60.

[2] Haas, M. and Hassell, J., A proposal for a measure of program understanding, SIGCSE Bulletin 15 (Feb. 1983) 7-13.

[3] Kernighan, B. W. and Plauger, P. J., The Elements of Programming Style, 2nd ed. (McGraw-Hill, New York, 1978).

[4] Lemos, R., Measuring programming language proficiency, AEDS J. (Summer 1980) 261-273.

[5] Lemos, R., FORTRAN programming: an analysis of pedagogical alternatives, J. Educational Data Processing 12 (Aug. 1975) 21-29.

[6] Lemos, R., An implementation of structured walk-throughs in teaching COBOL programming, Comm. ACM 22 (June 1979) 335-340.

[7] Nunnally, J. C., Psychometric Theory (McGraw-Hill, New York, 1967).

[8] Brooks, R., Using a behavioral theory of program comprehension in software engineering, in Proc. 3rd International Conf. on Software Engineering (IEEE, New York, 1978).

[9] Brooks, R., A theoretical analysis of the role of documentation in the comprehension of computer programs, in Proc. Conf. Human Factors in Computer Systems (Washington, D. C. Chapter ACM, Washington, 1982).

[10] Deimel, L. E. and Makoid, L. A., Measuring reading comprehension: the search for methods, in Proc. 6th Annual National Educational Computing Conf. (Univ. of Daton, Dayton, O., 1984).

[11] Bloom, B., et al., eds., Taxonomy of Educational Objectives: Handbook I: Cognitive Domain (David McKay, New York, 1956).

[12] Bloom, B., Hastings, J., and Madaus, G., Handbook of Formative and Summative Evaluation of Student Learning (McGraw-Hill, New York, 1971).

[13] Deimel, L. E., The uses of program reading, SIGCSE Bulletin 17 (June 1985).

[14] Kunen, S., Cohen, R., and Solman, R., A levels-of-processing analysis of Bloom's taxonomy, J. Educational Psyc. 73 (Apr. 1981) 202-211.

[15] Miller, H. G., Williams, R. G., and Haladyna, T. M., Beyond Facts: Objective Ways to Measure Thinking (Educational Technology Publications, Englewood Cliffs, 1978).

[16] Deimel, L. E., Kunz, L., Makoid, L. A., and Perry, J., The effects of comment placement and reading times on program reading comprehension, in Proc. 1985 Conf. Info. Sci-Sciences and Systems (Dept. of Electrical Engineering & Computer Science, The Johns Hopkins Univ., Baltimore, 1985).

[17] Ahmann, J. S. and Glock, M. D., Evaluating Student Progress: Principles of Tests and Measurements (Allyn and Bacon, Boston, 1981).

ACKNOWLEDGEMENTS

The authors would like to thank Jo Perry and Lynda Kunz for their help in developing some of the questions in this paper.

COMPUTERS IN EDUCATION, K. Duncan and D. Harris (eds.)
Elsevier Science Publishers B.V. (North-Holland)
© IFIP, 1985

How to Teach Programming:
A Cognitive Perspective

Dr. Elliot Soloway, Yale University. (Session Chair)
Dr. Roy Pea, Bank Street College of Education.
Dr. Harold W. Lawson Jr., Linkoping University.
Dr. Arthur Luehrmann, Computer Literacy, Inc.

What This Session Is About:

There is beginning to be a body of theory and experiment on how novices learn to program. Based on this literature, prescriptions for teaching programming can begin to be made that have some principled basis. Inasmuch as programming education is becoming an integral part of today's schooling, such practical observations should enable teachers to provide more effective instruction. Panelists at our session are some of the people who have been most instrumental in carrying out the cognitive research upon which prescriptions can be made. At the session, these people will venture forth and provide such prescriptions that are derivable from their theoretical and empirical research.

The objectives of this session are to:

1) *present state-of-art research in the cognitive underpinnings of novice programming,*

2) *present prescriptions based on this research that can be applied by the teacher in the classroom.*

****

Bridging the Gap: From Problem to Code

Dr. Elliot Soloway
Yale University
Dept. of Computer Science
New Haven, Ct. 06520

Most texts for introductory programming attempt to teach some form of top-down, stepwise refinement. Typically, examples are given that attempt to show the student how such a process proceeds. However, one key question is largely left unanswered: why did the author break the problem down into *those* 3 parts -- how did he/she know that *that* decomposition is a (the?) good one? Our approach to teaching programming attempts to answer this question; moreover our goal is to provide students with an *explicit problem solving language* that enables them to move from problems to code.

****

A Modern Approach to Teaching "Programming"

Harold W. Lawson Jr
Department of Computer and Information Science
Linkoping University
S-58183 Linkoping, Sweden

A modern approach to teaching programming should aim at providing fundamental knowledge that can be utilized in understanding various problem solving approaches and utilizing a variety of procedural, non-procedural and object-oriented programming languages. In order to accomplish this goal, the main abstract ideas of problem solving approaches and their concrete programming languages must be introduced. The *common denominators* of the various approaches and languages must be considered in order to provide an understanding instead of confusion based upon programming languages details.

A process oriented view of problem solving approaches provides a useful common denominator metaphor. Within this framework, the principles of procedural, non-procedural and object oriented programming can be taught. Several pedagogical methods for abstract and concrete representations will be considered.

Tools and Techniques for Guiding the Novices' First Steps Towards Programming Expertise

Dr. Roy Pea,
Bank Street College of Education
New York, N.Y.

Classroom observations and experiments involving students from elementary through high school reveal that many novice programmers have difficulty attaining minimal proficiencies in program design, analysis, and debugging. These difficulties appear in part due to the open ended nature of the programming environment often used by novices in instructional settings. Unproductive programming practices of novices will be described. We then discuss how our studies of the development of programming skills motivated the design and implementation of a set of LOGO programming games for children that provide *guiding tools* for achieving fundamental programming proficiencies. With tools to guide the attainment of foundational programming concepts and skills, and active monitoring of programming practices by the teacher, we expect students will find the conceptual hurdles of beginning programming easier to surmount.

****

Session Discussant:

Dr. Arthur Luehrmann,
Computer Literacy, Inc.
Berkeley, California

Dr. Arthur Luehrmann will serve as discussant for this panel and provide his on-line reactions to the presentations.

COMPUTERS IN EDUCATION, K. Duncan and D. Harris (eds.)
Elsevier Science Publishers B.V. (North-Holland)
©IFIP, 1985

A COMPARISON OF PROBLEM SOLVING APPROACHES:
PROCEDURAL, NON-PROCEDURAL AND OBJECT ORIENTED

Harold W. Lawson, Jr.

Department of Computer and Information Science
Linköping University
S-581 83 Linköping, Sweden

Computer related education and training programs frequently concentrate on problem solving in the context of a single programming language or one class of programming languages. By restricting the problem solving approach, many students tend to become restricted in their views of the use of computer systems for problem solving. One aspect of this situation is frequently referred to as "the first programming language syndrome". There is no one single best programming language or even class of programming languages to utilize in all problem solving situations.

It is considered to be an important educational goal, even at the introductory computer education and training levels, to provide a fundamental understanding of a spectrum of computer based problem solving approaches.

In this tutorial, we will focus on a comparison of problem solving approaches as well as the pedagogical methods for achieving the educational goal in introductory computer related education and training.

COMPUTERS IN EDUCATION, K. Duncan and D. Harris (eds.)
Elsevier Science Publishers B.V. (North-Holland)
© IFIP, 1985

Bugs In Novice Programs And Misconceptions In Novice Programmers

James C. Spohrer, Edgar Pope, Michael Lipman, Warren Sack
Scott Freiman, David Littman, Lewis Johnson, Elliot Soloway

Department of Computer Science
Cognition and Programming Project
Yale University
New Haven, Connecticut 06520

In this paper we propose a new scheme for classifying bugs in novice programs. The goal of this approach is to pinpoint where misconceptions occur in students' thinking. Key in this analysis is the identification of the knowledge --- the goals and plans --- underlying the creation of the program. We then demonstrate the application of our scheme to the analysis of actual buggy student programs.

1. Introduction: Motivation and Goals

We all have had the experience of running a computer program and receiving the following run-time error message: Bug in line 14. Moreover, we probably knew that the bug was not in line 14; rather, the bug was in some other piece of code and manifested itself in line 14. Unfortunately, novice programmers typically haven't had the experience to make this observation about run-time error messages: they proceed to line 14 and spend considerable time scratching their heads and wondering how there could be a bug in line 14.

The goal of this paper is to provide a method of program analysis such that we can (1) identify the bugs in a program, and (2) suggest where the students' misconception(s) that caused the bugs might lie. The motivation for this work lies in the belief that observable bugs provide a window into the mental, and otherwise non-observable, conceptions that the student has developed (Brown, 1978). Armed with an analysis of the student's misconceptions, instruction can be tailored to provide specific assistance. In fact, we have used the analysis described here in the development of a computer program, PROUST, that can correctly identify about 75% of the *non-syntactic* bugs in novice programs, for a class of moderately complex introductory programming assignments (Johnson & Soloway, 1983). Thus, we see significant utility in developing techniques that improve our ability to analyze buggy novice programs.

In what follows, we first illustrate our technique of bug analysis by comparing our approach to the one most

This work was sponsored in part by the National Science Foundation, under NSF Grant DCR-8302382 and NSF Grant DPE-8470014.

commonly used for bug analysis today. Next, we present a brief overview of a scheme for bug categorization that we had previously developed, but which is not adequate. We remedy the old approach by proposing an alternative scheme for bug analysis, and provide a number of examples of this new approach.

2. An Example: Getting at the REAL Bug

Consider the problem specification and program fragments in Figure 2-1. More standard bug description techniques (Ostrand & Weyuker, 1982) would describe the bug in the *Buggy Fragment* by comparing it to the *Correct Fragment*, and noting the differences. In Figure 2-1 the difference would be: Missing Assignment Statement. If one were to base remedial instruction on such a bug categorization, one would be missing the point. Notice that the student was able to form one type of assignment statement correctly: sum := sum + new. Thus, saying that the student does not understand assignment statements is simply too coarse an analysis.

What, then, is the bug? Based on the bug categorization scheme outlined in our previous work (Johnson et al, 1983), we would say that the *Buggy Fragment* is missing a Counter Update statement. By Counter Update statement we mean a statement that increments, by 1, a variable that keeps track of a count. Note that the notion of a counter is not "in" the specifications, nor is it "in" the code. Rather, to accomplish the problem, real world knowledge tells us that in order to compute an average we need to have the goal of counting how many numbers are read in. Moreover, as programmers, we have a programming plan for realizing this goal: initialize a variable to zero, and update that variable inside the loop each time a new value is read in.

A description of the bug in terms of a Missing Counter Update statement now provides something that remedial instruction can dig its teeth into. For example, questions immediately arise such as: did the student include in his program a Counter Initialization statement, e.g., count := 0? If so, then the student may have a misconception concerning how or when the update by 1 should occur. However, if there is no Counter Initialization statement the bug may be deeper: the student may not have even realized he/she needed a variable that kept track of how many numbers were read in.

From this example, we conclude that bug descriptions developed by comparing a potentially buggy program with a correct program simply do not get at the misconceptions that the student may be laboring under. However, when bug descriptions are developed with respect to the *goals and plans* underlying a correct solution, then there is some potential for pinpointing a true conceptual problem. In the next section we describe what we mean by goals and plans in more detail.

Problem Specification: Write a program that outputs the average of a set of numbers. Terminate reading the numbers when 99999 (the sentinel value) is input; do not include this stopping value in the calculation.

Correct Fragment
```
------------------
while new <> 99999 do
  begin
     sum := sum + new;
     count := count + 1;
     read(new);
  end;
```

Buggy Fragment
```
---------------
while new <> 99999 do
  begin
     sum := sum + new;
     read(new);
  end;
```

Figure 2-1: A Sample Bug

3. Goals and Plans: The Knowledge Underlying Programming

We have been developing a theory of (1) the knowledge that programmers use in programming, and (2) the process by which they use that knowledge to both read and write programs. We have carried out a number of empirical studies to evaluate our theory; to date, the data we have gathered has supported our view (Soloway et al, 1982) (Soloway & Ehrlich, 1984) (Soloway et al, 1984). In this section, we will describe the portion of our theory that is particularly relevant to the identification of bugs.

Consider, then, the problem statement in Figure 3-1, that was assigned to students in an introductory Pascal programming course. We can identify four main goals that

The Reformatting Problem

```
01 In this problem, you will read in "raw data" collected by the
02 experimenter and entered into the computer. The objective of
03 this program is to read through the data and:
04    1. Kick out all bad data; a human typist often makes
05       little typos that need to be corrected.
06    2. "reformat" the data; convert the data into another
07       form that is more easily analyzed.
08
09 The experiment in which the following data was generated asked
10 subjects to answer a problem. The experimenter collected data
11 on how long it took the subject to solve the problem, and
12 whether or not the subject was correct. The format of the data
13 will be as follows:
14    SUBJECT_NUMBER PROBLEM_TYPE START_TIME END_TIME ACCURACY
15    1. where the START_TIME and END_TIME are specified as:
16       hours minutes seconds (e.g. 4 32 16, means 4 o'clock,
17       32 minutes, and 16 seconds).
18    2. SUBJECT_NUMBER is an integer.
19    3. PROBLEM_TYPE is a char; there are ONLY 'a', 'b', 'c'
20       problem types -- all other inputs are bad data
21    4. a correct solution for ACCURACY is represented as a '+',
22       while an incorrect solution is represented as a '-'.
23
24 The goal of your program is to:
25    1. if data is found that is "bad" then ask the user to
26       retype the data item; ASSUME that on this retyping that
27       the user will type in the data item correctly!!!!!
28    2. calculate the elapsed time IN SECONDS from the start and
29       end times.
30    3. output a new record of information that contains:
31       SUBJECT_NUMBER PROBLEM_TYPE ELAPSED_TIME ACCURACY
32
33 So here is data on which your program should be tested (that
34 is, we will test your program on this data... and any other
35 data we feel will make your program cough.)
36    (1) 23 a 4 23 13 4 25 1 -        (6) 73 b 12 58 10 12 59 20 +
37    (2) 33 b 4 32 20 4 31 45 +       (7) 83 c 12 59 50 1 2 20 +
38    (3) 43 c 4 40 13 4 44 44 +       (8) 21 a 7 30 30 7 32 32 +
39    (4) 63 a 12 56 12 12 57 2 +      (9) 31 d 7 34 2 7 35 10 -
40    (5) 41 c 7 36 10 7 37 10 +
41 The output for the line (1) of data would be: 23 a 108 -
42
43 THE STOPPING CONDITION ON THE LOOP TO THIS PROBLEM
44 SHOULD BE A SENTINEL VALUE (SEE THE TEXTBOOK).
```

Figure 3-1: The Assignment

must be achieved:

- G:LOOP:[1]   This goal corresponds to the intention of reading through many records of input data.
- G:VDE: The goal of "G:VALID-DATA-ENTRY" corresponds to the intention of getting "good" data from the user.
- G:CALC: The "G:CALCULATION" goal corresponds to the the intention of computing the elapsed time in this problem.
- G:OUTPUT: This goal corresponds to the intention of writing out the reformatted data.

Each of the above goals can be achieved using a number of different *programming plans*. A programming plan is a fragment of code that accomplishes a stereotypic action. For example, there are a number of stereotypic ways in

[1]Throughout this paper the names of goals and plans will be capitalized. Goals will have the prefix "G:" and plans will have the prefix "P:".

which to realize the G:LOOP goal in the above problem. Below, we list two:

- P:RD
  (P:READ-INDIVIDUAL-DATA-ITEM-SENTINEL):
  Most commonly the data item used as the sentinel in this plan is the subject number. To achieve the G:LOOP goal, the plan must first read in the subject number, then test to see if it is not the sentinel value, in which case the contents of the loop are executed. The final part of the contents of the loop is a read statement to get the next subject number to be tested. The section of code below implements this plan, and also shows the subgoals it organizes.

```
G:INPUT --------> 01  read(Subject_Number);
G:GUARD --------> 02  while Subject_Number <> -1 do
                  03    begin
                  04      ....
G:REPEAT-INPUT -> 05      read(Subject_Number);
                  06    end;
```

- P:RC
  (P:READ-SPECIAL-STOPPING-CHARACTER-FOR-SENTINEL): Sometimes instead of using one of the input data items as a sentinel, a separate variable will be used. This plan spawns the same goals as the previous plan, but its major advantage is that it keeps the input of the data items all together in the same READLN. Code that implements this plan is:

```
G:INPUT --------> 01  writeln('Enter the letter "N" to stop');
                  02  writeln('Any other (ie. "Y") for more');
G:GUARD --------> 03  read(Sentinel);
                  04  while Sentinel <> 'N' do
                  05    begin
                  06      ....
G:REPEAT-INPUT -> 07      read(Sentinel);
                  08    end;
```

The program in Figure 3-3, which is a solution to the problem in Figure 3-1, employs the P:RD loop plan to achieve the G:LOOP goal (see Figure 3-3, Lines 9-16 and 55-61; notice too that the sentinel variable is Subject_Number). The P:RD loop plan must accomplish three subgoals: G:INPUT, G:GUARD, G:REPEAT-INPUT. In turn, there are stereotypic ways in which to achieve these goals, i.e., there are programming plans that can be used to achieve these goals.

We can represent the *space of possible correct solutions* to the Reformatting Problem through the use of a Goal and Plan Tree (GAP tree) (see Figure 3-2). A GAP tree encodes the set of goals and subgoals that are needed for a solution, and it encodes all of the different plans that could achieve those goals. One solution subtree[2] of a GAP tree, then, is a solution to the problem. We now present a more detailed description of the goals and plans at the top level of the GAP tree for the Reformatting Problem.

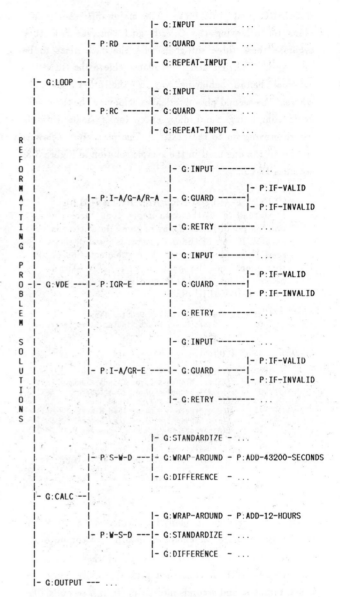

Figure 3-2: Simplified Goal-and-Plan Tree (GAP Tree) For the Reformatting Problem

The GAP tree in Figure 3-2 shows there are three plans for achieving the G:VALID-DATA-ENTRY goal. The plans for achieving the G:VALID-DATA-ENTRY goal all give rise to the same three sub-goals: G:INPUT,

---

[2]By solution subtree, we mean a tree which is extracted from the full GAP tree by committing, at each level down the tree, to a particular plan for achieving each goal. The solution subtree is a much less *bushy* version of the full GAP tree.

G:GUARD, and G:RETRY. The major difference in the plans for achieving the G:VDE goal concerns how they organize these three sub-goals with the data items to be processed. The first and third plans achieve the G:INPUT sub-goal before achieving any of the other sub-goals, whereas the second plan interleaves achieving the three sub-goals completing valid data entry for a single variable before moving on to the next.[3] The plan given below is similar to the one used in the sample solution in Figure 3-3; see lines 17-45.

- P:I-A/G-A/R-A
  (P:INPUT-ALL/GUARD-ALL/RETRY-ALL):
  First read in all the data items, then check (in one big conditional) if any of these data items is invalid. If any of the data items is invalid, then read them all in again. An implementation of this plan and the goals it spawns is shown below. (The G:GUARD goal is achieved using the P:IF-INVALID plan.)

```
G:INPUT-->  01  readln(Subject_Number, Problem_Type,
            02       Start_Hour, Start_Minute, Start_Second,
            03       End_Hour, End_Minute, End_Second,
            04       Accuracy);
G:GUARD-->  05  if (((Problem_Type <> 'a') and (Problem_Type <> 'b')
            06       and (Problem_Type <> 'c')) or
            07       ((Start_Hour   < 1) or (Start_Hour   > 12)) or
            08       ((Start_Minute < 0) or (Start_Minute > 59)) or
            09       ((Start_Second < 0) or (Start_Second > 59)) or
            10       ((End_Hour     < 1) or (End_Hour     > 12)) or
            11       ((End_Minute   < 0) or (End_Minute   > 59)) or
            12       ((End_Second   < 0) or (End_Second   > 59)) or
            13       ((Accuracy  <> '+') and (Accuracy  <> '-')))
            14  then begin
            15       writeln('Bad Data... Try Again.');
G:RETRY-->  16       readln(Subject_Number, Problem_Type,
            17            Start_Hour, Start_Minute, Start_Second,
            18            End_Hour, End_Minute, End_Second,
            19            Accuracy);
            20       end;
```

All of the calculation plans have three sub-goals which they must organize (or combine) in order to compute the elapsed time of the experiment. One of these sub-goals, G:STANDARDIZE, is concerned with converting a time in hours, minutes, and seconds into a time in just seconds. To do this standardization one needs to know how many seconds there are in an hour and a minute, and how to multiply and accumulate a sum. The G:WRAP-AROUND sub-goal is concerned with the problem which arises when, for instance, an experiment starts just before one o'clock (say 12:58:09) and ends just after one o'clock (say 1:02:35). In order to achieve this sub-goal, one must first detect that

wrap around has occurred (i.e., start time is greater than end time), and then compensate by adding to the end time one full clock period (i.e., 12 hours in some units). Clearly, depending on when one attempts to do wraparound with respect to standardization, the test and full-period add will be different (as illustrated in the two plans below). The G:DIFFERENCE sub-goal is concerned with the final step of the calculation, which is just subtracting start time from end time to find the elapsed time of the experiment. The first plan described below is the one in the program in Figure 3-3; see lines 46-51. We include a description here of both plans since it is relevant to the discussion in a subsequent section of this paper.

- P:S-W-D
  (P:STANDARDIZE-WRAP-AROUND-DIFFER-ENCE): When G:STANDARDIZE is achieved before G:WRAP-AROUND, the start and end times are each represented as a single number in seconds, so achieving G:WRAP-AROUND is particularly simple given that there are 43200 seconds in a 12 hour clock period. The plan used to achieve G:WRAP-AROUND in this example is P:ADD-43200-SECONDS.

```
01  Start_Time := 3600*Start_Hour +
02            60*Start_Minute + Start_Second;
03  End_Time := 3600*End_Hour +
04            60*End_Minute + End_Second;
05  if Start_Time >= End_Time
06    then End_Time := End_Time  + 43200;
07  Elapsed_Time := End_Time - Start_Time;
```

- P:W-S-D
  (P:WRAP-AROUND-STANDARDIZE-DIFFER-ENCE): When G:WRAP-AROUND must be achieved before G:STANDARDIZE, the plan is a bit more complex because start time and end time are still represented in their original form as six separate variables and three different time units (i.e., hours, minutes, and seconds). The plan used to achieve G:WRAP-AROUND in this example is P:ADD-12-HOURS.

```
01  if ( (Start_Hour > End_Hour) or
02       ((Start_Hour = End_Hour)
03       and (Start_Minute > End_Minute)) or
04       ((Start_Hour = End_Hour)
05       and (Start_Minute = End_Minute)
06       and (Start_Second >= End_Second)))
07    then End_Hour := End_Hour + 12;
08  Start_Time:=3600*Start_Hour +
09            60*Start_Minute + Start_Second;
10  End_Time   :=3600*End_Hour +
11            60*End_Minute + End_Second;
12  Elapsed_Time := End_Time - Start_Time;
```

4. Relating the GAP Tree to Students' Intentions and Programs

As we said above, the GAP tree represents the space of correct programs: a particular correct program would be derived from one solution subtree of that tree. We as

---

[3] A complete description of the first of these plans, the P:INPUT-ALL/GUARD-ALL/RETRY-ALL plan, is given. In Figure 6-1, a correct program fragment illustrates the second plan, the P:INPUT-GUARD-RETRY-EACH plan. The third plan, P:INPUT-ALL/GUARD-RETRY-EACH, first reads in all the data like the first plan, but then guards and retries each data variable like the second plan.

```
01  Program Reformat(input,output);
02  Var Subject_Number : Integer;
03      Start_Hour, Start_Minute, Start_Second : Integer;
04      End_Hour, End_Minute, End_Second : Integer;
05      Sentinel, Problem_Type, Accuracy : Char;
06      Start_Time, End_Time, Elapsed_Time : Integer;
07
08  Begin
09  +----------------------------------------------------------+
10  |  writeln('Do you want to reformat some data?');          |
11  |  writeln('YES: Type a "Y".');                            |
12  |  writeln('NO: Type an "N" (to STOP the program).');      |
13  |  readln(Sentinel);                                       |----------- G:LOOP
14  |  while Sentinel <> 'N' do                                |
15  |   begin                                                  |
16  +----------------------------------------------------------+
17  +----------------------------------------------------------+
18  |  |writeln('Enter Subject Number, Problem Type,           |
19  |  |writeln('Start Hour, Minute, Second, End Hour,         |
20  |  |writeln('Minute, Second, and Accuracy on one line.');  |
21  |  |writeln('FOR EXAMPLE: 1 a 3 30 2 3 36 59 +');          |
22  |  |readln(Subject_Number, Problem_Type,                   |
23  |  |       Start_Hour, Start_Minute, Start_Second,         |
24  |  |       End_Hour, End_Minute, End_Second,               |
25  |  |       Accuracy);                                      |
26  |  |if ((Subject_Number <= 0) or                           |
27  |  |   ((Problem_Type <> 'a') and                          |
28  |  |   (Problem_Type <> 'b') and (Problem_Type <> 'c')) or |
29  |  |   ((Start_Hour   < 1) or (Start_Hour   > 12)) or      |
30  |  |   ((Start_Minute < 0) or (Start_Minute > 59)) or      |----- G:VDE
31  |  |   ((Start_Second < 0) or (Start_Second > 59)) or      |
33  |  |   ((End_Hour   < 1) or (End_Hour   > 12)) or          |
34  |  |   ((End_Minute < 0) or (End_Minute > 59)) or          |
35  |  |   ((End_Second < 0) or (End_Second > 59)) or          |
36  |  |   ((Accuracy <> '+') and (Accuracy <> '-')))          |
37  |  |then                                                   |
38  |  |  begin                                                |
39  |  |    writeln('Some data bad.  Try again.');             |
40  |  |    readln(Subject_Number, Problem_Type,               |
41  |  |           Start_Hour, Start_Minute, Start_Second,     |
42  |  |           End_Hour, End_Minute, End_Second,           |
43  |  |           Accuracy);                                  |
44  |  |  end;                                                 | G:CALC
45  +----------------------------------------------------------+
46  +----------------------------------------------------------+
47  |  |Start_Time := 3600*Start_Hour + 60*Start_Minute + Start_Second;  |
48  |  |End_Time   := 3600*End_Hour + 60*End_Minute + End_Second;        |
49  |  |if End_Time <= Start_Time then End_Time := End_Time + 3600*12;    |
50  |  |Elapsed_Time := End_Time - Start_Time;                           |
51  +----------------------------------------------------------+
52  +----------------------------------------------------------+
53  |  |writeln('Output:',Subject_Number,Problem_Type,Elapsed_Time,Accuracy);|
54  +----------------------------------------------------------+
55  +----------------------------------------------------------+
56  |  writeln('Do you want to reformat some more data?');     |  G:OUTPUT
57  |  writeln('YES: Type a "Y".');                            |
58  |  writeln('NO: Type an "N" (to STOP the program).');      |------- G:LOOP
59  |  readln(Sentinel);                                       |
60  |  end;                                                    |
61  +----------------------------------------------------------+
62  End.
```

Figure 3-3: A Solution to the Reformatting Problem

experts developed the GAP tree for this problem; no novice programmer would know about all the different plans in the GAP tree. What we do claim, however, is that:

- We can infer from the student's buggy program what solution subtree of the GAP tree the student was intending to realize.
- The student did have in his mind the goals and plans that we posit for him/her based on the GAP tree.

There are, of course, some programs for which there is some ambiguity as to which solution subtree the student was using. The number of such situations is, however, reasonably low.

Of course, in order to more accurately assess our hypotheses as to the student's goals and plans, we would need to interview each   student as they were engaged in the process of creating their program. As a middle ground, we have conducted numerous interviews with novice prorammers, and analysis of those protocols

shows that our non-interview based judgments are indeed most often correct (Bonar & Soloway, 1983).

One final caveat: we are not claiming that we can necessarily identify precisely what misconception a student had, nor can we identify why the student had that misconception. Rather, we are only arguing that we can reliably infer where in the goal and plan structure the student's misconception must lie. For instance, in the example at the start of this paper, we argued that the student had a misconception about Counter Updates; from looking only at buggy program data, we can not *necessarily* know what specific misconception was operative, nor why that misconception was there in the first place.   Nonetheless, we can often make reasonably principled conjectures as to what misconception the student had and why they had it. Examples of such conjectures, and their basis, are given in the sections on bug descriptions.

5. The Source of Data: On-Line Protocols

The buggy program data that will be analyzed in subsequent sections are actual student generated programs. We augmented the VAX 750 operating system that the students were using, and, with their permission, obtained a copy of each syntactically correct program they submitted for execution. We call such data *on-line protocols*. We have collected this type of data from students from a number of introductory Pascal programming courses in universities settings. The data reported in this paper was collected during the Spring 1984 semester at Yale University in an introductory Pascal programming course specifically designed for non-science, humanities-oriented students. The analysis reported here was based on the first syntactically correct version of the Reformatting Problem produced by the students. We have analyzed data from other problems and from later versions; see (Spohrer et al, 1984) and (Johnson et al, 1983) for a more complete analysis of this data.

6. The Old Scheme for Bug Categorization

In (Johnson et al, 1983), our group developed a scheme for classifying program bugs based on differences between the buggy program and the plan that was being attempted. We described an example of this approach in the Introduction. In this section we review that work, and point out its weaknesses, and in the next section propose a revised scheme for bug classification that seeks to remedy those weaknesses.

There are four types of differences that can be captured: a plan component can be missing, malformed, spurious, or misplaced. In addition, there are seven types of plan components:

- **INPUT**: READ and READLN statements.
- **OUTPUT**: WRITE and WRITELN statements, for writing out either messages or variable values.
- **INIT**: Initialization type assignment statements that give variables their initial value.
- **UPDATE**: Assignment statements that change variables values.
- **GUARD**: IF statements and the termination test of WHILE, REPEAT, and FOR statements.
- **SYNTAX**: Syntactic connectives which delimit the scope of blocks of code such as BEGIN, END, THEN, ELSE, and DO.
- **PLAN**: Complex plans, composed of the above micro-plan components.

For example, in Figure 6-1 a buggy program fragment that is an attempt to achieve the G:VDE goal of the Reformatting Problem is displayed. By counting plan component differences, we can, as shown, identify six bugs in this program: missing guards for the six time variables (i.e., start hour, minute, second; end hour, minute, second).

Using the above "plan difference" approach, 28 categories of bugs are produced (4 types of differences times 7 types of plan components). In Figure 6-2 we present an analysis in terms of these categories of bugs from our sample of 46 student programs for the Reformatting Problem. Notice that almost half of the bugs are in the Missing or Malformed Guard categories (265 out of 549 bugs).

The bug description shown in Figure 6-1 is intuitively unsatisfactory: while the bug count would say that there are six bugs in this program, it would seem that they all follow from the same conceptual bug; namely, a misconception about whether to check the time data items to see if they were valid. On the other hand, the fact that our scheme points out that half of the bugs were guard bugs is also not satisfactory: there is simply not enough detail in that type of description. Since there are many places that a guard could have been used in the program (e.g., detecting when to stop in G:LOOP, detecting when to retry input in G:VDE, and detecting when to do wraparound in G:CALC), it is quite reasonable to suppose that the misconception underlying the improper use of a guard in one plan of the program is different from the misconception underlying the improper use of a guard in

another plan of the program. In other words, there are two basic weaknesses with the categorization scheme briefly outlined here, and more extensively described in (Johnson et al, 1983):

- The above scheme does not, in some cases, group bugs together that stem from a common cause: in effect, the scheme makes too many distinctions.
- The above scheme does not, in some cases, differentiate the plans from which the plan components are missing, malformed, etc. In effect, the scheme does not make enough distinctions.

The next section describes a bug categorization scheme that seeks to remedy these weaknesses.

7. A New Scheme for Bug Categorization

In Figure 7-1, we present a breakdown of the 28 bug categories originally described in Figure 6-2, in terms of the four top-level goals that need to be accomplished in the Reformatting Problem. Notice in particular that the distribution of errors in guard plan components is not even with respect to the four goals: while three of these goals had plans that required guard plans, the majority of bugs occurred in the plans for achieving the G:VDE goal. This suggests that the misconceptions that the students had were more focused than simply misunderstanding guard plans; rather they seemed to have difficulty with guard plans only in a specific context.

The strategy employed in Figure 7-1 can be extended: we can further breakdown the bug categories into finer subcategories based on the goals and plans in the GAP tree. For example, we can determine if the errors on the guard plans occur within a specific plan for realizing a subgoal of the G:VDE goal. We feel such a bug classification scheme would have some advantages, and would specifically address the two weaknesses of the previous scheme:

- *Bug Dependencies*: Often an individual student will have many bugs in a single program and this will artificially boost the bug count. However, upon closer inspection it will be clear that all the bugs have one common underlying misconception.
- *Finding The "Easy" And The "Hard" Plans*: There may be many different plans to achieve the same goal. If nearly all of the students who chose one plan were successful in implementing it and nearly all the students that chose another were unsuccessful in implementing it, then this provides a basis for collecting "easy" and "hard" plans. Again, we have the basis for pinpointing where the students' misconceptions lie.

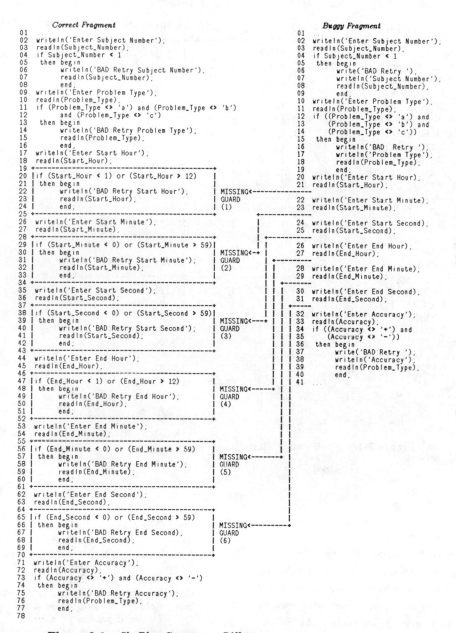

Correct Fragment

```
01   ...
02   writeln('Enter Subject Number'),
03   readln(Subject_Number),
04   if Subject_Number < 1
05    then begin
06         writeln('BAD Retry Subject Number'),
07         readln(Subject_Number),
08         end,
09   writeln('Enter Problem Type'),
10   readln(Problem_Type),
11   if (Problem_Type <> 'a') and (Problem_Type <> 'b')
12        and (Problem_Type <> 'c')
13    then begin
14         writeln('BAD Retry Problem Type'),
15         readln(Problem_Type),
16         end,
17   writeln('Enter Start Hour'),
18   readln(Start_Hour),
19 +--------------------------------------------+
20 |if (Start_Hour < 1) or (Start_Hour > 12)   |
21 | then begin                                |
22 |        writeln('BAD Retry Start Hour'),   |     MISSING<---------
23 |        readln(Start_Hour),                |     GUARD
24 |        end,                               |     (1)
25 +--------------------------------------------+
26   writeln('Enter Start Minute'),
27   readln(Start_Minute),
28 +--------------------------------------------+
29 |if (Start_Minute < 0) or (Start_Minute > 59)|
30 | then begin                                |
31 |        writeln('BAD Retry Start Minute'), |     MISSING<--+
32 |        readln(Start_Minute),              |     GUARD
33 |        end,                               |     (2)
34 +--------------------------------------------+
35   writeln('Enter Start Second'),
36   readln(Start_Second),
37 +--------------------------------------------+
38 |if (Start_Second < 0) or (Start_Second > 59)|
39 | then begin                                |
40 |        writeln('BAD Retry Start Second'), |     MISSING<----+
41 |        readln(Start_Second),              |     GUARD
42 |        end,                               |     (3)
43 +--------------------------------------------+
44   writeln('Enter End Hour'),
45   readln(End_Hour),
46 +--------------------------------------------+
47 |if (End_Hour < 1) or (End_Hour > 12)       |
48 | then begin                                |
49 |        writeln('BAD Retry End Hour'),     |     MISSING<------+
50 |        readln(End_Hour),                  |     GUARD
51 |        end,                               |     (4)
52 +--------------------------------------------+
53   writeln('Enter End Minute'),
54   readln(End_Minute),
55 +--------------------------------------------+
56 |if (End_Minute < 0) or (End_Minute > 59)   |
57 | then begin                                |
58 |        writeln('BAD Retry End Minute'),   |     MISSING<-------+
59 |        readln(End_Minute),                |     GUARD
60 |        end,                               |     (5)
61 +--------------------------------------------+
62   writeln('Enter End Second'),
63   readln(End_Second),
64 +--------------------------------------------+
65 |if (End_Second < 0) or (End_Second > 59)   |
66 | then begin                                |
67 |        writeln('BAD Retry End Second'),   |     MISSING<---------+
68 |        readln(End_Second),                |     GUARD
69 |        end,                               |     (6)
70 +--------------------------------------------+
71   writeln('Enter Accuracy'),
72   readln(Accuracy),
73   if (Accuracy <> '+') and (Accuracy <> '-')
74    then begin
75         writeln('BAD Retry Accuracy'),
76         readln(Problem_Type),
77         end,
78   ...
```

Buggy Fragment

```
01   ...
02   writeln('Enter Subject Number'),
03   readln(Subject_Number),
04   if Subject_Number < 1
05    then begin
06         write('BAD Retry '),
07         writeln('Subject Number'),
08         readln(Subject_Number),
09         end,
10   writeln('Enter Problem Type'),
11   readln(Problem_Type),
12   if ((Problem_Type <> 'a') and
13       (Problem_Type <> 'b') and
14       (Problem_Type <> 'c'))
15    then begin
16         writeln('BAD  Retry '),
17         writeln('Problem Type'),
18         readln(Problem_Type),
19         end,
20   writeln('Enter Start Hour'),
21   readln(Start_Hour),
22   writeln('Enter Start Minute'),
23   readln(Start_Minute),
24   writeln('Enter Start Second'),
25   readln(Start_Second),
26   writeln('Enter End Hour'),
27   readln(End_Hour),
28   writeln('Enter End Minute'),
29   readln(End_Minute),
30   writeln('Enter End Second'),
31   readln(End_Second),
32   writeln('Enter Accuracy'),
33   readln(Accuracy),
34   if ((Accuracy <> '+') and
35       (Accuracy <> '-'))
36    then begin
37         write('BAD Retry '),
38         writeln('Accuracy'),
39         readln(Problem_Type),
40         end,
41   ...
```

Figure 6-1: Six Plan Component Differences

	INIT	INPUT	GUARD	UPDATE	OUTPUT	SYNTAX	PLAN ||
MALFORMED	[0]	[53]	[162]	[19]	[64]	[0]	[21] || [319]
MISPLACED	[0]	[19]	[1]	[0]	[1]	[2]	[1] || [24]
MISSING	[1]	[22]	[103]	[0]	[18]	[11]	[23] || [178]
SPURIOUS	[1]	[1]	[2]	[0]	[2]	[22]	[0] || [28]
	[2]	[95]	[268]	[19]	[85]	[35]	[45] || [549]

Figure 6-2: Breakdown Of Bugs By

Plan Component Differences

	INIT	INPUT	GUARD	UPDATE	OUTPUT	SYNTAX	PLAN	
MALFORMED	[0]	[53]	[162]	[19]	[64]	[0]	[21]	[319]
G:LOOP	0	0	3	1	0	0	0	4
G:VDE	0	53	159	9	0	0	11	232
G:CALC	0	0	0	9	0	0	10	19
G:OUTPUT	–	–	0	–	64	0	0	64
MISPLACED	[0]	[19]	[1]	[0]	[1]	[2]	[1]	[24]
G:LOOP	0	0	0	0	0	1	1	2
G:VDE	0	19	1	0	0	1	0	21
G:CALC	0	0	0	0	0	0	0	0
G:OUTPUT	–	–	0	–	1	0	0	1
MISSING	[1]	[22]	[103]	[0]	[18]	[11]	[23]	[178]
G:LOOP	1	4	0	0	6	2	9	22
G:VDE	0	18	103	0	4	9	0	134
G:CALC	0	0	0	0	0	0	12	12
G:OUTPUT	–	–	0	–	8	0	2	10
SPURIOUS	[1]	[1]	[2]	[0]	[2]	[22]	[0]	[28]
G:LOOP	1	0	0	0	1	0	0	2
G:VDE	0	1	0	0	0	18	0	19
G:CALC	0	0	2	0	0	4	0	6
G:OUTPUT	–	–	0	–	1	0	0	1
	[2]	[95]	[268]	[19]	[85]	[35]	[45]	[549]
	2	4	3	1	7	3	10	30
	0	91	263	9	4	28	11	406
	0	0	2	9	0	4	22	37
	–	–	0	–	74	0	2	76

Figure 7-1:   Breakdown Of Bugs By

Top-Level Goals

7.1. Benefit 1: Bug Dependencies

The table in Figure 6-2 shows that there were 103 missing guard bugs, while the table in Figure 7-1 indicates that all of those missing guard bugs occurred in the plans to achieve the G:VDE goal. A still finer breakdown in terms of the plans to achieve the subgoals of the G:VDE goal is also illuminating. In the table in Figure 7-2 we see that relatively few students were responsible for all the time data bugs. Moreover, one specific bug type stands out: when a student missed a guard to check for valid timing data input (start and end time), then the student missed all the guards for that set of data (e.g., see Figure 6-1).

Viewing the data at this fine-grain level results in two advantages:

- The count of bugs becomes more realistic: there were not really 103 missing guard bugs on the G:VDE goal. Rather, we can see that 13 students were responsible for at least 78 of those bugs.

- The analysis of where the student's misconception lies now becomes more focused: no longer do we tell that student that he had, say 6 missing guard bugs, but rather, we say that the student had a misconception about how to check for valid timing data input. This type of "bug dependency" analysis is precisely what was missing from the bug categorization scheme described in the previous section.

Thus, we can see that continuing to represent the bug counts at finer and finer levels of the GAP tree can provide a more effective basis for understanding how the bugs in a student's program relate to his/her misconceptions.

MISSING VDE GUARD SUB-GOALS	No. of Bugs	No. of Students
G:SUBJECT-NUMBER	23	23
G:PROBLEM-TYPE	0	0
G:TIME-DATA --->(missing all 6)	78	13
--->(missing just a few)	2	1
G:ACCURACY	0	0

Figure 7-2:   Breakdown Of Missing Guard Bugs

By Sub-Goals

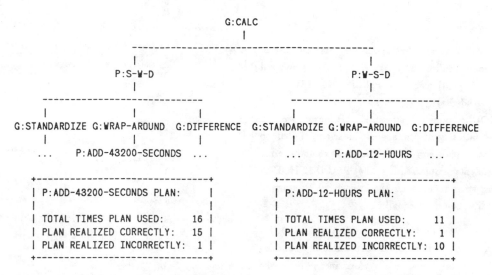

Figure 7-3: Portion of GAP Tree for the G:CALC Goal

Why would so many students (more than 25%) neglect to guard the time data, and no student omit the guards for problem type and accuracy? One explanation is that the bug arose during the interpretation phase of the program writing process, the phase in which the student is reading the assignment and forming goals. The values which the problem type and accuracy data items could take on were *explicitly* mentioned in the Reformatting Problem assignment (see Figure 3-1, Lines 15-22), whereas the values which the time variables could take on were only *implicitly* alluded to using examples (e.g., 4 32 16, means 4 o'clock, 32 minutes, and 16 seconds). Even though all the students probably knew the range of acceptable values for the time variables, this acceptable range was not stated explicitly in the assignment, and as a result many students simply did not form the goal of guarding against bad time values. There may be other possible explanations, but the point is that any explanation for this bug would have to explain the absence of all and only the time variable guards.

7.2. Benefit 2: Identifying The "Easy" And The "Hard" Plans

An analysis based on a GAP tree allows us to pinpoint where the students' misconceptions might lie by identifying which goals and plans they had difficulty realizing. In what follows, we provide an example in which this analysis serves to highlight a troublesome plan for achieving the G:CALC goal.

Consider the section of the GAP tree shown in Figure 7-3. The high level goal (G:CALC) of computing the correct elapsed time can be achieved using either the P:S-W-D plan or the P:W-S-D plan, which basically provide two different orderings on the three sub-goals of G:CALC, namely G:STANDARDIZE, G:WRAP-AROUND, and G:DIFFERENCE. The plans available for achieving the G:WRAP-AROUND goal are different depending on whether G:WRAP-AROUND is achieved before or after G:STANDARDIZE. If G:WRAP-AROUND is done after G:STANDARDIZE then the P:ADD-43200-SECONDS plan should be used; if G:WRAP-AROUND is done before G:STANDARDIZE the P:ADD-12-HOURS plan should be used.[4]

Figure 7-4 shows a possible implementation of the plans P:ADD-43200-SECONDS and P:ADD-12-HOURS. For each plan, a correct implementation and an incorrect one are shown. A correct implementation of P:ADD-43200-SECONDS requires that it be done after the G:STANDARDIZE goal has been achieved, and using the correct value of the constant. A correct implementation of P:ADD-12-HOURS requires that it be done before the G:STANDARDIZE goal is achieved, and that it check the possible case in which starting hour equals ending hour and a wrap-around should still be done (e.g., start is 4:32:04,

---

[4]We have simplified our description here: Actually the P:ADD-43200-SECONDS plan and the P:ADD-12-HOURS plan are realizations of more general plans for achieving the G:WRAP-AROUND goal. However, for expository purposes we chose to give the ɪ names more closely related to the particular problem.

and end is 4:26:35).

From Figure 7-3 we see that about the same number of students chose to realize the G:WRAP-AROUND subgoal (of the G:CALC goal) using the P:ADD-43200-SECONDS plan (16 students) as those who chose the P:ADD-12-HOURS plan (11 students). However, we can see that the latter students almost invariably failed to realize this latter plan correctly! The most common error made by students implementing the P:ADD-12-HOURS plan was forgetting to consider the case in which starting hours and ending hours are equal.

Clearly, then, we can say that the P:ADD-12-HOURS plan is the more difficult plan. Two possible explanations for the students' poorer performance on the P:ADD-12-HOURS plan are: (1) most students didn't consider the equal-hour case, and (2) even if they did intend to handle the equal-hour case, the logic was much more complicated than in the other plan.

8. Concluding Remarks

At first glance the huge amount of variation that exists in novice programs may appear chaotic and random. However, we have argued that by using a GAP tree representation, we can provide considerable structure to that data, and consequently identify where the students' misconceptions lie. Currently, there is no mechanical procedure for taking an arbitrary problem and producing a GAP tree for that problem. However, once developed, by experts, the GAP trees specify possible solutions to programming problems in terms of underlying knowledge, and facilitate bug analysis which is neither too fine-grained, nor too coarse-grained. As we pointed out earlier, our approach reliably only points to where the students are having difficulties, not what precisely those misconceptions are. Nonetheless, the clear utility of this approach to the analysis of student programs suggests that research on developing a method for producing GAP trees and research on identifying the sources of misconceptions is warranted. In sum, a systematic analysis can be provided for buggy programs, based on the knowledge and processes underlying their creation.

REFERENCES

Bonar, J., Soloway, E. (1983) Uncovering Principles of Novice Programming, SIGPLAN-SIGACT Tenth Annual Symposium on Principles of Programming Languages, Austin, Tx.

Brown, J.S. and Burton, R.R. (1978) "Diagnostic Models for Procedural Bugs in Mathematics." Cognitive Science 2 (June), 155-192.

Correct and Incorrect Code for P:ADD-43200-SECONDS *Calculation Plan*

```
CORRECT:    01 Start_Time := 3600*Start_Hours +
            02              60*Start_Minutes + Start_Seconds;
            03 End_Time := 3600*End_Hours +
            04              60*End_Minutes + End_Seconds;
            05 if Start_Time >= End_Time
            06   then End_Time := End_Time + 43200;
            07 Elapsed_Time := End_Time - Start_Time;

INCORRECT:  08 Start_Time := 3600*Start_Hours +
            09              60*Start_Minutes + Start_Seconds;
            10 End_Time := 3600*End_Hours +
            11              60*End_Minutes + End_Seconds;
            12 if Start_Time >= End_Time
            13   then End_Time := End_Time + 4320;
            14 Elapsed_Time := End_Time - Start_Time;
```

Bug in Incorrect Version: Incorrect value of constant.

Correct and Incorrect Code for the P:ADD-12-HOURS *Calculation Plan*

```
CORRECT:    15 if ((Start_Hours > End_Hours) or
            16    ((Start_Hours = End_Hours)
            17     and (Start_Minutes > End_Minutes)) or
            18    ((Start_Hours = End_Hours)
            19     and (Start_Minutes = End_Minutes)
            20     and (Start_Seconds >= End_Seconds)) )
            21   then End_Hours := End_Hours + 12;
            22 Start_Time := 3600*Start_Hours +
            23              60*Start_Minutes + Start_Seconds;
            24 End_Time := 3600*End_Hours +
            25              60*End_Minutes + End_Seconds;
            26 Elapsed_Time := End_Time - Start_Time;

INCORRECT:  27 if Start_Hours >= End_Hours
            28   then End_Hours := End_Hours + 12;
            29 Start_Time := 3600*Start_Hours +
            30              60*Start_Minutes + Start_Seconds;
            31 End_Time := 3600*End_Hours +
            32              60*End_Minutes + End_Seconds;
            33 Elapsed_Time := End_Time - Start_Time;
```

Bug in Incorrect Version: Not enough wraparound cases tested.

Figure 7-4: Correct And Incorrect Code For

Two Calculation Plans

Johnson, L. and Soloway, E. (1983) *PROUST: Knowledge-Based Program Understanding.* Technical Report 285, Dept. of Computer Science, Yale University, August.

Johnson, L., Soloway, E., Cutler, B. and Draper, S. (1983) *BUG CATALOGUE: I.* Technical Report 286, Dept. of Computer Science, Yale University, October.

Ostrand, T., and Weyuker, E. (1982) *Collecting and Categorizing Software Error Data in an Industrial Environment.* Technical Report 47, New York University, Dept. of Computer Science.

Soloway, E., Ehrlich, K., Bonar, J., Greenspan, J. (1982) What Do Novices Know About Programming?, In *Directions in Human-Computer Interactions,* B. Shneiderman and A. Badre, Eds., Ablex, Inc.

Soloway, E., Ehrlich, K. (1984) Empirical Studies of Programming Knowledge, *IEEE Transactions on Software Engineering,* to appear.

Soloway, E., Adelson, B., Ehrlich, K. (1984) Knowledge and Processes in the Comprehension of Computer Programs, in *The Nature of Expertise,* Chi, M., Glaser, R., Farr, M., (Eds.), to appear.

Spohrer, J., Pope, E., Lipman, M., Sack, W., Freiman, S., Littman, D., Johnson, L., and Soloway, E. (1984) *BUG CATALOGUE: II,III,IV.* In preparation.

COMPUTERS IN EDUCATION, K. Duncan and D. Harris (eds.)
Elsevier Science Publishers B.V. (North-Holland)
© IFIP, 1985

A Tale of One Little Program

Elliot Soloway

Department of Computer Science

Yale University

P.O. Box 2158

New Haven, Connecticut 06520

In this paper, we present a trace of an Idealized Expert Programmer writing a simple computer program. The trace clearly demonstrates that one needs to know more than the syntax and semantics of a language in order to write a computer program. In particular, we show how programming plan knowledge and rules of programming discourse play a key role in the construction of a program. The objective of this paper is to make explicit a substantial portion of the knowledge used by programmers that has by and large unfortunately remained implicit.

1. Introduction

What must a novice programmer know in order to write a computer program? Most certainly, the novice must know about the syntax and semantics of the programming language in which he/she is writing -- but that knowledge is only the tip of the iceberg. In particular, we have argued that expert programmers have and use at least the following two kinds of knowledge:

- *programming plans* which represent the stereotypic action sequences in programming. (Also see [7, 2].)
- *rules of programming discourse* which guide the composition of plans into understandable and executable programs.

We have carried out a number of empirical studies with novice and advanced programmers to evaluate the above claims; data do in fact support these claims [9, 4, 10, 11].

While we all may nod our heads and say yes, knowledge of the above sorts are needed to write programs, it is less clear exactly how much knowledge is necessary, and what that knowledge actually is. In what follows we have attempted to explicitly articulate a substantial percentage of the knowledge needed to write a simple program. The goal of this exercise is to raise our collective consciousness: learning to program is hard, and one reason for this being so is the sheer amount of knowledge that needs to be learned.

This work was sponsored by the National Science Foundation, under NSF Grant IST-8310659.

One major caveat needs to be voiced before we begin: with one exception, we will sweep under the rug detailed discussion of the *process* of solving the programming assignment. That is, we will defer to a later time questions such as: how does a programmer know when to use what knowledge; how does a programmer get access to that knowledge; how does a programmer know to structure the design in a particular manner. These are clearly all critical questions that do warrant considerable research (see [1] for a first-order theory of this process). Thus, we are only painting a portion of the picture. Nonetheless, we feel that there is still considerable utility in identifying a considerable portion of knowledge used in programming which has heretofore remained only tacit. For example, we have used knowledge analyses, of the sort about to be described, as the basis for better understanding the bugs and misconceptions students produce in writing programs (e.g., [13, 12, 14, 6]). In fact, we have constructed a program, PROUST, that uses such analyses to identify the majority of non-syntactic bugs in students' programs, for a class of moderately complex looping programs ([5]).

The method we use to present the knowledge analysis is to provide a "mental trace" of an Idealized Expert Programmer (IEP) who is writing a program for our example problem. More than likely there is no human expert who is exactly like IEP; rather, IEP is an amalgam of the expert programmers we have observed and analyzed. Moreover, the knowledge IEP uses may not be the knowledge that a novice would use in writing the same program, since the novice may not have as yet acquired the knowledge that IEP uses. Thus, we are only presenting a lower bound on the amount of knowledge that is needed to write a program. Most certainly, novices will need to use more knowledge than IEP.

2. The Tale: Knowledge Underlying Program Construction

Consider the following problem:

> Write a Pascal program that will read a set of integers and output the average of those numbers. Stop reading input when the number 99999 is read.

The first task that our Idealized Expert Programmer (IEP) would perform would be to abstract the essential goals of the problem.[1] Using knowledge about what characteristics of a problem statement indicate major problem goals, IEP would abstract the following two key goals from the problem specification:

```
Goal:compute average ---> Goal:output average
```

What we mean by the above notation is that achieving the goal of computing the average is a necessary precondition of being able to achieve the goal of outputting the average. Thus, we can view the former goal as enabling the latter goal to take place.

Notice that the stopping condition on the loop is not being considered yet. Based on IEP's experience, he recognizes that a loop stopping condition is a detail that will be handled once decisions about how to realize the main goals have been made. Also, notice that issues such as type declarations and actual looping construct are not being considered: those are lower-level concerns.

Once the major goals have been decided upon, these can be further transformed. In particular, IEP uses world knowledge about what it means to be an average in order to generate the following subgoals:

```
Subgoal:compute          Subgoal:compute
sum of input numbers     count of numbers input
         |                       |
         |                       |
         v                       v
```

```
Subgoal:compute sum divided by count
```

Again, we have goal enablement here: computing the sum

and computing the count enable the achievement of the subgoal of doing the division.

Since it is important to separate out the types of knowledge being used by IEP, we stress the fact that the knowledge about averages comes from world knowledge, and is not a programming specific set of facts. However, at this point IEP decides to straighten out the types of data. In order to carry out this task, programming specific knowledge plus world knowledge must be used. For example, programming knowledge suggests that a count of discrete items should be of type integer. World Knowledge, on the other hand, suggests that dividing two numbers might not necessarily result in a whole number; programming knowledge would suggest that the result variable be of type real. The problem statement itself says that the numbers read in are integers.

The next task that IEP undertakes is to retrieve from his memory a programming plan that will enable the program to achieve the subgoal of computing the sum of the numbers input. The activity of summing successively read inputs is one that is used in many, many programs. Thus, it is not surprising that IEP has a "compiled" routine for carrying out such an activity. We have called this plan the *running total loop plan*.[2] A representation of the *running total loop plan* is given below:

```
goal: achieve initialize (running_total := 0)
loop until stopping condition = true
   goal: achieve input (new_value)
   goal: achieve update
         (running_total := running_total + new_value)
endloop
```

Notice that this plan is not specified in terms of Pascal. Rather, a form of goal-language/pseudo-code is used. The transformation of this relatively language independent representation into Pascal requires additional knowledge. As we shall see soon, even making this transformation from a language-independent representation into Pascal requires more than just a knowledge of the syntax and semantics of Pascal.

Notice also that the *running total loop plan* has buried

---

[1]Knowing that this should be the first task is an aspect of IEP's processing strategy; however, as we mentioned in the Introduction, we will not focus (except as noted below) on processing issues.

[2]We are not claiming that IEP or even a human expert would necessarily retrieve this plan using its formal name: we, the researchers, have assigned a label to the plan to facilitate our understanding. However, it is quite possible that experts do in fact have names for plans and use the names for retrieval. It is more likely, however, that plans are accessed via key features, such as function, stereotypicality, etc.

in it two variable plans: a *new value variable plan* and a *running total variable plan*. The former plan specifies a variable whose role it is to hold each successive input value. The latter plan specifies a variable whose role it is to hold the accumulated sum. By the very definition of what it means to be a running total variable, this plan specifies, in describing how it should be updated, that the value to be accumulated is the new value variable.

Still pursuing the subgoal of computing the sum of the input, IEP returns to the problem specification and determines what the stopping condition of the loop is. In our case, the read and sum loop is to be terminated when the value 99999 is read. This form of loop termination is a standard one: it uses a sentinel value. Programming knowledge tells IEP that the sentinel value should not participate in the actual computation. In some circumstances, of course, the sentinel value could very well still participate in the actual computation. However, the normal, default expectation is that unless otherwise told, assume that the sentinel value has only 1 role, namely, that of signifying end of input.

Since sentinel termination is a standard way to stop a loop, IEP can index into his database of stored programming plans, and retrieve a *running total loop plan* that has already been customized to handle sentinel termination. We call such a plan a *sentinel controlled running total loop plan*:

```
goal: achieve initialize (running_total := 0)
goal: achieve input (new_value)
loop until sentinel value = new_value
  goal: achieve update
        (running_total := running_total + new_value)
  goal: achieve input (new_value)
endloop
```

The translation of this plan, in its abstract representation into Pascal, requires knowledge of the "pragmatics" of Pascal, in addition to knowledge of its syntax and semantics. In particular, the most appropriate looping construct in Pascal for realizing a *sentinel controlled running total loop plan* is the while construct. Of course, one can coerce any of Pascal's looping constructs to work in this particular case. However, IEP understands that each of Pascal's three looping constructs has a context in which it is most appropriate, and this context is determined by the type of stopping condition. For example, a for construct is most appropriate when the loop will be terminated on the basis of a counter. A repeat loop should be used when the

loop must definitely be executed at least once, because the terminating condition is based on some variable being computed in the loop whose initial value can be guaranteed not to be the terminating value. This sort of knowledge goes beyond syntax and semantics in that one needs to understand the goal behind each of the constructs; we have labeled this sort of knowledge as pragmatic knowledge: knowledge of when to use a construct in contrast to knowledge of how to use it (see also [9]).

After applying the specific pragmatic knowledge described above to choose Pascal's while construct, the resultant instantiated *sentinel controlled running total loop plan* looks like:

```
total := 0;
read(new);
while new <> 99999 do
  begin
      total := total + new;
      read(new);
  end;
```

The translation of the goal to get input from the user also requires additional programming knowledge. While the problem specification makes no mention of it, IEP knows that he needs to prompt the user to input a number on each pass through the loop. In effect, IEP is adding additional goals to the problem specification. As we have already seen --- and as we will continue to see --- the augmentation of the problem specification based on programming and world knowledge is a continual process. Note that if this program were written to run in a batch mode, not an interactive one, the inclusion of a prompt goal (and a prompt statement) would not be appropriate. Incorporating the prompt would result in the following code:

```
total := 0;
writeln('please input a number');
read(new);
while new <> 99999 do
  begin
      total := total + new;
      writeln('please input a number');
      read(new);
  end;
```

Now, IEP attempts to realize the subgoal of counting the number of numbers read in. Programming knowledge permits IEP to retrieve a programming plan for achieving this goal: the *counter loop plan*:

```
goal: achieve initialize (count := 0)
loop until stopping condition = true
    goal: achieve input (new_value)
    goal: achieve update (count := count + 1)
endloop
```

Embedded in the CLP is the variable plan for a *counter variable*: counting can be achieved by starting at 0 and updating by 1. Termination of the CLP is the same as that for the *running total loop plan*; thus, a CLP customized for sentinel termination can be retrieved and instantiated for Pascal:

```
count := 0;
while stopping_value <> 99999 do
  begin
      count := count + 1;
  end;
```

A major problem solving feat is about to take place. IEP realizes that he can't simply first use a followed *sentinel controlled running total loop plan* by a *sentinel controlled running total loop plan*, since each plan assumes that the data will be available. However the data is coming in as a stream, and thus can only be read (accessed) once. This understanding suggests to IEP that both looping plans need to be combined. Here we see for the first time the need to integrate two plans. We do not mean "compose" two plans; rather, we see that two plans need to be woven together into one piece of code. In order to weave together these two plans, we claim that IEP must "decompile" both plans, and reason causally about the elements of each plan. The following are examples of the type of reasoning that IEP needs to carry out in order to be assured that the two plans can be integrated:

- IEP must realize that the goal of each loop plan is the same, namely: process just one item on each iteration.[3]
- IEP must realize that it is OK to put the counter update anywhere in the loop for the following reason: the flow of data in the loop is such that the counter update will not interfere with any calculation in the loop.

___

[3]It is interesting to note that the integration of the two loop plans is, in effect, an optimization: since the data needs only to be input and summed, there is no need to keep the data around in an array. Thus, only 1 variable is needed to hold all the elements. This optimized algorithm is really for the computer's benefit: the more natural human algorithm is to make several sweeps over the data, e.g., one for counting the number of numbers, and one for summing the numbers. Since the optimized algorithm is not one that is commonly used, it is not surprising that novices have trouble realizing why one needs to integrate the plans in the first place; the novice would most likely not solve the averaging problem by hand using the optimized algorithm.

The reader may rightfully point out that if IEP is really an expert then he would have already compiled a looping plan that would both sum and count. Thus, the integration scenario just described would not take place. However, for the following reasons we felt it to be critically important to include, in a discussion of the knowledge used in programming, a description of the process of integrating two plans:

- In the initial creation of a looping plan that did combine both the summing and counting actions, the expert would most likely have had to go through the sort of reasoning process outlined above.
- We felt it instructive to see how plans are integrated together, since most programs are not built from totally standard components that can simply be composed together: some new construction must take place.
- We wanted to illustrate the legitimate use of "double duty", i.e., a situation in which one piece of code is used for two purposes. In this case one loop is used to both for computing a count of the numbers input and a sum of those numbers. We say that the use of the double duty is legitimate in this context because both activities are readily apparent. We have previously argued that an illegitimate use of double duty occurs when only one of the actions, and not both, is readily apparent ([11]).
- We would also like to point out that many bugs in novice programs appear at just those points in the design of the program that requires the integration of two plans. Typically integrating two plans is a non-trivial task: as we saw, IEP needed to return to the initial goals of both plans and had to follow through some data flow analysis in order to be confident that the integration would result in a correct program. We have found that novices would much prefer to simply compose two plans --- even when this would result in a buggy program ([6]).

Let us return to still another issue with respect to integrating the two loop plans. In particular, while the counter update can theoretically go anywhere in the loop, we claim that no expert would write the following code:

```
count := 0;
total := 0;
writeln('please input a number');
read(new);
while new <> 99999 do
  begin
      total := total + new;
      writeln('please input a number');
      read(new);
      count := count + 1;
  end;
```

The reason we claim that an expert wouldn't write such code is because it violates a rule of programming discourse that says: group code together that have a common role. Since the update of sum and the update of count both are referring to the same item, while the read is inputting the next item, we would argue that the sum update and the counter update share a common role and thus should --- and would --- be grouped together, as shown below:[4,5]

```
count := 0;
total := 0;
writeln('please input a number');
read(new);
while new <> 99999 do
   begin
      total := total + new;
      count := count + 1;
      writeln('please input a number');
      read(new);
   end;
```

IEP can now turn his attention to the subgoal of computing the average itself, since the looping code would enable the achievement of the subgoals of counting the number of items input and summing them. Performing the actual division is essentially a simple action:

```
count := 0;
total := 0;
writeln('please input a number');
read(new);
while new <> 99999 do
   begin
      total := total + new;
      count := count + 1;
      writeln('please input a number');
      read(new);
   end;
average := total/count;
```

However, programming knowledge comes into play again: one needs to be careful not to allow a division by zero to take place, since that would most likely cause a run-time error.

The need to prevent such a run-time error is a standard piece of programming knowledge. This knowledge thus

---

[4]Clearly, there will be times when a rule of discourse needs to be violated in order to satisfy another rule or some higher level goal. Moreover, we recognize that the above rule is very general, and is probably both too strong and too weak. Nonetheless, we claim that a rule something akin to the one given above is being obeyed when the counter update and the sum update are grouped textually together in the program.

[5]We also want to note that programmers find it difficult to effectively use the while construct in precisely the situation described above. The problem stems from the fact that the loop is out of synch: it is processing the ith element while reading the next-ith element, instead of reading and processing the ith element on the same pass. ([10]).

generates a new subgoal: guard the average calculation. Notice that this subgoal is also not given in the problem statement; it is an implicit goal that is generated based on the need to write a correct program. A standard plan for achieving this subgoal is to wrap a guard plan around the desired calculation. Notice again, that two plans are being integrated, and not composed: the average calculation is being embedded inside a guard plan:

```
count := 0;
total := 0;
writeln('please input a number');
read(new);
while new <> 99999 do
   begin
      total := total + new;
      count := count + 1;
      writeln('please input a number');
      read(new);
   end;
if count > 0 then average := total/count;
```

Before leaving this discussion, we would like to point out one further subtle inference that needed to take place. In particular, the decision to include a guard plan is based on the fact that the problem implies that it is possible to have zero inputs (and hence a count of 0). The inference of this possibility stems from the decision to use a *sentinel controlled running total loop plan*: an initial read of a data item is done outside the loop and if this read inputs the sentinel value then the test at the top of the loop will prevent the loop from even being executed once. Thus, it is clearly possible for the counter to have a value of zero. On the other hand, if the problem statement directed IEP to take the average of the first 10 numbers read in, then there would be no need for the guard plan on the average calculation, since it would be impossible --- by definition --- for the count to be 0.

Finally, IEP can attempt to achieve the second of the top-level goals, that of outputting the average. A straightforward implementation of that goal would not, however, be correct:

```
count := 0;
total := 0;
writeln('please input a number');
read(new);
while new <> 99999 do
   begin
      total := total + new;
      count := count + 1;
      writeln('please input a number');
      read(new);
   end;
if count > 0 then average := total/count;
writeln('average is ', average);
```

What if the count were zero? Since the average would not be calculated, the program would attempt to print out the value of a variable that in fact had not been assigned a value. Depending on the particular implementation this would either result in a run-time error, or the printing out of a random value (perhaps zero).

The solution, of course, is to wrap a guard plan around the output statement. However, again, plans must be integrated: the output goal, which is realized by a simple output plan, must be integrated into a division by zero guard plan, which in turn has been integrated with a simple calculation plan. This integration again requires a dataflow analysis in order to know where to put the average output statement.

We are still not done, however. Integrating the output plan with a division by zero guard plan requires that something be printed out when a division by zero might occur. Thus, what appears to be a simple plan to output a value becomes more complicated because another print statement is needed in the leg of the guard plan in which the error might occur:

```
count := 0;
total := 0;
writeln('please input a number');
read(new);
while new <> 99999 do
  begin
     total := total + new;
     count := count + 1;
     writeln('please input a number');
     read(new);
  end;
if count > 0 then
           begin
              average := total/count;
              writeln('average is ', average);
           end
         else
           begin
              writeln('no valid inputs;');
              writeln('no average calculated');
           end;
end.
```

As presented above, the program is now complete: it will solve the problem it was intended to solve.

3. Summarizing the Knowledge: The Goal-and-Plan Graph

A summary of the knowledge described in this paper is given in Figure 4-1. The graph structure attempts to relate the goals to subgoals, subgoals to plans, and plans to code. Interpretation of the connecting links is as follows:

- The picture

means that goal b is a subgoal of goal a; in order to achieve goal a, goal b must be achieved.

- The picture

means that PLAN B is used to realize goal a.

- The picture

means that goal b is a subgoal of PLAN A; PLAN A introduced a new subgoal that needs to be achieved.

In particular, note that the graph depicts where plans need to be integrated in order to realize a set of goals.

The graph in Figure 4-1 provides only one solution to the example problem. We have, in fact, constructed more elaborate tree structures that describe a space of correct solutions. These tree structures aid us in understanding the bugs students make in their programs ([13, 12, 14]). For example, we would predict that bugs would crop up at those points in the tree representation of the knowledge where two plans need to be integrated; data we have collected do in fact support this prediction ([14]).

4. Concluding Remarks

We have attempted to give a detailed account of a portion of the knowledge that was used writing what we all would agree should be a simple program. Frankly, we feel that the amount of knowledge and the types of inferences necessary to write this program borders on the staggering. Moreover, as we acknowledged at the outset, our discussion was not even a complete picture: missing from our discussion is a description of the knowledge needed to control the process of program generation.

It is an axiom of instruction that we, as teachers, need to

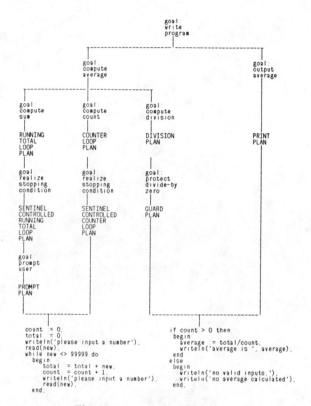

Figure 4-1: Goal-and-Plan Graph

know the subject matter in order to teach it effectively. The goal of this paper is to point out how much there is to know about writing programs. While the enterprise of making explicit what has more typically remained tacit is a difficult one, we feel that pursuing such a goal will certainly lead to improved programming instruction.[6]

Acknowledgements

The work that Lewis Johnson has done on PROUST has helped to identify a significant amount of knowledge underlying the creation of programs such as the one described here; this paper is deeply indebted to his efforts. We would also like to thank the Summer Bug Exterminators, who plowed through mountains of buggy programs with a religious fervor, and whose insights into why students make bugs also played an important role in the development of this paper: Jim Spohrer, Edgar Pope, Michael Lipman, Warren Sack, Scott Freiman, David Littman.

---

[6]Fortunately, some programming textbooks have begun to make such knowledge explicit (e.g., [3, 8]).

References

[1] Adelson, B., Soloway, E. .
A Cognitive Model of Software Design.
1984.
in *The Nature of Expertise*, Chi, M., Glaser, R., Farr, M., (Eds.), to appear. Also Technical Report #242, Dept. of Computer Science, Yale University.

[2] Barstow, David.
Knowledge-Based Program Construction.
Elsevier North Holland Inc., 1979.

[3] Dale, N., Orshalick D.
Introduction to PASCAL and Structured Design.
D.C. Heath and Co., 1983.

[4] Ehrlich, K., Soloway, E.
An Empirical Investigation of the Tacit Plan Knowledge in Programming. Ablex Inc., New York, 1984.

[5] Johnson, L., Soloway, E.
Diagnosis and Understanding in Novice Programs.
In *Proc. of AAAI-84*. American Association for Artificial Intelligence, Austin, Texas, 1984.

[6] Johnson, W. L., Soloway, E., Cutler, B., Draper, S.
Bug Catalogue: I.
Technical Report 298, Dept. of Computer Science, Yale University, 1983.

[7] Rich, C.
Inspection Methods in Programming.
Technical Report AI-TR-604, MIT AI Lab, 1981.

[8] Shneiderman, B.
Teaching Programming: A Spiral Approach to Syntax and Semantics.
Computers and Education 1:193-197, 1977.

[9] Soloway, E., Ehrlich, K., Bonar, J., Greenspan, J.
What Do Novices Know About Programming?
Ablex, Inc., 1982, .

[10] Soloway, E., Bonar, J., Ehrlich, K. .
Cognitive Strategies and Looping Constructs: An Empirical Study.
CACM 26:853-861, 1983.

[11] Soloway, E., Ehrlich, K.
Empirical Studies of Programming Knowledge.
IEEE Transactions on Software Engineering SE-10(5):595-609, 1984.

[12] Spohrer, J., Pope, E., Lipman, M., Sack, W., Freiman, S., Littman, D., Johnson, L., Soloway, E.
Bugs In Novice Programs and Misconceptions In Novice Programmers.
1984.
To appear: World Educational Computer Conference, 1985.

[13] Spohrer, J., Pope, E., Lipman, M., Sack, W., Freiman, S., Littman, D., Johnson, L., Soloway, E.
Bug Catalogues: II and III.
1985.
in preparation.

[14] Spohrer, J., Soloway, E., Pope, E.
Where the Bugs Are.
1985.

COMPUTERS IN EDUCATION, K. Duncan and D. Harris (eds.)
Elsevier Science Publishers B.V. (North-Holland)
© IFIP, 1985

TEACHING PROGRAM VERIFICATION WITH THE HELP OF AN
INTERACTIVE SUPPORT SYSTEM

Pentti Hietala

University of Tampere
Department of Mathematical Sciences
Computer Science, P.O.Box 607
SF—33101 Tampere 10, Finland

Research in program verification has contributed to the fundamental understanding of computer programming. However, there is not a consensus on how the program verification issues should be conveyed to future programmers. In this paper we report on a course on program verification where we employed an interactive verification support system. The experiences from this course advocate a greater use of support tools in teaching program verification and in teaching programming as well. The main benefits from the usage of this kind of tools culminate in motivating the students and in helping them to concentrate on the central issues instead of a myriad of details.

1. INTRODUCTION

Program correctness is one of the most essential issues in programming. On the other hand, program verification, i.e. the question of establishing the correctness by mathematical rigor (possibly by using a special program called the verifier) is a much more debatable issue, and is usually considered to have only academic interest. Opinions of this kind have partly their grounds in the unrealized expectations from the late sixties and early seventies, when verification enthusiastics envisioned automatic verifiers for the near future. As we all know, today it is still true that the complete automation of the verification of program correctness is not feasible for practical programs. However, in our opinion there are also other contributors to the unpopularity of program verification. One reason might be that there has been too much reliance on formality and theoretical aspects in presenting and demonstrating program verification. In this paper we try to show that the use of appropriate tools in teaching verification issues will greatly alleviate the difficulties in their learning and also in their acceptance.

As recently stated by J.L.Bentley [5], "the research on program verification has given us something far more valuable than a black box that gobbles programs and flashes 'good' or 'bad' — we now have a fundamental understanding of computer programming". There is a growing consensus that this understanding and the ideas of program verification should be conveyed to future programmers as early in their programming career as possible, because it is much more difficult "after they have become hackers" (a panel statement by H.D.Mills [16]). Especially the so called "science of programming" approach (led by Edsger Dijkstra and David Gries) advocates the teaching

of formal aspects to future programmers [8]. The verification of a program should not be a separate checking of a complete program; on the contrary, "a program and its proof should be developed hand—in—hand, with the proof usually leading the way" [9]. These ideas are manifested in the textbook of Gries [9] which excellently promotes the rigorous approach in teaching early programming.

There are several other examples how the concepts derived from verification research can be applied to the teaching of programming. For example, in the education of IBM programmers [15] this knowledge is brought to bear according to a textbook on structured programming [13] which emphasizes verification aspects. As for entire courses on program verification, there are only a few reported (one is discussed in [14]); the concepts of program verification are usually included as a small subsidiary on courses on programming methodology (see e.g. [4]). This trend has long been embodied in the curriculum recommendations (see e.g. [1], which does not seem to consider theoretical aspects very important). The prerequisites for successful inclusion of verification principles into the computer science curriculum, supplementary courses in mathematics and logic, are not either properly paid attention in the recommendations, as Ralston [18] notes.

The advocating of the increase of formalism in the early teaching has also aroused criticism. For example, Culik [6] points out that the "logical" formality of proofs should be replaced by the informality of "mathematical" proofs. However, the main problem seems to be the question of how to convince the programmers on the value of rigor and thus motivate them to employ these concepts. One solution might be the use of computerized tools (e.g. program verifiers) to illustrate the verification techniques and to clarify the meaning of proofs. If this system would be flexible enough, also the degree of formality could be adjusted according to the user of the system.

There are quite a few program verifiers constructed during the last decade, but their use in teaching is very little reported. Their application to assist teaching is usually found at the level of a comment, e.g. Wolfgang Polak notes briefly in [17] that "the Stanford Pascal Verifier is frequently used in class work". Another specification and verification system, the IOTA system [12], is also used in teaching essential issues of rigorous program analysis, but detailed results are not given.

In this paper we propose that computers should be brought to bear more extensively in the teaching of program verification. Our hypothesis is that the use of a computer as an assistant to attend to the tedious (although necessary) bookkeeping work in the verification would give the user more time to concentrate on the essentials. This is of most importance in a teaching environment. Furthermore, the immediate reinforcement of a new concept explained in class – now the student himself carrying out tasks on terminal – is a well-known factor to motivate learning. In this paper we describe a course on program verification [11] where we used an interactive support system called I3V. The system I3V is an experimental system to facilitate the incremental and iterative construction of a proof for program correctness [3,10]. Our emphasis on the user interface and bookkeeping issues of the verification process seemed to be well-accepted by the students who participated in the course. In addition to evaluating the learning of the students by examinations, their opinions were collected using questionnaires. They also kept a diary on their experiences of the course. This response shows that the motivation of the students increased considerably when they started the "hands-on" work with the support system after the introductory theory lessons.

This paper is organized as follows. In the next section we outline the teaching of program verification and the role of a computer system in assisting it. Section 3 describes our course on program verification and the teaching methods used. Section 4 discusses the results obtained from examinations and also from the comments of the students in their diaries and in the questionnaires. We conclude with a few recommendations for future courses on verification and programming.

2. ON TEACHING PROGRAM VERIFICATION

The course on program verification held in March–April 1984 at the University of Tampere had three goals: (1) to teach program verification using a technique called invariant oriented programming, (2) to investigate the use of a program verification support system for assisting the instruction, and (3) to evaluate the support system itself. This paper mainly reports on the first two goals.

Program verification can be seen as a process where one wants to check whether the program text conforms with the program specifications that are usually embedded among the program text as assertions (invariants). Using these assertions and proof rules (supplied for each statement type) it is possible to generate lemmas that must be established for the program to be correct. As with program construction, we think that practical verification will proceed incrementally, step by step, updating previous decisions when necessary. The both processes, program construction and verification, should be in fact conducted and taught together.

Let us next consider the role of computer assistance in the teaching. In this discussion we will use the following model for the phases of learning (see Gagne [7]): (1) motivation, (2) apprehending, (3) acquisition, (4) retention, (5) recall, (6) generalization, (7) performance and (8) feedback. These phases are not strictly sequential; they are iterated as the learning proceeds.

The use of a computer system as an assistant will have mainly influence on the phases 1,2 and 5 of the above model. Demonstrations with a support system will arouse motivation in the early learning of a theoretical subject (such as verification). Moreover, the availability of a support system will make it easier to initiate the application of the verification methodology in the other learning phases, too. This follows from the fact that when you know that there is a system that will do part of the job for you the starting threshold will not be so high (provided that the system is easy to use). In the phase 2 (apprehending) the learner can make use of the system when forming his own model of the verification process. The I3V system helps you to concentrate on the essentials and lets the learner choose the level of proof detail by himself. This influences also the phase 3 (knowledge acquisition) of learning.

In the phase 5 (recall) where the learner reinforces his model of the verification process by applying his knowledge to concrete problems, the support system comes also to help. It is important to have a tool to manage and control the wealth of detail that arises during the verification process. I3V systematizes the processing of this data, while at the same time providing the learner with plenty of degrees of freedom on how to use the system. A support system will also assist the phases 7 and 8 of learning (performance and feedback). For example, the log–playback facility of the I3V system makes it possible to observe the cognitive processes of the learner as he is solving a problem and to give him feedback on the basis of his performance, not only according to the outcome.

Next we describe our support system in more detail. It is a prototype version of the I3V system (an Interactive system for Incremental and Iterative program Verification) and is based on the use of invariants in programming [2]. In this methodology you first construct a set of invariants to specify the problem and after that design the program code to confirm with the invariants. The solution is then refined from one level to another with the invariants leading the way. The I3V system is intended to assist the user in verifying the correctness of a program built according to the above methodology. The system allows the correctness proof to be constructed in an incremental and iterative fashion while the system records the proof being constructed and keeps track of the status of the proof (what has already been proved, what still needs to be proved and so on). The I3V system supports the verification of partial correctness, proper termination and the absence of run—time errors of a program. The prototype version of the system that was used in the course provided only the possibility to modify program invariants and all the proofs were given by the user. The inclusion of additional facilities (e.g. program code modification and a theorem prover) would considerably extend the power of the I3V system in the verification domain, but with the teaching aspects in mind we feel that already this version is a rather useful tool.

The I3V system emphasizes the use of display terminal. In figure 1 we present a snapshot obtained from a session with the I3V system. The user is inspecting his program at location 12, or, in other words, the window into his program is positioned at location 12. A few adjacent locations are also displayed around the window on the terminal screen. The window itself is composed of three subwindows: assumptions, lemma and the proof part. The proof is written into the lower—part subwindow with an editor—like facility. In the proof one should establish the lemmas shown in the right—hand upper subwindow from the known facts on the left. There are operations available to support this activity: scrolling and suppressing the information in the subwindows.

```
LOCATION 12:

10:*              k:=1;
11:*              x:=A[k]
-------------------------------------------------
ASSUME:                :   PROVE:
                       :
(1) A = A#,            :   (1)  Perm(A,A0)
(2) x = A#[1],         :   (2)  Biggest(A,j-1,k)
(3) i = i#,            :   (3)  1 <= k <= j-1
(4) j = j#,            :   (4)  j-1 <= i
(5) k = 1,             :   (5)  x = A[k]          (OK)
(6) r >= 1,            :   (6)  (i,i-j+1) <= (i#,i#-j#+1)
(7) Perm(A#,A0),       :
(8) 1 <= i# <= r,      :
(9) Ordered(A#,i#+1,r) :
..................................:...............
PROOF:
Lemma (5) follows directly from assumptions (1), (2)
and (5).
-------------------------------------------------
12:+              goto loop2
13:      // (i <= 1) then
```

Figure 1. A window into a sort program in an example session with the I3V system.

After supplying a proof for a location the user can move the window to another location, and continue the verification. The proof for a program can be constructed location by location, because proofs for one location are independent from the other proofs. Proof construction can also be divided into several sessions with the system,

which assists the verification process in practice.

Furthermore, our system supports the iterative nature of verification: programs intended for verification are usually not correct in the first place, or the program invariants supplied for the proof are incomplete or incorrect. With the I3V facility to modify invariants the user can iteratively find the correct invariants. The effects of changes to invariants are propagated by the system to all the appropriate places (assumptions, lemmas etc.) in the program, as in spread sheet calculation.

An earlier implementation of the I3V system is described in [10] and the user interface issues of the system are elaborated in [3]. The system is running on DEC2060, the mainframe computer of our university and is written in SIMULA 67.

3. A COURSE ON PROGRAM VERIFICATION

This section describes the participants, teaching contents and methods used on a verification course held at the University of Tampere in March—April 1984.

3.1. Participants

There were six third—year undergraduate students who participated the course from the beginning to the end. They were all computer science majors; their previous studies in computer science comprised e.g. of courses in elementary programming, data structures and compiling techniques. It was possible for the students to include this verification course in their degree program, although the course is not a compulsory one in our curriculum. (Program verification had been introduced very briefly to them at their first programming course, but otherwise it is not regularly covered in our curriculum.) Their background in mathematics consisted mainly of introductory courses in calculus, set theory and matrix computing. Many useful courses like that of algebra and almost all from logic seemed to be missing from the studies of the participants: only one had taken the first course in logic. On the other hand, no more than two of them lacked work experience; the others had been working as programmers in the industry at least for three months.

3.2. The contents of the course

The course comprised of 30 hours of lessons in nearly six week's time. This included at the end a period of one and a half week for the final take—home exercise after which there was a session for each of the students separately with the instructor. The nature of the lessons was mainly lectures at the beginning of the course but near to the end there were also demonstrations and test sessions with the system. The contents of the course are explained in detail elsewhere [11], so here we only outline the course topics in figure 2.

```
Week #1
1.day (3 hours)
- motivation: syntactic vs semantic correctness;
  scope, content and goals of the course
- organization of the course (scheduling
  the course days)
- program verification in a nutshell:
  history, principles, tools and achievements
- verification of a flowchart program for
  the gcd problem
2.day (3 hours)
- more motivation of the need for verification
- introduction to invariants
- I3V: language, style and proof rules
- home exercise 1: factorial
3.day (3 hours)
- I3V proof rules revisited
- home exercise 1: discussion
- example program initiated (the parse program)
- home exercise 2: right justifying text

Week #2
1.day (3 hours)
- questionnaire
- on finding invariants
- I3V system: principles
2.day (3 hours)
- home exercise 2: discussion
- classroom exam: positive sequence on integers,
  and discussion
- demonstration of I3V system on the terminal
- home exercise 3: analysis of an existing sort
  program using the I3V system

Week #3
1.day (3 hours)
- special properties of I3V system
- terminal work with the teacher available
2.day (3 hours)
- termination of programs
- home exercise 3: discussion
- home exercise 4: minimum sum section
- terminal work with the teacher available

Week #4
1.day (3 hours)
- questionnaire
- home exercise 4: discussion
- first terminal exercise: fast exponentiation
2.day (3 hours)
- final take-home exercise: swapping sections
- evaluation of the first terminal exercise:
  playback session

Evaluation session (after 1 1/2 weeks, 3 hours)
- discussion of the final take-home exercise
- final questionnaire
- second terminal exercise: merge, using log
- evaluation of the second terminal exercise:
  playback session
```

Figure 2. The course contents

3.3. On the teaching and research methodology

In our teaching we encouraged the students to participate actively during the lectures. Also the structure of the course and the methods applied were supporting this kind of approach (cf. figure 2). For example, the course diaries that were kept by the students, produced immediate feedback that could be used to navigate the course. The students were supposed to write down their experiences into a computer file as soon as possible after each day. These notes were then inspected by the teacher and utilized in directing the course, i.e. issues that had proved difficult were revisited and given a more thorough treatment. Two questionnaires were conducted to focus on specific questions that had arisen from the diary notes. The final questionnaire after the course summed up the experiences of the students.

Another methodological aspect worth mentioning was the use of the log-playback facility of the I3V system. It was possible to log the session keystrokes of a user into a file and later on give this log file as input for another I3V session. In this way we could reproduce the terminal session afterwards exactly in the same form as in the original situation. This facility was employed to monitor the problems that the students have when working at the terminal. In the playback session the student explained his/hers way of thinking during the actual session. This procedure gave us information on how the students were able to grasp and organize the verification process in their minds.

4. RESULTS FROM THE COURSE

In this section we discuss the response from the students as well as the outcome of the examinations organized during the course.

4.1. Opinions of the students

Opinions of the students were gathered using questionnaires at three occasions: two questionnaires during the early lectures and the third at the final session after they had completed the final exercise (see figure 2).

The first two questionnaires gave a good picture of the learning process of the students and suggested possible issues the instructor should return to in the teaching. The notation of the proof rules, the rules itself and the question of how to invent invariants were considered difficult at the beginning of the course. However, the I3V system turned out to be easy to learn and use; the slowness of the system and the bugs found seemed to be the main obstacles when the students started to use the system.

Especially interesting were the answers to an open-ended question in the second questionnaire (the students had been using the system over one week): "how the use of I3V system has influenced your learning of program verification?" Answers included the following: the use of the system had
- clarified the idea of incremental proof construction and also the modularization principles in practice,
- clarified the "whole nature of verification",
- given time to concentrate on the actual verification while the system is attending housekeeping tasks,
- clarified the concept of "invariant".

The third questionnaire was posed to the students at the final session. At this stage the students had been working with the system for approximately three weeks. In the questionnaire we presented several statements about the I3V system and the participants answered how well these corresponded to their own opinions. The results are summarized in figure 3.

Statement (I3V supports...)	well	moderately	poorly	very poorly	don't know
1. invariant method	4	2			
2. incremental proof construction	4	2			
3. automatic program verification	1	2	2		1
4. finding errors in invariants	5	1			
5. fixing errors in invariants	1	4	1		
6. finding errors in program text	2	1	1		2
7. fixing errors in program text		3	2		1
8. being aware of the status and its evolving	5	1			
9. to divide the proof process into more manageable parts	5	1			
10. recovers from its own error situations				4	2
11. the learning of program verification	5	1			

Figure 3. Student comments at the final questionnaire

We can see from this response that the students were quite pleased with the system; their answers to questions number 1 and 2 show that they think that the system supports well our approach to verification. The answers to questions dealing with error locating and correcting (4-7) point out the direction where to extend the system. This response seems also to give evidence to our hypothesis that I3V assists the learning of verification by making the proof process more manageable (questions 8, 9 and 11).

The students' response as a whole revealed that they found the course to be a source of new ideas and a nice one especially because it was different from the ordinary courses. The diary and questionnaires seemed to clarify also the minds of the respondents.

4.2. Results from the examinations

Tests and programming assignments were scheduled throughout the course so it was possible to monitor the learning progress of the students and the impact of the support system to it.

The students had a one-hour classroom exam on programming and verification using the I3V methodology after the first third of the course. Up to that point the course had covered the essential topics of the methodology together with small classroom and take-home exercises; the I3V system had not yet been introduced. In this exercise they had to construct with paper and pencil a simple program and verify it using the invariant method. The construction of invariants and verifying according to the proof rules seemed to cause the most difficulties: only one managed to produce a nearly correct solution with respect to these issues, the others gave rather incomplete answers. Supplying the proof as a tree skeleton (instead of ordinary textual form) seemed to be most favoured.

Another test point was the final take-home exercise the end of the course. After the lecture part of the course the students were given the final exercise which was to be completed in one and a half weeks' time (this time included one-week easter holidays). The exercise turned out to be hard only for one student; the other five got it together in due time: they delivered the program with embedded invariants and had also verified their programs using the I3V system. The success in completing the final exercise seemed to correlate with the total amount of time spent with the I3V system: those students who had spent less time with the system had also the most difficulties with the exercise.

The log-playback facility of the I3V system was employed twice during the course. In the first of these terminal exercises the students were supposed to locate erroneous spots in a given program while trying to verify it. Although this exercise took place in the middle of the course the students found rather soon the inconsistencies between the invariants and program code. This led them to correcting the errors by modifying invariants. In the second terminal exercise (at the end of the course) they were to strengthen existing program invariants (i.e. they used the system to assist in adjusting the specifications). The one-hour time was insufficient for getting the job done but all the students managed to construct a few invariants correctly. The playback session held after this exercise revealed that the students had trouble in finding the most logical strategy to apply when trying to invent intermediate invariants: they usually preferred to progress lexically in the program text instead of starting from the goal of the program (exit invariant).

4.3. Discussion of the results

We have tried to adopt "a middle of the road" approach between the two extremes of verification support: completely automated proofs or proofs by paper and pencil. In the teaching domain it is especially suitable that the user has the responsibility of creating the proof. From the didactic point of view it should of course be the students who conduct the proving, not the system doing that for them. Anyway, with a tool systematizing the proof process and reminding the user of all the details he has to attend to, the lengthy process of verification is kept manageable. Furthermore, because the proof construction is not completely automatized the user can choose the level of detail he wants to have in his proof.

The students' comments in the diary and questionnaires show that the use of the I3V system helped them to form their inner model of verification (the apprehending phase of learning) as well as encouraged them to apply the issues explained in the classroom (support for the motivation and recall phases of learning). The log-playback sessions assisted both the students and the instructor (the performance and feedback phases): one could obtain a true picture of the behavior when solving a problem and adjust the corrective feedback to a real situation.

5. CONCLUSIONS

Our course on program verification can be seen as one of the first steps to shed light on a rather little investigated area of computer science education. Although we employed an experimental prototype system on our course, we feel that the results lend support to our hypothesis concerning the positive effect of interactive tools upon the learning of program verification. For more sophisticated conclusions, additional work is needed with a more advanced support system.

However, we feel that the I3V system contains some essential features that should be incorporated into the support systems to be used when teaching program verification in the future (and programming, too). First, the system should be inherently interactive, and utilize concepts of immediate feedback. Second, facilities for stepwise construction of proofs (cf. the incremental construction of programs) turned out to be a highly recommendable feature. Finally, we advocate increased support for the iterative nature of the problem-solving processes we are dealing with. This means encouragement of progressing by "trial and error" where the support system should take care of the updates in the manner of spread sheet calculation. This feature combined with immediate feedback will appeal to and motivate the coming students who have grown up in the age of personal computers.

Acknowledgements

This work was supported by the Academy of Finland. The constructive comments of Marja Vehvilainen are gratefully acknowledged.

References

[1] Austing, R.H., et.al., Curriculum 78. Comm. of the ACM 22, 3, March 1979, 147–166.

[2] Back, R.J.R., Invariant based programs and their correctness. In Biermann, Guiho, Kodratoff (eds.), Automatic program construction techniques. MacMillan 1983.

[3] Back, R.J.R., Hietala, P., A simple user interface for interactive program verification. In the Proceedings of the INTERACT '84: First IFIP Conference on Human–Computer Interaction, London, September 1984.

[4] Beforooz, A., Sharma, O.P., A foundation course in computer science. In the Proceedings of the Fifteenth SIGCSE Technical Symposium on Computer Science Education, Philadelphia, February 16–17, 1984. ACM SIGCSE Bulletin 16,1, February 1984, 159–163.

[5] Bentley, J.L., Writing correct programs. Section "Programming pearls". Comm. of the ACM 26, 12, December 1983, 1040–1045.

[6] Culik, K., On formal and informal proofs for program correctness. ACM SIGPLAN Notices 18, 1, January 1983, 23–28.

[7] Gagne, R.M., The conditions of learning (5th edition). Holt, Rinehart and Winston, Hong Kong, 1977.

[8] Gries, D., Educating the programmer: notation, proofs and the development of programs. In S.H.Lavington (ed.), Information processing 80, North–Holland Publishing Company, 1980, 935–944.

[9] Gries, D., The science of programming. Springer–Verlag, New York, 1981.

[10] Hietala, P., An interactive program verification system: first version of the MESS verification environment. University of Tampere, Department of Mathematical Sciences, Report A97, February 1983.

[11] Hietala, P., A course on program verification. University of Tampere, Department of Mathematical Sciences, Report A137, December 1984.

[12] The IOTA programming system. A modular programming environment. Nakajima, R. and Yuasa, T. (eds.), Lecture Notes in Computer Science 160. Springer–Verlag, 1983.

[13] Linger, R.C., Mills, H.D., Witt, B.I., Structured programming: theory and practice. Addison–Wesley, 1979.

[14] Mili, A., A case for teaching program verification: its importance in the CS curriculum. In the Proceedings of the Fourteenth SIGCSE Technical Symposium on Computer Science Education, Orlando, February 17–18, 1983. ACM SIGCSE Bulletin 15, 1, February 1983, 2–6.

[15] Mills, H.D., et.al., The management of software engineering. IBM System Journal 19, 4, 1980, 414–477.

[16] Mills, H.D., Panel discussion on "Teaching formal methods for program development and verification". In the Proceedings of the Fourteenth SIGCSE Technical Symposium on Computer Science Education. Orlando, February 17–18, 1983. ACM SIGCSE Bulletin 15, 1, February 1983, 50.

[17] Polak, W., Program verification at Stanford: past, present, future. In the Proceedings of GWAI–81: German Workshop on Artificial Intelligence, Bad Honnef, January 26–31, 1981. Informatik–Fachberichte 47, Springer–Verlag, 1981, 256–276.

[18] Ralston, A., Mathematical education for computer scientists and for mathematicians. In Lewis, R., Tagg, D., (eds.), Computers in Education, North–Holland, 1981, 753–759.

COMPUTERS IN EDUCATION, K. Duncan and D. Harris (eds.)
Elsevier Science Publishers B.V. (North-Holland)
© IFIP, 1985

T U T O R I A L

COMPARISON OF PASCAL, MODULA-2, ADA, AND C

John Beidler and Paul Jackowitz

Univ. of Scranton, Scranton, PA 18510

Objectives: Present a programming practices/software engineering framework of desirable features and characteristics of programming languages and use this to make a comprehensive evaluation and comparison of the relative merits of these four important programming language.

Audience: For college and pre-college level educators who have some familiarity with one of these four languages, perhaps Pascal, and are interested in learning about the features, strengths and weaknesses of these four programming languages.

Session 1: 8:30 AM - 10:00 AM

- Historic background, structure, and distinctive features of each language with representative sample programs.

- Programming practices, software engineering requirements for a programming language.

Break: 10:00 - 10:30 AM

Session 2: 10:30 AM - 12N

- Typical criticisms of standard Pascal

- Comparison of language features - syntactic structure, data structures, control structures, data abstraction, coroutines, generics, access to low level facilities, environment development, and other software engineering and system development considerations.

- Compilation/execution considerations and support - separate compilation, libraries, portability, etc.

COMPUTERS IN EDUCATION, K. Duncan and D. Harris (eds.)
Elsevier Science Publishers B.V. (North-Holland)
©IFIP, 1985

USING COMPUTERS TO TEACH CRITICAL THINKING
SKILLS AND FITTING CRITICAL THINKING INTO THE CURRICULUM

Chairperson: Susan D. Markey, Public Relations Director, Sunburst Communications, Inc.

Participants: Marge Kosel, Vice President, Microcomputer Courseware Division, Sunburst
Communications, Inc.; Beverly Hamilton, teacher, Skyline Elementary School,
Ann Lathrop, Library Coordinator, San Mateo County Office of Education
and Coordinator, California Statewide Evaluation Project; Jay Sivin,
Coordinator, Microcomputer Courseware Evaluation, Educational Products
Information Exchange (EPIE) Institute; Tom Snyder, President, Tom
Snyder Productions, Inc.

Problem solving is, and should be, a major objective in schools and home. But problem
solving in most textbooks is ambiguous. "Problems" in most math textbooks aren't really
problems. They are computational exercises disguised in words: "Two boys each ate four
hamburgers..." Such activities are trivial so far as problem solving is concerned.
Most of us rarely have to solve a "word problem" in our adult lives.
So what is problem solving? It is the ability, willingness and confidence to make sense
out of a novel situation and devise alternatives to reach a goal. The construction of
alternatives, not the repeating of formulas, is what thinking and problem solving are
all about. But what are the specific skills of problem solving? How do we teach them?
And how do we fit problem solving into our curriculum? Teachers already complain of so
little time to teach the basics. And the public is putting pressure on educators to
get back to basics. How do we justify   problem solving as a critical part of education? How do we then approach the teaching of this sometimes abstract skill in a
more concrete way?
These questions will be the basis for a panel discussion, representing viewpoints from
the practical classroom level, software development and publishing, courseware evaluation,
and state legislation.

Marge Kosel, Sunburst, is designer of the award-
winning problem-solving programs, The Factory,
The Pond and The Incredible Laboratory. Her
career includes math teacher and then instructional administrator of research and evaluation
in Hopkins, Minnesota. Later, she was instructional computing coordinator and manager of
development at Minnesota Educational Computing
Consortium (MECC). She has designed over 60
computer programs and manages the development
of over 150 software packages. She will focus
on the research and subsequent Sunburst matrix
which details skills used in critical thinking.
Next, she will discuss how to teach these skills
through classroom activities and computer
software.

Beverly Hamilton, fifth and sixth grade teacher,
has been using problem solving software in the
classroom for seven years. Her work with
colleage Beverly Saylor was the basis for a
Stanford University case study entitled,
"Successful integration of micros in an elementary school." They won the San Mateo county
award for their work, which led to the state-
funded project, COMPUTHINK. As co-project
developer for COMPUTHINK, she is developing a
taxonomy of cognitive skills. She will discuss
this research, as well as her experiences with
student learning, teacher training, and implementing a problem-solving curriculum.

As coordinator for the California Statewide
Evaluation Project, Ann Lathrop is actively
involved in setting up systems on a regional
level for training teachers to evaluate software.   She is coauthor of Courseware in
the Classroom; editor of Digest of Software
Reviews: Education; founder and editor of
SOFTSWAP, the Computer Using Educators (CUE)
exchange of public domain software; and author
of a library search software program, How Can
I Find It if I Don't Know What I'm Looking For?
She will discuss the problems and considerations
for introducing new policies for computer instruction on a district and state-wide level.

Jay Sivin coordinates the microcomputer courseware evaluation process for EPIE, the Educational
Products Information Exchange. EPIE's national
evaluation network evaluates software in cooperation with the Urban Superintendent's Technology
Consortium and other cities and universities
around the country. As part of the review
process, courseware is evaluated by classroom
teachers and curriculum specialists and is
tested with students. Mr. Sivin will discuss
the difficulties and pitfalls of evaluating this
new breed of software (problem solving). He will
also discuss the appropiate/inappropriate use of
computers and EPIE's six-month project to obtain
long-term user feedback of the EPIE evaluated
software.

An elementary school teacher for 10 years,
Tom Snyder is now developing educational
software as president of Tom Snyder Productions
Inc. (TSP). He is creator of the problem-
solving software, Snooper Troops 1 & 2, Agent
USA and the Search Series. Mr. Snyder will
discuss his new conflicts resolution game,
The Other Side, which requires students to use
many critical thinking skills in an effort
to avoid nuclear war, including balancing long
and short term goals and working with insufficient information. He'll also discuss how the
computer can be used in the classroom to create
an interactive learning and problem solving
environment.

COMPUTERS IN EDUCATION, K. Duncan and D. Harris (eds.)
Elsevier Science Publishers B.V. (North-Holland)
© IFIP, 1985

CAN WE CONSCIOUSLY TEACH EXCELLENT PROGRAMMING?

Peter Molzberger

Dept. of Computer Science
HSBw-University of the German Federal Armed Forces
8014 Neubiberg/W.Germany

ABSTRACT

In the field of software development there exist a small number of extremely excellent
people, superseding the performance of the average programmer, quantitatively as well
as qualitatively, by a factor up to 30. Facing the current situation in Software
Engineering individuals like them would be a powerful means of overcoming our
difficulties, provided we are able to teach these faculties to more people.
The study of these "superprogrammers" /4/ (not to be confused with the so called
hackers) shows that these individuals demonstrate a large variety of unusual skills
based on intuition and creativity rather than exclusively on rational thinking. There
are many indications that Superprogramming qualities are not acquired be learning
something new but by establishing coherence between existing mental faculties which
may be assigned to different hemispheres of the brain.
Based on this assumption special training methods have been developed giving people a
chance to start a growth process, leading to a mastery of programming. First
experiences with two of these techniques are very encouraging.

The Phenomenon of "Superprogramming"

A Superprogrammer is what we call a person
showing extraordinary performance in the field
of software development. Faculties are not restricted to coding a program in a programming
language but embrace all the necessary steps
from systems analysis, specification and design
to implementation and maintenance of the final
product. (We emphasise the coding phase here
because performance measurement is easier than
in the other phases.)

Superprogrammers work very fast. In coding a
program they may achieve a factor of 10 to 30
in lines of code, compared with an average
programmer. The quality of their products is
significantly better.

At one time programs were far more transparent
to other people and had a very low rate of
errors.

Programs of Superprogrammers may be seen as
"works of art" combining optimum layout parameters which normally are considered to be
competing. Superprogrammers, as we understand
them do not restrict themselves to communication with machines (like hackers). They show
much interest in their environment and take
responsibility for themselves and their work as
well as for the team and organization they are
engaged in or work with. Most of those we
studied were freelancing or running a small
company of their own.

Superprogrammers are of very great value in
large software projects. They can do (and are
interested in doing) extremely ambitious and
difficult jobs to save a crisis project. Though
they are strongly individualistic people, they
are well able to work in teams organized in an
appropriate way.

Software Engineering and Human Faculties

The software crisis since the late 60's is well
known. It is the common experience that, after
overcoming the bottlenecks and lack or
reliability of the hardware, we find ourselves
unable to build large software systems in a
satisfactory way:
Products usually become far more expensive than
estimated, deadlines are rarely met; and, worst
of all, the reliability of the systems is poor.

The first reaction to this situation was the
emergence of what we call Software Engineering
/7/. As the human being was found to be the
main source of trouble, the philosophy of Software Engineering tends to eliminate these
influences.

The software produced should be independent of
the individual attributes of the programmer.
This meant that methods, tools and programming
les had to be provided which restrict the
ssibilities for individual expression. The
most powerful instrument to support this
intention turned out to be the computer itself.
So the leading role in software development was
assigned to the machine, at least hypothetical-
ly: The ideal was seen in a software development process, comparable to the assembly line
in the automobile industry, where human
activity is reduced to that kind of work which,

up to this moment, cannot be taken over by
automated tools. The dream of building software
by means of general purpose standardized modules
was stimulated by ideas from the mass production
industry.

There is no doubt that the elimination of un-
disciplined tinkerers and artists with prima
donna attitudes was a most necessary step and we
should not be surprised that, by putting
emphasis on this goal, little attention was
given at that time to the existence of really
excellent individualistic software people.

During the last few years more and more
practitioners and scientists in the DP field
feel that mechanization and the development of
more efficient tools for average programmers
will not be the ultimate answer to our problems.

We still have enormous difficulties today
building really good software, but these
difficulties no longer have their origin in the
primary field of the coding of algorithms. They
are concentrated in areas not controllable by
mechanical means.

This general feeling of dissatisfaction is
clearly mirrored in the rediscovery of the
human being in the computing field which is
taking place at the moment. There is a fast
growing number of conferences on topics like
"Human Factors", "Software Psychology", and
"Software Ergonomy" all around the world.

Looking at the phenomenon of Superprogrammers we
find that they could make a real difference in
solving our problems if we would be able to
train very many of them. It seems to us that
time has come to move away from our ideal of the
average programmer who fits into our machinelike
organizational schemes and look for real
excellence in software development.

Some strange Features of Superprogrammers

The study of Superprogrammers was encouraged by
Gerald Weinberg in his guest talk at the first
conference on Human Factors in Computing
Systems, Gaithersberg 1982. Weinberg who started
the movement by publishing his book "The
Psychology of Programming" /8/ in 1971 pointed
out that the extraordinary of today has always
been the normal of tomorrow.

> "There must be some strange people some-
> where doing strange things. Watch for
> them!"

Looking for the extraordinary we found strange
people with strange faculties indeed.

The following list is a summing up of attributes
we found in more than one of the programmers but
not necessarily in all of them. Of course a lot
of further investigation is necessary.

- Altered mental states:

  o An experienced neurophysiologist diagnosed
    alpha brainwave patterns. (Measurements have
    not yet taken place.)
  o A grossly altered perception of time is
    commonly reported (shrinking the span of a
    night to one hour or less).
  o Several programmers claimed out-of-body
    experiences: "I was looking over my
    shoulder."

  o Many of the persons reported a state in
    which emotions are totally cut off. Never-
    theless the experience of being in that
    state is highly satisfactory and seems to
    be necessary from time to time for the men-
    tal and physical well-being of the person.
  o All highly skilled programmers claimed to
    be able to concentrate totally (not
    restricted to programming). "I become the
    program. Everything else is shut off."

- Using dreams and sleep intentionally:

  We have a lot of reports of programmers who
  take their problems with them into sleep.
  Some claim that they work on them in the
  dream state. Some of them get the solution
  immediately after they wake up. "It is simply
  there, but only when I wake up without an
  alarm clock."
  Most of them get the solution some time later,
  perhaps when stepping into the shower.
  "Suddenly the solution pops up."

- Precognitive faculties:

  Some programmers seem to have a strange knowledge about whether a very complicated
  solution will work or not, long before this
  can be seen on a rational basis. These people
  rely heavily on their feelings and claim that
  in doing so they have failed.

- Use of aesthetic faculties:

  This is a feature which, as far as we
  remember, all good programmers reported to a
  greater or lesser extent. It is discussed in
  greater detail in /4/.

Superprogrammers do not experience themselves as
technicians. Asked what they feel like in doing
their job we got answers like 'architect', 'composer' and the like. One of them said for
example:

a) in a position outside the program which allows for keeping the general view.
b) in a movable position inside the coding. "I myself am the processor. I become a point. That is how I run through the program: through loops, jumps, etc. I execute the program. Afterwards I am completely sure that the program is correct. It cannot be wrong, because it has been carried out correctly!"

Logical errors in programs are experienced time and again as a disruption of the aesthetic harmony. Logical correctness and good solutions manifest themselves in aesthetic elegance.

Georg: "Before I find a mistake I become aware that something is wrong with the aesthetics. I work very essentially with aesthetics."

Georg, too, uses this aesthetic feeling in a calculated way to test programs, when he says:

"There are programs which practically cannot be tested. There I simply have to look at it and know that they are o.k. When I see that, I'm convinced of their correctness."

Generally these people are not aware of the strangeness of what they are doing. A remark typical of them is: "So what! How can anyone write a good program without doing in that way?"

Can we teach "Superprogramming"?

Working with these people intensively we found that Maslow's pyramid of Human needs /3/ seems to be a good model to explain our group of "Superprogrammers". They seem to be opposed to those computer-minded people we call Hackers. Fig. 2

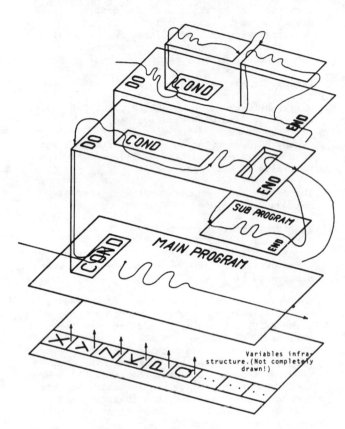

Figure 1: Example: Program mountain with calls, loops, subprogram, branching and infra-structure of the variables (The lines show the possible ways through the program)

Georg: "I am like a sculptor or a potter, I design something! But I cannot see any pots. Conceptualizing a program is not an intellectual, but an emotional performance for me. My difficulty is to express in words what I design. I am having problems furnishing an understandable description."

Most people do not really know what they see. A person able to visualize programs clearly told us:

Edwin: "For me, a program is a three dimensional structure of stairs around which I can walk and into which I can enter."
Fig. 1

Edwin can do even more with these three dimensional structures: He can test them by moving through them. He claims to "exist twice at the same time":

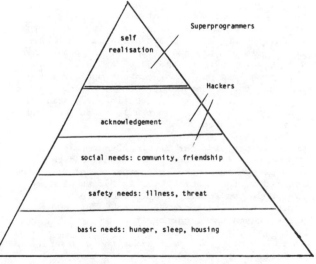

Figure 2: Maslow's Pyramid of Human Needs

Hackers are people fleeing from common reality. The computer replaces their engagement in social activity. When - as an example - a young man is too afraid to fall in love with a girl, he may find his satisfaction in an intimate relationship to a computer. Weizenbaum /9/ has pointed out the needs of a hacker to fulfill his urge for power in a self created artificial world.

In contrast to this, our "Superprogrammers" are fully integrated in their families and social groups. For them programming is a way of self-expression and self-realization, a behavior we find at the top of Maslow's scheme. Programming is a real art for them /6/.

The creative faculties of this group of people are specialized in the field of software production by many years of practical work, but they are in no way restricted to it. All of them said they could well imagine themselves working in totally different fields such as being an architect, scientist or manager.

The phenomenon we are dealing with here is not an excentric faculty of a genuis compensated by inabilities at some other place. It is a powerful general potential applied to a very specific field.

So the answer to our question whether we can teach superprogramming qualities is 'yes' and 'no'! For an explanation we should take a short look at what neurophysiology tells us about the two hemispheres of the brain /1/. We have two sets of functions within our brain; one of them - in most cases - is located on the left hemisphere while the other one is located in the right. Whatever the exceptions and the limitations of this model are, the right brain is said to be the residence of holistic recognition, creativity and intuition. The strange faculties of Superprogrammers listed above have to be assigned to this set.

There can be no doubt that programming is a highly rational and logical activity and is to be carried out by the left brain. If this hemisphere is not trained properly, the programmer will be unable to do the job. (At least it would require a long period of conventional training, but this is not the point of this paper.) So the answer is 'no', if the person is not a skilled and experienced programmer able to do the kind of work requested.

On the other side our findings show that programming is far beyond the rational and that Superprogrammers make intensive use of faculties located in the right brain. As far as we know, everybody has seemingly unlimited creative capabilities and there seems to be no need at all to teach the right brain.

So to become a Superprogrammer there is no need to learn anything additional. All that is necessary to provide access to blocked

resources which apparently have been available to us since early childhood. This can be achieved by breaking the dominance of the left hemisphere, which is blamed for suppressing the faculties of the right one. The goal is not the dominance of the right brain (this would mean an artist without predilection for rational activities or a regression to childhood) but coherence and harmony of the two hemispheres.

During the last several months we have obtained experimental results from no less than 5 different methods to establish this. The reader can easily (and with great value to himself) convince himself of the principal feasibility of these ideas by doing some experimental work in a totally different area: learning to draw portraits of human faces /2/.

The following 2 chapters deal with special methods we developed in Germany.

The Total Immersion Technique

To give an impression of how this technique works, we'll tell the story of how Josef Thum discovered it:

Several years ago, Josef, freelancing and overworked at that time, was looking for help. He found Ralf, a young man, ready to work for him. Ralf was a novice, one of the many attendees of DP schools offering a more or less intensive education to anyone able to write his name. He knew the features of some programming languages and he had tested a few small routines at the computer. Josef was struck by Ralf's tremendous willingness to learn whatever he could and to to any job requested.

Josef started working with Ralf at one terminal. Josef typed in the code explaining everything he was doing. Ralf had to keep track of the process and was told to ask questions whenever he was not clear about something. Soon Josef found out that these questions were of great value for himself. When Ralf couldn't follow, there was almost certainly a reason for it which Josef had been overlooking. He felt inspired by Ralf's questions and became more clear about what he was doing. So they went on for hours and hours. Slowly they found a way to share their job so that Ralf would take over more active auxilliary functions. It was an enjoyable experience for both of them.

After about 10 hours without any more interruption than going to the bathroom or having a cup of coffee, Ralf became totally exhausted. He was not able to keep his attention on the work anymore. He broke down mentally, as Josef calls it. As we know Josef from long experience, he is not willing to stop his work when in full swing. And with Ralf he had a companion who was not willing to give up no matter what happened: he literally gave everything he could.

After 12 hours a strange thing happened: Ralf became very alert and even more aware of what was going on than before. He not only took over a larger and more responsible part of the work but they also established a state of cooperation which Josef describes as "resonance of minds". They found that they thought the same things at the same time. When they had forgotten about something they remembered it simultaneously and the same held true for errors that occured. Even the smallest functions of the program were walked through at the same time.

Josef: "Two brains switched together and working at the same problem simultaneously - an extremely efficient mode of operation, led to extremely fast progress and to extremely reliable programs. And at the same time it was a very desirable experience for both partners. Time passed very quickly.

They called it a working day after 16 hours of continued efforts and went on after a period of sleep for another 16 or 18 hours. After three days the process began to peter out. They didn't actually stop but they found that 3 days are a natural span which should not be exceeded. It would have been best to relax completely for a couple of days, as Josef found out in the mean-time. The project had made an unexpected leap forward and Ralf now was described by Josef as a programmer, who had acquired unusual skills for a novice. "During our work, he just took over my way of seeing and formulating things which it took me at least 15 years to get to", Josef said, "and afterwards he was able to use them for himself."

This technique has been applied by the inventor several times with great success in his own com-pany. He is now expanding it to 4 trainees simultaneously to make it available on a commercial basis.

Total Immersion was first used with novices, but it is in no way restricted to them. It does not seem to be restricted to coding a program, either. We have credible reports about similar effects in the specification phase of a system, but this has not been studied until now.

In Total Immersion there still seems to be some-thing to learn: skills are acquired rapidly. This is not the case in our second technique, the Superprogramming Training.

The Superprogramming Training (SP)

This training has been developed in Germany by Dr. F.D. Peschanel in cooperation with the author. First practical experiments started in the fall of 1983 and at the moment the training is being tested in the environment of a large computer manufacturing company. So until now we have neither reliable scientific results nor has anything been published about the method. Never-theless, participants report extremely encouraging results.

A training period will take 2 1/2 days plus an additional day of relaxation where the participant is requested not to do any mental or stressful work. At the moment, the number of participants is restricted to 15-18 people.

In contrast to the intention of the Total Immersion Technique, the Superprogramming Training is not meant for beginners. It is a training for people with a well developed left hemisphere of the brain, mainly for qualified and well trained professionals in the DP field. They have a chance to reintegrate their right hemisphere faculties, to become "wholebrained". So essentially there is nothing to learn for the left brain. The core of the training consists of a quiet process with the participants sitting in their chairs and doing some mental exercises with their eyes closed. It's a very relaxing experience.

The first day, after warming up, participants are prepared for what will happen in the training. After some introductory exercises they are free to leave or to stay.

The third day is mainly dedicated to the transfer problem: how can the participant take home what he experienced; how he can use it at his job and how he can amplify the effect by regular exercises.

The training in principle is not restricted to software people but is applicable to all kinds of highly skilled mental workers such as scien-tists and engineers. It's not restricted to the domain of work either but, as far as we can see, has a harmonizing effect on all aspects of life.

Conclusion

As we have pointed out Superprogrammers seem to be largely equivalent to the group of people at the top of Maslow's pyramid: self-realizing people or individuals showing a very high degree of maturity and responsibility in life. This is a general state of mind, not a specific skill to be acquired in a seminar of 2 or 3 days.

On the other hand we have just been working out seminars to get people into that state. There seems to be a contradiction between our model and what we claim what we can do.

To be sure, a single seminar will hardly be able to convert an average person into a most excellent worker. What we can do in the seminar is to give the participants an experience of their true ability. This may start a process in life leading step by step to an increased trust in their innate faculties to be more auto-nomous.

That's exactly what software people participating in the Superprogramming exercises reported: "I'm now able to do ... (some specific skill like writing a program free of errors) ... I never thought I would be able to before." Participants find out that their limitation to do things are largely limited by their own beliefs and not by their true faculties. We found them very interested in having more of these experiences in order to expand their personal limits further.

So this training is not a panacea, something that makes people better automatically. It is a chance for individuals to take responsibility for what they do.

On the other hand, the method is in no way restricted to work in the DP Field, not even in its widest context. Personal growth may start in the field people are working in (and we think it's a good starting point) but sooner or later there will be found a growth process of the whole personality.

It was Pythagoras, about 2000 years ago, who recommended engagement in pure mathematics as a way to enlightenment. Nowadays we may well find out that dealing with the most abstract and complicated formal structures of a computer program may be a means to more integration and participation in real life.

REFERENCES

/1/ Blakeslee, T.R.,   'The Right Brain', Anchor Press/Doubleday, Garden City New York, 1980.

/2/ Edwards, B.,   'Drawing on the Right side of the Brain', J.P. Tarcher, Inc., Los Angeles, 1979.

/3/ Maslow, A.A.,   'A Theory of Human Motivation' in: Management and Motivation Vroom and Deci (Ed.) Penguin.

/4/ Molzberger, P.,   'Und Programmieren ist doch eine Kunst', in: H. Schelle und P. Molzberger (Hrsg.), Psychologische Aspekte der Software-Entwicklung, Oldenbourg, München-Wien 1983.

/5/ Molzberger, P.,   'Aesthetics and Programming', in: CHI '83, Dec. 12-15, Boston.

/6/ Molzberger, P.,   'Transcending the Basic Paradigma of Software Engineering', Report No. 8405 of the Dept. of Computer Sciences, HSBw, 8014 Neubiberg, W-Germany, March 1984.

/7/ Naur, P.,
    Randel, B.,   Ed: 'Software Engineering' NATO Conf. Garmisch 1968 Brussels 1969.

/8/ Weinberg, G.M.,   'The Psychology of Computer Programming', Van Nostrand Reinhold Company, New York 1971.

/9/ Weizenbaum, J.,   'Computer Power and Human Reason', Freeman and Co., 1976.

COMPUTERS IN EDUCATION, K. Duncan and D. Harris (eds.)
Elsevier Science Publishers B.V. (North-Holland)
© IFIP, 1985

SOFTWARE TOOLS IN COMPUTER ENGINEERING EDUCATION

M. Caboara, E.I. Giannotti

Department of Communication, Computer and System Sciences
University of Genoa - Via Opera Pia 11A
16145 Genoa - Italy

The paper describes the VISAL system, which has been developed to provide engineering students, in the area of computer programming, with a flexible and powerful software tool for assisting them during problem-solving and execution. This system allows the user to monitor the dynamic behaviour of an algorithm trough the evolution of its data structures. Students can interact with VISAL in an active way, according to their capabilities, both to better understand the behaviour of algorithms and to facilitate the debugging of their programs. The paper presents some considerations about the use of VISAL as support for a first-year course in computer programming. Preliminary experiments indicated the feasibility of the approach followed and suggested that VISAL be improved to meet various requirements.

1. INTRODUCTION

In the last few years, many research projects have adopted new approaches and points of view which are entirely different from the traditional ones in the field of software development. This trend is particularly interesting in computer-aided education, where early tutorial tools can be replaced or enforced by new software tools of great utility and flexibility.
The basic idea is to develop some programming environment that can be of help to problem solving design, program developing and coding, testing and debugging. High interaction is a basic feature for a friendly use of these tools.
As a result, the student is enabled to interact at different levels in understanding, developing and testing algorithms that have previously been implemented by the teacher or written by himself.
The specific software tools that several authors have developed in the educational field are aimed at meeting the following specific education requirements:

- Interactive programming environment with integrated facilities to create, edit, execute and, in some case, debug programs (1,2).

- Particular programming language to support top-down approaches (3).

- Graphic facility to visualize syntactic diagrams, program structures, recursion (4) and data structures (4,5).

Other research projects show a tendency for using pictorial representations to convey the structure and levels of abstraction of a program (6).

Besides their general importance in computer science, these new approaches are particularly useful in engineering education. In fact, informatics methodologies should be taught keeping in mind that the engineer will be confronted with highly technological environments and will be asked to use his expertise (including computer science) to solve new, complex problems in an integrated way. Therefore, all these new software tools should help the user, specifically the engineer, in learning to associate mental models (of an abstract or physical process) with mathematical models, graphic representations, and so on. The possibility of easy interactions in changing data or visualization characteristcs can also be used to develop skill in engineering design practice.

Concerning this subject, it is worth nothing that there are two interesting analogies between learning computer programming and solving engineering problems: the first is that both are faced with trials and errors, the second is a tendency for developing structured approaches for solving problems.

This paper presents a software tool which has mainly been developed to learn algorithms in the first year of a university electrical engineering curriculum. The concepts mentioned above were adopted in the design of the tool, which has been fully implemented and experimented.

2. OBJECTIVES AND FUNCTIONS

In the past two years, a DIST research group has worked on a project (7) for attaining the following goals:

- To produce software tools which can follow the steps of a first-year engineering course in problem solving and computer programming, and stimulate students to perform exercises and experimental work by themselves.

- To make, at the same time, a comparison with computer-aided engineering work.

- To obtain a real implementation to meet the different needs of a large number of students (about 500 students); such implementation should be made modular and improved according to specific requirements.

Along this line, our objective has been to develop, in a short time, a working system based on the programming language currently used for teaching (Pascal). To assist students in the different phases of their course, the following features have been implemented:

a) During the first approach to problem solving, when the teaching of programming begins by introducing the concepts of types, variables, data structure, we put at the student's disposal a library of instrumented algorithms. He can explore them in a guided way and select different examples. The behaviour of these algorithms should suggest to the student the mechanism of a solution by induction.

b) While learning the concepts of structured programming (control structures, procedures), the student goes on exploring the library and is stimulated to choose different algorithm values and parameters as well as to change the "granularity" of the algorithm evolution for a deeper comprehension of the related strategy.

c) Once the student has learned several basic algorithms, he is helped to design his own algorithms, equivalent to the library ones, and code them in the programming language. He can instrument his programs to obtain the algorithm visualization; he can use the available examples or devise his own examples, and then compare the behaviour of his algorithms with that of the corresponding library algorithms.

d) Finally, he is allowed to interactively test and debug any developed program according to some known process.

As a further guideline, we chose to use a standard programming language and did not adopt any application-oriented language: in this way, the student's attention can be focused on learning the solution technique and the standard language.

We implemented the project by a package (called VISAL) made up of library modules, which the user can easily link with his application program. Great flexibility and portability are achieved which are not peculiar to merely educational applications.

3. SYSTEM DESCRIPTION

A detailed system description is given in (7,8).
The student interacts with the system by its commands, whose tree structure is shown in figure 1. The commands (described in the Ref. 8) perform many functions, some of which are discussed below.

a) Step-by-step, algorithm evolution with data-structure display on the screen. The choice of the "clock" variables and the use of the CLOCK

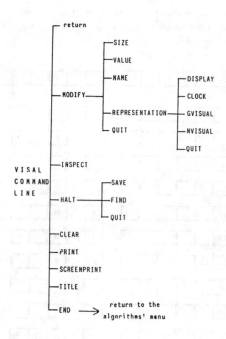

Figure 1. Tree Command structure

Type		Standard Name	Graphic Representation	Special Effect
two dimensional array	real integer char Boolean	ARn AIn ACn ABn		
one dimensional array	real integer char Boolean	VRn VIn VCn VBn		
scalar	real integer char Boolean	SRn SIn SCn SBn		
scalar parameters associated with a one-dimensional array used as a pointer: integer marker: integer marker: integer		Pn, Sn Ln, Fn Hn, Rn	∧ , ∧ ∧ ┃ , ┃ ┃ , ┃	
scalar parameters associated with a two-dimensional array used as an index: integer		In, Jn	> , ∧	

Figure 2. Data-Structure Representation in VISAL

procedure determine the definition of each algorithm step or "grain".

b) Evolution pause to operate on file: storing the data-structure real state on file; recovering a state previously stored on file; observing its display on the screen in order to compare it with the real state of the related algorithm or to determine new starting conditions (useful, in particular, for numerical-method algorithms (8)).

c) Modifications to values; representation parameters (graphical, numeric, iconic); "clock" variables.

d) Utility functions: listing and display of data structures; screen clearing; name of the algorithm under study, etc.

4. DATA-STRUCTURES SUPPLY

The available data structures are shown in figure 2.

It can be noticed that these structures are perfectly adequate to dealing with a large number of algorithms. These algorithms can be autonomously implemented by the user to interface them with the system: a certain number of fundamental algorithms are also provided by the libraries. Two libraries have already been implemented, one for non-numerical algorithms (sorting, merging, searching, ...) and the other for numerical method algorithms (linear algebra; Gaussian elimination method, etc.).

From a theoretical standpoint, we do not see any severe limitations to the extension of this approach to more complex data structures (e.g. trees, graphs, linked-lists, etc.), without modifications to the package structure. This feature makes VISAL an evolutionary tool which can meet the requirements of every user.

A very important aspect of the package concerns the ways in which a data structure can be represented on I/O peripherals. In a CAI system, not only the data structures supplied by the internal representation are important, but also their external aspects. Consequently, the system offers a certain number of pictorial possibilities, according to the kind of problem considered.

The modalities to visualize the evolution of an algorithm are defined by the following information:

- DS, the set of variables constituting the data structure on which the algorithm operates and which must be visualized.

- C, the set of variables for controlling the visualization evolution (C ⊂ DS). Whenever such variables (called "clock" variables) are modified, they allow the visualization of the variables contained in DS.

- Graphic modalities for representing the DS variables. The instrumentation of a user-developed program can be easily performed by using the CLOCK procedure (7).

5. EXAMPLES OF ALGORITHM VISUALIZATION

To illustrate the behaviour of VISAL, some examples of visualization are given in the following.

A first example shows the conversion of an algebraic expression from infix to postfix. We propose two different solutions: the first (9) uses a stack for operators, while the second (10) is based on the recursive definition of algebraic expressions. Both algorithms are not trivial and make use of several procedures.

The evolution of the first algorithm is shown in figure 3. DS is constituted by: the infix expression (IN), the postfix (PF), the symbol (SB) in scanning, the stack (OP) to "remember" the operators encountered previously, the symbol (TS) on the top of the stack. As far as the "clock" variables are concerned, different choices are possible which give rise to different representations of the algorithm evolution. In figure 3a, the choice C = {OP} gives a more detailed representation of the role played by the operators which pop or push in the stack. In figure 3b, the choice C = {PF} produces

a more compact representation and indicates how many time a symbol has been transferred to postfix PF.

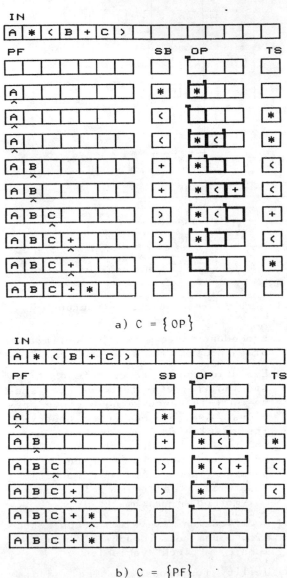

a) C = {OP}

b) C = {PF}

Figure 3. Visualization of the first algorithm by different choices of the clock variables.

The evolution of the second algorithm is illustrated in figure 4. DS is constituted by: the infix IN, the postfix PF, the current symbol SB of the infix, and CP, which does not correspond

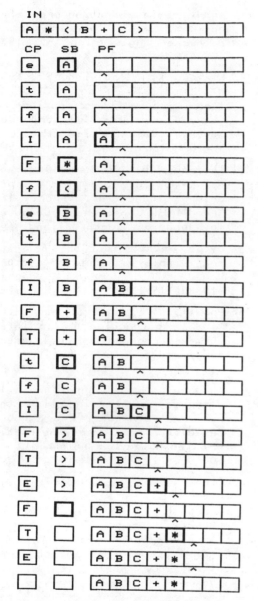

Figure 4. Visualization of the recursive algorithm with C = {CP}

and understand how recursion is implemented.

The second example shows the Quicksort algorithm, expressed as a recursive procedure (11). In this case, the data structure consists of the vector A, which contains initially the unsorted list; the two indices, I and J, which indicate the scanning of the vector; the two indices, L, R, which delimit the part of the unsorted list. The choice C ={A} highlights the swapping process, as shown in figure 5.

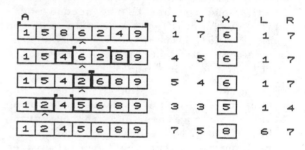

$$C = \{A\}$$

Figure 5. Visualization of the Quicksort algorithm

While the choice C = {I,J} would point out the scanning and swapping processes.

Additional examples using other data structures (also two-dimensional arrays) are given in refs. (7,8).

6. FIRST EXPERIENCES WITH VISAL

To evaluate the capabilities of the project and decide how to improve it, some first experiments were carried out by a small group of students during the academic year 1983-84. These experiments were mainly aimed at testing the user's interaction with a program, to verify how many examples of algorithms are necessary to evaluate how students are stimulated to work in an autonomous way and to face a sufficient number of problems by themselves. For these reasons, some first-year students were allowed to use the program, but only after they were given a two-mounth theoretical teaching of Pascal language and an introduction to problem solving.

to any significant variable of the algorithm but has been added to indicate which recursive procedure is running. This task is performed as follows: if CP takes on the values e, t, f, it means that the procedure EXPR, TERM, FACTOR are being accessed respectively, if CP takes on the values E, T, F, exit from the same procedure occurs; if CP takes on the value I, an identificator is found. By choosing C = {CP}, it is possible to follow the recursive chain

In such a way, the students' interest was focused on algorithm planning rather than on language learning.

Two modalities of use were adopted:

1. Guided exploration of algorithms present in the system libraries.

2. Free exploration of any user-written algorithms.

We observed that not all the students performed these two steps in a given time, as suggested by the teacher. In fact, someone (generally very skilled) chose to pass to the second modality very rapidly, to develop and run his own algorithm, while others, who had some difficulties, preferred to prolong the first modality.

We observed that no difficulty was encountered by the students in running library algorithms and instrumenting their own algorithms: it took only one hour to master the tutorial system. The program flexibility, which allows the student to skip from the first to the second step, whenever he deems it necessary, was shown to be a very important feature. In fact, the experimental results pointed out the necessity that our educational tool be flexible to enable the student to fit it to his particular needs.

Another valuable system feature is that the student can be relieved of minor details related to I/O of data structures in his program so that he can focus his attention on the correct solution of a problem. In particular, this facility is very important for beginners because I/O operations involving data structures may be the source of many errors. The experimental results confirmed the availability of the system, which will be experimented by all the first-year students during the academic year 1984-85.

REFERENCES

/1/ Teitelbaum, T. and Reps, T. The Cornell Program Synthesizer: A Syntax-Directed Programming Environment, CACM 9 (1981) 563-573.

/2/ Medina-Mora, R. and Feiler, P.H. An Incremental Programming Environment, IEEE Transactions on Software Engineering 5 (1981) 473-482.

/3/ Kleine, K., Jähnichen, S., Koch, W. Hommel, G., Program Construction with abstract notions in ELAN, Proc. IFIP 3rd World Conference, Computers in Education, North-Holland. 1981.

/4/ Thalmann, D., Magnenat-Thalmann, N., Graphical Tools for Computer Science Education, Proc. IFIP 3rd World Conference, Computers in Education, North-Holland, 1981.

/5/ Myers, B.A., INCENSE: A System for Displaying Data Structure, Proc. ACM, Computer Graphics (1983) 115-125.

/6/ Powell, M.L. and Linton, M.A., Visual Abstraction in an Interactive Programming Environment, ACM Sigplan Notices 6 (1983) 14-21.

/7/ Caboara, M., Giannotti, E.I., Olimpo, G., Learning Algorithms by CAL Techniques, Proc. Fourth Canadian Symposium on Instructional Technology, Winnipeg, Canada (October 1983).

/8/ Caboara, M., Giannotti, E.I., Ricci, F., A Personal Computer Approach for Learning Numerical Methods, Proc. Twenty Fourth I.S.M.M. Int. Symposium, Mini and Microcomputers and their Applications, Bari, Italy (June 1984).

/9/ Tenenbaum, A.M. and Augenstein, M.J., Data Structures Using Pascal (Prentice-Hall, 1981).

/10/ Jensen, K. and Wirth, N., Pascal-User Manual and Report (Springer-Verlag, 1975).

/11/ Wirth, N., Algorithms + Data Structures = Programs (Prentice-Hall, 1975).

COMPUTERS IN EDUCATION, K. Duncan and D. Harris (eds.)
Elsevier Science Publishers B.V. (North-Holland)
© IFIP, 1985

Experience and Hindsight

A.M. Burton, H.T. Smith and R.B. Henry
Human Computer Interaction Group
University of Nottingham
England

This paper reviews experience gained in trying to teach high level programming concepts to undergraduate psychology students. An AI-type software environment is described and the accomplishments of the students discussed. Some of the practical and conceptual difficulties in teaching this kind of material are elaborated.

1. Introduction

In the last few years the interests of many Cognitive Psychologists have extended to the use of computers for modelling 'knowledge-based' systems as an aid to understanding human thinking and behaviour. Researchers with a background in behavioural science have made significant contributions to the field of Artificial Intelligence in such areas as language understanding, computational aspects of vision, associative memory networks and such red-hot topics as expert systems. It is very difficult to teach psychology students about this work without providing a detailed introduction to the methods and tools that are used. For, like other people, our experience has been that students only begin to see the relevance, and the difficulties, when they are exposed to the tools themselves. However, this approach means a relatively painful period of learning that, with programming, you have to walk a very long way before you can fly.

During the last six years members of the Psychology Department at Nottingham University have been trying to teach their undergraduate students to utilise computers as tools for modelling, or just reasoning about, information processing in human cognition. The aim throughout has been to get students to focus on applications in cognitive science rather than programming per se. This paper outlines the directions that were taken and discusses the difficulties that have been observed in attempting to teach high level information processing concepts in limited time.

The paper does not describe empirical studies, these have not proved possible in our environment; what it does report are the kinds of experiences that other educators will face in attempting to teach similar material.

1.1 Teaching

In setting out to teach an appreciation of the artificial intelligence/ cognitive science field from an application perspective we were faced with the difficulty of finding the right vehicle. The kinds of material that we wanted to get across to our students included such topics as, how to model relationships between objects and events, the importance of the choice of representation, organisation and flow of control, and pattern matching. However, an important constraint was that our students had no prior programming experience and, in the majority of cases, no special aptitude. (Indeed one of the most considerable obstacles proved to be their lack of self-confidence.)

The time available for teaching was also severely limited. For the first four years the programming teaching had to be fitted within an existing practical-session teaching slot. This meant that students were available only for a five week period in which it was possible to mount a (very) intensive course based around fifteen formal contact hours. The course now occupies two terms and a notional twenty hours staff contact. In both cases it is unlikely that the students would spend less than fourty hours on their work assignments.

1.2 Facilities

In 1979 the department had a time-shared PDP 11/34 running V6 Unix. It was necessary that the teaching took place on this machine and, given the constraints, it was obviously critical to choose the right programming language and environment. At that time there were fewer choices than now; on the one hand a conventional compiled language (e.g, Pascal, FORTRAN), on the other an interactive interpretive language (e.g., BASIC, LISP). Given that most of the techniques in the AI field draw on symbol manipulation as opposed to numerical methods, there was really no serious consideration of the former class of languages for the purpose in hand. In choosing amongst the latter kind it was clear that LISP was much more suitable than BASIC in terms of the desired functionality (i.e., list and string handling, language extensibility). However LISP syntax is arcane and offputting to the beginner. Alternatives available were LOGO and POP2/POP11. The former corrected some of LISPs syntactic horrors but versions available at that time were not particularly adapted to doing much beyond turtle geometry. However, most of our interests were oriented towards language and simulation of information processing systems. The other options were POP-2 *[Burs71a]* which originated at Edinburgh and POP-11 an alternative implementation from Sussex University. Both gave similar facilities to LISP, but with an ALGOLish flavoured syntax.

The Sussex POP-11 system was chosen as it seemed to provide the most attractive environment for novice users. This version came complete with a library of teaching demonstrations and an extensive help documentation - the latter indexed compatibly with the system error messages (carefully called 'MISHAPS'). It also contained a simple line-based editor which overwrote, inserted and deleted lines of text. As the terminals used for teaching at that time could not support screen editors, this was not seen as a limitation of the programming environment.

In Section 2 of the paper, we describe our experiences of teaching on this system. In Section 3, we discuss the current course - this being based on POPLOG - a programming environment mounted on a VAX which supports an enhanced version of POP-11 and, among other features, a window screen editor.

2. Initial Teaching Experiences

The basic structure of the initial programming course was straightforward. For the first three weeks of the five week course, students were provided with teaching handouts, successively introducing more complex language concepts. Small-group tutorials were given weekly, and students were permitted to seek individual help from tutors when they needed it. In order to demonstrate understanding of the concepts introduced during this period, students were required to work through and hand-in a set of programing problems. During the last two weeks, students worked on a project of their own choosing and although they were encouraged to choose a topic of psychological interest, this was not compulsory.

We encountered many problems in the early days of POP11 teaching, not least a general computer phobia. Unwittingly, we occasionally reinforced this phobia. For example, as an aid to clarity our handouts used the stylistic device of representing general explanations and instructions in the normal case conventions, and POP-11 code in upper case - though actually typing POP-11 code in upper case produced an error. Students who had not grasped this convention would occasionally come to the conclusion that they had "broken the computer".

A LOGO-like turtle package was used to introduce first concepts - these being 'variables' and 'procedures'. POP-11 is primarily a list processing language, so list primitives were introduced very early in the course and our examples tended to focus on list construction and manipulation. After two or three sessions at the terminal students usually began to appreciate the need to save work from one session to another; at this stage, basic file editing and handling was introduced. Following the use of the editor, control structures (conditionals and iteration syntax) were taught. Finally, the students encountered procedure inter-communication and recursion, which intro-

---

EXAMPLE 1

```
define double(number)
number+number;
enddefine;

double(double(5))=>
```

EXAMPLE 2

```
define itoyou(list);
 if list = [] then
    []
 elseif hd(list) = "I" then
    [you] <> tl(list)
 else
    [^( hd(list) )] <> itoyou(tl(list))
endif
enddefine;
```

EXAMPLE 3

```
define doubleitoyou(list);
itoyou(itoyou(list))
enddefine;
```

KEY: vars   variable declaration;   ->   assignment;
     ⇒   print;   []   listdelimiters
     ^   evaluate;   <>   concatenation;
     hd(list) 1st element;   tl(list) everything else.

---

duced the notions of global versus local variables, and the explicit use of the stack.

The ideas which students found most difficult in this phase were the use of the stack and recursion. Example 1 shows the use of the stack to pass values between procedures. The following two examples illustrate the use of recursion. Example 2 shows a procedure that changes the first instance of the word "I" in a list to the word "you". Example 3 shows a procedure that calls the previous one resulting in the first <u>two</u> instances of "I" being changed to "you". A number of our students had difficulty in fully grasping and exploiting these techniques. However, mastery was required in order to be able to progress to the kinds of program we were encouraging them to tackle. (In fact we were not able to improve matters much until the introduction of new syntax for pattern matching assignment. This obviated the need for explicit use of certain techniques at an early stage in learning - particularly recursion -

and the difference this made is discussed in section three.)

In the second phase of the course the students worked on a project to construct a small program. A number of sample handouts were made available as a source of ideas. Most of these made use of a simple database package incorporated within the POP-11 environment which provided facilities to store information in lists structures. To complement this database store there are pre-defined procedures which aid retrieval and addition of information. The database package assumed an important role in our teaching; it was used as the vehicle for building 'knowledge based' programs, in the sense that states of different kinds of micro-worlds could easily be represented by lists manipulated by the database procedures. These were flexible enough to enable the user to impose many different kinds of structure on the store. We hoped then, that students would exploit this facility to build interesting models for the project assignment.

On the whole, we were disappointed with the progress made on the projects. Furthermore, the submission rate was lower than for other courses in the syllabus. Although some students did think carefully about issues such as knowledge representation and database structure, the majority settled for a program which performed some relatively trivial task. A sample of projects retained from this course shows the following breakdown by topic (n=38): unguided database search accounts for 32% of projects (e.g. simple linear searches through bibliographies); sequential guessing games (e.g. hangman) account for 18%; more 'intelligent' database search (always hierarchical) accounts for 16%; ELIZA-type dialogues account for 18%. The remaining projects tend to be more imaginative (and less common). These include: combination generators (menus, sentences); shape recognisers (using turtle); and dynamic databases with more sophisticated interfaces.

Clearly the course needed changes if we were to achieve our goal of inculcating an appreciation of AI-type modelling techniques. The following issues were suggested as causing the most problems: (i) students had little time in which to overcome early difficulties; (ii) there still existed a resistance to computers in general; (iii) the programming environment – particularly in relation to editing – was somewhat uncongenial; (iv) we were not sure whether we were indeed teaching programming skills at the right level.

In terms of the last issue, we were unsure as to whether we should be teaching fundamental elements of the programming language, or concentrating more on inbuilt high-level tools. The problem with starting at the existing level was that the majority of the students spent all their time concentrating on the nuts-and-bolts of the language, and never reached the stage at which they could write interesting models. On the other hand, we felt that starting at too high a level would mean that students would never really understand what was going on in a program, and would not be able to cope with the lower level programming necessary to 'glue together' the high level elements with which they would be provided.

Attempts to address the above issues were tackled by changing the course and the programming environment and these changes are described in the next section.

3. The Present Course

The last fifteen months have seen a change in the manner of our teaching and the facilities that are used. Students now receive a course split into two ten week blocks. In the first block they are given an 'Introduction to Programming Concepts' Course (one lecture hour + one tutorial per week); in the second block they work on an assessed project with weekly tutorial contact. This gives a much more satisfactory balance than the previous intensive five week course. This change was timed to coincide with a move from the original POP11 system on the departmental Unix machine to a later version – POPLOG *[Hard84a]* mounted on a VAX.

We had long wished for a better program development environment – one which used more sophisticated editing and error recovery procedures. The POPLOG environment offers both of these. It also tidied up some changes to the syntax of the language that had been under development – in particular, those relating to list structure matching and assignment.

As discussed below, the net result has been that the performance of our students has improved. However, we found that some of the ideas implemented in the new system worked very well and others, rather unexpectedly, did not work well at all. The features of the language and the environment will be discussed separately.

3.1 The Programming Environment

The POPLOG programming environment consists of the following elements:

1. VED – A Window Editor enabling the screen to be split into horizontal sections each containing a separate file.
2. POP11 – the language environment and run-time system.

3. An extensive help, tutorial and demonstration library

Users normally access all system facilities through the window editor VED. The system is introduced chronologically; users type program text into an edit window. In order to execute the program text, they first MARK all (or some section) of the program text with the screen cursor and a function key; then via a DOIT function key the marked text is passed automatically to the POP11 system. At this stage, an output file is created and displayed in a new window on the screen. If the program contains a syntax error, an appropriate error message is written to the output file and the cursor is positioned close to the incorrect statement in the source file window. If the program produces no error, then its output is written into the output file. (The only exception to this creation of an output file is the circumstance in which a user executes legal code which produces no output.) The default version of the editor allows just two windows on the screen at any one time although many more files may be open. The window manager keeps the two most recently used/activated windows on the screen, non-active windows being scrolled off. This system is about as close in spirit to the multi-windowed workstation programming environment (e.g, Sun, Lisa) as it is possible to get with conventional technology.

Somewhat surprisingly, the window environment proved to be one of the major causes of problems to our students. The first, and perhaps most immediately obvious, problem was that the window manager was insensitive to the last position of a scrolled-off window when it was brought back. People tend to like spatial order and were unimpressed when a window that had been at the bottom of the screen re-appeared after some delay at the top. Further, the use of 'least recent activation' as a criterion for de-selecting windows was too simple minded. It is almost always the case that only the user, and not the machine, is in a position to determine what should and should not be displayed at a given moment. The window manager should therefore have given the user more appropriate means of control. (A more recent version of POPLOG provides a halfway house in this respect.)

The second problem was more subtle. The students frequently became confused as to which of the **edit** or **execution** states they were in. To them, the windows all looked the same. For example, when MARKED program text was automatically passed to the POP11 system an outcome was observed only when output was produced or an error occurred. Thus the students never acquired a strong feeling for the distinction between the editor and the underlying POP11 system. A partial solution to this problem has been to abandon the concept of staying in the edit window and making use of the MARK and DOIT keys in favour of exiting from the editor to the POP11 system each time a new fragment of code is ready to be compiled. The editor then loses it's superordinate identity and becomes just another sub-system of POP11 run-time system. Although this seems to confuse students less, a certain amount of the bath water has been tossed out with the baby. Compiling just an extra few lines of code now involves recompiling the whole file. Whilst it is possible to get students to switch to the original method when they become more experienced, the problem of identifying different states of the programming environment remains.

3.2 Language Syntax

Changes to the POP11 language have resulted in apparently easier ways of implementing useful pieces of program code. In particular those relating to matching lists or elements of lists via pattern assignment statements. For example,

> [this is a true statement]
> **matches**
> [?firstbit ?middle ??lastbit]

In this piece of code, the variable 'firstbit' is assigned the value of the word "this"; 'middle' is assigned the word "is"; and 'lastbit' is assigned the list [a true statement]. Using this notation, consider a version of the procedure 'itoyou', defined recursively in section 2.

EXAMPLE 4

```
define itoyou(list);
vars pre post;
if list matches [??pre | ??post] then
    [^^pre you ^^post]
else
    list
endif;
enddefine;
```

KEY: ??x   assign a list of elements to x
     ^^x   evaluate the list 'x' and remove list brackets.

The major improvement has been that of reducing the need to write recursive procedures that chain up and down lists looking for matching expressions. Once the pattern assignment syntax and its operation is understood, it becomes quite easy to write simple parsers and dialogue systems.

The net result has been to decrease the amount of nuts-and-bolts learning that has to take place before a student can actually produce a program that does something. Taken together with improvements in the programming environment, this has meant that the projects submitted at the end of the course this year were more interesting (See table 1). More importantly perhaps, compared with previous years, the great majority of the students completed their assignment without feeling aggrieved at us.

4. Reflection

During the changes to our programming course, we have been forced time and again to ask why we want to teach psychology students to program. Our prime aim, as stated above, is to provide useful modelling tools for investigations into cognitive science. We feel that the new course moves us closer to this goal. Despite early problems with the POPLOG systems, its nature does facilitate a deeper understanding of underlying concepts of both computing and modelling onto students.

As for the elements of the language itself, the higher-level constructs taught have produced more interesting projects. However, there remains the problem of assessment. Having taught students the rudiments of model-building one has two choices of what should be assessed: grasp of the elements taught and resultant models. Of course, the clever student will try to build a model which shows off his/her grasp of the various elements, but both over-ambitious and under-achieving students can produce the same sorts of garbled program.

The kind of system we expose our students to now differs little from one on which serious AI work is undertaken. We can therefore demonstrate quite sophisticated programs and move away from emphasising low level mechanisms. However, this opportunity has given rise to another kind of phenomenon which is best evidenced by the remark of one of our students. The student was being

Project Type	Proportion of projects (n=41)	(examples)
Conversation Dialogues	7%	(Hardwired Dialogues, Eliza's)
Simple Script Dialogues	15%	(databases – bibliographies)
Search-based Dialogues	20%	(ancestors, memory simulations)
Simple Diagnosis	10%	(Branching control, discrim nets)
Complex Diagnosis	7%	(Production System control flow)
Parsers	10%	(translators)
Games/Teaching Devices	17%	(Chess Trainer, Hangman)
Simulations of various kinds	7%	(Addition Processes)
Problem Solving	7%	(Maze tracer, propositional logic)

Table 1: Categories of Project, 1984

shown a parser which, given a typed input sentence within a particular context, would analyse and draw the corresponding parse tree on the screen. "Oh", she said after some 30 seconds, "is that all it does?". In other words, the greater the complexity of the system, the more we risk hiding from the students. Now they do not see clearly the difficulties and limitations that were previously so evident.

To summarise then, we have refined our course over the last six years in terms of both our teaching, and the programming environment used. Although we feel that these changes have been beneficial to our students, they have also raised their own problems. The adoption of more sophisticated technology has, of course, been important, but it is by no means clear that this is the primary reason for our (still limited) achievements. We believe that success with more refined technology can only be achieved with a corresponding refinement of teaching philosophy.

References

Burs71a. R. Burstall, D. Collins, and R. Popplestone, *Programming in POP-2,* Edinburgh University Press (1971).

Hard84a. S. Hardy, "A New Software Environment for List Processing and Logic Programming", in *Artificial Intelligence,* ed. T. O'Shea & M. Eisenstadt, Harper & Row (1984).

COMPUTERS IN EDUCATION, K. Duncan and D. Harris (eds.)
Elsevier Science Publishers B.V. (North-Holland)
© IFIP, 1985

FOURTH-GENERATION LANGUAGES IN THE CLASSROOM

PANEL MEMBERSHIP

Boulton B. Miller Ph.D.
Professor, School of Business
Southern Illinois University
Edwardsville, IL 62026 (Chairman)

A. Milton Jenkins Ph.D.
Professor, Graduate School of Business
Indiana University
Bloomington, IN 47402

Anita Kollenbauer
PRINCESS Project
Dept. of Admin. Data Processing
University of Stockholm
Stockholm, Sweden, 10691

Colonel Wendell O. Jones Ph.D.
Professor, Dept. of Computer Science
United States Military Academy
West Point, NY 10996

The objectives of the panel presentations and audience discussions to follow are to understand the concept of prototyping for developing application systems; appreciate the capabilities and limitations of fourth-generation languages (4GL); and discuss to what extent prototyping and 4GLs should be taught in the classroom.

Expansion of end-user computing, recognition of 4GLs, improved communications-connected workstations, and acceptance of information centers are increasing the recognition of prototyping as an essential methodology. Experienced information center computer professionals are witnessing user development of many applications beyond their expectations. Development centers are gaining acceptance for more sophisticated applications. Both centers demonstrate the need for a greater understanding of the capabilities and limitations of 4GLs.

Professor Miller will provide examples of 4GLs used in a cross section of information centers, describe the trend toward the use of development centers, explain the nonprocedural and procedural uses of 4GLs, review the software, hardware, and data communications available to end-users, and discuss how these resources can be expected to expand in the future. His presentation will focus on end-user computing and the need for improved understanding of 4GLs. Dr. Miller will draw on the use of information centers by the members of the St. Louis Information Center Exchange (SLICE), and other examples in government agencies and the private sector.

Prototyping, a relative new phenomenon in the field of management information systems (MIS), was made possible by recent hardware and software technological developments. The principles of prototyping are currently being applied in both computer science and MIS, but in somewhat different ways.

Professor Jenkins will comment on the application of the prototype philosophy to the development of computerized information systems from the MIS perspective. Prototyping and user-developed methodologies provide the first real alternative to the Systems Development Life Cycle (SDLC) methodology for developing application systems. His comments will focus on: 1) a prototyping design and development methodology, which has been implemented in several large U. S. corporations and produces as its output an operational prototype--a working system that satisfies the user's information needs, and 2) the ways in which the operational prototype may be used: e.g.: "as is," as a pilot system, as an initial prototype for a subsequent prototyping process, as a design specification for the SDLC methodology, or abandoned.

Professor Kollenbauer will bring into focus the comments of the two previous panel members by explaining how the concepts presented are applicable within her areas of interest. She will also identify the differences and point out other concepts not included.

Colonel Jones will synthesize the presentations of the three previous speakers and establish a setting for a discussion of end-user computing within the prototyping concept, the issues related to fourth generation languages, and the question of inclusion of both subjects in the classroom.

Audience/panel participation in the discussion of end-user computing, 4GLs, and prototyping is important to the success of this panel and will be encouraged from the outset.

LOGO

COMPUTERS IN EDUCATION, K. Duncan and D. Harris (eds.)
Elsevier Science Publishers B.V. (North-Holland)
© IFIP, 1985

NOVEL USES OF COMPUTERS IN SECONDARY SCHOOL CLASSROOMS

J.A.M. Howe

Department of Artificial Intelligence, University of Edinburgh,
Forrest Hill, Edinburgh, UK.

INTRODUCTION

Twelve years ago, we began our investigation of novel uses of the computer in the secondary school classroom. Our objective is to enrich teaching of a subject by providing pupils with a symbolic notation for mechanizing processes. Just as a child learns about mechanical mechanisms by building and running physical models using Meccano parts, we believe that he can learn about symbolic mechanisms by constructing symbolic models from symbolic parts (5).

Our approach has its roots in an active child-centred view of knowledge acquisition which postulates that learning takes place when a child does something and gets information fed back to him about the outcome. The teacher's job, if he wants to introduce this child-centred approach in his classroom, is to conceive situations where the learner can get access to a process producing an effect or a result. However, it is much easier for the teacher to build a 'black box' program which produces an outcome, like a magician pulling a rabbit out of his hat, than it is to build a 'glass box' program which shows unambiguously how an effect is produced. Even when the learner has access to a process, if that process has been implemented by someone else (e.g. his teacher), he is still faced with the problem of understanding it so that he can come to terms with any discrepancy between an outcome which he predicts and an actual outcome. Yet detecting the existence of discrepancies and understanding why they occur is one of the most crucial functions of any knowledge representation system which is applying higher-order knowledge handling mechanisms such as abstraction and generalisation. The break through occurs by arranging for the child to devise the program that models the process. By "teaching the machine how to solve the problem", not only must the child state his thoughts in a precise, unambiguous form that can be translated into instructions in a rigorous modelling language, but it also involves him in an active learning cycle wherein he makes changes to his conceptualization of the problem (and his program) until the desired outcome is achieved.

In our work, we have identified two key problems that must be tackled before any subject can be taught successfully in this way. The first is the problem of designing an appropriate notation, and the second is the problem of devising a method of teaching a child, or adult, to use it creatively. In the remainder of this paper, we will focus on the first problem. The reader who is interested in the second one should consult recent papers (6, 8).

DESIGNING AN APPPROPRIATE NOTATION

Just as the designers of a mechanical modelling system such as Meccano or Fishertek had to decide what mechanical parts should be provided, and how they would be combined to form meaningful structures and mechanisms, the designer of a computer-based modelling system has to decide what symbolic parts (i.e. instructions) should be included in the notation. While particular choices will depend upon the problem domain, they can be fabricated readily in one of the high level modular programming languages, such as LOGO or Pascal. In the case of LOGO, each part is a procedure; parts are combined as collections of procedures forming a more powerful super procedure, and so on.

Let us take a simple example: the task is to teach a 12-year old some of the mathematical properties of regular plane shapes. Papert has provided 'turtle geometry' for this purpose (10). Turtle geometry is a kit of parts, in the form of commands like move FORWARD <a distance>, turn LEFT (or RIGHT) <an angle> for defining the motion of a pen around a drawing surface. Using these commands, a child can learn about the properties of regular plane shapes by experimenting with 2-D patterns, ranging from simple patterns such as squares, triangles, hexagons, to complex patterns reminiscent of the shapes made by Spirograph drawing wheels.

A child's early efforts usually take the form of a series of single commands, each of which is immediately executed by the computer, so a particular pattern is built up in piecemeal fashion. However, once familiar with the actions of the basic parts, he can learn how to put together single commands into chunks of commands (i.e. procedures) before checking their correctness by running them as a program. In this way, the program design and construction is separated from program execution, enabling the child to give full attention to the program's behaviour at run time.

APPLICATIONS IN THE CLASSROOM

Our work at Edinburgh in applying the model building approach to secondary school mathematics has already been well documented (7, 8).   Here, we will briefly examine several other applications, beginning with engineering control.

Although the automatic control of processes and machines is becoming increasingly pervasive in our everyday lives, control methods and concepts are taught only to senior pupils in UK schools. Our aim is to produce an environment in which younger pupils, in the 14-16 year age range, can acquire some appreciation of control technology (3).

As before, the task can be broken into two parts, the design and implementation of an appropriate kit, and the production of written materials to guide a pupil's discoveries. Here, we will concentrate on the former only. In this case, there are hardware and software components.   The hardware is a Buffer Box, linked to a microcomputer via a parallel link. It is equipped with eight switches for sending out signals to operate external devices, such as motors, and eight receivers for taking signals from external devices, such as mechanical switches.   The switches and receivers are software controlled.   Thus, the computer can change the state of a switch directly, discover its existing state, or make its state conditional on something. It can also discover the state of a receiver and record the number of times that it has changed its state.

The children's task is to build a plant, such as a crane, from a mechanical construction kit. To this, they attach motors and sensors, connected to the microcomputer via the Buffer Box.   Next, they write a program to schedule the operation of the motors and sensors. The essence of scheduling in this case is the control of, or response to, ongoing external processes which occur in an unpredictable way. This can be translated into a specification for a modelling language for control. Two features are critical, namely a fast response time and a multi-programming facility.   The latter is needed to deal with situations when more than one process is active (i.e. concurrent processes).   The implication is that the modelling language must be able to run a process, suspend its operation until something happens, run another process instead, return to the original process on demand, and so on. Also, it has to arbitrate in situations where two events happening at the same time compete for the computer's attention.

Chung has constructed a modelling language, with these features (4).   Called Concurrent-LOGO, it is designed to be used by children with some prior experience of working with the LOGO language, but providing additional facilities for creating objects and guards. For example, each switch, receiver, motor and sensor is an object.   But many objects are sufficiently similar to be treated as instances of a more general class.   Thus, each individual receiver

is an instance of the class receivers.   Also, each object can accept information (a message) from another object, or send a message to another object e.g. sensor-to-receiver, switch-to-motor.   The guard facility enables the user to create instructions that watch for some process to change its state and react appropriately.

A simple application is to a mechanical turtle controlled by switches operated by a child. The turtle is made from Meccano parts.   Two DC motors are used, one for driving the left wheel and one for the right wheel.   The motors are mounted back-to-back.   The left-hand motor is MOTORA and the right-hand motor, MOTORB. MOTORA and MOTORB are instances of the class MOTORS, which is a user defined class accepting the messages:

INIT (i.e. initialisation)	Each takes two
CLOCKWISE	inputs: the
ANTICLOCKWISE	first is the
	switch number for
	controlling the
	motor's direction
	of rotation, and
	the second is the
	switch number for
	turning it on and
	off.
HALT	Takes one input:
	the switch number
	for turning it on
	and off.

MOTORA is connected to switches 1 and 2 on the Buffer Box.   Switch 2 turns it on and off; switch 1 controls the direction of its rotation. If switch 2 is on and switch 1 is off then the motor rotates clockwise.   If switch 2 is on and switch 1 is on then the motor rotates anti-clockwise.

MOTORB is connected to switches 3 and 4. Switch 4 turns it on and off; switch 3 controls the direction of its rotation.   If switch 4 is on and switch 3 is off then the motor rotates clockwise.   If switch 4 is on and switch 3 is on then the motor rotates anti-clockwise.

A button box is used for controlling the turtle. It is also made out of Meccano; it has six switches on it.   Each switch is connected to a receiver on the Buffer Box.   Button 1 is connected to receiver 1, button 2 to receiver 2, and so on.

Responses to the buttons are as follows:
    Button 1 : the turtle moves forward.
    Button 2 : the turtle moves backward.
    Button 3 : the turtle turns left.
    Button 4 : the turtle turns right.
    Button 5 : the turtle stops.
    Button 6 : not used.

The program is as follows:
```
TURTLE;
MOTORA! INIT 1 2;
MOTORB! INIT 3 4;
WHENEVER EQU? RECEIVER 1! STATE 'ON
        (MOTORA! CLOCKWISE; MOTORB!
         ANTICLOCKWISE) //
WHENEVER EQU? RECEIVER 2! STATE 'ON
        (MOTORA! ANTICLOCKWISE; MOTORB!
         CLOCKWISE) //
WHENEVER EQU? RECEIVER 3! STATE 'ON
        (MOTORA! CLOCKWISE; MOTORB!
         CLOCKWISE) //
WHENEVER EQU? RECEIVER 4! STATE 'ON
        (MOTORA! ANTICLOCKWISE; MOTORB!
         ANTICLOCKWISE) //
WHENEVER EQU? RECEIVER 5! STATE 'ON
        (MOTORA! HALT; MOTORB! HALT)
```
The five WHENEVER statements run in parallel.
Each watches for a condition to occur, i.e. for
a particular button switch to be pressed, and
then carries out some appropriate actions.

We have just completed trials with COLOGO, in an
Edinburgh school, working with 14-16 year old
children, and are assessing the results.

My next example is an environment in which
pupils can construct, test and compare models of
either real or hypothetical computer processors,
or of selected parts of a processsor, in order
to study particular concepts of computer
architecture (9).

The environment offers a kit of parts in the
form of functional software representations of
common digital hardware components, including
various types of registers, random-access and
read-only memories, data buses and adders. A
particular processor is modelled by creating
instances of the required building blocks and
specifying their interconnections. After a
model has been defined, it can be tested by
executing a simple microprogram, written by the
pupil. Three types of microinstructions are
provided
- a control instruction
- a branch instruction (unconditional or
    conditional)
- a stop instruction.

For example, consider the arrangement in which
two registers, R1 and R2, are connected via a
common bus. Control signals allow data to pass
in or out of the registers. A configuration
can be created, using the statements
```
DATABUS = BUS(4)
R1 = REGISTER (4/DATABUS)
R2 = REGISTER (4/DATABUS)
```
where 4 signifies 4 bit wordlength. The
microinstruction:
```
R2(OUT) R1(IN)
```
when executed will cause the contents of R2 to
be transferred along the bus and into R1.

This configuration is easily extended to include
an adder unit, A1, and an additional register,
R3, to perform simple addition. The
microinstruction
```
R1(OUT) R3(OUT) R2(IN)
```
will result in the contents of registers R1 and
R3 being stored in register R2.

The next step might be to add a random-access
memory unit and a second bus. Suppose the
contents of a particular storage location in the
random access memory are to be added to the
contents of register R1. Register R4 holds the
storage location's address to be accessed. The
microinstruction needed is:
```
R4(OUT) READ R1(OUT) R2(IN)
```
The READ signal causes the contents of the
memory location, whose address appears on the
address bus, to be transferred to the databus,
from where they will then travel to input B of
the adder unit. The signal R4(OUT) ensures
that the required memory address is available on
the address bus, and R1(OUT) allows the second
operand to be transferred to input A of the
adder. The addition takes place and the result
is placed in R2.

Suppose the next step is to put the contents of
register R2 into a memory location whose address
is given in Register R4. A 'WRITE' control
signal will cause the binary pattern on the
databus to be stored in the memory location
whose address is held in the address bus. This
is accomplished by the microinstruction
```
R4(OUT) WRITE R2(OUT)
```
The next step might be to investigate how
successive machine language program instructions
may be fetched from the memory unit and stored
in the instruction register. A program counter
(binary counter) is used to store the address of
the next instruction to be fetched from memory.
The microinstruction
```
PC(OUT) READ 1R(IN) PC(INC)
```
causes the required instruction to be copied
from the memory unit to the instruction
register and increments the program counter.
Now we are in a position to put together a
complete, if simple, processor. The
instruction register has two roles
- it contains the instruction code
    that is output to the processor's
    control unit (not relevant in this
    case)
- it holds the address of an operand
    in a memory unit and is therefore
    output to the address bus.
The complete model is created with the
statements:
```
DATABUS = BUS(4)
ADDBUS = BUS(4)
R1 = REGISTER (4/DATABUS/ADDUNIT)
R2 = REGISTER (4/ADDUNIT/DATABUS)
ADDUNIT = ADDER (4/R1, DATABUS/R2)
PC = COUNTER (4//ADDRBUS)
IR = INSTREE (4/DATABUS/CONTROL : 2,
        ADDRBUS : 2)
MEM = RAM (4/16/ADDRBUS/DATABUS)
```

This processor has the instruction format

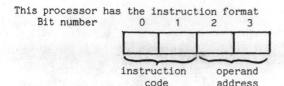

Bit number   0   1   2   3

instruction   operand
code   address

and the instruction codes are

    00   LOAD R1 from specified memory location
    01   STORE contents of R2 into specified
         memory location
    10   ADD contents of specified memory
         location to contents of R1
         (result placed in R2)
    11   HALT processsor

A microprogram that will interpret and execute a program written in this simple machine language on the configuration is given below:

```
1.  PC(OUT) READ        Get next instruction
    1R(IN) PC(INC)
2.  JUMP(7, 1R, 0, 0)   Interpret instruction
3.  JUMP(5, 1R, 1, 0)
4.  STOP                Halt processor
5.  1R(2, OUT) READ     Add
    R1(OUT) R2(IN)
6.  JUMP(1)             Next instruction
7.  JUMP(10, 1R, 1, 0)  Interpret instruction
8.  1R(2, OUT) R2(OUT)  Store
    WRITE
9.  JUMP(1)
10. 1R(2, OUT) READ     Load
    R1(IN)
11. JUMP(1)
12. END
```

Microinstruction 1 transfers a copy of the next instruction in sequence to the instruction register, after which the conditional branch instructions 2, 3 and 7 interpret the instructions and cause a branch to the microinstruction that performs the required machine operation, and so on until a halt is encountered.

A simple machine language program to add two numbers 3 and 2 is given below. Memory locations 0-2 are used to store the data values, while program instructions are stored in locations 3-6.

Address	Contents	Assembly language equivalent
0	00 11	A
1	00 10	B
2	00 00	C
3	00 00	LOAD A
4	10 01	ADD B
5	01 10	STORE C
6	11 00	HALT

This is loaded into the memory unit, the program counter is set to instruction 3, then the program is executed.

The system is on trial with pupils at present.

Enhancements planned include the use of a graphics display to illustrate the configuration of parts during assembly, and data transfers during program execution, and the implementation of an assembly language for the system.

My last two examples are drawn from school Physics. Brna (1, 2) has built two learning environments, a Dynamics Laboratory and an Electricity Laboratory, within which a pupil can set up experiments to explore basic concepts. In the case of learning Dynamics, there is growing evidence that one of the major difficulties is that learners bring to the classroom an intuitive pre-Newtonian model of dynamic behaviour. In many cases, the existence of this model seems to interfere with the acquisition of a formal Newtonian model. This suggests that the teaching of Dynamics should be organized as a confrontation between non-Newtonian and Newtonian explanations of phenomena. The Dynamics Laboratory is, in Bork's terminology, a controllable world, where these confrontations can take place. To illustrate this, let us take a simple problem:

JIM is playing football when he receives a fast pass straight across the goal mouth from FRED. He wants to hit the ball into the gap at the end of the goal mouth.
Indicate roughly the direction in which he should strike the ball.

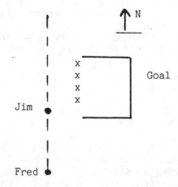

To model this situation, the pupil has to specify
    -        a map,
    -        a journey,   and
    -        a force
where map describes the territory over which an object is moving, journey describes features of the object, and force describes how the object is driven.

A record of the pupil's program is given below:

```
        BUILD GOAL                    GOAL is the name of the situation to be
                                      recorded in the Physics Database

        MAKE MAP ONE                  ONE is the name of the MAP
        DISPLACEMENT FRED JIM 10M 0   Displacement has magnitude 10 metres on
                                      bearing of 0 degrees
        DISPLACEMENT JIM GOAL 10M 90  Displacement has magnitude 10 metres on
        END                           bearing of 90 degrees

        MAKE JOURNEY BALL             BALL is name of the journey
        START FRED                    FRED is starting point
        MASS 1KG                      Mass of ball is 1KG
        VELOCITY FRED 0 M/S 0         Initial velocity at FRED is 0M/S on
        END                           bearing of 0 degrees

        MAKE FORCE CORNER             CORNER is the name of the force
        ACTS BALL                     Corner acts on ball
        KICK ONE FRED 1ONS 0          Starts ball moving from FRED
        KICK TWO JIM 1ONS 180         Stops the ball temporarily at JIM
        KICK THREE JIM 1ONS 90        Moves it to GOAL
        END
```

When the program is run, the computer displays a trace of the body, in the form of three places marked on the screen and a flashing object moving from the start, turning at the middle place and moving to the third one. If the ball does not turn the corner, the force can be re-defined by typing

```
    CORNER KICK TWO JIM    ?NS 180       or
    CORNER KICK THREE JIM ?NS 90
```

where ? is given a new value. The data written to the screen is stored in a trace file that can be displayed, or printed out, for re-examination.

The concepts handled by the Dynamics include Mass, Displacement, Velocity, Acceleration, Force, Impulse and Gravity, applied to one (or two) objects. Following our normal practice, a pupil is guided by worksheets built around the cycle, build-run-debug. As yet, we have had little opportunity to class test and refine the environment and worksheets.

When pupils are learning electrical concepts, intuitive electrical models also introduce confusions. For example, the fluid flow model encourages them to think of electrical current as flowing through conductors, an analogy frowned upon by James Clark Maxwell. Again, the purpose of the Electricity Laboratory is to provide a learning environment within which a pupil can set up a simple electrical circuit, apply steady state analysis to it and, if necessary, modify his design until the required result is obtained. The concepts that can be investigated include power, potential difference, current, electromotive force, resistance, capacitance and inductance.

To set up a circuit, a pupil transacts with three menus displayed on the computer's screen, as shown in the drawing below:
The left-hand menu is a list of components, denoted by icons.

The right-hand menu is a list of components in use in a particular circuit.
The third menu is a list of operations that can be performed, e.g. <u>Move</u> Battery (to a position on the screen by using the cursor).

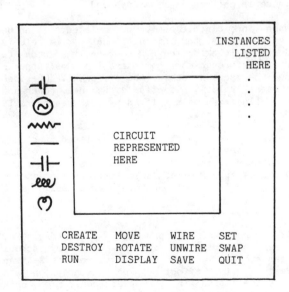

Let us look at a simple example: building a simple circuit, comprising a battery and a resistance, connected in series. The first step is to select components, and position them on the screen, using the CREATE command. This is done by placing the cursor at the left-hand side of its label and by pressing the space bar. Now, the circuit symbols in the left-hand menu are highlighted, with a new cursor appearing at their left.

To copy a battery symbol, the space bar is pressed and an instance of a battery, identifiied by the name 'bat1', appears at the top left-hand corner of the screen. Its name is also recorded in the list at the top right-hand side of the screen, so that it can be referred to later for editing. Now, the system is waiting for the battery symbol to be <u>positioned</u> on the screen. This is done by using the cursor keys which drive the symbol directly. The same procedure is followed to CREATE a resistor.

The second step is to insert the wire links. To <u>wire</u> between the battery and resistor, the command <u>WIRE</u> is invoked. Now, the user moves the cursor to the bat1 symbol, and presses RETURN to connect the wire to the battery. Next, the cursor is moved to res1. When RETURN is pressed, the wire linking one pole of the battery to one end of the resistor appears on the screen. Exactly the same procedure is followed to connect the other pole to the other end of the resistor.

The third step is to supply values for battery and resistance. This is done by activating the <u>SET</u> command which highlights the menu on the right recording the components. The cursor is used to activate a component, and an appropriate value is entered via the keyboard.

When the circuit has been completed, it can be evaluated by the circuit analyser. This is done by invoking the RUN command, whereupon the current through each component (in amps) appears on the screen beside the component. Besides current values, potential difference, power and V/I values can be displayed by using appropriate DISPLAY commands.

In accordance with our established practice, pupils are introduced to the facilities of the laboratory through the use of structured worksheets. A brief field testing programme is being carried out in an Edinburgh school.

CONCLUSION

The purpose of this paper was to identify novel uses of computers in the secondary school classroom. Each example represents 2-4 man years of effort from conception to experimentation in the classroom. Yet, each only scratches the surface of possibilities. Nevertheless, they give a taste for what can be done to put the power of the machine into pupils' hands.

ACKNOWLEDGEMENT

Our thanks are due to our sponsors, past and present: the Nuffield Foundation, the Scottish Council for Research in Education, the Leverhulme Trust and the Economic and Social Research Council.

REFERENCES

1. Brna, P. (1983a) Engineering Science and Dynamics. <u>DAI Working Paper : 141</u> Department of Artificial Intelligence, University of Edinburgh.
2. Brna, P. (1983b) Learning about Electrical Circuits via a Computer. <u>DAI Working Paper : 131</u>, Department of Artificial Intelligence, University of Edinburgh.
3. Chung, W.M. (1982) A Proposal for an Object-Oriented Control Language for Children. <u>DAI Working Paper : 136</u>, Department of Artificial Intelligence, University of Edinburgh.
4. Chung, W.H. (1984) Concurrent-LOGO. User's Manual. <u>DAI Occasional Paper : 49</u>, Department of Artificial Intelligence, University of Edinburgh.
5. Howe, J.A.M. (1979) Learning Through Model-building. In <u>Expert Systems in the Micro-Electronic Age</u>. (Ed.) Michie. Edinburgh: Edinburgh University Press.
6. Howe, J.A.M. (1984) Edinburgh LOGO: A Retrospective View. In <u>An Attitude of Mind</u>, (Ed.) W.B. Dockrell. Edinburgh: Scottish Council for Research in Education.
7. Howe, J.A.M., O'Shea, T. and Plane, F. (1980) Teaching Mathematics Through LOGO Programming : An Evaluation Study. In <u>Computer Assisted Learning : Scope, Progress and Limits</u>. (Eds) Lewis, R. and Tagg, E.D. Amsterdam: North Holland.
8. Howe, J.A.M., Ross, P.M., Johnson, K.R. and Inglis, R. (1984) Model Building, Mathematics and LOGO. In <u>New Horizons in Educational Computing</u>, (Ed.) Yazdani, M. Chichester: Ellis Horwood.
9. Lees, B. (1983) An Interactive Modelling System to Assist the Teaching of Computer Architecture. In <u>Proceedings of 4th Canadian Symposium on Instructional Technology</u>.
10. Papert, S. (1980) <u>Mindstorms : Children, Computers, and Powerful Ideas</u>. Brighton: Harvester Press Limited.

COMPUTERS IN EDUCATION, K. Duncan and D. Harris (eds.)
Elsevier Science Publishers B.V. (North-Holland)
© IFIP, 1985

DEVELOPMENT OF A K-12 COMPUTER SCIENCE CURRICULUM
UTILIZING THE LOGO COMPUTING LANGUAGE AS A PRIMARY VEHICLE

J. Thomas Burnett, Assistant to the Superintendent for Computer Technology
Charles D. Friesen, Educational Technology Consultant

Lincoln Public Schools
Lincoln, NE 68510

This paper describes a subset of a K-12 computing curriculum that has been developed and implemented which utilizes the LOGO computing language as an important vehicle. The curriculum stresses hands-on computer activities for students at all levels. Curriculum materials have been developed which can be utilized by teachers with a minimal amount of training. The LOGO curriculum and associated curricular materials are tied to a set of computing objectives which are a subset of a comprehensive set of computing objectives from areas including computer awareness, computer operation, utilizing the computer as a tool, and a computer science.

INTRODUCTION

School districts across the United States are hurrying to develop and implement computer curriculums for various grade levels. The Lincoln Public Schools in Lincoln, Nebraska, U.S.A, are no different. In 1981 preliminary work was done to address the issue of a formalized computer curriculum. Many ideas were exchanged and difficult questions were asked: Was a computer curriculum really needed? Given that a computer curriculum was needed or had been mandated, at what grade levels should the curriculum begin and end? What computing experiences were appropriate for all students? Should computer operations, computer awareness, computer-assisted instruction, computer programming, and/or using the computer as a tool be emphasized?

From the Lincoln Public Schools, the answers to these questions were that a computer curriculum was definitely needed. The curriculum should be implemented beginning at the kindergarten level and that common computer experiences should be provided to all students in grades K-12 with specialized computing experiences also occurring at the 7-12 grade levels. While it was felt that student experiences should include all aspects of computing, the areas of computer programming and utilizing the computer as a tool should be emphasized. This paper focuses upon those aspects of the comprehensive K-12 computer curriculum related to developing and implementing a K-12 computer programming curriculum utilizing the LOGO computing language as an important vehicle.

RATIONALE

Once it was decided to utilize computer programming as an important part of a comprehensive computer curriculum, it was necessary to find a programming language with features and capabilities appropriate for use in kindergarten through grade 12. The language chosen for use in the curriculum was LOGO.

LOGO was selected for several reasons. It had a structure which meshed well with the Pascal programming language which was being taught at the senior high school level. Being an interactive language, it put control of problem-solving activities at the fingertips of younger students. LOGO's turtle graphics orientation provided the visual stimulation felt necessary for younger children. Being a mathematics-oriented language, LOGO provided students with expanded and enriched experiences in a basic skills curricular area. LOGO, as well as all computing languages, provided students with a tool for not only solving problems, but developing problem-solving skills. This focus on developing student's problem-solving skills was one of the priorities of the mathematic's consultant in the school district as well as a primary recommendation of the National Council of Teachers of Mathematics (NCTM, 1980).

While not the most obvious of reasons, LOGO provided a vehicle to implement the curriculum and provide for equity. At the earlier grades, pictorial symbols could be used instead of words in learning to utilize the language. This allowed the problem-solving experiences, which were important aspects of the curriculum, to be taught almost immediately. The facility of using pictorial representations also provided special needs students the tools necessary to write programs to solve problems. While it has not yet been researched, it was felt that providing girls with motivating mathematics and computing experiences early in their formal education would begin to break down whatever barriers have limited them from pursuing further mathematics and computer science courses. In his book, Mindstorms: Children, Computers, and Powerful Ideas, Seymour Papert (1980) gives support to the concept that positive early experiences in a mathematics environment may have an effect on girls' perceptions of mathematics. Finally, the language also did not possess any characteristics that would tend to adversely influence its learning by minority populations.

With all of the positive reasons for selecting LOGO as the language to implement the curriculum, as well as the fact that LOGO was rapidly gaining in popularity, it became critical that the LOGO curriculum not attempt to do more than was practical, appropriate, and effective. It had been noted in various publications that the LOGO language could be utilized for many purposes including word processing, creative writing, and writing computer-assisted instructional programs. While these activities were indeed capable of being done utilizing the LOGO language, they were not strengths of the language and seemed inappropriate topics to be covered via the language. It was determined that the most appropriate and effective uses of the language were in the areas of mathematics, problem solving, and computer science.

The philosophy of utilizing the language where its strengths existed and where it appropriately fit with the goals and priorities of the school district served as a guiding principle. With this philosophy and the previously mentioned reasons in mind, the K-12 LOGO computing curriculum and associated curricular materials were developed.

BACKGROUND OF THE PROJECT

In the summer of 1982, a LOGO staff development course was taught to a group of curriculum consultants and teachers from all grade levels. Originally, this course was designed to be a follow up to a beginning computer literacy course for teachers. The teachers and consultants who took the LOGO course were excited about the possibility of utilizing the language with their students. What they asked for were some guidelines to follow as to what students should be expected to learn and curricular materials to assist students in meeting those objectives.

At that time, commercially available LOGO curricular materials were sparse and guidelines for implementing LOGO were non-existent. LOGO was still somewhat new in the public schools of the United States. The language had not yet experienced widespread adoption in the schools. Furthermore, original implementors of LOGO in the schools were clinging to Seymour Papert's notion of using the discovery approach in teaching LOGO to students. These original adopters did not accept the notion that traditional types of curricular materials, such as workbooks and activity cards, were necessary or appropriate for use with LOGO.

After a year of experimentation by the early adopters in the Lincoln Public Schools, curricular materials loosely tied to objectives were developed in the summer of 1983. These materials consisted of two sets of LOGO activity cards (Appendix A) along with a modified subset of LOGO . One set of cards was targeted for students in grades 4 through 6 using M.I.T. LOGO. A second set of LOGO cards was developed for kindergarten through grade 3 which were based on a subset of LOGO developed by teachers in the Lincoln Public Schools. This subset of LOGO was named One Key Logo (OKL). The OKL program and associated activity cards allowed students in the primary grades to begin to

work on problem-solving activities without needing extensive training in the LOGO language and keyboarding skills.

At this same time, work was being done in the secondary schools to develop and implement LOGO activities in computer literacy, computer science, and mathematics courses. Using the M.I.T. version of LOGO, curriculum modules were developed that targeted specific topics where the utilization of the LOGO language was most appropriate and effective.

In the fall of 1983, the elementary LOGO curriculum was implemented in a majority of the 33 elementary schools in Lincoln. The secondary school modules were pilot tested in geometry and algebra classes in two secondary schools during the fall of 1983. During the spring and summer of 1984, modules developed for the junior high school level were implemented. These modules were extensions of the primary and intermediate LOGO curriculum levels. Information gathered during the implementation process at the elementary and secondary school levels led to curriculum and materials revision.

The major curriculum revision occurred at the elementary level. The LOGO activity cards originally developed for kindergarten through grade 3 required students to be able to read. This was appropriate for some students but posed problems for others. A new set of activity cards was developed that eliminated the necessity to read as much as possible. The cards utilized pictures rather than words, thus allowing students to look for meaningful symbols on the keyboard.

After having worked with a majority of the LOGO curriculum for a year, a group of teachers, consultants, and administrators from the school district gathered during the spring and summer of 1984 to complete the development of a formalized LOGO curriculum and accompanying curricular materials for grades kindergarten through 12.

THE CURRICULUM

The LOGO curriculum is organized into four components based on student grade levels. The components are primary (kindergarten through grade 3), intermediate (grades 4 through 6), junior high school (grades 7 through 9), and senior high school (grades 10 through 12). The curriculum provides a set of structured activities for all students to work at accomplishing. Recognizing the fact that students progress through individualized curriculum activities such as those in the LOGO curriculum at various rates, enrichment activities were developed at each grade level to provide students additional opportunities to learn.

The following taxonomy of LOGO problem solving objectives are utilized at the elementary school level in both the primary and intermediate grade levels. This set of problem solving objectives are a subset of LOGO objectives which in turn are a subset of a comprehensive set of computing objectives for the district.

500	The student will analyze problem solving strategies by using LOGO to:
501	interpret precise directions.
502	discover and explore geometric properties.
503	manipulate control over the computer.
504	develop estimating skills by logical deduction.
505	develop modular approaches to solving problems.
506	predict outcomes of procedures.
507	respond constructively to error messages.
508	establish logical sequence.
509	define procedures in computer language.
510	evaluate and modify existing procedures.

Many other LOGO objectives are covered in the elementary school curriculum such as utilizing the editor, syntax of the language, screen layout, and others. However, the primary focus of the curriculum is the problem solving objectives listed previously. The curriculum is designed so that students are working on the problem-solving objectives from the very beginning. It was for this reason that the OKL activities were originally developed and the pictorial OKL cards were produced. These materials allow students to begin addressing the problem solving objectives very early in the curriculum.

In addition to specific LOGO objectives covered at the primary and intermediate levels, general computing objectives are covered via programming with LOGO. These include the handling and usage of various types of computing equipment, the keyboard, and computer terminology.

To assist teachers in implementing the LOGO curriculum, various curricular materials are provided. These materials include LOGO activities cards, transparency masters, LOGO workbooks, OKL diskettes, LOGO diskettes, Lincoln Public Schools LOGO Utilities Diskettes, and student disks. Teacher's guides are also provided to help teachers organize and present the elementary school LOGO curriculum.

While the LOGO curriculum at the elementary school level focuses on problem solving and mathematics, the junior high LOGO curriculum focuses on LOGO as a computing language. The objectives at the junior high level specifically address objectives related to computer science.

LOGO activities at the junior high level are implemented through a junior high school "computer literacy" course. This course includes various aspects of computing and provides students with usable skills in word processing, information management, and computer programming. While this one semester course is not presently required of students, all junior high school students are strongly encouraged to take the course.

The junior high school LOGO curriculum builds on the elementary curriculum. Many of the problem-solving objectives in the elementary school curriculum are also included in the junior high school curriculum. In addition to the problem solving objectives, computer science objectives are also addressed. These include structured design, top-down and bottom-up strategies, data structures, program design methodology, and file handling.

Advanced LOGO features are also utilized at the junior high school level. These include nested repeats, if-then-else statements, multi-variable procedures, parameter passing, list processing, local/global variables, and recursion.

Students who have progressed through the LOGO curriculum at the elementary and junior high school levels will have the skills needed to appropriately utilize the LOGO language to solve problems. Students will also have the experiences necessary to progress into the senior high school computer science curriculum which utilizes the Pascal computing language as a primary vehicle.

At the senior high school level, the LOGO curriculum branches in two directions. The first is the computer science curriculum. Student computing experiences with LOGO are used as building blocks to progress into Pascal programming language. The second branch involves the use of LOGO as a tool in other curricular areas.

In the senior high school Pascal course, the LOGO concepts which serve as building blocks for learning Pascal are stressed. The early sessions of Pascal utilize LOGO and Karel and Robot activities as an introduction.

In other curricular areas, LOGO modules were developed to aid student learning of various concepts. These modules were originally developed in the science and mathematics areas. Abelson and diSessa's book, Turtle Geometry: The Computer as a Medium for Exploring Mathematics (1981), along with textbooks in science and mathematics, were extensively utilized in developing the modules.

In the mathematics area, modules were developed for geometry, algebra, and calculus classes. Modules developed for geometry classes included length and midpoint of segments, supplementary/complementary angles, angle measure, properties of regular and irregular polygons, circles, parallel and perpendicular lines, reflections, translations, and rotations. Modules for the algebra classes include distance between points, linear equations, and parabolic equations. The primary module in calculus courses dealt with the idea of limits. All of these modules involve student programming using the LOGO language. The student projects include pictures as well as text. These activities serve to reinforce topics typically covered in these courses.

In science, a limited number of modules have been developed. Most of these modules are based on the Dynaturtle program developed by diSessa (Abelson, 1982). These modules serve to stress the concept of velocity as well as position.

As stated previously, LOGO can be utilized in many curricular areas. It has been our intent to use the language for purposes where it was most appropriate. At the secondary level, the areas of science, computer science, and mathematics were originally most appropriate. However, as innovative and effective modules are developed for other curriculum areas, they also will become part of the LOGO curriculum.

CONCLUSIONS

The results, after working with the LOGO curriculum for over one year, have been great. Students have gained in their knowledge of problem-solving strategies, attitudes toward computers, computer programming skills, and their appreciation of mathematics. Teachers have responded to inservice training with great enthusiasm. Teachers indicate seeing an excitement in students they rarely ever see. Students see teachers learning right alongside them. This concept of working together on a problem that is not judged as right or wrong has provided students as well as teachers with a new and positive view of their relationship.

The Lincoln Public Schools LOGO computing curriculum has been successful for several reasons. One major reason is the input from teachers. Many teachers have been contributors in the organization, development, and implementation of the curriculum. Concerns over time, materials, and organization have been carefully addressed. Teachers have a great sense of ownership in the curriculum and have worked very hard to help other teachers implement the curriculum in their classes.

Another reason the curriculum has been successfully implemented is the ongoing curriculum monitoring and revising which have occurred. The curriculum has been revised several times already. The mechanism is in place to see that it is updated when necessary. Monitoring is done via site visits by central administators, consultants, teachers, and principals as well as by surveys, questionnaires, and pre-post tests.

The Lincoln Public Schools staff has worked very hard to develop a viable, effective computing curriculum which will meet the needs of students both today and in the future. The dedication of teachers, administrators, and board of education members has been the strength of the computing efforts in Lincoln. This dedication coupled with a formalized plan for the development, implementation, evaluation, and revision of the computing curriculum should provide the school district with a firm foundation for implementing and institutionalizing the curriculum throughout the district.

REFERENCES

1. Abelson, Harold. Logo for the Apple II. (Byte/McGraw Hill. Peterborough, NH. 1982).

2. Abelson, H. and diSessa, A. Turtle Geometry: The Computer as a Medium for Exploring Mathematics. (MIT Press, Cambridge, MA. 1981).

3. National Council of Teachers of Mathematics. An Agenda for Action: Recommendations for School Mathematics of the 1980's. (1980).

4. Papert, Seymour. Mindstorms: Children, Computers, and Powerful Ideas. (Basic Books, Inc. New York, 1980).

Example OKL Pictorial Card

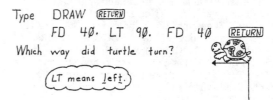

Example OKL Card

COMPUTERS IN EDUCATION, K. Duncan and D. Harris (eds.)
Elsevier Science Publishers B.V. (North-Holland)
© IFIP, 1985

LOGO AND THE INTELLIGENCE

Paul Laridon

University of the Witwatersrand, Johannesburg, South Africa.

An eclectic model of intelligence (the π-model) is briefly described.

Examples of children using Logo are then used to show how the processes inherent to
the model are enhanced. Some cases of resultant personal and intellectual development are described.

1. INTRODUCTION

Over the past four years, due to my involvement
with the Witwatersrand Micro Logo Project, I
have had many occasions to observe, to project
and reflect on the value of Logo to education.
My enthusiasm for Logo and the future it points
to, in my vision of the role of computers in
education, stems mainly from the intellectual
processes Logo integrates with so well and the
intellectual development which it, as a consequence, stimulates.

What disturbs me is when I hear of or observe
actual or intended implementations of Logo
which, in a shortsighted manner, see Logo only
in the context of computer awareness, or computer literacy, or programming or computer
science or mathematics, or providing for the
development of drill and practice type CAI with
-in a school. Granted, Logo can provide for
the items on this menu admirably. I consider
them to be mere entrée to a far more radical
and holistic view of computers in education and
of the educand.

To me Logo is a person and mind expansion tool.
This tool can do a tremendous amount for the
educand in the cognitive, affective and psycho-
motor domains. The essential rider is that
Logo needs to be used with these goals in view,
by educators prepared to implement it in the
appropriate style.

In this paper I intend to show how the use of
Logo can be made to integrate with the essential features of my π-model of intelligence.
I will do this by drawing on illustrations
taken from various Logo classrooms in and
around Johannesburg.

2. THE π-MODEL OF INTELLIGENCE

This model of intelligence is an eclectic one
drawing on the work mainly of cognitive psycho
-logists (Piaget, Bruner, Skemp, van Hiele,
Dienes, Kafka) yet incorporating important

insights from the behaviourists (Skinner, Gagne,
Ausubel). What follows is a very brief outline.

2.1 Schema

An integrated cognitive structure developed by
the process described below. A schema organises into an equilibrated whole the knowledge
(and approaches related to this knowledge) the
intelligence has built up in a specific area.

2.2 The Processes

New knowledge is integrated into the web of
schemata existing in the mind, or new schemata
are brought into existence by the following interactive processes :
(a) *Assimilation* whereby the new information is
preliminarily accepted on the basis of a schema
already existing in the mind.
(b) *Accommodation* occurs when the schema, as a
result of apparent conflict due to this new information, is forced to alter in order to attain
a satisfactory reorganization. The drive to
reorganization is a result of the tension generated by the conflict. This process is crucial
to learning for without it nothing new is established in the mind.
(c) *Application*. The mind subsequently verifies its newly attained organization by referring back to the original sources of this conflict arousing information. This source could
be within the mind (see π_3 below) or in the
external physical world. Implications arising
out of the new schema formed are tested, so as
to exhibit the solution of the original problem.
Only then does the mind finally accept the reorganization which has occurred.
(d) *Accumulation*. The structure established
by processes (a), (b) and (c) could be rather
evanescent. A structure once established
needs to be made stable by fixing the interrelationships constituting the structure. This
occurs by way of a continued cycling of related
information through the newly formed schema by
way of repeated assimilation, accommodation and
application. This cycling results in the

schema becoming richer, deeper, broader, but above all, of a more permanent nature.

An 'accumulation cycle', comprising the four processes described above, is represented schema -tically in Figure 1.

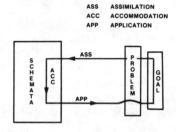

Figure 1 : An accumulation cycle

2.3 The π - Model

The processes described enable the intelligence, by action and interaction (either physical or mental), to develop schemata experientially, in three phases.

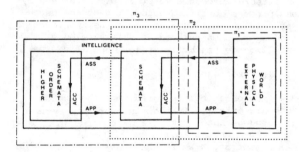

Figure 2 : The three phases

The three phases may be briefly distinguished as follows (see Figure 2):

- π_1 The objects acted on are in the external world. No schemata are involved in inter-actions.
- π_2 The objects acted on are in the external world. Schemata are built up as a con-sequence of accumulation cycles.
- π_3 Schemata now constitute the 'objects' of action, which is primarily internal. In-teraction is between existing schemata and the higher order schemata resulting.

For the purposes of this paper the processes assume greater importance. The phases will only briefly be mentioned as appropriate.

It is essential to be aware that the processes described are central. These processes are goal directed. The attainment of the goal is initially blocked by some problem (lack of an appropriate schema or of a sufficiently develop-ed schema). The intellectual tension set up drives the processes initially. The intellec-tual satisfaction resulting from successful

application (the aha! experience) supplies moti-vation to continue cycling ever deeper into fur-ther schemata-building and so into higher phases.

Homo sapiens has that quality of intelligence : adaptation, which has enabled the species not only to survive in, but to master its environ-ment. The emotional and sociological well-being of man is inextricably tied to the proper functioning of the intellect. Let us see evi-dence of how Logo is designed and can be used to work hand in hand with the processes described, so enabling the learner to progress through the phases involved in attaining an ever deeper understanding and appreciation of any particular topic.

3. LOGO AND THE PROCESSES

3.1 Assimilation

The immediate examples arising here are related to the use of the Turtle.

The robot-physical-turtle is used as a device whereby new concepts to be learned are ascribed, in the first instance, to problems related to the physical turtle. Learners of all ages very soon make the assimilation device their own bodies. In a standard-one class (± 8 years of age) I visited, I saw pupils being put through their 'body-work': Hands and shoes become the 'turtle-flippers', marked appropriately left and right. The teacher called out "left 90; forward 5, right 90 ---" to which her responsive brood of baby turtles marched off (not always in unison). Many teachers assured me that this 'playing turtle' did wonders for the children in their readiness to work with the screen turtle when it came to programming. Adults too play turtle when faced with problems. One need only watch for shoulder and body movements to pick out those programming in Logo from amongst a group working at keyboards. What better a way to build up schemata related to the explor-ation of space than by assimilating via one's own body through which one naturally first ex-periences space.

3.2 Accommodation

Ask a novice (older) Logo programmer to get the turtle to draw an equilateral triangle. What usually happens is this :

FD 50

RT 60

FD 50

The problem has been assimilated to the schema dependent on interior angles. Due to the ef-ficient offices of the turtle in immediate mode, the unexpected turn of events soon results in an accommodation to the local vantage point of progress so that a reorganisation results (often with the help of attendant 'body-work'):

```
        FD  50

        RT  120

        FD  50

        RT  120

        FD  50
```

What programmers refer to as a 'bug' becomes the
key to efficient accommodation.   The fact that
Logo, in immediate mode, here straight-away made
visual the effect of assimilation to an incorrect
schema, set in motion the equilibration procedure which resulted in an adaptation of the schema
to bring it into the overall organisation which
refers space to the turtle's location and direction.

The 'bug' is not viewed as a 'mistake' to be
avoided at all costs.   Learners soon come to
realise that the 'bug' is the key to a proper
understanding.   The 'bug' indicates where the
crucial accommodation has to be made.   I recall
observing Toby (a standard 3 pupil) working at
the problem of producing two concentric circles.
Though somewhat upset (fists pounding on the
desk) at getting the result
at right, there was nevertheless a look of relief
and mischievous antici-
pation on his face as he
realised what accom-
modation had to be made.
His frustration at having
to wait for the turtle to finish drawing before
he could get his corrected program was evident.

3.3 Application

This process serves to verify a newly arrived at
accommodation.   While working in immediate mode
this verification is continually being done.
In most Logo classes I have gone into, children
are presented with a problem which they have to
solve : draw a square; draw a triangle; draw two
concentric circles etc.   The resulting program
or procedure is then executed to "see whether
it has worked or not".

In a particular Logo session I have recollections of, pupils were working with the TRI procedure: REPEAT 2[FD 50 RT 120] FD 50, in order
to solve various problems, one of which was to
get the turtle to draw :

HILLS :
I will use this as background to illustrate how
one of three crucial things now happens within
the application process
(a) The accommodation was not a success.   This
initiates the search for the bug.   The manner
in which the program is executed helps the learn
-er to pinpoint where the further accommodation
has to be made.

Peter and John observing how the turtle executed
their ideas

```
RT  30
REPEAT  6[TRI]                                  (Turtle
                                                 Traverses
                                                 picture twice)
```
soon saw that they needed to take their turtle
back 50 so:

```
RT  30                                      (Turtle traverses
REPEAT  6[TRI BK 50]                         picture 6 times)
```
This they now saw needed a corrective resetting
of heading.
(b) The problem is solved.
In Peter and John's case:

```
REPEAT  6[RT 30  TRI  BK 50  RT 90]
```

This caused Peter a genuine aha or eureka experience "Yeah!" he shouted, "come and see our
Hills".   This regardless of the fact that
others had solved the problem before they had.
(In fact various different successful solutions
resulted.)
(c) Jenny and Kelly had come up with:

```
REPEAT  6[RT 30  TRI  BK 50  RT 150]
```

which they immediately to their delight called
STAR and called others over to see.

Notice how, in application, motivation to continue is always generated.   In (b) and (c)
intellectual satisfaction results, confidence in
one's own intellectual abilities is built up
with the resulting willingness to continue to
new challenges.   In (c) a spark of creativity
has taken over.   Is it not true that genuine
discoveries are so often made en route to the
solution of initially different problems?

I consider the manner in which Logo works hand
in glove with the application process to be at
the core of its success in promoting the development of the intellect.

3.4 Accumulation Cycles

The pupils in the previous session continued to
use their fundamental TRI procedure to solve the
following problems[2].

In a standard 4 class the following accumulation cycling occured:

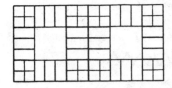

TO SQUARE
REPEAT 4 [FD 40 RT 90]
END

TO LADDER
REPEAT 6 [SQUARE FD 20]
END

TO FRAME
REPEAT 4 [LADDER FD 20 RT 90]
END

TO DOUBLE
FRAME LT 90 FD 140 RT 90 FRAME
END

TO SQUARE
REPEAT 4 [FD 30 RT 90]
END

TO SQUARE1
REPEAT 4 [FD 60 RT 90]
END

TO SQCIRC
REPEAT 36 [SQUARE RT 10 SQUARE1
RT 10] HT FS
END

Note how the fundamental procedure SQUARE is used to build ever more complex procedures which in turn are called to extend, enrich and integrate the schema relevant to these accumulation cycles.   The SQCIRC procedure was a particularly pleasing bit of freelance creative work produced by Sheila but nevertheless the result of accumulation cycles encompassing existing schemata.

4. THE PHASES

Logo, given an aware classroom practice, clearly promotes the cognitive processes. I now briefly (due to lack of space) wish to investigate cases where Logo was being used to promote progress through the phases of concept formation.

4.1 Case 1

The computers of a standard 2-class (8 - 9 years of age) had prodecures entered which enabled them to draw circles, squares, triangles and stars of various sizes on the screen ("playshapes"). The class was given two assignments:
(a) Use the playshapes to illustrate halves and quarters.
(b) Use the playshapes to draw any picture you like.

Here are some of the results for (a)

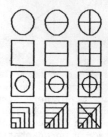

These children had as yet not been taught these fractions formally in any arithmetic lesson. They were operating in a π_1 mode. The girls were allowed to talk about what they were doing. The talk was excited busy talk, so essential for the subconscious integrative assimilation which it promotes.   In the arithmetic lesson which followed more rapid progress was made in building up the appropriate π_2 formalities and in achieving understanding within the scope of the schema being formed.
(b) Practically each group drew a different picture.   Some combined (a) and (b).   Here are two interesting examples of what emerged.

STAR 15
STAR 20
STAR 25
STAR 30

BUTTERFLY

Jane was exploring and so gaining Logico-mathematical experience of sequences and variables (amongst other things).

Belinda's picture is largely based on symmetry which was attained in an arithmetical way.

4.2 Case 2

Here a group of standard 2 girls were experimenting with the 'black boxes' PACKMAN and ANGLE-WORLD (preprogrammed in Logo).

AN ANGLE
OF 30 DEGREES

AN ANGLE
OF 90 DEGREES

AN ANGLE
OF 120 DEGREES

Some girls wanted to see what PAC 400 would do. Teacher decided they needed some bodywork so got them up to do RIGHT 90 RIGHT 90 RIGHT 90 RIGHT 90.   This helped them realise that the best they could get out of PACMAN was PAC 360

ANGLE: N   shows a flashing rotating arm which
rotates from the vertical

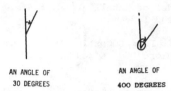

| AN ANGLE OF | AN ANGLE OF |
| 30 DEGREES | 400 DEGREES |

through any inputted angle.

Again these girls were gaining experiences, in a
π_1 mode which allowed them to understand without
difficulty once π_2 formalities were wanted.

4.3 Case 3

The following approach is being used in a number
of schools to provide an experiential basis for
a π_2 appreciation of the integers.

Essentially, by the use of 'black-box' procedures, the turtle is made to move up and down a
number line.   The turtle is then sent on a
journey, for example:

        (+60) - (+120)
    Arithmetical description

                    Destination
            (Turtle starts from HOME)
    FD 60   BK 120

    Turtle commands

Pupils are allowed to experiment.   The interest
-ing journeys are of course
(a)   +70 + (-70)   (c)   -70 - (+50)
(b)   +70 - (+70)   (d)   -70 - (-50)

Subsequently when very formal proofs (π_3)   depen
-dant on the distributive law, the additive iden
-tity and the additive inverse are presented,
pupils can the more easily find their way
through these proofs due to the experiences
they can assimilate from to arrive at the necess
-ary π_3 abstractions.

4.4 Case 4

The following is an outline of a worksheet some
standard six (11-12) pupils were using.[3]   Having
drawn a triangle (regular) and a square

pupils are required to draw a regular pentagon
and a regular hexagon:

The procedures invariably were (essentially)
something like

REPEAT 4[FD 40   RT 90]   (Square)
REPEAT 5[FD 40   RT 72]   (Pentagon)
REPEAT 6[FD 40   RT 60]   (Hexagon)

The worksheet now required the deduction of the
following conclusion :

Number of Repeats	n
Angle through which turtle was to turn	$360/n$

Pupils were then asked to formulate a procedure
by which any polygon could be drawn.   This is
what one particular boy used:

            DEADPARROT : N
            REPEAT : N[FD 40   RT 360/:N]

The pupils were then directed to experiment with
their polygon procedures.   The crunch came
though when the problem faced was that of getting the turtle to draw a circle.

Suprisingly (?) even the slowest pupil was able
to get up a good approximation.   Various solutions were of course proposed and executed.
For example

        REPEAT 100[FD 40   RT 360/100]
        REPEAT   36[FD 5   RT 360/36]
        REPEAT 360[FD 1   RT 1]
        REPEAT 1000[FD 1/10   RT 360/1000]

(Most using the DEADPARROT : N procedure)

From here the worksheet extrapolated to The
Total Turtle Trip Theorem (T^5) and to a descrip
-tion of the "perfect circle".

Notice the progression through π_1 (basic unrelated shapes) to π_2 (POLYGON : N) to π_3 (T^5,
limit concept, curvature, differential geometry,
relativity)[4].

5. EVIDENCE OF INTELLECTUAL AND PERSONAL
DEVELOPMENT

Any teacher involved with children and Logo can
mention case after case of evident personal and
intellectual development.   Fully documenting
these cases and other data is a research project
in itself.   Here are a few bits of evidence.

Psychological tests showed Rowan (a standard 3
pupil) who was old for his class (age 10) to be
introverted.   He lagged by $4\frac{1}{2}$ years in reading

age, in fact was a non-reader.   Rowan, working
with Logo, progressed to the upper quartile of
his class.   In Geography be tied for top place.
Rowan changed in demeanour, becoming outgoing
and a leader.

A standard 5 teacher at a certain school would
often set her mathematics class 'word-sums'.
Before a regular exposure to Logo, very few pupils even attempted to solve these problems.
After a term's exposure to Logo practically the
whole class made good attempts at the problem
she set in her test, with 80% success.   The
manner in which pupils set out their work showed
that they were breaking the problem down into
'mind-sized bytes'.   Their solutions were stepwise and structured.

All the pupils from The Ridge Preparatory School
were put through the Stanford Arithmetic Achieve
-ment Tests on the TOAM system.   The standard
4 class, which had a previous year of exposure
to Logo performed better than the standard 6
class (no Logo experience).

6. CONCLUSION

Finally I must again re-iterate that to me LOGO
IS A PERSON AND MIND EXPANSION TOOL.

Artificial Intelligence researchers hold that
"thinking involves the processing and changing
of symbolic structures in memory"[5].   The π-
model pin-points the processes involved.   The
child, working in a correctly controlled Logo
environment is continually made to overtly
employ these processes.   Evidence exists that
intellectual and personal development results,
in the psychomotor, cognitive and affective
domains.

Piaget stresses that spontaneous interaction
with the environment is the key to mental growth.
The task of the teacher is to foster conditions
under which each child can think freely.   Logo
provides for this admirably.

"A very important feature of work with computers
is that the teacher and the learner can be engaged in a real intellectual collaboration; together they can try to get the computer to do
this or that and understand what it actually
does.   New situations that neither teacher nor
learner has seen before come up frequently and
so the teacher does not have to pretend not to
know.   Sharing the problem and the experience
of solving it allows a child to learn from an
adult not "by doing what teacher says" but "by
doing what teacher does".   And one of the
things that the teacher does is pursue a problem
until it is completely understood.   The LOGO
environment is special because it provides
numerous problems that elementary schoolchildren
can understand with a kind of completeness that
is rare in ordinary life."(Papert-MINDSTORMS).[6]

REFERENCES:

[1] For a fuller description see: Laridon, P.E.,
    The π-model of Intelligence, *S Afr J Educ*.
    3(1983).138-142.

[2] See: Micro Logo Education, *Lets Learn Logo
    Book 1* (Micro Logo Education, Johannesburg,
    1983). 32-33.

[3] See: Brown, Judith, *The World of Logo* (McGraw
    Hill, Johannesburg, 1985). 14-15.

[4] See: Abelson, H.and di Sessa, A., *Turtle
    Geometry: the Computer as a Medium for
    Exploring Mathematics*. (MIT Press,
    1981).

[5] O'Shea, T. and Self, J, *Learning and Teaching
    with Computers* (The Harvester Press, 1983)
    54.

[6] Papert, Seymour, *Mindstorms* (The Harvester
    Press, 1980). 115.

COMPUTERS IN EDUCATION, K. Duncan and D. Harris (eds.)
Elsevier Science Publishers B.V. (North-Holland)
© IFIP, 1985

LOGO FOR PRIMARY GRADE TEACHERS - AN IN-SERVICE MODEL

Jeri Cohen, Rivka Elkin

Project for Computing in Education
Computation Center
Ben-Gurion University of the Negev

This paper describes an in-service training program which has as its objective not only to develop an effective method to teach Logo programming skills but to demonstrate to teachers how Logo can be integrated into a broader teaching, learning environment.

INTRODUCTION

Computing in education is increasingly becoming an integral part of the curriculum in schools and academic institutions throughout the country. The rush to teach children this new curriculum has resulted in a burst of computer literacy courses designed to train teachers in this new technology. The fact that computer literacy training is a very real need is not disputed. However, what should be taught, how it should be taught, whether the emphasis should be on CAI, CMI, Basic or simply developing an 'awareness' level on the part of teachers is still very much of an open and controversial question.

At the basis of this controversy lies the fundemental question of how a person views the computer; i.e. whether as an effective drill master which controls and directs children's activities or, rather, as a tool for children to control, to help them formulate and solve problems.

The newest and perhaps the most exciting of all the approaches used to teach computer literacy is the programming language Logo.* Logo represents a new direction in educational computing. It presupposes that interaction with the computer should be a dynamic process and that a person will learn by doing and thinking about what he did. Within the Logo context of learning, computer literacy becomes the ability of a student to think through problem solving strategies and communicate these strategies clearly to the computer. Because the user receives immediate visual feedback in the form of a graphics image, he is able to improve his strategy as he works through a problem. Computer literacy, in this context, anticipates much more than learning 'about' computers; how they work or how they are used. It becomes in a very real sense a well-defined technological extension of mental structures and thought processes.

Presently, in-service courses in Logo have as their objective teaching teachers the programming skills needed to introduce children to the Logo language. The major controversy surrounding the teaching of Logo stems from the didactic method a teacher should choose when teaching children. On the one side are those proponents of Logo who believe that because Logo is a very special learning experience which provides a problem solving environment where children learn how to think there should be a minimum of teacher intervention. Learning activities, therefore, should be open-ended and exploratory. The child interacts with the 'Logo environment' according to his ability and learning style. At the other end are those who believe that the teaching of Logo should be directed and consist of a graded sequence of learning activities. This approach is based on two assumptions; one, that computer time is limited and that all children should be exposed to the same activities in order to reach a minimum level of programming competency; and, two, that children will fall into a 'hacking' kind of programming if not given guidance. (Martin 1984) (Leron 1984).

In both of these approaches, however, the emphasis is on teaching programming skills. There is little, if any, attention paid to developing specially designed assistance materials to support young children in their initial programming efforts. In addition, the use of Logo as a vehicle to develop cognition has not seemed to be a major objective in existing training models in Logo.

This paper will describe an in-service training program which has as its objective not only to develop an effective method to teach Logo programming skills but to demonstrate to
* Logo is a high level language which allows easy entry into programming by children. It is interactive and has graphic, string manipulation and numerical capabilities.

teachers how Logo can be integrated into a broader teaching, learning environment.

THEORETICAL BACKGROUND

It has been said that the Logo learning environment simulates the Piagetian concept of learning whereby simple mental structures are assimilated into more complex and abstract structures in order to generate a higher level of cognition. This hierarchial building of thought processes is paralleled in Logo through the building of individual procedures. These procedures are eventually incorporated as sub-procedures in a 'super-procedure'.Since sub-procedures are independent entities, they can be used in different constellations to create new and different 'super-procedures'. The new knowledge in the form of the 'super-procedure' is subsequently assimilated and used as a sub-procedure in creating another super-procedure and so on. Knowledge, therefore, in both the Piagetian and Logo sense is hierarchial and modularizable.

In Logo a child's interaction with the "turtle" becomes a 'concrete' extention of the child's own thought processes, something he can manipulate, receive feedback and reflect upon. In addition, he practices working with systematic procedures. These procedures are named, stored, retrieved and used as building blocks. Developing procedures in this way provides the foundation for the understanding of structured programming, the proper way of developing a computer program. In this process they also take on a 'concrete' character. This ability to 'concretize' the abstract can have real relevance when young children are working through developmental concepts as spatial orientation, sequencing, reversibility, estimating and patterning.

DESCRIPTION OF TEACHER POPULATION

A total of 90 teachers were enrolled in the in-service program which was carried out at the Computation Center, Ben-Gurion University of the Negev, Beersheva, Israel. Beersheva is a city of 120,000 population and lies 70 km south of Jerusalem and 100km southeast of Tel-Aviv. It is the capital of the south and is called the "Gateway to the Negev". Beersheva is primarily a 'workers' city which was originally settled in 1948 by immigrants from North African countries. It supports a large chemical industry. Teachers participating in the program were chosen by the Ministry of Education as being representative of teachers teaching in development towns. The decision to enroll teachers from these areas was based on social equity issues. It was felt that if these teachers could by given computer literacy skills, these skills could possibly produce a

significant change both in the method as well as the level of teaching in schools with a culturally disadvantaged population.

TRAINING PROGRAM

During the training sessions that we conducted at Ben-Gurion University, teachers were actively involved in discovering key Logo concepts. Modularity became a major focus. It was our intention to demonstrate to teachers that modularity leads not only to flexibility in thinking but also promotes divergent thinking, an essential component in creativity. At the end of the training program teachers were able to systematically use individual procedures as the building blocks of a large project which demanded the inclusion of several different sub-procedures.

Another 'powerful' idea that received considerable attention was the idea of hierarchial organization. We tried to show that this idea not only permeates the organization of knowledge but is also relevant to the understanding of social and political structures as well as biological systems. Furthermore, we felt it was extremely important to emphasize that a complex system can be understood by breaking it down into a series of comprehensible steps which makes it possible to use a top down approach as a general problem solving strategy.

'Debugging' as a means of improving logical problem-solving strategies was compared to the process of assimilating and accomodating new knowledge in an existing mental structure. The process of 'debugging' was shown to lead to new levels of understanding and strengthened our argument that 'debugging' is another of the 'powerful' ideas in Logo.

As an educational philosophy Logo makes the assumption that if learning is to be meaningful it must involve intellectual exploration and discovery learning. In the Logo experience the child develops strategies for purposeful exploration. These explorations eventually lead to a hierachy of well thought out procedures by which a problem can be solved. It is important to note that in Logo the emphasis is on the "process" by which strategies are chosen and acted upon and not on the answers themselves. In contrast to "rule" learning, the Logo philosophy stresses that the child should reflect on what he has done and try to relate the new knowledge to existing knowledge.

While Papert takes the rather utopian view that by simply placing children in a 'computer rich environment' children will be stimulated towards meaningful learning, we along with other researchers, recognized the inherent problems and limitations in such a method. Personal observations by Leron (1984) have shown that "most children fall into a 'hacking' kind of programming which does not seem to be conducive to learning deep and sophisticated ideas." Moreover, Martin and Heller (1984) cite several cases of teacher frustration using an entirely open-ended approach.

Taking into account the observations made by Leron as well as the negative responses to teacher workshops organized by Papert "purists", we designed our teaching to include directed activities as well as open-ended explorations. It was important for us to demonstrate to teachers that an open and reflective approach can promote more meaningful learning but that this approach does not necessitate an unstructured learning environment. We felt that intelligent interventions were needed at critical points of learning in order to avoid the danger of teachers remaining at the same level. By intervening we were able to provide teachers with the means to move to a higher level of understanding. In addition, we were very cognizant of the danger of teachers reacting to Logo as a graphics generator only and during the course teachers were asked to reflect on the differences between Logo and a graphics program. Very rarely were teachers given a set formula to reach a specific goal. This we felt would be directly opposed to the Logo philosophy and could lead to "rule" learning. In addition, teachers were encouraged to share with one another how they reached their objectives. In this way we were able to demonstrate that there are many different approaches and many possible answers to exploratory questions; that the learning goal is the process of developing problem solving strategies. Results obtained by students were seen as being the culmination of this process rather than as an end in themselves.

One of the major considerations in this program was to try and show teachers that Logo can be taught to very young children if the necessary support materials are provided. These support materials would serve as the scaffolding upon which actual Logo programming could take place. Therefore, an integral part of our training program involved teachers in the building of these materials. After each session, participants were asked to develop a set of games or activities which would illustrate the

Logo principle under consideration for that week. At the following session teachers brought their games and shared them with one another. This part of our program proved to be extremely successful. Teachers were enthusiastic since they saw the immediate relevance of their training and felt they were being given tools which fostered not only computer literacy but basic concept development as well. Areas of learning which had not seemed to them to be of particular importance took on new meaning. Developmental concepts such as sequencing, patterning, estimating and spatial orientation were systematically explored. The games and activities were subsequently compiled into a workbook.

SYLLABUS

1. Pre-programming Activities in Logo

2. Exploring the Logo Environment

3. Developing Geometric Concepts using Logo

4. Procedures and Sub-procedures in Logo

5. Logo - Not only a Graphics Generator

6. Modularity - A Key Concept in Logo

7. Using Variables in Logo

8. Hierarchial Organization as the Focus of Program Design in Logo

9. Single Keystroke Logo - a program for very young children

10. Logo Without a Computer - Logo games and activities for primary grade children

STRUCTURE OF MODEL

UNIT	PROGRAMMING SKILLS	COGNITIVE SKILLS	GAMES AND ACTIVITIES
1	Algorithms	Giving Insructions Spatial Orientation	1. Playing Robot 2. Yard games 3. Inside Floor games 4. "Direct Me"
2	LOGO Commands Syntax	Understanding Differences between Position in space heading Estimating	1. Big Track 2. Maze games 3. "Turtle Goes Home"
3	_____	Geometric Concepts Patterning	1. Transparancies 2. "Pessach Plate"
4	Procedures Sub-procedures Debugging Editing	Hierarchial Organization Sequencing Reversibility	"Each Animal finds his Home"
5	--------	----------	------------
6	Modularity in a Structured Procedural Language	1. Divergent thinking 2. Flexibility 3. Changing Relationships 4. Sequencing 5. Same elements in different constellations	Transparancy Games Tracing Games
7	Use of Variables- How Stored in Memory	Function of Variables- Influence on Size, Shape, etc.	-----------
8	Program Design	Parts and Pieces Induction vs. Deduction Analysis and Synthesis	Project work
9	Program Design	---------	"Instant" Program with Limited Commands

CONCLUSIONS

Participating teachers included those enrolled in a 200 hour general Computer Literacy course of which Logo was taught for 25 hours and those enrolled in a 60 hour Introductory Logo course specifically designed for kindergarten and primary grade teachers. The 200 hour course had an extremely heterogeneous population and resulted in a wide range of programming competencies. The course designed specifically for teachers in the primary grades had a much more homogenous population and teachers exhibited a higher level of understanding both in the acquisition of programming skills as well as in recognizing the relevance of Logo as a tool to promote cognitive development. At the completion of the course teachers enrolled in the Introductory Logo course were given an evaluation sheet in which they were asked to reflect on what they had learned during the course and its relevance to their teaching. Over 90% of the respondents reported that the course not only provided them with a basic understanding of computers but that it had forced them to rethink previous ideas on how to teach basic cognitive skills. Perhaps the most significant response was that all participants enrolled in this course submitted a petition to the Ministry of Education requesting that the course be extended for another year. Although, as yet, no formal evaluation of the course was carried out it is our definite impression that the major objectives of this course were achieved.

REFERENCES

1. Hall,G.E. "Issues related to the implementation of computers in classrooms: Where now?, NIE Conference on Issues Related to the Implementation of Computer Technology in Schools, Washington,DC February 19-20, 1981.

2. Laurendeau, M. and Pinard, A. The Development of the Concept of Space in the Child. New York, International Universities Press, 1970.

3. Leron, Uri "Some Problems in Children's Logo Learning" (Working Paper, University of Haifa, 1984)

4. Martin, C.D., Heller, R. "Teaching Logo to Teachers: A Look at the Issues"; IFIP Working Conferences Informatics and Teacher Training, July 16-20, 1984.

5. Piaget,J. The Child's Conception of Space, Routledge and Kegan Paul, 1956.

6. Papert, S. Mindstorms, Basic Books, New York, 1980.

COMPUTERS IN EDUCATION, K. Duncan and D. Harris (eds.)
Elsevier Science Publishers B.V. (North-Holland)
© IFIP, 1985

PHRASEBOOKS AND BOXES: MICROWORLDS FOR LANGUAGE

Mike Sharples

School of Social Sciences
University of Sussex
Brighton, BN1 9QN

Turtle geometry, a computer-based environment which children can control and explore, has been a successful tool for helping children to learn mathematical concepts and processes. This paper describes computer programs for language exploration that have the desirable features of turtle geometry. The programs allow a child to model linguistic processes and to pose and solve interesting problems. The paper outlines the programs and their application and concludes with an outline description of a system that combines text with animated pictures.

Background

To most people, language is a nebulous substance. In everyday speech and writing we create patterns of words without being aware of their form, nor the process of shaping them. Research on the development of writing abilities (Britton et al. 1975, Bereiter & Scardamalia 1982, Sharples, 1984) suggests that an awareness of thought and language can help a child to make the transition to mature reflective writing. A conscious attention to a new technique appears to be as important to a writer as the rehearsal of a new activity to a gymnast; it allows her to explore its applications and limitations before incorporating it into an existing routine.

Aspects of Logo: Turtle Geometry and Lists

In order to develop the techniques of writing a child needs tools to shape and examine language. Papert (1980) has coined the term 'microworld' for a computer-based environment that a child can use to explore a complex abstract domain such as mathematics, dynamics or language. The 'turtle geometry' subset of the Logo computer language (Papert, 1972) is an example of a microworld for mathematics. Gains in mathematical ability by children who used Logo have been reported by Milner (1973), Howe (1983) and Finlayson (1984).

Logo is more than turtle geometry; it is also a general purpose list processing language. At first sight list processing seems to be a handy tool for language. A list may represent, for example, a string of words - [THE CAT SAT ON THE MAT] - a dictionary - [[[CAT][LE CHAT]][[DOG] [LE CHIEN]]] - or a structured grammar - [[NOUN-PHRASE [DETERMINER [THE] NOUN [CAT]]].

Attempts to teach list processing to children and adults have not been successful. Learners who enjoyed and profited from turtle geometry were bored and confused by lists. Some of them abandoned powerful ideas such as recursion and fumbled with long chains of FIRSTs and BUTFIRSTs.

Others inserted global assignment statements inside procedures, rather than returning lists as results.

Lists are flexible, elegant, abstract structures and it is precisely these qualities that cause difficulties for a novice. The success of turtle geometry as a mathematical tool is not due to its computational elegance, but to more pragmatic features (figure 1). Turtle geometry rests uneasily on the Logo language. Turtle commands (FORWARD 100 RIGHT 90 etc.) rely on procedural side effects (instructions to move the turtle) and are more like Smalltalk 'messages' than the functions of Lisp, on which the rest of Logo is based.

Turtle commands, are, however, powerful aids to learning because they act as instructions for a 'notational drawing machine' (du Boulay et al. 1981) whose state is represented by the position and orientation of the turtle. A turtle command causes an observable change of state and the child can detect immediately whether his intentions have been carried out.

The floor turtle is both a captivating toy and a concrete representation of the abstract 'drawing machine'. A great advantage of turtle over cartesian geometry is that it is a natural extension of a child's body movements; its repertoire of moves is familiar to the child as are the meanings of the basic commands: LEFT, RIGHT, FORWARD, BACKWARD, HOME. Within minutes of beginning turtle geometry a child can enter the turtle world and investigate interesting mathematical issues. Lastly, turtle geometry is only the gateway to the rich area of procedural mathematics (Abelson & DiSessa, 1981).

List Processing

By contrast, list processing is a poor introduction to exploring language. The list processing primitives - FIRST,

Commands not functions.
State apparent.
Concrete representation.
Models familiar skills and concepts.
Easy entry.
Can be used to represent and solve
    interesting problems.
Extensible.

Figure 1: Features of Turtle Geometry

BUTFIRST, FPUT, LPUT etc. - are functions rather
than commands, so creating or altering a list
requires an assignment command:

MAKE "NEWLIST FPUT "CAT :OLDLIST

Studies by Finlayson (1983) indicate that children aged eleven find difficulty in understanding
the concepts of assignment and variables. Since
Logo does not, by default, indicate the state
of each list after assignment, the child may be
deeply confused about the workings of the notional 'list machine'. For example, novice
users, children and adults, commonly believe
that the assignment above adds CAT to the front
of both OLDLIST and NEWLIST.

The word 'list' evokes familiar images: 'shopping
list' and 'list of instructions' for example.
Although these are superficially similar to Logo
lists, containing a linear ordered sequence of
elements, the differences are fundamental. A
shopping list is only a partially ordered
structure - we frequently add or cross off items
at arbitrary points - and a list of instructions
is normally read-only. Railway trains, stacks
of plates and 'Chinese boxes' have all been
offered as accessible metaphors for lists, but
they are all cumbersome or misleading, particularly as representations of embedded lists.

To understand most of the interesting list
projects (such as building a conversation
program, an 'Adventure game', or a sentence
generator) described in books on Logo programming, a child needs to know recursion and its
termination, a concept that most novice programmers find extremely difficult. About the
only merit of the list as a tool for learning
is its flexibility as a means of representing
knowledge, but there is a wide gulf between
playing with words and learning the skills of
knowledge engineering.

The remainder of this paper outlines two data
structures, the Phrasebook and the Box, that
form a language microworld with the positive
features (shown in Figure 1) of turtle geometry.

All the procedures described below have been
implemented in Apple Logo. The aim is, empha-
tically, not to set the implementation as a
task to the child, but to offer the procedures
(TEACH, FIND, etc.) as primitives.

The Phrasebook

A Phrasebook is a direct analogy of a tourist's
foreign language phrasebook. As well as phrases
and their foreign equivalents, the book may
contain any information that a child might want
to look up: questions and their answers; words
and synonyms; mnemonics and Logo commands. The
same data structure serves as a dictionary,
thesaurus, look-up table and on-keypress Logo
interpreter.

Three commands are needed to operate the phrasebook: TEACH, FIND and FORGET. TEACH adds an
entry to the book (i.e. the child 'teaches' the
computer a phrase and its pair). It accepts
either words or lists as arguments (the user's
typing is underlined):

TEACH "CAT "CHAT

CAT   CHAT

TEACH [THE DOG] [LE CHIEN]

CAT   CHAT
THE DOG   LE CHIEN

By default, the state of the Phrasebook is
printed out after each new entry. FIND looks
up its argument in the Phrasebook and prints
the result (or results, if more than one
entry is matched):

FIND [THE DOG]

LE CHIEN

FIND [THE HORSE]

THE HORSE IS NOT IN THE PHRASEBOOK

The third command, FORGET, deletes an entry:

FORGET [CAT]

DOG   LE CHIEN

Even in this elementary form, the phrasebook
provides an introduction to references aids and
to the techniques of table loop-up and pattern-
matching. For example, the child might be
given a core dictionary or thesaurus that she
can extend:

```
FIND "SAD
```

UNHAPPY, MOROSE, MELANCHOLY, DEPRESSING,
UNFORTUNATE

```
FIND "WILD
```

WILD IS NOT IN THE PHRASEBOOK

```
TEACH "WILD [UNTAMED, SAVAGE, UNRULY,
BOISTEROUS]
```

With the additional commands READLIST and FOR-
EVER (primitives in some versions of Logo;
easily written in others) a child can produce
quizzes or 'conversations':

```
TEACH [WHAT IS THE CAPITAL OF FRANCE] "PARIS
TEACH [HELLO] [HI THERE]
FOREVER [FIND READLIST]
HELLO
```

HI THERE

WHAT IS THE CAPITAL OF FRANCE

PARIS

'Wild cards' for pattern matching are simple,
but important, extensions to the Phrasebook. A
single question mark - ? - matches any single
word; a double question mark - ?? - matches a
series of words; a question mark followed by one
or more letters - ?X for example - matches a
single word and assigns it to a variable (in
this case to X); two question marks followed
by one or more letters - ??PHRASE for example
- matches and assigns a series of words. The
child can now create a more general-purpose quiz,
or a simple 'Eliza' (Weizenbaum 1976) conversation:

```
TEACH [?? MY ?X HURTS ??][YOUR ?X LOOKS
    VERY PAINFUL]
TEACH [MY ?X LIKES ??Y][TELL YOUR ?X TO
    STOP ??Y AND TAKE UP JOGGING INSTEAD]
FOREVER [FIND READLIST]
DOCTOR, MY KNEE HURTS
```

YOUR KNEE LOOKS VERY PAINFUL

MY CAT LIKES PROGRAMMING COMPUTERS

TELL YOUR CAT TO STOP PROGRAMMING COMPUTERS
    AND TAKE UP JOGGING INSTEAD

A further extension to the phrasebook turns it
into a one-keypress Logo. If a phrase contains
Logo commands, then FIND executes the commands
as well as printing them (the READCHARACTER)
primitive returns a single keypress as a word):

```
TEACH "F [FORWARD 100]
TEACH "R [RIGHT 90]
FOREVER [FIND READCHARACTER]
```

FORWARD 100	The child has pressed the F key and the turtle moves forward
RIGHT 90	The child has pressed the R key and the turtle turns

The Box

The Box is simply a data structure equivalent
to a physical box, labelled with a single word
name and holding an assortment of paper slips,
each bearing a string of one or more words.
Any of these words may be the names of other
boxes and, together, the set of boxes can
represent, for example, a taxonomy (Figure 2)
or a set of grammar rules (Figure 3).

The command PUT adds a new list of words to the
box:

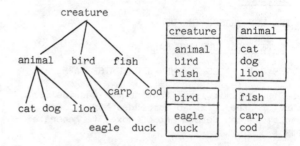

Figure 2: Box representation of a taxonomy.

```
nounphrase → article noun/article adjective noun
article → a/the
noun → cat/dog
adjective → friendly/hairy
```

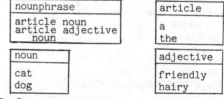

Figure 3: Box representation of grammar rules.

```
PUT "CAT "NOUN
```

NOUN

CAT

```
PUT "DOG "NOUN
```

NOUN

CAT
DOG

```
PUT [THE NOUN] "NOUNPHRASE
```

NOUNPHRASE

THE NOUN

CREATE scans the 'word pattern' given as its argument and replaces every box name by a word list taken, at random, out of the box. The scanning is repeated until no box name remains:

CREATE [NOUNPHRASE CHASES NOUNPHRASE]

THE CAT CHASES THE DOG

CREATE [NOUNPHRASE CHASES NOUNPHRASE]

THE DOG CHASES THE DOG

REMOVE deletes a box and its contents. As with the Phrasebook we can write a controlling FOREVER command:

PUT "HEN "NOUN
PUT [NOUNPHRASE CHASES NOUNPHRASE] "SENTENCE
FOREVER [CREATE READLIST]
SENTENCE

THE HEN CHASES THE DOG

SENTENCE AROUND THE FARM

THE CAT CHASES THE HEN AROUND THE FARM

There is no limit (save that of the machine's memory) to the levels of embedded boxes. For example, we can form a set of boxes to generate poems:

PUT [LINE1 & LINE2 & LINE3] "HAIKU
    <an ampersand is interpreted as a
    'newline' character>
PUT [ADJECTIVE ADJECTIVE NOUN VERB] "LINE1
PUT [ADJECTIVE NOUN VERB CONJUNCTION] "LINE2
PUT [VERB A ADJECTIVE ADJECTIVE NOUN] "LINE3

Given suitable contents for the NOUN, VERB, ADJECTIVE and CONJUNCTION boxes a call of CREATE [HAIKU] might produce the following:

HUNGRY LIFELESS BIRD FALLS
WHITE ROCK SINGS THEN
OPENS A STILL FRAGILE PETAL.

The poems may not always be grammatically correct, but children above the age of 8 or 9 are well able to judge the grammaticality of text. When they see that words do not tumble automatically into sentences and that there are many levels of correctness - syntactic order, tense and number agreement, meaning - then 'bugs' in language can be a source of inspiration and understanding.

Many other patterns of language - other forms of poetry, sentence forms, synonyms and antonyms, the ordering of adjectives - can be investigated with just the elementary forms of PUT and CREATE, but extensions can increase their scope. One is to specify affixes as additions to box names, for example:

PUT [NOUN + S] "PLURALNOUN

The affix is appended to the word generated from

'noun'. Another extension is to add a set of 'meanings' to each box entry, which define its semantic features, for example:

PUT "SNOWBALL "NOUN [INANIMATE AIR MOVING]

CREATE generates words as before, but picks those with the greatest overlap of meaning. A third improvement is to generate 'interactive text' (Sharples 1983) whereby the reader must complete the word pattern.

Features of the Box and Phrasebook Microworld

Phrases and boxes have most of the qualities of turtle geometry. They are operated by commands, not functions, which can display the state after each change and the child can be given familiar concrete representations of the data structures. We have used plastic components boxes to represent the Boxes microworld. The child labels the boxes and, for each PUT command, writes its input on a slip of paper and drops it into the appropriate box. To simulate the CREATE command, the child writes down the word pattern and then draws out, blind, a slip of paper for each box name in the pattern. For the phrasebook microworld, the child can keep record in a two columned notebook. The processes involved are both useful and generalisable. They are a training in the use of reference aids and in pattern recognition. Boxes are not restricted to holding English words, they could form a grammar to generate foreign phrases, mathematical expressions, or computer programs.

However worthy, a program should also capture a child's imagination and lead him to pose and solve interesting problems. Two fifteen year old boys worked with an early version of the Boxes microworld (Sharples 1978). The plan was to generate words at random and then add more and more constraints to the program until it produced only 'sensible' poems. The boys filled a small cardboard box with slips of paper, with a single word written on each slip and then drew out the words at random. They then repeated the process on the computer and at the end of the session they suggested improvements.

This led them to sort the words into part of speech boxes and then to produce 'part of speech patterns' for the CREATE procedure. Still dissatisfied with the results, they suggested that not only should the parts of speech be in the right order, but also 'the poems should make sense'. The final set of Logo procedures matched the words according to meaning lists and an example poem is shown below:

Dry Path

Lonely moon fades subtly
In cold plains
Black clouds
Frost fades by wish

We feed slowly

Black path fades to red rocks
I feed

The boys attempted to carry out the process
using actual boxes, but when a box contains ten
or more words then it becomes tedious in the
extreme, a task far better left to the computer.
By the end of the project they were talking
fluently about sentence structure, grammatical
categories and word function.

Another trial of the Boxes microworld has been
in a school for the deaf. Deaf children miss
out on verbal language games and word play, so
the aim has been to offer them similar experiences
with written language. The Phrasebook has been
tested with adults (who wrote entries to perform
a 'barman' conversation) but not yet with children.

The two microworlds are combined in a recent
program called Movie Maker written in Apple
Sprite Logo. With Movie Maker the phrasebook
becomes a film script. The child adds an entry,
such as THE COW JUMPS OVER THE MOON and then
animates the scene by calling up and moving
pictures around the screen with the aid of a
joystick. To rerun a scene, the child types
FIND and then the entry. The next stage is to
make the scripts more general. Rather than
teaching the computer a series of similar scripts
- such as THE CAT RUNS TO THE DOG, THE DOG RUNS
TO THE CAT, THE CAT RUNS TO THE COW - a child
can group words into categories. She might,
for example, put 'cat', 'dog' and 'cow' into an
'animal' box. Then she need only teach the
program one example script, say THE CAT RUNS TO
THE COW. Thereafter it will recognise and animate
every sentence with the same syntax pattern:
THE COW RUNS TO THE CAT, THE DOG RUNS TO THE
COW etc.

Learning by teaching is a powerful and effective
strategy. The child needs a deep understanding
of a subject to communicate it, even to a
computer, and she can gain confidence from being
a purveyor rather than a consumer of knowledge.
But, for a young child to be a successful teacher,
she needs a domain that is familiar yet extensible, and a set of tools that allow her to
represent and build on her existing knowledge.
The Boxes and Phrasebook microworlds are attempts
to provide such an environment for language.

Implementation

The original Boxes microworld was written in
Edinburgh Logo and has since been revised and
reimplemented in Pascal for the Terak micro-

computer (an improved version of the Logo program,
with graphics and a screen editor for the boxes),
in POP2 for the Vax minicomputer in BBC Basic for
the BBC B microcomputer and in Apple Logo for
the Apple 11 microcomputer. The Movie Maker
program is written in Apple Sprite Logo for the
Apple 11 microcomputer.

Acknowledgements

The work described in this paper was carried
out at Edinburgh University, Department of
Artificial Intelligence. My thanks to Helen
Finlayson, Ken Johnson, Peter Ross and Jim Howe
for their comments and support and to the
Social Science Research Council for financial
assistance.

References

[1] Abelson, H. & diSessa, A., Turtle Geometry
(MIT Press, Cambridge, Mass., 1981).

[2] Bereiter, C., Scardamalia, M., From
Conversation to Composition: the Role
of Instruction in a Developmental Process,
in Glaser, R. (ed.), Advances in Instructional Psychology, Volume 2 (Lawrence
Erlbaum Associates, Hillsdale, N.J., 1982).

[3] Britton, J., Burgess, T., Martin, N.,
Mcleod, A., Rosen., The Development of
Writing Abilities (11-18), Schools Council
London (1975).

[4] Du Boulay, B., O'Shea, T., Monk, J., The
Black Box Inside the Glass Box: Presenting
Computing Concepts to Novices, I.J.M.M.S.,
14 (1981) 237-249.

[5] Finlayson, H., The Development of Mathematical Thinking Through Logo, Greater
Manchester Primary Contact, Special Issue
2, December 1983.

[6] Finlayson, H., The Transfer of Mathematical
Problem Solving Skills from Logo Experience.
Paper submitted to WCCE (1985).

[7] Howe, J.A.M., Learning Middle School
Mathematics through Logo Programming: an
Evaluation Programme, Paper presented at
the conference The Challenge of Changing,
Montreal, (1983).

[8] McDougall, A., Adams, T., Adams, P.,
Learning Logo on the Apple 11 (Prentice
Hall of Australia, 1982).

[9] Milner, S., The Effects of Computer Programming on Performance in Mathematics.
Paper presented at the American Educational
Research Association. ERIC Reports ED 076
391 (1973).

[10] Papert, S., Teaching Children to be
Mathematicians vs. Teaching Children about
Mathematics, Int. Journal Math. Educ. Sci.

Technol., 3, 249-262, (1972).

[11]   Papert, S., Mindstorms: Children, Computers
       and Powerful Ideas (Harvester Press,
       Brighton, 1980).

[12]   Sharples, M., Poetry from Logo, Working
       Paper No. 30, Department of Artificial
       Intelligence, University of Edinburgh,
       (1978).

[13]   Sharples, M., A Construction Kit for
       Language, Exploring English with Micro-
       computers, Chandler, D. (ed.), Council
       for Educational Technology, London (1983).

[14]   Sharples, M., Cognition, Computers and
       Creative Writing, Ph.D Thesis, University
       of Edinburgh (1984).

[15]   Weizenbaum, J., Computer Power and Human
       Reason: From Judgement to Calculation
       (Freeman, San Francisco, 1976).

Footnotes

[1]   My thanks to McDougall, Adams and Adams
      (1981) for the example.

COMPUTERS IN EDUCATION, K. Duncan and D. Harris (eds.)
Elsevier Science Publishers B.V. (North-Holland)
© IFIP, 1985

APPROACHES TO TEACHING LOGO PROGRAMMING

Anne McDougall

Faculty of Education, Monash University, Clayton, Victoria, 3168, Australia

A variety of approaches to teaching programming in the Logo language is becoming
evident. Teachers develop various methodologies based on their particular aims and
audiences, and on their models of how learning does or should take place in their
students.
In this paper three different approaches to teaching Logo which have been documented
in book form are described and compared. The existence of other approaches is noted.
Some research comparing outcomes from different approaches is mentioned, and attention
is drawn to the importance of recognising the emergence of different approaches to
teaching Logo, particularly when evaluative research is being planned.

INTRODUCTION

Since Logo has become widely available on microcomputers, many Logo books and teaching resource
materials are appearing. While some of these
use Logo as a tool to explore other curriculum
areas such as mathematics (1,2), most have been
designed to teach the concepts and skills of
programming itself in the Logo language. It is
this latter area with which this paper is
concerned. I shall argue that already a considerable variety in approaches and strategies for
teaching (or encouraging learning of) Logo
programming is evident. No doubt more will
appear as more teachers develop experience with
the language.

A teacher develops a distinctive methodology for
many reasons. These include particular curricular
aims, different student audiences and the
teacher's own model of the ways in which learning
does or should take place in his or her students.
Three such teaching approaches which I have
observed, and perceive to be different from one
another, are described below. In each case I
shall outline the techniques used, referring to
published materials illustrating the approach
more fully. I shall then compare these approaches.
The following are used as bases for comparison:
the order in which students encounter parts of
the language; the extent to which students using
the approach work toward specific goals; and the
amount of teacher intervention and of student
autonomy implied by the approach, in initiating
activities and in subsequent work.

In outlining teaching approaches in a paper this
size I am forced to simplify somewhat. I shall
concentrate on features which are distinctive to
each particular approach, and endeavour in doing
so not to misrepresent the teachers and authors
to whom I refer.

Inevitably there are differences between a teaching method as practised with students and the
documentation of this method in a book. I believe

the argument of this paper to be valid despite
such differences.

A SYNTHETIC APPROACH

The first approach considered is a synthetic or
bottom-up approach, used in the earliest Logo
teaching (3). Variations of this approach are
evident in many Logo books (see for example
(4-9)). The approach is exemplified in
Australia in the work of Wills (10) and in her
book, Doodle Design Debug (11). In this
approach the individual turtle commands,
FORWARD, BACK, LEFT and RIGHT, are introduced
first, usually in the context of controlling a
robot turtle. Students explore and practise
using these and other primitive commands for
navigational and other turtle driving projects.
Wills refers to this as Doodling. Then students
begin to plan outcomes for their turtle drawings,
moving into the Design phase of their Logo
learning. This usually involves using groups
of primitive commands, and leads into the
building of procedures and subprocedures which
can be combined, built on and modified in the
Debug phase. Wills argues that in reality the
phases merge one into another, and their order
is not preordained inasmuch as a student might
slip into doodling or exploration at any stage
in a project (12). Nevertheless this synthetic
approach, combining and building onto mastered
primitive commands and concepts, is a clearly
established methodology for teaching and
learning Logo.

What assumptions about learners and learning
are implied by this approach? There is an
emphasis on not attempting too much at first,
and on becoming confident with concepts at a
very concrete level before attempting more
abstract material. These techniques are
particularly suitable for young, naive or
apprehensive learners.

In the very early stages the activities here
are teacher initiated, but the method aims to

give students confidence so that quite soon they should be able to explore more independently with little teacher intervention, until their planned projects require programming techniques or commands beyond their present level.

The approach is goal oriented, in that it assumes students are motivated to achieve particular planned ends as they program the turtle, though these ends might be various: navigational goals, designs or drawings for example. There is now good evidence that this assumption is justified for many students (see for example (13)).

This approach is not prescriptive, in that students are allowed to develop their own ways of grouping the primitives. The approach is thus designed to suit students of a variety of learning styles and preferences, and there is evidence that it achieves this (see for example (14)).

AN ANALYTIC APPROACH

An analytic or top-down approach has been advocated and used for teaching programming in other languages (see for example (15,16)). Here complete procedures are presented to the learner, to be read, typed into the computer and used, even if they are only partly understood at the time. The primitives and concepts of the language are encountered in the context of working procedures.

This approach was first used with Logo in work based at the University of Edinburgh (17). The influence of Howe is acknowledged and this method is used in the book Learning Logo, versions of which have been written for the Logo implementations on several microcomputers (18-21).

> This book is written in such a way
> that at times you might be typing into
> the computer commands that you only
> partly understand. It is possible to
> use Logo procedures without completely
> understanding their details. In fact
> experimenting with these pre-written
> procedures is a good way of learning
> how they work. (22)

After the usual preliminaries about setting up the system and loading the Logo language, the learner is presented with detailed instructions on how to type and use his or her first Logo commands, the complete procedure (23):

```
TO SQ
REPEAT 4 [FD 50 LT 90]
END
```

The procedures presented are carefully chosen and deliberately ordered to illustrate particular concepts, increasing in complexity as the learner progresses. By reading, using, modifying and extending these procedures the learner is to develop his or her own understanding and knowledge of the language and of the programming concepts

embodied therein. The learning model assumed here has been described as bearing some similarity to that occurring in natural language acquisition (24), and thus is seen as being compatible with the learning model advocated by Papert (25).

This approach differs from the synthetic one in that, to some extent, it "throws the learner in at the deep end" (see the review by Wills (26)). However it shares with the synthetic approach the attributes of being goal oriented, and of using teacher initiated projects at the outset while encouraging student exploration and independence as skills and understanding develop.

The analytic approach might be seen as more prescriptive than the synthetic one, in that in its "pure" form it deliberately shows procedures written with what are regarded as "good" programming techniques or style. Howe reports the development of a "style conscious" stage in his student programmers. "Correct Logo programming style . . . seems to be mostly derived from the worksheets which explicitly recommend particular programming, debugging and editing methods". (27) Logo itself is designed to encourage use of modularity and other good programming techniques, and this approach might almost be expected to preclude students writing any but well structured programs, by never showing inefficient or poorly structured examples. However Howe shows that this is by no means a certain outcome (28) and more research using this method is needed before any real evaluation can be made.

While the top-down teaching approach is used almost exclusively in the parts of the Learning Logo books where the language and programming concepts are being shown, a variety of planning styles emerge in the applications projects later in the books. These projects are presented as they were developed (and are generally shown without the "polishing" that would produce exemplar code). This is a result of the authors' (teachers') view that a top-down approach to teaching the language itself need not be tied subsequently only to a top-down style of planning and project design. Thus, as examples, top-down design is evident in multiple turtle games projects (29); a bottom-up highly exploratory development is used in some drawing projects (30) and in writing poetry generating procedures (31); and a middle-out, almost cyclic development is used in an interactive data base project (32).

TURTLE HUMMING

The next approach to be considered is "turtle humming", devised by Nevile and Dowling (33) and fully documented in their book, Let's Talk Turtle (34). The hums of A.A. Milne's Winnie-the-Pooh were fragments of melody which "came suddenly into his head". Similarly a turtle hum is a fragment of turtle path.

Its origins lie with the computer user. As a result of a user entering a message such as FD 25 RT 37 FD 26 LT 74, the screen Turtle sets off on what is seen by the user as a trip but to the Turtle is a hum. The 'trip' creates a visual display which may be a recognisable shape, a fancy squiggle, or merely a line. ... Hums can be successfully called without careful planning and without any understanding of the likely outcome in visual form. All that is needed is the simplest vocabulary (RT, LT, and FD), and the most elementary keyboard skills. ...Once a hum has been called, it is very easy to repeat it with the screen split so that the hum-call being copied can still be seen while it is being re-typed. (35)

Once the learner is familiar with the primitive commands and the entering of hum-calls, these are used to explore concepts such as similarity, reflection, repetition, rotation and reversal. The musical analogy continues.

The Turtle's hum is closely allied to other musical forms. Full-scale musical works are frequently developed from simple melodies. These melodies may be found throughout a piece of music in a range of recognisable forms - the melody may have changed key, speed, or been inverted or contorted, and yet still be the cohesive element throughout the musical work. The visual form of the hum will vary with each change in the hum, and therefore with each hum-call. The benefit here is that a hum which has been called without any particular purpose can be varied bit by bit and the results can suggest techniques for further change.

The hum lends itself easily to the teaching of the concepts of rotation and reflection. Just as a hum-call can be repeated by simply re-typing what is still written on the screen, the hum-call can be repeated with an extra turn first and, if this is done several times, the visual display will be rotated about the starting point. Rotation is "an extra bit" before the hum-call. Reflection is just changing all lefts for rights and all rights for lefts. This is easy for even a young child. (36)

Nevile argues that turtle humming does not teach programming as such (37), and perhaps in a formal sense this is so. However children using this approach are using the computer as a tool for independent exploration and experimentation, and as such are learning Logo in a very real sense.

Turtle humming, like the synthetic approach, is a bottom-up method, beginning with very concrete,

low level, single-command activities, and building onto these. However there is a major contrast between these two bottom-up methods. While in the synthetic approach the student directs the turtle with particular navigational, design or drawing goals in mind, that is not the case in turtle humming. In most turtle humming work the learner need have no idea or plan for the outcome to be produced by the turtle commands being entered. "There are no 'wrong' hum-calls, so the children cannot experience failure". (38) Advocates of more goal oriented approaches would argue that students pay for this avoidance of "failure" by never reaching the Design and Debug phases described earlier. It will be interesting to see how this is handled in the subsequent books promised in the turtle humming series (39).

Turtle humming probably has learners working independently sooner than is the case with the two methods described previously, since exploration can begin with so little pre-requisite knowledge. Nevile clearly believes that teacher intervention in Logo learning should be relatively limited.

When children are let free to control the Turtle, even in the most restrictive way, they cannot produce pictures which do not in some way reflect themselves. Tidy minds make tidy pictures, scatty minds make scatty pictures, inability to conserve length makes funny images, etc. The children see direct representations of their actions, and the teachers see them too. The mind-mirroring of the computer is an aid to understanding at both levels: the teachers understanding the children and the children understanding their work. If the children were told in advance to draw a square, and taught how to do it, what learning could really take place at either level?

I suggest that one cannot be empowered and directed at once. (40)

DISCUSSION

Which then is the best approach to Logo teaching for a particular teacher to use? The answer, as is so often the case in education, is - it depends. In situations where students' confidence, motivation and variety of learning styles are important, teachers might use techniques from the synthetic approach. If good programming style and efficiency of learning are desirable, then the analytic approach might be valuable. For development of an investigative style of working, the turtle humming approach has much to offer. And quite apart from criteria such as these, which are determined by the nature of the learners or the educational aims in a given situation, teachers will choose or devise teaching methods which match their models of learning processes in their students, an issue beyond the scope of this paper.

Some research studies using the synthetic and
analytic approaches were mentioned earlier.
However there is not yet sufficient research done
to make a full evaluative comparison of the
different Logo teaching approaches described in
this paper. To this end a current study comparing
some outcomes for students learning Logo with
the synthetic approach and others using turtle
humming is of interest(41).

Clearly the three methodologies considered here
are not the only possible approaches to teaching
and learning Logo. A fourth quite different one
has been devised by Richardson (42). In his
approach, which I refer to as "Logo on the Run",
there is a strong emphasis on student autonomy;
the teacher is called on to prepare, "on the
run", procedures required by the learner to
carry out particular activities. The learner
effectively specifies his or her programming
requirements (when they are beyond his or her
own programming skills) to the teacher who writes
to those specifications. The teacher aims to
exploit learning opportunities which may arise
through the learner's explorations or suggestions.
To use this approach with any success, a teacher
must be a very competent and quick Logo
programmer. No doubt many more and different
methodologies are being devised as Logo is used
more widely, by different teachers in different
situations.

If it is not yet possible to make evaluative
comparisons between the approaches described,
what then is the value of discussing them? An
awareness of the very existence of different
teaching and learning approaches, and the
likelihood that they could produce differences
in student outcomes, is vital now as research
studies are being designed in attempts to evaluate
Logo itself and the claims made by its advocates.
Let me use an extreme example to make the point.
To teach children Logo using the turtle humming
approach in an investigation of children's
development of top-down planning skills would be
absurd. And yet relatively few studies in which
children are "taught Logo" report details of the
way in which this was done or the materials or
resources used. Logo, like most other things,
can be taught and learned in different ways, and
research in which outcomes from Logo learning
are being studied must take account of these
differences if it is to have any meaning at all.

REFERENCES:

(1) Abelson, H. and di Sessa, A., Turtle
    Geometry (The MIT Press, Cambridge, 1981).

(2) Thornburg, D., Discovering Apple Logo
    (Addison-Wesley, Reading, Mass., 1983).

(3) Papert, S., Watt, D., di Sessa, A. and
    Weir, S., Final Report of the Brookline
    Logo Project, Part II: Project Summary and
    Data Analysis, Logo Memo 53, Massachusetts
    Institute of Technology (1979).

(4) Bearden, D., Martin, K. and Muller, J.,
    The Turtle's Sourcebook (Reston, Reston,
    Va., 1983).

(5) Bitter, G. and Watson, N., Apple Logo
    Primer (Reston, Reston, Va., 1983).

(6) Brunett, J.D., Logo: An Introduction
    (Creative Computing Press, Morris Plains,
    N.J., 1982).

(7) Conlan, J. and Inman, D., Sprites, a Turtle
    and TI Logo (Reston, Reston, Va., 1984).

(8) M.E.C.C., Apple Logo in the Classroom
    (Minnesota Educational Computing Consortium,
    St. Paul, 1983).

(9) Watt, D., Learning With Logo (McGraw-Hill,
    New York, 1983).

(10) Wills, S., Computers in Tasmanian Schools,
     The Australian Computer Bulletin (August,
     1980), 22-28.

(11) Wills, S., Doodle Design Debug (forth-
     coming).

(12) Wills, S., Doodle, Design, Debug, in
     Salvas, A. (ed.), Computing and Education -
     1984 and Beyond (Computer Education Group
     of Victoria, Melbourne, 1984).

(13) Papert, S. et al., op. cit.

(14) Watt, D., Final Report of the Brookline
     Logo Project, Part III: Profiles of
     Individual Students' Work, Logo Memo 54,
     Massachusetts Institute of Technology
     (1979).

(15) Dwyer, T. and Critchfield, M., BASIC and
     the Personal Computer (Addison-Wesley,
     Reading, Mass., 1978).

(16) McDougall, A., Teaching Computer
     Programming, in Rogerson, A. (ed.),
     Mathematics: Myths and Realities
     (Mathematical Association of Victoria,
     Melbourne, 1981).

(17) Howe, J., Developmental Stages in Learning
     to Program, Research Paper No.119,
     Department of Artificial Intelligence,
     University of Edinburgh (1978).

(18) McDougall, A., Adams, T. and Adams, P.,
     Learning Logo on the Apple II (Prentice-
     Hall, Sydney, 1982).

(19) Adams, T., Adams, P. and McDougall, A., Learning Logo on the TRS-80 Color Computer (Prentice-Hall, Sydney, 1984).

(20) McDougall, A., Adams, T. and Adams, P., Learning Logo on the Commodore 64 (Pitman, Melbourne, 1984).

(21) Squires, D., McDougall, A., Adams, T. and Adams, P., Learning Logo on the RML 480Z (forthcoming).

(22) McDougall A. et al., Learning Logo on the Apple II, xiii.

(23) Ibid., 9.

(24) Richardson, J., Turtle Talk, COM-3 33 (1983) 21.

(25) Papert, S., Mindstorms: Children, Computers and Powerful Ideas (Harvester, Brighton, 1980).

(26) Wills, S., Turtle Talk, COM-3 33 (1983) 19-21.

(27) Howe, J., op. cit., 6.

(28) Ibid., 7.

(29) Adams, T. et al., op. cit., ch.8.

(30) McDougall, A. et al., Learning Logo on the Apple II, ch.3.

(31) Ibid., ch.8.

(32) McDougall, A. et al., Learning Logo on the Commodore 64, Appendix D.

(33) Nevile, L., Of Crab Canons and Turtle Hums: A Conceptual Approach to the Teaching of the Logo Language, COM-3 33 (1983) 25-27.

(34) Nevile, L. and Dowling, C., Let's Talk Turtle: Teachers' and Parents' Edition (Prentice-Hall, Sydney, 1983).

(35) Nevile, L., Of Crab Canons and Turtle Hums, 26.

(36) Ibid., 27.

(37) Nevile, L. and Dowling, C., Let's Talk Turtle, iv.

(38) Ibid.

(39) Nevile, L. and Dowling, C., How Turtles Talk (Prentice-Hall, Sydney, in press).

(40) Nevile, L., Turtle Talk, COM-3 10:2 (1984) 17-19.

(41) Malone, T., Master of Educational Studies Project, Faculty of Education, Monash University (forthcoming).

(42) Richardson, J., Master of Educational Studies Project, Faculty of Education, Monash University (1985).

COMPUTERS IN EDUCATION, K. Duncan and D. Harris (eds.)
Elsevier Science Publishers B.V. (North-Holland)
© IFIP, 1985

TEACHING AND USING LOGO IN THE EDUCATION OF 5-12 YEAR OLD CHILDREN

Patricia F. Campbell, June L. Wright, and Shirley S. Schwartz

Department of Curriculum and Instruction
University of Maryland
College Park, MD   20742

This tutorial will present a suggested scope and sequence for teaching Logo to
5-12 year old children which is based upon cognitive development research as well
as research regarding children's acquisition of Logo. In addition to a
demonstration of materials used in classrooms for Logo instruction, this tutorial
will offer participants the opportunity to review microcomputer activities designed
to promote identified Logo programming concepts. Discussion will highlight
professional decision-making regarding classroom management, the monitoring of
instruction, the infusion of Logo in other content areas, and teaching strategies
to encourage student reflection upon programming decisions. Participants will
receive a collection of printed materials.

With the advent of the microcomputer, computer literacy and programming have become increasingly prominent in elementary and middle schools. Recent research reports have argued that learning to program a computer will promote cognitive benefits such as facility with problem-solving heuristics and experience with procedural thinking tasks. The Logo language is being used with increasing frequency in schools. Advocates cite Logo as a programming language which may promote programming skills applicable for other high-level languages while being accessible by young children. The purpose of this tutorial is to consider a scope and sequence for teaching Logo to 5-12 year old children which is based upon current research.

Initially the tutorial will focus on the potential of Logo for classroom use, managing its impact on the classroom environment, and implementing pre-computer activities. This section will include a description of sample activities and a demonstration of instructional materials.

Subsequently, participants will be introduced to a sequence for Logo language instruction which emphasizes hands-on experiences. Time will be provided for each participant to explore instructional activities using Instant Logo as well as transitional activities to Turtle Graphics. Participants will preview microcomputer activities designed to facilitate understanding of Logo programming concepts such as use of the editor, procedural style, use of variables, and applications of words and lists. Discussion will highlight the rationale supporting the design of these activities, the possible modifications which a teacher may consider in order to make selected activities more appropriate for older or younger children, and teaching strategies to encourage students to critically reflect upon and modify their programming projects. In addition, the tutorial will demonstrate the potential of curriculum enrichment via Sprites and robots.

A collection of printed materials including sample lesson plans, guidelines for integrating Logo within the existing elementary school content areas (e.g., social studies, language arts), suggested bibliographic references, and commercial sources will be distributed to participants.

COMPUTERS IN EDUCATION, K. Duncan and D. Harris (eds.)
Elsevier Science Publishers B.V. (North-Holland)
©IFIP, 1985

LOGO IN THE UNITED STATES

Tom Lough, Dennis O. Harper, Joyce Tobias,
David Thornburg and Steve Louie

International Council for Computers in Education,
National Logo Exchange, and University of California, Santa Barbara

This panel will focus on four aspects of Logo in the United States.
1. Teacher Training--Discussion of efforts throughout the United States to train both preservice and inservice teachers to use the Logo language.
2. Logo in the Schools--Discussion of ways Logo is being implemented in the classrooms of the United States.
3. Logo in the Home--Discussion of ways Logo is being used and learned in the homes of the United States.
4. Logo in Research--Results of Logo research projects and a needs assessment of Logo research.

Tom Lough, Chair
National Logo Exchange
Charlottesville, Virginia

Dennis O. Harper
University of California
Santa Barbara, California

In general, there is a very low level of Logo knowledge among teachers in the United States. Reasons for this include lack of interest, low level or training of Logo instructors, reluctance of teacher education centers to integrate Logo into their curricula, and lack of time required to establish Logo cultures. However, workshops, college courses, books, conferences and consultants are being used to educate teachers throughout the nation. Discussed will be the results of a national survey report on these efforts and possible directions for teacher education in the use of Logo.

Joyce Tobias
Public Schools of Brookline, MA
  and Boston University

Computer use in the classrooms of the United States has increased and with it the use of Logo, both as a philosophy and as a programming language. Based on results from a survey that was distributed to members of National Logo Exchange and participants of the Logo '84 conference, a discussion of how Logo is being implemented in the classrooom will be presented. It will include the grades where Logo is being taught, how it is integrated into the curriculum, the versions of Logo being used, and the books that have been most helpful. A summary of areas of Logo in which respondents would like help will also be included. The presentation will conclude with information on the inclusion of Logo in the first computer competency assessment conducted by the National Assessment of Educational Progress.

David Thornburg
Stanford University and Koala Technologies

Millions of computers are finding their way into homes in the United States. Logo can be a valuable asset to students at home as well as in the schools. Dr. Thornburg will discuss activities and Logo projects aimed at home use.

Steve Louie
Arizona Learning Center
Tucson, Arizona

Issues concerning Logo research, their interpretation and application in classroom practice are discussed. Curriculum objectives, development of higher order thinking skills, promotion of critical thinking, and issues related to teacher-training and Logo are emphasized in this presentation. Teachers (K-12), researchers, inservice education coordinators, and computer coordinators will find this presentation essential in school planning and classroom implementation.

A synopsis of research findings, resource materials and samples of research designs will be provided to participants. Trends in the Logo language, the incorporation of Logo words and lists as data bases for future robotics and classroom applications, and the use of Logo robotics with the handicapped will be touched upon.

COMPUTERS IN EDUCATION, K. Duncan and D. Harris (eds.)
Elsevier Science Publishers B.V. (North-Holland)
© IFIP, 1985

LOGO ON THE SIX CONTINENTS: ISSUES AND USES--1

Tom Lough, Hillel Weintraub, Hiroyoshi Goto
Richard Noss and Isidore Ngosso Nkakey

International Council for Computers in Education,
National Logo Exchange and University of California

Panelists will discuss how Logo is begin taught and used in Asia, Europe and Africa. Issues facing countries on these continents will also be discussed.

Tom Lough, Chair
National Logo Exchange
Charlottesville, Virginia

Asia
Hillel Weintraub
Doshisha International High School

Hiroyoshi Goto
Japan Logo Users' Group

After a general report on the use of Logo throughout Asia, the panelists will discuss the use of Logo in Japan. The Research Group of Logo Education in Japan is developing a standard and uniform Japanese Logo language. The group has been designing an ideal form (as to primitives, messages, grammar and features) of Japanese Logo. They are also developing epoch-making features of future Japanese Logo. Two possibilities under consideration are three dimensional graphics and file compatibility of other computer languages with Logo.

Members of the Research Group are proposing a new classification of subjects based on the stages of development of children's thinking ability and on some of the ideas of Logo such as interaction, environment and dynamics.

Realizing that most English Education in the Japanese schools is dissociated rather than syntonic, some experimental efforts are being made in the classroom and in seminars and training courses to develop teachers' awareness of the potential for using Logo to develop an engaging environment in which the English language can be used in a variety of ways.

A brief report on Dr. Yamanishi's work with autistic children using Logo will be given.

Europe
Richard Noss
University of London Institute of Education
London, England

Three issues relating to the implementation of Logo within UK and European schools will be discussed.

1. The relationship between the organization and curriculum of schools and the introduction of Logo within the specific education systems.
2. The role of teachers in extending the scope of the implementation of Logo within schools.
3. The elaboration of a suitable research perspective which will assist in the implementation of Logo within school curricula.

In the short term at least, the major tasks hinge around the integration of Logo into the school curriculum. This does not imply an uncritical acceptance of present curricular approaches into which Logo may be "inserted." On the contrary, the challenge is to incorporate Logo as a central facet of the curriculum--not merely to encourage schools to "do Logo," but rather to encourage a Logo-based approach to school learning. Such a perspective has repercussions for the focus of research, and in particular for a clarification and illumination of some of the claims made for the learning of Logo.

Africa
Isidore Ngosso Nkakey
Association des Professionale Africannes de
  l'Informatique
Cameroon, West Africa

A report on the uses of Logo in Africa will be given followed by a specific report on the science education project in the Cameroon and the Logo project in the Sudan.

COMPUTERS IN EDUCATION, K. Duncan and D. Harris (eds.)
Elsevier Science Publishers B.V. (North-Holland)
©IFIP, 1985

LOGO ON THE SIX CONTINENTS: ISSUES AND USES--II

Tom Lough, Anne McDougall,
Horacio C. Reggini and William Higginson

International Council for Computers in Education,
National Logo Exchange and University of California, Santa Barbara

Panelists will discuss how Logo is being taught and used in Australia, South America and North America. Issues facing countries on these continents will also be discussed.

Tom Lough, Chair
National Logo Exchange
Charlottesville, Virginia

Australia
Anne McDougall
Monash University
Clayton, Victoria

After early work in Tasmania, including development of the internationally used Tasman Turtle robot, Logo use has spread to all the states. A recent report of the Schools Commission's National Advisory Committee on Computing in Schools recommended support of Logo along with Pascal and BASIC for both student programming and software production. In Victoria, Logo is one of the recommended languages for the Year 12 Computer Science course, and a full implementation of Logo is one of the requirements for approval as a supplier of computer equipment to government schools in this state. Several Logo books have now been published in Australia, and research and development work at several universities and in many schools is producing a steady output of articles and reports appearing in computer education conference proceedings and journals.

South America
Horacio C. Reggini
Asociacion Amigos de Logo
Buenos Aires, Argentina

South American countries have a common root and similar characteristics. They have great natural resources and human potential, but they also share political instability and serious economical and social problems. Quite often, new technologies are rejected as they are considered as instruments alien to our own needs.

Nevertheless, South American countries have realized that not to take into account the changes produced by computers would mean an increasing gap in the economical and cultural orders. This assumption is especially valid in reference to future generations. For these reasons and because Logo implies a new computational and educational concept, it has won more and more advocates in the last years.

Logo is spread over the whole continent. The beginnings have been small in scale, but the offsprings are growing in a natural and progressive manner, so that they are smoothly assimilated by the social and cultural order. Now is the time to integrate all the efforts of isolated groups into stronger and financially supported plans. I will discuss the reasons why Logo has advanced as a social phenomenon within South America.

North America (Canada)
William Higginson
Queen's University at Kingston

The use of Logo in those parts of North America outside the United States has over the last three years followed the same general sorts of directions it has in the United States. There has been an uneven but widespread adoption of Logo at the elementary school often following the leadership of an enthusiastic teacher or computer coordinator. Secondary school use has been much more limited and almost always limited to math and science classes. There are indications that teachers need substantial and ongoing support if they are to realize the potential of the language as envisioned in Mindstorms. At the university level Logo has come to be an important part of many teacher education programs both inservice and preservice and has been the focus of attention in a large number of research studies examining the impact of technology on educational cognitive structures.

COMPUTERS IN EDUCATION, K. Duncan and D. Harris (eds.)
Elsevier Science Publishers B.V. (North-Holland)
© IFIP, 1985

LOGO AND THE WORLD OF EDUCATION

Tom Lough, Brian Harvey, Seymour Papert and Sylvia Weir

International Council for Computers in Education,
National Logo Exchange and University of California, Santa Barbara

Panelists will give their thoughts on the previous three panels and discuss what they see as Logo's place in the future of education throughout the world.

Tom Lough, Chair
National Logo Exchange
Charlottesville, Virginia

Brian Harvey
University of California
Berkeley, California

There has been some debate among Logoites about the relative importance of the learning environment and the intellectual content which is to be learned. I have a foot in both camps! I'm writing books which take a very intellectual approach to computer programming, emphasizing ideas like "evaluation" and "locality", but when I set up a computer center in a high school, most of my effort went into social issues like student self-government. I think this dichotomy is related to another issue, which is the broader social meaning of computer education. Why are we teaching programming, anyway? To whom should we be teaching it? Logo's designers have always understood the tremendous power of a strong metaphor. I think that many mistaken ideas in computer education have arisen out of the "computer literacy" metaphor, which has been completely disastrous for educational planning. In particular, I think that a computer is _not_ the first thing every child needs. Computer training is not the key to employability, nor to social power. The computer as tool (as word processor, for example) can be helpful to every child; the computer as object of study, though, seems to me more like drama or the school newspaper: something which is an outstanding educational experience for a minority of students.

Seymour Papert
Massachusetts Institute of Technology
Cambridge, Massachusetts

The ways computers are used in schools today are not even remotely related to the uses we can expect in the next decade. Higher density of computers, high levels of computer cultures among teachers and new understanding of the learning process will make possible very different uses.

I shall focus on some previews of the school of the future and on how educators today can prepare for tomorrow.

Sylvia Weir
Massachusetts Institute of Technology
Cambridge, Massachusetts

Developing Computational Environments for Teaching. I am concerned about communication and control in education, about restoring some control to teachers over the computer tools they use, and about exploiting the power of the technology to give both students and teachers control over the learning process. Computers can be assimilated into, and generate good educational practice, but good things don't happen automatically. They need careful nurturing. The development of many and diverse computer environments as a joint activity between educators and computer experts needs to be accompanied by ongoing teacher training and support, since it is no use talking about the wonders of Logo unless we find ways of bringing the teachers along with us.

Computational Environments that Match Individual Needs and Learning Styles. Some of the more interesting observations we have made over the past several years concern the wide range of styles of working shown by students in a Logo setting. Some of the academic failure that occurs in schools is as much induced by the inappropriate arrangements for learning provided in our institutions as by the lack of ability of the students. Different needs can be accommodated more easily using the versatile computer than by regular classroom tools.

Graphics

COMPUTERS IN EDUCATION, K. Duncan and D. Harris (eds.)
Elsevier Science Publishers B.V. (North-Holland)
© IFIP, 1985

637

A Comprehensive Computing System for Architectural Education

Ulrich Flemming, Omer Akin, Robert Woodbury

Department of Architecture, Carnegie-Mellon University
Pittsburgh, PA 15213, U.S.A.

A multi-year plan for the introduction of computing into the professional curriculum of the Department is outlined. The basic model of rational decision making is used to identify a series of projects for software and course development which can be independently funded and completed over a series of years. Together with the hardware specified, they constitute a comprehensive computing system for architecural education.

1. Introduction

Today, computers are used in architectural practice to execute repetitive routine tasks more efficiently, a use that is spreading rapidly, with the obvious goal of increasing productivity in architectural offices (and the less obvious goal of building a progressive public image for the firm). The design process itself, however, has remained essentially unchanged: neither is the computer used as a truly new *medium*, nor is the *nature* of design affected in any substantial way.

Similarly, the new technology has had very little impact on the way design is taught. To be sure, computer programs are occasionally used to back up support courses, for example, in energy analysis or design economics. Furthermore, computer-aided design is an area in which students can specialize, notably at institutions with ongoing research in the field [13]. But no school known to us has succeeded in integrating computers into its professional curriculum, especially the design studios. There seems indeed no need for this as long as the design process itself remains untouched by the new technology.

Traditionally, increased productivity has been the first goal when computers entered new fields. But once these tools were made available, they started to have a more profound impact; finite element analysis is a prime example from structural engineering. Based on these precedents as well as on prevailing trends within the field itself, similar developments have to be expected for architectural design. Such an evolving situation presents a formidable challenge to schools if they intend to prepare graduates for change and leadership in the profession. Architectural education, in North America at least, is based on hands-on experience (as exemplified by the studio system). If the new technology is to enter this system, appropriate educational software must be available, software that is carefully designed to demonstrate the possibilities of the medium and to make students familiar with the appropriate techniques and applications [1].

To a large extent, such software is not available at the present time. This paper describes a conceptual framework for the development of a comprehensive computing environment for architectural education. It also outlines the software and hardware components for a system scheduled to be implemented by the Departmant of Architecture at Carnegie-Mellon University over five years. This system certainly reflects the specific situation of the Department

and its long history of research in computer-aided architectural design. We believe, however, that the principles underlying our plans are of general interest; they will be stressed in the following sections.

2. Conceptual Framework

It appears highly desirable to develop educational software not as a collection of unrelated programs, but within a conceptual framework indicating how the programs relate logically to each other and to the overall design process. This section outlines such a framework and forms the basis for subsequent sections.

2.1. A Model for Design

Traditional design strategies aim at the generation of a single acceptable solution. They are constrained by the use of manual methods both for the creation of solutions and the prediction of their performance. Computer technology has made possible, for the first time, a more rapid and accurate evaluation of individual designs according to various criteria, including aesthetic ones, and this approach can be extended to the evaluation and comparison of design alternatives. Studies in which solutions to architectural design problems were explored in a systematic way [21] [24] [28] suggest that the design process can indeed benefit from a systematic exploration of alternatives. All of these studies are predicated, in one form or another, on the basic model of rational decision making, which consists of the following steps:

1 *Generation* of the alternatives to be considered.
2 *Prediction* of consequences for each alternative (or its analysis according to individual criteria).
3 *Evaluation* of each alternative, where the criteria are now considered simultaneously.
4 *Selection* of an alternative or alternatives.

This model is a cornerstone of our conceptual framework. It provides, first of all, a basis for assessing the role of existing computer programs and explains the logical relations between them (it is noteworthy that existing programs can typically be assigned to exactly one of the steps listed above). The model also helps in the evaluation of current trends and in the anticipation of future developments. Most importantly, it suggests an agenda for the development of educational software which will be outlined in the next chapter.

2.2. A Systems Environment

Users of today's computer systems must generally know a great deal about the computation environment if they are to use the system effectively. The concepts and commands needed to perform related tasks, such as editing and file manipulation, often differ widely from each other. This causes problems whenever primary attention should focus on the task at hand and not on technical issues related to the use of the machine. The programs that constitute a system for architectural education should be designed and be perceivable as parts of a single, unified environment with the following characteristics:

- Users should not have to assimilate much specialized knowledge about the system in order to use it effectively.
- There should be convenient ways for different parts of the system to communicate with each other.
- The communication should be at as high an organization level as is possible without becoming specific to particular applications.
- The interfaces should be based on a uniform syntax and allow students to switch easily from one program to another.

Software that is to be used in an educational context must have specific characteristics if it is to fulfill its purpose [23]:

- The underlying models and algorithms should be transparent; programs should be designed with this goal in mind, independent of the documentation accompanying them.
- Each program should be applicable to a sufficiently large class of applications. It should aim at the exploration or demonstration of aspects of architectural design, not at a demonstration of the tool itself.
- The results should have sufficient accuracy and power so that they do not distort the developing intuition of students.
- The input to any particular program should reflect a sufficiently high level of abstraction so that the use of the program is not unduly inhibited.
- The output from any program must be presented in an easily understood form.
- Carefully designed manuals and tutorials must be provided for each program.

The requirements listed above assure that the programs function as parts of a whole from both a *psychological* and *technical* point of view, whereas the model introduced in the previous section indicates the *logical* relations among these parts.

3. Theory and Software Development

The model of rational decision making is used in this chapter to identify a set of system capabilities, presented here as *projects*, which together form a comprehensive computing system for a professional architectural curriculum (a more detailed description can be found in [2]). It is important to note that the knowledge needed to implement each of these projects is available and does not require further research. But this is not to say that the general area to which some of these projects belong has been sufficiently explored. We also plan to contribute to further research in these areas, but this work is not included in the present plan.

3.1. Generation of Designs

Galle [16] classifies approaches toward the computer-assisted generation of floor plans in a way which reflects the model of rational decision-making. In a slightly augmented form, we use this classification to identify several areas of work dealing with the generation of design alternatives:

1. Automated evaluation of designs which are generated by traditional means
2. Interactive generation of designs using computer-assisted media
3. Stepwise interactive generation
4. Non-exhaustive generation of feasible solutions
5. Exhaustive generation (i.e. complete enumeration) of feasible solutions
6. Generation of (sub)optimal designs

The approaches are ordered according to the degree of automation involved. The first two recognize that large portions of the design process are not (yet) well-understood and extremely difficult to formalize and replicate through computer programs. Approach 1 therefore concentrates on the prediction of consequences; we deal with this approach in section 3.2. In approach 2, emphasis is placed on using the computer as a *medium* to develop and specify design alternatives; section 3.1.1 deals with this topic. We are also convinced that there exists a broad range of recurring, restricted design problems for which partial or complete automation, as implied by approaches 3, 4 and 5, becomes interesting from a theoretical and practical point of view; this topic is dealt with in sections 3.1.2 and 3.1.3.

3.1.1. Interactive Generation of Designs

Traditionally, designers create solutions by recording their ideas on some external medium. This process is informal and interactive: *informal* because the techniques used to generate and modify designs are not specified explicitly in advance; *interactive* because this process relies on an external medium to record the developing design. With the advent of computer modelling systems, designers are offered a new medium which is potentially interactive and powerful enough to replace, to a certain degree, traditional design media such as pencil and paper.

The user interface, so far, has had low priority in the design of modelling systems: the operations available to *describe* designs to the system have little resemblance to the ones used by designers to *generate* them. This is one of the reasons why computers have not yet assumed the role of a truly new medium in practice. But recent developments in other fields, such as office document preparation (Xerox Star, Apple Lisa), have demonstrated the power added to a system by a carefully designed interface [5]. Comparable developments for architectural design are presently under way in connection with a new generation of drafting systems offering users a broad range of facilities for the description and modification of drawings.

Work on the design of interfaces has been going on at the Department for some time [17] [29] and is closely related to investigations of the design process itself [3]. We plan to continue this work within the context of a drafting system and a solids modelling system.

Project A: Drafting System. We plan to acquire a commercially available drafting system and make it available for general use by students. The development costs for such systems are so high that a school can hardly afford to develop its own (this also means that the system adopted will define the *de facto* standard hardware and, to some extent, software environment of a school). Little is known about how designers use their media. A large group of students using an interactive drafting system as a design medium presents an excellent and much needed opportunity to study the interaction between designers and machines and to gain insights into the types of interactions that *should* be supported by such systems. We plan to observe the users of the system in a systematic way and to draw conclusions from our observations.

We believe that an integrated (or partially integrated) design environment must ultimately be based on a robust three-dimensional modelling system which is not restricted to a specific application domain. An analogy to a text editing program, such as EMACS, can be drawn. A text editor enables users to define, format and manipulate words regardless of the end purpose of the text. A three-dimensional modelling system can provide analogous capabilities for three dimensional solids.

The three-dimensional modeller VEGA is presently under development in the Department; it reflects a long history of work in geometric modelling [4] [10] [17] [29]. Several of the projects identified in this chapter can be implemented and related to each other as parts of this system. We will therefore return to VEGA on several occasions and describe planned extensions of the system. The following project deals specifically with the user interface.

Project B: VEGA Interface. VEGA represents solid objects as a collection of planar faces. Like other current solid modelling systems, it provides operations to describe and modify shapes that are very general precisely because they are defined on a purely *syntactic* level. These operations accommodate natural and intuitive modes of describing shapes only poorly when these modes rely heavily on the *semantic* properties of the objects under consideration (this becomes particularly obvious when site-related data such as contours are to be specified). We plan to expand the existing modelling facilities to allow, first of all, for an easy specification of sites through established techniques; we also plan to add facilities for the specification of building elements (such as pitched roofs) that occur frequently and can be described with greater ease if pre-programmed knowledge about the expected shapes is utilized, a technique known as *parameterized design*.

3.1.2. Stepwise Interactive Generation of Designs
A very useful paradigm describes the design process as a sequence of transformations which start from an initial configuration and terminate with a feasible solution to the problem at hand. This paradigm is not only useful for modelling empirically observed design procedures, but also provides a good starting point for automating certain aspects of that process.

In the *stepwise interactive* generation of designs, the trans-formations to which a current configuration can be subjected are found by a computer program; these possibilities are then displayed to the user, who makes a specific selection and thus re-starts the cycle. In early programs, the methods to find all possible transformations were pre-programmed and restricted to a particular problem context (mainly space allocation). A more recent program, the shape grammar interpreter SGI [19] [20], allows users to define their own rules for transforming given configurations into new ones. The program is an implementation of the shape

grammar formalism [26], which has been used successfully, by researchers in the Department and elsewhere, for the analysis of various corpora of designs [7] [14] [27]. We consider programs of this type excellent educational tools to explore the process of form generation.

Project C: Shape Grammar Interpreter. We plan to acquire SGI and and to adapt it to a suitable configuration. For educational purposes, it is highly desirable to provide students with sample grammars that can be used for demonstrations. The development of such grammars is planned as part of this project.

3.1.3. Automated Generation of Designs
Work on design automation has shifted from an early concentration on the generation of sub-optimal or single feasible solutions to the enumeration of entire solution sets; emphasis has been placed on a rigorous treatment of the problems involved, with important contributions by faculty in the Department and the University [8] [12] [18] [22]. Essential features of the emerging paradigm are exemplified by the program DIS, a floor plan generator designed especially for educational purposes. Its use is limited, however, to the generation of 'densely-packed' arrangements of rectangles under a pre-determined, limited set of constraints. But we consider the underlying principles capable of generalization to larger classes of problems or solutions [15].

The emphasis on the *enumeration* of designs becomes particularly important within our conceptual framework which stresses the comparison of design *alternatives* (which have to be generated before they can be compared). We consider further work within this area useful especially when it moves away from traditional, 'procedurally-oriented' styles of programming and starts to incorporate some of the techniques developed for the design of *expert systems*. These systems deal specifically with problems solved by experts using knowledge that is, for the most part, not explicitly stated anywhere (e.g. in textbooks) but internalized and based on the experience gained over years of practice. Architectural design relies, to a considerable degree, on such knowledge.

Expert systems are vehicles to extract this knowledge from experts who observe the behavior of the system over a series of realistic applications and suggest modifications. The systems are programmed so that the experts' knowledge and subsequent modifications can be encoded with ease. It is not surprising, then, that work on expert systems is emerging as an area of research concentration at various schools of architecture. This work is interesting not only for practical but also, and specifically, for educational purposes. An important part of design education consists in transferring to students the implicit knowledge needed to design successfully. Experts systems seem to be an excellent tool to discover this knowledge and to communicate it to students.

Project D : Design Generators. We plan to generalize the theory on which DIS is based to include 'loosely-packed' arrangements of rectangles. This will form the basis for creating a robust generator that can be used in a variety of contexts, especially as the backbone of generative expert systems for architectural design. The systems will be observed over a series of realistic applications. The ultimate goal is not only to discover the underlying design knowledge, but also to develop the principles of a general, programmable expert system for architectural design.

3.2. Prediction of Consequences

It has been argued in section 2 that the availability of analysis programs can influence the design process in two ways: a) by making the analysis of individual designs along selected criteria more efficient and potentially more thorough; and b) by making the comparison of design alternatives feasible where manual techniques prove too time-consuming and tedious. In order to introduce these possibilities to students, we intend to develop or acquire educational software in various areas.

3.2.1. Quantitative Analysis of Designs

Considerable effort has gone into the development of programs for the quantitative analysis of designs, especially for the various engineering disciplines involved in the design of buildings. Consequently, we intend to keep development efforts of our own to a minimum.

The nature of the programs listed in the following project illustrates particularly well the advantages of the specific framework adopted for our plans: Using any one of these programs outside this framework (which stresses the importance of evaluating solutions according to *multiple* criteria) would create the danger that particular criteria, namely those analyzed by the program at hand, are overemphasized at the expense of other criteria which cannot be analyzed with the same accuracy or depth, simply because the appropriate programs are not available or a formalized analysis is impossible to begin with.

Project E: Quantitative Analysis. We plan to acquire or, in a few cases, develop analysis programs in the areas of structural analysis; energy load analysis and energy simulation; acoustical analysis; daylight analysis; quantity surveying and cost estimation; and site analysis.

3.2.2. Visual Analysis

Computer graphics has great potential for facilitating the preparation of architectural representations. Applications in practice have remained limited, however, since much hand-crafting is still needed for the preparation of an image. In order to become useful in a more general way, the image generating algorithms have to become part of a system which allows a) the geometry of a large class of designs to be modelled; b) the shape of a specific design to be specified in a convenient manner; and c) complex viewing parameters to be specified interactively.

VEGA was designed with these goals in mind. Its potential usefulness for instruction, particularly in design studios, was demonstrated by a small trial project which also suggested certain features that should be added to the system. Most of these concern the interface and have been incorporated in Project B. To these should be added the capability for creating 3-dimensional images using advanced imaging techniques. An intermediate solution is specified by the following project.

Project F: Visual Analysis. In order to avoid a major programming effort of its own, the Department recently acquired MOVIE.BYU, a system designed for the preparation of 3-dimensional images using advanced techniques [6]. We plan to establish a link between this system and VEGA so that it can be used to create images of the models generated by VEGA.

3.2.3. General-Purpose Building Model

The data needed by various analysis programs overlap to a considerable degree, especially when it comes to building geometry. The programs, however, are usually developed as stand-alone-programs independent of each other and unable to share data. It has long been recognized that considerable gains in efficiency could result from integrating these programs into a system containing a project-dependent data base, set up and maintained independent of any application program. The data base must be able to record a building in all its relevant aspects, to model a design at various levels of resolution and allow access by multiple users. Work on such a database has been an area of concentration over the last decade at the Department [9] [11] [25]. Some formidable theoretical problems remain to be solved and cannot be addressed within the context of the present plan. But the *concept* of a project-oriented database for building design can be demonstrated to students through appropriate additions to VEGA. In this expanded form, VEGA can be used to analyze designs along selected criteria and to make comparisons between alternatives.

Project G: General-Purpose Building Model. At the present time, VEGA has only limited capabilities for storing non-geometric attributes associated with solid objects representing, for example, building elements. We plan to expand these capabilities and to add computational routines making use of these data in the analysis of designs along selected criteria.

3.3. Evaluation and Decision

The evaluation of architectural designs undoubtedly involves multiple criteria and has to deal with uncertainties. This gives rise to an intricate set of questions, especially when alternative designs are to be compared with each other. Similar problems are known from other fields and have led to the rise of multiple-attribute utility theory and decision theory. The work described before would remain incomplete if basic concepts and results from these fields were not reviewed and introduced to students. Suggestions for further research might come out of this effort.

Project H: Evaluation and Decision. The principles of optimization or the concept of an efficient or Pareto-optimal solution set [24] can effectively be demonstrated with the help of demonstration software, which we plan to acquire or develop. This project complements Project K described in section 4.

3.4. Systems Environment

Section 2 states that all of the programs made available through the proposed projects should be developed as part of a unified systems environment. The specification of this environment constitutes a project of its own.

Project J: Systems Environment. The systems environment characteristics are specified in a general way, probably in connection with the first projects nearing completion.

4. Computers in the Architectural Curriculum

The projects listed in the previous section will result in a collection of programs and systems that are logically linked to each other and able to communicate with each other to some degree. Students using these programs should not consider them as black boxes, but should be familiar with the underlying principles and models. This applies to both the particular application area of a program and the computational concepts and structures used. The use of a sophisticated system such as a programmable solids modeller might, in fact, require programming skills on the part of users who wish to use the full range of facilities offered by the system.

Preparatory courses introducing background knowledge and skills should be distinct from courses, such as design studios or certain support courses, which concentrate on the proper applications of the software. This separation avoids overloading certain courses as well as duplication of efforts.

It is impossible to predict in advance the precise effects that a comprehensive computation environment will have upon the curriculum of the Department. The projects suggest, however, certain courses that should be available to students, and the present section outlines these courses. To a large extent, the types of courses needed are already taught in the Department and need only to be modified, if at all, as our plans materialize. In a few instances, however, a new course must be developed, which will be the topic of a specific project distinct from the *software* development projects outlined in the previous section.

4.1. Preparatory Courses

All students should be familiar with basic concepts and structures of computing. These have been taught in the past within the context of a high level programming language (Pascal). The course, *Introduction to Computing*, is a required course in the undergraduate curriculum and scheduled for the second year of study. It is intended to give students basic literacy in computing. Those who wish to go beyond this goal and become competent application programmers, can take follow-up courses, predominantly in the Computer Science Department.

Areas such as geometric modelling or design generation have developed concepts, theories and modes of reasoning that are extensive enough to warrant introductory courses of their own. At the present time, modelling systems are introduced to students in the course *Computer Modelling in Design*, a crucial prerequisite for other courses, especially design studios, in which the possibilities of the new medium are explored.

The particular models underlying approaches towards design automation have been taught in the past in *Rules and Representations in Design*, an advanced seminar reserved for students with a particular interest in this area and a good background in mathematics. The significance of this course will increase as projects C and D get under way.

Some crucial issues of rational decision making are best discussed in the context of an application; it might however be desirable to introduce basic notions in a separate introduction, which is to be developed in the following project.

Project K: Course Module - Rational Decision Making. We plan to develop a new course module focusing on evaluation and decision from an architectural point of view.

The creation of effective CAD systems depends on contributions from various disciplines, such as architecture, computer science, cognitive psychology, operations research and engineering design. The CAD courses that have been offered by the Department require expansion and redesign if they are to reflect the growing expertise in the field of CAD.

Project L: Course Modules - Design and Implementation of CAD Systems. We plan to develop two new course modules dealing with the design and implementation of CAD systems.

4.2. Application-Oriented Courses

The programs listed under project E deal with the quantitative analysis of designs and serve a double function: to support the specific courses in which a particular type of analysis is taught, and to facilitate its application in studio projects. The proper place for teaching the underlying principles and models are the support courses themselves, which are already established in the curriculum.

Clearly, the projects outlined before are aimed ultimately at introducing computers as a medium and tool into the design studio. As a first step in this direction, we plan to offer computer-oriented elective studios in the middle part of the design sequence. In these studios the primary design generation and representation medium will be the computer. Sufficient capacity will be provided to enable all students to make maximal use of the new medium; that is, 24-hour access to relevant computing facilities will be guaranteed to every participating student. According to our experience, such studios have to be planned with care and need a prior trial run.

Project M: Computers in the Design Studio. We plan to develop syllabi and supporting materials for two intermediate design studios. At the present time, we envisage one of the studios to concentrate on rational decision making in the design process without emphasizing any particular aspect of design; a second studio will deal with particular aspects of design, such as the prediction of specific performance variables, at a level of detail unattainable without the help of computers. With these studios, we shall enter new terrain. It seems highly desirable, therefore, to observe the course of the studios closely, to evaluate the results and to communicate our findings to interested educators and practitioners.

5. A Computation Environment for Architectural Education

The plans outlined in sections 3 and 4 have important implications for the hardware and systems facilities needed.

Architectural design places high demands on computer systems in four categories: response speed, graphics, peripherals and memory. For our purposes, networked or distributed computing appears to be most suitable. A distributed computing system consists of individual dedicated processors sharing peripheral resources. Such a system allows each user to have the full capabilities of a processor available at all times, a feature required to guarantee fast response times. Since memory resources are shared, multiple users may theoretically access the same data simultaneously, which is a feature important for team design work.

The system software in a distributed computing system should support the network fully. No special user action should be required to distinguish between local and remote devices. The user interface itself should be powerful and conceptually clean. Several new machines support graphic interaction at the operating system level, particularly multi-tasking in separate windows. Such features greatly enhance the functionality of a system.

Software for architectural applications has been written in many languages. A system useful for architecture should support, at the minimum, Pascal, Fortran, and C programming languages. Other language development efforts, particularly object-oriented programming languages, are beginning to have a profound effect on computer science and will in the future provide more general, powerful programming environments. The choice of a system for architectural applications should not preclude use of these new developments. Artificial intelligence techniques have a long history of use in CAD, especially in Great Britain, where the main emphasis seems to be placed on their uses. Special languages, notably LISP and Prolog, are required to support such work.

The quality of system tools available to the software developer can have a large effect on the end product. Important features are facilities for multiple module compilation, a good debugger, tree structure filing systems, screen oriented text editors and mail systems. The UNIX operating system satisfies most of these requirements admirably and has proven to be a powerful support environment for system development. In spite of its few vices, UNIX enjoys wide use in academic computing and is becoming a standard operating system for today's micro computer systems. It is exceptionally clean and clear and under continuous development. Recent developments at several firms give UNIX a bright future.

Today, several new computer systems are under development which have all of the requisite features. An example is the Sun microcomputer manufactured by Sun Microsystems. It can serve as a model for the minimally acceptable configuration needed in architectural design studios. The software developments projects presently under way are all implemented for these machines.

The users expected to work with the system outlined above place stringent demands on its friendliness and reliability. Human support is needed to comply with these requirements and to supply the needed maintenance and assistance.

6. References

[1] Akin, O., Computer-aided education in architecture, *Proceedings of ACSA West Central Regional Conference*, Association of Collegiate Schools of Architecture (November 1983)

[2] Akin, O., Flemming, U., Woodbury, R. Development of Computer Systems for Use in Architectural Education, Internal report of the Department of Architecture, Carnegie-Mellon University (1984)

[3] Akin, O., *The Psychology of Architectural Design*, London: Pion (1985)

[4] Baer, A., Eastman, C., Henrion, M., Geometric modeling: a survey, *Computer Aided Design* 11(1979) 253-272

[5] Card, S.K., Moran, T.P., Newell, A., *The Psychology of Human-Computer Interaction*, Hillsdale, N.J.: Lawrence Erlbaum Associates (1983)

[6] Christiansen, H. and Stephenson, M., *MOVIE.BYU Training Text*, Provo, Utah: Brigham Young University (1983)

[7] Downing, F. and Flemming, U., The bungalows of Buffalo, *Environment and Planning B* 8(1981) 269-293

[8] Eastman, C.M., Automated space planning, *Artificial Intelligence* 4(1973) 41-64

[9] Eastman, C.M., General purpose building description systems, *Computer Aided Design* 8(1976) 17-26

[10] Eastman, C.M. and Weiler, K., Geometric Modeling Using the Euler Operators, Technical Report 78, Institute of Physical Planning, Carnegie-Mellon University (1979)

[11] Eastman, C.M., Database facilities for engineering design, *IEEE Proceedings* (October 1981)

[12] Flemming, U., Wall representations of rectangular dissections and their use in automated space allocation, *Environment and Planning B* 5(1978) 215-232

[13] Flemming, U., Computer-Aided Architectural Design at North American Universities, Technical Report, Department of Architecture, Carnegie-Mellon University (1981)

[14] Flemming, U., The secret of the Casa Giuliani Frigerio, *Environment and Planning B* 8(1981) 87-96

[15] Flemming, U., On the representation and generation of loosely-packed arrangements of rectangles, *Planning and Design* 12(1985) [forthcoming]

[16] Galle, P., An algorithm for exhaustive generation of building floor plans, *Communications of the ACM* 24(1981) 813-825

[17] Glass, G.J., The Definition of Dynamic Menus, Technical Report, Department of Architecture, Carnegie-Mellon University (1983)

[18] Grason, J., A dual linear graph representation for space-filling location problems of the floor plan type, in Moore, G.T. (ed.), *Emerging Methods in Environmental Design and Planning*, Cambridge, Mass.: M.I.T. Press (1970) 170-178

[19] Krishnamurti, R., The arithmetic of shapes, *Environment and Planning B* 7(1980) 463-484

[20] Krishnamurti, R., The construction of shapes, *Enviroment and Planning B* 8(1981) 5-40

[21] Olgyay, V., *Design with Climate*, Princeton, N.J.: Princeton University Press (1963)

[22] Pfefferkorn, C.E., The design problem solver, in Eastman, C.M. (ed.), *Spatial Synthesis in Computer-Aided Building Design* London: Applied Science Publishers (1975) 98-146

[23] Purcell, P., Computer education in architecture, *Computer Aided Design* 12(1980) 239-251

[24] Radford, A.D. and Gero, J.S., Tradeoff diagrams for the integrated design of the physical environment in buildings, *Building and Environment* 15(1980) 3-15

[25] Rasdorf, W.J. and Kutay, A.R., Maintenance of integrity during concurrent access in a building design database, *Computer Aided Design* 14(1982) 201-207

[26] Stiny, G., Introduction to shape and shape grammars, *Environment and Planning B* 7(1980) 343-351

[27] Stiny, G. and Mitchell, W.J., The Palladian grammar, *Environment and Planning B* 5(1978) 5-18

[28] Woodbury, R., Sun Sensitive Housing Aggregations, School of Architecture, Carleton University (1979)

[29] Woodbury, R., VEGA. A geometric modelling system, *Graphics Interface '83* Canadian Man-Computer Communications Society (May 1983) 103-109

COMPUTERS IN EDUCATION, K. Duncan and D. Harris (eds.)
Elsevier Science Publishers B.V. (North-Holland)
© IFIP, 1985

ENGINEERING GRAPHICS + COMPUTER GRAPHICS = COMPUTATIONAL ENGINEERING GRAPHICS ?

Harold P. Santo

Departamento de Engenharia Civil, Instituto Superior Técnico, CMEST -
- Centro de Mecânica e Engenharia Estruturais da Universidade Técnica
de Lisboa, 1096 Lisboa Codex Portugal

The role of the traditional counterpart of Computer Graphics (on the applications side), Engineering Graphics, has not been thoroughly understood or considered within engineering education, except for the general tendency to be relegated to a lesser position or merely eliminated from the programs.
In this paper a "solution" is proposed that can help overcome the problems that engineering schools encounter nowadays, concerning the unquestionable need to provide students with adequate background in graphics: the merging of Engineering and Computer Graphics, resulting in a brand-new discipline, herein called Computational Engineering Graphics, that can bring together the best of both worlds.
The traditional Engineering Graphics will have to "adapt or die" for most of its contents, objectives and scope is outdated. Engineering Graphics today has to be viewed as an introduction to the graphical methods, concepts and tools that form the basis of CAD/CAE, so its emphasis should veer towards a computational approach, accounting for Computer Graphics, as well as Computational Geometry, recent achievements.
The proposed 'new' discipline is therefore defined and assessed with detail. A four-year successful teaching experience is described and the course program is introduced. The importance of special-purpose software is discussed and the problem-oriented language ENGOL is outlined.
It is hoped that this paper will help motivate the engineering community to the constantly overlooked problems that Engineering Graphics - probably the most underrated subject of any engineering curriculum - has long been facing and for the need to gradually mold it into Computational Engineering Graphics, if it is to survive and play the part it has always been supposed to play.

1. INTRODUCTION

"Engineering is a graphics-oriented discipline in which drawings, sketches and graphs have always played an important role and required enormous manpower to produce." (H.A. Kamel [21])

In 1967 the Goal Committee of the American Society for Engineering Education (ASEE) completed a controversial report [49] that introduced important graphics recommendations, which in turn inspired early experiences concerning the inclusion of Computer Graphics (CG) in the fresh man Engineering Graphics (EG) program [5].

Ten years after a consistent progress apparently had not been achieved in that direction and the most cherished expectations did not seem to have been fulfilled satisfactorily in general. This can be appreciated by the results of an excellent survey conducted in 1978 [27]. In it several educators expressed relevant opinions such as :

"As science and technology grow ... there are pressures to eliminate some of the courses which the engineering faculty feel are less important..."

"...reason for the lack of hours in the graphics area is respectability."
"...educators believe graphics is not rigorous enough to be included in the college curriculum"
"Modern mathematical methods and computers have replaced graphical methods...graphics has very little of the theoretical."
"As those professors who are now involved in teaching engineering graphics retire will...
... courses in drafting [be reduced or eliminated] from the curriculum?"
"...what type of training should the new graphics teacher have?"
"...we will see that more theoretical graphics will be required."

Conclusions drawn from the review stressed that

"...there definitely must be a change in our presentation of the engineering graphics to the modern day engineering student...utilizing the concept of Computer Graphics in the Engineering Graphics curriculum."
"...there is indeed a need for Engineering Graphics in the engineering student's curriculum and a necessity to up-grade or revise the methods of teaching Engineering Graphics. Computer Graphics is one method of up-grading the curricula."
"...it seems necessary that these concepts be introduced to the students during their educational experience...computer graphics in association with introduction to Design is a necessary part of the engineering freshman's education and should be experienced by engineering students of all disciplines."
(underlined text by the author)

Other writers produced statements in the same

vein, like :
"Computer Graphics is becoming a topic of major
interest to the engineering graphics educator.
To some extent, this interest has been prompted
by the rising application of computer-aided
design and drafting in the industrial environment." [18]
"1. The last of our few remaining engineering
graphics faculty were nearing retirement. As
there are no Ph.D. programs and no 'leading edge'
research being done in this area, it was impossible to hire new faculty to replace them.
2. Industry is moving toward increased use of
computer graphics and computer aided drafting
systems.
3. Engineering Graphics has traditionally been
'boring', and we hoped computer graphics would
increase student interest (especially in their
first engineering course)." [33]

In spite of the 5 to 7 years hiatus, most certain
ly no other set of statements could summarize so
perfectly the "status of affairs" regarding the
teaching and learning of EG, probably the most
underrated course of any engineering curriculum.
They moreover actually best express the author's own
personal views and preoccupations on the subject,
as well as the guidelines he has been following in the
application of CG in an EG environment [37,39,42].

Engineering Graphics/Drawing/Drafting (it is
assumed that the non-specialist reader is familiar
with its character, exhibited in countless
treatises [10,15,26]), as a university level
discipline, faces the major dilemma, akin to so
many other traditional fields of knowledge or
activity : to "change or die", for most of its
contents, objectives and scope has for long been
out-of-date. Though it has been known for quite
awhile that "the times they are a-changin'",
graphics and drawing courses have been rarely
reflecting the changes accordingly, one of the
main reasons being the fact that computers/comput
ing and computer graphics evolved faster than
schools and educators could ever keep up with.

But EG today has to rely on the technological
advances, just as any other field, if it is to
survive and play its inherent role, providing
adequate graphics and geometry background for
would-be professionals, researchers and educators.
Noting also that it is estimated that there is a
need to train over 100,000 designers/drafters, in
the fundamentals and advanced features of CAD in
the next 3/4 years in the United States alone
[23], it is easy to comprehend the urgency that
there exists to turn EG into a wholly computer-
oriented subject or, more exactly, into an
introduction to the graphical and geometrical
methods, concepts and tools that form the basis
of CAD/CAE. This can be achieved by carefully
combining the traditional Drawing with CG and
Computational Geometry, an effort that will lead
to an overall computational approach to EG or,
more likely, to a practically brand-new
discipline, in tune with the current times, here
in, most naturally, christened Computational

Engineering Graphics (CEG), although it can be
reasonably objected that one more acronym is
already too much to take.

Anyway, the real heart of the matter is a concept,
which can encompass all the aspects and ideas
briefly outlined, as well as bringing a solution
to all the problems raised. CEG, correctly focus
ed on, is the solution proposed in this paper.

It should be justly said, however, that some
educators have taken parallel routes, which,
although adressed as Computer-Aided Graphics,
relate almost only to Automated Drafting, representing, therefore, no entire answer, from
the author's viewpoint, to all the questions
brought up herein [36,16].

Nevertheless, the long quotes presented above
prove that originality is far from claimed and,
while the author has been independently advocating and spreading the same ideas, for the select
ive merging of Computer and Engineering Graphics [37,42], it is important to indicate the
works that, to the best of his knowledge, follow
almost the same basic philosophy and that
constitute probably the best examples of what is
being successfully, and brilliantly, done nowadays, regarding the principal topic of these
notes : the efforts of mainly Juricic and Barr,
at the University of Texas [3,18,20] and of Riley
and others, at the University of Minnesota [22,
33].

Not with surprise these works come from the
mechanical engineering environment. The concern
of the author is aimed, however, at civil
engineering education, where probably proportional attention has not been paid and similar
objectives not pursued as should be. In the
Proceedings of the Annual ASEE Conferences from
the past few years, and in 52, outstanding
contributions in this domain can be appreciated,
though.

2. THE ROLE OF COMPUTER GRAPHICS IN ENGINEERING
   EDUCATION

"The role of computer graphics in the engineering curriculum is to provide a creative environment in which to learn...Computer Graphics allows
students to visualize and more clearly understand
complex geometric concepts associated with many
engineering disciplines. The ability to visually
interpret complex relationships and understand
global trade-offs as parameters are varied is
basic to an engineering education." (M.J. Wozny
[35])

It is a relatively well-known fact that CG has
already long come of age, while the same cannot
be exactly said of CAI/CAL. This subject has
been assessed in a former paper [41], in the
context of Structural Analysis (where CG is
particularly useful. See, for instance, 21, 25 &
50), but the overall concepts involved apply to
any other field, much obviously to Engineering
Graphics.

The basic ideas concerning the role of CG in engineering education, which help to set CEG into the right perspective and understand the arguments in its favor, can be summed up in the notion that, through a computer graphic aid, a student will gain a 'feeling', train the intuition, grasp the fundamental aspects and apprehend the underlying theory - of whatever field of study - - better and faster than by any other means.

With the arrival of low-cost micro-computers and peripherals with graphic capabilities, the computer-knowledgable instructor's job has become easier and the implementation of CG-based courses a much more feasible task. And, indeed, most computer-aided educational experiences rely on micro-computers, a fact which has to do with economic shortcomings that universities suffer, but that, in many cases, are simply a rational choice, considering the practical use that the micros allow and the anticipation of professional procedures they make possible [8,46,47].

CG constitutes also a tremendous contribution to bridge the gap between academic training and professional requirements, mainly for providing an instant visual guide to the learning process. The students can thus get "closer to reality", if aided by adequate CAI/CC packages, gathering information and tools which can be of enormous utility in later years of undergraduate or graduate instruction, as well as in their engineering practice.

To the unfamiliar reader a valuable collection of papers, 35, can best give the flavor, and show relevant applications, of CG in engineering education, while reference 31 is a very note-worthy summary of general computer assisted instruction.

The incorporation of CG and CAI material into engineering courses, though an unquestionable necessity these days, faces however several obstacles, which - inclusive of the economic drawbacks - are part of a wider panorama, recently very well synthesized this way by a notable educator :
"We are beginning a fundamental change in the way people learn, one of the few such changes that has ocurred in all of recorded history. This change is based on modern computer technology. The change is likely to occupy primarily the next quarter century. At that point we will have a very different educational system that we have at the present time". (A. Bork [6])

It is up to the dedicated and enthusiastic educator to inspire and promote the changes, of minds and status, relative to engineering education, a change that cannot come outside computers, CG and carefully developed CAI systems, that, in conjunction, certainly represent the major breakthrough in education since the advent of the slate.

3. COMPUTATIONAL ENGINEERING GRAPHICS

"The future of graphics is expanding and exciting. Computer graphics will continue to be developed and refined, increasing the power of graphics as a thinking and action tool. People in the Engineering Graphics field will be influential in furthering scientific and engineering knowledge for the betterment of mankind, and the social consciousness and responsability of scientists, engineers and technical educators". (S. Slaby [45]).

Strange as it may seem, the cases cited in §1 aside, the EG scene has not really lived up to those remarkable words, from the far-reaching vision of a noted professor in the field.

Still, anyone would certainly agree that no course can be more suitable than EG for the introduction of CG to engineering students. EG and CG (the applications side of it) are like twins and - observing as well that computers, along with their graphical features, are presently within reach of even children [17] - their merging appears to be the logical, and long over due, step in the evolution of graphics instruction.

So, drawing on the considerations made in §1 and §2 - and remembering that EG is a term that "describes the broad field that uses drawings as a means of solving problems and presenting their solutions", consisting of three major divisions : working drawings, Descriptive Geometry and specialty areas [10], and that CG is concisely referred to as "the art or science of producing graphical images with the aid of a computer" [4] - CEG can be tentatively defined as the discipline which "involves the solution of geometric problems, and its presentation; the representation, manipulation, input, output, analysis and synthesis of engineering shapes, forms, models, systems and structures, through computational means". CEG results, of course, not only from a weighted combination of CG and EG but also from a thorough concatenation of various other branches of the applied and pure sciences, mainly, Euclidean, Analytic and Projective Geometries, Linear Algebra, Numerical Analysis, Computational Geometry and Computer-Aided Geometric Design, assuming implicitly the character of an introduction to engineering design, CAD and CAE.

Though interdisciplinary in nature, CEG should be regarded as an endeavor with its own principles, emphasis and purpose. It is a sum much greater than the parts with unique approaches and scope, covering a wide spectrum of techniques and applications, highlighted by its educational goal, which should naturally lean heavily on CAI/CAL procedures.

The undeniable need to provide students with an adequate background in graphics can therefore be guaranteed by a discipline of this kind, in accordance with the contemporary age, one which will (gradually) substitute the traditional Engineering Graphics/Drafting, maintaining, though, the latter one's overall attributes.

It is certainly hard to overemphasize the fact that Graphics will always be indispensable to the engineering profession. The assertions "a picture is worth a thousand words" and "a graph is worth a thousand numbers" signify more than mere clichés, for the outcome of an engineer's talent will be nothing without a compatible means of visual communication, just like a composer will not be able to express his mind (and heart!) without the aid of a musical instrument. We live in a 3D world whose reality is, and will always be, graphic/geometric in nature, so any engineering work (of art!) will be immaterial without a corresponding graphical basis.

It is the part of a discipline like CEG to develop a clear 3D-vision and build a solid geometric foundation in the heads of prospective professionals and provide the background for a specialty advanced CAD course, another indispensable subject these days, best placed in the senior year of graduation.

3.1. A Syllabus

The definition of a program structure for CEG depends of course on several parameters : area of engineering, school facilities and available equipment, faculty preparation and, most of all, the general instructional objectives and educational philosophy, not alien to the region or environment in question.

Due to the characteristics of CEG, it is the writer's opinion that the traditional manual methods and conventional procedures of Graphics should be best left for secondary instruction, even though this cannot be considered apart from the whole organization of a country's educational system.

On the other hand, the global prerequisites should ideally include, besides elementary calculus, geometry and graphics, at least Linear Algebra, Analytic Geometry and computer programming, which will also depend on the particular school and environment.

With these factors in mind, a model syllabus, in very broad terms, could be arranged as follows :

1 – Review of basic geometry and graphics, Descriptive Geometry, general theory of planar projections, matrices and homogeneous coordinates.
2 – Introduction to Engineering Design and Graphics. Scope, methods and systems. Standards. Specialty areas. Applications.
3 – Overview of Computational Geometry and Computer Graphics. State of the art. History. Fields of application. Components and related disciplines. Standards. Conferences and associations. Basic literature.
4 – Introduction to the hardware of CG, peripherals, graphic capabilities of micro--computers. Graphical extensions of programming languages. Basic graphics techniques. Graphs and diagrams.
5 – Introduction to the geometric/mathematical tools. Representation of objects, data bases, modeling, coordinate systems. 2D and 3D transformations. Concatenation. Clipping, covering, mapping.
6 – Matrix formulation of the planar geometric projections. Detailed derivation of each type of projection. Manipulation of viewing parameters. 3D visualization. Plotting and display. Efficient computational techniques.
7 – Introduction to Computational Geometry and Computer-Aided Geometric Design. Approximation, interpolation, fitting and display of curves and surfaces. Coons and Bézier curves and surfaces. Contouring techniques.
8 – Hidden-line and surface algorithms. Overview and fundamentals. Basic geometric techniques and tools. Sorting. Coherence. Review of significant and classic algorithms.
9 – Complementary topics. Shading. Shadows. Stereoscopy. Animation.
10– Introduction to Graphics systems and packages. Languages. Writing of simple programs. Programming aids and techniques. Standard subroutines. Advanced graphics programming. Examples and case studies (including all other EG's relevant topics : vector graphics, nomography, dimensioning, etc.).

The above structure, directed more specifically towards a civil engineering curriculum, adaptable to particular constraints and divided eventually in individual modules or levels, illustrates the guidelines that ruled the implementation of the basic course described in the next section and is, in fact, a summary of the author's own course notes [42].

Justice should be done too, to the work that, better than any other, as far as the author is aware of, integrates the fundamental geometric concepts and ingredients pertaining to CEG : a recent book by P. Gasson [16], an extraordinary synthesis of engineering geometry, that should belong to every serious EG, and CG for that matter, educator's shelf. Some other books will also contribute significantly for the enhancement of the body of a CEG program : 1,2,11,12 & 51.

3.2. CEG Software

The experiences already referred to all take advantage of special purpose software, which is essential to CEG.

CEG software should basically fulfill two aims : provide students with a learning tool and instructors with a teaching tool.

Of course the structure of a CEG system or

program will depend on available equipment but it is important to stress that the students should not merely be exposed to a canned package as a 'black box', from a user's point of view. Not only the underlying features and algorithms should be familiar to them but they must be capable of developing their own programs, applications and projects, utilizing, preferably, a graphics-oriented language.

CEG instruction is much more than just CAI/CAL in EG so a mixture of utilization of existing systems and programming of new ones is required if a CEG course is to accomplish its ultimate goals.

3.3. What's in a Name ?

"I am nothing if not critical"
        W. Shakespeare (Othello, Act II, Scene 1)

Some people may argue that a discipline like CEG already exists, under other names and contents, and that one more term is not only needless but superfluous and undesirable.

The first objection should have hopefully vanished by the comments and evaluation produced so far. In fact, more than just a matter of labels, it is the innovation and a revolutionary change in the engineering education trends - to which a conceptual subject like CEG, with scope, tone and boundaries as marked, can, debatably more than and other, contribute - that is at stake. As for the second one, a little bit more has to be said.

Any scientific or technical designation must be simultaneously concise and accurate. It is a principle that unfortunately is much less confirmed than it should. The stunning example is that of Descriptive Geometry (DG), in all likelihood the worst case of a bad name. Indeed, DG is not a Geometry itself, for starters, but just a set of rules and procedures to solve problems of Classical 3D Euclidean Geometry, through the graphical aid of concurrent views (mainly front and top). Moreover, the purpose of DG is hardly that of describing space (which is the aim of "stereography" - from the Greek : description of space - - sometimes mistakenly identified with stereoscopy), its principal end being, in this regard, simply the presentation of solutions to geometric problems. (Any suggestions for a more precise name ?)

In these times, the often used terms "computer--aided" and "computer-assisted", in many occasions barely typify the respective subject areas. A thorough discussion of the terms involving Graphics can be found in 20 (this author does not agree completely with the definitions of CG and CAE expressed there, though), but the point wished to be made herein is that, in some instances, the distinction between the computational approach and nature of a certain discipline and the application of computers to an existing body of (applied) science, intricate as it may be, is of

an utmost importance that cannot be reduced to a mere question of names, let alone concepts, for reasons expectedly apparent at this point.

Just like the aptly titled Computational Geometry [12,14] (as opposed to the not so Computer--Aided Geometric Design [2]), CEG does not result simply from the addition of CG, or some computer applications, to an EG course or, in other words, from the mere aid of computers. It represents an original updated approach to graphics, so interweaved with computing techniques and mathematics, that only the qualifier "computational" can correctly specify its characteristics and range.

The term Computer-Aided Graphics, or Engineering Computer Graphics at that, cannot therefore adequately imply the same philosophy and approach of CEG, being just synonym with Computer-Aided Drafting, which is a whole different, more elementar and restricted, field. Computer-Aided Graphics/Drafting, as it has been considered and taught, corresponds to an intermediary phase, towards CEG, which is no longer justified *per se*, for it will be actually encompassed by the latter. And, in reality, CEG as a term, would just as well as be intermediary itself, for the 'computational' tag will probably be dropped in the long run, from the moment the computer-oriented character becomes taken for granted, just like it is being predicted, for years, for "(computer) graphics" (actually a shortened 'interactive graphics' is probably most widely used than 'I Computer G'). In short, EG must always exist as such - though occasionally disguising its name - - but its survival will rely on its ability to mold its shape, more or less in step with the corresponding stage of technical evolution.

4. A TEACHING EXPERIENCE

"Engineering educators everywhere can use educational research to plan and build for change. Every institution, department and faculty member has an opportunity to conduct some 'shirt sleeves' research. Retain what is good from the past, but be responsive to the present; be innovative, but evaluate and re-evaluate; use evaluative feedback to keep what is effective and discard what is not." (W.K. LeBold [24])

The concern and ideas expressed in the previous sections have been governing the author's teaching experiences at Instituto Superior Técnico (IST), the College of Engineering of the Technical University of Lisbon.

Engineering Graphics/Drafting has been part of IST's civil, mechanical and electrical engineering curricula for about seven decades. For many years it was divided in two yearlong courses (freshman and sophomore levels, if these designations can be applied to the then 6-year undergraduate structure), complemented by an also yearlong DG freshman course.

About 15 years ago a new curriculum organization,

closer to international standards, was effected, with semester-long courses and 5-year duration, within which the Drafting contribution was squeezed down to 2 semesters in the first year, and DG was purely and simply eliminated (an unfortunate measure, not unlike what was sadly happening throughout the world).

The civil engineering curriculum comprised, from then on, disciplines arranged in 4 main groups : basic, core, interdisciplinary and complementary, the first year basic group offering the ones indicated in Table 1.

Drawing I was basically a discipline through which students were introduced to the graphic representation techniques, learning how to use appropriate tools to comprehend or communicate ideas, forms and shapes, while exercising spatial relationships by means of carefully developed manual works of increasing complexity.

Drawing II, on the other hand, introduced the students to the graphics and graphical methods and computations of civil engineering, including a brief introduction to DG, to compensate in part for the suppression of the respective course.

4.1. A First Experience in Portugal

It can be noticed that the EG syllabuses described followed a conservative approach to the subject, almost in opposition to the Computational EG. A transition from one to the other had to be carried out, therefore, in a gradual manner, and not without the verification of the primordial basic assumptions : existence of proper equipment, sufficient know-how of the faculty and adequate background of the students.

Considering the overall educational context and the implicit difficulties of the developing country in question, the implementation of a CG-based EG program had to proceed in a few stages, a pioneering action started in 1981, and already reported elsewhere [37,39].

Observing the freshman curriculum, it can be seen that the first semester guaranteed the prerequisites of the students for an introduction to CG, so it was decided, in a first phase, to rearrange and up-grade the program of Drawing II, incorporating CG in the existing structure, following didactic tutorial-like schemes, allowing students to develop simple applications of all learned in Drawing I and II till then. Due to the experimental nature of the syllabus, a special class of only 30 students, picked up among the best, was formed.

An Apple II micro-computer configuration was adopted to surmount the equipment restrictions, and the course outline shown in Table 2, was defined, dropping nomography entirely, for evident reasons.

4.1.1. Lectures and workshops

The course had a 16-week duration with three 2-hour lectures a week. Theory was taught over a 12-week period, as indicated in Table 2, and the remaining 4 weeks were reserved for the finishing of programs and elaboration of assessment projects.

Computer workshops had to be introduced as early as possible (4th week), to allow the students to gain enough ease and experience with the Apple, Applesoft and its graphical features, becoming able to write the basic programs and evaluation works at their turn. The students were gathered in groups of three, using the computer in daily 2-hour block-times, which ran in parallel with the theoretical sessions, receiving assistance as needed.

4.1.2. Assessment and marking

The formal assessment of the students was based, in equal parts, on two major components : a mid-semester two-hour test and the CG works. The mid-semester test versed only on the strict drafting part of the course and it followed the usual Drawing exam format. It was divided in two sections : a half-hour 'theory' paper and an hour-and-a-half free-hand drawing execution.

The CG evaluation was also divided in two parts: discussion of the particular assessment projects with the entire group and an individual oral examination on the theoretical portion of the subject.

Prior to this, the projects - composed by full report, figures, program listings and hard-copies of results - were carefully appreciated and a preliminary mark was appointed, taking into account the relative quality and value of each. This appraisal obeyed the following guidelines :

Topic	Weight
. Overall presentation, form and completeness	0.1
. Report (writing, clearness, completeness, flowcharts, figures, diagrams)	0.2
. Program (legibility, structure, special subroutines, algorithms developed, speed, correction, validation, use)	0.5
. Creativity (solids and objects created, innovations, originality, form of output, messages, explaining texts, comments)	0.2

After this stage another confrontation of the project was carried out to refine the group grading and, in the final computations, the introductory exercises, interest shown and work performance were also accounted for to determine the individual marks.

4.1.3. Examples of exercises and projects

- Create a plane figure and, using the 'shape-table' facility and corresponding instructions,

write a program to rotate, change scale, move the figure and change its color at will or randomly.
- Write a program to draw a colored picture, mix ing geometric shapes with landscape, introduc ing an animated figure to 'bring life' to it.
- Create a simple geometric solid. Write a pro gram to draw its isometric projection by a 'brute force' approach, by direct generation and through the homogeneous coordinates tech nic. Compare all results. Try other objects and projections.
- Write a program do draw sectional views and floor-plans of buildings, using only the follow ing geometric elements : straight-line segments, rectangles (shaded or cross-hatched if neces sary), circumference arcs.
- Consider the roof of a building with rectangu lar top view, each side of it corresponding to one slope. Write a program to draw the complete projection, with the slopes intersections auto matically determined. In the text window pre sent the data and the calculated top level of the roof.
- Consider a two-story, one-span frame, with col umns of constant and equal cross-sections. Assuming the floors infinitely rigid, their displacements, due to horizontal forces F1 and F2, can be expressed respectively by

$$D1 = (F1 \times H1^3 + F2 \times H2^3) \times 10^{-6} \text{ m} \quad \text{and}$$
$$D2 = (F1 \times H1^3 + 2F2 \times H2^3) \times 10^{-6} \text{ m}.$$

Write a program to draw the deformed and un deformed frame, given the forces, heights (H1 and H2) and span. Use the text window to out put the data and the calculated displacements.
- Create a geometric solid. Using the matrix for mulation, write a program to generate any of its central projections, axonometric projec tions and multiple views.

4.1.4. Further comments and results of the experience

A set of course notes, with theory, description of the Applesoft graphic features and introduc tory exercises, was distributed and a complemen tary basic bibliography was suggested for further reading [12,30,34].

Throughout the notes various routines were given or delineated (dashed line generation, matrix multiplication, a simple hidden-line elimination technique, etc.) in order to avoid a duplication of efforts, saving students time. Attention was paid to speeded-up execution and memory saving tricks, distinguishing a compact execution-only version of a program from an extended, full of comments, form for ease of reading purposes.

Most of the text was naturally devoted to the transformations in two and three dimensions, in the homogeneous coordinates formulation, taking special care with concatenation and scaling.

Being the main concern to bridge the gap between the traditional graphics and the recent computer advances, exploring the micros as a new important tool in the EG environment, special emphasis was

placed on planar projections.

To facilitate the students job, a simple 3D com puter program and structuring scheme was suggest ed. It came to make part of most of their pro grams, permitting them to concentrate on other features such as model generation, mix of text and graphics, simple animations, optimal manipu lation, use of dashed lines, color differentia tion, hidden-line elimination and so forth.

The 'shape-table' facility motivated the stu dents enormously, having some of them developed programs with moving vehicles and figures, games, automatic generation and filing of 'shapes', and other interesting applications. Noticing that it was a first undergraduate year and they possessed a relatively limited background, this was a re markable accomplishment.

The outcome of the whole experience was plainly positive. The success, highlighted by the inter est and enthusiasm shown by the class, proved the viability of the CG introductory program and, furthermore, brought a bit of fresh air to a stale environment. It demonstrated also the great potential CG has, even at its lowest lev el, to reshape a well established discipline. Considering the shortcomings of the unexplored territory, perhaps the greatest merit was having done an omelet, so to speak, (almost) without breaking eggs.

4.2. Stage II

After the satisfactory experience reported in the previous item, the next step was to extend the course to the whole civil engineering fresh man level.

For this purpose a seminar with parallel work shops was organized to form the faculty involved in all classes, enriched by an enlarged version of the course notes, a tutorial text [19] and the standard literature [30,34].

With this event the remaining prerequisites-mini mum faculty expertise -was assured and, addi tionally, the old ingrained attitude towards the role of EG commenced a 180-degree turn.

4.2.1. Hardware and software

"The pen is mightier than the sword ... particu larly a plotter pen." (Guess Who)

The considerable increase in the number of stu dents, from 30 to about 250, brought a new ob stacle, fundamentally the need to provide enough computer time to each working group. IST is not a lucky American school [32,48], however, and, with the unpracticability of an adequate CG lab, advantage had to be taken solely of the Benson 1222 drum plotter installed at the university's computing center.

The accompanying software of the plotter was,

unfortunately, far from practical utilization, especially by freshmen, so, considering the goals in view, a student-oriented system was built on top of it, to facilitate the programming of appli cations and development of evaluation projects.

The system was baptized SIMPATICO - from the Portuguese 'Sistema SIMplificado PAssivo para Trata mento de Informação Gráfica por COmputador', which freely reads 'Simplified Passive System for Processing Graphical Information by Computer' - a word meaning kind, nice, sympathetic and helpful, at the same time, properly implying, not by chance, the spirit which presided its creation.

The system consisted of only 10 FORTRAN-callable subroutines with straight, easy to memorize, names and passing arguments, when unavoidable, very reduced in number : START, DATA, SCALE, MOVE, DRAW, TEXT, CIRCLE, ELIPSE, MATMUL and FINISH [38].

A standard layout (as shown in Figures 1 and 2), including eventual identifications, was produced by the system at the start of each run, within which the drawings were presented, auto- matically clipped, when necessary, to fit a maxi mum of 4 user-selected 'viewports'.

4.2.2. Course contents and lectures

In this second phase an improved program was applied, comprising, broadly, points 3 to 10 of the syllabus presented in §3.1, still only within Drawing II.

The lectures were given accordingly, much similar ly to the scheme of Stage I, except that, due to the equipment at disposal, no computer workshops were needed, but a suitable introduction to the SIMPATICO system and assistance for its use.

It should be stressed that the passive nature of the available hardware did not cause a conflict with the character and CAI-like approach of the course's concepts.

Introductory exercises (drawing of simple geomet ric figures) were proposed early to allow stu- dents to become familiar with the system in time. It was left to their convenience or imagination the execution, in parallel with the theoretical lectures, of those or any other applications, un til the assignment of the evaluation projects.

To arouse interest and provide a visual contact with the subject, a computer-generated film and sets of SIGGRAPH slides were shown in especially prepared sessions.

4.2.3. Projects and assessment

The assessment and marking in this stage follow- ed the same rules of the former, except that a written paper was required for the CG theory.

Examples of proposed theoretical questions are :

. Derive the 2D rotation matrix.

. Define concatenation. Indicate its advantages. Explain why the order of transformations is not always arbitrary.
. Define shearing and derive its matrix represen tation.
. Derive in detail the perspective matrix.
. Explain how to increase the dimensions of a polygon keeping the coordinates of one vertex unchanged.

The projects were arranged in 8 different types, covering the following topics :

1 - Sections and plans of houses and buildings
2 - Special structures (bridges, chimneys,...)
3 - Roofs
4 - Construction sites
5 - Dams and roads
6 - Urban systems
7 - Contour maps
8 - Structural detailing (connections, staircases, ...)

4.3. Current Stage

The favorable students response and the relative success of the previous step led to the consolidation of the CG program and a corresponding improvement, taking advantage of the gathered know-how and lessons learned with past mistakes.

Experience had shown that the bulk of working time was devoted to the testing and fine-tuning of programs, which enraged and deviated the stu- dents from the true goals of the course and proj ects. The computer then was more like a burden, not an educational attractive instrument, in spite of SIMPATICO, and CAI/CAL literally got lost in the proceedings.

4.3.1. The ENGOL language

The main issue of this third stage, that began in 1983, was the development and implementation of a special-purpose command-structured lan- guage, profiting from the SIMPATICO system, nam- ed, much too inevitably, ENGOL (for ENgineering- -Graphics-Oriented Language).

This language clearly helped to overcome the problems mentioned, providing the students with a speedy way to do their work, without losing precious time with programming tasks.

But, common sense can tell, without graphics programming a CG course has no substance; conse quently an improved SIMPATICO was kept at dispos al to allow students to write applications at their wish. Two such applications, developed by student Luis Antonio Silva and used with permis- sion, are demonstrated by Figures 1 and 2. Fig- ure 1 shows the result of a hidden-surface algo rithm, based on the 'covering' concept, while Figure 2 exemplifies a better version of the same algorithm, applied to the automatic genera tion of two interlocking tori.

Works of this kind were a delight to this

enthusiastic educator, making every effort worth while and giving him the zest and confidence to go on. And it is also worth saying that a great deal of students have done splendid "homeworks" on their own micro-computers, some above the level demanded for the proposed projects.

A detailed description of ENGOL is beyond the scope and space of this paper and, because it is still in an early stage anyway, only a subset will be discussed in the next item.

4.3.2. Planar geometric projections

The principal feature of ENGOL is the possibility it offers the user to choose any planar geometric projection to represent the objects or scene desired.

The current version, appropriately labeled PGP (from 'Planar Geometric Projections of Polyhedral Surfaces'), constitutes, not surprisingly, the core of the system.

The combination of the conventional Technical Drawing with computational techniques is best accomplished by the matrix formulation of the planar geometric projections, number 6 of the syllabus outlined in §3.1. A thorough treatment is introduced in 42 which, for certainly filling the gap that exists in the current CG and EG literature, despite the excellent works of Ingrid Carlbom, et al. [7,28], and of what is presented in 13 & 34, is the subject of forthcoming articles [43].

In actuality, important as it may be, enough attention has probably never been paid to this subject, a fact ascertained in several occasions. (One such instance took place at a high-ranking CG conference, during a renowned lecturer's invited paper. Showing a cube's oblique projection, he convincingly named it an 'isometric view', to the astonishment of this writer. Someone in the audience called his attention to the misstep, but he could not point out the difference even so. Surprise : the paper was about 3D visualization! Another incredible example is the following definition, appearing in the manual of a package from a famed university :"An isometric projection is a simple mechanism for showing the third axis as being at an angle to the other two axes."!?) Although it is understood that geometric transformations and projections form a small part of CG concerns, and that a computer science specialist is more preoccupied with other, more complex, matters, a lack of expertise of EG or CG educators in the general theory of projections is hard to accept or comprehend.

To make up for skill flaws and present students with a useful learning tool, ENGOL was initiated with the PGP subset. With it anybody can literally play with projections, changing parameters at will to see what comes out, checking the own inner 'feelings'. It is an invaluable aid for the strengthening of one's intuition and sharpening

the space vision, a formative factor rather overlooked in recent times.

PGP encompasses all types of planar projections, requested by the user through adequately-defined commands, namely, in short form :

FRON, SUPE, INFE, POST, LEFT, RIGH, for multiview, ISOM, DIME, TRIM, for axonometric,
CABI, CAVA, GENE, for oblique parallel projections and
PARA, ANGU, OBLI, for perspective projections (i.e., 1 , 2 and 3-point perspectives).

An additional command, STAN, is used for a 'standard' arrangement, composed of isometric, front, top and left-side views, in accordance with the first-angle convention, in effect outside USA.

The user must specify the parameters necessary to properly define a projection, including the hidden-line elimination option, input right after the corresponding command (though some can assume default values – e.g., for the dimetric projection the rotation angles are set to 19.454 and 20.684 degrees, x and y axes, if no other data is assigned) or no parameters whatsoever (e.g., for the isometric projection).

All projections are presented inside the layout drawn by SIMPATICO (PGP is implemented on top of it) and the user can request a maximum of 4 projections in each run. The projections are automatically scaled to fit a fourth of the layout's inner area, thus avoiding clipping. Figure 3 shows four projections of a bridge structure, obtained from an Apple II version of ENGOL (structure conceived by Luis Antonio Silva).

A line-printer output is also part of each run. In it the input data, all parameters, the transformation matrix, the final coordinates and the global scale calculated, of each projection required, are presented.

A detailed description of PGP can be found in 42 and will appear in extended format in 43 .

4.4. Further Developments

Despite the considerable progress accomplished so far, the total implementation of CEG is still in need to be achieved.

Requisites to be fulfilled, or problems to be solved, include the existence of a CG lab with adequate student/utilization-time ratio, and an advanced version of ENGOL in operation.

Interactive graphics terminals, or stand-alone systems, providing instantaneous feed-back to the students' geometric manipulations and experiments, are unquestionably a must for an up-to-date graphics course, but useless without a powerful graphical language.

ENGOL can suit the needs on focus and offer also

an indispensable introduction to the graphics standards, a feat that, as a matter of fact, is in store for ENGOL will be furthered upon a GKS implementation.

Above all, the establishing of a definitive year long CEG, paving the way for a 'specialty CAD/ /CAE' upper-level course, will help to bring a 'certain environment' closer to the 80's and somehow will prepare it for the Engineering of the 21st century.

5. CONCLUSIONS

"The role of the universities should be to concentrate on the basics with more reliance on computers and computer graphics to support some level of computer assisted training." (H.G. Schaeffer [44])

The advent of computers caused an impact on sensible educators nearly overnight, a fact sampled by some early sources [9]. The potential effect of CG on engineering education was felt even more profoundly from the very beginning (that is, from the seminal work of Ivan Sutherland [29,40]), but throughout the sixties and seventies, in spite of elaborate efforts like PLATO and TICCIT [31,41], a plain and effective utilization of CG in education had not been fully realized and, today, still much is left to be desired.

If it cannot be proclaimed, unhappily, that "CAI/ /CG in Engineering Education" has at last come of age, surely no one will disagree that computers represent one of the greatest ever accomplishments of mankind, whose revolutionary changes and influence at all levels of society have been felt only slightly yet. 2001 is at the door, notwithstanding, and the quest for better, deeper, faster, more complete, widespread instruction will lead to nothing without the compatible resources of technology.

It is somewhat sad to observe the more or less stale attitude of the CG industry relative to the prominent role it should have been playing in the world of education. The motivation of educators is undoubtably hindered by the lack of proper, easy -to-handle, devices. Though it should be stated, in due justice, that the development of sophisticated but accessible equipment still requires a lot of research investment, it would be a feast to a teacher's eyes to see , for example, flat- -panels, connected to a micro-computer system including a tablet, in place of the secular black- -or-any-other-color-board, chalks and desk. An educator's task and performance would be hugely eased and enhanced by such devices : pre-written 'pages' of lessons would be easily displayed and interrupted at will by sketches drawn on a tablet, saved if desired for later use, all eventually put out through hard-copy units; pre-programmed graphics and animated sequences could complement lectures, not forgetting the students 'computer- ized' desks, permitting direct access to pertinent data and communication with the instructor,

computer-operated video-disks, and so on.

This is how a "school of the future" will certainly look like, hard- and softwarewise, a suitable scenario for engineering classes, with liable lab experiments replaced with advantage by computer simulations and where the lecturer will be able to dedicate more time to explanations, intuition - training and expertise-forming.

Taking into account the crystal-gazing truth that the engineer of soon-coming years will work as closely with computers and CAD/CAE systems as they do with pocket calculators today, that they will be freed more and more from calculating, 'mechanical' and manual tasks, being allowed to concentrate themselves on the conceptional aspects, the graphic/geometric side of their craft might as well be second nature.

The revolution stirred up by computers and CG within engineering education will unreel its full potential when universities curricula world wide become wholly computer-oriented, with state -of the-art hard- and software to support faculty and students, with a corresponding modernization of theories and courses taught, improvement of teaching and learning methods and thorough preparation for investigational, educational and professional activities. This 'shape of things to come' will not come true outside a strong graphics-based instructional system.

It is believed, therefore, that the spread and implementation of CEG, helping to convey future professionals to the 'real world of their career' from the very start, is not only a valid answer to the questions approached in this essay, but what will give back the scientific interest, theoretical background and respectability to the graphics of engineering.

In a word, CG can insufflate a second life into a struggling-to-survive old-aged EG, that watched the world pass it by without a warning.

Unlike CG, which some years ago used to be referred to as "a solution looking for problems", CEG, as defined and assessed herein, appears to be "a solution to which the problems have long been looking for."

6. ACKNOWLEDGEMENTS

The experiences reported in this paper would not have been possible without the agreement of the Civil Engineering Department's Graphic Methods Section coordinator, Prof. Jaime de Oliveira,and the receptiveness of the faculty involved in the classes, Assistant Professors Arnaldo Frias, Carlos Ribeiro, Isabel Guilherme, João Costa, Mário Correia, Mário Roldão and Pedro Henriques.

The support of CMEST - Center for Structural Mechanics and Engineering of the Technical University of Lisbon, in the preparation of this document is also gratefully acknowledged.

The flawless typing is the product of Mrs. Sílvia Santos patience and utmost care.

7. REFERENCES

[1] Adler, C.F., "Modern Geometry", McGraw--Hill, 1967

[2] Barnhill, R.E., Riesenfeld, R.F., editors, "Computer Aided Geometric Design", Academic Press, 1974

[3] Barr, R.E., Wood, B.H., Juricic,D., "Computer Graphics and CAD in a Freshman Engineering Program", Engineering Education, Feb 1984.

[4] Beatty, J.C., Booth, K.S., "Tutorial : Computer Graphics", IEEE-CS, 1982

[5] Bechtold, C.W.,"An Introduction to Computer Graphics", Engineering Education, Jan 1971

[6] Bork, A., "The Computer in Education in the United States : The Perspective from the Educational Technology Center", 4th Canadian Symposium on Instructional Technology, Winnipeg, Canada, 1983

[7] Carlbom, I.B., Paciorek,J., "Planar Geometric Projections and Viewing Transformations", ACM Comp. Surveys, Dec 1978

[8] Charles, B.S., et al.,"Microcomputer Based Computer Aided Design System Applications in Engineering Education", Engsoft III,1983

[9] Clough, R.W.,"Use of Modern Computers in Structural Analysis", Convention ASCE, Oct 1957

[10] Earle, J.H.,"Drafting Technology", Addison--Wesley, 1982

[11] Eves, H.,"A Survey of Geometry", Allyn & Bacon, 1965

[12] Faux, I.D., Pratt, M.J.,"Computational Geometry for Design and Manufacture", Ellis Horwood, 1979

[13] Foley, J.D., VanDam, A.,"Fundamentals of Interactive Computer Graphics", Addison--Wesley, 1982

[14] Forrest, A.R.,"Computational Geometry", Proc. Royal Soc. London, 1971

[15] French, T.E., et al.,"Graphic Science and Design", McGraw-Hill, 1984

[16] Gasson, P.,"Geometry of Spatial Forms", Ellis Horwood, 1983

[17] Golden, F., et al.,"Here Come the Micro-kids", TIME, May 3, 1982

[18] Hamilton, P.S., et al.,"Implementation of Computer Graphics Exercises in Freshman Engineering Graphics Education", Computers & Graphics, Vol 6, no 1, 1982

[19] Hubbold, R.J., et al.,"Computer Graphics Fundamentals", Eurographics 82 Tutorial Notes

[20] Juricic, D., Barr, R.E.,"Graphics and CAD -A Systematic Approach", Mechanical Engineering, Sept 1982

[21] Kamel, H.A.,"Interactive Computer Graphics as a Tool in Teaching Structural Engineering", ASCE, JSTD, Vol 104, no 8, 1978

[22] Kelso, F., Riley, D.R., "Teaching Computer--Aided Drafting", Mechanical Engineering, Oct 1982

[23] Lazear, T.J.,"The Challenge of CAD Training", Computer Graphics World, Jan 1984

[24] LeBold, W.K., "Research in Engineering Education : An Overview", Engineering Education, Feb 1980

[25] Lubkin, J.L., Bigelow, R.H., "Computer Assisted Instruction in Structural Engineering - A Case Study", ASEE Conf., 1979

[26] Luzzader, W.J.,"Fundamentals of Engineering Graphics", Prentice-Hall, 1977

[27] McDougal, R.N.,"Engineering Graphics Teaching Aids", ASEE Conf., 1978

[28] Michener, J.C., Carlbom, I.B.,"Natural and Efficient Viewing Parameters", Computer Graphics, Aug 1980

[29] Miller, C.L.,"Man-Machine Communication in Civil Engineering", ASCE Conf. on Elect. Comp., June 1963

[30] Newman, W.M., Sproull, R.F.,"Principles of Interactive Computer Graphics", McGraw-Hill, 1979

[31] Nievergelt, J.,"A Pragmatic Introduction to Courseware Design". IEEE Computer, Sept 1980

[32] Osgood, D.,"A Computer in Every Desk", BYTE, June 1984

[33] Riley, D.R., Erdman, A.G.,"Computer Graphics and CAD in Mechanical Engineering at the University of Minnesota", Computers & Education, Vol 5, 1981

[34] Rogers, D.F., Adams, J.A.,"Mathematical Elements for Computer Graphics", McGraw-Hill, 1976

[35] Rogers, D.F., editor, "Computer Graphics in Engineering Education", Pergamon Press,1982

[36] Ryan, D.L.,"Computer-Aided Graphics and Design", Marcel Dekker, 1979

[37] Santo, H.P.,"The Teaching and Application of Computer Graphics in an Engineering Graphics Environment : A First Experience in Portugal", Report DUI 84/82, CMEST, Lisbon,1982

[38] Santo, H.P., Costa, J.M., "SIMPATICO - Sistema Simplificado Passivo para Tratamento de Informação Gráfica por Computador", AEIST, Lisbon, 1982

[39] Santo, H.P., panel 'Computer Graphics in Education', Eurographics 82 Conf., Manchester, UK, 1982

[40] Santo, H.P.,"Overview and Brief History of Applications of Computer Graphics to Structural Analysis and Engineering" (in Portuguese), JPEE, LNEC, Lisbon, 1982

[41] Santo, H.P.,"MABEL - A Micro-Computer Program for the Modal Analysis of Buildings under Earthquake Loads", EngSoft III, London,1983

[42] Santo, H.P., "Métodos Gráficos Computacionais - Iniciação Orientada, Vol 1 : Conceitos Básicos" (Computer Graphics -A Guided Initiation), Dinalivro, Lisbon, 1985

[43] Santo, H.P.,"An Educator's View of the Planar Geometric Projections Matrix Formulation", to appear

[44] Schaeffer, H.G., "A Futuristic View of Computer Assisted Education in Engineering", WC
on FEM, LA, 1981

[45] Slaby, S., letter in Graphic Science, Oct 1968

[46] Sommer, H.T., et al., "Computer-Aided Engineering Education", Mechanical Engineering, Dec
1982

[47] Vawter, D.L., "Microcomputers in Mechanics
of Materials", Mechanical Engineering, Sept
1982

[48] Wagner, P.M., "CG in Higher Education", CGW,
Jan 1984

[49] Walker, E.A. (chairman), "Final Report : Goals
of Engineering Education", Engineering Education, Jan 1968

[50] Proceedings of the ASCE Conferences on Civil
Engineering Education, Computing in Civil
Engineering and Electronic Computation

[51] Bowyer, A., Woodwark, J., "A Programmer's
Geometry", Butterworths, 1983

[52] International Conference on Engineering and
Computer Graphics, Aug 1984, Beijing, China

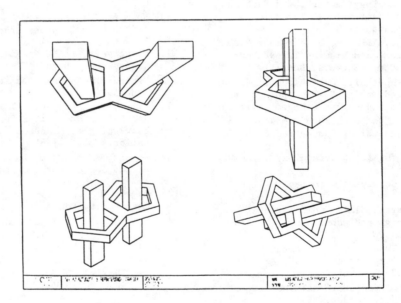

Figure 1

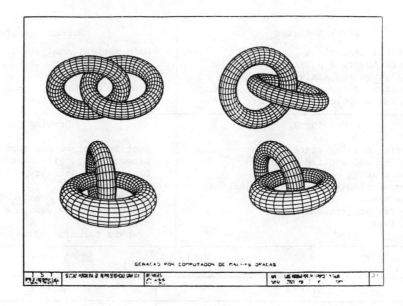

Figure 2

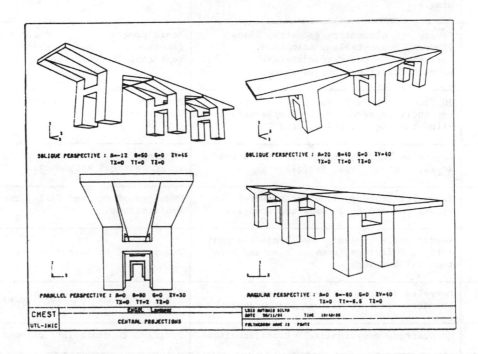

Figure 3

First Semester	Second Semester
Mathematical Analysis I General Chemistry I Linear Algebra and Analytical Geometry Introduction to Computers and Programming Drawing and Graphic Methods I	Mathematical Analysis II General Chemistry II History of Science Drawing and Graphic Methods II
Drawing I	**Drawing II**
Engineering drawing standards Engineering and applied geometry Freehand drawing and sketching Overview of planar geometric projections Multiple views Axonometric projections Perspectives	Sectional views and conventions Dimensioning. Size description Descriptive Geometry. Projections with elevations Topographic and construction drawing Introduction to design and project organization Graphic calculus. Nomography

Table 1

Week	Theory	Assignment Works
1	Overview and aims of the course.	Drawing of sectional multiple views from isometric projections with dimensions.
2	Sectional views. Conventions.	Drawing of isometric/dimetric projections with sections from multiple views with/without dimensions.
3	Dimensioning.	
4	Overview and aims of CG. History. Applications. Bibliography. Associations. Hardware. In/Output devices. Vendors. Micros. Languages. Basic graphics programming.	Micro-computer workshops. Operation and programming.
5	Review of elementary geometry. Plane figures. Shape-tables. Animation. Cartesian and polar coordinates. 2D math functions. Dashed lines.	Basic programs to draw plane figures, generate and animate 'shapes' and to represent 2D graphs and diagrams.
6	3D functions. Surfaces. Basic algorithms for their representation. Simple hidden-line techniques. Color. Art.	Programs to plot 3D functions. Visual arts applications.
7	Review of DG. Projections with elevations. Roofs. Contour maps. Profiles.	DG exercises. Horizontal projections of roofs. Vertical alignments.
8	Earthwork boundary lines of construction sites. Cut and fill. Dams and roadways.	Drawings of cut and fill limits in several applications.
9	Fundamentals of design and project organization. Buildings, construction and architectural drawings.	Drawings of buildings and detailing.
10	Overview of Computational Geometry. Geometric transformations in two dimensions.	Programs to manipulate figures in 2D.
11	Homogeneous coordinates. 3D transformations.	Programs to manipulate objects in 3D
12	Central, axonometric and multiview projections. Programming techniques.	Programs to draw projections of objects.

Table 2

COMPUTERS IN EDUCATION, K. Duncan and D. Harris (eds.)
Elsevier Science Publishers B.V. (North-Holland)
© IFIP, 1985

COMPUTER GRAPHICS AND TEACHING DESCRIPTIVE GEOMETRY

Manjula B. Waldron, Ph.D.
Associate Professor

Richard I. Hang
Professor Emeritus

Department of Engineering Graphics
The Ohio State University
Columbus, Ohio 43210

A software algorithm to teach descriptive geometry in the classroom is presented. The method of rotation is revisited. The ease of rotation of objects using computers makes this method very powerful and eliminates messey construction lines necessary in conventional methods of teaching descriptive geometry. The philosophy in developing the software is to allow the student to visualize the object as it rotates in space rather than getting lost in the mechanics of constructional detail. The design is modular and problem entry is easy. The high resolution of the Tektronix screen and the computational capabilities of the IBM 3277GA hosted by a 4341 computer is utilized to its fullest.

Introduction

Engineers require visualization of complex objects not only for the design conceptualization but also for communication and comprehension of complex objects and problems. Descriptive geometry is a tool used extensively to enhance this visualization through rotating objects in space and viewing from different angles. The study of descriptive geometry allows the projection of three dimensional objects into two dimensional plane of paper in a manner so as to allow geometric manipulation in determining true lengths, angles, shapes and other geometric information in graphics. The setting up of problems use principal views of orthographic projection (1).

Recent introduction of CAD/CAM techniques and three-dimensional represnetations of objects on the computer screen requires a knowledge of this visual manipulation technique. However, engineering college curricula of late have given less prominence to this aspect since, teaching this topic by traditional paper and pencil methods required a lot of students time with correspondingly limited benefits when weighed against other topics in the student's major area of study. It was generally felt that, yes, the descriptive geometry concepts are important but the curriculum can spare only one hour instead of four as was done say two decades ago.

Computers provide just such a vehicle to reduce the drawing time, without reducing the focus on the instruction of descriptive geometry concepts. Two methods are traditionally used to rotate the object in space to obtain specific information. Since all objects can be defined as lines, planes , cylinders and cones, most descriptive geometry introductory topics deal with finding specified views of lines, planes, cones and cylinders. The two methods used currently in teaching these concepts are 1) auxiliary view and 2) revolution.

In the auxiliary view method the observer shifts position for each view. Hence, reference planes are installed requiring a lot of construction lines for the projectors, a very time consuming process on paper. The software developed using the auxiliary view method is fairly involved and requires an extensive manual for user to interact (2-3). However, it does take away the tedium of drawing many projector lines on paper, especially if the student made an error to begin with in the first step.

In the revolution or rotation method the object is revolved into a new position in each view. Since rotation algorithms are very easy to use in computer graphics this method is far superior to auxiliary view method on the computer. In this paper the use to computer to explain this method is presented.

Method of Revolution

There are three fundamental principles of revolution:

1. The view of an object which shows the axis of revolution as a point will change in position only and not in size or shape.
2. All dimensions parallel to the axis of revolution will remain unchanged in the revolved views.
3. A point revolving about an axis lies in a plane perpendicular to the axis. A view showing the axis as a point will show the path of the point as a circle. This circle will appear as a line in all views perpendicular to this view.

Hence if there are lines whose point view are to be obtained one can revolve them so that they are parallel to one of the principle views. Hence the student only needs to know of this fact to solve his problems. This fact was exploited in the development of the software.

Hardware and Software

The system on which the software was developed consists of IBM 3277GA terminals attached to the tektronix 618 storage tube for graphical output. Each screen was connected to a hard copy device so the facsimile of the screen image could be obtained on a reduced 8 x 11 paper size. Each workstation was connected to the IBM 4341 computer running under VM/CMS and using RPQ graphics package.

The software design used the interactive features and high resolution screen to its fullest extent through a menu driven program. Student required no knowledge of any VM/CMS commands except how to log on and off. Through the profile EXEC file when the student logs on the menu displays the choices on the type of problem to be solved e.g., intersection of cylinders and lines. The program prompts for the student to enter his name. When this choice is made the software prompts the user with the problem definition like: "In this program you are to find the intersection points between lines and cylinders. The solution is to rotate the cylinder in such a manner so that the point view of the axis of the cylinder is available. The problem is now, reduced to intersection of line and a circle. The program can be asked to draw the points of intersection." The software then prompts with the menu shown in Figure 1 and the graphics screen displays the problem statement (Figure 2). The student at this point will make the selection by typing 1 and pushing enter key to rotate the axis of the cylinder.

The software then prompts with the following menu:

    Type 1 to rotate in top view
    Type 2 to rotate in front view
    Type 3 to rotate in side view

When the student makes his selection the software prompts with a prompt "Enter the position in degrees of the axis after rotation, 0-360". The student will enter 0 or 90 so as to get the end view of the axis in the adjacent view (Figure 4). At this point the student is ready to find the intesection point in the "I see it view" (the view which has the point view of the axis). Hence he/she makes the menu selection 2 in Figure 1. The menu will prompt the student to identify this view (Top, Front or Side). If the correct view is selected, crosses are placed at the point of intersection (Figure 5). The student can now choose menu selection 3 (Figure 1) to obtain a hard copy for submission. If at any point the student is confused he/she can always go back to the original problem by selecting option 4 thereby erasing all their work and leaving no smears. If frustrated, the student can make selection 5, which will return the student to the main menu for another problem selection.

Software Evaluation

Descriptive geometry is taught to freshman engineering students at The Ohio State University using paper and pencil techniques. The method used therefore, is auxiliary view method, since the method of rotation using paper and pencil is somewhat confusing (as the object is harder to move here). However, on the computer this latter method is extremely easy, since the basic rotation algorithm (which is heart of this software) consists of

$$X_{new} = X_{old} \; cosine(TH) - Y_{old} \; sine(TH)$$

$$Y_{new} = X_{old} \; sine(TH) + Y_{old} \; cosine(TH)$$

where   is the angle of rotation, X and Y are each X Y coordinates on the line computed for the rotated line. Each problem is built simply by calling a subroutine BUILD which generates the 2-dimensional representation of the data for the problem in Top, Front and write Side views. The rotate subroutine computes the present angle and then rotates it to the required angle. The software is modular in design; hence it is easy to generate new software for other topics in descriptive geometry.

To use the software the student does need to understand the concept of visualization through rotation. By the time the student has worked through a few problems, the concept of object in space becomes very clear to him. True lengths of lines, normal views of planes can be obtained in a matter of seconds and on making an error it is no major crisis. The stuent can easily make a clean start with no frustration.

The software developed so far has only been tested with a select group of students. All reactions have been positive. It is now ready to be used by the entire class. The problems which can be currently solved on the system are intersection of lines, lines and planes, planes and planes, lines and cyliners. Angles between lines & planes, and the shortest distance between planes. The example of intesection of lines and cylinder was chosen for this presentation, since on paper and pencil the elliptical views of the cylinder are not easy to draw. However, on the computer this algorithm is easy to implement. The strength of the software is easy to demonstrate using this problem.

Conclusion

computers have not been fully explored in the field of teaching descriptive geometry. Yet, this concept is of great importance in the new and upcoming field of CAD/CAM software, which depends on the engineer being able to specify the operations to be performed on the design concepts. To represent complex parts and objects, several rotated views of the objects are necessary to specify. Hence the

students must learn to mentally visualize the object in space and rotate these so that the features of interest are visible. The software presented here was developed with the novice user in mind and the requirement of teaching the visual rotation techniques. In using paper and pencil this method seems confusing to the student, while the computer the same method becomes extremely powerful. Full classroom evaluation has not been obtained. However, the preliminary reaction from the students are very favorable.

The software still needs some improvement in documentation entry of new problems under each category. However, the ease of use and the power behind the concept has been demonstrated. The modular design of the software and the high resolution of the screen is used to its fullest. The data base used is very simple and easy to generate.

References

[1] Earle J.H. *Engineering Design Graphics*. Ma: Addison Wesley, 1983.

[2] Hopkins, M.R. The IBM/OSU Project in Engineering Graphics. Proceeding of the 8th IBM University Studies conference. North Carolina, 1983.

[3] Smith, L.F. Computer Aided Instruction of Descriptive Geometry, submitted to 26th International conference on Computer Based Instruction to be held in Philadelphia, March 1985.

Acknowledgement

This research was partially supported by IBM Corporation and The Ohio State University.

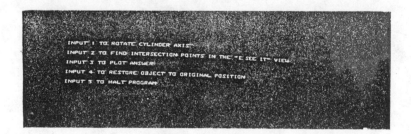

Figure 1. The student selection menu

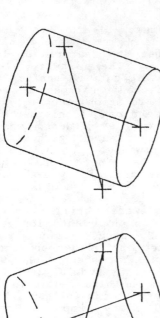

Figure 2. The problem as presented

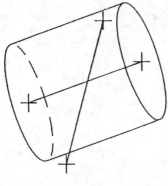

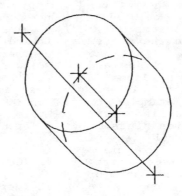

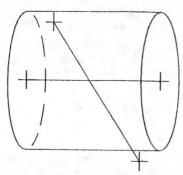

Figure 3. After selecting rotate axis option
(axis horizontal in top view)

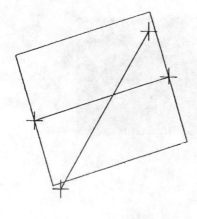

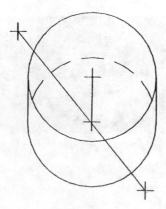

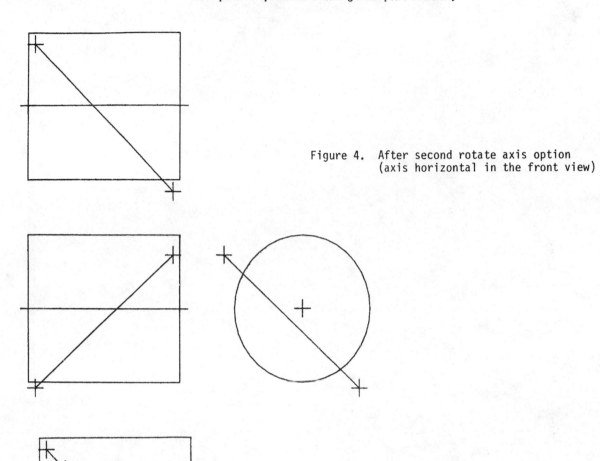

Figure 4. After second rotate axis option
(axis horizontal in the front view)

Figure 5. After selecting "find intersection" option
in the side view.

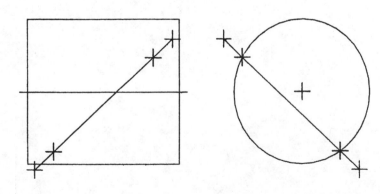

COMPUTERS IN EDUCATION, K. Duncan and D. Harris (eds.)
Elsevier Science Publishers B.V. (North-Holland)
© IFIP, 1985

HIGH PERFORMANCE COMPUTER GRAPHICS IN THE CLASSROOM

Chair
Dr. Lynne O'Brien, Brown University

Panelists
Nan Garrett, Brown University
David Laidlaw, Brown University
Steven Maker, Dartmouth College
Banu Onaral, Drexel University

The availability of high-resolution graphics-based computers at affordable cost has changed the ways people are using computers in education. The members of this panel represent universities where faculty have been experimenting with computer graphics in a variety of ways in conjunction with college-level courses. The subject matter of the courses using these graphics programs includes fine arts, social sciences, and engineering and the hardware environments range from VAX to Macintosh. Panel members will discuss the techniques used in the programs and address issues in the development and use of such techniques.

Nan Garrett, David Laidlaw, Brown University

Since the early 1970's, Brown has explored uses of computers in education. Brown's educational software authors have emphasized the computer's ability to aid students in visualizing abstract concepts and complex processes. Educational software, implemented on hardware ranging from a VAX 11/780 to a network of Apollo workstations to a Macintosh, has contributed to the curriculum in fine arts, political science, mathematics, neuroscience, and computer science (Figures 1 and 2).

Research currently is under way at Brown to develop a software environment that will allow good teachers to create educational software including graphics without becoming good programmers.

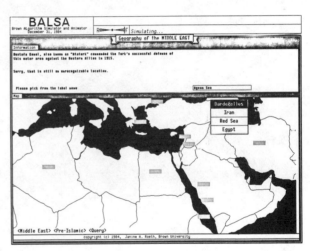

Figure 2 : Screen from a program designed to help anthropology students learn the geography of the Middle East.

Steven Maker, Dartmouth College

Because Dartmouth freshmen are encouraged to buy their own Apple Macintoshes, virtually all students have access to one. We are taking advantage of the fast, high-resolution graphic display to create courseware programs which would have been impossible or impractical before.

The benefits of the new programs include drastic reduction of learning time, reduced scope for errors, nearly instantaneous feedback, the feasibility of purely pictorial interaction, requirement of more complex decisions. The typing burden can often be removed completely, and student motivation is high because the programs are fun.

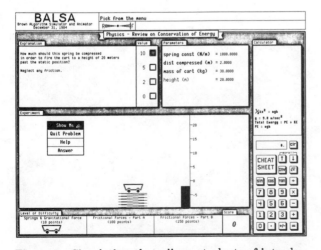

Figure 1 : Simulation that allows students of introductory physics to make multiple parameter changes and request a dynamic animation of proposed solutions.

Banu Onaral, Drexel University

Dr. Onaral will demonstrate and discuss the Signal and Systems package consisting of Signal Operations, Fourier Analysis and System Operations modules (Figure 3). The package provides an interactive environment within which the student can experiment with a multitude of theoretical and applied concepts while routine computations and display tasks are performed by the computer. The approach, akin to the "Engineering Workstation" concept, takes full advantage of Macintosh's user interface tools. Signal generation and selection of specific time and frequency domain operations are facilitated by the screen design, which also permits visual storage of signals. Signals can also be saved on disk.

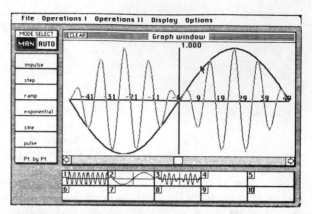

Figure 3 : The product of a higher frequency sinusoid with a lower frequency sinusoid serves to illustrate the modulation of a carrier.

COMPUTERS IN EDUCATION, K. Duncan and D. Harris (eds.)
Elsevier Science Publishers B.V. (North-Holland)
© IFIP, 1985

COMPUTER GRAPHICS AND THE ARTS

Terry Genin, Richard Dean

Northumberland Park School
Tottenham, London, England

The session will divide equally into
a) A demonstration of software
b) A talk by R. Dean on some of the problems in creating user friendly
   software which confront the Aesthetic/Artistic aspect of the user
   rather than the Intellectual/Cognitive.
c) A talk by T. Genin on the problems of program design when an
   aesthetic is to be developed.
d) A joint talk on the particular problems of using computer graphics
   in an 11 to 18 Art Department. Ways in which measurement techniques
   might be designed in order to assess the development of a user in
   terms of facility and their Aesthetic judgement as well as general
   creativity.

This presentation will concern itself with the particular problems of the user as observer. How observation skills may be developed in conjunction with carefully designed program displays. How those skills might be assessed together with the assessment of user understanding. Is promoting the use of computers in Art Departments advisable and if so how might that promotion be affected? Peculiar problems in translating the subjective response to the teacher measuring that development of that response.

The production of any worthwhile software depends heavily on close co-operation between the designer and the programmer as well as the maximum use made of all of the hardwares capabilities. In part of the session the particular problems of producing graphical software for use in a School Art Department will be outlined along with the solutions that were developed. Also, the problems associated with the spreading of the uses of microcomputers in schools, trying to reach parts of the curriculum where such devices were thought to be of very limited uses.

Course and Curricula Recommendations

COMPUTERS IN EDUCATION, K. Duncan and D. Harris (eds.)
Elsevier Science Publishers B.V. (North-Holland)
© IFIP, 1985

CURRICULA DEVELOPMENT AND TEACHER EDUCATION IN INFORMATICS

Peter Bollerslev, Denmark; Ulrich Bosler, Federal Republic of Germany
and David Tinsley, United Kingdom

Since the late 1960s, Working Group 3.1 has been helping informatics teachers through the publication of booklets and the proceedings of working conferences.

Main concerns of the group have been the impact of informatics on mathematics education, the introduction of microcomputers in secondary schools, computer assisted learning and the development of informatics in elementary schools.

The most recent working conference, held in Birmingham, UK, last summer returned to the key theme of informatics in the training of teachers and reviewed fifteen years of international development work.

Three members of WG 3.1 will be serving on this panel, all of whom are well experienced in the organisation and development of informatics in schools and teacher education centres.

David Tinsley, UK, will present the history of WG 3.1.

Ulrich Bosler, FRG, will give follow-up to the conference "Informatics in Elementary Education" held in 1983.

Peter Bollerslev, DK, will report on the work carried out with relation to teacher education.

COMPUTERS IN EDUCATION, K. Duncan and D. Harris (eds.)
Elsevier Science Publishers B.V. (North-Holland)
© IFIP, 1985

A HIGH SCHOOL COURSE IN INFORMATION AND
COMPUTER TECHNOLOGY

W. Atchison and R. Austing, University of Maryland; J. Berry, Fairfax
County (VA) Public Schools; G. Carruth, Wayzata (MN) Public Schools;
S. Charp, Philadelphia (PA) Public Schools; E. Daniel, University of
Syracuse; C. Harris, University of Texas at Dallas; M. King, Oak Park
and River Forest High School (IL); J. Rogers, University of Texas at
Austin; R. Schneiderhan, Roseville (MN) Schools.

This presentation reports on the curriculum development efforts of the Working Committee funded by the AFIPS (American Federation of Information Processing Societies) Education Committee.
In particular, topics are being developed which
could be presented in a one year course on computing and information technology.

RATIONALE:

The growth of new knowledge and technologies in
today's society is increasing rapidly. The computer is one of these technologies.

Also, as a part of the logical progression of
academic efforts in computer instruction, a
course is needed at the 9th and 10th grade
levels to give all students an understanding of
our information age and what it means to live
and work in it. Acquiring the technological
concepts and tools to process information are
essential for secondary students to know how to
live and function as competent adults and productive citizens.

The material presented in Computing and Information Technology and the teaching methodology
used will equip secondary students to cope with
the changes brought about by the emerging com-
puting/information technologies.

COURSE DESCRIPTION:

Computing and Information Technology is recommended for all Freshmen and Sophomore students.
Students will learn the importance of information in today's society and will have hands-on
experience to access and work with a variety of
computer-based information resources. The way
humans process information is contrasted to the
way computers process information. Human/com-
puter interaction demonstrates the use of information technology to enhance human capabilities.
Students will learn how to use information in
problem solving and decision making. Knowledge
of information processing strategies learned in
this course can benefit school performance in
other areas.

The materials for this course could be presented
in a full year, a semester, or in individual
modules. The range of assignments and activities accommodate the needs of each student,
whatever his/her previous experience and intellectual gifts.

GOALS:

Students will understand:

1. The impact of information technology on
today's society.

2. The importance of effective use of information, both to the individual and to society.

3. How information is processed: by humans, by
computer and related technologies, and by
human/computer systems.

4. How to obtain and use information for problem
solving and for decision making.

5. Their roles and responsibilities for living
and working in an information age.

Members of the Working Committee will discuss
details of the course outline and objectives as
well as examples of activities and resources
appropriate to the course.

A proposal for funding is being submitted for
the next stage of the project - teacher training
and pilot testing.

COMPUTERS IN EDUCATION, K. Duncan and D. Harris (eds.)
Elsevier Science Publishers B.V. (North-Holland)
©IFIP, 1985

COMPUTER SCIENCE FOR SECONDARY SCHOOLS: COURSE CONTENT

Jean B. Rogers, Chair
Department of Computer Sciences
University of Texas at Austin

John C. Arch
Computer Science Department
Shippensburg State University

John D. Lawson
Computer & Information Science
University of Oregon

Anthony Jongejan
College of Education
Western Washington University

Samuel F. Tumolo
Mathematics Department
Cincinnati Country Day School

During 1983-84, a task group under the direction of the Association for Computing Machinery's Elementary and Secondary Schools Subcommittee developed recommendations for content for computer science courses in secondary schools. The draft report was presented at numerous conferences and reviewed by both computer scientists and educators. The final report has been accepted by the ACM Education Board and by the Education Committee of the Institute of Electrical and Electronics Engineers/Computer Society. A summary of the report was published in the March, 1985, issue of the Communications of the ACM and the complete report is available through the ACM order department as part of Computer Science in Secondary Schools: Curriculum and Teacher Certification, order number 201850.

Session Summary

Computers and computing are topics of discussion in many curriculum areas in secondary school. The four courses recommended in this report, however, have computing as their primary content. The courses are:

1) Introduction to Computer Science I
   (a full year course)
2) Introduction to Computer Science II
   (a full year course)
3) Introduction to a High-level Computer Language
   (a half-year course)
4) Applications and Implications of Computers
   (a half-year course)

Courses 1 and 2 are designed for students with a serious interest in computer science. Course 1 can serve as a single introductory course for some students and also act as a prerequisite for Course 2. At the end of two years of study, students should be prepared to be placed in second level computer science classes in post-secondary educational institutions or to take the Advanced Placement Exam available through the College Entrance Exam Board.

Courses 1 and 2 will require a significant amount of equipment for each student enrolled. Computers, either microcomputers or a timesharing system with convenient storage for files (disks) and high-speed printers are necessary.

Courses 3 and 4 are designed to be of general interest to any student at the secondary level. Course 3 is a course about programming. It is a general introduction to the process of writing programs in a high-level computer language. It requires extensive hardware facilities, as students will need to practice using whichever computer language is chosen for the instruction.

Course 4 includes information about the ways computers are used and about the impact of computer use on people's lives. Because students in this course will be using a computer to learn about applications, teaching this course requires extensive software in addition to hardware.

Courses 1, 3 and 4 have been designed assuming no prerequisite courses and are not interdependent.

Teachers of all four of these courses should be qualified in the content area and preferably certified to teach about computing and computer science. The discipline of computer science has been evolving over several years and will continue to change. Courses in computer science will similarly continue to change. Well-trained teachers are the cornerstone of effective instruction in such a fluid environment.

COMPUTERS IN EDUCATION, K. Duncan and D. Harris (eds.)
Elsevier Science Publishers B.V. (North-Holland)
© IFIP, 1985

THE ADVANCED PLACEMENT (AP) COMPUTER SCIENCE (CS) PROGRAM

Philip L. Miller, Chairman AP CS Development Committee (session chair)
Computer Science Department, Carnegie - Mellon University
Pittsburgh, Pennsylvania 15312 (412-578-3560)

Henry M. Walker, AP CS Table Leader
Department of Mathematics, Computer Science, Grinnell College
Grinnell, Iowa 50112 (515-235-6181)

David C. Rine, Chief Reader AP CS Program (session organizer)
Department of Computer and Information Sciences
George Mason University
Fairfax, Virginia (previously at Western Illinois University)

The Advanced Placement (AP) Program is a cooperative educational endeavor of the
College Board. The goals of an Advanced Placement Computer Science course are com -
parable to those of a first-year course offered in college and university computer
science departments. An AP Computer Science course can be offered by any secondary
school that has faculty who possess the necessary expertise and that has access to
appropriate computing facilities. The teacher should be prepared to present a college
-level first course in computer science. The major emphasis in an AP Computer Science
course is on programming methodology, algorithms, and data structures. Applications
are used to develop student awareness of the need for particular algorithms and data
structures, as well as to provide topics for programming assignments to which stu -
dents can apply their knowledge. A particular programming language constitutes a
vehicle for implementing computer-based solutions to particular problems. Treatments
of computer systems and social implications of computing are integrated into the
course and not isolated as separate units. The Advanced Placement Computer Science
Examination seeks to determine how well a student has mastered the concepts and
techniques developed for the course.

' Issues in Advanced Placement Computer
Science '

Philip L. Miller
Carnegie-Mellon University

In this talk the difficult issues that faced,
and in some cases still face, the College
Board and its AP/CS Development Committee are
addressed. Topics included are the following:

. whether and what sort of involvement in
  computer science

. course content and language(s)

. examination format

. lack of experienced teachers

. hardware disparities

Key Addresses.

. Harlan P. Hanson, Program Service Officer
  The College Board, 888 Seventh Avenue
  New York, New York 10106.

. Carl Haag, Director
  Advanced Placement
  Educational Testing Service
  Princeton, N.J. 08541.

' Developing and Teaching an AP CS Course '

Henry M. Walker
Grinnell College

This talk will present many of the issues
involved in organizing and teaching an AP CS
Course, from the initial selection of mater -
ials to the final testing and evaluation of
students. Topics in this presentation will
include planning aids, recent and forthcoming
textbooks, major themes to be stressed, and
primary teaching objectives, Further, the talk
will present the format and grading of the
AP CS Examination itself, including expecta -
tions, issues of program organization and
style, and themes raised in the first two
years of grading. Major topics are the following:

. AP CS supporting materials

. AP CS examinations

. current text materials

References.

. Advanced Placement Program of the College
  Board. 'Advanced Placement Course Descrip -
  tion: Computer Science'. Educational Testing
  Service, Princeton, N.J. 1985.

(continuation) THE ADVANCED PLACEMENT (AP) COMPUTER SCIENCE (CS) PROGRAM

Michael Clancey, Director   (fourth author)
Introductory Programming Courses
Computer Science Division
University of California, Berkeley
Berkeley, California 94720

'Study of Large Programs as Part of
the Advanced Placement Computer Science (AP CS) Course'

Michael Clancey
University of California, Berkeley

I believe that the study of relatively
large programs (between 500 - 1500
lines) should be part of the AP CS
course. Certain aspects of the design
and development of such programs can
easily be included in the course, and
tested on the AP CS examination. For
instance, programming templates weighs
that good style facilitates good understanding, comparison of data structures
and program implementations, instrumentation of a program, tracing and analyzing a program, and incremental development of a program's routines. In this
talk I will discuss why and how we
teach these concepts in our introduction to computer science course at
University of California, Berkeley.

COMPUTERS IN EDUCATION, K. Duncan and D. Harris (eds.)
Elsevier Science Publishers B.V. (North-Holland)
© IFIP, 1985

CURRICULA IN COMPUTING FOR POST-SECONDARY INSTITUTIONS

Moderator: John Beidler, University of Scranton

Panelists: Nancy Ide, Vassar College
Arthur I. Larky, Lehigh University
John Meinke, University of Scranton
A. James Wynne, Virginia Commonwealth Univ.

There is great variation in curricula in computing at post-secondary institutions ranging from associate degree programs through various graduate programs. At the center of this are the various possibilities for undergraduate degree programs. Several professional societies have published model curricula for various programs. The panelists in this session present four types of undergraduate degree programs. Each presentation consists of background, model curriculum, and philosophical considerations along with considerations that are specific to the curriculum at the panelist's institution.

Nancy Ide presents the curriculum model for an AB program in computing that is under development through a grant from the Sloan Foundation.

Arthur I. Larky describes the computer engineering program currently offered in the Electrical Engineering Department at Lehigh University. This program is based upon the computer science and engineering model curriculum of the IEEE. This presentation describes considerations that are relevant both to the curriculum model and to the unique circumstances at Lehigh.

John Meinke presents a curriculum based upon the ACM Curriculum '78 model along with considerations which anticipate future revisions of the ACM curriculum model. This curriculum includes a freshman level discrete mathematics course and the use of a programming language in CS2 which more directly supports such software engineering concepts as data abstraction.

A. James Wynne describes the Information Systems degree program at Virginia Commonwealth University. There are two model curricula in Information Systems, one published by the ACM and one by the DPMA. Prof. Wynne describes both models and their relationship to the program at VCU

The panel concludes with observations about the common core of courses and concerns the models have in common. The panel concludes with an open discussion and questions from the audience.

COMPUTERS IN EDUCATION, K. Duncan and D. Harris (eds.)
Elsevier Science Publishers B.V. (North-Holland)
©IFIP, 1985

AN IFIP/BCS CURRICULUM FOR INFORMATION SYSTEM DESIGN

Chairperson: Prof. R.A. Buckingham, University of London

Participants: Prof. Frank F. Land, London School of Economics
                Prof. Gordon B. Davis, University of Minnesota
                Another speaker from Europe

In 1974 IFIP issued a report entitled 'An International Curriculum for Information System Designers'. At that time it was expected that education and training in information systems would be mainly confined to studies at graduate level, and the report contained guidelines for such studies. Since then immense changes have occurred in the technology available, in the variety of systems being developed, and in the role of the system designer. What has now been prepared is a much broader curriculum which encompasses these changes, and recognises that the development of a professional information system designer is not accomplished in a year or two; indeed if implemented at all fully the curriculum is likely to extend to 4 or 5 years. However the material assembled may be adapted by designers of courses to meet many other requirements and situations. The preparation has relied substantially on the knowledge and experience of members of the British Computer Society.

The aims of the session will be to explain the rationale behind the present work, to make some comparison with other approaches in North America and Europe, and to stimulate discussion.

F.F. Land: Development of a discipline of information systems management

From the early days of computer use the academic community invented the discipline of computer science for research and teaching related to the development of the technology. Over the years topics concerned with data processing and the design of information systems began to be introduced into the syllabuses of computer science courses, but because of the apparent fuzziness of the subject matter, and the "hints and wrinkles" level of methodology, it received scant respect from the academic community. At the same time, however, the growth of business computing was phenomenal, and the users needed trained staff to analyse, design, operate and manage the new data processing systems.

The outcome was the establishment of a new academic discipline - Information Systems Management - rooted not only in the older discipline of computer science, but in organisation and management theory, in

sociology and psychology, and having to look to theories of scientific method and philosophy for its intellectual justification.

Because of the rapid changes in the technology, and in the use that is made of the technology, the new discipline is itself undergoing constant scrutiny and change. The IFIP curriculum is the second version of a curriculum first published during the IFIP conference in Stockholm in 1974. It is not merely a second edition. It is a radical redesign in the context of a developing technology. Although it passes beyond the "hints and wrinkles" of earlier days, its authors are aware of the slow progress in defining a true theory of Information Systems.

G.B. Davis: A comparison of the IFIP/BCS curriculum for information systems and North American information systems curricula

The diversity in colleges and universities in North America also leads to significant diversity in information systems curricula. Two North American efforts to provide curriculum guidance for information systems are the Association for Computing Machinery (ACM) and the Data Processing Management Association (DPMA). Curriculum recommendations were made in 1972 by the ACM and revised in 1982. These are viewed as guidelines rather than absolute requirements. The DPMA model curriculum, published in 1981, is prescriptive and a school can be "certified" as meeting the requirements. The ACM model tends to be the one used by graduate schools; the DPMA model is followed more by junior colleges and undergraduate programs. These models and North American practices will be contrasted with the IFIP/BCS curriculum. Future curriculum developments will be forecast. For example, information systems programs are expected to respond to a significant change in information systems in organizations - the emergence of end-user facilities and the changing role of the central information systems organization. The IBM grant program in support of the "management of information system" will be an important stimulus to this curriculum response.

Computer Literacy

COMPUTERS IN EDUCATION, K. Duncan and D. Harris (eds.)
Elsevier Science Publishers B.V. (North-Holland)
©IFIP, 1985

IMPLEMENTING AN INNOVATIVE COMPUTER EDUCATION PROGRAM
IN LARGE SCHOOL DISTRICTS

STEPHEN SHULLER, MODERATOR
BANK STREET COLLEGE OF EDUCATION

In 1984, Bank Street College and the University of South Florida coordinated a major computer education program in 28 of the nation's largest school districts, with financial support from IBM. The Model School program involved 700 teachers representing many different disciplines and grade levels in using computers as tools for learning and instructional support. IBM supplied about 90 computers to each site, along with peripherals, applications software, and financial support for administration and staff development.

The program used a layered approach to staff development. Bank Street and the University of South Florida worked directly with Professional Staff Development Teams (PSDTs) from 14 school districts, who in turn worked directly with five key teachers in each of five local participating schools. The key teachers in each school were charged with involving their colleagues after an initial period of their own involvement.

Securing support from local school district administrators was an important feature of the program. Before beginning, IBM sponsored a conference for the participating district superintendents, and the PSDT members involved the building principals and school faculties in as much of the initial planning as possible. This groundwork seems to have been very important in facilitating the local implementations of the program.

For most of the participating school districts, the Model School program provided a focus or model for a much larger-scale computer education program taking place in the district. Many districts found that the Model School program enabled them to concentrate resources on a small number of schools in a way not possible in the district as a whole. The program also served as a catalyst for some districts to move from a CAI or programming based approach to computer education to one concerned with integrating computers into the curriculum using applications programs such as word processors, spread sheets, filers and graphics utilities.

This session will be a panel discussion of the Model School program, focusing on some of the issues in implementing computer education in large school districts. The panelists are all PSDT members from school districts in the program.

PANELISTS

Sharon Bell
New Orleans, LA

Bill Booz
Fairfax County, VA

Chuck Dulaney
Charlotte-Mecklenburg, NC

Ron Dries
Jefferson County, CO

Randy Johnson
Anoka-Hennepin, MN

Nancy Lebron
Commonwealth of Puerto Rico

Jenelle Leonard
District of Columbia

Stephen Shuller, Moderator
New York, NY

COMPUTERS IN EDUCATION, K. Duncan and D. Harris (eds.)
Elsevier Science Publishers B.V. (North-Holland)
© IFIP, 1985

DESIGNING A COMPUTER LITERACY CURRICULUM: AN INTEGRATED APPROACH

Shirl S. Schiffman

Curry School of Education
University of Virginia

During the 1983-84 school year, the Charlottesville Public School system began an eighth-grade computer literacy program in which all teachers from the four basic disciplines participated: social studies, reading/language arts, science, and mathematics. This particular approach is called an "integrated" curriculum because the responsibility for teaching the computer skills is divided among the regular classroom teachers rather than being delivered in a "computer class" by a "computer teacher".

This paper discusses: (1) the philosophy behind the selection of the integrated approach (2) the inservice and curriculum development activities and (3) the first year of implementation and plans for the future.

1. DERIVING A MODEL FOR TEACHING COMPUTER LITERACY

1.1 Introduction

Despite the myriad of articles, books, and workshops that purport to define computer literacy, school systems across the country find that they must finally come to grips with the issue on their own terms. State Departments of Education may issue guidelines and objectives, national organizations may offer suggestions, but ultimately an individual or a group from within a school system must decide exactly what will be done, how it will be done and who will do it. This leads to tremendous diversity in computer literacy definitions and curricular development. The most popular "model" for implementing a computer literacy program is to set up a special class, exploratory, or some other activity in which students participate to learn what are deemed essential computer literacy skills. This model has many advantages: (1) It usually requires only one instructor to be trained in the use of the computer, alleviating inservice problems. (2) One room equipped with all available computers and other resources can be kept under the direct supervision of the computer teacher, possibly cutting down on security problems. (3) The only scheduling problems involve arranging what times students will attend their computer class. (4) Finally, curriculum development is a relatively simple matter, since only one teacher may actually be involved.

The model just described represents the computer literacy model for many school systems, obviously with some variations. But, how were these decisions made? How does the model itself relate to the goals of computer literacy? Is it possible that this kind of approach may distort students' view of computers in some way? In order to answer these questions, one must arrive at a definition of computer literacy. How can we know if we have arrived if we don't know what we are shooting at?

1.2 Establishing a Valid Definition

In their book Needs Assessment: Concept and Application (1979)[1], Kaufman and English describe the concept of "external" needs assessment which suggests that in order to determine what schools should be teaching, an external referent point must be established as a planning guide. In other words, to determine what skills, knowledge, and attitudes students will need when they leave the educational system and enter society, it is essential to study society! What is required to become a person who can function in and contribute to society? Kaufman and English suggest that this kind of analysis yields an appropriate perspective for evaluating our K-12 curriculum goals for adequacy and relevancy.

This same kind of long-range planning can be used to make some critical decisions about the content and the format of our computer literacy programs. An observation of how people outside the school system are using computers yields the fact that many different people are using many different computer applications, but their choices are not random! They make use of those that are genuinely relevant to their personal or professional goals. Authors, journalists, secretaries -- all those involved in the production of printed materials are making tremendous use of word processing. Scientists and researchers are using computers to help conduct and analyze their studies. Large and small businessmen as well as many private individuals are using the computer for financial planning, forecasting, and recordkeeping. Cinematographers and other artists are experimenting

in ever astounding ways with computer-generated
graphics. Everybody, it seems, makes more and
more use of database management: banks,
libraries, the credit agency, the grocery store,
etc.

How might this cursory examination of how
computers are used in society help to determine
a definition and, therefore, a model of computer
literacy? The Charlottesville Public School
system felt that there were several very important implications. First, observing societal
use of computers would suggest that a wide
range of applications should be presented in a
computer literacy program. As previously
stated, many different people use computers in
many different ways. It would seem, then, that
a computer literacy program should attempt to
give students exposure to as many applications
as possible, emphasizing the versatility of the
tool in meeting diverse needs.

Second, using the external referent point seems
to suggest emphasizing the "tool" applications
of the computer. According to Robert Taylor's
well-known book, The Computer in the School:
Tutor, Tool, Tutee (1980)[2], tool applications
are those that help you do something better,
faster, more economically, or with less frustration than you could without the computer. An
analysis of societal use of computers certainly
shows heavy use of the "big three" software
tools: word processing, spreadsheets and other
data analysis software, and database management.
These applications account for the majority of
computer usage for individuals and companies.
Therefore, giving students experience with these
applications would seem a logical step in
preparing them for the future.

Third, programming would seem to be something
to de-emphasize. Of the millions of people
using computers outside the school system,
relatively few of them actually program their
own materials. Those who do are generally paid
professionals (computer scientists, staff or
free-lance programmers) or hobbyists. The
majority of people locate "canned" software that
suits their purposes or have software created
for them. Hence, having programming as a major
emphasis of a computer literacy unit would seem
to be presenting an inaccurate view of how the
computer really functions in society.

The Charlottesville teachers also felt that
using the external referent point gave them some
direction in determining how the curriculum
should be implemented and by whom. In order for
students to see how professionals in many
different disciplines make use of the powerful,
varied attributes of the computer, it seemed
necessary to model this for them. Since the
professionals with whom school children come in
contact are teachers, the questions were asked:
How do people in science use computers? How do
people involved in language, social sciences,
and math use computers? At this point it became
evident that having one or even a few teachers

to do all of the computer teaching would not be
as effective as a multi-discipline approach in
which the teachers in the different areas introduce applications that are related to their
subjects and needs.

Although this is but a brief summary of the
kind of philosophical decision-making that
preceded the ultimate development of an eighth-
grade computer literacy curriculum in the Spring
of 1983, it should be clear that the overall
guideline was to show the computer as a tool
with many different applications and to actually
model this by having the "regular" teachers be
an integral part of the teaching of computer
literacy. Earlier in this paper the advantages
of the "traditional" (special computer class/
special computer teacher) approach to computer
literacy were listed. The pros and cons of the
"integrated" approach that evolved from the
Charlottesville Public Schools' external needs
assessment are now listed.

1.3 The Integrated Approach: The Pros

.An integrated approach would model how the
computer has actually affected our lives:
people turn to it to solve personal or professional problems, to make their lives easier and
more productive, their work more professional,
more accurate, more time and cost effective.
.An integrated approach has the potential for
demonstrating more different kinds of applications because more teachers will be involved,
each looking for the ways the computer can best
be used in his or her area.
.An integrated approach will actually show
students that all kinds of different people are
using computers. First period Mr. Jones uses it
one way in English, second period Mrs. Carter
uses it another way in math. In science class
the computer is used as part of an experiment,
in social studies the teacher has the class
create a database to demonstrate issues of
privacy of information and piracy. This should
help to avoid a number of the stereotypes about
who uses computers (e.g. only math people, only
people with a computer science background, only
people who are male!)
.An integrated approach will lead to grassroots
faculty involvement: all teachers will be in it
together! At the same time, nobody will have to
do it all, but only the section of computer
literacy relevant to his or her area. An additional advantage here is that once subject area
teachers have gained some computer literacy
skills themselves, they are in a better position
to look for how the computer can specifically
help them in the teaching and management of
their classes.

1.4 An Integrated Approach: Possible Cons

.An integrated approach will require everybody
who is going to participate to get some
training.

.An integrated approach will require consensus and coordination among faculty in determining what will be taught and by whom.

.An integrated approach will require teachers to share computers, resources, and to schedule lab time.

After viewing the pros and cons and determining that at the middle school level where multi-discipline planning was viewed as a positive force, the Charlottesville Public School middle school teachers opted for taking on the challenge of developing and implementing an integrated computer literacy program at the eighth grade level.

2. A PROCEDURE FOR DEVELOPING AN INTEGRATED CURRICULUM

2.1 Initial Inservice Training

The actual sequence in which the eighth grade curriculum was theorized and developed extended from November, 1982 to August, 1983. Beginning in November, 1982, representatives from the four major discipline areas (two each from both middle schools in the system for a total of 16) along with several building level and central office administrators began a three-semester hour class at the University of Virginia. The first goal of the class was to bring the participants (many with no previous computer training) to a general awareness level of the computer and its capabilities. The second goal was to begin to analyze how the computer could be helpful in the various disciplines. Finally, the class was introduced to the concept of computer literacy and given the responsibility of participating in deciding how computer literacy would be taught.

Despite such extensive goals, the course succeeded in bringing all participants to a stage of being knowledgeable of the computer and many of its applications. Although many teachers still felt they needed much more time to be truly comfortable in using the computer (obviously true), they were prepared to discuss using the computer in the instructional program by the last few weeks of the course. At this point the external needs assessment planning approach was discussed and ultimately viewed as the most desirable philosophy. The course participants recognized that their decision meant they would not only have to continue their own learning, but would be responsible for bringing along the other members of their team who were unable to attend the class. Such was the enthusiasm and commitment on the part of the teachers and administrators in the course that this potentially overwhelming obstacle was viewed as a positive factor: they decided to learn together!

2.2 Curriculum Development

Following the class, a committee of one subject area representative from each school met with

several administrators to hash out exactly what the curriculum would be. These meetings were held during school hours, with substitute time being provided. Using the guidelines established during the course and recommendations from the Virginia Department of Education, the committee laid out what essential computer literacy skills would be for the upcoming eighth graders. The spectrum of skills broke down into the same four categories usually listed as computer literacy skills: computer operation and technology, computers in society, computer programming, computer applications.

These areas were then perused to see where they most logically might dovetail with the regular curriculum. For example, one major application, word processing, was felt to be most logically linked with language arts instruction. Discussing the implications of how computers have impacted our society was assigned to the social studies classrooms, where such topics are normally presented. Although programming was not viewed as a major emphasis, some experience with programming was viewed as essential to understanding the creation of software. The math teachers introduced Logo to provide the concept of programming while they simultaneously looked for ways in which Logo could be used in conjunction with the regular mathematics curriculum. In short, the goal was to divide up the essential computer literacy skills among the disciplines, where they were most appropriate and could benefit the existing objectives. After this, each teacher was encouraged to locate additional software related to the objectives of his or her subject. A final task for the committee was to arrange the topics in a logical order and plan for the acquisition of hardware and software.

Once the committee had devised the scope and sequence of skills, this was communicated to the other members of the class. At this point each school knew who was responsible for doing what and when. Course members undertook individual inservice work with other teachers who were to be involved. A lab with 15 computers for each school was established. Software was purchased.

During the first nine weeks of the 1983-84 school year the computer literacy program was begun. The concluding section of this paper will highlight both the strengths and the problems of the first year of implementation.

3. INTEGRATED COMPUTER LITERACY: THE FIRST YEAR

3.1 Positive Results

There is no question but that both middle schools were overwhelmed with the response from the students. To be sure, any introduction of computers into a school is bound to generate enthusiasm. However, the fact that so many teachers were involved seemed to make it a total school project. Indeed, the team approach must be seen as one of the major advantages. The faculty members became a support group for each other. People who had never really worked together before were suddenly sharing successes and frustrations in getting used to the new equipment, in seeing Johnny get interested in something for the first time, in marveling over the speed and ease with which the majority of students mastered the computer literacy skills. Students excitedly shared what they had done in their social studies class with their math teacher and vice versa. A real feeling of community was established because so many teachers and students were taking on this adventure at the same time. For the teachers there was comfort in knowing that they only had a few topics to cover; hence, preparation time was kept to a minimum. For the students, however, there was the excitement and benefit of learning different skills from different teachers, sometimes while simultaneously working on regular curriculum objectives. Many people commented on the fact that the computers seemed to be so much a part of the various subjects. This was generally viewed favorably by parents unsure of the value of computer classes that pull students from basic skill work. In response to parental interest, one middle school ran an evening class for parents and their children.

One initial concern, that of having to schedule and share the computer lab facilities, proved to be no problem. Perhaps because of the feeling of ownership they had in the overall program, teachers seemed to have no friction in working out arrangements.

Another major benefit was the interest on the part of the other teachers in both schools. Both middle schools conducted several inservice classes which included music, shop, home economics, sixth- and seventh-grade teachers-- all interested in how they could eventually use the computer in their areas. Members of the original class conducted these courses.

All in all, the first year was considered a success. Problems that surfaced are being analyzed to revise the program for next year. Some of these concerns are explained in the concluding section of this paper.

3.2 Some Problems and Future Plans

Teachers did experience a feeling of pressure because of the time they spent teaching the computer literacy skills. Even with an attempt to integrate this into the regular curriculum, some time had to be spent just teaching the students basic operations. This is viewed as only a temporary problem, however, because the 1984-85 school year will see the seventh grade begin a computer literacy unit, the following year the sixth grade will begin. As more of the computer operation skills are mastered at earlier grades, the subject area teachers at all levels will find they are more able to look for ways to truly use the computer as a tool in their particular disciplines.

There was not enough software available to support some of the goals set by the committee. This was an economic problem which will be alleviated for the 1984-85 school year. A continued emphasis on tool applications will be mounted. Several middle school teachers attended another class during the summer of 1984 to design student activities using spreadsheets, database management systems, and other utility software.

The need for continual inservice of teachers was directly felt when several of the original course members left the system or were transferred to other schools. However, because no one teacher is responsible for the entire program, remaining teachers seem confident of bringing new people on board.

Finally, teachers did indicate a wish that one person could act as coordinator--not to do the teaching of all the areas, but to help with communication, planning new activities, and to help supervise the computer lab. Realistically, this is somewhat unlikely in the near future, and the teachers survived. However, it is one of the disadvantages of the integrated approach.

4. SUMMARY

In conclusion, this paper has described the development and implementation of an eighth-grade computer literacy curriculum in which the computer literacy skills were integrated into the regular school curriculum. This approach is viewed as modeling more realistically the way computers are used in society. The Charlottesville Public School system is pleased with its middle school project and will systematically expand it downwards to the lower grades. In so doing, the final goal is a coherent sequence of skills that will prepare the students for even more sophisticated applications at the high school level and ultimately to be prepared to use computers in the world beyond the schools. In the process, all of the teachers will gradually become more expert in determining the ways in which the computer best supports their field.

[1] Kaufman, R. and English, F., Needs assessment: Concept and application (Educational Technology, Englewood Cliffs, 1979).

[2] Taylor, R., ed., The computer in the school: tutor, tool, tutee (Teachers College Press, New York, 1980).

COMPUTERS IN EDUCATION, K. Duncan and D. Harris (eds.)
Elsevier Science Publishers B.V. (North-Holland)
© IFIP, 1985

A MODEL TO DEVELOP COMPUTER LITERACY IN EDUCATION

RALPH STUCKMAN

Western Ohio Branch Campus
Wright State University
Celina, Ohio 45822, U.S.A.

People meet problems in developing computer literacy competencies. Literature sources are almost nonexistent on how people learn on the computer. Computer literacy needs to be interrelated with learning theory. A Model to Develop Computer Literacy in Education has been developed to fuse the nature of computer instruction with learning theory.

The model consists of five parts including psychological trust, demonstration, hands-on experience, capsulization and knowledge of results. The psychological trust component frees the learner to control the computer. Demonstration provides an overview of computing concepts and skills. Hands-on experience is the significant model part whereby the person is paced at a natural learning rate. Capsulization is a sharing process of computer learning events. Knowledge of results involves noted learning progress. This model is a systematic approach to increase computer learning efficiency.

SCENARIO

The professor is working with a group of people in a computer room. The group consists of fourteen people learning to be computer literate. The mentor says, "The computers that you see in this room will not blow up and will not smoke. As we work with the computers, there is really nothing that we will do that may damage the equipment. Of course, if we took this printer and slammed it to the floor, the printer would likely be damaged. In our work with these computers, we will get to know them and experience what they can do."

The mentor continues, "Let us gather around this TRS-80 model 3 microcomputer. I'm going to play with the keyboard and see what happens." After several practice runs with the keyboard, a person inquires, "May I try what you have done?" The mentor replies, "Sure, let us get you started." The rest of the group gives a sigh of relief as Greg begins to experiment with what the keyboard can do. Bob inquires, "Why does that blinking light dart across the screen?" The mentor replies, "The cursor is being moved by Greg who is holding down the spacebar."

Greg says, "This is fun." Mary questions, "Why is the computer so fast?" The mentor replies, "The computer has a lot of power which we will learn to appreciate." The mentor looks at the group and asks who would like to be the computer user. No volunteers emerge from the group. As Miriam begins to smile, the mentor notes Miriam's willingness to participate. Miriam begins with some operations that Greg and the mentor did.

Miriam states, "Now I am going to try some ideas on my own. What is that up arrow?" As she tries the key, nothing seems to happen. The mentor says, "Print 5↑2 and see what happens."

"It gave me 25...Why?" Another participant suggests that the up arrow probably deals with exponents. Another person suggests that 5 is the square root of 25. Suddenly Miriam says, "The up arrow gave me a power of two. Now I am going to try 5³. Yes, 125...that up arrow works. See how fast we got 125...almost instantly!"

Greg is becoming impatient and wants to work on another computer in the lab. The mentor notices this inclination and says, "Greg, I want you to now work on this computer in the middle of the room. Miriam, please work with Greg as a partner." The mentor has Miriam and Greg demonstrate the desired hands-on approach for computer instruction. After the other people observe how the two people work together, the other four people are split into two groups of two to work on the computer keyboards. The mentor is now serving as a floating resource person giving help and encouragement to the groups as needed.

In this scenario, the mentor is dealing with the anxiety levels of the people. He mentioned that the users really could not harm the computer with normal usage. He demonstrated how a person could experiment with the computer keys. He accepted Greg's offer to do some computer operations. He nudged Miriam to try the computer. He answered some questions quite directly. He allowed experimentation for participants to gain insights from group dialogue. The people were free to ask questions in a natural sense of inquiry.

REDUCING COMPLEXITY

Common problems emerge as people begin to use information with the computer. These problems are inherent in persons trying to learn too quickly. Learners may try to read computer

articles in the professional journals and feel
overwhelmed. Participants frequently try to run
programs full of bugs and errors.

We live in an informational society where data
may be delivered in an instant. Yet, we may
need to take five hours just to cope with getting the information on line. We may feel fur-
thur perplexed that our recently acquired
knowledge is now outdated due to new technological advances.

GAP

Although the literature has numerous listings of
titles describing the "what" of computers for
the educators, there is an apparent vacuum in
the studies on "how" people learn the computer.
During my sabbatical leave, I cross-referenced
learning theory and computer listings and found
no articles. I then searched the ERIC Documents
and found twelve potentially useful references.
It was my finding that the twelve chosen ERIC
Documents only alluded to learning theories.

PURPOSE

The purpose of this model is to interrelate
computer literacy with learning theory. My
major reference for developing computer literacy
comes from Miller and associates who wrote Basic
Programming for the Classroom Teacher in 1982.(1)
The learning theory for this model became my
synthesis work of the material presented in
Models of Teaching of 1980.(2)

VALIDATION EFFORTS

After my initial work of combining computer
literacy with learning theory, I undertook validation efforts. I worked experimentally with
six people who ranged in ages from ten to sixty.
Literacy and my emerging model became more fused
as I led six people in a public school project
on the computer language of logo for five weeks.
The logo project was further field tested in a
half day in-service session for thirty elementary teachers. This model became refined and
validated with twenty fifth-through-eighth
graders during fifteen hour instructional settings. This model was again validated with six
senior citizens for one-hour weekly sessions in
March of 1984.

INTENT

This model is written as a specific mechanism for
teaching computer literacy. It places special
emphasis upon a person's readiness to learn. It
has a structure to challenge a human being to
learn continually about computer awareness. It
has a major approach where people learn from
one another. It involves a vehicle whereby
people realize that computer literacy can be an
on-going process in a changing computer world.

SOCIAL SYSTEM

The mentor creates a moderate structure for
learning. Mentor encourages active participation. Interaction of people to people with the
computer is highlighted. The structure by the
mentor becomes less moderate as people increasingly gain control of their confidence and
mastery of computer usage.

PRINCIPLES OF REACTION

1. The mentor gives verbal and nonverbal en-
   encouragement to people.
2. The mentor gives a small task for the small
   group to accomplish.
3. The mentor gradually challenges people in
   their accomplishments.
4. The mentor takes clues from the group for
   readiness to assume more complex tasks.

SUPPORT SYSTEM

Optimal support is the grouping of people to
solve problems in a cooperative approach.

ORIENTATION TO THE MODEL--
GOALS AND ASSUMPTIONS

People have ranges of attitudes toward computer
literacy ranging from fear to curiosity. Fear
is a block which causes computer literacy to be
impeded. Curiosity is a natural phenomenon conducive to computer competency. The general goal
of this model is to help people obtain computer
knowledge and skills necessary for their daily
uses. Thus, people become computer users
through an increasingly independent approach.
People learn to adapt to changing ways of the
computer field so they feel in control of the
computer. The learner automatically uses
strategies to solve problems so that computers
are tools to enrich human lives.

Computer literacy begins with psychological
trust so that people may value a computer.
Secondly, the mentor chooses a computer con-
cept(s) and/or skill(s) for a presentation to be
given to the learners. Usually the people in
small groups practice their assigned tasks on an
actual computer. Fourthly, the people engage in
a capsulizing session with their mentor. Fifth-
ly, knowledge of a result becomes a cooperative
adventure with the involved people.

THE MODEL

Computer literacy has been described as to how
it could be developed into parts of a teaching
model. Now I will become more specific in terms
of model development. This model consists of
five parts including the concepts of the psychological trust, demonstration, hands-on, capsulizing and knowledge of results. I will build
each concept on how it works from an actual
classroom scenario.

Psychological Trust

The mentor is working with sixteen beginning computer students. He is about to introduce the concept of the GOTO statement. He wants to relieve tension and anxiety levels before a short demonstration. I have a question for us. What is the computer like? Think of an analogy. The wilder the analogy the better. My analogy is that the computer is like a skyhook. I grab a skyhood and wonder where I might be going!

Mentor: What are some of your analogies?

Greg: The computer is like a tiger.

Mentor: Why?

Greg: If you know how to handle a tiger, it will do what you want it to do. I hope that I will be able to tame my computer.

Mary: I have a personal analogy.

Mentor: Fine. What is it?

Mary: I am like a wild horse. I need to be harnessed to use the computer.

Jim: Where is that harness? I need it too!

Mentor: Do you have an analogy?

Jim: Mary's harness is okay with me.

Mentor: Anyone else?

Miriam: I would rather not tell my analogy.

Bob: Come on, Miriam Let us have it.

Miriam: Okay. The computer is like a scarecrow. It is scary at first and then the birds take the scarecrow for granted.

The mentor is working in the affective domain. His purpose was to get people to think above and beyond the computer. He realized that people would become relaxed through the dialogue. This calming effect on the class paved the way for the next phase in this model. The broken lines in the following diagram represent an openness and a flexible structure inherent in psychological trust.

```
 ┌ ─ ─ ─ ─ ─ ─ ─ ─ ─ ┐
 ┆   Psychological Trust  ┆
 └ ─ ─ ─ ─ ─ ─ ─ ─ ─ ┘
```

The mentor timed the first phase to coincide with the needs of the class. He was prepared to lengthen, shorten or eliminate this psychological trust portion of the model. He is now ready to do a demonstration. He uses a projectural with the following information:

```
10 Print "You"
20 Print "are"
30 GOTO 10
40 END
```

He made a smooth transition from psychological trust to the demonstration part of this lesson.

Demonstration

The mentor moves from the projectural of his demonstration computer unit to type the GOTO program. It runs. The people are engrossed. The computer is not stopping. Why? A person wants to know how long it will last. Another person wants to know what is happening. Another learner states that a little information was used in the program while the computer response did not end.

Mentor: We have just seen an endless loop. The GOTO statement in line 30 takes the program to line 10 and then line 20 appears and 30 takes us back to 10. We are continually getting the following:

> You
> are
> You
> are

This program would last until we pressed the break key or turned off the power.

In groups of two, you are to do some hands-on work with the computer. I have some work sheets involving GOTO statements with various programs. Try the programs and see what happens. Feel free to experiment with the GOTO statement. Hit the break key to escape from any endless loops. Talk with your partner about what is happening on your computer. I will now circulate around the classroom.

The mentor has completed the first two portions of this model. The model format looks like the following:

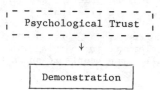

Hands-on

Group 1 is working on a chosen GOTO exercise. It runs. The group goes on to other given exercises with the GOTO statements. The mentor notices the group could use a challenge. He gives a few more difficult exercises to practice. He then urges them to change GOTO line numbers to predict what will happen. The mentor notices that persons rotate turns on the computer.

Group 2 finished their first given program and
find a syntax error. The group calls for help
from the mentor. The mentor points to line
number 10 of the syntax error. The group member
notices that Print is spelled as Pront. The
mentor mentions that Print is a command and that
Pront isn't understood by the computer. The
line is corrected and the program runs. The
group then continues their work with other GOTO
programs.

Group 3 is having difficulty. The program won't
run. The mentor has them go through the exercise step by step. He notices that the enter
key is lightly touched and the cursor is still
on the last character printed. The person is
urged to press firmly on the enter key. It
takes. The group notices a syntax error. Why?

The mentor encourages them to look over their
spellings. They notice that GOTO is spelled
GGTO. The GGTO is corrected and the program
runs. The group is continuing their work with
GOTO statements.

After an hour and fifteen minutes of GOTO practice, the mentor calls the whole group together.
He states that the computer will only handle the
information that we give it. The model has
added the hands-on component so that the model
diagram looks like the following:

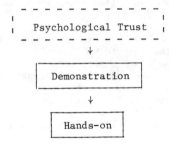

Capsulizing

The mentor shares with the group what he observed
during the hands-on practice session. He is
proud of the cooperative small group work. He
noted progress. He also observed some frustration. He relates that progress and frustration
are normal elements in learning computer literacy. He calls upon people to share their
reactions.

The whole group engaged in sharing their progress.
One person related that after initial trials
their work seemed to go quite well but there was
some confusion on the additional practice sheets.
Another class member said that her small group
was okay once they got over their many initial
clusters of syntax errors. The third group members related they needed additional practice time
and more help. The four model parts are included
in the following diagram:

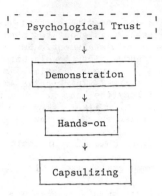

The first four model parts were aimed at getting
to the fifth model phase of results. The mentor
prepared himself with information and urged the
learners to keep a diary of their progress. The
mentor timed the results session to be the midway point of an eleven-week workshop.

Results

The mentor held a conference with each small
group. He gave a list of accomplishments that
the group made during the half-way point. He
had each small group member give an important
item from the diary. The conference was concluded with an exchange of ideas based on the
mentor's notations and participant diaries.
The mentor tallied the nature of accumplishments
from his notations to participants. The mentor
specified the kinds of recurring items found in
the diaries. These tallies were kept in the
records of the mentor. The tallies and frequency of distribution of the tallied items
were given to participants during the first
session after the midway point. The model parts
have been developed from psychological trust to
model results. The parts are like the following
diagram.

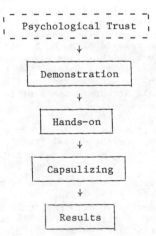

USE

This model may be used time and time again for computer instruction. The parts have recurring patterns which help a mentor to understand past, present and future instruction. The learning experiences begin at very concrete stages of development. Concrete instructional approaches provide a base for learning abstract aspects of computer uses. The recurring patterns found throughout this model provide a framework of consistent and coherent approach to computer literacy.

PHASE STATEMENTS

The following statements provide summary conclusions to the major aspects in the development of this model.

I   Psychological trust
    1. The computer will not explode
    2. People control computers
    3. The mentor provides psychological trust
    4. Small groups provide human security

II   Demonstration
    1. The mentor gives an overview of computer concepts and skills
    2. The people learn to role-model computer usage
    3. The people learn a way of doing
    4. The mentor energizes human groups to hands-on learning

III Hands-on
    1. One person works on the computer while the other person functions as a guide
    2. The small group chooses provided material to be learned
    3. The small group interacts with each other and the computer
    4. The small group paces themselves at their own rate of learning

IV   Capsulization
    1. The mentor reacts to what happened
    2. The mentor asks questions about hands-on session
    3. Mentor and people share insights
    4. Mentor and people set goals

V   Results
    1. The mentor notes progress of each person
    2. Learners keep diaries

FOOTNOTES

(1) Miller, Joan M. Basic Programming for the Classroom Teacher (Teachers College Press, New York, 1982).

(2) Joyce, Bruce, and Weil, Marsha. Models of Teaching (Prentice-Hall, Englewood Cliffs, N.J., 1980).

COMPUTERS IN EDUCATION, K. Duncan and D. Harris (eds.)
Elsevier Science Publishers B.V. (North-Holland)
© IFIP, 1985

COMPUTER LITERACY COURSE FOR FACULTY

ANTHONY Z. COLE, Ph.D. and ROBERT R. RISER

Department of Computer and Information Sciences
East Tennessee State University, Box 23830A
Johnson City, Tennessee, USA 37614

A two semester faculty development computer literacy course at East Tennessee State University is discussed. Tuition grants-in-aid are awarded annually to twenty selected faculty from a cross section of disciplines. The approach is best characterized as "the computer as a tool."
Specific objectives are presented. Though the content varies according to available facilities, detailed syllabi, structure, and policies are given.
While the measure of success will be the extent to which participants subsequently utilize the computer as a tool in their respective faculty roles – in the classroom and in service, administrative, personal, and research/professional areas – some preliminary observations and conclusions are presented.

1.0 INTRODUCTION

In June of 1982 the Tennessee State Board of Regents (SBR), the governing body for the State University and Community College System of Tennessee, endorsed a general computer literacy program for selected SBR faculty as a part of its faculty development activities. Graduate credit was to be given to faculty completing the program. Grants-in-aid covering tuition were to be provided jointly by the SBR and the participants' home institutions.

East Tennessee State University (ETSU) has been one of the participating institutions since the program's inception. The Department of Computer and Information Sciences was approached by the administration in July, 1982 to develop and teach a two semester computer literacy course for faculty development to begin in the Fall semester, 1982. The Vice-President of Academic Affairs, in consultation with the Deans of various schools and colleges at ETSU, would solicit and select faculty to participate.

Beginning with a set of objectives provided by the SBR, the course policies, objectives, content, and expectations have evolved significantly over the past two years. There have been four sections taught, each section has a limited enrollment of 20. Out of the total 80 faculty members who have started the four sections, 68 have finished the two semester course. This paper reports on the present status of the course, in particular the objectives, policies, syllabus, and sample assignments. The course that has evolved is neither a "programming" course, a "computers and society" course, nor an "introduction to data processing" course. It could more appropriately be characterized as a "computer as a tool" course. It is felt that this approach is most appropriate in fulfilling the primary objective, i.e. exposing faculty to ways in which the computer may be used as a tool in fulfilling their roles as university faculty.

2.0 OBJECTIVES

The primary purpose of the computer literacy program, as a faculty development activity, is to improve faculty performance. The specific course objectives are to:

(a) provide sufficient exposure to allow the participants to begin using the computer as an effective tool in their role as faculty members, including teaching, research, service, and administrative aspects,

(b) provide participants with sufficient background to enable them to appropriately integrate the computer into the classroom/laboratory environment within their own discipline,

(c) provide a level of understanding of key terms and concepts sufficient to converse intelligently with colleagues concerning computers and to read and understand computer related literature within their own discipline,

(d) provide an appreciation of the applications of computers within their own disciplines; provide sufficient expertise to distinguish between tasks which are or are not amenable to a computer solution; provide an appreciation of the differences between mainframe, mini, and micro computers and to recognize appropriate applications of each,

(e) intelligently consider the computer's role in our society; its past and potential impact; the history of computing; the social, ethical, and legal implications,

(f) encourage/increase interdisciplinary activity as well as attempt to head off "territorial" barriers to such activity, and

(g) provide an appreciation of the factors to be considered in the selection and/or use of discipline-related hardware and/or software.

Perhaps it is appropriate to note some things that are NOT included in the course objectives and to point out that they are deliberate omissions. First, the development of a proficiency in programming is not among the objectives. The original SBR definition of computer literacy included a "moderate proficiency in a high level language" as well as the "ability to read and write well structured programs that work." The authors consider this inappropriate and potentially counterproductive to the stated objectives. While computer literate faculty may choose to explore programming, programming is certainly not a prerequisite. It was found that those who became comfortable computer users often became curious about programming. Secondly, the course is NOT intended to train faculty to teach introductory computer science courses.

3.0 COURSE STRUCTURE

The course is structured as a combination lecture and laboratory class. Selected chapters from the text, Computers and Data Processing, Capron and Williams (1), and additional reading assignments from current articles are required of all participants, as well as completion of a take home examination on the assigned reading. In particular, participants are encouraged to become aware of computer related literature within their discipline. BASIC Fundamentals and Style, Quasney and Maniotes (2), is a required reference for the language portion of the course. Handouts have been developed internally for each software package used.

The basic layout for the class begins with an overview of computers and some necessary terminology. Then a description of the computing facilities and access policies at ETSU is presented. The course then takes the form of demonstrations and the presentations of packages, i.e. lecture one day and laboratory work the next class period. The syllabus described below is the present structure of the course after four revisions.

3.1 SYLLABUS

FIRST SEMESTER:

A. Introduction (1 period)

    1. Objectives and expectations
    2. Course Policies

B. Overview, Terminology, History of Computers and Computing (4 periods)

    1. Basic terms - hardware, software, program, input, output
    2. Hardware
        a. Processor (CPU) - control unit, arithmetic/logic unit
        b. Input devices, Output devices - examples
        c. Memory - bits, bytes, words, types and characteristics of memory devices, RAM, ROM, PROM, EPROM, usage of each
        d. Storage devices - examples, purpose; compare and contrast access speeds, costs, type of access (sequential, random)
    3. Software
        a. Programs, application programs
        b. Operating systems
        c. Translation process - define, compare, and contrast machine languages, assembly languages, high level languages, non-procedural languages; define, compare and contrast compilers, interpreters, assemblers
    4. History
        a. Early history - Babbage, Lovelace, Hollerith, von Neumann, MARK I, ENIAC, etc.
        b. Modern history - (hardware)
        c. Modern history - (software)
        d. Survey of languages (general and special purpose)

C. ETSU Computing Facilities (1 period)

    1. The "Mainframe" IBM 4341 - capabilities, usage, access, policies
    2. The "Mini" PDP 11/70 - capabilities, usage and access policies
    3. The "Micro" Apple II's, IBM's, and TI's - capabilities, usage and access policies

D. Introduction to the Apple II Microcomputer (1 period)

    1. Hardware
        a. Components - processor, memory, monitor, disk drive(s), printer
        b. "Cards", "slots"
    2. Software
        DOS, Integer, and Applesoft BASIC

E. Word Processing (3 periods)

  1. General overview, capabilities, applications
  2. APPLEWRITER

F. Spreadsheet (5 periods)

  1. General overview, different types, capabilities, applications
  2. VISICALC and LOTUS 123

G. Database Systems (5 periods)

  1. Personal Filing System (PFS) & dBASE II
  2. Lecture and demonstrations by library personnel of data base searches

H. CAD/CAM - Demo (1 period)

I. Graphical/Image Processing (2 periods)

J. Artificial Intelligence (AI) (1 period)

  1. AI definition, overview
  2. AI applications - expert systems
  3. Language - LISP

K. Computers in Education (6 periods)

  1. Computer Assisted Instruction (CAI)
  2. Computer Managed Instruction (CMI)
  3. Pilot authoring language
  4. Authoring system

SECOND SEMESTER:

A. Orientation to the PDP 11/70 (2 periods)

  1. Timesharing, concept of private libraries, files
  2. Response time, CPU time, "clock" time, file naming conventions
  3. "Logging-on" and "logging-off" - HELLO, BYE
  4. General utilities - DIR, PIP, QUE

B. MINITAB - An introductory interactive statistical package (3 periods)

  1. Overview, purpose, capabilities, applications
  2. Worksheet concept; MINITAB's worksheet
  3. MINITAB syntax
  4. Entering data into the worksheet
  5. Operating on the worksheet; statistical procedures available
  6. Miscellaneous commands

C. Wordprocessing on PDP 11/70 - RUNOFF (2 periods)

  1. Overview, purpose, capabilities, applications
  2. Commands

D. Orientation to the IBM 4341 (2 periods)
  1. Concept of virtual machines
  2. MOTEL (accessing the system, file manipulations)
  3. Full screen editing
  4. File concepts and file utilities

E. Word processing on the IBM 4341 (1 period)

  1. Overview of word processing, purpose, applications, hardware, and software components
  2. SCRIPT
  3. Assignments

F. A large general purpose statistical package (3 periods)

  1. Overview, capabilities of available packages
  2. Statistical Analysis System (SAS)
     a. Capabilities, examples of SAS generated reports
     b. SAS terms - observations, variables, variable name conventions
     c. Accessing SAS (cards, RJE)
     d. Required JCL
     e. SAS syntax
     f. Getting data into SAS data sets (DATA, INPUT, CARDS, etc.)
     g. Computing new variables
     h. Logical decisions (IF/THEN)
     i. Common SAS Procedures - PRINT, PLOT, CHART, UNIVARIATE, SORT
     j. Other SAS Procedures

G. BASIC (15 periods)

  1. Introduction to DOS
     a. Overview
     b. Some DOS Commands - CATALOG, FP, INT, INIT, PR#6, Control, Run
  2. Creation and Maintenance of BASIC Programs
     a. Overview of BASIC language
     b. File naming conventions
     c. NEW, LOAD, LIST, RENAME, SAVE, DELETE, RUN
     d. Editing BASIC programs

  3. APPLESOFT BASIC - Standard BASIC terms

3.2 ASSIGNMENTS

The assignments for the first semester are to:

  1. use APPLEWRITER to write a one page report on selecting a computer for home or office use,
  2. use VISICALC to set up some type of financial forecast for stocks or bonds,
  3. use VISICALC to set up a sheet for keeping student grades on tests,
  4. use PFS to store research bibliographies and abstracts, and
  5. use PILOT to set up a CAI lesson in their discipline.

The assignments for the second semester are to:

1. use the PDP 11/70 and learn about the utilities,
2. use MINITAB to analyze the response to a questionnaire,
3. use RUNOFF to print a one page report,
4. work through examples on IBM 4341 using utilities,
5. compare SCRIPT with RUNOFF and APPLEWRITER,
6. use SAS,
7. write a menu-driven program in BASIC to allow the selection of at least two options and make several calculations, and
8. write a BASIC program to read and write a Random Access file.

To successfully complete the course a faculty member must complete 80% of the assignments with a 70% proficiency on each assignment. The course grades are Pass/Fail.

4.0 OBSERVATIONS, CONCLUSIONS & FUTURE ACTIVITY

This course content is dynamic; as new facilities (hardware and software) become available on campus they must quickly be integrated into the course. A follow-up study is made to see whether the objectives were met. This is based on an analysis of:

(a) the material covered,
(b) the evaluation by the class participants, and
(c) the extent to which participants continue to use the computer after completing the course.

Course content changes are made with one major objective – to improve faculty performance through knowledge of and use of the computer in teaching, service, research, and professional activities.

It is critical that the objectives of the course are made clear to the administration and to the participants. This was not clear during the first offering of the course, leading to problems with a few participants who were not aware of the nature of the course and the time commitment involved. It is also very important to make clear the course policies and expectations to the participants, i.e. grading, attendance, policies, etc. A Pass/Fail grading policy with a predetermined percentage (80%) of the assignments required for successful completion of the course has been found to be most comfortable. The university must have the appropriate facilities to teach this course to the faculty. The faculty cannot be expected to compete with students for terminals or to do all of their work in student laboratories. A policy of liberal access to the computer is recommended and a 1 to 1 ratio of participants per laboratory work station for class sessions.

If this is not possible, a 2 to 1 ratio should be the maximum for optimum comprehension.

Futhermore, the assignments and topics covered in the course must have meaning and relate to the faculty's present or potential needs. Where possible, open-ended assignments that can be directed toward each participant's discipline or that can enable computer application explorations within his/her discipline are recommended. Also, that portion of the course, if any, devoted to a computer language should be placed at the end of the syllabus. By this time many of the participants are curious about programming and seem to gain a better appreciation of the software packages previously covered. It should also be noted that faculty have attendance problems that normal university students do not have. Teaching loads, committee assignments and other commitments leave limited time for the participants. An appreciation of these problems is essential in teaching this class. Careful consideration should be given to the spacing of various topics. In particular, demonstrations and lecture should be placed between software packages so that the participants are not overwhelmed with the commands and/or syntax of two packages at once.

The faculty has responded positively to this type of self-development. Most of the assignments, once completed provide the faculty with a useable tool for teaching or personal use. Most faculty members have incorporated what they have learned and used the computer as a tool in the teaching, research, service and/or administrative aspects of their role as a faculty member. An unexpected benefit has been the interaction of faculty from differing disciplines (helping each other with assignments, class interaction, etc.) who probably would otherwise never have met. This has enhanced overall cooperation, communication and goodwill throughout East Tennessee State University.

REFERENCES:

[1] Capron, H.L. and Williams, B.K., Second Edition, *Computers and Data Processing* (Benjamin/Cummings Publishing Co., Menlo Park, California, 1984).

[2] Quasney, J.S. and Maniotes, J., *BASIC Fundamentals and Style* (Boyd and Fraser Publishing Co., Boston, Massachusetts, 1984).

COMPUTERS IN EDUCATION, K. Duncan and D. Harris (eds.)
Elsevier Science Publishers B.V. (North-Holland)
© IFIP, 1985

ALGORITHMS AND PROGRAMMING AS PART OF COMPUTER LITERACY - SOME ASSESSMENT RESULTS WITH
IMPLICATIONS FOR SECONDARY SCHOOL MATHEMATICS

Johnson, D.C., U.K., University of London, London, England
Anderson, R.E., U.S., University of Minnesota, Minneapolis, Minnesota, U.S.A.

Data collected from two studies of computer literacy in Minnesota, U.S.A., include performance on a subset
of items designated 'programming and algorithms'. These items have a mathematical flavor and one is able
to identify pupil difficulties and strategies specific to some mathematical aspects of this component of
computer literacy. The data suggest many pupils experience difficulty with such tasks as 'processing a
(simple) algorithm/program' and modifying an algorithm to do a new but related task , particularly when the
algorithm involves concepts such as assignment (or replacement) with more than one variable. The paper
concludes with suggestions for the teaching of introductory programming.

The U.S. National Council of Teachers of Mathematics (NCTM)
in their report Recommendations for School Mathematics of
the 1980s (1980) note that 'pupils and teachers should
obtain a working knowledge of how one interacts with
computers and uses their capacities'. A group of
mathematics educators at a recent conference in the U.K.
(DES/MEP, 1983) agreed the recommendation that 'mathematical programming and the explicit study of algorithms should
be an integral part of the school mathematics curriculum'.
Such a recommendation is not new as individuals and
organisations have been espousing the importance of the
topic, algorithms and computer programming, for school
mathematics over the past 20 years (e.g. see SMSG (1966),
NCTM (1968), Committee on Computer Education (1972), NCTM
(1973), Johnson and Tinsley (1978), Engel (1979), Dwyer
(1980), Abelson and di Sessa (1981), NCTM (1984)). It is
also the case that there now exists a quite reasonable base
of research evidence to support the position that writing
programs to study selected mathematical topics can make a
significant contribution to the learning of these concepts
and to the development of mathematical problem-solving
ability (e.g. see Hatfield and Kieren (1972), Johnson and
Harding (1979), and Soloway, Lockhead, and Clements
(1982)).

While there is growing support for the inclusion of
mathematical programming in secondary school mathematics it
is also the case that the research or assessment data
regarding pupil 'difficulties' or 'strategies' specific to
the mathematical aspects of this activity is still somewhat
limited. This paper reports on a selected subset of the
data collected in two relatively large scale studies of
computer literacy (these are described briefly in the next
section). The present discussion is based on a secondary
analysis of secondary school pupils performance on a small
set of items designed to assess specific aspects of
knowledge and understanding of 'programming and algorithms'. The items have a numerical 'bias' and are very
much mathematical in nature (see Table 2). This report is
primarily descriptive and focuses on those aspects of
computing tasks (items) which have (hypothesised) links or
relationships with school mathematics.

THE MINNESOTA COMPUTER LITERACY ASSESSMENT

The February 1980 issue of the Mathematics Teacher included
an article (Johnson, et al, 1980) which lists objectives
for computer literacy. These objectives were devel-
oped/compiled as part of an NSF supported research project
and served as the basis for the development of test items
which were used in the Minnesota (USA) Computer Literacy
Field Study (selected aspects of this study were reported
at WCCE 81, Johnson et al (1981) and the full report is

also available, Klassen et al, 1980)). This research,
which was designed to ascertain the relative impact of
certain computing experiences on computer literacy, was
conducted during the year 1978 and involved testing of over
1100 secondary school pupils, ages 12 to 18, in junior and
senior high schools in Minnesota. The Field Study research
was followed in 1979 with the inclusion of computer
literacy testing in a Minnesota statewide assessment
program. The Field Study test, the 'Computer Literacy
Questionnaire', was modified and extended and the new
version, the 'Minnesota Computer Literacy and Awareness
Assessment', was administered to a sample of over 6000
secondary school pupils in grades 8 and 11, ages 13 and 16
(see Anderson et al, 1979 and Anderson, Krohn, and Sandman,
1981).

The Field Study and State Assessment Program both included
Programming and Algorithms as one of the five major
categories of objectives in the cognitive domain of
computer literacy. The set of objectives for this
category, which is designated P, is reproduced in Table 1.

Table 1
Minnesota Computer Literacy Study:
Programming and Algorithms (P) Objectives

Note: The student should be able to accomplish objectives
1.2-2.5 when the algorithm is expressed as a set of
English Language instructions or is in the form of a
computer program.

P.1.1 **Recognize** the definition of "Algorithm".

P.1.2 **Follow** and give the correct output for a simple
algorithm.

P.1.3 Given a simple algorithm, **explain** what is
accomplishes (i.e. interpret and generalize).

P.2.1 **Modify** a simple algorithm to accomplish a new, but
related task.

P.2.2 **Detect** logic errors in an algorithm.

P.2.3 **Correct** errors in an improperly functioning
algorithm.

P.2.4 **Develop** an algorithm for solving a specific
problem.

P.2.5 **Develop** an algorithm that can be used to solve a set
of similar problems.

Test items were developed for a subset of the objectives for each major category of objectives. In the case of Programming and Algorithms, items were produced for objectives P1.2, P1.3, P.2.1 – all items are given in Table 2. Five of the seven items were included in the 1978 Field Study and all seven were used in the 1979 State Assessment.

The structure of the set of items is such that two of the items, 82 and 83, are considered to be algorithms expressed in 'English language form', although 83 also involves following a flow diagram, and the remaining five, items 65, 70, 74, 77, and 80, are algorithms expressed in the form of a short computer program. The language BASIC was selected because it was, and still is, the language most used in secondary schools.

THE RESULTS

As indicated by the statements of objectives in Table 1, the P items were designed to assess performance at three levels. While it would seem that these three levels are indicative of a hierarchy it is not within the scope of this paper to attempt to validate such a proposed ordering. It is also the case that facilities or difficulty varied within each level. For example, the inclusion of sequential replacement in the context of generalization, item 80, made this task more difficult than, say, item 77, which asks for a reasonably straightforward modification.

A summary of the performance of the different samples in the Field Study and the Minnesota State Assessment is given in Table 3.

DISCUSSION

The data in Table 3 are first discussed in terms of each objective with particular attention given to the major errors or misconceptions – as indicated by quite large numbers of pupils selecting a particular (incorrect) alternative. This is followed with some general points specific to the two studies, the State Assessment and the Field Study.

Objective P.1.2: Processing an Algorithm (Items 65, 70, 82)

In considering groups of items by objective it is clear that items related to reading or processing an algorithm were easier than those which assessed the ability to generalize or modify an algorithm. However, even in the case of the English language item, 82, performance was not very high, ranging from a low of 29% for eighth-grade pupils to 55% for the Field Study Programming and Computer Studies pupils. No single distractor predominated although answer a was slightly more popular than c and d. The selection of a and to a lesser extent d, might have resulted from an inability to execute the decision and loop structures or, alternatively, and there is considerable informal 'discussion' data to support this, the error was due to a quick reading with particular attention to the phrase 'alphabetical order'. Hence many of the pupils tended to anticipate a result on the basis of a general perusal of the statements.

The two programming items at this level are clearly quite different in their demand. The relatively high performance on item 65 indicates that even for students who had not

written BASIC programs the notion of numerical substitution in an 'algebraic' expression seemed a reasonable thing to do. It is the case that this enables one to answer the question correctly without actually reading through the program. This, however, suggests that performance should possibly have been higher than it actually was – 57% for eleventh-grade and 32% for eighth-grade. The relatively high percentages for 'I don't know' might be explained in terms of individuals expectations – they may have decided they couldn't do the item since they had not done any programming[1].

Item 70 is more demanding in that it requires processing an algorithm in program form with sequential replacement (or assignment); lines 40 and 50 require assignment of updated or current values of variables, an important computing concept but clearly one that was difficult for most pupils. Nonetheless, one would have expected quite high performance from the Field Study Programming and Computer Studies group as these students had received formal instruction in BASIC programming. However, even for this group only 34% selected c, the correct response, while 26% selected a, the most popular distractor. Thus, the assignment concept was often not applied in processing the algorithm – the PRINT was executed on the basis of initial assignment of values to A and B (3 and 4 respectively), again an indication of 'anticipating a result'.

Overall performance on the items associated with processing a given algorithm, while relatively high compared to other objectives, was still low.

Objective P.1.3: Generalize (items 74, 80)

This objective was not assessed with an item in English language form; however, data were collected for two BASIC programming items. Item 74 deals with a reasonably straightforward algorithm to calculate the sum and average for any five numbers. The sum is calculated in one step (i.e. does not use a 'counter' to successively add new values to S; $S = S + A$), the mean M is calculated, and the values for S and M are printed as output. As no actual numbers are provided, the student needs to consider the general nature of the routine, which uses seven variable names (A, B, C, D, E, S, and M). It would appear that like item 65, some knowledge of mathematical ideas should enable one to make a quite reasonable choice from the alternatives given. Except for the relatively high number of 'I don't know' responses in the State Assessment (a possible reaction to the item being presented as a computer program, see footnote 1) and the number selecting response a which might seem reasonable since a computer can 'store' numbers, the level of performance was not unexpected, but percentages were still not very high. As noted previously, there is also the problem associated with the number of variables and this aspect of the mathematics accounted for some of the errors, e.g. the 4%-6% choosing b, and some of the 'I don't know's.

Question 80 is more intriguing. This item was only included in the State Assessment so one is unable to look at the performance of that subset of pupils who had received formal or planned instruction in programming. On the other hand, actual performance is so low relative to other items, that even those with programming experience, see footnote 1, found this very difficult. The item involves generalization, but with the added concept of assignment with variables and operations on these

Table 2

Programming and Algorithms Items[a]

OBJECTIVE P.1.2	Item[c]	Comment
[b]65 Choose the correct output for the computer program shown below:		BASIC (not included in Field Study)

```
10  LET C = 6          Output  a.  6
20  LET D = 8                  b.  14
30  LET E = C+D+2              c.  8
40  PRINT E                    d.  16
50  END                        e.  I don't know
```

		BASIC, includes concept of assignment using two variables

70   Choose the correct output for the computer program shown below:

```
10  LET A = 3          Output  a.  3 4
20  LET B = 4                  b.  4 3
30  LET C = A                  c.  3 3
40  LET B = C                  d.  4 4
50  LET A = B                  e.  I don't know
60  PRINT A,B
70  END
```

82   Choose the correct output[d] for the procedure described below.

English language form

1. List the three names Brown, Anderson and   Output a. Anderson, Brown, Crane
   Crane in alphabetical order   b. Brown
2. Remove the last name from the list   c. Anderson, Brown
3. If only one name is left, stop. Otherwise,   d. Anderson
4. List the remaining names in reverse order   e. I don't know
5. Go back to step 2.

OBJECTIVE P.1.3

74   What is the <u>main</u> purpose of the following program:

BASIC, linear with seven variable names

```
10  INPUT A, B, C, D, E    Output  a. store A, B, C, D, and E in
20  LET S = A+B+C+D+E                  the computer
30  LET M = S/5                     b. print the letters S and M
40  PRINT S,M                       c. print the sum and average
50  END                                of five numbers
                                    d. calculate large sums
                                    e. I don't know
```

80   When the following program is run, the user enters numbers for A and B. The computer will:

BASIC, includes idea of assignment with operations (not included in Field Study)

```
10  INPUT A,B      Output  a. print the two input numbers,
20  LET A = A+B                the smallest first
30  LET B = A-B             b. print the two input numbers,
40  LET A = A-B                the largest first
50  PRINT A,B              c. print the two input numbers in
60  END                        reverse order from the way they
                               were input
                            d. print the two input numbers in the
                               same order as they were input
                            e. I don't know
```

Table 2 continued

OBJECTIVE P.2.1

77   This program instructs the computer to count by two: BASIC, with loop
                                                                             and decision

     10 LET M = 0   Output a. 5 READ A
     20 LET M = M+2   7 DATA 3,5,8
     30 print M   b. 5 LET M = A
     40 IF M<100 THEN 20   30 PRINT A
     50 END   c. 5 INPUT A
                                                 20 LET M = M+A
    Which change will produce a program which   d. 5 LET X = A
    can be used to count by A? (For example,   20 LET M = X+A
    A=3, 5 or 8.)   e. I don't know

83   An algorithm (flowchart) to determine the weekly wages of employees in a bakery is shown below. Employees are paid
     $4 per hour up to 40 hours per week.

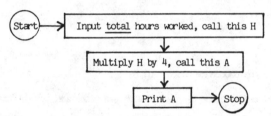

Employees are now to be paid "time-and-a-half" ($6 per hour) for overtime (hours worked over 40). How would you extend
the flowchart below to include overtime pay? Select answer a, b, c, d, or e.

ANSWERS

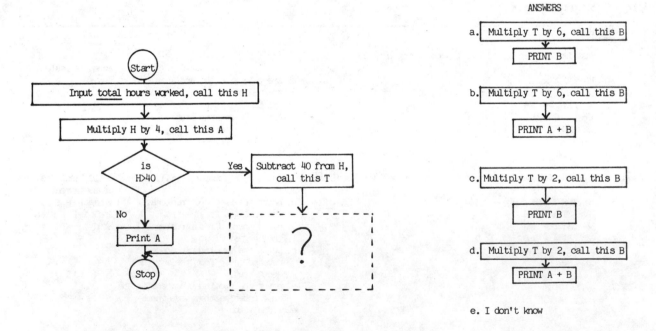

e. I don't know

---

a. Test directions tell students to 'select the best response' for each item.
b. Item numbers are those which correspond to the most recent version of the test.
c. Answers are d, c, b, c, c, c, c, d.
d. More recent feedback suggests that the word 'result' would be more appropriate than 'output' (although trials data
    indicated that pupils did not find the word output confusing).

Table 3

Student Responses to Programming and Algorithm Items
in MECC Field Study and Statewide Assessment

OBJECTIVE P.1.2	Description	Possible Answers[a]	State Assessment		Field Study All Computing Subjects[b]		Field Study Programming and Computer Science Subjects Only	
			Eleventh N=2535	Eighth N=3615	Pretest	Posttest N=929	Pretest	Posttest N=620
			%	%	%	%	%	%
Item 65	Read a linear program and substitute for variables in an expression.	a	3	4				
		b	4	8				
		c	4	9				
		d	57	32				
		e	31	46				
		NR	1	1				
Item 70	Read a linear program; includes assignment with two variables	a	35	25	8	21	9	26
		b	6	7	1	5	1	7
		c	17	11	8	26	9	34
		d	4	5	2	2	2	2
		e	37	49	8	6	8	6
		NR	1	3	73	40	71	25
Item 82	Read and rearrange a list; includes a decision and loop.	a	8	20	16	10	16	10
		b	49	29	34	53	36	55
		c	10	11	7	8	7	9
		d	14	11	11	12	11	13
		e	16	19	23	10	22	9
OBJECTIVE P.1.3		NR	3	10	9	7	8	4
Item 74[d]	Generalize; linear sequence.	a	9	16	2	3	2	4
		b	5	6	2	4	3	6
		c	45	20	7	20	8	26
		d	5	11	7	23	8	29
		e	35	42	7	9	8	10
OBJECTIVE P.1.3		NR	1	5	75	41	71	25
Item 80	Generalize; with assignment, more than one variable and operations.	a	7	10				
		b	7	8				
		c	8	8				
		d	32	21				
		e	44	45				
OBJECTIVE P.2.1		NR	2	8				
Item 77[e]	Modify a program; includes a decision and loop.	a	6	6	2	7	72	10
		b	11	11	3	6	2	8
		c	17	12	7	24	3	32
		d	6	5	1	7	8	9
		e	59	60	12	14	2	16
		NR	1	6	75	42	13	25
Item 83[f]	Modify a flowchart; involves aspect of generalization and includes a decision.	a	8	8	7	7	7	9
		b	32	16	25	41	28	46
		c	8	13	5	9	5	10
		d	13	7	6	8	6	9
		e	36	45	4	18	42	16
		NR	3	11	53	17	12	10

a. Correct answer is underlined.
b. This includes students in CAI and Computers in Society (without programming) Computer Programming and Computer Studies courses – the students were told they could omit responses to programming (BASIC) items if they had not done any BASIC programming.
c. This subset of students in the Field Study were in courses which included instruction in BASIC programming.
d. There was a major change from Field Study to State Assessment – hence responses a-e for Field Study students were not the same as those given in Table 2.
e. The eleventh-grade test had a misprint which quite likely accounts for some e responses.
f. There was a small change in wording in eighth and eleventh grade assessments.

variables. In addition, the programming notation (A = A + B) is not consistent with the usual algebraic statements of equality. Thus it is probably not unexpected that many pupils would opt for answers d or e, 76% at grade eleven and 65% at grade eight. The percentages of pupils responding a, b, or c were uniformly distributed, all about 8–9%, and this suggests that these were quite possibly random guesses.

The concept of assignment using two variables appears in item 70 (objective P.1.2) and item 80 and the corresponding performance levels suggest the concept is quite difficult, and indicates a need for careful attention in introducing and using the idea in school mathematics. Courses or units on programming should probably consider the concept in a variety of contexts, not merely as a counter, e.g. LET X = X + 1. This aspect, counting, is a feature of item 77, discussed in the next section of this paper.

Objective P.2.1: Modifying an Algorithm (Items 77, 83)

The English language item for this objective, item 83, was one of the most difficult items of the test with percentages correct ranging from 7% to 13%. It would appear that most students, even those in Programming and Computer Studies courses, tended to 'second guess' the question and opt for response b calculate overtime by multiplying by the overtime rate of $6 per hour – a natural way of thinking or of working out a solution to such a problem in real life. However, if one takes the time to actually use the flow diagram to process some data, say for example 41 or 50 hours, and contrast this with 'the usual' approach of calculating base pay then overtime, the error in applying answer b should be detected quite readily. This checking of course may not be consistent with the usual behavior of pupils taking a test –but alternatively this was the last actual 'test' item and pupils were given sufficient time to complete all items. Again, for this particular item there was a high proportion of 'I don't know' responses (from 16% to 45%) and a number of these pupils experienced difficulty with the use of variables – the final algorithm uses H, A, T, and B – or with the use of the inequality in the conditional 'H<40?'. Mathematically, however, it does seem reasonable to expect that by age 17 pupils should be able to complete such a task successfully. [Note that these data are consistent with the NAEP data for a flow chart item reported by Carpenter et al (1980), who state that the NAEP data suggests 'either that students have had little opportunity to develop knowledge about flow charts in general, or, more specifically, about flow charts containing a loop' (pg. 670).]

One phenomena which was suggested from further (more recent) informal trials of the full set of items with individuals and small groups in the U.K. is that the reading of a procedure or algorithm in either English language or program form is usually characterized by 'reading all lines with an attempt to comprehend or generalize – but without actually processing some trial data'. In other words students attempt to gain a sense of what is going on and as a result 'second guess' the procedure. This is certainly consistent with the choice of distractor for item 83 (as well as responses to items 70, 80 and 82).

The programming item for objective P.2.1 was item 77. The pupil was asked to modify a given algorithm which 'counted by two' to 'count by A'. This item was used in both the State Assessment and in the Field Study. The high percentage of 'I don't know' in the State Assessment (about 60% for each age group) suggests unfamiliarity with the mathematical idea and/or with programming – and in regard to this latter point the item and answers included a number of the BASIC statements, INPUT, LET, READ-DATA, PRINT, IF-THEN and END, as well as the idea of a loop. [The item is similar to the 'read a program' item in the NAEP assessment, Carpenter et al (1980, pg.671), which had a similar percentage for 'I don't know' for 13- and 17-year-old pupils.] Of particular concern on item 77 was the performance of the Programming and Computer Studies group in the Field Study. Posttest performance was only 32% with a somewhat uniform distribution of the remaining 68% over the other possible responses. It would seem that for these students facility in reading through and modifying a relatively straightforward numerical algorithm would represent some sort of minimal competency or expectation.

Eighth- and Eleventh-Grade State Assessment: Some General Observations

The relative performance, correct responses, of the 13- and 17-year-old samples for items 65 (P.1.2), 74 (P.1.3), and 82 (P.1.2) was not unexpected. The students had had the opportunity to study more mathematics (algebra in particular) and as computing has been a part of Minnesota education for many years it is quite likely that they have also had more opportunities to come in contact with computer programming during secondary schooling (45% said they had written computer programs). It is also the case that the English language form for objectives P.1.2 and P.2.1 had a reading factor and one would expect these to be easier for the older pupils.

On the other hand, data for items 70 (P.1.2), 80 (P.1.3), 77 (P.2.1) and 83 (P.2.1) did not show much difference in performance –all percentages were quite low, ranging from 8% to 17%. With the exception of item 70 these are items with a somewhat higher level of cognitive demand, but still it seems they should be amenable to solution by someone with some minimal proficiency in programming.

Field Study: Some General Observations

The data in Table 3 with the headings 'Field Study All Subjects' and 'Field Study Programming and Computer Studies Only' give results for the Field Study sample excluding a Control group – a group with no planned computing or computer related instructional activity. The pupils all had some exposure to computing, concepts and/or applications. The first set 'All Subjects' includes pupils whose exposure was CAI or Computer Appreciation (without programming) as well as pupils who had instruction in BASIC programming, either programming as a single focus or programming in a broader context of computer studies which included aspects of hardware, applications, and impact or issues. The last column in Table 3 gives the data for the subset of the sample who were in courses which provided instruction in BASIC programming. In this regard it is this latter group which is of most interest in terms of algorithms and programming items. On the other hand one can compare performance on the algorithms in English language form items (82 and 83) for the total sample and the subsample. Since the total includes the subsample one can infer that the CAI and computer appreciation subjects performance was actually less than the table entries, i.e.

the percentages were increased by the Programming and Computer Studies subsample performance since the subsample performance was greater than the total group performance on all items. This suggests the programming instruction contributed to an increase in performance (note that while the data here have not been corrected for initial differences in groups, these differences in pretest were very small).

As indicated previously, if we now look at the programming and computer studies group, it appears that even those who had written programs experienced considerable difficulty with the mathematical and programming concepts. While the increase in the percentages from pre-to posttest was statistically significant, the posttest percentages (item - %: 70 - 34%, 74 -29%, 77 - 32%, 82 - 55%, 83 -9%) were still quite low. It is acknowledged that 1) the questions are not easy, 2) the time and concentration demands of this type of activity is such that a testing environment does not provide optimum conditions for obtaining a true measure of ability, and 3) the small number of questions for each objective restricts making broad generalizations. However, even with these points in mind, it is still the case that the relatively low percentages were somewhat unexpected. One needs to ask what instruction was in fact provided —were the pupils merely taught the words and programming concepts for coding in BASIC or was there actually an emphasis on reading, generalizing, modifying and finally designing algorithms for processing by machine. Subjective analysis of some of the course syllabuses suggests more of the former than the latter. There is certainly a need for further research on the questions of 'a best balance of activities' and 'best approach' - as the data here suggest there is room for considerable improvement.

IMPLICATIONS

What does this all mean? The results are not inconsistent with the statement made by Carpenter et al (1980) 'results ... indicate that most 13- and 17-year-old pupils have had little firsthand experience with ... programming computers either inside or outside the mathematics classroom' (pg.673). However, the data reported in the present paper provides some additional insights into particular difficulties experienced by students. This in turn suggests that there are certain aspects of computing, algorithms and programming, which need more attention. It is quite clear that a mere knowledge of the BASIC vocabulary and some selected programming concepts is inadequate for some 'reasonable' facility in programming.

It is also suggested from the data presented here that there is a need for an emphasis on careful step-by-step processing in the reading of algorithms expressed as programs and in particular algorithms which include some of the more difficult programming concepts —assignment, loops (iteration and recursion), and conditionals (decisions). The skill is important both in terms of using a new algorithm or procedure, i.e. able to follow directions, and for modifying or debugging an algorithm. Accompanying this is a need for a firm foundation in some of the mathematics of elementary algebra, facility with the use of variables (including the concept of replacement) and the ability to generalize. Further, the idea of testing a procedure with data for which one knows the result is an important notion in both mathematics and computing. This enables one to at least provide a partial check on whether or not an algorithm is functioning properly.

Finally, it would appear that the intermediate step of modifying algorithms to do a new but related task would warrant a more substantial portion of the time now spent on teaching programming (time data were also collected in the studies, but these are not reported here). This activity has the added feature that it also provides additional practice in reading and generalizing. While the present research was not intended to ascertain how best to teach programming it does seem that from the data available a piecemeal or 'building up with a statement at a time' approach is inappropriate and (as many others have noted) a better approach would be to base an instructional sequence on key concepts embedded in complete blocks or modules which accomplish a particular task - a task which is of interest and demonstrates the 'power' of the machine. Such an approach has the added benefit of promoting a more structured approach to the design of an algorithm/program as well.

Included in all of the above is one other important aspect for the teacher - that is the need to consider the difficulties experienced by pupils, i.e., errors, misconceptions and inappropriate strategies. This can be assisted through the use of test items, such as those reported here, for diagnosis followed by one-to-one discussion. Particular attention needs to be given to assisting the learner in moving from where he or she is now to a better understanding of key concepts and strategies.

1. Note: Part III of the test, pupil self-report items, included a section on 'Computer Experience'. One of the items, number 85, asked whether the pupil had written computer programs. Percentages of pupils responding yes to this question were 35% and 45% for the Eighth- and Eleventh-grade State Assessment samples respectively.

References

Abelson, H. and di Sessa, A.A. Turtle Geometry: The Computer as a Medium for Exploring Mathematics, The MIT Press, Cambridge, Massachusetts, 1981.

Anderson, R.E., Hansen, T.P., Johnson, D.C., and Klassen, D.L. The Minnesota Computer Literacy and Awareness Assessment (test). Minnesota Educational Computing Consortium, St. Paul (Minnesota), 1979.

Anderson, R.E., Krohn, K. and Sandman, R.S., Technical Report and User's Manual for the Minnesota Computer Literacy and Awareness Assessment, Form 1. Minnesota Educational Computing Consortium, St. Paul (Minnesota), 1981.

Anderson, R.E., Krohn, K. and Sandman, R.S. User's Guide for the Minnesota Computer Literacy and Awareness Assessment Test. Minnesota Educational Computing Consortium, St. Paul (Minnesota), 1980.

Carpenter, T.P., Corbitt, M.K., Kepner, H.S., Lindquist, M.M., and Reys, R.R. "The Current Status of Computer Literacy: NAEP Results for Secondary Students". Mathematics Teacher, 73 (December 1980): 669-673.

Committee on Computer Education. Recommendations Regarding Computers in High School. Washington, D.C.: Conference Board of the Mathematical Sciences (CBMS), 1972.

DES/MEP (Department of Education and Science/ Microelectronics in Education Programme). Mathematics and Microcomputers: A Pendley Manor Report: London, May 1983 (report to be published in 1985).

Dwyer, T. (4 chapters) in R.P. Taylor, Ed., The Computer in the School: Tutor Tool, Tutee. Teachers College Press, New York, 1980.

Engel, A. "The Role of Algorithms and Computers in Teaching Mathematics at School". in New Trends in Mathematics Teaching, Volume IV (prepared by the International Commission on Mathematics Instruction, ICMI). UNESCO, Paris, 1979: 249-277.

Hatfield, L.L. and Kieren, T.E. "Computer-Assisted Problem Solving in School Mathematics". Journal for Research in Mathematics Education, 3 (March 1972): 99-111.

Johnson, D.C., Anderson, R.E., Hansen, T.P. and Klassen, D.L. "Computer Literacy – What Is It?". Mathematics Teacher, 73 (February 1980): 91-96.

Johnson, D.C., Anderson, R.E., Hansen, T.P., and Klassen, D.L. "The Impact of CAL on Computer Literacy in Schools." Computers in Education, 3rd WCCE 81 Conference Proceedings. IFIP. North Holland. 1981.

Johnson, D.C. and Harding, R.D. "University Level Computing and Mathematical Problem-Solving Ability". Journal for Research in Mathematics Education, 10 (January 1979): 37-55.

Johnson, D.C. and Tinsley, J.D., Eds. Informatics and Mathematics in Secondary Schools: Impacts and Relationships. IFIP Working Conference, Varna, Bulgaria, September 1977. North Holland, New York, 1978.

Klassen, D.L., Anderson, R.E., Hansen, T.P., and Johnson, D.C. A Study of Computer Use and Literacy in Science Education (Final Report). Minnesota Educational Computing Consortium, St. Paul (Minnesota), 1980.

NCTM An Agenda for Action: Recommendations for School Mathematics of the 1980s. National Council of Teachers of Mathematics, Reston, Va., 1980.

NCTM "Teaching Mathematics through Programming". Computers in Mathematics Education (Part III). National Council of Teachers of Mathematics, Reston, Va., 1984.

NCTM Computer Oriented Mathematics Committee. Introduction to an Algorithmic Language (BASIC). National Council of Teachers of Mathematics, Washington, D.C., 1968.

NCTM Computer Oriented Mathematics Committee. "The Role of Electronic Computers and Calculators". Instructional Aids in Mathematics, pp.153-201. Thirty-fourth Yearbook of the National Council of Teachers of Mathematics. Reston, Va., 1973.

SMSG Algorithms, Computation, and Mathematics. A.C. Vroman, Pasadena (Calif.), 1966.

Soloway, E., Lockhead, J. and Clements, J. "Does computer programming enhance problem solving ability? Some positive evidence on algebra word problems." In R. Seidel, R. Anderson and B. Hunter (Eds), Computer literacy. New York: Academic Press. 1982.

COMPUTERS IN EDUCATION, K. Duncan and D. Harris (eds.)
Elsevier Science Publishers B.V. (North-Holland)
© IFIP, 1985

COMPUTER SCIENCE/INFORMATICS - A CHALLENGE TO MATHEMATICAL EDUCATION - AND VICE VERSA

Klaus-Dieter Graf

Freie Universität Berlin
Institut für Didaktik der Mathematik und Informatik
Berlin (West), Federal Republic of Germany

The rise of computer science and informatics in the last thirty years has caused vivid and powerful developments in general and in vocational schools in Germany. Two main lines have to be distinguished: the introduction of a new, independent subject "informatics" and modifications of subject matter and methods in traditional school subjects. Mathematical education in the lower secondary grades plays a very important part in these developments since education in computer science and in its applications depends most essentially on mathematical and logical qualifications. Thus it seems inevitable to aim at a complete integration of the two subjects, mathematics and informatics, at school. In this paper first we want to give a survey of the arguments about this assertion, some from educational policy, some from didactics. Second we want to describe some of the curricular attempts and their implementation.

1. THE GENERAL SITUATION IN GERMANY, ESP. IN LOWER SECONDARY EDUCATION

1.1 Many mathematics teachers at schools and and mathematics professors at universities now view informatics as a general challenge to mathematical education. Thus the chairman of the "Gesellschaft für Didaktik der Mathematik", Professor Winter, said in an interview (1): "At present the computer is the greatest challenge to math education (also to other subjects) ... Hardly any situation in the history of mathematics could be compared to this. Math education must be reconsidered and redefined as to intentions, subject matter, methods and ways of learning." On the other hand, he also has some reservations: "The actions in the classroom must not be dictated by the development in computer technology, however. Not everything which can be done is reasonable from a pedagogic point of view. Possibly school has to resist and not to adapt."

1.2 An understanding about information technology as a general problem of education has meanwhile reached high ranking political decision makers. As a consequence many impulses and measures are flowing back into the field of education. According to an interview with the Secretary of Education and Science measures will be taken to introduce the teaching of basic skills in information technology to all schools and to develop teacher training as well.

1.3 Availability of computers in schools is growing rapidly. Many pedagogical objections are no longer valid because of high speed, large storage and efficient operating systems.

1.4 When computers began to enter the classrooms, problems related to subject matter and methods of informatics dominated the discussion. Now problems of 'didactics' are being considered more and more carefully, e.g. demands are made to put more emphasis on practical aspects of informatics. Generally, there is a discussion whether areas like micro-electronics, robotics, information technology, man-machine-communication should be dealt with in schools along with algorithmic methods which have dominated the field so far.

The solution of many problems will depend on a settling of the relation between education in mathematics and informatics. Many correspondences are obvious, differences as well. Possibly a new subject called "Systematic solution of problems" would be the best answer, unifying aspects of logic, algorithms and computation.

Very often the relations between teachers and students change completely when working with computers. Due to a quicker - since more naive - access to computers, many students outdo their teachers in certain respects. Thus a new way of cooperative learning will become inevitable.

Great progress has been made in settling the formal conditions for teacher education in informatics by the state authorities. Some federal states have issued regulations for exams on different levels. The universities are working on regulations for studying. Fundamental research on how the learning of informatics takes place is a very important point. An example is the work of Cohors-Fresenborg about "algorithmic thinking" (1). Slogans like "problem solving by programming" are analyzed in detail, attempts are made to find out if "interactive programming" is really more than problem solving by trial and error.

Here the specialist for math education mentioned above can appropriately be cited again: "The most urgent request in today's situation is a careful exploration of the possibilities, limits and dangers of computer use in school. For instance we do not know today how intensive working with computers will influence the total intellectual setting of students (development of intuitive thinking, of phantasy, of perception etc.). This can only be found out by research which is laid out widely and sensitively."

1.5 Four different formal ways of incorporating informatics into sylabuses for "Sek. I" are possible:
- informatics as a compulsory course to be chosen among others like French or gymnastics
- informatics as a voluntary course or in a working group
- elements of informatics in other courses like mathematics or natural science
- computer use in other courses.

These solutions are generally applied in grades 9 and 10.

2. CURRICULAR ATTEMPTS AND THEIR IMPLEMENTATION

2.1 The model of Berlin (West) for "Sek. I"
In 1975 official "outlines of a curriculum for informatics in the field of compulsory elective subjects in Sek. I" were published and admitted for testing.

The outlines started from the fact that graduates from 'Sek. I' are soon going to be users of the numerous products of information technology in their vocational lives. For this reason it is not important for them to know very much about the theoretical foundations of informatics. What is required for them is a sound knowledge about possibilities and limits of using the computer as a tool, which would enable them to judge this technology critically and to master problems in vocational life connected with the use of the computer.

The introduction of informatics into courses at school is not intended to result in a mere addition of subject matter. It will eventually lead to a redefinition of many contents of education, so that informatics can be integrated with other disciplines. Basically there are three tasks to fulfill:
- teaching ways of thinking which can be applied between different disciplines
- de-mystification of information technology by discovering its tool-like character
- discussion of the social consequences of the introduction of information technology.

These tasks demand a way of teaching informatics which is oriented towards application.

The integration of algorithmic and applied aspects of informatics in class can be achieved by dealing with modelling processes in five steps:

1. Formulation of the problem and the aims
2. Analysis of the problem and design of a model
3. Design of an algorithm
4. Computer programming
5. Application of the system and analysis of the consequences.

Examples are "simulation of an ecological system" or "rationalizing of office work by microelectronics".

The teaching of informatics in the way sketched above takes place in a so-called compulsory elective course in grades 9 and 10, three lessons a week. At present 21 of 65 'Realschulen' and 'Gesamtschulen' (comprehensive schools) offer these courses. The main difficulties in extending the concept are the lack of equipment and the lack of qualified teachers. 3 of 62 'Gymnasiums' offer a reduced course in grade 10, since there students can carry on with informatics in the upper grades 11 to 13.

Approximately 25 % of the students in a school opt for informatics, if a course is offered at all.

2.2 The Bavarian model for "Sek. I"
Recent activities on informatics in "Sek.I" in Bavarian schools were inspired by the public demand of widespread "computer literacy". Some people consider these skills to be equally important as reading, writing and calculating. Many parents expect their children to get better chances in their vocational lives.

A start in higher secondary education would be too late for those graduating after grade 10. Also, due to the course system, many would miss an informatics course. So one has to start in lower secondary education. The demands of the subject matter can be adapted to this period. They turned out to be very motivating for most students.

According to a study from 1980/81 250 'Gymnasiums' with emphasis on mathematics and natural sciences ran courses in informatics of 35 lessons within mathematics education (four lessons a week) in grade 10. Two lessons of informatics per week for the period of half a year turned out to be more effective than one lesson per week throughout the year. In other Gymnasiums 140 teachers run this course as a voluntary course.

The general intentions of the courses are:
- to enable students to solve certain problems by using algorithms, to program these and test them with a computer
- to teach students how to apply the methods and the ways of thinking of informatics and to consider consequences and limits of data processing.

Work in the classroom should be oriented towards real problems, practical work with the computer should begin early, opportunities for extra practising should be given.

The syllabus contains
- the notion of algorithm, starting from every-days-life algorithms with repetitions and choices, easy programs
- more complex algorithms with subroutines and nested structures, relying on structured programming
- algorithms on structured data, including non-numeric examples
- social consequences of data processing, data protection, historical aspects.

The syllabus tries to avoid dominance of numerical problems. File processing, searching algorithms and sorting algorithms are essential subject matter.

2.3 Other models
For a number of years students in grades 9 and 10 in Northrhine-Westfalia have had a choice of computer oriented mathematics instead of a third foreign language. These courses can deal with the algebra of switching circuits as well as with special algorithms like the simplex algorithm for linear programming in application to problems with more than two variables. For a pilot project there will be an optional course at 30 schools beginning in 1984 in grades 9 and 10 as a choice. This course is not intended to deal with programming only. It will in addition demonstrate applications of data processing using simple examples from real life. One example is planning a competition in sports at school with computer assistance.

In Baden-Württemberg an interesting model for the integration of basic facts about computers and informatics into different other subjects has been worked out, also for the Hauptschule. Under the heading of 'technology' "application of computers to the solution of practical problems, construction and use of simple electronic devices, construction of a computer controlled device and design of a programm" (grade 9) are typical examples.

'Mathematics' includes "work with a computer on applied calculus". 'Social science' deals with "division of labour and automation" (grade 8).

Similar aspects are dealt with at Realschule and Gymnasium in mathematics, physics, natural sciences, technology and social science, carrying as far as "chances and limits of modern information technology".

3. CHANGES IN THE INTENTIONS OF LOWER
    MATHEMATICAL EDUCATION

3.1 New methods available
It is obvious that due to calculators and computers the "skill to do numerical calculations by hand" has lost its great importance as an intention of mathematics education in Germany. More attention can be given instead to skills in formulating algorithms, in exact preparation of input data and in checking the plausibility of output data.

Teachers and educational authorities do also agree that far more essential changes will happen in math education. Some aspects are
- a far better visualization of mathematical objects and methods will be possible by using the computer, especially by graphics
- more practical ways of problem solving can be taught, also by using software-packages as "black boxes"
- an integration of different fields of mathematics can be achieved, e.g. analysis and probability theory
- cooperation with other subjects in school will be possible
- real applications of mathematics can be dealt with and demonstrated.

The intentions become attainable since due to computers new methods and also contents are available:
- algorithmic approach when looking for problem solutions
- effective means of representation of algorithms like flow charts or Nassi-Schneiderman diagrams (structograms)
- fast trial-and-error methods to check conjectures
- simulation of dynamic systems basing on simple models
- practical training courses which allow for sufficient free or guided individual or teamwork
- forms of teaching or learning like experiments, simulation, discovering, discussion.

3.2 Mathematics and informatics in school
The relations between math and informatics in school will be of great importance.
Since 1980 intentions for informatics education in lower sec. education have been formulated by several institutions in Germany. It turns out that many of these are very close to corresponding intentions of math education, some using different terms. There is no use in cancelling such intentions in math education, since they have proven important for many generations already. If they are mentioned in the discussion about informatics education, this only means that they have been neglected in mathematics at school. Thus they have to be put into the centre of attention again.

What are such intentions? A fundamental paper of Uwe Beck from 1980 (2) lists for instance:
- systematic finding of algorithmic solutions of problems
- formulation of algorithmic solutions of problems in programms
- dealing with problems close to real life, using adequate data structures and forms of date processing organization.

These intentions imply more detailed aspects for the ways of teaching:
- teaching should be oriented towards application
- non-numerical problems should be considered, also complex ones

- solutions should be constructed in an en-
  gineer-like way
- solutions should be found in groups and
  working on projects
- programming should be preceded by structuring

The paper outlines that most of these demands
are fulfilled today (and before) in mathematics education in German schools. As to algorithms one even can go back to F. Klein, who
pointed out their importance in 1935. But
there are more points: In math education the
"genetical principle" plays an important part.
It leads to viewing instruction in school as a
process. Also, math education today is oriented clearly towards applications, beginning in
primary schools. Modelling is an important
step in this area and it is done in a way very
similar to structured programming. It is done
less strictly 'top down' than in programming
but it admits different levels of precision at
each step of the process. Math education is
also dealing with complex problems and it admits work in a group.

The work of H. Löthe (3) about different
methods of programming (from FORTRAN via LOGO
to FP) also proves that mathematics and informatics should not be taught independently in
school. A right combination of their methods
will arm students with effective strategies
for problem solving. One of these will be
using the computer not only for executing solutions of problems but first for finding and
formulating the solutions.

Thus mathematics teachers can rely on strong
resources in the theory of math education, but
also in reality, when facing the challenge of
informatics. Many intentions just have to be
reformulated and have to be attacked with new
means, e.g. another language for describing and
solving problems, maybe a programming language.
Two examples of textbooks for teachers and
teacher students following these ideas are (4)
and (5).

3.3 Some examples for illustration
A paper of J. Ziegenbalg (6) describes, how
the following methodological intentions can
be enforced by using computers or methods of
informatics:
- empirical founding of mathematical notions,
  contents and methods by many examples
- elementarization and simplification of
  problems.
Here he deals with the problem of finding out
when a loan will be paid off, if you know the
annuity. Normally you need means of analysis
for this problem, available in upper grades
only. Using a computer you can solve it with
elementary mathematical means in lower grades
already.
- Operative working. The fundamental question
  of this method is "what if?" In real data
  processing so-called "spreadsheet-software"
  has been developed to go along this way.
  This method can be adapted to math education and should be taught there. The example given handles the drawing of a car

answering different requirements. It depends upon using the "turtle" from the
programming language LOGO.
- Constructive working. Here examples for applying the computer in geometry in Sek. I
  are given.
- Modular working. This method of working
  with modules when finding the solution of
  problems requires a careful study of the
  interfaces. It is illustrated by an application to a strategic game, using recursion
  also.

A paper of K. Menzel (7) points out, that numerical topics in math education have to be
reduced. One of the reasons is the fact that
today real applications of data processing
mostly deal with non-numerical problems.
These problems will also motivate students
again to deal with mathematics at all. As an
example, he proposes to study and to implement the procedures for school administration including school data bases. It is also
stressed that application of programs is
more important than developing programs
since software-packages are getting standard
tools in many areas.

As a last point a paper of D. Werner (8)
shall be mentioned. It starts from the observation that computers today are more 'if-
then-machines' than calculators. This is exemplified by the real application of controlling a robot in production. His work in the
classroom in grade 10 has four phases: manipulating the robot; teaching the robot; applying the robot; limits, problems and background of the robot.

4. THE ROLE OF MATHEMATICS TEACHERS

Due to their background and their experiences mathematics teachers have to fulfill
important tasks in the process mentioned
above. The following statement from a working group on computer and teacher education
at the 5th International Congress on Mathematical Education in 1984 shall prove that
they are prepared for this:
"The group noted that we are training teachers in computer science who will teach for
30 or 40 years. We cannot give them a definitive body of knowledge, but we have to
enable them to adapt and evolve. At the present state of development there is a strong
link between pre-service and in-service
training. In-service training is in fact
"pre-service because of the constant evolution of informatics and of pedagogy.

Computer Science is more than a technical
tool. It is also a tool for thinking, reasoning, and problem solving; it can lead to different thinking styles; questions of means
are as important as ends. Computer Science is
embedded in the curricula, it is not a complement to it. Student teachers must be
taught:
1. Not only computer science but also pedagogical aspects of its use.

2. Not only programming but also algorithmic thinking
3. To re-centre in mathematics the role of algorithms
4. To stress the main algorithmic concepts and methods for problem solving
5. The different ways informatics appear: data banks, word processors, expert systems etc.

Computer Science changes the philosophical foundations of mathematics. For example:
1. Impact on what mathematics is to be taught
2. The development of symbolic systems
3. More experimental mathematics
4. New skills - observation, visualisation, simulation, conjecture and numerical verification etc.

Computer Science changes pedagogical styles. The computer must not be used in only one way; we have to carry out a multi-useage approach. Nor must the computer be used to do things that can be better done without one. The computer does not replace the teacher but will alter the pupil-teacher relationship. The teacher must become a partner of his pupils.

<u>Classically:</u>

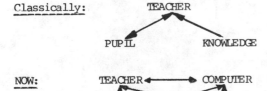

NOW:

Several problems exist:
1. How to convince our colleagues of the role computer science plays in mathematics
2. The need for serious reflection upon the relationship between mathematics, computers and education
3. How to disseminate our findings knowing that we are already <u>late</u> with respect to the social dissemination of computers themselves.
The working group expects considerable turbulences in the development of mathematical and computer science education due to the rise of information technology. Many problems cannot even be foreseen. National and worldwide meetings will be helpful in identifying true directions. We must also identify blind alleys, fads, and those directions wasteful of our time, energy and resources and destructive to students learning and mathematics.

The working group is also aware of deep philosophical questions which information technology raises in our society. Teachers have to be alert and ensure that students learn how to use information technology as a powerful tool and how to control it completely.

5. REFERENCES

(1) Cohors-Fresenborg, E.: The understanding of algorithmic concepts on the basis of elementary actions.
In: Proceedings of the Sixth Conference PME, Antwerpen 1982.

(2) Beck, U., Ziele des zukünftigen Informatikunterrichts.
In: Journal für Mathematik-Didaktik 1, H. 3 (1980) 189-197.

(3) Löthe, H., Arten des Programmierens und Programmiersprachen - ihr Stellenwert im Mathematikunterricht.
In: Zentralblatt für Didaktik der Mathematik 15, H. 5 (1983) 220-224.

(4) Graf, K.-D., Informatik. Eine Einführung in Grundlagen und Methoden, Verlag Herder, Freiburg (1981) 256 p.

(5) Graf, K.-D. (Hrsg.), Computer in der Schule - Perspektiven für den Mathematikunterricht, Verlag Teubner, Stuttgart (1985) 203 p.

(6) Ziegenbalg, J., Informatik und allgemeine Ziele des Mathematikunterrichts.
In: Zentralblatt für Didaktik der Mathematik 15, H. 5 (1983) 215-220.

(7) Menzel, K., Computereinsatz in der Sekundarstufe I - Die bisherigen Ansätze reichen nicht aus.
In: Zentralblatt für Didaktik der Mathematik 15, H. 5 (1983) 225-228.

(8) Werner, D., Ein Robot-Modell als Beispiel zum Thema "Reale DV in der Schule".
In: Zentralblatt für Didaktik der Mathematik 16, H. 1 (1984) 2-5.

COMPUTERS IN EDUCATION, K. Duncan and D. Harris (eds.)
Elsevier Science Publishers B.V. (North-Holland)
© IFIP, 1985

RETHINKING COMPUTER LITERACY

Jane M. Fritz

University of New Brunswick

Fredericton, New Brunswick, Canada E3B 5A3

A current, generally accepted definition of computer literacy is the acquisition of the knowledge, attitudes and skills necessary for a person to function effectively in an information-based society. This definition clearly has different interpretations for different age groups and different interest groups. As well, the implications of this definition are bound to continually change as technology and its effect on society changes. This paper attempts to analyze the content of some of the computer literacy programs that have been put in place and to assess the programs' success in fulfilling the definition of computer literacy. As well, a brief look is taken at the overall educational process to identify other areas in the curriculum that have an impact on our children's ability to function in a changing world.

Introduction

The public at large has become convinced that exposure to computers is a necessary element of modern education. Massive news media attention to the "computer revolution" has spread the message that some form of computer knowledge is essential for today's students to function as responsible and employable citizens. This is a unique phenomenon in the history of education, where the will of the public for an untried and expensive new subject is placing it in many curricula before the educators are either convinced about its place in education or prepared to handle the subject completely and in a coordinated fashion. Public approval is forthcoming for the expenditure of large sums of money to put microcomputers in school at a time when money is hard to come by, the quality of our public school education is being seriously challenged (1,2), and teachers are being laid off. Is this pressure to include computer literacy in our educational system justified? Are we headed in the right direction? Are there evaluation procedures in place to allow us to steer the computer literacy programs in new directions as new directions arise? Do these computer literacy programs really go a long way towards making our children more able to cope in our information-based society?

Computer literacy programs are found in two distinctly different forms: as a continuing part of the educational process, encompassing many grade levels, and as a discrete course or learning unit at a specific grade level. Within these two methods of presentation there are two basic approaches, either integrating the computer literacy material into the existing curricula or presenting the material as a distinct course, separate from existing subject matter. It is generally agreed that the ideal approach is a continuing, integrated one. After all, literacy, computer or general literacy, is something best acquired gradually and with exposure to it from many vantage points. However, ideals are not always easy to achieve, and this ideal approach to computer literacy is no exception.

The major components of computer literacy have been identified as (3,4,5,6,):

- How Computers Work (an introduction to hardware and software)
- Computer Applications
- History of Computers
- Societal Impact of Computers
- Careers in Computing
- Computer Programming

These topics were developed as a starting point by pioneers who worked hard to include areas that seemed appropriate at the time and for that time. But as new programs are developed, those responsible for the new programs naturally look to the existing programs for guidance and find these topics. As new textbooks are written to compete in a burgeoning market, and a lucrative market it is too, these topics are recognized as being de rigour for a computer literacy text. For many school systems struggling to put computer literacy programs in place, the existing programs have become the definition of computer literacy.

This paper will attempt to analyze the suitability of these computer literacy programs and this set of topics as vehicles to satisfy the mandate of computer literacy. As well, we will discuss some questionable consequences of the introduction of computers in the schools, consequences that are too often overlooked in the rush to put programs in place.

Is the Content Meeting the Perceived Need?

The acknowledged reason for computer literacy in the schools is to ensure that our children are fully prepared to function in our information-based society. Are the topics that are generally considered part of computer literacy fulfilling this need?

1. How Computers Work.
    An introduction to hardware and software is a useful exercise for anyone today, regardless of age. Having some hands-on experience, learning some of the basic terminology that is bandied about in ads and news articles continually, and running a few turnkey programs will go a long way towards alleviating the mystique that exists about computers. Removing the mystery of computers will remove some of the exaggerated value now attached to anything that is done by computer.

2. Computer Applications.
    This is a broad item requiring a clear understanding of its intent. Computers are a tool, one of the most powerful tools imaginable. The use of computers as a tool in many diverse areas is definitely changing the way many traditional disciplines are carrying out their tasks. Writers, scientists, statisticians, secretaries, travel agents, cashiers, etc. are all finding that computers as specialized tools are changing the way they do their jobs. Eventually computer literacy will more or less mean being able to use the computer as a specialized tool in one's work life and, optionally, home life. In the interim, while more and more specialized applications are evolving, there are two possible approaches to studying about computer applications.

    One approach is a general, discussion-oriented survey of some wide-spread, well-known current applications that we might all encounter, eg. computers in banking, point-of-sales terminals in shopkeeping, computers in police work, computers in medicine, etc.

    The other approach is quite different and more directly connected to the student becoming computer literate. It involves using some available software tools in applications that arise in existing subject areas; using a data base to find or rearrange information being used in an assignment, learning to use a spreadsheet to help solve problems that crop up in a class, learning to use a word processing package to write essays, letters, etc.

    Both of these approaches have some merit. The first approach is a transient one.

These applications will be too commonplace to warrant attention 5 to 10 years from now. The second approach is very worthy of inclusion. One challenge is to encourage the relevant subject teachers to become involved and learn to use these tools themselves so that computer literacy does become just that, literacy, and not a separate subject. The application tools will continue to improve and proliferate. We have a responsibility to expand our user group in the educational community.

3. History of Computers.
    It is questionable whether the study of the history of computers has any bearing on a person's ability to function in an information-based society. Do we study the history of communication in general; printing-press, telegraph, telephone, television, satellite technology? The computer is really just a part of this larger picture. The history of computers is interesting, but no more so than the rest of the history of science and technology.

4. Societal Impact of Computers.
    This is an interesting, thought-provoking topic, usually including such areas as data privacy and security, computer crime, computer ethics, and the necessity for people to be aware of the subjective value attached to the analysis and use of data. While it is important for students to recognize that vigilance is necessary to prevent the misuse of computers and the abuse of data, is it not equally important for students to learn of other perils in our information-based society? For example, we are constantly fed biased information from the news media; our news is controlled by other people who decide what is important and then put their own interpretation on it. In order to have well-informed citizens at the end of our educational process, we should probably spend as much time developing a perspective on individual interpretation of all the information coming our way as we spend discussing computer implications. Teaching students to become alert, responsible citizens who can analyze information intelligently requires a broader platform than merely the repercussions of the use of computers. This is an expansion to the subject of civics, social studies, etc.

5. Careers in Computing.
    This topic is misleading at best. Most teachers have little first hand knowledge in this area (except that teachers should now have some computer background) and so naturally rely on the available textbooks. Unfortunately, this is a very volatile area of employment, so that the textbook information is usually either out of date

or too general to be of any use. One significant problem lately has been that students appear to be convinced that any computer experience at all is going to assure them of a well-paying job. Unfortunately, this is not the case.

6. Computer Programming.
This is a controversial area. Some people maintain that it isn't necessary for everyone to learn to program, since only a small percentage of people will be involved in actual programming. This can be easily debated. While the premise is true, our educational system is supposed to be more than just a training program, it is meant to educate. We teach many things that are not going to be directly used by every student, but still have skill value or conceptual value. The fact is that there is no better way to understand how a computer does its job than to have to develop the logic to solve a small problem and then complete the translation into a computer program that will successfully solve the problem. As well, the logic and problem solving skills learned are invaluable.

The main problem with handling the unit on computer programming is that the problem-solving component, which is so important for everyone, tends to play second fiddle to language syntax. The message that the programming language is merely a tool which allows us to use the computer to solve a problem seems to get lost. The programming language and its syntax rules usually become the main focus of this area, when in fact being able to understand a problem and describe it as a programmable algorithm is the vital learning objective.

One unfortunate but widespread product of computer programming in schools is the glorification of students who perform any trivial task on a computer. Because of the preponderance of teachers who are teaching computer courses with minimum background, students often have little guidance as to the value of their accomplishments. Usually in an educational setting we try to give positive reinforcement, giving praise for results and effort. But in this strange world of King Computer, this praise is creating an undesirable side effect, the students who think they know more about computer programming than they really do. This effect is also reinforced by parents, who often have no background with which to measure the relative merit of computer work.

Obviously, there are schools with rigorous programming courses. The problem of

what students with extensive computer backgrounds do when they get to college is another matter. Such a situation far exceeds the definition of computer literacy anyway.

Computer programming has a definite place in a computer literacy curriculum. But there are two points which we must not lose track of:

(1) the problem-solving, or algorithm development, component of the unit is more important than whatever programming language is used,

(2) the students should be made aware, without taking a negative approach, of just how introductory their programming exposure is.

Three topics within the set of those generally included in a computer literacy program have been identified as having strong justification for their inclusion;

- How Computers Work (general terminology and hands on time),
- Computer Applications,
- Computer Programming.

These three topics can be identified as being worthy of helping to satisfy the goal of providing our students with the skills and concepts they will need to cope in our computer-oriented society. Wherever possible these topics should be integrated into existing programs so that the point is made very clear that, for most of us, computers will be another tool that we use in various ways to make life easier, just the way we use cars and washing machines.

Problem Areas Inherent in Existing Programs

There are some side effects of the existing computer literacy programs that are worth considering. By being aware of unplanned problem areas that are inherent in existing programs, we can hopefully improve our approach.

Some very innovative software is available (8,9) which hides much of the frustration involved in using most of today's programming languages and operating system commands. This software fulfills the purpose of allowing the underlying concepts to be learned without being constrained by awkward syntax and man-machine interfaces. These products are very useful as teaching tools, but they aren't making students truly computer literate. While this approach is very useful, the students should at least be aware that they are dealing with an "ideal" system, not a real one. The reason this point is made is that using computers today is not the trivial, straight-forward process we hope it will eventually become. Every system one uses is different, and learning to use each non-ideal system requires patience and a methodical approach. These are two qualities that students are not strong on, but are very important to being a good computer user.

We should teach a little more of the reality of computer science. We have encountered too many students who have not been forced to develop the discipline of reading through manuals or of using the fundamentals they have been given to find the information they need. By making it "easy" we may be doing the students a disservice. These skills are vital to success in a changing society. One excellent way of reinforcing these skills is to have different students responsible for reading and understanding specified sections of a manual appropriate to their school work. These students should then be required to write an instruction sheet or short user's guide for their fellow students and be able to instruct others in how to perform the tasks they have learned. These are the very skills that people in the work force are expected to use often, especially where new hardware and software is being introduced . Such exercises could be conducted appropriately in language arts classes.

A new phenomenon that is a side effect of the introduction of computers in the schools is something we might call "computer anxiety". It is a first cousin to the well-documented condition called "math anxiety" (7,10,11,12). The irony in the situation is that we introduce anxiety in students who are forced to deal with computers, when the whole point of introducing computers into the schools is to prevent this anxiety. Math anxiety is a phenomenon that is identified as affecting girls more than boys, although it affects large numbers of students, including plenty of boys. There are four general types of explanations for math avoidance (10),

1. lack of ability,
2. negative attitude toward the subject,
3. perceived lack of usefulness in future life,
4. discouraging social milieu.

It has been found that girls are less confident of success and quicker to give up than boys when confronted with the possibility of failure, possibly because there has been the view that girls won't need math anyway. This is no longer true. Math has been identified as a strong career filter; that is, without math many career paths are automatically closed, and if girls don't want to continue to settle for the traditional, lower-paid female jobs, then they are going to have to accept the math

challenge. Computer knowledge of some kind is becoming an equally strong career filter (13). The fourth type of math avoidance, a discouraging social milieu, seems to be the strongest factor in computer anxiety in girls. Boys tend to gravitate towards the computer, at least at the outset. In general, boys seem to thrive on the challenge of winning a computer game and that gives them a positive start. For some reason, girls don't seem to care as much about computer games, either for fear of not doing well or because of socialization factors we don't understand well. Ironically, those female students who learn word-processing and accounting packages in vocational education classes are learning at least as many computer concepts as those in the other computer classes. And they perform well. In that setting those students feel less threatened and perform accordingly. Somehow, we must learn how to interject the interest and motivation into math and computer classes that will bring more students along. This is a big challenge to educators, but a worthy one.

What Skills will be Vital to Function Effectively in the Future

If we are going to be concerned with whether our students will be prepared to function in this information-based society, then we should be taking a closer look at what skills other than computer skills these students should have and how the computer can act as an educational tool to strength some identified weaknesses in the existing general curriculum.

Technological advances have been coming with increasing rapidity. In this light, we have evaluated our role as educators and determined that computer skills of some description should be covered. But because technology is changing, the details of what we teach can change just as quickly. We have to come to terms with the difference between the details, which can change quickly, and the concepts, which don't change very fast at all. For example, at the postsecondary level, industry complains that the languages we teach are obsolete, that we should forget about procedural languages and teach 4th generation languages. But this is both unreasonable and ill-considered. It is unreasonable because the current 4th generation languages are in a state of evolution themselves, are all very different, tied to different types of data bases or sometimes tied to no data base and are specific to different hardware installations. Learning one 4th generation language is not going to make learning another one much easier. The computer industry is going to continue to introduce new hardware and new software. We in education cannot hope to keep our students or ourselves abreast of every new product. The point is that in this area we all must expect to be involved in a continual learning process. The request is ill-considered because what employers should be expecting are students who are well equipped to continue to learn once they have left the educational system.

Never has the notion that learning is a life-long activity been more apparent than now. All we can hope to give our children to allow them to function in this complex world are the fundamentals upon which they can continue to learn. The fundamentals include:

- Reading and comprehension skills
- Communication skills (writing and speaking)
- Mathematical concepts and problem-solving
- Fundamentals of scientific principles
- Computer skills

Computer skills will vary, but should include knowing how a computer can be used as a tool when applicable, basically knowing how to be an effective computer user.

The real effort necessary in education to produce useful citizens is not in the area of computers, but in the area of adaptability. We must be able to adapt to continual change. In order to keep up with constant change, people have to be able to read manuals and understand them, possibly be able to write them so they can be understood. People need to have more analytical skills than many have now. They need to know what kind of questions to ask when they are exposed to something new. We need less rote learning of facts and more learning of concepts. Learning concepts must go beyond just parroting back the wording of the "concept"; students must have experience in going one step beyond and applying the learned concepts to new situations. In fact, one of the biggest challenges to the developers of educational software is to produce software that stimulates the student to think for himself, to make "new" discoveries. If we can produce more imaginative, high quality software, the computer can be a valuable tool to help the teachers prepare the students for the future. The potential is there.

Conclusion

Both educators and the general public have recognized the need for the introduction of computer skills into the education system. Because technology is advancing rapidly, the precise requirements of computer literacy will continue to change. We must be vigilant in regard to what computer literacy components are valid at any point in time and what parts should be stressed. Two areas of concern that need to be resolved before the presence of computers in schools can be a true success are teacher readiness and the appearance of more innovative educational software. The first

issue is largely a matter of time and exposure. We should train teachers to the point where the computer is an integrated part of their "educational toolkit", along with dictionaries and encyclopedias (10). The second issue, better software, probably requires introducing more teachers to the potential of the computer and then forming working teams of teachers and programmers.

In this interim period, while we are feeling our way, we should not lose sight of the larger picture of preparing our students for this new world. Our teaching strategies in all subject areas, through both traditional classroom teaching and new educational software, must encourage students to ask for relevant information, allow students to build up intuition and insight, and encourage students to attempt to arrive at their own conclusions. We must try to make the learning process, or more specifically the thinking process, a joy.

References

1. The National Commission on Excellence in Education, A Nation at Risk: The Imperative for Educational Reform, U.S. Government Printing Office, Wash., D.C., April 1983.

2. Science Council of Canada, Science for Every Student, Government Documents, Ottawa, May 1984.

3. Computer Literacy: An Introduction, Center for Learning Technologies, State Education Department, Albany, N.Y., 1983.

4. TIES, Computer Literacy Curriculum: Grades K-9, Minnesota School Districts Data Processing Joint Board, St. Paul, Minn., Sept. 1982.

5. Computer Literacy Curriculum Guides: Elementary, Junior High, and High School, Alberta Education, Edmonton, Alberta, 1983.

6. Program Guide for Computer Literacy, The Penn-Harris-Maddison School Corporation, Osceola, Indiana, Aug., 1982.

7. Tobias, Sheila, Overcoming Math Anxiety, Norton, N.Y., 1978.

8. Computer Discovery, SRA, Inc., Chicago, 1981.

9. Pattis, Richard, Karel the Robot, A Gentle Introduction to the Art of Programming with Pascal, John Wiley & Sons, N.Y., 1981.

10. Brush, Lorelei, <u>Encouraging Girls in
     Mathematics</u>, Abt Books, Cambridge, Mass.,
     1980.

11. Skolnick, J., Langbort, C., Day, L., <u>How
     to Encourage Girls in Math and Science</u>,
     Prentice-Hall, Englewood Cliffs, N.J.,
     1982.

12. Buxton, Laurie, <u>Do You Panic About Maths?
     Coping With Maths Anxiety</u>, Heinemann
     Educational Books, London, 1981.

13. Menzies, Heather, <u>Computer Technology and
     the Education of Female Students</u>, Canadi-
     an Teachers' Federation, Ottawa, 1982.

COMPUTERS IN EDUCATION, K. Duncan and D. Harris (eds.)
Elsevier Science Publishers B.V. (North-Holland)
© IFIP, 1985

EDUCOM COMPUTER LITERACY PROJECT: INTEGRATING COMPUTING THROUGHOUT THE
CURRICULUM IN COLLEGES AND UNIVERSITIES -- TRENDS AND ANALYSIS

Steven W. Gilbert, Managing Director
Kimberly S. Wiley, Manager
EDUCOM Computer Literacy Project
EDUCOM
PO Box 364
Princeton, New Jersey 08540

The central mission of the EDUCOM Computer Literacy Project (ECLP) is helping
colleges and universities increase the availability and use of cost-effective
information technology for those not specializing in computing, regardless of
whether or not this effort is called "computer literacy." Results and
analysis, including survey data, from the first two years of the ECLP will be
presented. A conceptual framework for the integration of computing throughout
the curriculum, for learning about computing, and for thinking about academic
software in higher education will be offered.

I. TRENDS AND ANALYSIS -- SURVEY RESULTS

The ECLP has been carefully observing the
computer literacy movement in higher
education for more than two years --
identifying trends and studying
innovations. The trends have become
clearer, even though "computer literacy" is
a phrase that will never have a precise
definition. Focus on finding a definition
for "computer literacy" has shifted to a
focus on implementation.

Illustrative survey data: More than 90% of
institutions responding offer activities
that encourage faculty members to learn
about computing. About 10% offer promotion
or tenure incentives for the development of
instructional software.

II. CONCEPTUAL FRAMEWORK FOR "INTEGRATING COMPUTING THROUGHOUT THE CURRICULUM" -- STAGES, STEPS, AND PITFALLS

A sequence of needs (and how to meet them):

1) Faculty access to computers (and
   how to meet them):

2) Faculty development

3) Access to academic software
   (faculty development of software,
   evaluation and selection of
   software, distribution of software, and software site
   licensing

4) User support services.

III. CONCEPTUAL FRAMEWORK FOR LEARNING ABOUT COMPUTING

In the evolution of computing systems,
watch the transitions: from concepts to
implementations, from implementations to
idiosyncrasies, from idiosyncrasies to
standards, and from standards to
obsolescence.

IV. CONCEPTUAL FRAMEWORK FOR ACADEMIC SOFTWARE DEVELOPMENT AND DISSEMINATION IN HIGHER EDUCATION

Context: EDUCOM, a consortium of 500
colleges and universities, began in
October, 1984 to examine current practices
and future opportunities related to the
development and dissemination of
"academic" software -- software intended
to support academic activities -- in
colleges and universities. This focus
reflected the ECLP's recognition that
faculty access to "good" software for
academic purposes was a major obstacle to
rapid "integration of computing throughout
the curriculum."

Classifications for academic software:

1) SOFTWARE THAT IS COMMERCIALLY
   SUCCESSFUL OUTSIDE OF HIGHER
   EDUCATION, BUT THAT HAS
   SIGNIFICANT APPLICATIONS
   WITHIN HIGHER EDUCATION (E.G.,
   SPREADSHEETS, WORD
   PROCESSING).

2) SOFTWARE THAT IS COMMERCIALLY
   VIABLE ENTIRELY WITHIN HIGHER
   EDUCATION (NO EXAMPLES KNOWN
   YET; MANY HOPED FOR).

3) "DEVELOPMENTAL SOFTWARE" OR
   "AMATEUR SOFTWARE" OR
   "MANUSCRIPT DRAFT SOFTWARE" --
   SOFTWARE DEVELOPED WITHOUT A
   COMMERCIAL OBJECTIVE (AT LEAST
   INITIALLY). THE DEVELOPMENT
   OF SUCH SOFTWARE SHOULD BE
   ENCOURAGED AND ITS
   DISSEMINATION FACILITATED.

INCENTIVES SHOULD BE OFFERED
TO MAKE WORK ON SUCH PROJECTS
FALL WITHIN THE ACADEMIC
TRADITION, AND MOVE PEOPLE
ALONG THE TENURE TRACK. THIS
"GRASS ROOTS" LEVEL COULD
BECOME THE SOURCE OF SOME OF
THE MOST CREATIVE SOFTWARE
THAT EVENTUALLY APPEARS IN
CATEGORIES 1 AND 2 ABOVE; BUT
ONLY IF MECHANISMS FOR THE
TRANSITION BETWEEN THE
CATEGORIES ARE ALSO AVAILABLE.

GOAL: FACILITATE FACULTY MEMBERS'
EFFORTS TO DEVELOP AND DISTRIBUTE
ACADEMIC SOFTWARE. PROVIDE EFFECTIVE
SOFTWARE DISTRIBUTION CHANNELS AND
SOURCES OF information about academic
software. [If separate information
sources and distribution channels for
each of the above categories of software
are necessary, then coordination and
linkages among them will also be
essential.]

***

What are the unmet needs and the
possible future roles for EDUCOM and
similar organizations?

COMPUTERS IN EDUCATION, K. Duncan and D. Harris (eds.)
Elsevier Science Publishers B.V. (North-Holland)
© IFIP, 1985

SO YOUR DISTRICT HAS MANDATED COMPUTER LITERACY--WHAT DO YOU DO NOW?

Tony Jongejan, Sheila Cory and Vicki Smith

International Council for Computers in Education

The debate over the definition of computer literacy continues. Yet states, provinces, districts, etc. are mandating computer literacy for their students. How are the implementors handling the mandates for a subject computer educators can't agree on? Computer Literacy has three possible components:
* Applications (word processing, spreadsheets, data bases, etc.)
* Computer Science and Computer Programming (BASIC, Logo, etc.)
* Computers and Society (history, computer components, issues, and impacts of computers on society)

Computer educators can't agree on how much, if any, of each component should be included in the computer literacy curriculum. Another issue to resolve is whether the computer literacy curriculum should be integrated into the K-12 curriculum or just into 1 or 2 required courses and at what level.

After the Computer Literacy curriculum is determined, planning needs to be done in four other areas: hardware, software, teacher training and support services. Three panelists will be discussing these planning areas and how their district or state has implemented computer literacy into the curriculum.

Tony Jongejan, Chair
Western Washington University
Bellingham, Washington

I will discuss the process the Everett School District followed in K-12 planning for Computer Literacy. The first task--to determine how Computer Literacy would be defined--resulted in a list of computer competencies. The next task was to develop curriculum for various district units and provide for necessary hardware, software, teacher training and support service for implementing this curriculum. I will draw parallels between the process and outcomes used in Everett and by the School of Education at Western Washington, where I have also been involved in a Computer Literacy mandate.

Sheila Cory
Coordinator of Educational Computing
Chapel Hill-Carrboro City Schools
Chapel Hill, North Carolina

I will outline the process that our school system went through to define computer literacy, develop a philosophical position on computer literacy, develop a scope and sequence to achieve some degree of computer literacy for all students in the system, develop curriculum materials, train teachers, present instruction to students, and then to evaluate for future decision-making. Implementation of a full computer literacy program will be discussed as a developmental process, with emphasis placed on careful evaluation at each stage of development.

Vicki S. Smith
Coordinator for Computer-Based Instruction
Region IV Education Service Center
Houston, Texas

The state of Texas has mandated that all seventh or eighth grade students will receive one semester of instruction in computer literacy. The essential elements for this course include programming, applications, and computers and society.

Included in implementation of this course has been:
* development of a curriculum guide
* competency testing of identified teachers
* laboratory planning
* student testing
* a regional training network

I will discuss strategies utilized in accomplishing the above as well as plans for expanding this initial focus to extend towards either end of the grade spectrum. Legislative, state and local district concerns will be addressed.

COMPUTERS IN EDUCATION, K. Duncan and D. Harris (eds.)
Elsevier Science Publishers B.V. (North-Holland)
©IFIP, 1985

714

IMPLEMENTATIONS OF CAMPUS-WIDE COMPUTER LITERACY PROGRAMS

Gabriel G. Balazs-Chairperson
Director Computer Services
Virginia Military Institute
Lexington, VA 24450

Charles E. Fraley
Director Academic Computing
Virginia Military Institute
Lexington, VA 24450

Peter Adman
Assistant Director
Computer Centre
University of Hull
Hull HU6 7RX England

Ulrich Bosler
IPM
Universität Kiel
Olshausenstrasse 40-60
D-2300 Kiel 1 Federal German Rep.

Anthony Halaris
Department of Computer Science
Iona College
New Rochelle, NY 10801

The implementations of establishing, running and equipping a campus-wide computer literacy program will be discussed by each participant. Each panelist will discuss how his campus developed its program summarizing both positive and negative aspects. Discussions will include administrative, organizational, choice of hardware/software and other problems or solutions. A question and answer period will follow.

MICROCOMPUTER IMPLEMENTATION AT A SMALL
ENGINEERING AND LIBERAL ARTS COLLEGE:
THE VMI APPROACH

Dr. Fraley

VMI's new computer program is designed to give every student a working knowledge of computers and the ability to use them in every academic discipline--to make computer users of all students, but not necessarily programmers. This new emphasis on computer use is designed to improve academic quality and produce better prepared graduates. The new program introduces microcomputers to be used in addition to a mainframe computer. Do on micros what they do best and on the mainframe what it does best.

A UNIVERSITY CAMPUS COMPUTER LITERACY PROGRAMME

Dr. Adman

This is a long established programme in computer literacy for the undergraudates at Hull University, two-thirds of whom are Humanities/Arts based.

The courses are almost exclusively of practical nature, following a compact but nevertheless immensely enjoyable syllabus covering: Basic Introduction, Elementary Programming, Use of Files, followed by various applications, including, Word Processing, Mailmerge, Ideas Processing, Spreadsheet, Mailbox, Graphics, Icons, Use of Sound and Colour, and whole range of Software Tools.

Departments participating in this programme include, amongst others, European Studies, Linguistics, Theology, Drama, Psychology, Geography, Economics, French, English and History.

Some administrative and operational problems arising from such a large programme are also discussed.

Dr. Bosler

SUMMARY WAS NOT RECEIVED IN TIME FOR PUBLICATION

Dr. Halaris

SUMMARY WAS NOT RECEIVED IN TIME FOR PUBLICATION

COMPUTERS IN EDUCATION, K. Duncan and D. Harris (eds.)
Elsevier Science Publishers B.V. (North-Holland)
© IFIP, 1985

FROM COMPUTER LITERACY TO INFORMATION LITERACY

Bram van Weering, Tineke Zeelenberg and Ard Hartsuijker

National Institute for Curriculum Development (SLO),
Enschede, The Netherlands

Some results of the national project for the development of a curriculum on computer
and information literacy for students and teachers of Junior High Schools in The
Netherlands will be presented.

In 1983 the Dutch Department of Education initiated an experiment on defining the content of
computer and information literacy in Junior High
Schools and the content of the teacher training
as regards this subject.
The aim was to introduce computer and information literacy during the next few years as a
compulsory subject of the curriculum of all
Junior High Schools in The Netherlands and forming a part of a National Information Technology
Stimulation Plan.
The coördination of this project was given to
the Dutch Institute for Curriculum Development
(SLO). About a hundred schools were equipped
with microcomputers and the teacher training
institutes received some extra money in order to
start inservice training.

In the first part of the session the major
choices and decisions made in this experiment,
their reasons and consequences will be discussed and the proposed curriculum, both for the
Junior High Schools and the teacher training,
will be presented.

In the second part of the session the change in
thinking as regards the content of computer and
information literacy during the first two years
of the experiment (August 1983 - July 1985)
will be discussed. All this is based on the
experiences in the 102 schools.

Finally some conclusions will be drawn concerning the experiment as a whole and some proposals, plans and recommendations for the future
will be presented, based on the first two years
of the curriculum development in this experiment.

Non-traditional Education

COMPUTERS IN EDUCATION, K. Duncan and D. Harris (eds.)
Elsevier Science Publishers B.V. (North-Holland)
© IFIP, 1985

TEACHING THE BLIND TO READ TACTILE GRAPHICS BY COMPUTER

Waltraud Schweikhardt

Institut für Informatik Universität Stuttgart
Azenbergstr. 12, D-7000 Stuttgart 1
Federal Republic of Germany

Not long ago it became possible also for blind people to use public communications networks, i.e. videotex-systems. In addition to text, graphics can be shown in a tactile form. This results in a new motivation for the blind to get familiar with tactile graphics.
In this paper we introduce a program to teach the blind to understand tactile graphics, and we present the devices we use at Stuttgart. Finally we report about our experience and initial results in testing this learning environment with blind children and students.

1. INTRODUCTION

Nowadays communications networks such as for example videotex-systems represent messages in colour and with graphics. These networks can also be used by blind subscribers (1). This is possible since we have implemented programs to convert the contents of the screen into a representation which can be displayed tactually on suitable devices connected to the user-terminal.

Though for blind people videotex-systems can open a door to much more knowledge about the world we live in, there still remain problems. Much of the information included in a page on the screen is represented in colour graphics. These graphics cannot just form letters and numbers, but also diagrams, maps, or pictures. Many blind people, however, have never been taught to read tactile graphics. One reason for this is that the production of reliefs is very expensive. Another one is the troublesome teaching of reading figures by touch, which even differs from person to person.

This situation has often resulted in blind students with a poor knowledge of geometry and science. Moreover many of them are not familiar with figures and pictures of our everyday-life. This lack, however, is often only the result of not having adequate teaching facilities.

In this paper we introduce a program which enables blind students to learn by computer how to read tactile graphics. We explain the devices which are used in this learning environment and report on results in testing the program with blind subjects.

2. DEVICES TO REPRESENT TACTILE GRAPHICS

For about 5 years electronic braille-output-devices for computers are available (2). Most of these devices work with raisable metal pins to represent 6- or 8-dot-braille characters (see figure 1) (2).

Figure 1: MBT Braille Output Device

In addition to these paperless braille-devices, there exist electronic braille-printers which emboss the output of a computer in 6-dot-braille or in 8-dot-braille. The braille-printer shown in figure 2 can also be programmed to skip the inter-line gap.

This makes it possible to emboss graphics as shown in figure 3.

In cooperation with the German companies Metec in Stuttgart and Papenmeier in Schwerte, we have developed the first paperless electronic graphics display for the blind (see figure 4). On this device tactile graphics can be represented without inter-character gaps. Moreover each pin can be addressed and raised individually, facilitating the output of graphics and the alteration of a displayed figure. The latter is necessary to enable a blind reader to elaborate on the information included in a graphic in a dialogue with the computer. The reader might ask to show only the outline of a figure, or to show only those parts of a graphic which are displayed in the colours specified by him. This means he can look at different layers of a picture, where the attributes to describe the layer are specified by the reader (1).

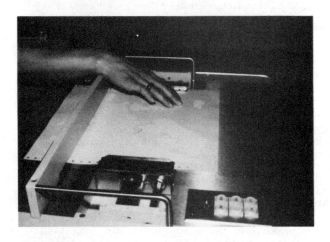

Figure 2: Electronic Braille-Printer

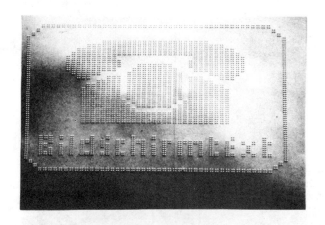

Figure 3: Embossed Copy of a Videotex-
          graphic

All the above mentioned devices receive a sequence of alphanumeric characters and display or emboss the corresponding braille-characters. Thus all embossed dots within a graphic must be grouped to braille-characters and the sequence of the corresponding alphanumeric characters is sent to the braille-printer.

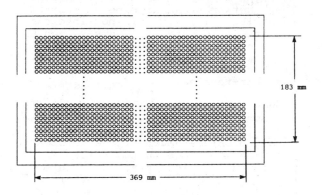

Figure 4: Graphics Display for the Blind

The display consists of a 59x119 pin-matrix. This number of pins represents the text of one half of a videotex-page, i.e., 12 lines with 40 characters each. For each character we provide 8 pins arranged as a 4x2-matrix. The distance between two characters is one pin-column of the height of the braille-character (3 or 4 pins, respectively).

3. COMPUTER-ASSISTED TEACHING TO READ
   TACTILE GEOMETRIC GRAPHICS

In order to enable the blind to understand a tactile graphic, it is first necessary to explain the connection between objects in the real world and a special series or a field of tactile dots.

Children who are blind from birth must basically learn methods to represent objects two-dimensionally. If they have grown blind later on in their life they must re-learn and re-discover by touch what they knew only from reading with the eyes until then.

One approach to teach reading graphics is to teach geometric objects such as the point, line, angle between lines, circle, etc. These are elements which occur in more complex pictures as well. Their understanding is often based on detecting such basic elements in a figure. In parallel it is necessary to teach the blind to recognize objects from their everyday life, represented as reliefs.

3.1 Components of the Program RAPRO to Teach Blind Students in a Computer Based Learning and Working Environment

In 1980 we implemented the learner-controlled frame-program RAPRO (Rahmen-programm) to teach blind students in a computer based learning and working

environment (4). The program is written in APL. It has proved to be good for teaching different subjects of algebra at highschool-level. Now, the availability of the graphics-display for the blind (see Section 2) has allowed us to use RAPRO teaching the blind to read tactile graphics in geometry.

For each lesson $i(i\epsilon|N)$, the author of a teaching-program based on RAPRO has to fill the four functions

- ΔiTEXT
  ΔiFRAGE (question)
  ΔiBSP   (Beispiel = example)
  ΔiUEBUNG (exercise)

with text, questions, exercises, help, and examples. Moreover, in a dictionary the author puts together the important terms of the lessons and their explanation. A student can ask for them while working with the program.

The interaction of the components of RAPRO are shown in Figure 5.

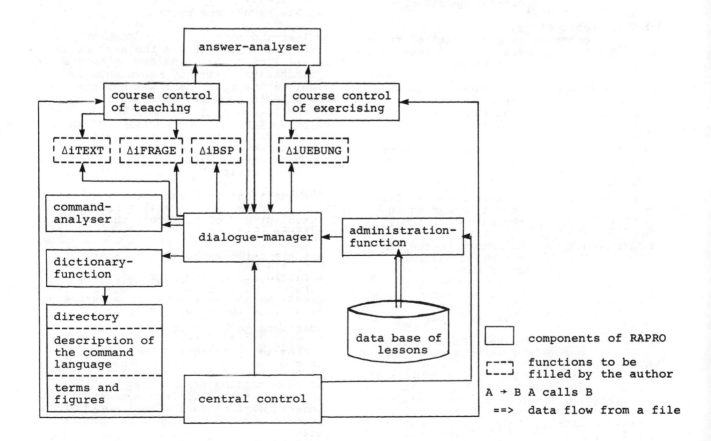

Figure 5: Components of the Strategy RAPRO to Teach Blind Students

It should be stressed that all output
to the addressee can be generated at run-
time dependent on the input of the student. To make this possible, the author
provides the appropriate variables and
the necessary algorithms as generating
or analysing functions. Their names must
be inserted within the text of the Δ...-
functions.
Whenever the learner is asked for input,
he can affect the control of the course.
The commands which are available for the
student are

$ANTWORT (answer)   to get the result of
                      the last exercise or
                      the answer to the
                      last question,

$BSP (example)   to get an example
                      for the current sub-
                      ject,

$ENDE (end)   to terminate the work
                      on the current lesson
                      or the teaching pro-
                      gram, respectively,

$FRAGE (question)   to re-display the
                      current question,

$INHALT (table of
        contents)   to get a list of the
                      subjects the lessons
                      deal with,

$SPRINGE (jump)   to change to another
                      lesson or exercise
                      from which one returns
                      with $ZURÜCK (back),

$TIP (hint)   to get help to solve
                      the current problem,

$WDH (repeat)   to return to the last
                      lesson according to
                      the author control,

$ZURÜCK (back)   to return to the les-
                      son which was left
                      by $SPRINGE

$?   to get a listing of
                      the commands and
                      their effects,

$|<term>   to get the definition
                      of <term.>

3.2 The teaching-program GEOMGRAFIK

The program GEOMGRAFIK (geometrische
Grafiken) consists of 11 lessons which
deal with the following subjects:

- straight line, position and length of
  a straight line,

- line, points of intersection, parallel
  lines,

- angle

- quadrangle, square, rectangle,

- special quadrangles,

- triangle,

- circle, ellipse,

- cube, ashlar looking at them from the
  front,

- prisms and ashlar looking at them from
  different visual angles,

- cylinder

- sphere, cone, and pyramid.

The learning objectives of GEOMGRAFIK are
on the one hand to train the student in
the skill of recognizing new objects and
of identifiying already known ones by
touch. On the other hand the student
should learn to distinguish efficiently
different geometric objects. The student
learns to find out the position of an object as well as the relative positions
of two objects (e.g. do two circles which
have been displayed intersect, is one of
them in or beside the other one?).

Since questions and exercises are generated dynamically, there is a nearly unlimited variety of different shapes and
positions.

There are three types of questions:

- questions to be answered by yes or no,
- questions to be answered by a number
  (written with letters or digits),
- questions to be answered by terms.

Mistakes in spelling are recognized and
do not cause a rejection of the answer.

3.3 The Hardware Configuration

GEOMGRAFIK is implemented on an IBM-PC. The students use the normal keyboard, since most of them are familiar with typing and prefer it to a braille-keyboard. However, a braille-keyboard could be connected to the micro-computer as well.

The output is displayed on an MBT 80 if it is text, and on the pin-matrix-device if it is graphic. A protocol of a session can be produced on the braille-printer shown previously in figure 2. The dialogue and all figures can also be printed for the sighted. The configuration which is in use in our Institute is shown in figure 6.

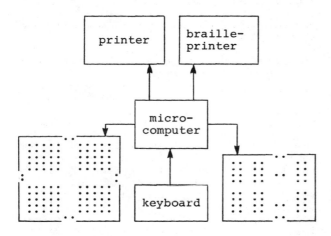

Figure 6: Hardware Configuration to Teach Reading Tactile Graphics

4. EXPERIENCE IN TESTING GEOMGRAFIK

Up to this time, we have tested GEOMGRAFIK with three 9 year-old children who attend a school for the blind and a 17 year-old girl who is student at a "Gymnasium" (college) for the sighted. All these subjects have been blind from birth.

For the children the first important step was to identify a series of embossed dots as a line. The girl, however, was already familiar with this representation. It was easy for all of them to recognize whether a line was horizontal or vertical, rising or falling. The hint from the program not to count the dots in order to find the longer one of two straight lines proved to be necessary.

Figure 7 shows an example for this difficulty. Of course, the problem is more apparent if one reads the dots with one's fingers.

Figure 7: Straight Lines of Different Length

All subjects liked to detect the polygons, circles, and ellipses, though different perceptive faculties could be observed. In this first session, only one of the children was eager to go on to the three-dimensional objects which, however, could not be understood at first glance. Further training is necessary.

The 17 year-old girl already knew polygons, circles and ellipses but up to that time she had less experience in reading them by touch. She had no idea of how to represent cubes and other three-dimensional objects two-dimensionally. She could, however, identify the different shapes after they had been explained to her.

All of our subjects worked with the program for about 3 hours. All of them wanted to continue.

These first results show that teaching facilities, such as the one presented here, are urgently needed to give blind students the means and the motivation to concern themselves more with geometry than they have up to now. Since the newly introduced devices are still very expensive, session protocols can be produced with the braille-printer and thus made available to more blind people already now.

5. CONCLUDING REMARKS

Our first results in testing GEOMGRAFIK with blind subjects have shown the necessity of such new facilities to teach the blind to read graphics. The subsequent continuation of GEOMGRAFIK to a program which teaches the recognition of pictures seems to be worth-while.

Beside gaining the possibility and the ability to understand more about the world we live in, examining tactile graphics turns out to be an enjoyable task for the blind reader.

6. ACKNOWLEDGEMENT

I wish to thank Thomas Fehrle who implemented the first version of GEOMGRAFIK as the project for his "Studienarbeit". Special thanks are also due to Dipl. Inform. Klaus Klöpfer for his helpful assistance and to all the boys and girls who patiently learned with our program. The discussions with the blind programmer, Alfred Werner, of our research group were and continue to be invaluable to our work.

REFERENCES

(1) Schweikhardt, W. and Klöpfer, K., Computer Aided Conversion of Videotex-Graphics into a Tactile Representation, Proceedings of the Internatinal Conference on Reliefs for the Blind, Berlin, GDR, 1984.

(2) Schweikhardt, W., The Impact of Micro-Computers on the Education of Blind Students, in Lewis, R. and Tagg, D. (eds.), Computers in Education (North Holland, Amsterdam 1981) 461-467.

(3) Schweikhardt, W., 8-Dot-Braille for Representing Information from Computers, in Proceedings of The IEEE Computer Society Workshop on Computers in the Education and Employment of the Handicapped (IEEE Computer Society Press, 1984) 85-88.

(4) Kohns, M., Implementierung einer Lehr- und Übungsstrategie für blinde Schüler und deren exemplarischer Einsatz im Bereich der Bruchrechnung, Diplomarbeit, Institut für Informatik, Universität Stuttgart (1980).

COMPUTERS IN EDUCATION, K. Duncan and D. Harris (eds.)
Elsevier Science Publishers B.V. (North-Holland)
© IFIP, 1985

AN ELECTRONIC APPOINTMENT BOOK FOR THE BLIND

Klaus Klöpfer
University of Stuttgart
Department of Computer Science
Azenbergstr. 12
7000 Stuttgart 1
West Germany

There is a shortage of employment for blind people. In the office, the growing automation and the evolution towards a paperless office help to establish a working environment suited to the needs of blind persons. By the example of an electronic appointment book, this paper describes how such a working environment can be established. Special output devices for the script of the blind are presented, and dialogue methods for interactive computer programs which have been adapted to the needs of blind people, are explained.

1. INTRODUCTION

There always has been a shortage of employment for the visually disabled with higher qualifications. Further, for several years there has been a reduction in professions traditionally practiced by visually disabled persons. For example, typists writing texts previously spoken on tape are replaced because of the use of text processing systems in the office, and telephone operators are replaced by electronic direct dialing devices.

The main difficulty in employing the blind in factories has been their reduced mobility. In the office, the main problem has been that they could not read the information printed or written by hand or typewriter. Office automation and the evolution towards a paperless office may help to overcome this problem. By example of an electronic appointment book, this paper describes how the blind could work in a modern office. Special output devices and interactive computer programs with dialogue methods tailored to their needs are used.

The electronic appointment book is part of the integrated office work-station for the blind as it exists in Stuttgart. Further components are an electronic mail system and a data base system, both of which are based on the German videotex system, a calculator, a text-editor and a graphics-editor. The components of this work-station are shown in figure 1. The user communicates with these interactive programs via a window system /1/. The programs of the work-station are implemented on a personal computer. The work station could be used by sighted persons too, but in this paper only those aspects relevant to blind users are considered.

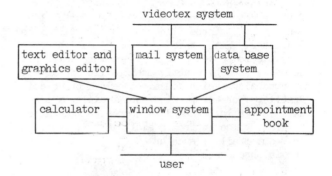

Figure 1: Components of the Stuttgart integrated office work-station for the blind

2. INTERFACE FOR BLIND USERS

The visually disabled cannot read directly the output of a computer program on a TV-screen. Distinctive output devices and further special dialog methods are required.

2.1 Display devices

In Stuttgart we are using an electronic pin board as the output device. We developed it in our research project "Videotex as Computer Aided Means of Communication for the Blind" in cooperation with a company situated in Stuttgart /2/. The project is sponsored by the "Deutsche Forschungsgemeinschaft". On the pin board there are metal pins, which can be raised and lowered electronically. When raised, they protrude out of the surface of the board and become touchable. Thus a tactile script can be displayed on the pin board.

The tactile script of the blind is called Braille, being named after its inventor Louis Braille. It is based on 6 dots arranged in two columns and three lines. Usually these dots are embossed into thin cardboard and are read with the finger-tips. Various combinations of dots represent letters and digits. The following is an example of Braille.

```
   b      r      a      i      l      l      e

  ●●     ●○     ●○     ○●     ●○     ●○     ●○
  ○○     ●●     ○○     ●○     ●○     ●○     ○●
  ○○     ●○     ○○     ○○     ●○     ●○     ○○
```

For work with computers, the 6-dot-Braille has been enlarged to an 8-dot-Braille /3/. The two further dots are concatenated as a fourth line beneath the three lines of a 6-dot-Braille character. With this enlargement it becomes possible to represent all characters which are normally used by exactly one Braille character, a condition which does not hold for 6-dot-Braille. For example in 6-dot-Braille, a capital letter is preceded by a special character to distinguish it from a small letter, whereas in 8-dot-Braille, such an extra special character is unnecessary.

On our pin board, 12 lines can be displayed, each line being 40 8-dot-braille characters long. This corresponds to the contents of half a videotex TV-screen. There are other devices capable of representing Braille with movable pins, but they are only able to display up to 80 characters at a time /4/.

In addition we are using a voice synthesizer, but most blind people capable of reading Braille prefer Braille. Synthetic speech may disturb other people and not all information may be destined to be heard by the public. Particularly when working with an appointment book privacy should be protected. Using earphones is rejected because they prevent the blind from hearing the sounds of their surroundings: hearing these sounds is very important since it is their main sense for getting information about their environment. But for those blind persons not able to read Braille, synthetic speech is the only possible way of getting access to digitized information. (In West-Germany there are about 70,000 blind people of which only 27% are able to read Braille. Of those blind people younger than 45 years of age, 71% can read Braille /5/.)

2.2 Dialogue methods

The blind are forced to read text sequentially. They are not able to get a survey at a "glance" or to recognize quickly changes. Reading by finger takes longer than reading by eye. Therefore explanations, hints and error messages ought to be brief and precise and should be displayed in an easy to find region. Blank lines and leading blanks ought to be avoided because they make it more difficult to pick up information. To make very sure that a line is empty, the blind person has to touch the whole line. In this way after reading several continuous blanks following a piece of text he may believe that the remaining line is empty although there can still be more text.

When reading by touch it is difficult to recognize precisely the relationship between parts. For example it is difficult to trace a column of a table with many narrow columns. Hence too many narrow columns should be avoided, or there should at least be a clear border betweeen the columns.

There exists no correspondence in Braille to visual effects such as half-brightness or reverse video. The reverse of a combination of dots may be represented on a Braille display but this is impractical since it would be very hard to read. Underlining can be displayed on the pin board too, but this does not attract the attention as much as for the sighted. Only blinking represented by the pins moving up and down continuously is a means of highlighting something important.

3. THE ELECTRONIC APPOINTMENT BOOK

For the blind it is hard to keep an appointment book because there are no special appointment books offered to them. Time and date of meetings, conferences, lectures, invitations or other events must be embossed on Braille-paper sheets. But with this, for example it is hard to insert a new entry in chronological order. Therefore an interactive appointment-book program is especially valuable for the blind.

The user of our electronic appointment-book system is able to inform himself of all general calendar subjects. The appointment book "knows" about week-days, about Easter, Christmas and other holidays, about phases of the moon, etc. He may also ask for a survey of a particular month or week. As an example, figure 2 shows the pin board with raised and lowered pins after asking for a survey of the month of July.

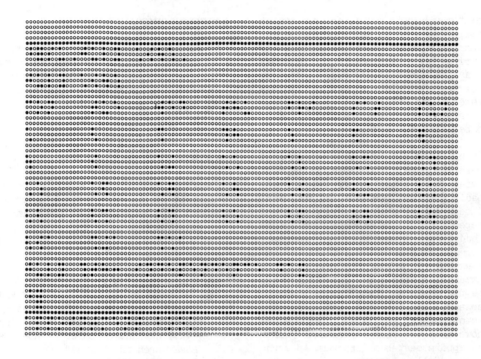

Figure 2: Pin board after asking for a survey of the month of July

The characters are 8–dot Braille characters but only small letters are used because the less dots one has to read the faster and securer one can read. Figure 3 shows the contents of the pin board of figure 2.

```
>%su 'july 1985'
july 1985
mon    tue   wed   thu    fri    sat   sun
1      2     3     4h     5      6     7
8      9     10    11     12     13    14
15     16    17    18     19     20    21
22     23    24    25     26     27    28
29a    30a   31a
july 4th: independence day
>█

appointment book
```

Figure 3: Contents of the pin board of figure 2

The letters indicate holidays (h) or appointments (a). The holidays are explained beneath the survey. Dates are explained in detail on demand. In the survey, names of weekdays are abbreviated and listed horizontally. Compared to a vertical notation, this has the advantage that the days are numbered line by line and if the user is searching a special day, say the 12th, he can touch the lines from left to right as he usually reads text until he reaches the day for which he is searching. For a blind person this is easier to do than to search along columns where it is difficult to find the next column's top after reaching a column's bottom. In the survey, no blank lines are used the way they would have been used in a survey for the sighted in order to group the output and to make it more readable. Between every pair of adjacent columns there are at least two blanks. With such spacing, columns can reliably be distinguished from one another, and there are not too many unnecessary character positions to read.

The appointment book is able to draw the attention of the user to a future appointment. While entering an appointment, the user is asked whether he wants to be reminded of this appointment. If so, he may enter a date from when on he would like to be reminded of this appointment and if he wants to be reminded every day after this date or only once. The user is reminded of such future appointments when he enters the appointment book for the first time on that day. Later on he will only be informed of these appointments on demand. This prevents him from reading the same messages several times a day.

An appointment may be entered as an appointment at a specific time or as an appointment at several recurring times such as for example by the week, during the next three months or every year (such as for a birthday). Every entry may be changed or deleted. If a recurring appointment is deleted, the appointment book will ask if all recurring instances of this appointment should also be deleted.

The user communicates with the appointment book via a command language. The commands are mnemonic abbreviations for actions with a distinguishing leading symbol. For example, %en, %su, %ch and %de mean enter, show survey, change and delete, respectively. Some commands are specified with additional parameters, for example %su 'july', and some commands initiate a dialogue, for example %en. With %he, explanations to all commands possible at this time are listed. The pin board's first line is reserved for error messages and the last line indicates the actual state of the work station. For example, it shows that the user is presently working with the appointment-book program. An error message is optionally accompanied with a sound to let the blind know that an error has occured.

The appointment-book program has been implemented on a personal computer in the programming language APL. The appointment book manages 20 months: 2 in the past, the current month and 17 in the future /6/. At the beginning of a new month, the very last month is deleted and a new month, the 17th in the future, is calculated and generated. This month is put at the beginning of the sequence. In this way there is no break at the end of a year. The appointment book moves with the flow of time.

4. CONCLUSION

The electronic appointment-book we have described shows that there are devices and dialogue methods by means of which the blind are able to work in modern offices, and we believe that with these aids the visually handicapped are able to do their office work as effectively as the sighted. It is to be hoped that the existing possibilities indeed will be used for the establishment of work-stations for the blind.

ACKNOWLEDGEMENT

I wish to thank Dr. Schweikhardt, Prof. Dr. Gunzenhäuser and Mr. Werner for many valuable discussions and advice and Miss Herrmann for implementing most of the electronic appointment-book program.

REFERENCES

/1/ Weber,G.
"Ein Fenstersystem für Blinde"
("A window system for the blind")
Diplomarbeit Nr. 287
Department of Computer Science, University of Stuttgart 1984

/2/ Schweikhardt,W., Klöpfer,K.
"Computer Aided Conversion of Videotex-Graphics into a Tactile Representation"
to be published in the proceedings of the "Internationale Konferenz über Reliefdarstellungen für Blinde"
Ost-Berlin 1984

/3/ Schweikhardt,W.
"8-Dot-Braille for Representing Information from Computers"
Proceedings of The IEEE Computer Society Workshop on Computers in the Education and Employment of the Handicapped
Minneapolis 1983 pp. 85-88

/4/ Description of the Braille display MBT80
Gemeinnützige Gesellschaft für Elektronik und Hilfsmittel mbH der deutschen Blindenstudienanstalt e.V.
Brunnenstr. 10
7240 Horb/Neckar 1983

/5/ Herzog,H.W., Kügle,M.
"Untersuchung zu technischen Hilfsmitteln für Blinde" ("Investigation of technical aids for the blind")
Infratest Gesundheitsforschung
München 1982

/6/ Herrmann,B.
"Ein Terminverwaltungssystem für Blinde"
("An appointment management system for the blind")
Studienarbeit
Department of Computer Science, University of Stuttgart 1984

COMPUTERS IN EDUCATION, K. Duncan and D. Harris (eds.)
Elsevier Science Publishers B.V. (North-Holland)
© IFIP, 1985

A DISTANCE LEARNING PACK FOR TRAINING TEACHERS TO ASSESS SOFTWARE

Jenny Preece and Ann Jones

Institute of Educational Technology
The Open University
Walton Hall
Milton Keynes
England

1. INTRODUCTION

One of the pressing problems for teachers wanting to get to grips with microcomputers is the lack of good educational software. Most teachers have now reached the 'awareness' stage of using computers: that is, they can run programs with their pupils. Many teachers, however, are surprisingly uncritical about the software they use. There are several reasons for this; firstly many teachers are still unaware of the potential of teaching with computers; secondly most teachers do not have experience in designing educational software; thirdly, they are not well versed in critically analysing the design of software and finally they do not have much programming experience. We argue that, whilst it is not necessary for teachers to learn to program, it is essential for them to know sufficient about program design and the capabilities of microcomputers to develop a framework within which to judge educational software.

In this paper we describe an Open University course (Open University Press, 1984) which attempts to tackle the problem of training teachers to be critical software consumers. First, the course provides a grounding in fundamental programming concepts; it then examines the process of designing software, and considers what kind of programs are possible (e.g. simulation, tutorial, etc) - and the role of these programs in different learning environments. The different styles of software are illustrated by including sample programs which the teacher can run, and which are written so that they can be examined easily. We shall also report the findings of a formative evaluation study in which 18 teachers worked through a second draft of the course.

2. THE OPEN UNIVERSITY SYSTEM

The Open University (O.U.) was set up in 1970 to provide both undergraduate courses and courses outside of the degree programme which include inservice education courses for teachers, (INSET courses). In 1983 around 100,000 students enrolled on Open University courses and 23% of these students were teachers. Thus, the O.U.'s role in the professional development of teachers is already well established. O.U. courses are open to everyone regardless of qualifications and are designed to be studied part-time whilst the student continues with his or her full-time employment. Correspondence texts provide the chief medium of study for Open University students but most courses have other components such as television, radio, audio-cassettes, home kits, computer assisted learning, residential one week or weekend courses, integrated into their structure.

3. THE COURSE

Educational Software (P541) is produced by the Open University's Micros in Schools Project and funded by the Microelectronics Education Program (MEP). The course is a 40-50 hour inservice teacher training pack for primary and secondary teachers with some experience of microcomputers. The main aim of the course is to give teachers sufficient expertise to evaluate the design of existing software, - and this involves an understanding of some fundamental programming concepts which are introduced at the beginning of the course. Our reasons for including this section are best summarised by an extract from the course itself:

"Why do we think you should know something about programming?.....

Here are some practical reasons why knowing a little about programming might help you:

It will help you to give advice on the design of educational software, or even work as a member of a local software design group.

Many good ideas for educational software come from teachers; knowing something about programming might prevent your own ideas from being unrealistic or uninspired.....

You might be able to modify existing software. Sometimes a program does not quite do what you would like. You might want to adapt it, or improve it, or even remove a bug. If the change is simple, you may be able to do it yourself.

But the real reason why these early sections concentrate on the nature of programming is that it is for teachers the main new skill involved in the production of educational software. To understand how computers could be used."

[Educational Software. Study Book. Open University Press, 1984].

The Educational Software pack consists of a study guide (the main study text), an activities book, a reader, audio and video cassette, and of course, software. Programming concepts are introduced through activities where students run, examine and modify small programs written in LOGO. Full listings of the programs are provided and the student examines the design and structure of the programs by working through a series of structured exercises where she changes the program and observes the effects.

In the next part of the course teachers run a number of "sampler" programs which illustrate different styles of educational software. These include simple drill and practice, modelling, information retrieval and an adventure game. (Tutorial CAL and intelligent CAL are discussed in Reader articles). The teachers examine the design of each program and consider the educational role that it plays. Finally the concepts and skills that have been learnt in these early sections are put into practice in evaluating three commercially produced software packages. Throughout the course a distinction is made between software evaluation which involves examinating software in use in the classroom and software selection (which the course deals with). The final part of the course consists of a discussion of the principles of software design used by national software development projects. The reader includes articles written by experts on tutorial computer assisted learning systems such as PLATO and TICCIT, simulations, using Logo in the classroom, and intelligent computer based teaching systems such as MYCIN and SOPHIE.

Articles about various programming languages (e.g. PROLOG, SMALLTALK, BASIC and authoring languages) introduce the debate on programming languages and are also included for those teachers who wish to extend their knowledge of programming.

4. FORMATIVE EVALUATION

As with the other Micros in Schools packs, we carried out a formative evaluation which included critical commenting from internal and external readers, and from practising teachers who worked through the pack in a draft form and commented on it. Educational Software was tested by two groups of teachers. It formed the basis of an inservice teacher training course run over two weekends and it was also used by six teachers working independently. It might seem that using distance learning materials as the basis for a face to face course is a strange thing to do! However, at this stage of development, having direct and immediate contact with teachers and being on hand to sort out any real difficulties can be very helpful. In this case we discovered that we had pitched some of the course at too high a level. Having one of the course team members present enabled us both to get detailed feedback on what the problems were, and to help the teachers over difficulties so that they could continue to the next part of the course. In

general the teachers' reactions were very positive, but they indicated some areas which needed to be changed. In the next section we focus on some of the problems we discovered and on how we addressed them.

4.1 Programming concepts

This part of the course is divided into several sections. The first activity is a short case study in which students run, examine and modify a Logo program called MENDEL which simulates the inheritance of the height characteristics in peas. The program is modular in structure and is designed so that it is relatively easy for students to take it apart and 'to see what's going on'.

The second section describes the process of program design, and is followed by another hands-on activity, which introduces and illustrates a number of programming concepts, again with reference to the MENDEL program. In particular, it introduces students to the following concepts: procedure, parameter, function, conditional instruction, loop, variable and assignment.

Finally, the teacher is led through a worked example, to develop an algorithm and an outline of a small program which she then, in the final hands-on activity, develops into a working LOGO program.

Although the teachers' reactions were positive, they did find this section difficult; several of them described it as the most difficult, most frustrating, most challenging but also the most rewarding, stimulating, – and sometimes enjoyable part of the pack. The message was that we had included too much, it was too hard and was developed too fast. We needed to reduce the difficulty whilst maintaining the challenge.

There were 5 types of problems which the teachers found when they were working through these activities. The first type of problem was logistical and the others were conceptual.

(i) Logistical problems

Even though all the teachers had 'awareness level' experience, some teachers still had problems loading and running programs. For example, disks were inserted the wrong way around into the disk drives and the load command was specified incorrectly. These sorts of problems should not be surprising: it's all too easy to forget the details of connecting up and loading, and furthermore we cannot expect teachers to have had experience on a specific machine. Some of the teachers in our sample had used different micros previously whilst others had not used disc drives.

The other problems were conceptual in nature, and although they're inter-related, we'll discuss them under the following headings: error messages, previous experience, understanding programming concepts and "conceptual leaps".

(ii) Error messages

There were a few error messages which our teachers did not understand. Ideally, error messages should be couched at the right level; i.e. they should 'match' the understanding of the student (see du Boulay, O'Shea and Monk, 1981, for a detailed discussion of levels of presentation). However there are two problems. Firstly, if a student gets an error message very early on in the activity she won't have the conceptual framework to understand it. Suppose she is exploring turtle commands and gets 'FORWARD DIDN'T OUTPUT TO RIGHT". Not surprisingly, this wouldn't make sense as she would need to know about procedures that return results, - which she wouldn't know about at this stage. This leads to the second problem, the extent to which we could alter error messages to make them as helpful as possible in locating and correcting the error. We are able to do this with our own programs, and LOGO generally has very helpful messages, but the BASIC messages aren't at all diagnostic, and include helpful messages like: "?SYNTAX ERROR"!

(iii) Previous experience

Some teachers found LOGO initially confusing because they knew some BASIC and were thinking in BASIC and got confused. The worst cases consist of trying to translate from BASIC to LOGO.

(iv) Understanding programming concepts

Programming is hard, (Jones, 1981) and some programming concepts are conceptually quite difficult to get a grasp of, especially in a limited amount of time. Our teachers had difficulty understanding parameters, variables, functions and assignment.

(v)   Conceptual leaps

We discovered that some of our programming activities required the teachers to make conceptual leaps; that is, the steps were too big, and the material moved too fast.

Addressing the problems

In order to address the logistic problems we had to find a balance between too much hand-holding - suitable for awareness levels but not here, - and leaving our teacher-students without hand-rails at all! We therefore included just enough information to guide the teachers through connecting up the computer and getting programs running and provided references to help if they got stuck. We addressed the conceptual problems by making the exercises more structured and more graded, and including extra steps to reduce the conceptual leaps. We also reduced the amount that we were trying to teach. Where we were able to, we changed the error messages to make them more helpful, and where this was not possible, we helped the students to decipher them by

including them in the trouble-shooting guide. Like the activities book (see O'Shea, 1984), the trouble-shooting guide has a 3 column format: the first describes the error and how it may occur, the second has a photograph of the screen with the error and the 3rd column gives the user a possible solution.

We could not alleviate the confusion which previous BASIC experience might lead to, but we did try to encourage teachers to think of themselves as starting again from scratch, if possible. We were encouraged to find that the developmental testers came to appreciate LOGO and enjoyed their experience with it, although some of them found it initially hard.

4.2 Software Selection

Before she starts the software selection activities, the teacher examines a wide variety of educational programs which we have already described. The aim of the selection criteria activities which come next, is to help teachers to decide "what makes good software good?" In doing this she is applying the knowledge and skills that she has learnt in earlier parts of the course. Not surprisingly, the teachers experienced few problems in actually carrying out the software selection activity compared to the programming activities. They were, however, far less critical and insightful than we had hoped they would be. In the account that follows we describe each of the three packages that were examined and present data showing the rating that teachers gave the packages.

(i)   The programs

The three packages used in the activity were: FARM, (Walker and Watson, 1979), CLIMATE (Preston M. and Horton, A. 1981), and PIRATES (ITMA, 1981). The FARM package is a simulation game in which the player chooses which crops to plant on a farm in a particular region of the British Isles. The program simulates the weather conditions which are typical of the chosen region, and also calculates profits, losses and net income. Pupils play to make the most profit.

The CLIMATE package contains a drill-and-practice program which has more sophisticated graphics than the other two programs. It provides rainfall and temperature data for weather stations all over the world. The teacher selects data for a particular weather station, and the pupil interprets this data, and answers a series of questions in order to identify the climate type. When the pupil makes a mistake the program gives simple clues as help. It is not adaptive, and if the pupil answers the same question incorrectly a second time, she will get the same clue.

The third program, PIRATES, has been designed for use by a teacher with a whole class. It is a treasure hunt game in which pupils specify the coordinates of either a 2-d or 3-d grid to indicate where they think the treasure is hidden.

The three programs were selected because they are quite different in their content and in their educational aims. They also vary in terms of their user control, the use of graphics and their help facilities.

The teacher examines each of these packages in turn by working through a structured series of exercises. In the first exercise she reads a short case study written by a teacher who has used the package about how it can be used with a class and answers some questions. Next she is asked to read the documentatation and to run the program on the micro, filling in a selection criteria sheet as she works through the program. These sheets (see Figure 1) are introduced and discussed in the text. Our aim is using the sheets is to encourage teachers to focus upon different aspects of package design and to consider and evaluate them. After working through the three packages, the teacher is asked to summarise the good and bad features of each of the programs and then to compare her own ideas with the discussion in the text.

Software Selection Criteria

Complete this sheet by awarding a score for each aspect which describes how well you consider it has been achieved by the package: place a √ in the appropriate column. 5 is highest, 1 is lowest, N/A is not applicable. Use the blank space to record your additional comments.

You may wish to photocopy this sheet.

Name of package _____

Name of program _____

	5	4	3	2	1	N/A	*Additional comments*

1 Educational documentation
- 1a Statement of aims and objectives ☐ ☐ ☐ ☐ ☐ ☐
- 1b Information about the content and background ☐ ☐ ☐ ☐ ☐ ☐
- 1c Statement of intended type of use and audience ☐ ☐ ☐ ☐ ☐ ☐
- 1d Suggestions of ways to use the program ☐ ☐ ☐ ☐ ☐ ☐
- 1e Pupil activities or worksheets ☐ ☐ ☐ ☐ ☐ ☐
- 1f Instructions for running the program ☐ ☐ ☐ ☐ ☐ ☐
- 1g Presentation of a typical run ☐ ☐ ☐ ☐ ☐ ☐
- 1h *General impressions* ☐ ☐ ☐ ☐ ☐ ☐

2 Achievement of stated aims
(as far as you can tell without actually using the program with a class)
- 2a Aims/objectives ☐ ☐ ☐ ☐ ☐ ☐
- 2b *General impressions* ☐ ☐ ☐ ☐ ☐ ☐

3 Appropriateness of the micro and program
- 3a For teaching this topic ☐ ☐ ☐ ☐ ☐ ☐
- 3b For the suggested audience and type of use (e.g. group whole class, etc.) ☐ ☐ ☐ ☐ ☐ ☐
- 3c *General impressions* ☐ ☐ ☐ ☐ ☐ ☐

4 Screen presentation
- 4a Use of graphics ☐ ☐ ☐ ☐ ☐ ☐
- 4b Use of colour and animation ☐ ☐ ☐ ☐ ☐ ☐
- 4c *General impressions* ☐ ☐ ☐ ☐ ☐ ☐

Figure 1. Part of a checklist of selection criteria for educational software.

In general the teachers commented favourably about FARM's educational documentation, and whether it achieved its stated aims and the appropriateness of the medium and the program. The screen presentation was, however, heavily criticised. Their comments about the friendliness of the program were rather negative, and they thought that the program was inflexible and should provide positive feedback.

The teachers gave CLIMATE average and above average ratings on most criteria. Most of them thought that the instructions for using the program were excellent, but that more educational material and in particular pupil worksheets would be helpful. Comments on whether the program had achieved its stated aim were also mixed and ranged from "very boring, a button pressing exercise" to "very good". Few teachers had anything to say about the appropriateness of the media for teaching this topic, which is rather surprising as CLIMATE is a rather unsophisticated drill and practice program. They did however criticise the screen presentation and disliked its lack of friendliness and flexibility: "The program is very distant with no human touch, although it does offer a reasonable amount of control and feedback to the pupil". Finally some teachers commented on the underlying model, in particular the classification of the climates: "The British Isles can be listed three times, once in the Southern Hemisphere and twice in the Northern Hemisphere. Is this a mistake?"

Most teachers liked PIRATES and gave it high ratings, especially on the first three sections of criteria. They also thought that the package achieved its aims and that it was a good use of the media. The teachers were less complimentary about the screen presentation. No comments were made about the friendliness of the program but two teachers commented that it was difficult to use and to modify.

In general the teachers identified the main strengths and weaknesses of each package and were able to compare the different designs of the packages. They realised that the pedagogy of FARM was sound despite its out-dated design and poor graphics. They recognised CLIMATE as a glossy drill and practice program and were not over-impressed by the pedagogy underlying the package design. PIRATES was well received and most of the teachers thought it was a very good package. The most sought after feature was good graphics but sound pedagogy was also important. Program flexibility was not a key issue although several teachers wanted to be able to tinker with the program code to make it suit their own requirements. Experience of using the programs with a class might have produced a different response.

The most surprising feature of this study was that even after doing the earlier parts of the course, which were designed to encourage teachers to examine the structure of educational software, the teachers were not very critical. We had hoped that the teachers would make more constructive criticisms which would include suggestions of ways to improve the programs but very few suggestions were made. The results of the formative evaluation did not provide any pointers for improving this part of the course but it clearly showed that discriminating between good and bad features in software design is not a trivial task.

5. CONCLUSIONS

Many people who have developed sound software selection skills, have done so over a long period of time, and consequently greatly underestimate the difficulty of helping others to develop similar skills. Having analysed how the teachers performed on our activities we argue that it is essential to provide them with a sound basis from which to make judgements. Merely showing teachers several software packages and then leaving them to work through others for a few hours, as is practised in many inservice training courses, is not sufficient. Providing checklists on their own is also inadequate as it takes time and experience to use these lists well. The selection criteria sheets were valuable in focussing their attention upon specific aspects. We are sure, however, that the success of this kind of activity depends upon the teacher having a sound framework of the main issues involved in programming and program design.

REFERENCES

du Boulay, B. O'Shea, T. and Monk, J. (1981). The black box inside the glass box : presenting computing concepts to novices. Int. J. Man-Machine Studies, 14 pp 237-249.

ITMA, (1981) PIRATES, Longman Group Limited.

Jones, A. (1981) How do novices learn programming. CAL Research Group technical report No. 25, Open University.

Open University Press, (1984), Micros in Schools Educational Software (P541).

O'Shea, T. (1984) The Open University Micros in Schools Project, in Informatics and Teacher Training, proceedings of the IFIP working conference, ed. F. Lovis, to be published by North-Holland Press.

Preston, M. and Horton, A. (1981). CLIMATE, Heinemann, Computer in Education Limited.

Walker, D. and Watson, D. (1979). FARM GAME in Computers in the Geography Curriculum, edited by Watson, D. Schools Council Publications.

ACKNOWLEDGEMENTS

We would like to thank all our colleagues in the
Micros in Schools Project.

The Micros in Schools Educational Software
Course (P541) was produced by the Open University
P541 Course Team, chaired by John Self and
Jenny Preece. The Micros in Schools Project is
funded by MEP, and directed by Tim O'Shea.

COMPUTERS IN EDUCATION, K. Duncan and D. Harris (eds.)
Elsevier Science Publishers B.V. (North-Holland)
© IFIP, 1985

735

COMPUTER ASSISTED TELEVISION - A JOINT DEVELOPMENT

Sophie McCormick

Assistant Director (Sciences), Computers in the Curriculum Project
Centre for Science and Mathematics Education
Chelsea College, University of London.

The Chelsea College, Centre for Science and Mathematics Education, Computers in the
Curriculum (CIC) Project, one of the largest national government funded software
development groups in the United Kingdom, and the Schools Television section of the
British Broadcasting Corporation (BBC) are working together on a new area of software
development. Funded by BBC Publications the CIC Project is designing and developing a
range of computer assisted learning (CAL) packages in close collaboration with the
BBC, to accompany the BBC's educational schools science television series, Science
Topics. The complementary resource material will bring together the use of television
and CAL in the classroom and will provide the opportunity to explore the potential of
the interaction and combined use of the two media. This paper describes the rationale
behind the work, the development methods employed and the implications for future
developments.

1 INTRODUCTION

Educational television has become well
established in the United Kingdom over the last
twenty five years and its effectiveness and
influence on learning has been studied in a
variety of contexts, from the Children's
Television Workshop and the 'Sesame Street'
series (Reeves, 1970) to the work of the Open
University and the distance learning studies
(Gallagher, 1977). As a classroom teaching tool
it has powerful features providing high quality,
memorable images, attracting attention and
increasing motivation. It is however a passive
learning medium, a linear sequence of film
material demanding little to no active student
involvement. The presentation of ideas and
information can be exciting but as with other
forms of mass communication the type of response
elicited is often unpredictable, depending on
the viewers past experience and individual
interpretation. The increasing use of video
recordings of broadcasts is now changing the
range of classroom uses of educational
television. A programme need no longer only be
viewed as a whole but can be interrupted, paused
or replayed as appropriate. In this way film
sequences can provide excellent teaching
material giving the teacher the freedom to
highlight issues, relate to the familiar and
direct towards specific goals.

Computer assisted learning material on the other
hand is usually interactive and demands a far
greater level of active student participation.
Although some CAL is tutorial in style and
linear in structure it need not be so; it can be
flexible and provide sufficient control so that
learning routes related to the requirements and
needs of the user can be identified and selected.
However for the student the presentation of most
computer software is unexciting and often quite
difficult to interpret. Compared to the quality
of television, the resolution of most micro-

computers used in the classroom is relatively
low and the graphics and animation consequently
comparatively poor.

The advantages of combining these two well
established media to use high quality film with
computer flexibility has initiated great interest
in the development and potential of interactive
video material. The cost of production of
interactive video material however is high and
there is little to no appropriate hardware in
schools in the United Kingdom (Duke, 1983).

> "In marrying the two media, we make the
> assumption that they are compatible and
> complementary and together they will form
> something like a complete individual
> learning system. This is the ideal: what
> is the reality?" (Laurillard, 1982)

The objective of the BBC/CIC work was to develop
complementary material which, using common
themes and educational aims, made appropriate use
of the advantages of both television and computer
material. The results of this work will be a
set of resource materials that can be used and
tested with the hardware already available in
schools but which will allow a more detailed
study of the potential educational links between
film and computer software, the ways that both
can be used and integrated together and the role
of the learner in using the two media.

2 THE SCIENCE TOPICS SERIES

The work has been centred around a BBC schools
television series, Science Topics, which was
undergoing a major rewrite and updating. The
themes and topic areas were already defined but
the approach and coverage was to be decided. The
series aims to bring the modern world of science
and technology into the classroom by concentrating on the work of real scientists and the every
day applications of scientific knowledge. Twenty

Title	Television Coverage	CAL Approach
Ecology	The interaction of living things and the problems related to conservation versus preservation as shown through a nature reserve.	A management game based on the running of a nature reserve with various, conflicting interest groups.
Food and Population	Improving food production and some of the political and economic issues that arise.	Planning the food crops needed for an isolated population in an imaginary world.
Relationships	The interrelationship of living things illustrated by the life cycle of the malarial parasite.	Playing the role of medical officer with the task to reduce the level of malaria in a village.
Electronics in Action	Modern electronics in everyday applications.	The analysis of control systems and the function of microprocessors using and writing simplified assembly code programs.
Electromagnetic Spectrum	An introduction to the range of radiation beyond the visible.	An Adventure Game using a knowledge of the properties and applications of different radiations.
Newton and the Space Shuttle	Newton's law of motion illustrated through the Shuttle and Space Laboratory.	A simulation based on a real NASA mission to rescue a satellite.
Waves	The nature and properties of sound waves illustrated through various real life situations.	A simulation of a ripple tank demonstrating various properties of plane and circular waves.
Bonding	An introduction to the way scientists develop theories about the structure of atoms and how they join together.	An exercise in establishing patterns of how elements combine related to their electronic structure.
Macromolecules	The use of natural and synthetic materials in industry today.	A decision making game to find the most appropriate and economic polymers for the manufacture of different objects.
Periodic Table	The ideas of atomic structure and periodicity as explanations used by chemists to make sense of a vast range of reactions.	Constructing a classification using a 'filing' system to encourage an active investigation of periodicity.

new television programmes were to be produced and ten of these were selected, to be developed in parallel with computer software. The topics covered are listed in Table 1.

The aim was to experiment with the different ways that audio visuals and computer software could be used to explore a common theme, (McCormick, 1985) but at the same time to develop resource material that could be used independently. In most cases the television provides a broader coverage and the CAL, a study of particular aspects of the theme in greater depth.

To maintain the educational continuity through- out a number of basic principles were established:

1   The television and software is aimed at the same target audience, average to above, 14-16 year old students working on Certificate of Secondary Education (CSE) or Ordinary level (OL) examination courses but not related to any one syllabus.

2   The material is designed and developed for use in an educational context but is sufficiently adaptable in style to be used in a number of different ways. To maintain flexibility the software is not tutorial in style but based on menu driven, option structures. It is assumed that the

television programmes would be recorded on video cassettes and could be used select- ively. However the television and CAL are not designed in such a way that a predetermined order of use is imposed so it is not necessary to view the whole or any part of the television programme before using the computer software. Opportunities for moving freely between the two media are included wherever possible but no direct guidance is provided in either the television or software, with the aim of making the material as open ended as possible in its potential use.

For example the television programme 'Relationships' deals with parasites and their life cycles. It considers in detail the malarial parasite and its relationship to mosquitos and man. The television shows an African village where the disease is endemic. The effects it has on the inhabitants and their way of life, the control measures that can be implemented and the task of medical control officers are illustrated. The scene is set for the CAL in which the user plays the role of a medical control officer. Control measures can be selected and implemented annually within the constraints of limited manpower resources and a restricted budget from the World Health Organisation. Decisions must

be made to achieve the desired goal -
significant reduction in the level of
infection after a 6 year term of office with
the minimum expense. (Figure 1).

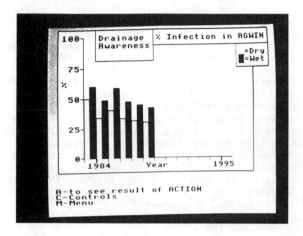

Figure 1   A gradual decrease in the malarial
infection level using various control
measures (from 'Relationships').

Such decisions can be based on information
provided in the television or on information
available within the program, in a database,
which provides details of what has been done
in local neighbouring villages and the
consequences. (Figure 2).

The television provides visual interest and
an awareness of the local conditions making
the village a reality; the CAL allows the
students to participate actively and find
out "What would happen if.......?"

3   Visual continuity is maintained whenever
possible. All the television graphics
including animation sequences are computer
generated and similar in style to that of
the appropriate software. For example after
a pop concert film sequence the television
programme, 'Waves' uses computer generated
animated sequences to illustrate the motion
of the sound waves in relation to the loud-
speaker systems used by the pop group. The
computer software uses the same type of
graphics to allow students to interact with
the animated sequences by changing various
features of the system and to explore the
behaviour of such wave motion in much greater
depth. Figures 3 and 4 show various stages
in one of the animation displays from the
diffraction section of the 'Waves' programs.
The width of the slit, the velocity of the
medium and the animation are under user
control.

Similarly in 'Newton and the Shuttle'

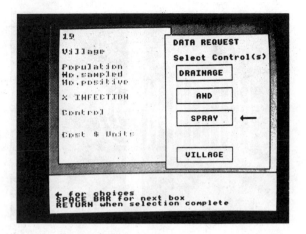

Figure 2   Setting up a data search about the
use of drainage and spray, control
measures in neighbouring villages
(from 'Relationships').

computer generated sequences are used with
real film material in the television. With
the computer the student is able to interact
directly with the graphics to build up an
understanding of the laws of motion.
(Figure 5).

4   Each theme has been treated separately and
as most appropriate for each topic.
Consequently the software is quite varied
and does not reflect any one type of
structure, mode of operation or teaching
style. The material ranges from role playing
activities such as the Medical Control
Officer as in 'Relationships', decision making
and planning for the conservation of an area
as in 'Ecology', to an adventure game through
the solar system to collect and investigate
a mysterious rock sample in 'The Electromagnetic Spectrum'. (Figure 6).

It also includes much more open ended utility
style material such as 'Electronics in Action'
where simple assembly language is used to
introduce the control of systems and the
role of a microprocessor (Figure 7) or where
the development of a filing system introduces
the principles of classification.

3   THE DEVELOPMENT PROCESS

The development of such material required
bringing together not only a range of different
'experts'; those experienced in the design and
production of the two media, subject specialists
and practising teachers but also dovetailing two
different development processes.

The design and development of the software

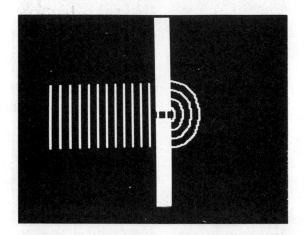

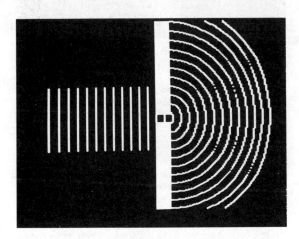

Figures 3 and 4   Various stages in an animation
                   display from 'Waves' showing
                   diffraction waves through a
                   slit.

reflected the Computers in the Curriculum
development model and the ground rules
established through the Project's experience.
(D.M. Watson, 1983). Such a model involves a
team approach with the active involvement of
subject teachers.

"The Computers in the Curriculum Project (CIC)
believes that it is the subject specialist
and the classroom teacher who can best
identify appropriate areas in the curriculum
for resource development and who are best
qualified to guide the educational course of
such material. Innovative ideas are generated
through teacher writing groups with an understanding and appreciation of the role of CAL
materials. Such groups need support and
encouragement from specialist CAL developers
and programmers who have stepped out of
classroom teaching and have the time to

assess methods and styles in greater depth".
(S. McCormick, 1984)

However, whereas the CAL developer brings
together both pedagogic and computing skills,
this 'Science Topics' work also required an
awareness and understanding of the audio visual
medium and hence close collaboration with the
television production so that limitations and
restrictions inherent in each media were matched
with the potential and scope of the other.

Television production also involves teamwork but
operates in a different way. Rather than a
network of individuals all working towards the
development of the whole, television production
tends to be based on a 'top down' approach. The
television producer is the one individual with a
vision of the whole. Specialists are consulted
and technical staff used in the development but
it is the producer who brings together the parts.
Inevitably the collaboration between the software
and television was focussed on the interaction
between the television producer and the CAL
development team.

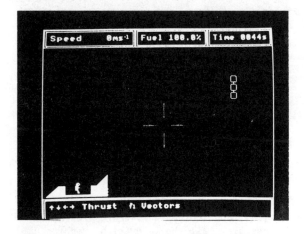

Figure 5   Recovering the satellite in 'Newton
            and the Shuttle.'

The critical stage for collaboration was at the
initial design. Outline specifications of both
the television and computer programs were
discussed and modified together. Subsequent
coding of the computer programs and filming and
editing the television programmes were kept in
parallel as far as possible although difficulties
were inevitably encountered because of the
difference in the overall development time.
Television programmes can be produced much more
quickly than computer software and the timing of
the various production schedules were controlled
by television broadcast times and software
publication dates. Such imposed schedules were
not ideal because of the very different nature
of development in the two media. Filming and

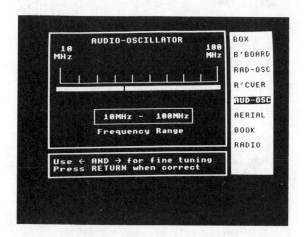

Figure 6   Tuning the radio in the adventure on
'Electromagnetic Spectrum'.

video editing are expensive processes and once
completed it is very difficult to change. Film
commentaries and computer screen displays
however could be modified at various stages in
the development process to maintain consistency
and continuity where necessary. Inevitably it
was usually the software that had to be made to
fit the television rather than the other way
round.

4   SCHOOL TRIALS AND EVALUATION

An important stage in the development process
was to test the material with students in
schools. However this material was unusual in
that there were two levels of testing needed:

a) A school trials and/or an independent
    assessment of the television and the software
    separately as stand alone resource materials,
    to check the content was appropriate and that
    they could be used successfully in the
    classroom.

b) An evaluation and assessment of the effects
    of the combined uses of the two resources
    materials.

The trials mechanism of Computers in the
Curriculum Project was employed using selected
teachers in various parts of the country who
tested the material with students in their
schools and reported back on the results.
Modifications were made to the software in the
final stage of development in the light of trials
feedback.

The BBC have no formal school trials of their
television programmes before transmission.
However, a network of evaluators and education
officers provide comments on early rough cut
versions of the material and more detailed
feedback is collected from teachers soon after
transmission to be fed into the general

development process. An interesting additional
element was introduced with this new work. The
close involvement with teachers in discussion on
the design and content of programmes provided an
extra level of interaction for the television
producer. The material was being critically
analysed and discussed by teachers at the
development stage, issues were raised and
modifications were made. The role of the
education field officers in the BBC will continue
to be valuable. These officers liaise between
schools and the production teams and monitor
teacher's opinions and the classroom success of
materials. The timing of the work over a two
year period is such that information gained
from the use of the first packages available to
schools can be fed back into the development
mechanism and modifications for improvement made
where appropriate.

An evaluation of the combined use of the
material is more difficult since the variables
and expected outcomes are so uncertain. However
an evaluation study was set up in September 1984.
The study is being undertaken by practising
teachers, one of the many local working groups
of the Secondary Science Curriculum Review, a
national project currently underway in the
United Kingdom considering the present state and
forward directions of secondary science education.
These teachers over the next year will be using
the ten linked television programmes and
accompanying software in their schools to
consider the advantages and disadvantages of the
use of such linked resource material for the
teacher and the implications it may have for the
learner.

5   COMPUTER ASSISTED TELEVISION AND THE FUTURE

This work is one of the first coordinated
attempts to develop educational resource
material that brings together television and
computer software designed to be used together

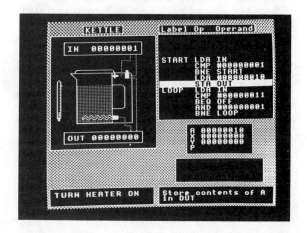

Figure 7   The operation of a thermostatically
            controlled kettle in 'Electronics'.

and to explore the ways that visual sequences, commentaries, interactive graphics and computing and information handling facilities can be drawn into a common theme.

There are two important future directions for this work:

a) Telesoftware: the transmission and down loading of computer software through the various teletext facilities.

The BBC have already introduced a telesoftware service. The natural progression would be for the appropriate computer programs to be transmitted during the week of transmission of the television programmes. This would allow continual maintenance, updating and improvement of the software although careful consideration would need to be given to the role and distribution of any accompanying written material. At present the main barrier to further developments in this field is financial and the balance between development costs and the publishers' return on sales.

b) the design of educational material for the interactive video disc medium.

The work has brought together a team of television and design experts, CAL developers, teachers and subject specialists: a range of skills frequently recognised as necessary for interactive video development (Duke, 1983).

It has also highlighted some of the difficulties related to attempting to bring together two different development processes based within different institutions and some of the problems that could arise with the 'balance of power' in an interactive video disc team, when computer controlled video material "implies a dominant role for computer programmers compared to television producers" (Fuller, 1984).

The product of this work will provide material that can be used to consider in greater depth the potential links between audio visual material and computer software in terms of educational design, presentation and user access.

"Even if interactive video itself is ultimately not feasible, the research projects it inaugurates, if they happen, will be invaluable for what they tell us about how people use and learn from the technologies". (Laurillard, 1984)

6   REFERENCES

[1] Duke, J., Interactive Video: Implications for Education and Training, Working Paper 22. (Council for Educational Technology for the United Kingdom, 1983).

[2] Fuller, R.G., Videodiscs in Bates, A.W., (ed.), The Role of Technology in Distance Education. (Croom Helm, London, 1984).

[3] Gallagher, M., Programme Evaluation Methods at the Open University, in Bates, T. and Robinson, J. (eds.), Evaluating Educational Television and Radio. (Open University Press, Milton Keynes, 1977).

[4] Laurillard, D.M., The Potential of Interactive Video, Journal of Educational Television, Vol. 8., No. 3., (1982).

[5] Laurillard, D.M., The Problems and Possibilities of Interactive Video, in Jones, A., Scanlon, E. and O'Shea, T. (eds.), New Technologies in Distance Teaching. (Harvester Press, Brighton) (in press).

[6] McCormick, S.J, The Development of CAL Materials: The Computers in the Curriculum Model, in Watson, D. (ed.), MEP Readers 3, Exploring Georgraphy with Microcomputers. (Council for Educational Technology, London, 1984).

[7] McCormick, S.J., Software and Television - A New Approach, paper presented at the CAL 85 Conference, University of Nottingham, England.

[8] Reeves, B.F., The First Year of 'Sesame Street': the formative research, New York: Children's Television Workshop (1970).

[9] Watson, D.M., A Model for the Production of CAL Material, Computer Education, Vol. 7, No. 3, (1983) 167-176.

COMPUTERS IN EDUCATION, K. Duncan and D. Harris (eds.)
Elsevier Science Publishers B.V. (North-Holland)
© IFIP, 1985

FINDINGS OF THE HOMEBASED COMPUTER ASSISTED ADULT EDUCATION PROJECT (1980-83)

Rolland L. Broussard, Ed.D., Project Director
Professor of Education
Charles E. Blanchard, M.S., Curriculum Coordinator
Assistant Professor of Mathematics
P. O. Box 43091
University of Southwestern Louisiana
Lafayette, Louisiana U.S.A. 70504

The purpose of the multi-year, multi-agency project was to develop a homebased CAI delivery system for ABE and GED. The project was conducted by U.S.L. in cooperation with the Lafayette Parish Adult Education Program and the E.S.E.A. Title I Project. which provided computer facilities to couple with a commercially available adult education curriculum. A total of 83 students received substantial CAI services. For the modest field testing component students were provided with terminals and acoustical couplers to interface with the centrally located computer. The program was found to be appropriate for drill and practice (and some tutorial instruction) for adult education students.

1. INTRODUCTION

The purpose of the multi-year, multi-agency project was to develop a delivery system for adult education utilizing contemporary educational technology. The appropriateness and feasibility of computer assisted instruction (CAI) and computer managed instruction (CMI) for undereducated adults in a homebased context was to be determined. Undereducated adults were adults who had not completed elementary or secondary school. The project was to accomplish the following objectives:
1. Development of a homebased computer assisted instruction delivery system for use with undereducated adults.
2. Preparation of a curriculum guide for instructors which will correlate the computer program lesson material with commonly available resource material in adult education programs in Louisiana.
3. Determination of the effectiveness of computer assisted instruction in a normal adult education context.
4. Field testing of the homebased computer assisted instruction delivery system developed in the first objective.

2. PROCEDURE

The special experimental demonstration project was conducted by the University of Southwestern Louisiana in cooperation with the Lafayette Parish Adult Education Program and the E.S.E.A. Title I Project. The project conducted the following program in order to accomplish its objectives. This paper provides information for Phases I and II (1980-82) and, or, Phase III (1982-83) and, or, for all three phases (1980-83).

In Phase I of the three year project, planning, development, and testing of computer assisted instruction in a traditional adult education part-time class setting was conducted. The project capitalized on the availability of computer facilities of the Title I Project at no cost and rented ABE/GED curriculum software. During Phase II this experience was continued and the classes expanded to two sites. A selected class, emphasizing CAI, was conducted during Phase III along with a limited homebased component.

In all phases a regularly available computer assisted instruction (CAI) and computer managed instruction (CMI) system was coupled with an ABE/GED curriculum available from Computer Curriculum Corporation, Palo Alto, California, (regionally represented by Southern Educational Media, Inc., Pearl, Mississippi) to provide CAI on a supplementary basis to students enrolled in an adult education program. The CMI component provided information on the students' progress in various reporting formats. Remote terminals were connected to the centrally located computer via direct telephone lines or through an acoustical coupler. The hardware was a Data General system. A curriculum coordinator and usually one aide were employed to conduct the CAI sessions and prepare a curriculum guide which would correlate the ABE/GED curriculum with normally available adult education instructional materials. The guide was intended to assist adult education instructors in teaching concepts for which controlled drill and practice was provided by CCC's CAI curriculum.

During Phases I and II of the project emphasis was placed on determining the feasibility of using CCC's computer system with undereducated adults, determining the effectiveness of the ABE/GED curriculum, and preparing a revised curriculum guide. During Phase III a regular CAI supported class was conducted and a homebased CAI component was field tested.

3. RESULTS

Over the three-year period of operations the adult education students received computer assisted instruction during 180, two and one-half hour sessions usually meeting on Tuesday and Thursday evenings. The program of instruction was for an academic year, excluding summer classes. The students were enrolled in a regular adult education program and received CAI on a supplementary basis with the option to elect how much time they would spend working at the monitors. It was anticipated that students would average about 30 minutes of CAI per session. During Phase III students receiving CAI services spent their entire time in the computer lab, but still elected how much actual time they would spend at the monitors.

Approximately 83 students received substantial CAI services, which was operationally defined as spending at least a minimum of 90 minutes working with the CAI curriculum. Some students worked as long as 44 hours and some only met the minimum requirement of 90 minutes. The average CAI time over the three years was 10 hours and 31 minutes per student. Tables 1 and 2 indicate student participation and the amount of time devoted to CAI at the monitors.

Adult students manipulated the computer hardware as they studied the ABE/GED curriculum materials. The lab assistant and curriculum coordinator were available to assist students during CAI

sessions. Regular adult education teachers and paraprofessionals were assisted by project personnel in working with the adult students. Emphasis was placed on the need for instructional services by regular adult education personnel and correlating normally available adult education instructional materials to the CAI curriculum.

	Received at least 90 minutes of CAI	
Phase I		27
Phase II		
Site 1	27	
Site 2	12	39
Phase III		17
TOTAL		83

Table 1 : Number of students receiving CAI instruction during class sessions

	Range		Average
	Low	High	
Phase I	90min.	17hrs.	6hrs.30min.
Phase II	90min.	27hrs.	9hrs.38min.
Phase III	125min.	44hrs.	15hrs.24min.
Overall Average	–		10hrs.31min.

Table 2 : Amount of "CAI time" per phase

Lesson materials were adult oriented and did not seem to be psychologically offending to adults by including "childish" material. The adult age level in the classes was relatively low and hence material which might be appropriate for middle and late teens was useful in the project. During all phases very few enrollees were beyond 25 years of age.

The Computer Curriculum Corporation's ABE/GED curriculum was deemed appropriate by project personnel for use with adult education students. It was the only curriculum which could be used with the available hardware but it seemed usable for supplementary purposes in ABE/GED programs.

The effectiveness of CAI was determined by comparing California Achievement Test grade equivalence score elevations between "CAI students" and "non-CAI students" in Lafayette Parish and the State. Average time spent in class between the two groups differed and scores were extrapolated in order to make adequate comparisons. During each year the scores of the "CAI students" either virtually equaled those of the "non-CAI students" or substantially exceeded them. The project staff felt that the comparisons demonstrated that CAI with undereducated adults was not deleterious at worst and was perhaps superior at best. Rigorous research design was not possible with the resources available to the project and no statistical significance was claimed. Figures 1 and 2 summarize the comparisons with Lafayette Parish and Louisiana "non CAI students".

Efforts were also made during Phases II and III to determine the affective disposition of students towards CAI. The attitudes of the adult education students who had received substantial CAI services were measured using the "Revised Brown Scale". The scale, modified (for preparing a Master's thesis by Mrs. Ann Justice, an adult education teacher) to measure attitudes of adult education students toward CAI, was administered to participants in the CAI project. Scale responses includes responses by both students in the classes and homebased (except for items 34 through 36 which apply only to homebased students).

The "Revised Brown Scale" consisted of thirty comments concerning attitudes towards CAI, one question on what is most liked about CAI, one question on what is most disliked about CAI, and one question soliciting suggestions for CAI

in adult education. Three items (34 - 36) measured the attitudes of students who received homebased CAI services. The scale is referenced in the bibliography.

Very briefly, results from scoring and analyzing survey responses to the "Revised Brown Scale" were summarized as follows;
1. They were not awed by the computer or its terminals.
2. They did not think CAI impersonal, boring, or a waste of time.
3. They found computer assisted instruction individualized, effective, better than other instructional methods, flexible, interesting, satisfying, and fun.

A rough draft of a curriculum guide was prepared during Phase I and revised. Additional sections were prepared by a selected consultant with experience in adult education instruction. The guide is Appendix B of the Final Project Report listed in the bibliography. The exercises referenced in the guide provided another form of study, and drill and practice in areas correlated to the CAI lesson topics.

For some students a deliberate effort was made to supplement the CAI activities with other adult education materials. Teachers "followed-up" on the assignments either by checking student work or providing tutoring services when appropriate.

The homebased component of the CAI

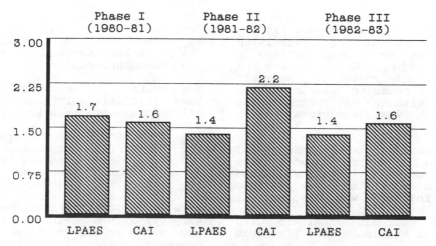

Figure 1: Average grade equivalence elevation scores for Lafayette Parish adult education students and CAI students (extrapolated)

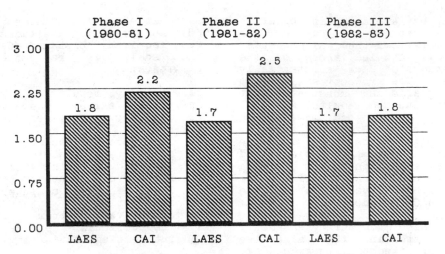

Figure 2:   Average grade equivalence elevation scores for
             Louisiana adult education students and CAI
             students (extrapolated)

project was modified from the original
planning.   Circumstances beyond the
control of the project staff affected
the amount of time that could be
dedicated to CAI in home sites.

The circumstances which affected the
planned procedures ranged from late
funding notification to relocation of
the computer facilities in the Title I
lab due to a school plant construction
project. No deviations in plans were
caused by the lessee who delivered the
four home terminals and other Phase III
equipment. Late approval of extra phone
equipment delayed the installation of
the phone line and modem to February,
1983.

The end of the school year was rapidly
approaching.   Instead   of   recruiting
students who had never been enrolled in
adult education or CAI classes a
decision was made by the project staff
to enroll adult students who may have
been familiar with the CAI program. The
first terminal was placed in a home on
March 7, 1983.

After experiencing the establishment of
one home site the staff planned for the
installation of the remaining three
terminals.   A small table was provided
to a participant who lacked an
appropriate desk or table for the
terminal and equipment. Within two
weeks two more terminals were placed in
home sites.

The four terminals were placed in six
different homes.   One terminal was

virtually not used by one adult student
who had seemed enthusiastic about
enrolling. This terminal was relocated
to another home site and was not counted
in the total of six homes. In another
home site the student was diligently
pursuing CAI via the homebased terminal
but became ill and was forced to
discontinue participation.   This
terminal was counted in the six homes
but was relocated to another home.

Some of the final relocations came after
the regular adult education program was
closed for the year. Two students were
willing to enroll in the homebased
component even if just for a few weeks
since they could continue their adult
education program. This continued until
June 7, 1983, when CAI equipment had to
be relocated from the Title I lab and
the phone line needed to be relocated
(and disconnected).

Most of the terminals were placed in the
homes of older adult education students.
All of these students were females.

Active participants diligently worked
through the CAI curriculum.   During a
period of approximately two months the
average computer time was 27 hours and
36 minutes. One student worked as much
as 67 hours and 2 minutes. The minimum
time was 12 hours and 53 minutes which
was logged in a period of approximately
two weeks close to the end of the
homebased component.

Pre-post testing was not feasible for
the   students   who   participated

exclusively in the homebased program. Virtually, only one student was exclusively enrolled in the homebased component and pre-post test scores were not available for that student due to the limited time available during the homebased component.

The curriculum coordinator was responsible for supporting instruction for the homebased program. He was available for tutoring students by telephone. He also monitored student progress via the computer management capability of the centrally located computer. The coordinator initiated telephone contact with students and followed-up with home site visits for instructional or equipment operation difficulties. Students were also invited to attend the regular class sessions for tutoring purposes.

The Revised Brown Scale responses by homebased students were included among the class responses. However, three items were added to the scale for students who participated in the homebased component. Space does not permit a detailed analysis of their responses. However, the students were found to be very supportive of CAI in their homes.

4. PROBLEM AREAS

Although the objectives were accomplished (except for limitations during Phase III), improvement in one area could produce substantial differences. Many adult education programs have experienced attendance problems and the CAI project was, again as in prior Phases, no exception. This seems to be a continuing problem in adult education programs.

In the homebased component the terminals and related home site equipment were somewhat large and participants needed sufficient space and, or, appropriate furniture for operating the equipment. A more serious potential problem is the availability of telephone models which will fit the respective acoustical couplers.

5. CONCLUSIONS

Objective 1 addressed the development of a homebased CAI delivery system for use with adults. During all phases of the project, CAI developmental work for use with undereducated adults was studied with a class of adult students.

Experience with the software (ABE and GED curriculum from the Computer Curriculum Corporation) produced results in terms of academic growth which compared favorably or exceeded that of non-CAI groups in Lafayette Parish and the State. The computer system which accommodates this software was readily usable by adult education students both in a class environment and in a homebased context.

Objective 2 called for the development of a curriculum guide which would correlate the CAI curriculum to normally available adult education materials. A curriculum guide was revised and expanded and was prepared as an instructors handbook. The guide correlates the CAI curriculum to commonly available adult education materials in Louisiana's Adult Education Program. The guide can be used in either a class setting or in a homebased context.

Objective 3 was concerned with the determination of the effectiveness of computer assisted instruction in a normal adult education context. It was found that adults continue to work satisfactorily at the CAI terminals and that many were motivated by the learning format. The data shows that students in CAI experienced academic growth which generally equaled or exceeded those of selected reference groups. Readers are again cautioned about the absence of statistical tests for significance due to certain project limitations. In addition, adult students had very positive attitudes towards CAI. At this time it seems safe to conclude that CAI with undereducated adults, coupled with normal adult education materials and instruction, is an effective learning format especially with the assistance of an adult education teacher. However, it must be kept in mind that some adults may not be attracted to this learning format and that CAI is not a panacea for all undereducated adults.

Objective 4 was to determine the effectiveness of the homebased computer assisted instruction system developed in Objective 1 by means of field testing. A modest field testing of homebased CAI was conducted with four to six students over a period of eight to ten weeks. Only one or two students were enrolled for the entire period. Only limited conclusions can be drawn from this experience. The effort required in placing terminals (and related equipment) in individual homes warrants a commitment to several months of CAI.

Homebased students were enthusiastic about the ability to work virtually any time of the day or night every day. However, the need for telephone linkage to the computer complicated the use of homebased CAI. As was carefully pointed out in the assessment of Objective 3 it seemed unreasonable to draw any conclusions about the academic effectiveness of homebased CAI. There is evidence that students will successfully participate in attempts at providing CAI in their respective homes.

6. RECOMMENDATIONS

The study initiated in this project should be continued. CAI has been in use in an increasing number of adult education programs (largely experimentally). This special experimental demonstration approach to the implementation of CAI with these adults (and extended to home sites) is vital and should be continued.

The accelerated development of microcomputers may provide an alternative to the substantial logistical problems involved in placing remote terminals of a centrally located computer in home sites. For this reason an effort should be made to study the potential of microcomputers in adult education in both a class and homebased context.

The curriculum guide, developed as an instructor's handbook, should be used in conjunction with computer assisted instruction. The curriculum guide should be studied further.

The limited homebased component extended CAI and CMI to home sites. While statistical differences in achievement test scores were not determined in the project enough experience was gained to believe that adult education students could benefit from homebased CAI with the assistance of an adult education teacher. Due to certain limiting factors it may be that the CCC curriculum coupled with a microcomputer would be more feasible for extending adult education services to individual homes of regular or special needs adult education students.

A brief bibliography has been included in this paper. It identifies sources for persons interested in CAI and CMI, especially with undereducated adults. One of the references which contains detailed information not found in this paper is the Final Project Report which is listed in ERIC.

7. SELECTED REFERENCES

Broussard, R. L. (Project Director), Homebased Computer Assisted Adult Education Project - Phase III. Final Project Report, September 1, 1982, to August 31, 1983. Lafayette, La.: University of Southwestern Louisiana, 1983. Published in Resources in Education, ERIC Clearinghouse on Adult, Career, and Vocational Education, February, 1984. ED 234 181

Brown, B. R., "An Instrument for the Measurement of Expressed Attitude Toward Computer-Assisted Instruction". In H. E. Mitzel and G. L. Brandon (Eds.), Experimentation with Computer-Assisted Instruction in Technical Education. (Semi-Annual Progress Report, Project No. OEC-5-85-074), University Park, Pa.: The Pennsylvania State University, Dec. 31, 1966. (Revised and revalidated by A. Justice for Master's thesis research, University of Southwestern Louisiana.)

Buckley, E. (Project Director), Pilot Project in Computer Assisted Instruction for Adult Basic Education Students (Final Three Year Report, 2/77 - 6/79). Great Neck, N. Y.: Adult Learning Centers, Great Neck Public Schools, 1979.

Caldwell, R. M., "Designing Effective Computer-Based Education to Teach Reading to Nonliterate Adults". Journal of Instructional Development, 1980, 3 (4), 16-18, 23-24.

Guide to the Adult Skills Courses. Palo Alto, Calif.: Computer Curriculum Corporation, 1979.

Guide to the GED Curriculum. Palo Alto, Calif.: Computer Curriculum Corporation, 1979.

Siegel, M. A., "Computer-Based Education in Prison Schools". Journal of Educational Technology Systems, 1978-79, 7 (3), 239-56.

COMPUTERS IN EDUCATION, K. Duncan and D. Harris (eds.)
Elsevier Science Publishers B.V. (North-Holland)
© IFIP, 1985

Computer Science Education for All Students

Kunio Takahashi, Kunihiro Suetake, and Sadaki Hirose

Faculty of Engineering
Kanagawa University
3-27 Rokkakubashi, Yokohama 221, Japan

Abstract As large scale computers and micro computers are used in all areas, needs for information processing curricula are rapidly increasing. In Kanagawa University, the Information Processing Center was established in 1982 and introductory computer science education for all students has been provided. The total number of students who take this curriculum comes to 1,200 this year. The curriculum is taught at an audio-visual demonstration room (exercise) with video system and an educational TSS room (laboratory work) with 51 TSS terminals (one is for a teacher and others are for 100 students) every other week. After visual education in the audio-visual demonstration room, comprehensive education in the TSS room is given step by step. Therefore, there are few students, especially in engineering, who drop out of the curriculum.

In this paper, we introduce our university and introductory computer science curriculum for all students.

1. Introduction of the university and computer science education

Kanagawa University comprises 4 faculties, a Junior College and several institutes. The total number of undergraduate students is about 15,000. Detailed figures are as follows : Faculty of Law, 2,800; Faculty of Economics, 5,900; Faculty of Foreign Language, 1,000; Faculty of Engineering, 4,700; Junior College, 600.

There is no specific department specializing in computer science or information science. Such research and education are being done partly by Electrical Engineering and Management Engineering in the faculty of Engineering. But, there is no such course provided in other faculties.

The Information Processing Center was established in 1982 with the following purposes ; computer science education for all students, computing service for all members in the university, and EDP service and research in information science.

2. Purpose of introductory computer science curriculum by TSS

The spread of micro computers is surprisingly rapid. Students in all the faculties, especially those in engineering, have some sort of experience with programming languages and key board operations of micro computers.

By development of time sharing system, the use of a computer has become easier and is spread throughout business areas other than technology. It has been strongly required that all students should use the time sharing system and have knowledge of information processing without cards.

The reasons that the students should know about computer science are as follows.

(1) In all the faculties, especially in engineering, information processing is a necessary tool for their research. Accordingly, the freshmen must finish an introductory computer science curriculum. In this curriculum students must acquire methods of computing by using TSS and elementary programming techniques. After that, students take specified curriculum in their faculties and use miscellaneous software packages.

(2) An increasing number of graduates, whether their major is engineering or the humanities, participate in information processing. By rapid development of computer application, even the students in the departments of traditional mechanical and electrical engineering have to attempt software engineering, system software, CAD/CAM, AI and EDP. Of course, the students in the humanities have to study EDP.

(3) Nowadays in order to get employment, most students, even those in the humanities, are required to have knowledge or experience concerning information processing technology. Women students with experience in programming can find employment relatively easily, and they could contribute to the development of software engineering, as women are generally apt at programming.

Actually, the number of students who wish to take the introductory computer science curriculum in all faculties has been increasing.

3. Computer system, educational TSS room, demonstration rooms and faculty members

In order to meet those requirements, the

Information Processing Center (IPC) was established in 1982.

3.1 Computer system

A large scale computer system **FACOM M-180II AD** was installed in IPC, with 16 MB main memory. It is also equipped with 5 GB of disk, MT equipment, digitizer, ordinary line printer, laser printer and x-y plotter.

3.2 Educational TSS room

The educational TSS room with 51 terminals (one is for a teacher and others are for 100 students) and 5 local printers for laboratory sessions is also located inside IPC. This room is equipped with 2 OHPs for explanation of program and key board operations.

When this room is not occupied for regular classes, it is open for any students from 8:45 A.M. to 10 P.M. Monday through Friday and 9 A.M. to 12:00 P.M. on Saturdays.

3.3 Demonstration rooms

There are two audio-visual demonstration rooms outside IPC. At first, each room was equipped with a TSS terminal and a large scale video screen. The video system can show the image on TSS terminal, television camera, slide projector, and video tape to 120 students. Programming statements in the curriculum are projected on a large screen through the TSS terminal. However, it was insufficient because the characters of a program statement were so small that the students in the room could not see them clearly. So we altered one of the rooms, say room A.

Now, in the room A, two video projectors are fixed to the ceiling wall, and two associated 100 type concave screens (2 meter X 1.5 meter) are fixed to the wall in the shape of letter V, then we have a jumbo screen (4 meter X 1.5 meter) as shown in Figure 1. Those two video projectors can be easily controled by a instructor.

On the lecture table, 2 overhead television cameras, 2 monitors associated to those cameras, and a monitor for computer display are set. Another monitor for display is kept in the closet in which two high quality television cameras are provided to focus on the right and left parts of the monitor's screen in order to give detailed information of the computer program on the display.

Two OHPs and two associated screens are also provided in the corner of this room, and parallel or comparison presentation can be given to students when the instructor wish to show his transparencies.

The room is also furnished with an air conditioner, and several down-lighting apparatus are provided to avoid direct illumination onto the video screens by regular lighting.

3.4 Faculty members

Three full-time faculty members and four technical staff members are assigned to this curriculum. Three part-time teaching staff members cooperate with them.

4. The multi-screen video system

Supposing that an instructor likes to transfer one idea to his students, and the idea is composed of three informations, say A, B and C; then he prepared three slides A, B and C for his lecture.

The lecture room condition allows him to use only one slide projector for his presentation, so he is obliged to show his slides to his students one after another sequentially.

This presentation is not good for his students, because, when he shows the last slide C after showing the first slide A, then the next slide B, student's impression about the A may disappear, and the B may be shadowy.

However, if he is allowed to use 2 slide projectors, his presentation would become very understandable for his students, even though he uses the same slides A, B and C.

The reason is very simple, because one glance to Figure 2 may be enough to explanation.

Miscellaneous modes can be available. For example, five modes on presentations can be available as shown in Figure 3.

Those five modes can be easily switched over from one to the other with just pushing the controlling buttons by the instructor.

The presentation done by those five modes can give understandable information to the students.

Five Modes for better instruction

	LEFT SCREEN	RIGHT SCREEN
1	Textbook	Instruction note
2	Video material	Instruction note
3	Key board	Text book
4	Key board	Display
5	Enlarged display	Enlarged display

The multi-screen video system has miscellaneous advantages for comprehension of the curriculum as follows.

(1) Algorithms and short program statements are displayed at once on the multi-screen. In this way, sufficient explanation for the programming technique is given with explanation of the algorithm.

(2) Video text tape and instruction note are displayed at once. Further explanations of the program can be added to video text tapes.

(3) One of the overhead television cameras has two ways of presentations, one for taking a page of text book, and another for taking the face of the key board which can be easily shifted to the appropriate position just under the lenze of the overhead camera along the rail on the table.

(4) The movement of the cursor on the display is clearly projected to the left screen of the video projector, while the operator (instructor) touches on the key on the key-board which is shown in the right screen, and such a parallel presentation gives a strong impression to

students.

(5) An image on TSS terminal is divided into halves, the left and the right side, and each side of the image is respectively projected on the two screens.

5. Significant features of curriculum

The significance of the introductory computer science curriculum is shown as follows.

(1) Education by TSS

The laboratory work is given to get practical experience by actually using 51 TSS computer terminals and 5 local printers. All the students must submit reports for exercise problems every week. As each terminal has to be shared between two students in the regular session, they must operate TSS terminals outside the regular sessions for submitting their reports.

Through learning to use computer methods by TSS and introductory programming technique, students would be stimulated to greater interest in advanced information processing, e.g. CAD/CAM, database and expert system. Therefore, complete computer science education should be offered to all the students who wish to take this curriculum. At present, it is difficult to offer such a large scale curriculum. Such a curriculum is offered by the departments of Electrical Engineering and of Management Engineering.

(2) Alternative execution of exercise and laboratory work

In computer science, the computer programming lecture (exercise) in the demonstration room and laboratory work in the TSS room are given every other week. With this method, students can remember what they have learned in the exercise when they execute laboratory work.

(3) Comprehensive education by 2 OHPs in the TSS room

After the lectures at the demonstration room, students use TSS terminals at the educational TSS room. In this case, students are given instructions of key board operations on OHP screen step by step. Further, students are given sufficient explanation about program on OHP screen again.

(4) Visual education

(a) The demonstration room is used for the computer programming lecture (exercise).

(b) To avoid occupation of TSS terminals in the TSS room and to give sufficient explanation of the program, a teaching staff member operates the key board of the TSS terminal in the demonstration room and shows those operations on the large video screen by television camera. And, also teacher shows an image of TSS terminal for 120 students.

(c) Also, video text is displayed on a large

screen.

(d) And, slides are displayed on a large screen.

(5) Strong recommendation by faculty members to the students in engineering

Students in the faculty of engineering are encouraged by strong recommendation by faculty members. In a department in engineering where the faculty members recommend the curriculum, almost all the students take this curriculum.

(6) Semi-compulsory curriculum for students in the humanities

Introductory computer science curriculum is added as the semi-compulsory subject for the students in the humanities. The students who hope to take this course number 1,500 this year.

(7) Slow and steady execution of curriculum for the students especially in the humanities.

The students in the humanities are taught much more slowly than the students in engineering.

Computer science is a full-year course which includes 28 lectures in two semesters for the students in the humanities. One lecture lasts for 90 minutes. Six sections per week are being held this year. Also, computer science is a half-year course for engineering students, and ten sections are being held this year.

(8) The registration fee is needed

The registration fee is set at 40$. These curriculum are well-attended voluntary.

There are few students who drop out of the course, especially in engineering. The number of registered students for the course is 666 in engineering and 520 in the humanities as shown in Table 3, 1; the percentage of attendance is 95 % in engineering and 80 % in the humanities.

The students in engineering show better comprehension of the laboratory work, while those in the humanities show better understanding of the lecture.

6. Subjects of curriculum

Topics in computer science are selected based on the following considerations.

(1) Through experience in using the TSS terminal, students learn the characteristics of computer software and simple programming method.

(2) As the computer develops and the use of computer spreads through all areas, non-numerical problems are recognized as an important part of information processing. Students study non-numerical problems, e.g, character processing, graphic processing, file processing and simulation.

(3) Finally, students study the detailed algorithm of particular numerical method : ordinary differential equations,

partial differential equations, simultaneous equations and Fourie transform.

    The following subjects are options;

(1) History of computing
(2) Computer systems
(3) Method of using the TSS terminal
(4) Editing and executing programs using the screen editor
(5) Execution of Batch Jobs
(6) Fundamentals of Fortran 77
(7) Exercise in Fortran 77
(8) Graphics by plotter
   (a) Sine wave
   (b) Drawing of house
(9) Filing methods
(10) Statistical Analysis
   (a) Calculation of variation
   (b) Sorting
   (c) Generation of random numbers
   (d) Scientific library
   (e) Monte Carlo methods
   (f) Music composition
(11) Simulation
(12) Numerical Analysis
   (a) Simultaneous linear equations
   (b) Ordinary differential equations
      Euler method
      Lunge-Kutta method
      Milne method
   (c) Partial differential equations
   (d) Fast Fourie transform

7. Conclusion

    Need and demand for computer science curriculum are increasing. Actually, students who wish to take introductory computer science curriculum number 2,000 as shown in Table 2 and Table 3. Through the significant features of the curriculum as mentioned above, satisfactory results are obtained. Miscellaneous considerations for the future development of the information processing curriculum must be done as follows;

(1) Advanced computer programming and advanced computer science courses must be provided to all the students.

(2) Education by CAI must be developed.

(3) Effective audio-visual educational text tapes must be produced.

(4) Effective educational software system must be produced.

Acknowledgement

    The authors heartly appreciate the encouragement of Prof. Hisao Takeyama (Emeritus Professor of Tohoku University).

Figure 1. Demonstration room A

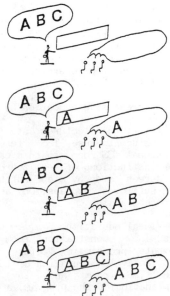

Figure 2. Multi-screen effect

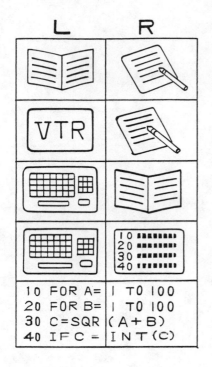

L   R

```
10 FOR A= | TO 100
20 FOR B= | TO 100
30 C=SQR (A+B)
40 IF C = INT(C)
```

Figure 3. Examples of display

Table 1. Number of students enrolled in the introductory computer science curriculum

Faculty	Grade				
	Freshman	Sophomore	Junior	Senior	Total
Law	22	19	32	49	122
Economics	106	37	41	69	253
Trade	23	10	21	39	93
Language	2	3	6	12	23
Junior college	14	15			29
Total	167	84	100	169	520

Table 2. Number of students wished to take the curriculum in the Humanities

Freshman	Sophomore	Junior	Senior	Total
448	266	292	320	1326

Table 3. Number of students enrolled in the introductory computer science curriculum

Department	Grade				
	Freshman	Sophomore	Junior	Senior	Total
Mechanical E.	50	0	19	2	71
Electrical E.	263	6	1	0	270
Chemical E.	0	97	33	18	148
Architecture	0	0	60	18	78
Management E.	0	53	37	9	99
Total	313	156	150	47	666

COMPUTERS IN EDUCATION, K. Duncan and D. Harris (eds.)
Elsevier Science Publishers B.V. (North-Holland)
© IFIP, 1985

SOFTWARE ENGINEERING EDUCATION IN ACADEMIA AND INDUSTRY: SYNTHESIS OF SOME PRACTICAL EXPERIENCE

Pierre N. Robillard   Marcel Dupras   Ali Mili

Ecole Polytechnique   Département d'Informatique   Département d'Informatique
C.P.6079, Succ."A", Montréal, Université Laval, Québec,   Université de Tunis,
Qc., Canada, H3C 3A7   Qc, Canada, G1K 7P4   El Menzah, 1060, Tunisie

Software engineering spans a wide range of topics, from such technical matters as the mathematics of structured programming and programming language semantics to such non-technical matters as team organization and programmer psychology. In this paper we report on our experience in teaching some of these topics in regular university courses and in industrial short courses. We try to draw some conclusions.

1. INTRODUCTION: The problem of software engineering education

Following (MILL80), we recognize two parts in the problem of software engineering education: university education and industrial education; university education refers to (typically) one-term credit courses given to university students whereas industrial education refers to (typically) one-week non-credit courses given to practicing software professionals. In a field more stable than software engineering, the role that each part plays in educating professionals of the field is clearly definable: while university education deals with scientific foundations and fundamental principles, industrial education deals primarily with technological advances. The youth of the field of software engineering blurs the distinction between these two parts and generally makes their definition difficult.

The problem of university education in software engineering can be formulated in the following terms:
- Determining the scientific foundations of software engineering is difficult: many proposals for dealing with the various aspects of the field have been made in the past; few have earned wide acceptance and many are subject to heated controversy.
- Dealing with fundamentals while keeping a practical perspective is difficult: the gap between the technological needs of software engineering and the capability afforded by its state of the art is such that many fundamental solutions to software engineering problems seem woefully inadequate or overly simplistic; at the same time this gap provides a strong temptation to seek ad hoc solutions lacking theoretical basis.
- Sorting through the software engineering literature is difficult: most books are analytic rather than synthetic; many are oriented toward reference use by the practicing software professional rather than textbook use by the student.

In addition to some of the difficulties mentioned above, industrial education in software engineering suffers from the following difficulties:
- Participants vary considerably in backgrounds (university degrees, on-the-job training, professional experience, etc...), abilities (ease with abstraction, ability to reason logically etc...), and interests (types of problems they face on the job, types of solutions they are most interested in, etc...). This difficulty is discussed in (MILL80).
- Participants are very concerned about the short-term benefits of what they learn. They are more interested in technology transfer than in actual education; in the current state of the art, software researchers have some actual education to offer, while they have little technology to transfer (in a recent software engineering conference, a participant in a birds of a feather session on Technology Transfer suggested that the major problem with technology transfer in software engineering is that there is no technology to transfer).

In this paper, we report on the experience we gained teaching various software engineering courses in university environments and industrial environments. Generally, we have taken a rather hardline pro-fundamentals attitude in designing our courses, though we had to find compromises with regard to industrial courses.

The courses discussed in this paper are given in the appendix. They are classified as follows: University Education

Technical Aspects of Software Engineering

Managerial Aspects of Software Engineering

Industrial Education

Technical Aspects of Software Engineering
Managerial Aspects of Software Engineering

The plan of the paper will basically follow this classification.

2. UNIVERSITY EDUCATION: Technical Aspects

2.1 Discrete Mathematics

It has been our experience that some students are attracted to computer science studies by its glamour, as perceived through computer games, computer graphics, computer music and the like; for the computer science instructor, it is difficult to draw the student's attention away from the glamourous appearances and toward the foundations of the field (of course, computer graphics, computer music and computer games have interesting foundations of their own --which students may not know). This creates a strong temptation on the part of the instructor (and textbook author) to spend a great deal of time and effort explaining to the student (reader) what the material being taught is useful for the practice of computing. We feel that this defensive attitude is an impediment to sound education. By contrast, we adopt a more assertive attitude in teaching course AA1: We concentrated more on teaching concepts rather than applications and we figured that if we did a good job of teaching these concepts properly, the students would like them for what they are rather than for what they can be useful for. Using C.L. Liu's Elements of Discrete Mathematics helped us reach our goal.

The success of this approach can perhaps be summarized in the following anecdote: Many a student were so interested in the material that they made a habit of doing all the exercises of each chapter of Liu's book and bringing them to the teaching assistant (TA) for checking; the TA was so swamped with work (some chapters have nearly forty exercises, some of them difficult) that the instructor had to give him the solutions manual during each help session.

2.2 Program Design and Construction

In (DUPR84), we have discussed in detail our experience with teaching a calculus of programming to beginners (no previous programming experience) as well as to non-beginners. The conclusion we have drawn from our experience is that as much as teaching a formal calculus of programming to beginners is feasible and productive, teaching the same material to senior level students who have been exposed to (polluted by?) an informal introduction to programming can be frustrating to the instructor as well as to the student; in particular, we have encountered serious problems of motivation on the part of students, who did not understand why they had to struggle through heavy mathematical formalisms while they have been programming without them for a few years.

2.3 Program Correctness and Fault Tolerance

Motivation was not an issue in these courses. Graduate students who signed up for these courses were typically aware of the necessity of formal mathematical models to grasp the problems of correctness and fault tolerance.

The course on program verification (AC1) covers such topics as: elements of discrete mathematics; elements of logical expression and reasoning; programming language semantics; formulas of program correctness; program verification by induction. The students usually appreciated the interest and novelty of the topics covered in this course; yet we find unsettling that some of the material we are teaching at the graduate level could actualy be taught at the freshman/sophomore level (see course AB1).

In addition to the background material of mathematics, logic and program correctness, the course on fault tolerance covered such topics as: error detection in programs; program validation by assertions; damage confinement and assessment; forward error recovery; backward error recovery. This course was offered to electrical engineering majors who typically had some programming experience but were not previously acquainted with formal approaches to programming. We were surprised by how fast they could catch up with novel ideas of program correctness and program fault tolerance; we were also pleased by the amount of interest they have shown for a topic so distant from their major.

3. UNIVERSITY EDUCATION: Managerial Aspects

3.1 Software Engineering Economics

We covered all thirty three chapters of Barry Boehm's book (BOEH81). The material was generally well received, well understood and appreciated. It was felt that the book used has been successful in motivating the students to problems of Software Engineering they had not experienced themselves.

4. INDUSTRIAL EDUCATION: Technical Aspects

4.1 Education of the programmer and analyst

In course CA1, the topics covered are: mathematical background; Mills approach to program correctness and design; Hoare's approach to program correctness; elements of program design. In course CA2, the topics covered are: mathematical background; the nature and properties of specifications; specification languages; Hoare's approach to program correctness.

Two conclusions have emerged from our experience with these courses.
- First, motivation is a key ingredient to the sucess of such courses. In course CA1, we organized an optional session on Monday (May 9) evening in which we read some articles advocating the need for a mathematical approach to programming ((GRIE80), (MILLL80), (MILL82)); as it turned out the students who could not attend that particular session were the only ones who had a great deal of difficulty following during the rest of the week (they were criticizing the material as being too abstract and of little use). In course CA2, the first session (Monday morning)

was set aside to make a strong case in favor
of a mathematical approach to programming.
The session included four parts: quotations
from well-known authorities (Dijkstra, Mills,
McCarthy); success stories showing the superiority of a mathematical approach (New York
Times, Census Bureau 1980, Gries experiment
(GRIE80)); articles on the education of the
programmer ((GRIE80), (MILL80)) advocating a
strong mathematical background; finally the
students were presented with a simple 3/4 of
a line program and were asked questions about
it, which nobody could answer correctly (hu-
mility generates a learning attitude).
- Second, the Mills approach has proven more
popular with the participants than the Hoare
approach. While designing course CA2, we had
planned to spend more time on Hoare's approach
than on Mills approach because, we felt, the
former -with its preconditions, postconditions,
verification rules- is more tangible, hence
would be more appealing to practicing programmers. As it turned out, virtually all participants preferred the latter, for they found
it more structured; also, they had a difficult
time generating loop invariants (creative step
of Hoare's approach) while they had no problem
determining the function of while statements
(creative step of Mills approach). Incidentally, no such preference was noticed in graduate level courses on the same subject (AC1).

5. INDUSTRIAL EDUCATION: Managerial Aspects

5.1 Education of the Software Manager

Practicing software managers found the material
of course DA1 relevant to their concerns as well
as being easily applicable. They followed the
course with interest and compared COCOMO equations with data from their projects. A survey
conducted at the end of the course did find that
they were very prudent as to how much they will
rely on COCOMO; a major source of concern has
been the evaluation of KDSI (chapters 22 and 23
did not answer all the questions we had).

5.2 Managing the Software Project

This short course was oriented toward software
professionals. It introduced the participants
to systematic means of managing software projects.
Because they come from an industrial background,
participants were already familiar with the practical realities of software design; they found
the techniques and tools presented in the course
quite helpful in harnessing the complexity of the
problems they face.

6. CONCLUSION

Our disparate experience spanning many universities, semesters and topics has given us some basis for drawing conclusions about software engineering education in the industrial and university environments; we will avoid being assertive
about our conclusions because we feel that we do

not have a long enough background to back our
conclusions.

It seems fair to say that a short course should
be anything but a shortened regular course.
When an instructor must teach a short course on
the basis of the textbook used for a regular
course, he is strongly tempted to take the book
and go through it quickly; this practice is nearly fatal for the success of a short course.There
are two main   reasons for this:
- In a regular course, students have a much
  longer time (semester) to gradually digest
  what they learn in class; this possibility is
  not provided for in a short course.
- Because they have more time to think about
  what they are learning, students in a regular
  university course are likely to have more in-
  depth questions than participants in a short-
  course; hence a regular course instructor
  needs to provide his students with means to
  answer their questions. This need does not
  exist for short-course participants who would
  be encumbered by what they perceive as a solution without a problem.

As far as regular university courses go, we have
had some success teaching fundamentals. In the
perennial debate regarding how to balance theory and practice in a university course, we happen
to have hardline views in favor of theory: we
feel it is not a university's business to try
and guess a student's future problems and tell
him how to solve them (his problems are his, by
definition); rather a university must arm the
student with the necessary modelling and structuring tools and let him tune these tools to his
particular concerns. Our experience reported on
here tends to support our view, as does -to some
extent- the discussion of the next paragraph.

The problem of motivation is posed in different
terms for industrial education and university
education. The reason for the difference is
that industrial students are familiar with the
problem and attend the course to seek solutions
they -supposedly- ignore, whereas university
students are best motivated by the intrinsic appeal of solutions (elegance, rationality,...)
whereas industrial students are best motivated
by being shown the adequacy of the proposed solution to their problem. The latter form of motivation is made difficult by the diversity of the
participants problems and -most dangerously- by
the diversity of their interpretation of the
course description.

To our surprise, we have found that, when properly motivated, industrial participants in a
short course can learn a great deal of material
usually viewed as "theoritical"; this was the
case of course CA2, in particular. What heightened our surprise (puzzlement?) in that course
is that the participants favored a program verification method whose superiority is based on
theoritical (rather than practical) considerations. It is noteworthy that in that particular

course, a special motivation session was set a-
side culminating in an experiment consisting of
asking the participants simple questions about
a simple short program and noticing that none
answered correctly or diligently enough. To the
group of successful professional programmers and
analysts that they were, this session served a
twofold purpose: first it makes them humble, an
ideal attitude for learning; second, it has vi-
sibly created a sense of emergency, fueling the
participants desire to find sound solutions.

APPENDIX: Courses Discussed in this Paper

A. University Education: Technical Aspects
AA. Discrete Mathematics for Programming
AA1. "Structures Discrètes" (Discrete Structures).
     Fall 83. Université Laval. Junior level.
     Text: (LIU77).
AB. Program Design and Construction
AB1. "Eléments d'Algorithmique" (Elements of Al-
     gorithmics). Spring 83, Fall 83 and Spring
     84. Université Laval. Sophomore level.
     Text: (MILL80).
AB2. "Conception de Logiciel, I" (Software De-
     sign, I). Fall 82. Université Laval. Senior
     level. Text: (MILL80).
AB3. "Conception de Logiciel, II" (Software
     Design, II). Spring 83. Université Laval.
     Graduate level. Text: (GRIE81).
AB4. "Theory of Computer Programming". Spring
     84. McGill Univerity. Graduate level.
     Text: (GRIE81).
AB5. "Méthodes de Spécifications et de Concep-
     tion" (Specification and Design Methods).
     Spring 84. Ecole Polytechnique. Graduate
     level. Text: (PRES82).
AB6. "Programmation Structurée" (Structured Pro-
     gramming). Each semester since 1980. Ecole
     Polytechnique. Undergraduate. Text: (HOLT
     80).
AC. Program Correctness and Fault Tolerance
AC1. "Special Topics on Formal Program Verifica-
     tion". Fall 82 and Fall 83. McGill Univer-
     sity. Graduate level. Text: manuscript of
     (MILI84).
AC2. "Program Fault Tolerance". Spring 84.
     McGill University. Graduate level. Text:
     (ANDE80).
B. University Education: Managerial Aspects
BA. Software Engineering Economics
BA1. "Aspects Economiques du Génie de Logiciel"
     (Economic Aspects of Software Engineering).
     Fall 83. Université Laval. Graduate level.
     Text: (BOEH81).
C. Industrial Education: Technical Aspects
CA. Education of the Programmer and Analyst
CA1. "Analyse et Conception de Logiciel" (Soft-
     ware Analysis and Design). Ecole d'Eté
     d'Informatique de l'Université Laval 83.
     May 9-13 1983. Text: (LING79).
CA2. "Program Specification, Verification and
     Testing". McGill Summer Institute of Com-
     puter Science 84. July 9-13 1984. Text:
     manuscript of (MILI84).
D. Industrial Education: managerial Aspects
DA. Education of the Software Manager
DA1. "Aspects Economiques et Humains du Dévelop-

pement de Projets Logiciels". Ecole d'Eté
     d'Informatique de l'Université Laval 84.
     June 11-15 1984. Text: (BOEH81).
DB. Managing the Software Process
DB1. "Conception de logiciels" (Software Design).
     Centre de cours intensifs, Ecole Polytech-
     nique de Montréal. April 25-27 1984. Text:
     (ROBI84).

BIBLIOGRAPHY

(ANDE81): Anderson T. and P.A. Lee. Fault Toler-
     ance Principles and Practice. Prentice-
     Hall International, 1981.
(BOEH81): Boehm B. Software Engineering Econom-
     ics. Prentice-Hall, 1981.
(DUPR84): Dupras M., F. Lemay and A. Mili. Some
     Thoughts on Teaching First Year Program-
     ming. SIGCSE Bulletin, 16(1) (February
     1984), pp 148-153.
(GRIE80): Gries, D. Educating the Programmer:
     Notation, Proofs and the Development of
     Programs. Invited paper, Information Proc-
     essing. (S.H. Lavington, editor). North
     Holland Publishing Company.
(GRIE81): Gries, D. The Science of Programming,
     Springer-Verlag, 1981.
(HOLT80): Holt R.C., J.P. Hume, J.Lavoie, P.N.
     Robillard, Programmation structurée et
     exercices, Gaétan Morin, 1980.
(LING79): Linger, R.C., H.D. Mills and B.I.
     Witt. Structured Programming: Theory and
     Practice. Addison-Wesley, 1979.
(LIU77): Liu, C.L. Elements of Discrete Mathe-
     matics. McGraw-Hill, 1977.
(MILI84): Mili, A. An Introduction to Formal
     Program Verification. Van Nostrand Rein-
     hold, 1984 (to appear).
(MILL80): Mills, H.D. Software Engineering Educa-
     tion. Proceedings of IEEE, 68(9) (September
     1980), pp1158-1162.
(MILL82): Mills, H.D. The Intellectual Control
     of Computers. Keynote Adress in Interna-
     tional Symposium on Current Issues of Re-
     quirements Engineering Environments. Kyoto,
     Japan, September 20-21 1982.
(MILL84): Mills H.D. et al. The Calculus of Com-
     puter Programming. Allyn and Bacon, 1984
     (to appear).
(PRES82): Pressman R.C. Software Engineering: A
     Practitionner's approach, McGraw-Hill, 1982.
(ROBI82): Robillard P.N.,R. Plamondon, Planning
     for Software Tool Implementation: Experience
     with SCHEMACODE. National Computer Con-
     ference, Houston, June 1982.
(ROBI84): Robillard P.N., Conception de Logi-
     ciels, Gaétan Morin, 1984 (to appear).
(ZELK79): Zelkowitz M.C., A.C.Shaw, J.D.Gannon,
     Principles of Software Engineering and
     Design, Prentice-Hall, 1979.

COMPUTERS IN EDUCATION, K. Duncan and D. Harris (eds.)
Elsevier Science Publishers B.V. (North-Holland)
© IFIP, 1985

DIAL-A-DIPLOMA DOWN UNDER

Reginald Daly Pearson

Deakin University
Victoria 3217
Australia

The aims and structure of a fully accredited Australian Graduate Diploma of Computing
are outlined. The Diploma program, which has been offered in the off campus mode
since 1980, features the use of home computers being linked via the telephone network
to the University. The various modes of interaction are explained together with the
enrolment procedures and student characteristics. As a result of recent advances in
technology, this mode of teaching in distance education is encouraged.

1. INTRODUCTION

Deakin University is situated at Geelong, a city
of almost 160,000 people 80 kilometres southwest of Melbourne, the capital of the state of
Victoria. It is Victoria's fourth, youngest and
only University outside the Melbourne
metropolitan area. It has developed into
Australia's "Open University" in which 4043 of
the 6345 current enrolments in all academic
schools are students studying various programs
in the Off Campus mode.

The School of Sciences at Deakin University
conducts a Graduate Diploma of Computing which
has since 1976 been offered On Campus and has
since 1980 been offered as an Off Campus
program.

2. THE GRADUATE DIPLOMA OF COMPUTING

The Diploma is designed to provide data
processing and computer studies for graduates
from disciplines generally considered to be
outside the ambit of EDP or computer science
courses. Its main objectives are to allow
graduates in other fields to become
professionally qualified in the computing field
and to give teachers who may be required to
teach computing an opportunity to acquire the
necessary background knowledge. On completion
of the course, students should be competent in
the techniques of computer programming using
both commercial and scientific languages, and
have a working understanding of the applications
and interactions of computers in the commercial,
industrial, educational and social environment.
The Diploma is accredited with The Australian
Computer Society as an appropriate qualification
for membership.

The Diploma is comprised of 8 semester units
which can be completed in a minimum of two
years' and a maximum of five years' study. Off
Campus units currently available are:

SCP710   Introduction to Programming
SCP711   EDP Systems
SCP712   Machine Level Concepts
SCP713   Computers and Society
SCP715   EDP Audit
SCP717   Computer Applications in Education
SCP720   Data Base and Data Communications
SCP723   Data Structures
SCP725   Project

The units SCP710, SCP711 and SCP725 are
compulsory, with SCP710 and SCP711 being prerequisites for the rest of the units in the
program. For students living in close proximity
to the University, 5 additional and alternative
units available by attendance at lectures are:

SCP714   Optimisation techniques
SCP721   Systems Software
SCP722   Real-Time Systems
SCP724   Computer Graphics

Off Campus students study in their own home,
with occasional face to face contact with
academic staff occurring when staff visit area
study centres to conduct tutorials and
workshops. Students are located in study areas
centred on major country towns at distances of
up to 1000 kilometres from Geelong.

3. COURSE REQUIREMENTS

In the course of the Off Campus Program, each
student uses a stand-alone microcomputer. This
must have as a minimum:
(a) on board BASIC
(b) 16K RAM
(c) screen width output of 80 characters
(d) interface into which an acoustic coupler
can be plugged to provide, via the telephone
network, communication with Deakin University's
mainframe computer.

The telephone connection using an acoustic coupler is a necessary requisite to attempt the Graduate Diploma. The program is structured around the use of the University's computer providing a regular communication link with respect to electronic mail, electronic course material, data, files, data bases, packages, languages, assignments and assessment. It enables the course to be common to all students and provides uniformity and consistency in approach, presentation and assessment.

Whilst the make and type of computer the student uses is invisible to the University, experience has shown that there are some computers which have significant cost, reliability and user friendliness advantages over others. This applies in particular to the operation of the communications interfacing, where file to file transfer of data and programs can produce significant cost savings to STD telephone connect times. As technology changes, the University requirements and recommendations are modified. This is best illustrated by the fact that in 1980 when preparing for the introduction of the Off Campus presentation of the Diploma, a microcomputer was built on campus as there was none suitable or available for the type of communications required. This was quickly superseded by "off the shelf" microcomputers, one of which fitted the specifications and price structures required. This in turn is now no longer available and new equipment configurations are now recommended.

Course notes were initially written, typed into computer files, computer edited, computer formatted and computer printed by the academic staff developing the course. The computer printout was reproduced and collated into book form in the University printery. The majority of the material for Off Campus courses offered in 1981 was developed at night and at home by academic staff using a student home computer configuration and linking via the telephone network to Deakin University's mainframe computer. The course notes are now professionally typeset, edited and produced and supplemented by prescribed texts, manuals, audio and video tapes.

4. COURSE ADMINISTRATION

Each course consists of a semester of 13 weeks and is based on an average work loading of 8 hours per week. This time is associated with the study of course material, prescribed reading and completion of course work which is submitted for assessment. For example, the first course SCP710 requires through the progression of the unit, the submission of 11 assignments including major programming exercises. SCP711 requires the submission at regular intervals of 6 assignments. In these courses, submission of assignments is mostly electronic via the Telecom network.

Assessment is by a combination of course work and examination. Examinations are conducted at the end of each semester at regional study centres. In general, assessment is 30% assignment and 70% examination with the requirements that there be a pass in the submitted assignments and at least 40% obtained in the final examination. Precise assessment detail is provided in the course material distributed at the commencement of each semester.

Where appropriate, the semester units have one or more tutorials and/or workshops which are conducted at regional study centres or on the main campus. Students who are unable to attend these are at a distinct disadvantage owing to the technical nature of some of the courses. In some cases assessment includes work done at these workshops. Because of the progressive, sequential nature of the courses in the Graduate Diploma, students are advised to take 3 years to do the program, attempting 2 courses in the first year and 3 in each of the following 2 years.

Prior to enrolment, academic staff visit the study centre regions to test and confirm the suitability of the telephone network for computer data transmission, to demonstrate the application of the technology and to explain to prospective students the diploma program, course commitments and requirements. The successful operation of the Off Campus program is dependent upon the reliability of the transmission of data over the Telecom telephone network. Some country areas are serviced by telephone equipment which provides an unacceptable degrading of data transfer signals and if this is the case students find it impossible to successfully proceed with the program. Since this connect time can be up to 25 hours per year, its reliability is of prime importance.

When an assignment is ready for assessment or help or advice is required, the student advises the staff member by a special brief "mail" facility on the computer. When the staff member makes a regular link to the computer, the backlog of students' "mail" can be read. In 1984 for the introductory unit SCP710, 1262 such "mail" messages were logged in the lecturer's directory. Student's assignments, developed on and stored by the computer, are then viewed and assessed by the staff member. Test data can be used to check the validity of the student's work. A line printer copy of the assignment is forwarded to the student by conventional mail and thus the student has individual feedback within 24 hours and hard copy of work done within 2 or 3 days. This aspect of the course is a very time consuming exercise. Computer satatistics for 1984 indicate that for the 13 week first semester course SCP710, the lecturer's directory was used in this way for 299 hours during the period 8am to 5pm, 44 hours from 5pm to midnight and 42 hours on weekends or between midnight and 8am.

All students enrolled in a particular course are allocated user file space in a common course directory on Deakin's mainframe. The staff member involved also has filespace allocated in the directory and in addition, has access to all students files. Students can only access their own files in their own user directory and those files in the lecturer's directory which have had file protection modifed to allow read and execute access.

Due to STD charges, and to effectively utilize available computer time, most students computer work is done during night and weekend hours. The Diploma is thus largely supported by otherwise unused out-of-hours computer availability. The over-riding fear of an excessive telephone account due to long connect times, has prompted students to take more care in planning, checking and presenting their work. Compilation and execution of programs tend not to be the regular hit and miss approach adopted by On Campus students who have "unlimited free use" of computing facilities.

It would appear that because of maturity and dedication, the majority of students produce and present work of a very high standard. Table 1 indicates the level of achievement in the first unit SCP710 Introduction to Programming over the years 1981 to 1984 inclusive. This semester course has as its content an introduction to computers and computing together with detailed study and application of the programming languages BASIC and COBOL. A brief appreciation and application of the Pascal language is also covered.

Table 1 : SCP710 Assessment Distribution (by %).

Grade	HD	D	C	P	N
Mark Range	>80%	70-79	69-60	50-59	<50%
1981	9	39	18	18	16
1982	10	28	31	23	8
1983	12	24	44	15	5
1984	28	32	18	14	8

In addition to having access to all the system components of a large mainframe computer, there are other software components which have been developed specifically for the operation of the Graduate Diploma program. A student can for example, after an assignment has been assessed, run a computer program (called MARK) which indicates the mark given, together with a personalised message and statistics on class average and number of assignments assessed. Those students who make personal details available also have access via another program (called CONTACT) which provides other students names, addresses, telephone numbers, occupation and make of home computer used. This encourages contact between students and has resulted in one group of 8 students in one provincial town meeting in private homes every two weeks as a self help group.

5. ENROLMENT

Enrolment in most programs of study in Australian Universities is restricted by application of quotas imposed by limitations in available resources. Students do not pay tuition fees with education being basically free and funded by the Federal Government. Costs which need to be met by the student in the Graduate Diploma program include purchase of text books and manuals, postage, STD telephone connect time to the mainframe in Geelong and a University general service fee of approximately $50. All course materials generated and provided by the University are free to the student.

For the first three years of the Off Campus program, a resource imposed intake quota of 50 students applied. For 1984, with the added availability of two part time tutors, part time secretarial support and additional resources, the quota was extended to 100 students. Each year a number in excess of the quota is enrolled to take into account those students who either do not commence work in the program or through a variety of reasons, drop out in the first eight weeks. This means that mid way through the first semester (the University statistical cut-off date), those continuing are approximately equal to the allocated intake quota. Table 2 supplies figures relating to the Graduate Diploma of Computing in the first 4 years of operation.

Table 2 : New Enrolment Statistics.

	Quota	Applicants	Offers	Acceptances	Mid Semester
1981	50	120	58	50	43
1982	50	270	65	49	46
1983	50	470	60	50	48
1984	100	690	136	124	102

Table 3 gives an indication of the total University enrolment trend over the same 4 year period and compares the trend with the quota allocations made to the Graduate Diploma. Table 4 indicates that this quota imposition and demand for such a course is not peculiar to Deakin University, even though two of the other Victorian Universities offer their Graduate Diplomas on campus.

Table 3 : Deakin University Enrolment Statistics

	1981	1982	1983	1984
On Campus	2254	2126	2202	2302
Off Campus	3024	3253	3576	4043
On Campus % increase	-	-5.7%	3.6%	4.5%
Off Campus % increase	-	7.6%	9.9%	13.1%
% of Off Campus enrolled in Diploma	-	1.4%	1.4%	2.4%

Table 4 :   Victorian Universities application -
             quota ratio for Graduate Diplomas of
             Computing.

	1982	1983
Melbourne University	120/15	120/15
LaTrobe University	300/75	250/75
Deakin University	270/50	420/50

6. SELECTION CRITERIA

To be considered for selection into the quota, a student must be a graduate from a 3 year (at least) full time tertiary program of an approved educational institution. In selecting students, the selection committee may determine and make geographically based decisions in order to maximise the effect of the program from both the student's and University's point of view. Such decisions are influenced by University resource implications and the ability of Telecom to provide STD network data transmission paths free of signal degradation. Subject to these geographical and operational constraints, selection is primarily based on academic merit. Where a group of applicants has equal ranking, preference is given to those who have made previous application, the remaining places being allocated by ballot.

Criteria for selection certainly does not take into account the sex, age or occupation of an applicant. By far, most of the applicants are teachers who require formal qualifications to become qualified in the teaching of computing in schools, this application distribution being reflected in the quota intake. Most other applicants recognise the necessity of a formal education at an appropriate level as they are being enveloped in their careers by ever growing technology and its applications. The percentage distribution as indicated in Table 5 is also typified in similar data for the previous three years.

Table 5 : 1984 Occupation and Age Distribution.

Teacher	54%	20-22	1%
Engineers	15%	23-25	10%
Technical Officers	6%	26-28	19%
Medical Profession	6%	29-31	15%
Legal/Accounting	5%	32-34	21%
Clerks	4%	35-37	15%
Surveyors	3%	38-40	8%
Librarians	3%	40+	11%
Remainder	4%		

                                    Average Age = 32.6

The course content of the Graduate Diploma, its professional recognition and convenient mode of operation are all recognised by students as significant criteria for enrolling in the program. With the average age of students being 32.6 years, they are typically married and face the pressures of establishing a home, providing for and being an active, caring member of a family including young children, being involved in community and social organisations and pursuing a demanding career. Whilst application into the Graduate Diploma is career motivated, work commitments, family pressures and insufficient time are the reasons most often given for withdrawing (see Table 6).

Table 6 : Reasons Given for Withdrawal (1984).

Work commitments/insufficient time	57%
Family commitments	22%
Communication problems	14%
Overseas travel	7%

The increasing retention rate indicated in Table 7 implies that those in the program are doing so through career motivation and are thus dedicating themselves to complete the Diploma. While a retention figure of 76% may seem low, it is certainly better than the 70% retention for all Off Campus programs offerred by the University in 1983.

Table 7 : Graduate Diploma Retention Figures.

	1981	1982	1983	1984
Returning	30	40	55	71
Enrolment	73	86	103	173
Graduating	8	12	9	-
Retention	-	62%	74%	76%

7. CONCLUSION

Deakin University's Graduate Diploma of Computing has been offered in the Off Campus mode for the past four years. During this time a unique approach to computer teaching was pioneered, resulting in a level of expertise and method being developed to take into consideration the changing technology and student needs. This is a process which is constantly being monitored and acted upon. It is evident that there is an overwhelming and growing demand for such vocation oriented programs given the advancements taking place in the workplace, and it is with regret that Deakin University cannot satisfy this demand, the intake quota imposed on the course being resource based. Supplied with the extra manpower, equipment and funds required, the University, using the tried and tested infrastructure already in place, would be in a better position to satisfy student demand and make a significant contribution to the technological advancement within Australian education, commerce and industry.

It can only be hoped that those in control of
the purse strings in educational institutions
(whether they be in Australia or any other
country), can appreciate the trends developing
in this form of education and act quickly to
meet the demands of the community. For
government authorities, educators and education
administrators to ignore new technology, its
uses and the resulting implications it has on
society is both negligent and irresponsible.

COMPUTERS IN EDUCATION, K. Duncan and D. Harris (eds.)
Elsevier Science Publishers B.V. (North-Holland)
© IFIP, 1985

TRAINING AND EDUCATION OF THE USER

Drs. F.H. Lindhout

Ministry of Home Affairs,
Government Training Institute,
Postbox 20011,
2500 EA The Hague,
The Netherlands.

TRAINING AND EDUCATION OF THE USER

User-training is the in-thing for end-users, as well as for managers and material experts. Many organisations are involved with this type of training using various methods of approach. Some are concentrating on computerisation, on the resources made available and on the methods and techniques to be used while others concentrate more on the possible uses, on the organisational consequences of both the management and different categories of users.

Many training courses are presented in the traditional form. These are often open courses allowing the registration of trainees from different companies. Besides this, there is a growing interest in closed courses aimed at a particular company, a company department or a group of employees within a company. This is motivated by a need to relate the automation training courses to the policy and circumstances of that company. Often, a more integral approach toward automation is also required, corresponding to the objectives and culture of that special company.

A new development is taking place within the field of new educational aids. Self-training packages are being developed with increasing frequency, making use of both video and computed aided instruction. Besides this, there is also a growing number of educational packages available in which a micro/home computer is supplied as an integral part. There are also various companies which have allowed their employees to take home a computer complete with software for several months, giving them a chance to become familiar with the new technology.
All in all, many new developments wich raise the question as to which is the best method? Is it one of the methods mentioned above or, more probably, a mixture: and on which conditions is the correct structure of such a mixture dependant?

Besides all these activities, in some countries a more systematic mehod of approach is applied to user training. Recommandations are made, and in some cases even studies are carried out. An example of this is the User-training Working Party in the Netherlands. This working party, which is part of the Netherlands Society for Informatics (NGI), has published several reports concerning user training during the last few years. The second report entitled "What should the user know?" (1981) was presented at the last WCCE conference in Lausanne. The third report entitled "Computer user training: how and to what end?" was published in late 1982.
This report, compiled by more than 20 computer experts, is principally concerned with the instructional objectives and the educational aspects of these training courses. This report was presented at the IFAC/IFIP conference "Training for Tomorrow" (Leyden, the Netherlands, 1983).

This part of the program attempts to initiate a discussion about the various subjects covered above. This with regard to questions related to the content of the user-training courses as well as the form which they take. It will be organised as a panel discussion preceeded by 2 or 3 speakers, each giving their own opinion on the subject in about 5 to 10 minutes (no case treatments), with a view to giving the discussion a good start and making the issue more concrete. The discussion will be led by the chairman of the above mentioned User training Working Party from the Netherlands, Drs. F.H. Lindhout (head of the Government Automation training sector).

Teacher Training

COMPUTERS IN EDUCATION, K. Duncan and D. Harris (eds.)
Elsevier Science Publishers B.V. (North-Holland)
© IFIP, 1985

A SELF-STUDY GUIDE IN COMPUTER LITERACY FOR TEACHERS

Sally Vogel and Robert Aiken*

Oak Ridge City Schools
Oak Ridge, Tennessee

The development of a self-study guide for teachers based on a Concerns-Based Model for
the delivery of inservice is presented. This prototype is proposed as a means for
delivering cost effective on-going training so teachers can make effective use of
microcomputers. Emphasis is placed on relating activities to teachers' assessed
concerns and interests. The materials are arranged so teachers can proceed on their
own time at their own pace based on their background and level of motivation.
Procedures for evaluating the prototype are suggested.

1. INTRODUCTION

Most teachers in the United States have had
little or no computer training. However, schools
are purchasing computer hardware at an incredible
rate, and pushed by parents and students, administrators are expecting teachers, at the very
least, to use educational software programs with
their students. The inservice job is immense
and there aren't enough trainers or training
programs to go around, nor is there enough
money to pay teachers for the training time. In
fact a recent study by Market Data Retrieval,
Inc. of Westport, Connecticut, has shown that the
number of schools using microcomputers in the
United States for instruction doubled in 1983.
Talmis, a Chicago based market research firm,
predicts that by 1988 there will be two million
microcomputers in the U. S. public schools with
an average of 20 per school. Thus a means for
providing introductory material regarding the
use of microcomputers to a large number of teachers is greatly needed. This paper discusses
one possible means for doing this.

Since adults seem to need to practice skills in
a safe situation before using them on the job
[Joyce and Showers (1980); Dormant, (1980)], the
authors emphasize this approach. This seems to
be especially true for teachers who don't like
to make mistakes in front of their peers, let
alone in front of their students.

Some authors have suggested that a computer be
made available in the school for teachers to use
in privacy during their planning periods. Another suggestion is that schools loan computers
for use at home on weekends and/or during school
vacations. This latter strategy seems to be a
good idea for several reasons including:

-the time teachers spend at home learning
 saves the schools a large part of the

expense involved in providing inservice
training - paying for teachers' time!

-teachers can better schedule time to use the
system

-they can learn on their own without comments
from administrators, teachers and students,
and

-they can work with fewer interruptions
(hopefully!)

2. RELATED RESEARCH

2.1 Effective Inservice Education

Joyce and Showers (1980) have identified five
components of inservice training and have
investigated the impact of these on teachers.
The components are:

1) presentation of theory;
2) modeling or demonstration of skills;
3) practice in simulated and classroom settings;
4) structured and open-ended feedback about
   performance;
5) coaching for application (hands-on,
   in-classroom assistance with the transfer
   of skills and strategies to the classroom.

They looked at how each of these components
affected:

a) awareness of a particular topic;
b) acquisition of concepts and knowledge
   about the topic;
c) development of skills; transfer of skills
   to the classroom.

They found that:

-presentation of theory and modeling (1 and
 2) affected awareness and knowledge (a and
 b) but had little affect on skills or transfer (c).

*Robert Aiken, Computer Science Department,
 Temple University

-practice under simulated conditions (small groups or practice with peers) (3) seemed to be an efficient way to acquire skills (b) and some teachers transferred these to the classroom (c);

-structured feedback (4), that is, regularly utilizing a system of observation (by self, peer, or supervisor) and reflecting on the results of the observation can affect the teacher's awareness of his/her practice and also impact skills and their use in the classroom (c);

-assistance from a peer, consultant, or supervisor is needed by some teachers (5) to develop a specific plan to utilize a new approach (c).

The research by Joyce and Showers suggests that it is best to include all components in a training program since this assures that the maximum number of teachers will progress to the transfer level. It is only after this level that any impact on children can be expected.

2.2 Microcomputer Inservice Programs

Although there are some articles on providing inservice education for teachers about microcomputers [Bork (1981; Archer (1981) ; Hopping (1983); Sadowski (1983); Electronic Learning (1983-84)] they are, for the most part, recommendations for topics to be included or descriptions of activities.

Most articles about providing microcomputer inservice education for teachers assume the familiar delivery system of a trainer and a series of one or more workshops [Electronic Learning (1983-84); Sadowski (1983)]. Bork (1981) strongly recommends using the computer itself as the vehicle for providing training. He does not, however, address the question of teachers' readiness to learn the material he would include in the six topics he suggests for inclusion in a computer inservice sequence. He does say that not all teachers will want to cover everything and that they should be encouraged to select on the basis of interest.

In a recent letter, Bork (1984) says that a project designed to identify teacher characteristics associated with successful uses of computers found few such uses. In fact, he and a colleague found that "current classroom usage is often a tragedy."

An article by Wells and Bitter (1982) discusses a four-week summer institute that was presented at the University of Arizona. The article includes a set of recommendations for changes in the program based on their experience, but it does not assess the effectiveness of the institute in terms of how microcomputers were later used in schools. The authors do suggest increasing the amount of time spent on user skills such

as loading, saving and running programs, as well as using educational software and demonstrating class management programs such as Genis I or programming techniques. The authors go on to say that special programming classes should be offered for teachers who want to learn this skill.

2.3 The Process of Innovation Adoption

The previous recommendations might have been anticipated, if the authors had used a "Concerns-Based Model for the Delivery of Inservice" developed by Hall, Loucks & Hord (1980) as shown in Appendix 1. The model rests on the assumptions that change is:

A process
Made by individuals first
A highly personal experience
Entails developmental growth in feeling and skill

All teachers, both preservice and practicing, go through a developmental sequence in adopting any innovation. Different activities are appropriate for each Stage of Concern. Appendix 2 summarizes some of the work of Hord and Loucks (1980) showing types of training related to each stage.

Leary's (1983) research has demonstrated that an inservice program geared to teachers' assessed Stages of Concern (SoC) has a predictable influence on their Stages of Concern about an innovation, their Level of Use (LoU) of that innovation (See appendix 3) and the way the innovation is adapted for use by the adopting teachers (Configuration of the Innovation).

There is some evidence that changes in attitudes reflected in Stage of Concern, precede changes in behavior evidenced in Level of Use of an innovation (Leary, 1983). At both the early and later stages of an innovation adoption, the Concerns of the adopters and their Levels of Use are related. In the middle ranges LoU cannot be predicted from SoC. Hall, Loucks, and Hord (1979) state that, "Only in a well-planned and supported change effort will Stage of Concern 4 and above concerns become more intense. Otherwise, either Stage of Concern 3 concerns remain high, or all stages gradually decrease with no apparent peak, thus indicating relatively little concern."

Dormant (1980) lists some of the mistakes which can lead to the rejection of an innovation. Rejection may occur if:

-stages are skipped;

-the sequence of training activities is not the same as the sequence of SoC (e.g., providing skills training before giving a demonstration of how the innovation can be used;

-not enough time is provided at each stage;

individual differences are ignored in the rate at which teachers move through the stages.

If teachers are to use computers successfully with students they will have to reach the higher Stages of Concern about the use of microcomputers in schools and also be able to use them in ways that demonstrate that they are at the routine or higher Levels of Use. To reach these stages, the inservice programs designed for classroom teachers need to be geared to each teacher's current Stage of Concern. Provisions must be made for appropriate activity for that Stage so each teacher can progress to the next stage as he/she is ready. Teachers will vary in:

-the amount of previous training and experience that they have had with computers;

-their level of interest in and/or fear of computing;

-the rate at which they learn;

-their approaches to teaching students.

An individualized approach is needed for training teachers just as it is appropriate for other learners. To the greatest extent possible, this inservice should be self-deliverable so that teachers can move at their own rates and so the greatest number of teachers can be reached. In addition, the cost of inservice materials needs to be kept at a minimum if both impoverished school systems and/or individual teachers are to be willing participants.

3. A CONCERNS-BASED SELF-STUDY GUIDE

The authors have developed a prototype for a self-study guide that will be used by teachers during the 1984-85 school year. Specifically it will be tested and revised by teachers in Oak Ridge, Tennessee, where the school system has recently established a procedure for loaning computers to teachers and where a computer will be set aside for teacher use in each building during this next school year.

The Guide directs the teacher user to certain activities on the basis of his or her responses to two questionnaires. The first is the thirty-five item Stages of Concern Questionnaire (see Appendix 4 for a sample of this questionnaire). It can be used for any innovation, but in this project teachers will respond about microcomputers. The teacher then follows scoring directions which include determining the amount of concern he/she has at each Stage and determining the specific Stage he/she is at. The Research and Development Center for Teacher Education at the University of Austin in Texas will soon make this questionnaire available in a

computer-based form that will be scored for the user.[1]

Next the teacher will respond to the Awareness Checklist (see Figure 1). First the teacher will place a check next to the statements which describe conditions the teacher would like to exist in his/her classroom. Next the teacher will check those conditions that do exist. If there is a check in the first column (would like) but not in the second (existing conditions) teachers will be directed to a topic that is correlated with their statements "would like for condition to exist." The Awareness Checklist is designed to tie the inservice to teachers' current classroom interests (see Stage 0 AWARENESS in Appendix 2). Also, it should inform teachers about possible uses for microcomputers.

Please put a check on the first blank in front of each of the statements below if it is something you would like to have happening in your classroom. After you have completed the checklist go back and fill in the second blank in front of each item if it is something which is already done effectively in your classroom.

WOULD   ALREADY
LIKE   EXISTS

____ ____   Student answers are corrected immediately. (Microcomputer and Computer Managed Instruction)

____ ____   Directions are repeated for those that need them but not for others (Microcomputer and Selection of Software)

____ ____   The number of examples on assignments are varied on the basis of student need.

____ ____   The amount of time students have to do examples is varied.

____ ____   Each student is given enough examples so that each practices until they are giving correct answers.

____ ____   Each student gets enough instructional time.

____ ____   Student work is often corrected without the teacher having to do it.

____ ____   Students use instructional and supplementary learning materials on their own which cover the same content that is taught in the classroom.

____ ____   Students can apply their learning in life-like situations.

____ ____   Students have opportunities to examine the consequences of their choices without risk to themselves or others.

____ ____   Students accurately follow written directions.

____ ____   Students are aware of ways in which the world is being changed by technology.

____ ____   Students locate resources and organize information effectively.

____ ____   Student written work is of good quality and neat appearance.

____ ____   Students use a variety of strategies for solving problems.

____ ____   Students locate and correct their own mistakes.

____ ____   Students analyze data they collect to support or disconfirm their predictions.

____ ____   A variety of materials are available for practice that do not require excessive amounts of teacher time to prepare.

Figure 1 : Microcomputer Awareness Checklist

---

[1] A scoring program is already available for the Apple II, II+, and IIe systems. Specific information can be obtained from the senior author.

At the present time, the following topics are planned for inclusion in the guide:

- Computer Literacy (including history and social impact)
- The Microcomputer: Components, Capabilities, and Educational Uses (including keyboard, peripherals, branching, drills, tutorial, games, simulations)
- Software Selection and Evaluation
- Computer Managed Instruction
- Management and Utility Programs for Teachers
- Computer as Tool (word processing, data base management, electronic spreadsheet)
- Designing and Writing Computer-Based Educational Materials (discussed in Figure 2)
- Programming (including reading and understanding programs and algorithm development)
- LOGO (beginning and intermediate)
- BASIC (beginning and intermediate)
- Pascal (beginning and perhaps, intermediate)

The topics are quite inclusive since this guide is designed to be used by teachers at all Stages of Concern about microcomputer use. Since teachers will progress through different stages and will wish information on different topics, the guide needs to be broad. A search for software and other materials related to these topics is continuing but other than material from the Minnesota Educational Computing Consortium not much has yet been found.

It may be that certain topics are more appropriate for certain Stages of Concern than others. As more teachers use the guide and more modules are completed, specific topics may be suggested for certain stages. At this time, no evidence is available to make a judgment about which topics may be appropriate for the stages. At some point the checklist may be produced in a computer-based form and descriptions of the topics will be provided on the basis of the responses of the teachers.

Figure 2 is an example of one module in the Concerns-Based Microcomputer Inservice Self-Study Guide prototype. For each Stage of Concern there is, if available, at least one computer program or program writing activity that is selected or designed to be an appropriate activity for that stage. Some of the programs and accompanying documentation are available to school systems and hence to teachers at minimal cost from the Minnesota Educational Computing Consortium (MECC). Other materials are in the public domain. Future work will include an examination of how well the various programs correlate with the different Stages of Concern.

In addition, the success of the program will be measured in two ways. First, the Stage of Concern can be determined. Second, a Level of Use interview will be conducted with teachers choosing to test the prototype both before their use and at the end of the year. A change in Level of Use will be related to training since LoU remains the same unless there is an inter-

vention (Leary, 1983).

AWARENESS
   Activity: See if someone in your school has written a computer program to teach a concept or provide skill practice? Ask that teacher about why they wrote the program and how he/she has used it. Ask the teacher to let you try the program.
INFORMATIONAL
   Activity: Use the Designing and Writing a Computer-Based Tutorial diskette to see how a lesson you might develop would look.
   Activity: Review the checklist of types of computer-based lessons and advantages of using computer-based instructional materials.
PERSONAL
   Activity: Practice sheet such as SkillMaster 3: The Computer as a Tool for the Teacher (Electronic Learning, October 1983 p. 90, 5b)
   Activity: Review examples of teacher-made programs available from the State clearinghouses. (Some specific ones may be suggested.)
   Activity: Read description of the process of developing a computer-based lesson to get some idea of the time it takes and other alternatives.
MANAGEMENT
   Activity: Use CoPILOT diskettes that are included with the SuperPILOT package.
   Activity: Use Designing Instructional Computing Materials and Design diskettes I and II available from the Minnesota Educational Computing Consortium.
   Activity: Read What Makes a Good Educational Program, by Dan Isaacson, 1982.
   Activity: Write your own lesson. Ask the teacher who wrote the computer-based lesson you saw earlier to help you if you get stuck.
CONSEQUENCE
   Activity: Contact your local computer store to see if they know of others who are writing educational software. Join or create such a group.
   Activity: Subscribe to a magazine that includes programs of interest.
   Activity: Find a computing conference you would like to attend and request district support to go. Offer to help others when you return.
COLLABORATION
   Activity: Write a computer-based lesson with some other teachers. Divide up the work: perhaps the art teacher can design the graphics, the reading specialist can help with working to maintain the correct reading level, etc.
   Activity: Demonstrate a computer-based lesson you have written for others.
REFOCUSING
   Activity: Volunteer for a systemwide computer committee.

Figure 2 : Designing and Writing Computer-Based Educational Materials Module

The senior author has written a program in Super-PILOT for the Apple II systems which is a demonstration of how to write a computer-based lesson that is educationally sound.[2] The program has the teacher develop the beginning of a lesson during the course of the tutorial by taking their responses to questions and execut-

---

[2] This program may be obtained from the senior author by sending a blank 5¼" floppy diskette and a self-addressed stamped return mailer for the diskette to Sally Vogel, Computer Education Specialist, Oak Ridge Teacher Center, Oak Ridge City Schools, Oak Ridge, TN 37830. Note on the package: SuperPILOT Tutorial.

ing them as a short SuperPILOT program. The end result is a program which allows the teacher or someone else to actually use this lesson (prepared by the teacher) without the teacher having to write any code. Topics such as starting with objectives, using cues and making sure the student practices a correct response are included. This program is not designed to help teachers develop the skills necessary for writing software but rather to involve them in seeing how a computer tutorial can be created using their own familiar content.

The Guide suggests other activities for each Stage of Concern. Often these involve talking with others or sharing information and ideas with them. Such activities help to develop and maintain the supportive environment needed to continue the change process. As many resources as possible are being explored to find appropriate activities for each stage and topic. Emphasis is on locating software that stands alone, but some print and low cost audio-visual materials are included. Material is not included which is:

1) not appropriate for a particular state/ topic block;
2) too costly for use by a teacher;
3) inconvenient (such as 16mm film) or
4) not of interest to teachers who have previewed it.

4. CONCLUSION

There is a need for an effective, ongoing inservice effort to improve teachers' implementation of microcomputer use in schools. The inservice activity must be related to the teacher's stage in the process of adopting the use of microcomputers in his/her instruction. Although there are many inservice programs presently being conducted about microcomputers, there seem to be none which first determine what concerns teachers have about microcomputer use and then fit the activities to these concerns. Research cited earlier would suggest that inservice programs that do not provide this match will result in teachers only reaching the lower levels of use of microcomputers and at these levels there is likely to be little or no impact on students. In some cases there may actually be some negative impact.

To promote continued growth in the process of the adoption of microcomputers in schools the inservice effort needs to be sustained over a period of time (usually three to five years). Most schools cannot afford a full-time computer coordinator or the cost of consultants for a variety of inservice offerings. One inservice course is not appropriate for all teachers unless they are all at the same stage in the process of change. Also, most schools will not purchase an expensive commercially produced set of computer programs for teacher training. Even if they were willing, multiple copies of such

material would be necessary if all teachers in a system were to have access to the software.

Thus, this paper discusses the development of a self-study inservice guide which attempts to meet the needs just cited, that is to provide a means for organizing widely available resources that can be duplicated for use in schools and can be updated with new (hopefully teacher created) computer-based materials. In this way one can establish a cost-effective, ongoing, in-house microcomputer inservice which is available to any and all teachers whenever they have time to use it.

5. ACKNOWLEDGEMENT

The authors would like to thank the Research and Development Center for Teacher Education at The University of Texas, Austin, for permission to use their material in this article.

BIBLIOGRAPHY

Archer, Doug. Microcomputer CAI-ASE: An In-Service Module. Computer Assisted Instruction: Applications for Special Education. Paper presented at the Annual Conference of the Association for Educational Data Systems (1981: Minneapolis, Minn). ERIC document ED 226 718

Bork, Alfred. Computer Literacy for Teachers. In Robert J. Seidel, Ronald E. Anderson and Beverly Hunter (Eds). National Computer Literacy Goals for 1985 Conference (1980: Reston, Va.) Computer Literacy: issues and directions for 1985. New York. Academic Press, 1982

Bork, Alfred. Letter of May 25, 1984 to the senior author.

Dormant, Diane. A Trainer's Guide to Change Agentry. Unpublished, 1980.

Electronic Learning, EL's In-Service Workshops, Parts I-VII. September, 1983 to April 1984 issues.

Hall, G.E., Loucks, S.F. and Hord, S.M. Concerns-Based Consulting Skills Workshop. CBAM Project. Research and Development Center for Teacher Education, University of Texas at Austin, 1979.

Heines, Jesse M., Screen Design Strategies for Computer Aided Instruction, Billerica, MA. Digital Press, 1983

Hopping, Lorraine, Do-It-Yourself In-Service Training Packages. Electronic Learning, 1983 vol.2 no. 5 pp. 38, 43.

Hord, S.M. and Loucks, S.F., A Concerns-Based Model for the Delivery of Inservice. Research and Development Center for Teacher Education, University of Texas at Austin, 1980.

Issacson, Dan, What Makes A Good Educational Program? Fresno, CA. School and Home Courseware Inc., 1982.

Joyce, Bruce and Showers, Beverly, Improving Inservice Training: The Messages of Research. Educational Leadership, 1980 vol. 37 no. 5 pp. 369-385.

Leary, Jim, The Effectiveness of Concerns-Based Staff Development in Facilitating Curriculum Implementation. Paper presented at the Annual Conference of American Educational Research Association, Montreal, April 1983 ERIC document ED 231 788.

Minnesota Educational Computing Consortium. St. Paul, MN.
     Designing Instructional Computing Material, 1983
     Instructional Computing Presentations, 1983
     The Three R's of Microcomputing (The Glass Computer), 1983.

Sadowski, Barbara, A Model for Preparing Teachers to Teach with the Microcomputer. Arithmetic Teacher, February, 1983 pp. 24-25 62-63.

Wells, M. and Bitter, G., The First Step in Utilizing Computers in Education: Preparing Computer Literate Teachers. 1982 ERIC document ED 218 703

Appendix 1 STAGES OF CONCERN ABOUT THE INNOVATION

0 AWARENESS: Little concern about or involvement with the innovation in indicated.

1 INFORMATIONAL: A general awareness of the innovation and interest in learning more detail about it is indicated. The person seems to be unworried about himself/herself in relation to the innovation. She/he is interested in substantive aspects of the innovation in a selfless manner such as general characteristics, effects, and requirements for use.

2 PERSONAL: Individual is uncertain about the demands of the innovation, his/her inadequacy to meet those demands, and his/her role with the innovation. This includes analysis of his/her role in relation to the reward structure of the organization, decision-making and consideration of potential conflicts with existing structures or personal commitment. Financial or status implications of the program for self and colleagues may also be reflected.

3 MANAGEMENT: Attention is focused on the processes and tasks of using the innovation and the best use of information and resources. Issues related to efficiency, organizing, managing, scheduling, and time demands are utmost.

4 CONSEQUENCE: Attention focuses on impact of the innovation of students in his/her immediate sphere of influence. The focus is on relevance of the innovation for students, evaluation of student outcomes, including performance and competencies, and changes needed to increase student outcomes.

5 COLLABORATION: The focus is on coordination and cooperation with others regarding use of the innovation.

6 REFOCUSING: The focus is on exploration of more universal benefits from the innovation, including the possiblity of major changes or replacement with a more powerful alternative. Individual has definite ideas about alternatives to the proposed or existing form of the innovation.

Appendix 3 LEVELS OF USE OF THE INNOVATION

0 NONUSE:	Stage in which the user has little or no knowledge of the innovation, no involvement with the innovation, and is doing nothing toward becoming involved.
I ORIENTATION	State in which the user has recently acquired or is acquiring information about the innovation and/or has recently explored its value orientation and its demands upon users and user system.
II PREPARATION	State in which the user is preparing for first use of the innovation.
III MECHANICAL USE	State in which the user focuses most effort on the short-term, day-to-day use of the innovation with little time for reflection. Changes in use are made more to meet user needs than client needs. The user is primarily engaged in a step-wise attempt to master the tasks required to use the innovation, often resulting in disjointed and superficial use.
IVA ROUTINE	Use of the innovation is stabilized. Few, if any changes are being made in ongoing use. Little preparation or thought is being given to improving innovation use or its consequences.
IVB REFINEMENT	State in which the user varies the use of the innovation to increase the impact on clients within the immediate sphere of influence. Variations are based on knowledge of both short and long-term consequences for clients.
V INTEGRATION	State in which the user is combining own efforts to use the innovation with related activities of colleagues to achieve a collective impact on clients within their common sphere of influence.
VI RENEWAL	State in which the user re-evaluates the quality of use of the innovation, seeks major modifications of or alternatives to present innovation to achieve increased impact on clients, examines new developments in the field, and explores new goals for self and the system.

Appendix 2 APPROPRIATE TRAINING ACTIVITIES BY STAGES OF CONCERN

Stage 0: AWARENESS

Tie the innovation to an area that the teacher is concerned about.
Encourage the teacher to talk with others about the program.
Share information in hopes of arousing some interest.

Stage 1: INFORMATIONAL

Share descriptive information: brochures, short media presentation, conversation.
Contrast what teacher is now doing with what he or she might do if using innovation.
Provide opportunity to visit a site where innovation is in use.

Stage 2: PERSONAL

Establish rapport, encourage and assure the teacher she/he can do it.
Clarify how innovation relates to other priorities.
Introduce innovation gradually.
Provide personal support through easy access to facilitator.

Stage 3: MANAGEMENT

Provide hands-on practice with innovative materials.
Provide classroom management and organizational tips.
Ask users to share successful and unsuccessful practices.
Establish buddy system/consulting pair or support group.

Stage 4: CONSEQUENCE

Encourage and reinforce regularly.
Send written information about topics of interest.
Advertise the teacher's potential for sharing skills with others.
Send teachers to a conference or workshop on topic of interest and usefulness.

Stage 5: COLLABORATION

Arrange a meeting for idea exchange.
Provide time and support on the school level for collaboration.
Facilitate training in organization development skills.
Use teacher to assist others in use of the innovation.

Stage 6: REFOCUSING

Involve teacher as trainer
Encourage and facilitate teacher to take action related to his or her concern.
Provide resources to access other materials and encourage to pilot test other programs or ideas.

Appendix 4 SAMPLE PAGE FROM STAGES OF CONCERN QUESTIONNAIRE

0	1	2	3	4	5	6	7
Irrelevant	Not true of me now		Somewhat true of me now			Very true of me now	

1. I am concerned about students' attitudes toward this innovation. 0 1 2 3 4 5 6 7

2. I now know of some other approaches that might work better. 0 1 2 3 4 5 6 7

3. I don't even know what the innovation is. 0 1 2 3 4 5 6 7

4. I am concerned about not having enough time to organize myself each day. 0 1 2 3 4 5 6 7

5. I would like to help other faculty in their use of the innovation. 0 1 2 3 4 5 6 7

6. I have a very limited knowledge about the innovation. 0 1 2 3 4 5 6 7

7. I would like to know the effect of reorganization on my professional status. 0 1 2 3 4 5 6 7

8. I am concerned about conflict between my interests and responsibilities. 0 1 2 3 4 5 6 7

9. I am concerned about revising my use of the innovation 0 1 2 3 4 5 6 7

10. I would like to develop working relationships with both our faculty and outside faculty using this innovation. 0 1 2 3 4 5 6 7

11. I am concerned about how the innovation affects students. 0 1 2 3 4 5 6 7

12. I am not concerned about this innovation. 0 1 2 3 4 5 6 7

13. I would like to know who will make the decisions in the new system. 0 1 2 3 4 5 6 7

14. I would like to discuss the possibility of using the innovation. 0 1 2 3 4 5 6 7

15. I would like to know what resources are available if we decide to adopt this innovation. 0 1 2 3 4 5 6 7

16. I am concerned about my inability to manage all the innovation requires. 0 1 2 3 4 5 6 7

17. I would like to know how my teaching or administration is supposed to change. 0 1 2 3 4 5 6 7

18. I would like to familiarize other departments or persons with the progress of this new approach. 0 1 2 3 4 5 6 7

COMPUTERS IN EDUCATION, K. Duncan and D. Harris (eds.)
Elsevier Science Publishers B.V. (North-Holland)
© IFIP, 1985

BRIDGING THE GAP : POST AWARENESS TEACHER TRAINING

Ann Jones, Jenny Preece and John Wood

Institute of Educational Technology
The Open University
Walton Hall
Milton Keynes
England

1.   INTRODUCTION

The term 'Awareness' is commonly used to
describe the aims of first level training courses
in new technology for practising or trainee
teachers. Providing such courses is an important aspect of introducing computers into schools,
but the complexity and magnitude of this training task have made it more difficult to achieve
than installing hardware and software. This
paper describes an attempt by the Open University
'Micros in Schools' project to provide not only
a first level 'Awareness' course but also
several second level courses. If there is little
consensus about the content and methodology for
'Awareness' courses there is even less about
what should come next; indeed it is likely that
a variety of approaches are necessary to meet the
various needs of the teaching profession.
Within the Micros in Schools project, there will
be four courses which can be studied, in any
order, after the 'Awareness' course. Two of
them: 'Inside Microcomputers' and 'Discovering
Microelectronics' are concerned with technical-
ities of hardware and may therefore be considered to be aiming at a specialised audience.
This paper considers the other two: 'Micros in
Action in the Classroom' (MAC) and 'Educational Software' (ES) which are aimed at a general
audience of teachers.

All these courses are distance-learning packs
and provide the student support demanded by that
medium; for example key presses are clearly
identified, and likely error messages are carefully explained and corrected. The overall
project design and production philosophy are
described in O'Shea (1984).

MAC and ES differ in their aims: ES aims to
develop teachers' understanding and critical
faculties with respect to software design and
MAC does the same but with respect to its uses
in the classroom. They differ more fundamentally in the way they capitalise upon teachers'
perceived needs, experience and expectations of
the course to achieve their aims.

For each pack the major issue is concerned with
whether to start with teachers' existing
practice and develop new or theoretical issues
from that context or to present the necessary
theoretical material prior to examining its
practical implications. Realistically this

becomes a question of acquiring a balance between
these two approaches.

2. THE ISSUES

Producing packs for second level training raises
issues which are quite different from those which
need to be considered in basic awareness training. The main difference is that awareness
training is aimed at an audience of teachers who
have no experience of using microcomputers, and
so is concerned with how to build up teachers'
confidence and competence with the technology.
The emphasis, therefore, is on the mechanics of
getting the machine working, and this acts as a
bridge between the other two elements of training: building on teachers' own experience, and
drawing in 'educational perspectives'. Teachers
need to at least be able to use a microcomputer
before they can engage in debates such as 'how
could program x be used with class y?' Such
questions are part of what we are calling educational perspectives. This relationship between
the three aspects of awareness training are
shown in figure 1.

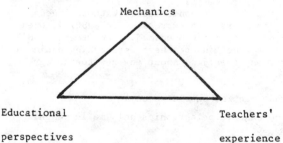

Figure 1 : Three aspects of awareness training.

The problem in post-awareness training is that
teaching about the mechanics of the system is no
longer a major issue. The emphasis therefore,
shifts to focus upon the other two strands. For
example, in both of the courses that we shall
discuss, we wanted the teachers to develop a
sound framework from which to make informed
judgements. In the case of the Educational Software pack, the aim is to help teachers to develop
software selection skills. The Micros in Action
in the Classroom pack, on the other hand, aims to
develop a framework from which teachers can plan
and evaluate the use of software in the classroom. In order to develop the frameworks necessary to make these judgements we needed to bridge

the gap between discussing educational perspectives, and the teachers' experience. Focussing on educational perspectives, for example, might lead a history teacher to ask questions such as: 'what kinds of skills and knowledge will my pupils develop through interrogating a census data base compared to the way I would usually teach the topic?' (MAC) and, 'what features make this information retrieval program more suitable than that one for my pupils?' (ES).

In post awareness courses there is a tension between training about educational perspectives and drawing on teachers' own experiences. It is this tension which raises questions about the balance between theory and practise, and how they are introduced and integrated, which is discussed in relation to the MAC and ES packs. Before we do that however, we shall describe the structure and underlying pedagogy of the Awareness pack which forms the foundation for these two packs.

3.   THE AWARENESS PACK

The Awareness Pack is designed for teachers who have no knowledge or expertise in using microcomputers in the classroom. The aims, as stated in the pack, are to train teachers to:

° connect up, switch on and run a microcomputer;

° use educational material on the microcomputer;

° evaluate the educational potential of the microcomputer;

° understand enough computer jargon to be able to communicate with a local computer expert.

These aims correspond closely with the needs that teachers were expressing in 1980/81, when the pack was being produced. (See Preece, 1981). At this time many teachers were asking basic and pertinent questions about the new technology, such as:

° what machine should we buy?

° how can microelectronics help me in teaching my subject?

° what kind of software is available and how should I use it?

The question about which machine to buy was, for many teachers, the most important issue of all, and one which the authors of the pack made no attempt to answer. It was clear even at this stage that a government or local educational authority policy would be formed to deal with this problem and, in fact, both were developed. The other questions were all given serious consideration, and a key objective of the production course team was to address these concerns. We believed that the best approach for doing this was through the knowledge and skills that the teachers had acquired in their professional training and experience. In other words our foremost consideration was that we were preparing

materials for professionals who needed training in order to get the best out of the technology but who already had a well established training in educational practice. In order to capitalise upon the teachers' expertise, we realised, at a very early stage, that the teachers needed to be helped to acquire confidence and competence to use the new technology effectively, and that the only way to do this was through extensive 'hands-on' experience. The three column format, boxed key presses, and extensive trouble-shooting guide were, therefore, developed to provide a high degree of 'hand-holding' in order to facilitate the teachers' development of the basic skills, knowledge and confidence needed to use the equipment. Like all Micros in Schools packs the Awareness Pack has a study book which directs the teacher through the pack and introduces basic concepts. In this pack the study book also introduces the first hands-on activities and a project book provides extended hands-on experience in the form of two long projects (taking 4 hours and 6 hours respectively) which are based on a queuing simulation and an information retrieval program. Disks containing the software are provided with the pack and there is a book of short case studies written by teachers to provide background information about how different kinds of software are currently being used by practising teachers.

On first impressions, the Awareness pack appears to have a high 'practice:theory ratio' because of the apparent predominance of 'hands-on' work, but in fact all the activities are firmly embedded in an 'educational perspective'. This approach requires the teachers to use their professional judgement to assess the potential of the software and technology for their own teaching and also provides a firm foundation for raising theoretical issues concerned with the educational philosophy underlying the activities.

The role of the computer and the educational potential of the software are given high priority and issues about software design, the integration and interaction of pupils, teachers and machines are also considered. Although the software included in the pack is not sophisticated, it is designed to exemplify some features of friendly, flexible, well designed software, and the teachers' attention is drawn to these design principles.

In essence therefore, the role of the Awareness Pack is to take teachers from a basis of 'no knowledge' and to provide a foundation upon which to develop the skills and knowledge necessary to select software and to plan and evaluate its use in the classroom. The two post-awareness packs 'Educational Software' and 'Micros in Action in the Classroom' deal with these two aspects and are discussed in the following two sections of this paper.

4. MICROS IN ACTION IN THE CLASSROOM

The audience for this course is all teachers
who have followed our Awareness course or an
equivalent course. The aims of the course are
to increase understanding of the range of
applications of computers within the classroom,
and the potential of microcomputers to support and
enhance teaching and learning styles and the
logistical problems associated with achieving
this potential. This may be paraphrased as
'learning to become critical users of computers'.

To realise these aims the course team needed to
shift the training emphasis. Teachers often
perceive that their need is for greater technical expertise but the aim of this course was to
focus on pedagogical, cognitive and curriculum
issues with hardware and software taking an
explicit but secondary role. These are, of
course, areas in which teachers possess considerable professional expertise and it is arguable
to what extent those skills need further
development to cope with the impact of new
technologies. The reactions of teachers who
tested the pack during its development and early
users support our belief that, far from feeling
patronised, the users of the pack were pleased
to be working from this familiar territory.

The pack consists of the following items:

° Study Book - containing the discussion and
  exercises;

° Case Studies - classroom experiences of 29
  teachers;

° Activity Book, software and Program Notes -
  to support the practical work;

° Video and Audio Tapes and associated Notes -
  showing parts of another 8 lessons.

The majority of the discussion and exercises
within the Study Book has been based on the
Case Studies. These were written by teachers
who were contacted by the course team. The pupil
age, subject, teaching style and aims described
within the studies varies, the only common
element in all the studies being the use of
computers. We feel that real classroom case
studies can provide an accessible starting
point for the students but were careful to
ensure that their diversity was used to positive
effect and to discourage students from using
only those case studies where the classroom
parameters matched their own. Typically the
Study Book demands that the student reads three
or four of the studies and analyses the difference
and similarities with respect to the role of the
computer. This technique is used to develop the
following areas (amongst others):

° Motivational, social and emotional benefits,

° The computer as simplifier,

° Children as problem solvers,

° Teaching versus learning,

° Classroom organisation and grouping,

° The teacher's role,

° School-wide development.

Video case studies are used in a similar way to
support work on learning style, group dynamics
and classroom management. These materials are
therefore starting with existing practice and,
by directed analysis, helping teachers to develop
a theoretical framework to apply to their own
situations. But is such a framework, however
carefully developed, sufficient? For several
important reasons the course team decided that
teachers needed to be given practical experiences
and throughout the course of study the teachers
are referred to tutorial sessions in the 'Activity Book' using the software we have provided.
(The software includes a Logo interpreter, a
versatile data-handling program, a simple 'word
processor' and other programs).

The first reason for integrating these types of
activities into the work with case studies was
to allow the students to gain the confidence and
competence to use the software in their own
classrooms and generate personal case studies to
augment and enhance the ones supplied. They are
encouraged to do so at the end of the practical
sessions and even, at one point, asked to
classify their experiences using the same categ-
orisations and format as is used in the Study
Book. This is an iterative process which, we
would argue, supports the modification of teaching styles. This contrasts with attempts to use
computer technology to affect rapid and dramatic
changes, in the curriculum or in teaching styles,
without such support. Secondly, many important
issues, raised by several of the case studies
and considered in the Study Book, are generated
by powerful software 'tools' such as Logo and
QUEST (the data-handler). We needed to ensure
that our students had a real understanding of
this type of software.

Thirdly, we felt that there was an opportunity to
allow teachers to experience learning situations
similar to those of their pupils. We use this
experience within the course to provide a personal
reference point for the study of learning styles
and teachers' roles. (There was, of course, an
insurmountable difficulty providing any range
of teacher intervention strategies from the
printed page, which was most apparent in the
early Logo sessions; despite entreaties to
explore with Logo and various attempts to be a
'non-interventionist' printed page, many students
are motivated to move on to the next part!)

Developing theoretical work from the practical
case studies is, then, the underlying philosophy
of this course. The computer-based activities
act not only to support, but also to drive this
development.

5. EDUCATIONAL SOFTWARE

'Educational Software' is designed to give some

insights into the nature of educational software
and how it is produced. If the aims of 'Micros
in Action in the Classroom' can be paraphrased
as learning to become critical users of computers,
then ES's aim can be paraphrased as helping
teachers to become critical selectors of software.

Its other aims include:

° providing an appreciation of fundamental
  programming concepts,

° introducing some principles underlying
  educational software design,

° helping to develop an appreciation of which
  kinds of software are suited to which
  learning tasks.

Like MAC the only prerequisite for this pack is
to have studied the Awareness Pack or have
equivalent experience.

To what extent does this pack address teachers'
perceived needs? There is widespread agreement
that the main problem in this area is the
paucity of good educational software, and the
resulting difficulty in selecting it from the
heterogenous range of available software. There
is a key question which must be asked and it is:
how can teachers be trained so that they will
develop the necessary selection skills. Whilst
many teachers claim that what they need is more
technical skills and more and better software,
we believe that being able to judge the educational value of software without being prejudi-
ced by the technical whizardry and glossy
graphics is more valuable! This depends on
developing a sound understanding of the
principles underlying the program, which in turn
requires an appreciation of program structure
and design, and of the potential application of
the microcomputer.

Briefly, the route through the Educational Software pack is as follows:

° Introduction.

° Case study - looking in detail at one educational program.

° Programming - how educational software is
  designed and written introducing programming
  concepts, - (mainly using LOGO).

° Styles of educational software - Introducing
  different kinds of educational programs, how
  they're written, and what they're used for.

° Selecting Educational Software - Developing
  criteria for selecting educational software,
  by looking at commercial software.

° Developing educational software - by examining
  how educational software is produced in
  Britain.

The key issue in our rationale of including this
material and in following this particular route
is the need to develop teachers' understanding
of the potential role of the microcomputer. This
potential can be viewed as operating on different levels; firstly an understanding of the
different types of educational software, the
pedagogical principles underlying them, and the
role that they play in the learning/teaching
process; this is the 'macro' level. Secondly,
an understanding of the potential of an individual piece of educational software which involves
an understanding of both program structure and
design, and of some fundamental programming
principles. We can think of this as the 'micro'
level. Whilst many people would argue quite
rightly that it is the former which is important;
we believe that it is not possible to develop a
sound understanding at the 'macro' level without
a good feel for the 'micro' level. This rationale
determined both what was included in the pack,
and the route which is taken through the material. The activity which is in many ways the
most accessible (and relevant) to teachers, that
of examining commercial software, has to be left
until the end of the pack when the teacher has
formed a basis from which to analyse the programs,
and the pack begins with examining the structure
of an educational program and learning some
fundamental programming concepts. In order to
support these initial activities it made sense
to use LOGO, - although to some of our critics,
the most obvious languages to use at the time
(1982) was BASIC, which many teachers had some
familiarity with. However, if teachers are to
gain an understanding of what is possible in an
educational program, they need to appreciate
which parts of the program reflect the underlying educational design - and which are manifes-
tations of how the program is written. LOGO was
designed for novices, and its readability and
modularity make it ideal for writing programs
which teachers can dissect in order to examine
the structure. This, in fact, is exactly what
one of the first activities in the pack consists
of: the teacher is given a partly written LOGO
simulation program and guided through a series of
exercises in which she examines and modifies the
procedures that make up the program and in doing
so develops an understanding of the role that
each procedure plays in the program, and gets a
feel for how big a job making various different
modifications would be. Our decision to use
LOGO led to some production problems early on as
LOGO was not available for all the different
micros for which the pack would be written.
Since then, however, LOGO has enjoyed a growing
popularity in schools, - and indeed the teachers
who developmentally tested our pack found LOGO
used in this way a very stimulating and challenging starting point.

The balance between theory and practice in
Educational Software tends to be weighted towards
the theoretical, because of our belief in the
necessity of theoretical underpinning for software selection. For example, many of the
Reader articles draw on a wide theoretical base
including Computer Science, Artificial Intelligence, and Cognitive Science. Some of the

developments discussed in the Reader will be
somewhat removed from teachers' own experiences:
for example, some of the work emphasizes the
need and difficulty of modelling the learner in
intelligent computer assisted learning. This is
a consideration which is usually totally ignored
in the context of schools, and one possible
reason for the gap between the exciting potential of micros in education and the drab reality
of Skinnerian drill-and-practice found in many
schools.

Although these articles may not reflect teachers'
own experiences, they are able to explore what
some of these principles mean in practice through
the use of several sampler programs which
illustrate different types of software, and are
again written in LOGO so that teachers can
look 'underneath the bonnet'. In the final
section of the course the two 'levels' of looking at the potential of the microcomputer -
macro and micro levels are brought together.
Three commercial programs are provided for the
teachers to run and examine. These are not
seen as exemplary programs, but were chosen to
illustrate a diversity of styles (covering
simulation, drill-and-practice and a mathematical gaming environment), user interfaces (menus,
command languages and a 'drivechart') and
technical diversity (from fancy graphics to
nothing). Through a series of guided activities our students bring together their 'micro'
knowledge and their 'macro' knowledge in a very
practical way to develop criteria for selecting
educational software. In this way they come
to address their perceived needs - albeit by a
different route.

6. CONCLUSIONS

In this paper we have discussed 3 in-service
training packs provided by the Open University
Micros in Schools Project. Whilst the main
thrust of awareness training is towards competence and confidence, this is not true of post
awareness courses. One of the main functions of
these second level courses has been to help
teachers to develop sound frameworks from which
to make informed judgements. We, as trainers,
have adopted the role of 'question raisers'
rather than attempting to provide answers. In
order to do this, we have had to search for the
right balance between introducing and discussing
educational perspectives (theory) and building
on teachers' own experiences (practice).

For courses to be motivating and relevant at all
levels they must relate to teachers' own
experiences. Using teachers' own experiences
provides a powerful starting point, but it is
not always possible to take this route as we
have shown in our discussion of the ES pack. It
is clear, however, that in planning courses the
most important consideration is to interrelate
practise and theory.

REFERENCES

° The Open University Press. Micros in Schools :
  An awareness pack for teachers, P540, 1982.

° The Open University Press. Micros in Schools :
  Educational Software, P541, 1983.

° The Open University Press. Micros in Schools :
  Micros in action in the classroom, P542 (in
  press).

° The Open University Press, Micros in Schools :
  Discovering Microelectronics, P543, 1984.

° The Open University Press, Micros in Schools :
  Inside Microcomputers, P544, (in press).

° Preece, J. Inservice teacher training about
  microcomputers : An Open University initiative
  in distance learning, in Lewis R, and Tagg,
  E.D. (editors), Computers in Education, WCCE
  81. North-Holland, Part 2. pp. 697.

° Jones, A. and Preece, J. The Educational software pack for the Open University project
  'Micros in Schools' in Lovis, F. and Tagg, E.D.
  (editors) Informatics and Teacher Training
  North-Holland, 1984.

° O'Shea, T. The Open University Micros in
  Schools Project in Lovis, F. and Tagg, E.D.
  (editors) Informatics and Teacher Training
  North-Holland, 1984.

ACKNOWLEDGEMENTS

We wish to acknowledge all our colleagues in the
Micros in Schools Project and particularly the
following people:

Marc Eisenstadt (Chairman of the Awareness Pack
production team).

John Self (Academic chairman of the Educational
Software pack).

Ann Floyd (Chairman of the Micros in Action in
the Classroom pack).

Tim O'Shea (Director of the Micros in Schools
Project).

The Micros in Schools Project is funded by the
British Microelectronics Education Programme.

COMPUTERS IN EDUCATION, K. Duncan and D. Harris (eds.)
Elsevier Science Publishers B.V. (North-Holland)
© IFIP, 1985

SOFTWARE TOOLS FOR CURRICULUM CHANGE
IMPLICATIONS FOR TEACHER EDUCATION

by

Mike Aston and David Squires

Microelectronics Education Programme

The Advisory Unit for Computer Based Education

Endymion Road
Hatfield
Herts AL10 8AU
United Kingdom

Microcomputers have penetrated the primary and secondary school systems in the United Kingdom to give an unprecedented opportunity for teachers of all aspects of the curriculum to embrace the new technology and allow pupils the chance of using the computer as an aid to learning.

The authors have both been concerned with the problems of synthesising curriculum development and changing classroom practice by way of in-service teacher education.

The key to effective change is good educational software. This paper addresses the problems created by the rapid advances in hardware and the slow response of educational software producers.

The authors argue for a few good software tools rather than a thousand limited programs and look at the consequences for teacher education and curriculum change. An attempt is made to survey the variety of models for INSET which have been adopted in Britain and, in some cases, overseas. A plan for the future is proposed in which educational software tools play a dominant role.

Preamble/Background

The UK Microelectronics Education Programme (MEP) was launched by the Department of Education and Science in 1981, initially to run until March 1984, but now extended to March 1986. The aim of the Programme is to help schools to prepare children for life in a society in which devices and systems based on microelectronics are commonplace and pervasive. The programme is administered through 14 regions (excluding Scotland which has its own programme) and concentrates on in-service teacher education, curriculum development and information services to teachers. The scope of activity includes computer based learning, electronics, control technology, communications, information systems and computer studies. Alongside this programme, the Department of Trade and Industry has sponsored microcomputer hardware in primary and secondary schools on a matched funding basis. This scheme has proved so successful that it can be assumed that virtually every school in the UK has at least one microcomputer - in fact the average number in secondary schools (ages 11 - 18) is estimated (January 1985) to be well over ten.

The British Broadcasting Corporation (BBC) has also been very active in promoting computer awareness amongst the general public. The corporation has sponsored a microcomputer, the BBC Acorn, and has screened a number of series with titles such as "The Computer Programme", "Making the Most of the Micro" and "Computers in Control". Currently, the BBC is sponsoring the Computers in the Curriculum Project to develop educational software in conjunction with a TV series entitled "Science Topics". All of this activity adds up to an unprecedented interest by all sectors of the community in microelectronics and computer applications. Evidence of interest is shown by the home ownership of over one and a half million personal computers.

YEAR	CSE	GCE O LEVEL	GCE A/O LEVEL	GCE A LEVEL	CEE	TOTAL
1975	8,785	1,335		1,340		11,460
1976	13,181	3,217	116	1,512		18,026
1977	15,218	6,091	109	1,764		23,182
1978	15,489	8,417	511	1,769	233	26,419
1979	16,210	11,635	765	2,323	591	31,524
1980	18,001	14,907	1,049	2,819	635	37,411
1981	23,590	22,546	1,374	3,947	1,250	52,707
1982	32,261	37,868	1,524	5,825	1,531	79,009
1983	44,653	50,219	2,143	7,310	3,180	107,505
1984	*52,000	60,951	2,396	8,610	1,464	125,421

* Estimate.

Figure 1 : COMPUTER STUDIES
ENTRIES FOR FORMAL EXAMINATIONS

(source : ICL/CES and Acorn/CES)

Curriculum Development

Curriculum development is the 'applied branch' of curriculum study. It is an attempt to bring educational realities closer to educational intentions. Ralph Tyler, in a work published 35 years ago, summed up his ideas on curriculum development by asking four questions:

a) What educational purposes should the school seek to attain?

b) What educational experiences can be provided that are likely to attain these purposes?

c) How can these educational experiences be effectively organised?

d) How can we determine whether these purposes are being attained?

MEP is concerned with how new technology can support the existing curriculum by providing better educational experiences and, perhaps more importantly, how new technology can act as an agent for change.

MEP sponsors curriculum development by funding projects at national, regional and local level. In many projects, the key outcome is a number of software packages or, perhaps, just a single program. Others may produce some hardware, a case study or a report. In the case of software, MEP may account for say 30% of the total portfolio available for educational use in schools. The number of programs on the market far exceeds two thousand, and teachers find the selection of appropriate software a bewildering experience. Unlike books, which have covers, contents lists, chapters, page numbering and indexes, there are no acceptable standards for software. Many of the 2,000 programs have a limited application in the classroom and are often only of benefit when used by the author.

One of MEP's roles is to identify exemplar software and incorporate it into the in-service teacher education programme. The fourteen regional computer based learning co-ordinators are each linked to specific curriculum development projects with a view to identifying key software for this very purpose. About once every three months, they meet under the auspices of the national co-ordinator and the relevant project directors present the software product. Trials and positive evaluation may result in the software being included in the national INSET strategy.

Software Tools

As teachers are becoming more aware of software
potential across the curriculum and having tried
a few specific programs in their classrooms,
their attitudes are changing. At first, the
demand was for large numbers of programs to
support a particular subject area e.g. Physics or
Home Economics. Now the mood has changed.
General purpose software which can be used in a
variety of learning situations is fast becoming a
key to effective curriculum change and a relevant
and powerful use of the microcomputer in the
classroom.

We can categorize this general purpose software
to some extent and it may be helpful to consider
a few of the main types in turn:

High Level Languages   e.g. PROLOG and LOGO

LOGO allows children to learn by teaching the
machine and at the same time provide a problem
solving environment. PROLOG offers a new way of
thinking about the relationships between
attributes, characteristics and objects.

Database Systems   e.g. SEEK, QUEST and INFOVIEW

Three ways of providing a structure for
information e.g. binary, arrayed and hierarchial
menu, are now available for all the common
microcomputers. Some the most significant
learning appears to come through collecting,
sifting and ordering the information itself
rather than in the later interrogation.

Word Processing

e.g. VIEW, WORDWISE, ALPHA
and EDWORD

There must be dozens of text manipulation systems
on the market today. We are just beginning to
realize the potential they have for stimulating
children to write creatively and to offer an
alternative to pen and paper - a medium which
sometimes is seen as a huge stumbling block by
children who wish to communicate but are very
unhappy about their own untidy style of writing.

Spreadsheets   e.g. MULTIPLAN and VIEWSHEET

An opportunity here for children to build up
their own simple management system and project
the results of their decisions into the future.
They also enable children to observe the
behaviour of complex systems which can be
expressed as multi-variant models when displayed
as a spreadsheet.

Modelling Packages   e.g. DYNAMIC MODELLING SYSTEM (DMS)

Developments in this area are in their infancy,
but some attempts have been made to produce
general purpose modelling tools.

Graphics Packages   e.g. TESSELATIONS and MOSIAC

The electronic paintbox allows artistic
impression not previously available to many
children. Creative designs for weaving, printing
and purer aesthetic pleasure offer a whole range
of new opportunities, as yet hardly explored at
all.

This list is not exhaustive but gives a general
view of the wealth of software tools which we
already possess but have yet to exploit. The
list reflects a concern for information
processing and support for the 'new' curriculum -
perhaps giving children a new set of skills.

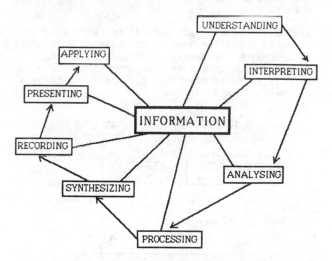

Figure 2 : The Information Cycle

With acknowledgements to Jean Beck

CAIS co-ordinator, MEP Capital Region.

Our thesis is that we are now moving out of the
software stone age in education. We are evolving
a bridge towards the design of a real learning
machine. For our own education we cannot make
leaps in the dark; we must understand each step
in software evolution in order that firm
foundations exist for future developments.

We must ask the question - 'Do we really want ten
or a thousand software packages?' It is our
belief that the right ten will show us the way
and the thousand can be considered as useful
learning experiences for teachers.

Models for In-Service Teacher Education

The effective use of software tools in the class has significant implications for the education of teachers, both in-service and pre-service. The cost of re-training the teaching profession for any nation is going to be prohibitive in current economic climates.

The model adopted in the U.K. as being the most cost effective can be described as being a cascade (or pyramid). The area of Computer Based Learning has a national co-ordinator who, in turn, has a team of regional co-ordinators operating in the 14 MEP Regions which cover the whole of England, Wales and Northern Ireland.

This group of 15 In-Service Teacher Trainers together with a National Working Advisory Group supported by subject panels, are responsible for the Computer Based Learning INSET strategy. Each regional trainer runs courses for local trainers in their own region and this cascades to local authority and school based courses in the community.

The whole cascade is supported by nationally produced INSET resource packs covering such areas as Geography, Mathematics, Physical Sciences, Careers Education, Home Economics etc. etc. Locally produced materials are also encouraged to be used by the trainers.

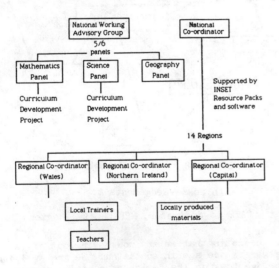

Figure 3

The Computer Based Learning INSET structure.

Some measure of the numbers of teachers and trainers who were part of this cascade is given in the table:

	Teachers	TDCUs*
General Awareness	5057	5129
Primary	6112	6005
Science	2398	3709
Mathematics	1314	1941
Geography	961	1491
Head Teachers	1013	1037
Home Economics	345	360
History	337	446
Trainers	288	1053
Art and Graphics	162	239
Other**	2589	3796
TOTAL:	20576	25206

Figure 4

*   A TDCU is a Teacher-Day Course Unit i.e. a measure of length of course.

**   Others include :- English, Modern Languages, Religious Education, Economics, Road Safety, Careers Education etc.

Figures for January 1982 - March 1984

It is possible to identify three levels of course namely:

Familiarization - awareness level
The target audience at this level consists of primary and secondary school teachers in any discipline, who have a computer facility in their school but, as yet, have not been made aware of its relevance in the classrooms. They probably see it as a resource for computer studies and mathematics but will have heard somewhere about its use in their subjects. They are interested enough to investigate further but worried by 'experts' and problems of actually getting time on the system for (a) hands-on experience and (b) use in their classrooms.

Understanding - intermediate level

The target audience here consists mainly of secondary school teachers, advisers, inspectors with subject responsibilities who have attended an INPUT course (an induction course for teachers qualifying under the UK Department of Trade and Industry Micros in Schools scheme) or similar familiarization course. They have probably seen one or two programs or computer-based packages which are relevant to their disciplines but are not able to judge whether they are 'sound', robust and worth using in the classroom. They are motivated to find out more, prepared to try new materials in their schools, but not necessarily to be involved in a curriculum development group. They have few programming skills, beyond understanding the structures of the programs they are using.

Application - advanced level

At this level are teachers, advisers, etc. who have used CBL materials in the classroom, feel the need for more resources in their own subject and are prepared to collaborate with others to generate subject-based or inter-disciplinary packages with software support. They are sufficiently motivated and skilled to look objectively at new material and report back on its educational effectiveness and the quality of the user interface, documentation and any other criteria outlined by an evaluation group. They will probably have simple programming skill, i.e. sufficient to alter data statements, user messages, etc., and at least enough knowledge to specify their developmental ideas in terms that a programmer can understand.

Objectives

Familiarization

1. Raise the level of awareness of the teaching profession such that CBL materials will be seen as a realistic option when a teaching strategy is being designed.

2. Make critical use of catalogues of software and associated CBL materials available to relevant subject areas.

3. Provide a sufficient range of activity to enable a teacher to progress from the initial awareness level to one of innovation.

Understanding

1. Establish a number of standards in the CBL domain which can be interpreted and applied by subject teachers when considering the use of CBL material in the classroom.

Application

1. Provide a framework for curriculum development based on sound knowledge of good practice, software standards and appropriate resources (e.g. programming support).

2. Create an environment in which innovation can take place - innovation which could have implications for examinations, the curriculum and the role of the teacher.

As a general rule teachers are encouraged to work in small groups supported by tutors. All courses are evaluated both by the participants and the course leaders and the results are fed back to the subject panels. Ideally, teachers are visited by advisers some time after the course and a longitudenal evaluation can take place, so trying to answer Tyler's fourth question.

Transferability of the Strategy

By invitation of the Finnish authorities, a team of three teacher trainers and an information officer/software librarian from the UK ran a national course for 60 educational decision makers in Helsinki. Finland, a small country in terms of population compared with the U.K., had been considering a computer education strategy and the course was designed to highlight the opportunities afforded by information technology in the classroom and also to give the Finnish educationalists a chance to look at a range of software and in-service training materials produced by another nation. As you can see from the programme, software tools played a large part in the practical sessions.

INFORMATION TECHNOLOGY ACROSS THE CURRICULUM
                    PROGRAMME

Day 1	1200	Finnish and British Tutor Meeting
Day 2	0900	Welcome and Introduction
	0930	Looking at Computer Aided Learning
	1300	Information Handling
	1700	Practical Work on CAL and I/H
Day 3	0900	Word Processing
	1300	Hardware Issues, Input / Output devices
	1500	Turtle Geometry - Introduction to LOGO
	1630	LOGO Practical Work
Day 4	0900	Selecting Software
	1000	OPTIONS: A. Language Teaching
		B. Science Teaching
		C. Humanities Teaching
		D. Mathematics Teaching
	1300	Software Distribution Models (telesoftware)
	1700	OPTIONS: A. Video Workshop (looking at classroom practice)
		B. Control Technology
		C. Visit to Primary School Computer Club
Day 5	0900	OPTIONS: A. School / Classroom Management
		B. In-Service Training
		C. Pre-Service Training
		D. Running a Software Library
	1000	Information Technology: the impact on education in school and after
	1100	OPTIONS: as above (repeat)
	1300	Panel: The Finnish Model for Innovation
	1600	Practical Work and/or Video Workshop
Day 6	0900	Keeping the Teachers Informed
	1000	Models for Software Production
	1100	Discussion on above to sessions
	1300	Plenary Session - Presentation of Project Work
	1445	Presentation of Certificates

Figure 5

The spoken language barrier was easily overcome
and software translations were apparent by the
end of the course.

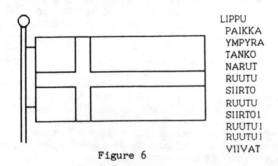

LIPPU
 PAIKKA
 YMPYRA
 TANKO
 NARUT
 RUUTU
 SIIRTO
 RUUTU
 SIIRTO1
 RUUTU1
 RUUTU1
 VIIVAT

Figure 6

This Finnish Flag was designed by
a group of participants in the
Helsinki ITAC course. The listing
beside it is of the LOGO procedures
used to construct the flag.

What does the future hold?

We cannot afford to reinvent software wheels. As
the cost of hardware falls, so the cost of
software rises.

If teachers and schools are to keep abreast of
technological developments in our information
based society, there must be much greater
collaboration between nations and the fostering
of software and teacher training exchanges on a
large scale.

References

*   Fothergill R. et al, Microelectronics
    Education Programme Policy and Guidelines,
    London : Council for Educational Technology,
    1983 (ISBN 0 86184 114 X)

*   Tagg Dr W. et al, The Daily Telegraph Guide
    to Educational Software, London : The Daily
    Telegraph, March 1985 ISBN 86367 040 7

*   Aston M. H., Can we really learn from
    computers? The 1984 Annual Systime Lecture
    publ. University of Leeds, June 1985

*   Aston M. et al, Computer Education in
    Finland, Hatfield : Advisory Unit for
    Computer Based Education, 1983 Reprint and
    Update 1984

*   "Selecting CAL Packages : Helping Teachers
    to Recognise Quality Software", Preece J.
    and Squires Computer Education No 46
    February 1984 pp 20 - 21

*   Variety of authors, Computer Based Learning
    INSET Resource Packs, Hatfield : MEP, 1983/5

*   Question in the House Hansard House of
    Commons, London : Vol 55 No 109 Col 175 29th
    February 1984.

*   Aston M. "Whatever Happened to 'Talk and
    Chalk'" Computer Education No 41 June 1982
    pp 14.

COMPUTERS IN EDUCATION, K. Duncan and D. Harris (eds.)
Elsevier Science Publishers B.V. (North-Holland)
© IFIP, 1985

AN INTRODUCTORY COMPUTER TRAINING COURSE
FOR UNIVERSITY PERSONNEL AND STUDENTS

G.J. Roebersen

SARA (Amsterdam Universities' Computing Centre)
P.O. Box 4613
1009 AP Amsterdam
the Netherlands

Preparing a general introductory course for the widely varying audience of a university computing centre poses a number of problems. In the design of such a course, emphasis was laid on three elements:
- the course was directed at interactive use of the central computer system;
- broad and specific instructional objectives (cognitive and affective) were formulated;
- high integration between instruction and practical work was obtained by a so-called "classroom terminal connection".
After two years experience, student satisfaction with the new course appears to be high. Particularly, nine out of ten trainees think they can independently use the computer system after the training process.

1.   Introduction

SARA, the Amsterdam Universities' Computing Centre, provides its users with computer hardware and software and maintains the systems software. Most users belong to the personnel and the students of both universities at Amsterdam, and a few related institutions. The task of SARA is limited to the aforementioned; i.e., users should develop their own programs with little or no assistance from the computer centre.
SARA's computer system for general use consists of a dual-mainframe CDC Cyber 170-750 system with two ModComp Classic front-end computers, used as a multiplexer and an editor, respectively. The operating system is NOS/BE 1; the interactive subsystem is Intercom 4 with many local modifications.

SARA has a few thousand users with very different backgrounds (e.g., physical sciences, social sciences, medical sciences, administration) and a wide variation in computer knowledge and experience. A large part of them uses only standard software (e.g., SPSS); another part writes their own (mostly small) programs using languages like Fortran or Pascal.
Since 1978, SARA has given a few courses for new users, introducing the use of the system. After such a course, users could attend an SPSS or a programming course. Also, some courses for experienced users were presented.

After a few years experience, some severe problems showed up with respect to the introductory courses:
- For many novice users, the old-fashioned and rather unfriendly operating system appeared very difficult to master.
- Mainly for historical and practical reasons, the introductory courses were divided in a "batch" (punched cards) course and an interactive one. The growing number of interactive terminals available for users made this distinction obsolete.

- Most new users wanted to use the computer as a tool (or were even demanded to do so by their employers), and were not interested in the computer as an object of study.
- The largely different backgrounds of the users prevented us from improving their motivation by presenting examples and problems related to their field of study.
- Especially for those users who wanted to use standard programs, the courses contained superfluous subjects and lasted too long (five days batch, three and a half days interactive).
- The growing number of new and inexperienced users caused capacity problems with facilities for practical work. Due to those limited facilities, only little "hands-on" experience at a terminal could be provided.

2.   The new introductory course

The above-mentioned problems led us to the development of a new introductory course, with emphasis on interactive use.
Full integration between instruction and practical work was reached by providing the students with a terminal that could be used either to show the teacher's examples or for their own work.

2.1   Program

The aim of the new course was providing the users with enough knowledge and experience to be able to run standard programs on the computer system. They should work independently, i.e. recognize and correct frequently occurring errors without resort to the advisory service. The trainees were assumed to have no previous experience with computers. The contents of existing courses were screened with this purpose in mind, and a completely new sequence of topics was arranged. For a clear view on the purpose and contents of the course, broad and specific instructional objectives were formulated (cf. next section).

The course starts with a short general introduction to computers, which serves for gaining some insight in the computing process and for demystification of the computer. The main part is dedicated to interactive use: the terminal keyboard, interactive commands, editor usage and file handling. As in some instances the use of batch jobs is necessary, the construction of batch jobs and submitting them from a terminal is treated next. The course ends with some special subjects and an introduction to magnetic tape usage.

Practical work constitutes an essential part of the course. After some hours of instruction and examples in the classroom, trainees may work out a number of problems at their terminal. If they are ready with these, they are stimulated to try their own variants of the problems or play computer games. This makes trainees familiar with the terminal, and teaches them to handle unexpected situations.

The course is given in a relatively short time: 14 hours instruction and about 15 hours "lab", spread over six days.

2.2   Instructional objectives

Mager (1) defines instructional objectives as "a description of a perceptible behaviour (performance) that the student must be able to show after the training process."

Good instructional objectives must contain an activity component (a perceptible activity, like "describe") and a concrete content component.

As is stated in a report of the Working Party on User Education of the Dutch Informatics Society (2, 3), explicit instructional objectives have a number of advantages in course development. They make the purpose of a course element clearer for course-designers, course-users, teachers and students. Use of accurate instructional objectives leads to better-informed consultation with the clients and a better evaluation of achieved results in relation to intended effects.

The general objective of our course was stated as:
"After the training process, the student is able to:
- independently use standard software on the SARA computer system, by applying the right control statements for interactive as well as for batch processing;
- use commands for entry, storage and retrieval of data."

"Education is not for knowing more but for behaving differently" (John Ruskin). An important purpose for an introductory course is giving the trainee enough self-confidence when working with the computer. Therefore, besides cognitive objectives a number of "affective" instructional objectives have been defined. Some of these are:
- value the possibilities and limitations of the computer;
- appear self-assured and pragmatical with respect to automation;
- state the responsibility of the user (especially in the SARA situation);

- tackle problems in the right way; state that an error is less important than the choice of the way of job processing.

2.3   Means

The course objectives could only be fulfilled when the trainees could easily follow the teacher's examples and get much "hands-on" experience themselves.

This was reached by using a classroom with 15 interactive terminals for instruction as well as practical work. Each terminal was shared by two students. For the instruction sessions, the terminals were "chained" by connecting the auxiliary port of one terminal to the main port of the next one. So all students could see the teacher's commands and the response from the computer system on their own terminal display. During practical work, all terminals were independently connected to the computer system.

3.   Discussion

3.1   Experiences

In the academic years 1982-1984 the course has been given thirteen times by three teachers. The new course was a success from the beginning: it was received enthusiastically by participants and teachers alike. The SARA users showed much interest in this course, which led - alas - to long waiting times due to capacity problems. This forced us to increase the number of trainees per course (from 20 to 30) and to insert extra courses.

We believe that the large number of interested users is caused by three factors:
- growing need to use the computer for work or study, and the requirement that the introductory course be followed before other courses;
- a lower threshold, as the course demands little fore-knowledge and does not take much time;
- a growing awareness of the importance of computers, which made students choose the course to obtain general information about computers (although it is intended primarily for users of the SARA computer system).

3.2   Evaluation

At the larger part of the courses given, evaluation forms were filled out by the trainees. The results are summarized here.

For a large majority the motive for following the course is the need to use the computer for an application in their professional area. A minority shows general interest in computers; some hope to increase their chances on the labour market. 57 percent of the participants had no practical experience with computers before; about a quarter had some Cyber experience.

The contents of the course fulfilled largely the participants' expectations. The level and the pace of the course were considered "good". The grouping of subjects was not always clear to the trainees (it was slightly changed after some time, which led to a somewhat better rating).

In the first year, the trainees got the available general documentation (somewhat out of date) together with some supplementary material. This written material received rather much criticism. The mean qualification of the old manuals was only "reasonable".

A new syllabus, covering all course material, was completed only one year after the start of the course. This time-lag was due partly to the requirement that the book could be used also as a written instruction, apart from the course. This new course-book was rated "good".

The various aspects of the practical work (problems, assistance and especially terminal facilities) were judged positively.

At last, it is important to know to what extent the instructional objectives (cognitive and affective) have been reached. So, trainees were asked: Do you think to be able to apply the course contents independently now?

The answers were (149 respondents):

Yes	37%
Yes, after some training	52%
I still need assistance in the beginning	9%
No	1%

3.3 Conclusions

1. Just for a course introducing an incoherent system, consisting of many loosely related parts, it is essential to formulate instructional objectives very carefully.
2. Demonstration of the actual application of control statements, followed by "hands-on" experience at the terminal, leads to better performance of trainees in shorter time.

Footnotes:

[1] The classroom was equipped by the Inter-faculty Working Party on Informatics at the University of Amsterdam.

[2] This was done by hand at first, later with a switch-cupboard developed by the Data Communications department of SARA.

References:

(1) Mager, Robert F., Preparing instructional objectives (Fearon Lear Siegler, Belmont, 1962).
(2) Working Party on User Education, Computer-user training: How and to what end? (Dutch Informatics Society, Amsterdam, 1982). English translation scheduled to appear in 1985.
(3) Lindhout, F.H., Computer-User Training: For Whom, How and to What End?, in Rijnsdorp, J.E. and Plomp, Tj. (Eds.), "Training for Tomorrow" (Pergamon Press, Oxford, 1984).

COMPUTERS IN EDUCATION, K. Duncan and D. Harris (eds.)
Elsevier Science Publishers B.V. (North-Holland)
© IFIP, 1985

COMPUTER TRAINING PROGRAMME FOR COLLEGE TEACHERS

Paul Kang Hoh Phua

Department of Information Systems & Computer Science
National University of Singapore
Kent Ridge
Singapore 0511

This paper is intended to describe some of the important experiences
gained through the provision of a Diploma Course in Computer Science for
College Teachers in Singapore, and to pursue some thoughts of a more
general nature which may be applicable to other countries in the region.
Within a period of three years (1980-82), there were altogether 69
teachers who went through the training programme and they were posted to
respective Junior Colleges to teach 'A' level Computer Science subjects
after their graduation. The total number of students taking computer
science at 'A' level is more than 1000 (including the first and second
year students) and which represents 10% of the student population each
year.

1. INTRODUCTION

This paper is intended to describe some
of the more important experiences gained
through the provision of a diploma
course in Computer Science for teachers
in Singapore, and to pursue some thoughts
of a more general nature which will be
applicable to other countries in the
region. Just like any other modern
country, Singapore is experiencing the
impact of the Information Revolution. To
cope with the rapidly growing demand of
computing expertise, Singapore is building up a local computer education system
which can be found at secondary, Pre-
University and University levels.

In Singapore, computer education was
started as early as in 1968, at the
University level. Computer courses were
offered by the Computer Centres and made
it possible for the teaching departments
to offer computer related courses to
their students. These courses were
treated as electives and in themselves
did not lead to a degree. At that time,
the prupose of offering these courses
was to make students intelligent users
of computer systems and not to train
them as computer professionals. In 1975,
the Department of Computer Science was
established. It offered a three-year
B.Sc. degree in Computer Science and
produced about 100 graduates for the
first few years. Employment opportunities for these graduates have always been
so good that a lot of final year students
have had their jobs offered even before
their final examination. Over the past
few years, the intake of Computer Science
students to the University had been increased to about 200 students each year.

In 1979, the Ministry of Education
decided to introduce Computer Science as
an 'A' level subject for Junior Colleges
in Singapore. The immediate problem
faced in the implementation was the
difficulty in getting qualified teaching
staff to teach this particular new
subject. A practical solution would be
to get the assistance of some well-known
organisation with experience in the
training of computer professionals. The
organisation would provide experienced
staff to take part in the training of
the few batches of selected teachers. It
was hoped that within a short period of
time, the organisation would be able to
train sufficient teaching staff to fulfil
the manpower requirement for the Junior
Colleges in order to offer computer
science subject at 'A' level.

In October 1979, the Department of
Computer Science of the National
University of Singapore was approached
by the Ministry of Education to hold a
diploma course in computer science for
graduate teachers. The aim of the course
was to train teachers to teach the
computer science subject at G.C.E. 'A'
level. The Department undertook this
assignment and came out with the suggestion of implementing a whole-year fulltime
Educational Programme in Computer Science
for selected graduate teachers. This
programme implemented at the beginning
of 1980 and it was continued for another
two consecutive years. Within these
three years (1980-82), about seventy
graduate teachers were trained under this
programme.

2.   CURRICULUM

The education system in Singapore traditionally follows the British system. In
their final year of study in Junior
Colleges, Pre-University students are
required to take the Cambridge 'A' level
external examinations. Besides preparing
students for the 'A' level examinations
it is however also our objective to
provide students with good general knowledge in Computer Science and prepare
them to pursue further study at the
University level. It is therefore in the
design of the curriculum for this training programme, the following reports have
been the sources of reference:

(a) Detailed syllabus of the Cambridge
     'A' level examinations for the
     Computer Science subject.

(b) Detailed syllabus of Parts I and II
     Examinations of the British Computer
     Society.

(c) Curriculum '78. Recommendations for
     Programme in Computer Science.
     Comm. ACM 22, 3 (March 79), pp 147-
     166.

(d) A Recommended Curriculum in Computer
     Science Engineering, IEEE Computer
     Society Report, November 1976.

(e) Curriculum Recommendations for
     Undergraduate Programmes in Inform-
     ation Systems. A report of the ACM
     Committee on Computer Education for
     Management, Comm. ACM 6, 12
     (December 73), pp 727-749.

The course structure of this training
programme is included in Table 1. The
detailed syllabuses of these courses are
included in Appendix A. The Programme
usually began on the second week of
January and ended by the third week of
December each year. First and second
terms of the programme consisted of 14
weeks each, while there were 19 weeks in
the third term. Examinations were held
at the end of each term, and following
that there was a one week's break.
Lectures were usually conducted in the
morning, while in the afternoon students
attended their tutorial classes or
practical sessions. As students were
all full-time graduate teachers coming
from different secondary schools or
junior colleges, they were provided with
one year full-pay leave by the Ministry
of Education in order to undergo this
full-time training programme.

3.   ADMISSION AND EXAMINATIONS

For admission to the training programme,
teachers were required to take an
aptitude test held by the Ministry of
Education. From 1980 to 1982, there were
about 150 to 200 teachers applied for the
course and sat for the aptitude test each
year. But only 25 teachers were selected to attend the course every year. For
the year 1980, the selection was based
entirely on the aptitude test, i.e. the
top 25 candidates were selected from the
aptitude test results. Basing on the
knowledge of the performance of the
teachers on the first course and their
academic backgrounds, it was felt that
the aptitude test should not be the sole
criteria for selection. It was generally
felt that the candidate's academic
results at 'O', 'A' and University levels
ought to be examined as well. It was for
this reason that the second and third
batch of teachers were selected through
these criteria. In order not to create
a shortage of teaching staff of the
schools, only one teacher per school was
selected each year. In view of the
result of selection, it is interesting
to note that most of the selected
teachers were graduates either in
Mathematics or Physics, for which there
was already a shortage of school teachers
in those fields at that time.

Examinations were held at the end of
each of term of study. Each examination
comprised two papers as follows:

Term I

| CD 11 | Introduction to Computer Science | } 1 paper |
| CD 12 | Scientific Programming I (BASIC) | |

| CD 13 | Business Programming (COBOL) | } 1 paper |
| CD 14 | Data Management | |

Term II

| CD 21 | Assembly Language Programme | } 1 paper |
| CD 22 | Computer Organisation | |

| CD 23 | Scientific Programming II (FORTRAN) | } 1 paper |
| CD 24 | Data Structures | |

Term III

CD 31   Programming Languages ⎫
CD 32   Operating Systems   ⎬ 1 paper

CD 33   File Processing   ⎫
CD 34   Systems Analysis and   ⎬ 1 paper
           Design   ⎭

On completion of the course, these grad-uate teachers were required to fulfil a project which was assessed upon a written report and an oral presentation. The written reports were required to include a brief survey of literature, a discuss-ion of algorithms and a description of methods used. A user's manual and list-ing of the running program should also appear as appendices in the report. An oral presentation was held before a panel of two or more staff members.

Each candidate was required to pass all six papers and the report in order to pass the Diploma in Computer Science Examination and qualify for the award of the Diploma. A candidate who failed in any paper(s) at each of the first and second term examinations were permitted to carry forward the paper(s) in which he had failed and proceeded to read courses in the next term. He was re-quired to take supplementary examination in the paper(s) in which he had failed, together with such other paper(s) in which he might have failed at the third term examination. The supplementary examination was held within a period of three months from the end of the third term. A candidate who failed the Examination (the main examinations and the supplementary examination taken as a whole) would be refused re-admission to the programme.

Statistics on the passes and failures in the Examination over the three years (1980-82) are summarised in Table 2.

4.   DISCUSSION AND CONCLUSION

Over the past three years (1980-82), there was a total of 69 graduate teachers who went through the training of the Diploma Course in Computer Science and out of these there were 57 teachers who completed the course successfully, while there were 12 fail-ures.

For teachers who had obtained the Diploma, they were posted to respective Junior Colleges to teach 'A' level computer science subject. For teachers who did not complete their study successfully, they either returned to their original positions or they were posted to the secondary schools to assist the operations of Computer Clubs. In the secondary schools students do not receive formal education in Computer Science. Many of them join a Computer Club or Society and acquire some programming experience by joining the activities organised by the Club. Presently, all secondary schools in Singapore are equipped with at least three microcomputers. Each school runs a Microcomputer Club which conducts computer appreciation courses for students of the school.

In 1980, the National Junior College was the first college in Singapore to start offering computer science as an 'A' level subject to their students, and the intake was limited to only 50 students. In 1981, the first batch of graduate teachers which had completed their training programme were posted to the respective Junior Colleges. The number of students who had opted for Computer Science as an 'A' level subject shot up to 450 at that year. It is however the policy of the Ministry of Education to restrict the number of students taking Computer Science to about 50 to 100 in each college each year. Among the nine Junior Colleges eight of them are equip-ped with a mini-computer and various microcomputers. The total number of students taking Computer Science at 'A' level is more than 500 per year, which represents 10% of the student population at that level.

Table 1. Course Structure of the Graduate Teachers' Training Programme

First Term

Course Number	Course Title	Lecture Hours	Tutorial Hours	Practical Work (Hrs)
CD 11	Introduction to Computer Science	30	15	0
CD 12	Scientific Programming I (BASIC)	30	15	45
CD 13	Business Programming (COBOL)	40	20	45
CD 14	Data Management	20	20	0

Second Term

Course Number	Course Title	Lecture Hours	Tutorial Hours	Practical Work (Hrs)
CD 21	Assembly Language Programming	30	15	45
CD 22	Computer Organisation	40	20	20
CD 23	Scientific Programming II (FORTRAN)	30	15	20
CD 24	Data Structures	30	15	20

Third Term

Course Number	Course Title	Lecture Hours	Tutorial Hours	Practical Work (Hrs)
CD 31	Programming Languages	35	17	15
CD 32	Operating Systems	35	18	15
CD 33	File Processing	35	17	20
CD 34	Systems Analysis & Design	35	18	20
CD 35	Project	60		
Total		450	195	285

Table 2. Number of Graduate Teachers Passed/Failed the Examination

Batch	Number of Passes	Number of Failures
1980	21	4
1981	22	3
1982	14	5
Total	57	12

APPENDIX A. DETAILED SYLLABUS

CD 11 Introduction to Computer Science

History of computers: early devices, development of computing systems. Hardware: central processing unit, main memory, input/output devices, auxiliary storage devices, computer network. Software: programming languages, operating systems, system software, data processing systems. Data representation: number systems, data types. Boolean Algebra: true tables, minimization procedures for Boolean functions including the use of Karnaugh maps. Logic design: logic gates, flip-flops, counters, registers, memories, and applications. Computer technology development: hardware and software. Types of computer applications.

CD 12 Scientific Programming I

Fundamentals of programming in BASIC. Elementary BASIC statements: assignment statement, input and output statement, GO TO statements, IF statement, FOR statement, DIM statement. BASIC subroutine, GOSUB statement. Sequential access files, virtual arrays, and direct access files. Advanced BASIC features: character strings manipulation, file handling techniques. Applications: random numbers, statistics, simulation, etc.

CD 13 Business Programming I

Overview of COBOL language. Structured programming. Data organisation. The identification division. The environment division. The data division. The procedure division. Table handling. Magnetic tape files. Sorting and merging of sequential files. Organisation of files on disk. Modular programs and subroutines.

CD 14 Data Management

Internal data representation. Alphanumeric data representation in I/O devices and mass storage devices. Record structures: record formats and record type. Data management functions: blocking, buffering storage usage efficiency. Data editing. Disk storage technology: disk formatting, access mechanism, access time. Data management structure: data sets, volumes, catalog structure. Data management operation. Data protection: transfer checking,

truncation and rounding errors.

CD 21 Assembly Language Programming

Machine instruction formats. Input/Output, registers. Data and instruction formats. Arithmetic, shift and branching. Address modification, indirect addressing and indexed addressing. Subroutine linkages. Floating-point subroutine. Symbol table, code generation and relocatable assembly.

CD 22 Computer Organisation

Basic Computer Design. Hardware Organisation, System Software. Principles of Programming. Functions and characteristics of storage media. Input/output device control. Direct memory access. The characteristics and performance of peripheral equipment. Data transmission.

CD 23 Scientific Programming II

Introduction to FORTRAN. Structured programming concepts and flow chart. FORTRAN component: data types, constants, variables, arrays, expressions, assignment statements. Control statements: GO TO statement, IF statement, DO statement, etc. FORTRAN subprogram, BLOCK DATA subprogram. Specification statements: COMMON statement, EQUIVALENCE statement, EXTERNAL statement, DATA statements, etc. Input/Output statements and format statements. Trucation and rounding of numeric values, loss of significance, overflow and underflow. Applications: numerical integration, system of linear equations, linear programming, etc.

CD 24 Data Structures

Character strings. Arrays, Stacks, queues, deques. Linear data structures: sequential storage allocation, linked lists. Trees: tree traversing, binary trees, tree sort, applications. Internal sorting methods: bubble, shell, insertion, selection, etc. Searching methods: sequential search, binary search. Hash table methods.

CD 31 Programming Languages

Development of high level languages. Assemblers, compilers, interpreters. Formal language concepts including

syntax, sematics and grammars. The
specification of a language by using
BNF. Features of high level languages:
variable names, data types, arrays,
arithmetic expressions, control statements, subprograms, etc. Implementations of some features will be discussed.
Evaluation and comparison of programming
languages in the scientific, data processing and text processing application
areas. examples from BASIC, FORTRAN,
PASCAL, PL/I, ALGOL, COBOL, RPG, SNOBOL,
LISP, etc.

CD 32 Operating Systems

Types of operating systems: batch,
simple multiprogramming, complex multi-
programming, multiprocessing, real-time
systems. Operating System Services: I/O
services, error recovery, language processors, loaders, utilities, accounting
for resource usage, security and protection. Memory management: partitioned
allocation, paged scheduler, traffic
controller, race condition, multiprocess
systems. Information management: basic
file systems, general file systems.

CD 33 File Processing

File organisation: file sequence, serial
access, random access. Basic file
structure: sequential file, direct file,
indexed sequential file. Other file
structures: list, inverted file, ring,
VSAM file. File I/O operation. I/O
programming: creation, addition, deletion, updating. File merging: 2-way
merge, polyphase merge. File maintenance: file protection, recovery
management utilities. Concept of database systems.

CD 34 System Analysis and Design

A system study. Concept of analysis.
Data collection. Systems flowcharts and
decision tables. Analysis of current
system costs. Problem definition.
Feasibility study. Concept of design.
Data communication. Management information systems. File design and form
design. Systems evaluation and costs of
the proposed system. Systems documentation. System implementation and
follow-up. Case studies.

COMPUTERS IN EDUCATION, K. Duncan and D. Harris (eds.)
Elsevier Science Publishers B.V. (North-Holland)
© IFIP, 1985

FACULTY TRAINING AND SUPPORT FOR COMPUTER-BASED INSTRUCTION

Jeanette Cates

Austin Community College
P.O. Box 2285 Austin, TX 78768
United States of America

The success of computer-based instruction is dependent on the support and participation of the faculty. Austin Community College recognizes this and provides training and support for its faculty with a variety of workshops, mini workshops, mini grants, a rescue squad, and other activities. This paper describes the faculty training and support programs for The College.

I. BACKGROUND

Austin Community College (ACC) is located in Austin, Texas, one of the fastest growing "high tech" cities in the United States. The College is a multi-campus college, with over 20,000 students. There are 200 full-time faculty members and 450 part-time faculty members.

The Computer-Based Instruction program at ACC was begun in the Fall of 1982. In addition to the general support given to faculty members, it included the establishment of a Computer-Based Instruction (CBI) Lab at one of the campuses. The success of the CBI Lab depends on the support of a variety of instructors to maintain its usage figures and to support the CBI program in general.

II. TRAINING

From the beginning, the emphasis of the CBI program has been in training faculty members so that they could, in turn, train students to make computers an integral part of their lives. Training for the faculty has been accomplished through two types of workshops: Instructional Development Workshops and Mini Workshops.

The Instructional Development (ID) workshops are sponsored by the Instructional Development Office of The College. These workshops are scheduled and advertised in the same way as all of the other ID workshops. Each is two to three hours long, usually given on a Friday afternoon, either by the CBI Coordinator or a consultant. Several workshops per semester are also scheduled for evenings or Saturdays so that more part-time faculty can attend. All of the ID workshops require preregistration and are often full weeks in advance. Of the 15-20 workshops presented in a semester, approximately one-third of them are CBI-related.

In addition to the incentive of learning more from the workshops, faculty members are given Professional Development Units (PDUs) for attendance. To a part-time faculty member, a

PDU translates to $4. To a full-time faculty member, PDUs can be accumulated and applied to the salary and promotion scale in a ratio of 20 PDUs equal to 1 graduate credit hour. Though the PDUs do not amount to much individually, the faculty is appreciative of the fact that they are recognized for their efforts to increase their knowledge and skills through development activities.

There have been a variety of CBI-related workshops sponsored by the Instructional Development Office. Topics have included Basic Concepts of CBI, Commercial Software for Your Classroom, Introduction to Authoring Systems, Introduction to SuperPILOT, Introduction to Interactive Video, How to Evaluate Software, and BASIC programming (an unusual 24-hour long course, instead of the usual 3-hour course). In addition there have been workshops on specific word processing software, as well as grade programs and data base programs. In the case of specific packages, there are usually courses for beginners, as well as courses for faculty members who have been using the package for a while. Topics for future workshops are Graphics, Telecommunications, Advanced Super-PILOT, and A Comparison of Computers--by faculty owners of different brands.

While the ID Workshops have provided a great deal of formal training for the faculty, the CBI Lab has offered a number of informal workshops for faculty, staff, and students. These informal workshops, known as Mini Workshops, were developed with the idea of presenting information that could be used immediately. Staff members were included because of their requests and the fact that they work so closely with the faculty. Students were addressed with the hope that even if their particular instructor did not present computers to them, they would still have a chance to learn and use them.

Each mini workshop is 45 minutes long. They are scheduled one topic per week, with each topic offered six times per week at varying times. There is no preregistration required, so users can attend on a walk-in basis. This also encourages users to come back to a specific topic if they want to listen again. The typical workshop provides instruction on how to insert the disk, turn on the computer, choose from the menu, produce a short product, save it, then print it. Handouts of the commands are provided, as well as a "sample session". However, the workshop never attempts to cover all the intricacies of a package or all the "what-ifs" that may come up in typical use. These potential problems would be handled by the CBI Lab staff when a user returns to use a package individually. If it is practical, users are given a chance to use the package being taught during the mini workshop.

Topics that have been addressed in mini workshops are Introduction to Word Processing, Introduction to Spreadsheets, Introduction to Electronic Filing, How to Improve Your Typing with Software, How to Design a Data Base File, How to Prepare Your Term Paper with a Word Processor, Math Software, Grammar Software, and Health Games. As new software packages arrive in The Lab, a mini workshop is designed to highlight them, thus increasing use. In addition to the special topic mini workshops, an Orientation to the CBI Lab is offered every Monday and Friday. This includes a short "tour" of the computer keyboard, an explanation of the sign-in and reservation procedures, and the chance to use the computer for 30-40 minutes. Like mini workshops, these orientations are given to as many or as few users as arrive.

III. SUPPORT ACTIVITIES

Though training is the basis for success, the continued and varied support of the faculty in CBI activities has enhanced the use and relevance of the program. Support is provided in a variety of ways: computer and software checkout, mini-grant program, the rescue squad, software review policy, and direct support.

Faculty members have access to computers at several locations: at their office, at the CBI Lab, and at Learning Resource Services. However, there are times when a computer is needed elsewhere. In these cases, every effort is made to check out a computer to a faculty member. The LRS keeps one computer for checkout to classrooms; the CBI Lab has several that can be checked out over a holiday period. In addition to checking out an entire computer, faculty members can also use a disk drive or other peripheral for short periods of time. Likewise, software is available for faculty check-out so that it can be used at various campuses.

Most of the software used in the CBI program at ACC is commercial software. However, a few programs have been and are currently being produced by faculty members. These production efforts are supported by the Mini Grant program. Administered by the Instructional Development Office, the mini grant program supports the development of materials to enhance instruction in existing courses. This may range from preparing slides for an art course to making a videotape for a Spanish course to producing research handouts at the Library. Although a specified percentage of the mini grant money was set aside for CBI grants in the first year of the CBI program, CBI-related grants now compete on the same basis as other grant requests. Grants may be requested for a course reduction (for full-time faculty), a course reimbursement (for part-time faculty), supplies, typing support, and other materials. CBI-related mini grants have included reviews of math software, grammar software, physics software, and statistics software, production of tutorials for history, a medical terminology course, an advanced French grammar course, a job cost accounting problem set, and the repurposing of nutrition videotapes for interactive video.

Another means of faculty support has evolved in the form of the Rescue Squad. The Rescue Squad is activated by a telephone call from a frantic user. Since the CBI Lab tries to maintain a copy of every program that is used on all campuses, one of the staff members can either answer a question directly or work through it while on the telephone. If that does not work, or if they are on the same campus, the Rescue Squad makes an office call. The Rescue Squad does preventive maintenance, such as inspections and routine cleaning, while on special missions or on a rotating basis. An informal call to visit will often raise questions about particular software packages and provide ideas for additional training. The Rescue Squad also maintains an informal network of users of particular machines and software packages. Thus, a new user can be put in touch with an "experienced" user in order to have a source of direct help.

One of the most productive support services has been the software review program. Using the procedures established by the LRS staff, faculty members can request any software package for a 30-day review. Since the LRS had had experience in doing this, most publishers have been glad to cooperate with this system. When the package arrives, at least two faculty members review it for its applicability to their courses, as well as to its quality of content. When requested, the CBI Coordinator also reviews the package for instructional design considerations. This review procedure has done two things: it has saved The College a lot of money that might have been spent on poor software and it has guaranteed that at least two instructors know how to use the program and already know where it will "fit" if it is purchased.

Direct faculty support includes consultations
in what software might be appropriate, as well
as developing instructions that are useable for
students. The CBI Coordinator suggests packages by reviewing computer periodicals, education periodicals, and software review data
bases and catalogs. Faculty members, in turn,
suggest software they have seen advertised in
professional journals or by word of mouth from
other instructors in their field of study. In
addition to consultations, the CBI Staff gives
orientations to classes that will be using the
CBI Lab. These orientations are conducted
either in the instructor's classroom or in the
Lab. Other in-class presentations are also
given, highlighting a specific package, as
requested by the instructor. If an instructor
wants to present a computer demonstration, a
member of the CBI Staff will assist in producing the transparencies, slides, or videotape
that is to be used, as well as making certain
that the equipment is properly connected.

IV. CONCLUSION

The Computer-Based Instruction program at
Austin Community College has provided a variety
of training modes, as well as a great deal of
support for the faculty members who want to use
CBI. In turn, the faculty has supported the
CBI program and contributed to its overall
success.

COMPUTERS IN EDUCATION, K. Duncan and D. Harris (eds.)
Elsevier Science Publishers B.V. (North-Holland)
© IFIP, 1985

OLLIE - an On-Line Library for Inter-campus Exchange

Sharon M. Cubbin, Principal Consultant
Inter-Campus Service
5503 Windmill Court
Lansing, Michigan 48917
U.S.A.

RESEARCH AND DEVELOPMENT OF
A MASTER EDUCATIONAL COMPUTER PROGRAM
TO BE PLACED ON A WORLDWIDE, COMMERCIAL,
COMPUTER TIME-SHARING NETWORK;
GOAL BEING TO PROVIDE
ACCURATE COURSE INFORMATION FOR STUDENT TRANSFERS

OVERVIEW

In researching Articulation (student transfer procedures), the following statistics warranted relentless action to develop OLLIE: 12% of the students enrolled in the U. S. educational institutions lose an average of 10 credits when transferring, thus students are witnessing a minimum total annual tuition waste of $270 million. Additionally, 40% drop-out within 5 years and never return. If one-half of those students could be professionally encouraged to pursue at least two years of further education, the U. S. institutional income would increase annually by $540 million. Counselors need to resume their productive role of counseling.

The basic objective is to reduce comments such as, "Yes, Mike, 60 of your business credits from the community college are accepted; however, only 40 of those credits apply to our bachelor of business administration curriculum." Counselors need accurate information as well as relief from their current "sort and suffer" clerical activity in order to return to their professional responsibilities of recruitment, retainment, and personal career advisement.

OLLIE will be a master national computer program placed on a worldwide, commercial, computer time-sharing network; long-range goal being global computerized articulation communication. Course equivalencies, curriculum guides, automated student transcript evaluations, transcript forwarding, graduate resumes, and catalogs will be available. The project management group, Inter-Campus Service (ICS), will be responsible for the development, pilot, implementation, maintenance, user training, and expansion of OLLIE. Articulation areas will also include nursing, business, and military credits of the public and private, two- and four-year schools.

A three-hour slide presentation/computer demonstration accompanied by a 100-page proposal describe the three-year project plan in its entirety. Contact Inter-Campus Service.

PROBLEM

Institutions offer an array of courses and a multitude of curriculums in order to fulfill the ambitions of the diversified student body. The mutual respect and appreciation for the privilege of autonomous school systems is not to be forfeited because of the disharmony with which they are faced. The discord before them can be summarized in one word: transferring.

There lies considerable waste of money and time at present when students transfer from one school to another. This is being circumvented by the endless cycle of new policy loop-holes counselors must decipher daily. The gamut includes the 4-to-4, the 4-to-2, the 2-to-2, and the dominant community college transfer to the four-year institution. One of the intents of the two- to four-year college program was to reduce costs of higher education. Differences between the acceptance of credit for "admission purposes" and the applicability of credit for "degree purposes" increase the difficulty of counseling. Add to the imponderables the underemphasized distinction between an Associate degree and the utilization of the community college to accomplish two years of courses applicable to a Bachelor's degree at a predetermined college. These should be matters of full and emphatic disclosure, consumated with easily accessible, up-to-date information from our fellow schools. That information is not easily accessible and is constantly changing. The discouraging, ballooning counseling clerical workload regretfully prompts passive guidance of students' money and time.

Determining a student's knowledge in required subject areas poses another dimension of time-consuming transcript evaluation: recognition of extra-institutional learning. Documentation and testing programs (CLEP, GED, etc.) are used in the assessment of military courses plus civilian non-collegiate sponsors such as businesses, corporations, government agencies, and labor unions. Institutions of postsecondary education that are not accredited by COPA-recognized accrediting bodies may lack that status for reasons unrelated to questions of quality. Once again, special steps are needed to validate credits previously earned.

Improvement in transfer-of-credit methods should encompass all of the aforementioned, concentrating on the lower level activities, merging to the upper level process. Severely needed attention should be extended to the high school transfer procedure. Foreign exchange information is yet another conglomerate of confusion. With coordination, incentive, existing knowledge, and today's technology, an increase in staff and student productivity will result through the use of a popular and proven tool: a commercial, computer time-sharing network.

Solution

The initial determination necessary would be, "Which courses at the other school(s) would be acceptable in lieu of our courses?" Gathering that data, which is now repeatedly pondered in one transcript after another, and joining that data with curriculum listings, the student transcript evaluation process will become expedient and accurate. Relieved of the massive clerical burden, each autonomous school can redirect it's internal resources. Less paperwork reduces administration. Counseling can resume its personal intent, directing the individual as no computer can do. Recruiting can be the focal target. Drop-outs can be delicately pursued. Creativity to provide a better educational environment can be released.

An artificial or short-sighted "quick fix" can result in an alarming loss of time, energy, and dollars. The concept of computerization having rooted, the development of autonomous state computer systems which cannot meld together in the decades ahead will provoke a catastrophe. Evolving from a cottage industry, Inter-Campus Service (ICS) has researched the current activities of "the computer articulation communication revolution" within the American higher educational structure. ICS conclusions show the need for not only a national network evolving from a state pilot project, but the inevitable long-range goal of a worldwide network.

Precautions have been taken. Each autonomous institution determines and owns their equivalency and curriculum data; the receiving school has the final authority in all student applications; the counseling responsibility is borne by the institutions, not an outside agency; the motivation to create, maintain, promote, and expand OLLIE is the responsibility of the middleman, ICS; the

talents of the institutions very own experts residing at each autonomous campus will be exploited through the unique "Inter-Campus Service/On-Site" staff; the challenge to make the transition from "grant supported" to "independent" activity is not only the destiny but simply common sense.

Developing various articulation programs on established educational time-sharing networks has been a conservative "step forward" and the beginning of a perpetual headache. The institutions (particularly the engineering and medical departments which aspire to a worldwide pool of applicants) do not want to isolate themselves from other states' transfer information nor do they want to get caught-up in numerous interfacing programs; they are overwhelmingly responding to the sound approach of using an establishment created for the very type of communication sought.

A MASTER PROGRAM called OLLIE (an On-Line Library for Inter-campus Exchange) will be placed on ONE, WORLDWIDE, COMMERCIAL, COMPUTER TIME-SHARING NETWORK. Each institution, via the terminal/personal computer and modem, connects with the major time-sharing computer; this procedure does not effect the institution's internal computer staff nor functions. The major time-sharing companies have multi-lines, are capable of extremely large data bases, have minimal downtime, provide the most advanced technology, and are in business to serve. Renewable contracts and competitors are foremost in their minds, thus they will be acting in the same service capacity to ICS as ICS is to the institutions.

The following examples of the proposed computer program are typed versions of the actual input/output from operational Demonstration Programs developed by ICS.

MAIN MENU

0. ADDITIONAL HELP

1. COURSE EQUIVALENCIES

2. CURRICULUM GUIDES

3. STUDENT TRANSCRIPT EVALUATIONS

4. MINI-CATALOGS

5. PERSONAL PRIVILEGES

6. EXIT THE PROGRAM

ENTER SELECTION: 3

<u>STUDENT TRANSCRIPT EVALUATIONS INPUT</u>
<u>(all demo data is simulated)</u>

DEGREE SCHOOL:?   <u>THE UNIVERSITY OF MICHIGAN</u>

DEGREE:?   <u>B.B.A.</u>

PRE-DEGREE SCHOOL:?   <u>FERRIS STATE COLLEGE</u>

SCHOOL OF COMPLETED CLASSES:?   <u>MACOMB COMMUNITY COLLEGE</u>

COURSE:?   <u>DPR 110</u>

COURSE:?   <u>ECON 104</u>

COURSE:?   <u>DONE</u>

SCHOOL OF COMPLETED CLASSES:?   <u>OAKLAND COMMUNITY COLLEGE</u>

COURSE:?   <u>ECON 261</u>

COURSE:?   <u>ART 155</u>
INPUT ERROR OR COURSE NOT ON FILE

COURSE:?   <u>ART 156</u>

COURSE:?   <u>HIS 251</u>

COURSE:?   <u>POL 151</u>

COURSE:?   <u>ENG 151</u>

COURSE:?   <u>ANTH 271</u>

COURSE:?   <u>DONE</u>

SCHOOL OF COMPLETED CLASSES:?   <u>FERRIS STATE COLLEGE</u>

COURSE:?   <u>DPR 209</u>

COURSE:?   <u>ENG 500</u>

COURSE:?   <u>DONE</u>

SCHOOL OF COMPLETED CLASSES:?   <u>DONE</u>

The student's goal is to obtain a Bachelor's in Business Administration from
the University of Michigan. The student wishes to continue taking classes
at Ferris State College before transferring to the University. The student
has completed two courses at Macomb Community College, six courses at Oakland
Community College, and two courses at Ferris State College.

STUDENT TRANSCRIPT EVALUATION OUTPUT

(all demo data is simulated)

BBA/U. of M.	PRE-DEGREE/FERRIS STATE	EVALUATION

freshman-sophmore level courses:

BBA/U. of M.	PRE-DEGREE/FERRIS STATE	EVALUATION
ACC 350	NO EQUIVALENCY	---
DPR 190	DPR 209	COMPLETED AT FERRIS STATE
ENG 105	ENG 151	COMPLETED AT OAKLAND COMMUNITY COLLEGE
MAT 150	MAT 200	TO BE TAKEN AT FERRIS STATE

junior-senior level courses:

BBA/U. of M.	PRE-DEGREE/FERRIS STATE	EVALUATION
ACC 500	NO EQUIVALENCY	---
ACC 501	NO EQUIVALENCY	---
ENG 620	ENG 500	COMPLETED AT FERRIS STATE
ENG 621	NO EQUIVALENCY	---
MAT 600	MAT 575	TO BE TAKEN AT FERRIS STATE
MAT 700	MAT 675	TO BE TAKEN AT FERRIS STATE

electives-humanities(3 credits required):

BBA/U. of M.	PRE-DEGREE/FERRIS STATE	EVALUATION
ART 207	ART 156	COMPLETED AT OAKLAND COMMUNITY COLLEGE
MUS 207	NO EQUIVALENCY	---

electives-natural sciences(3 credits required):

BBA/U. of M.	PRE-DEGREE/FERRIS STATE	EVALUATION
BIO 191	NO EQUIVALENCY	---
PHY 181	NO EQUIVALENCY	---

electives-social sciences(3 credits required):

BBA/U. of M.	PRE-DEGREE/FERRIS STATE	EVALUATION
HIS 300	HIS 251	COMPLETED AT OAKLAND COMMUNITY COLLEGE
POL 320	POL 151	COMPLETED AT OAKLAND COMMUNITY COLLEGE

Neither of the Macomb Community College courses apply to the BBA degree. Four of the six courses from Oakland Community College apply. Both courses taken at Ferris State College apply. Three courses (residency requirements not considered in this example) may be taken at Ferris before transferring. History 251 is a Humanity at Oakland Community College; Political Science 151 is a Behavioral Science at Oakland Community College; History and Political Science at the University of Michigan are both Social Sciences; therefore, the two courses are both "acceptable" (equivalent) and "applicable" (listed on the cirriculum guide desired), yet one of the courses is a surplus. Departmental classifications for electives is a major confusing factor for the student who is attempting to complete Distribution Requirements at a school other than his degree school. Our example student lost five courses.

OLLIE ...
...will include comments (for example, "non-transfer of 'D' grades") advising the student of appropriate conditions.

...will generate the common courses between an Associate (two year) Degree and a "pre-Bachelor program," allowing the student maximum postponement of the decision to set an Associate or Bachelor Degree goal for him/herself. Also, decisions regarding field of study can be prolonged as well by the generation of common, core courses between selected curriculums.

...will, with the inclusion of a complete tuition data base, generate an institutional-comparison-cost-study. Financial advantages of completing their education at one institution versus the financial advantages of attending two or more schools can be examined by the student.

...will receive transcripts (via the terminal/personal computer and modem) and incorporate them directly into the computerized Student Transcript Evaluations.

...will analyze the Input (courses taken and chosen degree school) and produce the curriculum which maximizes the application of those courses previously completed; beneficial to students desiring "a degree" as soon as possible in order to return to the job market.

...will handle local, statewide, regional, national, and/or worldwide information exchange.

The tangible information (computer print-out) encourages students to seek professional guidance rather than turn towards peer guess-work.

Negotiations are underway to fund the three-year project. The costs to develop, pilot, and implement the master program varies depending on the number of pilot schools. If two universities and eight feeder schools pilot the project, total start-up costs are estimated at $1.5 million; two universities and sixteen feeder schools, $2.3 million; four universities and sixteen feeder schools, $2.7 million; four universities and thirty-two feeder schools, $4.3 million. Upon completion of the three-year research and development period, operational costs are offset by institutional cost-savings; therefore, the result is a financially self-sustaining system.

The key element to OLLIE's positive reception lies in the fact that every individual entity of the educational structure chooses their communication partner; it is not mandatory that all participants exchange information with all other participants though that option does exist. Computerized articulation communication is permitted between two or more educational units without restraint of geographic parameters, thus OLLIE will serve an infinite number of situations ranging from two neighboring campuses to articulation communication between distant countries.

COMPUTERS IN EDUCATION, K. Duncan and D. Harris (eds.)
Elsevier Science Publishers B.V. (North-Holland)
© IFIP, 1985

PLANNING, IMPLEMENTING AND EVALUATING A MASTERS PROGRAM IN EDUCATIONAL COMPUTING

Terence R. Cannings and Stephen W. Brown

Pepperdine University
3415 Sepulveda Blvd.
Los Angeles, CA 90034

Computers, computers, computers . . . Will they really have an impact on teachers and the way they teach? Will they create a new learning environment for students? Of more importance to people in the profession - will they replace the classroom teacher?

The answer to these questions must be "yes", "yes", and "no". But such answers depend on how you view the use of computers. If you view them as a piece of technology which can organize, store and analyze informatin you will use them as a resource in a learning environment. If you view computers as a complete substitute for a teacher you won't use them at all. If you foresee ways in which they help children learn in new and excitng ways you will consider adding them to your list of teaching resources.

With these thoughts in mind, we began looking for a way our Graduate School of Education and Psychology could stimulate the acceptance and use of computers as a part of the teaching-learning process. We were firmly convinced that computers offered education a potential resource that would be beneficial to everyone involved in the process.

As we talked among ourselves, it became apparent that the kinds of ideas and skills we wanted to disseminate would require more than a workshop or a single course; rather, it would require a whole new master's program. Thus the idea of a master's of Science in Educational Computing was born. This idea appeared to have great timing:

• The University was committed to information technology literacy.

• The President stipulated that students graduating beginning in 1985 would be computer literate.

• The School was assessing its programs, pending some reorganization.

Armed with our ideas and much enthusiasm, we then encountered some fundamental and very practical questions that needed to be answered:

1. How do we get started?

2. Who should be our audience?

3. What should be the goals of our program?

4. What assumption should we make concerning our students, and the methods of instruction?

5. Would we need an advisory committee?

6. What specific courses should we teach?

7. What hardware and software resources would we need?

8. Would the program fulfill our goals? What problems would we encounter?

The remainder of this article addresses these questions.

GETTING STARTED

Getting started was actually a fairly easy matter, as in all colleges and universities, we did what comes naturally -- we appointed a committee. This committee consisted of 4 people in addition to ourselves: Diana Hiatt, an early childhood/curriculum specialist; Chet McCall, a researcher/statistician, Jack McManus, a computer specialist/educational psychologist; and, Cara Garcia, a reading/literacy specialist and educationa psychologist. These people combined with the two of us, Terry, a school administrator/ futurist curriculum specialist and Steve, a psychologist/researcher. We began meeting on a weekly basis to plan our new M.S. program. We began our task by defining our "target audience".

THE TARGET AUDIENCE

We clearly agreed that we wanted to focus on educators. However, did we want people who would be full time software developers, teachers, administrators, or whatever? Clearly, we could not design a program that would meet all people's needs so we had to identify a fairly specific "target audience".

With the use of computers in schools growing at an exponential rate classroom teachers were obviously the number one priority for our target audience. But not far behind, were industrial trainers and others directly involved in the instructional process. Further, we wanted to design a program that might appeal to people in higher education as well as K-12 teachers. We also believed that such a program would attract individuals outside of the classroom, such as school administrators, educational consultants, and educational publishers. In short, we felt we could do a good job of preparing "generalist education computer practioners"; we had no intention of preparing would-be hardware specialists or machine language programmers. We eliminated "computer science" as our arena.

OUR GOAL

The development of any program always requires a clear statement of its goals. As such, the committee spent considerable time working on a statement of goals. We needed this in order to specify the types of skills we hoped our graduates would develop. Further, a goal statement would help us to plan the scope and sequence of our curriculum. After much deliberation, the following statement from the University Catalogue was agreed upon as our "general goal statement":

> The Master of Science degree program in Educational Computing is designed for teachers, administrators and parents who wish to develop and expand their skills in the educational application of computers. Although emphasis is given to the use of computers in the instructional process, students will also learn how to use computers in non-instructional and administrative settings. As part of the program, students will also be taught how to develop evaluation criteria and evaluate educational software; to write general-purpose programs using one or more programming languages; to plan a computer system for an educational site using existing hardware; and to assess current and future technological trends in education.

Using this broad statement of goals, we then proceeded to look at the assumptions we would need to make about our students and the program in order to meet these goals.

WHAT DID WE ASSUME?

Constructing a program for a wide audience is difficult. However, we identified some assumptions that made this task a little more manageable. In summary, we assumed:

1. All students would be interested in education and/or training.

2. The majority of course work should be computer related. That is, although traditionally all master's programs include some basic or foundation courses, these should be kept to a minimum. Also, whenever possible, information directly relevant to educational computing should be inserted into the traditional educational foundation courses.

3. A problem-solving approach would provide the commonality for teacher K-adult and trainers. They would all see that we deal with the same processes. This saved us from having to conduct elementary sections of the same class.

4. Most of our students would be working adults. Thus, classes needed to be offered in the evening hours and on weekends. Further, since travel in Southern California is often quite difficult, classes should be scheduled so that students could complete the 30 unit program in approximately 18 months.

5. Current applications of computers in educational settings would not be sufficient. Analysis of future trends and its implications for education would need to be incorporated into the program.

6. Students would need to be exposed to several types of microcomputers and a wide variety of software. Since schools and districts differ in their hardware configurations, we needed to train students so they would be familiar with several different computing systems. Similarly, we wanted our graduates to have a high degree of familiarity with software that could and would be used in a variety of different settings and disciplines.

7. A high level of computer anxiety would exist among many new students. Introducing these people to computers must begin on the first night of their first class.

8. Teachers would be interested in practical applications. For practitioners, theory and knowledge is of little value without practical application. But because we believe that the current practical knowledge about computers is most likely to change fast in the information explosion, we had to intergrate the practical with the theoretical which will be the more lasting and which will give our students

the independence to make suitable decisions for themselves with future generations of hardware. "There's nothing as practical as a good theory." - Kurt Lewin.

9. Similarly, a hands-on approach during class time would be essential. In addition, students would require additional hands-on experience following class time.

10. The range of entrant expertise would vary but as computer education was relatively new, this gap should not be too wide.

THE ADVISORY COMMITTEE

After laboring through the issues above, we developed a preliminary draft of our program. It was quite apparent to all of us, however, that the program needed input from people who were already working in the field. As such, we posed the rhetorical question: Can an advisory committee help? It certainly can and did! We invited educators, computer specialists, and software developers from within California to form a program advisory committee. The advisory committee critiqued our first draft of the proposed program and several issues were raised:

- Did the program emphasize too heavily the production of software?

- Was it necessary to include a programming language? If so, which one?

- Did the university possess sufficient resources to train students on several types of microcomputers?

- How much software, and of what variety, did we possess and plan to obtain?

- Did the program include staff development strategies and change theory?

- How could the core courses reflect an educational computing emphasis?

- Should electives be introduced?

Needless to say, these issues forced us back to the drawing board. Several difficult and tedious months were spent trying to address the issue: many of which had strong budgetry implications. Thanks to some strong administrative support from our Dean we achieved what we felt were satisfactory answers to the advisory committee's questions, and we prepared a second draft of the program. We then took this second draft back to the

advisory committee. Some success was achieved--they liked it. Further, by wrestling with the issues raised by our advisory committee we had reached an agreement that we wanted to train people who could be good practitioners as well as effective change agents.

THE COURSES

A very important result of our work with the advisory committee was the development of the courses that would be taught in the program. These are presented below. See Table 1 for course descriptions. Table 2 presents the competencies for each course while Table 3 highlights the resources used.

Table 1

COURSE DESCRIPTIONS

ED 600 Historical, Social and Philosophical Foundations of Education (3)

Students will gain a better understanding of the development of the American educational system from colonial to modern times, with a special emphasis upon the emergence of the computer as an integral part of the teaching-learning process. Further, students will increase their understanding of the major philosophies which underlie current public and private schools in America, and, in particular, will examine from a philosophical viewpoint the increasing use of computers in the educational setting.

ED 601 Psychological Foundations of Education (3)

A study of psychological principles as applied to teaching/learning process. Learning theory, motivation, individual differences, retention, and transfers are included in this course.

ED 602 Introduction to Educational Research (3)

This course will cover the location, selection, and analysis of professional literature as well as methods of investigation, data analysis, and reporting. Practice in definition of problems, formulation of hypothesis, construction of samples, control of variables, and the interpretation of results are presented. Students will critique several computer education research studies.

ED 603 Principles of Curriculum Development (3)

This course will emphasize the concepts and processes in curriculum building and renewal. Steps in curriculum planning, organizing for curriculum change, and forces affecting curriculum development will be applied to practical situations. Students will develop and critique a computer literacy curriculum.

ED 654   Introduction to Computer-Based
         Education (3)

An overview of the application of computers in education. Fundamentals of hardware, software, classroom and administrative applications and computer literacy will be presented. Field trips and computer assisted instruction will be used in this course. Students will be introduced to LOGO to create turtle graphics.

ED 655   Instructional Application of
         Computers I (3)

This course focuses on the use of computers and related technology in the instructional process. Students will design evaluation criteria for software, apply those criteria to existing software, and design a classroom using computer technology. The topics of computer assisted instruction (CAI), computer managed instruction (CMI), and teaching computer literacy will be considered.

ED 656   Fundamentals of Programming (3)

An introduction to user-oriented computer programming languages. Students will be expected to develop proficiency in at least one programming language such as BASIC or PASCAL and one authoring language or system such as PILOT or EASE.

ED 657   Instructional Application of
         Computers II (3)

Operations research and system analysis techniques, such as modeling and programming, will be applied using such strategies as drill and practice, simulation, and tutorial instructional techniques. Students are required to design, program, (using BASIC, Logo or an authoring system of language) field test, and evaluate their own computer-based educational program. Students will assess the use of the micro vs mini vs mainframe in the classroom setting. They will assess the advantages and disadvantages of using a laboratory vs individual classroom usage.

ED 658   Non-instructional and Administrative
         Applications of Computers (3)

Application of computers in such areas as data-based management, word processing, scheduling, attendance, record keeping, reporting, electronic and spreadsheet

calculation, budgeting, personnel, counseling, and testing. Field trips will be required.

ED 659   Information Technology (3)

Present and future trends in technology such as developments in microcomputers, the video disc, and other communication systems. Emphasis is on the application of this technology to the educational process. Research on school improvement and effective staff development strategies are presented. Analysis of several case studies will promote a greater understanding of the role of the change agent in educational institutions.

COURSE REQUIREMENTS:

The Master of Science degree program in Educational Computing consists of thirty units. Courses Ed 654 – Ed 659 must be taken consecutively or, in some cases, concurrently.

ED 600   Historical, Social, and Philosophical
         Foundations of Education   (3)
ED 601   Psychological Foundations of Ed   (3)
ED 602   Introduction to Educational
         Research   (3)
ED 603   Principles of Curriculum Develop. (3)
ED 654   Introduction to Computer-Based Ed (3)
ED 655   Instructional App of Computers   (3)
ED 656   Fundamentals of Programming   (3)
ED 657   Instructional App of Computers II (3)
ED 658   Non-instructional and Administrative
         Applications of Computers   (3)
ED 659   Information Technology   (3)

The program can be completed in four trimesters. A typical sequence would be:

Trimester I   Ed 600, 601, 654

Trimester II   Ed 603, 655, 656

Trimester III   Ed 657, 658

Trimester IV   Ed 659, 602

It should be noted that the program emphasizes Logo and software evaluation in the early courses. Students also are introduced to "applications programs" (e.g. word processing) quite early in the program, and the core courses (i.e., History and Philosophy, Educational Psychology, Curriculum Development, and Education Research) are spread out over the four trimesters. Attempts are made to intergrate the content of the core courses and the content of the computer courses. Students also study programming and information technology. To be consistent with out goals, major emphasis is given to the instructional applications of computers.

HARDWARE AND SOFTWARE RESOURCES

Currently, the Masters of Science in Educational Computing is offered at two of the university centers. One of these is located in West Los Angeles and the other in Orange County. The resources at Pepperdine University Plaza (West Los Angeles) include two electronic classrooms and a computer laboratory. One electronic classroom contains 7 Commodore 64s, 1 CBM 8032, 1 Commodore PET, 1 TRS-80 Model III, 1 Atari 800, 9 Franklin 1200s linked by a network but with individual disk drives. The second electronic classroom contains "16 bit" machines: 12 IBM PCs and 7 Victor 9000s. For assignments to be completed outside of class time, students have access in the computer lab to 4 Apples, 3 IBM PCs, 2 Victor 9000s, 1 Osborne, and a Commodore PET. The academic laboratory is open late in the evenings and on Saturdays to provide students with access to a range of microcomputers. The electronic classrooms are opened if demand exceeds lab resources.

In Orange County we have 9 Franklin 1000s networked through a Corona hard-disk drive, 6 commodore 64s, 1 TRS80 Model III, 1 Atari 800, 2 Apple IIs and 7 Victor 9000s.

We were very fortunate: Pepperdine was selected as one of the 12 teacher training institutions across the nation to participate in the "IBM Model Schools Project". As a member we received 15 IBM PCs, 5 printers and over $20,000 in software. Commodore also donated 12 Commodore 64s, 12 datasettes, 4 disk drives and 3 printers. Panasonic loaned a complete interactive videotape set-up and Videovision donated several video-discs and accompanying software. This equipment has been incorporated into our program.

In the software area we currently have available all the MECC and "Softswap" materials. In addition, funds are budgeted each year to purchase a variety of new software. Further, some publishers have generously donated, or provided extended loans of their materials. Additionally, some

TABLE 2. COURSE COMPETENCIES FOR M.S. EDUCATIONAL COMPUTING

	COMPUTER AWARENESS	PROGRAMMING AUTHORING	SOFTWARE EVALUATION	USE GENERIC APPLICATION	SOFTWARE DEVELOP	PLANNING & IMPLEMENTION	HARDWARE EVALUATION
600	History, sociology, philosophy—Discussion of ALL these areas focusing on "problems" and "benefits" computer brings to Education						
601	Analyze features of computer literacy program - Intro to Artificial Intell.		Create portion of evaluation sheet related to learning theory			Analyze features of computer literacy program	
654	Overview history, use, ed. applications, terminology, philosophy overviewing computer	• Logo I turtlegraphics to adv. graphics, music	Use of 3 existing forms 1. Inventory 2. Scholastic 3. Other			Analyze factors to intiate "start-up" at site	Identify criteria to select approp. computer
655		• Logo II • Classroom authoring systems to prepare lessons	• Design own evaluation sheet • Learn participant observation to evaluate software	Using a word processor in designing lessons		Design alternate classroom configurations	
656	Role of programming in comp. literacy. Application of programming in an elemen./ sec. classroom	BASIC Codes (opt) Private Tutor (opt)			Flowcharting Top-down programming. Edit pubic domain soft.		
603	Create a computer based curriculum from a logically-devised position			Integrating computers into existing school curriculum			Classroom set up & budget
657		Use of authoring language and/or BASIC CLASS (opt)	Evaluate latest software package. Field test		Develop software Design computer lab.		Lab vs. classroom? Mainframe vs mini vs micro
658	Specific administrative problems. Political implications of Admin. applications		Ed. Admin. packages. Attendance Reporting Grades Counseling Compare Apple	Spreadsheet Data Base Mgt. Word Processing Graphics Individual applications PC DOS	Gradebook & budget on spreadsheet or DBMS	Utilization of admin. software in school setting	Professional computers Establishing admin. configurations
659	Teleconferencing Telecommunication	BASIC Authoring Systems	Evaluate latest software Videotape & Videodiscs		Future developments awareness	Program develop. implementation strategies Impact of tech. on ed. Analysis of case studies	Future developments Videotape Videodisc Peripherals
602	Role in Research & Evaluation	Data Manipulation Data Files SPS	Process Evaluations Evaluations			Outcome Assessments	Effectiveness Analyses

students purchase their own software, or they are able to borrow software from their school district or other places of employment that they bring into class and lab for demonstration purposes. One other source of software has been software that the students develop themselves.

AN EVALUATION OF THE PROGRAM

We accepted our first students into the program in January, 1983 at the West Los Angeles campus. Our first students were accepted in Orange County in April of 1983. Since that time we have accepted four additional classes in Los Angeles each averaging 25 students. In Orange County we have accepted 3 classes with an average class size of 18 students.

Our students have quite diverse backgrounds. As predicted most have been elementary and secondary school teachers. However, we have had several administrators, people from higher education, industrial trainers, publishers, and software developers. Interestingly, many of our students have already earned masters or doctorate degrees, and they are returning to school to upgrade and expand their skills in the computer area.

Students anonymously complete course evaluation forms, and they are encouraged to talk with faculty members and administrators regarding the program. These data indicate a high degree of satisfaction with the course and with the instructors. Similarly, members of the advisory committee seem to be quite satisfied, and even impressed with the program.

In summary, student and faculty evaluation highlight the following:

• Using Logo in the first course proved to be a winner. Students programmed the turtle to draw a house, their initials, a flower and a design of their own choosing. They learned primitives, procedures, subprocedures, and recursion. But many of them wanted more. Logo list processing was introduced into Ed 655, the second computer class.

• The amount of hands-on time can never be enough. In some classes, half of class time was spent on the computer; others used small groups on computers for the entire session. No matter how much we offered, it could always be extended.

TABLE 3. MATERIALS/RESOURCES USED IN M.S. EDUCATIONAL COMPUTING

	COMPUTER AWARENESS	PROGRAMMING/ AUTHORING	SOFTWARE EVALUATION	USE GENERIC APPLICATION	SOFTWARE DEVELOP.	PROGRAM PLANNING & IMPLEMENTATION	HARDWARE EVALUATION
600					Victor-data base program		
601					CONDUIT AI Programs		
654		• Terrapin Logo • Apple Logo • Commodore Logo • Dan Watt text	Softswap Commodore MECC Scholastic IBM				Evaluate 2 or 3 microcomputers in electronic classroom
655		Logo - Text edit EASE Pilot Ezy Pilot	MECC & Commercial Software	Bank Street writer Wordstar Victorwriter Easywriter			
656		BASIC					
603							
657		CLASS BASIC BLOCKS			MECC Manuals Graphic Pads		Network/hard disk systems
658			Commercial - e.g., Equip, Bursar, CERF,	Administrative appli- e.g., Easywriter, pfs: Apple-athletics Multiplan, pfs: Graph Wordproof, Typefaces, Wordstar DBII	Budget applications, and planning File Visicalc, some	IBM PC Victor Some Apple Some	Commodore
659	The Source/Compu-Serve Modems-software programs	• Videovision authoring system • McGraw-Hill authoring system	Videovision video-Commercially prepared videodiscs			Analysis of several studies Speech Digitizer/	Pioneer/Sony Video-tape, videodisc Synthesizer
602	V 9000 IBM/PC UNIVAC						

- Programming in BASIC is a required course. Some students came to the class with some BASIC knowledge, some with none. The class could not be taught as a single unit. Two different levels of instruction were required. But this presented a longer range problem – perhaps two classes should be offered? One immediate solution: one course dealing with "Introduction to BASIC Programming" for those with no previous experience, and "Advanced BASIC Programming" for others will be offered in future trimesters.

- All students in the program recently evaluated the M.S. in Educational Computing. Their assessment was similar to ours: a) reorganize the BASIC Programming course to meet individual differences; b) provide more electives within the program. It appears that these electives will initially occur in the "programming" area. We are now considering four electives. In addition to the above two courses we may offer "Introduction to Pascal" and "Logo II" (word and list processing).

- The introduction of a teaching assistant's program will be continued. Each instructor selected one student to assist with grading papers, organizing resource material and laboratory support. As one professor stated, "this (teaching assistant program) is the best thing we have ever done." Teaching assistants received a scholarship equivalent to three units of credit for their efforts.

It is quite apparent that we have come a long way from the ruminations of two rather quixotic professors. In our opinion, the results have been quite favorable, and we look forward to the continued growth and development of our program. It is our opinion that the graduates will be on the forefront of the computer revolution in education---and we sincerely hope that they will make significant contributions that will benefit all. As with any educational program, the real evaluation of the program is assessed by the quality and the proficiency of its graduates. Based upon this criterion, we really hope and believe that we have a winner.

COMPUTERS IN EDUCATION, K. Duncan and D. Harris (eds.)
Elsevier Science Publishers B.V. (North-Holland)
© IFIP, 1985

COMPUTERS IN EDUCATION: A COURSE FOR TEACHERS

Neil Hall

School of Education
Riverina College of Advanced Education
Wagga Wagga, Australia

Riverina College of Advanced Education offers a course on computers in education for
qualified and experienced school teachers. This course is available only through
correspondence study.
The content of the course emphasises the application of microcomputers across the
curriculum, taking into account what we know about learning, teaching and curriculum
development. The course caters for all teachers regardless of the grades they teach.

Since July 1983 Riverina College of Advanced
Education has offered a two year part-time,
correspondence course on computers in education
for experienced teachers. To be eligible for
this course applicants must have at least a
three year academic qualification in teaching
and have taught for at least two years. Intending students must also have regular access to a
microcomputer with a disk drive. At present the
College is able to cater only for Apple II,
Commodore 64 and Atari 800XL microcomputers.

The course involves four semesters of part time,
correspondence study, with two subjects studied
each semester. There is a July intake each
year, so as to allow students to attend a
residential school in the August/September
school vacation, early in the course. Compulsory residential schools are held during school
vacations for four days in each of the first
two semesters, with an optional two day
residential school in the third semester.

The course had been planned over a three year
period: in some ways this was unnecessarily
long, but much time had to be spent convincing
various individuals, groups and official
committees both within and outside the college
that there was a need for the type of course we
had in mind. The whole exercise has been
littered with financial, economic, educational,
philosophic and computerese arguments as well as
a good selection of red herrings. One could
summarise these different views in this way:
the computer scientists' belief that such a
course should have computer programming as its
major emphasis, together with a heavy loading of
esoteric computerese and electronic paraphenalia
versus the educationalists' view that it is
more relevant for teachers to learn about the
educational applications of computers in a
broader context. This broader context would
include some computer programming, but would
also include significant work on how children
learn, on a variety of teaching strategies, and
on curriculum development. The latter view
held sway.

The course attempts to blend aspects of
computer technology with aspects of the field
of education, to provide an educationally
justifiable synthesis of these two fields. The
course caters for both primary and secondary
school teachers, with teaching specialisations
being taken into account within subjects rather
than by separate elective subjects.

AIMS

The course had the following aims

> To develop an awareness of the impact of
> computers on society in general, and on
> education in particular.

> To provide insights into the ways in which
> computers can be used across the school
> curriculum to meet desired educational
> objectives.

> To develop skills of organisation which
> facilitate the effective utilisation of
> computers when such use is seen as an
> appropriate means of achieving curriculum
> objectives.

> To identify the limitations and possible
> abuses of computers, in society in general
> and in the educational setting in partic-
> ular.

> To develop competence in operating
> computers in schools, and in managing
> computer resources.

> To give basic skills in writing and
> adapting computer programs to meet
> specific educational needs.

> To develop competence in responding to the
> inservice needs of colleagues in the field
> of computers in education.

To provide knowledge and skills in the use of computers for management and administrative purposes in the school to which the student is attached.

SUBJECTS TO BE STUDIED

1.   Teaching, Learning and Computers
      (Semester 1)

A study of models of teaching and learning, and theories of human development, together with an examination of the characteristics of educational computer software that satisfies various models and theories.

This subject tries to assist students to look at educational software in broader terms than simply content. We know a good deal about how children learn, and we use various models of teaching: do computer programs exist, or are we able to design educational computer programs that effectively reflect this knowledge.

2.   Computing Skills in Education
      (Semesters 1 and 2)

This subject begins with a look at computer technology, and then turns to programming in Basic. The second semester starts with a study of computer applications and the social implications of these applications. Students are then able to select three options from twelve: options include Logo, authoring languages, further Basic, modifying educational software and documenting educational software.

As is mentioned later, the initial version of this subject was much more mathematically and business oriented and caused a good deal of student reaction.

3.   Computers and the Curriculum
      (Semester 2)

The application of computers to a variety of curriculum areas, particularly through the trialling and evaluation of educational computer software.

In this subject students are encouraged to look at a variety of content areas, regardless of their professional background, so as to ensure that they have some feeling for the use of computers across the curriculum. Assignments in this subject include evaluating software from a curriculum point of view, together with planning units of work for use in classrooms.

4.   Computers and the School
      (Semester 3)

Examining those aspects of classroom and school operations for which a computer might provide an effective tool. Through analysis of the school situation, students attempt to answer the question "does my school need a computer?".

The assignment for this subject is cumulative in nature: students initially describe their school situation, and eventually have to prepare a report to be put to the School Council/Parent group outlining the computer needs of the school, with both detailed resource requirements and justifications.

5.   Designing Educational Packages
      (Semesters 3 and 4)

This subject requires students to bring together their educational, curricular and programming knowledge, understandings and skills to carry out a project of their own choice. Projects may involve programming, particularly if the project involves creating educational software, but many non-programming possibilities exist too. The subject seeks to provide students with the opportunity to pursue a topic of their own choosing, one that is of practical use to them.

6.   Leadership and Computers in Education
      (Semester 4)

Attempts to help students develop those qualities of educational leadership that will enable them to become more effective leaders in the field of computers in education. In addition to looking at some theoretical aspects of educational leadership, this subject requires students to prepare a teacher in-service activity.

TEACHING THE COURSE

As has been mentioned before, this course is taught by external study. Students live at varying distances from the college, and rely on text books and teaching notes to guide their studies. An assumption underlying the preparation of these teaching materials was that the course should have a practical orientation. That is, rather than communicating a body of knowledge much of which may not be relevant to a given student's circumstances, the emphasis was on providing flexible learning activities for students: activities that students could adapt to suit their own situations.

The subject Computing Skills in Education was initially based on a modified version of an introductory programming subject taught else-where in the college. This led to a great deal of ill feeling from students who felt they were being asked to learn skills which were of no long term benefit to them: this was made worse by the nature of many of the assignments which were mathematical or business oriented. Students' reactions to this subject were so strong that it was altered part-way through its first teaching session: and received a major revision prior to its being taught for the second time. The subject is now much more oriented to microcomputers, and to the school situation. The assignments are more education-ally oriented, and a range of options have been

provided to allow students some choice in the
direction they take.

Students have been complimentary in expressing
their support for the practical nature of the
course. Unsolicited remarks often accompany
assignment submissions, generally referring to
the valuable nature of the assignment concerned.
Reactions to the programming assignments aside,
students have felt very positive about the
orientation and value of the course.

The first residential school was held in
August/September 1983. Some students found the
programming aspect of the residential school
hard going. They felt there was too much
content covered too quickly, with too few
computers available. The equivalent residential
school for 1984 has not yet been held, but the
comments made by these students in 1983 have
been or will be acted upon. The May 1984
residential school was concerned only with the
subject Computers and the Curriculum, and so
emphasised the use and evaluation of computer
software suitable for schools. Students rated
this residential school highly.

The course sets out to provide teachers with
the kinds of knowledge and experiences that
will make them critical users of computer
technology, users who seek to apply computers
to maximise the value of a learner's educational experiences. Graduates from this course
will know a good deal about computers per se,
will have some insights into computer programming and will know a great deal about the
effective application of computers in
educational settings. Our first intake of
students are still involved in the course and
will not have graduated until mid-1985; all the
same, it is clear that these students are
moving towards the successful achievement of
the set aims and objectives.

COMPUTERS IN EDUCATION, K. Duncan and D. Harris (eds.)
Elsevier Science Publishers B.V. (North-Holland)
© IFIP, 1985

MODEL SYLLABUS FOR LITERACY FOR ALL TEACHERS

Prof.Peter Gorny
University of Oldenburg
Federal Republic of Germany

drs.Tom J.van Weert
Institute for Teacher Education
"Ubbo Emmius"
The Netherlands

The model syllabus "Literacy in Information Technology for all Teachers" was developed by the Working Group on New Information Technologies of the Association for Teacher Education in Europe (ATEE) [x]. It is the feeling of the Working Group that the ideas on the definition, requirements and implementation of the concept of Computer Literacy, as currently developed in the United States of America, can be added to, thereby arriving at a notion of literacy in Information Technology that is tailored to European needs and perspectives. The model syllabus is intended to serve as a basis for discussion.

Four classes of educational use of Information Technology can be identified:
- learning about Information Technology,
- learning with the aid of Information Technology,
- learning by means of Information Technology,
- Information Technology as an aid to school management.

The priority, as the Working Group sees it, is to help teachers understand the new technology and use it appropriately from a fundament of knowledge (literacy) about Information Technology.

The central need in the teaching of literacy in Information Technology is to create insights which enable the teachers to develop a reasoned and balanced attitude towards Information Technology and which enabels them furthermore to react appropriately to situations in which contact with automated systems takes place.

Moving from environment to machine, four subject areas can be discerned:
- Social Impact,
- Use of Application Systems,
- Problem Solving by Algorithmic Methods,
- Principles of Software and Machine Architecture.
A fifth subject area is the methodology of teaching about Information Technology.

All teachers should be provided with a basic literacy in Information Technology in courses covering five course areas related to the five subject areas mentioned:
  i Information Technology and Society,
 ii Practical Work with Applications Software,
iii Introduction to Problem Solving by
       Algorithmic Means,
 iv Introduction to the Architecture of
       Information Technology Systems,
  v Methodology of Teaching Information
       Technology.
The model syllabus contains descriptions of the first four course areas.

[x] ATEE
   Association for Teacher Education in Europe
   51, Rue de la Concorde
   1050 Brussels
   Belgium

COMPUTERS IN EDUCATION, K. Duncan and D. Harris (eds.)
Elsevier Science Publishers B.V. (North-Holland)
© IFIP, 1985

RECOMMENDATIONS FOR THE TRAINING AND CERTIFICATION OF TEACHERS

Task Group on Teacher Certification and
Teacher Certification Committee

Association for Computing Machinery and
International Council for Computers in Education

This session will be reports by the ACM Task Group on Teacher Certification and the ICCE Teacher Certification Committee. Following the reports, there will be a panel discussion by committee members about their recommendations. Audience participation is encouraged.

Report of the ACM Task Group on Teacher Certification

A program of study leading to certification of computer science teachers at the precollege level will be presented. Recommendations for required and elective courses are provided. The objectives of each course are listed, with greater detail supplied for courses not commonly found in a university level computer science curriculum. The recommendations are the product of an ACM task group effort and were accepted by the ACM Education Board and the IEEE Computer Society Education Committee.

Committee Members:

James Pcirot, North Texas State University
Arthur Luehrmann, Computer Literacy
Cathleen Norris, North Texas State University
Harriet Taylor, Louisiana State University
Robert Taylor, Columbia University

Report of the ICCE Teacher Certification Committee

The proliferation of computers in the schools and of computer-using educator programs has resulted in a need to establish certification requirements. Competencies and course requirements need to be established for the following groups:

1. all teachers
2. teachers by grade level or subject
3. teachers of computer science
4. computer specialists (coordinators, etc.)

The ICCE believes that the determining of certification requirements should be a grassroots development with practitioners formulating their own recommendations.

Individual states are beginning to address the issue of teacher certification, and some states have legislation in process. The ICCE committee has formulated recommendations and guidelines for state committees to use in developing their own teacher certification requirements.

Members of the ICCE committee will discuss the process of establishing certification requirements and report their results.

Committee Members:

Tony Jongejan, Western Washington University
Bobby Goodson, ICCE
Margaret Moore, Oregon State University

COMPUTERS IN EDUCATION, K. Duncan and D. Harris (eds.)
Elsevier Science Publishers B.V. (North-Holland)
© IFIP, 1985

EXAMINING THE RETRAINING STRATEGIES FOR OBTAINING COMPUTER FACULTY

Moderator: John Beidler, University of Scranton, Scranton, PA

Panelists: Carter Bays, Univ. of South Carolina
             Janet Hartman, University of Evansville
             Zaven Karian, Denison University
             William Mitchell, Univ. of Evansville
             Lawrence E. Levine, Stevens Institute of Technology
             Darrell Turnridge, Kent State University

This session presents both a status report and a forum for discussing the issues and impact of formally retraining faculty from other disciplines to teach undergraduate computer science. A data base on participants and graduates of full-time summer retraining programs has been established at the University of Evansville, and the session commences with a summary of the collected data on nine classes from five programs. This is followed by short presentations on three current retraining thrusts, IFRICS, the State of New Jersey plan, and the program at the University of Evansville by panelists, who are deeply involved in these programs. Several participant in these retraining programs will act as respondent to the panel and provide insights from the point of view of the retrainees.

Dr. Carter Bays, of the University of South Carolina, established the first retraining program in 1979 with the assistance of a government grant. After six summers the program was discontinued. Dr. Bays will act as a "devil's advocate" on this panel.

Dr. Janet Hartman reports on the characteristics of retrainees and their attitudes toward the retraining experience and their new responsibilities as instructors in undergraduate computing programs.

Dr. Zaven Karian of Denison University is a member of the MAA/ACM Joint Committee on Retraining for Computer Science which oversees the various programs offered through the Institute for Retraining in Computer Science (IFRICS). In addition, Dr. Karian has participated in computer programs at Ohio State University which sought to provide growth opportunities in computer science for a consortium of nearby small colleges.

Dr. Lawrence E. Levine, Stevens Institute of Technology, describes the program established by the State of New Jersey to provide for greater access to computing science instruction within the State. Although housed at Stevens, this program was designed in consultation with computer science departments at three other State institutions and has as its goals the preparation of a faculty member competent to present any core undergraduate course in computer science.

Dr. William Mitchell established the Masters of Computer Science Education program at the University of Evansville a year before the IFRICS program was established at Clarkson University. The program was established for many of the same concerns, namely, that small colleges have a great demand for computing faculty and are unable to currently meet this demand in the marketplace. This program seeks to prepare experienced faculty who are able to establish and present quality lower division computing courses in computer science, information systems, education, or data processing. Although the participants are drawn from many different disciplines, they must be experienced programmers and demonstrate a concern for curricular considerations.

Dr. Darrell Trunridge of Kent State University is the Director of the second program established under the auspices of IFRICS. The curriculum and selection criteria at Kent State mirrors that developed for the original IFRICS program at Clarkson University, which has already selected and trained two classes. IFRICS focuses on the retraining of mathematicians, particularly those from smaller colleges with a liberal arts emphasis and intends to infuse into those institutions a balanced understanding of the theory and practice of computer science. Unlike the other programs presented in this panel, IFRICS does not award a degree.

Issues and Ethics

COMPUTERS IN EDUCATION, K. Duncan and D. Harris (eds.)
Elsevier Science Publishers B.V. (North-Holland)
© IFIP, 1985

EQUITY ISSUES IN THE INFORMATION AGE

Dr. Robert L. Caret
Dean of Natural and
  Mathematical Sciences
Smith Hall
Towson State University
Towson, MD. 21204

Dr. Doris Lidtke
Department of Computer and
  Information Sciences
Cook Library
Towson State University
Towson, MD. 21204

Reports that the number of microcomputers in schools have been doubling each year and that colleges and universities report large increases in the amount of computer hardware should encourage us all. However closer examination indicates that access to this equipment is not at all uniform. It is therefore important to determine who is attaining access to this equipment. In this dawn of the information age, are we creating an information rich and an information poor through our educational system? Are the socio-economic, racial and sexual inequities of the past influencing the computing education of today? What evidence is available? What solutions can we suggest?

Each panelist will address one of the important questions concerning equity of access to computing in education. The panelists will cover the spectrum of elementary, secondary and post-secondary education in both public and private institutions. Evidence from studies and surveys will be presented.

1. Ms. Beth Lowd
    Specialist for Computers in
      Instruction
    Lexington Public Schools
      System
    Lexington, MA. 02173

2. Dr. Robert L. Caret
    Dean of Natural and Mathematical
      Sciences
    Smith Hall
    Towson State University
    Towson, MD. 21204

CLASSROOM EQUITY AT THE PRE-COLLEGE UNIVERSITY LEVEL

In elementary schools, there are many inequities related to computer use. In my community, the most striking difference is between students who use a computer at home (most, but not all, of whom are white males) and those who do not. Required courses can never make up for their advantage. This appears to be fundamentally an economic inequity, though parent prejudices often make it sexist as well. Taken more globally, we can see that my students whose parents routinely use computers at home and at work have an immense advantage over those in the rural farm town where I used to teach, whether they have used home computers or not. To my students computers are everyday tools.

At a disadvantage are students in some communities who never are allowed to be in control of this new technology, who are always forced to respond to it. Their teachers have been seduced by the false promise of faster rote learning, rather than seeing ways that the computer can empower children to learn how to become lifelong learners in the information age.

and

Dr. Doris Lidtke
Department of Computer and
  Information Sciences
Cook Library
Towson State University
Towson, MD. 21204

CLASSROOM EQUITY AT THE COLLEGE AND UNIVERSITY LEVEL

The "Information Age" has come upon us at a time when higher education is in a difficult position to respond appropriately.

1. The demographics are working against us; the cohort of high school age graduates is shrinking on a year by year basis and will continue to do so through the 1980's.

2. Government is cutting back.

3. And the private sector is not responding to fill the void.

This presentation will concentrate on these forces and their potential effect on computer education in the decade ahead. The relative effects on three

major classes of the four-year higher
education institutions will be contrasted: research universities, comprehensive universities, and liberal
arts colleges. Particular emphasis
will be focused on the role of the
private sector: what it is doing in
contrast to what it should be doing.

3. Mrs. Carol Edwards
   Director of Project MICRO
   75 Marietta Street, N.W.
   Suite 308
   Atlanta, Ga. 30303

SOCIO-ECONOMIC EQUITY: HAVES VERSUS HAVE NOTS

Technology holds promise for the future.
Whether that promise translates to progress depends in part on the quality of
social decisions we, as educators, make.
In educational computing the haves and
have nots can already be distinguished.
If minorities, the economically disadvantaged and girls are to have future
equal opportunity, educators must set
policies and implement actions which
result in qualitative as well as quantitative access to instructional computing. In this presentation we will first
explore how institutional racism affects
educational computing. We will also
examine some of the practices being
tried to meet this challenge focusing
upon innovative approaches such as
Project MICRO.

4. Ms. Marlaine Lockheed
   Educational Testing Service
   Princeton, N.J. 08541

GENDER EQUITY IN COMPUTER USE: LIMITED STUDY ON GENDER ISSUES IN THE CLASSROOM

Recent large scale surveys have found
that girls are more likely than boys to
have (or to believe that they have)
access to computers in school, out of
school, and at home. Is this the case?
The purpose of this presentation will
be to review recent evidence regarding
four factors that effect girls' access
to and use of computers:

1. Gender Segregation;

2. Direct Socilization Regarding The
   Gender Appropriateness of Computers;

3. The Quality and Relevance of
   Computer Courses;

4. Economic Factors.

In addition, this conception about
gender differences in computer competence will be laid to rest through a
review of current research.

5. Mr. Fred Weingarden
   Office of Technology Assessment
   Communication and Information
   Technologies Program
   Congress of the United States
   Washington, D.C. 20510

EDUCATIONAL TECHNOLOGY AND SOCIAL EQUITY

Equitable access for all of the benefits
of education has been a basic guiding
principle of American education policy
for well over a century (of course,
interpretations of who should be included under the term "all" have
changed drastically over time). Educational technology interacts with these
equity issues in four basic ways.

1. Many of the stresses now felt by the
   educational system are created by
   society's demand for equal educational opportunity. Technology can
   play a major role in helping schools
   meet these demands.

2. If educational technology is the
   powerful and cost effective tool
   that proponents argue, inequity of
   access among schools or ability to
   use technology may result in inequity
   of education. This imbalance can
   be of particular concern to the
   extent that private and for-profit
   institutions are more able to obtain
   and utilize technology.

3. Information technology and the
   evolving information industry provides many alternate forms and
   institutional mechanisms for delivering education. These new forms and
   mechanisms, if successful, could
   challenge public schools by drawing
   off middle class students eroding
   public support.

4. Educational technology may, itself,
   be self-selecting and create new
   classes of disadvantaged -- those
   students whose cognitive styles or
   ability to adapt to automated
   learning systems is limited. Schools
   that use technology heavily may
   stress subjects and approaches that
   are most easily taught on those media.

COMPUTERS IN EDUCATION, K. Duncan and D. Harris (eds.)
Elsevier Science Publishers B.V. (North-Holland)
©IFIP, 1985

EQUITY ISSUES--2

Antonia Stone, Vicki Carver, Leslie Leath,
Susan Rappoport and Jo Shuchat Sanders

International Council for Computers in Education

The danger that the growth of computer technology will widen the gap between rich and poor and between male and female, increase the problems of obtaining employment by changing the definition of "entry-level job" and exacerbate the social and gender-based problems of poverty and unemployment has received increasing national attention in the press and even in the halls of Congress.

"Floppy Disk" and "Modem" are becoming household words in the homes of those who can afford personal computers, whose children attend "computer-rich" schools. Where is the school dropout, the unwed mother, the ex-offender to go to acquire the degree of computer experience and knowledge that may make the difference between being on welfare and paying taxes? Will computer avoidance by girls in school handicap their education and job potential?

This session will focus on projects underway to ensure that opportunities for computer learning are made available to people who are disadvantaged socially, economically, geographically, and by gender.

Antonia Stone, Chair
Playing To Win
New York, New York

Jo Shuchat Sanders
Women's Action Alliance
New York, New York

The federally funded Computer Equity Training Project will be described. Project staff have researched the causes of the computer gender gap and are now conducting a nationwide test of school-based strategies to encourage greater computer use by girls. The book containing the strategies, The Neuter Computer: Why and How to Encourage Computer Equity for Girls, will be published in September. Ms. Sanders will also discuss a common misconception among educators: that improving the overall quality of a computer education program is sufficient to deal with the computer equity problem.

Vicki Carver
Playing to Win Computer Center
New York, New York

One response to the lack of opportunities for computer learning and use in poverty areas is the establishment of open access computer learning centers. The Playing to Win East Harlem Computer Center, opened in 1983 in the Washington Housing Project, is just such a pioneering effort. With 24 microcomputer systems, an abundance of application and learning games software and a lending library, the Center serves 600 plus preschoolers, school children, teenagers and adults from East Harlem, Harlem, the Bronx and surrounding neighborhoods. Because it is

unprecedented, much of the Center's programs and operation have had to be invented from scratch and on the spot. This presentation will describe that process and what has been learned from it, as well as current center programs and projections for the future.

Susan Rappaport
The New York Public Library
New York, New York

Since 1983, the New York Public Library has been involved in a microcomputer project in the branch libraries. The purpose of the project is to provide computer access to people who don't normally have that access. The results of these beginning stages were excellent. It was discovered that computer services fit very well into the mainstream of standard library services. Appointments for computers were booked weeks in advance, and people who did not ordinarily use the library were attracted because of the computer access.

Now the number of computers in the library has more than doubled. We have also just begun a new program using computers to teach adults how to read. In this way, adults learn not only basic skills, but also computer skills adaptable to the work situation.

Because the library is an information center, it is becoming increasingly important to give people hands-on access to computers for various educational purposes.

Leslie Leath
Director of Education
Massachusetts Department of Corrections

Since 1983 the Massachusetts Department of Corrections has supported and implemented a computer assisted instructional program in five major correctional facilities. The program consists of integrating the use of Logo, word processing, graphics and drill-and-practice software into the school program in these facilities.

The typical inmate has either been turned off by or dropped out of traditional educational programs. Correctional educators are consistently faced with the responsibilities for designing programs and using instructional methods which will attract and retain these inmates. Computers are seen as a means of producing a new and different learning environment. Incorporation of microcomputers into prison education is a way to attract more inmates to the education programs.

Inmates are isolated from the world in an environment which maintains total control over their lives while incarcerated. In addition many of them have failed in a traditional education environment. Microcomputers are used in ways that provide experiences both with success and control and real world applications.

A team of two teachers from each participating institution was involved in a week long workshop, followed by site visitations and inservice days as well as occasional general meetings. Each team was responsible for training other staff members thus broadening the project. Sites visits, sharing sessions, the general meetings and the journal that the project staff are keeping have provided us with many anecdotes. The inmates have responded favorable to Logo. The teaching of Logo has kept the project alive and moving as other software is added to the project activities.

COMPUTERS IN EDUCATION, K. Duncan and D. Harris (eds.)
Elsevier Science Publishers B.V. (North-Holland)
©IFIP, 1985

SOFTWARE--COPYRIGHT AND MARKETING ISSUES

LeRoy Finkel, Bodie Marx, Carol Risher and Leslie Wharton

International Council for Computers in Education

This session will discuss the impact of copyright law interpretation and the educational use of microcomputer software, the impact of vendor marketing policies on schools, and the ICCE Policy Statement on Network and Multiple Machine Software.
There are no definitive answers to most questions regarding copyright law interpretation. The copyright law is vague in places, and there have been no court cases to set precedent. Nevertheless, copyright attorneys, court watchers and lawmakers all seem to agree on the likely interpretation for issues of back-up copies, networks, and multiple-loading or booting from one disk into multiple machines at the same time. School districts must recognize that software authors, developers and vendors are entitled to a fair return on their investments. They need to pass software policies and enforce them to ensure only legal uses of software on school campuses.
Educators have a valid need for quality software and reasonable prices. They also need accurate and up-to-date information on marketing policies such as multiple-copy discounts, special licenses for multiple-loading software, networking, etc. Software publishers/distributors seem reluctant to publish this information.
Some panelists are members of an ICCE Software Policy Committee which drafted a policy statement on Network and Multiple Machine Software. This committee has been reconvened to examine the current state-of-the-art (things in law tend to change over time) and review the current policies. Members of that committee will report on their progress and seek input from the audience.
LeRoy Finkel, Chair
San Mateo County Office of Education, California

Bodie Marx, Vice President
Mindscape, Inc., Northbrook, Illinois

Educational software publishers and educators appear to be at a impasse regarding equitable policies for purchase and use of software in schools with multiple computers. Educational software publishers must be able to forecast a reasonable return of their investment to develop, market and support quality educational software that educators are demanding. Educators must recognize the high development, marketing and support costs associated with educational software. This presentation will try to offer some compromise solutions without which this nascent publishing industry might never fulfill earlier expectations.

Carol A. Risher, Copyright and New Technology
Association of American Publishers, Inc.
Washington, D.C.

The Association of American Publishers represents software and book publishers. It is the position of the Association that the U.S. Copyright Act clearly specifies what can and what cannot be done with computer software in an educational setting. AAP has established an enforcement fund to actively see that compliance with the law is achieved. The presentation will summarize those aspects of the copyright law

relevant to the use of computers in education and will seek to assist attendees in determining how they can make maximum use of computers in education while still adhering to the copyright law. The presentation will include comments on policy statements adopted by schools and universities around the country in an effort to ensure that faculty members and students comply with the copyright law.

Leslie Wharton, Attorney at Law
Matthews & Branscomb, San Antonio, Texas

I will discuss copyright law as it applies to computer software (programs and accompanying documentation) and data bases as prepared for and used in the educational environment. In particular, I will focus on problems associated with the use of software on network systems, multiple-loading or booting of a single disk into several machines at the same time, possible applications of the fair use doctrine to educational uses of software, and S 117 of the Copyright Act as it may affect the right of educators to make back-up copies, alterations, translations, or other "derivative" works based on copyrighted software. I will also discuss some of the perceived differences between copyright law as it applies to the "owner" of a copy of a program, and the "licensee" or "lessee" of a copy of a computer program.

COMPUTERS IN EDUCATION, K. Duncan and D. Harris (eds.)
Elsevier Science Publishers B.V. (North-Holland)
© IFIP, 1985

"HOW SHOULD ETHICS BE TAUGHT?"

a question for a
PANEL DISCUSSION

JOHN McLEOD, Moderator
Society for Computer Simulation

In 1983 the Moderator was awarded a National Science Foundation grant to study "Ethical Issues for Computer Simulation Under Conditions of Uncertainty." The primary purpose of that investigation was to develop a set of "Ethical Guidelines for the Professional Conduct of Simulationists" which would help simulationists to -- among other things -- cope with the hazards of "soft" data. However, during the course of that study I was interested to find that it seems that most of us acquire what sense of ethics we have by some kind of osmosis.

True, there are courses taught on the subject, and some individuals and organizations, notably the EVIST (Ethics and Values in Science and Technology) Program at the National Science Foundation, the Ethics Resource Center in Washington, and the Center for the Study of Ethics in the Professions at the Illinois Institute of Technology in Chicago, are funding, conducting and/or promoting studies of ethics. Others are concerned, but there certainly does not seem to be any consensus as to how ethics should be taught in existing educational institutions.

It is the Moderator's hope that the panelists and audience will thresh this matter out and help separate the wheat from the chaff. There is probably no _one_ best way to teach ethics, but I believe that the more the subject is discussed by people who are concerned and knowledgeable about the matter, the better our chances of instilling a sense of the importance of teaching ethics, and in practicing ethical behavior in our professions.

To this end I have invited several professional educators to participate in a discussion of the subject. As a result, the following preliminary comments have been elicited.

From DANIEL RADELL, Associate Professor; Management Information Systems; Norfolk State University; Norfolk, Virginia.

"How Should Ethics Be Taught?"

By _example_ -- e.g. when, and if, our actions are ethical they provide clear-cut, unequivocal individual and collective examples of what is meant by or expected from ethical behavior.

In this sense, of course, the proposition that ethics should be taught is accepted as a given (neither subject to nor requiring discussion) and individual differences of opinion as to the meaning or definition of _ethics_ are disregarded.

1.	SITUATION	Identification of situation requiring a decision and the possible alternative courses of action.
2.	ETHICAL ACTION	Definition/ identification of the "ethics" at issue and the choice of action (in keeping with ethical guidelines).
3.	FOCUS	Focus of attention on the action taken; identification of rejected alternatives.
4.	EXPLANATION	Discussion and explanation of action taken; dissemination of pertinent facts to the widest extent possible.
5.	REINFORCEMENT	Coupling of action taken with particular ethic (or moral standard involved); discussion of the necessity for such action in terms of existing standards/ethics.

*   *   *

From EDWARD KOROSTOFF, Ph.D., 6421 Overbrook Avenue, Philadelphia, Pennsylvania 19151.

I have always had an interest in the ethical (and more often, in the unethical) behaviors of people, and in society's acceptance of a very low standard for human behavior. Most of the bile I secrete (if that is what is emitted during anger) has to do with my feelings about the immoral commissions by lawyers, politicians, and other institutionalized liars (that is a bit strong, and I do not mean, of course, to include _all_ in those professions). Of course, being perfect, I do not even have the occasional occasion to require rationalizations for my own acts!

How is ethics taught? I am not sure. Perhaps a definition is first required of the content of what is to be taught. Properly defined, it may point the way to the teaching.

I believe that many if not most ethical violations stem from the general acceptance and use of untruth as an operative parameter. Is it not a lie for a writer of software to place a value of $500 on a program (which is really the successor to a book that may be priced at $20-$50) and then use the power of the law to prosecute users, for whom the act of copying is so trivial to carry out? The lie about the value, combined with the ease of copying, provides a discontinuity so great as to defy any common-sense application of either outrage or legal recourse.

But application of the foregoing logic has to be modified for any circumstances that may determine the real value to the user of the 'pirated' program. For an individual, e.g., an educator, who wants to possess a number of programs for general informational input, there is no compensating dollar income to pay for the $400 times ten programs that he might want to study. On the other hand, a corporation (or other profit center) that makes its operations more efficient by the use of programs, does have an increased bottom line from which to pay for the real added value that the software provides.

So, does this mean that the principles of ethics are compromised by less lofty considerations, such as price? You bet! To deny that softening factor means that violations of principle, which have no inherent consequences, should merit the same punishment as infractions that result in dire consequences.

The discussion of software [covers] only one small corner of ethics. There are other issues that have been discussed, and recognized as being fearfully important, e.g., privacy for the individual and the right of institutions to hold creative and business information for their own uses. And the right of governments to keep information away from potential enemies.

How does one teach ethics? I do not believe that it can be done with a list of do's and don't's that is supplied to an adult who has already formulated his ethical concepts (probably in childhood). If he has routinely used the lie to others, and to rationalize his own behavior to himself, then, as they say in Yiddish, "zoll gornisht helfin" [roughly, "Nothing will help"]. You give such a person a list, and he will simply use it as an avoidance guide. What is required for ethical behavior is a mindset, a super ego, that has embedded in it at least a few of the religious commandments such as: do not bear false witness; do not steal; do not bring harm to other people. With a few of these, one does not need detailed lists of how to behave in specific situations, for the

answers are either self-evident or can be constructed without outside intervention.

We have people among us, perhaps a large number, who are borderline ethical cripples -- either by virtue of not enough early ethical training (religious, or by example) or because they cannot easily apply ethical principles to concrete situations. Such people may, indeed, be educable by the cookbook listing.

*   *   *

From **DONALD FAIRBURN**, P.E., Department of System Analysis, Miami University, Oxford, Ohio 45056

In the interests of involving others -- while expressing my _own_ views, I would like to ask three questions that are intended to focus attention on the _assumptions_ which are implied in the title "How Should Ethics Be Taught?"

*   Do students _want_ to be taught ethics?

Not necessarily. While students may agree in the abstract that the achievement of high ethical standards is a good thing, my experience is that when something of importance is at stake they become quite willing to make accommodations and compromise personal integrity in order to reach their objectives more directly. I guess that makes them not unlike the rest of us. My point is that leading the ethical life will assuredly demand sacrifice, and we must be prepared to meet resistance when our students realize that we are, in a behavioral sense, teaching something more demanding than well-structured programming.

*   _Should_ we teach ethics?

Yes; but not necessarily by instruction. Given the premise expressed in my first answer, and assuming that we want to do more than merely discuss comparative ethical systems, our success should be measured in terms of the effect we have on the student. By "effect" I do not mean the loudness with which the student decries the latest injustice perceived by the teacher. Our success should be measured in terms of the silent effect which our teaching has had on their ethical behaviour, and this is done best by example rather than by indoctrination. A seminar course on "Professional Problems" can serve to raise instances of ethical conflict for discussion purposes, but the most effective way to convey ethics if for the teacher to _be_ ethical.

*   Can we teach ethics in an _ethical_ _way_?

Only if we resist the compelling urge to transmit our personal philosophical basis for ethics. _While_ _in_ _the_ _classroom_ let's teach the non-controversial fact that a lie is wrong. But let each of us come to that truth by any one of the many different paths that lead there.

COMPUTERS IN EDUCATION, K. Duncan and D. Harris (eds.)
Elsevier Science Publishers B.V. (North-Holland)
© IFIP, 1985

WHAT IS DIFFERENT IN BRITISH CLASSROOMS?

Richard Fothergill, John S.A. Anderson, Bill Broderick, John Coll,
Mike Doran, Ann Irving, Mike Page, Hilary Pitts, Alistair Ross

Microelectronics Education Programme, United Kingdom

In the past four years the United Kingdom has
experienced the most rapid coordinated and overall development of microcomputer and microelectronics education in recent years. This presentation reveals three strands of innovation
which are very different from earlier classroom
practise and from that in most other countries.

The National Director of the renowned UK Government's Microelectronics Education Programme
(MEP) first sets the scene, describing a nationally inspired, teacher-led grassroots programme
of developments which encompasses a national
information service, and programmes of teacher
education and of curriculum change.

MEP's influence has brought about changes, not
just in the content of single technology-related
subject areas, such as computing and electronics,
but also in most other parts of the curriculum.
However, it is changes in methods of LEARNING
which predominate in British schools at all
levels. In this presentation we show examples
of children aged 5 through to 18 in integrated
curriculum work at primary/elementary level and
at secondary level in information technology
awareness courses and also in english, geography,
history, maths, science, foreign languages,
computing, craft design technology and electronics. All these examples are of work from real
classrooms, not from curriculum laboratories or
development project settings. They are presented today through three themes.

1. PROBLEM-SOLVING (through curriculum use of
information retrieval, through basic electronics
awareness for 11-14 year olds, and through
robotic control for elementary age learners).

2. LANGUAGE COMMUNICATIONS, AND INFORMATION
   HANDLING SKILLS DEVELOPMENT (through experience with word-processing creative writing and
electronic mail packages, electronics "design
and make" projects).

3. EXPLORATORY LEARNING (through data-acquisi-
tion, data-logging and the use of databases in
science, social sciences and humanities,
through robotic control and adventuring).

We believe that Conference participants can only
really appreciate the differences in learning
approach through 'hands-on' experience. In addition we shall offer workshops of these practical
sessions and examples to illustrate each of these
themes at all age and curriculum levels in the
Conference "Birds of a Feather" sessions.

COMPUTERS IN EDUCATION, K. Duncan and D. Harris (eds.)
Elsevier Science Publishers B.V. (North-Holland)
© IFIP, 1985

MAKING STUDENTS AND TEACHERS AWARE OF SOCIAL AND ETHICAL ISSUES OF COMPUTER USE

J. Michael Dunlap, LeRoy Finkel, Larry Hannah and Linda Roberts

International Council for Computers in Education

The rapid growth of information processing technologies has left our society, in particular our schools, unprepared to deal with the ethical, moral and social issues involving this technology. This panel will discuss the ethical, moral and social questions involved in using information processing technology in our schools. In particular, attention will be given to questions of copyright, copying of software and the teaching of values in the classroom. Panel members are knowledgeable about copyright issues, dilemmas currently facing teachers, students and society, and values clarification. Suggestions will be made as to effective methods of teaching values in the classroom. After brief presentations, the moderator will ask for written questions from the audience.

J. Michael Dunlap, Chair
Willamette University, Salem Oregon

LeRoy Finkel
San Mateo County Office of Education
Redwood City, California

There are no definitive answers to most questions about software copyright laws, since the copyright law is vague in places and there have been no court cases to set precedent. Nevertheless, copyright attorneys, court watchers and lawmakers all seem to agree on how a court would interpret the current law if and when a case came before it. School districts need to pass software policies and enforce them to ensure only legal uses of software on school campuses. It is the responsibility of each of us to be a role model to fellow teachers and students alike and allow only legal uses of software on our campuses.

Larry Hannah
California State University
Sacramento, California

Advances in science and technology, including the widespread use of microcomputers, have brought with them new social and moral issues; issues that must be faced by young people as well as adults. These range from personal ethical issues, such as piracy, to broader social issues, such as the ownership and control of information. How can teachers introduce these topics in the classroom? What teaching strategies will effectively prepare students to develop answers to such issues? This talk will review the research and curriculum development efforts that pertain to the topic.

Linda Roberts
Office of Technology Assessment
Washington, D.C.

The Office of Technology Assessment is presently conducting a study on "Intellectual Property Rights in an Age of Electronics and Information." In this study OTA is looking at how the new information and communications technologies might affect United States laws and practices regarding intellectual property--laws and practices designed to provide incentives for the creation and distribution of creative and inventive works. The study will look at how the changing social and economic role of information might affect how we, as a society, view intellectual property in the future.

As part of its study, OTA is examining differing attitudes and practices toward intellectual property. Of particular interest to the education community are the attitudes and practices of teachers and their students about computers. The deployment of computer and information technologies provides new opportunities for teaching and learning in our nation's classrooms and at the same time creates moral and ethical dilemmas for its use. To what extent is there confusion and a lack of understanding about appropriate and fair use? To what extent is copying and sharing of computer programs appropriate? What steps are being taken to clarify school use of software? How might school practices be supported or undermined by practices in the home and community? What role can educational institutions and teachers play?

COMPUTERS IN EDUCATION, K. Duncan and D. Harris (eds.)
Elsevier Science Publishers B.V. (North-Holland)
© IFIP, 1985

PREDICTING ACADEMIC SUCCESS IN COMPUTER SCIENCE

William S. Curran and Janet Melancon

Loyola University
6363 St. Charles Avenue, Box 191
New Orleans, LA 70118   USA

A computer science-specific aptitude test has been developed to determine entry level for prospective computer science students. Previous tests have relied heavily on mathematical questions, disregarding the fact that many students have math anxiety while others are interested in the data processing (less mathematical) side of computer science. The present test provides an objective means of predicting success without the use of mathematical questions. It is superior to ACT math scores as a predictor and if students had enrolled on the basis of the test, the dropout/failure rate would have dropped from 40-50% to 10-15%.

1. INTRODUCTION

There is a great need for a Computer Science - specific Aptitude Test to determine the entry level for prospective Computer Science students. Such a test would provide a basis for the proper advising of students who are unsure of their goals, drives, or abilities, and would alleviate the unusually high dropout/failure rates in computer science courses.

Previous studies have attempted to correlate past academic performance, gender, hours worked per week and semesters at school. Mazlack (4) reported low correlation between success and semesters at school, gender and academic program. Wileman et.al. (7) reported some significant correlation with hours worked and high school performance but such results are not surprising and are not peculiar to computer science: surely a student working long hours will show reduced performance in all demanding disciplines.

The Konvalina test (3) is a good test but relies a great deal on questions of mathematical sequences and algebraic word problems. Without entering the controversy regarding the mathematical nature of computer science (6) the following points should be noted:

A. Many universities offer a degree in Computer Information Processing, which is specifically designed for students more interested in the business aspects of Computer Science than in the mathematical aspects.

B. There is no reason in principle why a computer science test cannot be devised without resorting to mathematical questions.

C. Most universities require all students to take placement tests for English and Math. It makes sense to administer yet another test for computer science placement only if the test is computer science specific.

Bearing these points in mind, the authors have developed a test which aims at capturing the kinds of thinking found in Computer Science, while eliminating mathematical questions altogether. It provides an objective means for predicting success for all students regardless of their math background, age, sex, or past academic performance.

2. TEST DESCRIPTION

The predictor consists of 24 questions and was not divided into sections although similar questions were grouped together. The questions were designed to test the basic concepts of computer science, reflecting the kinds of examples encountered in textbooks, none of which presupposed any knowledge of computer programming or languages.

The fundamental concepts of looping and conditional action were tested, along with flowcharts, recursion, and de-bugging. Simple logic problems involving conjunction, disjunction and implication were included as were questions with complicated sets of instructions.

3. PROCEDURE

The test was administered in the first week of class to all sections of Introduction to Computer Science (COSC 220) over the past two years (119 students). COSC 220 is not a service course and there are several other beginning courses in computer science at a lower level. It is, however, normally the first course for computer science majors. Computer Information Processing majors are advised to take COSC 110 as a first course with COSC 220 as the second course. Consequently, most of those tested were computer-related majors.

All sections were taught by Ph.D.s with considerable teaching experience. To avoid the possibility of a self-fulfilling hypothesis, students were not appraised of the results of the test. Teachers were likewise kept uninformed to insure impartiality. The test itself was evaluated using the Kuder-Richardson method (2), and produced a reliability coefficient of .842, a high figure indicating that the internal coherence of the test is quite respectable.

The predictive ability of the test was measured by correlating test scores with final grades for the course.

4. RESULTS AND DISCUSSION

The results to date are very encouraging. The correlation coefficient between pretest scores and course grades for all data was .5196 (the average of coefficients by semester was .6266). Thus there is good correlation between high test scores and high grades. But the bottom line is that by using the test we were able to predict passing or withdraw/fail with 69.7 percent accuracy. We are able to say that if all who fell below the cutoff for the predictor had been advised to not take the course (and if they had followed the advice), the withdrawal/failure rate would have fallen from about 40-50% to 10-15%.

It is worth noting in passing that previous authors have ignored comparisons between their predictor and ACT math scores. To satisfy ourselves that we had not merely produced another math I.Q. test, a correlation was run between the predictor and ACT math scores (where available). The result was a correlation of .709. This figure fits nicely with previous results and with most intuitions about the topic. It is high enough to support the view that math and computer science are interrelated, yet is low enough to dilineate between the two. Consequently, it is safe to say that the test is a measure of computer science per se, and not merely another math test.

These results also shed light on other related points: Many professional programmers are not particularly adept at mathematics, and yet produce programs in many ways superior to their math oriented colleagues. The present results explain this and more importantly they explain why most universities offer two curriculae: one for majors who take calculus through differential equations, and a second program which places much less emphasis on math. Both programs produce talented graduates and now it is possible to detect those students who may have been overlooked or screened out by other methods. It is also worth noting that having a subject-specific test helps to advise students who argue that math scores are not indicators of computer

science ability and who insist on entering the program at a high level.

The test was designed to predict success, not failure, and was intended to encourage those with computer science ability to do well. Hence the most satisfying results come from a few students who scored poorly on math ACT but did well on the predictor and who also did well in the course.

REFERENCES

(1) Alspaugh, C.A., Identification of some components of computer programming aptitude, Journal of Research in Mathematics 3 (1972).

(2) Ferguson, G.A., Statistical Analysis in Psychology and Education (5th Ed. McGraw-Hill, 1981 438-439).

(3) Konvalina, J., Wileman, S. & Stephens, L.J., Math proficiency: a key to success for computer science students, Communications of The ACM 26 (1983).

(4) Mazlack, L.J. Identifying potential to acquire programming skills, Communications of The ACM 23 (1980).

(5) Peterssen, C.G. & Howe, T.G. Predicting academic success in introduction to computers, Association for Educational Data Systems Journal (1979).

(6) Ralston, A. & Shaw, M. Curriculum'78 - is computer science really unmathematical?, Communications of The ACM 23(2) (1980).

(7) Wileman, S., Konvalina, J. & Stephens, L.J. Factors influencing success in beginning computer science courses, Journal of Educational Research 74(4) (1981).

COMPUTERS IN EDUCATION, K. Duncan and D. Harris (eds.)
Elsevier Science Publishers B.V. (North-Holland)
© IFIP, 1985

COMPUTING IN A SOCIAL CONTEXT

Valerie A. Clarke

Division of Cognitive Science and Psychology,
School of Sciences,
Deakin University,
Australia, 3217

Gender inequities in computer education were considered in relation to the social
context in which computers are being introduced. Data derived from the comparison
of primary school children from a co-educational school with girls from a single-sex
school showed that the sex-typing by girls from the two schools was markedly
different.   These differences were more evident at the higher grade levels.   Girls'
perceptions of boys' and girls' relative liking of computers related to their general
attitudes to computing and to their computing performance.   The implications of
these findings were discussed in relation to the social context in which computing is
introduced.

INTRODUCTION

The introduction of computers into schools
provides an opportunity for all children to
utilise new technology to enhance a range of
general and academic skills as well as being a
"superb motivating force in education" (1).
However, research in the U.K., U.S.A. and
Australia shows that girls are not participating
fully in this new technology, being well
under-represented in computer courses (2-4),
computer camps (5) and computer clubs (2), and
being less likely to own or use computers at
home (6).

When girls are involved in computing programs,
their interests and option choices lie in word
processing and business applications, in
contrast to the boys' preference for programming
languages (6).   These interests are reflected
in later employment opportunities in the
computer industry where women predominate in the
unskilled data entry section and men in data
analysis and programming (7).

If girls are going to share equally with boys in
the educational and employment opportunities
provided by computers, it is essential to
understand the reasons underlying their apparent
lack of interest and participation.   However,
most computer research ignores the social
context in which computers are being introduced,
focussing on the "man-machine" interface or on
making systems "user friendly", but

> Computing is more than a set of skills.   It
> is embedded in a social system consisting of
> shared values and norms, a special
> vocabulary and humor, status and prestige
> ordering, and differentiation of members
> from non-members.   In short, it is a
> culture.   (1, p.3).

The nature of this culture needs to be
researched, described and understood.
Generally, computer manufacturers and promoters

are promulgating the myths that computers are
predominantly for men, and that computing is
about machines.   Studies of illustrations and
advertisements in computing magazines show that
they generally depict males rather than females
(5,6).   Analyses of computer and video games
9,10), commercially available software (5) and
so-called educational software (10) show a
strong male-orientation, with most activities
designed to appeal to boys, rather than to
girls, concentrating on aggression,
competition, rapid and violent action, loud
noises, racing cars and rocket blasts.

Similarly, ratings of commercial software yield
a general consensus that the majority of
software is designed to appeal to males rather
than to females (10).

Within the classroom, computers are often
introduced within the mathematics and science
curriculum by male teachers who have a personal
interest in computers which they see as
"machines for men and boys" (2, p.7), a bias
reflected in their tendency to choose boys as
"volunteers" to operate the machines (10).
Girls' low participation rates and negative
attitudes to mathematics and science courses
have been well documented (11-13).   By
introducing computing within the context of
mathematics and science, these negative
attitudes may be being transferred to computing
where they are further reinforced by the total
classroom context, a context in which girls must
compete for scarce resources.

The problem of competition for resources within
classrooms is also well documented.   In
mixed-sexed classes boys demand, and receive,
more than their fair share of resources,
including books, space, laboratory materials and
teacher attention (10, 14-16).   This competition
is magnified in computer classes where the
resources are usually more limited than in other
school activities.   Boys tend to be competitive
and aggressive (17), rapidly deciding to move in

and take over the machines, whilst the girls
tend to defer to the boys, preferring to avoid
hostility and competition (10, 18). Generally,
children from kindergarten to about year 9 tend
to remain relatively segregated for most
activities (6). Once an activity or area has
been identified as a "male" domain, the girls
tend to avoid it. Within most schools, the boys
move in and dominate the computer centre, which,
due to male competition and aggression (17) and
female default, soon becomes identified as a
male domain (6).

Thus it is the cultural context in which
computers are being introduced, rather than the
nature of the computers per se, that is turning
girls away from this new technology. Despite
the widespread emphasis on the mechanical
aspects of computers, technical expertise is not
an essential requirement for computer literacy.
Rather, Papert (19) argues that the essence of
computer literacy lies in procedural thinking.

There is no evidence to suggest that girls are
inferior to boys in this respect, nor that they
lack the necessary general ability or interest
in computing (1). The failure of girls to
participate fully in this area may be
principally a social phenomenon, arising
predominantly from their unwillingness to
compete with the boys for scarce resources or to
penetrate an area which has become identified as
a male domain.

One way to reduce this phenomenon within the
educational system might be to introduce
computers at the primary level where one teacher
is generally involved most of the time with the
same grade, subject boundaries are not clearly
defined, the curriculum tends to be
child-centered rather than subject-centred, and
there is freedom from pressure of examination
requirements or employers' demands. At this
level it should be possible to introduce
computing as part of the general curriculum,
avoiding links with mathematics and science.
The class teacher should be able to develop
strategies which ensure that girls have an equal
opportunity to actively participate in computing
activities (2).

Another way to reduce the social disadvantage of
girls may be to introduce computers to girls in
a single-sex setting, where it is likely that
most, if not all, the role models will be female
(20). In this context the social costs of
computer involvement for girls will be
reduced. The computer centre will be seen as a
girls' domain, and possibly teachers will select
software that will appeal to girls.

The present paper presents data relevant to
these possibilities by focussing on a number of
specific questions. Do primary school children
see computing as being more for boys than for
girls? If sex-typing occurs in the primary
school, at which year level does it start to
emerge? If there are differences between boys

and girls in the sex-typing of computing, are
these differences due solely to differences in
general ability, attitudes to mathematics and/or
attitudes to science? Does sex-typing of
computing affect girls' attitudes to computing
or their computing performance?

METHOD

Sample

The sample of 118 children was drawn from two
local primary schools. It was an accidental
sample, utilising schools which were introducing
Logo into the curriculum. All children from
years 1, 3 and 5 in both schools participated in
the project. One school was a girls' school
with 16 girls in year 1, 15 in year 3 and 12 in
year 5. The sample from the second school, a
co-educational school, consisted of 42 boys and
33 girls. There were 26 children from year 1,
23 from year 3 and 26 from year 5. The
children were aged approximately 5 to 11 years
when the project began.

The sample was drawn from predominantly middle
class families. Paternal occupational status
was assessed using Congalton's (21) 7-point
scale on which an occupational rating of 1
denotes a high status occupation (e.g. medical
practitioner, civil engineer) and a rating of 7
denotes a low status occupation (e.g. unskilled
manual worker). The status ratings for paternal
occupations ranged from 1 to 5, with a mean
score of 2.2 and a standard deviation of 1.0
indicating that the majority of children in the
sample came from families where the father had a
relatively high status occupation. However,
there were no significant differences between
the mean scores for paternal occupational status
for the three sub-samples - girls from a
single-sex school, girls from a co-educational
school and boys from a co-educational school.

Procedure

Children were tested in February 1983 before the
computing classes were introduced, using both
standardised tests and non-standardised
measures. During the school year each class
had two sessions of Logo per week, each session
being approximately 20 minutes in duration.
Class sizes varied from 12 to 26 children. The
number of Apple II computers available at any
class session varied from 5 to 9. Towards the
end of the school year, after approximately 50
computing sessions, further testing was carried
out.

Measures

1. Sex-typing   Sex-typing was measured in
   February by two items included in a 26-item
   general questionnaire. This questionnaire
   was designed to assess sex-typing of
   computing, previous experience with

computers and knowledge of computers. The questionnaire took approximately 30 minutes and was completed in class, with the teacher reading the items and children recording their answers. The first sex-typing item asked "Who is better at using computers?" and provided the three response categories, "girls", "boys", and "both are the same."

The second item asked "Who likes computers most?" and again provided three response categories, but changed the order of the responses - "boys", "girls" and "both the same."

The sex-typing measures used in November were included in a 20-item questionnaire designed to measure attitudes to computing. This questionnaire took approximately 20 minutes and was also completed in class. It presented pairs of alternative statements in a manner which suggested that either alternative was equally socially acceptable. Children were asked to select one of the pair of statements and then to indicate whether the chosen statement was "Partly true for me" or "Really true for me." The first sex-typing item stated that "Some children think girls like computing more than boys do BUT Other children think boys like computing more than girls do." The second sex-typing item focussed on boys being better than girls.

2. Prior Computer Experience and Knowledge: Computer experience and knowledge were assessed using the questionnaire completed in class in February. Three questions focussed on previous experience with computers and 13 questions tested knowledge about computers. The scores on these measures are presented as percentages.

3. General Ability: To assess whether any sex or school differences in attitudes or performance could be solely attributed to differences in ability, two general measures of ability were included before computing began. Children completed the appropriate level of the Raven's Progressive Matrices Test, which was included as a non-verbal measure of intelligence that is generally considered to be relatively free from cultural or educational influences. Secondly, they completed the appropriate level of the Otis-Lennon School Ability Test which was designed to measure verbal, figural and quantitative reasoning, and verbal comprehension.

4. General School Attitudes: The Hogan's Survey of School Attitudes (SSA) was completed in February 1983. This test was designed to measure children's interest in each of four curriculum areas, providing separate percentile scores for attitudes to mathematics, reading, science and social science. For present purposes, only the

attitudes to mathematics and science will be considered.

5. Attitudes to Computing: The SSA provided a section in which 12 additional items might be included. Items were developed to assess children's attitudes to computing and to working individually or in groups. To remain consistent with the SSA scoring format these items were scored 0, 1 or 2 giving a range of possible scores of 0 to 16.

The November measure of attitudes to computing consisted of 8 items from the 20 item general measure. Four of these items asked about the children's general evaluation of computing as to whether it was liked/disliked, easy/hard, fun/boring, useful/waste of time; two items asked whether they did or did not want to learn computing this year, or next year; one asked about spending more or less class time on computing and one asked about their time on the computer in relation to other children in the class. To compute a single attitude score the response categories were dichotomised and the responses indicating a positive attitude were summed to give a raw score with a possible range of 0 to 8.

6. Computing Performance

A 16-item written test was developed to assess children's knowledge of computing and understanding of Logo commands at the end of the school year. Fourteen items were in a multiple-choice form, each with four alternative answers. One item contained a bugged program and asked children to circle the bugs and one item required them to complete a set of commands. The test was completed in class, taking approximately 30 minutes. Scores are presented as percentages of items correct.

Results

The pre-computing measures of sex-typing of computing showed there were clear differences between the three samples (See Table 1). In response to the question "Who likes computing most?" differences were significant, $\chi^2 = 57.76$, 4 d.f., p <0.001. For the children at the co-educational school over half the children suggested that boys and girls like computing equally, whilst of those expressing a preference boys selected boys and girls were fairly equally

Table 1. Responses to the pre-computing measure of children's perceptions of boys' and girls' relative liking of computing.

	Respondents (%)		
	Boys (Co-ed) N=38	Girls (Co-ed) N=32	Girls (Single-sex) N=39
Boys	42	16	5
Girls	3	19	77
Same	55	65	18

divided. These responses are in marked contrast to those of the girls in the single-sex school where most girls perceived girls as liking computing more.

Do these differences increase or decrease with age? Table 2 shows the numbers of children at each year level giving each response. Numbers are used in preference to percentages due to the small expected cell frequencies. For the boys, there was a clear year effect whereby boys in higher grades were more likely to reply boys, $\chi^2 = 7.68$, 4 d.f., p = 0.01. The same trend was less marked for the girls in the co-educational school, $\chi^2 = 6.81$, 4 d.f., N.S., whilst the opposite trend occurred for girls at the single-sex school with all year 3 and all except one of the year 5 girls seeing girls as liking computing more, $\chi^2 = 15.43$, 4 d.f. p <0.01. Although the numbers of children in each of the three samples are relatively small, year differences are evident for the boys at the co-educational school and the girls at the single-sex school.

Table 2. Numbers of children at each year level who gave each response to the pre-computing measure of girls' and boys' relative liking of computers.

	Year Level	Respondents		
		Boys (Co-ed)	Girls (Co-ed)	Girls (Single-sex)
Boys	1	3	1	1
	3	4	0	0
	5	9	4	1
Girls	1	1	2	7
	3	0	3	14
	5	0	1	9
Same	1	9	9	7
	3	8	6	0
	5	4	6	0

When children were asked "Who is better at using computers?" similar sex-typing and year differences were found.

General ability, attitudes to mathematics, attitudes to science, attitudes to computing, computing knowledge and computing experience were measured before the Logo program was introduced to assess the comparability of the three samples and the possible contribution of these factors to the development of sex-typing of computing. However, there were no significant differences between groups on any of the measures except computer knowledge. (See Table 3).

The scores on the computer knowledge test ranged from 0% to 85% with a mean score of 32% for boys, 26% for girls (co-educational) and 15% for girls (girls), F(2.83) = 9.78, p <0.001. There was a significant difference between the two schools, t(86) = 4.14, p <0.001, but not between

Table 3. Mean scores for the three samples on the measures of general ability, attitudes, computing experience and computing knowledge, before the Logo program began.

Measures	Boys (Co-ed)	Girls (Co-ed)	Girls (Single-sex)
Ravens Percentile	74	74	77
Otis-Lennon DIQ	106	110	105
SSA Mathematics (Percentile)	33	40	36
SSA Science (Percentile)	49	42	39
Computing Attitudes, (Raw Score)	10.3	10.4	10.5
Computing Experience (Percentage)	23	27	20
Computing Knowledge (Percentage)	32	26	15
Computing Knowledge (Percentage) (Yrs. 1,3)	22	13	12

* P < 0.01

the boys and girls at the co-educational school, t(43) = 1.35, N.S. This difference between schools might reflect the fact that the children in year 5 at the co-educational school had some Basic programming experience during the year prior to the commencement of the study. The possible effect of this experience was assessed by comparing the scores for the three samples for the children from years 1 and 3 only. Although the boys' score of 22% for this group was higher than the girls' scores of 13% (co-educational) and 7%, (girls) the differences were not significant, F(2,49) = 1.93, N.S.

Turning to the measures taken after a year of Logo experience, the differences were again evident between the three samples in the children's sex-typing of computing. Table 4 shows the percentage of children at each level and of the total sample who replied "boys" when asked whether boys or girls liked computing more. For the total sample, 86% of boys chose boys, the option selected by 52% of the girls (co-educational) and 12% of the girls (girls), $\chi^2 = 64.44$, 2 d.f., p <0.001. Again year differences were apparent, with older boys choosing boys, $\chi^2 = 4.13$, 2 d.f., N.S. and more of the older girls at the co-educational school choosing boys, $\chi^2 = 5.07$, 2 d.f. p <0.10. These trends contrast with those for the girls at the single-sex school where fewer of the older girls chose boys, $\chi^2 = 6.74$, 2 d.f., p <0.05. When asked about computing performance, rather than liking, similar response patterns emerged.

Table 4. Percentages of children from each
sample and from each year level who
replied "boys" when asked whether
girls or boys like computing more.

Year Level	Sample		
	Boys (Co-ed)	Girls (Co-ed)	Girls (Single-sex)
1	73	21	31
3	79	21	0
5	100	57	0
Total	86	52	12
N	42	33	43

Do children's perceptions of sex-typing affect
their attitudes to computing and their computing
performance? For the boys it is difficult to
answer this question using the present data as
only 13% of boys suggested that girls might like
computing more than boys do. As computing is
generally seen as a male domain, it probably
presents little problem for boys. However, for
the girls it is possible to examine the
relationship between their perception of boys'
and girls' relative liking of computing and
their attitudes to computing or their computing
performance. Such comparisons show that girls
who perceive girls as liking computing more than
boys (female-oriented girls) do achieve more
positive scores on the computer attitudes scale
and higher scores on the computing test than
girls who perceived boys as liking computing
more (male-oriented girls). On the measure of
attitudes to computing, which had a possible
range of 0 to 8, the female-oriented girls
achieved a mean score of 7.0 whilst the male
oriented girls scored 6.0, $t(65)$ = 2.76,
$p<0.01$. On the computing performance test, the
female-oriented girls scored 64% in contrast to
the male-oriented respondents' score of 43%,
$t(69)$ = 3.09, p <0.01. Similar trends emerged
for the girls' perceptions of "being better".

Discussion

Prior to the introduction of the Logo program
there were significant differences between the
three samples of children in their perceptions
of boys' and girls' relative liking of computers
and relative computer performance. These
differential perceptions cannot be attributed to
differences between the samples in SES origin,
general ability, attitudes to mathematics,
science or computing, or computing knowledge or
experience. Hence explanations for these
responses must be sought within the social
environment, rather than in terms of differences
in attitudes to school subjects, general ability
or previous computing experience. For the
children within the co-educational school, the
pattern of responses is fairly consistent with
societal expectations. Although a considerably
large proportion of the children perceive girls
and boys as liking computing equally, there is a
tendency for those expressing a preference to
choose boys rather than girls, a tendency which
is more evident among boys than among girls, and

more evident at the higher grade levels than at
the lower grade levels.

The main differences in attitudes obtained in
the co-educational school are consistent with
those reported by other studies of the attitudes
of primary school children to computing in the
U.K and Australia (2, 22). These trends may be
seen as a gradual acceptance of the male
stereotypes being promulgated by computer
manufacturers and promoters and the media in
general.

However, the wider social context, with its
male-orientation, provides little explanation
for the strong female-orientation shown by the
girls in the single-sex school. Perhaps the
answer lies in the social context within the
school. Generally, children in single-sex
schools show less sex stereotyping of curriculum
areas and achievement patterns (20). Shaw (23,
24) argues that single-sex schools probably
offer the only genuine opportunity for equality
in a highly unequal society. Theoretically,
co-educational schools offer equality of
opportunity to both girls and boys. In reality
they may reduce the opportunity for equality,
creating an educational context which reflects
the gender-based power structures evident in the
wider social context, a context which is
generally characterised by male dominance and
male assertiveness, a world in which men are
encouraged to be aggressive, competitive and
independent and women to be more submissive and
domestically-oriented. Within a single-sex
school, girls are not required to compete with
boys, but function in a more female-oriented
social system where the role models are
predominantly female, and all educational
pursuits are seen as being provided solely for
girls (20). Within this environment, any
curriculum area is seen as being relevant for
females, a perception clearly evident in the
responses of the girls from the single-sex
school.

After a year of Logo class, these differences
between the three-samples persisted.
Experience within computing classes seemed to
reinforce, rather than negate, the sex-typing
evident at the beginning of the year, suggesting
that classroom experiences were probably
consistent with the children's expectations.
These differences in attitudes between girls in
different social contexts, demonstrate the
important role played by the social environment
of the school in influencing the development of
attitudes to particular curriculum areas and
subsequent performance in these areas. The
current findings provide support for those who
recommend the provision of separate classes for
girls in subject areas commonly perceived as
male preserves (e.g. 25). In single-sex
classes girls can develop positive attitudes to
these curriculum areas and confidence in their
ability to participate.

For the girls, the perception of boys as liking computing more is related to their end of year attitudes to computing and their computer performance. From the present data it is not clear whether these girls obtained lower attitudes and performance scores because they rejected computing as a male domain, or whether they experienced difficulty in working with computers and used the popular male stereotype as an explanation for their own inferior performance. However, the existence of sex-typing before the introduction of classroom computing activities offers some support for the suggestion that sex-typing may be the cause rather than an effect of differential attitudes and performance. The nature of this relationship is being investigated in the next phase of the project.

Although the current findings need to be replicated using a larger sample of children drawn from a broader range of socio-economic backgrounds and including boys from single-sex schools, they imply the need to focus greater attention on the social context in which computers are introduced into schools if all children are going to derive equal benefit from this new technology.

References

[1] Kiesler, S., Sproull, L., & Eccles, J., (1984) Poolhalls, chips and war games: women in the culture of computing, Psychology of Women Quarterly, (in press).

[2] E.O.C., (1983) Equal Opportunities Commission, Information Technology in Schools: Guidelines of Good Practice for Teachers. Report prepared by the London Borough of Croydon.

[3] Watt, D., (1982) Education for citizenship in a computer-based socity. In R. Seidel, R. Anderson & B. Hunter (eds.), Computer Literacy, N.Y., Academic Press.

[4] Firken, J., (1984) Girls and computers in schools, Unpublished paper. VISE.

[5] Muira, I.T., & Hess, R.D., (1984) Enrolment differences in computer camps and summer classes, The Computing Teacher, Vol. 11, No. 8.

[6] Lockheed, M.E., and Frakt, S.E., (1984) Sex equity: increasing girls' use of computers, The Computing Teacher, Vol. 11, No. 8, 16-18.

[7] Game, A., and Pringle, R., (1983) Gender at work, Sydney, George, Allen.

[8] Kiesler, S., and Eccles, J., (1983) Second class citizens? Psychology Today, March.

[9] Reinecke, I., (1983) Microcomputers, Penguin, Melbourne.

[10] Fisher, G., (1984) Access to Computers. The Computing Teacher. Vol. 11, No. 8, 24-27.

[11] Harding, J., Switched Off, (1983) EOC/Schools Council, Longmans.

[12] Kelly, A., (1982) The Missing Half, Manchester University Press.

[13] Fox, L.H., (1977) The effects of sex role socialization in mathematics participation and achievement. In L.H. Fox, E. Fennema, and J. Sherman (eds.), Women and Mathematics : research perspectives for change. N.I.E. Papers in Education, No. 8.

[14] Spender, D. & Sara E., (1980) Learning to Lose, Great Britain, The Women's Press, 1980.

[15] Becker, J., (1981) Differential treatment of females and males in mathematics classes, Journal for Research in Mathematics Education, Vol. 12, No. 1, 40-83.

[16] Whyte, J. (1984), Observing sex stereotypes and interactions in the school lab and workshop, Educational Review, Vol. 36, No. 1, 75-86.

[17] Ward, R., (1984), Boys are elbowing girls off the school computer, Acorn User, May.

[18] Boss, J., (1982) Sexism among the micros, The Computer Teacher, Jan.

[19] Papert, S., (1980) Mindstorms, computers and powerful ideas, N.Y., Harvester Press.

[20] Marland, M., (1983) Should the sexes be separated? In M. Marland (ed), Sex Differentiation and Schooling, Lond, Heinemann Educational Books.

[21] Congalton, A.A., (1969) Status and prestige in Australia, Melbourne, Cheshire.

[22] Chambers, S.M., and Clarke, V.A., (1984) Sex-related differences in attitudes and achievements of a fourth grade class learning computing. Unpublished paper. Deakin University.

[23] Shaw, J., (1976), Finishing school - some implications for sex-segregated education. In D. L. Barker and S. Allen (eds.), Sexual Divisions and Society: Process and Change, Tavistock.

[24] Shaw, J., (1984) The politics of single-sex schools. In R. Deem (ed.), Co-education Reconsidered, Open University Press, Milton Keynes.

[25] Smith, S., (1984) Single-sex setting. In R. Deem (ed.), Co-education Reconsidered, Open University Press, Milton Keynes, ch. 5. Spender, Dale and Sara, Elizabeth, (1980) Learning to Lose, Great Britain, The Women's Press.

COMPUTERS IN EDUCATION, K. Duncan and D. Harris (eds.)
Elsevier Science Publishers B.V. (North-Holland)
© IFIP, 1985

SOFTWARE FOR GIRLS: A SEXIST SOLUTION?

Twila Slesnick

Classroom Computer Learning Magazine
19 Davis Drive
Belmont, CA 94002

Proponents of sex equity should not have as their goal equal numbers of men and women in computer careers or equal numbers of boys and girls in computer classes. Their goal should be equal opportunity. This certainly means giving girls equal access to computers, to classes and to careers. But it also means providing them with enough computer experience to make an informed decision about the role computers will play in their lives. Making sure that girls take advantage of these opportunities may require some enticement. Historically software has been an enticement for boys and it might serve the same function for girls. It would be a mistake, however, to develop a line of software just for girls. Rather we should create programs that appeal equally to boys and girls--true nonsexist software.

Why is it that female participation in computer studies and computer careers is well below male participation? Some educators suggest that this condition stems from a lack of ability or confidence on the part of women when dealing with technology. Others argue that women are given fewer opportunities to learn about and use computers. And still others say that women just aren't as interested in what's on the screen.

Research doesn't provide many answers yet as to what's really going on, but we have some leads. We know that girls and boys do equally well in computer classes and, for the most part, they have equal access to computers during school hours. In fact, until junior high, there isn't even much difference in attitude or perceived utility of computers.

The key difference between boys and girls crops up most noticeably in voluntary use of the machines. Boys sign up for elective computer classes. They seek out and use computers outside of school more than girls do (they take extra courses and they "play" with the computer in their spare time).

There are several plausible explanations for this disparity in interest. For one thing, more boys than girls are coming home to computers. (Parents seem more willing to spend money on computers for boys than for girls.) Through ads, role models, and sex-segregated school activities, society suggests to kids that the computer is a male machine. But perhaps the most significant factor is the lack of software appeal for women. There's just nothing for girls that stimulates the same kind of software infatuation currently drawing boys into the world of computers.

Before we begin scrambling to write software for girls, we should decide just what it is we want to accomplish. Do we want equal numbers of girls and boys hanging out in computer arcades? Do we want a one-to-one ratio of males to females in programming classes and in computer-related careers? Do we want girls and boys to spend the same amount of time on computers outside of class? Probably not. Individuality and diversity are highly valued in our society. But we do want to be sure that boys and girls have equal opportunities (with similar enticements) to make an informed decision about whether or not to become involved with the technology.

In other words, we need to encourage girls to check out computers and see what they have to offer. How do we do this? One inclination is to develop "girl" software to compete with "boy" software. But this solution is fraught with traps. On the one hand, suppose we misguess in our attempt to infuse software with qualities that appeal to girls; then, in all likelihood, we will have created a bastardized kind of software that reinforces inaccurate stereotypes and appeals to no one. On the other hand, let's assume that we

successfully identify what boys seem to
like (violence, power, high adventure,
slick graphics) and what girls seem to
like (safe choices, approval, artistic
expression, spelling). Have we solved
the problem? Not at all. In fact, we
have exacerbated it. We have used an
attractive medium not to expand students'
horizons, but to perpetuate certain
learned values in our children--values
that are not only sexist, but often
destructive as well.

And while software companies might be
commended for their concern, their
feeble attempts to create non-sexist
software convince us that there must be
a better way. Let's see what can be
learned from some failures.

Few publishers admit that they sell software aimed specifically at girls, but
Rhiannon is an exception. Although they
are aware that many boys are enamoured
of adventure games and many girls are
not, the authors believe that the adventure concept has inherent appeal to all
children. They feel that any sex bias
comes from the storyline and the decision-
making choices a child is offered. They
hypothesized that if they altered the
setting of the standard adventure game,
they could produce a computer game attractive to girls.

So Rhiannon created Jenny of the Prairie,
an adventure game with a female protagon-
ist. Since the developers believe girl
software should be non-violent, Jenny
can only kill for food or clothing. She
may not kill animals that threaten her,
but must run away from them instead.
The entire adventure proceeds slowly
because, according to Rhiannon, girls
feel "bombarded by faster visual stimuli
that seem to jump out at them."

And here we have it--a piece of "girl"
software that is slow (watered down) and
passive (girls don't fight to protect
themselves). This is not to say that
good software must be fast and promote
aggressive behavior, but it need not be
dull and atypical of human behavior. In
attempting to accommodate girls, the
developers have unveiled their own sex
biases and produced as sexist a program
as any piece of "boy" software. Worse,
Jenny of the Prairie affirms to the world
that "girl" software is boring.

Many publishers recognize that attaching
a gender to their software is not wise,
but they still seek ways to tap into the
female market. Some have employed
female designers and programmers in the
belief that products of females automatically appeal to other females. Spell

Diver, for example, was programmed by
a woman. Nowhere in the promotional
literature for Spell Diver is there a
claim that the program is for girls or
was developed with girls in mind. Yet
prominent in the literature is the fact
that the programmer was female. Also
prominent is the apparently serendipi-
tous discovery that the program has
great appeal for girls.

Curiously, even though the publishers
were not thinking about girls when they
put the package together, the front of
the package and the cover of the documentation both show a female diver. Is
it also coincidental that the focus of
the program is on spelling and word
recognition--"female" topics?

Girls may like Spell Diver, but as far
as intellectual stimulation goes, it's
a lightweight. Moreover, it further
entrenches spelling in the female domain
and reinforces the notion that math and
science and other "hard" subjects must
be removed from software that girls use
because it might scare them off.

Finally, the most prevalent approach to
combatting sexism in software is to put
a woman on the cover and change all pro-
nouns in the documentation to she or her.
"Fay: That Math Woman" does this. According to the developers, this drill
and practice arithmetic program is
"non-violent and employs a woman who is
good at math." But drill is dull and
let's face it--who cares if a woman is
good at dull stuff? Furthermore,
violence should never be an issue in a
drill program. Such programs are not
inherently violent; violence appears
when developers try to jazz them up.

The above approaches to involving girls
with computers fail because the solution
lies not in creating software for girls
or boys, but developing software that
appeals to both boys and girls. But
what is non-sexist software? It seems
that non-sexist software need not be
used by equal numbers of boys and girls.
Nor must kids use it for the same tasks
and with the same frequency. Rather,
these programs are tools that provide
an open-ended and flexible framework
within which a person can work in individual ways to accomplish individual
goals. These tools don't promise to
deliver students to level three of a
scope and sequence chart, to make them
music literate or to teach them about
rotational symmetry. There are no
right answers built in, nor are there
predetermined methods for interacting
with the software. Instead, these programs inspire questions and encourage

users to dig around for their own answers or insights. Furthermore, the software is not self-contained. Used optimally, it requires input from the outside world. Here are some examples of such programs.

PatternMaker, Movie Maker and MusiCalc are all programs that can be used for a tantalizing variety of activities. PatternMaker, for example, is an art tool. It provides an environment--a grid, some colors and textures and a set of commands--in which students can create a picture and then manipulate it. In the process, students might learn about balance, symmetry and counter-change. But PatternMaker is also a tool for mathematics--for exploring estimation, visual patterns, and geometry. Then there's weaving, architecture, and animation.

Movie Maker is similar in many respects. It is an animation tool through which learners can experiment with sound, sequence, color and motion (speed and acceleration) to create a harmonious whole. One of the most appealing aspects of the program is that it offers kids several different levels at which to get involved. They can simply observe prefabricated movies on the disk, they can put together prefabricated frames or they can create their own movie right from scratch.

Finally, there is MusiCalc. This program allows youngsters to listen to, create and change musical pieces. They can even add harmony to their compositions if they want an extra challenge. These seem like simple enough activities, but can you imagine a child sitting at a piano, pencil in hand, trying to experiment with different sounds and eventually recording a song on a sheaf of staff paper? Only girls would have the patience!!!

With such tools, we may have the key to non-sexist software and perhaps even non-sexist education. There are other computer tools we already know about: word processors, data base managers, and spreadsheets. These, too, are non-sexist (although the domains in which they are commonly used may not be). There are simulations like Simpolicon--a tool with which students construct a society and monitor or control its growth and survival. And there is computerized equipment for the science laboratory (Atari Lab, for example) that will record and graph readings from instruments like thermometers or barometers.

The trend toward tools is a good one and the next step is to expand our collection. But there remains an interesting question: Even if we identify and develop non-sexist programs, will they necessarily attract girls to computers? Certainly we don't want girls to use computers if they find them neither helpful nor interesting. We don't worry much about boys who don't like computers. But how do we differentiate between avoidance and lack of interest?

I would be quite satisfied to see girls using the computer when they have papers to write, when they want to show off their music skills to a friend, or when they want to illustrate a poem. I would check to see if they ever investigate what the computer might have to offer in new areas. If they never do, the teacher's role then becomes critical. She must step in with activities that demonstrate the utility of computers in new areas as well as in the child's established areas of interest.

National Systems
and Policies

INTERNATIONAL ACTIVITIES OF THE TECHNICAL
COMMITTEE FOR EDUCATION (IFIP)

Chairperson: J. Hebenstreit, Ecole Superieure d'Electricite, France;
W. F. Atchison, University of Maryland; S. Charp, Phildelphia, PA;
R. Lewis, Institute for Educational Computing, St. Martin's College,
United Kingdom; F. B. Lovis, The Open University, United Kingdom;
D. H. Wolbers, University of Technology, Delft, The Netherlands.

This panel session will review past and present
activities of the Technical Committee for Education (TC-3) of the International Federation
for Information Processing (IFIP). Future plans
of the Committee and its Working Groups will be
discussed.

COMPUTERS IN EDUCATION, K. Duncan and D. Harris (eds.)
Elsevier Science Publishers B.V. (North-Holland)
© IFIP, 1985

IMPLEMENTING CAL IN DEVELOPING COUNTRIES - SOME CONSIDERATIONS (WITH EXAMPLES FROM SRI LANKA)

Peter Chandra

Educational Computing Section
Chelsea College, University of London
552 Kings Road, London SW10 0UA
United Kingdom

This paper looks briefly at a developing country in the East (Sri Lanka) and highlights some real and concrete examples of the problems and considerations that will be involved in introducing CAL into schools in the country. An important aspect of this paper is the critical examination of the urgent needs and problems of the country, and the government's main considerations for deciding whether or not to introduce computers into its schools. The role that international aid and links play and should play in introducing CAL into the country is also examined.

1.0 INTRODUCTION

Within developing countries there is a broad spectrum of needs, with each country at a different stage of its development. It is essential first to ask what the specific educational needs are for a particular developing country and then to ask the question as to whether CAL would be able to help meet some of those needs. At the same time, it should be borne in mind that the impact of the introduction of a new technology or innovation may create secondary effects to those that was initially intended. What would the impact of such a technology be with a country that is far removed from it ? Would people accept the use of computers in their schools and to see it as part and parcel of their education ? How does one go about introducing the use of computers for education in developing countries ?

In this paper, the author hopes to look at only some of these issues and to select relevant examples as seen in a developing country like Sri Lanka. Time and paper does not allow such an extensive discussion on all of the issues mentioned to be written. A more extensive discussion on the different considerations needed is made in another paper by the author (1).

2.0 WHY CAL IN DEVELOPING COUNTRIES ?

One of the most urgent needs of education in developing countries is the adequate training of teachers. This would directly influence the quality of teaching in schools which has generally been critisized to be poor in developing countries (2). Computers could firstly beused for the training (or re-training) of teacher-trainers. As funds and resources are limited in developing countries, it would be wise to concentrate our most powerful resources to upgrade the skills and expertise of our educators. CAL may be one of those ways of ensuring that.

Another urgent need of education in developing countries is that of providing basic literacy and numeracy skills for the masses (3). It is in this area that CAL could be seen to be most effective. This is due to the ability of the computer to be able to work at the pace of the learner and to perform repetitive tasks. The computer (if programmed wisely) would be able to assess the response of the student and guide the learner along a route which is matched to his present ability.

There is also the problem in developing countries where a majority of the people do not attend any form of institutionalised schooling, especially at the secondary school level (4). This is due to many reasons, one of which is the fact that children at this age are mostly needed in the home or in the fields to work. CAL could be used with other distance-learning methods, for example, in correspondence courses where it could work side by side with other forms of instructional media like radio, television, study guides etc., to reach the majority who are not in school. The possibility of broadcasting not only radio and television programmes but also CAL programs economically (for eg. BASICODE developed in Holland) is a strong possibility.

Microcomputers could be placed in easily

accessible places to provide a more equitable distribution of educational resources for use by the general public, for example, in community centres or public meeting halls. The use of small, light and portable, battery or solar-powered microcomputers could be a feasible form of appropriate computer technology. A basic and primitive example of this would be "Speak & Spell" manufactured by Texas Instruments. However, this could be modified whereby modules (and hence lessons) could be varied (by the changing of a chip) and where different levels of difficulty are achieved with sound and visual reinforcements. The same basic equipment could then be used for an entire class or school. This may work out to be cheaper than purchasing different textbooks for different classes. These portable "talking books" could even be brought home and used to carry out one's homework.

One of the most urgent needs of education must be the need to encourage its people to think and not to learn by rote. There must be something wrong with an educational system that encourages students to gear all their efforts to the passing of examinations for the sole purpose of gaining entry into wage employment in the modern sector of the economy. The tragedy is that so many of them will never in fact achieve this goal. Can the computer be one of the ways of providing a creative way of learning ? Creativity must be encouraged among our students, the lack of which would hinder future change and development.

"Should we rely on existing educational systems to carry out the tasks which lie ahead ? The present day world is marked by a population explosion; the imperative requirements of economic development and the fight against hunger; the scientific and technological revolution; the multiplication of knowledge; the rise of the masses.....the extension and proliferation of information and communication media. This world is making and will make new demands on education. Does it not contain new means which education may and must use of, if it is not to fail in its task ? " (Learning to Be, UNESCO Publication).

3.0 SRI LANKA

Sri Lanka is an island-republic and a member of the British Commonwealth. Recently it has received attention because of the racial disturbances in the small island. Prior to that, Sri Lanka had a growing economy with an ever-expanding tourist industry. Being a former British Colony (formerly known as Ceylon), Sri Lanka has inherited government bureaucracies staffed mainly by the English educated, who were schooled in the same tradition.

The education system of the country has been modelled after the British system. The country conducts their own versions of the "O" and "A" level examinations which are very similar to those of the British. However, in Sri Lanka, the educational system is centralised, with full power and responsibilities resting on its Ministry of Education. At all levels, English is taught (or at least, made available) in the schools and is recognised as the main language for business and communication.

3.1 The Use of Computers in Sri Lanka

The use of computers in Sri Lanka was largely pioneered by the public sector. The public sector comprises not only the Ministries and Departments dealing with the functions usually associated with the government such as law enforcement, health, education and public utilities, but also industrial corporations. The public sector dominates the economy of Sri Lanka and employs half of the working force in Sri Lanka.

The actual number of computers in Sri Lanka is small compared to the size of the public and private sectors but the rate of computers being purchased is steadily increasing. Most of the computers are being used for administration (for eg. in accounts, billing) and for the analysis of huge amounts of data (for eg. in economic surveys, census surveys and in analysing examination results). The main computers used are those of IBM, Wang and ICL. In the microcomputer scene, Radio Shack, Commodore, Sinclair Spectrums and BBCs are becoming more popular particularly with small businesses (with burgeoning computer tuition establishments). They are also slowly being bought and used in middle-class homes. Recently, the government has adopted a National Computer Policy in 1983 with help from the United Kingdom Council for Computing Development (5) and formed the Computer and Information Technology Council in 1984, to coordinate and maintain high standards in the use of computers in the country.

In education, computers were used mainly at the tertiary level based in the main engineering faculties of the Universities of Sri Lanka. They were mainly used for project work and for statistical analysis, for example, in the Statistical Unit of the University of Colombo (6). In recent years, there has been a major push in the universities to use computers with the setting up of computer centres in the different universities in the country and in organising courses and training appropriate staff from these universities. This was initiated by the University Grants Commission with help from the University of Colombo and the British Council.

3.2 Urgent Educational Needs & Problems in Schools in Sri Lanka

One of the main problems of education in schools in Sri Lanka is a shortage of teachers in Science, Mathematics and English. The shortage of teachers in the Science areas is mainly due to the fact that in a developing and industrialising country like Sri Lanka, the attraction for Science graduates to work in the commercial sector is very great. The teaching profession normally obtains the remnants of these graduates. This situation in Sri Lanka is compounded by the exodus of teachers in these subject areas to Nigeria and the Middle East as a result of very aggressive and attractive recruiting campaign made by these countries.

Education in Sri Lanka is free and there are about 9,500 schools, which the government feels is adequate at present. However, the facilities provided for adequate teaching is far from satisfactory. For example, there is still a large number of schools, especially in the rural areas, without proper buildings and playing fields, and with the minimum basic equipment like furniture, chalkboards, science equipment, laboratories and textbooks. Also, only about 1,000 of the 9,500 schools in Sri Lanka are linked to some source of electricity supply.

There is also the problem of providing an equal distribution of educational resources in the different schools throughout the country, say for example, between the private and the government schools. For example, some of the schools in Colombo (the capital of Sri Lanka), where former ministers and government officials were educated, seem to have better equipped buildings, laboratories, playing fields and even swimming pools, whereas certain rural schools are unable to afford decent toilets for their teachers and pupils. If measures were introduced to even out this distribution of educational resources, there may be political repercussions.

Can computers be used to solve some of these educational problems and needs in Sri Lanka ? Some of these problems are complex and require not single solutions but a combination of strategies.

3.3 Main Considerations

Some of the Sri Lankan government's main considerations for deciding whether to introduce or not to introduce the use of computers in schools includes the fact that the educational plan of the country must go hand-in-hand with other economic and social developmental plans of the country. For example, the nation's present priorities include the modernisation and industrialisation of the country. Hence, the educational priorities must include the emphasis of teaching and equipping its students in Science, Mathematics and English, for these are essential for the national development of the country. The introduction of educational technology (which includes the use of computers) was seen as a step towards achieving the nation's goal of modernisation. The question was not so much as to introduce or not to introduce computers, but more on when to introduce computers into the schools and to what extent and level. The other important factor considered was that in developing countries, the greatest asset of the nation is still her people. Hence, the use of technology must be so as to enhance the capabilities and contribution that her people could make to the nation, and not to replace them.

3.4 Implementation Strategy

With a centralised system of education, any new innovation to be introduced in the schools would first have to be initiated by the Ministry of Education. They would then be the ones who would provide the financial resources to implement such an innovation. The design of the curriculum and the formulation of suitable training programmes would also be the responsibility of the Ministry. This is done at a central level because there is a common curriculum and examinations board throughout the country. Any new innovation or "idea" would have to go through the appropriate "Special Advisor" of the Ministry of Education. He is the one that would carry out the initial groundwork and preparation, and would prepare a paper of his findings and recommendations to the appropriate Ministers for consideration. Once a decision has been made at the ministerial level to proceed with such an introduction, financial resources are then allocated, a suitable curriculum is designed or adapted from another country, and an implementation strategy drawn up. Pilot work is normally carried out first with a few schools to examine the best way of introducing such an innovation and to analyse its effects.

With the introduction of microcomputers in Sri Lanka, the Ministry of Education started off by purchasing 200 Sinclair Spectrums with tape recorders and colour televisions as monitors, for use in 100 government schools that was specially selected. These schools were situated chiefly in the major towns. A wise move by the Ministry was to encourage computer awareness (for example, in information technology, data-handling, word-processing) by starting computer awareness clubs in these schools instead of introducing a Computer Science/Studies courses per se. These microcomputers were also used for the 6th form (16-18 year olds) and especially for scientific simulations in subjects like Physics and Chemistry (as laboratory equipment is very scarce in these schools).

The training of teachers was also a special emphasis and 7 training centres were set up in the schools (mainly in the "prestigious" schools that were already open to the use of computers). In these centres, more computers were purchased (including BBCs and Commodores). Training sessions (in the form of a 2-day introductory course where elementary BASIC programming and keyboard experience was covered) was conducted for these teachers (one teacher from each of the 100 schools chosen, to be covered at about 20 a time) with help from the University of Colombo, the British Council and some interested commercial firms (7). These courses were also attended by teacher trainers from colleges, educators from the Curriculum Development Centre, and representatives from the Ministry of Education (including the representative for educational television).

The Ministry of Education would obviously like to do much more in the way of encouraging the use of computers in schools by providing the necessary hardware, software and training but, like most developing countries, do not

have sufficient resources to provide such a positive back-up. Hence, help is needed from other ministries or from other organisations and countries.

3.5 Foreign Aid

Sri Lanka has, at present, links with UNESCO, UNDP, Sweden, Norway, Japan and the Commonwealth Secretariat. These organisations and countries send experts and provide finance for training programmes and equipment. Most of the aid is given for specific projects. There are however no formal links with governments to provide aid in the area of using computers in schools in Sri Lanka. The government has only recently approached the British Council and the Overseas Development Administration (ODA) in the United Kingdom to provide a substantial grant with the aim of providing a microcomputer for each school in Sri Lanka.

One of the main problems of accepting overseas aid is that of continuity, especially with respect to personnel and equipment. Expertise is provided from different institutions of the donor countries at different stages. That is why clear, long-term objectives and plans are needed so that whatever aid is received will fit into the overall development plan without major adjustments to various projects just to accommodate the aid programs.

Another way of alleviating this problem is to have an "adoption" scheme whereby two institutions are linked on a long-term basis. For example, in the training of computer analysts, the University of Colombo has been "adopted" by the University of Reading Statistical Unit in England. In the past eight years, Reading has sent six of their staff members to Colombo for summer visits where they have been able to set up the Statistical Unit at the University of Colombo, conduct relevant courses for the training of its new staff and formulate courses for the new students. At the same time, Colombo has sent, in return, six of its own staff to Reading for more extensive training. The advantage of this adoption scheme is that the organisation and the situation at the Unit of the University of Colombo is well known by the staff in Reading and hence appropriate training courses could be planned and carried out. Also, whenever a problem arises in Colombo which cannot be solved by the staff there, a communication could be sent to Reading and suitable and accurate advice could be made as the person handling the enquiry would be familiar with the set-up in Colombo. Even if half of the staff in Colombo or Reading would leave in five or ten years time, there would still be the other half who would be familiar with the situation. Hence this ensures continuity in the long-term. In this particular scheme, the British Council has provided a major portion of the funding (travel and maintenance costs for the staff). What is also important is that one does not keep away either staff for too long and hence do not alleniate them from their main jobs. Summer visits also encourage the up-dating of knowledge, skills and awareness of staff on either side.

Can a similar scheme be done for teacher-training colleges where colleges in Sri Lanka are adopted by teacher-training colleges in the developed countries ? In this way, continuity is achieved in the long-term with relevant and immediate expertise provided for teacher-trainers and teachers.

In the end, it would be helpful for the donor countries to have extensive discussions with the country to which it is giving aid, and to identify areas of priority in the country's own development programmes. It is not sufficient to have money or equipment "dumped" onto a country. Instead, long-term exchange programmes as described above should be encouraged not only between academic institutions but also between centralised agencies and organisations. This will ensure that there will be continuous graduation and mid-course adjustments of the project that are being carried out in the developing country.

4.0 CONCLUSION

Whether CAL would be suitable or unsuitable for a developing country should be seen in relation to the emphasis and forms of educational policies and systems of the developing country. The considerations of such emphasis and forms in-turn depend on the needs of the individuals and the country as a whole. As the needs of the individuals and the country change, so must the emphasis and forms of the educational policies and systems of the country.

Although this paper focusses on the considerations of introducing CAL for specific needs of education in developing countries, it has been emphasized that the overall policies of the country play an important role. Whether one agrees as to whether these policies are right or wrong is another matter altogether. One can only hope that the use of computers especially in education will not be mis-used or even abused in developing countries.

REFERENCES

1. CHANDRA, P. (1983) "Missions for Regional Computer Cooperation in Education and Research". Proceedings of the Regional Computer Cooperation in Developing Countries Conference. Stockholm, Sweden. 14-16 September. To be published by North-Holland.

2. THOMAS,J. (1975) World Problems in Education: A Brief Analytical Survey. International Bureau of Education: Studies and Surveys in Comparative Education. Paris. The UNESCO Press.

3. FAURE,E. et al. (1972) Learning to Be: The World of Education Today and Tommorrow. UNESCO. Paris. Harrap London. p39.

4. See s/no.6, p43.

5. BOGOD,J. (1982) "Sri Lankan Government Follows-Up UKCCD Initiative". Bulletin No.2, UKCCD. London.

6. SAMARANAYAKE,V.K. and ABEYASEKERA,S. (1984) "Microcomputer Applications in Sri Lanka: A Case Study of the Activities of the Statistical Consultancy and Data Processing Servive of the University of Colombo". Proceedings of the First International Symposium on Microcomputer Applications in Developing Countries. University of Colombo. Sri Lanka.

7. AVIS,P. and HATHAWAY,M. (1984) Report on the Seminar on Computer Literacy in Education in Sri Lanka, Colombo, Sri Lanka. 17-27 Sep.1984. Report obtainable from Peter Avis, South Yorkshire and Humberside, MEP, Donchaster DN2 4PY, UK.

ACKNOWLEDGEMENTS

I would like to thank the Sri Lankan Ministry of Education officials and the staff of the Univ. of Colombo; my supervisors, Dr. Margaret Cox and Dr. Joan Bliss for their help and support; and to the Queen Anne Street Ed. Trust and the Leonard Cohen Fund for their financial help. Finally, a special thank-you to the Family, whose concern, encouragement and love I value so much.

COMPUTERS IN EDUCATION, K. Duncan and D. Harris (eds.)
Elsevier Science Publishers B.V. (North-Holland)
© IFIP, 1985

A MODEL FOR THE PRODUCTION OF EXEMPLARY EDUCATIONAL SOFTWARE
THREE YEARS EXPERIENCE

Luella Egerton, Lorne R. Smith

Computers in Education Centre,
Ontario Ministry of Education,
Toronto, Ontario, Canada
(416) 965-0692

In 1982 the province of Ontario, Canada, through its Ministry of Education and supported by funds from the Board of Industrial Leadership and Development (BILD), embarked on a one million dollar plan to fund the development of quality computerized learning materials for Ontario elementary and secondary schools. The purpose was twofold: To provide exemplary computer lessonware (short educational programs) and to stimulate a Canadian based software industry. This software production model formed the basis for a multi-million dollar software initiative in 1984-85 and subsequent years. This original production model, its results, and the revised model presently in use are discussed.

1. INTRODUCTION

An official memorandum issued by the Ministry of Education for the province of Ontario, Canada, in February, 1982 stated:

> There will be two fundamentally different ways to use computers in the process of teaching and learning. The more significant way will be the creative use of the computer by individuals; writing, composing, designing, analyzing, and other extensions of original thought. All students must be given opportunities to use computers in this way. (1)

Given a lack of quality software and hardware and using this as a philosophical base, the Ontario Ministry of Education took two bold initiatives:

a. Functional Requirements (2) for an educational microcomputer capable of encouraging creative extensions of original thought were published;

b. A Call for Proposals (3) to develop computerized learning materials was issued.

2. THE EDUCATIONAL MICROCOMPUTER

The Canadian Education Microcomputer Corporation (CEMCORP) was the first manufacturer to meet the functional requirements. Its 16-bit ICON microcomputer and LEXICON fileserver is an Ontario Approved Education Microcomputer (OAEM) system.

3. THE CALL FOR PROPOSALS

Two purposes were to be served by this Call for computerized learning material proposals:

a. The development of exemplary educational software to achieve curricular goals while pushing the microcomputer's capabilities to their limit;

b. The development of authoring skills to stimulate the Canadian software industry.

Over five hundred (500) proposals came from teachers, students, colleges, universities, publishers, and software companies. Proposals were received for French and/or English lessonware for all areas of the curriculum from kindergarten through secondary school.

3.1 Evaluation of These Proposals

More than seventy (70) curriculum specialists within the Ministry of Education and teachers' organizations, along with educational computing experts principally from the Educational Computing Organization of Ontario (E C O O), evaluated these proposals. Three screenings were employed:

a. To determine whether or not the proposal complied with the parameters of the Call;

b. To determine whether or not the submission met Ministry curriculum guideline requirements;

c. To determine whether or not the proposed lessonware would demonstrate an exemplary use of the computer.

Fifty-nine proposals were selected for development at a cost of $1 million. These formed the 1982 Exemplary Lessonware Project.

4. THE CONTRACT

A contract signed with each developer provided full funding by the Ministry for the lessonware. The Ministry holds the licence for use of these programs in educational institutions within the province of Ontario. The authors retain the copyright and the rights to sell the programs outside Ontario.

4.1 Stages of The Contract

There were three stages in the development process:

Stage 1:
   The design and specification stage called for the objectives of the lessonware, its description, hardware and peripheral details, the program logic, complete scripting and screen layouts. Drafts of teacher, programmer, and student manuals (where appropriate) plus hardcopy student worksheets accompanied this stage.

Stage 2:
   This stage involved programming of the lessonware. Formative evaluation through field-testing with teachers and students was carried out. All revisions for the software and accompanying manuals were completed before submission of the final program.

Stage 3:
   Commercial production of all components of the program including disks, manuals, worksheets, etc., formed this final stage.

The contract provided the right to terminate, by either the Ministry or the developer, at the conclusion of any stage.

Each stage was evaluated by the Ministry and approval of the work given before final payment for that stage was approved. Approval of a stage did not automatically imply approval to proceed to the next stage. These were separate decisions.

4.2 Production and Distribution

Because at the time the contracts were signed (summer of 1982) very few of the authors had any experience with commercial education software production, Stage 3 was carried out by only a few developers.

It became evident as the project continued that the reproduction of the disks and hardcopy materials would be very closely tied to the distribution of these.

In order to accommodate this, the Ontario Educational Software Service (OESS) was initiated as a joint service from the Ministry of Education and TVOntario, Ontario's educational communications authority. TVOntario contracted to reproduce and to distribute all licensed educational software funded by the Ministry, thus handling Stage 3 of the lessonware contracts.

5. LESSONWARE MONITORS/EVALUATORS

Since the central purpose for undertaking this unique model of software development was to satisfy the Ministry's desire to provide quality and innovative computerized learning materials which would challenge students to extend their thinking and problem-solving abilities, close evaluative monitoring was used.

Lessonware monitors, the majority of whom were Ministry of Education curriculum specialists, worked with the developers to ensure that both the content and the design of the software met the Ministry's expectations for exemplary material.

Technical experts also reviewed the programs at the conclusion of Stage 1 and Stage 2. Their comments and suggestions played an important role in helping developers improve their software.

6. DEVELOPERS'/MONITORS' MEETINGS

One of the most dynamic and exciting aspects of the entire project was the interaction among developers and monitors. This was facilitated by a number of meetings where developers demonstrated their programs and received feedback from their peers.

7. STANDARDS

The thrusts of this particular model for software production were to provide exemplary programs and to encourage a thriving, creative software industry. Therefore, strict formatting and programming standards were not imposed. The position taken was that such restrictions would inhibit imaginative and inventive directions, particularly in this first project.

8. RESEARCH

Research in a number of important areas was undertaken parallel to the development.

For example, a report focusing on formative evaluation entitled *Evaluating the Effectiveness of Lessonware Prototypes: Some Guidelines for Use in the Development* of Education Software (4) was prepared. Two modes of evaluating were examined - the case study and student assessment. Recommendations on where to field test, what to look for, how to collect information and how to write the evaluation report were outlined.

A concentrated examination of the field-testing and revision work of a number of developers was carried out. The premise of this examination was that this evaluation process is very different from that used for text books. The report Developing Exemplary Software: Lessons from the Evaluation of Four Software Projects (5) is being used for background information in field testing in the present round of software development.

A major report A Formative Evaluation Plan for Exemplary Software (6) grew out of the experiences of this 1982 Exemplary Lessonware Project. This plan provides the field testing model now being used by the educational software developers under contract to the Ministry.

9. FINDINGS

When this model for the production of exemplary educational software was initiated in the spring of 1982 few guidelines were established. This was intentional since a principal aim was to encourage developers to explore the potential of the microcomputer in an educational setting, to push this tool to its limits.

As developers worked and reworked their ideas and programs, striving to make them exemplary as they interacted with each other and with their monitors, and as they field tested, evaluated, and revised their lessonware, certain trends emerged:

a. The timelines developers originally established were much too short, and the amount of work involved was much greater than many had anticipated. This was especially true of the design stage.

b. Some developers had difficulty transforming what appeared to be a dynamic proposal into a dynamic interactive exemplary software program.

c. Book writing experience tended to be a liability; it proved difficult to move from linear, page-turning programs to meaningful interactive ones.

d. Completion of Stage 1 (the design) without complementary development of Stage 2 (programming) proved difficult with some programs.

e. Development teams which included a

practising teacher were, on the whole, most successful in meeting the lessonware project's objectives.

f. Field testing the software with students revealed unexpected results in many cases. Things developers and/or educators thought would occur did not; unanticipated things did. Formative evaluation with students and classroom teachers proved valuable in creating exemplary programs.

g. Developers created strategies to improve their programs which would not have occurred without the pressure and stimulation of this project.

h. Monitors, who were principally Ministry curriculum experts, gained invaluable experience with computers in educational settings.

i. The enthusiasm of the developers remained throughout the project; in some instances it increased as they met the challenges of producing the very best of which the machines were capable.

10. RESULTS

Each grade level, from kindergarten through secondary school, has programs which enhance its curriculum.

Of the original fifty-nine (59) contracted projects, forty-five (45) continued to completion. A number of these are examined below.

10.1 The Puzzler

This reading strategies program, based on the Goodman and Burke (7) reading theory of predicting, confirming, and integrating, presents a choice of five short stories for junior grade students.

Each story is no more than six pages (screens). When each page is read the student is presented with a screen where s/he types in one or more predictions as to what the person or object in the story is. As each subsequent page is read the student may change, delete or add to his or her predictions thereby developing the skills of confirming and integrating.

This program has received wide acclaim as it has been demonstrated at reading and computer conferences in the United States, Britain, and Canada. Wheeler, in an article The Puzzler... An Answer to the Reading Riddle? (8), writes:

"The computer's power is used to

encourage the reader to take responsibility for active reading and comprehension monitoring. With The Puzzler, active reading is both learnable and engagingly fun." (p49)

10.2 Flame Life

This simulation of burning candles in a beaker where the student can control such variables as the size of the beaker, the number, and the height of the candles is an excellent program to teach data collection and interpretation skills.

Not only can junior grade students experiment safely with burning candles, they also have the opportunity to record data, to change the variables, to present this information in graph form, and to draw their own conclusions.

This rather simple simulation then becomes a tool for students to manipulate data and thereby actively participate in the learning process.

Both Flame Life and The Puzzler won awards at the 1984 Association for Media and Technology in Education in Canada (AMTEC).

10.3 IZZIT

The computer has been presented by Papert(9) and others as a tool that can alter and enhance the ways in which learning takes place. IZZIT is a program which attempts to do this. It is a game to develop primary children's thinking skills.

IZZIT is a two part activity. It helps to develop visual and verbal memory, classification skills and the ability to make generalizations. Problem-solving skills are developed by encouraging children to discover relationships, to classify by sets, and to use question and answer techniques to form hypotheses, and then revise them on the basis of feedback. The student learns to differentiate between three classes of shapes with nonsense names (zoz, zob, and zod) while doing the first part of the program. This knowledge is used in the second part to play a twenty (20) questions-type game.

10.4 Musicland Games

This program, a series of four "games" - Music Doodles, Timbre Painting, Music Blocks and Sound Factory - illustrates the capacity of the computer to accommodate different grade levels and different curriculum areas through the same program.

Dr. Martin Lamb of the University of Toronto has broken the traditional barrier of creating music by using notes. This software permits even preliterate children to compose by "drawing" music on the staff using a joystick. They may then use colours to "paint" their music. Each colour represents an instrument; for example, blue plays a flute while red sounds a trumpet. The computer plays the composition; changes can be made easily to the pitch, the time, and so on.

Sound Factory, the most sophisticated of the "games", permits manipulation of sound waves and can be used in secondary physics.

This one program satisfies a wide range of needs in the music curriculum, as well as other subject areas.

10.5 Human Settlements

Networking, which allows students to share information to cooperatively make decisions, is an important feature of educational computing. The program Human Settlements for secondary students makes use of this technique.

With this software, up to six students can network and use the shared information for consensus decision-making. The task is to come to a decision on the route for a new throughway in a large metropolitan area.

In this simulation each student chooses one of six roles (engineer, housewife, developer, etc.). Each role has variations. For example, if a student decides to be the developer s/he must choose whether to be a residential or commercial builder.

During the first part of the program the students individually make certain decisions which they feed onto the central disk. When this is complete they access the decisions of their classmates, alter their own decisions if necessary and finally come to a conclusion agreeable to everyone.

Such a simulation not only provides students with information about human settlements, but also permits them to gain an understanding of what is involved in making decisions affecting large numbers of people.

10.6 Features of The Software

Each of the programs developed under this 1982-84 Exemplary Lessonware Project exploits some feature of computerized learning. The five discussed above highlight their significant characteristics.

The forty-five (45) lessonware programs were originally developed for 8-bit machines, including the Apple, Commodore, IBM, and TRS-80. During 1984 they have been converted and enhanced to run on the 16-bit ICON microcomputer, an Ontario Approved Educational Microcomputer (OAEM). These OAEM programs have also been placed within a pointing-oriented "ambience" which makes them easy to use even for very young children.

Information about these programs is available from the Ontario Educational Software Service. (10)

11. THE 1984-85 LESSONWARE PROJECT

A number of important changes were incorporated into the new project as a result of the 1982-84 experience:

a. The objectives of the software programs may not only support the present Ministry curriculum guidelines, but may also extend and/or enhance them.

b. The design stage (Stage 1) and the programming stage (Stage 2) may proceed concurrently if the lessonware will benefit from this arrangement.

c. Field-testing with students and teachers in classrooms was found to be of such vital importance it became a separate stage (Stage 3). Specific guidelines contained in the Gillis report A Formative Evaluation Plan for Exemplary Software (6) apply to the field-testing.

d. Closer monitoring of the progress of each project is taking place to ensure timelines are adhered to.

12. SUMMARY

These lessonware projects have been undertaken by the government of Ontario, Canada, in the belief that the nature of the educational process will be increasingly affected by the new microelectronics and communication technologies. The availability of quality software consistent with learning and curriculum objectives is essential if education is to obtain the maximum educational benefits of these technological advances.

The experiences have demonstrated that education and computer experts working co-operatively, with close supervision and close attention to educational objectives, will produce materials which can significantly enhance the learning of children and assist them in using the computer creatively.

REFERENCES

1. Podrebarac, G. R. Computers in Education. Memorandum to: Directors of Education, Principals of Schools, Ontario Ministry of Education, Memorandum No. 31, February 23, 1982.

2. Ontario Ministry of Education. Functional Requirements for Microcomputers for Educational Use in Ontario Schools - Stage 1. Queen's Park, Toronto: March, 1983.

3. Ontario Ministry of Education. Request for Proposals for Exemplary Computer-based Learning Materials. Queen's Park, Toronto: March, 1982.

4. Pike, Ruth. Evaluating the Effectiveness of Lessonware Prototypes: Some Guidelines for Use in the Development of Educational Software. Queen's Park, Toronto: Ministry of Education, 1983.

5. Gillis, Lynette. Developing Exemplary Software: Lessons from the Evaluation of Four Software Projects. Queen's Park, Toronto: Ministry of Education, 1984.

6. Gillis, Lynette. A Formative Evaluation Plan for Exemplary Software. Toronto: TVOntario, 1984.

7. Goodman, Y. and Burke, C. L. Reading Strategies: Focus on Comprehension. New York: Holt, Rinehart and Winston, 1980.

8. Wheeler, Fay. The Puzzler... An Answer to the Reading Riddle? Classroom Computer Learning, 1983, 4 (4), 46-49.

9. Papert, S. Mindstorms. New York: Basic Books, 1980.

10. Ontario Educational Software Service. TVOntario Customer Service, Box 200, Station "Q", Toronto, Ontario M4T 2T1.

COMPUTERS IN EDUCATION, K. Duncan and D. Harris (eds.)
Elsevier Science Publishers B.V. (North-Holland)
© IFIP, 1985

THE PRODUCTION OF EDUCATIONAL SOFTWARE IN FINLAND

Jukka Rantanen

Technical Research Centre of Finland
(VTT/ATK) Vuorimiehentie 5
02150 Espoo, Finland

The production of educational software is one of the major issues that slows down the advancement of educational computing. In a small country like Finland one has to consider a national strategy to promote the production of educational software; the independent efforts of publishers, small software companies or public projects are insufficient to solve the many problems involved. This paper considers a general strategy of educational software production for Finland. First, a survey of introduction of microcomputers to Finnish schools and homes is presented, followed by a survey of educational software needs. Finally some measures are suggested to promote the production and evaluation of educational software in Finland; these recommendations represent a proposal for national strategy.

1. INTRODUCTION

During the past few years microcomputers have been introduced to Finnish schools, homes and companies in great numbers. This microcomputer boom has increased the demand for software and literature, which could guide users to useful and productive activities. Microcomputers in schools and homes are, for the time being, used mainly for learning BASIC programming and playing games. Everybody agrees that the promotion of educational software development is one of the major issues in educational computing; teacher training being certainly the first priority.

More and more teenagers, teachers and professionals are interested and involved in the development of microcomputer software. During the 1980's it seems to become one of the most innovative fields, which demands both technical, intellectual and artistic creativity. But it is not easy to develop high quality microcomputer software. It is less and less a hobby business, it will demand more expertise of the application area and of the software engineering. The new authors of the telematic society would need new kind of training and support that is not yet provided in educational institutions.

This paper describes a proposal for a national strategy of educational software production for Finland. It will deal with issues such as the introduction of microcomputers to schools and homes, the needs of educational software and the measures to promote domestic production of educational software. The proposal is based on a project that was recently conducted by the Technical Research Centre of Finland in co-operation with the National Board of Schools and a few publishers (1).

2. MICROCOMPUTERS IN FINNISH SCHOOLS AND HOMES

The introduction of computer literacy into the secondary education has begun in Finland. About 85 % of high schools had an optional computer literacy course during the term 1982-83, when it was just included into the curriculum. Information technology will have also great impact on the vocational education curriculum. By the year 1988 all students in vocational schools will take the obligatory informatics course. Since 1960´s there has been EDP-courses in technical and commercial schools. According to a recent proposal an optional computer literacy course will be included into the primary school curriculum; this course will be given beginning the school year 1987-88. Already now there are quite many computer clubs in primary schools, that often share their microcomputers and software with high schools.

During the next years a major effort will be to introduce computer literacy education in the secondary and primary level education. Most of the resources will be directed to teacher training, the purchase of hardware and software as well as experimental work.

Since the year 1982 there have been working groups in the school administration that have annually specified requirements for school microcomputer systems and asked for bids for volume purchases. The systems offered have been tested against the specifications given by the Technical Research Centre of Finland. Recently a working group specified that school microcomputers should have CP/M or MS-DOS operating system, BASIC and Pascal languages available. Also it must be possible to connect the individual microcomputers to a network that shares a mass memory and a printer. The recommendation of the spring 1984 included the following microcomputers: Auditek AMC-100, DEC PC-100, MikroMikko 1G, MicroSpectra, ABC-806, Apple IIe, and Commodore 8032. Despite the recommendations there is currently a wide variety of different microcomputers in schools, which causes problems for software development. However, most of the microcomputers have CP/M operating system.

According to recent estimates there were about
2000 microcomputers in high schools and vocational schools in the end of the year 1984;
this means about 4 microcomputers per school.
By the year 1988 there will probably be at least
8 microcomputers in every high school and vocational school by a cautious forecast; the
total amount will be 10.000 meaning a tenfold
increase. It is probable that after five years
in every primary school (for the ages of 10-16)
there will be a computer class with 8-10 microcomputers.

Because of the extensive introduction of computer literacy to the secondary and primary
level curriculum, the foremost need is software
and literature for computer literacy and informatics. One needs uptodate software and literature, because the computer and communication
technology is developing rapidly. The needs of
educational software are the following:
1) software for computer literacy and informatics education: programming tools, personal
   computing tools, courseware for the user
   training of personal computing and programming tools.
2) general-purpose software: personal computing
   and problem solving tools (calculation,
   information handling, word processing, presentation graphics) that can be used with
   different subjects.
3) software for class demonstrations and for
   laboratory work: including science simulations, and control and measurement applications.
4) courseware for remedial teaching: drill and
   practise programs for mathematics and
   languages.
5) software for professional training: commercial and technical applications software
   (accounting, Computer Aided Design etc.).
6) personal computing tools for teachers:
   including general-purpose software (word
   processing etc.) and educational applications
   (test banking etc.).
7) software and literature for teacher training:
   software and literature suitable for both
   self-studies and coursework.

Computer literacy education in schools is
already now affected by the home computers, that
are now in fashion among the young people. Some
primary school pupils use their own home computers in computer clubs of their schools. Yet
it is difficult to foresee how home computers
will affect the teaching of computer literacy
and other subjects in schools. The potential is
great, but formal education system is still
unprepared to utilize the new learning tool and
resource.

In the end of the year 1984 there were about
60.000 microcomputers in households or in individual use; that is 3 % of households. This has
a great influence to computer literacy, because
each home computer often has many users:

youngsters, friends, and grown-ups. If the
trends are similar to the U.S.A. and the U.K.,
there will be over half a million home computers
in Finland by the 1990; that will be 30 % of the
households. At present there are tens of different kinds of microcomputers, so production of
software for home computers is often not feasible. There are demands for consumer information service that could give advise in hardware and software purchases and could set some
standards for hardware and software quality.

There are many needs for home computer software
that are common to those for schools:
1) games for teaching reasoning skills and basic
   skills.
2) self-instruction packages for computer literacy.
3) courseware for teaching mathematics,
   languages, self-development skills (such as
   study and memory skills), typing and word
   processing.
4) personal and home computing software.
At present domestic producers of consumer software and users of home computers do not yet
realize the potential of microcomputers in homebased education.

3. THE PRESENT PRODUCTION OF EDUCATIONAL SOFTWARE

The production and publishing of educational
software is now starting in Finland. Most of
the major publishers support some authors that
develop educational software. There are also
about ten small companies dedicated to the
production of educational software. But many
problems remain to be solved before educational
and consumer software development becomes a real
business:
- There is not enough visible and convincing
  evidence of usefulness of educational or
  consumer software.
- There are no general plans for the educational
  software development; authors are developing
  simple programs that cannot be integrated into
  larger units.
- There is a tendency to develop software for
  the same purpose by different authors; thus
  there is a need for some kind of
  coordination.
- There are no general guidelines for the
  designing and implementation of educational or
  consumer software, and authoring tools are not
  utilized; without proper procedures and tools
  the productivity remains low.

Many of these problems cannot be solved easily
and independently by the domestic publishers and
small companies themselves. In a small country
like Finland a general strategy and cooperative
actions are needed to promote the production of
educational software.

4. A STRATEGY FOR EDUCATIONAL SOFTWARE DEVELOPMENT

The following recommendations are included in a national strategy to promote domestic production of educational software. Some of the proposed measures are already being carried out. These recommendations are intended for publishers and producers of educational software as well as for school authorities.

RECOMMENDATION 1) Specification and development of basic software.

At first one should specify the software that could be used most extensively and then either develop it or purchase it in volumes. A recommendation should be made that every school purchase the specified basic software in addition to hardware. This guarantees a better start to educational computing in schools.

The basic software consists of
a) general-purpose software for personal computing and problem solving, including word processing, data management, calculation, and presentation graphics. This so-called toolware may be used in different subjects as well as in personal computing by teachers and pupils. At first they are used in computer literacy and then gradually integrated into other subjects, too. The toolware supports a new approach to the introduction of computer literacy to schools: the emphasis of computer literacy is changed from programming to the use of personal computing and problem solving tools.

On short term one should specify the educational requirements for these tools and select the software from what is available. Instead of developing the demanded toolware from the scratch one should put most efforts to apply the toolware already available to different subjects. This emphasizes the development of literature, user interfaces and self-instruction packages that support the use of selected toolware.

On long term projects one should develop problem solving and open learning environments for different subjects. These may be based on integrated software packages that are applied to different subjects.

In order to introduce personal computing and problem solving tools to high schools, the National Board of Schools will during the fall 1984 ask bids for volume purchase of these software. Then a recommendation will be made of those CP/M or MS-DOS based packages that are suitable to schools.

b) courseware for different subjects, including drills, games and simulations. On short term one should try to introduce "break-through"

courseware to different subjects. This should be high quality courseware that will give convincing evidence of the educational potential of the computer. This courseware for exploratory use should not be too complex, because the medium is new to the users. One may rapidly create a collection of exploratory courseware by selecting the best pieces of domestically and internationally available courseware. Authors and publishers will get useful feedback from this courseware, showing the kind of courseware that is accepted and seen most useful.

On long term projects one should develop more extensive courseware packages. These are more integrated into the curriculum and provide remarkable solutions to instructional problems. It may take many years to develop these packages, so they have to be done in cooperation with producers and school authorities.

RECOMMENDATION 2) Setting up educational software development groups.

Long term projects are necessary in order to integrate educational software into curriculum and in order to develop new approaches to teaching different subjects. Feasible efforts demand people who have been involved in the development of educational software at least for a few years. Therefore it is recommended that one should set up educational software development groups that are able to work for many years. In addition to producing software these groups could give on-the-job training for new authors and test different development procedures and tools. They should have good contacts with teacher training and didactic R & D and of course with schools where they evaluate the software and experiment with new approaches. It is improbable that publishers could alone start such groups doing pioneer development work for different subjects. These groups need support from public fund as well as from publishers.

During the past two years a few such educational software development groups have been started in Finland. At present they are working in close co-operation with teacher associations: Association for Mathematics, Physics, Chemistry and Computer Literacy Teachers, Association for Foreign Language Teachers, and Association for Finnish Language Teachers. The groups have got some support from public funds and publishers.

RECOMMENDATION 3) Collecting good examples of educational software.

Maybe the best learning material for new authors is good examples of educational software. So one should set up collections of good software for different subject-matters. These represent models for different pedagogical designs, good user interfaces and supporting materials.

Recently a collection of good domestic and
foreign software has been set up by a project
(1). It has turned out to be very useful in the
training of new authors.

RECOMMENDATION 4) Evaluation of educational
software.

From the beginning educational software should
be of high quality, because teachers are at
first very critical and there is little money
available for the purchase of software. For the
benefit of both authors and users one should
establish quality standards or evaluation criteria for educational software.

In the end of the year 1983 an educational software evaluation procedure was started by the
National Board of Schools. The software provided by publishers or individual authors is
checked against quality criteria that deal with
pedagogical value, user friendliness and technical quality. The first catalog of approved
educational software was published in the spring
1984 and sent to all high schools. The schools
will get some public funds for the purchase of
approved software. During the next years the
evaluation procedure has to be improved.
Opinions vary on what is good software and what
are proper criteria for quality evaluation.

RECOMMENDATION 5) Establishing of information
services and distribution channels for
educational software.

Users of educational software need guidance in
the selection, introduction and maintenance of
the software. They need to have adequate information service and software distribution organisations that are able to give enough support to
them. Commercial software producers and distributors often are not able to provide proper
support for schools.

In Finland information is currently disseminated
only by the catalog of approved educational
software of the National Board of Schools. In
addition to this the National Board of
Vocational Schools is setting up software libraries for technical, commercial, and other
vocational schools. The software libraries are
located in a few vocational schools that shall
have resources to distribute software and
support users. These software libraries and
distributors will also study software offerers
and evaluate software for educational use. They
will also ask bids for volume purchases of software.

RECOMMENDATION 6) Agreeing about standards for
educational software and hardware.

It is very important to agree about standards
for educational software and hardware in order
to allow development of portable software and

volume purchases of software. In Finland it is
recommended that schools should purchase microcomputers that have CP/M or MS-DOS operating
system available. It is also recommended that
educational software is implemented by CP/M- or
MS-DOS-based programming languages and graphics
subroutine libraries that conform to the GKS
(Graphics Kernel System) standard. Currently the
graphics extension software (GKS) of CP/M is
implemented to most of microcomputers that are
recommended for schools. An alternative will be
the forthcoming graphics extensions of MS-DOS
that are not yet available. Concerning new
programming languages for education, such as
LOGO and PROLOG, one should introduce versions
that are available for CP/M or MS-DOS operating
systems.

RECOMMENDATION 7) Organizing training for
authors and teachers.

Because there are very few experienced authors
of educational software, training has to be
organized for new authors. At present publishers, teacher associations, universities, and
some public organizations have given some training. Also during the spring 1984 a successful
course to Finnish authors and teacher educators
was given by a training staff of the
Microelectronics Education Programme of Great
Britain. It seems that such international
courses are an important means to stimulate
local thinking and activities.

During the next years in Finland the foremost
problem is organizing teacher training for computer literacy and for applications in different
subjects. One solution will be distance education by television and radio, supported by
local courses. A project is now proposed to
develop materials for the distance education.

RECOMMENDATION 8) Developing authoring tools.

In order to improve author's productivity one
should provide them proper authoring tools and
systems. Currently most authors of educational
software in Finland are using only BASIC
language and do not utilize or create standardized subroutine libraries for common routines. One should introduce them to more advanced authoring tools and give guidelines to
implementation of software.

RECOMMENDATION 9) Asking bids for volume
purchases of software.

It is recommended that national or local school
authorities ask for bids for volume purchase of
software for computer literacy, personal
computing and problem solving, and school administration. The volume purchases are beneficial
both for producers and for users because of
volume discounts and better support. The
schools should invest enough money to purchasing
software; for example each school might purchase
software every year by at least USD 1500.

RECOMMENDATION 10) Encouraging national co-operation.

In order to get a good start in educational software development one should have national co-operation projects. These should include participants from publishers, companies specialized to educational software production, microcomputer vendors, universities, and representatives of national or local educational authorities. So far there have been no such projects developing other learning materials. However, the markets for educational software are so limited in Finland that it seems improbable for individual publishers to be able to start any major undertakings alone.

RECOMMENDATION 11) Promoting internationalco-operation.

International co-operation in the advancement of educational computing is necessary for Finland. The resources for educational software development are so scarce in Finland, that they should be used reasonably . There is much educational software available on international markets that may be adapted to Finnish schools. Especially it is feasible to try to adapt general purpose packages for personal computing and problem solving, and authoring tools for educational software development. However, the licence agreements for translating and distributing commercial software are not favourable for small countries. The costs of licences are often too high to distributors and schools and the translation procedures may take long time to complete because of copy protection issues.

At present, it is best for Finnish author groups and publishers to aim at co-operative projects with the producers of educational software in other countries. In addition to adapting foreign software to Finland, domestic producers should try to develop software for international markets. Even though it is more difficult to develop this kind of software, it is good to try to reach better quality and originality as well as common standards for software portability. First co-operative projects in Scandinavia are now starting to develop educational software. Also some Finnish publishers are interested to co-operate with European publishers in this field. It remains to be seen what kinds of problems these projects will have, since there is no previous experiences of such international co-operation.

5. SUMMARY

This paper describes a national strategy for educational software development. The proposal will be further refined in a working group of a national project "computer in education" which outlines a long-term national scheme for computer literacy education and computer-based learning. The project started in the beginning of the year 1985 in co-operation with the National Boards of Schools and Vocational Schools.

ACKNOWLEDGEMENTS The project referred in this paper was supported by the National Fund for Research and Development (SITRA).

REFERENCES

(1) Rantanen, J., Tietokonepohjainen oppimateriaali: markkinat ja tuotanto. Computer-based learning materials: markets and production. SITRA B77, Kyriiri Oy,Helsinki,1984.

COMPUTERS IN EDUCATION, K. Duncan and D. Harris (eds.)
Elsevier Science Publishers B.V. (North-Holland)
© IFIP, 1985

Meeting Tennessee's Computer Literacy Requirement for Higher
Education

Gene Bailey and Rebekah Tidwell
East Tennessee State University

Introduction

This year, the Tennessee State Board of Regents (TSBR) passed down requirements which would set a mandate for "computer literacy" for all sixteen schools of higher education within its jurisdiction. The requirements will apply to all students entering as of the Fall, 1984 term who are seeking either a baccalaureate degree or an associate degree and must be met prior to graduation. The decision to implement the requirement was announced shortly before the start of the Fall semester. Thus, many institutions had little opportunity to acquire either equipment or additional faculty. This paper outlines the plan developed by East Tennessee State University which makes use of existing faculty and staff. It is set apart from its sister universities in the interdisciplinary and non-programming approach.

The TSBR recommended that the term "computer literate" be defined as one who has the knowledge of and skill to be competent in the following:

1. A communicable knowledge of the history of computers and of the social, ethical, and legal implications and limits of computer use.

2. A working knowledge of computer equipment and technology.

3. The ability to discriminate between problems that can and those that cannot be appropriately solved on a computer.

4. A modest capability in a programming language.

5. The ability to use the computer effectively in educational and career tasks.

East Tennessee State University's Policy on Computer Literacy

Effective as of the academic year 1984-85, all incoming students seeking a degree must demonstrate a level of "computer literacy" equivalent to the level of knowledge required in other general education courses. ETSU has adopted the definition of "computer literacy" as stated above. The policy will apply to students as follows:

1. Students who are seeking an associate degree in a curricula designed for transfer must meet the computer literacy requirement by graduation.

2. Students who are seeking a baccalaureate degree must meet the computer literacy requirement within the first sixty semester credit hours of their program.

3. Students transferring to ETSU with sixty or more hours of credit must meet the computer literacy requirement within the first thirty hours at ETSU.

4. Students transferring to ETSU with less than sixty hours of credit must meet the computer literacy requirement within their first thirty hours of credit received at ETSU or by the time their total number of hours has reached sixty.

In order to meet the requirement a student must achieve one of the following:

1. Satisfactory completion of an approved course or the transfer of a course equivalent to an approved course.

2. Successful performance at a level of 70% or higher on a challenge exam. The challenge exam was designed by the Department of Computer and Information Sciences and has been approved by the Computer Literacy Review Panel. The exam will cover the five competencies previously identified.

A Computer Literacy Review Panel has been established with its members being appointed by the Vice President of Academic Affairs. The panel consists of one faculty representative from each school/college, one representative from the Office of Admissions and Records, and one undergraduate student representative. This panel will be responsible for:

1. Reviewing all proposals for existing courses which schools/colleges wish to have approved for meeting the computer literacy requirement as described and making recommendations to the Academic Council for final approval.

2. Approving petitions from students who wish previous experience or non-credit study to qualify as meeting the computer literacy requirement.

All students must submit documentation to the Office of Admissions and Records prior to completion of thirty semester hours of study, indicating either completion of an approved course, successful performance on the challenge examination, appropriate transfer credit, or plans for attainment of the above under the time restraints given.

ETSU's Undergraduate Course in Computer Literacy

The course is divided into two distinct areas; theory and "hands-on" training. Students spend half of the semester studying topics related to competencies 1), 3), and 5). This is accomplished in a lecture environment accommodating approximately one hundred students. This part of the course is taught by a faculty member of the Department of Computer and Information Sciences. The topics include history, terminology, storage devices and file processing, input/output devices, data communications, security and privacy, and the impact of computers on society.

The second half of the course is designed to permit "hands-on" experience and is taught in a lab environment. Twelve IBM Personal Computers have been purchased specifically for this purpose. Students work in pairs, thus allowing twenty-four students to enroll for each lab.

It is in this area of lab training that a marked difference is seen in ETSU's plan and that of other schools/colleges. Three primary software applications are studied; wordprocessing, databases (filing systems), and spreadsheets. The topics

are presented by faculty from disciplines other than Computer Science. Although all lab sections use the same software, instructors can use examples from their respective areas of interest. Students have the opportunity to enroll for a lab that will best suit his/her individual needs.

Advancements in computer technology have permitted the development of software that is very easy to use. As a result, it is no longer necessary for the ordinary user to be proficient in or even knowledgeable about programming. In a paper presented at the ACM National Computer Science Conference, February, 1984, Dan McCracken cautioned against teaching programming to individuals who were not planning on a career in computer science. Dr. Louis Robinson, Director of University Relations for IBM Corporation, defines computer literacy as the ability to _use_ computer technology in a discipline. He feels that it does not imply an accomplished capacity to program. These are only two of a growing number of experts who are de-emphasizing programming for the non-computer science major.

The emphasis, then, of the Computer Literacy course at ETSU is placed on the use of generally applicable software packages. The desired effect is that students will learn to use the computer as a tool throughout their education and career. This exposure should give them a base for learning to operate other packages easily and usefully.

Expected enrollment for this course is approximately two hundred per semester. The theory and lab portions will run concurrently with half of the students attending lecture and half attending lab. Midway through the semester, the two groups will exchange, thus allowing both groups equal exposure in both disciplines.

Future Research and Development

Implementation of ETSU's Computer Literacy Course has exposed unforseen problems which will require additional study before they can be resolved. The problems seem to be primarily in staffing and scheduling the labs, purchasing software, and awarding appropriate credit to faculty for teaching.

The logistics have been very involved for scheduling faculty and labs. Typically, faculty who have been actively involved with using the computer for their respective research are the same faculty who are in top demand by students in their own departments. Therefore, department chairmen are reluctant to "give up" their popular faculty to the Computer and Information Sciences. In addition, schedules for the following semester must be prepared within the first few weeks of the current semester. This makes it difficult to try to anticipate which faculty member could be released for one-quarter time to an outside department.

Awarding appropriate credit for teaching the lab courses has proved to be a political burden. Faculty who teach outside their own departments actually damage the department's funding potential. This is because the means by which funds are allocated depends on enrollment in the respective programs. It has been difficult to formulate a policy which would enable the hours generated by teaching the labs to be awarded to the faculty member's own department.

Adhering to the copyright laws has placed a tremendous financial burden on East Tennessee State University and many others across the state and country. Instead of purchasing one package and duplicating it for use on the other eleven machines, it is necessary to purchase twelve originals. If a package proves to be inappropriate (as did the integrated packaged purchased at ETSU), it will probably still have to be kept used because the cost in replacing it is prohibitive. If the package does prove to be useful, it will still be outdated in six months.

The Computer Literacy Review Panel is currently working on possible solutions to the previously stated problems. The Computer and Information Sciences Department has decided against using integrated packages, but will use instead separate packages. This will allow the freedom to pick a wordprocessor, a spreadsheet, and a filing system (data base) which best suits the needs of the students and of the university. This means, too, that texts for the course that rely on specific packages will not, in all probability, be selected.

Conclusion

ETSU is making every effort possible to meet the growing and changing needs in the field of computer literacy. It has been determined that through the cooperation of all departments within the university, a sound policy of computer literacy can be developed and implemented to meet the requirements of students enrolled in each discipline. Even though the program is new, feedback from students is already showing that there is a need and a desire among them to be able to use the computer as a tool.

References

1. *Proceedings of the ACM Computer Science Conference*, February, 1984.

2. "Computers in Education: Implications for Schools and Colleges," *Regional Spotlight*, January, 1984, p.3.

COMPUTERS IN EDUCATION, K. Duncan and D. Harris (eds.)
Elsevier Science Publishers B.V. (North-Holland)
© IFIP, 1985

STATUS OF COMPUTER SCIENCE EDUCATION IN USA HIGHER EDUCATION: THRU 1982-83

John W. Hamblen

Computer Science Department
University of Missouri-Rolla
Rolla, MO 65401 USA

Tremendous growth has occurred in enrollment in four-year computer related degree programs in USA institutions of higher education since 1977. Yet in 1983 the number of graduates from four-year programs numbers about half of the estimated annual need, the number of master's degrees awarded were about one sixth of those needed and the production of doctorates was still at only one fifth of those needed.

1. INTRODUCTION

By 1981 nearly a quarter of a million students were pursuing undergraduate curricula in Computer Science and related programs in post-secondary institutions in the USA [1]. This amounted to about 2% of all students enrolled in these institutions. Data are not available for the years following 1980-81, but we do know that significant increases have occurred. In publications [1,2] data are presented on production at all levels for years prior to 1980 as well as estimates of the demand for such personnel on a state by state basis. Reference [3] presents the production data up thru 1983 and [4] gives projections through the 80's based upon data contained in [2].

2. POST-SECONDARY VOCATIONAL AND TWO YEAR PROGRAM COMPLETIONS

Post-Secondary Vocational and two year programs tend to serve local, or at most regional needs. In many areas of the U.S. these programs have been producing surpluses for several years [4]. The better two year programs provide transfers into four year programs. Nationwide there appears to be near balance in demand vs. production at a level of 27,000 completions per year. However, there could still be extreme shortages in some locations and large surpluses in others.

3. GRADUATES OF FOUR YEAR PROGRAMS

Data on production of four year programs prior to 1980 were obtained from surveys which asked for the numbers of graduates of programs rather than departments. Therefore, graduates of computer science programs in departments of mathematics and graduates of programs in information systems in business administration were included. Since 1980 the only data available are those obtained by the U.S. Department of Education's National Center for Educational Statistics (NCES). Their data is department oriented, hence the numbers are smaller. Since more and more of the programs in other departments are either becoming separate departments or are causing a change in department name their graduates are becoming included in the NCES data. Therefore, I will use NCES data in this paper for 79-80, 80-81,

and 81-82. Estimates for 1982-83 were obtained from NCES figures for 1981-82 and the results of a survey conducted by the Quad Data Corporation in late 1983. NCES data are not yet available for 1982-83. Table I shows that the numbers of recipients of bachelor's degrees have been increasing at about 34% per year since 1980.

Table I

Numbers of Bachelor's Degrees Awarded
in the Computer and Information Sciences (0700)

Year	Degrees Awarded
1979-80	11213
1980-81	15193
1981-82	20267
1982-83	28203*

*Estimated

If this growth rate continues through 1985-86 we may soon see a surplus of four year graduates. It is unfortunate that we do not have data available on numbers of majors by level so that we could anticipate what the productions will be for future years by a better method than extrapolation. There are already some indicators that we are approaching saturation. The poorer students are having difficulties obtaining jobs and the average student gets fewer offers. However, since there is still an extreme shortage at the master's level the market will absorb extra four year graduates to fill in the gap.

4. GRADUATES OF MASTER'S PROGRAMS

Since 1980 the rate of growth in Master's degree awards has been around 20%. If this rate continues we could see a surplus of Master's degrees by 1993. At present we are producing about one sixth the annual need for M.S. graduates. However, since many of the Master's degrees are being awarded to persons already employed the surplus may be delayed somewhat. New personnel come primarily from the ranks of full time graduate students who require financial support via teaching and research assistantships. Since such support is limited there is a built in ceiling on the number of personnel entering the computer fields from Master's programs independent of supply and demand. It is likely that more than half the Master's degrees awarded are to those who are working full time and attending school evenings. Although these do not provide new entrants into the computer manpower pool, they are likely to be promoted and this may open up entry positions at the bachelor's level. The interaction here is complex and there are no data available for a more detailed analysis of this interaction. Table II presents the data on productions of M.S. degrees in Computer and Information Sciences from the same sources as mentioned in the previous section with the same caveats.

Table II

Numbers of Master's Degrees Awarded in the Computer and Information Sciences (0700)

Year	Degrees Awarded
1979-80	3647
1980-81	4143
1981-82	4395
1982-83	5961*

*Estimated

5. GRADUATES OF DOCTORAL PROGRAMS

Although the numbers of new doctorates each year are much smaller than required at the lower levels, the numbers being produced are only one fifth the annual need. The numbers are smaller but the negative impacts resulting from this shortage are enormous. Not enough qualified faculty are available for the rapidly expanding undergraduate departments to attain and maintain quality programs. The resulting heavy teaching loads have in many cases brought research to a standstill and caused discontent among those who want to, or must, do research to achieve promotion and tenure. A large number of those who do complete Ph.D.'s in the Computer and Information Sciences are from other countries and return home afterwards. More than half of the others are employed by government and industry. Some have camouflaged the real solutions to the shortage problem by recommending that more money be given to universities for equipment so that jobs there will be more attractive. This only increases the competition between industry and the universities for the too few graduates and causes inflation in salaries. The only sensible solution is to increase the number of Ph.D. candidates in the pipeline and that will take a large number of good fellowships over an extended period. Other disciplines will oppose this since the extreme shortage of Ph.D.'s in the Computer and Information Sciences combined with the huge enrollments in undergraduate courses has provided job opportunities for some of their colleagues and this in turn opens up positions for their new Ph.D.'s. The production of Ph.D.'s in the Computer and Information Sciences (0700) has been level at about 250 for

the past four years (see Table III). A lot of concern is expressed about keeping pace or ahead of other nations in computer technology, yet we are passing up a relatively cheap opportunity to enhance our position by producing more Ph.D.'s in Computer Science by providing a few hundred good fellowships.

Table III

Numbers of Ph.D.'s Awarded in the Computer and Information Sciences (0700)

Year	Degrees Awarded
1979-80	240
1980-81	252
1981-82	251
1982-83*	254

*Estimated

6. SUPPLY VS DEMAND

Demand for computer personnel has been estimated by the author via a static manpower model developed in 1973. [2], [3]. Until now the shortages have been so great that a more accurate and sophisticated model has not been necessary. As we approach equality between supply and demand it would be very desirable to have a dynamic model which could more accurately track the demand side. At present, the resources required to do this are beyond those available to the author and no one else seems to be interested in such a model. Therefore, we will find out the same way that other disciplines have in the past when supply catches up with demand and that is when graduates cannot find jobs. Unfortunately this is three to four years too late for some. To track supply and demand properly we also need to know the numbers of majors in the pipeline at each level in addition to having a dynamic demand model. Such data is not being collected by NCES or anyone else and the institutions appear unwilling to supply this information to an independent surveyor such as the author.

Table IV compares estimates of demand with production estimates for 1982-83 at all levels.

Table IV

Estimates of Annual Computer Manpower Needs vs Estimates of Productions for 1982-83

	Post Sec, Voc & 2-year	B.S.	M.S.	Ph.D.
	Level of Education			
Annual Needs	26,376	54,351	34,153	1309
Estimated 1982-83 Production	27,085	28,203	5,961	254
Prod/Need	1:1	1:2	1:6	1:5

ACKNOWLEDGMENTS

The author is indebted to the Quad Data Corporation of Tallahassee, Florida, and in, particular to Dr. Jesse Poore and Dianna Newsome for their support in publishing [3]. The cooperation of Mr. Tom Synder of NCES in supplying NCES data is also very much appreciated.

REFERENCES

[1] Hamblen, John W.; Status of Computing and Computer Science Education in USA Higher Education: 1978-79, Proceedings of 1981 World Conference on Computers in Education, North-Holland Publishing Co., Amsterdam, 1981.

[2] Hamblen, John W., Computer Manpower – Supply and Demand – By States; Information Systems Consultants, Rolla, MO, 1973, 1975, 1971, 1981.

[3] Hamblen, John W., Computer Manpower – Supply and Demand – By States; (Fifth Edition), Quad Data Corporation, Tallahassee, Florida, 1984.

[4] Hamblen, John W.; Computer Manpower Production at the Post-Secondary, Non-proprietary Institution Level: Projections Through the 80's, T.H.E. Journal, November, 1983.

COMPUTERS IN EDUCATION, K. Duncan and D. Harris (eds.)
Elsevier Science Publishers B.V. (North-Holland)
© IFIP, 1985

MICROCOMPUTERS AND EDUCATION IN THE UNITED KINGDOM: TOWARDS A FRAMEWORK FOR RESEARCH

David Smith and Morley Sage

The Computing Service
University of Southampton
Southampton
England

The evolution within the United Kingdom of a policy for the support of research into educational applications of Information Technology (IT) is discussed. This development is presented in relation to a high level of practitioner activity which is inadequately based on theoretical foundations. A proposed programme of research activity directed towards providing theoretical underpinning for current and future development activity is outlined and discussed.

1.   INTRODUCTION

This paper arises from a study (Sage & Smith, 1983) carried out within the Computing Service at Southampton University on behalf of the Social Science Research Council (SSRC), a major British research funding agency. The object of the investigation was the identification of research funding priorities in the field of educational applications of Information Technology (IT), with particular reference to the primary and secondary sectors. The study was undertaken in the context of Government programmes which had stimulated a high level of practitioner activity, but where a concommitant stimulus to basic research was absent: a situation referred to below as "theoretical impoverishment". A range of areas for high priority research and development are here identified and outlined. Some progress towards the elaboration of a national infrastructure for the support of appropriate research is described, and probable future progress is indicated.

2.   BACKGROUND

Every backpacker soon learns the hard but very important lesson that distant horizons have a terrible habit of remaining obdurately distant! This has also been the case with educational applications of what we now choose to label "Information Technology". Despite our apparent conviction that awareness of the power of IT to transform both the processes and content of education is a special insight peculiar to our own (enlightened) times, the fact is that part at least of this potential has been apparent to visionaries of one sort or another since before the technology as such even existed (as witness the more famous passages of "Gulliver's Travels" or "Erewhon") and was certainly clearly evident in the writings of the very first generation of computer pioneers. Despite this early interest, however, the high cost and attendant difficulties of implementing educationally worthwhile computer supported learning environments caused researchers to turn their attention towards less distant horizons and more readily attainable versions of Nirvana. In the UK at least, relatively little substantial academic research was carried out in this field much before 1970.

During the early 1970's, however, the pace of research and development accelerated for a time. Fuelled by perceptions of national economic decline, there were moves to increase the use of CAL and related techniques in higher education. A notable initiative in this respect was the National Development Programme for Computer Assisted Learning NDPCAL (Hooper, 1978). At the same time, and in opposition to this process, there were one or two rather curious decisions, such as the effect of the Lighthill Report (1972) in cutting off Government funding for the great majority of research into Artificial Intelligence (AI). Since this time, the UK academic establishment has been rather slow to respond to either the challenges or the opportunities inherent in new technologies, and a recent official report (Computer Board, 1983) has focussed attention on what can only be described as a parlous state of affairs in the use of computer-based media for the support of learning in higher education in Britain.

In schools, though innovators such as Donovan Tagg and his colleagues were using computers in the early sixties, the pace of development of educational computing was quite slow, due largely to heavy reliance on remote mainframes. It was the advent of the microcomputer, putting cheap and relatively powerful computers at the immediate disposal of 'ordinary' classroom teachers, which created a climate of concern in which pressure began to mount for national programmes of research and development relating to the educational implications of modern IT. The small voices who had been crying in the wilderness for so long suddenly found themselves with powerful allies! Somewhat belatedly, a variety of enabling programmes, such as the Microelectronics Education Programme (Fothergill, 1981), designed to facilitate the acquisition of computers by schools, were instituted. Suddenly everybody had computers and everybody had problems!

This explosion of demand for information and ideas at the practitioner level was accompanied by growing awareness and interest among academic researchers. One particularly important organisation which began to take a long close look at its actual and potential role in relation to educational IT applications was the (then) SSRC. This is a government-funded body charged with the following objectives:

> To encourage and support by any means research in the social sciences by any person or body;
>
> To provide and operate services for common use in carrying out such research;
>
> To carry out research in the social sciences;
>
> To make grants to students for postgraduate instruction in the social sciences;
>
> To provide advice in and disseminate knowledge concerning the social sciences.

SSRC had already over the years supported much important research related specifically or generally to computer applications in education (see for example Pask, 1975). In 1979, a working group was set up to review potential future activity in this field.

In April 1981, after extensive consultation, the working group proposed a research programme directed towards "The use and applications of microelectronics technology in education". The Council subsequently agreed in principle to the allocation of funds for research in this area. Morley Sage and David Smith (the present authors) were commissioned to review the field and to make specific proposals as to support priorities for a five-year programme. After various delays, the project got under way in May 1982.

3.   THEORETICAL IMPOVERISHMENT?

The extent to which the teaching profession in the UK (as elsewhere) has risen to meet "The challenge of the chip" could hardly have been anticipated only a few years ago. Quite apart from the low priority which the field formerly enjoyed, the problem of access to the technology or information about it was substantial. Hubbard (1981) reported that as recently as 1980 there were only about 700 microcomputers in British schools (and those were mainly used for maths and 'computer studies'). In the same year in the USA, there were over 30,000 microcomputers available for school use (Goor, Melmed and Farris, 1981), though these were not necessarily being put to best use! (Sheingold, Kane, Endreweit and Billings, 1981) Since then, the availability of computers in British schools has increased enormously, to the point where the percentage of educational institutions with computers is probably higher in the UK than in most other countries. This is clearly a major feat of educational logistics, and one of which the parties involved may justly be proud.

However, although the government intervention referrred to above has dramatically increased the availability of IT hardware in the UK, educational thinking does not seem to have advanced at the same pace. To some extent this must reflect the age-old "moving target" paradox, where classroom practise may evolve too fast for ideas and developments to be evaluated and disseminated before being outmoded in their turn. Nevertheless, much of the computer-related development activity in Britain can be characterised as "Innovation without research", based (often very loosely) on professional intuition and personal insight, with no overt (or even discernible) relation to a body of theory or to valid formal models of process, product or organisation of knowledge. A great wealth of expertise has been amassed within the UK teaching profession, but the bulk of this is not supported by a systematic information base or by any depth of theoretical understanding. What is more, the fact of this deficiency is not generally acknowledged in Britain, where an attitude of 'intellectual Luddism' is well entrenched.

As teachers have acquired expertise in the use of computers, and as competition has intensified within the "Education Industry" (Smith and Sage, 1984), the programming and coding of teaching packages have become increasingly competent and elegant, such that a tendency to smug complacency regarding the "excellence" of British software is widespread. However, this apparent sophistication probably conceals fundamental weaknesses in the educational design and classroom application of these materials (see Self, 1984). The persistent absence, at least within the UK educational tradition of a satisfactory theoretical rationale for the design and curricular implementation of IT based educational materials has led to a situation where much currently available (and even highly praised) courseware is based on naive and quite inadequate models of teaching, learning and the organisation of knowledge. It is interesting to note a similar observation regarding the position in the USA (Kurland, 1983). For the most part, the production of educational IT materials is a "cottage industry", devoid of an adequate design base, starved of resources and with the exploittion of its products largely dependent on 'grapevining', personal enthusiasms, charismatic 'salesmanship' and with post-hoc justification thinly disguised as evaluative research.

Some responsibility for this situation may lie in the original conception of the enabling infrastructures such as MEP, but apportionment of blame is a sterile exercise. Attention should be directed instead to the extent of the problem and to its mitigation. It is certainly true that a substantial edifice has been built in a remarkably short time; it is built (so to speak) on sand, its foundations are shallow and it is in desperate need of underpinning. There is still no secure base of theory or even a hardcore of information on which future developments at this level may be based. We have only the most inadequate basis for the design of school curricula or of specific educational experiences within their general framework.

To argue in terms of the theoretical impoverishment of UK educational IT application is not in any way to belittle the practical value of much of the present corpus of 'practitioner lore' or clinical case knowledge, far less the pioneering spirit and enthusiasm which have led to its accumulation. All the same, this impoverishment could become a major impediment to the renewal of the curriculum in the face of the many conflicting pressures of the "Information Society". The curriculum for the new social and economic order will develop from present-day experiences, processes, practices and structures, yet there is a great deal about all of these which is understood only poorly (if at all). There is a considerable danger that the inevitable (and largely blameless!) mistakes and false trails of early innovators will become institutionalised. Compromises and short-cuts forced on innovators by the limitations of early generation technologies or by the lack of an R&D tradition may become securely enshrined in routine structures and practices. The persistence of BASIC and the current plethora of "Hangman-Assisted-Education" may be cases in point. It is vitally important to sustain the momentum of curriculum renewal, and not to dissipate our efforts in the over-refinement of early successes. The initiative reported here must be seen in such a light.

4.   RESEARCH STRATEGIES

The technological 'quantum leap' which brought stand-alone microcomputers within the financial grasp of most schools has sharply highlighted many defects and deficiencies in our understanding of education in the general sense, rather than in its relation to any particular technology. It became clear early in the course of the study to which this paper refers that a number of potential entry-points existed for research in this field, and that in fact the number was too large to concentrate the attentions of a small and chronically under-financed research community in any single direction. Indeed, a 'straw poll' conducted informally among academics and other interested people in Britain, the USA and Canada pointed up a whole host of largely unconnected foci for interest within this community. It soon became apparent that there was an immediate need for a very large amount of research into all aspects of IT and education. The problems to be faced were complex, demanding inputs from a wide array of research traditions and academic disciplines. Consequently there was (and there remains) a high risk that both effort and funds might be dissipated ineffectually. Therefore a programme of commissioned research, targetted into specified areas of concern, was proposed.

The matter of **exactly** what research should (or should not) be promoted under such circumstances is of course wide open to debate, not to say acrimony. The whole field has been starved of

funds for many years (a sitation which seems as true for the USA as elsewhere), and only quite small-scale work has been possible. Too much of this has been of the "Justificatory Evaluation" type, often based on quite inappropriate methodological paradigms. This is, of course, a highly problematic field - described by Gerhold (1980) as a "can of worms"!, with only a fraction of what we teach in any case capable of evaluation by formal comparative testing. It was decided, therefore, not to recommend evaluative research narrowly targetted on specific software or hardware environments, but to attempt to identify problems which were central to the understanding of certain generalised aspects of educational processes.

It was concluded that there was a fundamental strategic need for research which would contribute to the information base and the theoretical models which could inform the design and implementation of learning experiences based on the application of IT in a variety of contexts. At the same time, note was taken of past experience with curriculum development in the UK, and it was felt that there was a parallel need for an understanding of management structures and information-flow within the education profession, leading to effective management of changes in practice and organisation.

Two directions for research were identified within this overall strategic framework:

Learning Processes and **Information Technology:** giving attention to styles, strategies and processes of IT-based learning;

Curriculum and the Information Society: concerned with the effects of IT both on and in the curriculum, and with the formal and informal channels through which knowledge and ideas are transmitted within, into and out of the education system.

5.   PROBLEM AREAS FOR RESEARCH

From the strategic perspective outlined above, a number of significant problem areas were found, and provisionally related to the two programme directions as follows:

5a. Learning Processes and IT

1.   Effects of IT on Childrens' Thinking

We have little idea how childrens' minds may be affected by the experience of growing up in an IT society (Lepper, 1982). Young people today live in an environment where computers are all-pervasive, even to the point of forming part of Popeye's stock-in-trade (gone are the days when spinach alone was enough!). It would be valuable to know what effects this sub-cultural exposure may have. We lack the baseline data against which future change may be measured or interpreted, and the opportunity of studying a "computer-naive" cohort will soon be lost forever, just as we have already lost the chance of understanding the influences on children of 'non-educational' television.

We are almost equally ignorant of the effects and influences of the **planned** exposure of young children to IT. Much research in this context has been trivial and poorly designed, and yet, according to Papert (1980), this is a question of the utmost significance for the future development of education. We need, for example, to know about the effects on childrens' thinking of the linguistic and procedural structure implicit in computing environments, and about which teachers might not even be aware.

2.   Investigative Learning

Independent heuristic knowledge creation ("Investigative Learning") is likely to be a valuable life skill in the Information Society. Little is known, however, about the design and management of appropriate learning experiences through which this and related cognitive skills may be developed. In the past, the whole area of the study of thinking processes was inhibited by the inaccessibility of the basic processes (which could only be inferred from putative products). But now computers permit more direct (though still inferential) access to cognitive process (Colbourn, Smith & Light, 1984).

3.   Cognitive Impoverishment

Visually and aurally handicapped people may incur varying degrees of 'cognitive impoverishment' due to their perceptual difficulties. Comparable problems may arise through restrictions placed on experience by social or ethnic customs or practices, or through experiential constraints imposed by mental or physical handicaps. The results may be to cause individuals to be unjustly excluded from effective participation in IT-based educational, occupational or leisure activities because of imperfect communication with various devices. It is the problems of cognitive interaction with IT systems which are referred to here, rather than the (very real!) obstacles to physical communication. The underlying problem is in the nature of learning processes and the construction and organisation of knowledge where input is deficient or otherwise inadequate.

4.   IT and Motivation

The axiom that computers are intrinsically motivating is, despite Malone's (1980) seminal study, largely unsupported by hard evidence. Indeed it might even be

justly considered to be part of the folk-lore of education! Nevertheless, the question of motivation is central to the business of education, and this surely deserves early and intensive study. Motivation is a complex and idiosyncratic phenomenon, depending on the interaction of many personal and contextual factors which can hardly even be identified, let alone subjected to experimental control. Research here is not likely to reveal global truths, but any insights could illuminate the design and organisation of IT-based learning materials and environments.

5.   Social Interactions in Schools

The capacity of new technologies to mediate new styles and strategies of teaching, learning and even thinking may bring about many changes in social structures and interactions within schools. These changes, which might include new patterns of deference and esteem, as well as modified friendship structures and routes for peer-group influence, could have great effects on the social and cognitive effectiveness of schooling. Moves towards independent, collaborative or peer-mediated learning will affect the management practices of teachers, and could indirectly influence the role and authority of the teacher and even childrens' general attitudes towards authority and authority figures. Such affective realignments could have significant consequences for social structure and stability.

5b. Curriculum and the Information Society

1.   Adoption of IT by Schools

Factors which promote or inhibit the adoption of IT by teachers are not well known or understood in the UK. This is an area where statistically-oriented paradigms are unlikely to be specially fruitful in disentangling the plethora of social, personal and professional interactions which may be involved. Case Studies could both contribute to our understanding of the dynamics of curriculum diffusion and also provide teachers with aids to the analysis of their own immediate problems.

2.   Management of Curriculum Change

The pace of changes already in train and the accelerated pace of change to be expected in years to come will demand effective and even inspired management if systems are not to succumb to what Pogrow (1983) called "Environmental Collapse". The need for change management is well appreciated in industry and commerce, but the UK has seen little use of ideas and insights from outside education in the management of curriculum change. There is a need to evaluate resource and personnel management strategies whatever their origin.

3.   Special Interest Groups

Despite large-scale government interventions, and the longer-standing interest of bodies such as ESRC and the former Schools Council, the diffusion of ideas and information about educational IT has been a periphery-periphery process. Interest groups such as MUSE, SIGCUE etc have played what may prove to have been crucial roles. The dynamics of such influences are well worthy of attention.

4.   Courseware and the Curriculum

Software of all kinds embodies structures and models (eg implicit student models) which may not be apparent to naive users (or even to their writers!). Some of these hidden structures may even be quite incompatible with the curriculum and ethos of schools in which the material is used. This could lead to complex dissonance problems. Research is needed into the influences which software styles and structures may have on teachers' curricular thinking.

5.   Resource-Rich Environments

Once the application of IT is no longer limited by resource availability, attention will have to be given to specific tactical issues associated with resource-rich learning environments. The problems and opportunities inherent in such situations cannot even be guessed at in the climate of one computer per school.

On the basis of the priorities outlined above, a programme of research was proposed to last 5 years. It was clearly recognised that this could only scratch the surface of a massive problem for a society in transition. Many urgent and pressing areas of research were omitted (a serious defect was lack of reference to gender-role issues). There was never at any time an assumption that spectacular breakthroughs were to be gained at the cost of minimal short-term investment. There is no room here for the "big push" mentality.

6.   SUBSEQUENT DEVELOPMENTS

The report was published in July 1983 as a discussion document. Comments were invited from any interested parties. The vast majority of replies were highly favourable. There was widespread acceptance of advocacy of research into cognitive processes at a fundamental rather than phenomenological level. Espousal of the cognitive modelling approach was more controversial, but still

gained wide approval. Some specific ideas were challenged, but there was no evidence of a strong contrary consensus.

It was in fact generally agreed that the issues to which research should be addressed transcend technocentric problems. One respondent noted:

> "Many aspects... are those to which any resource-based innovation would be addressed. ...IT... has created a level of concern about models of education that are equally appropriate to, say, laboratory-based science education."

In November 1983, a residential workshop was held to bring together a representative cross-section of the concerned research community (Smith, 1985). It emerged that the apparent concord evident in the broad acceptance of the Report masked deep divergences of opinion and interpretation. The Report had emphasised the potential value of synergetic multidisciplinary collaboration in this research field, but it was quite obvious that no sort of synergesis could be expected without much prior attention to the achievement of a convergence of perspective within the research community. The chief contribution and aim of the workshop was to initiate this convergence.

The Report somewhat tentatively floated the idea of a formal infrastructure which would bring together researchers and others, and which might initiate studies into educational IT applications. This was far from a major cornerstone of the Report's case, but it appears to have struck some sort of chord within the community. The workshop and other events highlighted the diffuseness and lack of focus or common perception among concerned researchers to such an extent that the need for mutual support, information and communication was seen to be of paramount importance in lifting any new major research programmes off the ground. A series of discussions and consultations through the first half of 1984 culminated in the Research Council's acceptance that some sort of support infrastructure ought to be established and funded.

In July 1984, the Council (now, for various reasons transmogrified into the Economic and Social Research Council, ESRC) advertised for a Coordinator who would set in train the various structures and mechanisms needed by the research community. The person is now in post, and facing an enormous uphill task. For the first time, the UK is moving towards a policy for the support and encouragement of R&D activities in at least one restricted area of education which is not piecemeal, which does not rest uncomfortably on the immediate interests of a small handful of enthusiasts and which will carry significant funding for a reasonable number of years. It remains now for the research community as well as administrators and teachers to respond to this new situation and to work together to bring the seedcorn to a successful harvest.

One rather dark cloud on the horizon is the small
size of the available research community. Years
of severe financial constraint and university
faculty cuts have pruned the numbers of trained
workers to a bare minimum. Research finance is
for various reasons woefully inadequate, whilst
the attitude of much of the IT industry to education is that of the Great White Shark to the
Californian Sea Lion! Also, the industrial
orientation of recent initiatives in cognitive
science and artificial intelligence rising from
the Alvey Report (1982) has directed the attention of the small handful of high-grade workers
in those fields away from poorly funded and
methodologically "dirty" educational research
towards the relative golconda of more profitable
horizons elsewhere. In such a situation, educational research is in the position of a small
football club which constantly loses its best
players to larger, richer clubs without itself
advancing in the process: and we don't even get
transfer fees!

Now there's a thought!

In the long run we can begin to feel a certain
optimism. The significance and magnitude of the
problems before us are being faced. But time is
short. Gutenborg's IT revolution was nearly 500
years ago, yet we still have not come to terms
with the optimal design and presentation of
printed materials. The present IT revolution will
not grant us half a millenium of leeway. Even
five years wasted will be five years too many.
The security and happiness of the next generation
of our citizens could depend to a large extent on
the way in which our research effort comes together
in the very near future.

7.   REFERENCES

Alvey J (chmn) A Programme for Advanced Information Technology (The Alvey Report) London. Her
Majesty's Stationery Office. 1982

Colbourn C, Smith D J and Light P H (1984) Peer
Interaction and microPROLOG. IT, AI and Child
Development Conference. British Psychological
Society. Brighton.

The Computer Board for Universities and Research
Councils. Report of a Working Party on Computer
Facilities for Teaching in Universities. The
Board. London 1983

Fothergill R (1981) Microelectronics Education
Programme: the strategy document. London. D.E.S.

Gerhold G (1980) Teacher Produced CAI. in R Lewis
and D Tagg (eds) CAL Scope, Progress, Limits.
North Holland. Amsterdam. 1980

Goor J, Melmed A & Farris E (1981). Student Use
of Computers in Schools: Fall 1980. Fast Response
Survey System. USDEd. Washington DC.

Hubbard G (1981). Education and the New Technologies. Proc. Roy Soc. Arts CXXIX. 5297

Hooper R (1977) National Development Programme
in Computer Assisted Education: Final Report of
the Director. London. C.E.T.

Kurland D (1983) Software for the Classroom.
Technical Report 15. Center for Children and
Technology. Bank Street College. New York.

Lighthill Sir James (1972). Artificial Intelligence. London. Science Research Council.

Lepper M (1982) Microcomputers in Education:
Motivational and Social Issues. Invited address
to American Psychological Association 90th
annual meeting, Washington DC.

Malone T (1980) What Makes Things Fun to Learn?
A study of intrinsically motivating computer
games. PhD Thesis, Dept of Psychology, Stanford.

Papert S (1980) Mindstorms. Brighton.
Harvester Press.

Pask G (1975) Conversation, Cognition and
Learning. Amsterdam. Elsevier.

Pogrow S (1983) Education in the Computer Age.
Beverley Hills. Sage.

Sage M W and Smith D J (1983) Microcomputers in
Education: A Framework for Research. London.
Social Science Research Council.

Self J (1984) Microcomputers in Education: A
critical appraisal of educational software.
Brighton. Harvester Press.

Sheingold K, Kane J, Endreweit M & Billings K
(1981) A Study of Issues Related to the Implementation of Computer Technology in Schools.
Childrens' Electronic Laboratory Memo 2.

Smith D J (ed) (1985) Information Technology
and Education: Signposts and Research Directions
London. Economic and Social Research Council.

Smith D J & Sage M W (1984) Computer Based
Education and the Education Industry. Micros in
Education Conference. Loughborough. England.

COMPUTERS IN EDUCATION, K. Duncan and D. Harris (eds.)
Elsevier Science Publishers B.V. (North-Holland)
© IFIP, 1985

877

PANEL SESSION

VOCATIONAL EDUCATION AND TRAINING

Chairperson: Patrick Raymont, National Computing Centre UK

Participants: Ben Barta, Ministry of Education, Israel
                 Joyce Currie Little, Towson State University, USA
                 Konrad Klöckner, Bureau of Mathematics & Computing, FRG.

This panel session will describe the situation in vocational education and training
in each of the participants countries and will, drawing on this shared experience,
seek to suggest how improvements might be made.

The field of vocational education and training deals with courses, sometimes of quite short duration,
aimed at imparting specific computing skills related to employment. It covers both the computing
specialisms (eg programming and systems) and the skills needed by specialists in other fields to make
use of computers (eg CAD for engineers, spreadsheets for accountants).

The participants will describe the situation in their countries in respect of:

-    the organisational arrangements (eg in which types of institution is the
     work done; how is it funded; how do pre-employment training for young
     people and in-service training for mature adults compare?

-    curricula and qualifications; their acceptance by industry; the problem
     of keeping up-to-date

-    national planning relating to the supply and demand for skilled manpower

-    problems limiting the effectiveness of vocational education and training
     (eg resource problems, shortages of skilled teaching staff, constantly
     changing technology)

COMPUTERS IN EDUCATION, K. Duncan and D. Harris (eds.)
Elsevier Science Publishers B.V. (North-Holland)
© IFIP, 1985

INFORMATION TECHNOLOGY IN EDUCATION: PLANS AND POLICIES IN THE NETHERLANDS

Tjeerd Plomp and Bert van Muylwijk

Department of Education
Twente University of Technology
Enschede, The Netherlands

Education is playing a key role in the preparation of people for functioning in society. Because Information Technology (IT) is growing more and more important in our
societal functioning, education has to prepare for that as well. In The Netherlands
the national government has made IT in education a major priority in her policy, in
both a financial and a organizational sense. Mainlines, goals and priorities are discussed in this paper. The Advisory Committee for Education and Information Technology (AEIT) has published several reports for the Dutch Minister for Education and
Science. The reports that discuss IT in general compulsary education and IT in vocational education are elaborated. As far as appropriate all topics in this paper are
discussed from a educational viewpoint.

1. INTRODUCTION

When talking about information technology (IT)
in education it is important that there is no
misunderstanding about what we mean by information technology and more generally by technology. Galbraith's definition of technology is
generally accepted. He states that technology
is "the systematic application of scientific or
organized knowledge to practical tasks"
(Galbraith, 1967, p. 12). Starting from this,
we may define information technology (IT) as the
application of scientific and technical knowledge about storing, retrieving and processing
of data for the purpose of gaining information
in order to satisfy needs. It is commonly
accepted that the term technology is not only
referring to the specific knowledge which can
be applied, but also to products, machines and
instruments which are produced based upon scientific and technical knowledge. This means that
IT refers not only to the knowledge about or the
techniques for distributing and processing data
via TV-channels, satellites or computernetworks,
for example, but that those "things" are very
often also called examples of information
technology. In most situations this twofold use
of the term is not causing trouble.

As a consequence of recent development in microelectronics, computer design and communication
technology, IT has changed so drastically that
many people are speaking of new information
technology or technologies when referring to
the instrumental aspect of it. However, in this
paper we will stick to the use of the general
term information technology (IT) when referring
to new information technology.

In The Netherlands several advisory committees
have drawn up reports for the government. The
Advisory Committee for Education and Information
Technology (AEIT) was installed by the Minister
of Education in May 1981 to advice the government about the introduction of information

technology in Dutch education. The AEIT has published several reports since then (AEIT, 1982,
1984 a, b). During this period the Minister of
Education in cooperation with his colleagues of
Economical Affairs and Agriculture and Fishing,
prepared two white papers in which he presented
his plans for an overall policy.

In the present paper the overall policy and the
financial framework of the Dutch government is
summarized in section 2. In the remaining sections the reports of the AEIT are summarized.
In section 3 a description of possible application of IT in education is presented, followed
by a discussion of how learning about IT should
be operationalized in lower general education
(section 4) and in vocational education (section
5).

2. A NATIONAL POLICY ON EDUCATION AND INFORMA-
TION TECHNOLOGY

In September 1982 the Dutch government published
a white paper titled "Education and Information
Technology". In this paper a plan for the introduction of IT in education in 1983 - 1988 was
presented, which can be characterized as a strategy of projects in every sector of the educational system. The financial framework consisted of a yearly amount of Dfl. 6 million. In
January 1984 a new white paper, titled "Information Stimulation Plan", was published containing
a proposal for an overall national policy for
introducing IT in Dutch society. In a separate
appendix the plans for an educational policy
with respect to IT was presented, including a new
financial framework. This appendix, replacing
the 1982 paper, is summarized in this section.

2.1 Education as the key for the future of the society

Education is playing a key role in the preparation of people for changes in society. There is no doubt that the use of IT in society will result in great changes. Both the demands from the labour market and the functioning of people in society and their personal development are asking for educational programs in which ample attention will be paid to IT. Giving information technology a place in education is serving two aims:
- making all people (citizens) acquainted with IT (in The Netherlands this basic education is often called: "citizen informatics"[1])
- the creation of "human capital" to strengthen the market sector, as well as to let societal provisions function better and more efficient.

Although the second aim is also directed on all levels and all sectors of education, the accent is on vocational education. For the labour market is demanding now and will demand in the future a diversity of professional knowledge of informatics. Many existing professions will change, new professions will arise. A better tuning of education to the labour market has to be realized by increasing the number of specialists on informatics as well as by adapting the vocational education for all possible types of professions to the demands of tomorrow's society. To realize this tuning gradually we must get more specified signals from industry, from the labour market more generally and from the industrialisation policy to enlarge the effectivity of education and educational policy. The policy which approach is elaborated in the informatics stimulation plan will give all possible changes for this process. By tuning the demands of education and industry, these proposals can give a substantial contribution to the strengthening of the market sector. The plan is also offering the industrial sector possibilities for the development of software, while also an important market for hardware will be created.

2.2 Mainlines, goals and priorities

The Dutch government is striving that within 5 till 10 years all pupils will be taught about and with computers for their future profession, for participation in society and for their personal development. Everybody needs a general knowledge of information systems. Many people must be taught informatics, some in an advanced study, others as a preparation on a profession, because the use of computers (more general: of programmable components and systems) is becoming more and more important. For many pupils education will be more varied and more efficient when the computer will be used as a tool (e.g. for simulation). Some groups of people will profit much from computer based instruction. One can think of pupils in special education or slow learners or children who are otherwise disadvantaged.

The government would like to bring together the already available experience and the existing policy elements and combine them to a policy which can be characterized as unorthodox and innovative. The goal of this policy is that in 1988 we have attained a situation in which the educational institutions, which are educating people (e.g. continuing education) are able to penetrate the remaining part of the educational field without further support.

With a long term policy as a perspective, now on a shorter term two types of measures have to be taken:
- The development of an educational computer network; a material infrastructure in which organizations from education and industry can work together to develop and disseminate software or, more general, instructional materials. The goal of this development is the improvement of the quality of software. A large emanation (on a voluntary base) can be expected.
- To pay attention quickly and on a large scale to training, inservice training and educational support. This is a necessary condition for a broad introduction and a meaningful use of hardware and software.
Further, for the various educational sectors, the financial priority on the short and middle term is given to:
- Courses in which pupils in the 9th and 10th grade of the lower vocational education and the middle vocational education are prepared for their future profession, especially within the technical streams and in agricultural education; the accent is in particular on applications of informatics;
- the professional preparation in the higher vocational education, again in particular in the technical schooltypes and the agricultural education. In these sectors on the short term a great effect is possible by better and more hardware provisions and inservice training; the emphasis will be put on applications in informatics besides more specialistic informatics courses;
- introductory information and computer science ("citizen informatics"), as a basic education for everybody (i.e. the first 3 grades of secondary education);
- an optional course in informatics in the upper general secondary education;
- the use of the computer in other courses than informatics in secondary education;
- specific applications of the computer in special education;
- the use of the computer, for example as computer assisted instruction, especially in the part of primary education with large numbers of children which are in a draw back situation (for example cultural minorities) and for remedial use in vocational education.

In summary, a breadth strategy for introducing IT in both sectors of vocational education and the first phase of secondary and special education is proposed in this white paper.

The Minister of Education and Science states that such a broad introduction of computer based education will be <u>only possible in connection with a reallocation of money within the existing budget</u>. The total amount of money involved adds up to Dfl. 267.5 million (appr. US$ 83.5) over a period of five years.

3. INFORMATION TECHNOLOGY (IT) IN EDUCATION [2])

In the same period in which the Minister of Education and Science was preparing the framework for an overall national policy, the Advisory Committee for Education and Information Technology (AEIT) was preparing its reports. Although the AEIT worked independently, its proposals are fitting in the policy framework prepared for the sectors of lower general secondary education and vocational education.

In this section the conceptual framework which the AEIT developed is summarized, while in the following sections some of the main conclusions of the reports are summarized. A categorization often used to describe possible applications or uses of IT in education is:
A. Learning <u>about</u> IT,
B. Learning and teaching <u>with</u> IT, espec. the computer.
C. Learning and teaching <u>through</u> IT, espec. the computer.
D. The computer as a tool for organizational purposes.
Before describing briefly these four applications, two remarks have to be made. Although IT encompasses more than computers, e.g. also interactive videotex systems, the present applications in education concern almost exclusively the computer. We therefore will use in this and the following sections learning with and/or through IT interchangeably with learning with and/or through computers. This does not hold for learning <u>about</u> IT, which comprises more than learning about computers, as will be explained later on in section 4. Further, in practice the distinction between learning "about", "with" and "through" the computer will not be as clear as in our analysis; very often mixed forms of applications will be found.

A. Learning and teaching about IT
Information technology refers to a set of knowledge domains, all of which have to do with automatic information processing or the <u>processing of data</u> with the help of machines, such as informatics (computer science), micro-electronics, and telecommunication. Information processing, also by means of computers, is a purposeful activity and can change drastically if its purpose changes. Often information-processing is <u>ludicrous</u> or meant for leisure. But often its purpose is <u>exploration</u>: e.g. acquiring knowledge, diagnosing probabilities or checking hypotheses by computer based calculations, simulations, learning, etc. Information processing can also be used for <u>controlling</u> and <u>directing</u> processes: almost all human activities and almost all functioning of machines, systems, processes and or-

ganizations are directed and controlled by data, nowadays frequently automatically processed. Learing about IT will in principle mean learning about all its knowledge domains and all its applications. What will be taught and what will be learned is dependent on the age and the level of the students and the type of school. We will elaborate on the topic of learning about IT later on in this paper.

B. Learning and teaching with the help of the computer
Characteristic for this application is the use of the computer as an aid or a tool in the learning and teaching process. Here, the computer is used in a way similar to the already existing resources in education, like blackboard, calculator, encyclopedia or laboratory equipment. Examples are the computer as an aid in spelling, in sorting, storing and retrieving data, in generating data and displaying them graphically, in creative writing (wordprocessing), in testing, etc. In these cases the computer is used for only one support function or type of application at a time by either the teacher, the pupil, or by both. The computer can also be used multifunctionally: This means that in a computer program more than one of the possible support functions of the computer will be used. In this way learning with the help of the computer evolves gradually to learning by means of or "through" the computer, which is the next application we will describe.

C. Learning and teaching through the computer
Characteristic for this application is that the teacher delegates "teaching intelligence" to the computer. The teacher leaves to the machine certain decisions about the courses of the (individualized) teaching-learning process, at which information about the progress of the pupil is used. Yet, the ultimate decision about the use of the computer remains mostly in the hands of the teacher. In this type of application three functions of the computer can be distinguished:
- the computer as a teaching machine: the student learns in interaction with the machine; the computer controls the learning process and directs the presentation of new subject matter;
- the computer as a testing machine: the result of testing can be that the computer will present additional instruction or other test items; the testing can be either for diagnostic use or for grading;
- the computer as a monitoring machine: depending on the results of teaching and testing, the system directs the student to a new part of the course or to the earlier or additional instruction.

D. The computer as a tool for organization purposes
This application is referring to the use of the computer for administrative purposes (financial, personnel and student administration) as well as for organizational goals (e.g. time tables, surveys of progresses of students).

The last application of computers in education will not be discussed further, because it is beyond the scope of this paper. Considering application C: learning and teaching through the computer, one must say that an application of this type of multi-functional use of the computer is not to be expected on a large scale on a short term. This application asks for very complex software, in combination with more complex, and therefore expensive hardware. Moreover, this type of computer use can have drastic consequences for the role of the teacher, the learning of the student, the organization within the schools and the classrooms, and teacher education. On all these aspects, much research and development work is needed before a large scale implementation of this application in education can be justified. All these arguments lead to the conclusion that this application must have a low priority when thinking of a short term policy for the introduction of IT in education.

An ongoing OECD study provides us assistance for a further elaboration of application A: learning about IT and B: learning with IT, especially computers. In analyzing the forces underlying the technological demands for and on education, the following arguments are put forward for introducing IT in education (OECD, 1984):

1. The needs of the economy: to produce specialised manpower.
2. The need to prepare the young to be functional in a society permeated with IT by giving them also a basic education in IT.
3. The improvement of the teaching/learning process: IT adds new powerful tools to education, by which its quality and effectiveness can be improved; especially low achievers and gifted may profit from this advantage.

The third argument refers to application B about the use of the computer as an aid in education. We will not discuss this application further, only for reasons of limiting the length of this paper.

In considering the two other needs (arguments 1 and 2) one can conclude that both are referring to the application of IT in education, which we have labelled with A: learning and teaching about IT. The "need of economy" is referring primarily to learning about IT in vocational education, which will be further discussed in section 5. The second need is dealing with the general preparation of all pupils to be functional in our society. Considering the preparation of all pupils leads us to the question of what place learning about IT should have in education. This will be discussed in section 4.

4. IT in general education[3])

The information environment in our society is changing, which will result in a new balance of storage, retrieving and processing of data between human beings and machines. Many human activities (manual and cognitive skills) will be taken over by IT-systems (see e.g. Häfner, 1981 and Naisbitt, 1984). As it is one of the goals of education to prepare the young people for their future functioning in our society. This preparation also has to extend itself to the characteristics of a society permeated with information technology. A characteristic of the so-called "information society" is the presence of large numbers of data, which can easily be made available to individuals via IT-equipment. However, the availability of data does not imply automatically that one has information at one's disposal. The drawing of information form data (or messages) is a goal-oriented activity. There is a fundamental difference between data or messages at one hand and information at the other. This difference can be learned from the description of these terms.
- "data" = facts, from which one can draw conclusions which may lead to the solution of a problem (e.g.: the inflation rate in the USA in 1983 was x%);
- "message" = an objectified communication or text, physically recorded, e.g. a text in a newspaper or on tape (e.g.: the Minister noticed that inflation of x% is too high and that the policy of the government need to be changed):
- "information" = the meaning or interpretation which the receiver of data or message(s) attaches to them (e.g.: the interpretation which the receiver of the message about the x% inflation attaches to it).

From the preceding it may be clear that there is no direct causal relation between the computer as processor, manipulator and retriever of data at the one hand and information as the meaning or interpretation which one may attach to the available data at the other side. One can speak of an instrumental relationship between the computer and information, i.e. with the help of a computer one can derive information from data and messages. (See figure 1).

The relationship between information science and computer science is complementary. From the angle of information science one can indicate which processed data or messages are needed to provide information for a certain goal. From the angle of computer science one can indicate how the computer, or more general information technology, should be used to produce from raw data and messages the desired data and messages.

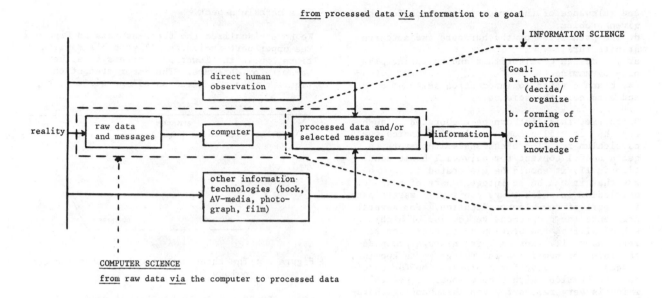

from processed data via information to a goal

Figure 1 : The relationship between information science and computer science (from AEIT, 1984 b)

Let us now return to the central question of this section. If education has to prepare people for their future functioning in our society, what could then be the place of IT in education? We have seen that our society is changing as a consequence of the developments in IT. Routine work and processes will be automated; the job market will change; the prestige and the necessity of certain types of knowledge and skills will diminish. People not only have to learn to live with more free time, but also have to be prepared for lifelong learning. Our society is becoming an information society. Many people believe that we are dealing with a change in our society which is comparable to the discovery of the printing in the 15th century. Only the speed with which IT makes its influence felt is much faster.

The present developments are also threatening to some extent. Many people fear that the speed of the developments will exclude the interests of the non-experts or those citizens who are not involved in this process and that they will no longer play a role. In this context, people refer to problems of "privacy" and of the "control" of the management and supply of information: who will decide which data will be stored and where e.g. in hospitals, banks, insurance companies, tax offices, local authorities? Who will decide which data will be accessible to whom. How many data banks be combined into a network? Every citizen will also be confronted with these aspects of the information society.

This brings us to the role of compulsory education. With approval we would like to cite from the recent "white paper" of the Dutch Minister

Education and Science (Informatics Stimulation Plan, January, 1984) in which he states that education not only has to create "human capital" to strengthen the market sector (as discussed in the following section on vocational education), but also has as its goal the familiarization of all citizens with information technology.

This is a plea for some basic education. Not a basic education in computer literacy in the sense of learning some programming skills and how to operate the (micro)computer. Such a narrowly oriented education cannot contribute to a real understanding of the characteristics of the information society. From the first part of this section (see e.g. Figure 1) it may be clear that, when talking about a basic education for everybody, we are referring to basic skills about the field of information and computer science including the underlying knowledge. Given the fundamental changes in our society and given the new balance of storage, retrieving and processing of data between human beings and machines, we then have to master the skills and knowledge which are a necessity for responsive functioning in the information society[4]).

A first operationalization of these skills and knowledge is given by AEIT (1984 b): a. The selection, production, collection, storage, processing, retrieval and distribution of data and messages given a certain problem or defined need for information, with or without the help of a computer; b. The drawing of information from data and messages; c. The assessing of the reliability and the precisoin of data and messages and of the validity

and relevance of the drawn information for the given problem;
d. The principles of the hardware and software architecture;
e. The design of algorithms and the principles of programming.
(a, b and c refer to information science; a, d and e to computer science.).

Of course, this list can be elaborated in such a way that it will become the list of topics for a curriculum for IT-professionals. However, to get a useful content for universal basic education in IT, it should be elaborated in such a way that it can be an integral part of a school curriculum in which every pupil will participate, i.e. part of compulsory education. For several arguments the comprehensive (or junior high) school will be the best phase in education to learn about IT. Not only is this age group accessible for new facts and things worth knowing, it can also provide for a preparation for continuing education, either vocational or general, which is very relevant given the changing character of many jobs.

It is beyond the scope of this paper to discuss all apsects of implementation or this new universal basic education, such as the size, the place in the curriculum (separate course or not), the further development of the content, the problem of getting every pupil (girls as well as boys) involved, the teacher training component, the software development and the hardware supply. In the Netherlands, these questions are being studied in a project from 1983-1985 in which 100 schools are taking part.

5. IT in vocational education[5])

In information technology as such three fundamental parts or aspects can be distinguished: hardware, software and application.
- Hardware consits of computers with their peripherals, micro-processors (more generally microelectronics), computer networks and interfaces (e.g. sensors).
- Software consists of operating systems, interpreters, standard programs for datafiles and databases, procedures (the human component in information systems), programs for specific applications such as the collection and processing of data e.g. for stock administration or for trends in blood pressure.
- Applications consist of hardware and software which perform a specific function, usually as parts of a larger system. Many examples can be found: in intensive care units in the health sector, in laboratory automation, in automated hotel administration, in salary administration, in food distribution systems for cattlefarms. None of these three fundamental aspects can be considered while neglecting others. Vocational education which restricts itself to one or two of these main points would fail its mission. Yet, certain sectors or programs within vocational education may differ in degree of emphasis

on a certain aspect.

We have visualized the three aspects in Figure 2. The upper part indicates all possible applications, while the lower part refers to either hardware or software. The inner area of this figure can be conceived as all possible IT topics

Figure 2 : The three aspects of information technology

which can be taught in vocational education to prepare students adequately for their future professional life. Points which are in the upper part refer to specific applications of IT in technical professions, agriculture, administration, health, etc. Points more to the left in the lower part refer to topics in which great emphasis is laid on the design and development of hardware and little to the other aspects. The reverse holds for points more in the right lower part, where the emphasis is much more on the design and development of systems software. If we understand by IT-education all the teaching (and learning) which pertains to IT, then we may learn from the figure that not all vocational IT-education can be the same. A first distinction we can make is between education of IT-users (end-users) and of IT-professionals.

Education of IT-users

Most students in vocational education will not get a job as designer or developer (or maintainer) of hardware or software systems. For them it will be sufficient to become capable and responsive users of IT in their profession, whether it will be in technical fields, administration, health, social welfare, agriculture, shopkeeping or others. Because IT will be an integrated part of a job or a profession it is important to teach IT not separately from job preparation. Therefore all (or almost all) courses concerned in job preparation should deal in an appropriate way with the application of IT on user's level. This IT-user education should strive for the following goals:
- Having knowledge about the meaning of IT for the particular sector and ability in handling the most important and characteristic applications;
- being able to consult with IT-professionals and to judge their proposals;
- understanding the societal consequences of IT. For this type of IT-user's education, it is neces-

sary to modernize the curricula of all sectors
in vocational education to develop relevant software, to bring the ability requirements of teachers up-to-date and to provide for adequate in-
service training of teachers.

Education of IT-professionals

We have seen earlier that in business and industry many new jobs are created which are concerned with design, development and presumably also
the maintaining of hardware and software systems.
Generally one can distinguish here between two
types of educational goals, viz. product innovation and production innovation. Product innova-
is concerned with the improvement of instruments,
equipment and machines or with the design and
development of new ones. IT-professionals in
this field will be the designers (and maintainers) of advanced hardware and software systems
based upon the application of micro-electronics,
control theory and computer design. As systems
designers they will study topics near the baseline of Figure 2; very often they will hardly be
interested in applications. Production innovation comprises IT-applications, which are directed at a better functioning of production machines as well as processes making those cheaper,
and with less dropout. The technical aspects of
these applications concern the automatic control
of machines and processes. They are known as
computer aided design, computer aided manufacturing, numerical control of machines, process
control and robotics. There will be an increasing demand for professionals who are competent
designers of the types of IT applications.

Both types of IT-professionals need special curricula which may partly consist of existing ones
and partly of new courses in computer science
and informatics. The curriculum for product innovators, i.e. for builders and maintainers of
hardware and software systems has to contain
courses in micro-electronics, control theory,
computer science, informatics and supporting
theoretical and practical courses. The production innovators, i.e. the designers of IT-applications, need in their curriculum a fair mix of
courses just mentioned and courses in their field
of application, which can be mechanics, administration, agriculture, etc. It is clear that
next to the development of new curricula, courses and software, new teacher requirements and
certifications have to be formulated, followed by
an adequate teacher training program and a suitable provision of hardware for schools.

Finally, we are able to refine Figure 2 with different manifestation of IT in vocational education. The sectors represent IT-users and both
types of IT-professionals (see Figure 3).

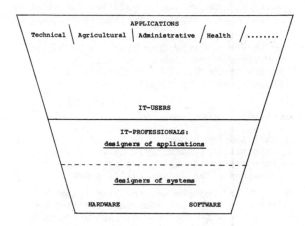

Figure 3 : IT in vocational education

6. Concluding remarks

This paper deals with only some aspects of the
application of IT in education. Attention is
given to what learning about IT should encompass
in general compulsory education and in vocational education. In may countries (see e.g. OECD,
1984) equal or more importance is given to the
application which can be characterized by "learning with the computer". But even the topic of
learning about IT is not discussed exhaustively.
As stated earlier, aspects like the place in the
curriculum, the operationalization of the general goals into course content, the problem of
equal involvement of all pupils, courseware development etc. are not discussed. A first elaboration of these can be found in the reports of
the Advisory Committee for Education and Information Technology (in Dutch, see references).
Another source for "learning about IT" for general compulsory education is Van Weert (1984), of
which an English and a German version is published.

FOOTNOTES

[1]) In this summary this basic education is translated as: introductory information and computer science.

[2]) The sections 3, 4 and 5 are largely based on
the reports, which the Advisory Committee for
Education and Information Technology (AEIT)
presented to the Dutch Minister of Education
and Science (AEIT, 1982, 1984 a, b).

[3]) This section is largely based on a second report which the Advisory Committee for Education and Information Technology (AEIT) presented to the Dutch Minister of Education and
Science, March 1984 (AEIT, 1984 b).

[4]) It is important to state that the preparation
for the so called information society implies
more than just learning about IT. It also has

to imply issues like the possibilities of
self-realization and preparation for lifelong
learning in a constantly changing society.

[5]) This section is largely based on a report
which the Advisory Committee for Education
and Information Technology (AEIT) presented
to the Dutch Minister of Education and
Science, March 1984 (AEIT, 1984).

REFERENCES

(1) AEIT (Advisory Committee for Education and
Information Technology), Learning about
information technology: a necessity for
everybody. The Hague, 1982 (in Dutch).

(2) AEIT, Information and computer science: about
the content of and equipment for "informatics for all". The Hague, 1984 a (in Dutch).

(3) AEIT, Information technology in middle vocational education. The Hague, 1984 b (in
Dutch).

(4) Education and Information Technology. White
paper of the Dutch government, September
1982 (in Dutch).

(5) Häfner, K., Challenge of information technology to education: the new educational crisis, in Lewis, R and Tagg, D. (eds.), Computers in education. North Holland, Amsterdam,
1981.

(6) Informatics Stimulation Plan (Appendix on
Education). White paper of the Dutch government, January 1984 (in Dutch).

(7) Naisbitt, J., Megatrends (Warner Books, New
York, 1984).

(8) OECD, The introduction of the new information technology in education: policy trends
and developments in member countries. Report
presented at the International Conference on
Education and New Information Technologies.
Paris, 9-12 July, 1984.

(9) Weert, T. van, Modell-Lehrplan Informatische
Grundkentnisse für alle Lehrer. Brussels,
Association for Teacher Education in Europe,
1984 (also in English).

COMPUTERS IN EDUCATION, K. Duncan and D. Harris (eds.)
Elsevier Science Publishers B.V. (North-Holland)
© IFIP, 1985

THE MANAGEMENT INFORMATION SYSTEM OF HIGHER EDUCATION IN THE GDR

Franz Stuchlik

College of Advanced Technology Otto von Guericke
Section Informatics
3010 Magdeburg, German Democratic Republic

In the higher education system of the GDR a management information system has been developed and used giving assistance in the process of management on all levels of higher education. The aims of this system, its architecture, the poly-hierarchical structure, the subsystem "education, instruction and further education" and its environment, some vital relations between the subsystems and the development and the preparations for the utilization are described.

1. INTRODUCTION

At the beginning some remarks as to the development of computer applications in the higher education system of the GDR are given. These remarks are intended to facilitate understanding of the development and of the present situation. Computers have been used for more than twenty five years. A modern university or college is an establishment where didactic, scientific research and management activities are integrated. Variable user needs, as well as the development of various computer systems and computer application systems create new problems of wide-range computer application within the university. Therefore, for a period of twenty years, the process of informatics development and computer application has been controlled by the relevant ministry. This process concerns the construction of new computer centres, the extension of existing ones, the foundation of new sections or departments of informatics, the development of specialized software and computer application in teaching, research, library affairs, medical treatment and management in the higher education system.

The base for these control activities is given by a global model of informatics development and utilization adapted continuously to social and consequently scientific requirements. Due to this, a relatively unified development, satisfying the requirements of the individual user categories is obtained.

The following strategy is utilized for implementing the global model (Fig. 1):

a) Each university and each college with university status has got a computer centre except for a few small specialized colleges.

b) All computer centres have hardware (mainframe computers) of the same kind.

c) As a rule, the basic software (operating systems, compilers etc.) of the computer manufacturer is used (Fig. 2).

d) Software made by companies, research institutes etc. which can be used by the higher education system will be bought by a representative of the Ministry of Higher Education (M.H.Ed.).

e) The exchange of software developed within the universities is free of charge (Fig. 3).

f) Computing by staff, students and members of technical staff is free of charge.

g) Mainframe computers are used for education, scientific research, management, medical treatment, library affairs etc. (Fig. 2).

h) The main from of software production is a collective, members being repressentatives from several universities. These collectives are charged with the responsibility of maintaining these products.

Software is developed
- collectively or individually for teaching [1]
- individually for scientific research
- exclusively collectively for management and medical treatment.

i) Pre-requisites for work in the active as well as interactive dialogue are extended step by step (time sharing systems, teleprocessing, multicomputer systems, intelligent terminals, personal computers, local area networks) [2, 4, 5].

2. COMPUTER UTILIZATION IN THE HIGHER EDUCATION SYSTEM

Within the universities (with the exception of highly specialized colleges) there is a wide spectrum of computer

utilization. Many colleges of advanced
technology have computers and microcomputers in use across all sections.
A survey is given by the rough general
model of centralized computer utilization of a university computer centre
(Fig. 1), this consisting of two parts:
- the general application system which
  is the basis for all other systems,
- the specialized systems.

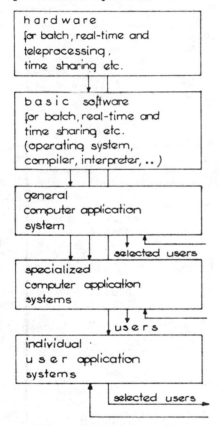

Fig. 1 General model of computer
utilization of a university

Fig. 2 gives a simplified survey on the
functional structure and the utilization form of a centralized computer
application system.
Depending on the type of university and
its specific requirements, this system
has been partially applied, modified
and extended.

3. DESCRIPTION OF THE MANAGEMENT INFOR-
   MATION SYSTEM (MIS)

In the course of the last 18 years, an
effective computer application system,
called MIS, has been created. This system provides support in the process of
management on all levels of higher education. The most important objectives

of the MIS are:
- Qualification of management and decision processes by thoroughly preparing the same on the basis of efficient models and methods of informatics
- Intensification and increasing the
  efficiency of the processes of management, prognosis, planning etc. by
  rationalization and computer-aided
  implementation of the latter
- Stabilization in the execution of
  many processes by making the latter
  independent of office workers
- Unification of process sequences in
  connection with an increase in correctness, security and controllability
- Improvement of working and living
  conditions of people involved in
  these processes by relieving them
  from physical strain, above all from
  tiring routine work.

Finally it was again found that a number of processes could be implemented
by computers only, since time available
for the particular job did not permit
manual execution. Apart from these relatively general objectives, it was
above all the quantity of data to be
processed and the complex relations
between the same which justified the
construction of MIS.
This system is characterized by a poly-
hierarchical structure since not all
universities are directly assigned to
the M.H.Ed.. MIS provides the following
levels:
- Ministry of Higher Education (1)
- Higher education system (a)
- Universities and colleges located
  within one region (b)
- University or college (2)
- Section, institute (3)
- Processes.
Out of them only (1), (2) and (3) are
managerial levels. On level (a) the
processes are centrally implemented for
all universities and colleges independent of their assignment to ministries.
On level (b) the process is supported
for the universities and colleges of
one region independent of their assignment. This level (b) has been established to provide assistence by MIS
also to those universities or colleges
which are not in possession of powerful
computers.

Fig. 4 shows the general structure of
MIS in a very simplified form.
In addition Table 1 gives a survey of
some vital subsystems of MIS.

Fig. 5 shows the functional structure
and some vital relations between these
subsystems.
Due to the hierarchical structure,

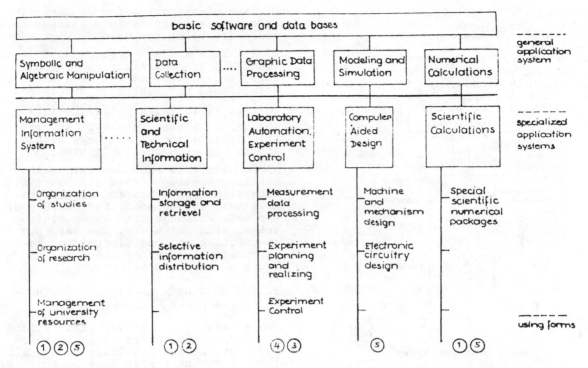

Fig. 2 Functional structure and the utilization forms of a university computer application system
(① batch mode   ② inquiry mode   ③ interactive mode   ④ real-time mode
⑤ interactive conversational mode)

there exists a great flow of information from level to level in both directions and within the levels of the higher education system. In addition, there is a rich flow of information to and from other areas of society.

Fig. 6 shows a general diagram of information flow among three types of computer centres.

In recent years, a number of great data bases have been established which can be extended in the future. Due to the high requirements for resources and maintenance by man, the main part of these data bases will be centrally operated in the future also. On the other hand, data bank systems have been established at the university computer centres (CC1, CC2, CC3). To ensure continuous updating of all their data, these data can operated only in a decentralized way. Data bases working simultaneously for more than one university or college are being established at the regional university computer centres (b1, b2, ...). Updating and utilization of these data bases require a very extensive data exchange and the
- decentralized access to central data bases an the

- centralized access to decentralized data bases.

Examples for centralized data bases are:
- the centralized data bank system of higher education system including data for time series, modelling, simulation etc.
- the catalogue of large-scale units and devices for research and medical treatment of the population
- the central catalogue and specialized catalogues of the two largest scientific central libraries of the GDR.

These data bases are operated by specialized computer centres (a1, ...).

Examples of decentralized data bases are:
- the data bank system of students and their performances
- the data bank system of all fixed assets of one university
- the data bank sytem of material economy of one university
- the data file for accounts and statistics
- the catalogues of the university libraries.

These data bases are operated by university computer centres (CC1, ... or b1, b2, ...).

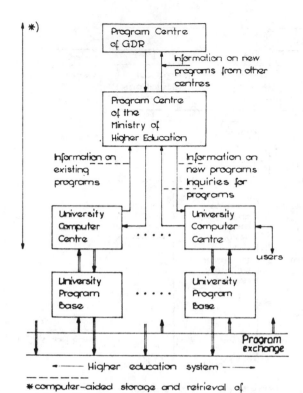

* computer-aided storage and retrieval of information about programs

Fig. 3 Cooperation of the university program bases

4. DEVELOPMENT AND PREPARATIONS FOR THE UTILIZATION

From the very beginning, the following measures are being implemented as part of a global strategy:

a) The centralized and unified architecture and development of the entire system MIS by central and collective management are the pertinent directions of the Minister of Higher Education.

b) From the very beginning, some restrictions have been introduced as to the implementation of MIS in order to facilitate introduction and the general utilization of this system.

c) Ministerial directives lay down which subsystems and elements of the same shall be used in any given case at all universities and colleges, and which elements or subsystems can be used in a facultative way.

d) After their completion and during their time of routine utilization all subsystems are maintained exclusively in a central way and adapted to new requirements. Due to this fact, the uniformity of the total system will be ensured.

e) Data dictionaries for designers, operators and the various classes of users are being prepared.

f) All keys and key systems used in the total MIS are uniformly and formally described. A central key data basis is established and centrally maintained only. It is only the updated copies of this key data basis which are used at the universities. This will ensure unified application of all keys within the entire higher education system.

g) For the data exchange within the higher education system and between the subsystems protocols and interfaces have been established. For years also the data exchange with other ministries, with banks etc. has been put into practice on most diversified machinereadable data carriers on the basis of agreed protocols.

5. THE SUBSYSTEM EDUCATION, INSTRUCTION AND FURTHER EDUCATION

The subsystem education, instruction and further education is the largest and most sophisticated one within MIS [3]. At the beginning some general remarks are made to facilitate understanding:
- The M. H. Ed. is responsible for management and planning within its sphere and the coordination of the whole higher education system.
- All processes of education, instruction and further education are controlled hierarchically by the management levels.
- These processes are planned and accounted for several planning periods (five-year plan, one-year plan, semester plan). Planning at all levels is based on a well-knit system of prognosis.
- Long-term processes are managed, planned and accounted for by the M. H. Ed. taking into account all needs of proportionate development of

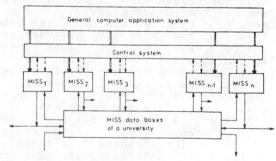

Fig. 4 Rough structure of MIS of a university
(MISS : MIS subsystem, see Table 1)

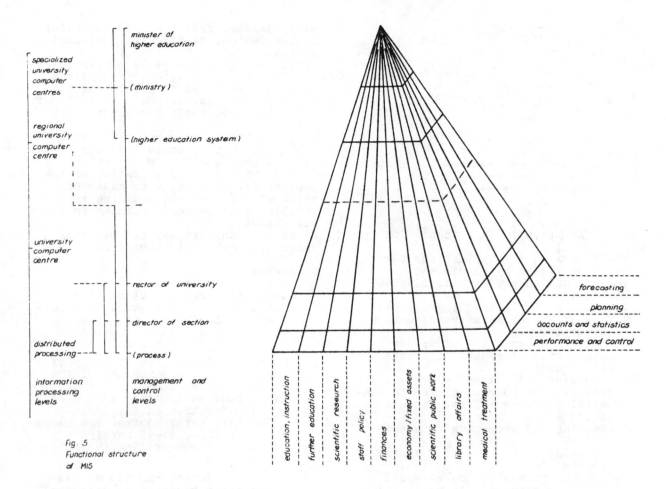

specialized
university
computer
centres

regional
university
computer
centre

university
computer
centre

distributed
processing

information
processing
levels

management and
control
levels

minister of
higher education

(ministry)

(higher education system)

rector of university

director of section

(process)

forecasting

planning

accounts and statistics

performance and control

education, instruction

further education

scientific research

staff policy

finances

economy/fixed assets

scientific public work

library affairs

medical treatment

Fig. 5
Functional structure
of MIS

the national economy.
- The majority of these processes are connected with management processes of other areas of society (Ministry of Planning, Ministry of General Education, Ministry of Science and Technology etc.).
- Short-term processes are managed, planned, implemented and accounted for by the universities and their sections taking into account tasks of the national economic plan and the perspective plan.

Processes concerning the entire higher education system are implemented in a centralized way by one specialized university computer centre.
Examples in this connection are:
- the elaboration of long-term fore-casts for the demographic development of population by simulative methods
- the elaboration of long-term fore-casts for changes in the number and structure of the working population is based upon a highly complex model and simulation system

- the planning of the long-term devel-opment of universities and their training facilities (numbers of admissions in all specializations of the subject nomenclature)
- the centralized collection and ana-lysis of pupils' desires concerning their prospective study subjects. This is a base for an orientation to extended secondary schools, pupils and their parents as to the next phase of application for enrolment at a university by the M. H. Ed.
- the centralized control of the treat-ment of application for study submit-ted by pupils of the extended secon-dary schools, workers, employees etc.
Thus the training facilities of all universities are totally used
- the centralized control of directing all graduates after their studies into practical work.

Processes concerning one university or all universities of a region are im-plemented in a university computer

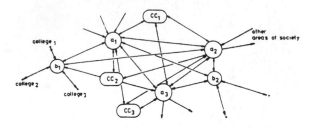

Fig. 6 General diagram of information flow
(a_1; a_2, a_3 : specialized university computer centres,
b_1; b_2 : regional university computer centres,
CC_1; CC_2; CC_3 : university computer centres)

centre. Examples in this connection
are:
- the treatment of applications for
  study submitted by pupils etc.
- the support in the organization of
  studies:
  . planning of all teaching activi-
    ties of the university as to time
    and location
  . decision on granting of grants
  . calculation of amount of grants for
    all students
  . recording and analyzing students'
    performances (marks, prizes in com-
    petitions, innovations, patents
    etc.)
  . planning and preparing of examina-
    tions
  . supervision of the entire course of
    studies
- support in directing the graduates
  after their studies into practical
  work taking into account tasks of the
  M. H. Ed.

Processes concerning only one section
are implemented either in the relevant
university computer centre or within
the section by microcomputers.
This subsystem renders remarkable
advantages to pupils, undergraduates,
graduates and postgraduates as well as
extensive assistance to the members of
the staff and to the university administration.

6. CONCLUSIONS

The long-term utilization of the MIS
has led to many useful results as well
as to number of new probleme for the
designers and for the users, for which
there are several reasons. In this respect, designers as well as users faced
the new tasks jointly. For this purpose
it is important to keep alive the conviction in the user that with this
design and implementation "his future
tool" will be established.
Hence, in recent years, the potential
user of the individual subsystems has

been included from the very beginning
in the design, testing and introduction
processes.
Small user communities have been established for the individual subsystems.
These are intended to jointly tackle
difficulties occurring and to work out
collective proposals for further development.
Of vital importance are user instruction and training activities during the
various phases of design as well as
during the time of utilization of the
subsystems. Especially in cases of
major adaptations and modifications,
detailed and thorough training is in-
dispensible.
It is only in this way posible that
users will not feel overstrained.

7. REFERENCES

[1] Stuchlik, Franz, A Stand-Alone
    C.A.L. System, Computers in educa-
    tion, R. Lewis & D. Tagg (edi-
    tors), North-Holland Publishing
    Company, IFIP, 1981, p. 263

[2] Stuchlik, Franz, The strategy of
    preparing the application of the
    computer network DELTA by the
    management information system of
    higher education in the GDR,
    CONMET'81, Networks from the users
    point of view, 11-15 May 1981
    Budapest, North-Holland Publishing
    Company, 1981, p. 3-63

[3] Stuchlik, Franz, Funktionen des
    Informationssystems des Hochschul-
    wesens der DDR, 6th Int. congress
    on data processing in Europe,
    Vienna 1980, Conf. Proc., part 1,
    p. 575

[4] Bazewicz, M., Stuchlik, F., Der
    Einfluss neuer Technologien gei-
    stiger Arbeit auf die Architektur
    und Projektierung informationsver-
    arbeitender Systeme, 7th Int.
    congress on data processing in
    Europa, Vienna 1984, Conf. Proc.,
    p. 68

[5] Bazewicz, M., Stuchlik, F., Pro-
    blems of computer system/network
    design and application methods,
    Wiss. Z. Techn. Hochsch. Magdeburg
    27 (1983) Heft 8, p. 1

EDUCATION AND INSTRUCTION:

- analysis of pupils' desires concerning their prospective study subjects
- treatment of applications for study
  submitted by pupils, workers, employees etc.
- organization of studies:
  . planning of teaching activities as

to time and location (timetable)
- decision on granting of grant
- calculation of amount of grant
- recording and analyzing students'
  performances
- planning of examinations
- directing the graduates after their
  studies into practical work

SCIENTIFIC RESEARCH:

- control of research contracts
- accounting of research projects
- analysis of results of scientific investigation and of research expenditures

STAFF POLICY:

- employing of staff
- preparation of appointments
- social services

FINANCES:

- financing
- salaries and wages

ECONOMY OF FIXED ASSETS:

- material economy
- utilization units
- investments
- maintenance of fixed assets

LIBRARY AFFAIRS:

- acquisition of library items
- lending services for library items
- analysis of user processes
- maintenance of several general and
  specialized catalogues
- preparation of bibliographic information for printing etc.

SCIENTIFIC PUBLIC WORK:

- congresses and similar events
- scientific publications
- scientific exhibitions

Table 1: Survey on some subsystems of
         MIS and their elements

COMPUTERS IN EDUCATION, K. Duncan and D. Harris (eds.)
Elsevier Science Publishers B.V. (North-Holland)
© IFIP, 1985

COMPUTER EDUCATION IN HONG KONG

Douglas S. Tung,   PhD

Department of Computer Science,
The Chinese University of Hong Kong
Shatin, Hong Kong

This article describes the environment, the manpower needs and the computer educational programmes available in Hong Kong. There are four categories of institutions offering computer education, the computer vendors, the vocational institutes of sponsored or trade associations, the agents of overseas companies and profit-making institutes, and the non-profit-making institutes. Three computer professional organizations have their examination centers established in Hong Kong. Keywords: computer curriculum, computer education, computer professional examinations.

1. ENVIRONMENT

The first computer in Hong Kong was installed in an utility company (China Light and Power Company) in 1963. In 1968, there were about twenty mainframe computers. With the advent of minicomputers in the 1970's, growth in data automation is astounding. The number of computer installations in the local commerce, industry, government and educational organizations has grown steadily in the recent years as shown in table 1.

The term "computer installation" refers to an in-house set up of computer equipment to provide computing service to the organization. Of the 1,005 installations, the number of mainframes is small, being around 50. However, there are around 950 minicomputers installed, with the major suppliers being IBM and Wang. In micros, there are in excess of 30,000 illegitimate Apples believed to exist, mostly at homes, and with an average cost of under US$400 for the processor, there is a rapid spread of computer literacy. There are around 3,000 legitimate 16-bit microcomputers, and a rather larger number of legitimate 8-bit machines.

The large applications are in the obvious areas of banking, transportation, utility companies and government administration. Medium sized systems and minis cover all business areas, but with a surprisingly small penetration in manufacturing, which is Hong Kong's major employment sector. The reasons are the small size of very

many of the organizations, and their desire to retain flexibility.

Year	Number of installations
1976	119
1977	231
1978	276
1979	461
1980	551
1981	684
1982	718
1983	1005

Table 1. Growth of Computer Installations in Hong Kong (1976-1983)

2. MANPOWER NEEDS

The expansion in the use of computer facilities in the local industry and business have created the staffing requirements for a decade. People with the necessary programming, systems analysis and design skills have to be imported to fill the needs. For the past years, there has been a great demand for computer education by the white collars, technicians and students because it is believed that computers could pervade so many areas that a person will be at a disadvantage without some knowledge of this field in the competitive job markets.

A recent manpower survey shows that there are about 2,720 systems development staff, i.e. EDP managers, analysts and programmers in 1980. The

numbers of staff grew by 21% in 1980-81,
22% in 1981-82 and 12% in 1982-83,
leading to an annual growth rate of 18%.
By the end of 1983, there were around
4,500 systems development staff. It is
estimated that the growth rate of staff
will be between 15% and 20%. (1)

There is, however, a serious outflow of
skilled computer personnel, estimated to
be about eight percent of the work force
in computer field. It may well cause an
underestimation of the staffing needs in
the coming years.

The manpower survey of all computer
installations and education institutions
in Hong Kong has enabled us to make
projections of the demand and supply of
computer personnel for the next several
years. This is tabulated in table 2.
The demand was provided by each
installation giving two estimates, one
on the high end, and the other on the
low end. The means of these estimates
were then calculated. The supply
figures are rather deterministic. They
were provided by the Universities,
Polytechnics Technical Institutes and
Post-secondary Colleges.

The survey shows that a shortfall of 572
trained EDP personnel by the end of 1984

alone, and the present number of EDP
systems development staff employed must
more than double by the end of 1989 to
keep pace with the projected number of
computer installations which will by
then be in place. (2)

3. COMPUTER EDUCATION INSTITUTIONS

In Hong Kong, there are four categories
of institutions offering computer
education.

3.1 Computer Vendors

They have two purposes in training the
various personnel levels of the user:

(a) They educate the user's staff to
operate the computer, giving courses on
operating systems, programming and job
control languages, software and
peripheral usage, all heavily oriented
to their own products. This education
is usually free to customers, specified
in the sales or lease contract.

(b) Appreciation courses designed to
brief EDP (Electronic Data Processing)
concepts to line managers so as to win
their involvement are also conducted.
Vendors may charge for this extra
service on a break-even basis.

	Year						
	83	84	85	86	87	88	89
Demand							
High end	4477	5290	6251	7386	8731	10320	12199
Low end	4477	5114	5709	6304	6900	7495	8091
Mean	4477	5202	5980	6845	7816	8908	10145
Estimated demand based on mean		725	778	865	971	1092	1237
Supply							
Estimated supply from Universities & Polytechnics		153	302	330	618	701	745
Supply as percent of demand (in %)		21	39	38	64	64	60
Taking into account supply from post-secondary institutes		282	432	480	788	881	945
Supply as percent of demand (in %)		38	55	55	81	80	76

Table 2.   Demand and Supply of Systems Development Staff
in Hong Kong for 1983-1989

3.2 Vocational Institutes of Sponsored or Trade Associations

The Hong Kong Productivity Centre has been very active in offering vocational training to the public. It is administered by the Hong Kong Productivity Council, a government financed body for the promotion of industrial productivity. Regularly, courses on programming languages, systems analysis and EDP management are given. Students are awarded certificates on passing examinations.

The Hong Kong Management Association plays also an active role in promoting EDP education, offering courses with emphasis on EDP organizational functions and knowledge.

3.3 Agents of overseas companies and profit-making institutions

Agents of overseas companies with bases in the U.K. or U.S.A. offer both very technical computer courses to a captive market, and public courses on Computer Appreciation, System Analysis and O & M (Organization and Management) Programming, and EDP Management Training.

With the implementation of the Pilot Scheme to teach Computer Studies to the secondary schools in 1982, data processing education has become a boom industry in Hong Kong. Private schools set up to teach computer courses have mushroomed. Their training is oriented toward microcomputers. However, the problem is that nobody is quite sure about the quality of these schools. In addition, there has been an ebb and flow of these schools. They lack the consistency, and therefore they cannot secure high ratings for their courses.

3.4 Non-profit Educational Institutions

Universities, Polytechnics, Technical Institutes, Post-secondary Colleges, secondary and primary schools fall into this category.

Tertiary education in computing began in 1968 when the two universities in Hong Kong, the Chinese University of Hong Kong and the Hong Kong University offered computer courses. In October 1970, the Joint Universities Computer Centre (JUCC) was established. Since then, extra-mural computer science, programming and EDP management courses have been offered to the public.

In 1973, in due recognition of the importance to provide computer education, the Chinese University set up the Department of Computer Science to offer a Minor Programme in Computer Science and to oversee further development in this area of studies. The Minor Programme required students to take FORTRAN Programming, Introduction to Computer Science, and elective courses such as Data Processing, COBOL Programming and Numerical Analysis in their first two years. In the third and fourth year, the programme was divided into three streams - Pure Computer Science, Information Systems and Numerical Methods. Students were required to take core courses, and to make their own choice of the curricular stream based on their aptitude and interest.

Soon, the Chinese University recognized the future need in Hong Kong for some computer scientists with a more specialized training than that provided by the Minor Programme. In view of the need, the implementation of the Major Programme in Computer Science began in 1978 and was completed in 1982 when the first batch of the majors graduated with honour degrees in Science. It is a four-year programme. Currently, the annual intake of students is 55. The number of qualified applicants for admission is around 300. Students major in Computer Science can take Minor Programmes in business administration, science, social science or arts subjects according to their interests. The curriculum was constructed by consulting other British Commonwealth Universities and the Curriculum Recommendations of the Association for Computing Machinery (ACM) 1973. (3)

In 1982, a Graduate Programme leading to the degree of M.Phil. in Computer Science was introduced to enable local qualified students to pursue research-oriented studies. The Department has also been involved in training teachers to teach Computer Studies in the secondary schools.

In the academic year 1983-84, the enrollment figures are: 6 for M.Phil. Programme, 147 for Major Programme, 320 for Minor Programme, and around 1200 students taking elective courses. There are plans to increase the intake of major students, minor students, and to launch additional programmes of studies in the foreseeable years.

In the University of Hong Kong, since early 1970's, the Computer Center has offered courses on computing. In the academic year 1976-77, a small number of computer science courses were offered in the BSc degree curriculum. The courses were selected by students in combination with mathematics and statistics to form a programme of studies in applied mathematics.

In 1982, the Center of Computer Studies and Applications was established to take the first batch of approximately 30 students. It is a three-year programme. In general terms, a computer studies student must take and successfully complete approved courses in which not less than half must be offered by the Center.

In the Hong Kong Polytechnic, courses at the computer appreciation and the computer user levels were offered in almost all departments in the mid 1970's. The Computing Studies Department was then established to offer a two-year diploma course and a three-year higher diploma course in Systems Analysis. The entrance qualification for these diploma courses was Hong Kong Certificate of Education. Students graduating in the diploma course can proceed on to a higher diploma in Computer Studies which requires one year of practical work and another year of study. In 1983, a four-year programme leading to the bachelor degree in Computer Studies was implemented with the admission of 40 students. The entrance qualification is successful completion of two advanced level subjects and three ordinary level subjects. This is a sandwich programme, requiring students to work in their third year.

Some Post-secondary Colleges participate in computer education, for instance, the Hong Kong Baptist College, Chu Hai College and Lingnan College. The Lee Wai Lee Technical Institute also conducts computer studies courses. The City Polytechnic of Hong Kong, founded in 1984, and other technical institutes will play an increasing role in computer education, taking over the diploma courses in Computer Studies from the Hong Kong Polytechnic.

Starting in October, 1984, the City Polytechnic began to offer a three-year professional diploma course for 100 students on a full-time basis, and a four-year higher diploma course for 60 students on a part-time basis. The entry requirement for the professional diploma is two advanced levels and for the higher diploma is based on the Hong Kong School Certificate Examination results.

In 1982, the Education Department implemented the Pilot Scheme to teach computer fundamentals to thirty secondary schools. Courses were offered to the Form 4 (Grade 9) students, and then to both the Form 4 and the Form 5 (Grade 10) students in 1983. These Forms are equivalent to Grades 10 and 11 in the U.S.A. Today, there are about forty-five secondary schools offering computer courses on their own budgets. The total number of students taking the courses is around 4,800. In the summer of 1983, some schools advertised to teach primary school children computer, or to teach English language using microcomputers equipped with sound.

In early 1984, the Director of Education of the Hong Kong Government announced the number of secondary schools able to offer computer courses will be more than trebled in the next academic year. Some \$9.4 million had been set aside to equip 75 additional schools with microcomputers systems, bringing the total number of schools equipped to 105.

3.5 Summary of Educational Programmes

A summary of the computer educational programmes of the several institutions in Hong Kong is shown in table 3.

4. PROFESSIONAL EXAMINATIONS

There are three professional organizations offering computer certification examinations which are available in Hong Kong. Certification is an useful means to give recognition to computer personnel with skills up to the standards. It also serves as good reference for employers in their recruitments.

(1) The British Computer Society (BCS),

(2) The Institute of Data Processing Management, U.K., and

(3) The Institute for Certification of

Computer Professionals, U.S.A., which sponsored the CDP (Certificate in Data Processing) and the CCP (Certificate in Computer Programming) Examinations.

The BCS Examination is a popular qualifying examination in Hong Kong. A few private schools claim to offer course geared to it and some correspondence schools offer home study course for part of the Examination.

In November 1983, the British Computer Society granted exemption from both Parts I and II of the Society Examinations to graduates of Computer

Institute	Programme	Duration (in years)	Department
The Chinese University	BSc(Hons) (Computer Science) M.Phil.	4	Computer Science (Faculty of Science)
Hong Kong University	BSc (Computer Studies)	3	Center of Computer Studies & Applications
Hong Kong Polytechnic	BA(Hons) Computer Studies Higher Dip. S.A. ^ Higher Dip. C.S. + Diploma C.S.	4* 3 2+2 2	Computer Studies
Lee Wai Lee Technical Institute	Diploma C.S.	2	General Studies
City Poly- technic	Professional Diploma Higher Diploma C.S.	3 4@	Computing Studies
Post-secondary schools	Elective courses in Computers	-	Computer Centers
Secondary schools	Computer Studies courses	2	

```
* Sandwich course
^ Systems Analysis
+ Computer Studies
@ Part-time
```

Table 3. Summary of Computer Educational Programmes Available in Hong Kong

Science major of the Chinese University of Hong Kong, with BSc honour degree and at least Grade C in the final year project. Graduates with pass degrees will be given exemption from Part I Examination only. This accreditation enables eligible graduates who have been exempted from the Society Examination to become Associate Members of the Society (AMBCS) after at least one year's practical experience in the use and application of computers. The Chinese University is the first institution outside United Kingdom which has ever been accredited by the Society.

5. FUTURE PLANS

The proliferation of computer usage in the local industry, commerce, education and contemporary life strongly supports the issue of promoting computer education in Hong Kong. The Chinese University, being the pioneer in computer education in this region, began to revise its curriculum in 1984, making it compatible with the recent curricular recommendations of several computer professional bodies, such as the British Computer Society, the Association for Computing Machinery and the Institute of Electrical and Electronics Engineers (IEEE).

Essentially, in the Years 3 and 4, there are four streams: Computer Science, Applied Computer Science, Information Systems and Computer Engineering. The streams Computer Science and Applied Computer Science are natural consequences of the existing programme. Graduates in these streams are expected to further their studies, or to work as systems programmers and programmers. Hong Kong is mainly a business community. The demand for information systems graduates is even more intense than it is in U.S.A. Accordingly, the Information Systems stream is set up as recommended by the 1979 report of the ACM Curriculum Committee on Information Systems.(4) The design of the Computer Engineering stream was based on "A Curriculum in Computer Science and

Engineering" by IEEE in 1977. (5) It is envisaged that topics of microprocessors will meet the upsurging needs of the local, technology bound industries.   .

In 1985, a School of Informatics will be established in the Chinese University to achieve autonomy in planning, organization, allocation of resources and control. Informatics is an interdisciplinary subject of metadisciplinary import, such as computer science, business management, engineering, mathematics and social sciences.   It is felt that this will be the orientation for preparation of students to meet the challenges and needs for computer personnel in the 1990's.

The future plans of the computer educational institutions in Hong Kong are summarised in table 4.

6.   CONCLUDING REMARKS

With the proliferation of higher quality computer education available in the local environment, computer use will win more acceptance.   This, in turn will lead Hong Kong's commerce and industry into progressively greater profitablity by the intelligent use of the technology.   Because of the importance of the issues involved, a well conceived plan for monitoring computer education and Government support are essential.

REFERENCES

[1] Strickland, J. E., EDP Training in Hong Kong, Hong Kong Computer Society, Yearbook 1983 (Hong Kong, 1984) 3-4.

[2] Asian Computer Monthly, Shock Manpower Figures from Hong Kong Survey, 78 (April 1984).

[3] Association for Computing Machinery, Curriculum Committee, Curriculum Recommedations for Undergraduate Programs in Information Systems, Comm. ACM, 16, 12, (December 1973) 727-749.

[4] ____. Curriculum '78, Recommendations for Undergraduate Program in Computer Science. Comm. ACM, 22, 3, (March 1979) 147-165.

[5] Institute of Electrical and Electronics Engineers, A Curriculum in Computer Science and Engineering, Committee Report (IEEE, California, Long Beach, 1977).

Institute		Plans
The Chinese Univ. of Hong Kong	86	Launch One-year Full-time MSc Programme in Informatics
	86	Launch Part-time Degree Programme (6 years)
	87	Take PhD students
University of Hong Kong	85	Launch Postgraduate Diploma in Data Processing
HK Polytechnic	85	Take a limited number of M.Phil students
City Polytechnic	86	Convert Diploma course to degree course
Technical Institutes	85	Increase Diploma student numbers
Post-secondary Colleges		Computer Literacy Programmes; Data Processing Certificates; Diplomas in Systems Analysis

Table 4.   Future Plans of Educational Institutions

COMPUTERS IN EDUCATION, K. Duncan and D. Harris (eds.)
Elsevier Science Publishers B.V. (North-Holland)
© IFIP, 1985

COMPUTERS IN THE ISRAELI EDUCATIONAL SYSTEM (1980-84)

BEN ZION BARTA

MINISTRY OF EDUCATION AND CULTURE*
JERUSALEM, ISRAEL

The paper presents an overview of the main developments in educational computing in the period 1980-84 in Israel. The fields of priority for new development are stated, followed by short descriptions of the main projects. Most details are given about: curricula for computer awareness and literacy, introduction of informatics and computer applications into professional training curricula, teacher's training and updating, courseware development by de-centralized, coordinated teams. Other aspects of educational computing development in Israel are shortly mentioned. As for future trends, not only that the already on-going activities have to be continued, but, perhaps, we have to be prepared for several new issues like: advanced technologies being integrated into educational and training computerized systems; a shift of typical computer-activities along the years of schooling; the start of more profound changes in the organization of learning activities and, perhaps of the whole schooling environment.

Keywords: Computer Literacy, Teaching of Informatics, Informatics in Vocational Education, Courseware Development, Teacher's Training in Informatics.

1. INTRODUCTION

The state of computer applications in the Israeli educational system, as it developed from the late 60's to the late 70's, is described in a paper presented to WCCE-81 (Barta, 1981). It is the purpose of this paper to report on the next four years of activity in this so fastly expanding field.

The closing section of the mentioned paper discussed trends for the future and set the main lines of action as being the following ones:

(i) An intensive action to introduce learning of Basic Computer Concepts, of Computer Sciences and of Computer Based Education Methodology at schools of education of any kind. This action must include involvement of the teaching staff into research and development and promotion of educational computing subjects as thesis work of graduate students.

(ii) To influence the design of hardware to be better adapted to education needs.

(iii) To promote basic research of educational and social effects of the use of computer-based educational systems.

(vi) To promote development and production of courseware, using the (micro) computers to improve and enrich the teaching process and to integrate it into the daily activities of teachers and students.

(v) To teach basic computer concepts and programming at the junior high school level and to have most high school students able to use computers freely.

(vi) To review curricula for training professionals and update them. To promote training of data processing and computer professionals.

(vii) To promote computer-oriented extracurricular activities.

(viii) To prepare for the large scale growth of computing within the whole school system with all its aspects of hardware, software, communications, maintenance, etc.

Out of the eight items listed, only for items 2 and 3 there is not much action to be reported. Considerable progress did occur within the other six lines of action, and, some more, not mentioned in 1981. This paper provides information on the policy about Computers in Education in our school system and highlights some of the activities and achievements.

2. GENERAL POLICY ON COMPUTERS IN EDUCATION

The first years of development in the field of computers in education in Israel were mainly directed by initiatives from institutes and schools not directly belonging to the Ministry of Education. In 1978-79 a first small budget was dedicated for computers in education and during the same period the Ministry started to coordinate the plans of the institutes active in this field. A substantial increase in funding - equivalent to $2.25 million per year was granted for 1983-84 and towards this expected expansion of activities a series of seminars and discussions were held during fall and winter 1982. Participants at these meetings were most executives of the Ministry, some of them knowledgeable in the field of computers in education, as well as several specialists from research and development institutes and from academies.

As a result of these discussions a general policy was concluded, stating the main purposes for using the budget. The author of this paper was active to define this policy, together with a small team of specialists and, after its approval, he was assigned the responsibility for its execution. He is reporting to the chairman of the Pedagogical Secretariat of the Ministry - the top executive in educational matters. A special committee appointed by the Ministry, accompanies the execution of this policy. The chairman of the Pedagogical Secretariat is heading this committee.

Curricular development was selected as the main issue for using the budget. It was decided to use only a small part of the budget for purchasing equipment and

---

*While completing this paper, the author was at WAYNE STATE UNIVERSITY in Detroit, Michigan, USA, as a Visiting Professor with the DEPARTMENT OF ELECTRICAL AND COMPUTER ENGINEERING. The help and environment provided to work on this paper are fully appreciated.

that this part should be kept as low as possible. Expenses for actual implementation of activities (e.g., teaching hours) are not included in this budget.

A special committee appointed by the government, to deal with national planning for computer, communications and information technologies, checked our development plans and recommended to provide funding for large scale, nation-wide implementation of some of the proposed programs. It is hoped that this funding will be available for the 1985-86 budget.

As regarding curricular development, the efforts are directed towards six areas. They are not covering all matters in computers in education - but priority is given to them. However, initiatives in other possible areas are not prohibited.

The six selected areas of development are the following:

a. Teacher's training and updating: introductory courses to computers and their educational applications, methodology, courseware evaluation, and authoring, qualifying courses to train teachers of Informatics, of professional Computer Applications and of Computer Literacy.

b. Introducing a nation-wide curriculum for teaching Computer Literacy, at the grade span from 1st to 8th grade.

c. Further development and implementation of Drill and Practice in basic skills, mainly in the primary education.

d. Computer-related Vocational Education - development of new curriculae for vocations specializing in computers (software and hardware) and updating curriculae of most professions, as regarding computer applications specific to each one.

e. Teaching of Computer Sciences in high-schools as a general sciences education subject, part of the matriculation examinations.

f. Development and implementation of various approaches of Computer Aided Learning (other than drill and practice).

All of the mentioned topics are accompanied by adequate research and evaluation. Most of them have to deal with aspects of hardware selection and standardization, courseware and software portability, etc.

3. OUTLINES OF CURRICULAR DEVELOPMENT AND RESEARCH

Most of these activities fall into one of the following two:

a. Development of curriculae for teaching informatics, computer applications and computer-related subjects;

b. Development of educational computer applications.

Some efforts are directed toward evaluation and research as well as to applications to educational administration.

3.1 CURRICULA FOR INFORMATICS AND COMPUTER APPLICATIONS

3.1.1 Computer Awareness and Literacy

The curricula on Computer Awareness and Literacy is on its way to the status of a national project, intended to reach all pupils before leaving junior high school.

It started by the general policy statement mentioned in Sec. 2. Next a professional committee was appointed to define actual actions and a first outline for a sylabus (Barta and Osin, 1983). The recommendations of this committee led to the initiation of two, coordinated but independent, curriculum development projects, one at the Hebrew University of Jerusalem, the second at the Oranim College of Education in Tivon, for developing contents, teaching materials, methodologies and their formative evaluation in 7th and 8th grades. An interim report of the National Council for Research and Developments recommends to provide founding for the implementation of this program to about 25%-35% of the pupils in 1985-86 toward its complete implementation in the few forthcoming years (Subcommittee on Telematics, 1984). A third project, at the Tel-Aviv University deals with development of computer related activities, intended to provide computer awareness at younger ages, up to the sixth grade (Nachmias, 1985). Apart from the regular classroom activities, there is much interest in informal, extracurricular computer related activities, for pupils, ranging from 8-9 years old and up to high school pupils. These activities may be a first encounter with computers but in many cases, they provide for advanced computer applications. They are provided by six academic institutions dedicated to the promotion of science education and by many schools and community centers. A team at the Ben-Gurion University in Beer-Sheba is active in developing, collecting, publishing concepts, guidelines and materials for these extracurricular activities (Regev, 1985). This same team helps implementing in the Southern part of Israel the regular 7th grade classroom Computer Literacy curriculum, as developed by the two just mentioned teams.

The framework for the Computer Awareness and Literacy curriculum is characterized by the following main points:

a. The approaches will be different according to the age of the pupils. Up to sixth grades (perhaps from Kindergarden), computer awareness will be indirectly attained, by various activities providing a first contact and practice with computer technologies - games, simulations, a variety of other computer aided learning activities, inquiries about computer applications and their influence and, at the higher grades, operation of hardware and software. All these activities, integrated within the regular school schedule without special class time dedicated to computer studies.

At 7th grade formal Computer Literacy studies should start. The programs being under development and evaluation are based on two weekly hours for two years. These hours are to be delivered in the computer-laboratory providing direct hands-on experience, as needed, during the study hours (a workstation available for two pupils).

At higher grades, especially in the Senior High School, the use of computers should be integrated within the study of most subject matters, as a natural use of high technology computing and communication resources, when needed and as needed.

b. The contents, from the Informatics point of view, are divided into five main divisions, namely:

Computer uses and applications
Human and social implications of computers
Principles of computer operation
Hardware and devices
Software and programming principles

c. Regarding the pupil-audience, the curricula should find answers to the whole pupil population, regardless of the intellectual and social background of each pupil, or of his previous knowledge or experience. Accordingly, various approaches and materials are produced for the variety of needs.

In 1984-85 about 25 schools use these materials, some of them directly related to the development team and providing the possibility for larger scale field tests and formative evaluation. The teachers for these classes are qualified to teach Informatics and they recieve on-going methodological support. A committee, headed by Prof. Y. Schueika from Bar-Ilan University in Ramat-Gan supervises and coordinates the curricula development and its implementation.

3.1.2 Advanced, General Studies of Informatics

Informatics studies at general high schools are still along the same lines as described in the past (Barta, 1981 and Pelles, 1975). There are four 90 hours modules that can be taken within the 10th-12th grades, as an elective subject. About a quarter of the contents of the four modules available, was changed, mainly as an update of microcomputer technologies.

A major change of these curricula will be carried out within the next few years, as a result of the implementation of the Computer Awareness and Literacy program described in 3.1.1.

The Center for Educational Technology in Tel-Aviv produced most of the courses delivered at high schools. Courses specific for vocational education (partly delivered by CAL materials) were produced by the Institute for Teaching Aids in Tel-Aviv. The actual implementation of these courses within the school system is coordinated by a team at the Technological Education Institute in Holon.

3.1.3 Informatics in Vocational Education

A 60-hour introductory course to computers, usually taught at the 11th grade, is compulsory to most pupils learning technical and business professions. Advanced, profession-specific studies were developed and are delivered as continuation to the introduction.

Courses on computerized bookkeeping and office automation were developed for 12th grade in business professions. This development included syllabus, teaching materials, methodology, teachers' training, etc. (Adereth, 1984). It is compulsory, but maybe only in 1985-86 will all vocational high schools teach it.

Similar packages were developed for teaching an Introduction to Computer Controlled Systems. They are intended for those specializing in mechanical engineering, but are useful also to students of electronics and computer programming (Cohen, 1984).

Teaching of CAD/CAM principles in the vocational high school is on its way too. The main obstacle is the lack (in 1983-84) of adequate quality software packages on low cost microcomputers. Syllabuses were prepared and experimentally delivered in two forms: an introduction to computer aided drafting as an add-on to technical drafting courses in the 11th grade; an in-depth learning of a professional CAD package in the

13th grade of pupils leaning towards qualification as practical engineers; these pupils will use CAD when preparing their final projects in the 14th grade (Sagiv, 1984).

The use of software packages for problem solving as a natural part of the technical studies is being integrated within studies of electricity, instrumentation, building and architecture professions at the technical high school.

The changes are more profound in the curricula of profession directly related to computer technology. Within the curricula of the electronics department and that of instrumentation and control, the time dedicated to computer hardware and software is steadily increasing. The departments for automatic data processing which were dedicated to train programmers, are in a process to augment the teaching of principles of hardware components of computer systems and the approaches for programming and maintenance of real-time systems. The additional subjects of these departments require at least one additional year of study, the 13th grade, to reach an acceptable level of training. Its graduates are qualified as technicians.

Most curricular development on Informatics within the Vocational Education is carried out by: The Institute for Teaching Aids, The Center for Information Systems of the Israel Institute for Productivity, The Center for Educational Technology, The ORT-Moshinsky Pedagogical Center - all located in Tel-Aviv; The Central Technological Laboratory in Beer-Sheva; The Technion, Israel Institute of Technology in Haifa.

3.1.4 Teachers' Training and Updating

1. Certification of Informatics Teachers

As in any educational activity, the actual implementation of the variety of programs just mentioned is highly dependent upon the teachers that have to provide teaching, counseling, coordination as well as practice of the use of computer-equipment and related laboratory instrumentation.

There was no doubt that teachers, already qualified and acting in schools have to be prepared for teaching the new subjects. From one point of view, this is the only possible way to have new curricula introduced within the whole schooling system in a few years; from another point of view, teachers are highly interested and motivated to learn and teach these new, interesting and prestigious subjects.

To qualify for teaching Informatics, 450-hour courses are offered to qualified teachers (mostly of mathematics, sciences or technology). They are organized as one day per week in-service courses, seven hours per day, for two years. After completion of the course, the teacher is qualified for teaching up to the first two modules of the advanced Informatics studies at high schools. At the completion of the first year, they qualify to teach Computer Literacy. These courses are provided as regular activity at four centers, within the main districts of Israel. About 150 hours of the course are dedicated to hands-on programming practice and laboratory activities - the rest is dedicated to provide a sound knowledge of Computer Structure and Operation, Programming and several more theoretical aspects of Informatics, as well as Teaching Methodology.

To prepare for teaching specific computer applications like Office Automation, Computerized Bookkeeping, Data-Entry, use of engineering software pack-

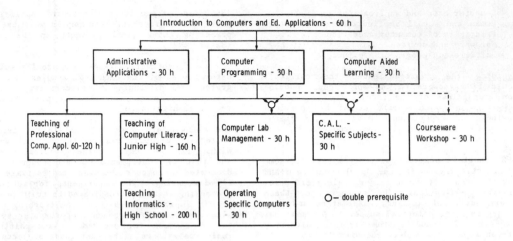

Fig. 1. The overall scheme of teachers' training and updating courses

ages - courses ranging from 120-240 hours are given. About one third of such a course is dedicated to general computer studies, the rest of it, to the specific subject matter and methodology.

During their first year of teaching the new subjects, especially when the curricula being taught is also new, close support and advice is provided for the teachers.

Courses developed for in-service teacher training are gradually adopted by colleges and schools of education, so that new graduating teachers are already prepared for teaching Informatics and Computer Applications.

2.   Teachers' Initiation to Computers and CAL

A variety of modular courses, in the range of 30-60 hours per module, are offered to teachers, as updating, informative courses with no intention to qualify for teaching of new subjects. The first module usually taken is a Computer Literacy module, including an introduction to computer applications in education. Others may provide better knwoledge of programming, or specific subjects, like an introduction to Computer Aided Design and Manufacturing Systems.

Many of these courses are taught by the Institutes already mentioned, which deal also with the development of the various curriculae. Some details on the content of these courses have been published (Millin, 1984). An overall scheme of the possible sequences is given in Fig. 1.

Colleges of Education, mainly those preparing teachers for the primary education, included in their curricula, as a compulsory subject, the first 60 hours introductory course. Others may be offered as elective ones or left for in-service updating, after completion of college. A similar, but somewhat slower process, occurs at the colleges belonging to universities, preparing teachers mostly for the secondary education.

3.2 EDUCATIONAL APPLICATIONS OF COMPUTERS

Most research and development of educational applications is done either directly by the Ministry of Edu-

cation or by public, non-profit institutes, some of them owned by the state - most of the funding being by the Ministry. Only limited activity is carried out by private institutes - it is not reviewed in this paper.

3.2.1 Computers in the Kindergarten

This research and development project is directed towards the youngest children within the educational system. It started in 1982-83 at the "Oranim" College of Education as a joint initiative of their Center for the Study of the Child's Activities and their Educational Computing Laboratory (Levyn, 1983). The computer system is based on LOGO, adopted for the kindergarten. It is limited to graphic display, using a few keys, each one activating a pre-programmed procedure, controlling the movement of the turtle on the screen. Other keys are disabled. The program is not intended to teach any computer awareness issues. The computer based activity may provide an advanced environment for the development of children's logical and intuitive thinking. It provides a tool allowing the child to try out his ideas and to discover facts which are not directly tangible. Problem solving in this environment is not fit to automatic solving, without understanding, without thinking. Accordingly, these activities may help developing the childrens' capacity to define problems, to plan solutions and test them, to be able to think about the results of a sequence of actions. The 1983-84 school year was mostly dedicated to develop activities, to test them, to observe the children as they act during these activities, to prepare and test evaluation-tools for the possible effects of the computer-activities on the development of the children. In 1984-85 more basic evaluation is to start.

3.2.2 Courseware Development

If a few years ago most courseware was drill and practice oriented and mostly in arithmetics, presently the range of subjects in much wider and more sophisticated applications are developed. However, most of the effort is still for the basic skills in the primary education.

ated reports for individual/group assignment of instruction. MACAL was developed by a joint effort of the Ministry of Education and Culture, the Ministry of Labor and Social Affairs, The Institute for Teaching Aids and BOSMAT, the Junior Technical College of the Technion. It is presently promoted by the Institute for Teaching Aids with professional and financial support of the Ministry of Education.

Available courses include elementary high school algebra, an Introduction to Computers for high school pupils. Under development are packages for Hebrew Composition at high school level, Geometry and Statistic for high school level and an Introduction to Programming for Computer Literacy courses to be delivered to teachers and students in education.

MACAL is actually implemented on a variety of mini and micro computers, courseware being automatically transferred from the authoring system to the different users.

Courseware is developed mostly by central teams, accompanied by steering committees. Representatives of the Division for Curricula Development and of the Ministry's inspection team are part of these committees.

SML (Hebrew acronym for Computer Assistance to Teaching) is a micro-computer system intended to assist teachers to deliver individualized instruction to their pupils. It allows the teacher to have full control on the learning activities of his students; to provide group or individual learning paths using available courseware; to modify available courseware or generate new one according to his/her decision; or to use pre-loaded sequences of existing courseware.

SML started as a local project by a team of teachers and computer professionals in the township of Kiryat Schmonach, supported by the Ministry of Education. It is presently used by some 100 primary schools around Israel. The support for the users is provided by the Institute for Teaching Aids. The courseware development teams are not more self standing - they are now integrated within the regional team approach of Department for Computer-Based Curricula.

Authoring and delivery tools exist for drill and practice, tutorials, remedial learning, simulations, educational games. Courseware, existing and under development covers mainly elementary school material.

Both MACAL and SML have a basic alpha-numeric orientation, with limited graphic capabilities. A new software system, developed in 1983-84, allows for advanced facilities - good graphic, animation, sound, color, etc. The two existing systems are in their way to merge into a single one, which, while providing all tools of common interest, will still allow each team to work according to his own philosophy.

iv. Computers in Special Education

Until recently, the use of computers in special education for the handicapped and retarded children was limited to the usage of existing courseware, considered adequate to the special needs.

A team at the Tel-Aviv University (Margalit, 1984) is dedicated to study and develop methodologies and courseware, specially fit for these children. At the first stage, they are not dealing with special hardware, but this aspect may be added at some later stage.

Field tests and implementation first started during 1984-85 school year.

v. Private Initiative

Several commercial firms are active in courseware production and marketing in Israel. They are selecting their own fields of activity, subjects and quality criteria. Some of them produced software packages for authoring and delivery of learning systems, as well as learning sequences intended for school use. Others, developed limited size, self-standing courseware packages, usually programmed in BASIC and intended either for school use or for home learning on personal computers. Adaptation and translation of courseware produced in foreign countries, is mostly done by private firms.

There is no control by educational authorities on the private production of courseware. The decision for using it is of the school principal and the teachers of each school. Some of the privately produced software tools are in use by teams of the Division for Curricula Development.

The possibility is considered to set up a Ministry directed mechanism for checking and testing privately produced software, as for its approval for school use. However, there is yet no decision to implement this idea.

3.3 RESEARCH AND EVALUATION OF COMPUTER AIDED LEARNING

Most work in this field started with evaluation - formative and summative - but is changing gradually to more basic aspects of the research of computer based activities of learning, of the learning process and its strategies, of social and individual effects of large-scale exposure to computers.

Any large scale courseware producing project is requested to care for its own intrinsic, formative evaluation, as an integral part of the development process to check and improve the teaching materials and the methodologies.

Apart from this, there are three teams at Hebrew University in Jerusalem, at the Tel-Aviv University and at the Ben Gurion University in Beer Sheva dealing only with evaluation and research aspects.

At the Hebrew University, the first step was a survey of five computer aided learning systems used in our schools (Davis, 1983). Presently, they are dealing with CAL in three directions:

a. A study of capabilities of computers to improve the learning of basic skills as compared with conventional means at equal costs.

b. Field observation of learning and teaching activities, school operation and organization at primary schools using CAL systems.

c. Quasi-laboratory study of CAL: a "laboratory" having different systems installed in the same room, was set up in a school, geographically not far from the University. This is an adequate place for observation and study of the learning activities and processes, as well as comparative studies of a variety of systems and approaches.

First reports of these studies are expected in 1984-85.

The team at the Tel-Aviv University deals with formative evaluation tools for CAL systems, intended for use by courseware development teams. A branching of this project, will develop procedures for approval-

i.   The TOAM System

TOAM (Hebrew acronym to Computer Assisted Testing and Practice) is one of the first CAL systems implemented in Israel and the most widespread in our primary schools. It is based on a hardware system developed and produced by the Center for Educational Technology (Osin, 1984) - up to some 40 terminals driven by centralized, common computing power.

The operation of the TOAM system is based on the interaction of three models represented by adequate data bases: a model of the knowledge-subject matter, facts, procedures; a student's models representing his achievements and his relevant aptitudes; a pedagogical model, embodying the teaching strategy. Based on these models and on preliminary pupil's test, the system will deliver to each pupil an individualized sequence of practice and on-going testing.

The reports provided to the teacher help him to conduct his/her classroom activities, as well as to deal with the pupils on a small group or individual basis.

Subject matters, from the elementary school curricula, covered by the TOAM system are Arithmetic, Hebrew Reading Comprehension, English as a second language. The benefits of using TOAM, towards the progress in arithmetics are well accepted. For other subjects, large-scale evaluation is just under way (1983-84, 1984-85). Courseware is under development for similar subjects for the junior high school level and for several technical and scientific subjects at the high school level.

ii. The Ministry of Education Department for Computer Based Curricula

One of the main divisions within the Ministry of Education is the Division for Curricula Development - in charge of the development of curricula for the Israeli School System. Part of this development is done by teams employed directly by the Ministry, but the division has also the responsibility to coordinate activities of several institutes involved in curricular development.

As from 1983 a separate department within this division, is dedicated to the development of computer-based curricula (Feinstein, 1984).

One of the roles of this department is to help teams working in different areas to integrate adequate usage of computers, within the media selected for teaching. To accomplish this task, curricula-development teams had to learn about computers and their educational applications, methods of courseware production and methodologies for integrating the use of computer in curricula. At the time of writing this paper, this stage is completed and the first outputs of these teams are expected.

In many subject matters the syllabus is already available and steady, as well as teaching materials and methodology. However, even without major changes to the syllabus, the use of computers may be added to the existing materials, to improve teaching in general, the individualization of learning and the better adaptation of the teaching process to heterogeneous classes.

The approach for including computer usage into existing curricula seems to be quite innovative. It is not done by central dedicated teams. It is a decentralized, coordinated project, based on regional teams. The team members are acting teachers, dedicating mostly two days per week for courseware development.

Most of the work of these teams is concentrated in three main subject matters:

Hebrew (as a mother tongue): reading comprehension, vocabulary, language constructs, composition, grammar - grades 3-9.

English (as a foreign language): reading comprehension, grammatical constructs, vocabulary, language constructs - grades 5-10.

Arithmetics, Algegra and Geometry - grades 2-9.

Other subjects covered, but presently at a relatively small scale: Judaism, History, Biology, Physics, Chemistry, as well as some interdisciplinar integrative courseware packages, intended to help develop understanding of inter-relations between distinct subjects. When working with these integrative packages, the pupil has to use and coordinate the knowledge-domain of several, "separate" subject matters.

For each subject matter, there is a national coordinator, usually the head of the curricula development team for the specific subject, at the Division for Curricular Development at the Ministry of Education. For each one of the main subject matters, there is a regional coordination, working directly with the regional team of teachers. These teachers usually are from different schools, invited to join the teams accordingly to their teaching achievements, dedication and the estimated courseware production capability.

The national coordinator is working intensively with his regional partners but he will also meet periodically the whole regional team.

As in each region there are teams working on several subjects, there are locations dedicated to the work of the teams and local coordinators, dealing with common problems like computer facilities, software services and general administrative support.

This descentralized organization seems to be less efficient then having one centralized team using the same amount of manpower. However, it was adopted because of several advantages it offers:

a.   The possibility to use the talents of the school teachers without removing them from the schools.

b.   The on-going interaction between the acting teacher, the courseware team and the central curriculum specialists.

c.   The immediate effect on the school activity and the opening of the school to the penetration of computers - due to the influence of the teachers involved in courseware development.

Presently, this approach seems to be promising, but at least three years of activity may be required for being able to evaluate its merits.

iii. The MACAL and SML Systems

These two systems are among the pioneers of computer assisted learning in Israel (Barta and Behar, 1983).

MACAL (Multimedia Approach to Computer Aided Learning) is based on an overall approach to the teaching process, integrating teacher presentations, advice, discussions and problem solving; use of books and booklets; student-computer interaction for drill and practice, tutorials, remedial learning, simulation; use of other media under computer control or by teacher/computer assignment; use of computer gener-

testing of available courseware, mainly of commercial.

The Ben-Gurion University teams are going to look for answers to questions arised by the Ministry of Education about the implications and consequences of large scall penetration of computers into the entire range of institutions for education and culture. This project, executed by one institute, is to develop to a national project involving specialists from several institutions and hopefully providing results which may influence the educational and instructional philosophy at a national scale.

3.4 COMPUTERS IN EDUCATIONAL ADMINISTRATION

Even if several schools are using computers to help their educational administration the number of projects in this field is rather limited.

A project carried out by Institute of Teaching Aids in 1983-84 was involved with two aspects: the human and social aspects of introducing computers into the educational administration of schools of different types; survey of problems related to the use of such systems and checking to what extent their features are adequate to school needs.

For 1984-85 a systems analysis and feasibility study is planned towards a national network of computerized educational administration. Such a network should provide facilities at school level, as well as at local, regional and national levels.

4. OUTLINE OF IMPLEMENTATION

The main goal of this paper is to present the development and research efforts in Israel. Going into details of the implementation in the school system may result in a second paper of similar length.

The educational system in Israel is organized on a regional basis, centrally coordinated by the Ministry of Education. The framework of curricula, syllabuses and matriculation examinations are set by the Ministry. However, each municipality and township has its educational authorities, not directly dependent but cooperating with the Ministry. Accordingly, quite a big difference exists between the extent of the activities, the support and the development of local initiative at different parts of the country.

Three teams of the Ministry provide supervision, advice and support in the field of computers, to:

a.   high schools, dealing with grades 7 and up;
b.   elementary schools, up to the 6th grade;
c.   teachers training and updating.

There are some 1600 primary schools in Israel, out of them, 500-550 have computer systems (8-40 terminals or micro's, mostly 16 or more) in 1984-85. These systems are mainly used for computer aided learning and at some extent for computer literacy and computer clubs.

At the high school level, out of some 550 schools, computers are available in 1984-85 at about 400 (8-40 terminals per school, some having 16-20, a few schools more than 20).

The uses of computers in high-schools: teaching of Informatics at various levels, from introductory courses to advanced computer studies, vocational training of software and hardware professionals; vocational training related to computer applications in different professions. Computer-aided learning is not so widespread at the high school level, but its use is steadily broadening.

Out of 39 teachers training colleges, 37 are equipped with computers and provide computer studies to future teachers, the first course being a compulsory one.

All universities having Schools of Education are involved, even if at very different extents, with teaching, development and research of educational applications of computers. Teaching of educational computing is provided at graduate and undergraduate levels, but only two of the schools decided to have some of these courses compulsory for part of their students.

A network of teachers' computing centers is on its way to implementation. These centers have to provide a meeting place for teachers, where they may exchange ideas, but as well, find updated materials and computer equipment for their use and technical and pedagogical advice.

5. TRENDS FOR THE FUTURE

Considering the present extent of implementation of computers in our school system and the large-scale effort for development and teacher training, one may conclude that computers in education are well established and no one can more consider them as "another gadget -that may disappear within one or two years."

Most of the development and research described in this paper has to continue and to be brought to a successful completion - among them, most important and relatively slow and hard to accomplish, is the effort to bring the whole teaching body to a good knowledge of computers and their educational applications.

However, some new issues have to be considered and their implementation prepared:

Advanced Technologies. From the technological point of view, present systems are not yet using last technological development - advanced man-machine interaction (video, audio, etc.), mass-storage communication systems, advanced-integrated-intelligent learning delivery systems. One should expect to have all these (and other similar ones) entering schools, perhaps, as present equipment gets out-dated and changed, even if they should be first expected in training systems for advanced professional applications.

The Changing Emphasis of Computer Applications. It seems that in a gross way, the educational applications of computers can be divided into three main categories:

a.   CAL in its variety forms;

b.   Learning computer sciences at all levels;

c.   Free use of computers as an integral part of the study of different subjects.

Out of these applications, it seems clear that use of CAL can start at early stages, from first or second grade. Nevertheless, as already mentioned, some applications may develop from kindergarten already. CAL seems to be well established at elementary school. Its use may drop at higher grades - except if new developments may justify its widespread use at higher grades in high school.

Learning of Informatics may be rather limited at low grades, augment at 7th-10th grade and drop again at the higher ones.

The free use of computer is an application still to be defined and developed. It should start at about 7th-9th grade and be more dominant at the higher grades.

The School Environment and the Organization of Learning. Even if a lot of computing power is already available it is still far from being enough to allow free use for all types of educational activity at any time. Presently, few school can allow more than an average of one hour/week of terminal time per student. Also, not enough good quality applications and not enough initiated teachers are available to allow much broader use. We can foresee to have enough equipment and enough contents available to allow several weekly terminal hours to each student. At this stage, profound and far reaching changes of the whole learning process may occur.

On the other hand, computer-aided learning is pushing towards individualized learning, much stronger then existing non-computerized approaches. In places where most of the schooling is still based on conventional frontal class room teaching, this fact may cause overall changes of the whole school organization.

Nevertheless, as home computers linked to communication systems become available, one can foresee a much stronger link between the school based and home based activities of pupils and teachers as well.

The ideas raised in the last few paragraphs are not really new. The innovation is that one may feel such profound changes of the educational system, being on their way to happen, under our eyes, within time lags not much bigger then between the writing of a paper and its presentation at a World Conference.

6.   SUMMARY AND ACKNOWLEDGEMENT

The intention of this paper is to provide information about the main trends of the development and implementation as it can be seen from a national overview. It did not attempt to present a more profound, scientific or philosophical approach to the whole issue.

Much effort was invested to mention institutes and references to those involved in developing and implementing these ideas. Even if many of the ideas and actions described in this paper were proposed and developed in full cooperation with the author of this paper and other persons from the Ministry - it is clear that the main part of the work was done by the teams in charge of the projects and the respective team leaders. All persons involved have to be acknowledged for their work and dedication.

Finally, full acknowledgement is given to all personalities deciding upon the educational policy, administration and budgeting, who did appreciate the importance of the new technologies, provided the necessary funding and support to enable these important actions.

REFERENCES

1.   Adereth, A., Barta, B.Z., Naaman, S. and Telem, M., Integrating Informatics Within the Vocational High School Curricula for the Business Professions. IIVCE,* 1984.

2.   Barta, B.Z., Computers in the Israeli Educational System, Proc. of World Conf. on Computers in Education (WCCE-81), North Holland, 1981.

3.   Barta, B.Z., Behar, Z., Shorek, M. and Schlesinger, C., Adapting Microcomputers to Medium Scale Educational Uses, Microcomputer: Developments in Industry, Business, and Education (Proceedings - Euromicro 1983), North Holland, 1983.

4.   Barta, B.Z., Osin, L., Nahmias, R., Snir, J. and Pery, A., Computer Literacy Within the Educational System, internal report (in Hebrew), 1983.

5.   Cohen, D., An Introduction to Computer Controlled Systems Using a Laboratory Trainer. IIVCE,* 1984.

6.   Davis, D., Heller, A., Finkelstein, T. and Kaufman, L., Computed Aided Learning, A Survey of Five Systems (in Hebrew), Pub. No. 94, NCJW Research Institute for Innovations in Education, the Hebrew University in Jerusalem, Dec. 1983.

7.   Feinstein, B., Integrating the Computer into Curricula Design (in Hebrew), Maase Hoshev, Vol. 11, No. 2, May 1984.

8.   Levyn, G. and Snir, J., Computer Activities in the Kindergarten (in Hebrew), Oranim internal reports, June-December 1983.

9.   Margalit, M., Trends of Courseware Development for Children with Special Needs (in Hebrew), internal report, Tel-Aviv University, 1984.

10.   Millin, D. and Barta, B.Z., In-Service and Pre-Service Training of Primary School Teachers in Informatics and Computer Applications in Education. Working Conference on Informatics and Teaching Training, U.K., July 1984.

11.   Nachmias, R., Miodusar, D. and Chen, D., Cognitive and Curricular Model for Teaching Programming to Children, in these proceedings.

12.   Osin, L., Toam: C.A.I. on a National Scale, Proceedings of 1984 Jerusalem Conference on Information Technology, North Holland, 1984.

13.   Pelles, Y., Computer Literacy in Israeli High Schools, Computers in Education, North Holland, 1975.

14.   Regev, J., Teaching and Thinking and Computers in Problem Solving Methodology, WCCE 85, in these proceedings.

15.   Sagiv, A., Barta, B.Z. and Behar, Z., Integrating CAD/CAM Concepts into Curricula for Vocational and Continuing Education. IIVCE,* 1984.

16.   Subcommittee on Telematics in Education, Employment and Society, Interim Report (in Hebrew), National Council for Research and Development, March 1984.

17.   Waks, S., Courseware Development - An Essential Ingredient of Technological Teacher Education Curricula. IIVCE,* 1984.

*Impact of Informatics on Vocational and Continuing Education (Proceedings of 1984 Jerusalem Working Conference), North Holland, 1984.

COMPUTERS IN EDUCATION, K. Duncan and D. Harris (eds.)
Elsevier Science Publishers B.V. (North-Holland)
© IFIP, 1985

CREATING A NATIONAL COMPUTER EDUCATION PROGRAM: THE AUSTRALIAN BEGINNING

JUDITH H. HAMMOND, F.A.C.S.

Curriculum Development Centre,
Canberra, Australia

Computers have been incorporated into educational practice by most States in
Australia for more than a decade, but their penetration has not been even
across all States nor in all schools. The problems of lack of coordination in
the massive introduction of computers into schools in the 1980's and the
inequity that has arisen in the opportunities that all students have to learn
about and with computers have become increasingly apparent. In 1983, the
Federal government took initiatives to address these problems. This paper
Program, its recommendations and the initial activities being undertaken.

1. INTRODUCTION

Australia is sometimes described as "The Big
Country", and this is indeed true. The total
land mass is about the same size as the U.S.A.
Most of Australia is an extensive inland semi-
desert, with very few inhabitants other than
farmers (mainly cattle and sheep), miners
(coal, iron ore and many other minerals) and
aborigines (the original inhabitants of the
island continent). The great majority of people
live along the coastal areas, particularly on
the east and southeast coasts. These areas are
becoming more and more urbanised with the State
capital cities being the largest centres of
population in each State. In fact, the two
capitals of Sydney and Melbourne account for
nearly half the country's total population of
14.3 million (3.3 million and 2.7 million respectively). Therefore, education for all Australians means that educational programmes must be
able to be used in both large concentrated
cities and towns and in isolated farmsteads and
places where children may only be able to
receive lessons by radio and correspondence.

Australia operates as a Federation, with seven
States and the Australian Capital Territory (the
location of the national government). In the
Australian Constitution, education is identified
as a State responsibility. Each State therefore
has its own Education Department and conducts
its own system of schools, independent of other
States. To compound the situation, in each
State there are non-government school systems.
These systems are independent of the State education systems, but interact with them when necessary, such as for the preparation and conduct
of public examinations at the end of secondary
schooling. They receive some grants and subsidies from Federal and State treasuries.

One of the Australian federal government departments is that of Education within which lies the
Commonwealth Schools Commission with a particular responsibility for school age children, aged
from 5 to 18 years. A prime concern of the

Department is to provide and disperse money for
all aspects of Australian education in the form
of funds and grants. It undertakes research and
development work seen as beneficial for education throughout Australia. From time to time the
Department may initiate new programs and projects in cooperation with the States, usually
acting as coordinator, and frequently as the
principal funding body.

2. COMPUTER EDUCATION IN THE STATES

By 1983, most secondary and some primary schools
in Australia, particularly in the secondary
area, had acquired computers to enhance the
processes of learning and teaching. Initiatives
had come from a variety of sources - enthusiastic teachers and teacher associations, parents,
community groups and some State education authorities. At best, the computer was seen as a
way of improving the whole educational process.
More frequently computers were purchased
because:

(a) they were fun;
(b) a neighbouring school had acquired
    one;
(c) it was a generally held notion that
    children learned better, even
    though there was little evidence
    to prove this;
(d) there was a generally held view
    that it was essential for children
    to learn about computers, as
    computers were found everywhere
    else in society and therefore
    should also be in schools.

The choice of microcomputer brand used in each
State has generally been left to the individual
schools to decide. After long and careful
assessment of hardware and supporting software,
each State has placed some microcomputers on
government contract for a period of one or two
years, guaranteeing maintenance and software
support. The only brand of microcomputer to be
used in every State is the Apple IIE. Other

machines on contract are the BBC microcomputer
(6 States), the Microbee - an Australian made
micro (3 States), and a variety of other brands
in individual States, such as Atari, Commodore
and IBM-PC.

The first education authorities to coordinate
computing activities within their States were
the smaller States, and in particular, Tasmania.
Starting before the advent of microcomputers,
they have developed computer education to an
advanced state. Tasmania, in particular, now
has an extensive network using minicomputers
supporting terminals in schools, colleges and
other educational institutions throughout the
State, with all activities being focused on the
Elizabeth Computer Centre.

Individual schools at many locations throughout
Australia have been incorporating computers into
their classroom teaching for a number of years.
However several States have only just taken
steps to support these computing practices by
promoting computer education to an area of high
priority and by introducing the systematic
development of computer education. This has
generally been accomplished by the production of
policy documents and by the establishment of a
central agency in the form of a Computer Centre
or Computer Unit. Table 1 summarises factors
relevant to the State situation.

State	Policy Document	Computer Centre/Unit Established	Staff Employed
NEW SOUTH WALES	Yes	1983	7
VICTORIA	Yes	1983	7
QUEENS- LAND	Yes	1983	9.5
SOUTH AUSTRALIA	Yes	1976	13
WEST AUSTRALIA	Yes	1978	11
TASMANIA	Yes	1974	22
NORTHERN TERRITORY	Yes	1984	4
AUSTRALIAN CAPITAL TERRITORY	Yes	1985	4

Table 1.   Commitment of Australian States
           to Computing in Schools

From the recent date of the policy documents in
several States it can be seen that the initial
planning of courses is still being undertaken.
It is interesting to note that all States are
committed to developing, or are already
teaching, Computer Awareness or Computer Literacy courses and that on the whole, Computer
Studies courses are confined to the senior
secondary years, or being given a lower priority
than Computer Awareness/ Computer Literacy.

The more active States have had time to develop
their own areas of expertise. South Australia
is placing a major emphasis on integrating computers across the curriculum. Western Australia
is working extensively on Computer Assisted
Learning and has moved its emphasis toward the
European model of "informatique", by introducing
a course in Information Processing rather than
Computer Studies. Tasmania has been working
vigorously on databases and their uses in particular subject areas. It has provided two very
popular packages, Birds of Antartica and The
First Fleet, for distribution to secondary
schools throughout Australia. These curriculum
materials, which include teachers' guides and
student work sheets, were undertaken as Information Technology Week initiatives (1).

3.   THE NATIONAL INITIATIVE

3.1 In The Beginning

In February 1983, the Commonwealth Schools Commission released its recommendations for 1984
and stated that a program of computer education
in all Australian schools was of vital importance to Australia's future. The Commission saw
this national program being directed toward

    (a) the development of computing skills in
        teachers and students,

    (b) an awareness of the importance and
        possibilities of high technology,

    (c) the use of computers in the teaching
        and learning practices of schools.

3.2 Funds for the Computer Education Program

The Commonwealth Schools Commission felt that it
was not possible for the States to provide all
the necessary resources to implement an adequate
program within the short time span they planned,
and concluded that the Commonwealth Schools
Commission itself should assist by providing
the substantial additional financial resources
necessary. The sum of $125 million over 5 years
was seen as being the amount needed to achieve
their objectives.

Australia held an election in March 1983, and
both major political parties promised support
for computer education. At about the same time
that the government changed, with the Labour
Party being successful in the 1983 election,

the Commonwealth Schools Commission appointed the National Advisory Committee on Computers in Schools. The Committee was requested to provide a report by 30 September, 1983. The new Minister for Education, Senator the Hon. Susan Ryan, announced the Guidelines for the 1984 Schools Commission Programme and indicated that $18.7 million would be available in equal amounts for each of the years in the 1984-86 triennium for a Computer Education Program. Thus, the amount of financial assistance was significantly reduced. In 1984, $A4.987 million of that total was provided for government schools and $A1.247 million for non-government schools, making $A6.234million in all. This was a significant reduction in the money actually made available from that proposed originally and will no doubt affect the number and possibly the quality of the outcomes from the Report.

3.3 Structure and terms of reference

The National Advisory Committee on Computers in Schools was made up of 23 various State educational representatives. The membership included education department officers from all States and Territories and from the Commonwealth Schools Commission, and representatives from the Department of Science and Technology, the non-government and Catholic school organisations, the Teachers Federation, and the Australian Parents Council. The Schools Commission gave the Advisory Committee the following terms of reference:

" * The use of computers in schools as they relate to the educational needs of boys and girls enrolled in primary, secondary and special schools;

 * The rationale for a national program, including desirable short and long term educational, social and economic outcomes;

 * An implementation plan, and associated guidelines, for the introduction of a national Schools Computing Program into primary, secondary and special schools, including its integration with State and non-government schools policies and provisions. This plan will include options for the allocation of funds among States and sectors, advice on the minimum standards of provision, and on ways of achieving an equitable sharing of resources and services across Australia;

 * A plan for generating and supporting discussion and awareness within the community and especially within school communities of school computing and its applications;

 * Evaluation activities relating to computing in schools and to the provision and operation of the proposed national program" (2).

The Schools Commission immediately formed six working parties to provide expert advice in a number of broad areas. It is interesting to note that whilst the Advisory Committee was representative in nature, members of the Technical Working parties were chosen for their expertise. The Advisory Committee also sought consultations with a range of national organisations involved with, or interested in, the use of computers in schools.

3.4 The Working Parties' Task

There were 46 people spread over the Technical Working Parties, with some Schools Commission personnel participating in several Parties. Their task was to advise the Advisory Committee on the following areas:

 * Professional Development
 * Curriculum Development
 * Software/courseware
 * Hardware
 * Evaluation
 * Support Services

These Working Parties met several times over four months and produced comprehensive reports for the Advisory Committee in August, 1983. As a member of the Curriculum Development Working Party, I found the meetings with fellow experts who were drawn from various parts of Australia to be most stimulating, as I had never previously had the opportunity to meet them all in a working atmosphere. It is interesting to reflect that although the time frame was short, and the nature of the task so wide-ranging, the final documents were of a consistently high quality. It is unlikely that their reports would have been much more comprehensive had the Parties been given several more months to complete the task.

3.5 Producing The Report

The Advisory Committee was then set the task of creating the Report for the Commonwealth Schools Commission. Fifty two recommendations came from the Working Parties' reports, as shown in Table 2. Evaluation was included throughout the reports.

Working Party	No. of Recommendations
Curriculum Development	8
Professional Development	9
Support Services	10
Software/Courseware	11
Hardware	8
Organisation	6

Table 2. Recommendations from the Working Parties

These recommendations were debated and agreed to by the National Advisory Committee on Computers

in Schools, except for two statements of diss-
ent. The dissents were specifically concerned
with the hardware recommendations, which were
advising short-term support in terms of purchase, provision of maintenance, and development
of software and courseware for three specific
brands of microcomputer. These recommendations
were not endorsed by the Commonwealth Schools
Commission.

The number of recommendations is too numerous to
discuss individual ones in this paper. They can
be found in the Commonwealth Schools Commission
report mentioned in (2). The most important
aspects of the recommendations endorsed by the
Schools Commission are the need to:

* move towards more equal educational
  outcomes for students, particularly when
  involving the new technologies in education;

* give priority initially to the professional development of teachers,
  particularly in terms of inservice
  courses, as well as preservice training
* at the school level, involve parents,
  teachers and students in the decision-
  making processes, especially in relation
  to the purchase and use of computers in
  schools.

The Commonwealth Schools Commission's view of
the introduction of new technologies into the
school situation is that there should be a close
examination of the social, economic, political
and cultural consequences of the new technologies, and it identifies that the most important
courses to introduce are those relating to computer awareness and computer literacy.

4. IMPLEMENTATION OF THE COMPUTERS IN SCHOOLS REPORT

There was little visible activity evidenced
between the time the Commonwealth Schools Commission endorsed the report in October 1983 and
its acceptance by the Government in mid-
February, 1984. Since that time, much initial
organisation has been put in place, at both the
Federal and the State levels.

The Commonwealth stance is one of being a partner, ready to support the initiatives already
undertaken within the States, and being sensitive to

" the emerging needs which can best be met by
  central support and co-ordination" (3)

as stated by the Federal Minister for Education,
Hon. Susan Ryan. She emphasises the following
points:

" * We are making a national effort to bring
    a high standard of technological aware-
    ness and skill among all Australian

children, which is the way towards sharing the rewards of technological change
among all Australians.

* We are going to approach computer education in terms of a broad computer educational program, rather than simply as
  an exercise in hardware provision. The
  central themes here are building a capacity to generate Australian content with
  sound educational values across the broad
  range of school subjects; and developing
  a teacher force capable of using computers to the advantage of all children in
  school." (4)

5. THE INITIAL DIRECTION

The structure of the National Computer Education
Program has now been put in place. The Commonwealth Schools Commission has formed a new
National Advisory Committee on Computers in
Schools, which is deliberating on various aspects of the Report's recommendations and how
they can be implemented. Four Working Parties
have been set up to discuss the following issues
and present their findings to the National
Advisory Committee early in 1985. The areas
covered are:

* software
* educational specifications of hardware
* technical specifications of hardware
* extension of the program to encompass
  primary schools

Each state has now appointed Advisory Committees, a separate one for the government and non-
government education sectors although in some
States these Committees have been combined.
These Committees work on a state level in conjunction with the National Advisory Committee.
Money granted to the States for 1984 has been
allocated to particular tasks by State Committees, with the approval of the Commonwealth
Schools Commission. First priority has been
given to teacher training with the acquisition
of computer hardware being seen as having the
least case for the use of grant moneys.

The State Committees are currently assessing the
1985 projects which will receive grants once the
proposals have been reviewed by the National
Advisory Committee. Professional Development
programs have already been substantially expanded in the States to enable more teachers to gain
inservice training on many different aspects of
computer education.

In 1984, the Curriculum Development Centre was
established as a Division of the Commonwealth
Schools Commission. It is primarily concerned
with researching into curricula matters; devising, developing and publishing school curricula
and school educational materials; and providing
information relating to these materials. In
early 1985, plans had been approved and funds

granted to create an Information Technology in the Curriculum Program, within the Curriculum Development Centre. This Program will develop and produce software and courseware materials of high quality for use in all Australian schools and will undertake research into various aspects of computer education which are of national importance. For example, a project has been established to research into the feasibility of establishing a national software clearinghouse. Initial software and courseware materials developed and produced by the Curriculum Development Centre will include a handwriting program and an economics and geography package. Many of these materials will be suitable for use by educators in countries outside Australia.

It is not possible to report any substantial results from the National Computer Education Program yet. However, there are two observations that can be made. The first relates to the general feeling of consensus that now exists in all States in Australia. The Commonwealth Schools Commission Report has been very favourably received in most quarters. It builds on initiatives which were already taking place, thus confirming, in each State's pre-existing philosophy, the directions that they were already taking. This has acted as a stimulus to some State governments to provide additional money for their own systems to further enhance computer education. It has also introduced additional considerations for teachers and educational systems to explore within the framework of computer education with some degree of certainty that they will be supported by the Commonwealth Schools Commission.

Secondly, planning for the national program has enabled many experts from many areas of computer education to come together for the first time, and discuss issues and directions in a working environment. In a country where there are great distances between major population centres, this interaction is not common, and thus this has been a most valuable outcome in itself.

REFERENCES:

[1] Hammond, J., The Challenge of Change: Information Technology and the Community, in Mason (ed.), Information Processing (North-Holland, Amsterdam, 1983).

[2] National Advisory Committee on Computers in Schools, Teaching, Learning and Computers: a report (Commonwealth Schools Commission, 1983).

[3] Commonwealth Schools Commission, Teaching, Learning and Computers: 1984 Information Kit (Commonwealth Schools Commission, 1984)

[4] ibid

COMPUTERS IN EDUCATION, K. Duncan and D. Harris (eds.)
Elsevier Science Publishers B.V. (North-Holland)
© IFIP, 1985

LARGE-SCALE MULTI-MEDIA COMPUTER COURSES IN BELGIUM

Prof. Dr. Carlos R. DE BACKER, director computer center

Antwerp University - UFSIA, Prinsstraat 13,
B - 2000 ANTWERP, BELGIUM

In most Western countries the unemployment level is very high. Besides the
economic situation in the world, the poor adaptation of some people to the new
technologies has widely been accepted to be another main reason.

In order to meet these important needs of computer education, the Belgian
Ministery of Employment started a large scale educational project. In this
presentation I would like to present the actual situation of the project. All
comments will be helpful in order to improve this ambitious project in the next
few years.

1. OBJECTIVES.

The objectives of the project can be summarized
as follows :

1. To give the opportunity to a large group of
   people to study an introductory computer
   course in order to minimize the fear for
   new technologies ;

2. To give a practical computer knowledge to
   unemployed people in order to improve their
   employment chances in the near future ;

3. To give the opportunity to employed people
   to study various computer courses in order
   to let them understand the fast changing
   working conditions ;

4. To give the opportunity to computer
   professionals to broaden their general
   computer knowledge.

So the project aimed at four different groups
of people :

1. the unemployed people ;

2. the employed people with minor computer
   knowledge ;

3. the computer professionals ;

4. a secondary (but very large) group of people
   without computer education.

2. THE EDUCATIONAL PROGRAM

   Three separate initiatives have been taken :

   1. an introductary course on computers ;

   2. an educational program on week days ;

   3. an educational program on saturday.

SCHEMA

INTRODUCTION TO COMPUTERS

I

I

PROGRAM LOGIC

I

MANAGEMENT	ANALYSIS	PROGRAMMING
computer audit	systems analysis	BASIC
office automation	systems design	COBOL
design of packages		PASCAL
		PL/I
		RPG

2.1 The introductory course

The objective of this introductory course
was to give a general understanding of
computer technology. In order to reach
a large group of people various communication
media have been used : television, radio,
books, oral presentations.

Television : twelve 30' programs on thursday
              (7.00 P.M.) giving a general
              introduction and illustration
              of computers
              topics :
              1. computers in society
              2. What's a computer ?
              3. Input devices - input
                 instructions in programming
              4. Output devices - output
                 instructions in programming
              5. CPU - arithmetic and logic
                 instructions
              6. programming (structured
                 charts)
              7. external memory
              8. system software
              9. systems analysis
              10. networks
              11. office automation
              12. the future ?

Radio   : twelve 30' live programs used
             to answer various questions

Book   : study and reference guide for
             students. Television programs
             were illustrations of the
             chapters in the book.

Presentations : hands-on experience for
              students (programming, spread-
              sheet applications, ...)

Results   : 25000 books have been sold
              10000 people came to the
              hands-on sessions

2.2 The educational program on weekdays

The educational program on computers running
on weekdays is limited to unemployed people.
Two main initiatives have been taken :
   1. A condensed program on computers
      (12 weeks)
      curriculum : programming logic
                   programming languages
                      (Basic, Pascal, Cobol,
                      RPG)
                   systems analysis
                   introduction to data bases
      results : 120 students - employment
                rate 75% (June 1984)

   2. specific computer training in
      cooperation with computer manufacturers.
      Students are trained to manage mini and
      microcomputers in business administrations.
      results : 500 students - employment
                rate 95% (June 1984)

2.3 The educational program on saturday

The educational program on computers running
on saturday is open for all people : employed
and unemployed. Only regular students
registered at schools or universities are
the only exceptions.

Various courses are offered :

- programming logic (flow-chart, structured
  chart ...) ;
  duration (16 hours)

- programming languages (25% theory -
  75% exercices)
  BASIC (32 hours)
  COBOL (80 hours)
  PL/I   (80 hours)
  RPG   (48 hours)
  PASCAL (48 hours)

- systems analysis (96 hours)
- systems design (96 hours)
- introduction to data bases (96 hours)
- introduction to data communications

                  (32 hours)

- computer audit (48 hours)
- analysis and programming of an accountancy
  package (96 hours)
- office automation and text processing

                  (32 hours)

All courses are taught by members of Belgian
undergraduate and graduate institutions.
Courses run on saturday from 8.00 a.m. -
5.00 p.m.. Admittance to a course is
controlled by a preliminary test. Registration
to all courses is free.

results : 5000 students a year

3. PLANNING

In the next few years considerable efforts
must be done to improve the curriculum
in order to guarantee the quality of the
programs. Very probably new courses must
be offerred in order to meet the changing
requirements of our society.

Ackowledgements

I would like to thank Mr. Boudeweel and
Mr. Demeyere for the numerous discussions
on the topic and Mrs E. Vandenbergh for the
fast and accurate typing of this manuscript.

COMPUTERS IN EDUCATION, K. Duncan and D. Harris (eds.)
Elsevier Science Publishers B.V. (North-Holland)
© IFIP, 1985

COMPUTER EDUCATION IN ECUADOR:
AN ECONOMIC, SOCIOLOGICAL, AND POLITICAL ANALYSIS

Janet Palmer, Ed.D.

Western Kentucky University
Bowling Green, Kentucky 42101 U.S.A.

Economic, sociological, and political implications of computer education in Ecuador
are examined. Because similarities exist regarding the use of hardware, software,
programming languages, and instructional applications, computer education is seen as
a means of promoting greater international understanding. Ecuadorean problems include
a shortage of qualified computer instructors, insufficient computer equipment, lack of
Spanish software and documentation, economic resources for the funding of computer education programs, and fears of job displacement because of automation. Computer education is suggested as a viable means for enabling "have not" nations to join the "have"
nations. Computer educators are challenged to play control roles in this process.

This paper presents the results of an investigation made of the status of computer education
in Ecuador during May, 1984. The investigation
was conducted as part of an assignment from
Partners of the Americas, a United States Government agency which aids developing nations.
The agency had received a request to send an
educational consultant in computer education to
Ecuador to help a school there establish such a
program. Acceptance of that assignment provided
a unique opportunity to observe first hand the
efforts of a "have-not" nation trying to ensure
that its children receive an education to enable
them to compete with the "have" nations.

METHOD

The investigation was conducted in some of the
major cities of Ecuador. These cities included
the capital, Quito, and Santo Domingo de los
Colorados, Otavalo, and Cuenca. The method
employed in the study involved empirical observation and personal interviews. Visits were
made to the organizations employing the largest
number of computer personnel--banks. These
banks included the Banco Central, Ecuador's
national bank and its largest, and the Filan-
banco, the second largest bank in Ecuador.
Several educational institutions were visited
which offered computer instruction--Centro de
Programacion de Sistemas Electronicas and the
Colegio Alberto Einstein. In addition, students,
graduates, or directors representing other educational institutions which offered computer
education were interviewed. These included the
University Central, Ecuador's largest national
university, Catholic University, Polytechnic
Institute, and the Binational Center Ecuatoriano
Norte Americano. Two representative computer
vendors were also visited--IBM and Apple.

Discussions were held with directors of two
government agencies. One of these interviews
was at the Ministry of Education with the Supervisor for Pichincha, the province which includes
the capital city. The other interview was with
the director of SECAP (Servicio Ecuatoriano de
Capacitacion Profesional). This agency, comparable to the former CETA operation in the
United States, was interested in establishing
computer training as one of its programs.

AVAILABILITY AND QUALITY

In the United States computer education is
rapidly becoming available at all educational
levels and in almost all educational programs of
study. In Ecuador computer education can be
found at the postsecondary level, the private
secondary school level, and at private commercial schools. Thus far, the public elementary
and secondary schools have not begun programs in
computer education.

The majority of computer scientists and information systems professionals in Ecuador receive
their training at Ecuadorean universities, both
public and private, the Polytechnic Institute,
or the Government Military School. Some computer professionals receive their training at
universities in the United States or Europe.

Just as in universities in the United States,
students in computer science in Ecuador complain
about the lack of sufficient terminals with
which to do their work. For example, at what is
generally regarded to be the best place at which
to study computer science in Ecuador--the Polytechnic Institute--one student said that all
students in the program had access to only two
terminals. This limited access, however, did
not seem to affect the quality of instruction.
All of the employers appeared to have the highest respect for graduates of these computer
science programs in higher education. These
graduates were employed as systems directors and
analysts in the largest and most prominent
organizations in Ecuador, in both the public and
private sectors.

Interestingly, no sexual division of labor seems to exist in either the study of computer science or in the practice of it. Both men and women were found employed in the field. In the United States, especially at the secondary-school level, females often shun technical/mathematics oriented programs of study. Such an inclination among females did not seem prevalent in Ecuador.

Postsecondary training in computers can also be obtained at private computer schools. At these small institutions the amount of equipment was limited too. For example, at one school with an enrollment of 250 students, only one Atari microcomputer using tape cassettes and two IBM dumb terminals were available. This school, however, was expecting a shipment of twelve Commodore 64 microcomputers, which could be expected to improve the quality of instruction.

Unlike the fine comments heard from Ecuadorean employers regarding the quality of computer instruction in higher education, no such favorable comments were heard about these private commercial computer schools. Employers indicated that graduates of these proprietary schools generally were only prepared to handle routine, entry-level positions, such as data-entry operator.

To compensate for the lack of a large pool of highly trained computer specialists, many organizations offered on-the-job training in computers. Employees were selected for such training on the basis of test scores for numerical aptitude and general level of educational attainment. The on-the-job computer training also included secretaries using word processors. Just as is common in the United States, secretaries received a few days training either on- or offsite and a hefty manual with the purchase of such equipment. The use of word processing was observed to be quite limited in business in Ecuador unlike in the United States. For example, in the capital city of Quito there are only twenty IBM Displaywriters. In a similar vein, Ecuadorean organizations are not offering instruction to their employees in the use of personal computers because these are also notably absent from business desk tops. The use of computers in Ecuador is still very much a mainframe-to-terminal operation. One area, however, where the microcomputer is rapidly making some inroads is at the private secondary school level.

A MODEL PROGRAM

A model computer education program was observed at the Colegio Alberto Einstein in Quito. This Hebrew institution has an enrollment of 400 students in grades 9-12 and a faculty of 16. The school began its program in computer instruction in May, 1984, after a six-month planning period. The decision to incorporate computer education into the curriculum was done because of the experiences of the school's curriculum director,

who received her doctorate in educational administration at The Ohio State University. During her doctoral study period in the United States, she became familiar with the use of computers in education and carried back with her the desire to implement such a curriculum in Ecuador. As part of the planning, she and the school's chief director visited the head-quarters office in the United States of the Southern Association of Secondary Schools and Colleges. The Colegio is accredited by this agency. The agency assisted the directors in gathering information about implementing a computer education program and suggested model programs to visit in the New Orleans area. With this assistance the directors have implemented a computer education program.

The curriculum consists of instruction in BASIC and PASCAL computer programming languages. In addition, computers are used for instruction in mathematics, keyboarding, and teaching English as a second language. Word processing is taught to secondary-school age students using Applewriter II software (80 columns), and the elementary-age students use Bank Street Writer (40 columns).

The computer laboratory is a modern, well-equipped facility. The equipment was purchased through fund-raising activities of the PTA and friends of the school. The equipment consists of ten modular student work stations with ten Apple lle microcomputers in a Corvus network with four Imagewriter dot matrix printers. Other equipment includes a large Sony television monitor for demonstration teaching, a dust-less board, and a surge protector. As additional funds become available, plans include the purchase of additional microcomputers.

Instruction on the computers is provided by a native of Ecuador who received his Bachelor's degree in Computer Science from Arizona State University. He was recruited for teaching by an advertisement in the Quito newspaper. In addition to instructing students, he is also conducting in-service training for the faculty. Two, ten-hour courses have already been given, and more courses are planned.

Obtaining appropriate instructional materials in Spanish has been a difficult problem for the Colegio. The relatively few English-speaking instructors must spend long hours translating English programming instructions and equipment manuals into Spanish. The computer laboratory material shown in figure 1 displays a small portion of a translated equipment manual. According to the curriculum director, students have shown a dramatic increase in their desire to learn English because of the lack of Spanish software and documentation.

LABORATORIO DE COMPUTACION.- Guia de Practica

LAB #1   NOMBRE: _____

FECHA: _____   CURSO: _____

CONOZCA A SU "APPLE IIe"

OBJETIVO

- Familiarizarse con el uso del teclado y el monitor de
la computadora.

TABLERO DEL TECLADO

El tablero se usa para entrar y editar informacion e
instrucciones.

El tablero se usa de la misma manera que una maquina de
escribir. A medida que se escribe, la informacion
aparece en su monitor. El tablero de teclado es
similar a una ordinaria maquina de escribir; sin
embargo las teclas de la computadora tienen una
ventaja: si ustedes sostienen una tecla aplastada por
mas de un segundo, el caracter (letras, numeros,
puntuacion y otros) generado se repite.

Figure 1 : Translated computer manual

The Colegio Alberto Einstein appears to be developing a high-quality program, which could be the envy of many schools in the United States. The Colegio's curriculum, instructional materials, methodology, and equipment could easily be compared favorably with any computer education program in the United States. With so many similarities existing among programs and approaches, computer education might have the potential to become a great unifying force for international understanding. Several obstacles must be overcome, however, before that potential can become a reality, at least in Latin America.

OBSERVATIONS

One serious obstacle to the implementation of computer education programs in Ecuador that schools must contend with relates to the overall economic condition of third world nations. The Government of Ecuador is in deep debt and is not likely to spend its limited funds on the purchase of computers for its nation's public schools. This lack of funds also impacts on the number of teachers than can become computer literate and aware of the potential of the computer in the classroom. Elementary teachers in Ecuador are trained in two-year "normal" schools and do not receive training in programs in computer education. Secondary school teachers

receive their education in their subject matter disciplines at the universities. Consequently, students trained in computer science are recruited typically by business, government, and industry. Salaries in Ecuador for teachers are very low--about $200 a month or less; therefore, schools cannot compete in the marketplace for computer science graduates. Many schools are requesting help in training teachers in computers from international agencies and universities. The private commercial schools solve this problem of a lack of qualified computer instructors by using employed computer professionals to teach on a part-time basis.

Besides a shortage of computer instructors, Ecuadorean schools have faced difficulties in obtaining computer equipment. Until March, 1984, a Government ban existed for two years on the sale of imported computers. This restriction was in effect because of the problem with Ecuador's trade deficit. With the lifting of this ban, schools with funding will at least be able to acquire computer equipment without resorting to unusual means.

Another good indicator of the willingness of Ecuador to enter the computer age was exhibited during the last election in May, 1984. The winning candidate used on his campaign posters

a slogan which stated that through technology
Ecuador could achieve greater economic development. In general, Ecuadoreans, both public and
private citizens alike, seem enthusiastic and
confident that computers will play a leading
role in the nation's future.

One exception to this confidence was expressed
by a Government official concerning the effect
of automation on job displacement. In a developing nation with a large, unskilled population,
automation could lead to even greater unemployment and class division than exists now. The
United States has greater economic resources
and a work force with a higher educational level
than does Ecuador. Yet job displacement and job
retraining remain a big issue among companies
and union officials as well as among private
individuals confronted with the problem of job
loss. No easy solution has become apparent for
the United States. The issue is not likely to
be dismissed lightly either by third world
nations in considering the future directions for
education in their respective countries.

CONCLUSION

A first-hand observation of the emerging computer education movement in Ecuador provided an
opportunity to witness some of its driving
forces. These forces include the economic,
sociological, and political implications of computer education. While these forces might well
affect any educational movement, they appear
particularly critical for third world nations.
Computer educators are in effect equipping students with a powerful tool with the potential to
change their world. How computer educators
respond to this challenge might profoundly
affect the course of world history.

COMPUTERS IN EDUCATION, K. Duncan and D. Harris (eds.)
Elsevier Science Publishers B.V. (North-Holland)
© IFIP, 1985

UNIVERSITY EDUCATION IN COMPUTER SCIENCE AND TECHNOLOGY: THE NEW IRANIAN PLAN

Behrooz Parhami

Sharif University of Technology
Tehran, Iran

The closure of Iranian universities for 2.5 years starting in June of 1980 was unfortunate in many respects, but it did provide an opportunity for revising the academic curricula and sketching a master plan for university education in the field of computer science and technology. The plan, which is described in this paper, comprises integrated hardware/software programs for training computer specialists at three levels: (1) Technicians for routine activities -- 2 to 2.5 years; (2) Experts for non-routine engineering work -- 4 to 5 years; and (3) Senior Experts for R&D and education -- 6 to 7 years. Each program is designed with a view on projected job market demands and with the aim of training specialists who possess the common language needed for effective communication among team members. The programs described in this paper are being offered by seven major universities in Iran.

1. BACKGROUND

In a 1977 paper [1], it was proposed that three bodies must be established in order to deal with the unpleasant state of informatics affairs in Iran:

a. The Informatics High Council for coordinating informatics projects, conducting standardization activities, and supporting large-scale research and development programs.
b. The Council of Informatics Education for planning and coordinating all educational programs in informatics at a national level.
c. The Iranian Computer Society for maintaining a high standard of work within the computing profession and promoting cooperation and exchange of ideas among computer specialists.

All three bodies have since been established in one form or another.

The Informatics High Council, initially called "The National Commission for Informatics", was officially formed in June of 1979. The functions of the second proposed council have been delegated to a special "Computer Committee" within the "Cultural Revolution Headquarters" (C^3RH). Finally, the Informatics Society of Iran (ISI) was inaugurated in September of 1978, following two years of planning by a group of concerned computer specialists, and presently has more than 600 members.

Many of the inadequacies, for which these bodies were created, are still with us. There are also additional problems resulting from the new socioeconomic order. Nevertheless, these bodies have managed to take important steps for the solution of the most pressing problems. The educational planning of C^3RH, which is reported in this paper, is one such example.

The sociopolitical closure of Iranian universities, under the "Cultural Revolution" slogan, in June of 1980 provided an opportunity for revising the academic curricula and sketching a master plan for university education in the field of computer science and technology. The plan slowly evolved over a period of two years. It was finalized and approved in February of 1983, just in time for the reopening of the universities.

2. AIMS OF THE PLAN

Early in the process of C^3RH's planning, the following principles were agreed upon:

a. Computer technology is important for the welfare of a country, regardless of the state of its development. Computers will soon become as basic to our way of life as the telephone and television are today, and we cannot afford not to prepare ourselves for this eventuality. Thus, computer education is an important cornerstone of the movement towards technological progress and self-sufficiency.
b. Our educational programs in computer science and technology must be goal-oriented and based upon projected future needs. Education for the sake of education is a luxury we cannot afford in view of the extreme scarcity of resources, especially high-quality college-level educators.
c. Since the post-revolutionary climate and lack of planning excludes an accurate and detailed projection of needs, we must rely on the best judgements of our experienced computer professionals and educators, validated by extensive peer reviews.
d. The simplistic hardware/software dichotomy must be challenged in view of new developments in computing. No longer can a software specialist completely isolate him/herself from hardware details, nor can a hardware specialist get along without substantial knowledge of software. This is especially true in the developing world, where manpower shortage causes each university graduate to confront varied tasks.

It was noted that the above principles could be
best served through the establishment of a handful of strong computer departments within major
universities, since the level of needs did not
justify, nor did the amount of resources support,
continuing with a dozen or so "degree mills" in
computer science and engineering. These departments must have close ties to both mathematics
and electrical engineering departments but should
be independent of both.

Accordingly, the Ministry of Culture and Higher
Education was advised to initially limit the annual intake of the entire program to about 150
students nationally. The above figure was somewhat inflated by the Ministry as a partial compen-
sation for the three-year interruption of student
flow through the higher education system. In addition, it was recommended that universities with
strong (applied) mathematics and electrical engineering programs as well as good laboratory and
computing facilities should be selected as the
homes of computer science and technology departments.

The aim was to establish a tradition of high-
quality computer science and technology training
for the newly entering students as well as to provide an acceptable level of education to some 1500
existing students at the various stages of the
higher education pipeline. Most of these existing
students were trained within mathematics or electrical engineering departments (with little emphasis on computer courses) or in academically low-
ranking computer applications colleges and were
thus inadequately prepared for serious work in
computer science and technology.

3. THE OVERALL STRUCTURE

As shown in Figure 1, the proposed program will
train computer specialists at three levels:
   a. Technicians -- 2 to 2.5 years.
   b. Experts -- 4 to 5 years.
   c. Senior Experts -- 6 to 7 years.
These programs are roughly equivalent to, though
somewhat heavier than, the two-year colleges or
professional schools, B.S. or engineering programs, and M.S. programs elsewhere. The establishment of doctoral-level programs was judged to be
inappropriate in view of the present needs and
resources.

The relation of the above programs to the projected needs of the job market is as follows:
   a. Usage, operation, and maintenance of hardware
      and software systems:
      1. Routine, preplanned, or guided activities:
         Technicians.
      2. Non-routine, unpredictable, or unique
         problems: Applied experts.
   b. Design, development, and construction of
      hardware and software systems: Design experts
      (Computer Engineers).
   c. Innovation, research, and education in the
      field of computer science and technology:
      Senior Experts.

Of the programs depicted in Figue 1, all but the
digital electronics technician program (which has
been planned by a joint committee due to its
interdisciplinary nature) will be discussed in
this paper. It must be noted that the following
programs have been developed according to the
guidelines and constraints posed by the Cultural
Revolution Council. These included the maximum
and minimum allowed duration of programs, number
of required and elective units, general university
and social science requirements, etc. Several
disadvantages of this rigid framework have been
pointed out and may affect the future development
of the said programs.

One feature of the program shown in Figure 1 deserves special emphasis. Students entering the
Expert program study for at least two years before
choosing between the hardware and software orientations. This is an excellent way of providing
these experts with the common language so badly
lacking between today's hardware and software people. It also provides the student (totally unaware of the hardware/software distinction upon
graduation from high school) with an opportunity
to assess his or her strengths and potentials before making the choice. Those unable or unwilling
to continue with either orientation are given the
opportunity to take several applied courses in an
"adaptation" semester in order to enter the job
market as technicians.

4. TRAINING OF TECHNICIANS

Computer technicians can be classified into two
groups according to their job functions:
   a. Computer operations, coding, routine program-
      ming, and periodic running of application
      software.
   b. Routine maintenance, repair, and construction
      of digital electronics and computer circuits.
The needed skills are developed by the "Computer
Applications" and "Digital Electronics" technician
training programs, respectively.

Table I shows the coursework for the two-year
computer applications technician program. These
technician programs are highly applied and skill-
oriented programs. Therefore, their graduates are
discouraged, though not totally banned from entering the "Expert" program. Instead, an "Applied
Expert" program has been specially developed to
sharpen the skills and broaden the knowledge of
these technicians for tackling more challenging
non-routine problems.

Our higher education system has traditionally been
weak in the training of technicians. The reason
is a combination of inadequate resources at the
two-year technician-training institutes and an
abundance of demotivating factors (salary structure, job classification and benefits, social sta-
ture, etc.) preventing talented high-school graduates from entering these programs. Significant
technological progress will be impossible with the
present knowledge gap between engineers and technicians. It has, therefore, been recommended that

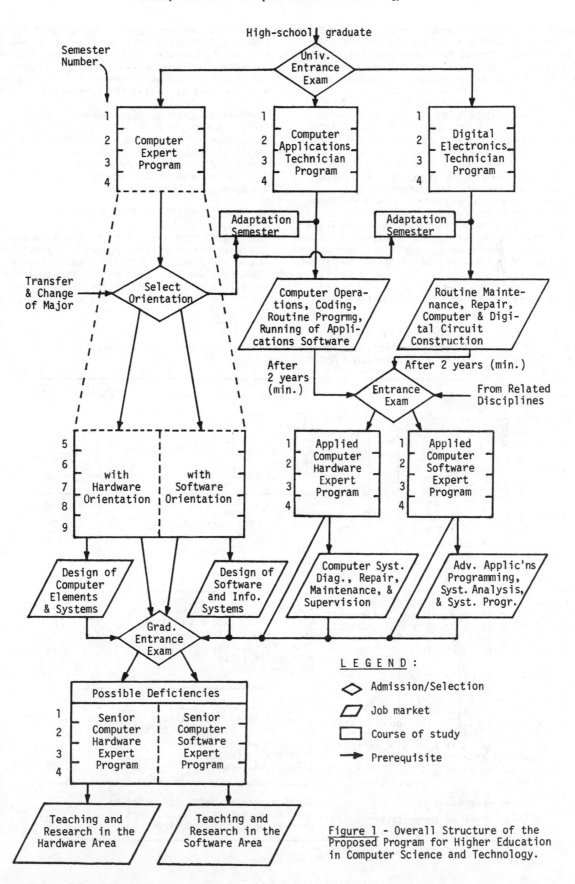

Figure 1 - Overall Structure of the Proposed Program for Higher Education in Computer Science and Technology.

technician training programs be viewed as important components of our higher education system.
Running these programs at major universities will
provide them with adequate resources. It will, at
the same time, alleviate some of the demotivating
factors.

5. APPLIED COMPUTER EXPERTS

Applied computer experts are envisaged as filling
in higher level skill-oriented jobs in two categories:
  a. Advanced applications programming, systems
     analysis, and systems programming.
  b. Computer system diagnosis, repair, mainte-
     nance, and supervision.
They may be viewed as "executive engineers," in
contrast to "design engineers" resulting from the
knowledge-oriented expert program, and must therefore have a sound general knowledge of computing,
as well as vast practical experience and skill in
their own specialization (Table II). Applied
computer software experts will normally assume

positions such as "senior programmer," "systems
analyst," "systems engineer," and "systems programmer." However, they are also given a chance
to enter the "Senior Expert" program upon passing
an entrance exam and compensating for possible
deficiencies by taking extra non-credit courses.

Applied computer hardware experts will normally
assume positions such as "maintenance engineer,"
"customer engineer," "manufacturing engineer," and
"operations manager." Applied hardware experts
can enter the "Senior Expert" program if they are
willing to make up for academic deficiencies
through non-credit courses.

6. THE COMPUTER EXPERT PROGRAM

The aim of this program is to train hardware and
software design experts possessing broad theoretical and practical knowledge as well as a common
language, enabling them to act as members of effective and productive design teams. Computer
experts will also participate in acitivities such

Table I

Model Four-Semester Schedule of Courses and the Prerequisite Structure
for Computer Applications Technician Program

Course Name	Units	Total
General Mathematics 1	4	
Elementary Probability & Stat.	3	
General Physics 1 + Lab.	5	
Fund. of Computers & Programming	4	
English 1	3	
Physical Education	1	20
General Mathematics 2	4	
Elective Mathematics Course	3	
General Physics 2 + Lab.	5	
Advanced Programming	4	
Special English	2	
Arabic 1	2	20
Computer Logic Circuits + Lab.	4	
Machine Structure & Language	3	
Fund. of Data Structures	3	
Prog. for Business Systems	4	
History of Islam	2	
Persian 1	4	20
Computer Hardware + Lab.	4	
Computer Systems Operations	3	
Applications of Systems Software	3	
Computer Software Lab.	3	
Programming Project	3	
Islamic Culture 1	3	19

Stat.   Numer.
Meth.   Comput.

→ Prerequisite

*
⇒ Pre- or Corequisite

Total Number of Units (64 units of
specialty courses + 15 units of
general university requirements)   79

as the following:
a. Planning for effective use of computing resources.
b. Adapting hardware and software systems to
   changing needs.
c. Improving the performance of hardware and
   software systems.

The "Expert" program (Figure 2) consists of two
parts:
a. The common or "base" part, comprising the
   general university requirements plus some 60
   percent of the specialty courses.
b. The "orientation" part, comprising roughly
   40 percent of the specialty courses.

Table II

Model Four-Semester Schedule of Courses for Applied Computer
Hardware and Software Expert Programs

Applied Computer Hardware Expert		Applied Computer Software Expert	
Units	Course Name	Units	Course Name
3	Fund. of Computer Organization	3	Fund. of Computer Organization
4	Electrical Machines + Lab.	3	Elective Mathematics Course
			(Stat. Meth. or Numer. Comput'n)
3	Computer Software Lab.	4	Operations Research
2	Technical Presentation	2	Technical Presentation
2	Arabic 2	3	Info. Storage & Retrieval
3	English 2	3	English 2
3	Islamic Culture 2	3	Islamic Culture 2
3	Fund. of Operating Systems	3	Fund. of Operating Systems
3	Computer Elements & Technology	3	Systems Design & Analysis
4	Microprocessors + Lab.	2	Elementary Hardware Lab.
3	Advanced Hardware Lab.	3	Advanced Software Lab.
3	Persian 2	3	Persian 2
2	Present Iran & the Islamic Revol.	2	Present Iran & the Islamic Revol.
2	History of Science	2	History of Science
		2	Arabic 2
3	Summer Practical Training	3	Summer Practical Training
4	Computer Peripheral Devices + Lab.	4	Microprocessors + Lab.
3	Industrial Appl. of Computers	3	Computer Simulation
3	Fault Diagnosis in Digital Syst.	3	Software Engineering
3	Practical Work on a Particular	3	Comparative Study & Applic'ns of
	Computer System		Programming Languages
3	Logic and Methodology	3	Logic and Methodology
2	Philosophy of Science	2	Philosophy of Science
2	Islamic History of Science	2	Islamic History of Science
3	Computer System Installation	3	Computer Mangmnt & Social Aspects
3	Case Studies of Common Computer	3	Case Studies of Common Computer
	Hardware		Software
6	Elective Courses#	6	Elective Courses@
3	Hardware Project	3	Software Project
3	Astronomy	3	Astronomy
81	Total Number of Units (60 units of specialty courses + 21 units of general university req'ments)	82	Total Number of Units (61 units of specialty courses + 21 units of general university req'ments)
	# Possible Elective Courses		@ Possible Elective Courses
3	Microprogramming	3	Microprogramming
3	On-Line Computer Systems	3	On-Line Computer Systems
3	Operating Systems 2	3	Advanced Logic Circuits
3	Compilers 1	3	Computer Elements & Technology
3	Info. Storage & Retrieval	3	Numerical Analysis 2
4	Industrial Electronics + Lab.	3	Computer Graphics
3	Process Control by Computers	3	Data Privacy and Security
3	Computer-Aided Design & Manufac.	3	Computer Performance Evaluation
3	Fault Diagnosis & Tolerance	3	Software Reliability
3	Analog Computers		

928   *B. Parhami*

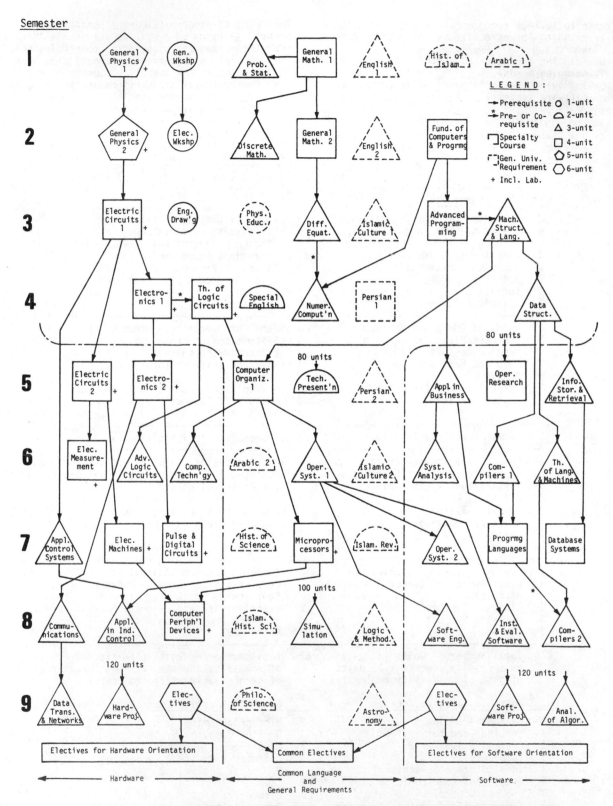

Figure 2 - The Computer Expert Program with Hardware and Software Orientations: Specialty Courses, General University Requirements, Prerequisite Structure, the Common Language Between Hardware and Software Experts, and Model Scheduling.

The importance of providing hardware and software experts with a common language was pointed out in Sections 2 and 3 of this paper.

After about two years of study in the "Expert" program, each student is assigned to one of the two orientations according to the following criteria:
 a. The student's own preference.
 b. The student's performance in the main courses related to the two orientations:
    1. Machine structure & language, Theory of logic circuits, electronics 1; Hardware.
    2. Machine structure & language, advanced programming, data structures; Software.
 c. The maximum capacity assigned to each orientation, based on job market needs forecast.
Other features of the "Expert" program include extensive laboratory and project work for both hardware and software courses, interaction between hardware and software students through common required and elective courses, and provision of some basic courses in each orientation as electives for the other orientation. The courses shown with dashed lines in Figure 2 are general university requirements, over which C^3RH had no control.

7. THE SENIOR EXPERT PROGRAM

The aim of this program is to train computer researchers and educators, as well as high-level specialists capable of assisting in the establishment of a national computer technology and planning for effective use of the available resources. The strategic importance of computer science and technology as a prerequisite of fundamental progress in scientific research, industrial control, and national planning underscores the necessity and priority of the "Senior Expert" program.

Coursework requirements for the senior computer expert program, including non-credit courses to cover possible deficiencies in the prerequisite structure, are given in Table III. The two-unit courses in Table III (a total of 6 units) constitute the general senior expert program requirements established by the Cultural Revolution Council. The rest of the program (31 units) has been planned by C^3RH.

The departments offering this program (currently two) can plan their own elective courses, provided such courses satisfy the following conditions:
 a. Elective courses in computer science and technology must be graduate-level: i.e., they should have prerequisites in the upper division undergraduate courses.
 b. Courses in related disciplines (electronics, communications, control, applied mathematics, statistics) should at least correspond to fourth-year courses in the respective undergraduate programs.
The 4-unit "Advanced Topics ..." course is designed to supplement the project and thesis units, limited to 6 by an unfortunate bureaucratic rule, which were judged to be inadequate for meaningful research in computer science and technology.

Selection of students for the "Senior Expert" program is based on a written entrance examination emphasizing main courses in the respective orientation, along with the following additional criteria:
 a. Undergraduate grade point average.
 b. Interview and oral exam.
 c. Letters or recommendation.
 d. English proficiency.
Only graduates of the "Expert" program in computer science and technology can enter the "Senior Expert" program, except for highly qualified candidates from disciplines with a significant amount of overlap (in specialty courses) with the computer expert program.

8. CONCLUSION

The programs described in this paper are being offered by seven major universities (two, in the case of the "Senior Expert" program) in Iran and should soon face their first major revision based on 2.5 years of operational experience. At present, it is not clear which direction the changes will take, but it appears likely that the length of the program (total number of units) would be reduced based on criticisms citing disadvantages such as student overloading, inadequate supply of specialists, and waste of scarce resources.

There is also a school of thought challenging the foundation of an integrated hardware/software program and favoring totally separate programs (rather than orientations) within engineering and science divisions, respectively. Total isolation of hardware and software programs has caused great damage in the past and will be even more harmful in future, in view of current developments in the field of computing.

There has been an increasing awareness of the need for closer links between hardware and software educational programs:

"... industry continues to hire programmers for software and engineers for VLSI and micro-code work, ... and only a few universities have the foresight to balance and cross-fertilize the education of hardware and software engineers."[2]

"At some universities, the difficulty of maintaining separate resources for two or more departments has led to a decision to merge the departments."[3]

"... the differences in background of the early workers in [computer science and engineering] led to the identification of programming, or software, as a discipline that differed from logic design, or hardware. ... The 1970s brought many rapid developments in computers that led to the realization that hardware and software had to be treated as an integrated whole."[4]

These are but a few examples of a general trend.

Table III

Coursework and Thesis Requirements for the Senior Computer Hardware
and Software Expert Programs

Senior Computer Hardware Expert	Senior Computer Software Expert
Units Course Name	Units Course Name

(a) Prerequisite (Deficiency) Courses

0 Computer Organization I	0 Computer Organization I
0 Computer Elements and Technology	0 Software Engineering
0 Computer Peripheral Devices + Lab.	0 Theory of Languages and Machines
0 Pulse and Digital Circuits	0 Database Systems
0 Computer Appl. in Industrial Control	0 Compilers II
0 Electronics II	0 Operating Systems II
0 Advanced Logic Circuits	0 Programming Languages

(b) General University Requirements

2 Islamic Culture	2 Islamic Culture
2 Logic (Ancient & Modern)	2 Logic (Ancient & Modern)
2 Statistical Analysis	2 Statistical Analysis

(c) Specialty Coursework and Research

3 Computer Organization II	3 Computer Organization II
3 Microprogramming	3 Microprogramming
4 Advanced Topics in Computer Science and Technology (Research)	3 Advanced Topics in Computer Science and Technology (Research)
3 Advanced Electronics	3 Self-Contained Information Systems
3 Computer-Aided Design and Control	3 Artificial Intelligence
3 Fault Diagnosis and Tolerance	3 Software Reliability
3 Theory of Finite State Machines	3 Theory of Programming Languages
2 Graduate Seminar	2 Graduate Seminar
6 Project and Thesis	6 Project and Thesis
9 Elective Courses	9 Elective Courses

| 45 Total Number of Units (39 units of specialty courses + 6 units of general university req'ments) | 45 Total Number of Units (39 units of specialty courses + 6 units of general university req'ments) |

An important ingredient of this awareness is the new meaning assigned to "computer engineering":

"Interinsic to computer engineering is the concept of _design_ as it applies to all aspects of a computer system -- the hardware, the software, and algorithms used -- and the application for which it is intended."[5]

Computer engineering has assumed a much broader meaning (application of known theories to the design of hardware and software) and is no longer synonymous with computer hardware and digital technology.

Educational programs in computer hardware and software have been moving towards each other steadily and their gradual integration appears inevitable. We in Iran have seized the opportunity provided by the disruption of the higher education system to do this in one giant step.

REFERENCES

[1] Mavaddat, F. and B. Parhami, "Informatics in Iran: Problems and Prospects," Proc. of Int'l Conf. on Computer Appl. in Developing Countries, Bangkok, Aug. 1977, pp. 121-133.

[2] Musa, J.D. (Editor), "Stimulating Software Engineering Progress," Software Engineering Technical Committee Newsletter, IEEE, Vol. 7, No. 4, pp. 1-26, May 1983.

[3] Zorpette, G., "CS/E Programs," IEEE Spectrum, Vol. 21, No. 11, pp. 50-54, Nov. 1984.

[4] Booth, T.L., "The Case for Two Distinct Disciplines," IEEE Spectrum, Vol. 21, No. 11, p. 53, Nov. 1984.

[5] Freeman, H., "Research Directions in Computer Engineering: NSF Workshop Report," Computer, Vol. 16, No. 5, pp. 80-82, May 1983.

# #

COMPUTERS IN EDUCATION, K. Duncan and D. Harris (eds.)
Elsevier Science Publishers B.V. (North-Holland)
© IFIP, 1985

THE NATIONAL INFORMATICS UP-DATE PROGRAMME FOR THE NETHERLANDS: CONSEQUENCES FOR THE GOVERNMENT

Drs. A. Bongers

Ministry of Home Affairs,
Government Training Institute,
Postbox 20011,
2500 EA The Hague,
The Netherlands.

Abstract. The Automation Training Sector of the Government Training Institute is responsible for user-training in automation within the Dutch civil service. Within this context the institute became involved in 1983 in a feasibility study with the aim of studying the possibility of starting a national informatics up-date programme for the government (i.e. central government and local government) and commercial industry.
The institute participated in the Steering Committee established for the purpose of directing the investigation and for carrying out quality control. This investigation resulted in a report which proposed several projects for different areas of which the government is one. The report was accepted by the cabinet in May 1984.
The institute will be responsible for coordinating the part of the programme for the government in collaboration with the central training organisation for the local government.
Following a short introduction and a description of the total framework of the national up-date programme as well as the included proposals, this paper continues with a more detailed description of the part of the programme for the government.

Keywords. Government; National programme; Informatics specialists-training; Management-training.

INTRODUCTION

The Government Training Institute (GTI) is a department of the Ministry of Home Affairs and is the central training organisation for the Dutch civil service.

The Automation Training Sector (AUTOP) is as a department of the GTI responsible for the user-training in automation within the Dutch civil service. AUTOP is also involved in the training of informatics specialists.
The activities of AUTOP have been described in the proceedings of the IFAC conference in 1983 (1).
One of the activities has been described as:
The setting up and supervision of a training programme for the "up-dating" of informatics specialists who have never followed a specialised training.

This activity is a result of the work of a committee, which established in 1981 that in both the government and commercial industry there existed a substantial shortage of informatics specialists and that there was also an important qualitative lack of know-how in this type of function (2).
The committee recommended in a report that these shortcomings be quickly eliminated by means of an up-date programme.

The conclusions of the committee can be summarised as follows:
a. there is a substantial -assumed but not quantifiable- shortage of informatics specialists.
b. there is a question of a substantial growth in computerisation and of the jobs involved.
c. there is only a limited output expected from regular informatics education.
d. there is an important qualitative gap in the knowledge of the present automation staff.

The ministers of Home Affairs, Economic Affairs, Education and Science, Social Affairs and Employment, have therefore initiated a feasibility study for a national informatics up-date training programme.
It was already clear during the formulation of the assignment for the feasibility study that it would not only be sufficient to develop proposals regarding the primary target group (the presently employed informatics specialists). Proposals were finally made aimed also at target groups for which automation is not a main task. The reason for this was that for the creation of conditions for the application of information technology other target groups (e.g. managers) must also be trained in this subject.

The state secretary of the Ministry for Home Affairs set up the "Informatics up-date programme study Steering Committee", to supervise the feasibility study.
The GTI has participated in this steering committee.

The tasks of the Steering Committee were:
- to give direction to the investigation, in the sense that its approval was necessary for the further completion of the assignment
- the supervision and direction of the methods used to carry out the assignment.

The results of the study are described in the next chapter (3).

RESULTS OF THE FEASIBILITY STUDY

Evaluation of the areas of application

As mentioned in the previous chapter, the original target group to be investigated was the group of informatics specialists. For this group a programme had to be set up. For better application of the new information technology, programmes for target groups from certain other application areas of information technology had to be set up as well.
The areas to be investigated are a selection of applications which could be very successful within the Dutch commercial industry. These applications have been investigated by the Advisory Commission for the Industrial Policy in 1983 (Wagner Commission(4)). From all possible applications from the report of the Wagner Commission the Steering Committee has made a choice of areas to be studied.

The choices include:

1. transit-informatics applications
2. production-automation applications including CAD/CAM systems
3. documentation information systems
4. automatic payment systems
5. electronic publishing systems
6. traffic (guidance) control systems
7. medical information- and automation systems
8. informatics for the government

It became evident that these areas of application could be divided into three groups, namely:
- areas suited for up-date activities
- areas only partly suited for up-date activities
- areas not suited for up-date activities.

Besides the up-dating of informatics specialists the following areas are regarded as suitable:
a. transit-informatics applications
b. production-automation applications
c. informatics for the government

The areas of application, "documentation information systems" and "automatic payment systems" are according to the following explanation only partly suitable for up-date activities.

Documentation information.

This area of application includes information systems for the storage and retrieval of information.
The Steering Committee has suggested that the main point of study for this area of application must be placed in information intended for public use, and more specifically for instructional tasks.
With the communicative information supply, therefore, the transfer of public information to various groups in society is a central issue.

It has emerged from talks that a good communicative information supply of public information is especially required by employers in middle and small industry. Concrete form has been given to an up-date action by including aspects of communicative information supply in the demonstration project for middle and small industry.

Automatic payment systems.

An up-date programme for the automatic payment systems is not considered as suitable by the representatives of banks because the knowledge of information-technology and the application of it is considered as a "strategic good". During the further working out of the up-date activities the accent has been placed on the preference of the bank representatives which is to aim the activities at particular client target groups such as the employers in middle and small industry.

Finally three areas of application, namely "electronic publishing systems", "traffic (guidance) control systems" and "medical information- and automation systems" appeared to be not suitable for the setting up of up-date activities.

Knowledge gaps in the government and commercial industry

From the many interviews and discussions held in the government and in commercial industry a picture has been formed of the shortcomings.

In this inventory the following points were determined:
a. the target groups in which the knowledge gaps exist
b. the main subjects from the field of informatics for which these shortcomings are relevant.

The findings from the areas of application within commercial industry will not be elaborated upon in this paper.
In the next part of this paper only the part the government plays within the national up-date programme will be explained further. The GTI is responsible for the training activities within the central government and the CIVOB (the central training organisation for local government) is responsible for the training activities within the local government.

The following findings (A and B) have resulted from the interviews which took place with civil service staff members.

A. The primary knowledge gaps for informatics specialists are found in the following target groups:

> **Target group: projectleaders/advisers information analysts**
>
> Type of knowledge gap:
> - knowledge of architectural problems of complex systems
> - knowledge of the design methods of large integrated systems
> - knowledge of the application of the latest technology
> - knowledge of the latest methods and techniques
> - knowledge of management aspects which are related to the introduction of large integrated systems
> - knowledge of organisational subjects.

> **Target group: systems designers**
>
> Type of knowledge gap:
> - knowledge of fields such as database design and management, data-communication, network design.

> **Target group: systems managers**
>
> Type of knowledge gap:
> - knowledge of the uses of informatics in their own work, especially concerning data management, approach and systems organisation.

> **Target group: trainers**
>
> Type of knowledge gap:
> - keeping up to date with the latest technology and organisational developments.

B. There is also a question of a knowledge gap for the non-informatics specialists. It concerns here especially the management functions, staff members, material experts who must function as specialists and the users at executive level.

> **Target group: users (executive)**
>
> Type of knowledge gap:
> - appreciation of computerisation in general
> - motivation for using the information technology
> - general change in attitude with regard to the use of informatics

> **Target group: material experts (specialists)**
>
> Type of knowledge gap:
> - capacity to think along when specifying applications, mainly in the administrative field
> - skill in carrying out elementary process and problem analysis and use of the necessary methods and techniques

> **Target group: management**
>
> Type of knowledge gap:
> - skill in judging project proposals/ planning
> - knowledge of the possibilities of modern information technology
> - knowledge of methods for investment study and policy decision, in which the application of informatics plays a part

Presently available informatics training courses (not regular education) for the traced knowledge gaps.

In deciding the necessary measures to be taken it is important to have an overall picture of the available training courses, relevant to the traced knowledge gaps. From the following summary it can be concluded that especially for the target group project leaders/advisers and information analysts a particularly insufficient supply of courses is available in the Netherlands.

Target group: project leaders/advisers information analysts	
Subject	Supply
Information planning	-
Organisation design	-
Evaluation standard packages	-
Integrated office automation	-
Methods and techniques	#
Prototyping	-
Management aspects	#
User participation	#
Project planning	+·

Target group: systems designers	
Subject	Supply
Design interactive systems	#
Data communication networks	#
Data analysis and data dictionary	#
Dialogue design	#
Knowledge of micro-computers	#

Target group: systems managers	
Subject	Supply
Systems manager courses	#

Legend supply
- = none or very limited supply
= limited supply (about 5)
+ = sufficient supply

Financial consequences

The total cost for all the government and commercial industry projects to be realised has been estimated at $ 60 million. In May 1984 the cabinet accepted the national up-date programme and agreed to contribute $ 12 million from the national budget. The remaining $ 48 million has to be paid by the participants. The plan is to complete the up-date programme within five years. The courses begin in January 1986.

In the following two chapters the respective projects for "informatics-specialists" and "non-informatics specialists" within the government will be described in more detail.

TRAINING PROJECT FOR INFORMATICS SPECIALISTS

Project description

The main objective of this project is to retrain the informatics specialists already working as project leaders/advisers, information analysts, systems designers,

systems managers or trainers by means of a training programme so that the latest developments in automation can also be used within their own work environment. The courses should be taken care of by principally non-regular educational institutions. This training project for government informatics specialists is the same as for commercial industry because knowledge gaps in both case appear to be nearly the same. For this reason the up-date programme for informatics specialists can be realised as one project.

Main elements of the programme

In realising this programme certain activities must be carried out. These activities as a whole form the knowledge transfer process.
a. determination of the subjects for which training requirements exist
b. the setting up of an organisation concerning itself with the transfer of knowledge at home and abroad
c. development of training courses for the stated subjects by non-regular training institutions
d. the recruitment and training of teachers
e. the giving of courses by non-regular training institutions
f. evaluation of the so-called "end-terms" of the training courses with an end to establishing how much knowledge has in fact been transmitted
g. the creation of acknowledgement mechanisms by including the courses in the programme.

Areas of attention and target groups

The programme suggested for informatics training courses is aimed at the following areas of attention and target groups:
a. application and implementation aspects of modern information technology:
   - at management level for project leaders/advisers;
   - at the level of execution for information analysts.
b. information systems design with the help of modern information technology (databases, networks etc.), chiefly for systems designers.
c. knowledge of the application of informatics in ones own work environment, mainly for systems managers.

On the basis of the knowledge gaps determined a basis block course is created for each of these target groups. To be able to satisfy the flexible knowledge requirements, a choice can also be made from several optional subjects.
The length of the course can, within limits, be determined by the training institution but will, generally speaking, be about 3 to 5 days for each subject.

Subjects can be followed spread over a period of time.
In the following lists the contents of the basic block and optional subjects for a number of target groups are shown.

Retraining project leaders/advisors

Subject
Basis block
1. information policy
2. integration of office and production computerisation
3. management aspects
4. organisational subjects
Optional subjects
5. information planning
6. organisation design
7. new methods and techniques of system development
8. prototyping
9. latest technology developments
10. preliminary study/applications study
11. development EDP standards
12. evaluation of standard packages

Retraining information analysts

Subject
Basis block
1. preliminary study/applications study
2. object system analysis
3. data analysis and data dictionary
4. prototyping
Optional subjects
5. organisation of the information supply
6. new methods and techniques of system development
7. management aspects
8. industrial accountancy
9. latest technological developments
10. evaluation of standard packages

Retraining systems designers

Subject
Basis block
1. DB/DC system design
2. data communication networks
3. dialogue design
4. distributed systems design
Optional subjects
5. flexible systems design
6. real-time operating systems
7. knowledge of micro computers
8. new methods and techniques for system development
9. testing methods

Retraining systems managers

Subject
Basis block
1. documentation
2. principles of programming
3. data management
4. operating systems
Optional subjects
5. query languages
6. principles of computers
7. technical management

Organisational framework of the programme for informatics specialists

The programme for informatics specialists will fall under the control of a (as yet to be established) foundation.

For the execution of its tasks the foundation will have to have the following at its disposal:
- a commission for informatics retraining
- an executive bureau.

The retraining committee is made up of a selected group of informatics managers from the government and industry. Three didactitians, preferably with informatics education experience, will complete the committee.

Expected results.

It is expected that within the next 5 years 50% of the informatics specialist target groups will have undergone a quality improvement whereby they will be able to make practical use of new methods and techniques in their own work environments. Given the size of the target group -about 15,000 persons with the function of project leader/adviser, information analyst and systems designer and systems manager- and the supposed restrictions of training space for this category, this will be the optimum effect of the programme.

THE GOVERNMENT INFORMATICS TRAINING PROJECT FOR MANAGERS

Project description

The aim of the project is:
- a training in informatics for managers in the government, organised so that existing knowledge gaps are quickly filled and that know-how and understanding of informatics technology and the organisational consequences related to its application develop on a large scale.

- an increase in the involvement of the most
  senior management and middle management in
  an expected more intensive use of
  computerisation, especially in the direct
  work environment.
- the gaining of experience with regard to
  the large scale retraining of various
  groups of government employees.

Project framework

Regarding the starting point to be chosen
for the up-date programme within the
government, a definite preference has been
stated for a "top-down" approach, which is
to say that training starts with the
official top followed by the various
functionaries filling managerial positions.
The training takes the form of a
theoretical/practical transfer of knowledge,
during a limited period, about informatics
subjects important for managers.
This management retraining can best be done
in the form of 3-day seminars, in which one
half of the time is spent listening to
presentations, while the rest of the time is
spent working on practical situations and
generally gaining experience of computerised
systems with the help of simple experiments
and demonstrations.

Two types of seminars can be predetermined:

"Top-management" seminars, aimed at the most
senior departmental management
(Secretary-general, Directorate-general,
Deputy Secretary-general and Deputy
Directorate-general), large services,
universities, and local government.
Group composition for these seminars should
be preferably open (interdepartmental
without distinguishing central/local
government, 12-15 participants per seminar).

"Management" seminars, aimed at the upper
management and management of organisation
units in the central government as well as
the local government (second echelon and
middle management).
Closed group composition for the various
grades of management occuring in the related
organisation unit, supplemented with a few
staff members (+ 20 participants per
seminar).

The following comments can be made regarding
the "top-management" seminars:
- the contents of these seminars will be
  adjusted to cover the communal problems of
  the most senior management.
- no differentiation between the subject
  contents for central government or local
  government.
- the total size of this target group is
  limited and consists of about 500 persons.
- the top management should be retrained
  before other management groups ("setting
  an example").

Within the central government a start has
already been made with the "top-management"
seminars, the programme of which is
described in the following paragraph.

The following comments can be made regarding
the "management" seminars:
- the contents will be adapted to the tasks
  and problems of the organisation unit.
- modular framework course material will
  have to be used for this type of seminar,
  making it possible to adapt the
  theoretical material and practical cases
  (limited) to the actual problems involved.
- the total size of the target groups for
  this type of seminar is large and consists
  of about 9500 persons.
- the seminar should be organised locally
  (by the organisation concerned). Support
  is given at a central level by making
  framework course material available,
  helping organise the course (hiring
  trainers, course adjustment) as well as
  general stimulation and an accompanying
  internal publicity plan.

Programme of the "Top Management" seminars

The programme occupies six successive half
days in which theory and practice
(demonstrations) are alternately dealt
with. Also a representative of a large
succesful company tells how the company put
computerisation into practice.

The following summary shows the subjects of
the seminar without going into detail about
the contents.
1.1 The importance of the (computerised)
     information supply
1.2 Computerisation, practical experiences
     - within a service, within a
       department, inter-managerial
     - length of project, exceeding costs,
       improving information supplies,
       personel and organisational
       consequences, use of hardware and
       software
1.3 Problems summary and project management
     discussions
     - relationship with involved persons
       who are not part of the organisation
     - relationship project group/steering
       committee
     - relationship with computer centre.
2.1 Why is planning and coordination
     necessary within a department and how
     should it be done?
     - analysis and solutions partly based
       on personel, financial and material
       resources
     - longterm computerisation plan and
       project plans.
2.2 Miniaturisation and the consequences of
     decentralisation, consequences of the
     role played by the Organisation and
     Informatics department.

2.3 Demonstration: management information systems, particularly in the field of office computerisation.

3.1 Why is interdepartmental coordination also necessary?
- the importance of an information supply for the government - which policy should be pursued in this area and what are the results of this policy?
- significance of the policy for ones own organisation within the departments.

3.2 Demonstration: management information systems in the field of data management.

4.1 How does a large enterprise tackle the problem?

5.1 What are the developments for the future?
- information systems also become outdated: how to determine this and what to do about it.
- technological developments: telecommunication, office computerisation.

5.2 Demonstration: individual and integrated use of the personal computer.

6.1 Can it now be done any better? What can we do about it?

6.2 Plenary discussion.

Organisational framework of the programme for managers

The coordination and support of the project are carried out from a central point (project bureau).

This project bureau is a cooperative venture involving the Government Training Institute and the central training organisation for local government (CIVOB). Considerations for this construction are:
- The Government Training Institute as well as the central training organisation for the local government are both organisations with a lot of training facilities and know-how.
- the proposed approach of using framework courses, which are then adapted to the relevant problem areas of the trainees, requires a central point of coordination.
- the fact that much of the course material and many trainers are taken on from outside makes it necessary that one has sufficient insight into the supply of trainers, and that attention must also be paid to quality control of the knowledge transfer process.

The participants involved in the project are:
- the computer departments of the various central government and local government bodies.

- the already mentioned project bureau as a central point for the project organisation.
- private training institutions, for the provision of trainers and (possibly)course material.
- members of staff from the government organisation who can give parts of the courses.

Expected results

On the basis of these proposals it may be expected that after a five-year period, a greater degree of involvement will arise, with regard to computer applications, by the public employees in management functions. This justifies the expectation that in the future there will be question of a positive effect on the quality of the realised systems and that more suitable systems will find their way into the government. Lastly is expected that the training of the management of the government will stimulate the training of all other public employees at all levels ("top-down" approach).

LITERATURE REFERENCES

1. Drs. A. Bongers, User-training Policy within the Dutch civil service, Proceedings of the IFAC/IFIP Conference, 1983, Leyden.

2. About education in informatics: a reconnaissance, Staatsuitgeverij, The Hague, 1981 (only available in Dutch).

3. Feasibility study for a national up-date programme for informatics, Bakkenist Spits & Co., Amsterdam, 1984 (only available in Dutch).

4. The Advisory Commission Report concerning the Progress the Industrial Policy (July 1982-January 1983, Wagner Commission), Ministry of Economic Affairs, The Hague, 1983 (available in Dutch and in English).

COMPUTERS IN EDUCATION, K. Duncan and D. Harris (eds.)
Elsevier Science Publishers B.V. (North-Holland)
© IFIP, 1985

COMPUTERS IN DANISH ELEMENTARY AND YOUTH EDUCATION

Peter Bollerslev

Direktoratet for folkeskolen og seminarierne
Danish Ministry of Education
Copenhagen, Denmark

As an introduction a description of the Danish education system is given. Next how the
application of computers in elementary education has developed in the last decade and
the present situation are described. Finally, the development and the state of the art
of the youth education are described in brief.

1. DENMARK, THE INFRASTRUCTURE

Denmark is a small country with a population of
5 million people occupying 43,000 square
kilometers of Northern Europe between the North
Sea and the Baltic.

The standard of living has reached a very high
level and in the other Scandinavian countries
the Danes have the reputation of being carefree
spenders. This may well be an exaggeration, but
there is no doubt that most Danes today
experience a strong sense of material comfort.

Social class differences exist but are little
commented upon - perhaps too little - and not
noticeably divisive. Much of the nation's
wealth has been used to build a "welfare state"
of which most Danes are intensely proud but
which has recently run into criticism. They
tend to think in terms of collective social
responsibility and to believe that everyone must
be properly cared for, so that public
expenditure on goods and services is at 24% of
GDP.

Virtually devoid of natural resources, Denmark
can survive and prosper only through energetic
and successful trading. Being thus acutely
aware of the need to cultivate close relations
with other countries in Europe besides the
Scandinavian group, it has elected, as the only
Scandinavian country, to join the European
Economic Community with all the political and
social implications that such an attachment
entails. In general, it recognizes the
necessity of bringing up the young with a strong
international awareness and of ensuring that its
citizens can command foreign languages and adapt
to living in and working with countries in all
parts of the world.

There is a dawning recognition that Denmark may
have been living beyond its means and that,
despite the goodwill of its commercial partners
and external investors, a harsh reckoning awaits
it unless some creative compromises can be
reached and unless entrepreneurial research and
development prowess can be applied to find new
outlets for its productive capacity and reserves
of human capital.

It is natural that in these changing
circumstances the future of education is being
seriously considered in Denmark, although most
of the discussion has centered less on
entrepreneurial and research and development
prowess than on the long-term goals of citizen's
education in a democracy. We are conscious of
dealing with an established, in some way unique,
education system which has been exceptionally
well supported financially but which itself is
now subject to scrutiny from inside and outside.

The Figure 1 gives an overview of the Danish
education system.

2. APPLICATION OF COMPUTERS IN DANISH ELEMENTARY EDUCATION

2.1 The "Folkeskole"

In Denmark there are, since 1972-73, nine years
of compulsory education, from age 7 to age 16.
This compulsory education may be given in the
home by the parents, but this is extremely rare.
Normally the compulsory education is obtained by
participation in school education and this will
normally be during first to ninth grade. CAI
has first and foremost been applied in so-called
special education to improve proficiency in the
Danish language and in arithmetic. CAI has also
been applied to a moderate extent in other
disciplines: physics, geography and biology.
In these disciplines CAI has been used for
simulation of experiments. It is mostly
mentally handicapped pupils who have benefited
from CAI, and this has contributed to the
integration (versus segregation) of the mentally
handicapped, which is the aim at present in the
Danish "folkeskole."

Some experiments have been aimed at application
of computers as an aid in teaching Danish
language for pupils with a foreign language as
the mother tongue. The results appear to be
successful, expecially for education of pupils
with high scholastic achievement. As an
example: Vietnamese immigrants.

In a survey carried out by the Ministry of
education in February 1984 it was found that
about 17% of Danish schools at the primary and

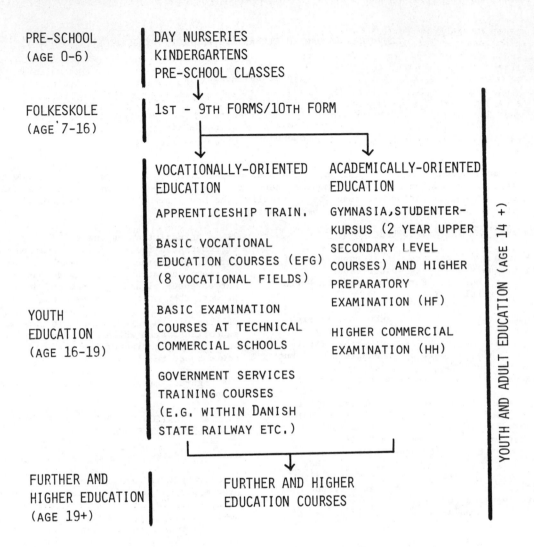

PRE-SCHOOL
(AGE 0-6)

DAY NURSERIES
KINDERGARTENS
PRE-SCHOOL CLASSES

FOLKESKOLE
(AGE 7-16)

1ST - 9TH FORMS/10TH FORM

YOUTH
EDUCATION
(AGE 16-19)

VOCATIONALLY-ORIENTED
EDUCATION

APPRENTICESHIP TRAIN.

BASIC VOCATIONAL
EDUCATION COURSES (EFG)
(8 VOCATIONAL FIELDS)

BASIC EXAMINATION
COURSES AT TECHNICAL
COMMERCIAL SCHOOLS

GOVERNMENT SERVICES
TRAINING COURSES
(E.G. WITHIN DANISH
STATE RAILWAY ETC.)

ACADEMICALLY-ORIENTED
EDUCATION

GYMNASIA,STUDENTER-
KURSUS (2 YEAR UPPER
SECONDARY LEVEL
COURSES) AND HIGHER
PREPARATORY
EXAMINATION (HF)

HIGHER COMMERCIAL
EXAMINATION (HH)

YOUTH AND ADULT EDUCATION (AGE 14 +)

FURTHER AND
HIGHER EDUCATION
(AGE 19+)

FURTHER AND HIGHER
EDUCATION COURSES

Figure 1. The Danish Education System

lower secondary level were in possession of computers for education. The typical equipment is a number of microcomputers with floppy disc and printer. The equipment is financed by each of the municipalities without subsidy from the state. There has been no provision for financial contributions from the state, and there has been no financial support from private industry.

At the moment every effort is being made to purchase equipment for the "folkeskole," and a reasonable guess is that 25% of the schools had their own equipment by the beginning of 1985.

2.2 Curriculum

In 1970 the Danish Ministry of Education set up a committee on the teaching of electronic data processing with a broad representation from all areas of education and training. The committee was required to make proposals for a rational distribution of tasks within the teaching of edp between the various stages and areas of education and training of students. And it was required to make proposals as to how computer science could be integrated into existing general and vocational curricula.

The committee submitted a very detailed report in 1972. This report has been of immense importance to the content and teaching that has taken place since then.

The recommendations of the committee say without reservations that the subject, now called "datalaere," should be introduced at all states of education and training. Thus the summary of the recommendations say:

As much seems to indicate that the results of datalaere are desired in our society as it already concerns everybody, and as experience with datalaere as a subject is positive with respect to motivation as well as learning, the committee found that it had to recommend that datalaere be introduced as a subject in the entire education system.

The general purpose of introducing datalaere is formulated thus:

(1) to provide a general understanding of the importance of the subject in combination with other subjects, including the general function of this subject.
(2) to provide such knowledge of the subject that it can be used actively in the vocational role which the education aims at.
(3) to provide such teaching of datalaere that on the basis of this the student may play an active vocational role in which datalaere is involved with other vocational skills.
(4) to develop further the subject of datalaere as a teaching subject.

The report comprises a detailed account of the consequences of these recommendations at the individual states of education and training. It is remarkable that today it is on the whole as topical as it was when it was drawn up. This applies to, e.g., the section on the introduction of datalaere in the Danish folkeskole.

In the Danish Folkeskole-Act in force at the time, the general purpose of the education was stated to be, among other things,

- that the individual pupil be provided with the opportunity of acquiring skills, knowledge and insight
- that the individual pupil be given an opportunity for independent and social development of his personality.

On the connection between this purpose and datalaere the committee says:

"It has often been stressed in public debate that the bureaucratization and technocratization of society can be countered in that already in the primary school pupils acquire knowledge of and are given an understanding of the possibilities and risks inherent in computers as an aid in administration, construction, problem solving and control.

Computing is increasingly used with the public sector and in private trade and industry. Thus computing is an important part of the every-day life of most people. One result of this in the view of the committee is that datalaere as a taught subject will contribute to further the achievement of the general purposes of the Danish folkeskole."

Note that in 1972 before the crisis a varied insight into possibilities as well as risks was the expression used, and note that computers are mentioned not only as an aid in administration, but that administration, construction and problem solving and not least control rank equal. As mentioned the committee recommended that the subject datalaere be introduced at all stages of education from the start of the primary school and on.

For the primary and lower secondary school (grades 1 to 10) the proposals for purpose and content look as follows:

The purposes of the subjects are:

- to give the pupils insight into fundamental, interdisciplinary topics and concepts of datalogical nature
- to give the pupils knowledge of the possibilities and limitations of the computer
- to inform the pupils of the fields of application of data processing and of the social advantages and disadvantages connected with extensive use of automatic data processing.

The contents of the subject are:

1. The concept of data
   a. Representation of data and varieties of notation
   b. Structure of data
   c. Organization of data
2. Setting and structuring of problems
3. Concept of models and types of models
4. Concept of algorithm
   a. Setting algorithms
   b. Descriptions of algorithms
   d. Problem-oriented programming language
   d. Reading, writing and testing of programmes
5. Construction of the computer in principle
6. Systems of data processing, use of and social aspects of data processing.

Since the publication of this report there have been a number of experiments which were all related to the concepts of the report. These experiments have mainly been in grades 8 to 10 (age range 14 to 17), where datalaere has been given either as an independent discipline or has been offered as integrated in other disciplines either mathematics, physics or social sciences.

Since 1982/83 there are already some experiments with datalaere as an independent discipline in grades 5 and 6 (age range 11 to 13).

The social consequences of more widespread utilization of computers in society are treated in the folkeskole in the discipline "samtids-orientering" (social sciences), which is a compulsory discipline in grades 8, 9 and 10.

Most of the software has been developed by the teachers. The computer suppliers have contributed only a minor part. Individual software houses and publishers have recently demonstrated some interest in this market.

BASIC was until recently the most widely used programming language, but lately the Danish version of "structured BASIC," called COMAL, has developed into the major programming language in Denmark. Today COMAL is dominant to the degree that it is impossible to sell a microcomputer to a Danish school if it cannot be programmed in COMAL.

2.3 The present situation

Recently a lot has happened in the area of computers in education. In the folkeskole an amendment of the Primary Education Act has given the local municipal authorities permission to establish an optional course in datalaere in grades 8 and 9 after August 1984 (until now this has been permitted only in grade 10, with pilot projects as an exception). Datalaere established as an optional course means that the local authorities can decide whether they want to offer this course to the pupils in the community or not. It is anticipated that the pressure from pupils and their parents to get these courses in datalaere established will be so strong that virtually all local authorities (in all 275) will offer the courses within a few years. The Ministry of Education has urged strongly that the local authorities starting with the optional course in datalaere now also establish some kind of education in datalaere at the lower grades. The local authority in a community can itself decide how this should be organized - either as a discipline integrated in existing subjects or by establishing a separate obligatory subject. The intention is clear enough: datalaere starting at grade 8 may very well become a new toy for the bright boys. It is indeed necessary to start much earlier in order to insure that the girls get a chance to get involved.

The instructional proposal for a curriculum, which the ministerial committee has worked out as a basis for the optional course in datalaere with 2 lessons per week in grades 8 to 10, follows.

2.3.1 Goal

1. The goal is that the pupils gain insight in electronic data processing and fields of application.
2. Pupils should have the opportunity for experience with problem-solving through the use of computers.
3. Pupils should develop a background for assessment of and attitudes toward the possibilities, influences and consequences of the use of computers.

2.3.2 Content

The content basis is computers and their uses.

The content should be chosen from the following main areas:

    Communications, information and data

    Problem-solving with the use of computers

    Fields of applications for computers

    Consequences of the use of computers.

The education should be organized such that elements from the four main areas support and throw light on each other such that practical work with computers is a part of the treatment of each group of subjects.

Communications, information and data

The coursework should be organized such that the pupils get an opportunity to acquire a broad knowledge of the relationship between data, information and communication. These relationships should be considered in a historical perspective and in connection with other subject areas. The pupils should work with different types of data and data carriers and with the important part that data and data carriers play in the communication of information and in problem-solving processes. Coursework should throw light on how the use of computers influences our perception of reality.

Problem solving with the use of computers

Different types of problems should be treated in order to determine which problems easily (or only) can be solved by the use of computers, and which problems it is difficult (or impossible) to solve by the help of computers. It is considered which external circumstances eventually influence the assessment of a computer as a suitable tool for the purpose.

Through the work on concrete problem solving with computers the pupils should get the opportunity of gaining insight into systematic procedures in problem solving processes.

The prerequisites for the program used in problem solving should be made clear, and the pupils should consider the relationship between these prerequisites and the interpretation of the results from dataprocessing.

Fields of application for computers

The pupils work with the relationships between the various types of computer use and the ways in which they involve a human being, in society and in economic life. Pupils shall be taught how computers are used in connection with most of the working processes of society, from superior decisions in connection with legislative work and management to solving routine problems at a specific place of work.

Pupils should be taught how computers enter into

different functions in working processes, for instance control, calculation, simulation and information-handling and retrieval.

It should be shown how computers are used in public life, in private business, by organizations and by individuals.

Consequences of the use of computers

It should be shown how the use of computers influences the human existence, with consequences for the individual, working life and society.

It should be shown that the computer is a valuable tool which can help solve many problems, for instance problems that earlier were difficult or impossible to solve.

It should be considered how thinking and patterns of action are influenced by the way in which one as a computer user chooses exactly those problems for which a computer is a suitable tool in the problem-solving process.

Finally, it should be shown how certain applications of computers may be an advantage for some but a disadvantage for others.

3. APPLICATION OF COMPUTERS IN DANISH YOUTH EDUCATION

3.1 The study-preparatory

By this term we mean the 3-year higher secondary education which is given in the so-called "gymnasier." The end examination qualifies students for entry to universities. The gymnasium follows immediately after the nine-years compulsory folkeskole. Approximately 30% of all 16-year olds attend this secondary school.

We also incorporate courses for higher preparatory examination. As day-courses they have a duration of 2 years. But they may be taken as part-time courses of longer duration, for instance by selecting a few subjects at a time.

Educational experiments in computer science were until now based upon the earlier mentioned report from 1972 from the Ministry of Education. On this basis computer science was introduced experimentally from 1975 to 1981. These experiments, however, for a number of reasons did not attract many students and teachers. Some found the subject too hardware-oriented and the courses not sufficient for the students to write their own programmes. After that, the Ministry of Education in a circular to all secondary schools dated October 1980 stated that an experiment in integrating computer science and computer-based teaching into social sciences and natural sciences and other subjects was to be carried out. As these courses were found to be a success radical changes have taken place

since August 1984. A course "Education in EDP" has been made obligatory for all students. This is valid whether the student is on one of the science-oriented branches or on one of the humanistic branches.

Some of the provisions of edp in education in the "gymnasium" follow.

3.1.1 Goal

The goal is

1. that the students obtain knowledge of the fundamental methods and concepts in computer science,
2. that the students obtain familiarity with the use of edp and ways of thinking through the work with edp in various subjects,
3. that the students gain insight in the relationship between edp and human beings, culture and society from scientific as well as humanistic and sociological viewpoints.

3.1.2 Organization of education

The education in edp consists of

A. an obligatory course of approximately 30 lessons, normally placed in grade 1,
B. a follow-up course placed in various subjects in grades 2 and 3. This part may be organized through cooperation between more subjects.

A. The obligatory course

The course consists of

1. examples of the scope and limitations of an edp system,
2. running of pre-written programmes on the equipment at the school, correction of pre-written programmes and writing of small and simple programmes,
3. information about software and hardware, including an explanation of the difference,
4. presentation of an edp system used in business or in an institution,
5. examples of the relationship between new information technologies and human beings, culture and society.

B. The follow-up

The education for each sequence (split up in some sequences) may be organized cooperatively among several subjects or as a part of just one subject.

A February 1984 report on hardware concludes that about 90% of Danish secondary schools have some kind of computer capacity, predominantly microcomputers, averaging 6 micros per school.

The most frequently used language in COMAL, but PASCAL is often preferred by teachers for its higher speed in computer-based teaching programmes.

3.2 The technical and vocational

By this term we mean the various types of
education and training which lead to employment
in industries and services. Some of them start
with full-time school-based education and
training and continue with alternating courses
at school and employment plus training in
industry and the service trades. Others are
apprenticeships, organized with reference to the
apprenticeship act and with alternating courses
at school and employment and training in
industry and the service trades. The third
major type is technician education.

We usually apply the term secondary vocational
schools to those schools which give education
and sometimes some workshop training of the kind
mentioned above.

In the basic year of the schools of economics
and business there is a compulsory course in
"datalaere," 100-200 lessons depending on the
branch. At all these schools there are at least
12 workstations.

In the basic year of the technical schools there
is a compulsory course in datalaere with 20-40
lessons, and besides that an optional 40-80
lessons course and some branch-specific courses.
At all these schools there is one workstation
per 3-4 students.

COMPUTERS IN EDUCATION, K. Duncan and D. Harris (eds.)
Elsevier Science Publishers B.V. (North-Holland)
© IFIP, 1985

COMPUTING IN SECOND-LEVEL EDUCATION IN IRELAND - A CASE STUDY
(STUDENT & TEACHER ATTITUDES)

Brendan Mackey

Computer Education Society of Ireland,
Vocational School, Westgate, Wexford, Ireland.

A. OVERVIEW - IRISH EDUCATION, CESI, WEXFORD
****

P R E V I E W

IRELAND

- has a centralised education system.   All
policy relating to education is formulated by our
Department of Education in Dublin.

SECOND-LEVEL Education (i.e. 12-18 age group)
is provided in the main by two types of school:

(i) SECONDARY SCHOOLS - the great majority of
which are private voluntary schools run by Roman
Catholic Religious Orders (though in recent years
the major part of their running costs is met by
the State). They provide approximately 66% of
second-level school places.

(ii) VOCATIONAL SCHOOLS - run by local stat-
utory education authorities, and financed
entirely out of public funds.   They traditionally
catered for technical and trade subjects, and
despite the fact that they now offer a full academic syllabus, still tend to attract the academically less-able student.

Recently, there has been a move towards
Comprehensive and Community Schools whose aim is
to provide a common approach, or "middle ground"
between the two systems.   Recent trends can be
seen from the following figures:

Number of Schools	1979	1983
Secondary	531	516
Vocational	248	245
Comprehensive/Community	45	57

CESI - THE COMPUTER EDUCATION SOCIETY OF IRELAND

The Computer Education Society is the national
body representing those interested in Educational
Computing in Ireland.   It was formed in 1973,
sprang from the interest of those who attended
the first Department of Education courses in
Computer Studies mainly on the initiative of
Professor Bajpai of Loughborough University.
It has a membership of around 700 - mainly second
-level teachers, though not exclusively so.   It
is open to anyone interested in the promotion of
Educational Computing.   It has, like the technology, undergone a number of changes in its
history.   It began by representing mainly Maths/
Science teachers, or budding Computer Scientists
from the Education sector, but has spread its
influence to practically all educational groups
and disciplines.   Recently, there has been a
strong move towards primary education.
Despite being a voluntary group with little
or no outside funding, it has been extremely

active and influential in promoting Educational
Computing.   It publishes a bi-monthly journal,
liases with the Department of Education, with
industry and other semi-state bodies, and is
generally regarded as the voice of Educational
Computing for Ireland.   It organises courses for
teachers, seminars and workshops on specific
topics relating to Educational Computing.   It
has strongly advocated the formulation of a
National Policy and the creation of a national
support network for the introduction of Computers
into Irish education.

Some years ago, its main objective was the
creation of a separate subject on the school
curriculum, but in latter years it has moved
towards dual objectives - Computer Studies on the
Curriculum plus the application of Information
Technologies to the education system, i.e. to the
teaching and learning processes.   The author was
Chairman of the Computer Education Society for the
years 1981 - 1984.

WEXFORD

Situated in the south-east corner of Ireland,
it has a population of 15,364.   In an Irish context, it would be in the "big town" category.

Second-level Education

It has five second-level schools - four Secondary, one Vocational.   The four Secondary
schools are run by religious and are single-sex
schools.   The Vocational school is run by the
local Vocational Education Committee andis a
mixed school.

School	Computer Facilities
St. Peter's College Numbers: 550 (boys)	1 x Apple II 2 x B.B.C. 1 x Vic 20 1 x TRS 80 (1)
Presentation Convent Numbers: 740 (girls)	8 x Commodore 64 (network) 1 x Apple II
Christian Brothers School Numbers: 500 (boys)	1 x Apple II
Loreto Convent Numbers: 550 (girls)	1 x Apple II
Vocational School Numbers: 384 boys · 261 girls	1 x B.B.C. 4 x Apple II ICL 2903 system (four terminals)

Why Wexford as a Case Study?

It is one of the few areas in Ireland where
five schools in the one town had courses designed

and run by teachers themselves and, therefore, provides a compact area of study. (The management of the five schools came together in 1980 to formulate a common approach.) The emphasis has been inter-disciplinary - i.e. we have attempted to involve teachers from all disciplines.

Our efforts have been two-fold - to teach Computer Studies (which is done in most schools) but also to integrate Computers/Information Technology into the formal education system.

Some schools in the area, in particular the Vocational school, were among the earliest to introduce Computers into the curriculum and, hence, have longer experience in this area.

The results, achievements and failures, have reflected so accurately the national picture as perceived by the Computer Education Society over the years.

WEXFORD VOCATIONAL SCHOOL

Computing was introduced to the School in 1975 when students taking Business Organisation were given a brief Computer Appreciation Course .

In the following year, 1976, Computer Studies was introduced to Secretarial students. This has been developed over the years and has resulted in the highly successful Senior Secretarial and Computer Studies course now being offered to school-leavers.

In 1976 also, optional courses were first provided for Senior students and Maurice Brosnan, Teacher of Mathematics and present National Treasurer of CESI, joined us. At this stage, the School had no hardware of its own, but processing was carried out on the Wexford County Council ICL 2903 system, using ICL* Computer Education in Schools (C.E.S.) materials. (*International Computers Limited G.B.).

In 1977, we purchased our first Apple II computer. Three others were added over the next few years.

In 1979, we began to provide Adult Education Courses in Computing (night classes for adults).

In 1981, we took over the complete computer system of Wexford County Council, due mainly to the efforts of their D.P. Manager, Mr. Ger Leahy. At this stage, we were one of the best equipped schools in the country and were further able to expand the number and scope of the classes provided both within the Day School and under the Adult Education scheme.

From 1980 onwards, we began to provide courses for teachers - firstly, for secondary teachers in the area and, later, for teachers in Primary and Special (handicapped) schools. The expertise and resources built up over the years meant that the School became an unofficial Resource and Information Centre for schools in the region.

Our objectives have been two-fold - Computer Literacy (to teach about computers) and the use of computers and Information Technology to enhance the Education (and especially the learning) process (to teach with computers).

Our approach has been inter-disciplinary, involving all subject areas and we have placed great emphasis on Remedial Education. The underlying philosophy here is that if technology is to benefit education then it should benefit those most in need of it. A lot of good work has been done by Maurice Brosnan and Richard Walsh, Remedial teacher, in this area.

At present, we have eight teachers out of a total staff of 35 directly involved in the use of computers, and quite a few others who wish to become involved if they could be shown the way. We are experimenting with the use of the Micros in English, Maths., Science, Business Studies, and Secretarial Studies. We hope to have a major network installed in the 1984/'85 school year so that we can further our research and expand into subject areas that we have not touched as yet.

B. STUDENT ATTITUDES - WEXFORD VOCATIONAL SCHOOL
****

STUDENTS' QUESTIONNAIRE: March '84

Preamble

Here I would like to express my gratitude to Dave O'Grady, teacher of Mathematics and English, for his work on the Questionnaire.

The Questionnaire was distributed among those pupils of Wexford Vocational School who had shown an interest in working with computers outside normal class hours. No direct pressure to furnish information was placed on the pupils.

Those who did respond, then, can be assumed to share a degree of motivation in this field which is above average. No influence was brought to bear on pupils while filling the sheet, so the responses reflect their own personal assessments of their competence vis-a-vis computer studies.

This aspect of self-assessment was crucial to the study, as we were attempting to establish the students' perspective on discipline of computer studies within Wexford Vocational School.

Objectives

These were three-fold:

1. To establish those factors (if any) which were shared by those students who displayed a greater motivation than the normal in computer studies.
2. To get the students to assess their own level of competence in different aspects of the discipline.
3. To discover how best to develop in directions which would meet the students' needs and interests.

The Questionnaire

Q. 1, 2 and 3 requested name, age and classgroup.
Q. 4 asked how long the student had been using computers (in terms of years).
Q. 5 asked who had taught the student most of what he/she knew of computers.
Q. 6 asked for an assessment of competence in

the following:
(a) running programmes from disks,
(b) programming in Basic,
(c) programming in other languages,
(d) machine code,
(e) input/output monitor and control,
(f) graphics,
(g) word processing,
(h) file handling.
Q. 7 asked if the computer had helped the student in English, Maths., Science or Business Studies, and to what extent.
Q. 8 asked if the student was a member of the Computer Club.
Q. 9 asked if the student had access to a computer outside school, who owned it, and what type it was.
Q.10 asked what areas the student would like to investigate further, of those specified in Q.6.
Q.11 asked for suggestions in improving the input from teachers and the School in meeting the student's needs.

Responses

88 students responded of 150 canvassed.

Q.2 Age:
13 yrs.	- 21 responses	- 23%
14 "	- 31 "	- 35%
15 "	- 12 "	- 14%
16 "	- 12 "	- 14%
17 "	- 4 "	- 5%
18+ "	- 8 "	- 9%

Q.3 Classgroup:
1st yr.	- 24 (27%)
2nd yr.	- 31 (35%)
3rd yr.	- 9 (10%)
Leaving Certificate I	- 12 (14%)
Leaving Certificate II	- 0 (0%)
Pre-Employment	- 7 (8%)
Secretarial	- 5 (6%)

Q.4 Number of Years working with Computers:
1 year	- 46 responses	(52%)
2 years	- 34 "	(39%)
3 years	- 7 "	(8%)
4 years	- 1 "	(1%)

Q.5 Who has taught you most?
Teachers	- 46 responses	(50%)
Friends	- 29 "	(39%)
Books, etc.	- 2 "	(2%)
Myself	- 15 "	(16%)

(92 here, as some indicated more than one source)

Q.6 Levels of Proficiency (as assessed by student)

Level Indicated	None	Some	A good deal	A great deal
(a) Running programs from disks	1%	43%	34%	22%
(b) Programming in Basic	22%	40%	26%	12%
(c) Programming in other languages	70%	24%	2%	4%
(d) Machine code	82%	16%	2%	0%
(e) Input/output monitor and control	64%	26%	10%	0%
(f) Graphics	44%	20%	25%	11%
(g) Word Processing	43%	34%	16%	7%
(h) File handling	61%	20%	14%	5%

Q.7 Computers as a Study Aid:

For:	Helped a little	Was Useful	Was Very Useful
English	23 (26%)	8(9%)	2(2%)
Mathematics	24 (27%)	19(22%)	15(17%)
Science	11 (13%)	2(2%)	2(2%)
Business Studies	14 (16%)	0(0%)	1(1%)

Q.8 Two-thirds of those who responded were members of the Club.

Q.9 Only 9 (10%) had access to a computer outside school, 4 had their own, and 5 were owned by friends.

Q.10 The students' priorities were in the areas of:
(a) Graphics (50%)
(b) Programming in Logo and other languages(47%)
(c) Programming in Basic (32%)
Though most options in Q.6 scored over 25% excepting -
(a) running programmes from disks, and
(b) input/output monitor and control.

Q.11 Few suggestions were offered, the most frequently mentioned being:
(a) More and better instruction/supervision (18)
(b) More time on machines (13)
(c) More books (10)

A separate sheet, made available to the members of the Computer Club only, asked what disks were used most often. The most popular were:
(a) Work disks, containing programmes written by students (99),
(b) Logo disks, comprising a logo primer (75),
(c) Smerc disks, containing educational games with graphics (67).

Remarks

1. The School

In 1984/'85, the first-year intake to Wexford Vocational School was assessed for reading ability on the Schonell 'B' Test. A total of 52% of that group had a reading age of less than 10 years, the entire group being 12 years old or more. This result is consistent with those of previous years.

Furthermore, the pupils tend to be from the lower end of the socio-economic scale and, being one of five secondary schools in Wexford, the "Tech." has traditionally catered for the children of the working class only.

Because an intensive remedial programme operates in the School, the Schonell Test at the end of first year consistently indicates an improvement in overall reading ability within that eight month period. By May, the 52% with a reading age of less than 10 is reduced by half.

Our experiences indicate that slow learners are very enthusiastic about working with computers. On this Questionnaire, the breakdown of reading ages of the 24 first years as of 1st September '83 was as follows:

Reading Age - Actual Age	Number
0	-

Reading Age - Actual Age	Number
- 1	3
- 2	4
- 3	7
- 4	2
- 5 or more	3

Clearly, the respondents are not all "in the fast lane". Of the second years, 7 are in a remedial class, all but one of the third years are in remedial classes, and the reading abilities of the Pre-Employment respondents are below average.

This perspective is further strengthened by the membership of the Computer Club where more than 50% of the regular participants are from "weaker" classes.

2. The Questionnaire

Q. 2 and 3: 58% of the respondents were under 15 and, thereafter, interest tended to be restricted to classgroups. Of the four classes in Leaving Certificate cycle, three were not represented at all.

Q.4: Again, the vast majority (81%) have worked with computers for two years or less. This indicates an initial enthusiasm which declines (due perhaps to lack of direction and guidance?) unless a peer group maintains an interest.

Q.5: The teachers are not as prominent as they might be here, but our experience has shown that students tend to "feed off" each other's ideas and experiments to great effect. The lack of reading material and its unattractive image is obvious.

Q.6: An objective assessment would yield very different results. What is significant here is the confidence and sense of achievement that many students derive from the experience. Rarely do you find "remedial" students claiming "a good deal" of knowledge or proficiency in traditional subject areas; yet here, only one respondent pleaded ignorance of all eight categories. Graphics and programming in BASIC would seem to be most popular and, again, this is borne out by our experiences.

Q.7: The poor response here was a surprise, and a reminder to us teachers of the perceived gulf between traditional subject areas and new technology. A coherent software input to these areas is required.

Q.8: The Club facilitates the use of machines at lunchtime and after school. The "missing third" use machines as part of their formal timetable, in Maths., Business Studies, etc.

Q.9: This reflects the economic background of the students. Spectrum AZ(6) and Commodore (3) were the machines used.

Conclusions:

1. Common Factors: The most significant is age. Those in first and second year exploit the material available and a threshold is reached after two years when students either drop out or main-

tain interest due to peer pressure. The older students had a good grasp of graphics, word processing and file handling which they explored largely on their own initiative.

2. The major advantage of using computers with weaker students is that it provides an alternative avenue to learning, one which is not hampered by the antipathy to the traditional school environment prevalent among this group. It enhances the pupil's self-image and gives a sense of achievement.

3. The students did not provide any real clues as to how the stucture in the School could be developed, and perhaps they should not have been expected to. The emphasis must be on doing, on immediate results, on building on the sense of achievement gained by the students in their initial contact with computers.

C. TEACHERS' ATTITUDES - WEXFORD TOWN
****

BACKGROUND

In 1980, the management of the second-level schools in Wexford Town came together to formulate some common approach to the introduction of Computing to their schools. As a result, it was decided to put on an Introductory Course in Computers for the teachers in these schools. This Course was run to the end of the school year (June) 1980, and was given by Brendan Mackey at the Vocational School. A Continuation Course was provided during the school year 1980/1981 by Mr. Mackey and Fr. Donal Collins of St. Peter's College, Wexford. In 1981, as a result of negotiations between the Town of Wexford Vocational Education Committee and Waterford, the local Regional Technical College, a two-year Diploma course was provided by Waterford R.T.C. in Wexford Vocational School for teachers. During this time, normal night class courses were provided, including Comal courses provided for teachers by Maurice Brosnan.

The object of the present Case Study is to analyse the reactions of those teachers who attended some or all of these Courses between 1981/'83 and to speculate on the prospects for the proper use of computers in education, based on these reactions. At the outset, it may be interesting to note the drop-out rate from these courses:

Course	Language	Number Started	Number Finished
Introduction (1980)	Basic	35	21
Continuation (1980/'81)	Basic	19	12
R.T.C. Diploma (1981/'82, 1982/'83)	Pascal	17	6

On the first course (Introduction), the 35 included a good number who came along on the first night "to see what it was like" and left. "Significantly, practically all of those who left were from the "non-Maths. and Science" disciplines.) After that, the attendance held remarkably high for the duration of the Course.

At the other end of the scale, when the Diploma Course went deeper into technology and programming there was a rapid fall-off in attendance.

As we were dealing with a compact, easily-identifiable group, we asked them to fill in a Questionnaire, and conducted informal interviews with a number of them in order to ascertain their attitudes.

The survey was carried out by Mary Daffy and Pat Lanigan, Maths. teachers at Wexford Vocational School, in April/May '84, a year after the last course ended.

SUMMARY OF TEACHERS' ATTITUDES

The aim in providing Courses was to familiarise teachers with the Microcomputer, and thus to encourage their use in schools.   All Courses, to a greater or lesser degree, emphasised not just the technology, but the application of the technology to education.   Hence we set out to ascertain whether they found them of benefit, what their Pre-Course expectations were, and to what extent they were now using Microcomputers in their teaching.   As the full results would be far too detailed for this paper, I will summarise the main ones, and our assessment of their significance.

Replies

50 Questionnaires were sent out - 32 replied. (N.B. 28 of the 32 who replied were in the Maths/ Science disciplines.)

I will take the two leading questions together as I believe the replies are significant.
Q. Did you find the Courses helpful?
    Yes: 27   No: 2   No Reply: 3
Q. Are you still using Computers?
    Yes: 15   No: 17

From these replies, it would appear that the majority found the Courses helpful, but less than half were actually still using computers one year later.   At this stage, we concentrate on those who are:

A. Not using Computers

The reasons are many: "Only one computer in the school - not getting a chance to use it"; "Time does not allow - too busy preparing students for exams."; "Can't see how it can be applied to my teaching"; "No good software available"; "Don't know enough yet"; "Maths. teacher monopolises the computer".   However, some interesting trends emerge (even if at first they seem contradictory):
    Over 80% of those not using computers intend to renew their interest in Educational Computing.
    70% expressed a belief that the use of computers could enhance the teaching of their subject.
    50% expressed concern that they were not using computers in their subject area.

Of those who:

B. Do Use Computers

(i) With the exception of one English and one Business Studies, all are Maths./Science teachers either teaching Computer Studies or using Computing in the teaching of Maths. or Science.
(ii) 11 of the 15 teach to Senior classes only.
(iii) The majority teach one class per week of Computer Studies, as per the Department of Education directive.
(iv) A big majority think that student proficiency in Programming is important.
(v) 3 use computers to help slow-learners.
(vi) The majority are dissatisfied with the amount and quality of Educational Software available.

Asked how they think computers could most effectively be used in education:
    7 said Computer Studies as a separate subject,
    9 said as an Educational Aid and Resource (CAL, etc.)
    7 said Computing as a part of existing subject material.
    Obviously, quite a few chose more than one option, did not see it confined to one.

Interim Conclusions

As mentioned earlier, this is not meant to be a detailed statistical analysis, more an overview of the attitudes of one group of second-level teachers.

1. Despite our efforts to widen the scope of Computing across the curriculum, it is still perceived by teachers as being the preserve of the Maths. and Science disciplines.   The "fall-out" rate of other teachers tends to confirm this. When questioned as to the reasons, many of them pointed to the concentration on programming, computational skills and technology in the course content, and the relationship which they see between the algorithmic problem-solving approach and Maths.   The courses hold very little interest for humanities teachers - the emphasis is on the Computational rather than the Information-processing aspects of the new technologies.

2. The majority of the teachers who finished the Courses and are now using Computers in school are Maths./Science teachers who are now teaching Computer Studies.   The main benefit they received from the Courses was the material which they are now passing on to their students. Very few of them are using computers as an aid in teaching their normal subjects.

3. The trend towards an "elitist" subject - i.e. Computer Science or programming proficiency for the minority "top-flight" students is already evident.

4. Whereas the majority believe that the use of Computers can enhance their own subjects, none of them seemed to know how this could be achieved. When asked what their pre-Course expectations were the answers, apart from the obvious "to learn about computers", were so vague that we must conclude that they expected the Courses to show them how the technology could be used in their own daily work - and, despite our best efforts, this the Courses failed to do.

Overall, whereas the Courses achieved the aim of familiarising teachers with computers, in their main objective of achieving some level of application of Computers to the education process the approach has not been successful.

We must remember that there is a great interest in, and curiosity about, computers in society generally, and a great demand for all courses in Computing.   In this context, we have to ask ourselves the obvious question: Are our Courses simply satisfying the curiosity of one particular group, in this case teachers, about the new technology?   If the answer is in the affirmative, then we can hardly claim to be laying the foundations for a system to use Information Technology effectively in education.   This will call for a completely new approach.

5. Perhaps the most discouraging result is the number of teachers who have been "turned off" computers.   Yes, it has to be admitted that in the case of quite a number of teachers (especially as shown above, those in the humanities areas), the Courses have had the opposite effect to that which was intended.   This negative effect is also evident through the involvement of the Computer Education Society in providing courses at national level.   Indeed, it is reflected in the "turnover" evident in the membership of the Society itself over the years.   The conclusion is inescapable: A very high percentage of teachers taking courses in "Computers in Education" either attend such courses simply to find out more about computers with no intention of using them in education or, having taken the courses, are convinced that the material, as presented to them, has no relevance to their everyday work in the classroom.   Whichever is the case, to those of us interested in promoting the use of Information Technology to enhance the education process it most surely indicates that a change of policy is called for.

What Went Wrong?

1. Lack of clearly-defined objectives

Courses, loosely defined as dealing with "Computers in Education", are being offered to teachers without any clear indication of just how they are to be applied in education; i.e. whether they are to equip teachers to teach about technology or whether the teachers are expected to apply Information Technology to their daily work.   We have, as yet, made no clear policy statement on this matter and so the best we have achieved is to give some limited, and often disjointed, information about the new technologies to teachers who then pass it on to their students.   This approach is very suspect("a little learning, etc.").   The relevance of Computing to Education has not been established.

2. Lack of Proper Teacher Training

Apart from the short In-service Courses, there is no clear policy of teacher training in the new technologies.   Various universities and other tertiary institutions are providing courses but these courses tend to reflect the independant outlook of the individual institutions.   Once again, there is no shortage of course material on Technology, or for that matter, on education

(provided by a different department) - what is missing is the application of Technology to Education.   There is no proper scheme for the release of teachers to study the possible applications of Information Technology to their work. Perhaps what is needed is less "raw technology" and more emphasis on the applications to the teacher's subject area.

3. Lack of Co-Ordination

There are many examples of individual projects being carried out in various areas, but generally they represent a wasteful duplication of effort. What is sadly lacking is a national body to co-ordinate these efforts, such as the Microelectronics Education Programme in Great Britain.

4. The Role of the Teacher

One of the most fundamental problems besetting the attempts to introduce Information Technology to the education system is a basic misunderstanding of the role of the teacher in the education process. In a country like ours, with a centralised system which is strongly curriculum and examination orientated, the teacher is involved mainly in transmitting information and preparing students for examinations.   Under the pressures of such a system, he has no time for research into teaching or learning methodology.   A great deal of prospective educational innovation has failed because of the different perceptions of this role by the Educationalist and the Educator.   Educational research tends to be done remote from both the classroom atmosphere and the classroom practitioner.   Some exciting theories have been expounded by Educationalists which either have never been heard of by Educators or have failed the test of exposure to the real world of education. Unfortunately, the indications are that research in Educational Technology is going the same way.

5. Machines before People

In common with many other countries, Ireland has suffered from the arrival of technology before the people in a particular occupation had been prepared for it.   In hindsight, the "Micro computer for every Secondary School" scheme was a mistake for this very reason.   Microcomputers were put into schools before anybody in the schools knew how to use them or, more importantly, how to use them in an educational context.   The disillusionment caused by such an exposure to technology may yet prove to be the greatest barrier to overcome in our future efforts.   If I may quote from a submission by our Department of Education to a recent European meeting: "The first step in setting up a Computer Studies Course is to supply the hardware.   The second is to select a suitable language."   No mention of people!   Our experience has shown that the introduction of Microcomputers into a school without the support structures necessary to establish their relevance to the daily work of that school can have a very negative effect, on the attitude of teachers and students alike, to the new technology.

6. The Nature of the Technology

The rapidly changing nature of the technology itself has caused problems for our system. Our education system tends to be extremely conservative, indeed, teachers themselves tend to be conservative. Such a system does not adapt easily to change and the indications are that we will have to adopt a far more flexible approach if we are to successfully adopt the new technologies. It seems inevitable that they will cause fundamental change and unless our formal education system is able to adapt to such change, many of our present structures will become obsolete.

7. The Relevance of Information Technology to Education

To summarise, I would suggest that while we are busy introducing computers into our schools and competing with private agencies in providing courses in Computing for our students, in the long term we will be unsuccessful so long as we fail to establish the real relevance of Information Technology to the education process, i.e. to the teaching and, more importantly, the learning process.

This we have so far failed to do. The new technology can help us to develop new learning strategies, new modes of instructional delivery and can, in fact, create a completely new mode of education more relevant to the needs of the Information Society. We must now work towards developing such systems.

COMPUTERS IN EDUCATION, K. Duncan and D. Harris (eds.)
Elsevier Science Publishers B.V. (North-Holland)
© IFIP, 1985

953

TO COMMENT ON DPS 8/52 HONEYWELL TIME SHARING SYSTEM AND
TO INTRODUCE THE SITUATION OF SEVERAL JOBS

Shen Wei-jun

Dept. of Computer Science & Engineering
Xi'an Jiaotong University, CHINA

This paper is based on experience and practice of using the DPS 8/52 Honeywell
TSS in the first month which arrived our university and introduced to the
situation of several jobs.
We familiarized something after conversation with TSS which enough commentted
on the advantages and disadvantages of DPS 8/52 computer.
Its ablity must be used to the best way.
We hope the related company and manufactory to provide the honest cooperation
and friendship including the honest price and the recent technology.

1. INTRODUCTION

Our undertaking is now going forward to
victory. Using world bank loan our university bought DPS 8/52 computer from American
Honeywell Company. It recently have built
in computer center of our university. Now
they can receive users. The work was
finished sooner than expected. To construct
a developing priority university we need a
very nice computer for education, research
work and administrative control.

According to experience and practice of
using the DPS 8/52 Honeywell TSS we are
talking about the situation of conversation
with GCOS completely in the view of users.

GCOS is operating system of DPS 8/52. Time
Sharing System is subsystem which belong to
GCOS. Using TSS users can directly interchange message with computer, input
program, operate program and see the
results at terminal, simultaneously debug
program in the form of converstion, make
the circulatory operation-remolding-opera-
tion circle shortly.

TSS has multiple and numerous dimensional
character, terminal can provided be batched
job, it is easy to use and suitable to
numerous computer language such as Fortran,
Basic, Pascal, Cobol, Lisp etc. System has
powerful ability and provide numerous
subsystem such as EDIT, ACCESS, CONVERT,
HELP, JOUT, DBUG etc.

Conneting electric source of terminal,
simultaneously pressing CRT and W key,
system demonstrate:

```
$*$ CN
USERID ── xxxxxxxxxxxx
PASSWORD
hhhhhhhhhhhh
```

* Star denotes to enter TSS. If you enter
an alphabet at "*" status system familiarized that it was command.

2. THE SITUATION OF SEVERAL JOBS

To participate examination for the new
computer you must prepare several source
programs. In order to giving job and
batched job to terminal author selected
three source programs as follow:

2.1 Using ASSIGN statement and ASSIGN
labeled GOTO statement we wrote the program
Pay and data Dpay (data file name) which is
used to distribute pay automatically. Its
flowchart is as follow. (include 40 rows,
already pass in Victor 9000 personal computer, you can see the reference (5)).

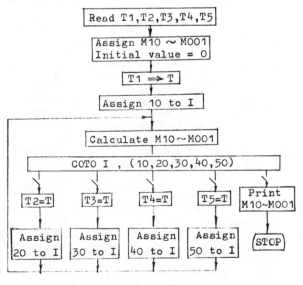

2.2 Computational Program for the Geometric Character of a Blade. It pass the
APPLE personal computer. You can see the

technical report of Xi'an Jaiotong University 84-132. Its flowchart is as follow.
(include 64 rows and three example results).

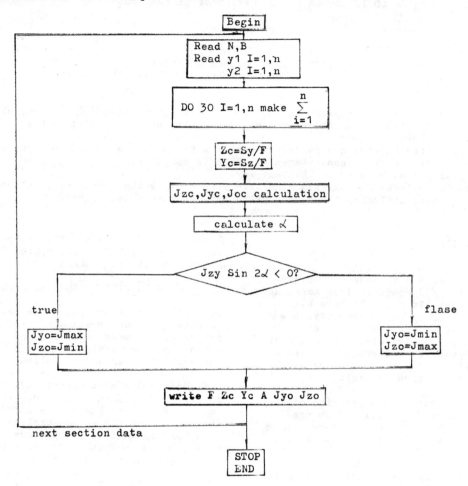

2.3 Thermal Elastic-Plastic Analysis and Computer Program for Turbine Blade Root Fastenings. It pass the West Germany Siemens 7760, include 935 rows, need storage element 133585. You can see Proceedings of the International Conference on Finite Element Methods P 958-960. Its flowchart is as follow:

From Siemens 7760 convert to Honeywell DPS 8/52 we must pay attention to the seven

symbols whose code holes is diffirent.

&
continuation
line sign

*
asterisk

<
less than

>
more than

+
plus sign

−
minus sign

=
equal sign

We can enter system EDIT and use the following command.

```
*-RVS:/xxx/:/yyy/  make local modification
*-RVS:/xxx/;*:/yyy/ make total modification
```

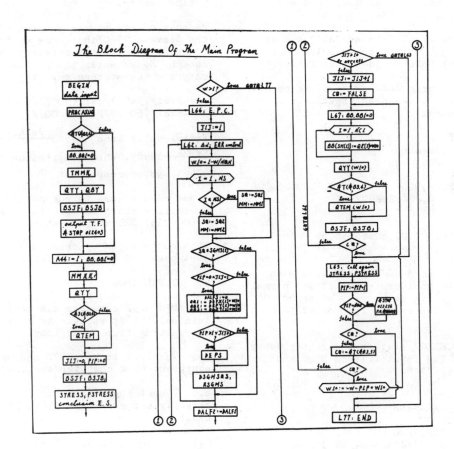

3. CREATE FILE SYSTEM

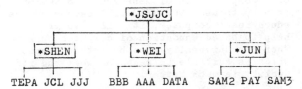

According to the file and record control manual file system was applied by tree structure. Generally you create catalog first, then create the file. Catalog and file are selected by a name which you can easy remember. In the figure the asterisk denotes catalog, other are file.

4. SUCCESSFUL SHARING DATA FILE AND BATCHED JOB

When you will creat data file, you can use the command *AUTO or *AUTO 10,10. After creating the line number you type your data line by line. Deleting line number use command *STRIP then storing as a data file use command *SAVE DPAY. For example the data file of program PAY named DPAY. Before runing the program use command *FRN, you must use command *GET DPAY "10",Q. "10" is the channel number of read stetement of source program. Checking *AFT and *RLMO"10" is necessary. Camma Q denotes priority, you can instead of R or W. On the other hand, Command *GET is prepareing that the data input automatically. If compilation discovers some error the form of error information is as follow:

```
SOURCE LINE 1350
<W> 1457 DO Loop Index N May not be
          Redefined in Call or Abnormal
          Function
SOURCE LINE 4060
<W> 1470 Equality or Non-equality Com-
          parison May not be Meaningful in
```

Logical If Expressions.

You must overcome the wrong until it have no syntax error. Computer inputs data automatically and does H* code file and prints results.

If you gave terminal batched job you must writing your job by job control language. Two successful batched job is as follow:

4.1 Source program JSJJC/JUN/PAY is as a permanent file. Other need input data at job control card.

```
$$ N,J,MONI
$:IDENT:123,AP-SHEN
$:USERID:JSJJC$xxxxx
$:OPTION:FORT77
$:FORT77:NFORM,NLNO
$:PRMFL:S*,R,S,JSJJC/JUN/PAY
$:EXECUTE
$:DATA:I*
  53.26,66.74,101.27,80.68,38.51
$:ENDJOB
```

This job card named JSJJC/SHEN/JJJ. When you operate to monitor (*JRN) it can normal termination. If it is correct at report 06 you can print the result by command "Direct Onl".

4.2 TO use SELECT statement directly debug object file. The input file is "10" and output file is "11".

```
$$ N,J,MONI
$:IDENT:123,AP-SHEN
$:OPTION:FORT77
$:FORT77:NFORM,NLNO
$$ SELECT (JSJJC/JUN/SAM2/OBJ)
$:EXECUTE
$:PRMFL:10,R.S,JSJJC/SHEN/DDD
$:PRMFL:**,W,S,JSJJC/OUT
$:LIMIS:100,250K,-5K,50K
$:ENDJOB
```

Which also can normal termination. It may be storage by means of a permanent file.

5. THE RESULTS OF EXAMINATION FOR COMPUTER

For the job 1. 2. you can creat program first, pass the syntax check, compilation, operation and get the correct results. For the job 3. syntax tells us:

    16   overflow fault
  *HELP ⟩ System response said:

The subsystem in execution encountered an overflow condition at the designated lacation and the subsystem did not specify a fault vector. The location is relative to zero (see edit map) unless it is a master subsystem. Then the location is relative to TSS zero, and one must determine the load address of the subsystem to determine the fault lacation in the master subsystem. Review your program input for incorrect data before requesting help from the computing center.

Because of the source program already pass the Siemens 7760 that make us trouble. We consider the storage capacity that is not enough. So we enter the system *EDIT and compress the storage capacity.

    -RVS:/(3600)/;:/(3000)/
    *-RVS:/(50000)/:/(40000)/

Individually from 133585 —reduce→ 109485 —reduce→ 82485. When compression reached to 99485 system responses:

    Not enough core to run job
    Compiler abort 000)80 in phase 4
    (006055) DRL abort - abort file written.

When compression reached to 82485 program just pass and become perfect.

6. CONCLUSION

6.1 DPS 8/52 computer has many sharing terminal. It is sutable to many users but the waiting time is so long.

6.2 We ought to buy FR7T and speed up the equipment of a computer center.

6.3 Computer provides each user the storage capacity not more than 256K. It was too small.

6.4 The computer play large role in education but restrict in research work.

6.5 Print spend so much paper.

6.6 Compare with Siemens 7760 TSS command is easy to use. DPS 8/52 will become a nice educational computer, it will give great help to based education of computer applied. Then our university must buy other computer which is suitable to research work and its quality is much better.

We hope the related company and manufactory to provide the honest cooperation and friendship including the honest price and the recent technology.

7. REFERENCES

(1) DPS8 GCOS8 On Time Sharing System
    Reference Manual
(2) DPS8 GOS8 On Job Control Language
(3) Honeywell Level 66 Fortran-77 User's
    Guide
(4) Jerrold L. Wagener
    Fortran 77 Principles of Programming

1980

(5) Question and Answer of Fortran Language. Tsing Hua University 1983

(6) Siemens 7760 User's Manual. 631 Research Institute. 1979.9.

(7) Shen Wei-jun "Computational Program for the Geometric Character of a Blade" Scientific Technical Report of Xi'an Jaiotong University 84-132 1984.4.

(8) Shen Wei-Jun "Thermal Elastic-Plastic Analysis and Computer Program for Turbine Blade Root Fastenings." Proceedings of the International Conference on Finite Element Methods. p958-960 1982

(9) Donald M. Monro "Computing with Fortran: A Practical Course".

(10) J.N.P. Hume "Programming Fortran 77: A Structured Approach".

(11) Frank L. Friedman "Problem Solving and Structured Approach".

(12) Willian R. Fuller "Fortran Programming: A Supplement For Calculus Courses".

(13) CP/M fortran-80 for APPLE2

(14) Honeywell Lever 66 TSS Pocket Cuide.

COMPUTERS IN EDUCATION, K. Duncan and D. Harris (eds.)
Elsevier Science Publishers B.V. (North-Holland)
© IFIP, 1985

TEACHING INFORMATICS AT VARIOUS LEVELS IN GENERAL EDUCATION -
A SURVEY OF THE SITUATION IN THE FEDERAL REPUBLIC OF GERMANY

Dr. Ulrich Bosler

IPN - Institute for Science Education
Olshausenstr. 40, D-2300 Kiel

This article provides a survey of various aspects of informatics in
general education. Detailed coverage of this subject in grades 11 to
13 (age 16 to 18) is given. The application-oriented content, together
with projects - many of which have been introduced and tested in
schools - bear witness to a high level of informatics education. The
formative stage of this subject at upper secondary level is now essentially completed.
Major changes are now taking place in lower secondary education (age
10 to 15). A long-term plan for pupils aged 13 to 18 is outlined here
and the features of the IPN computer literacy curriculum (for all 13
year old pupils) described.
The reasons for the small amount of informatics in Elementary Education
(age 6 to 10) are demonstrated, as well as those for the striking lack
of major projects in Computer Assisted Instruction.
The article also contains further details, information sources and an
exhaustive bibliography.

1. CONDITIONS RELATING TO SCHOOL

The Federal Republic including West
Berlin has a total of approximately 62
million inhabitants. The state ("Land")
of North Rhine-Westphalia, with 17
million, has the highest population,
while Bremen, with 750 000, has the
lowest.

Federally structured school system

The authority for the school system lies
with the 10 Länder and West Berlin.
Authoritative control includes regulations regarding the curriculum, time
schedules, professional requirements and
recruitment of teachers, school buildings and equipment. The system helps to
ensure that irrequalities in facilities
and teaching personnel are avoided to a
large extent.

The educational system in the FRG is
primarily characterized by its 4-year
elementary school ("Grundschule", age
6 to 10), followed by the tripartite
system of secondary education, with
"Hauptschule" (up to age 15), "Realschule" (up to age 16) and "Gymnasium"
(up to age 19). A minority of Länder,
most private schools and the several
dozen comprehensive schools spread
throughout the FRG either postpone the
decision as to which type of school a
pupil should attend, or use a setting
system.

Wide-ranging reforms have been applied
to upper secondary education at the
Gymnasium (age 16 to 19), where a
system of courses providing for various
optional subjects has been introduced.

*About 50% of Realschulen and Gymnasien
are equipped with computers*

Judging on the basis of various reports,
I would estimate that approximately 50%
of general schools - especially in upper
secondary education and exclusive of
Grundschule and Hauptschule - are well
equipped with microcomputers of different makes or have access to a large
computer.

2. THE USE OF THE COMPUTER AT THE UPPER SECONDARY LEVEL

2.1 Teaching informatics

The introduction of informatics in the
Federal Republic was at first concentrated on pupils aged 16 to 18. An
independent subject evolved. The application-oriented content in the syllabi
of many Länder, together with projects -
many of which have been introduced and
testes in schools - bear witness to a
high level of informatics education
(cf. SCHULZ-ZANDER, 1981). Approximately
10% of pupils take part in informatics
instruction, and the number is steadily
increasing (BURKERT, 1984), although for
many pupils it means additional lessons

used to develop proposals for computer
literacy for all pupils at the age of 13.

The following areas are to be dealt with
together:

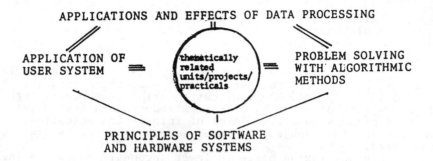

A project-oriented curriculum

The core of the 60-period curriculum -
approximately 30 periods - is thus to be
project-oriented. The pupils begin, for
example, by dealing with their own leisure
activities. They compile relevant lists
and try to classify the various items.
They produce a suitable program and feed
in the data. During this process, the
pupils deal with the principles of the
construction of software and hardware
systems. As the work progresses, the
pupils see the stored and evaluated data
about themselves. This can lead to treatment of issues such as data protection,
as well as the application and outcomes
of data processing. The project-oriented
approach is complemented by two phases
for introduction and extension of the
material, which can deal with topics not
ocuuring in the project. It is also
possible, however to include one or both
phases in the project-oriented section.
The following figure demonstrates this
tripartite division and refers to some
of the eight examples worked on so far.

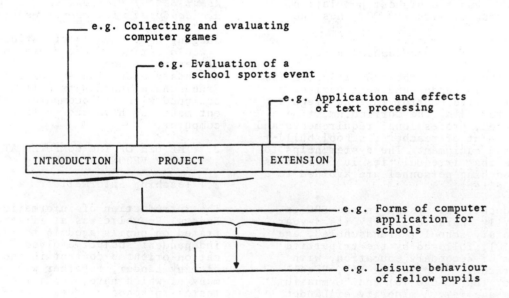

Detailed results are published in BOSLER,
HAMPE, WANKE, van WEERT, 1985.

on their timetable. All federal states offer courses up to Abitur (certificate of upper secondary education). The courses usually comprise 160 or more periods. The formative stage of this subject is now essentially completed.

Project instruction of up to one year

A special feature is that many Länder offer projects with themes chosen by the pupils themselves. Software projects are usually chosen, lasting between six months and a year (with 3 periods per week). The following example is based on syllabi in Berlin and Schleswig-Holstein.

1st year	application-oriented treatment of informatics Increasing complexity of case studies	
2nd year	Transition phase	one or two projects

Themes taken from the area of school administation are often used in such projects (cf. also BUHSE, 1983). In the teachers' book on Metzler Informatics is described how pupils at two schools produced in a professional way a computer forecast of the results of a parliamentary election (cf. BOSLER, BUHSE, HARBECK, MOLL, SCHLICHTIG, THODE, WILMS, 1984). Further examples can be found in LOG IN 3 (1983) No. 2.

What are the causes of the consolidation of informatics at upper secondary level?

It was possible to introduce a new subject to pupils aged 16 to 18. This new subject had no preconceived path to follow. Forms of instruction were introduced, which could not have been used to the same extent in other subjects, for example applications and carrying out wide-ranging projects.

In the last 15 years, experience has been gained with computer education, pioneered by Bavaria and Berlin. Initially, hardware-oriented syllaby were developed, later replaced by application-oriented syllabi. University-oriented computer science is not a significant feature in these revised syllabi. Emphasis is placed rather on orientation to practice and extensive software projects.

Establishment of infrastructure

The introduction was consistently carried out. Acquisition of hardware alone was avoided. Major innovations were based on pilot experiments ("Modellversuche"), each lasting three to four years. These were usually funded by the federal government in conjunction with one Land. For example the objective of one pilot experiment had been the development of teaching materials for a three-year course of informatics at upper secondary level in Schleswig-Holstein.

This material was prepared at one school and tested in four others. Guidance was provided by the IPN in its capacity as institute for science education (cf. BOSLER, LEHRKE, SCHULZ-ZANDER, 1983).

Important results of the pilot experiment went beyond the original objectives; hardware was procured and there was close co-operation between the teachers themselves as well as between teachers and persons acting as scientific advisers. Intensive training of the participant teachers resulted from the preparation of their own teaching materials. In one region, infrastructure was developed.

Examples are the development of a curriculum for computer science in the Rhineland Palatinate (cf. HOSSEUS, 1983), the development of teaching materials in North Rhine-Westphalia (cf. DRESCH, et al., 1979), for pupils aged 14 and 15 in Berlin (cf. ARLT et al., 1980-1984) and a supraregional pilot experiment coordinated by the IPN in which programming languages were evaluted and teaching materials prepared (cf. SCHULZ-ZANDER, BOSLER, HANSEN, LEHRKE, 1983).

In the past, pilot experiments have been the most important - but also the most expensive - instrument for the institutionalisation and recognition of informatics teaching.

This meant that the problem of insufficient in-service teacher training had less effect, due to the influence of certain "islands" within the FRG with a good infrastructure and a high standard of qualification among teachers.

In this way, the lack of good instruction material could also be countered.

Improved instructional material

Good instructional material was gradually produced (e.g. OCKER, SCHÖTTLE,
SIMON, 1979; BAUMANN, 1980 and DRESCH,
FROBEL, KOSCHORREK, 1983/84). In spring
1984, a school textbook was published,
which lays claim to a standard comparable
to that of established textbooks in
other subjects. The textbook by BOSLER,
BUHSE, HARBECK, MOLL, SCHLICHTIG, THODE,
WILMS, 1984 is intended for instruction
for the age range 16 to 19.

Further in-service training for teachers

The amount of in-service teacher training
is still limited. The trend is increasingly a progression from advanced training to a complete schedule of course
series (particularly in the states of
Berlin, Lower Saxony and the Rhineland
Palatinate).

2.2 The use of the computer in other
    subjects areas

In the FRG, as in other countries, computers in various forms are of course
used in a wide variety of subjects and
project groups. Further details can be
found in HANSEN, 1984.

3. COMPUER EDUCATION AT LOWER SECONDARY
    LEVEL

Computer education is currently undergoing considerable change at lower
secondary level. In the next few years,
intensive financial support will be given
to projects in this area.

3.1 Informatics in optional courses

Comprehensive subject options have been
developed for pupils aged 14 and 15 in
Bavaria and Berlin (cf. ARLT et al., 1980
to 1984). A number of pupils became acquainted with the use of microcomputers,
especially in mathematics, the sciences
and in project groups (cf. PESCHKE,
HULLEN, DIEMER, 1984).

3.2 Informatics for all pupils

In recent years, microcomputers have made
their way increasingly into the spheres
of work and everyday life. Home computers
were the best-selling Christmas presents
in recent years.

From 1983 onwards, educationalists increasingly discussed the issue of microcomputers and school. As in many other countries, a variety of views habe been expressed on this subject, which need not
to be repeated here (cf. BOSLER, HAMPE,

WANKE, van WEERT, 1984).

A new aspect which entered the discussion
is the demand for computer literacy for
all pupils at the lower secondary level.
The Land of Baden-Württemberg, for
example, allows for computer science
topics in various subject for pupils of
14 upwards (cf. MINISTERIUM FÜR KULTUS
UND SPORT, BADEN-WÜRTTEMBERG, 1984).
Following these initial approaches in
Bavaria, Berlin and Baden-Württemberg,
a major conference in March 1984 produced
long-term perspectives for computer
literacy and further instruction in this
discipline (cf. PESCHKE, HULLEN, DIEMER,
1984). This is demonstrated by the
following chart.

		age
computer literacy for all pupils (foundation I)		13
options	individual	14
	subjects	15
foundation II		16
subject	individual	17
informatics	subjects	18

The major recommendation of the experts
was for the development of a syllabus in
computer literacy valid for all pupils
at lower secondary level, which would be
introduced into schools within a few
years, and upon which subsequent instruction could build, either as an optional subject or as a topic within
various other subjects.

At present, concepts are still being
worked upon. If, in some 5-10 years'
time, all children are following a
basic computer literacy course, this
should have repurssions in the area
of vocational education, where only a
few lessons are currently set aside for
data processing.

3.3 IPN curriculum computer literacy

The Institute for Science Education (IPN),
which operates at national level, has
drawn particularly on work carried out in
Holland (cf. van WEERT, 1983) and by the
Association for Teacher Education in
Europe (ATEE) (cf. van WEERT, 1984). The
special tool of the curriculum conference
(cf. FREY, 1981, 1983 and 1984) was then

A clear delineation of the tasks of computer literacy and of further instruction was aimed at. During basic education, the pupil should play the role of a user and during further instruction rather the role of an expert.

Use of software tools

The pupil role adopted and the limit of 60 periods suggests that software tools such as data management systems (for example dBASE II) should used for the implementation of algorithms rather than the use of programming languages like BASIC or PASCAL.

If only 60 periods are available, a decision must eventually be taken as to whether a programming language course is to be offered, or whether time is to be taken to deal with the learning areas as interrelated topics, in which case limitations on the teaching time for programming languages would be necessary.

This limitation appears feasible, as the increasing use of microcomputers in all branches has led to the development of more specialized systems for users, comprising simple control structures. Limitations exist with data structures. Texts, formulae, summations and functions can be manipulated by spreadsheet systems more simply than by the use of programming languages. Data Management Sytems (such as dBASE II) are a further example. Detailed results are published in BOSLER, HAMPE, WANKE, van WEERT, 1985.

A comprehensive experiment has been started for schools in North Rhine-Westphalia, the Land with the highest population, in which syllabi and instruction material are to be developed for the various school types.

4. TEACHING INFORMATICS IN ELEMENTARY EDUCATION

In most Länder in the FRG, the elementary school attended by every child comprises only four years - in contrast to many other countries (e.g. folkeskole in Denmark). The educationalists have great reservations about the extensive introduction of informatics in these first four years. This became apparent at the IFIP-working conference, "Informatics in Elementary Education", in Malente near Kiel in 1983 (cf. TINSLEY, TAGG, 1984).

In my opinion, the reasons are as follows:

- The FRG has a well established curriculum of good quality, highly inter- culum of good quality, highly inter-

activ in its social, physical and emotive dimensions (cf. also, FREY, LAUTERBACH, 1981 and further literatur recommended there);

- It is based on the assumption that direct experience with people, nature and technology are the fundamentals of child development, including its cognition;

- The historical experience with the "book school" fosters the apprehension that informatics at too early an age may reduce direct experience for the case of its use, leading to "verbalism" void of understanding;

- International research has barely touched on the question of personality change and child development through extensive computer use. Projects such as PAPERT, 1982 have concentrated on cognition within highly favourable environments uncommon for the normal school setting.

5. PROGRAMMING LANGUAGES

A lively discussion has been going on about an appropriate programming language. This discussion could be settled by a pilot experiment involving 35 schools (SCHULZ-ZANDER, BOSLER, HANSEN, LEHRKE, 1983).

The choice of the language depends on the time available. If you have less time, an extended - often commercially-oriented - BASIC is useful. If you have more lessons available, languages like PASCAL, LOGO and ELAN are helpful.

The pilot experiment also made clear how important it is for the student to establish good communication with the computer.

PASCAL is spreading in the FRG. Denmark has had good experience with COMAL, an "extended BASIC with PASCAL-like control structures".

6. COMPUTER ASSISTED INSTRUCTION

In the FRG there is strikingly little use made of Computer Assisted Instruction (CAI) in comparison with, for example, the United Kingdom. Until 1975, a large amount of financial support had been given to the promotion of CAI (cf. DER BUNDES- MINISTER FÜR BILDUNG UND WISSENSCHAFT, 1971), with remarkable research results. However, these remained simply the products of research groups and were not disseminated further. One of the reasons for this is that expectations with regard to CAI had been much too high, with the result

that supporters were greatly disappointed when the expected success failed to
come. CAI using large computers was also
too expensive and the dissemination into
the schools was missing.

A reduction in the price of hardware and
improved graphic software have, however,
led to a renewed gradual increase in
minor research in this area.

7. FURTHER INFORMATION

The situation reports in PESCHKE,
HULLEN, DIEMER, 1984 provide a detailed
survey of the current level of informatics in the various Länder. In conjunction with the IPN curriculum computer
literacy material has been compiled
relating to various areas. It includes
discussions on educational policy, exposition of informatics topics, case
studies in the use of computer and a
great deal more (BOSLER, HAMPE, WANKE,
van WEERT, 1985; van WEERT, HAMPE,
1984).

A comprehensive bibliography and references to various institutions are contained in an introductory leaflet for
new teachers and parents (BOSLER,
KAPUNE, LEHMANN, 1985).

The specialist publication "LOG IN -
Informatik in Schule und Ausbildung"
provides a regular view of the situation
in the FRG.

8. REFERENCES:

(1) Arlt, W. (ed.), EDV-Einsatz in Schule
    und Ausbildung - Modelle und Er-
    fahrungen, Reihe Datenverarbeitung
    im Bildungsbereich, Band 1 (München/
    Wien, Oldenbourg, 1981).

(2) Arlt, W. (ed.), Informatik als Schul-
    fach, Reihe Datenverarbeitung im
    Bildungsbereich, Band 4 (München/
    Wien, Oldenbourg, 1981).

(3) Arlt, W., Fleischhut, J., Koerber,
    B., Peters, I., Riedel, D., Rohde,
    M., Modellversuch ECIS - Entwicklung
    von curricularen Elementen für das
    Fach Informatik in der Sekundarstufe I
    (Berlin (West), Freie Universität
    Berlin, verschiedene Broschüren und
    Manuskriptdrucke aus den Jahren 1980-
    1984, erhältlich über Prof. W. Arlt,
    FU Berlin, ZI 7, WE 3, Habelschwerd-
    ter Allee 45, D-1000 Berlin 33).

(4) Baumann, R., Programmieren mit
    PASCAL, Einstieg für Schüler, Hobby-
    programmierer, Volkshochschüler
    (Würzburg, Vogel, 1980).

(5) Bosler, U., Lehrke, M., Schulz-
    Zander, R., Abschlußbericht zur
    wissenschaftlichen Begleitung des
    Modellversuchs PIK, Projekt Infor-
    matik-Kurse (Kiel, IPN, Polyskript,
    1983).

(6) Bosler, U., Buhse, R., Harbeck, G.,
    Moll, G., Thode, R., Schlichtig, T.,
    Wilms, J., Metzler Informatik,
    Grundband (bearbeitet von G. Harbeck),
    Lehrerband (bearbeitet von G. Moll
    und R. Buhse), Sprachenband BASIC
    und Sprachenband PASCAL (bearbeitet
    von R. Thode) (Stuttgart, Metzler,
    1985).

(7) Bosler, U., Hampe, W., Wanke, I.,
    van Weert, T.J. (eds.), Grundbildung
    Informatik - Ziele, Anregungen, Bei-
    spiele (Stuttgart, Metzler, 1985).

(8) Bosler, U., Kapune, Th., Lehmann, B.
    (eds.), Computer in unsere Schule?
    (Weinheim, Beltz, 1985).

(9) Buhse, R., Projekt "Oberstufenver-
    waltung" - Ein Beispiel zur Durch-
    führung eines Projektes im Fach In-
    formatik, in LOG IN 3 (1983) No.2.

(10) Burkert, J., Zum Stand des Informa-
     tikunterrichts in der gymnasialen
     Oberstufe, in Peschke, R., Hullen, G.,
     Diemer, W. (eds.), Band 2, (1984).
     cf. LOG IN 4 (1984) No.2.

(11) Claus, V., Informationstechnologische
     Grundlagen in der Schule, in
     Peschke, R., Hullen, G., Diemer, W.,
     (1984).

(12) Der Bundesminister für Bildung und
     Wissenschaft, Zweites Datenverar-
     beitungsprogramm der Bundesregie-
     rung (1971).

(13) Der Kultusminister des Landes Schles-
     wig-Holstein (ed.), Lehrplan Gymna-
     sien Informatik - Erprobungsfassung
     für einen Modellversuch, AZ XL 120 -
     3243.074 (Kiel, 1979).

(14) Diepold, P., Borg, B. (eds.), Wirt-
     schaftsinformatik an kaufmännischen
     Schulen, Reihe Datenverarbeitung im
     Bildungsbereich, Band 5 (München/
     Wien, Oldenbourg, 1984)

(15) Dresch, P.J., Frobel, G., Koschor-
     rek, H.-J., Teufel, I., Hauf, A.,
     Sturm, L., Kursmaterialien Informa-
     tik, Band 1-7 (Paderborn, FEoLL,
     1979 and Paderborn, Schöningh).

(16) Dresch, P.J., Frobel, G., Koschor-
     rek, H.-J., Informatik S II, Band 1
     und Band 2 (Paderborn, Schöningh,
     1983 and 1984).

(17) Evangelische Akademie Loccum,
     Niedersächsisches Kultusministerium
     (eds.), Neue Technologien und Schule
     Loccumer Protokolle 23/1983 (Loccum,
     Evangelische Akademie, 1984).

(18) Frey, K. (ed.), Curriculum-Kon-
     ferenz, Gebiet Mikroprozessor,
     Arbeitsbericht Nr. 45 (Kiel, IPN,
     1981).

(19) Frey, K., Lauterbach, R., Primary
     Science Education in the Federal
     Republic of Germany. Italien-USA-
     Seminar on Primary Science Educa-
     tion (Kiel, IPN, Polyskript,
     1983).

(20) Frey, K., The Curriculum-Conference,
     an Approach to Curriculum-Develop-
     ment in Groups (Kiel, IPN, Poly-
     skript, 1983).

(21) Frey, K., The Curriculum-Conference
     as a New Approach to the Curriculum
     Development of a Mathematics Curri-
     culum in Technical Training, Welt-
     kongreß für Ingenieurpädagogik
     (Kiel, IPN, Polyskript, 1984).

(22) Hansen, K.-H., Informatikinhalte
     und Computernutzung im naturwissen-
     schaftlichen und technischen Unter-
     richt allgemeinbildender Schulen,
     in Peschke, R., Hullen, G.,
     Diemer, W. (eds.), Band 2 (1984).

(23) Gesellschaft für Informatik (ed.),
     Zielsetzungen und Lerninhalte des
     Informatikunterrichts (Stuttgart,
     Klett, 1976).

(24) Gorny, P., New Information Techno-
     logies in Education in Germany
     (Brüssel, Association for Teacher
     Education in Europe, Polyskript,
     1981).

(25) Gizycki, W., Weiler, U., Auswir-
     kungen einer breiten Einführung
     von Mikroprozessoren auf die
     Bildungs- und Berufsqualifi-
     zierungspolitik (Batelle-Institut,
     Frankfurt, 1979).

(26) Haefner, K., Die Herausforderung
     der Informationstechnik an Bildung
     und Ausbildung, in Evangelische
     Akademie Loccum, Niedersächsisches
     Kultusministerium, a.a.O.

(27) Hosseus, W. (ed.), Programmier-
     sprachen im Unterricht. Abschluß-
     bericht eines Modellversuchs zur
     Einführung der Informatik (Mainz,
     von Hase & Köhler, 1983).

(28) Koerber, B., Mikroelektronik und
     das Schulfach Informatik, in
     Bosler, U., Hansen, K.-H. (eds.),
     Mikroelektronik, sozialer Wandel
     und Bildung (Weinheim, Beltz, 1981).

(29) Kultusministerium Rheinland-Pfalz
     (ed.), Modellversuch zum Computer-
     einsatz in Unterricht und Verwal-
     tung. Entwurf eines lernziel-
     orientierten Lehrplans - Informa-
     tik Grundfach (Mainz, Hase &
     Köhler, 1978).

(30) Lewis, R., Tagg, D. (eds.),
     Computers in Education, 3rd World
     Conference in Computer Education
     in Lausanne, Part 2, Panel Dis-
     cussion (Amsterdam/New York, North
     Holland, 1981).

(31) Lovis, F., Tagg, D. (eds.), Infor-
     matics and Teacher Training.
     Working Conference in Birmingham,
     July 1984 (Amsterdam/New York/
     Oxford, North Holland, 1985).

(32) Ministerium für Kultus und Sport
     Baden-Württemberg, Grundkenntnisse
     über Computer und Informatik -
     Änderungen und Ergänzungen in den
     Lehrplänen der weiterführenden
     Schulen (Published in Schulintern,
     April 1984).

(33) Papert, S., Mindstorms - Kinder,
     Computer und Neues Lernen (Basel/
     Boston/Stuttgart, Birkhäuser,
     1982).

(34) Peschke, R., Hullen, G., Diemer, W.
     (eds.), Anforderungen an neue Lern-
     inhalte. Band 1, Ergebnisse der Fach-
     tagung "Mikroelektronik und Schule
     III", Band 2, Sachstandsberichte
     zum Informatikunterricht in der
     Bundesrepublik Deutschland, Schule
     und Datenverarbeitung in Hessen,
     Heft 20 (Wiesbaden, HIBS, Bodenstedt-
     str. 7, D-6200 Wiesbaden, 1984).

(35) Ocker, S., Schöttle, L., Simon, W.,
     Informatik, Algorithmen und ihre
     Programmierung (München, Olden-
     bourg, 1979).

(36) Schulz-Zander, R., Analyse curri-
     cularer Ansätze für das Schulfach
     Informatik, in Arlt, W. (ed.), EDV-
     Einsatz in Schule und Ausbildung -
     Modelle und Erfahrungen, Datenver-
     arbeitung im Bildungswesen, Band 1
     (München/Wien, Oldenbourg, 1978).

(37) Schulz-Zander, R., Ein didaktischer
     Ansatz für den Informatikunterricht,
     in LOG IN 1 (1981) No. 1.

(38) Schulz-Zander, R., Bosler, U.,
     Hansen, K.-H., Lehrke, M., Schul-
     spezifische Programmiersprachen im
     Informatikunterricht. Abschlußbe-
     richt der Modellversuche "Überregio-
     nale Erprobung und Vergleich von
     schulspezifischen Programmier-
     sprachen im Informatik- und Daten-
     verarbeitungsunterricht". IPN-
     Arbeitsbericht Nr. 52 (Kiel, IPN,
     1983).
     Empfehlungen in LOG IN 3 (1983) No.2
     Kurzfassung in LOG IN 3 (1983) No.3.

(39) Tinsley, D., Tagg, D. (eds.), Infor-
     matics in Elementary Education.
     Working Conference in Malente near
     Kiel, July 1983 (Amsterdam/New York/
     Oxford, North Holland, 1984).

(40) van WEERT, T.J., Projekt Informa-
     tionstechnologie im Unterricht,
     in LOG IN 3 (1883) No. 4.

(41) van Weert, T.J. (ed.), A model
     syllabus on literacy in information
     technology for all teachers (ATEE,
     B-1050 Brussels, 51, rue de la Con-
     corde) Deutsche Fassung, LOG IN 4
     (1984) No. 4).

(42) van Weert, T.J., Basislehrgang In-
     formatik - 'Bürgerinformatik' für
     alle Schüler, in Bosler, U., Hampe,
     W., Wanke, I., van Weert, T.J.,
     (1984).

(43) van Weert, T.J., Hampe, W., Curri-
     culum-Konferenz Grundbildung Infor-
     matik - Hintergrundmaterial zum
     Informationsangebot (Kiel, IPN,
     Polyskript, 1984).

COMPUTERS IN EDUCATION, K. Duncan and D. Harris (eds.)
Elsevier Science Publishers B.V. (North-Holland)
© IFIP, 1985

ODENSE   A TOWN IN DENMARK   WHY AND HOW

Emil Pedersen   and   Niels Tovgaard

Odense
DENMARK

The Danish primary school has a special outline. We shall have to start by drawing this, as it is the condition of replying to the questions why and how.

The Danish primary school is an integral part of our society, and thus a mutual influence takes place. In practice, the social influence is implemented through laws and guidelines defined by certain limits to the obligations and allowances of the primary school. Therefore, development in the primary school may contribute to influencing development in society on a long view.

The primary school develops from within between the Primary School Acts, and has often almost broken the limits of the Act, before a new bill has been passed. This is made possible by a very elastic preamble, and by the fact that, on principle, each primary school has its own syllabus.

Thus, the preamble reads:"It is the aim of the primary school to enable the pupils - in collaboration with the parents - to acquire knowledge, skills, working methods, and ways of expressing themselves which will contribute to the versatile development of each individual pupil. Subsection 2. In all its work, the primary school must seek to create such possibilities of experience and self-activity that the pupil may increase his desire to learn, display his imagination, and train his capability of independent evaluation and attitudes.
Subsection 3. The primary school pripares the pupils to understanding and taking an active part in a decocratic society, and to share the responsibility for the solotion of common tasks. Therefore, the instruction and the entire daily life of the scholl must build on freedom of spirit and decocracy."

This peculiar interplay between school and society has repeated itself in the field of technological development, although the formal wording of the school legislation in Denmark in the seventies should almost be characterized as restraining.

In Odense, the endeavours in 1971 and 1972 took place on the verbal level. In the schoolyear 1973/74 we started up with 3 classes in "datalære", growing to 8 in 1974/75. Already then it was clear to everybody that a continued offer to the pupils in grades 8, 9, and 10 of the optional subject "datalære" would cause an extensively increased interest with the pupils - if

not a "boom" in the subject.

Today (1984) it is almost the favourite optional subject, only exceeded by German (English is compulsory). Statistics show that there were 111 "datalære" classes in the school year 1982/83 and 147 in 1983/84. The pupils have realized that already now - in primary school - as well as later on as citizens, they shall need this knowledge, especially in view of the fact that "datalære", from being computer science (the science of data, their existence and use), via an extension also focussing on communication and problemsolving, now comprises the conseqences to man and society, so that the subject can be characterized most suitably by the consept "datalære"/informatics. School legislation has taken the conseqences so that now, with effect form 1st August 1984, the subject "datalære" has been legalized as an optional subject.

Parallel to this development the micro computer has been applied as a tool, an educational aid, in a long series of the school subjects. In this connection we must emphasize, howewer, that we regard it as an aid corresponding to blackboard/ chalk, paper/pencil, taperecorder, overhead projector, video, minitutor, languagemaster, etc. In this relation it should only be applied if it is a better tool, or at least just as good as the others, emphasizing that it is an aid in a teacher's and his pupils hands. It can never replace the teacher himself.

The following describes the results of a series of experiments, starting with experiments with "datalære" as an optional subject in grades 8, 9, and 10 in 1975/76, now concluded with experiments with "datalære" as a compulsory subject at lower secondary (grades 5 and 6) in 1982/84:

The aim of the experimental work in 1982/83 in the "datalære" instruction taking place at the Sct. Hans School (teacher Niels Tovgaard) and the Seden School (teacher Niels Askær and Christian Wang) is formulated as follows:

" - to plan, carry out, and follow up instruction in the subject "datalære" as a compulsary subject in grades 5 and 6, and as an optional subject in grades 8 and 9.

  - to work out a proposal for instruction - comprising edp-systems to be used by children.

- to gather practical, methodical, and pedagogical experience from the instruction in question."

Thus, the "datalære" must contain technical/
practical elements as well as social aspects, in
order that the pupils acquire a basis for independent attitudes in relation to the technological, economical, occupational, and human aspects,
positive as well as negative, connected with society's applikation of edp and computers.

THE CONTENTS OF THE EXPERIMENT was arranged in
such a way that it reflected the interaction
between man and technology. Therefore, the contents were divided into 3 main themes:

1. the functional principles behind micro-
   processor-based technology.

2. application of micro-processor-based
   technology.

3. human and social conseqences of the
   application of micro-processor-based
   technology.

One of the basic ideas in this experimental
work was to be as "universal" as possible. A
problem complex was to be considered from several points of view. This was illustrated by
the "datalære" house.

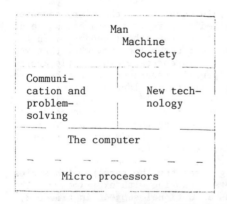

An instructional sequence comprises all
4 rooms.

Another of the basic attitudes assumed that the
instruction was to be based upon concrete materials. Furthermore, the instruction should have
the children's world of experience and consepts
as a starting point and deal with problem areas
from their own daily life.

From the wish to examine to what extend it would
be possible to give the pupils an understanding
of the development taking place in many working
processes, i.e. the development from manual via
mechanical to automatic processes, the project

"automatic control" was started up. This project was divided into two parts: control of
traffic lights, and control of industrial robots.

From the report of the experiment we quote:

"Computers are problem-solving machines. If you
are to "teach" a computer to solve a problem,
i. e. program it, you have to possess certain
general skills in solving problems.

One of the most important skills in this connection is the capability of structural thinking: to be able to work out a plan, a strategy,
or an algorithm for the procedure to be applied
in order to reach the solution of the problem.

Therefore, it is an obvious advantage to dispo-
se of a programming language which can reflect
the structure of the solving method itself (the
algorithm to be applied) and at the same time
contains linguistic structures which make it
easy to describe each individual part of the
solving method to other persons, and to the
computer, of course. The programming language
should assist the problem solver in structural
thinking.

In short we make two main demands on the programming languages to be applied in the "datalære" instruction: They must contain well-deve-
loped algorithmic structures and linguistic
structures.

In the following we shall describe two examples
of "concrete materials": control of traffic
lights and control of robots.

For the instruction sequence of control of traffic lights we developed concrete materials in
the form of a number of crossroads made in
chipboard and fitted with mini traffic lights.
Furthermore, a new programming language was de-
velopeded. In this language the pupil could instruct the computer what to do, using almost
his own terms. It was an essential point to us
that it should be easy to learn to use the language and that it was as close to the pupil's
everyday language as possible. To illustrate
this, a program activating a traffic light would
look like this:

```
1. ON RED (1)
2.    PAUSE (1)
3. OFF RED (1)
4.    PAUSE (1)
5. START AGAIN
```

It turned out that the pupils found no difficulty at all in using this language. They could use
all their imagination for solving the algorithmic problem itself, and it was not necessary to
spend much time on acquiring knowledge of a complicated language.

For the instruction sequence of control of an industrial robot, a toy robot was applied. It consisted of a conveyor belt and a crane. Being constructed of toys, the model gave the children the impression that "they could just play with it", which was why they were not afraid of making errors in their work with it. According to the same principles as mentioned for the traffic light, a language was developed for control of the robot. E. g. a control program might look as follows:

```
 1. CONVEYOR FORWARD (4)
 2. CRANE DOWN (3)
 3. MAGNET ON
 4. CRANE UP (3)
 5. CRANE LEFT (90)
 6. CRANE DOWN (3)
 7. MAGNET OFF
 8. CRANE UP (3)
 9. CRANE RIGHT (90)
10. START AGAIN
```

The purpose of the experiment was to reveal whether it was possible to teach children at primary and lower secondary "datalære". The reply to this question was an unconditioned 'yes'!

With the right instructional aids it is even possible to give the children a good basis for understanding the impact of technology to society, for the individual as well for the group. Furthermore, it is possible to make them reasonably competent in assessing the application of technology in various situations. Furthermore, the experiment has proved quite clearly that it is possible to start up instruction in "datalære" in primary and lower secondary and then follow up this basis instruction in grades 8-9. But this requires a large selection of suitable instructional materials, implying in this connection that they must be concrete — that they must be developed for children's use — and that the materials will lead to logical treatment of well-defined units in the instruction.

This experimental series has contributed to developing the "datalære" concept in Denmark. A new legislation — with reference to the introductory reflections of this contribution — can hereafter incorporate "datalære" /informatics as an independent compulsory subject in grades 5-6 (age 11-12) and as an optional subject in grades 8, 9 and 10 (age 14-16). In this case, the contents, both in grades 5 - 6 and 8 -10, should consist of the abovementioned main areas:

1. the functional principles of the microprocessor-based technology
2. the application of microprocessor-based technology
3. human and social consequences of the application of microprocessor-based technology

The treatment of these main areas should be integrated.

APPLICATION OF EDP IN EDUCATION

In continuation of the experimental work in primary and in an attempt to describe the spectrum of activities constituting the everyday life of the school, one of our collegues, Chr. Wang, Seden School, has lined up the activities as extreme ends, on one side activities the purpose of which is to increase the quantity of the pupil's specific skills and knowledge, on the other side activities aiming at increasing the quantity of the children's general possibilities of development:

ACTIVITIES AND INSTRUCTIONAL MATERIALS

SPECTRUM

practice	play
train	experiment
closed	open
convergent	divergent
competition	cooperation
problem solving	problem creating
fixed	flexible
error = negative	error = positive

specifik knowledge	general consepts and principles
specifik skills	general strategies

finished programmes	programming languages and games

Elaboration of the various keywords:

PRACTICE/PLAY: Small children practice all the time while they play. They practice over and over again — they seem to love repetition; and they get better, of cource, in no time. When they play with others it is typical that they often change the "rules" of the game. When the adults do not interfere, the children see to it themselves that the game offers appropriate challenges of suitable difficulty.

TRAIN/EXPERIMENT:"Training" seems a more purposeful activity than "practising". When one trains, one does so because one has a certain aim to attain - and fast. Similarly, "experimenting" is a more purposeful activity than playing.

CLOSED/OPEN: When someone trains, one's behaviour is closed in the sense that one "concentrates on the task" - shutting out all disturbances, so to speak. When experimenting, however, one is often bound to be open to thoughts and ideas from outside if the experiments are to lead to something useful that can bring one forward.

CONVERGENT/DIVERGENT:These terms cover almost the same as above. Divergent is to many people a better word than the loaded "creative". In a convergent activity, the teachers' replies for instance will differ considerably from the ones in a divergent activity.

COMPETITION/COORPERATION: Training activities lead to competition. We kvow that - is it hard to avoid. The experimenting activities, by contrast, invite coorperation. Many experiments can only be made through a coorperation with others - pupils and teachers.

PROBLEM SOLVING/PROBLEM CREATING: When the pupils are training, the activities almost always consist of problems that they have not decided themselves, (e.g. numeral training, spelling exercises etc.). This may be one of the reasons why it is difficult for the pupils to muster any great interest in the matter. When the pupils are afforded the opportunity to play and experiment suitable materials, they create new great and small problems for themselves all the time. "When it is possible to do this, couldn't I then just do like this instead?" The pupils will often be extremely interested in solving problems they have created and had a chance to influenze themselves.

FIXED/FLEXIBLE: Teaching materials available for training purposes are usually fixed programmes, sometimes with small ramifications where the author has anticipated (or tried to anticipate) how the pupil, the user, will behave underway. Normally, the pupil himself has no influenze on the training programme. Teaching materials for games and experiments, by contrast, must be designed in such a way that they constitute an open offer to the pupils. It is up to the pupils to decide what is going to happen. The benefit of the programme is the pupil's mutual discussions in which ideas and arguments are put to the test, rather than the resulting physical product.

POSITIVE AND NEGATIVE ERRORS: In a training programme, errors are something which must be avoided. Errors are conceived by the pupils as something negative. In this type of activity errors contribute to sorting the pupils. But when the pupils get the opportunity to participate in various games and experiments, errors occurred are not conceived as something negative in the way it was before. In pedagogical terms the errors can be characterized as something positive in the sense that they often occation invalidation of assumptions or theories and act as incentives for further experiments.

SPECIFIK KNOWLEDGE AND SKILLS/GENERAL CONCEPTS; PRINCIPLES AND STRATEGIES: When the children perform convergent activities they acquire knowledgeand skills that are associated with specific contexts. By and large, the knowledge can be put to use only in situations that are very similar to the one in which the teaching took place. On the other hand, when the children perform divergent activities the number of situations grows in which they can take advantage of and use the knowledge and skills they have acquired. It seems to be a fact that the children learn to use consepts, principles and solution strategies in a meaningful way in various contexts. The link between the two types of activities thus consists of the process (in the divergent activities) in which previously acquired knowledge and skills are used in new contexts; this must be the objective in large parts of our primary and lower secondary education. Throughout an entire school career the pupils spend their time primarily on convergent activities (left side of the listing); in fact, in special education, i. e. the teaching of pupils with special learning problems, so to speak all activities are convergent. Several reasons could be quoted for this, e. g. : 1) Only a small amount of teaching materials introduce divergent activities (right side of listing). 2) The school has to operate under tight economic conditions. 3) Demands on the part of pupils/parents that the choldren should qualify for future permanent jobs. The final tests certainly come into this context, too. Perhaps the lack of interest in the school evidenced by the older pupils is, in fact, also attributable to the excessive emphasis on convergent activities.

READY-MADE PROGRAMMES/PROGRAMMING LANGUAGE AND GAMES: So far, micro computers have (still apart from computer instruction) primarily been in use for convergent activities (app. 95 per cent according to the Ministry of Education) such as EDP programmes affording the pupils the opportunity to train on a specific topic, often individually. This tends to show that micro computers, so far, have only been used to strengthen the already predominant convergent activities in the school.

Hereby Chr. Wang has pointed at some possibilities (unprecedented to us) for the application of the micro computers, which may contribute to a pedagogical renewal of the everyday life in our schools, - probably applicable for the solution of pedagogical problems which till now we have not been able to solve satisfactorily.

COMPUTERS IN EDUCATION, K. Duncan and D. Harris (eds.)
Elsevier Science Publishers B.V. (North-Holland)
© IFIP, 1985

THE SWEDISH "COMPUTER IN SCHOOL" - COMPIS - PROJECT

Hans Svensson

Österängskolan
Kristianstad
Sweden

Sweden is one of the most computerized countries in the world, yet the arrival of the personal computer took the educational establishment by surprise. In the typical Swedish tradition, the problem ended up in an official committee, resulting in both modification of curriculums for the inclusion of computer programming and computer literacy, and a specification for a personal computer system and associated software suitable for almost every educational situation in the Swedish school system. This specification and the resulting computer system is the topic of this paper.

1. INTRODUCTION

The responsibility for setting up the requirements on the computer system was given to STU, the National Board for Technical Development of Sweden. It was obvious that none of the then commercially available computer systems were satisfactory from an educational viewpoint, and that their weaknesses were bound to become even more disturbing in the near future. The shortcomings were not only limited to the hardware, in fact the shortage of suitable educational software was even more embarassing.

Therefore, a specification was set up for a computer system where these shortcomings were eliminated, a contract for developing a suitable computer system, including the software - with STU giving financial support for the development costs - was proposed, and the manufacturers were encouraged to compete for the contract.
Meanwhile, considerable support was given to schools for buying hardware and sofware equipment which as far as possible fulfilled the specification, in return for which the schools had to report experiences from the equipment, so as to give a solid background for the proposed project and hints for improvements in the specification. A preliminary specification was completed in the autumn of 1981, a formal requirement specification half a year later, and the first systems bought with goverment support were installed another six months later.

To ensure a solid foundation in educational practise, STU formed a group consisting of three STU officials and four teachers representing towns where the evaluation of the later-to-be prototypes was to take place. Connected to this group was a reference group representing SÖ, the National School Supervising Board, Kommunfürbundet and Statskontoret, the latter two representing town districts and government that ultimately were to pay the schools´ computing equipment.

2. THE SPECIFICATION

A. Hardware and firmware

The workstations should have separate keyboards with Swedish standard layout. The monitors should display at least 24 by 80 characters with high legibility, little reflexes and low flicker. They should also have the possibility of graphics display. This latter requirement was considerably enhanced by the demand for a high-resolution graphics screen meaning at least 500 by 500 pixels. The demand for this high resolution originated in CAD/CAM requirements, but was adopted for all workstations.
General requirements for good ergonomics and sturdy design were made, without prescribing any details.
The workstations should have at least 32 K RAM, expandable to more than 128 K, and have an interpretative, structured high-level language built into the firmware.

Author's comment:
These requirements clearly indicate that only a 16-bit computer was practically possible. The graphics would require more memory and computational power than any 8-bit system could provide.

The demands for an interpretative, structured high-level language were at that time only fulfilled by COMAL, also known as COMAL-BASIC. COMAL is an acronym for COMmon Algorithmic Language, a Danish language which has its general structure common with BASIC, but which incorporates flow control and subroutine mechanism very similar to those of Pascal. Unlike Pascal, though, there is no user control of data structures. A particularly advantageous feature of COMAL for educational purposes is the ability to incorporate external subprograms which could be used by the student as tools. It was therefore required that a "toolbox", or subprogram library was to be created for the system as part of the system software.

B. Software

Two vital requirements vere made:

I) Educational software, chiefly written in COMAL and listable, was to be produced in parallel with the hardware and
II) The system should be able to operate in both a multi-user and a single-user environment. This requirement included all software delivered as part of the project.

The first requirement was further pinned down to the following topics:
Computer literacy, as defined in the new curriculum.
Science and mathematics (subroutine library, CAI, simulation programs)
Business (ledgers)
Office education (word processing)
Social sciences
Technology (computer supported experiments)
Measurement and process control
Structured programming

The latter requirement was based on the belief that a multi-user system was going to be a superior alternative to both minicomputers and separate personal computers from both economical and pedagogical standpoint. At that time though, there were few such systems installed in Sweden.

To gain experience from existing systems, schools were encouraged to install multi-user systems with government financial support as mentioned above. Even before that, a few schools had bought such systems of both Swedish and U.S. origin. The author's school - Österängskolan - has had a Corvus-Apple system operating since the end of 1981. Another group of schools bought Apple computers with Z80 Softcards, connected them in a similar Corvus network and tested COMAL on them. COMAL is available under CP/M but not

under Apple DOS.

The experiences gained with the Corvus-Apple multi-user system indicated that the system was quite workable, and offered great advantages in teaching situations, such as giving both student and teacher easy access to common utilities, very fast response, considerable work savings for the teacher when judging and correcting the student's programs, but also troubles caused by erroneous system software in the beginning and insufficient protection against misuse. The general conclusion was, however, that a multi-user system along these lines was the solution to be preferred.

C. Educational support

Requirement for teacher's manuals as well as textbooks and exercising material for the various programs were made.

3. THE CONTRACT

May 12, 1982, the complete requirement specification was sent out to a great number of producers of educational material and computers, urging them to leave a bid for producing the computer system, associated software and educational support. The deadline for bidding was August 31, 1982.

When the various bids were evaluated, special stress was put on their ability to conform with the requirements on the following points:

- The connection between teaching material (text material, exercising material, teacher's and student's manuals) and the hardware. The principle of one main deliverer even in a joint project was considered essential.

- System flexibility meaning that both single-user and multi-user environment should be possible and that delivered software should be portable between those environments.

- Graphic capability demand (500*500 pixels).

- Price/performance ratio.

On December 17, 1982, a contract was signed with one of the bidders, Esselte Studium as a main deliverer. Esselte Studium is one of Sweden's major producers of textbooks and other educational material, and also produces and markets a small computer, Esselte 100, primarily for measurement purposes, but two other

Swedish companies with more experience of sophisticated hardware were subcontracted for the delivery of the hardware. Prototypes of the computer were to be delivered to certain schools for evaluation during 1983/84, and maximum prices for schools within the next years were set up.

Author's comment:
The fact that the contract went to a renowned producer of educational material rather than to a computer manufacturer reflects the viewpoint that the machine itself is just a part of a large educational package, where the other components are of vital importance.

4. THE COMPUTER

After a name contest the selected computer was given its name COMPIS, being both an acronym for COMputer In School and the Swedish word for "pal". It was a 16-bit computer from the outset, being based on the Intel 80186 processor. The main board takes either 16 or 32 RAM chips, that is 128 or 256 K RAM with 64 K chips and up to 1 M - the full addressing space, with 256 K chips. Ample space is provided for ROM firmware.
The graphics is handled by an Intel 82720 graphics controller. This unit easily handles the required 500*500 pixels, in fact it handles 16 times as much memory, or up to 512 K display memory. For the Compis computer, either a lower resolution of 640*400 pixels in black and white, available on the prototype models or four times as much, 1280*800 pixels, also in b/w, and finally 640*400 pixels in colour. The first model requires 32 K display memory, the latter two 128 K. This display memory is entirely separate from the processor's work area. In textmode, 25 lines of 80 characters are normally used.

This layout must be considered quite sophisticated, even from an international viewpoint. The chips were at that time largely untried. However, the requirement for a low price necessiates a low chip count, which is precisely the advantage of these chips.

A modification was made shortly after the contract was signed, when the Intel 80150 chip became available. This contains Digital Research's CP/M-86 operating system, freeing in its turn the RAM from the operating system and also opening up a considerable amount of commercially available software.
Curiously, the problem of the operating system to be chosen had not been considered of enough importance to be included in the contract.

5. EDUCATIONAL MATERIAL

Programs, manuals and textbooks along the prescribed lines have been developed. A chief aspect has been that the material should be "inspiring" rather than "leading", and teach the student to use the computer as a creative educational tool rather than a device to be programmed.

Some examples:

In mathematics, one of the programs uses the graphics for quick display of function graphs and coordinate systems in randomly chosen intervals. Such programs were earlier developed for the Apple II computer, but the greater speed, higher resolution and additional features such as enlarging/diminishing and windowing technique of the new computer opens up far wider horizons.

In biology, a genetics simulation program also developed from an earlier Apple version, enables convenient studies of simulated heritage. The greater speed allows quite large amounts of data processing without undue waiting.

In chemistry, titration curves is a problem for which there is often too little time. But Compis both incorporates a very simple connection for a pH-meter - and other measurement apparatus as well - inherited from the above mentioned small Esselte 100 computer, together with firmware which enables measurement commands with very few program lines, and adds its own unique capability for displaying the curves with very high accuracy. A program for utilising these features has been developed. Thus, these experiments will be far easier to make.

For general computer literacy use, an integrated program with spreadsheet, word processor and data base manager has been developed. It is particularly simple to use, even for primary school pupils.

6. EVALUATION

The prototypes have been tested in 15 schools in four towns in Sweden. The evaluation was completed in the fall of 1984, and the delivery to other schools started at the same time. Educational material was to be evaluated before the end of 1984, but this evaluation is not yet published.

Single-user version of the Compis computer

Non-curricular Aspects
of Computing and Education

COMPUTERS IN EDUCATION, K. Duncan and D. Harris (eds.)
Elsevier Science Publishers B.V. (North-Holland)
© IFIP, 1985

976

COMPUTING COOPERATIVES AND RESOURCE CENTERS

E. Ronald Carruth   Minnesota School Districts Data Processing
Chairperson   Joint Board (TIES), St. Paul, Minnesota

Kaylene Smith Little   Northwest Ohio Educational Television Foundation
                            Computer Resource Center, Bowling Green, Ohio

Kevan Penter   Education Department, Schools Computing Branch
                            East Perth, Western Australia, Australia

Judith Morton   Regional Consortium for Education & Technology,
                            St. Louis, Missouri; Co-author with Robert Benson,
                            St. Louis University

Computing cooperatives and resource center consortiums are increasingly recognized as an effective means for educational institutions to share both financial and professional resources to explore, utilize and promote the application of technology to education. Cooperatives vary in their membership, mission, organizational structure, services and finances. Whether cooperatives focus their services on administrative, instructional or research/evaluation applications of technology, they share a common strategy i.e., to optimize the utilization of scarce resources through cooperation. This session will provide an overview of differing models, each of which may provide ideas for exploring the approach in other environments.

THE MINNESOTA TIES MODEL

The TIES (Total Information Educational Systems) cooperative was organized in 1967. TIES' membership includes 53 Minnesota school districts with a combined enrollment of 235,000 students. TIES provides an array of administrative, instructional and research computing services to its members including financial accounting, personnel, payroll, inventory, transportation, census, scheduling, mark reporting, attendance, health information, instructional courseware development, inservice and field research. TIES operates one of the largest microcomputer software resource centers in the U.S. The TIES model represents a transferable approach to the modern "information resource center" concept which has applicability for educational institutions at all levels. The presentation will overview TIES' mission, goals and services.

A NORTHWEST OHIO COMPUTER RESOURCE CENTER MODEL

Educators face many challenges. The computer technology and how it should be used in the school setting is but one more challenge to be met and solved. NWOETV Foundation's Computer Resource Center is committed to developing and coordinating the resources which will assist schools plan and implement a successful instructional computing program. The members of the Computer Resource Center are part of a network of professionals who will work together to develop the most beneficial computer education for today's students.

The presentation will explain the objectives and goals of the Computer Resource Center and how the center has assisted the schools in meeting the challenges of computers in education.

COOPERATIVE ACTIVITY IN AUSTRALIA

This session will provide an overview of current and planned activity in Australia with regard to computing cooperatives and resource centers. The session will compare and contrast needs and organizational strategies between Australian activities and those in the United States.

THE ST. LOUIS, MISSOURI CONSORTIUM

This session will overview a paper entitled "The Establishment of a Regional Consortium for Educational Technology in the St. Louis, Missouri Area".

The Regional Consortium for Education and Technology (RCET) was established in October, 1983, to serve the needs of public and private elementary and secondary districts and schools in new technology applications. It serves educators in the city of St. Louis and four surrounding counties, where the total student population is 350,000. The Consortium is a not-for-profit organization owned by its membership: schools and districts; universities; government agencies; business organizations. Each organization has one representative on the Board which governs the Consortium.

RCET is dedicated to providing focus and leadership in educational technology by encouraging, supporting, and promoting programs and activities at all levels of education. It is evidence of the new cooperative spirit among various groups interested in improving education during a time of dwindling resources and mounting pressures to demonstrate improvement and excellence.

COMPUTERS IN EDUCATION, K. Duncan and D. Harris (eds.)
Elsevier Science Publishers B.V. (North-Holland)
© IFIP, 1985

THE ESTABLISHMENT OF A REGIONAL CONSORTIUM FOR EDUCATIONAL TECHNOLOGY IN THE ST. LOUIS METROPOLITAN AREA

by Judith Morton and Robert Benson
Regional Consortium for Educational Technology
& Washington University
Box 1080
Lindell and Skinker
St. Louis, MO 63130

A new type of school organization has recently been evolving in the United States: the Educational Technology Center dedicated to assisting elementary and secondary educators apply new technologies to school settings. This type of organization characteristically serves several school districts, focusing on assisting them in applications of new educational technologies, specifically computers. Although the need for them is evident and schools demonstrate great interest in their services, it is difficult for schools to support them financially. As a result, these centers vary widely in organizational structure and financial support. This is the story of the successful establishment of one such center located in the St. Louis, MO., area. Accompanying the story are observations regarding what is essential in establishing a successful and potentially long-term educational technology center.

1. INTRODUCTION

"Schools have to be the glue of our society; they are our greatest means of social stability."

Shirley McCune

It is a well known fact that within the past 30 years we have changed from an industrial society to one based on exchange of information. Internalizing this and changing our organizations to adapt to it is not as easy as understanding the facts.

Beaurocracies, school organizations, were designed to prepare children to live in a culture based on industrialization. Now, due to the new information technologies, how and even what we teach and learn in schools is changing. It is difficult to let go of the familiar, to discard old solutions that previously worked. Making changes in a beaurocratic structure that once functioned successfully, and not being able to clearly define the new goals and methods, makes it more difficult.

Schools, well aware of their stabilizing force in society and the lack of clarity of the future, are justifiably hesitant to change. They need to adapt carefully and with direction to new ways of teaching and learning. It is with this perspective, with a proactive not a reactive spirit, that we propose a model for helping schools and districts adapt their organizations to the new information, technology-based society. Schools are able to change with a direction given through the eyes of their own Technology Center dedicated to providing the leadership training and support necessary for them. Schools may observe at a slight distance the changes necessary, and integrate them rationally. Districts and schools are able to cooperate with one another through a Center,

learn from each other and build on the vision and resources of the whole. In the St. Louis, Missouri, area we have successfully designed and built such a Technology Center.

2. DESCRIPTION OF THE ST. LOUIS, MO., EDUCATION COMMUNITY

The St. Louis metropolitan area encompasses approximately sixty square miles. Within this area, there are approximately 350,000 students in elementary and secondary schools. There is one large city public school district, St. Louis City, with a student population of 48,000, and 44 public school districts in four surrounding Missouri counties (St. Louis, Franklin, Jefferson and St. Charles) ranging in size from 350 to 25,000 students. Within this same area, there are two large religion-affiliated school districts: the Catholic School District with 68,000 students; and the Lutheran School District with 17,000 students. Scattered throughout the local area are some 65 small independent private schools ranging in size from 35 to 450 students.

Educationally, the St. Louis area is typically midwestern; regional, conservative, and protective. The state of Missouri does not exercise a strong leadership role with its public school districts. There is no influential super structure and local districts are not grouped into regions, which could report to a central state organization. Although there are some state controls, school districts are rather independent, fragmented, and competitive. Also, St. Louis City students are bused to St. Louis county districts under court-ordered desegregation. Private and religion-affiliated schools are popular in the region; one-fifth of the total student population attends these schools.

Sharing of ideas and resources has not been the standard for the St. Louis region in the past, especially across public and private schools.

When new technologies became affordable for elementary and secondary schools, many educators felt that they could not respond quickly enough to meet the challenge. They needed to make decisions and purchases for which there was little or no precedent or experience. They needed to design and implement programs with minimal training of personnel and not enough definition of long term goals. Scarce resources set the climate for willingness and enthusiasm to cooperate and share.

3. THE NEED FOR A TECHNOLOGY CENTER

Several individuals who were working with the St. Louis Public Schools, Judy Morton and Robert DeBlauw, were interested in the possibility of establishing a technology center to support elementary and secondary districts and schools in the St. Louis metropolitan area in their efforts to use the new technologies. In September, 1982, Dr. Gene Schwilk from the Danforth Foundation learned about this idea and in January, 1983, introduced Judy Morton and Bob DeBlauw to Robert Benson from Washington University in St. Louis. Mr. Benson had previous experience in the development of multi-organizational cooperative ventures with the Center for the Study of Data Processing (CSDP). This Center is a joint University-industry activity with thirty-five Corporate affiliates. The Corporate affiliates provide financial and staff support, while the Center provides training, information resources, and sponsors national speakers' forums. This model appealed to Dr. Schwilk as a possible basis for a cooperative regional technology center.

Dr. Schwilk discussed the Technology Center concept with several influential school superintendents in the local area. They supported the idea enthusiastically. A planning group of eight superintendents met in the spring of 1983 to discuss the possibility of the center. They supported the idea from the beginning for several reasons. They saw the need for technology support in their schools. The Danforth Foundation was willing to give some financial support. The planning group included Mr. Benson from Washington University and CSDP. This offered the potential involvement of a well-respected university. It also offered the possibility of using the highly successful and respected organizational model of CSDP; its structure could be used as a basis for the design of the regional technology center--a joint cooperative venture among the many school districts in the metropolitan area. Unlike the Center for the Study of Data Processing, however, the superintendents believed that a significant amount of external funding would be required to start up a cooperative technology center.

In order to build a case for such a cooperative center and to establish the basis for approaching foundations and corporations for support, the group determined to conduct a comprehensive needs assessment among the variety of metropolitan area schools and districts. To accomplish

this needs assessment and to support the development of the cooperative center itself, the Danforth Foundation agreed to provide a small grant for the spring and summer of 1983. This grant supported the needs assessment staffing and the full-time services of Judy Morton to conduct it during the summer.

The survey gave clear evidence that all schools and districts were most interested in the services of a technology center. The results of the survey showed that districts and schools were most interested in an educational technology center engaging in the following activities:

1. It should establish a resource center for educational technology.

2. It should publish and disseminate information regarding educational technology to all districts and schools.

3. It should offer inservice programs in instructional and administrative computing.

4. It should provide a mechanism whereby districts and schools can acquire hardware and/or software at the lowest prices possible.

5. It should collect available new technological resources and evaluate their quality and applicability to education.

6. It should disseminate information about other technological developments in the local area.

7. It should provide opportunities for districts and schools to learn about new technologies.

In retrospect, the key elements in initiating the activities and obtaining the initial funding seem to be:

* A number of Superintendents were directly involved in the planning process and provided real leadership in the development of plans.

* A successful model could be identified (the Center for the Study of Data Processing) and used to formulate initial plans.

* A commitment to doing a comprehensive needs assessment assured the development of a proposal to meet real needs and supported by a wide constituency.

* A University was directly involved with the prospect of future joint activities for the benefit of the schools.

4. STRUCTURE OF THE ORGANIZATION

The Center for the Study of Data Processing organizational structure was used as the basis for
the RCET organization. Briefly, these principles apply:

* Every organization joining RCET participates
  in its governance. Members include schools
  and school districts, groups such as the
  Regional Commerce and Growth Association
  (the metropolitan Chamber of Commerce) CSDP,
  area Universities, and individual businesses.
  Each organization has a member on the Board.

* The day-to-day management is conducted by an
  Executive Director. An Operating Committee
  is elected from the full Member Board and
  conducts month-to-month overseeing. A Chairman of the Board is the head of the organization, and a President is the individual to
  whom the Executive Director reports. The
  Operating Committee consists of the Chairman
  and ten other member individuals, all who
  serve for a two-year term. Budget/Finance
  and Nominating Committees are made up of
  Operating Committee members.

In effect, then, all member organizations participate in the overall governance through the
Board. From that Board, detailed guidance is
provided by an elected Operating Committee.
The Chairman and the President provide individual leadership and responsibility. The Executive
Director is the full-time manager of the organization.

Of equal importance is the manner in which program, technical, and educational leadership is
provided by RCET.

The principles that apply:

* Every program and activity exists to serve
  the educational community in the metropolitan area. To date these include:

      Colloquia
      Inservice Programs
      Educational Technology Resource Center
      Cooperative Purchasing

* For each activity, a Steering Committee governs its development and planning. This
  Steering Committee is made up of representation from the schools and universities who
  are members of RCET. The individuals directly involved in the areas affected by the
  RCET activity are generally selected for committee membership; this RCET activity serves
  its intended constitutencies by involving
  them directly in the planning of the activity.

The implementation of these principles has resulted in Steering Committees, each of about 15
individuals. They were nominated by their respective superintendents and appointed by the
Executive Director. To date, some sixty individuals have participated in various Steering

Committees of RCET. This heightens awareness of
RCET and builds a constituency base among the
schools involved.

5. INITIAL MEMBERS OF THE ORGANIZATION

The eight Superintendents who met in the spring
of 1983 to formulate the technology center a-
greed to serve as the initial Planning Board
for RCET. In addition, it was recognized that
others should participate in the planning and
development of RCET. Accordingly, the following categories of individuals were asked to
join:

   Representation from private school districts,
      including the Catholic, Lutheran, and the
      non-sectarian private schools.

   Representation from business organizations,
      including RCGA, CSDP, and one company sig-
      nificantly interested in computing and ed-
      ucation--McDonnell Douglas.

   Representation from the Universities in the
      local area, including Washington University,
      University of Missouri in St. Louis, Web-
      ster University, and Southern Illinois
      University.

   Representation from other education-related
      activities, including the Science Center
      in St. Louis and the director of a public
      school cooperative.

A twenty person Planning Board with a wide range
of representation and interests resulted. This
Board reviewed the original proposal, endorsed
the principles of RCET, and agreed to become
the first Board of Directors upon the successful acquisition of funding.

The role of the Planning Board cannot be over-
stated in the Development of RCET. Without
question this Board has demonstrated the breadth
of support for the ideas behind RCET.

This demonstration was critical in establishing
the credibility of the organization to the foundations to which the support requests were made.

At the same time, the individuals participating
on the Planning Board discovered mutual interests in education. Even beyond the accomplishment of RCET, the Planning Board resulted in a
community of individuals from many areas united
in support of education. It appears that the
emergence of a wide-spread support group will
have a positive impact on RCET and other potential cooperative activities in the metropolitan
area.

6. LONGTERM FUNDING

The original small planning grant permitted the
development of a Needs Assessment, conducted in
person by RCET teams, in every school district
and private school. The result of the Needs

Assessment was a clear vision of what role a regional technology center might play, the needs it might address, and a clear indication of the amount of support from the many districts and schools.

This permitted the development of a strong proposal for external funding. The key elements were: broad school support, coverage of public and private sector, involvement of superintendents in its development, involvement of business representatives through RCGA and individual companies in the planning effort.

Over and above all this was the realization by all concerned that an organization like RCET should develop service and support activities that could be sustained by its users. Thus the proposal emphasized the intention of RCET to achieve self-sufficiency over a period of three years. Based on this plan, the need for support for the start-up period was defined, and a request for three-year funding was made to the Danforth Foundation and to the James F. McDonnell Foundation. Fortunately, both responded positively.

7. GOALS AND ACTIVITIES

The initial goal of RCET was to assist elementary and secondary educators in the applications of new technologies in educational settings. As RCET developed, this goal was refined and broadened. Now RCET is dedicated to providing focus and leadership for technology in education by encouraging, supporting, and promoting programs and activities at all levels of education. The primary focus, though, remains the same: to serve the needs of public and private elementary and secondary districts and schools in their efforts to apply new educational technologies.

The RCET focus can be expressed in five general goals.

1. Provide leadership in the local area regarding the applications of new technologies in educational settings.

2. Identify and provide opportunities for educators to acquire information regarding new technologies.

3. Identify, promote and provide opportunities for training so that educators can develop expertise in the applications of new technologies in educational settings.

4. Promote, encourage, and provide opportunities and encourage educators to communicate and share ideas and methodologies with others regarding educational technologies.

5. Identify and provide support to educators in their efforts to apply new technologies in educational settings.

The objectives and activities for RCET have been

determined and follow from these five basic goals.

8. ESSENTIALS FOR ESTABLISHING A CENTER

Persons in other local areas may be interested in creating an organization similar to RCET. Several areas in the US do have Regional Technology Centers which are similar in activities to this organization. RCET differs in its organizational structure, its ownership, and its funding.

In terms or organizational structure, any elementary or secondary school or district, private or public, may join. Colleges and universities may be members. Business may join as members. As for ownership, the members are the owners of RCET. Through the Board and the Steering Committees the members have the final word on the direction and activities of RCET. It is privately funded, independent of government monies. It will eventually be self-supporting.

What are the necessary ingredients in setting up an organization similar to RCET? Through observations of other technology centers, and through the experience of setting up RCET, we have determined that a number of elements need to be present.

1. Set a clear goal for the organization, but be flexible with objectives. The goal must not be radically changed at any time. However, the way the goal is achieved will probably be very different than originally perceived.

2. Use initiative to search out the essential resources. Make goals and needs known to those with essential resources.

3. Be open to all resources. Approach potential resources, money, personnel, equipment, and information, creatively. See possibilities for a variety of resources. The most valuable resources may not initially be recognized.

4. Associate the project with a well-respected, neutral organization and have it host the project. Make the project as politically neutral, and yet as educationally sound as possible.

5. Acquire the cooperation, active support, and planning of key educational leaders in the local area. Establish member ownership immediately.

6. Solicit support from all local higher education groups. Involve them in the planning of the organization early in its formation.

7. Employ at least one person full time to do the work involved to initiate the project. Do not expect it to be accomplished in a

reasonable amount of time if someone is working on it part time or in addition to a regular job.

8. Design the organization to be multifaceted; that is, to serve all technology needs in some way.

9. Design it to be cooperative, not competitive. Involve all existing organizations which relate to it in any way. Organize it and promote it to complement other organizations, so that if a resource is not available elsewhere in the community it is available through the new organization.

10. Involve the business community as much as possible. Make membership in the organization possible for them. Design it so that businesses play an integral role and have a stake in the organization.

11. Plan for the organization to be self-supporting after several years. Then it has time to give evidence of its worth to the community. It will be able to show the quality and value of its product in the first few years. The community will then judge it worthy of their support.

COMPUTERS IN EDUCATION, K. Duncan and D. Harris (eds.)
Elsevier Science Publishers B.V. (North-Holland)
© IFIP, 1985

EDUCATING PARENTS ON THE EDUCATIONAL POTENTIAL OF MICROCOMPUTERS

KEVAN PENTER
Western Australian Regional Computing Cntre.
University of Western Australia.

C. DIANNE MARTIN
The George Washington University
WASHINGTON. DC

In many parts of the world parents have shown an extraordinary degree of interest in the educational potential of the microcomputer. There have been both positive and negative consequences from the high level of interest among parents. In their over-anxiety to ensure that children benefit from the educational potential of microcomputers, some parents (and schools!) have acquired micro-computers with no clear idea as to how the computers should be used.

Many of the microcomputer manufacturers have also recognized the extraordinary degree of concern that parents have about the use of microcomputers for educational purposes, either at home or at school. Currently we see an enormous effort going into the advertising and marketing of home computers on the basis of the educational potential of this technology. Much of this advertising can only be classified as deceptive. Unfortunately, it has persuaded many parents that what their children need is access to a cheap microcomputer and to the BASIC language. Parents need education which will enable them to be perceptive consumers and evaluators of microcomputer technology, otherwise home computers may continue to be more of a hindrance than a help. This potential for producing bad habits and misconceptions is one of the negative aspects of parents' anxiety about microcomputers.

A positive aspect of parents' interest has been their willingness to contribute towards the development of worthwhile programmes in schools. In some parts of the world, a substantial portion of the costs of providing computer equipment in schools has been met by parents acting either on an individual or collective basis. In countries such as Australia, Sweden and the United Kingdom, governments have adopted policies which exploit the high degree of parental involvement by offering matching government subsidies on monies raised by parent groups to assist with the purchase of microcomputers. These policies of course raise the question as to what should happen in those schools where parents lack the capacity to contribute additional resources with which to acquire computer equipment.

The interest and concern of parents in ensuring that their children have access to micro-computers is in many cases not matched by any personal understanding of the technology. Unless this situation is addressed, parents will be "locked out" of Microcomputer Revolution. There is the distinct possibility of a

"generation gap" opening up between the young who have the opportunity to become familiar and confident with microcomputer technology, and their parents who for the most part remain unfamiliar and lacking in confidence. There are dangers in the present situation. Public education must address the needs of parents for programmes which will provide them with the opportunity to learn about, and benefit from, the educational potential of microcomputers. Fortunately, this process has already started in many places and initiatives in parent education deserve close scrutiny.

COMPUTERS IN EDUCATION, K. Duncan and D. Harris (eds.)
Elsevier Science Publishers B.V. (North-Holland)
© IFIP, 1985

Instructional Computing Support Services:
State Models and Regional Implementation Strategies

Carol Klenow, Oakland Schools, Pontiac, MI
Patrick Rose, Oakland Schools, Pontiac, MI
Vickie S. Smith, Region IV Education Service Center, Houston, TX
John Vaille, Stanislaus County Department of Education, Modesto, CA

This panel brings together representatives from regional education centers in the states of California, Michigan, and Texas to discuss regional and statewide technology services and activities.

Since 1981 state education agencies have conducted needs assessments and implemented a variety of plans to support instructional computing within their states. While some plans focused on placing hardware in schools, others concentrated on software evaluation or the "computer literacy" curriculum. Many state agencies established teacher training centers and worked to facilitate state networks for sharing resources. The purpose of this panel is to provide information about instructional computing activities in California, Texas, and Michigan, three states in which these programs are at various stages of development. The following goals will be the target of this presentation.

GOAL: To provide models for regional centers that support instructional computing.

GOAL: To disseminate resource information about projects that are contributing to the effective use of computers in instruction.

GOAL: To create a forum for instructional computing issues relevant to state and regional education agencies.

Patrick Rose
Instructional Computing Consultant
Oakland Schools
2100 Pontiac Lake Road
Pontiac, MI 48054

The Interactive and Instructional Computing Department (IICD) of Oakland Schools, an intermediate school district, provides educational computing support services to the 28 school districts and over 75 non-public schools in Oakland County, Michigan. Department personnel provide consultations and in-service training to the many timeshare and microcomputer users who use more than 500 terminals and 6,000 microcomputers in their schools. As a service agency to local districts we act as a clearinghouse for information, a meeting place for special interest groups, and a catalyst for special projects relating to technology in education. Some of the projects and services provided include: a bimonthly newsletter; an annual conference, "Kids and Computers"; a software preview center; a software evaluation and documentation project, "DISC" (Documentation and Integration of Software into the Classroom); a international high school programming contest, "ComCon"; a technology in-service curriculum produced in cooperation with other subject area consultants, "OakTEC" (Oakland Technology Education Center); and user group meetings (e.g. Computing Coordinators, Logo Users, etc.).

Carol Klenow
Director of Interactive and
   Instructional Computing Department
Oakland Schools
2100 Pontiac Lake Rd.
Pontiac, MI   48054

The educational system in Michigan is made up of 529 local school districts. Consequently, emphasis is placed on local control of educational programs and policies. This environment of decentralization has nurtured a grassroots approach to educational computing in the state. Instructional planning and teacher inservice programs have been conducted in local school districts with the assistance of intermediate educational agencies, universities and the Michigan Association for Computer Users in Learning (MACUL). The growing need for statewide communication and shared resources among educators prompted action by the State Board of Education. In 1984, Michigan established five regional software/training to coordinate educational computing efforts throughout the state. In addition, a training project was initiated at the University of Michigan to develop teacher training materials for use in school districts, regional centers and other Michigan educational agencies. In my presentation I will highlight activities of the five software/training centers, the Training Michigan Teachers (TMT) project, the Michigan Microcomputer Network Committee which links the software/training centers and the Michigan Department of Education and MACUL.

John Vaille
Educational Technology Consultant
Stanislaus County
Department of Education
801 County Center Three Court
Modesto, CA   95355

California's educational support agencies are an interesting and sometimes complex mixture of local and regional institutions. Those which support the classroom use of technology are no less affected by and benefit from the complexity. The schools which I serve are located in rural/suburban Stanislaus County, 100 miles east of San Francisco. My role as Educational Technology Consultant is to provide technical expertise, software selection and use support, inservice education and coordination for teachers, administrators and staff in 38 school districts ranging in size from 13 to 21,000 students.

Support for technology (primarily computers and video) is also provided by the Teacher Education Computer Center (TECC) program, a state-funded regionally administrated agency responsible for many areas of teacher inservice. The combination of these two agencies has created a number of interesting applications of the computer and other technology to regular classroom programs.

Vicki S. Smith
Coordinator for Computer-Based
   Instruction
Region IV Education Service Center
P.O. Box 863
Houston, Texas   77001

The educational community, as it attempts to address technology and delivery of an equitable computer curriculum, continues to seek resources appropriate to such needs. In the state of Texas, recent legislation and curriculum mandates have further indicated the importance of strong delivery systems of information and training.

The panel member will focus on three such delivery systems being used in Texas:

- the Statewide Microcomputer Courseware Evaluation Network, a state funded project involving the twenty state education service centers;
- training vehicles offered in Region IV Education Service Center, Houston, to include a description of InterAct, an instructional television fixed service (ITFS) system; and
- the Texas Computer Education Association, a professional organization of over three thousand state educators involved in instructional computing.

COMPUTERS IN EDUCATION, K. Duncan and D. Harris (eds.)
Elsevier Science Publishers B.V. (North-Holland)
© IFIP, 1985

986

THE ROLE OF THE SCHOOL ADMINISTRATOR IN IMPLEMENTING COMPUTER SCIENCE COURSES INTO THE PRE-COLLEGE CURRICULUM

Ted Mims, Panel Chairperson, Louisiana State University

John Bristol, Lyons Township School System, George Culp and Jean Rogers, University of Texas, Harriet Taylor, Louisiana State University

School administrators are faced with the task of insuring that the instructional use of computers in their schools is productive and of the highest quality. This panel discussion should provide school administrators with valuable information. Topics which will be discussed are: role and responsibility of the administrator, teacher certification, selection and instruction of teachers, curriculum and course offerings, and problem areas.

John Bristol

Lyons Township School District's plan for instructional computing has received recognition at the national level. The role of the administrator in developing and implementing a plan for instructional computing in a school district similar to Lyons Township's will be discussed.

George Culp

The proliferation of microcomputers at the secondary school level has also resulted in the proliferation of BASIC as the most widely used language in pre-college computer science courses. At the collegiate level, however, PASCAL is the preferred language for introductory courses. Many computer scientists decry BASIC as a poor programming language; some go as far as proclaimming it causes irreparable harm. Should BASIC be discontinued in computer science courses at the pre-college level? Can <u>any</u> BASIC be taught in a pseudo-structured format? Is it the language per se, or the programming teaching method that is the issue? These and other questions will be discussed.

Ted Mims

Administrators must be competent in several areas related to the offering of computing courses in secondary schools. Results of a recent study concerning computing competencies for school administrators indicates instructional related competencies are very important to administrators. In this presentation instructional related computing competencies for administrators will be discussed.

Jean Rogers

School administrators are confronted with many important decisions when they are facilitating introduction of computing in their schools. Inevitably, priority must be given to some uses of or instruction about computers. Resources must be distributed between courses that focus on the computer itself (e.g. computer science) and on courses that integrate computing in other curricula (e.g. word processing in composition). Within courses that focus on the computer, choices may have to be made about the audience to be served (e.g. college bound or general education). Careful planning by administrators is required for effective use of staff and equipment.

Harriet Taylor

One of the major problems confronted by administrators planning to implement computer science courses has been finding qualified teachers. Until recently, few secondary teachers had any formal instruction in computer science. Many states are now considering the adoption of standards for the certification of secondary school computer science teachers. Typically, these standards call for at least 18 semester hours of computer science course work. Administrators must plan now for that time when certification is mandatory. The role of the administrator facing the demands of the present and future in terms of faculty recruitment, development, and retention will be discussed.

COMPUTERS IN EDUCATION, K. Duncan and D. Harris (eds.)
Elsevier Science Publishers B.V. (North-Holland)
© IFIP, 1985

USING COMPUTERS TO IMPROVE THE ADMINISTRATION OF ELEMENTARY AND SECONDARY SCHOOLS

Ted Mims, Panel Chairperson, Louisiana State University

John Bristol, Lyons Township School System, Richard Dennis, University of Illinois, Nolan Estes, University of Texas, and James Hecht, Hinsdale Township High School

School administrators are becoming more interested in learning how they can use computers to improve the administration of schools. This panel discussion should provide school administrators with valuable information. Topics which will be discussed by the panel members are: impact of computerizing administration, computing competencies, computing skills, courses and in-service instruction, planning and implementing for administrative computing, and problem areas.

John Bristol

Computers are being used effectively in the area of administration in Lyons Township School District. The role of the administrator in developing and implementing a plan for using computers in administration in a school district similar to Lyons Township will be discussed.

Richard Dennis

Since the 1960's, the use of computers in administration has become a relatively common phenomenon in schools. This presentation will focus on administrative uses of computers from the perspective of the school administrator. Topics of discussion related to administrative computing are: 1. What does the school administrator do?, 2. What does he/she need in order to accomplish his/her task?, 3. What are the types and sources of information involved in school administration?, and 4. What are the specific uses of information in administering "my" school(s)?.

Nolan Estes

The information age has arrived. To prepare young people to live effectively in the twenty-first century a corresponding change is needed in education. This means school administrators must be aware of the ways in which computers can be utilized to manage and analyze information. To effectively utilize information in the decision making process an administrator must be able to use computers. As a user of computers to manage information the administrator will need to be aware of related social implications. This presentation will discuss anticipated changes in school administration as a result of increased innovative uses of computers to manage information in schools.

James Hecht

In any school, a sizable amount of time and energy is devoted to gathering and reporting data on students. Computers have been utilized to manage student records in Hinsdale (Illinois) Township High School District 86 for more than ten years, initially through the facilities of an outside service bureau, and ultimately through an in-house data processing facility. This presentation will discuss some of the problems which a small district such as High School District 86 might expect to encounter in implementing automated student records management, and will describe solutions which have proven effective within District 86.

Ted Mims

Optimal utilization of computers by administrators will require that they master certain computing competencies related to managing and utilizing information. Results of a recent study indicate that some administrators may be placing emphasis on mastering non-user related competencies while neglecting competencies related to utilizing computers to help them manage and analyze information. A discussion of the importance of administrators mastering user related computing competencies will be presented.

COMPUTERS IN EDUCATION, K. Duncan and D. Harris (eds.)
Elsevier Science Publishers B.V. (North-Holland)
© IFIP, 1985

WHAT'S IN A NAME - SCAMP?

Carlo Tomasso

Schools Computer Administration & Management Project
Scottish Microelectronics Development Programme
74 Victoria Crescent Road
Glasgow G12 9JN SCOTLAND

This paper reviews the work that has been carried out over the past seven years in
developing a comprehensive computerised administration and management system capable
of being run on powerful stand alone microcomputers in Scottish schools and linking
to outside agencies as and when necessary.

INTRODUCTION

SCAMP is an acronym for SCHOOLS COMPUTER
ADMINISTRATION & MANAGEMENT PROJECT and is
aimed directly at the systematisation of
school administration taking full advantage of
the facilities offered by the very latest
advances in powerful 16-bit microcomputer
equipment. The system as it is currently being
developed is seen by many as pointing decidedly
in the direction in which schools will
ultimately have to move in order to remain
effective and efficient in their use of scarce
resources in meeting the challenges of both
present and future demands constantly being
made on the educational system.

BACKGROUND

The current state of developments within
Scotland is the cumulative result of much
effort and design which evolved over a period
of some seven to eight years of intensive work
and which involved the combined support of the
Scottish Education Department, Colleges of
Education, Scottish Regional Education
Departments and the Schools themselves. This
amalgamation of expertise recognised at an
early stage that if a concerted effort were not
made in tackling the whole question of applying
computer assistance to the administration and
management of the secondary school sector then
a state of chaos would quickly develop from
which it would become increasingly difficult to
redress the balance at a later stage. In
addition it was recognised that the job was non-
trivial and that to expect schools to cope with
such a problem was not a reasonable expectation
if the job were to be tackled in a professional
manner.

Throughout the early 70's and increasingly in
the late 70's due to the advent of the
microcomputer, a great deal of work was done by
active teachers each beavering away
independently in his own school programming the
variety of routine administrative tasks
commonly found in most schools. As a direct
consequence of the state of the art in

hardware/software availability at the time it
was not surprising to find that most of the
applications written for teachers by teachers
were of the non-integrated type, meaning, for
example, that if names were input for the
production of class lists then names were again
input for the production of attendance reports.
This illustration merely serves to uncover one
of the key factors which would cause real
problems in a developing environment.

On closer scrutiny the problems inherent in
having keen activists embroiled in independent
development and in many cases virtually
duplicating the work of other activists
magnifies enormously if viewed from the
standpoint of keenness on the part of the
developer. This however is not the only
requirement to do the job properly. The root
cause factors mitigating against the keen
activist developer within a school would appear
to be uncovered by the following:

Education System Factor

. Teachers are trained as teachers and are
  not trained in the skills to earn a
  living through programming computers.
  Additionally little if any training is
  given in the administration and
  management of a school. Training is
  basically considered to be an acquired
  skill usually gained on the job once in
  post after promotion is achieved and then
  only supplemented by short "in-service"
  courses provided for those who volunteer
  to attend.

. Schools in budgetary terms are, on the
  whole, large concerns and usually
  account for a significant proportion of
  National and Local spending. Many
  managers within Industry are quite
  envious of the large degree of autonomy
  that schools enjoy when they themselves,
  despite recognising the limitations
  imposed by conformity, have to discipline
  themselves to the administrative and
  management procedures imposed by Head

Office.

. In consequence of the points made above, schools are as diverse in their approach and style of management and administration as they are in number and as such are not presently in a position to benefit from economies and efficiencies to be gained from acceptance of at least some degree of standardisation imposed by the introduction of automated administration procedures.

Skills Factor

. Teachers are not in general skilled programmers although the programming "bug" exists in many cases. Because of their enthusiasm to program, many teachers unwittingly take on potentially very large and complex administration programming tasks and find, some to their surprise, that the hardware and or software cannot match their expectations. With such drive and effort one is tempted to think that this enthusiasm might have been better expended in the development of curriculum related program package production rather than in the direction of administration.

. Programs once written by teachers are rarely documented to the level which complex software demands and in consequence seeds many a problem which could have been avoided had the necessary documentation been provided. Maintenance and enhancement of such programs become increasingly more hazardous with increased complexity under such conditions. Indeed it is not uncommon to find that a school will find it easier to rewrite a program from scratch than to have to unravel the apparent incongruities of logic devised by the original author who has probably left the school for reasons of promotion and is no longer interested in past endeavours.

. In general programs written by teachers tend to become unstructured even in cases where an original structure existed since lack of time often forces the adoption of a "quick fix" approach to the update and enhancement of existing applications.

Equipment/Operating Systems Software/ Languages

. Hardware limitations embedded in 8-bitness, small capacity diskettes and relatively small amounts of memory lead schools into the position of devising systems that become awkward to use for the human operator especially if the operator is not the designer of the administration system. Maintaining data integrity across a number of diskettes for example is no easy matter in cases where two or more persons are involved in running the system within the one school. To counter this problem it is true to say that the latest equipment finding its way on to the open market is becoming more powerful, less costly, has higher disc capacities and more memory and which, if properly utilised, should ease the problems just described although all the other problems continue to lurk in the background.

. Operating systems as such are in general unfriendly and do not easily lend themselves for use by the non-expert, which implies that school office staff find it difficult if not impossible to use the computer. This often mitigates against the wider acceptance of the system to other members of staff.

. The languages on microcomputers have until now been somewhat limited and much attention has been focussed on Basic. Because of the diversity in different dialects of the Basic provided, many time consuming hours have been spent in conversion and rewriting existing administration applications for newer equipment. This of course could have been avoided if the language chosen in the first instance were one which was recognised for its portability characteristics.

The problems outlined above are not intended to be exhaustive in themselves but indicative of the kind of difficulty which was foreseen in the Scottish context wherein it was abundantly clear that the wheel was being re-invented and would continue to be re-invented over and over again if some initiative were not taken to counter such an eventuality.

WHY SCAMP?

Education, like many other organisations, is no stranger to the modern phenomenon of having to face up to changing demands which are brought about increasingly by more rapidly changing policies and goals aimed at responding to changing needs. This has in turn stimulated the demand for the supply of more information to be produced more rapidly for management within the schools themselves and for agencies outwith the school at both local and national level. Only if this information is timeous in its production and accurate in content can schools be better assured of more effective and efficient use of scarce resources in both human and other terms. In effect what has become clear is the rapid realisation that only the most modern techniques employed in information processing can match the modern demand and that the days when information handling was regarded as a trivial recording task have long since disappeared. Without properly organised information systems it is abundantly evident that effective control and organisation of a modern school is becoming an impossible task since a greater proportion of teachers' time could well be diverted to administration matters.

Attempting to develop information systems for schools which depend on making use of teachers' spare time or which depend on the use of inadequate equipment or which removed the microcomputer for any length of time as a computing resource from within the arena of the curriculum would clearly not produce the desired end result. Thus SCAMP has emerged as a serious attempt to rationalise a set of undesirable trends by providing an environment in which teachers can teach and write their own curriculum oriented program packages if they wish and administrators are freed to administer and manage their schools while SCAMP develops, maintains and enhances the information systems software as an ongoing process.

NEED FOR AN INTEGRATED APPROACH

Many schools in the ad hoc situation use their computer for a variety of single task administration uses such as Class Lists, Attendance, Assessment processing, Objective Test analysis and so on. What had not been explored to any significant degree was the processing of all such tasks in an integrated mode to circumvent numerous disc changes, redundant re-entry of data and in general all the many problems associated with the use of inadequate hardware and design of inadequate software. The need for the integrated approach was abundantly obvious and with this aim in view SCAMP set about developing a system of interrelated procedures called SUBSYSTEMS, all of which pivot on the "single entry of data - multiple use " concept. Only by so doing could a systematic approach to the collection, processing and reporting of information be assured.

The SCAMP application lends itself ideally to the employment of proper Database techniques. Many database products have been examined and many were found to be lacking in the facilities offered or the features provided. Those best suited for the job were clearly seen to be of the relational type such as RAPPORT but suffered the disadvantage of being too expensive at the present time to be acceptable.

DESIGN CRITERIA

Based on the experience which had been gained from the ad hoc developments described earlier

it became relatively easy to decide upon the essential features which should be present in a well designed school administration and management system taking account of people, hardware, operating systems and applications elements. The following points are therefore considered of major importance in developing a design strategy to meet the stated aims.

A PROJECT which

* is directed by education for education.

* is specified in applications terms by consultant school administrators, SCAMP users and computer professionals.

* is broad enough in scope to encompass the more general needs of Education Department, Local Education Department, Examination Boards and other interested agencies.

A SYSTEM which

* is capable of being mounted on a powerful microcomputer.

* is capable of being transferred to other suitable machines with the minimum of effort.

* is capable of operating in a distributed system environment.

* has sufficient flexibility for each school to impose its own identity.

* is easy to use and does not require the employment of specialised or extra staff to operate and use the system.

* is simple to back-up and recover in cases of machine malfunction.

* requires a minimum of training in making use of its applications.

* is menu driven throughout.

* has a standard and consistent user screen interface with each and every application.

* has wide security and access level capability.

* has all necessary data available at all times on-line.

* employs check digiting techniques as appropriate.

* has inbuilt on-line full screen validity checking.

* has flexibility in selection and sorting of information for specific

reports.

* operates on the principle that data is entered once and is thereafter available for the processing of all other applications.

* has communications facilities for electronic mail and access to Prestel type services, Examination Board systems and other available databases.

* has a data encryption facility for the transfer of data between sites if required.

In essence the SCAMP System is a structured administration and management system written and designed by professionals within education for professionals within education.

THE SCAMP DEVELOPMENT

The Main Menu

Initial entry to the system and main menu is achieved via a unique username and password applied to each authorised user of the system. This authorisation is tied inextricably to a set of applied access codes that define the set of menu items displayed to the user. Examination of the entire main menu shown below reveals a number of supporting items all of which, with the sole exception of Word Processing, have been developed by SCAMP.

        0   Return to previous menu
        1   SCAMP system
        2   MP/M-86 system
        3   Communications system
        4   Word Processing
        5   Configure printer
        6   Edit users
        7   Disc utilities

Each of the items above can be briefly described as follows:

* Return to previous menu

This item appears as the first element of every menu within the system giving access to the previous menu in the hierarchy of menus.

* SCAMP system

This element is described in the next section and forms the main entry point to all the SCAMP Subsystems.

* MP/M-86 system

This element permits limited access to the host operating system since full access to all the facilities of an

operating system is considered to be undesirable in a situation wherein non computer specialist personnel are expected to make use of the system. This window permits the user for example to display disc directories, spool output, compare files, attach and detatch processes but disallows the access to editors, system generation commands and the like for obvious reasons.

* Communications system

See SCAMP Subsystems for elaboration of this element.

* Word processing

This application permits all the usual facilities expected in a modern word processing applications package. Since SCAMP is not in the business of re-inventing the wheel, this application has been bought in and supplied with the system.

* Configure printer

Where a printer is of the type which permits remote set up under software control, then the control is achieved by accessing this element of the menu. Its use is mainly confined to setting up the speed/quality of print requirements for the particular job in hand.

* Edit users

This element permits the school administrator to maintain Usernames, Passwords and Access Levels applied to all users of the system. Dependent upon the access levels applied to a given user, that user will only be confronted with those menu items which apply in his/her case. All gaps caused by any denial of access are automatically closed so that the user is unaware of the fact that access has been denied.

* Disc utilities

The final element on the menu is concerned with formatting of discs, copying discs and integrity checking of all released SCAMP software.

SCAMP Subsystems

The core of the SCAMP system consists of a set of integrated modules referred to as Subsystems which are described in outline as follows:

Subsystem   &   Description
''''''''   '''''''''''

INITIALISATION

* forms the basis of the whole of the
  SCAMP system by providing the
  definitions against which all relevant
  input of data is checked for accuracy.

* defines the school in terms of its basic
  administrative parameters, eg
  associated feeder schools, register
  classes, house system, subjects and
  courses offered etc.

ADMISSIONS

* establishes the Basic Student Record
  which records essential data on each
  student in relation to such items as
  name, address, date of birth, sex,
  emergency contacts etc.

* permits the provision of many useful
  types of report such as Class Lists,
  Specific Disabilities Lists, Leavers
  Lists, Date of Birth Range Lists.

* caters for new entrant admission from
  primary school, secondary transfers and
  leavers.

* provides global statistics on the most
  frequently required male/female
  population groups within the school.

CLASS/COURSE ALLOCATION

* records the allocation of subjects and
  courses throughout the entire school
  career of each and every student from
  secondary 1 to 7. This system has
  particular relevance at the course
  options stage in a student's career.

* provides facilities to form mixed or
  streamed ability classes based on the
  new student intake and on school
  supplied criteria.

* enables mass movement of students in
  relation to classes and subjects
  allocated in transferring from one
  academic session to the next.

ASSESSMENT (MODE A)

* provides a comprehensive set of
  procedures for the organisation,
  collection, processing and reporting of
  school examinations using norm-
  referenced techniques.

* provides for numerous examination diets
  to be applied within any given school
  session.

* uses comment banking techniques for
  reporting purposes.

* provides internal school analysis of
  results as well as external reporting to
  parents.

ASSESSMENT (MODE B)

* as for ASSESSMENT MODE A but in this case
  all assessment is based on criterion
  referencing and student profiling.

REGISTRATION

* provides comprehensive facilities to
  record, analyse and report in detail on
  ALL aspects of a student's attendance
  over a given period.

* provides facilities for detailed roll
  analysis.

* links to the Assessment Subsystem to
  pick up report attendances.

COMMUNICATIONS

* permits the transmission and reception
  of electronic mail by way of text files.

* permits access to commonly available
  facilities such as Prestel, British
  Telecom Gold etc.

* permits interaction with Examination
  Boards for candidate entry and results
  update.

* permits statistical returns to
  Education Department or Local Education
  Authority as and when necessary.

TEACHER RECORD**

* establishes a basic teacher record which
  records essential data on each teacher
  pertaining to such elements as name,
  address, sex, qualifications.

* provides the ability to analyse school
  staffing in respect of teaching and
  non-teaching duties, experience,
  full/part time employment etc.

TIMETABLING AIDS**

* makes available a range of facilities to
  assist the school administrator in the
  preparation, planning and construction
  of the school timetable. This is NOT a
  timetabling system.

STATISTICS**

* provides a wide range of statistical
  information derived from the

information held within each of the Subsystems in use and is designed to assist in responding to the demands made upon the school from outside agencies eg Examination Board, Education Department, Local Education Authority and others.

SKETCHPAD**

* provides the school with the facility to define its own individual extensions to existing information within the system and create and maintain new files as needs arise.

* provides the capability to produce new reports by interacting with the screen in the design of new printouts.

NB Those subsystems marked with '**' have been designed and are now in the various stages of completion - summer 1984.

BEYOND OCTOBER 1985

The current phase of the project terminates in October 1985 with the set of Subsystems defined in the previous section. Looking beyond this, one can predict from suggestions already being made that future Subsystems would include:

* FINANCE & BUDGETING   - see NOTE below
* INVENTORY CONTROL   - see NOTE below
* LIBRARY SYSTEM
* CAREERS
* GUIDANCE
* DIAGNOSTIC ASSESSMENT & ITEM BANKING
* JIIG-CAL
* COMPUTER MANAGED INSTRUCTION

NOTE - within SKETCHPAD there exists a complete spreadsheet facility which could make the FINANCE & BUDGETING and INVENTORY systems redundant.

ACHIEVEMENTS TO DATE

The Project is now in its second phase having been in existence since 1978 and during which time has accounted for about 30 man years of development effort. Early work in Phase I of the Project on 8-bit Dacoll distributed equipment and mainframe batch equipment was quick to attract interest because of the extent of the collaborative development effort by Central and Fife Regions, the Scottish Education Department, Moray House College of Education, Dundee College of Education and all in association with the Scottish Microelectronics Development Programme.

Phase II, the current phase extending to October 1985, is heavily supported by national government through the Department of Trade & Industry which injected capital in excess of £250,000. With this help the system is currently on trial in almost every Region in

Scotland and has been operating in these Regions since April 1983. Although, as yet, it is too early for a comprehensive evaluation to have taken place, feedback already gleaned from the users suggest many of the hallmarks of success. Despite having only made use of the system for a period in excess of one academic year, all users without exception have made it known that they would not wish to revert to a pre-SCAMP situation and that SCAMP should continue into the future as a permanent on-going development/maintenance/support facility for schools.

Experience in phasing the system into a school quite clearly reveals that Subsystems have to be introduced in "drip feed" fashion. This is to say that only one Subsystem at a time is introduced into the school, since Subsystems tend to be large and the school requires time for assimilation of the module into its administration system. For example, the Admissions Subsystem requires on average 8 to 12 weeks to transfer approximately 1800 records from the existing manual system to the new computer system. Other Subsystems are normally assimilated in shorter time frames depending on the school. Training in any Subsystem to date has taken no more than two working days.

The languages chosen for portability reasons have been restricted to Microfocus Level II Cobol, C and the host machine Assembler. Work is already started on moving the system from Future Technology Series 88 and 86 equipment on to Dacoll Democrat, Sirius, Apricot, ICL PC, Cifer and IBM PC equipment.

In conclusion Authorities participating in SCAMP can now expect to be in a position to avoid duplication and repetition of effort and expenditure inherent in limited administrative packages whether devised at school or Authority level. Administrators within such Authorities can now proceed with confidence in the knowledge that the SCAMP product is one which is supported, maintained and which will adjust to changing administration requirements as time progresses. Correspondingly teachers in schools, relieved of the production and maintenance of their own computer administration applications, can now concentrate on managing the school and applying their computer skills to curricular requirements.

COMPUTERS IN EDUCATION, K. Duncan and D. Harris (eds.)
Elsevier Science Publishers B.V. (North-Holland)
© IFIP, 1985

A SYSTEMATIC MANAGEMENT STRATEGY FOR INTEGRATING TECHNOLOGY INTO THE WORKPLACE

Dr. Renee C. Barrett and Dr. Shirley J. McCann

Our society has been able to produce more communication and information exchanges because of the new technology. The United States economy is rapidly transforming from an industrial base to an information service base. Technical competencies continue to expand even in non-technical career fields. Managers and supervisors need to know how to analyze and computerize reports, communicate with technical staff, and use computers to process and manage information. However, reluctance to adapt to the increasing rate of technological change often effects the impact of the technology upon the workplace. The scenarios range from employees who claim that computers are dehumanizing and out of control to those who feel that a systematic organizational environment is impossible without the technology. Consequently, organizational strategies which increase technological competencies and decrease technological anxieties are crucial factors which influence the effective utilization of computers.

This paper will present a paradigm for implementation of computer technology in an organizational environment. A conceptual framework will be presented for illustrating individual and organizational responses to the new technology. Utilizing an innovative change process, strategies will be presented to facilitate positive responses to technological developments. The paradigm and strategies could be implemented within the public, private, corporate, and educational sectors.

As a society, we are in the process of moving from an industrial to an information age. The increasing demand and need for information has begun to restructure the workplace. The U.S. Department of Labor & Statistics reports that service producing industries such as accounting, data processing, and health care are expected to grow by twenty to twenty eight percent and will create more new jobs than any other sector between 1980 and 1990. The technology has created the proliferation of computers which has led to greater access to information and decentralization of systems.

One difficulty with assessing these new developments is that our knowledge of the technology outpaces our understanding of the social effects. Too often the human response to the technology is the least planned or anticipated in the design and implementation of computerized systems. Consequently, managers are faced with systems that under utilized. The organizational challenge is to design and implement computer systems that will lead to acceptance and effective utilization. This paper will introduce a paradigm for integrating technology with the human factor in the workplace.

Organizational research shows that a worker's willingness to accept technological changes will depend on more of his understanding of, attitudes toward, view of the organization and the environmental perspective he lives by than on organizational guidelines and regulations.

An employee's point of view will depend on his knowledge and experiences and how he uses them to organize his perceptions about change. In turn, these perceptions would shape an employee's receptiveness toward information systems.

According to Russell Ackoff, attitudes toward change vary but can be classified into four types of responses: inactive, reactive, preactive, and interactive. These attitudes illustrated in Figure 1 are found within individuals and vary within organizations and can change from situation to situation.

FIGURE 1: HUMAN RESPONSES TO TECHNOLOGICAL CHANGE

Each of these individual responses can have a significant impact on the successful implementation of a computerized system. They can range from rejection to acceptance of the technology.

Inactivists believe that most technological changes are superficial or temporary. They are satisfied with the way things are and the way they are going. Consequently, they believe that any change in the course of events is unlikely to improve them or make them worse. Their approach is conservative. They seek stability and survival. When change is forced upon them, they resort to using organizational structure to prevent change from occurring. For example, they will not make decisions but will instead relegate them to others. Through strategic delays, plans become eventually outdated or irrelevant. Inactivists do not want change and much of their efforts are spent keeping things as they are in the organization. They view technology as something to be avoided. They take a "Do Nothing" position or when forced to accommodate the technology will generate a lot of actions that lead to nothing constructive. Specifically they will tend to be prolific producers of policy statements, position papers, and any other kind of document that will be a substitute for action. They will resort also to the use of committees, commissions, study groups, and task forces to thwart efforts to bring about technological change. Inactivists will use any means necessary to maintain status quo.

Unlike the inactivists, the reactivists do not ride with the tide; they try to fight their way back to a familiar shore. Reactivists treat technological change as a scapegoat for whatever ills they perceive. They long to return to the "Good Ole Days". Reactivists not only resist technological innovations but they try to undo previous changes and return to where they once were. When change is introduced into an organization the reactivist response is "We've tried this before and it doesn't work." They will resist efforts to implement changes by using management-labor relationships to prevent organizational changes. Reactivists' actions are intended to challenge and redirect the momentum for change back to "tried and true" ways of doing things.

Preactivists view technology as the opportunity to grow and optimize. They seek to solve problems and exploit opportunities more through research and development of technology. Preactivists believe the future will be better than the present. Consequently, they are caught up in attempting to predict and prepare for it. Preactivists tend to view themselves as the ones to produce the plans and present them to those empowered to act. They seldom, if ever become involved in the implementation aspects.

Interactivists are beyond the theories, they seek to invent ways that will bring about change. Interactivists are willing to accept changes that alter a system's structure, functioning, organization, and personnel. They do not fear technological changes, they try to direct it for bringing about organizational development and advancement.

It is not enough to acknowledge that attitudes can vary toward change. Management needs to assess their employees to determine what the responses are to a proposed technological change. Individuals as well as work groups should be part of this assessment. This can be done through surveys, questionnaires, or structured interviews. Systematic strategies that would lead to interactive responses to technological innovation need to be included within a management perspective.

STRATEGIES FOR PROMOTING INTERACTIVE ATTITUDES TOWARD THE TECHNOLOGY

The management strategies illustrated in Figure 2 represent a continuum of techniques for assisting workers in positively adapting to the changing technology.

FIGURE 2:   MANAGEMENT STRATEGIES

DIRECTIVE STRATEGY

In the first quadrant, the inactivist attitude represents individuals who believe that change is either illusionary, superficial or temporary. These individuals spend most of their time defining functions, disputing technological advancements, and limiting technological development to committees and task forces. Managers must assume a directive managerial strategy for coping with this passive position.

Often these positions prevail because of unfounded fears and anxieties regarding high technology. Exposure to successful operational systems might dispel rejections and reservations. Carefully planned on site visits to other agencies, departments, or organizations who have successfully implemented the new technology provides an opportunity to respond to a realistic operation. After the immersion, a goal oriented plan of action might be executed. The "workmap" could include the development of strategies for minimizing technical anxieties. The inactivists could be given a technological problem to resolve which would benefit management and provide an opportunity to relate to the technology. The integration of these divergent needs would be rewarding and motivational. Although this strategy is directive and the tasks and perimeters have been predefined, opportunities are available for the inactivists to assume a more interactive attitude toward the technology.

COACHING STRATEGY

In the second quadrant, the reactivists attitude represents individuals who prefer a previous state and try to dispute currently operational systems. These individuals rely on decisions based upon intuition rather than proven data. They will resort to system sabotage and blame the technology for "any and all" organizational problems. Institutional managers must establish a coaching strategy for coping with this aggressive position. Because this position is represented by individuals who have a deliberate mission, an accepting but challenging attitude might be assumed. Due to the fact that many of their beliefs are unsubstantiated, a quantifiable project to investigate the impact of the technology on the workplace might discount their opinions. Through coaching and reassuring approval of their ability to analyze problems, they would be collecting data to substantiate and/or denounce the existence of technical systems. The compiled data might be organized into an incident report format so the style resembles the experienced-based approach of a reactivist. Because of an opportunity to verify perceptions about the system, this approach should be satisfying and motivational. The coaching (supportive and accepting) strategy provides the manager with data to evaluate the effectivness of the technology, but also provides an opportunity for the reactivists to relate to the technology in a more quantifiable manner.

SELF-DIRECTIVE STRATEGY

In the third quadrant, the preactivists attitude represents individuals who believe that technological changes are inadequate. These individuals want better, larger, and more powerful technology. Institutional managers must assume a self-directing management strategy for coping with this futuristic position.

In contrast to the reactivists' unsubstantiated perceptions about technological changes, preactivists substantiate their beliefs through logic, science, and experimentation. Because of their preoccupation with the future, the piloting of an innovative technological project might encourage the formulation of a prototype for a future state of the art system. Even if the project may not be feasible now, the process and/or parts of the prototype might be applied to current operational systems. Furthermore, technological forecasting and projections might be studied by preactivists to satisfy their interest in the future and to provide long range planning data for managers. Assuming a self-directive strategy allows the preactivists to explore, extrapolate, and experiment with the technology.

In the fourth quadrant, the interactivists attitude represents individuals who effectively utilize the operational system. These individuals interact directly with the system and invent ways of bringing about a supportive technological environment. Managers must assume a cooperative management strategy for these individuals.

Since a team effort is required for technical staff and their users, a cooperative strategy capitalizes on the full potential of the system. The decentralization of power stimulated by the advent of microcomputers necessitates team work among mainframe and microcomputer users. Communication lines must be established to develop networks for distributed systems. A cooperative management strategy provides a model for the interactivist to emulate in their own relationships with users and support staff. Because of the technical jargon and highly scientific nature of computing an aura of exclusiveness often prevails among computer staff. The cooperative management strategy tends to demystify the technology and encourages interactive responses to technological changes.

CONCLUSION

Individuals who are involved with the technology maintain a level of control and a sense of responsibility for changing the technology. They can be influential in fostering the creative potential of computing. Specifically, the results of participating interactively are...

Preparation for new roles in high tech careers

Facilitative decisions and directions for technological innovations

Increased knowledge about state-of-the-art technology

Confidence with computer interfacing

Competence in working with highly technical systems

These benefits are inherent in the outcome for management styles that include coaching, cooperative, directive or self directive

strategies will enable workers to accept and
utilize the technology.

REFERENCE

Ackoff, Russell L. REDESIGNING THE FUTURE.
New York: Wiley & Sons 1984.

COMPUTERS IN EDUCATION, K. Duncan and D. Harris (eds.)
Elsevier Science Publishers B.V. (North-Holland)
© IFIP, 1985

COMPUTER-GENERATED, GRAPHICAL AND STATISTICAL CHARACTERIZATION OF ADMINISTRATIVE
DATA: SPATIALLY-ORIENTED STUDENT ENROLLMENT TRENDS

Alan D. Smith

Department of Business Administration, College of Business, Combs 215
Eastern Kentucky University, Richmond, Kentucky 40475, U.S.A.

The research in the literature on the problematic effects of attrition in high education has been well documented in the past. Obviously, the nature and purpose of the
colleges/universities involved have a significant impace on the dropout problem, and
there may be many factors that post secondary institutions can control in order to
curb attention. The attempt to delineate those factors require models to be generated
to provide additional information on the interruption of student flow toward degree
completion, in order to produce forecasting tools. Since most the attrition appears
to be during the first year of college attendance, the spatial distributions of incoming freshmen students coming to Eastern Kentucky University, a large residential university were inspected to determine if detectable patterns or enrollment trends
existed. The University has a regional mission, thus spatial characterization of student flows are important to determine stability of enrollment in its service area and
surrounding counties. Student flow models were created and statistically tested for
enrollment data from 1979 through 1982, inclusively, as well as change in enrollment
from 1981 to 1982, based on data obtained from 117 counties in Kentucky. Three-dimensional modeling techniques as well as hypotheses testing and model comparisons of
polynomial trend surfaces were utilized in modeling the spatial distributions of incoming freshmen students.

INTRODUCTION

The use of statistical regression techniques to
enhance prediction for institutional fit or
congruence models, and student flow models have
accelerated in recent years. Several researchers have constructed models of institutional
fit or congruence through the years (1-9).
There is a documented need to collect data that
are specifically designed to identify factors
associated with eventual withdrawal from college. These data should not only include
easily college demographic characteristics
(sex, age, SAT scores, financial aid), but
also consider variable interactions. The
interactions may operate concurrently as mod-
erating, suppressing, or accentuating factors
relative to attrition. However, most of the
attrition appears to occur during the first
year and among those who are academically less
talented than their continuing-student counter-
parts (9-13). The nature and purpose of the
institution of higher education have a significant impact on the dropout problem and there
may be many factors that post-secondary institutions can control, both directly and indirectly, to curb attrition. Moreover, the
attempt to delineate these factors requires
models to be generated to provide additional
information on the interruption of student
flows towards degree completion. In referring
to institutional characteristics with the
effects of the institutional presses on student
behavior and development, rarely has a spatial-
dimensional element based on geographic location and their changes throughout the year been
incorporated into model research.

The primary purpose of this research effort is
to develop three-dimensional models portraying
the spatial distributions of first entering
students over a period of years and selected
changes to a regional institution of higher
education. In addition, polynomial-trend surfaces, coupled with hypothesis testing and
model comparisons of these trends to determine
the best fit, is to be used to statistically
verify any predictive trend that may exist on a
statewide basis. If these relationships exist,
they should prove useful in the incorporation
of spatial student-flows into previously established congruence models that an institution
may have already established.

METHODS

The major research tools used in the present
study are polynomial-trend surface analyses,
hypothesis testing and model comparisons of
trend surfaces, and three-dimensional models
generated from commercially available computer
software, via the incremental plotter.

THREE-DIMENSIONAL MODELS, RESPONSE, SURFACES,
AND MODEL COMPARISONS OF TRENDS

Basically, the response surface or three-dimensional surface can be thought of as the representation of a statistical surface consisting
of a series of numbers of which has an x, y,
and z characteristics. In terms of geographic
or spatial location and analysis, the x and y
values refer to the horizontal or planimetric

locations, and the z values are measured values with relative heights above some horizontal datum, such as the plane of a map (14). A trend, on-the-other-hand, is a statistically derived surface to explain variations in a given set of values, known as Z-values, such as total population or changes in student flows, that have a given geographic position, either regularly or irregularly distributed in the z-y plane. The surface is the representation of an equation using the least-squares criterion. This means that the generated surface will be fitted to the input data in such a way that the sum of the squared deviations between the data at their particular locations and the corresponding value of the computed surface are minimized. Thus, the least-squares criterion calls for the surface to be laid down in such a way that the sum of the squares of these discrepencies is as small as possible, as indicated by: $\Sigma d^2 = E$, where d^2 = deviation squared and E = minimum value. The basic reasoning behind minimizing the sum of squares of the deviations, and not minimizing the sum of squares of the deviations, and not minimizing the sum of the absolute magnitudes of the discrepancies, are: 1. It is extremely difficult to mathematically deal with the absolute discrepancies or deviations; while the treatment of the squared deviations provides the method of practical mathematical developments in the interpretation of the regression equation. 2. Useful and desirable statistical properties follow from using the least-squares criterion (15-17). The equation describing the surface can be linear (plane), quandratic (paraboloid), cubic (paraboloid with an additional point of inflection), to higher order degree surfaces, the more the residuals, or individual deviations, will be minimized and the more computation will be required. The higher-order trend surfaces may reflect the variation in Z-values more accurately if the study area is complex, but lower-order surfaces may be more useful in the isolation of local trends. The filtering mechanism allows the upper limit of variability to be determined by the order of the surface. The equation for a linear trend surface, for example, is: $Y = b_o + b_1X_1 = b_2X_2$, where Y = dependent variable, b_o = constant value related to the mean of the observations, b_1b_2 = coefficients, X_1X_2 = geographic coordinates. This linear equation generates 3 unknowns and 3 equations are needed to determine a solution. These equations are:

(1) $\sum_{i=1}^{n}Y = b_o n + b_1 \sum_{i=1}^{n}X_1 + b_2 \sum_{i=1}^{n}X_2$.

(2) $\sum_{i=1}^{n}X_1 Y = b_o \sum_{i=1}^{n}X_1 + b_1 \sum_{i=1}^{n}X_1^2 + b_2 \sum_{i=1}^{n}X_1X_2$, and

(3) $\sum_{i=1}^{n}X_2 Y = b_o \sum_{i=1}^{n}X_2 + b_1 \sum_{i=1}^{n}X_1X_2 + b_2 \sum_{i=1}^{n}X_2^2$.

where n = number of observations or data collected. Solving these equations simultaneously will give the coefficients of the best-fitting linear surfaces, where best fit is defined by the least-square criterion. As the degree of

the trend surface that is to be used increases, so does the number of equations that must be solved simultaneously. Higher order regression equations, in trend surface analysis, may reflect the variation in particular values with a geographic or spatial distribution with more accuracy than lower order surfaces, but the low order surfaces may be more useful in isolating important local or regional trends that may exist over a larger area. Thus, surface analyses can be considered a process of filtering an input signal (measured values or Z-values), where the surface represents the resultant signal after filtering. In this process, the order of the surface determines the upper limit of variability of frequency of the input data which will pass through the gate or filter. Localized or site-specific variation will be blocked by the filter when lower orders are used, and it will be increasingly transmitted as the order of the surface increases. This filtering process is in contrast to standard linear interpolation used in contouring, in which all the input data are taken in equal importance. However, a visual check on the accuracy of the filtering mechanism of trend surface analysis would be very helpful in localizing sources of noise or localized variation. In addition, visual inspection would be of great value in determining the effectiveness of increasing the order of the regression equations to account for additional variation of the spatially oriented data. The significance of a trend or regression may be tested by performing an analysis of variance, which deals with the separation of the total variance of a set of observations into components with defined sources of variation (18). In trend-surface analysis, the total variance in an independent variable may be divided into the trend itself, which is determined by regression analysis, and the residuals, or error vector. An analysis of variance table can be calculated (Table 1). By reducing the sum of squares, derived from the least-square criterion, an estimate of the variance can be computed by using the F-distribution (18). The F-test, like a t-test, is a very robust test and relatively insensitive to violations of the assumptions of random selection of observations and normal distribution of the variables (19, 20). Fraas and Newman (21) and Nunnally (22) looked at a number of investigations that dealt with the F-distribution assumptions and their violation and summarized by suggesting that no appreciable effect on the accuracy of the F-test from skewed sample distribution occurred. In addition, if sample sizes are equal, heterogeneity of variance has a negligible effect. The F-test for significance of fit is a test of the null hypothesis that the partial regression coefficients are equal to zero and, hence, there is no regression. If the computed F-value exceeds the F-value having a probability of a set alpha level (α = 0.01 to 0.05), then the null hypothesis is rejected. In polynomial trend-surface analysis, it is customary for investigators to fit a series of successively higher degrees to the data without statistically testing the higher order's contribution in additional variance. Davis(18) suggested that an analysis of variance table be expanded to analyze the contribution of the additional partial regression coefficients to give a measure of the appropriateness of each order equation. In regression work, the question often arises as to whether it was worthwhile to include certain terms associated with the order of the polynomial in the model. This question can be investigated by considering the extra portion of the regression sum of squares which arises due to the fact that the terms under consideration were in the model. If this extra sum of squares is significantly large, those terms should be included. However, if nonsignificant, they are judged unnecessary and should be deleted. For example, $SS(b_1 b_0)$ is the extra sum of squares owing to the $\beta_1 X_1$ term was included in a model which otherwise only contained β_0. If the F-test indicated significance, the model should include the the $\beta_1 X_1$ term. The full versus restricted model principle implies if that the null hypothesis, were H_0: $\beta_1 = 0$ were true, and if this condition is imposed on the model, the result would be that contribution of the $\beta_1 X_1$ term is zero. This is equivalent to discharging the $\beta_1 X_1$ term from the model, resulting in the restricted model. Hence, the restricted model to the model which results when the specific null hypothesis, which is assumed true, is imposed or restricted on the full model. The full model is the model which contains all the terms of the lower and higher order polynomial coefficients being tested. The sum of squares of the null hypothesis ($SS(H_0)$) is simply the difference between the degrees of freedom of the full and restricted models.

Computer-Generated Graphical Displays of Three-Dimensional Models

The three-dimensional plotting programs can be used via the incremental drum plotter to produce statistical surfaces of geographic units with assigned values of continuous data. There are a variety of options available to the user and these programs also produce their own diagnostic messages for common errors that the user may encounter. There are basically four programs under the three-dimensional plotting programs, each one designed to give either a completely different type of plot or flexibility in the presentation of its final form; these options are known as ZUSMO, QUSMO2, QUCRS, and QTAB (23). Quick Smooth (QUSMO) produces a smoothes surface over an input data matrix and places the surface on a base or plane. This program performs a nine-point quadratic interpolation between the input data points to give the plot a smooth appearance. QUSMO2 however, combines the features of QUSMO but allows for control over the size output, vertical scale, and read the data matrix from tape storage.

QUSMO2, similar in function to the commercially available SURFACE II software (24), was used to produce the three-dimensional plots found in this study, as previously outlined by Smith (25). Quick Crosscut (QUCRS) also produces a smooth surface over the input data as does QUSMO and QUSMO2. However, it does not put the interpolated surface on a plane. A base is drawn for the surface so that it can be visualized as if it was isolated in space. Quick Tabular (QTAB) produces a plot similar to a three-dimensional histogram. Each data point of the data matrix is assumed to be the center of a plotted cell and thus appears as many small squares at various levels. Since there is no interpolation between the input data points, the program produces a step-like surface. In addition, all four plotting routines have the option to view the surface from eight directions (north, south, east, west, northwest, northeast, southeast, southwest).

INSTITUTION UNDER STUDY

The institution under study is Eastern Kentucky University, a regional, coeducational, and public institution of higher education. The University offers traditional general and liberal arts programs, pre-professional and professional training in education and other disciplines at both the undergraduate and graduate levels. Situated in the heart of the Bluegrass, Richmond is 26 miles southeast of Lexington, Kentucky and is the county seat of Madison County, in a community of 21,000 people. The University currently enrolls more than 13,000 PTEs, and is still growing in student enrollment. Table 2 illustrates the first-time enrollment of freshmen students from Kentucky counties (120) for the years of 1979 through 1982, as well as the change in enrollment from 1981 to 1982. Table 2 is the basic database used in the present study to create the three-dimensional graphics and statistical models of student flow. However, as evident from the enrollments in the table, the counties of Jefferson, Fayette, and Madison, which are directly adjacent to Eastern Kentucky University, were not included in the present study so that the high enrollments from these counties do not skew the flow models generated from the other counties.

RESULTS AND DISCUSSION

Student flow statistics were analyzed and trend surface techniques were employed, via SYMAP(26) and a computer program suggested by Smith (14). Tables 3 and 4 summarize the results of the hypothesis testing and model comparisons of the polynomial trend surface, and Figures 1 through 12 are the computer-generated, three-dimensional graphics of the spatial distributions of incoming freshmen students into Eastern Kentucky University, as well as selected trend

surfaces and residual surfaces (differences between the actual and predicted number of students), for illustrative purposes. The results
of testing a sixth-degree, polynomial trend
surface over random variance, in traditional
analysis of variance (ANOVA) format are illustrated in Table 3. The sixth-order surface
accounted for 60.10 percent of the explained
variance in student flow as a function of spatial distribution in the state of Kentucky,
and was found to be statistically significant
at the 0.01 level (p = 0.0000). The results
found in Table 3 represent one entry in Table
4, which is a summary of F-ratios, probability
levels, R^2 for both the full and restricted
models, degrees of freedom-numerator, degrees
of freedom-denominator, and significance for
each trend surface for predicting student
enrollment/flow from counties in Kentucky to
Eastern Kentucky University, in standard multiple linear regression (MLR) format. The hypothesis and model comparisons of trend surfaces
are summarized in this table for incoming
freshmen for the years 1979 through 1982, inclusive, as well as the change in flow from
1981 to 1982, for comparative purposes. As
illustrated in Table 3 and 4, the sixth-degree
polynomial trend surface accounted for enough
explained variance (R^2 = 0.5632, p = 0.0069)
and 1982 (R^2 = 0.6099, p = 0.0160) student flow
models. However, no trend surface accounted
for enough explained variance in predicting
the change in student flow from 1981 to 1982,
as a function of spatial distribution in the
117 counties studied. The graphic displays of
the three-dimensional plots for the spatial
distribution for each of the years 1979 through
1982 may be found in Figures 1 through 8, either viewed from the southeast or northeast
direction, 30 degrees from the horizontal plane
of the state of Kentucky. Figures 9 and 10
present the three-degree polynomial surface
used in an attempt to predict the change in the
spatial distribution of incoming freshmen enrollment for the years 1981 to 1982. Figures
4 and 5 portray the three-dimensional distribution of the residuals (the difference between
the actual and predicted number of students)
from use of the third-order polynomial trend as
the predictive student flow model. As illustrated in Figures 1 and 2, large portions of
the incoming freshman class were derived from
extreme eastern Kentucky and a north-south
trend-line passing through Madison County, the
site of the University. The recruiting efforts
of the University, either through literature,
advisors, past graduates, or school visits must
be successful in attracting traditional-aged
students. This is not surprising, since the
University has a very strong teacher-training
program. The same basic trends are evident
for 1980, as presented in Figures 3 and 4. The
contribution of the north-south trend and eastern Kentucky to entering student enrollment is
strong, as well as increased student flows from
central portions of the state. The 1981 incoming student flows are also similar, except for
a slightly greater magnitude of inflows and

more contributions from middle-eastern Kentucky
(Figures 5 and 6). The three-dimensional distributions for the 1982 incoming freshmen-stu-
dent flows display a more decentralized flow
pattern, with the north-south trend and high
contribution of extreme eastern Kentucky still
evident. However, a large percentage of inflows are occuring in the central portions of
the state (Figures 7 and 8). In summary, Figures 1 through 8 portray the actual distributions of student flows in the state. They are
not models in the mathematical sense, although
the computer algorithm that generated them performed a nine-point quadratic interpolation for
smoothing purposes. Figures 9 through 12 represent the mathematical modeling results as applied to the difference or enrollment change
from 1981 to 1982. Figures 9 and 10 present
the best-fit model, based on the least-squares
criterion, in forecasting the student flows
change from 1981 to 1982. The polynomial equation was of the third-order, with the highest
exponential being three and containing all the
first-, second-, and third-degree terms. Figures 11 and 12 are the error or residual surfaces, showing the difference between the actual
enrollment change and the predicted enrollment
change between the years 1981 and 1982. The
three-degree represented a filter or regional
trend, and the residuals are the values that
passed through the filter and are anamolous to
the regional trend. As shown in Figures 11 and
12, the residuals are large in magnitude and
show a north-south trend as previously discussed. The residuals are relatively low for
eastern Kentucky, which indicates that the
third-degree surface explained the variance in
student flow changes in that region in good
fashion. However, as routinely performed in
regression and forecasting studies, if a trend
exists in the residual or error surfaces, that
a possibly higher-order polynomial trend (cur-
vilinear fit) may account for significantly
increased amounts of explained variance in
forecasting enrollment changes. As shown in
Table 4, the variability in enrollment changes
are highly predictable for each year viewed
separately but figures for 1981 to 1982 were
too randomly distributed to be modeled. This
is not the case, as previously discussed, for
modeling student flows for the years 1979
through 1982.

CONCLUSION

As evident from the statistical analysis presented in Table 3 and 4, and the computer-generated graphics in Figures 1 through 12, powerful and statistically significant, predictive
models of student flow can be generated for the
years studied, and may be used for constructing
models in the future, given other constraints.
However, no such relationship was established
for the change from one year to the next, as
evident from the results obtained from an attempt to forecast and model the 1981/1982
change in incoming student enrollment to East-

ern Kentucky University. The major benefit of modeling research is to be able to visualize the actual distributions of important parameters associated with student flows. Examples illustrated in this research allow the user to portray selected distributions of parameters in order to take administrative measures in the future to take corrective steps in the institution, either through retention/recruitment or to buffer the effects of such change in student enrollment. The use of plotting statistical as well as actual contour surfaces, allows the investigator a chance to actually visualize what the surface looks like and the residuals or errors in prediction and their magnitudes. This process can bring in the investigator's "common sense" and administrative judgement into play to determine the best fit. With the increasing use and availability or appropriate software and hardware, computer modeling should be used in conjunction with statistical models in estimating the usefulness and limitations of trend-surface analyses for predictive purposes in the construction of student flow models.

REFERENCES
(available upon request)

TABLE 1 – Typical Analysis of Variance Table for Polynomial Trend Surfaces.

Source of Variation	Sum of Squares	Degrees of Freedom	Mean Squares	F Ratio
Regression	SS_{Reg}	m	MS_{Reg}	MS_{Reg}/MS_{Res}
Residual	SS_{Res}	n − m − 1	MS_{Res}	
Total	SS_T	n − 1		

Note: In the table, m is the number of coefficients in the polynomial-trend surface equation, not including the constant term, b ; and n is the number of valid data points used in the regression equation.

TABLE 2 First-time Freshman Student Enrollment by County in Kentucky to Eastern Kentucky University for the Years 1979 to 1982, Inclusively.(partial listing only)

County in Kentucky	First-time Freshman Enrollment Years 1979	1980	1981	1982	1981/1982 (Change)
ADAIR	6	5	3	7	+ 4
ALLEN	0	1	1	0	− 1
ANDERSON	6	9	22	14	− 8
BALLARD	0	1	1	0	− 1
BARREN	11	10	4	4	0
BATH	7	7	9	8	− 1
BELL	37	64	38	30	+ 8
BOONE	36	34	19	31	+ 12
BOURBON	13	27	47	18	− 29
BOYD	35	40	30	18	− 12
BOYLE	38	61	54	58	+ 4

TABLE 3 ANOVA Table for Sixth Degree, Polynomial Trend Surface Predicting Student Flow of 1979 Incoming Freshman Students to Eastern Kentucky University.

Source of Variation	SS	df	MS	F-Ratio	Prob. Sign.
Sixth Degree Regression	16467.855	27	609.9206	4.9644	0.0000 s**
Error (Residual)	10934.453	89	122.8590		
Total	27402.308	116			

$R_f^2 = 0.6010$, $R_r^2 = 0.0$

** denotes statistical significance at the 0.01 level for a nondirectional, two-tailed test.

TABLE 4 Summary of F-Ratios, Probability Levels, R^2 for both the Full and Restricted Models, Degrees of Freedom-Numerator, Degrees of Freedom-Denominator, and Significance for each Trend Surface for Predicting Student Enrollment/Flow from Counties in Kentucky to Eastern Kentucky University.

Order of Trend Surface	R_f^2	R_r^2	df_n/df_d	F-Ratio	Prob. Sign.
STUDENT FLOW MODEL, 1979 INCOMING FRESHMEN STUDENTS					
1	0.1571	0.0	2/114	10.6230	0.0001 s**
2	0.1969	0.0	5/111	5.4443	0.0002 s**
3	0.2547	0.0	9/107	4.0619	0.0002 s**
4	0.3394	0.0	14/102	3.7426	0.0000 s**
5	0.4929	0.0	20/96	4.6652	0.0000 s**
6	0.6010	0.0	27/89	4.9644	0.0000 s**
1 vs 2	0.1969	0.1571	3/111	1.8359	0.1448 NS
2 vs 3	0.2547	0.1969	4/107	2.0712	0.0896 NS
3 vs 4	0.3394	0.2547	5/102	2.6159	0.0287 s*
4 vs 5	0.4929	0.3394	6/96	4.8435	0.0002 s**
5 vs 6	0.6010	0.4929	7/89	3.4439	0.0026 s**
STUDENT FLOW MODEL, 1980 INCOMING FRESHMEN STUDENTS					
1	0.1547	0.0	2/114	10.4289	0.0001 s**
2	0.2252	0.0	5/111	6.4544	0.0000 s**
3	0.2885	0.0	9/107	4.8211	0.0000 s**
4	0.3643	0.0	14/102	4.1758	0.0000 s**
5	0.4901	0.0	20/96	4.6136	0.0000 s**
6	0.6161	0.0	27/89	5.2905	0.0000 s**
1 vs 2	0.2252	0.1547	3/111	3.3709	0.0211 s*
2 vs 3	0.2885	0.2252	4/107	2.3787	0.0563 NS
3 vs 4	0.3643	0.2885	5/102	2.4330	0.0398 s*
4 vs 5	0.4901	0.3643	6/96	3.9466	0.0014 s**
5 vs 6	0.6161	0.4901	7/89	4.1737	0.0005 s**
STUDENT FLOW MODEL, 1981 INCOMING FRESHMEN STUDENTS					
1	0.1543	0.0	2/114	10.3959	0.0001 s**
2	0.2141	0.0	5/111	6.0491	0.0001 s**
3	0.2965	0.0	9/107	5.0103	0.0000 s**
4	0.3320	0.0	14/102	3.6217	0.0001 s**
5	0.4597	0.0	20/96	4.0842	0.0000 s**
6	0.5632	0.0	27/89	4.2503	0.0000 s**
1 vs 2	0.2141	0.1543	3/111	2.8194	0.0423 s*
2 vs 3	0.2965	0.2141	4/107	3.1311	0.0177 s*
3 vs 4	0.3320	0.2965	5/102	1.0861	0.3727 NS
4 vs 5	0.4597	0.3320	6/96	3.7808	0.0026 s**
5 vs 6	0.5632	0.4597	7/89	3.0125	0.0069 s**
STUDENT FLOW MODEL, 1982 INCOMING FRESHMEN STUDENTS					
1	0.1648	0.0	2/114	11.2503	0.0000 s**
2	0.2256	0.0	5/111	6.4677	0.0000 s**
3	0.3116	0.0	9/107	5.3809	0.0000 s**
4	0.3935	0.0	14/102	4.7273	0.0000 s**
5	0.5290	0.0	20/96	5.3913	0.0000 s**
6	0.6099	0.0	27/89	5.1526	0.0000 s**
1 vs 2	0.2256	0.1648	3/111	2.9036	0.0380 s*
2 vs 3	0.3116	0.2256	4/107	3.3405	0.0128 s**
3 vs 4	0.3935	0.3116	5/102	2.7361	0.0223 s*
4 vs 5	0.5290	0.3935	6/96	4.6029	0.0004 s**
5 vs 6	0.6099	0.5290	7/89	7.6366	0.0160 s*
STUDENT FLOW MODEL, 1981/1982 CHANGE IN INCOMING FRESHMEN STUDENTS					
1	0.0053	0.0	2/114	0.3017	0.7405 NS
2	0.0084	0.0	5/111	0.1880	0.9665 NS
3	0.0186	0.0	9/107	0.2257	0.9902 NS
4	0.0860	0.0	14/102	0.6854	0.7838 NS
5	0.1076	0.0	20/96	0.5785	0.9185 NS
6	0.1779	0.0	27/89	0.7131	0.8399 NS
1 vs 2	0.0084	0.0053	3/111	0.1173	0.9498 NS
2 vs 3	0.0186	0.0084	4/107	0.2789	0.6911 NS
3 vs 4	0.0860	0.0186	5/102	1.5033	0.1953 NS
4 vs 5	0.1076	0.0860	6/96	0.3880	0.8851 NS
5 vs 6	0.1779	0.1076	7/89	1.0862	0.3790 NS

Note. The counties of Jefferson, Fayette, and Madison, which are directly adjacent to Eastern Kentucky University, were not included in the present study so that the high enrollments from these counties do not skew the flow models generated from the data.

* denotes statistical significance at the 0.05 level, for a nondirectional, two-tailed test.

** denotes statistical significance at the 0.01 level, for a nondirectional, two-tailed test.

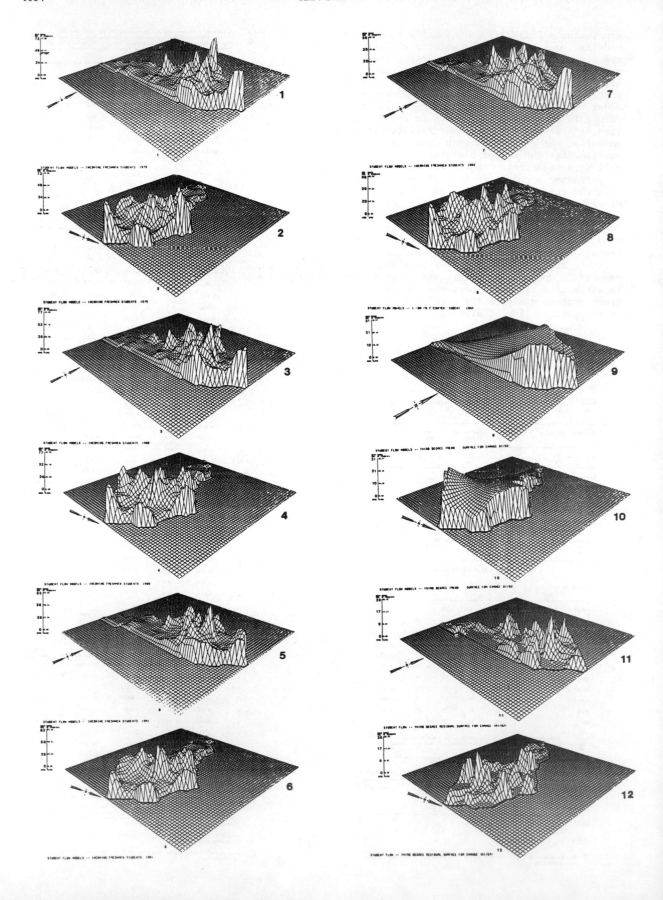

STUDENT FLOW MODELS -- INCOMING FRESHMEN STUDENTS 1978

STUDENT FLOW MODELS -- INCOMING FRESHMEN STUDENTS 1979

STUDENT FLOW MODELS -- INCOMING FRESHMEN STUDENTS 1980

STUDENT FLOW MODELS -- INCOMING FRESHMEN STUDENTS 1980

STUDENT FLOW MODELS -- INCOMING FRESHMEN STUDENTS 1981

STUDENT FLOW MODELS -- INCOMING FRESHMEN STUDENTS 1982

STUDENT FLOW MODELS -- INCOMING FRESHMEN STUDENTS 1982

STUDENT FLOW MODELS -- THIRD DEGREE TREND SURFACE FOR CHANGE 81/82

STUDENT FLOW MODELS -- THIRD DEGREE TREND SURFACE FOR CHANGE 81/82

STUDENT FLOW MODELS -- THIRD DEGREE RESIDUAL SURFACE FOR CHANGE 81/82

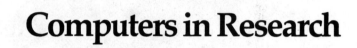

Computers in Research

COMPUTERS IN EDUCATION, K. Duncan and D. Harris (eds.)
Elsevier Science Publishers B.V. (North-Holland)
© IFIP, 1985

THE LOGO LANGUAGE AS A TOOL IN EDUCATIONAL RESEARCH

Tony   Adams

Department of Administrative Studies,
Royal Melbourne Institute of Technology,
Melbourne, Australia.

Logo has been widely used in a variety of educational research projects related to children's learning, and the learning of programming in particular.   This paper examines the specific features of Logo that make it accessible to researchers and students, and a research environment transparent to the learner is described.

INTRODUCTION

The Logo language can lay claim to be useful in two areas of educational research with computers.

Firstly as a language tool for carrying out educational research.   Logo has been used as a tool in research into learning with or about computers and into the development of children's mental processes.   Many researchers have reported that Logo provides an environment where children can articulate thought processes, making Logo a powerful tool for education.

Secondly, Logo has features which make it useful as a tool for studying and analysing educational computing environments.   For example building new language features as an object of research, or creating an environment for the observation by Logo itself of the learner's activities.

FEATURES THAT MAKE LOGO USEFUL IN EDUCATION

The features of Logo that make it suitable for educational use include the following (17, 10).

It contains a procedural view of the world. This view is seen as one where complex processes can be described in terms of sub-processes. These sub-processes either are simple enough to solve directly or in turn can be described further in terms of sub-processes.   These can then be combined together to solve the problem at hand.

The concrete nature of turtle geometry is a powerful problem solving tool allowing the development of metaphors, such as acting out the role of the turtle using the learner's own body movements.

Debugging is an activity in which children learn the process of learning, as well as about the problem to be solved.   Papert (13) states:

"Many children are held back in their
learning because they have a model of
learning in which you have either
'got it' or 'got it wrong'.   But
when you learn to program a computer
you almost never get it
right first time.... The
question to ask about a
program is not whether it
is right or wrong, but if
it is fixable.   If this
way of looking at intellectual
products were generalized to
how the larger culture thinks
about knowledge and its
acquisition, we might all be
less intimated about our fears
of being wrong."

(Papert, 1981, p. 84)

Logo is consistent with the educational philosophy of Piaget (Papert, 1980).   Papert sees children as "builders of their own intellectual structures" and argues that "like other builders, children appropriate to their own use materials they find about them, most saliently the models and metaphors suggested by their surrounding culture".   Important in this is that Logo becomes a means of representing and testing conceptual structures, naming concepts and discussing thinking processes.

Bornet and Brady (2) summarise the reasons why Logo is preferable to other languages such as Basic:

"An interesting problem domain which
doesn't rely on students having
extensive formula knowledge from
some other discipline.

An obvious program trace which
aids debugging, is a primitive
measure of efficiency and so on.

It encourages the notion of a
process as a representation of a
solution to a problem.

Its primitive commands are simple
to understand, being defined purely
in terms of actions in the problem
and not alterations to the internal
state of the machine."

(Bornet and Brady, 1974, p. 3)

Howe (8) sees Logo as consistent with artificial intelligence ideas and contrasts it to traditional classroom problem solving activity, which uses well known and understood algorithms as recipes to solve relatively brief tasks.

LOGO AS A RESEARCH TOOL

McDougall and Adams (10) see that Logo research has a number of facets:

> "Developments in the Logo language and in research into its use have, until now, been mainly based in university laboratories or in limited school settings, and have necessarily been exploratory in nature. Results from these studies suggest that Logo has great potential for use in a wide variety of educational settings... the availability of Logo on microcomputers now makes possible more extensive and sustained studies of the use of this language beyond the laboratories. Much of this research effort will be directed at evaluation of Logo itself, as a means of improving children's whole approach to learning, or as a resource in the teaching of traditional materials and skills. However there are other possible roles for the language in educational research... as a very powerful tool for studying learning processes as such."

> (McDougall and Adams, 1982, p. 126)

Logo research to date has been carried out in two main ways. Groen (5) identifies the first as being anecdotal in nature and concentrating on the reporting of case study observations, generally of a small number of students. This approach is that of the MIT Logo group and follows Papert (12, p. 994) who argues that "the diffusion of personal computation will cause the coming years into a giant experiment in developmental psychology" in which present research methods are irrelevant. According to Wills (18) "Comparative evaluation, he (Papert) believed, would be of little value in pinpointing the processes children use in learning and solving problems".

The second approach is that of traditional educational evaluation. Behavioral measures are subjected to statistical analysis. This approach is typical of work done at the University of Edinburgh under Howe, and work by Pea (14) at Bank Street College.

Higginson (7) says:

> "What happens when you inject 'x' units of substance 'y' into the blood stream of individual 'z'? is a very

different sort of question from What happens when individual 'p' is exposed to language 'q'? Despite this much of the discussion of what children learn from Logo is carried out as if the question were of the first type rather than the second."

> (Higginson, 1984, p. 34)

Groen observes that neither approach has been able to adequately interpret Logo claims. This he states is because Papert's writings on the benefits of Logo provide hints towards a theory of Logo but not the theory itself. He states:

> "Its (Logo's) educational value, especially with children, comes from the fact that it provides a way of exploring Microworlds. Powerful ideas are not generalized programming skills but ways of coordinating a microworld with its analogues in reality, or ways of coordinating between different representations of microworlds."

> (Groen, 1984, p. 51)

Groen further observes that the child doing Logo is not learning a programming language, but rather a way of establishing correspondence between a concrete world and one of abstract representations.

It is clear that sharp divisions exist within the Logo community on appropriate research methodologies.

A COMPUTER ENVIRONMENT FOR LOGO BASED RESEARCH

Solomon (16) provides an idea of what a Logo environment might be:

> "a computer,
>
> a programming language and an operating system,
>
> a collection of computer peripherals, usually including graphics and turtles;
>
> a collection of projects,
>
> a meta language - a consistent way of talking about the language, the projects, etc;
>
> a relationship between teacher and learner, and
>
> a collection of bridge activities, like juggling, puzzles, etc.
>
> All of these components are interdependent and the special virtues of the environment follow from their

coherence with one another".

(Solomon, 1978, p. 21)

Wills (18) argues:

"There is agreement that much more documentation of children's learning experiences must be made available, and that much of this must be documentation by teachers working with their students in natural classroom settings".

(Wills, 1984, p. 14)

If Wills' statement is to be taken seriously, the level of expertise required to operate the hardware and therefore the software must be consistent with the training and needs of the researchers. If educational research is to be carried out by teachers and specialists in children's learning, rather than by computer scientists, then a very convivial operating environment must be available.

An educational research environment has, in addition to the features outlined by Solomon, the following requirements:

a means of recording data dynamically as it is created by the student,

a means of storing student data for later analysis,

analysis and reporting software as required by the researcher,

the ability to retain control of error situations, and

the software being used should enable the development of research tools. Consistent with the idea of research being done in a natural environment is the idea that the computer language being used should also provide a means for developing transparent observing and measuring tools. In particular if the language is to be regarded as convivial then these tools should be accessible to the researcher and perhaps the student.

Consider research which is examining students' use of the features of a particular language. Tools which may be useful are those which would examine individual language commands entered by the student, their correctness, and the context in which they have been used. In a conventional system using Basic or Pascal these tools have to be either developed at an operating system level, by modifying the interpreter or compiler, or by developing a specific language compiler or interpreter.

Logo has features that provide the ability to build these tools. A RUN command allows a Logo procedure to execute data as a procedure.

Thus Logo commands entered by the user can be handled as data by another Logo procedure and so be analysed, modified, or saved for later analysis prior to their execution as Logo commands. The use of the Run command also allows new language constructs to be developed from existing ones. Foe example Abelson (1, p. 159) creates a WHILE construct similar to that which exists in Pascal, and Harvey (1984) demonstrates the construction of a range of iterative commands more powerful than those that exist currently in conventional computer languages in education.

The ability of both user procedures and many Logo primitives to output a result to another procedure is particularly useful with system primitives that can output information about the internal state of the Logo machine.

A feature available in versions of Logo derived from LCSI Apple Logo allows syntax and run-time errors to be intercepted by another Logo procedure. Thus tools can be provided which catch, analyse and report errors without resorting to the underlying operating system or interpreter. This feature allows the researcher to maintain control of the programming environment when errors occur.

Some Logo systems allow primitives to be redefined by the user. Thus the code for a primitive command can be altered by a Logo procedure to collect additional information, or to provide a new modified primitive.

Logo procedures can be created from within Logo, by primitives that create an executable procedure from data. The reverse process, of turning Logo procedures that have been already defined into data accessible from within another Logo procedure, enables the contents of the user's workspace to be accessed and analysed.

THE DEVELOPMENT OF AN EDUCATIONAL RESEARCH
    ENVIRONMENT

The following work has been carried out in collaboration with Anne McDougall of Monash University who is working with children of primary (elementary) school age, and Pauline Adams and Lesley Tann at the Melbourne College of Advanced Education, Institute of Early Childhood Development with pre-school children.

A research environment has been constructed for the Apple II using Apple Logo. Apple Logo was chosen instead of MIT Logo for the Apple because of the ability to maintain control after an error. We considered this important since it otherwise would have been necessary to develop a "front-end" syntax checking module that because of memory restrictions would have prevented the full implementation of Logo being available to the researcher.

The environment consists of four modules that run

as sets of Logo procedures.   The modules are a
data collection module, one key Logo module for
young children, a module to run a Tasman Robot
Turtle, an installation module, and an analysis
module.

The data collection module is the heart of the
system.   It is loaded as a startup file (this
means it is loaded automatically) and consists
of about fourteen core Logo statements that
maintain control of the environment.   The
functions of this "inner loop" are to read user
commands from the Keyboard, to add these to a
data list, to cause them to be run (executed),
and to maintain control when an error occurs.

Procedures as they are created or edited are
saved as data.   Since disk read and write
commands are also saved, a complete record of the
interaction between the student and Logo is
maintained.   The module simulates the toplevel
processing of Apple Logo, so the student is not
aware of its presence.

The data collection module, although loaded with
Logo, is not invoked until the user requires it.
This is necessary as the saving of commands takes
up scarce memory, and because the information
requires manual date stamping as no internal date
mechanism exists.   When data collection is
complete, the data is stored on disk for later
retrieval with a name constructed out of the date
and student name.   Data collected in this way is
called a dribble.

This method has been widely used in Logo research
carried out at MIT and the University of Edinburgh, but little about it has appeared in the
literature.   Feurzeig and Lukas (4) describe a
dribble system running with an early version of
Logo.   Ross (15) reports on the difficulty in
coping with the volume of data produced by a
dribble system.

The second module consists of one key Logo
procedures collectively called Toddler.   These
are described in McDougall, Adams and Adams (11,
p. 225) and are designed for pre-school children.
A similar set of procedures is also described in
Abelson (1982).

The third module is a set of driving procedures
for a Tasman robot turtle.   These can be used
in conjunction with the Toddler module or as a
freestanding set of procedures.

The installation module is used to control
changes to all the modules.   This is necessary
as multiple modules may exist in the user's workspace, so careful management of disk files is
required.

In its simplest form the analysis module enables
a dribble to be retrieved from disk and displayed
or printed.   It will contain all commands
entered by the student and procedures that have
been defined or edited.   Thus the dribble contains a dynamic picture of changes to the

student's workspace.   For many research needs,
this feature alone will provide a powerful
facility for reflection.

Two approaches could be taken in developing a
more significant analysis module.   The first
would be to create procedures that statistically
analyse the information in the dribble.   This
approach is consistent with the behavioural
approach to Logo research.   The second would be
to develop a set of tools that increase the
observational power of the researcher.   This is
the approach we have taken.   The metaphor we
have chosen is that of a video recorder.   The
watcher can view, stop on a frame, scan backwards, scan forward, or replay the material being
viewed.

This model when applied to dribble data enables
the researcher to replay, reflect, modify, or to
carry out a discourse with the student on previous
activities.   Commands can be retrieved one at a
time and selectively executed.   Because all
commands can be treated in the same way, the above
feature allows the student's workspace to be
directly entered whenever a procedure has been
defined or edited.   A quick scan feature enables
the researcher to go forward or backward or to
search for a particular attribute.   Because the
module is running in a normal Logo environment,
at any point modifications can be made to existing procedures or completely new explorations
begun.   The original dribble can be recommenced
later.   The analysis itself can be saved as a
dribble.

At the time of writing the above features are at
a developmental stage, but progress is promising.

PROBLEMS WITH PRESENT MICRO-COMPUTER ENVIRONMENTS

Our experience in developing software research
tools with Logo on current micro-computers is
that there are significant problems with the use
of the software and hardware by novices and users
with limited computer experience.   These include
the physical handling of devices, poor quality
error messages, the use of small capacity flexible
diskettes, multiple key keyboard sequences to
control the computer, poor resolution of screen
displays, and non integration of different software environments on the same computer.

A major difficulty working against the development of effective research tools is the lack of
memory in which to develop strategies that
limit the expertise required for effective
operation, in particular for the provision of
high quality user interfaces.

Our observation is that present eight bit technology even with very friendly languages such as
Logo, do not provide a completely convivial
operating environment for the non-expert
computer user.   Current research and development
involving sixteen bit hardware address these
difficulties.   We are optimistic that research

with the Boxer environment at MIT (3, p. 154), and the development of Smalltalk (9) with the consequential commercial release of integrated systems such as Apple's Lisa and Macintosh computers will provide new opportunities for extending the observational power of the researcher with convivial operating environments.

REFERENCES

[1]   Abelson, H., Logo for the Apple II (McGraw-Hill, 1982).

[2]   Bornet, R. and Brady, J. "The Linguistics of Logo", Computer Science Memo, No.4, University of Essex, (July, 1974).

[3]   di Sessa, A., "Notes on the Future of Programming", in Sorkin, R. (ed.), LOGO 84, Pre-Proceedings of the National Logo Conference, MIT, (1984), 149-155.

[4]   Feurzeig, W. and Lukas, G., "The Use of Dribble Files as Instructional Aids", Technical Report, Bolt Beranek and Newman Inc., Cambridge, Mass.,(1972).

[5]   Groen, G., "Theories of Logo", in Sorkin, R., (ed.), LOGO 84, Pre-Proceedings of the National Logo Conference, MIT, (1984), 49-54.

[6]   Harvey, B., "Iteration in Logo", in Sorkin, R. (ed.), LOGO 84, Pre-Proceedings of the National Logo Conference, MIT, (1984), 113-119.

[7]   Higginson, W., "About the Rose Garden: Remarks on Logo, Learning, Children and Schools", in Sorken, R. (ed.), LOGO 84, Pre-Proceedings of the National Logo Conference, MIT, (1984), 31-39.

[8]   Howe, J., "Artificial Intelligence in Education", in Hooper, R. (ed.), Computer Assisted Learning in the U.K., Council for Educational Technology, London, (1975), 295-317.

[9]   Kay, A. and Goldberg, A., "Personal Dynamic Media", Computer, Vol. 10, No. 3, (1977), 31-41.

[10] McDougall, A. and Adams, T., "Logo Environments: The Development of the Language and its use in Education and Research", Proceedings of the Ninth Australian Computer Conference, (1982), 115-132.

[11] McDougall, A., Adams, T. and Adams, P., Learning Logo on the Apple II, (Prentice-Hall, 1982).

[12] Papert, S., "Redefining Childhood: The Computer Presence as an Experiment in Developmental Psychology", in Lavington, S. (ed.), Information Processing 80, (North-Holland, 1980), 993-997.

[13] Papert, S., "Computers and Computer Cultures", Creative Computing, Vol. 7, No. 3, (1981), 82-90.

[14] Pea, R., "Symbol Systems and Thinking Skills: Logo in Context", in Sorkin, R. (ed.), LOGO 84, Pre-Proceedings of the National Logo Conference, MIT, (1984), 55-62.

[15] Ross, P., Personal Communication, University of Edinburgh, (1982).

[16] Solomon, C., "Teaching Young Children to Program in a Logo Turtle Culture", Sigcue Bulletin, Vol. 12, No. 3, (1978), 20-29.

[17] Solomon, C., "Language in the Logo Computer Culture", Proceedings Necc, June (1979), 250-254.

[18] Wills, S., "Evaluating Logo", unpublished essay, Faculty of Education, Monash University, (1984).

COMPUTERS IN EDUCATION, K. Duncan and D. Harris (eds.)
Elsevier Science Publishers B.V. (North-Holland)
© IFIP, 1985

COGNITIVE AND VISUAL ELEMENTS OF USING A COMPUTER FOR INSTRUCTION

Morrison F. Hammond

School of Education, Maquarie University
North Ryde, Sydney, New South Wales
Australia

When one looks at the literature relating to the use of computers in education, one finds articles about the ways in which computers or computing studies have been integrated into educational programmes. Little is found about research or opinion on the place of the learner as a receiver of the computerated teaching. Here, attention is paid to a consideration of the place of perceptual and cognitive aspects that bear upon the process.

If one draws back and looks at the teaching/learning situation in which computers are employed, one must recognise that what is really happening is that the learner is being subject to teaching, or education by television. When taken to its basics, the learner is being called upon to react to a range of symbols on a television screen, and with the new generation of computer generated and driven graphics it is almost impossible to identify a screen that has been generated by a computer and one that is showing camera derived television coverage of reality; particularly if a high definition screen is being used.

We have now had about thirty years of research into the effects of educational television and have a few indices of its effectiveness. We have also had the value of theoretical research into the possible effect on alpha waves by the scanning of the video tube (12).

In this paper I wish to address attention to some of the perceptual and psychological dimensions of using a computer in learning.

We are living and learning in a very visual age. There is evidence of that from the beginning of our day to its end with the newspapers, television, billboards, arcade games and other hard and electronic information providers that we attend to. Some of these are part of our work environment, some are part of the general environment and others are part of the educational and leisure environments. Some are attended to by choice, others by requirement and others, such as street billboards, quite involuntarily. To manage our psychological well-being, and to prevent information overload, we spend a great deal of our time filtering our visual world. Only the visually literate can make full use of the highly visual technology.

Twenty years ago, attention was drawn to educators' neglect of considering learners' visual capacities and visual preferences in learning. Dondis (12) claimed that "even the use of a visual approach to learning through the media is without rigour and purpose. In many instances, students are bombarded with visual aids - but the presentation reinforces their passive experience as consumers of television." So began the visual literacy movement.

Visual literacy may be thought of as a group of skills which enable an individual to understand and use visuals for intentionally communicating with others (4), or as consisting of two types of knowledge: lingual or non-lingual. Lingual knowledge involves the decoding of commonly shared symbols to acquire knowledge, and non-lingual knowledge is the learner's interpretation of reality as portrayed visually (29). The first sense emphasises intentionality, seeing visual literacy as a communication mode. The second position reflects a deeper interest in the type of symbol system used to transmit or acquire knowledge.

As the intrusion of the computer into the educational environment is said to have brought a new force to education, it must surely be important for us to assess the current operation of education so that this new era may be profitably embraced. Educators should recognise and respect the learner as an individual and be determining how an individual seeks meaning. In order for learners to participate in a communication situation, it is necessary for them to begin by cognitively structuring it. It can be shown that one of the stable differences among learners is their cognitive style (1, 25). Cognitive style can be linked to the development of visual literacy (19) and cognitive style can also be connected with factors related to the learner's involvement in a visual communication process (11).

The term cognitive style refers to individual modes of cognitive functioning (8) and it has been shown that these modes determine the amount and organization of information available to the individual at any particular time (18). These modes are seen as being pervasive and relatively stable traits in an individual (17). Cognitive style may be thought of as a construct that has been developed to explain the process of mediation between stimulation and response, or the characteristic ways in which individuals conceptually organise the environment (15). This structure emphasises how cognition is organised, rather than what content is available. "The human mind must contribute to the process of visual perception by its organizational function" (1).

The organizing must operate in terms of perceiving, remembering and thinking. That last attribute calls for the transforming and utilizing of information. This means that there is a quantitative as well as qualitative variation in the mental functioning of individuals which can be reliably measured.

A child's cognitive style is thought to develop from an interaction of the child's communication styles, human relational styles, incentive-motivational styles, and the child's ways of perceiving and thinking (learning styles) (14). The cognitive style that develops is not just an ability, but is rather a bipolar trait representing directions or preferences in information processing (18). Thus, cognitive style represents a preferred manner of dealing with material. Individuals differ in the strength of their preferred mode.

If we focus on some of the identified styles, it should become clearer how they are related to a learner interacting with a computer in say ,a drill and practice, or tutorial mode unit of CAI. A proposed listing can be found in Table 1.

Table 1: Commonly Identified Cognitive Styles.

1. Field independent - field dependent: involves the tendency to perceive a perceptual field either analytically or globally. It entails the ability to experience items as discrete from their background, and to overcome embeddedness.

2. Scanning - focussing: involves differences in the manner and extensiveness with which attention and concentration are deployed and distributed when dealing with a stimulus field.

3. Breadth of categorising: involves preferences for either broad inclusiveness or narrow exclusiveness in establishing ranges for categories.

4. Conceptualizing styles: involves preferred approaches to categorizing perceived similarities and differences among stimuli and with conceptualizing approaches as bases for forming concepts.

5. Cognitive complexity - simplicity: involves differences in tendency to construe the world in a multi-dimensional and complex way.

6. Reflectivity - impulsivity: involves the tendency, when faced with simultaneous response alternatives, to select either careful deliberation and relative certainty of response correctness or speed of response and high risk of

incorrect response. (Cognitive tempo.)

7. Levelling - sharpening: involves differences in the mode of assimilation of sequential stimuli in the memory, with preference given either to the merging of stimuli into relatively undifferentiated recollections or to maintaining discrete experiences in memory.

8. Constricted - flexible field control: involves differences in handling a stimulus field containing contradiction and cognitive interference. It entails the ability to withold attention selectively from irrelevant intrusions and focus on a central task.

9. Tolerance for incongruous or unrealistic experiences: involves the willingness to accept perceptions at variance with conventional experience.

10. Risk taking - cautiousness: involves differences in preference for high payoff - low probability or low payoff - high probability options.

11. Visual - haptic: involves preference for, and an ability in dealing with visual or kinaesthetic sensory input and processing.

after Ausburn and Ausburn (3)

Cognitive style can affect academic performance in a range of tasks such as reading, inductive reasoning, recognition memory and serial learning (2, 26). Traditional schooling which has an emphasis on printed material has been seen to advantage learners who display field independent, reflective behaviour (20). Because of these orientations, many learners have been disadvantaged, not through lack of ability, but because their preferred modes of acquiring, transforming and using information do not match the expectations and requirements of the educational process. Cognitive styles cut across traditional subject boundaries, making their effects more pervasive (30).

Moving toward the use of the computer in instruction, we need to examine a number of questions. It is apparent that there is an interaction between cognitive style and perception of the material displayed on the monitor/television screen. Two considerations immediately come into focus:

a) some intervention is needed to correct the apparent mismatch between the cognitive styles of some learners and the visual material that is presented, and

b) there is need for a systematic examination of the ways in which learning programmes may come to assist students who have difficulties with interpreting the visual inputs into their learning sequences.

It would seem that students cannot be trained into an alternative cognitive style (3, 6, 9). Training in trying to develop a more field independent approach, or any of the other more advantageous approaches, does not show a significant shift in orientation. While resistance to change makes training difficult, it could be that the stability of cognitive style can be turned to advantage.

Instructional material may be presented in the form which will provide a capitalization match with the learner's preferred cognitive style. While it may seem obvious that this matching is best for the learner, caution should be followed so that the learner's style is not given increased rigidity and inflexibility. The identified types of cognitive style given earlier in this paper should be thought of as a set of continua, and as such, most learners are not completely polar. By presenting a range of other matches such as challenge match, corrective or remedial match, or compensatory match, it may assist the learner to maintain some degrees of flexibility in approach. If these steps are to be used, they must be undertaken deliberately, and with the understanding of the learner so that students with particular cognitive styles are not placed in an hostile environment and then made to appear uncooperative and poorly motivated (9).

Interpretation of visual material does not have the use of visual short-term memory in the way that verbal content utilizes iconic storage. This means that memory strength for any visual object is a function of attention. Recognition of information in pictorial memory is a fairly high speed associative task that is reasonably accurate. This is linked to an individual's cognitive structure and the arrangement of their schemas. In recalling visual experiences there cannot be a recreating of physical objects; there is merely a symbolic representation of reality in, and comparison with, verbal symbols; the symbols are less abstract.

One must take into account the proposition that a learner presented with a variety of cues - visual, audio etc. - will select those cues most appropriate to their learning style and compound them to process the information successfully.

Such propositions that depend on a multi-channel theory (i.e. the mind can process information from several sources at the same time) are in conflict with the single channel theory that concludes that the mind can process only one channel of simultaneously presented information. This latter theory suggests that there is attenuation, or inhibition in other channels while one channel of input is being acted on.

Attention should also be paid to experimental work that is assessing the relative functioning of left and right hemispheres of the brain in relation to various abilities and skills that are developed through the educational process, and their correlation with the manipulation and interpretation of multi-channel sensory inputs.

Cognitive style inhibits learning when an incompatibility exists between an individual's information processing patterns and those patterns required by certain learning tasks. This may be thought of supplantation, which is an attempt to provide a link between the learner's characteristics and the task requirements. It is an "explicit performance of a mental task requirement which learners would otherwise have to perform covertly for themselves " (2).

It may be of several types. Conciliatory supplantation builds on a learner's preferred instructional mode. Here the content is conveyed through the symbol system that matches learner preference. Compensatory supplantation compensates for a learner's task-related deficiencies by providing the specific process that the learner cannot provide alone. For the use of computers for the delivery of instruction, one needs to accommodate to those who are strongly visual, and haptics who have difficulty in retaining visual images. The latter may need to have a set of screens presented simultaneously through another medium to simulate the retention capacity of those with strong visual retention.

With learner participation in computer assisted learning being so dependent on the reading of the monitor screen, it is worth noting that eye movement, and thus the decoding of the screen, is associated with cognitive style. Children who tend to be more reflective in style make more systematic eye movements when examining a visual display than do impulsive children (26), and field independent individuals show less organization in their eye movements than field dependent individuals by having more erratic movements, longer fixations, and more blinking behaviour under stress. Field independent individuals are more active scanners of visual material than are field dependent individuals 86).

There appears to be a tendency for field independent learners to score higher from instruction in either audio or written form, but field dependent learners consistently score higher from television presentations (10). Field dependent individuals when learning concepts remember the most salient cues, whether or not they are relevant to the concept. When the salient ones are relevant, concept acquisition is rapid. Field independent learners will apply a structure to the field and select out the relevant cues regardless of their salience (16, 17).

If one takes a range of the current software that is being offerred on the educational market, one finds that the potential learner is being bombarded with sight and sound, with a range of degrees of required interaction with the unit of instruction. The learner is being asked to cope with visual, and auditory inputs and make responses through manipulative behaviour, by typing in a response or positioning a cursor by using a joystick. Fine for most, but an hostile situation for many. These situations may be made much worse by having the content of the units at an inappropriate cognitive level.

If one takes a Piagetian approach to cognitive development, there is a definite order in which to expose the learner to material, concretely based experiences leading to abstract processes. It would seem that a great number of software makers are ignorant of this perspective and present units that have abstract material presented in a structure that is suited to a learner still working at a concrete level, and the reverse of this situation. It would seem that many producers of educational software take either an eclectic or a Brunerian approach to their work.

In designing software there is a need to work just as much from a communication point of view as from an educational. The learner, after all is going to watch television. Television is, as pointed out previously, a visually based language and as such shares the same basic principles of all languages. As written language depends on a balance between sender and receiver through a matching of encoding and decoding in an appropriate environment, so too is television or the content of the computer screen.

One can identify three stages in the process of communicating messages and each is subject to wide variation: 1) the nature of the messages, comprising both their content and structure, 2) the manner in which they are conveyed, and 3) the learning capacities of the receivers to whom they are directed. In the relationship between the coding systems of sender (software maker) and receiver (potential learner) with respect to computer software exists a very complex structure of symbols. The structure is concerned with the symbols of the content of the messages that make up the software package, and the symbols that come from the syntax of the medium itself.

The use to which computer software may be put in an educational setting may be categorized by their functional operation: 1) instructional, leading to gains in knowledge, 2) motivational, leading to the restructuring of some aspect of the learner, and 3) demonstrational, leading to changes in skill performance. In each of these, there are differences in symbolic structures. The level of success of the software is very much linked to the care with which it has been developed against current ideas and theory about the relationship of visual literacy and cognitive style and the findings of research on the effectiveness of television as a teaching medium. It should though, be recognised that the teaching of programming and computer science subjects that call for learner interaction with the computer to develop language and keyboard skills should be looked at from a different

point of view. There the computer is directly related to the task, whereas in computer assisted instruction or learning, it is merely the medium of communication.

It has been pointed out that "symbolically different presentations of information vary as to the mental skills of processing that they require......media's ways of structuring and presenting material, i.e. their symbol system, are media's most important attributes when learning and cognition are considered" (28). In discussing cognitive style and the role of computer assisted learning, future research will need to examine:

  a) how cognitive styles affect the way that a learner perceives and organizes the presentation, and

  b) how visual material can be used to overcome the disadvantages some students suffer because of strategy mismatch.

Along with this research there is the need to plan systematic programmes to teach people how to think visually.

References.

[1] Amery, L.J., Visual Literacy: Implications for the Production of Children's Television Programs (Dalhousie University School of Library Services, Halifax, 1978).

[2] Ausburn, F.B., Impact of learning styles on air force technical training: multiple and linear imagery in the presentation of a comparative visual location task to visual and haptic subjects (Air Forces Human Resources Laboratory, Oklahoma, 1979, ERIC No. ED174760).

[3] Ausburn, L.J and Ausburn, F.B., Cognitive styles: some inferences and implications for instructional design, Educational Communication and Technology Journal, 4, (1978) 337-354.

[4] Ausburn L.J. and Ausburn, F.B., Visual literacy: background, theory and practice, Programmed Learning and Educational Technology, 4, (1978) 291-297.

[5] Berry, C. and Unwin, D., A selected bibliography of production and audience variables in film and television, Programmed Learning and Educational Technology, 1, (1975) 54-70.

[6] Britain, S.B., Dunkel, J. and Coull, B., Visual perceptual training of field-dependent and field-independent 5 year olds: an increase in analytic visual ability (U.S. Department of Health, Education and Welfare, Washington (1979) ERIC No. ED190590).

[7] Cohen, P.A., Ebeling, B.J., and Kulik, J.A.,

A meta-analysis of outcome studies of visual-based instruction, Educational Communication and Technology Journal, 1, (1981) 26-36.

[8] Coop, R.H. and Sigel, I.E., Cognitive style: implications for learning and instruction, Psychology in the Schools, 2 (1971) 152-160.

[9] Cross, K.P., Accent on Learning (Jossey-Bass, San Francisco, 1976).

[10] Danielson, J.E., Seiler, W.J. and Friedrich, G.W., Learners' cognitive style and levels of learning in television and print instruction for use in open learning: an exploratory study (Paper presented at the 65th Annual Meeting of the Speech Communication Association, San Antonio, Texas, 1979, ERIC No. ED 180036).

[11] De Santis, L.B. and Pett, D.W., Visual literacy: an overview of theory and practice, (1980, ERIC No. ED 210036).

[12] Dondis, D.A., A Primer of Visual Literacy (M.I.T., Cambridge, 1973).

[13] Emery, N., Neuropsychological effects of TV: latest findings, in Broadcasting in Australia: Today's Issues and the Future, (Conference Papers, A.N.U., Canberra, 1982).

[14] Gardner, R.C., Learning styles: what every teacher should consider (Paper presented at the Rocky Mountain Regional Conference of the International Reading Association (5th Boise, Indiana) 1980, ERIC No. ED198059).

[15] Goldstein, K.M. and Blackman, S., Cognitive Style: Five Approaches and Relevant Research (John Wiley and Sons, New York, 1976).

[16] Goodenough, D.R., The role of individual differences in field dependence as a factor in learning and memory, Psychological Bulletin, 4 (1976) 675-694.

[17] Greco, A.A. and McClung, C., Interaction between attention directing and cognitive style, Educational Communication and Technology Journal, 2 (1979) 97-102.

[18] Guilford, J.P., Cognitive styles: what are they ? Educational and Psychological Measurement, (1980) 715-735.

[19] Hortin, J.A., Visual literacy and visual thinking (ERIC No. ED214522, 1980).

[20] Kirby, P., Cognitive style, leaning style and transfer skill acquisition (National Center for Research in Vocational Education, Ohio, 1979, ERIC No. ED186685).

[21] Kogan, N., Educational implications of cognitive style, in Lesser, G.S. (ed.) Psychology and Educational Practice (Scott, Forseman and Co, Illinois, 1971).

[22] McKim, R.H., Experiences in Visual Thinking (Brooks Cole Publishing, California, 1972).

[23] Mullally, L., Educational cognitive style: implications for instruction, Theory into Practice, 4, (1977) 238-242.

[24] Ragan, T.J., Insights on visual capacities from perceptual and cognitive styles (Paper presented at the National Convention of the Association for Educational Communications and Technology, Kansas City, Missouri, 1978, ERIC No. ED179228).

[25] Ragan, T.J., Visual literacy: the learner dimension (Paper presented at the Annual Convention of the Association for Educational Communications and Technology, New Orleans, 1979, ERIC No. ED180440).

[26] Rollins, H.A. and Genser, L., Role of cognitive style in a cognitive task: a case favouring the impulsive approach to problem solving, Journal of Educational Psychology, 3, (1977) 281-287.

[27] Salomon, G., What is learned and how it is taught: the interaction between media, message, task and learner, in Olson, D.R. (ed.) Media and Symbols: The Forms of Expression, Communication and Education (N.S.S.E., Chicago, 1974).

[28] Salomon, G., Interaction of Media, Cognition and Learning (Jossey-Bass, San Francisco, 1979).

[29] Sikora, P.A., Visual literacy, International Journal of Instructional Media, 2, (1980-1) 143-152.

[30] Witkin, H.A., Moore, C.A., Goodenough, D.R. and Cox, P.W., Field-dependent and field-independent cognitive styles and their educational implications, Review of Educational Research, 1, (1977) 1-64.

COMPUTERS IN EDUCATION, K. Duncan and D. Harris (eds.)
Elsevier Science Publishers B.V. (North-Holland)
© IFIP, 1985

THEORETICAL INFLUENCES ON THE DESIGN AND IMPLEMENTATION OF COMPUTER-MEDIATED LEARNING

D.F. Sewell and D.R. Rotheray

Educational Technology Research Group,
Department of Psychology,
Hull University, Hull, England, HU6 7RX.

The relationship between CAL environments and psychological models is discussed, in particular the need for explication of the theories of learning implicit in various styles of software.   It is argued that the design of the educational experience must take into account our knowledge of cognitive development, and a generalised 'schematic' model of cognition is proposed as an appropriate tool.   The educational implications of this paradigm are examined with reference to current CAL environments, in particular those with an explicit theoretical basis such as LOGO.   Emphasis is given to the need for environments which allow users to explore the implications of their own cognitive models.

Much has been said about the use of the micro-computer as an educational tool, but relatively little attempt has been made to place this use within particular models of cognitive develop-ment.   As Mills (1984) points out, not only can CAL be categorised according to the degree of user control permitted to the learner, but also particular implementations often reflect differing models of learning and, hence, of cognitive development.   It must be said, however, that these models are rarely made explicit by the program designers.

A notable exception to this general trend has been the development of LOGO and its use as en-visaged by Papert (1980).   Papert's view of LOGO and its origins owes much to the influence of Piaget, an influence which can also be found in other areas of AI (Boden, 1981).   These influences tend to draw on Piaget's view of children as epistemologists, rather than on his outline of cognitive development along well-defined stages.   The acceptance by Papert of the former model of knowledge acquisition led him to an emphasis on "discovery learning" via the medium of the microcomputer.   We thus find in "Mindstorms" an emphasis on children discov-ering knowledge through their exploration of "computer microworlds", which Goldenberg (1982) has defined as "a well-defined, but limited, learning environment in which interesting things happen and in which there are important ideas to be learned."   These "important ideas" are analogous to Papert's "powerful ideas" which are essentially cognitive skills valued by society.   Papert emphasises mathematical and physical concepts, and their discovery via the medium of LOGO.   Other Logophiles emphasise problem solving (Harvey, 1982) or the acquisi-tion of reading skills (Lawler, 1982).   The important linking feature of the learning of these particular cognitive abilities lies not so much in the fact that they have been emphas-ised in the context of LOGO, but more signifi-cantly on the fact that they reflect an adher-ence to the particular model of cognitive growth emphasised by Piaget and by other cognitive theorists.

Broadly speaking this model has the central proposition that learning takes place via inter-action with a learning environment which, in some sense, embodies what is to be learnt.   As a result of the interaction, the learner con-structs a set of internal hypotheses (or schemata) about the nature of the world.   These schemata then act as "a set of rules serving as instructions for producing a population proto-type" (Evans, 1967).   Subsequent information is then processed within the existing schema which adjusts in order to cope with dissonant informa-tion.   Although the schematic model of learning implied above is often associated with recent cognitive theorists, its origins can be traced to Piaget's ideas on assimilation and equili-bration.   For Piaget, assimilation was the integration of the experience of reality into an intellectual structure, and equilibration was the process of schema modification in order to compensate for the disturbances caused by novel information.

In the Piagetian model referred to above, devel-opment occurs as a progression through a series of stages, each characterised by its own form of equilibration.   An essential element in this model is that learning is only possible if a complex structure is based on a simpler struct-ure, a conclusion which finds echoes in Papert's discussion of "powerful ideas".   This notion remains one of the most significant aspects to emerge from Piagetian theory, yet it seems that the Piagetians themselves seemed to overlook its significance for the design of their own observ-ational studies.   Piaget's stage theory genera-ted a veritable mini-industry in psychological experiments examining the validity, or other-wise, of stage theory.   The overall conclusion to emerge from a wealth of studies was that many Piagetians failed to take account of the child's current mental state, the child's "world knowledge", or to pose questions that made sense to the child (i.e. could be processed within existing schemata). These failings resulted in an underestimation of children's mental abilities.

This research tradition, generally associated with Bruner's model of cognitive growth, has indicated that the claims made for the strict interpretation of stage theory have been un-founded, and that children are considerably less limited than originally supposed. In all cases this re-interpretation of children's abilities has been based on studies which have presented tasks to children in a manner which either made sense to the child or removed unnecessary confu-sing elements in the testing procedure (see Donaldson, 1978, for a review of such investi-gations).

Thus Piaget has made two important contributions to the present discussion, one positive and one negative. First, he laid the foundation stone of the constructivist, hierarchical model implicit in such approaches as encapsulated in LOGO. Secondly, by making striking claims about the cognitive limitations of children, a research tradition was generated which attacked those assertions by making explicit the limiting factors in the learning process. The work of Bruner and his followers has clearly demonstra-ted that the limiting factors have often been in the testing situation and task structure rather than within the learner.

Although Piagetian and Brunerian approaches are often considered to be at odds, there are essen-tial similarities between the models. Both are basically hierarchical models in which cognitive growth is an ordered process from simple to complex. In both models, this development is based upon interactions with the environment, and the learner is presumed to be an active participant in the learning process. Nor is this hierarchical framework restricted to Piaget and Bruner. It is implicit in the work of many cognitive and AI theorists. Norman and Rumel-hart (1975) categorised three modes of learning:
1. "accretion" - the addition of new knowledge to existing schemata. The framework exists, but new data are entered.
2. "structuring" - the formation of new concept-ualisations when existing schemata will no longer suffice.
3. "tuning" - the fine adjustment of knowledge to a task which occurs when the appropriate schemata exist and the necessary knowledge is within them, but they are inefficient for the task at hand because they are too general or not matched to the particular task.

In these terms, "accretion", the most common form of learning, is equivalent to "assimilation" and "structuring" to "accommodation".

Schank (1982) developed a theory of dynamic memory based on his work in AI. His main point is that memorising is not enough, but that the learner must have a context into which to place newly acquired information in order to make intelligent use of the incoming data. Schank refers to the existing frameworks as "scripts", and argues that the most efficient learning takes place when we remind ourselves of a previous script and modify it in accordance with a new learning experience. There are close similarities here with Norman's statement (1982) that "knowledge does not imply understanding". The latter comes when the former is interpreted in the light of existing conceptual frameworks.

The direct implication of these views for the design of learning experiences is that they should begin with a framework of knowledge with which the learner is already familiar, then show parallels between the existing framework and new material. Additionally, the learner should be able to explore the differences between new and old material, thereby allowing opportunity for conceptual restructuring. This is the basis of Papert's advocacy of LOGO. Turtle geometry is said to succeed because it can be related to "body knowledge" (i.e. a domain of experience with which a child is already familiar and to which the learner can relate). In the Piaget-ian scheme, "knowing" an object consists of acting upon it, manipulating it and discovering its properties. Note, however, that the "object" need not necessarily be a physical object, although in the early phases of cognit-ive growth it may well be. It can, for example, be a linguistic or conceptual "object" in the sense that these can be manipulated and their functions explored. The turtle, physical or screen based, is an example of such a hypothesis-testing object, or "object to think with". The turtle is fundamentally neutral (as is the micro-computer) in that its actions are dependent upon the input of the user, although this input is, in turn, constrained by the limits set by LOGO.

Gagne (1970, 1975) referred to those objects which stimulated learning as "objects of instruc-tion" - i.e. stimuli from which concepts could be taught or derived. Although Gagne is a psychologist in the learning theory mould, his is an essentially hierarchical model of learning in which complex cognitive abilities are based upon the mastery of simpler skills. In this scheme, as in Piaget's and Bruner's, the compo-nents of cognitive growth are to be found in the child's environment and in the nature of the child's interactions with the environment. The environment, populated as it is with objects and people, provides the necessary raw material for cognitive explorations.

Children growing up in modern technological societies are increasingly placed in an environ-ment in which the microcomputer is one of the "objects of instruction" or, more flexibly, one of the objects to think with - along with people, toys, games, sand, water etc.   Aaron Sloman (1978) has described the modern digital computer as "perhaps the most complex toy ever created by man."   His choice of the word "toy" is particularly apt.   As outlined above, cognitive growth can be seen as a process which is dependent on the nature of our interactions with the environment.   From early childhood on, many of these interactions can be viewed as "play" activities in that they involve manipulations and explorations of the environment. Sloman points out that from infancy we need to play with toys "be they bricks, dolls, construction kits, paint and brushes, words, nursery rhymes, stories, pencil and paper, mathematical problems, crossword puzzles, games like chess, musical instruments, theatres, scientific theories, and other people."   Out of these interactions comes understanding - i.e. cognition.   As implied earlier, the microcomputer is an essentially neutral "toy".   Its efficiency as a provider of stimuli for encouraging cognitive growth depends significantly on how the computer-mediated learning experiences are structured - i.e. on how the microworlds are designed, the nature of the interactions they permit, and on which powerful ideas they incorporate.   Lawler (op cit) has, in fact, referred to the process of designing microworlds as "cognitive engineering" and alludes to the designers of the computer learning environments as "architects of inner space".

Although the implications of the theoretical frameworks referred to above are readily perceived, it is worth considering the extent to which current educational software incorporates the principles of exploration, user freedom and active involvement.   LOGO has already been implicated as a learning environment which owes its origins to ideas in developmental psychology.   Although LOGO can be adapted for use in many ways (e.g. Howe's use of LOGO contains more imposed structure than does Papert's envisaged use), many of its proponents would maintain that "pure" LOGO requires a commitment to exploratory learning. Additionally LOGO allows users to impose their own structure on the environment.   The user freedom inherent in the language permits the user to combine and recombine the LOGO primitives in such a way as to change the immediate environment within the limits of user and LOGO potentials.   This considerable flexibility can be viewed as one of the major strengths of this particular language.   Indeed, it can be argued that such an imposition of one's will upon the environment is a major component of normal cognitive growth. Halliday (1973, 1975), in discussing the development of language, has argued that this is one of the major functions of language.   Via the growth of communicative skills, the child comes to comprehend the nature of the environment and to explore his or her own cognitive abilities through language, by giving instructions, describing situations, reflecting on the past, speculating on the future, and imagining the unknown (the fantasy element so prevalent in

children's literature).   The communication made possible thus becomes, amongst other things, a vehicle for testing possibilities.

In testing possibilities, whether via language, conventional play or through the medium of a microcomputer, we are basically exploring and developing our own cognitions or schemata. Through interactions with the environment these schemata can be examined, their implications and validity assessed, and the necessary modifications made - the processes of assimilation and equilibration referred to earlier.   In the context of microcomputer-based learning LOGO provides one such interactive possibility.   In manipulating the turtle, using the features of turtle geometry or LOGO's list processing capacity (McDougall, Adams and Adams, 1982) children are said to develop their own cognitive schemata and problem solving strategies. LOGO has been used as an exemplar in this discussion not least because it is a well known educational language (at least by reputation). More significantly, LOGO contains many of the elements already referred to.   It is one of the few computer-based learning tools which claims a theoretical basis, and for which major cognitive claims have been made. Although it must be stated, however, that many of these claims have yet to be substantiated by sound objective data.

In the present context, a major feature of LOGO is that it permits users to impose their own cognitive structure on the environment - e.g. by the definition and combination of new userdefined procedures.   A similar argument can be made for another current "vogue" language, namely PROLOG.   Although there has been some dispute about the relative merits of LOGO and PROLOG (Mellar, 1983), it is significant that amongst the advantages claimed for PROLOG is that it enhances logical thinking, a claim not far removed from the argument that use of LOGO improves problem solving strategies.

Although LOGO and PROLOG demonstrate significant differences - e.g. the former is best known for its graphics environment and for being a procedural language, whereas the latter is text based and declarative - both share the feature that their potential is best realised when the user is in control of the input, be it manipulating the turtle, or in constructing and querying a data base.   Ennals (1983) views an important feature of PROLOG as lying not in the fact that it is a programming language per se, but in that its use demands logical thinking.   For Ennals and others associated with the relatively embryonic use of PROLOG in the classroom, the associations between logic, clarity of thought and many areas of the school curriculum are self evident.   Ennals also reports that, notwithstanding criticisms about PROLOG's front end, children of 9 rapidly gain facility with its syntax.   These criticisms are, to some extent, nullified by both the "SIMPLE" front end, and by the "Man In The Street Interface"

(MITSI) currently being developed by Jonathan Briggs (Briggs, personal communication, 1984).

To many classroom users of PROLOG, its attractions lie not in the claims that it may form the basis of the 5th Generation languages, but in the nature of the cognitive skills that its use may promote. The development and expression of these abilities (i.e. those associated with logical thinking) are currently being explored through the use of PROLOG in the classroom.

It is no accident that its introduction in a classroom setting (see Ennals, op cit) involves the construction of data bases on material familiar to the users - e.g. football, friendship patterns, school meals, bus routes etc. As LOGO's turtle geometry relates to the child's "body knowledge", so use of PROLOG relates to "world knowledge". In both cases the programming language is a medium through which children can express and explore the implications of their own understanding. These then become a route to the cognitive "meta-skills" which underpin many everyday activities.

Bruner's contention that children's cognitive abilities are best examined in situations with which the child is familiar (i.e. are syntonic with their world knowledge) takes on an additional force when placed in the context of micro-computer-based learning environments which allow children to create their own personal microworlds.

This process of creation, which is analogous to the arguments presented earlier concerning the imposition of one's own cognitions onto the environment, can also be found in apparently less powerful computer environments, although it is, of course, not restricted to computers. The program "Animals" and its various derivatives (e.g. "Tree of Knowledge") has been widely welcomed by both teachers and children. In such programs the user can develop a tree-structure which grows as more objects are inserted. The user is thus able to create a personal data tree. It is not even necessary that the items in the data base are real "animals", although this is often the first use. The data base could be populated by orcs, goblins, dragons, giants, dwarves, elves etc. All that is necessry is that the child can cognitively identify the various items to be inserted and express their discriminating features. With each new addition the user has to provide a question which will discriminate between the new entry and one already included. In such a process, the user is not only required to reflect on possible salient discriminating features, but also to distinguish between a question enquiring about a difference and a statement declaring that difference. This latter procedure demands sophisticated linguistic and conceptual skills, as well as illustrating the close relationships which exist between thought and language.

The last 12 months have also seen a growing acceptance of a potential role for computer-based simulations and Adventure games in educational computing (Educational Computing, June and November, 1983). Although these are not creative environments in the same vein as LOGO and PROLOG they do allow users to impose their own strategies upon the task at hand. Thus, although the environments are essentially constrained, they do permit, and in fact require, exploration if their potentials are to be discovered. This limiting factor, however, may soon cease to be the case. The appearance of Adventure generators allows individuals to construct their own adventure, and to insert their own characters, clues, problems etc. Such developments may well reflect a significant move in Adventure games towards environments which can be tailored towards particular educational objectives. This could well prove to be a powerful tool in the hands of imaginative teachers and children.

Simulations represent a further exploratory style of program. A wide variety of simulations exist including ones on archaeology, history, economics, politics, exploration, pollution control, evolution, flying and military battles. The essence of these simulations lies not so much in their accurate reflection of reality, although there are some very accurate simulations, but in their facility to allow the user to experience a set of problems and to see the consequences of various decisions. Simulations enable the user to adopt different strategies - e.g. in running an imaginary country or in adopting different battle tactics. In this process, the user is forming differing hypotheses (in order to solve the simulated problem) and in testing out these hypotheses. The richness of the potential hypothesis-testing ultimately depends on the quality of the simulation - i.e. on the quality of the microworld.

As argued earlier, hypothesis-testing forms an important component of cognitive growth. The hypotheses reflect internal schemata and allow exploration of the implications of those schemata. The returning data, in turn, allow modification or equilibration. Hypothesis-testing is inherent in simulation. It is also built into the computer-mediated learning environments described above. In Burton and Brown's Intelligent Tutoring System "How the West was Won" (1982) the success of the computer tutor lay not simply in the quality of its intervention but in the fact that the users sought to "psych" the coach - i.e. to discover the situations which would result in the computer coach's intervention. In other words, hypotheses were formed about the way the tutor operated and those hypotheses were then tested. A significant potential of computer environments is that feedback about these hypotheses can be immediately apparent. Such a situation is not always to be found in the classroom.

This paper has argued that CAL can be examined in the context of models of cognitive development, and, in particular, within the broad context of a hierarchical model of learning. Not only can styles of CAL be regarded in this light, but also it can be argued that developments in this field need to take into account our understanding of the factors known to influence cognitive growth. The framework provided by modern developmental and cognitive psychology provides such an opportunity. However, it does more. Not only can it provide guidelines for the development, implementation and assessment of CAL, but it can also benefit from the data on the nature of children's interactions with the new technology - i.e. our observations may result in a better understanding of cognitive growth.

Our estimation of children's intellectual abilities is often clouded by pre-conceptions about those abilities, and by children's behaviour in environments which do not provide them with the opportunity to display sophisticated cognitive skills. Bruner's work has demonstrated the importance of providing children with the appropriate environment. Papert, coming from the Piagetian stable, has stated essentially the same thing. Olson (1976) argued that the expression of intellectual skills was critically influenced by the nature of the surrounding technology. The way in which we use the new technology and design the learning experiences may well have significant influences on the expression of intellectual skills.

(1) Boden, M.A., Minds and Mechanisms (Harvester, Brighton, 1981).

(2) Burton, R.R. and Brown, J.S., An investigation of computer coaching for informal learning, in Sleeman, D. and Brown, J.S. (eds.), Intelligent Tutoring Systems (Academic Press, London, 1982).

(3) Donaldson, M., Children's Minds (Fontana/ Collins, Glasgow, 1978).

(4) Ennals, J.R., Beginning micro-PROLOG (Ellis Horwood, Chichester, 1983).

(5) Evans, S.H., A brief statement of schema theory, Psychonomic Science, 8 (1967) 87-88.

(6) Gagne, R.M., The Conditions of Learning (Holt, Rinehart and Winston, London, 1970).

(7) Gagne, R.M., Essentials of Learning for Instruction (Dryden Press, Hinsdale, 1975).

(8) Goldenberg, E.P., LOGO - a cultural glossary, Byte, 7(8) (1982) 210-228.

(9) Halliday. M.A.K., Explorations in the Functions of Language (Edward Arnold, London, 1973).

(10) Halliday, M.A.K., Learning How to Mean : Explorations in the Development of Language (Edward Arnold, London, 1975).

(11) Harvey, B., Why LOGO?, Byte, 7(8) (1982) 163-193.

(12) Lawler, R.W., Designing Computer-based Microworlds, Byte, 7(8) (1982) 138-160.

(13) McDougall, A., Adams, T. and Adams, P., Learning LOGO on the Apple II (Prentice Hall, Australia, 1982).

(14) Mellar, H., Languages at Logoheads, Soft, July (1983) 82-106.

(15) Mills, G.M., Categories of Educational Microcomputer Programs, Theories of Learning and Implications for Future Research. Paper presented at ETIC '84 Conference, Bradford University (1984).

(16) Norman, D.A., Learning and Memory (W.H. Freeman, San Francisco, 1982).

(17) Norman, D.A. and Rumelhart, D.E., Memory and Knowledge, in Norman, D.A., Rumelhart, D.E. and the LNY Research Group (eds.), Explorations in Cognition (W.H. Freeman, San Francisco, 1975).

(18) Olson, D.R., Culture, Technology and Intellect, in Resnick, L.B. (ed.), The Nature of Intelligence (Lawrence Erlbaum Associates, Hillsdale, 1976).

(19) Papert, S., Mindstorms : Children, Computers and Powerful Ideas (Harvester, Brighton, 1980).

(20) Schank, R.C., Dynamic Memory (Cambridge University Press, Cambridge, 1982).

(21) Sloman, A., The Computer Revolution in Philosophy (Harvester, Brighton, 1978).

COMPUTERS IN EDUCATION, K. Duncan and D. Harris (eds.)
Elsevier Science Publishers B.V. (North-Holland)
© IFIP, 1985

EDUCATIONAL TECHNOLOGIES DATABASE PROJECT

Mary Grace Smith, Chairperson; Inabeth Miller

Educational Technologies Database Project
HGSE, Harvard University
Cambridge, Massachusetts

The Educational Technologies Database Project supported by a grant from the Fund for the Improvement of Post-Secondary Education is compiling a directory of information on the uses of microcomputers in educational settings nationwide. The database will be published electronically on Compu-Serve, a Consumer Information Service, and will be searchable.

Data will be provided about instructional, administrative, and research applications from pre-school through post-secondary institutions, both public and private, and in non-institutional settings as well. In addition to statistical information, the database will also be a compendium of the latest advances in educational technology in real life settings and will provide ready access to knowlegeable colleagues around the country, thus encouraging collegial consultation and networking among educators.

Each entry will include the name, address, and phone number of a contact person. In order to encourage communication an open forum will also be established on Compu-Serve.

We have found in our research that many educators, even those who use computers for instructional purposes and/or for word processing, are not yet familiar with personal computer communication capabilities. Our database is only one of many sources of information now available electronically which will eventually change research methods and questions. We see the dissemination of information about the Educational Technologies Database as serving the dual purpose of acquainting the educational community with the availability of the specific data contained as well as with the potential of communicating and performing research via personal computers.

This session will inform educators about the kinds of information available, train potential users in access techniques and search strategies, and encourage participation in on-line conferences. We will also solicit suggestions for forum topics.

AGENDA

INTRODUCTION:

Rationale and history of the Database

Inabeth Miller
Librarian to the Faculty

PRESENTATION:

Database content: explanation of design and data

Mary Grace Smith
Project Director

TRAINING:

How-to session covering both accessing the Information Service and searching the database

The project will provide how-to materials and bibliography on personal computer communications

Mary Grace Smith
Inabeth Miller

FORUM REPORT:

Statistics on use; topics discussed; analysis of usefulness to users; solicitation of suggestions.

Mary Grace Smith

QUESTIONS AND DISCUSSION

Future of Computing and Education

COMPUTERS IN EDUCATION, K. Duncan and D. Harris (eds.)
Elsevier Science Publishers B.V. (North-Holland)
© IFIP, 1985

NEW DIRECTIONS IN COMPUTER EDUCATION

Chairperson:

Elayne Schulman
Computer Coordinator
Staten Island Academy
Staten Island, NY 10304

Presentors:

Arthur Luehrmann
Co-Founder
Computer Literacy, Inc.
Berkeley, CA 94708

Martin B. Schneiderman
Director, Computer Education Programs
Educational Testing Service
Princeton, NJ 08541

Microcomputers are coming into our nation's schools at an accelerating rate as educators try to respond to the changing needs of the information age. Yet there is strong evidence that the influx of equipment is outpacing ideas about how to put it to effective use. The question, in short, is this: Are our schools teaching students the right things about computing? In this special session, the presentors will discuss critical issues concerning new directions in computer education at the elementary and secondary levels. At the conclusion of the presentation, questions and comments by session attendees will be invited.

Issues to be discussed:

Curriculum

● What will be important for all kids to know about computers and
information processing in the years to come?

  - What should the balance be between learning computer applications, computer
    programming, general computer knowledge and societal implications?

  - Should learning computer applications and computer programming be elective or
    required subjects?

Instruction

● How should students develop essential computing competencies?

  - How and when should computer applications (such as word processing, database
    management, graphics, spreadsheet analysis and telecommunications) be taught?

  - How and when should computer programming be taught?

  - What are important logistical considerations in teaching software dependent
    courses?

Curriculum Materials

● Do appropriate machine and software specific curriculum materials exist to teach
computer applications and computer programming?

● What effect will state approved computing curricula and textbook adoptions have on
the future of computing in our schools?

COMPUTERS IN EDUCATION, K. Duncan and D. Harris (eds.)
Elsevier Science Publishers B.V. (North-Holland)
© IFIP, 1985

Careers in Computing

A Panel Session

Joyce Currie Little, Chair
Towson State University
Towson, Maryland, United States of America

Patrick Raymont
The National Computing Centre Limited
Manchester M1 7ED, England

Cathleen Norris
North Texas State University
Denton, Texas, United States of America

Although much of the popular literature on "how to get ahead in the computer field" makes success in a computer career seem easy, the field has become more and more complex. As a new emerging discipline just beginning to gain maturity, the computer field is as rapidly changing than ever, and wide varieties of specialties continue to appear and evolve. Planning for careers, sometimes classified as either "top-down" or "bottom-up," has become more ad-hoc than ever, in spite of the need for improved career advisement. Efforts to better define the discipline and its many facets are critical to the career planning and advisement process. This panel session concerns areas of progress made toward improved education and advisement about careers in the computer field.

Joyce Currie Little, Panelist

Several theories of career planning and decision-making have been observed in the computer field. Dr. Little will describe several typical computer career ladders, and summarize some recent research studies describing computer personnel. An overview will be given of the wide spectrum of computer jobs and the varying levels of capabilities, talents, and education needed for each.

Patrick Raymont, Panelist

Career patterns and choices in computer jobs are often influenced by educational systems and environmental conditions. Mr. Raymont will give his impressions about computer careers in the United Kingdom, and will describe some of the differences he has observed in different locales. Efforts to promote improved education about computing careers through IFIP will be described.

Cathleen Norris, Panelist

The Association for Computing Machinery [ACM] recently initiated a Careers in Computing project, designed to provide information about careers in the computer field to pre-college students. Dr. Norris will describe the wide-spread participation of ACM members in this national effort, and give an overview of the type of materials likely to be made available upon its completion.

COMPUTERS IN EDUCATION, K. Duncan and D. Harris (eds.)
Elsevier Science Publishers B.V. (North-Holland)
© IFIP, 1985

Closing Session

LARGE SCALE NETWORKS FOR COMPUTER-BASED EDUCATION

Donald Bitzer
Computer-Based Education Research Laboratory
University of Illinois
103 S. Matthews
Urbana, IL

The recent influx of a large number of different types of personal computers has both widened the opportunity for exploration into computer-based education and also confused the issue with a variety of incompatible and inadequate courseware. Where is computer-based education heading? How will the coordination and management necessary to deliver effective computer-based education become possible? Potential solutions to these questions will be addressed in light of the past 24 years experience in computer-based education. A description will be given of a proposed large scale network that could connect and centrally operate as many as 400,000 terminals across the U.S. in schools, homes, and industry. The integration of terminals into the network will provide terminal to computer as well as terminal to terminal communications, making possible the sharing of large data banks and immediate dissemination of courseware and other information. An explanation will be given of how computer service and remote communication costs can be made very affordable utilizing a large network approach, while still providing the necessary management tools.

COMPUTERS IN EDUCATION, K. Duncan and D. Harris (eds.)
Elsevier Science Publishers B.V. (North-Holland)
© IFIP, 1985

IMPACT OF INFORMATION TECHNOLOGY ON EDUCATION

Klaus Haefner
Fachbereich 3, Universitat Bremen
Bremen, Germany

This talk surveys the consequences of information technology for European education and training. Four main areas are covered:

(1) The direct consequences of the use of information technology by students inside and outside schools and universities are discussed. In particular, learning programs and video-games are educational issues of increasing importance in Europe.

(2) Computer-based learning in vocational training as well as general changes in the vocational information environment are analyzed. European companies do not seem eager to adopt cheap personal computers and expert systems for "on-the-job- training"; they are still oriented toward basic knowledge and people skills.

(3) An analysis of the capacity of human information processing compared with technical information processing, however, shows that there is a decreasing need for "traditional" qualifications. Thus it is necessary to reconsider the relevance of all curricula. There is a need for an appropriate balance between human and technical information processing, and this must be supported at both school and university levels.

(4) Organization of knowledge is shifting from books and brains toward data bases and expert systems. This development has not been taken very seriously in Europe. Europeans are challenged to use their elaborate educational systems to contribute to the technical organization of knowledge.

The talk includes examples and suggests methods for approaching solutions to the various problems. An answer to many questions can be found only if there is an appropriate concept of a humanistically computerized society. This is summarized briefly.

Author List

WCCE '85 Paper Reviewers

Ada-Winter, Peter
Adams, J. Mack
Augustin, G. Cuevas
Alty, J.L.
Ariyama, Masataka
Atchison, William F.
Barta, Ben Zion
Bass, George
Bauer, F. Samuel
Baugh, Robert P.
Beck, James D.
Best, Anita
Bestougeff, Helene
Booth, Taylor
Bork, Alfred
Bosler, Ulrich
Boynton, G.R.
Brauer, Wilfried
Brennan, Joyce R.
Britton, Otha L.
Buoncristiani, A.M.
Burns, Hugh
Buswell, Cain
Cassel, Lillian N.
Castellan, N. John, Jr.
Church, Marilyn
Clark, Frank C.
Clark, Jim
Claus, V.
Close, Richard
Cody, Ronald
Connolly, Frank W.
Culp, George H.
Dale, Nell
Dalphin, John F.
Daniel, Millin
DeKock, Arlan
Deringer, Dorothy K.
Dershem, Herbert L.
Dubuc, Louise
Eickel, J.
Eldredge, David L.
Engel, Gerald L.
Ettinger, Linda
Evans, Sclloy
Fink, Frederick T.
Fletcher, Dexter

Fontell, Lauri
Foster, Susan J.
Frericks, Don
Friedman, B. Albert
Friedman, Frank L.
Frye, Helen B.
Fuhs, F. Paul
Garcia, Ric A.
Geist, Robert
Gersting, Judith L.
Gordon, Douglas
Gordon, Sheldon P.
Grady, Tim
Graf, J.D.
Grossman, Harold
Hall, Keith A.
Hammond, Judith H.
Harris, Mary Dee
Hassell, Johnette
Hebenstreit, Jacques
Heilmann, Heidi
Huntley, Joan
Ide, Nancy M.
Jehn, Betty
Johnson, Dale
Johnson, Jerry
Johnson, David C.
Jones, Vincent H.
Karush, Gerald
Keil, Karl-August
Keller, Sister Mary K.
Kerner, I.O.
Kessler, Gary
Klassen, Dan
Koffman, Elliot
Koontz, Marvin S.
Ladisler, Uncorsky
Lehtinen, Jukka
Lewis, R.
Lidtke, Doris K.
Lothe, H.
Lyle, William
Maharry, David E.
Mayer, Joerg
McAdams, Sister Joseph
McClain, Donald H.
McGregor, John

Monien, Burkhard
Morgan, Catherine E.
Moursund, David
Nishimura, Toshio
Norcross, Bruce E.
Oliver, Lawrence H.
Page, Edward
Peck, John C.
Petty, Linda C.
Poirot, Jim
Porterfield, W.W.
Ragsdale, R.G.
Randan, Alice F.
Ricardo, Catherine
Rickman, Jen
Rine, David C.
Riser, Robert
Roberts, Nancy
Rodriguez, A. Alvarez
Roecks, A.L.
Romaniuk, E.W.
Roquemore, Leroy
Sarmanto, Auvo
Schmitt, Alfred
Schoen, Harold
Schubert, D.
Scott, David
Seidman, Robert H.
Shostak, Robert
Shub, Charles
Simpson, Hassell
Sjoerdsma, Ted
Smr, Joseph
Spelt, Philip F.
Staman, E. Michael
Stevenson, D.
Tauber, Michael
Thomson, Robert A.
Ufo Mohri
Van Iwaarden, John L.
Vernon, Erwin C.
Waligorski, Stanislaw
Weingarten, Fred W.
Wiechers, G.
Wittlich, Gary
Ziegenbalg, J.

AFIPS Steering Committee

Sylvia Charp, Chairwoman
Ron Carruth
Seymour Wolfson

IFIP TC 3 Committee

TC 3 Chairman, J. Hebenstreit
TC 3 Chairman Elect, W. Brauer
TC 3 Secretary, G. Weichers
IFIP Cognizant Officer, B. Sendov
TC 3/WG 3.1 Chairman, P. Bollerslev
TC 3/WG 3.2 Chairman, W.F. Atchison
TC 3/WG 3.3 Chairman, R.E.J. Lewis
TC 3/WG 3.4 Chairman, P.G. Raymont
TC 3/WG 3.5 Chairman, F.B. Lovis

Australia, I.G. Pirie
Austria, H. Schauer
Belgium, R. de Caluwe
Bulgaria, T. Boyanov
Canada, R.S. McLean
Czechoslovakia, L. Uncovsky
Denmark, M. Koch
Finland, L. Fontell
German Democratic Republic, D. Schubert
Greece, G. Filokyprou
Hungary, M. Hamori
India, V. Rajaraman
Iraq, Al-Tarafi
Israel, B.Z. Barta
Italy, P. Ercoli
Japan, T. Nishimura
Morocco, M. Najim
Netherlands, D.H. Wolbers
New Zealand, C.R. Boswell
Norway, A. Staupe
Poland, S. Waligorski
Spain, R. Portaencasa
Sweden, L. Gunnarsson
Switzerland, R. Morel
United Kingdom, J.L. Alty
United States, S. Charp
Yugoslavia, A. Mandzic